Treaties in Force

A List of Treaties and Other International Agreements of the United States in Force on January 1, 2001

This publication lists treaties and other international agreements of the United States on record in the Department of State on January 1, 2001 which had not expired by their terms or which had not been denounced by the parties, replaced or superseded by other agreements, or otherwise definitely terminated.

Compiled by the Treaty Affairs Staff,
Office of the Legal Adviser,
Department of State.

FOREWORD

Treaties in Force is published annually by the Department of State for the purpose of providing information on treaties and other international agreements to which the United States has become a party and which are carried on the records of the Department of State as being in force as of January 1 of each year.

The title *Treaties in Force* uses the term treaty in the generic sense as defined in the Vienna Convention on the Law of Treaties, that is, an international agreement "governed by international law, whether embodied in a single instrument or in two or more related instruments and whatever its particular designation." The term "treaty" in its restricted usage in the United States denotes international agreements made by the President with the advice and consent of the Senate in accordance with Article II, section 2 of the Constitution of the United States. In addition to such "treaties," this publication covers international agreements in force for the United States which have been concluded by the Executive (a) pursuant to or in accordance with existing legislation or a prior treaty, (b) subject to congressional approval or implementation, and/or (c) under and in accordance with the President's Constitutional powers.

Arrangement

This publication is arranged in two parts, with an appendix. Part 1 includes bilateral treaties and other international agreements listed by country or other international entity with subject headings under each entry. Arrangements with territorial possessions of a country appear at the end of the entry for that country. In some cases, treaties and international agreements applicable to a territory prior to its independence are included in the entry for that country on the basis of its assumption of treaty obligations upon becoming independent, as noted at the beginning of the entry for that country.

Part 2 lists multilateral treaties and other international agreements to which the United States is a party, arranged by subject with a listing of the parties to that agreement. Information is based on the most recent data available from the government or organization that serves as the depositary for that agreement. Where countries are listed on the basis of their assumption of obligations under treaties and agreements applied to them prior to independence, a reference is included to the note at the beginning of the entry for that country in Part 1 of this publication.

While every effort is made to insure that the multilateral listings in *Treaties in Force* are accurate and up to date, the depositary has the ultimate responsibility for furnishing a current list of parties and information on other matters concerning the status of the agreement.

The appendix contains a consolidated tabulation of documents affecting international copyright relations of the United States. In addition to treaties and agreements listed in Parts 1 and 2 of this publication, the appendix includes proclamations by the United States with respect to copyright relations.

Status of Treaties and Other Agreements

Treaties in Force includes those treaties and other international agreements entered into by the United States which on January 1 of the specified year had not expired by their own terms, been denounced by the parties or replaced or superseded by other agreements, or otherwise definitely terminated. Certain agreements, particularly those concerned with World War II and the immediate postwar period, which contain continuing provisions or which have not been clearly terminated in their entirety are included even though operations under the agreements may have ceased. The absence of a listing for a particular agreement should not be regarded as a determination that it is not in force. Listings are based largely upon treaties and agreements published in the *Treaties and Other International Acts Series* (TIAS). Entries for these treaties and agreements show a TIAS designator. Other agreements that the Department of State will not publish in TIAS, pursuant to Section 138 of Public Law, 1 U.S.C. 112a, and 22 C.F.R. 181.8, are also listed in *Treaties in Force*. Each of these agreements is designated Not Printed (NP). Certain arrangements are not listed in *Treaties in Force*; these include, for example, project grants and loans made by the Agency for International Development and agreements that are considered as "implementing" other treaties and agreements.

Supplementary Information

Information on the current status of treaties and other international agreements is published regularly in the Department of State Dispatch, a monthly publication for sale by the Superintendent of Documents, United States Government Printing Office, Washington, D.C. 20402.

Inquiries concerning agreements a user believes may not have been included in *Treaties in Force* or requests for agreements that are not being printed in TIAS may be made to the Office of Treaty Affairs, Department of State, Washington, D.C. 20520.

References

NP	Not Printed in *Treaties and Other International Acts Series*.
Stat.	United States Statutes at Large.
UST	United States Treaties and Other International Agreements (volumes published on a calendar-year basis beginning as of January 1, 1950).
TS	Treaty Series, issued singly in pamphlets by the Department of State (until replaced in 1945 by the TIAS).
EAS	Executive Agreement Series, issued singly in pamphlets by the Department of State (until replaced in 1945 by the TIAS).
TIAS	Treaties and Other International Acts Series, issued singly in pamphlets by the Department of State.
Miller	Treaties and other International Acts of the United States of America, edited by Hunter Miller.
Bevans	Treaties and Other International Agreements of the United States of America 1776–1949, compiled under the direction of Charles I. Bevans.
Foreign Relations	Foreign Relations of the United States.
F.R.	Federal Register.
LNTS	League of Nations Treaty Series.
UNTS	United Nations Treaty Series.

CONTENTS

PART 1: BILATERAL TREATIES AND OTHER AGREEMENTS

AFGHANISTAN

AGRICULTURAL COMMODITIES

Agricultural commodities agreement, with exchanges of notes. Signed at Kabul May 22, 1965; entered into force May 22, 1965.
16 UST 1078; TIAS 5849; 579 UNTS 29.

Agricultural commodities agreement with exchange of notes. Signed at Kabul December 22, 1966; entered into force December 22, 1966.
17 UST 2229; TIAS 6161; 681 UNTS 123.

Agricultural commodities agreement with annex. Signed at Kabul July 19, 1967; entered into force July 19, 1967.
18 UST 1766; TIAS 6322; 692 UNTS 345.

Related agreements:
July 2, 1968 (19 UST 5413; TIAS 6523; 707 UNTS 111).
February 1 and March 15, 1969 (20 UST 520; TIAS 6660; 707 UNTS 120).
March 27, 1971 (22 UST 538; TIAS 7096; 792 UNTS 229).
August 23, 1971 (22 UST 2181; TIAS 7262).
February 21, 1973 (25 UST 245; TIAS 7793; 944 UNTS 73).

Agricultural commodities agreement, with minutes of understanding. Signed at Kabul August 8, 1976; entered into force August 8, 1976.
27 UST 3740; TIAS 8390.

Agricultural commodities agreement, with minutes of understanding. Signed at Kabul December 28, 1977; entered into force December 28, 1977.
29 UST 3321; TIAS 9014; 1124 UNTS 129.

CULTURAL RELATIONS

Agreement concerning cultural relations. Exchange of notes at Washington June 26, 1958; entered into force June 26, 1958.
9 UST 997; TIAS 4069; 321 UNTS 67.

DEFENSE

Agreement relating to the deposit by Afghanistan of ten percent of the value of grant military assistance furnished by the United States. Exchange of notes at Kabul May 24 and June 29, 1972; entered into force June 29, 1972; effective May 24, 1972.
23 UST 1219; TIAS 7389.

ECONOMIC AND TECHNICAL COOPERATION

General agreement for technical cooperation. Signed at Kabul February 7, 1951; entered into force February 7, 1951.
2 UST 592; TIAS 2210; 132 UNTS 265.

Amendment:
January 2 and 24, 1952 (3 UST 4683; TIAS 2624; 177 UNTS 341).

Agreement relating to a loan for the purchase of wheat and flour for famine relief in Afghanistan. Exchange of notes at Washington January 8, 1953; entered into force January 8, 1953.
4 UST 2941; TIAS 2896.

Agreement providing development assistance to Afghanistan. Exchange of notes at Kabul June 23, 1956; entered into force June 23, 1956.
7 UST 2047; TIAS 3606; 271 UNTS 295.

EDUCATION

Agreement for financing certain educational exchange programs. Signed at Kabul August 20, 1963; entered into force August 20, 1963.
14 UST 1218; TIAS 5421; 488 UNTS 41.

FINANCE

Agreement relating to investment guaranties under section 413(b)(4) of the Mutual Security Act of 1954; as amended. Exchange of notes at Kabul June 5 and 9, 1957; entered into force June 9, 1957.
8 UST 2507; TIAS 3972; 307 UNTS 97.

GENERAL RELATIONS

Provisional agreement in regard to friendship and diplomatic and consular representation. Signed at Paris March 26, 1936; entered into force March 26, 1936.
49 Stat. 3873; EAS 88; 5 Bevans 1; 168 LNTS 143.

INFORMATIONAL MEDIA GUARANTIES

Agreement providing for an informational media guaranty program. Exchange of notes at Kabul January 26 and February 15, 1961; entered into force February 15, 1961.
12 UST 378; TIAS 4726; 406 UNTS 235.

NARCOTIC DRUGS

Agreement concerning the prohibition of opium poppy cultivation in the project area of the Central Helmand drainage project (phase II). Signed at Kabul August 29, 1977; entered into force August 29, 1977.
29 UST 2481; TIAS 8951.

Agreement concerning the prohibition of opium poppy cultivation in the project area of the integrated wheat development project. Signed at Kabul September 29, 1977; entered into force September 29, 1977.
29 UST 2479; TIAS 8950.

PEACE CORPS

Agreement relating to the establishment of a Peace Corps program in Afghanistan. Exchange of notes at Kabul September 6 and 11, 1962; entered into force September 11, 1962.
13 UST 2100; TIAS 5169; 461 UNTS 169.

PUBLICATIONS

Agreement relating to the exchange of official publications. Exchange of notes at Kabul February 29, 1944; entered into force February 29, 1944.
58 Stat. 1393; EAS 418; 5 Bevans 3; 106 UNTS 247.

RELIEF SUPPLIES AND PACKAGES

Agreement relating to duty-free entry and defrayment of inland transportation charges on relief supplies and packages to Afghanistan. Exchange of notes at Kabul April 29 and May 29, 1954; entered into force May 29, 1954.
5 UST 1533; TIAS 3030; 234 UNTS 3.

Amendment:
December 27, 1960 and January 12, 1961 (12 UST 52; TIAS 4673; 402 UNTS 319).

AFRICAN DEVELOPMENT BANK

ECONOMIC AND TECHNICAL COOPERATION

Agency for International Development:
June 30, 1976 (28 UST 6963; TIAS 8698).

AFRICAN DEVELOPMENT BANK (Cont'd)

FINANCE

Cooperation agreement. Signed at New York May 29, 1986; entered into force May 29, 1986.
TIAS 11363.

ALBANIA

CLAIMS

Agreement on the settlement of certain outstanding claims, with agreed minute. Signed at Tirana March 10, 1995; entered into force April 18, 1995.
TIAS 12611.

COPYRIGHT (See APPENDIX)

DEFENSE

Agreement regarding grants under the Foreign Assistance Act of 1961, as amended, and the furnishing of defense articles, related training and other defense services from the United States to Albania. Exchange of notes at Tirana April 27 and May 6, 1994; entered into force May 6, 1994.
TIAS 12272.

Agreement concerning the status of U.S. military personnel and civilian employees of the Department of Defense who may be present in Albania in connection with the Search and Rescue (SAREX) joint military exercise. Exchange of notes at Tirana January 17 and 24, 1995; entered into force January 24, 1995.
NP

Security agreement. Signed at Washington October 16, 1995; entered into force October 16, 1995.
TIAS 12244.

Acquisition and cross-servicing agreement, with annexes. Signed at Tirana November 8, 2000; entered into force November 8, 2000.
TIAS

DIPLOMATIC RELATIONS

Memorandum of understanding concerning the re-establishment of diplomatic relations. Signed at Washington March 15, 1991; entered into force March 15, 1991.
TIAS 12428.

ECONOMIC AND TECHNICAL COOPERATION

Agreement concerning economic, technical and related assistance. Signed at Tirana June 10, 1992; entered into force June 10, 1992.
TIAS 12456.

EMPLOYMENT

Agreement relating to the employment of dependents of official government employees. Exchange of notes at Washington August 30 and September 30, 1993; entered into force September 30, 1993.
TIAS

EXTRADITION

Treaty of extradition. Signed at Tirana March 1, 1933; entered into force November 14, 1935.
49 Stat. 3313; TS 902; 5 Bevans 22; 166 LNTS 195.

FINANCE

Investment incentive agreement. Signed at Washington November 19, 1991; entered into force March 18, 1993.
TIAS 12441.

INVESTMENT

Treaty concerning the reciprocal protection of investment, with annex and protocol. Signed at Washington January 11, 1995; entered into force January 4, 1998.
TIAS

MAPPING

Basic exchange and cooperative agreement for topographic mapping, nautical and aeronautical charting and information, geodesy and geophysics, digital data and related mapping, charting and geodesy materials. Signed at Tirana March 25, 1994; entered into force March 25, 1994.
NP

PACIFIC SETTLEMENT OF DISPUTES

Arbitration treaty. Signed at Washington October 22, 1928; entered into force February 12, 1929.
45 Stat. 2728; TS 770; 5 Bevans 14; 92 LNTS 217.

Treaty of conciliation. Signed at Washington October 22, 1928; entered into force February 12, 1929.
45 Stat. 2732; TS 771; 5 Bevans 17; 92 LNTS 223.

POSTAL MATTERS

Express mail agreement, with detailed regulations. Signed at Tirana and Washington June 26 and July 15, 1996; entered into force September 15, 1996.
NP

TRADE AND COMMERCE

Agreement concerning most-favored-nation treatment and passports. Exchange of notes at Tirana June 23 and 25, 1922; operative July 28, 1922.
Foreign Relations, 1925, Vol. I, p. 511; 5 Bevans 9.

Agreement on trade relations, with exchange of letters. Signed at Washington May 14, 1992; entered into force November 2, 1992.
TIAS 12454.

VISAS

Agreement relating to waiver of passport visa fees for nonimmigrants. Exchange of notes at Tirana May 7, 1926; operative June 1, 1926.
5 Bevans 12.

ALGERIA [1]

NOTE:
[1] For the ''Declarations of the Government of the Democratic and Popular Republic of Algeria . . .'' initialed at Algiers January 19, 1981, see IRAN—CLAIMS.

AGRICULTURAL COMMODITIES

Agricultural commodities agreement with exchange of notes and related agreement. Signed at Algiers February 23, 1966; entered into force February 23, 1966.
17 UST 551; TIAS 6002; 592 UNTS 117.

AGRICULTURE

Memorandum of understanding concerning cooperation and trade in the field of agriculture, with annex. Signed at Algiers February 2, 1984; entered into force February 2, 1984.
TIAS 10936.

ALGERIA [1] (Cont'd)

CONSULS

Consular convention. Signed at Washington January 12, 1989; entered into force July 30, 1997.
TIAS

COPYRIGHT (See APPENDIX)

CULTURAL RELATIONS

Agreement on cultural cooperation. Signed at Algiers June 2, 1987; entered into force October 3, 1988.
TIAS 12016.

ECONOMIC AND TECHNICAL COOPERATION

Agreement establishing the United States-Algerian Joint Commission for economic, technical and technological cooperation. Signed at Washington April 17, 1985; entered into force April 17, 1985.
TIAS 11998.

FINANCE

Investment incentive agreement. Signed at Washington June 22, 1990; entered into force December 4, 1990.
TIAS 12075.

Agreement regarding the consolidation and rescheduling or refinancing of certain debts owed to, guaranteed by or insured by the United States Government and its agencies, with annexes. Signed at Algiers December 15, 1994; entered into force February 8, 1995.
NP

Agreement regarding the consolidation and rescheduling of certain debts owed to, guaranteed by, or insured by the United States Government and its agencies, with annexes. Signed at Algiers March 27, 1996; entered into force June 24, 1996.
NP

JUDICIAL ASSISTANCE

Agreement for mutual assistance in connection with the investigation of activities of International Systems and Controls Corporation and International Telephone and Telegraph Company, their affiliates and subsidiaries. Exchange of letters at Washington May 22, 1980; entered into force May 22, 1980.
32 UST 1411; TIAS 9780; 1234 UNTS 339.

Related agreement:
December 18, 1980 (32 UST 4491; TIAS 9960; 1266 UNTS 378).

POSTAL MATTERS

International express mail agreement, with detailed regulations. Signed at Algiers and Washington June 25 and July 26, 1994; entered into force September 1, 1994.
NP

SCIENTIFIC COOPERATION

Memorandum of understanding concerning scientific and technical cooperation in the earth sciences, with annexes. Signed at Algiers February 21, 2000; entered into force February 21, 2000.
TIAS

ANGOLA

COPYRIGHT (See APPENDIX)

DEFENSE

Agreement concerning the provision of training to military and related civilian personnel of foreign countries under the United States International Military Education and Training (IMET) Program. Exchange of notes at Luanda September 21, 1995 and January 24, 1996; entered into force January 24, 1996.
NP

ECONOMIC AND TECHNICAL COOPERATION

Economic, technical and related assistance agreement. Signed at Luanda April 9, 1996; entered into force April 9, 1996.
TIAS

FINANCE

Investment incentive agreement. Signed at Luanda July 27, 1994; entered into force August 18, 1994.
TIAS 12189.

POSTAL MATTERS

International express mail agreement, with detailed regulations. Signed at Luanda and Washington December 29, 1993 and October 17, 1994; entered into force December 1, 1994.
NP

ANTIGUA and BARBUDA

On November 1, 1981 Antigua and Barbuda became an independent state. In a note dated November 4, 1981 to the Secretary-General of the United Nations, the Deputy Prime Minister and Minister of Foreign Affairs made a statement reading in part as follows:

"I have the honour to inform you that Antigua and Barbuda became an independent nation on 1st November, 1981, and is now ready to participate with other nations in fulfilling obligations under international law with respect to treaties to which this Government succeeded upon independence. However, it is necessary to examine in depth such treaties to ascertain whether or not under customary international law any may have lapsed. Until this has been done the Government of Antigua and Barbuda wish:

"(a) that it be presumed that each Treaty has been legally succeeded to by Antigua and Barbuda; and

"(b) that future action be based on the presumption in (a) above.

"You will be notified in due course of those treaties this Government regards as having lapsed and those treaties which this Government wishes to terminate. Notice of lapse or termination in an appropriate form will also be given to the country or countries that is or are party to those treaties."

AVIATION

Agreement between the United States and the United Kingdom concerning air services, with annexes and exchange of letters. Signed at Bermuda July 23, 1977; entered into force July 23, 1977.
28 UST 5367; TIAS 8641.

Amendments:
April 25, 1978 (29 UST 2680; TIAS 8965).
December 4, 1980 (33 UST 655; TIAS 10059).
August 19 and October 7, 1991 (TIAS 11794).

CONSULS

Consular convention between the United States and the United Kingdom. Signed at Washington June 6, 1951; entered into force September 7, 1952.
3 UST 3426; TIAS 2494; 165 UNTS 121.

ANTIGUA and BARBUDA (Cont'd)

COPYRIGHT (See APPENDIX)

DEFENSE

Agreement regarding United States defense areas and facilities in Antigua, with annex, memorandum of understanding and agreed minute. Signed at Washington December 14, 1977; entered into force January 1, 1978.
29 UST 4183; TIAS 9054; 1135 UNTS 3.

Amendments and extensions:
December 4, 1985 and February 5 and 26, 1986.
October 28, 1988.
January 19, 1999.

Agreement concerning the provision of training related to defense articles under the United States International Military Education and Training (IMET) Program. Exchange of notes at St. John's December 7 and 10, 1981; entered into force December 10, 1981.
33 UST 4411; TIAS 10311.

ECONOMIC AND TECHNICAL COOPERATION

General agreement for economic, technical, and related assistance. Signed at St. John's June 17, 1983; entered into force June 17, 1983.
TIAS 10742.

EMPLOYMENT

Agreement relating to the employment of dependents of official government employees. Exchange of notes at Bridgetown and St. John's December 23, 1997 and January 27, 1998; entered into force January 27, 1998.
TIAS

EXTRADITION

Extradition treaty. Done at St. John's June 3, 1996; entered into force July 1, 1999.
TIAS

FINANCE

Agreement relating to investment guaranties. Signed at St. John's October 9, 1968; entered into force October 9, 1968.
19 UST 6060; TIAS 6567; 702 UNTS 253.

JUDICIAL ASSISTANCE

Treaty on mutual legal assistance in criminal matters, with exchange of notes. Signed at St. John's October 31, 1996; entered into force July 1, 1999.
TIAS

NARCOTIC DRUGS

Agreement concerning maritime counter-drug operations. Signed at St. John's April 19, 1995; entered into force April 19, 1995.
TIAS

Amendment:
June 3, 1996.

PEACE CORPS

Agreement relating to the establishment of a Peace Corps program in Antigua. Exchange of notes at Bridgetown and Antigua December 19 and 28, 1966; entered into force December 28, 1966.
18 UST 25; TIAS 6195; 681 UNTS 137.

PEACEKEEPING

Agreement for the furnishing of commodities and services in connection with the peace-keeping force for Grenada. Exchange of notes at Bridgetown and St. John's November 30, 1983 and January 27, 1984; entered into force January 27, 1984.
TIAS 10934.

Related agreement:
December 16, 1985 and January 28, 1986 (TIAS 11172).

POSTAL MATTERS

Convention for the exchange of postal money orders with Antigua. Signed at Antigua December 5, 1956 and at Washington March 22, 1957; entered into force December 1, 1957.
11 UST 1425; TIAS 4482.

PROPERTY

Convention between the United States and the United Kingdom relating to the tenure and disposition of real and personal property. Signed at Washington March 2, 1899; applicable to Antigua June 17, 1901.
31 Stat. 1939; TS 146; 12 Bevans 246.

Supplementary convention relating to the tenure and disposition of real and personal property of March 2, 1899. Signed at Washington

May 27, 1936; entered into force March 10, 1941.
55 Stat. 1101; TS 964; 5 Bevans 140; 203 LNTS 367.

TELECOMMUNICATION

Agreement between the United States and the United Kingdom relating to the reciprocal granting of authorizations to permit licensed amateur radio operators of either country to operate their stations in the other country. Exchange of notes at London November 26, 1965; applicable to Antigua December 11, 1969.
16 UST 2047; TIAS 5941; 561 UNTS 193.

Agreement between the United States and the United Kingdom extending to certain territories the application of the agreement of November 26, 1965 relating to the reciprocal granting of authorizations to permit licensed amateur radio operators of either country to operate their stations in the other country. Exchange of notes at London December 11, 1969; entered into force December 11, 1969.
20 UST 4089; TIAS 6800; 732 UNTS 334.

Memorandum of understanding providing for a radio relay facility in Antigua for relaying Voice of America programs to areas in the Caribbean. Signed at St. John's September 12, 1980; entered into force September 12, 1980.
33 UST 1541; TIAS 10130; 1560 UNTS 409.

Arrangement relating to radio communications between amateur stations on behalf of third parties. Exchange of notes at St. John's April 30 and May 24, 1982; entered into force June 23, 1982.
34 UST 1103; TIAS 10395; 1566 UNTS 117.

TRACKING STATIONS

Agreement between the United States and the United Kingdom concerning the establishment and operation of a space vehicle tracking and communications station on Antigua. Exchange of notes at Washington January 17 and 23, 1967; entered into force January 23, 1967.
18 UST 112; TIAS 6207.

TRADE-MARKS

Declaration by the United States and the United Kingdom affording reciprocal protection to trade-marks. Signed at London October 24, 1877; entered into force October 24, 1877.
20 Stat. 703; TS 138; 12 Bevans 198.

ARGENTINA

AGRICULTURAL COMMODITIES

Agreement providing for the sale and purchase of cottonseed oil, etc. Signed at Washington April 25, 1955; entered into force April 25, 1955.
6 UST 1085; TIAS 3247; 251 UNTS 283.

Amendments:
April 11 and 22, 1958 (9 UST 543; TIAS 4032; 316 UNTS 380).
September 19 and November 26, 1962 (13 UST 2621; TIAS 5230; 462 UNTS 344).

Agricultural commodities agreement to finance the sale to Argentina of edible oils and/or fat. Signed at Buenos Aires December 21, 1955; entered into force December 21, 1955.
6 UST 6077; TIAS 3459; 240 UNTS 329.

Amendment:
September 19 and November 26, 1962 (13 UST 2621; TIAS 5230; 462 UNTS 344).

Agricultural commodities agreement with exchanges of notes. Signed at Washington June 12, 1959; entered into force June 12, 1959.
10 UST 1068; TIAS 4246; 347 UNTS 59.

AGRICULTURE

Agreement for cooperation in the fields of agriculture, livestock and forestry. Signed at Washington May 20, 1981; entered into force May 20, 1981.
33 UST 1971; TIAS 10161.

Extension:
November 17, 1986.

ATOMIC ENERGY

Agreement providing for a grant to assist in the acquisition of certain nuclear research and training equipment and materials. Exchange of notes at Buenos Aires September 9, 1959 and May 23, 1960; entered into force May 23, 1960.
11 UST 1628; TIAS 4508; 377 UNTS 3.

Agreement providing for equipment to be used in nuclear research and training programs at La Plata University, Argentina. Exchange of notes at Buenos Aires November 8, 1962 and November 30, 1963; entered into force November 30, 1963.
14 UST 1907; TIAS 5504; 505 UNTS 131.

Memorandum of understanding for the exchange of technical information directly applicable to the safety of operating civil power and research reactors, with appendix. Signed at

Buenos Aires November 30, 1990; entered into force November 30, 1990.
TIAS 12147.

Arrangement for the exchange of technical information and cooperation in regulatory and safety research matters, with addendum. Signed at Vienna September 17, 1996; entered into force September 17, 1996.
TIAS

Agreement for cooperation concerning peaceful uses of nuclear energy, with annex and agreed minute. Signed at Buenos Aires February 29, 1996; entered into force October 16, 1997.
TIAS

Implementing arrangement for technical exchange and cooperation in the area of peaceful uses of nuclear energy. Signed at Buenos Aires October 16, 1997; entered into force October 16, 1997.
TIAS

AVIATION

Air transport services agreement, with annexes. Signed at Buenos Aires October 22, 1985; entered into force provisionally October 22, 1985; definitively December 29, 1986.
TIAS 11262.

Amendments:
April 11 and July 3, 1995.
October 26 and November 24, 2000.

Agreement relating to the reciprocal acceptance of airworthiness certifications. Exchange of notes at Buenos Aires June 22, 1989; entered into force June 22, 1989.
TIAS 11669.

COMMERCE

Treaty of friendship, commerce and navigation. Signed at San Jose July 27, 1853; entered into force December 20, 1854.
10 Stat. 1005; TS 4; 5 Bevans 61.

CONSERVATION

Agreement on cooperation in management and protection of national parks and other protected natural and cultural heritage sites. Signed at Buenos Aires October 16, 1997; entered into force October 16, 1997.
TIAS

CONSULS (See COMMERCE)

COPYRIGHT (See also APPENDIX)

Copyright arrangement. Exchanges of notes at Buenos Aires April 28, July 28, August 28, and September 3, 1934; operative August 23, 1934.
5 Bevans 72; 160 LNTS 57.

DEFENSE

Agreement relating to a military assistance program. Exchange of notes at Buenos Aires May 10, 1964; entered into force May 10, 1964.
15 UST 719; TIAS 5594; 527 UNTS 77.

Armed forces cooperative projects agreement. Exchange of notes at Buenos Aires May 5, 1970; entered into force May 5, 1970.
21 UST 1297; TIAS 6881; 752 UNTS 25.

Agreement relating to the deposit by Argentina of ten percent of the value of grant military assistance furnished by the United States. Exchange of notes at Buenos Aires April 4 and June 8, 1972; entered into force June 8, 1972.
23 UST 1324; TIAS 7414.

Memorandum of understanding on the exchange of officers between the U.S. Marine Corps and the Argentine Marine Corps. Signed at Washington October 7 and December 3, 1987; entered into force December 3, 1987.
TIAS 11559.

Memorandum of understanding on the exchange of service personnel between the United States Navy and Argentine Navy and on the general conditions which will apply to the exchange of such personnel. Signed at Washington July 13, 1992; entered into force July 13, 1992.
NP

Agreement concerning exchange of research and development information, with appendix. Signed at Washington July 22, 1998; entered into force July 22, 1998.
TIAS

Amendment:
October 17, 2000.

Agreement concerning security measures for the protection of classified information. Signed at Washington January 12, 1999; entered into force January 12, 1999.
TIAS

Acquisition and cross-servicing agreement, with annex. Signed at Miami and Buenos Aires January 11 and 15, 1999; entered into force January 15, 1999.
TIAS

ARGENTINA (Cont'd)

Agreement regarding the status of civilian and military personnel of the Armed Services of the United States of America temporarily present in the Republic of Argentina in connection with the peacekeeping exercise "Allied Forces Cabanas 2000". Exchange of notes at Buenos Aires July 21 and 31, 2000; entered into force July 31, 2000.
NP

ECONOMIC AND TECHNICAL COOPERATION

General agreement for a program of technical cooperation. Signed at Buenos Aires June 3, 1957; entered into force June 3, 1957.
8 UST 811; TIAS 3840; 291 UNTS 61.

Agreement concerning the establishment of an Americas Fund and Administering Commission. Signed at Buenos Aires September 27, 1993; entered into force September 27, 1993.
TIAS 12507.

EDUCATION

Agreement for financing certain educational exchange programs. Signed at Buenos Aires August 21, 1963; entered into force August 21, 1963.
14 UST 1236; TIAS 5423; 488 UNTS 61.

Amendment:
January 18 and March 20, 2000.

EMPLOYMENT

Agreement relating to the employment of dependents of official government employees. Exchange of notes at Buenos Aires May 28 and December 15, 1986; entered into force December 15, 1986.
TIAS 11414.

ENVIRONMENTAL COOPERATION

Agreement for cooperation in the Global Learning and Observations to Benefit the Environment Program, with appendices. Signed at Buenos Aires June 28, 1995; entered into force June 28, 1995.
TIAS 12671.

EXTRADITION

Treaty on extradition. Signed at Buenos Aires June 10, 1997; entered into force June 15, 2000.
TIAS

FINANCE

Agreement relating to investment guaranties under section 413(b)(4) of the Mutual Security Act of 1954, as amended. Signed at Buenos Aires December 22, 1959; entered into force provisionally December 22, 1959; definitively May 5, 1961.
12 UST 955; TIAS 4799; 411 UNTS 41.

Agreement regarding the consolidation and rescheduling of certain debts owed to, guaranteed by or insured by the United States Government and its agencies, with annexes. Signed at Buenos Aires April 8, 1986; entered into force May 19, 1986.
NP

Swap agreement between the United States Treasury and the Central Bank of the Argentine Republic/Government of the Argentine Republic, with related letter and amendment. Signed at Washington and Buenos Aires February 23, 1988; entered into force February 23, 1988.
TIAS

Swap agreement between the United States Treasury, the Central Bank of the Argentine Republic/Government of the Argentine Republic, with memorandum of understanding. Signed at Washington and Buenos Aires October 19, 1988; entered into force October 19, 1988.
TIAS

Agreement regarding the consolidation and rescheduling or refinancing of certain debts owed to, guaranteed by, or insured by the United States Government and its agencies, with annexes. Signed at Buenos Aires December 14, 1989; entered into force January 22, 1990.
NP

Agreement regarding the consolidation and rescheduling of certain debts owed to, guaranteed by, or insured by the United States Government and its agencies, with annexes. Signed at Buenos Aires December 5, 1990; entered into force January 16, 1991.
NP

Agreement regarding the consolidation and rescheduling or refinancing of certain debts owed to, guaranteed by or insured by the United States Government and its agencies, with annexes. Signed at Washington December 6, 1991; entered into force February 10, 1992.
NP

Agreement regarding the consolidation and rescheduling of certain debts owed to, guaranteed by or insured by the United States Government and its agencies, with annexes. Signed

at Washington January 13, 1993; entered into force March 8, 1993.
NP

Agreement regarding the reduction of certain debts related to foreign assistance owed to the Government of the United States and its agencies, with appendices. Signed at Washington and Buenos Aires January 13 and 15, 1993; entered into force February 14, 1993.
NP

INVESTMENT

Treaty concerning the reciprocal encouragement and protection of investment, with protocol. Signed at Washington November 14, 1991; entered into force October 20, 1994.
TIAS

Amendment:
August 24 and November 6, 1992.

JUDICIAL ASSISTANCE

Treaty on mutual legal assistance in criminal matters, with attachments. Signed at Buenos Aires December 4, 1990; entered into force February 9, 1993.
TIAS

MAPPING

Memorandum of understanding relating to cooperation and mutual assistance in mapping, charting and geodesy, with annex. Signed at Buenos Aires June 23, 1981; entered into force June 23, 1981.
33 UST 2097; TIAS 10175; 1529 UNTS 299.

Agreement relating to cooperation and mutual assistance in cartography and geodesy, with annex. Signed at Buenos Aires July 11, 1983; entered into force July 11, 1983.
TIAS 10730; 1578 UNTS 91.

Agreement concerning nautical cartography and geodesy, with annexes. Signed at Buenos Aires and Fairfax November 28, 1990 and June 18, 1991; entered into force June 18, 1991.
NP

MARITIME MATTERS

Agreement relating to the transfer to Argentina of certain United States naval vessels. Exchange of notes at Washington January 4 and 8, 1951 with memorandum of understanding dated January 11, 1951; entered into force January 8, 1951.
3 UST 2735; TIAS 2442; 165 UNTS 89.

Memorandum of understanding regarding certain maritime matters. Signed at Buenos Aires

ARGENTINA (Cont'd)

March 31, 1978; entered into force January 30, 1979.
30 UST 1054; TIAS 9239; 1152 UNTS 227.

MISSIONS, MILITARY

Agreement for a United States Air Force Mission to the Argentine Republic. Signed at Buenos Aires October 3, 1956; entered into force October 3, 1956.[1]
7 UST 2571; TIAS 3652; 279 UNTS 13.

Amendment:
October 16, 1959 (10 UST 1978; TIAS 4363; 361 UNTS 358).

Agreement relating to the appointment of officers to constitute a United States Army Mission to Argentina. Signed at Buenos Aires August 2, 1960; entered into force August 2, 1960.
11 UST 1964; TIAS 4546; 384 UNTS 105.

Amendment:
January 8 and June 7, 1962 (13 UST 1376; TIAS 5098; 458 UNTS 354).

NOTE:
[1] Article 17 suspended by agreement of November 27, 1972 (24 UST 279; TIAS 7550).

NARCOTIC DRUGS

Memorandum of understanding on cooperation in the narcotics field. Signed at Buenos Aires September 15, 1972; entered into force September 15, 1972.
23 UST 2620; TIAS 7450; 852 UNTS 97.

NAVIGATION

Treaty for the free navigation of the rivers Parana and Uruguay. Signed at San Jose de Flores July 10, 1853; entered into force December 20, 1854.
10 Stat. 1001; TS 3; 5 Bevans 58.

PEACE CORPS

Agreement establishing a Peace Corps program in Argentina. Exchange of notes at Buenos Aires July 18 and August 30, 1991; entered into force August 30, 1991.
TIAS 12102.

POSTAL MATTERS

Agreement for the exchange of insured parcel post packages. Signed at Buenos Aires Feb-

ruary 28 and at Washington April 8, 1939; operative October 1, 1938.
53 Stat. 2223; Post Office Department print; 198 LNTS 55.

International express mail agreement, with detailed regulations. Signed at Buenos Aires and Washington September 4 and 26, 1980; entered into force January 1, 1981.
33 UST 2509; TIAS 10193; 1529 UNTS 269.

Memorandum of understanding concerning the operation of the INTELPOST field trial, with details of implementation. Signed at Washington August 24 and October 12, 1982 and Buenos Aires September 16, 1982; entered into force November 1, 1982.
TIAS 10526; 1777 UNTS 355.

PUBLICATIONS

Agreement relating to the exchange of official publications. Exchange of notes at Buenos Aires September 30 and October 17, 1939; entered into force October 17, 1939.
54 Stat. 1855; EAS 162; 5 Bevans 83; 201 LNTS 273.

SCIENTIFIC COOPERATION

Agreement for scientific and technical cooperation. Signed at Buenos Aires April 7, 1972; entered into force August 11, 1972.
23 UST 2534; TIAS 7442; 852 UNTS 77.

SEISMIC OBSERVATIONS

Agreement on scientific and technical cooperation for a global telemetered seismograph network. Signed at Reston and San Juan December 28 and 29, 1987; entered into force December 29, 1987.
TIAS 12054.

SOCIAL SECURITY

Agreement relating to the payment of old-age, survivors, and disability benefits to beneficiaries residing abroad. Exchange of notes at Buenos Aires September 15, 1972; entered into force September 15, 1972.
23 UST 2660; TIAS 7458; 852 UNTS 91.

SPACE COOPERATION

Agreement for cooperation in the civil uses of space. Signed at Buenos Aires August 6, 1991; entered into force August 6, 1991.
TIAS 12214.

Extension:
February 29, 1996 (TIAS 12214).

Memorandum of understanding concerning the SAC-B Astrophysics Engineering Demonstration Mission. Signed at Buenos Aires August 6, 1991; entered into force August 6, 1991.
TIAS 12212.

Memorandum of understanding concerning the Scientific Applications Satellite-C Earth Observation Mission. Signed at Washington October 28, 1996; entered into force October 28, 1996.
TIAS

Memorandum of understanding concerning the flight of the SAC-A Mission on the Shuttle. Signed at Buenos Aires October 16, 1997; entered into force October 16, 1997.
TIAS

TAXATION

Agreement for relief from double taxation on earnings derived from operation of ships and aircraft. Exchange of notes at Washington July 20, 1950; entered into force July 20, 1950.
1 UST 473; TIAS 2088; 89 UNTS 63.

TECHNOLOGY TRANSFER

Memorandum of understanding on the transfer and protection of strategic technology. Signed at Buenos Aires February 12, 1993; entered into force February 12, 1993.
TIAS 12487.

TELECOMMUNICATION

Agreement relating to the reciprocal granting of authorizations to permit licensed amateur radio operators of either country to operate their stations in the other country. Exchange of notes at Buenos Aires March 31, 1967; entered into force April 30, 1967.
18 UST 361; TIAS 6243; 636 UNTS 95.

Agreement relating to radio communications between amateur stations on behalf of third parties. Exchange of notes at Buenos Aires March 31, 1967; entered into force April 30, 1967.
18 UST 365; TIAS 6244; 636 UNTS 103.

Agreement concerning the provision of satellite facilities and the transmission and reception of signals to and from satellites for the provision of satellite services to users in the United States of America and the Argentine Republic, with protocol. Signed at Washington June 5, 1998; entered into force June 5, 1998.
TIAS

TOURISM

Agreement on the development and facilitation of tourism. Signed at Buenos Aires September

ARGENTINA (Cont'd)

25, 1990; entered into force September 25, 1990.
TIAS 12420.

TRACKING STATIONS

Agreement relating to a cooperative program for the optical satellite tracking station at Villa Dolores, Argentina. Exchange of notes at Buenos Aires March 16, 1962; entered into force March 16, 1962.
13 UST 1385; TIAS 5100; 454 UNTS 3.

TRADE (See also COMMERCE)

Trade agreement with exchanges of notes. Signed at Buenos Aires October 14, 1941; entered into force provisionally November 15, 1941; definitively January 8, 1943.
56 Stat. 1685; EAS 277; 5 Bevans 102; 119 UNTS 193.

Agreement relating to the effectiveness of United States schedules to the trade agreement of October 14, 1941. Exchange of notes at Buenos Aires July 24, 1963; entered into force July 24, 1963.
14 UST 1046; TIAS 5402; 487 UNTS 183.

Amendment:
December 18 and 27, 1967 (18 UST 3102; TIAS 6402; 693 UNTS 370).

Agreement relating to the status of the trade agreements of October 14, 1941 and July 24, 1963. Exchange of notes at Buenos Aires August 3 and 8, 1966; entered into force August 8, 1966.
17 UST 1223; TIAS 6086.

Amendment:
December 18 and 27, 1967 (18 UST 3102; TIAS 6402; 693 UNTS 370).

Agreement concerning trade in women's and girls' wool trousers, with attachment. Exchange of notes at Buenos Aires May 14 and 31, 1991; entered into force May 31, 1991.
NP

VISAS

Agreement relating to the reciprocal waiver of nonimmigrant passport visa fees. Exchange of notes at Buenos Aires April 15, 1942; operative June 1, 1942.
56 Stat. 1578; EAS 266; 5 Bevans 117; 103 UNTS 307.

ARMENIA

For agreements prior to December 31, 1991, see UNION OF SOVIET SOCIALIST REPUBLICS.

COPYRIGHT (See APPENDIX)

ECONOMIC AND TECHNICAL COOPERATION

Agreement regarding cooperation to facilitate the provision of humanitarian and technical economic assistance. Signed at Yerevan December 15, 1992; entered into force December 15, 1992.
TIAS 12483.

FINANCE

Investment incentive agreement. Signed at Washington April 2, 1992; entered into force April 2, 1992.
TIAS 12451.

INVESTMENT

Treaty concerning the reciprocal encouragement and protection of investment, with annex. Signed at Washington September 23, 1992; entered into force March 29, 1996.
TIAS

PEACE CORPS

Agreement concerning the program of the Peace Corps in Armenia. Signed at Washington September 24, 1992; entered into force September 24, 1992.
TIAS 12082.

POSTAL MATTERS

Postal money order agreement. Signed at Yerevan and Washington June 28 and August 3, 1995; entered into force September 1, 1995.
NP

SCIENTIFIC COOPERATION

Agreement on science and technology cooperation. Signed at Washington February 28, 1997; entered into force February 28, 1997.
TIAS

Memorandum of understanding concerning scientific and technical cooperation in the earth sciences, with annex. Signed at Reston and Yerevan September 25 and November 2, 1998; entered into force November 2, 1998.
TIAS

TRADE

Agreement on trade relations, with related exchanges of letters. Signed at Washington April 2, 1992; entered into force April 7, 1992.
TIAS

ASIAN DEVELOPMENT BANK

FINANCE

Agreement relating to the United States contribution to the Multi-Purpose Special Fund of the Asian Development Bank. Signed at Manila April 19, 1974; entered into force April 19, 1974.
25 UST 1672; TIAS 7903.

Amendment:
December 23, 1974 and April 1, 1975 (26 UST 897; TIAS 8074).

ASSOCIATION OF SOUTHEAST ASIAN NATIONS (ASEAN)

AGRICULTURE

Agreement regarding the establishment of an ASEAN Agricultural Development and Planning Center. Exchange of notes at Kuala Lumpur June 28, 1980; entered into force June 28, 1980.
32 UST 1371; TIAS 9778; 1234 UNTS 399.

ECONOMIC AND TECHNICAL COOPERATION

Agreement concerning cooperation in economic development, education, culture, and narcotics. Signed at Denpasar and Kuala Lumpur July 2 and October 24, 1979; entered into force October 24, 1979.
TIAS

AUSTRALIA

AEROSPACE DISTURBANCES

Agreement concerning the transfer to the Australian National University of the facility for research on aerospace disturbances at Amberley, Queensland. Exchange of notes at

AUSTRALIA (Cont'd)

Canberra January 31 and February 26, 1975; entered into force February 26, 1975.
26 UST 446; TIAS 8043; 992 UNTS 139.

ATOMIC ENERGY

Agreement for cooperation regarding atomic information for mutual defense purposes. Signed at Washington July 12, 1957; entered into force August 14, 1957.
8 UST 1339; TIAS 3881; 290 UNTS 139.

Agreement concerning peaceful uses of nuclear energy, with annex and agreed minute. Signed at Canberra July 5, 1979; entered into force January 16, 1981.
32 UST 3227; TIAS 9893; 1217 UNTS 211.

Agreement concerning research and development in nuclear material control, accountancy, verification, physical protection, and advanced containment and surveillance technologies for international safeguards applications, with annex. Done at Washington October 1, 1992; entered into force October 1, 1992.
TIAS

Memorandum of understanding concerning the acceptance by the United States Government of spent fuel from the HIFAR research reactor, with attachment. Exchange of notes at Canberra October 30, 1997; entered into force October 30, 1997.
TIAS

Agreement for cooperation concerning technology for the separation of isotopes of uranium by laser excitation, with annexes, agreed minute and related exchange of letters. Signed at Washington October 28, 1999; entered into force May 24, 2000.
TIAS

AVIATION

Air transport agreement.[1] Signed at Washington December 3, 1946; entered into force December 3, 1946.
61 Stat. 2464; TIAS 1574; 5 Bevans 170; 7 UNTS 201.

Amendments:
December 22, 1987 (TIAS 11922; 1571 UNTS 480).
March 23, 1989 (TIAS 11990; 1820 UNTS 495).
February 22, 1994 (TIAS 12174; 1820 UNTS 468).

Related agreement:
March 23, 1989 (TIAS 11989).

Air service agreement relating to facilities at Eagle Farm and Amberley, Queensland. Signed at Canberra March 10, 1947; entered into force March 10, 1947.
61 Stat. 3843; TIAS 1732; 5 Bevans 181; 10 UNTS 89.

Agreement relating to the reciprocal acceptance of airworthiness certifications. Exchange of notes at Washington December 24, 1974 and June 11, 1975; entered into force June 11, 1975.
26 UST 1665; TIAS 8126; 1006 UNTS 241.

NOTE:
[1] Applicable to all territories.

CONSULS

Convention to regulate commerce (article IV) between the United States and the United Kingdom. Signed at London July 3, 1815; entered into force July 3, 1815.
8 Stat. 228; TS 110; 12 Bevans 49.

COPYRIGHT (See APPENDIX)

DEFENSE

Mutual defense assistance agreement. Exchange of notes at Washington February 1 and 20, 1951; entered into force February 20, 1951.
2 UST 644; TIAS 2217; 132 UNTS 297.

Mutual weapons development program agreement. Signed at Washington August 23, 1960; entered into force August 23, 1960.
11 UST 2089; TIAS 4565; 388 UNTS 232.

Agreement concerning the status of United States forces in Australia with protocol. Signed at Canberra May 9, 1963; entered into force May 9, 1963.
14 UST 506; TIAS 5349; 469 UNTS 55.

Agreement relating to the establishment of a United States naval communication station in Australia. Signed at Canberra May 9, 1963; entered into force June 28, 1963.
14 UST 908; TIAS 5377; 475 UNTS 331.

Amendments:
July 12, 1968 (19 UST 5445; TIAS 6527; 660 UNTS 401).
March 21, 1974 (27 UST 2667; TIAS 8338).
November 24, 1982 (TIAS 10610).
May 8, 1992 (1680 UNTS 494).

Memorandum of arrangement between the United States, Australia, and the United Kingdom to cover re-entry experiments in Australia (Project Sparta), with exchanges of notes. Signed at Canberra March 30, 1966; entered into force March 30, 1966.
17 UST 350; TIAS 5984; 593 UNTS 261.

Agreement relating to the establishment of a joint defense space research facility. Signed at Canberra December 9, 1966; entered into force December 9, 1966.
17 UST 2235; TIAS 6162; 607 UNTS 83.

Extensions and amendments:
October 19, 1977 (29 UST 2759; TIAS 8969).
November 16, 1988 (TIAS 12266).
June 4, 1998.

Agreement relating to the establishment of a joint defense space communications station in Australia. Signed at Canberra November 10, 1969; entered into force November 10, 1969.
20 UST 3097; TIAS 6788; 729 UNTS 17.

Extension and amendment:
November 16, 1988 (TIAS 12267).

Memorandum of understanding regarding the exchange training program of units from both forces. Signed at Washington November 4, 1976; entered into force November 4, 1976.
28 UST 8237; TIAS 8757; 1095 UNTS 91.

Agreement relating to operation of United States military flights through RAAF Base Darwin. Exchange of notes at Canberra March 11, 1981; entered into force March 11, 1981.
33 UST 1300; TIAS 10112.

Memorandum of understanding concerning the exchange of service personnel between the U.S. Marine Corps and the Royal Australian Air Force. Signed at Washington April 13, 1984; entered into force April 13, 1984.
TIAS 11131.

Memorandum of understanding on logistic support, with annexes. Signed at Washington and Canberra March 30 and April 23, 1985; entered into force April 23, 1985.
TIAS 12052.

Memorandum of arrangement relating to the provision of NOMAD aircraft and related services, with attachment. Signed at Washington April 2, 1987; entered into force April 2, 1987.
TIAS 11317.

Memorandum of understanding concerning exchange of service personnel between the U.S. Marine Corps and the Australian Army. Signed at Canberra and Washington August 31 and September 16, 1987; entered into force September 16, 1987.
TIAS 11550.

Agreement concerning cooperation in defense logistic support. Signed at Sydney November 4, 1989; entered into force November 4, 1989.
TIAS   ; 1571 UNTS 167.

Agreement concerning defense communications services, with annexes. Signed at Canberra November 6, 1989; entered into force November 6, 1989.
TIAS 12268; 1571 UNTS 189.

Agreement concerning Navstar Global Positioning System. Signed at Washington February 7, 1991; entered into force February 7, 1991.
TIAS 12269; 1642 UNTS 299.

AUSTRALIA (Cont'd)

Agreement concerning cooperation in radar activities, with project arrangements. Signed at Salisbury March 3, 1992; entered into force March 3, 1992.
TIAS 12270.

Arrangement for the exchange of military personnel between the Royal Australian Navy and the U.S. Coast Guard. Signed at Washington July 27, 1992; entered into force July 27, 1992.
NP

Agreement concerning the exchange of electronic warfare officers between the Department of Defense of the United States and the Department of Defense of Australia, with annexes. Signed at Washington August 26, 1992; entered into force August 26, 1992.
NP

Agreement concerning cooperative and collaborative research, development and engineering, with appendix. Signed at Washington October 21, 1994; entered into force October 21, 1994.
TIAS 12271.

Agreement concerning the establishment of certain mutual defense commitments. Exchange of notes at Sydney and Canberra December 1, 1995; entered into force December 1, 1995.
TIAS 12704; 1945 UNTS 263.

Memorandum of understanding for the production of the offboard active decoy Nulka, with annexes. Signed at Washington June 25, 1996; entered into force June 25, 1996.
TIAS

Agreement concerning defense communications services, with annexes. Signed at Washington October 14 and 30, 1998; entered into force July 13, 1999.
TIAS

ECONOMIC AND TECHNICAL COOPERATION

Agreement relating to training and other technical services to be furnished by the Bureau of Reclamation, Department of the Interior, in connection with proposed projects of the Australian Snowy Mountains Hydroelectric Authority. Exchange of notes at Washington November 16, 1951; entered into force November 16, 1951.
3 UST 2836; TIAS 2456; 168 UNTS 75.

EDUCATION

Agreement for financing certain educational and cultural exchange programs. Signed at Canberra August 28, 1964; entered into force August 28, 1964.
15 UST 1689; TIAS 5643; 510 UNTS 201.

Amendments:
May 12, 1967 (18 UST 493; TIAS 6255; 638 UNTS 300).
February 20 and 21, 1992 (TIAS 12449; 1680 UNTS 502).

EMPLOYMENT

Agreement relating to employment of dependents of official government employees, with related notes. Exchange of notes at Canberra November 5 and 9, 1984; entered into force November 9, 1984.
TIAS 11138.

ENERGY

Memorandum of understanding relating to coal information exchange in the areas of health, safety and environment. Signed at Canberra October 24 and 25, 1978; entered into force November 23, 1978.
30 UST 2208; TIAS 9328.

ENVIRONMENTAL COOPERATION

Memorandum of understanding for cooperation in the Global Learning and Observations to Benefit the Environment (GLOBE) Program, with appendices. Signed at Canberra April 21, 1995; entered into force April 21, 1995.
TIAS 12634.

EXTRADITION

Treaty on extradition.[1] Signed at Washington May 14, 1974; entered into force May 8, 1976.
27 UST 957; TIAS 8234.

Amendment:
September 4, 1990 (1736 UNTS 344).

NOTE:
[1] Applicable to all territories.

FISHERIES

Agreement concerning fishing by United States vessels in waters surrounding Christmas Island and Cocos/Keeling Islands pursuant to the treaty on fisheries between the United States and certain Pacific Island states. Exchange of notes at Port Moresby April 2, 1987; entered into force April 2, 1987.
TIAS 11295.

JUDICIAL ASSISTANCE

Procedures for mutual assistance in administration of justice in connection with the Lockheed Aircraft Corporation matter. Signed at Washington September 13, 1976; entered into force September 13, 1976.
27 UST 3424; TIAS 8372.

LEND-LEASE

Agreement relating to the principles applying to the provision of aid in the prosecution of the war. Exchange of notes at Washington September 3, 1942; entered into force September 3, 1942.
56 Stat. 1608; EAS 271; 5 Bevans 146; 24 UNTS 195.

Agreement on settlement for lend-lease, reciprocal aid, surplus war property, and claims. Signed at Washington June 7, 1946; entered into force June 7, 1946.
60 Stat. 1707; TIAS 1528; 5 Bevans 164; 4 UNTS 237.

Agreement relating to the investment of a portion of the trust account established under the lend-lease settlement agreement of June 7, 1946, and the education agreement of November 26, 1949.[1] Exchange of notes at Canberra July 9 and August 25, 1952; entered into force August 25, 1952.
5 UST 650; TIAS 2954; 229 UNTS 262.

NOTE:
[1] November 26, 1949 agreement (TIAS 1994) superseded by agreement of August 28, 1964 (TIAS 5643). See under EDUCATION.

MAPPING

Cooperative mapping agreement. Approved by Australia March 6, 1947 and by the United States April 4, 1947; entered into force April 4, 1947.
5 Bevans 183.

Agreement concerning cooperative development of the digital chart of the world. Signed at Washington June 22, 1990; entered into force June 22, 1990.
1598 UNTS 263.

Memorandum of understanding concerning geospatial information and services cooperation, with annexes. Signed at Bethesda and Canberra March 27 and 31, 2000; entered into force March 31, 2000.
NP

MARITIME MATTERS

Agreement relating to the furnishing of certain supplies and services to naval vessels. Ex-

AUSTRALIA (Cont'd)

change of notes at Canberra December 19 and 31, 1956; entered into force January 26, 1957.
8 UST 9; TIAS 3729; 266 UNTS 89.

Amendment:
March 28, 1963 (14 UST 347; TIAS 5319; 474 UNTS 338).

METEOROLOGY

Agreement concerning the conduct of a program known as the Equatorial Mesoscale Experiment, with related letter. Exchange of notes at Canberra January 5, 1987; entered into force January 5, 1987.
TIAS

Agreement concerning the conduct of a program known as the Stratosphere-Troposphere Exchange Project. Exchange of notes at Canberra January 5, 1987; entered into force January 5, 1987.
TIAS 12391.

PACIFIC SETTLEMENT OF DISPUTES

Treaty amending in their application to Australia certain provisions of the treaty for the advancement of peace between the United States and the United Kingdom signed at Washington September 15, 1914. Signed at Washington September 6, 1940; entered into force August 13, 1941.
55 Stat. 1211; TS 974; 5 Bevans 143.

PATENTS

Agreement to facilitate the interchange of patent rights and technical information for defense purposes, with exchange of notes. Signed at Washington January 24, 1958; entered into force January 24, 1958.
9 UST 5; TIAS 3974; 307 UNTS 105.

Agreement approving the procedures for reciprocal filing of classified patent applications. Exchange of notes at Washington September 13 and October 2, 1961; entered into force October 2, 1961.
12 UST 1359; TIAS 4857; 421 UNTS 318.

POSTAL MATTERS

Parcel post agreement and detailed regulations of execution. Signed at Melbourne May 16 and at Washington May 27, 1952; entered into force August 1, 1952.
3 UST 4305; TIAS 2580; 178 UNTS 113.

Memorandum of understanding for the exchange of international express mail, with details of implementation. Signed at Washington and Victoria June 5 and 16, 1981; entered into force July 1, 1981.
33 UST 3872; TIAS 10266; 1543 UNTS 89.

PROPERTY

Conventions between the United States and the United Kingdom applicable to Australia from April 3, 1902:
> Convention relating to tenure and disposition of real and personal property. Signed at Washington March 2, 1899 (31 Stat. 1939; TS 146; 12 Bevans 246).
> Supplementary convention extending the time within which notifications may be given of the accession of British colonies or foreign possessions to the convention of March 2, 1899. Signed at Washington January 13, 1902 (32 Stat. 1914; TS 402; 12 Bevans 261).

Supplementary convention relating to the tenure and disposition of real and personal property. Signed at Washington May 27, 1936 by the United States, the United Kingdom, Australia, and New Zealand; entered into force March 10, 1941.
55 Stat. 1101; TS 964; 5 Bevans 140; 203 LNTS 367.

SCIENTIFIC COOPERATION

Agreement relating to the establishment, maintenance and operation of a solar observatory at Learmonth, Western Australia. Exchange of notes at Canberra October 14 and 27, 1977; entered into force October 27, 1977.
29 UST 2747; TIAS 8968.

Agreement concerning the furnishing of balloon launching and associated services, with arrangement. Exchange of notes at Canberra July 16 and October 18, 1984; entered into force October 18, 1984.
TIAS 11166.

Agreement concerning the furnishing of balloon launching and associated services for long-duration flights. Exchange of notes at Canberra January 24 and July 24, 1985; entered into force July 24, 1985.
TIAS 11323.

Agreement concerning the use of Australian facilities by the National Aeronautics and Space Administration (NASA) for balloon flights for scientific purposes. Exchange of notes at Canberra June 15 and 19, 1992; entered into force June 19, 1992.
TIAS 12458; 1698 UNTS 393.

SEISMIC OBSERVATIONS

Agreement regarding the management and operation of the joint geological and geophysical

research station at Alice Springs, Australia. Exchange of notes at Canberra February 28, 1978; entered into force March 2, 1978.
29 UST 3040; TIAS 8995; 1120 UNTS 67.

Amendment:
February 17, 1984 (TIAS 10946).

SPACE COOPERATION

Agreement concerning cooperation on the use by the United States of facilities in Australia for launching, tracking and recovery of sounding rockets and their payloads. Exchange of notes at Canberra September 1, 1987; entered into force September 1, 1987.
TIAS 12215.

SURPLUS PROPERTY

Agreement regarding disposal of United States Government excess property in Australia. Exchange of notes at Canberra November 9, 1973; entered into force November 9, 1973.
24 UST 2280; TIAS 7750; 938 UNTS 375.

TAXATION

Convention for the avoidance of double taxation and the prevention of fiscal evasion with respect to taxes on gifts.[1] Signed at Washington May 14, 1953; entered into force December 14, 1953.
4 UST 2264; TIAS 2879; 205 UNTS 237.

Convention for the avoidance of double taxation and the prevention of fiscal evasion with respect to taxes on the estates of deceased persons.[1] Signed at Washington May 14, 1953; entered into force January 7, 1954.
5 UST 92; TIAS 2903; 205 UNTS 277.

Convention for the avoidance of double taxation and the prevention of fiscal evasion with respect to taxes on income. Signed at Sydney August 6, 1982; entered into force October 31, 1983.
TIAS 10773.

NOTE:
[1] Applicable to Norfolk Is.

TELECOMMUNICATION

Agreement relating to the reciprocal granting of authorizations to permit licensed amateur radio operators of either country to operate their stations in the other country. Exchange of notes at Canberra June 25, 1965; entered into force June 25, 1965.
16 UST 973; TIAS 5836; 541 UNTS 155.

Arrangement relating to radio communications between amateur stations on behalf of third

AUSTRALIA (Cont'd)

parties. Exchange of notes at Canberra May 21 and 26, 1982; entered into force June 25, 1982.
34 UST 1109; TIAS 10396; 1566 UNTS 133.

Agreement concerning the agreement of December 16, 1988 and January 20, 1989, and the transfer to the Government of Australia of the high frequency diplomatic radio communications facility in Uriarra. Exchange of notes at Canberra December 19, 1994 and March 22, 1995; entered into force March 22, 1995.
TIAS 12201.

TRACKING STATIONS

Agreement providing for the establishment and operation in Australia of a tracking station in connection with the transit navigational satellite program. Exchange of notes at Canberra June 5, 1961; entered into force June 5, 1961.
12 UST 789; TIAS 4779; 409 UNTS 279.

Agreement providing for the continuation of a cooperative program facilitating space flight operations. Exchange of notes at Canberra May 29, 1980; entered into force May 29, 1980; effective February 26, 1980.
32 UST 1417; TIAS 9781; 1217 UNTS 237.

Amendment:
January 17 and May 2, 1990 (TIAS 12413; 1571 UNTS 548).

TRADE AND COMMERCE

Agreed record of conclusions within the context of the multilateral trade negotiations with exchange of letters clarifying conclusions, and related letters of February 4 and March 26, 1980. Done at Washington March 29, October 22 and 26, 1979; entered into force March 31, 1980.
32 UST 5233; TIAS 9975.

Agreement relating to cooperation on antitrust matters. Signed at Washington June 29, 1982; entered into force June 29, 1982.
34 UST 388; TIAS 10365; 1369 UNTS 43.

Framework for arrangement on steel trade liberalization, with appendices, and related letters. Exchange of letters at Washington March 9, 1990; entered into force March 9, 1990.
TIAS

Agreement on mutual antitrust enforcement assistance, with annex. Signed at Washington April 27, 1999; entered into force November 5, 1999.
TIAS

VISAS

Agreement relating to the reciprocal waiver of visa fees for nonimmigrants. Exchange of notes at Canberra February 10, 1950; entered into force February 10, 1950; operative March 1, 1950.
1 UST 457; TIAS 2082; 51 UNTS 167.

Agreement concerning reciprocal changes in immigration regulations relating to nonimmigrant visas. Exchanges of notes at Canberra July 29 and August 9, 17 and 20, 1955; entered into force August 20, 1955; operative September 1, 1955.
6 UST 6225; TIAS 3472; 268 UNTS 133.

Agreement relating to the relaxation of nonimmigrant visa requirements. Exchange of notes at Canberra March 13, June 1 and August 19, 1959; entered into force August 19, 1959.
11 UST 2049; TIAS 4561; 388 UNTS 183.

WEATHER STATIONS

Agreement providing for the construction and operation of a weather station on Nauru Island. Exchange of notes at Canberra February 19 and 25, 1958; entered into force February 25, 1958.
9 UST 266; TIAS 4001; 317 UNTS 153.

AUSTRIA

AGRICULTURAL COMMODITIES

Agreement providing for emergency relief for Hungarians in Austria. Exchange of notes at Vienna May 10, 1957; entered into force May 10, 1957.
8 UST 709; TIAS 3825; 283 UNTS 33.

Agreement relating to the utilization of counterpart funds to provide assistance for Austrian program of permanent refugee housing. Exchange of notes at Vienna August 9 and October 3, 1961; entered into force October 3, 1961.
12 UST 1651; TIAS 4879; 426 UNTS 187.

Amendment:
May 18 and June 14, 1962 (13 UST 1306; TIAS 5084; 459 UNTS 314).

AVIATION

Agreement for reciprocal acceptance of certificates of airworthiness for imported aircraft. Exchange of notes at Washington April 30, 1959; entered into force April 30, 1959.
10 UST 796; TIAS 4219; 343 UNTS 41.

Memorandum of agreement relating to the provision of flight inspection services. Signed at

Washington and Vienna March 10 and June 22, 1978; entered into force June 22, 1978; effective April 1, 1978.
30 UST 288; TIAS 9200.

Air services agreement, with annexes. Signed at Vienna March 16, 1989; entered into force June 2, 1989.
TIAS 11265.

Amendment:
June 14, 1995 (TIAS 11503).

CLAIMS

Agreement regarding settlement for war accounts and claims incident to the operations of United States forces in Austria from April 9, 1945 to June 30, 1947, inclusive. Signed at Vienna June 21, 1947; entered into force June 21, 1947.
61 Stat. 4168; TIAS 1920; 5 Bevans 380; 67 UNTS 89.

Agreement providing for settlement of certain claims under article 26 of the Austrian State Treaty of May 15, 1955. Exchange of notes at Vienna May 8, 15 and 22, 1959; entered into force May 22, 1959.
10 UST 1158; TIAS 4253; 347 UNTS 3.

Agreement concerning the Austrian Fund "Reconciliation, Peace and Cooperation" (Reconciliation Fund). Signed at Vienna October 24, 2000; entered into force December 1, 2000.
TIAS

COMMERCE

Treaty of friendship, commerce and consular rights. Signed at Vienna June 19, 1928; entered into force May 27, 1931.
47 Stat. 1876; TS 838; 5 Bevans 341; 118 LNTS 241.

Supplementary agreement to the treaty of friendship, commerce and consular rights of June 19, 1928. Signed at Vienna January 20, 1931; entered into force May 27, 1931.
47 Stat. 1899; TS 839; 5 Bevans 372; 118 LNTS 259.

CONSULS (See COMMERCE)

COPYRIGHT (See APPENDIX)

CUSTOMS

Agreement regarding mutual assistance between the customs services of the United States and Austria. Signed at Vienna Sep-

AUSTRIA (Cont'd)

tember 15, 1976; entered into force July 3, 1978.
29 UST 1011; TIAS 8863.

Amendment:
April 2, 1986.

DEFENSE

Agreement relating to the purchase by Austria of certain military equipment, materials and services. Exchange of notes at Washington August 9, 1957; entered into force August 9, 1957.
8 UST 1241; TIAS 3875; 288 UNTS 299.

Acquisition and cross-servicing agreement, with annexes. Signed at Patch Barracks and Vienna March 15, 2000; entered into force March 15, 2000.
TIAS

ECONOMIC AND TECHNICAL COOPERATION

Economic cooperation agreement and supplementary note. Signed at Vienna July 2, 1948; entered into force July 2, 1948.
62 Stat. 2137; TIAS 1780; 5 Bevans 404; 21 UNTS 29.

Amendments:
October 21 and November 30, 1949, and February 20, 1950 (1 UST 145; TIAS 2020; 79 UNTS 288).
January 16 and March 7, 1951 (2 UST 1315; TIAS 2283; 141 UNTS 372).
May 11 and 15, 1951 (2 UST 2569; TIAS 2380; 139 UNTS 79).
October 15 and December 6, 1952 (3 UST 5300; TIAS 2731; 185 UNTS 322).

EDUCATION

Agreement for financing certain educational exchange programs. Signed at Vienna June 25, 1963; entered into force June 25, 1963.
14 UST 957; TIAS 5386; 479 UNTS 223.

ENVIRONMENTAL COOPERATION

Agreement for cooperation in the Global Learning and Observations to Benefit the Environment (GLOBE) Program, with appendices. Signed at Vienna April 20, 1995; entered into force April 20, 1995.
TIAS 12631.

EXTRADITION

Extradition treaty. Signed at Washington January 8, 1998; entered into force January 1, 2000.
TIAS

FINANCE (See also PROPERTY)

Agreement relating to the funding of the indebtedness of Austria to the United States. Signed at Washington May 8, 1930; operative January 1, 1928.
Treasury Department print; 5 Bevans 365.

Agreement modifying the debt funding agreement of May 8, 1930. Signed at Washington September 14, 1932; operative July 1, 1931.
Treasury Department print; 5 Bevans 376.

Agreement relating to guaranties authorized by section 111(b)(3) of the Economic Cooperation Act of 1948, as amended. Exchange of notes at Washington February 14 and 16, 1952; entered into force February 20, 1952.
3 UST 3874; TIAS 2516; 177 UNTS 299.

Amendment:
October 23, 1958 (9 UST 1345; TIAS 4127; 336 UNTS 336).

Agreement regarding certain bonds of Austrian issue denominated in dollars, with annex and protocol. Signed at Washington November 21, 1956; entered into force September 11, 1957.
8 UST 1457; TIAS 3903; 290 UNTS 181.

Counterpart settlement agreement, with related exchange of notes of March 10 and 28, 1961. Signed at Vienna March 29, 1961; entered into force July 12, 1962.
13 UST 1838; TIAS 5133; 459 UNTS 45.

GENERAL RELATIONS

Treaty establishing friendly relations. Signed at Vienna August 24, 1921; entered into force November 8, 1921.
42 Stat. 1946; TS 659; 5 Bevans 215; 7 LNTS 156.

JUDICIAL ASSISTANCE

Treaty on mutual legal assistance in criminal matters, with attachments. Signed at Vienna February 23, 1995; entered into force August 1, 1998.
TIAS

MUTUAL SECURITY

Agreement relating to the assurances required under the Mutual Security Act of 1951. Exchange of notes at Vienna December 14, 1951

and January 5, 1952; entered into force January 5, 1952.
3 UST 4525; TIAS 2600; 179 UNTS 73.

NARCOTIC DRUGS

Arrangement for the direct exchange of information regarding the traffic in narcotic drugs. Exchange of notes at Vienna April 10 and July 24, 1931; entered into force July 24, 1931.
5 Bevans 373.

OCCUPATION COSTS

Agreement relating to occupation costs of United States forces in Austria subsequent to June 30, 1947. Signed at Vienna June 21, 1947; entered into force July 1, 1947.
61 Stat. 4171; TIAS 1921; 5 Bevans 383; 67 UNTS 99.

PACIFIC SETTLEMENT OF DISPUTES

Arbitration treaty. Signed at Washington August 16, 1928; entered into force February 28, 1929.
45 Stat. 2752; TS 776; 5 Bevans 353; 88 LNTS 95.

Treaty of conciliation. Signed at Washington August 16, 1928; entered into force February 28, 1929.
45 Stat. 2756; TS 777; 5 Bevans 356; 88 LNTS 101.

POSTAL MATTERS

Agreement for collect-on-delivery service. Signed at Vienna November 8 and at Washington December 11, 1929; operative December 1, 1929.
46 Stat. 2427; Post Office Department print.

Money order convention. Signed at Washington February 18 and at Vienna March 14, 1928; entered into force May 1, 1928.
NP

Parcel post convention. Signed at Vienna February 16 and at Washington March 1, 1928; operative March 1, 1928.
45 Stat. 2468; Post Office Department print.

Agreement relating to international express mail with memorandum of understanding. Exchange of letters at Washington and Vienna August 6 and September 4, 1986; entered into force February 2, 1987.
TIAS 11391.

AUSTRIA (Cont'd)

PROPERTY

Agreement concerning the disposition of certain United States property in Austria. Signed at Vienna September 26, 1955; entered into force September 26, 1955.
7 UST 223; TIAS 3499; 272 UNTS 31.

Agreement regarding the return of Austrian property, rights and interests, with schedule and annex. Signed at Washington January 30, 1959; entered into force May 19, 1964.
15 UST 439; TIAS 5577; 511 UNTS 145.

PUBLICATIONS

Agreement for the exchange of official publications. Exchange of notes at Washington March 11 and 23, 1949; entered into force March 23, 1949.
63 Stat. 2434; TIAS 1927; 5 Bevans 422; 43 UNTS 127.

RELIEF SUPPLIES AND PACKAGES

Agreement relating to duty-free entry of relief goods and packages and standard packs and for defrayment of transportation charges. Exchange of notes at Vienna February 3 and 11, 1949; entered into force February 11, 1949.
63 Stat. 2420; TIAS 1922; 5 Bevans 419; 79 UNTS 113.

Amendment:
July 1 and 31, 1952 (3 UST 5042; TIAS 2685; 181 UNTS 326).

SOCIAL SECURITY

Agreement on social security, with administrative arrangement. Signed at Vienna July 13, 1990; entered into force November 1, 1991.
TIAS 12037.

Amendment:
October 5, 1995 (TIAS 12696).

TAXATION

Convention for the avoidance of double taxation and the prevention of fiscal evasion with respect to taxes on estates, inheritances, gifts and generation-skipping transfers. Signed at Vienna June 21, 1982; entered into force July 1, 1983.
TIAS 10570.

Convention for the avoidance of double taxation and the prevention of fiscal evasion with respect to taxes on income, with memorandum

of understanding. Signed at Vienna May 31, 1996; entered into force February 1, 1998.
TIAS

TELECOMMUNICATION

Agreement relating to the operation of amateur radio stations. Signed at Vienna November 21, 1967; entered into force December 21, 1967.
18 UST 2878; TIAS 6378; 634 UNTS 43.

TRADE (See also COMMERCE)

Arrangement within the context of the multilateral trade negotiations concerning agricultural products, and related letters of January 30 and April 14, 1980. Done April 12 and October 17, 1979; entered into force January 1, 1980.
32 UST 5257; TIAS 9977; 1265 UNTS 235.

Agreed record of discussions and memorandum of understanding within the context of the multilateral trade negotiations concerning the Austrian motor vehicle tax, and related letters of January 30 and April 14, 1980. Done at Geneva April 11, 1979; entered into force January 1, 1980.
32 UST 5225; TIAS 9974; 1265 UNTS 227.

VISAS

Agreement relating to the waiver of passport visas and passport visa fees. Exchange of notes at Vienna June 10 and 28 and July 12, 1949; entered into force July 12, 1949; operative July 15, 1949.
63 Stat. 2740; TIAS 1988; 5 Bevans 426; 84 UNTS 291.

AZERBAIJAN

For agreements prior to December 31, 1991, see UNION OF SOVIET SOCIALIST REPUBLICS.

COPYRIGHT (See APPENDIX)

DIPLOMATIC PROPERTIES

Agreement concerning the acquisition and retention of diplomatic and consular properties in the United States of America and the Republic of Azerbaijan. Signed at Baku March 5 and April 21, 1999; entered into force June 8, 1999.
TIAS

EMPLOYMENT

Agreement relating to the employment of dependents of official government employees. Exchange of notes at Washington February 10 and March 8, 1995; entered into force March 8, 1995.
TIAS 12608.

FINANCE

Investment incentive agreement. Signed at Washington September 28, 1992; entered into force January 17, 1995.
TIAS

POSTAL MATTERS

Postal money order agreement. Signed at Baku and Washington April 3 and May 17, 1996; entered into force July 1, 1996.
NP

TRADE

Agreement on trade relations, with exchanges of letters. Signed at Washington April 12, 1993; entered into force April 21, 1995.
TIAS

THE BAHAMAS

On July 10, 1973 The Bahamas became an independent state. In a note dated July 10, 1973 to the Secretary-General of the United Nations, the Prime Minister made a statement reading in part as follows:

"I have the honour, further to inform you that the Government of the Commonwealth of The Bahamas, conscious of the desirability of maintaining existing legal relationships, and conscious of its obligations under international law to honour its treaty commitments, acknowledges that many treaty rights and obligations of the Government of the United Kingdom in respect of The Bahamas were succeeded to by the Commonwealth of The Bahamas upon Independence by virtue of customary international law.

"Since, however, it is likely that in virtue of customary international law certain treaties may have lapsed at the date of Independence of the Commonwealth of The Bahamas, it seems essential that each treaty should be subjected to legal examination. It is proposed, after this examination has been completed, to indicate which, if any, of the treaties which may have lapsed by customary international law the Government of the Commonwealth of The Bahamas wishes to treat as having lapsed.

"It is desired that it be presumed that each treaty has been legally succeeded to by the

THE BAHAMAS (Cont'd)

Commonwealth of The Bahamas and that action be based on this presumption until a decision is reached that the treaty should be regarded as having lapsed. Should the Government of the Commonwealth of The Bahamas be of the opinion that it has legally succeeded to a treaty, and wishes to terminate the operation of the treaty, it will in due course give notice of termination in the terms thereof.''

AVIATION

Agreement between the United States and the United Kingdom relating to air services. Signed at Bermuda February 11, 1946; entered into force February 11, 1946.
60 Stat. 1499; TIAS 1507; 12 Bevans 726; 3 UNTS 253.

Agreement on preclearance for entry into the United States, with annex. Signed at Nassau April 23, 1974; entered into force April 23, 1974.
25 UST 646; TIAS 7816.

Related agreement:
December 28, 1977 and January 10, 1978 (29 UST 4645; TIAS 9072).

Memorandum of agreement for the provision of assistance in developing and modernizing the civil aviation infrastructure of The Bahamas. Signed at Washington and Nassau December 14, 1998 and January 8, 1999; entered into force January 8, 1999.
TIAS

CONSULS

Consular convention between the United States and the United Kingdom. Signed at Washington June 6, 1951; entered into force September 7, 1952.
3 UST 3426; TIAS 2494; 165 UNTS 121.

COPYRIGHT (See APPENDIX)

CUSTOMS

Agreement between the United States and the United Kingdom relating to the prevention of abuses of customs privileges at certain leased naval and air bases. Exchange of notes at Washington January 18 and February 21, 1946; entered into force February 21, 1946.
61 Stat. 2637; TIAS 1592; 12 Bevans 739; 6 UNTS 137.

DEFENSE

Arrangement between the United States and the United Kingdom relating to naval and air bases.[1] Exchange of notes at Washington September 2, 1940; entered into force September 2, 1940.
54 Stat. 2405; EAS 181; 12 Bevans 551; 203 LNTS 201.

Agreement between the United States and the United Kingdom regarding leased naval and air bases, and exchanges of notes.[1] Signed at London March 27, 1941; entered into force March 27, 1941.
55 Stat. 1560; EAS 235; 12 Bevans 560; 204 LNTS 15.

Agreement between the United States and the United Kingdom amending articles IV and VI of the leased bases agreement of March 27, 1941.[1] Exchange of notes at Washington July 19 and August 1, 1950; entered into force August 1, 1950.
1 UST 585; TIAS 2105; 88 UNTS 273.

Agreement between the United States and the United Kingdom concerning a long-range proving ground for guided missiles to be known as "The Bahamas Long Range Proving Ground", and exchange of notes.[1] Signed at Washington July 21, 1950; entered into force July 21, 1950.
1 UST 545; TIAS 2099; 97 UNTS 193.

Amendment:
July 17, 1967 (18 UST 1657; TIAS 6308; 619 UNTS 330).

Agreement between the United States and the United Kingdom regarding the establishment by the United States of a high altitude interceptor range in connection with the operation of the Bahamas Long Range Proving Ground.[1] Exchange of notes at Washington February 24 and March 2, 1953; entered into force March 2, 1953.
4 UST 429; TIAS 2789; 172 UNTS 257.

Agreement between the United States and the United Kingdom providing for regular use by civil aircraft of certain facilities in the Bahama Islands Long Range Proving Ground for guided missiles.[1][2] Exchange of notes at Washington July 11 and 22, 1955; entered into force July 22, 1955.
6 UST 3783; TIAS 3379; 218 UNTS 384.

Amendment:
December 6, 1956 and January 4, 1957 (8 UST 1; TIAS 3727; 266 UNTS 396).

Agreement between the United States and the United Kingdom amending the agreement for the establishment of the Bahamas Long Range Proving Ground by extending the flight testing range.[1] Exchange of notes at Washington April 1, 1957; entered into force April 1, 1957.
8 UST 493; TIAS 3803; 288 UNTS 364.

Agreement between the United States and the United Kingdom for the establishment of oceanographic research stations in the Bahama

Islands.[1] Signed at Washington November 1, 1957; entered into force November 1, 1957.
8 UST 1741; TIAS 3927; 299 UNTS 167.

Amendment:
May 12, 1960 (11 UST 1405; TIAS 4479; 372 UNTS 364).

Agreement between the United States and the United Kingdom concerning the establishment in the Bahama Islands of a long range aid to navigation station.[1] Signed at Washington June 24, 1960; entered into force June 24, 1960.
11 UST 1587; TIAS 4502; 377 UNTS 63.

Agreement between the United States and the United Kingdom for the establishment of an Atlantic Undersea Test and Evaluation Center in the Bahama Islands, with agreed minutes.[1][3] Signed at Washington October 11, 1963; entered into force October 11, 1963.
14 UST 1431; TIAS 5441; 483 UNTS 3.

Agreement between the United States and the United Kingdom relating to the transfer of certain real estate on Eleuthera Island to the United States Navy with annexes.[1] Exchange of notes at Nassau August 9, 1971 and February 17, 1972; entered into force February 17, 1972.
23 UST 155; TIAS 7286.

Understanding between the United States and the United Kingdom relating to the use by Bahamian organizations of certain land at the United States Navy Base, Georgetown, Great Exuma Island, with map and schedule.[1] Exchange of notes at Nassau June 19, September 12 and November 2, 1972; entered into force November 2, 1972.
23 UST 3688; TIAS 7514.

Agreement relating to the continuance of United States military rights in the Bahamas as well as existing maritime practices. Exchange of notes at Nassau July 10 and 20, 1973; entered into force July 20, 1973; effective July 10, 1973.
24 UST 1783; TIAS 7688.

Agreement concerning United States defense facilities in The Bahamas, with annex, agreed minute, exchanges of notes and implementing arrangement, with maps. Signed at Washington April 5, 1984; entered into force April 5, 1984; effective January 26, 1983.
TIAS 11058.

Amendment and extensions:
August 20, 1987, January 25, February 3 and 23, 1988.
January 27, February 6, July 27 and August 11, 1992.
September 22 and October 7, 1992.

Agreement concerning the provision of training related to defense articles under the United States International Military Education and Training (IMET) Program. Exchange of notes at Nassau March 11 and May 6, 1985; entered into force May 6, 1985.
TIAS 11103.

Implementing arrangement to the agreement of April 5, 1984, relating to United States defense

THE BAHAMAS (Cont'd)

facilities, concerning the provision of sites for United States defense purposes. Signed at Nassau January 25 and March 10, 2000; entered into force March 10, 2000.
TIAS

NOTES:
[1] Continues to apply *mutatis mutandis* by virtue of the agreement relating to the continuance of U.S. military rights in the Bahamas as well as existing maritime practices, effected by exchange of notes at Nassau July 10 and 20, 1973 (TIAS 7688).
[2] Paragraph 2(2) superseded by agreements between the United States and the United Kingdom of June 11, 1971 (TIAS 7446) and December 12, 1979 (TIAS 9711).
[3] See also agreement of April 5, 1984 under UNITED KINGDOM — DEFENSE.

EXTRADITION

Extradition treaty. Signed at Nassau March 9, 1990; entered into force September 22, 1994.
TIAS

FINANCE

Agreement on investment insurance and guaranties. Exchange of notes at Nassau April 5, 1983 and September 27, 1984; entered into force September 27, 1984.
TIAS 10997.

JUDICIAL ASSISTANCE

Treaty on mutual assistance in criminal matters. Signed at Nassau June 12 and August 18, 1987; entered into force July 18, 1990.
TIAS

Agreement correcting the text of the treaty on mutual assistance in criminal matters of June 12 and August 18, 1987, with attachments. Exchange of notes at Nassau January 27 and February 4, 1988; entered into force February 4, 1988.
TIAS

NARCOTIC DRUGS

Agreement for the interdiction of narcotics trafficking. Signed at Nassau March 6, 1985; entered into force March 6, 1985.
TIAS 11123.

Agreement on the control of narcotic drugs and psychotropic substances, with appendix. Signed at Nassau February 17, 1989; entered into force February 17, 1989.
TIAS 11602.

Agreement concerning a cooperative shiprider and overflight drug interdiction program. Exchange of notes at Nassau May 1 and 6, 1996; entered into force May 6, 1996.
TIAS

POSTAL MATTERS

Money order agreement. Signed at Washington June 22 and at Nassau July 7, 1921; operative August 1, 1921.
NP

Agreement concerning the exchange of parcel post, and regulations of execution. Signed at Nassau October 29 and at Washington December 21, 1936; operative November 1, 1936.
50 Stat. 1472; Post Office Department print; 176 LNTS 411.

International express mail agreement, with detailed regulations. Signed at Nassau and Washington June 24 and July 17, 1985; entered into force September 9, 1985.
TIAS 11153.

Memorandum of understanding concerning the INTELPOST service, with details of implementation. Signed at Nassau and Washington September 15 and October 7, 1987; entered into force November 1, 1987.
TIAS 11544.

PROPERTY

Convention between the United States and the United Kingdom relating to tenure and disposition of real and personal property. Signed at Washington March 2, 1899; applicable to the Bahamas February 9, 1901.
31 Stat. 1939; TS 146; 12 Bevans 246.

Supplementary convention relating to the tenure and disposition of real and personal property. Signed at Washington May 27, 1936; entered into force March 10, 1941.
55 Stat. 1101; TS 964; 5 Bevans 140; 203 LNTS 367.

SHIPPING

Agreement relating to jurisdiction over vessels utilizing the Louisiana Offshore Oil Port. Exchange of notes at Nassau September 23 and October 5, 1982; entered into force October 5, 1982.
TIAS 10888.

SOCIAL SECURITY

Agreement relating to United States participation in the national insurance scheme of The Bahamas, with related note. Exchange of notes at Nassau October 27, 1976, May 6 and Sep-

tember 23, 1977; entered into force September 23, 1977; effective October 7, 1974.
29 UST 2423; TIAS 8946.

TAXATION

Agreement concerning the reciprocal exemption from income tax of income derived from the international operation of ships and aircraft. Exchange of notes at Washington June 26 and July 16, 1987; entered into force July 16, 1987.
TIAS 11276.

TELECOMMUNICATION

Agreement between the United States and the United Kingdom relating to the reciprocal granting of authorizations to permit licensed amateur radio operators of either country to operate their stations in the other country. Exchange of notes at London November 26, 1965; applicable to the Bahamas December 11, 1969.
16 UST 2047; TIAS 5941; 561 UNTS 193.

Agreement between the United States and the United Kingdom extending to certain territories the application of the agreement of November 26, 1965 relating to the reciprocal granting of authorizations to permit licensed amateur radio operators of either country to operate their stations in the other country. Exchange of notes at London December 11, 1969; entered into force December 11, 1969.
20 UST 4089; TIAS 6800; 732 UNTS 334.

Agreement relating to pre-sunrise operations of certain standard broadcasting stations. Exchange of notes at Nassau January 30 and September 4, 1974; entered into force September 4, 1974.
25 UST 2478; TIAS 7929.

TRADE-MARKS

Declaration by the United States and the United Kingdom affording reciprocal protection to trade-marks. Signed at London October 24, 1877; entered into force October 24, 1877.
20 Stat. 703; TS 138; 12 Bevans 198.

WEATHER STATIONS

Agreement relating to the continuation of a cooperative meteorological program in the Bahama Islands with memoranda of arrangement. Exchange of notes at Nassau October 14, 1982 and August 25, 1983; entered into force August 25, 1983; effective July 2, 1982.
TIAS 10868.

BAHRAIN

AVIATION

Civil aviation security agreement. Signed at Manama November 15, 1992; entered into force November 15, 1992.
TIAS 11912.

COPYRIGHT (See APPENDIX)

DEFENSE

Agreement relating to the status of personnel of the Administrative Support Unit in Bahrain. Exchange of notes at Manama June 28, 1977; entered into force June 28, 1977.
28 UST 5312; TIAS 8632.

Agreement regarding grants under the Foreign Assistance Act of 1961, as amended, and the furnishing of defense articles, related training and other defense services from the United States to Bahrain. Exchange of notes at Manama July 18 and August 8, 19 and 29, 1992; entered into force August 29, 1992.
TIAS

Cross servicing agreement, with annexes. Signed at Washington January 20, 1994; entered into force January 20, 1994.
TIAS 12259.

FINANCE

Investment incentive agreement. Signed at Manama April 25, 1987; entered into force April 25, 1987.
TIAS 12091.

PEACE CORPS

Agreement relating to the establishment of a Peace Corps program in Bahrain. Exchange of notes at Manama April 24 and June 12, 1973; entered into force June 12, 1973.
24 UST 1762; TIAS 7684.

POSTAL MATTERS

International express mail agreement, with detailed regulations. Signed at Bahrain and Washington April 22 and July 28, 1982; entered into force August 1, 1982.
TIAS 10469.

TAXATION

Agreement to exempt from income tax certain income derived from the international operation of a ship or ships and aircraft. Exchange of notes at Manama September 1 and 12, 1999; entered into force September 12, 1999.
TIAS

TRADE AND COMMERCE

Agreement concerning trade in textiles and textile products, with annexes. Exchange of notes at Manama April 4 and June 6, 1993; entered into force June 6, 1993; effective January 1, 1993.
NP

BANGLADESH

AGRICULTURAL COMMODITIES

Agricultural commodities agreement. Signed at Dhaka August 6, 1973; entered into force August 6, 1973.
24 UST 1985; TIAS 7711.

Amendments:
August 28 and September 19, 1973 (24 UST 2017; TIAS 7715).
November 1 and 24, 1973 (24 UST 2313; TIAS 7756).
December 10 and 28, 1973 (25 UST 38; TIAS 7774).
March 23 and 25, 1974 (25 UST 307; TIAS 7807).
April 17 and 19, 1974 (25 UST 630; TIAS 7813).

Agricultural commodities agreement. Signed at Dhaka October 4, 1974; entered into force October 4, 1974.
25 UST 2833; TIAS 7949.

Amendments:
October 29 and November 8, 1974 (25 UST 2852; TIAS 7949).
December 2, 1974 (25 UST 3113; TIAS 7973).
January 27, 1975 (26 UST 117; TIAS 8016).
February 28, 1975 (26 UST 467; TIAS 8046; 992 UNTS 398).
April 11, 1975 (26 UST 470; TIAS 8046; 992 UNTS 398).
May 16, 1975 (26 UST 536; TIAS 8055; 992 UNTS 398).
June 5, 1975 (26 UST 1325; TIAS 8114).

Related agreements:
September 11, 1975 (26 UST 2738; TIAS 8191; 1045 UNTS 72).
February 23, 1976 (27 UST 1515; TIAS 8260; 1045 UNTS 79).
March 30, 1976 (27 UST 1523; TIAS 8260; 1045 UNTS 85).
April 26, 1976 (27 UST 1525; TIAS 8260; 1045 UNTS 87).

April 1, 1977 (29 UST 1549; TIAS 8898; 1115 UNTS 2).
June 30, 1977 (29 UST 1562; TIAS 8898; 1115 UNTS 10).
August 8, 1977 (29 UST 1567; TIAS 8898; 1115 UNTS 13).
September 21, 1977 (29 UST 1572; TIAS 8898; 1115 UNTS 16).
January 13, 1978 (29 UST 4510; TIAS 9065; 1148 UNTS 182).
March 3, 1978 (29 UST 4527; TIAS 9065; 1148 UNTS 191).
April 11, 1978 (29 UST 4529; TIAS 9066; 1148 UNTS 193).
May 23, 1978 (29 UST 4539; TIAS 9066; 1148 UNTS 201).
August 2, 1978 (30 UST 3205; TIAS 9389).
April 25, 1979 (30 UST 3912; TIAS 9435).
May 11, 1979 (TIAS 10642).
June 15, 1979 (TIAS 10642).
June 22, 1979 (TIAS 10642).
June 29, 1979 (TIAS 10642).
March 7, 1980 (NP).
September 5, 1980 (NP).
June 26, 1981 (NP).

Agreement for sales of agricultural commodities, with annexes and agreed minutes. Signed at Dhaka March 8, 1982; entered into force March 8, 1982.
TIAS 10483.

Amendments:
July 9 and 13, 1982 (TIAS 10483).
August 23 and 24, 1982 (TIAS 10483).
October 14, 1982 (TIAS 10483).
December 30, 1982 (TIAS 10899).
February 6, 1983 (TIAS 10899).
October 25, 1983 (TIAS 10899).
August 23, 1984 (TIAS 11048).
October 3, 1984 (TIAS 11048).
December 20, 1984 (TIAS 11048).
August 31, 1985 (NP).
December 10, 1985 (NP).
August 28, 1986 (NP).
May 15, 1988 (NP).
July 9, 1990 (NP).

Agricultural commodities agreement, with annexes. Signed at Dhaka April 17, 1987; entered into force April 17, 1987.
NP

Amendments:
August 3, 1987 (NP).
August 23, 1987 (NP).
September 1, 1987 (NP).
June 25, 1988 (NP).
September 14, 1988 (NP).
May 31, 1989 (NP).
July 24, 1989 (NP).
February 10, 1990 (NP).
June 14, 1990 (NP).

ATOMIC ENERGY

Agreement for cooperation concerning peaceful uses of nuclear energy, with annex and agreed minute. Signed at Dhaka September 17, 1981; entered into force June 24, 1982.
34 UST 63; TIAS 10339.

BANGLADESH (Cont'd)

Extension:
January 5 and February 16, 1993.

AVIATION

Agreement on aviation security. Exchange of notes at Dhaka November 23, 1992 and August 23, 1993; entered into force August 23, 1993.
TIAS 12160.

CONSERVATION

Agreement concerning the establishment of a Tropical Forest Fund and a Tropical Forest Conservation Board. Signed at Washington September 12, 2000; entered into force September 12, 2000.
TIAS

COPYRIGHT (See APPENDIX)

DEFENSE

Memorandum of understanding concerning an exchange of officers. Signed at Dhaka May 18, 1989; entered into force May 18, 1989.
TIAS 11680.

Memorandum of understanding to specify the legal status of the United States Pacific Command Disaster Relief Task Force. Signed at Dhaka May 20, 1991; entered into force May 20, 1991.
NP

Agreement regarding military assistance under the Foreign Assistance Act of 1961, as amended, and the furnishing of defense articles, related training and other defense services from the United States to Bangladesh. Exchange of notes at Dhaka September 18 and October 3, 1994; entered into force October 3, 1994.
TIAS 12273.

Agreement regarding the status of United States forces visiting Bangladesh. Exchange of notes at Dhaka August 10 and 24, 1998; entered into force August 24, 1998.
TIAS

ECONOMIC AND TECHNICAL COOPERATION

Economic, technical and related assistance agreement, with related letter. Signed at Dhaka May 21, 1974; entered into force May 21, 1974.
25 UST 1454; TIAS 7877.

Agency for International Development:
May 30, 1972 (23 UST 2540; TIAS 7443).
April 10, 1973 (24 UST 1374; TIAS 7646).
June 28, 1973 (24 UST 1786; TIAS 7689).
September 19, 1974 (25 UST 2817; TIAS 7948).
January 15, 1975 (26 UST 84; TIAS 8011).
February 12, 1975 (26 UST 385; TIAS 8040; 992 UNTS 145).
March 29, 1976 (28 UST 2103; TIAS 8536).
March 29, 1976 (29 UST 27; TIAS 8788).
April 15 and 19, 1976 (29 UST 49; TIAS 8788).
May 28, 1976 (28 UST 3209; TIAS 8583).
May 31, 1976 (29 UST 50; TIAS 8789).
September 29, 1976 (28 UST 3158; TIAS 8580).
September 29, 1976 (29 UST 76; TIAS 8791).
December 8, 1976 (28 UST 8787; TIAS 8772; 1095 UNTS 151).
August 31, 1977 (29 UST 3231; TIAS 9009; 1123 UNTS 141).
August 31, 1977 (29 UST 3287; TIAS 9013; 1123 UNTS 165).
December 15, 1977 (29 UST 4065; TIAS 9049).
March 16, 1978 (30 UST 3063; TIAS 9378).
May 31, 1978 (30 UST 4523; TIAS 9475; 1233 UNTS 151).
August 31, 1978 (30 UST 5247; TIAS 9505; 1170 UNTS 344).
June 25, 1979 (30 UST 3424; TIAS 9397; 1233 UNTS 179).
August 20, 1981 (33 UST 3688; TIAS 10250).
August 30, 1984 (NP).
August 31, 1987 (NP).
September 28, 1994 (NP).
May 9, 1997 (NP).
March 20, 2000.

FINANCE

Agreement relating to establishment of a trust account for payment by Bangladesh of certain development assistance program expenses, with related letter. Signed at Dhaka July 1, 1974; entered into force July 1, 1974.
25 UST 2403; TIAS 7918.

Agreement relating to consolidation and rescheduling of certain debts owed to the United States, with annexes. Signed at Washington March 3, 1976; entered into force May 11, 1976.
27 UST 4020; TIAS 8423; 1059 UNTS 21.

Investment incentive agreement. Signed at Washington May 19, 1998; entered into force May 19, 1998.
TIAS

Agreement regarding the reduction of certain debt related to agricultural trade owed to the Government of the United States and its agencies, with appendix. Signed at Washington September 12, 2000; entered into force September 12, 2000.
NP

INVESTMENT

Treaty concerning the reciprocal encouragement and protection of investment, with annex, protocol and exchange of letters. Signed at Washington March 12, 1986; entered into force July 25, 1989.
TIAS

PEACE CORPS

Agreement concerning the establishment of a Peace Corps program in Bangladesh. Signed at Washington July 13, 1978; entered into force July 13, 1978.
30 UST 1734; TIAS 9283; 1153 UNTS 95.

POSTAL MATTERS

International postal money order agreement, with schedules. Signed at Washington August 11, 1977; entered into force September 1, 1977.
29 UST 5431; TIAS 9120; 1148 UNTS 159.

International express mail memorandum of understanding, with detailed regulations. Signed at Dhaka and Washington April 9 and 17, 1987; entered into force June 1, 1987.
TIAS 11303.

Memorandum of understanding concerning operation of the INTELPOST service, with details of implementation. Signed at Dhaka and Washington May 16 and 24, 1989; entered into force June 15, 1989.
TIAS 11682.

TRADE

Agreement relating to trade in certain apparel categories. Exchange of notes at Washington February 19 and 24, 1986; entered into force February 24, 1986; effective February 1, 1986.
NP

Amendments and extensions:
September 15, October 8 and 17, 1986 (NP).
March 25 and 27, 1987 (NP).
August 10 and 18, 1987 (NP).
October 6 and 9, 1987 (NP).
July 14 and September 15, 1988 (NP).
June 23 and August 23, 1989 (NP).
March 6 and May 13, 1990 (NP).
January 20, February 3, March 29 and June 15, 1992 (NP).

BARBADOS

On November 30, 1966 Barbados became an independent state. In a note dated February 10, 1967 to the Secretary-General of the United Nations, the Prime Minister and Minister of External Affairs made a statement reading in part as follows:

BARBADOS (Cont'd)

"I have the honour to inform you that the Government of Barbados, conscious of the desirability of maintaining existing legal relationships, and conscious of its obligation under international law to honour its treaty commitments, acknowledges that many treaty rights and obligations of the Government of the United Kingdom in respect of Barbados were succeeded to by Barbados upon independence by virtue of customary international law.

"2. Since, however, it is likely that by virtue of customary international law certain treaties may have lapsed at the date of independence of Barbados, it seems essential that each treaty should be subjected to legal examination. It is proposed after this examination has been completed, to indicate which, if any, of the treaties which may have lapsed by customary international law the Government of Barbados wishes to treat as having lapsed.

"3. It is desired that it be presumed that each treaty has been legally succeeded to by Barbados and that action be based on this presumption until a decision is reached that it should be regarded as having lapsed. Should the Government of Barbados be of the opinion that it has legally succeeded to a treaty and wishes to terminate the operation of the treaty, it will in due course give notice of termination in the terms thereof."

AVIATION

Air transport agreement, with exchange of letters. Signed at Bridgetown April 8, 1982; entered into force April 8, 1982.
34 UST 439; TIAS 10370.

CONSULS

Consular convention between the United States and the United Kingdom. Signed at Washington June 6, 1951; entered into force September 7, 1952.
3 UST 3426; TIAS 2494; 165 UNTS 121.

Agreement continuing in force between the United States and Barbados the consular convention of June 6, 1951 between the United States and the United Kingdom. Exchange of notes at Bridgetown September 14, 1972 and May 10, 1973; entered into force May 10, 1973.
24 UST 1803; TIAS 7693.

COPYRIGHT (See APPENDIX)

DEFENSE

Agreement concerning the provision of training related to defense articles under the United States International Military Education and Training (IMET) Program. Exchange of notes at Bridgetown March 6 and April 3, 1980; entered into force April 3, 1980.
32 UST 960; TIAS 9743; 1234 UNTS 321.

ECONOMIC AND TECHNICAL COOPERATION

General agreement for economic, technical and related assistance. Signed at Bridgetown September 14, 1983; entered into force September 14, 1983.
TIAS 10829; 1590 UNTS 153.

EXTRADITION

Extradition treaty. Signed at Bridgetown February 28, 1996; entered into force March 3, 2000.
TIAS

FINANCE

Agreement relating to investment guaranties. Signed at Bridgetown March 11, 1968; entered into force March 11, 1968.
19 UST 4692; TIAS 6463; 698 UNTS 87.

JUDICIAL ASSISTANCE

Treaty on mutual legal assistance in criminal matters, with forms. Signed at Bridgetown February 28, 1996; entered into force March 3, 2000.
TIAS

METEOROLOGY

Agreement between the United States and the United Kingdom providing for a tropical meteorological research program (including Project Harp) in Barbados. Exchange of notes at Bridgetown January 7 and 15, 1963; entered into force January 15, 1963.
14 UST 109; TIAS 5276; 466 UNTS 181.

NARCOTIC DRUGS

Agreement concerning cooperation in suppressing illicit maritime drug trafficking.

Signed at Bridgetown June 25, 1997; entered into force October 11, 1998.
TIAS

PEACE CORPS

Agreement relating to the establishment of a Peace Corps program in Barbados. Exchange of notes at Bridgetown May 10 and June 8, 1982; entered into force June 8, 1982.
TIAS 10413.

PEACEKEEPING

Agreement for the furnishing of commodities and services in connection with the peacekeeping force for Grenada. Exchange of notes at Bridgetown November 25, 1983 and January 12, 1984; entered into force January 12, 1984.
TIAS 10922.

POSTAL MATTERS

Convention for the exchange of postal money orders. Signed at Washington September 27 and at Bridgetown November 30, 1933, operative October 1, 1933.
NP

Agreement for the exchange of parcels by parcel post, and detailed regulations. Signed at Washington September 13 and at Bridgetown August 14, 1939; entered into force November 1, 1938.
54 Stat. 1838; Post Office Department print; 199 LNTS 375.

International express mail agreement, with detailed regulations. Signed at Hamburg June 27, 1984; entered into force October 1, 1984.
TIAS 11006.

Memorandum of understanding concerning the operation of the INTELPOST service, with details of implementation. Signed at Bridgetown and Washington October 18 and 26, 1989; entered into force February 15, 1990.
TIAS 11704.

PROPERTY

Convention between the United States and the United Kingdom relating to the tenure and disposition of real and personal property. Signed at Washington March 2, 1899; applicable to Barbados February 9, 1901.
31 Stat. 1939; TS 146; 12 Bevans 246.

Supplementary convention relating to the tenure and disposition of real and personal property. Signed at Washington May 27, 1936; entered into force March 10, 1941.
55 Stat. 1101; TS 964; 5 Bevans 140; 203 LNTS 367.

BARBADOS (Cont'd)

TAXATION

Agreement for the exchange of information with respect to taxes. Signed at Washington November 3, 1984; entered into force November 3, 1984.
TIAS 11203.

Convention for the avoidance of double taxation and the prevention of fiscal evasion with respect to taxes on income, with exchange of notes.[1] Signed at Bridgetown December 31, 1984; entered into force February 28, 1986.
TIAS 11090.

Protocol amending the convention for the avoidance of double taxation and the prevention of fiscal evasion with respect to taxes on income signed December 31, 1984, with exchange of notes and understandings.[1] Signed at Washington December 18, 1991; entered into force December 29, 1993.
TIAS

NOTE:
[1] With reservation.

TELECOMMUNICATION

Agreement relating to the reciprocal granting of authorizations to permit licensed amateur radio operators of either country to operate their stations in the other country. Exchange of notes at Bridgetown September 10 and 12, 1968; entered into force September 12, 1968.
19 UST 5994; TIAS 6553; 702 UNTS 175.

TRADE-MARKS

Declaration by the United States and the United Kingdom affording reciprocal protection to trade-marks. Signed at London October 24, 1877; entered into force October 24, 1877.
20 Stat. 703; TS 138; 12 Bevans 198.

WEATHER STATIONS

Agreement relating to a cooperative program for operation and maintenance of a rawinsonde station at Seawell Airport, Barbados. Exchange of notes at Bridgetown October 13, 1975; entered into force October 13, 1975; effective July 1, 1970.
26 UST 2557; TIAS 8174; 1028 UNTS 37.

BELARUS

For agreements prior to December 31, 1991, see UNION OF SOVIET SOCIALIST REPUBLICS.

COPYRIGHT (See APPENDIX)

CUSTOMS

Agreement regarding cooperation and mutual assistance between their customs services. Exchange of notes at Minsk January 14, 1994; entered into force January 14, 1994.
TIAS 12531.

DEFENSE

Agreement concerning the provision of material and services for the establishment of a continuous communications link, with annexes. Signed at Minsk January 15, 1993; entered into force January 15, 1993.
TIAS

EMPLOYMENT

Agreement relating to the employment of dependents of official government employees. Exchange of notes at Washington June 14 and July 26, 1996; entered into force July 26, 1996.
TIAS

FINANCE

Investment incentive agreement. Signed at Minsk June 24, 1992; entered into force June 24, 1992.
TIAS 12460.

POSTAL MATTERS

International express mail agreement, with detailed regulations. Signed at Minsk and Washington September 21 and November 8, 1993; entered into force January 1, 1994.
NP

Postal money order agreement. Signed at Washington and Minsk May 1 and November 7, 1996; entered into force January 1, 1997.
NP

TRADE AND COMMERCE

Agreement on trade relations. Exchange of notes at Minsk January 6 and February 16, 1993; entered into force February 16, 1993.
TIAS 12488.

WEAPONS

Agreement concerning emergency response and the prevention of proliferation of weapons of mass destruction. Signed at Washington October 22, 1992; entered into force October 22, 1992.
TIAS

Amendments and extensions:
April 29, 1993.
July 22, 1993.
January 24 and 29, 1997.
January 14 and 21, 1998.

Agreement concerning the conversion of military technologies and capabilities into civilian activities. Signed at Washington July 22, 1993; entered into force July 22, 1993.
TIAS

Agreement concerning the environmental restoration of former Strategic Rocket Forces facilities and sites to promote the prevention of proliferation of weapons of mass destruction. Signed at Washington July 22, 1993; entered into force July 22, 1993.
TIAS

Agreement concerning the disposal of the remnants of dismantled conventional military equipment, with annex. Signed at Minsk August 12, 1994; entered into force August 12, 1994.
TIAS

Agreement concerning the elimination of strategic offensive arms. Signed at Minsk June 23, 1995; entered into force June 23, 1995.
TIAS

Agreement concerning control, accounting and physical protection of nuclear material to promote the prevention of nuclear weapons proliferation. Signed at Minsk June 23, 1995; entered into force June 23, 1995.
TIAS

BELGIUM

ATOMIC ENERGY

Agreement for cooperation on the use of atomic energy for mutual defense purposes. Signed at Brussels May 17, 1962; entered into force September 5, 1962.
13 UST 1995; TIAS 5157; 461 UNTS 3.

Agreement in the field of radioactive waste management. Signed at Mol and Washington January 7 and 19, 1981; entered into force January 19, 1981.
32 UST 4569; TIAS 9970; 1268 UNTS 83.

Agreement relating to severe nuclear accident research. Signed at Washington and Brussels March 29 and April 18, 1983; entered into force April 18, 1983; effective February 10, 1983.
TIAS 10692.

Arrangement for the exchange of technical information and cooperation in nuclear safety matters, with appendices. Signed at Wash-

BELGIUM (Cont'd)

ington May 2, 1988; entered into force May 2, 1988.
TIAS 12231.

Extension:
March 19 and 20, 1996.

AUTOMOTIVE TRAFFIC

Agreement regarding the facilitation of road travel in the United States for holders of Belgian driving permits and in Belgium for holders of United States driving permits. Exchange of notes at Brussels February 4 and 12, 1971; entered into force February 12, 1971.
22 UST 1525; TIAS 7172; 806 UNTS 281.

AVIATION

Agreement relating to the reciprocal acceptance of airworthiness certifications. Exchange of notes at Brussels February 12 and May 14, 1973; entered into force May 14, 1973.
24 UST 1720; TIAS 7675.

Air transport agreement. Exchange of notes at Washington October 23, 1980; entered into force October 23, 1980.
32 UST 3515; TIAS 9903; 1275 UNTS 103.

Amendments:
September 22 and November 12, 1986.
November 5, 1993 and January 12, 1994.

Memorandum of agreement concerning assistance in developing and modernizing Belgium's civil aviation infrastructure. Signed at Washington and Brussels June 19 and July 30, 1998; entered into force July 30, 1998.
TIAS

CLAIMS

Agreement relating to reciprocity on indemnification for war damages to private property. Exchanges of notes at Brussels December 5, 1949, March 17 and December 1, 1950, and March 12, 1951; entered into force March 12, 1951.
2 UST 943; TIAS 2248; 93 UNTS 109.

COMMERCE

Convention in addition to the treaty of July 17, 1858, with annexed declaration.[1] Signed at Brussels May 20, 1863; entered into force June 27, 1864.
13 Stat. 647; TS 22; 5 Bevans 468.

Treaty providing for the extinguishment of the Scheldt dues. Signed at Brussels July 20, 1863; entered into force June 27, 1864.
13 Stat. 655; TS 23; 5 Bevans 471.

Treaty of friendship, establishment and navigation, with protocol. Signed at Brussels February 21, 1961; entered into force October 3, 1963.
14 UST 1284; TIAS 5432; 480 UNTS 149.

NOTE:
[1] Articles I and IV remain in force perpetually; remaining articles terminated July 1, 1875 with termination of 1858 treaty (12 Stat. 1043; TS 20; 5 Bevans 454).

CONSULS

Consular convention with exchanges of notes. Signed at Washington September 2, 1969; entered into force January 5, 1974.
25 UST 41; TIAS 7775.

COPYRIGHT (See APPENDIX)

CUSTOMS

Arrangement relating to the granting to diplomatic and consular personnel, on a reciprocal basis, of exemption from duties and import taxes on merchandise imported for their personal use. Exchange of notes at Brussels February 26 and May 28, 1948; entered into force May 28, 1948.
5 Bevans 670.

Agreement regarding mutual assistance between customs services. Signed at Brussels June 26, 1991; entered into force May 1, 1993.
TIAS 12111.

DEFENSE (See also MUTUAL SECURITY)

Mutual defense assistance agreement. Signed at Washington January 27, 1950; entered into force March 30, 1950.
1 UST 1; TIAS 2010; 51 UNTS 213.

Agreement concerning export licenses for goods bought in the Belgo-Luxembourg Economic Union for common defense effort under the offshore procurement program. Exchange of notes at Brussels June 18, 1953; entered into force June 18, 1953.
4 UST 1; TIAS 2760; 222 UNTS 3.

Agreement relating to offshore procurement with exchange of notes. Signed at Brussels September 2, 1953; entered into force July 22, 1954.
5 UST 1311; TIAS 3000; 200 UNTS 127.

Agreement approving the standard offshore procurement contract with Belgium. Signed at Brussels November 19, 1953; entered into force July 22, 1954.
5 UST 1334; TIAS 3001; 233 UNTS 310.

Amendment:
May 13 and July 19, 1954 (5 UST 2254; TIAS 3085; 237 UNTS 342).

Agreement relating to the disposal of redistributable and excess property furnished in connection with the mutual defense assistance program. Signed at Brussels November 17, 1953; entered into force March 10, 1955.
6 UST 495; TIAS 3182; 251 UNTS 105.

Agreement concerning the participation of the Belgian forces in United Nations operations in Korea. Signed at Washington July 15, 1955; entered into force July 15, 1955.
6 UST 2829; TIAS 3325; 223 UNTS 3.

Agreement relating to a weapons production program. Exchange of notes at Brussels April 6 and 22, 1960; entered into force April 22, 1960.
11 UST 1368; TIAS 4472; 372 UNTS 277.

Arrangement pursuant to the mutual defense assistance agreement of January 27, 1950 relating to the disposition of equipment and materials furnished under the mutual defense assistance program. Exchange of notes at Brussels July 7, 1961; entered into force July 7, 1961.
12 UST 1174; TIAS 4830; 416 UNTS 301.

Agreement concerning certain communications facilities. Signed at Brussels April 19, 1963; entered into force April 19, 1963.
14 UST 414; TIAS 5334; 476 UNTS 29.

Memorandum of understanding concerning the principles governing mutual cooperation in the research, development, production, procurement and logistic support of defense equipment. Signed at Brussels December 12, 1979; entered into force December 12, 1979.
TIAS

Agreement concerning provision of mutual logistic support, with annexes. Signed at Brussels and Stuttgart May 6 and 11, 1982; entered into force May 11, 1982.
TIAS 12275.

Amendments:
July 1 and 10, 1991 (TIAS 12275).
May 1 and 22, 1992 (TIAS 12275).
October 27 and 30, 1997.

Memorandum of understanding on the exchange of officers between the United States and Belgian air forces. Signed at Brussels and Washington September 22 and November 2, 1983; entered into force November 2, 1983.
TIAS 10804.

Agreement concerning the status of a U.S. ground launched cruise missile (GLCM) unit to be located in Belgium. Exchange of notes at Brussels February 13, 1984; entered into force February 13, 1984.
TIAS 10943.

BELGIUM (Cont'd)

Implementing arrangement concerning mutual logistic support, with annexes. Signed at Evere, Belgium and Patch Barracks, Germany October 27 and 30, 1997; entered into force October 30, 1997.
TIAS

ECONOMIC AND TECHNICAL COOPERATION

Economic cooperation agreement. Signed at Brussels July 2, 1948; entered into force July 29, 1948.
62 Stat. 2173; TIAS 1781; 5 Bevans 678; 19 UNTS 127.

Amendments:
November 22 and 29, 1948 (62 Stat. 3776; TIAS 1906; 5 Bevans 703; 31 UNTS 485).
June 29, 1950 (1 UST 510; TIAS 2093; 76 UNTS 250).
September 10, 1951 (2 UST 2057; TIAS 2334; 140 UNTS 428).
December 11, 1952 and March 5, 1953 (4 UST 435; TIAS 2790; 207 UNTS 316).

EDUCATION

Agreement for the financing of certain academic and cultural exchanges and programs in the field of education. Signed at Brussels December 12, 1968; entered into force May 13, 1971.
22 UST 1538; TIAS 7175; 806 UNTS 231.

EXTRADITION

Extradition treaty. Signed at Brussels April 27, 1987; entered into force September 1, 1997.
TIAS

FINANCE

Debt funding agreement. Signed at Washington August 18, 1925; operative June 15, 1925.
Treasury Department print; 5 Bevans 531.

Agreement modifying the debt funding agreement of August 18, 1925. Signed at Washington June 10, 1932; operative July 1, 1931.
Treasury Department print; 5 Bevans 561.

Agreement relating to guaranties authorized by section 111(b)(3) of the Economic Cooperation Act of 1948, as amended. Exchange of notes at Washington May 7 and 12, 1952; entered into force May 12, 1952.
3 UST 4285; TIAS 2575; 179 UNTS 15.

JUDICIAL ASSISTANCE

Procedures for mutual assistance in the administration of justice in connection with the Lockheed Aircraft Corporation matter. Signed at Washington May 21, 1976; entered into force May 21, 1976.
27 UST 1966; TIAS 8292.

Treaty on mutual legal assistance in criminal matters, with attachment. Signed at Washington January 28, 1988; entered into force January 1, 2000.
TIAS

LEND-LEASE

Preliminary agreement regarding principles applying to mutual aid in the prosecution of the war against aggression. Signed at Washington June 16, 1942; entered into force June 16, 1942.
56 Stat. 1504; EAS 254; 5 Bevans 571; 105 UNTS 159.

Agreement relating to principles applying to the provision of aid to the armed forces of the United States. Exchange of notes at Washington April 17 and 19, 1945; operative June 16, 1942.
59 Stat. 1642; EAS 481; 5 Bevans 606; 139 UNTS 279.

Agreement relating to supplies and services, with memorandum of interpretation and exchanges of notes. Signed at Washington April 17 and 19 and May 19, 1945; entered into force April 17, 1945.
59 Stat. 1642; EAS 481; 5 Bevans 594; 139 UNTS 279.

LEND-LEASE SETTLEMENT

Memorandum of understanding regarding settlement for lend-lease, reciprocal aid, Plan A, surplus property and claims. Agreement relating to the transfer of United States surplus property in Belgium.

Memorandum of agreement regarding the purchase of Belgian francs for use by United States armed forces. Signed at Washington September 24, 1946. Exchanges of letters signed at Washington September 24, 1946. Exchanges of memorandums signed at Washington July 23 and September 24, 1946; entered into force September 24, 1946.
62 Stat. 3984; TIAS 2064; 5 Bevans 631; 132 UNTS 80.

Amendments:
May 12, 1949 (63 Stat. 2837; TIAS 2070; 5 Bevans 708; 132 UNTS 126).
January 20 and April 2, 1954 (5 UST 647; TIAS 2953; 229 UNTS 304).

MAPPING

Basic exchange and cooperative agreement concerning mapping, charting and geodesy cooperation. Signed at Fairfax March 1, 1994; entered into force March 1, 1994.
NP

MILITARY CEMETERIES AND MONUMENTS

Agreement concerning American military cemeteries, and related note of December 24, 1959. Signed at Brussels November 27, 1959; entered into force November 27, 1959.
10 UST 2124; TIAS 4383; 366 UNTS 331.

Amendment:
January 8, 1962 and October 24, 1963 (14 UST 1542; TIAS 5455; 489 UNTS 393).

MUTUAL SECURITY

Agreement relating to the assurances required under the Mutual Security Act of 1951. Exchange of notes at Brussels January 7, 1952; entered into force January 7, 1952.
3 UST 4529; TIAS 2601; 179 UNTS 81.

NARCOTIC DRUGS

Arrangement for the direct exchange of certain information regarding the traffic in narcotic drugs. Exchange of notes at Brussels February 6 and June 13, 1928; entered into force June 13, 1928.
5 Bevans 545.

PACIFIC SETTLEMENT OF DISPUTES

Treaty of arbitration. Signed at Washington March 20, 1929; entered into force August 25, 1930.
46 Stat. 2790; TS 823; 5 Bevans 547; 109 LNTS 267.

Treaty of conciliation. Signed at Washington March 20, 1929; entered into force August 25, 1930.
46 Stat. 2794; TS 824; 5 Bevans 549; 109 LNTS 261.

PATENTS

Agreement to facilitate the interchange of patent rights and technical information for defense purposes. Signed at Brussels October 12, 1954; entered into force October 12, 1954.
5 UST 2318; TIAS 3093; 202 UNTS 289.

BELGIUM (Cont'd)

Agreement approving the procedures for reciprocal filing of classified patent applications. Exchange of notes at Brussels May 6 and 18, 1960; entered into force May 18, 1960.
11 UST 1464; TIAS 4488.

POSTAL MATTERS

Money order convention. Signed at Washington November 20, 1882; entered into force January 1, 1883.
22 Stat. 1009.

Agreement concerning the exchange of parcel post, and regulations of execution. Signed at Washington January 5, 1939; entered into force May 1, 1939.
53 Stat. 2100; Post Office Department print; 199 LNTS 321.

Memorandum of understanding relating to the initiation of express mail/datapost service. Signed at Washington and Brussels March 6 and 28, 1975; entered into force March 28, 1975; effective April 1, 1975.
29 UST 95; TIAS 8796.

SCIENTIFIC COOPERATION

Memorandum of understanding concerning the furnishing of balloon launching and associated services. Signed at Washington June 8 and 15, 1983; entered into force June 15, 1983.
TIAS 10754.

SEABEDS

Agreement relating to the agreement of August 14, 1987 on the resolution of practical problems with respect to deep seabed mining areas.[1] Exchange of notes at Brussels August 14, 1987; entered into force August 14, 1987.
TIAS 11438.

NOTE:
[1] Parties to the multilateral agreement of August 14, 1987 are Belgium, Canada, Italy, Netherlands and Union of Soviet Socialist Republics.

SHIPPING

Agreement relating to jurisdiction over vessels utilizing the Louisiana Offshore Oil Port. Exchange of notes at Washington December 1 and 9, 1983; entered into force December 9, 1983.
TIAS 10853.

SMUGGLING

Convention for the prevention of smuggling of alcoholic beverages into the United States. Signed at Washington December 9, 1925; entered into force January 11, 1928.
45 Stat. 2456; TS 759; 5 Bevans 539; 72 LNTS 171.

SOCIAL SECURITY

Agreement on social security, with final protocol. Signed at Washington February 19, 1982; entered into force July 1, 1984.
TIAS 11175.

Additional protocol and administrative agreement for the implementation of the agreement on social security of February 19, 1982. Signed at Brussels November 23, 1982; entered into force July 1, 1984.
TIAS 11175.

TAXATION

Agreement relating to relief from taxation of United States expenditures in Belgium for common defense. Exchange of notes at Brussels March 18 and April 7, 1952; entered into force April 7, 1952.
3 UST 5245; TIAS 2719; 205 UNTS 3.

Convention for the avoidance of double taxation and the prevention of fiscal evasion with respect to taxes on income. Signed at Brussels July 9, 1970; entered into force October 13, 1972.
23 UST 2687; TIAS 7463.

Supplementary protocol modifying and supplementing the convention of July 9, 1970 for the avoidance of double taxation and the prevention of fiscal evasion with respect to taxes on income, with exchange of notes. Signed at Washington December 31, 1987; entered into force August 3, 1989.
TIAS 11254.

Agreement concerning relief from double taxation on income derived from the operation of ships and aircraft. Exchange of notes at Washington October 14, 1987 and March 21, 1988; entered into force March 21, 1988.
TIAS 11571.

TELECOMMUNICATION

Agreement relating to the reciprocal granting of authorizations to permit licensed amateur radio operators of either country to operate their stations in the other country. Exchange of notes at Brussels June 15 and 18, 1965; entered into force June 18, 1965.
16 UST 869; TIAS 5824; 549 UNTS 95.

TRADE (See COMMERCE; BENELUX)

VISAS

Agreement relating to the reciprocal waiver of visas and visa fees. Exchange of notes at Brussels May 3 and 23, 1962; entered into force May 23, 1962; operative June 22, 1962.
13 UST 1246; TIAS 5071; 434 UNTS 133.

Amendment:
March 9 and April 20, 1971 (22 UST 678; TIAS 7124; 778 UNTS 227).

BENELUX (BELGIUM, NETHERLANDS, LUXEMBOURG)

TRADE

Agreement providing trade concessions on certain items under the general agreement on tariffs and trade. Signed at Geneva June 8, 1955; entered into force July 24, 1955.
6 UST 6229; TIAS 3473.

Agreement supplementary to the general agreement on tariffs and trade, with exchanges of notes. Signed at Washington June 27, 1957; entered into force June 27, 1957.
8 UST 933; TIAS 3854; 284 UNTS 139.

Agreement providing compensatory concessions under the general agreement on tariffs and trade for certain tariff actions taken by the United States. Exchange of notes at Geneva January 29 and February 1, 1962; entered into force February 1, 1962.
13 UST 928; TIAS 5032.

BELIZE

On September 21, 1981 Belize became an independent state. In a letter dated September 29, 1982 to the Secretary General of the United Nations, the Prime Minister and Minister of Foreign Affairs of Belize made a statement reading in part as follows:

"I have the honour to inform you that the Government of Belize has decided to continue to apply provisionally and on the basis of reciprocity, all treaties to which the Government of the United Kingdom of Great Britain and Northern Ireland was a party, the application of which was extended either expressly or by necessary implication to the then dependent territory of Belize.

"Such provisional application would subsist until Belize otherwise notifies Your Excellency, the depository (in the case of a multilateral treaty), or the state party (in the case of a bilateral treaty.)"

BELIZE (Cont'd)

AGRICULTURE

Agreement confirming the cooperative agreement for the prevention of foot-and-mouth disease and rinderpest in British Honduras. Signed at Belize September 6 and 12, 1972; entered into force September 12, 1972.
23 UST 2592; TIAS 7447.

Memorandum of understanding relating to cooperative efforts to protect crops from plant pest damage and plant diseases. Signed at Washington December 8, 1976; entered into force December 8, 1976.
28 UST 8703; TIAS 8767.

AVIATION

Agreement between the United States and the United Kingdom concerning air services, with annexes and exchange of letters. Signed at Bermuda July 23, 1977; entered into force July 23, 1977.
28 UST 5367; TIAS 8641.

Amendments:
April 25, 1978 (29 UST 2680; TIAS 8965).
December 27, 1979 (32 UST 524; TIAS 9722).
December 4, 1980 (33 UST 655; TIAS 10059).

CONSULS

Consular convention between the United States and the United Kingdom. Signed at Washington June 6, 1951; entered into force September 7, 1952.
3 UST 3426; TIAS 2494; 165 UNTS 121.

COPYRIGHT (See APPENDIX)

DEFENSE

Agreement concerning the provision of training related to defense articles under the United States International Military Education and Training (IMET) Program. Exchange of notes at Belize and Belmopan December 8, 1981 and January 15, 1982; entered into force January 15, 1982.
34 UST 23; TIAS 10334.

Agreement concerning grants of defense articles and services to Belize from U.S. military stocks. Exchange of notes at Belize and Belmopan August 6 and 23, 1990; entered into force August 23, 1990.
TIAS 11743.

ECONOMIC AND TECHNICAL COOPERATION

Agreement relating to economic and technical cooperation. Signed at Belmopan March 8, 1983; entered into force March 8, 1983.
TIAS 10670.

EXTRADITION

Extradition treaty between the United States and the United Kingdom with protocol of signature and exchange of notes. Signed at London June 8, 1972; entered into force January 21, 1977.
28 UST 227; TIAS 8468.

FINANCE

Agreement relating to investment guaranties. Signed at Belize February 8, 1966; entered into force February 8, 1966.
17 UST 347; TIAS 5983; 685 UNTS 47.

HEALTH

Memorandum of understanding concerning a cooperative medical research program. Signed at Belmopan December 12, 1989; entered into force December 12, 1989.
TIAS 11729.

NARCOTIC DRUGS

Mutual cooperation for reducing demand, preventing illicit use and combatting illicit production and traffic of drugs. Signed at Belmopan February 9, 1989; entered into force February 9, 1989.
TIAS 11600.

Agreement concerning maritime counter-drug operations. Signed at Belmopan December 23, 1992; entered into force December 23, 1992.
TIAS 11914.

PEACE CORPS

Agreement relating to the establishment of a Peace Corps program in British Honduras. Exchange of notes at Belize July 26 and August 15, 1962; entered into force August 15, 1962.
13 UST 1868; TIAS 5137; 580 UNTS 189.

POSTAL MATTERS

Money order agreement. Signed at Washington August 1 and at Belize August 17, 1906; operative October 1, 1906.
NP

Parcel post agreement, with details of implementation. Signed at Belize City and Washington September 14 and 28, 1982; entered into force January 1, 1983.
TIAS 10512; 1777 UNTS 373.

International express mail agreement, with detailed regulations. Signed at Belize and Washington October 28 and November 13, 1992; entered into force December 14, 1992.
TIAS 11906.

PROPERTY

Convention between the United States and the United Kingdom relating to the tenure and disposition of real and personal property. Signed at Washington March 2, 1899; applicable to Belize February 9, 1901.
31 Stat. 1939; TS 146; 12 Bevans 246.

Supplementary convention relating to the tenure and disposition of real and personal property of March 2, 1899. Signed at Washington May 27, 1936; entered into force March 10, 1941.
55 Stat. 1101; TS 964; 5 Bevans 140; 203 LNTS 367.

TELECOMMUNICATION

Agreement between the United States and the United Kingdom relating to the reciprocal granting of authorizations to permit licensed amateur radio operators of either country to operate their stations in the other country. Exchange of notes at London November 26, 1965; applicable to Belize December 11, 1969.
16 UST 2047; TIAS 5941; 561 UNTS 193.

Agreement between the United States and the United Kingdom extending to certain territories the application of the agreement of November 26, 1965 relating to the reciprocal granting of authorizations to permit licensed amateur radio operators of either country to operate their stations in the other country. Exchange of notes at London December 11, 1969; entered into force December 11, 1969.
20 UST 4089; TIAS 6800; 732 UNTS 334.

Arrangement relating to radio communications between amateur stations on behalf of third parties. Exchange of notes at Belmopan and Belize May 3 and 23, 1984; entered into force June 22, 1984.
TIAS 11198.

Agreement concerning establishment of a radio relay station of the United States Information Agency (VOA) in Belize, with annexes.

BELIZE (Cont'd)

Signed at Belize September 20, 1984; entered into force September 20, 1984.
TIAS 11199.

TRADE-MARKS

Declaration by the United States and the United Kingdom affording reciprocal protection to trade-marks. Signed at London October 24, 1877; entered into force October 24, 1877.
20 Stat. 703; TS 138; 12 Bevans 198.

WEATHER STATIONS

Agreement relating to the establishment, operation and maintenance of an upper air (rawinsonde) observation station at Belize International Airport, with memorandum of arrangement. Exchange of letters at Belize and Belmopan August 26, 1981; entered into force August 26, 1981.
33 UST 3709; TIAS 10253; 1541 UNTS 71.

BENIN

COPYRIGHT (See APPENDIX)

DEFENSE

Agreement relating to the furnishing of military equipment, materials and services to Dahomey (Benin) to help assure its security and independence. Exchange of notes at Cotonou June 5 and 13, 1962; entered into force June 13, 1962.
13 UST 1285; TIAS 5078; 458 UNTS 219.

Agreement concerning the provision of training related to defense articles under the United States International Military Education and Training (IMET) Program. Exchange of notes at Cotonou May 15 and October 15, 1984; entered into force October 15, 1984.
TIAS 10988.

Agreement regarding military assistance under the Foreign Assistance Act of 1961, as amended, and the furnishing of defense articles, related training and other defense services from the United States to Benin. Exchange of notes at Cotonou September 26 and October 3, 1994; entered into force October 3, 1994.
TIAS 12276.

Agreement on the establishment of a joint commission for military cooperation. Signed at Cotonou January 19, 1996; entered into force January 19, 1996.
TIAS

Agreement regarding the provision of commodities, services and related training to assist the Republic of Benin's forces participating in the African Crisis Response Initiative. Exchange of notes at Cotonou June 24 and July 23, 1998; entered into force July 23, 1998.
TIAS

Agreement regarding the status of U.S. military personnel and civilian employees of the U.S. Department of Defense temporarily present in Benin in connection with the African Crisis Response Initiative and other activities. Exchange of notes at Cotonou June 24 and July 29, 1998; entered into force July 29, 1998.
TIAS

ECONOMIC AND TECHNICAL COOPERATION

Agreement relating to economic, technical and related assistance. Exchange of notes at Cotonou May 27, 1961; entered into force May 27, 1961.
13 UST 347; TIAS 4989; 455 UNTS 23.

EMPLOYMENT

Agreement relating to the employment of dependents of official government employees. Exchange of notes at Washington September 22 and December 3, 1998; entered into force December 3, 1998.
TIAS

ENVIRONMENTAL COOPERATION

Agreement regarding the Global Learning and Observations to Benefit the Environment (GLOBE) Program, with appendices. Signed at Cotonou April 28, 1995; entered into force April 28, 1995.
TIAS 12639.

FINANCE

Agreement regarding the consolidation and rescheduling of certain debts owed to, guaranteed by, or insured by the United States Government and its agency, with annexes. Signed at Cotonou November 20, 1989; entered into force December 28, 1989.
NP

Investment incentive agreement. Signed at Washington November 30, 1998; entered into force November 30, 1998.
TIAS

PEACE CORPS

Agreement relating to the establishment of a Peace Corps program. Exchange of notes at Cotonou June 30 and July 3, 1967; entered into force July 3, 1967.
18 UST 1606; TIAS 6302; 692 UNTS 323.

POSTAL MATTERS

International express mail agreement, with detailed regulations. Signed at Cotonou and Washington July 6 and 26, 1988; entered into force September 15, 1988.
TIAS 11590.

Postal money order agreement. Signed at Cotonou and Washington December 15, 1994 and January 10, 1995; entered into force April 1, 1995.
NP

BHUTAN

POSTAL MATTERS

International express mail agreement. Signed at Thimphu and Washington June 3 and July 6, 1993; entered into force August 1, 1993.
NP

BOLIVIA

AGRICULTURAL COMMODITIES

Agricultural commodities agreement. Signed at La Paz June 7, 1957; entered into force June 7, 1957.
8 UST 821; TIAS 3841; 291 UNTS 77.

Amendments:
June 17 and 21, 1957 (8 UST 866; TIAS 3847; 291 UNTS 86).
August 30, 1957 (8 UST 1427; TIAS 3897; 291 UNTS 89).

Agricultural commodities agreement, with exchange of notes. Signed at La Paz November 15, 1961; entered into force November 15, 1961.
13 UST 1197; TIAS 5064; 456 UNTS 191.

Agricultural commodities agreement, with exchange of notes. Signed at La Paz February 12, 1962; entered into force February 12, 1962.
13 UST 1042; TIAS 5047; 451 UNTS 281.

Amendments:
March 27, 1962 (13 UST 1042; TIAS 5047; 451 UNTS 281).
July 14, 1962 (13 UST 1773; TIAS 5121; 458 UNTS 368).

BOLIVIA (Cont'd)

December 6, 1962 (13 UST 2631; TIAS 5233; 462 UNTS 370).
March 29, 1963 (14 UST 349; TIAS 5320; 474 UNTS 367).

Agricultural commodities agreement with exchange of notes. Signed at La Paz December 17, 1962; entered into force December 17, 1962.
13 UST 3844; TIAS 5259; 469 UNTS 121.

Amendment:
June 24, 1963 (14 UST 1727; TIAS 5478; 494 UNTS 341).

Agricultural commodities agreement. Signed at La Paz February 4, 1963; entered into force February 4, 1963.
14 UST 172; TIAS 5292; 473 UNTS 65.

Amendments:
March 29, 1963 (14 UST 361; TIAS 5323; 473 UNTS 74).
June 24, 1963 (14 UST 1730; TIAS 5479; 494 UNTS 346).
November 20, 1963 (14 UST 1730; TIAS 5479; 494 UNTS 349).
April 27, 1964 (15 UST 392; TIAS 5569; 526 UNTS 343).

Agricultural commodities agreement with exchange of notes. Signed at La Paz March 25, 1964; entered into force March 25, 1964.
15 UST 2258; TIAS 5716; 532 UNTS 3.

Agricultural commodities agreement with exchange of notes. Signed at La Paz May 12, 1965; entered into force May 12, 1965.
16 UST 1191; TIAS 5866; 564 UNTS 143.

Agricultural commodities agreement, with exchange of notes. Signed at La Paz August 17, 1965; entered into force August 17, 1965. .
16 UST 1218; TIAS 5871; 587 UNTS 289.

Amendment:
November 30, 1966 (17 UST 2252; TIAS 6164; 681 UNTS 380).

Agricultural commodities agreement with exchange of notes. Signed at La Paz April 22, 1966; entered into force April 22, 1966.
17 UST 645; TIAS 6013; 578 UNTS 73.

Agricultural commodities agreement with annex. Signed at La Paz January 16, 1968; entered into force January 16, 1968.
19 UST 6153; TIAS 6571; 701 UNTS 285.

Amendment:
February 12 and April 16, 1971 (22 UST 568; TIAS 7101; 792 UNTS 388).

Related agreements:
January 16, 1968 (19 UST 6199; TIAS 6573; 701 UNTS 323).
March 7, 1969 (20 UST 481; TIAS 6652; 707 UNTS 167).

March 7, 1969 (20 UST 486; TIAS 6653; 707 UNTS 181).
March 24, 1971 and April 20, 1972 (23 UST 3192; TIAS 7497; 898 UNTS 327).

Agricultural commodities agreement with annex and memorandum of understanding. Signed at La Paz April 29, 1971; entered into force April 29, 1971.
22 UST 1861; TIAS 7231, 837 UNTS 3.

Amendments:
December 30, 1971 (22 UST 2122; TIAS 7257).
June 5 and 7, 1972 (23 UST 3221; TIAS 7500; 898 UNTS 344).

Related agreements:
December 20, 1972 (25 UST 156; TIAS 7777).
November 9, 1973 (25 UST 164; TIAS 7777).
December 28, 1973 (25 UST 166; TIAS 7777).
September 22 and October 18, 1976 (28 UST 8180; TIAS 8753).

Agricultural commodities agreement, with memorandum of understanding. Signed at La Paz February 4, 1985; entered into force February 4, 1985.
NP

Amendment:
August 20, 1985 (NP).

Agricultural commodities agreement with annexes. Signed at La Paz April 9, 1986; entered into force April 9, 1986.
NP

Amendments:
April 22, 1987 (NP).
June 8 and 10, 1988 (NP).
February 15, 1989 (NP).

Agricultural commodities agreement. Signed at Washington May 9, 1990; entered into force May 9, 1990.
NP

AVIATION

Agreement relating to the sending of a technical mission to Bolivia to assist in the development of Bolivian civil aviation. Exchange of notes at La Paz August 26 and November 3, 1947; entered into force November 3, 1947.
61 Stat. 3863; TIAS 1739; 5 Bevans 778; 51 UNTS 33.

Air transport agreement. Signed at La Paz September 29, 1948; entered into force November 4, 1948.
14 UST 2209; TIAS 5507; 505 UNTS 139.

Amendments:
May 4 and 17, 1967 (18 UST 2362; TIAS 6340).
June 28 and August 23, 1988 (TIAS 11642).

Memorandum of agreement concerning assistance in developing and modernizing Bolivia's civil aviation system, with annex. Signed at

Washington and La Paz March 1 and June 8, 1988; entered into force June 8, 1988.
TIAS 11587.

COMMERCE

Treaty of peace, friendship, commerce and navigation.[1] Signed at La Paz May 13, 1858; entered into force November 9, 1862.
12 Stat. 1003; TS 32; 5 Bevans 721.

NOTE:
[1] Article 34 terminated by the United States, effective July 1, 1916, in accordance with the Seamen's Act (38 Stat. 1164).

CONSULS (See COMMERCE)

COPYRIGHT (See APPENDIX)

DEFENSE

Military assistance agreement. Exchange of notes at La Paz March 21 and April 22, 1958; entered into force April 22, 1958.
9 UST 953; TIAS 4061; 317 UNTS 209.

Agreement relating to the furnishing of defense articles and services to Bolivia. Exchange of notes at La Paz April 26, 1962; entered into force April 26, 1962.
13 UST 2294; TIAS 5197; 461 UNTS 105.

Agreement relating to the deposit by Bolivia of ten percent of the value of grant military assistance and excess defense articles furnished by the United States. Exchange of notes at La Paz March 27 and May 2, 1972; entered into force May 2, 1972; effective February 7, 1972.
23 UST 892; TIAS 7352.

Agreement concerning payment to the United States of net proceeds from the sale of defense articles furnished under the military assistance program. Exchange of notes at La Paz May 31 and June 28, 1974; entered into force July 1, 1974.
25 UST 1557; TIAS 7893.

Agreement concerning United States Armed Forces technical personnel deployments to Bolivia. Exchange of notes at La Paz February 4 and 13, 1997; entered into force February 13, 1997.
TIAS

Agreement concerning security assistance matters and the provision of articles, services and associated military education and training by the United States Government for anti-narcotics purposes. Exchange of notes at La Paz October 27 and November 5, 1998; entered into force November 5, 1998.
TIAS

BOLIVIA (Cont'd)

ECONOMIC AND TECHNICAL COOPERATION

General agreement for technical cooperation. Signed at La Paz March 14, 1951; entered into force March 14, 1951.
2 UST 671; TIAS 2221; 132 UNTS 319.

Amendments:
December 14, 1951 and January 2, 7 and 8, 1952 (3 UST 4686; TIAS 2625; 180 UNTS 346).
August 27, 1953 and January 15, 1954 (5 UST 518; TIAS 2944; 229 UNTS 213).

Agreement providing economic assistance to Bolivia. Signed at La Paz November 6, 1953; entered into force November 6, 1953.
4 UST 2297; TIAS 2883; 222 UNTS 41.

Amendment:
August 24 and November 11, 1959 (10 UST 3023; TIAS 4395; 367 UNTS 319).

Agency for International Development:
December 29, 1975 (28 UST 437; TIAS 8475; 1071 UNTS 201).
March 24, 1976 (28 UST 1315; TIAS 8514; 1071 UNTS 279).
September 20, 1976 (28 UST 7529; TIAS 8714).
September 22 and October 18, 1976 (28 UST 8180; TIAS 8753).
August 30, 1977 (29 UST 2975; TIAS 8994).
November 24, 1977 (29 UST 3891; TIAS 9043).
January 9, 1978 (30 UST 1675; TIAS 9276; 1152 UNTS 69).
July 5, 1991 (NP).
August 21, 1992 (NP).

EMPLOYMENT

Agreement relating to the employment of dependents of official government employees. Exchange of notes at La Paz March 5, 1982; entered into force March 5, 1982.
34 UST 291; TIAS 10355.

ENVIRONMENTAL COOPERATION

Agreement concerning the establishment of an Enterprise for the Americas Environmental Account at the National Fund for the Environment. Signed at Washington November 26, 1991; entered into force November 26, 1991.
TIAS 11849.

Agreement concerning cooperation in the Global Learning and Observations to Benefit the Environment (GLOBE) Program, with appendices. Signed at La Paz April 22, 1995; entered into force April 22, 1995.
TIAS 12636.

EXTRADITION

Treaty on extradition. Signed at La Paz June 27, 1995; entered into force November 21, 1996.
TIAS

FINANCE

Agreement relating to investment guaranties under section 413 (b)(4) of the Mutual Security Act of 1954, as amended. Exchange of notes at La Paz September 23, 1955; entered into force September 23, 1955.
6 UST 3948; TIAS 3404; 256 UNTS 275.

Amendment:
March 4, 1964 (15 UST 260; TIAS 5548; 524 UNTS 312).

Related agreements:
December 19, 1985 (TIAS 12042).
May 20, 1992 (TIAS 12042).

Agreement regarding the consolidation and rescheduling of certain debts owed to, guaranteed by or insured by the United States Government and its agencies, with annexes. Signed at La Paz March 27, 1987; entered into force May 6, 1987.
NP

Agreement regarding the consolidation and rescheduling of certain debts owed to, guaranteed by, or insured by the United States Government and its agencies, with annexes. Signed at La Paz May 15, 1989; entered into force June 23, 1989.
NP

Swap agreement between the United States Treasury and the Central Bank of Bolivia/Government of Bolivia, with related letter. Signed at La Paz and Washington July 11, 1989; entered into force July 11, 1989.
TIAS

Swap agreement between the United States Treasury and the Central Bank of Bolivia/Government of Bolivia, with related letter. Signed at La Paz and Washington September 14 and 15, 1989; entered into force September 15, 1989.
TIAS

Extension:
December 15, 1989.

Swap agreement between the United States Treasury and the Central Bank of Bolivia/Government of Bolivia, with related letter. Signed at Washington and La Paz December 27, 1989; entered into force December 27, 1989.
TIAS

Agreement regarding the consolidation and rescheduling of certain debts owed to, guaranteed by, or insured by the United States Government and its agencies, with annexes. Signed at La Paz November 27, 1990; entered into force February 6, 1991.
NP

Agreement regarding the discharge of certain debts owed to the United States, with annex. Signed at Washington August 22, 1991; entered into force August 22, 1991.
NP

Agreement regarding the consolidation and rescheduling or refinancing of certain debts owed to, guaranteed by, or insured by the United States Government and its agencies, with annexes. Signed at La Paz October 13, 1992; entered into force December 3, 1992.
NP

Amendments:
March 2 and April 13, 1994 (NP).
August 9 and October 21, 1994 (NP).

Agreement regarding the consolidation and rescheduling of certain debts owed to, guaranteed by, or insured by the United States Government and its agencies, with annexes. Signed at La Paz January 23, 1996; entered into force March 7, 1996.
NP

Agreement regarding the reduction and reorganization of certain debts owed to, guaranteed by, or insured by the United States Government and its agencies. Signed at La Paz November 27, 1996; entered into force April 7, 1997.
NP

Agreement regarding the reduction and reorganization of certain debts owed to, guaranteed by, or insured by the United States Government and its agencies, with annexes. Signed at Santa Cruz December 2, 1999; entered into force February 23, 2000.
NP

INFORMATIONAL MEDIA GUARANTIES

Agreement providing for an informational media guaranty program. Exchange of notes at La Paz February 27 and March 10, 1956; entered into force March 10, 1956.
7 UST 440; TIAS 3528; 270 UNTS 199.

MAPPING

Cooperative arrangement for the production of topographic maps of Bolivia, with annexes. Signed at Washington and La Paz April 21 and 30, 1986; entered into force April 30, 1986.
TIAS 11375.

MISSIONS, MILITARY

Agreement for establishment of an Air Force Mission to Bolivia. Signed at La Paz June 30, 1956; entered into force June 30, 1956.
7 UST 2017; TIAS 3604; 271 UNTS 243.

BOLIVIA (Cont'd)

Amendment:
April 2 and 3, 1959 (10 UST 742; TIAS 4209;
342 UNTS 356).

Agreement for the establishment of an Army
Mission to Bolivia. Signed at La Paz June 30,
1956; entered into force June 30, 1956.
7 UST 2033; TIAS 3605; 271 UNTS 269.

Amendment:
April 2 and 3, 1959 (10 UST 742; TIAS 4209;
342 UNTS 356).

NARCOTIC DRUGS

Agreement concerning cooperation to combat
narcotics trafficking, with annexes and related
letter. Signed at La Paz February 24, 1987; entered into force August 13, 1987.
TIAS 12053.

Amendment:
May 9, 1990.

PACIFIC SETTLEMENT OF DISPUTES

Treaty looking to the advancement of the
cause of general peace. Signed at Washington
January 22, 1914; entered into force January 8,
1915.
38 Stat. 1868; TS 606; 5 Bevans 740.

POSTAL MATTERS

International express mail agreement, with detailed regulations. Signed at La Paz and Washington August 10 and November 21, 1988; entered into force December 15, 1988.
TIAS 11635.

Postal money order agreement. Signed at La
Paz and Washington February 26 and March
11, 1993; entered into force June 1, 1993.
NP

PRISONER TRANSFER

Treaty on the execution of penal sentences.
Signed at La Paz February 10, 1978; entered
into force August 17, 1978.
30 UST 796; TIAS 9219; 1150 UNTS 11.

PUBLICATIONS

Agreement relating to the exchange of official
publications. Exchange of notes at La Paz Jan-

uary 26 and 31, 1942; entered into force January 31, 1942.
56 Stat. 1436; EAS 242; 5 Bevans 753; 101
UNTS 138.

RELIEF SUPPLIES AND PACKAGES

Agreement providing for payment by the
United States of ocean freight costs on relief
shipments to Bolivia, and duty and tax-free
entry and payment of inland transportation to
point of distribution by Bolivia. Exchange of
notes at La Paz June 3 and 16, 1954; entered
into force June 16, 1954.
5 UST 1547; TIAS 3033; 234 UNTS 35.

Amendment:
December 14 and 30, 1970 (22 UST 211;
TIAS 7051; 781 UNTS 312).

SCIENTIFIC AND TECHNICAL COOPERATION

Memorandum of understanding for scientific
and technical cooperation in the earth sciences.
Signed at La Paz and Reston April 24 and
May 29, 1985; entered into force May 29,
1985.
TIAS 11214.

Amendment and extension:
November 20, 1991 (TIAS 11828).

SEISMIC OBSERVATIONS

Memorandum of understanding concerning the
installation and operation of a real-time seismic station. Signed at La Paz and Reston September 7, 1983 and June 14, 1984; entered into
force June 14, 1984.
TIAS 11250.

TAXATION

Agreement concerning reciprocal exemption
from income tax of income derived from the
international operation of ships and aircraft.
Exchange of notes at Washington July 21 and
November 23, 1987; entered into force November 23, 1987.
TIAS 11542.

TELECOMMUNICATION

Agreement relating to radio communications
between amateur stations on behalf of third
parties. Exchange of notes at La Paz October
23, 1961; entered into force November
22, 1961.
12 UST 1695; TIAS 4888; 424 UNTS 93.

Agreement relating to the reciprocal granting
of authorization to permit licensed amateur radio operators of either country to operate their stations in the other country. Exchange of notes at La Paz March 16, 1965; entered into force April 15, 1965.
16 UST 165; TIAS 5777; 542 UNTS 209.

BOSNIA–HERZEGOVINA

For agreements prior to the independence of
Bosnia-Herzegovina, see YUGOSLAVIA.

COPYRIGHT (See APPENDIX)

DEFENSE

Agreement related to the provision of defense
articles, related training or other defense services from the United States to Bosnia, with related exchange of notes. Exchange of notes at
Sarajevo January 6 and 7, 1996; entered into
force January 7, 1996.
TIAS

ECONOMIC AND TECHNICAL COOPERATION

Agreement concerning economic, technical and
related assistance for Bosnia and Herzegovina,
with related letters. Signed at Sarajevo May 3,
1996; entered into force May 3, 1996.
TIAS

EMPLOYMENT

Agreement relating to the employment of dependents of official government employees.
Exchange of notes at Washington March 7 and
15, 1995; entered into force March 15, 1995.
TIAS 12614.

FINANCE

Investment incentive agreement. Signed at Sarajevo July 12, 1996; entered into force December 10, 1996.
TIAS

Agreement regarding the consolidation, reduction and rescheduling of certain debts owed to,
guaranteed by, or insured by the United States
Government and its agencies, with annexes.
Signed at Sarajevo August 19, 1999; entered
into force October 21, 1999.
NP

BOSNIA–HERZEGOVINA (Cont'd)

TELECOMMUNICATION

Agreement relating to radio communications between amateur stations on behalf of third parties. Exchange of notes at New York September 24 and October 14, 1993; entered into force October 14, 1993.
TIAS 12511.

BOTSWANA

On September 30, 1966, Bechuanaland Protectorate became the independent state of Botswana.

In a note dated October 6, 1966 to the Secretary-General of the United Nations the President of Botswana made a statement reading in part as follows: "As regards bilateral treaties validly concluded by the Government of the United Kingdom on behalf of the former Bechuanaland Protectorate, or validly applied or extended by the said Government to the territory of the former Bechuanaland Protectorate, the Government of Botswana is willing to continue to apply within its territory, on a basis of reciprocity, the terms of all such treaties for a period of twenty-four months from the date of independence (i.e., until October 1, 1968) unless abrogated or modified earlier by mutual consent. At the expiry of that period, the Government of Botswana will regard such of these treaties which could not by the application of the rules of customary international law be regarded as otherwise surviving, as having terminated.

"It is the earnest hope of the Government of Botswana that during the aforementioned period of twenty-four months, the normal processes of diplomatic negotiations will enable it to reach satisfactory accord with the States concerned upon the possibility of the continuance or modification of such treaties.

"The Government of Botswana is conscious that the above declaration applicable to bilateral treaties cannot with equal facility be applied to multilateral treaties. As regards these, therefore, the Government of Botswana proposes to review each of them individually and to indicate to the depositary in each case what steps it wishes to take in relation to each such instrument whether by way of confirmation of termination, confirmation of succession or accession. During such interim period of review any party to a multilateral treaty which has, prior to independence, been applied or extended to the former Bechuanaland Protectorate, may, on a basis of reciprocity, rely as against Botswana on the terms of such treaty."

COPYRIGHT (See APPENDIX)

DEFENSE

Agreement concerning the provision of training related to defense articles under the United States International Military Education and Training (IMET) Program. Exchange of notes at Gaborone February 26 and March 21, 1980; entered into force March 21, 1980.
32 UST 957; TIAS 9742; 1221 UNTS 217.

Agreement regarding grants under the Foreign Assistance Act of 1961, as amended, and the furnishing of defense articles, related training and other defense services from the United States to Botswana. Exchange of notes at Gaborone May 21 and June 17, 1992; entered into force June 17, 1992.
TIAS 12277.

ECONOMIC AND TECHNICAL COOPERATION

Agency for International Development:
September 19, 1975 (28 UST 791; TIAS 8481).
May 13, 1986 (NP).

EMPLOYMENT

Agreement relating to the employment of dependents of official government employees. Signed at Gaborone June 15, 1984; entered into force June 15, 1984.
TIAS 11134.

Amendment:
August 16, 1999 and December 1, 2000.

Agreement concerning interpretation of the agreement of June 15, 1984, relating to the employment of dependents of official government employees. Exchange of notes at New York March 14 and April 27, 1989; entered into force April 27, 1989.
TIAS

FINANCE

Investment incentive agreement. Signed at Gaborone December 12, 1997; entered into force March 12, 1998.
TIAS

JUDICIAL ASSISTANCE

Agreement concerning an International Law Enforcement Academy. Signed at Gaborone July 24, 2000; entered into force July 24, 2000.
TIAS

PEACE CORPS

Agreement relating to the establishment of a Peace Corps Program in Botswana. Exchange of notes at Gaborone May 14, 1971; entered into force May 14, 1971.
22 UST 1025; TIAS 7145; 797 UNTS 13.

POSTAL MATTERS

International express mail agreement, with detailed regulations. Signed at Gaborone and Washington October 24 and December 29, 1988; entered into force January 16, 1989.
TIAS 11624.

SEISMIC OBSERVATIONS

Memorandum of understanding concerning the development, installation and operation of a seismic data acquisition system. Signed at Reston and Gaborone June 16 and August 13, 1986; entered into force August 13, 1986.
TIAS 11361.

Agreement concerning the operation of a seismic monitoring station in Botswana. Signed at Washington and Lobatse October 14, 1999 and February 16, 2000; entered into force February 16, 2000.
TIAS

TELECOMMUNICATION

Agreement relating to the reciprocal granting of authorizations to permit licensed amateur radio operators of either country to operate their stations in the other country. Exchange of notes at Gaborone November 7, 1978 and September 26, 1979; entered into force September 26, 1979.
32 UST 1357; TIAS 9776; 1221 UNTS 211.

Agreement providing for a radio facility for the purpose of relaying Voice of America programs to areas in Africa. Signed at Gaborone March 28, 1980; entered into force March 28, 1980.
32 UST 947; TIAS 9741; 1221 UNTS 223.

Extension:
March 13 and 20, 1990.

Agreement concerning the construction, operation and maintenance of a Voice of America radio relay facility in Botswana, with appendix. Signed at Gaborone September 5, 1985; entered into force September 5, 1985.
TIAS 11126.

BRAZIL

AGRICULTURAL COMMODITIES

Agricultural commodities agreement, agreed official minutes and related notes. Signed at Washington December 31, 1956; entered into force December 31, 1956.
7 UST 3475; TIAS 3725; 266 UNTS 151.

Amendments:
July 25, 1957 (8 UST 993; TIAS 3864; 290 UNTS 345).
June 30, 1958 (9 UST 1015; TIAS 4074; 321 UNTS 288).
December 12, 1958 (9 UST 1474; TIAS 4144; 337 UNTS 422).
March 2, 1959 (10 UST 200; TIAS 4183; 341 UNTS 405).
May 29, 1959 (10 UST 1033; TIAS 4239; 346 UNTS 339).
September 2, 1959 (10 UST 1638; TIAS 4311; 358 UNTS 320).
December 9, 1960 (11 UST 2532; TIAS 4639; 401 UNTS 284).
December 29, 1960 (11 UST 2559; TIAS 4644; 401 UNTS 288).
January 4 and April 18, 1961 (12 UST 728; TIAS 4775; 409 UNTS 316).
February 26, 1962 (13 UST 478; TIAS 5011; 435 UNTS 352).
October 5, 1967 (18 UST 2815; TIAS 6367; 701 UNTS 360).

Agricultural commodities agreement, with exchange of notes. Signed at Rio de Janeiro May 4, 1961; entered into force May 4, 1961.
12 UST 3151; TIAS 4918; 433 UNTS 91.

Related agreement:
October 5, 1967 (18 UST 2818; TIAS 6368; 701 UNTS 370).

Agricultural commodities agreement, with exchanges of notes. Signed at Brasilia March 15, 1962; entered into force March 15, 1962.
13 UST 1167; TIAS 5061; 456 UNTS 209.

Amendments:
October 4, 1962 (14 UST 405; TIAS 5333; 479 UNTS 402).
August 22, 1963 (14 UST 1248; TIAS 5425; 488 UNTS 310).

Related agreement:
October 5, 1967 (18 UST 2821; TIAS 6369; 701 UNTS 382).

Agricultural commodities agreement, with exchanges of notes. Signed at Rio de Janeiro September 11, 1963; entered into force September 11, 1963.
14 UST 1669; TIAS 5471; 493 UNTS 267.

Amendment:
May 15, 1964 (15 UST 650; TIAS 5585; 526 UNTS 354).

Agricultural commodities agreement with exchange of notes. Signed at Rio de Janeiro April 23, 1966; entered into force April 23, 1966.
17 UST 1622; TIAS 6118; 607 UNTS 117.

Agricultural commodities agreement with annex. Signed at Rio de Janeiro October 5, 1967; entered into force October 5, 1967.
22 UST 2125; TIAS 7258.

Related agreements:
May 14, 1968 (22 UST 2146; TIAS 7259).
August 28, 1969 (22 UST 2150; TIAS 7260).

Agricultural commodities agreement with annex. Signed at Brasilia October 21, 1970; entered into force October 21, 1970.
22 UST 2155; TIAS 7261.

Amendments:
December 30, 1970 (22 UST 2155; TIAS 7261).
April 28, 1971 (22 UST 2155; TIAS 7261).

AMITY

Treaty of peace, friendship, commerce and navigation.[1] Signed at Rio de Janeiro December 12, 1828; entered into force March 18, 1829; operative December 12, 1828.
8 Stat. 390; TS 34; 5 Bevans 792.

NOTE:
[1] All articles terminated December 12, 1841 except those relating to peace and friendship.

ATOMIC ENERGY

Agreement providing for a grant to assist in the acquisition of a subcritical assembly for the Aeronautical Institute of Technology. Exchange of notes at Rio de Janeiro October 20, 1959 and February 27, 1960; entered into force February 27, 1960.
11 UST 1977; TIAS 4547; 384 UNTS 131.

Agreement providing for a grant to assist in the acquisition of certain nuclear research and training equipment and materials. Exchange of notes at Rio de Janeiro October 10, 1960 and March 17, 1961; entered into force March 17, 1961.
12 UST 381; TIAS 4727; 406 UNTS 241.

Agreement providing for a grant for assistance in obtaining materials and equipment for use in developing the Instituto de Biofisica da Universidade de Brasil radio-biological and research program. Exchange of notes at Rio de Janeiro October 10, 1962 and March 29, 1963; entered into force March 29, 1963.
14 UST 424; TIAS 5337; 476 UNTS 67.

Agreement for cooperation concerning civil uses of atomic energy with appendix and related notes. Signed at Washington July 17, 1972; entered into force September 20, 1972.
23 UST 2477; TIAS 7439.

Arrangement concerning the exchange of technical information and cooperation in regulatory and safety research matters, with patent addendum. Signed at Rockville May 18, 1989; entered into force May 18, 1989.
TIAS 12228.

Agreement for cooperation concerning peaceful uses of nuclear energy, with annex and agreed minute. Signed at Brasilia October 14, 1997; entered into force September 15, 1999.
TIAS

Arrangement for the exchange of technical information and cooperation in regulatory and safety research matters, with addenda. Signed at Vienna September 30, 1999; entered into force September 30, 1999.
TIAS

AVIATION

Agreement relating to reciprocal acceptance of airworthiness certifications. Exchange of notes at Brasilia June 16, 1976; entered into force June 16, 1976.
27 UST 3700; TIAS 8384; 1054 UNTS 181.

Agreement on air transport, with annexes. Signed at Brasilia March 21, 1989; entered into force January 13, 1992.
TIAS 11780; 1668 UNTS 59.

Agreement replacing annexes I and II to the air transport agreement of March 21, 1989, as amended. Exchange of notes at Brasilia September 2, 1997; entered into force September 2, 1997; effective April 1, 1996.
TIAS

COFFEE

Agreement concerning Brazilian exports of soluble coffee to the United States. Exchange of notes at Brasilia April 2, 1971; entered into force April 2, 1971.
22 UST 654; TIAS 7118; 792 UNTS 305.

COMMERCE (See AMITY)

COPYRIGHT (See also APPENDIX)

Agreement providing for reciprocal copyright protection of literary, artistic and scientific works. Exchange of notes at Washington April 2, 1957; entered into force April 2, 1957.
8 UST 418; TIAS 3793; 290 UNTS 119.

CUSTOMS

Agreement granting reciprocal customs privileges for Foreign Service personnel. Exchange

BRAZIL (Cont'd)

of notes at Rio de Janeiro October 11, 1940; entered into force October 11, 1940.
54 Stat. 2419; EAS 185; 5 Bevans 897; 203 LNTS 261.

DEFENSE

Agreement relating to the presence of military personnel of the United States in Brazil and the presence of military personnel of Brazil in the United States. Exchange of notes at Rio de Janeiro December 15, 1947 and February 2, 1948; entered into force February 2, 1948.
62 Stat. 1957; TIAS 1759; 5 Bevans 1045; 67 UNTS 109.

Agreement for the establishment of the Joint Group on Emergency Supply Problems. Exchange of notes at Rio de Janeiro July 24, 1951; entered into force July 24, 1951.
2 UST 1594; TIAS 2301; 134 UNTS 195.

Military assistance agreement.[1] Signed at Rio de Janeiro March 15, 1952; entered into force May 19, 1953.
4 UST 170; TIAS 2776; 199 UNTS 221.

Understanding relating to military assistance. Exchange of notes at Rio de Janeiro January 30, 1964; entered into force January 30, 1964.
15 UST 163; TIAS 5534; 511 UNTS 77.

Agreement relating to the deposit by Brazil of ten percent of the value of grant military assistance furnished by the United States. Exchange of notes at Brasilia February 28 and June 27, 1972; entered into force June 27, 1972; effective February 7, 1972.
23 UST 1222; TIAS 7390.

Memorandum of understanding relating to the acquisition of military aircraft. Signed September 24, 1973; entered into force September 24, 1973.
27 UST 2810; TIAS 8350; 1066 UNTS 119.

Agreement relating to industrial and military cooperation, with memorandum of understanding. Exchange of notes at Brasilia February 6, 1984; entered into force February 6, 1984.
TIAS 12278.

Master data exchange arrangement for the mutual development of military equipment. Signed at Washington November 14, 1984; entered into force November 14, 1984.
TIAS 11164.

Memorandum of understanding regarding the exchange of scientists and engineers. Signed at Washington November 14, 1984; entered into force November 14, 1984.
NP

Amendment and extension:
June 13, 1990 (NP).

Agreement concerning the provision of training related to defense articles under the United States International Military Education and Training (IMET) Program. Exchange of notes at Brasilia April 19, 1988 and March 27, 1989; entered into force March 27, 1989.
NP

Agreement regarding grants under the Foreign Assistance Act of 1961, as amended, and the furnishing of defense articles from the United States of America to the Government of the Federative Republic of Brazil. Exchange of notes at Washington June 2, 2000; entered into force October 19, 2000.
TIAS

NOTE:
[1] Terminated March 11, 1977 except that the safeguard clauses to which articles I and III refer remain in force.

ECONOMIC AND TECHNICAL COOPERATION

Agreement relating to the mobilization of productive resources of Brazil. Exchange of notes at Washington March 3, 1942; entered into force March 3, 1942.
57 Stat. 1314; EAS 370; 5 Bevans 913; 105 UNTS 99.

Agreement relating to technical cooperation. Exchange of notes at Rio de Janeiro December 19, 1950; entered into force December 19, 1950.
2 UST 845; TIAS 2239; 141 UNTS 3.

Amendment:
January 8, 1952 (3 UST 4693; TIAS 2626; 200 UNTS 306).

Special services program agreement. Signed at Rio de Janeiro May 30, 1953; entered into force provisionally May 30, 1953; definitively November 3, 1959.
13 UST 1061; TIAS 5049; 460 UNTS 89.

Extension:
December 27 and 30, 1963 (15 UST 99; TIAS 5520; 511 UNTS 308).

Agreement on the cooperation for the promotion of economic and social development in the Brazilian Northeast, with exchange of letters. Signed at Washington April 13, 1962; entered into force April 13, 1962.
13 UST 356; TIAS 4990; 445 UNTS 227.

Complementary agreement for technical cooperation in the area of irrigation, with appendices. Signed at Brasilia November 6, 1986; entered into force November 6, 1986.
TIAS

Extension:
September 20 and December 2, 1999.

EDUCATION

Agreement for financing certain educational exchange programs. Exchange of notes at Rio de Janeiro October 5 and 19, 1966; entered into force October 19, 1966.
17 UST 2241; TIAS 6163; 680 UNTS 261.

EMPLOYMENT

Agreement relating to the employment of dependents of official government employees, with exchange of letters. Exchange of notes at Brasilia July 8, 1987; entered into force July 8, 1987.
TIAS 11529.

Extension:
June 21 and 25, 1999.

ENERGY

Implementing arrangement for cooperation in the area of energy technology, with annexes. Signed at Brasilia October 14, 1997; entered into force October 14, 1997.
TIAS

ENVIRONMENTAL COOPERATION

Memorandum of understanding concerning environmental cooperation. Signed at Washington November 16, 1990; entered into force November 16, 1990.
TIAS 11770.

EXTRADITION

Treaty of extradition. Signed at Rio de Janeiro January 13, 1961; entered into force December 17, 1964.
15 UST 2093; TIAS 5691; 532 UNTS 177.

Additional protocol to the treaty of extradition. Signed at Rio de Janeiro June 18, 1962; entered into force December 17, 1964.
15 UST 2112; TIAS 5691; 532 UNTS 198.

FINANCE

Agreement relating to investment guaranties. Signed at Washington February 6, 1965; entered into force September 17, 1965.
18 UST 1807; TIAS 6327; 719 UNTS 3.

Agreement regarding the consolidation and rescheduling of certain debts owed to, guaranteed by or insured by the United States Government and its agencies, with annexes. Signed at Brasilia April 15, 1985; entered into force May 28, 1985.
NP

BRAZIL (Cont'd)

Swap agreement between the United States Treasury and the Central Bank of Brazil/Government of Brazil, with memorandum of understanding. Signed at Washington and Rio de Janeiro July 15, 1988; entered into force July 15, 1988.
TIAS

Agreement regarding the consolidation and re-scheduling of certain debts owed to, guaranteed by, or insured by the United States Government and its agencies, with annexes. Signed at Brasilia March 14, 1990; entered into force April 19, 1990.
NP

Agreement regarding the consolidation and re-scheduling of certain debts owed to, guaranteed by or insured by the United States Government and its agencies, with annexes. Signed at Brasilia December 20, 1991; entered into force March 9, 1992.
NP

Agreement regarding the consolidation and re-scheduling or refinancing of certain debts owed to, guaranteed by, or insured by the United States Government and its agencies, with annexes. Signed at Washington September 23, 1992; entered into force November 9, 1992.
NP

INDUSTRIAL AND MILITARY COOPERATION (See under DEFENSE)

LEND-LEASE

Agreement on the disposition of lend-lease supplies in inventory or procurement in the United States. Signed at Washington June 28, 1946; entered into force June 28, 1946.
60 Stat. 1797; TIAS 1537; 5 Bevans 1019; 6 UNTS 327.

MARITIME MATTERS (See also SHIPPING)

Agreement relating to the transfer to Brazil of certain United States naval vessels. Exchange of notes at Washington January 4, 1951 with memorandum of understanding dated January 9, 1951; entered into force January 4, 1951.
3 UST 2738; TIAS 2443; 165 UNTS 97.

NARCOTIC DRUGS

Agreement on cooperation in the field of control of illicit traffic of drugs, with annex. Ex-

change of notes at Brasilia July 19, 1983; entered into force July 19, 1983.
TIAS 10756.

Amendments and extension:
October 4 and December 3, 1984 (TIAS 11056).
June 2 and 19, 1986 (TIAS 12388).

PACIFIC SETTLEMENT OF DISPUTES

Arbitration convention. Signed at Washington January 23, 1909; entered into force July 26, 1911.
37 Stat. 1535; TS 562; 5 Bevans 818.

Treaty looking to the advancement of the cause of general peace. Signed at Washington July 24, 1914; entered into force October 28, 1916.
39 Stat. 1698; TS 627; 5 Bevans 820.

PEACE CORPS

Agreement relating to the establishment of a Peace Corps program in Brazil. Exchange of notes at Brasilia June 18, 1973; entered into force June 18, 1973.
24 UST 1650; TIAS 7669.

POSTAL MATTERS

Money order convention. Signed at Washington September 1 and at Rio de Janeiro September 20, 1921; operative October 17, 1921.
NP

Memorandum of understanding concerning the operation of the INTELPOST field trial, with attachment and details of implementation. Signed at Brasilia and Washington December 18 and 28, 1984; entered into force January 7, 1985.
TIAS 11004.

International express mail agreement, with detailed regulations. Signed at Brasilia and Washington April 7 and May 11, 1988; entered into force May 11, 1988.
TIAS 11654.

Postal money order agreement. Signed at Brasilia and Washington July 19 and August 14, 1990; entered into force October 15, 1990.
TIAS 11740.

PUBLICATIONS

Agreement relating to the exchange of official publications. Exchange of notes at Washington June 15 and 24, 1940; entered into force June 24, 1940.
54 Stat. 2329; EAS 176; 5 Bevans 883; 203 LNTS 227.

Amendment:
May 16 and 23, 1950 (3 UST 387; TIAS 2402; 151 UNTS 141).

RELATIONS

Memorandum of understanding concerning consultations on matters of mutual interest. Signed at Brasilia February 21, 1976; entered into force February 21, 1976.
27 UST 1034; TIAS 8240.

REMOTE SENSING

Memorandum of understanding concerning the Landsat system. Signed at Brasilia May 8, 1984; entered into force May 8, 1984.
TIAS 11252.

Extension:
October 18 and November 28, 1996.

SATELLITES

Agreement relating to a program of joint participation in intercontinental testing in connection with experimental communications satellites. Exchange of notes at Rio de Janeiro October 27, 1961; entered into force October 27, 1961.
12 UST 3145; TIAS 4917; 433 UNTS 113.

SCIENTIFIC COOPERATION

Memorandum of understanding for scientific and technical cooperation in geological sciences and earth resources. Signed at Brasilia April 12, 1983; entered into force April 12, 1983.
TIAS 10746.

Agreement relating to cooperation in science and technology. Signed at Brasilia February 6, 1984; entered into force May 15, 1986.
TIAS 10990.

Amendment and extension:
March 21, 1994 (TIAS 12537).

Memorandum of understanding concerning scientific and technical cooperation in the earth sciences. Signed at Reston January 17 and 31, 1997; entered into force January 31, 1997.
TIAS

Supplementary agreement to the agreement of February 6, 1984, as amended and extended, relating to cooperation in science and technology. Signed at Brasilia March 31, 1998; entered into force April 30, 1998.
TIAS

Implementing arrangement to the agreement of February 6, 1984, as amended and extended, on scientific and technological cooperation concerning cooperative efforts in the field of

BRAZIL (Cont'd)

public health and science. Signed at Geneva May 12, 1998; entered into force May 12, 1998.
TIAS

Memorandum of understanding concerning scientific and technical cooperation in the earth sciences. Signed at Reston and Brasilia May 18 and November 4, 1998; entered into force November 4, 1998.
TIAS

Implementing arrangement for the biological control of the Aedes Aegypti mosquito. Signed at Washington February 29, 2000; entered into force February 29, 2000.
TIAS

SEISMIC OBSERVATIONS

Memorandum of understanding concerning the development, installation and operation of a seismic data acquisition system. Signed at Reston and Brasilia April 8 and May 5, 1986; entered into force May 5, 1986.
TIAS 11360.

SHIPPING

Agreement relating to establishment of a mechanism for consultation on maritime transportation problems. Exchange of notes at Rio de Janeiro September 18 and 20, 1968; entered into force September 20, 1968.
19 UST 6017; TIAS 6559; 702 UNTS 227.

SPACE COOPERATION

Agreement for use of the geostationary operational environmental satellite in the Brazilian national plan for data collection platforms. Signed at Brasilia June 14, 1982; entered into force June 14, 1982.
TIAS 10419; 1287 UNTS 73.

Memorandum of understanding concerning cooperation in aerospace experiments employing sounding rockets. Signed at Brasilia January 31, 1983; entered into force January 31, 1983.
TIAS 10643; 1305 UNTS 245.

Memorandum of understanding for the smoke/sulfate, clouds and radiation experiment – Brazil, with exchange of letters. Signed at Washington May 19, 1995; entered into force May 19, 1995.
TIAS 12213.

Memorandum of understanding for flight of the Humidity Sounder for Brazil (HSB) instrument on NASA's Earth Observing System PM–1 spacecraft. Signed at Washington De-

cember 5, 1996; entered into force December 5, 1996.
TIAS

Implementing arrangement for the design, development, operation and use of flight equipment and payloads for the International Space Station Program. Signed at Brasilia October 14, 1997; entered into force October 14, 1997.
TIAS

TELECOMMUNICATION

Agreement relating to radio communications between amateur stations on behalf of third parties. Exchange of notes at Washington June 1, 1965; entered into force June 1, 1965.
16 UST 821; TIAS 5816; 546 UNTS 195.

Agreement relating to the reciprocal granting of authorizations to permit licensed amateur radio operators of either country to operate their stations in the other country. Exchange of notes at Rio de Janeiro January 26 and Brasilia June 19, 1970; entered into force June 19, 1970.
21 UST 1960; TIAS 6936; 756 UNTS 109.

TRADE AND COMMERCE

Joint communique relating to trade, investment and financial matters. Issued at Brasilia May 11, 1976; entered into force May 11, 1976.
27 UST 4121; TIAS 8435; 1066 UNTS 131.

Agreement relating to the establishment of a United States Trade Center in Sao Paulo, with note of guarantee. Exchange of notes at Brasilia June 22 and October 20, 1976; entered into force October 20, 1976.
28 UST 8146; TIAS 8748.

Agreement relating to trade in cotton, wool and man-made fiber textiles and textile products, with annexes. Exchange of notes at Washington September 15 and 19, 1988; entered into force September 19, 1988; effective April 1, 1988.
NP

Amendments and extension:
October 12 and November 25, 1988 (NP).
April 16 and 23, 1992 (NP).
May 4 and June 27, 1994 (NP).

Agreement on steel trade liberalization, with appendices and related letter. Exchange of letters at Washington February 26 and March 5, 1990; entered into force March 5, 1990.
TIAS

TRADE-MARKS

Agreement for the protection of the marks of manufacture and trade. Signed at Rio de Janeiro September 24, 1878.
21 Stat. 659; TS 36; 5 Bevans 807.

VISAS

Agreement relating to the waiver of nonimmigrant passport visa fees. Exchange of notes at Rio de Janeiro December 16 and 17, 1937; operative January 1, 1938.
5 Bevans 874; 186 LNTS 413.

Agreement relating to the reciprocal issuance of nonimmigrant visas free of charge to diplomatic, consular, and administrative officers and employees serving in diplomatic missions, and career consular officers, as well as officers and employees of governmental agencies of both countries. Exchange of notes at Rio de Janeiro May 26, 1965; entered into force July 25, 1965.
16 UST 1006; TIAS 5843; 549 UNTS 125.

BRUNEI

On January 1, 1984, the former British protected state of Brunei gained full independence. In a letter dated January 1, 1984 to the Secretary General of the United Nations, the Sultan made a statement reading in part as follows:

"The Government of Brunei Darussalam recognises that it is desirable to maintain to the fullest extent compatible with the resumption by Brunei Darussalam of its status and emergence on 1st January 1984 as a fully independent and sovereign nation, legal continuity in treaty relations between Brunei Darussalam and other states. Accordingly, the Government of Brunei Darussalam makes the following declaration:

"1] As regards bilateral treaties validly concluded by the United Kingdom on behalf of Brunei Darussalam or validly applied or extended by the former to the latter, the Government of Brunei Darussalam is willing to accept, on a basis of reciprocity, the rights and obligations under the terms of all such treaties for a period of five years from 1st January 1984 until 31st December 1988 unless abrogated or modified earlier by mutual consent. At the expiry of that period, the Government of Brunei Darussalam will regard such of those treaties which could not by the application of the rules of customary international law be regarded as otherwise surviving, as having terminated.

"2] The Government of Brunei Darussalam acknowledges that the above declaration applicable to bilateral treaties cannot with equal facility be applied to multilateral treaties. As regards these, therefore, the Government of Brunei Darussalam proposes to examine each of them individually and to indicate to the depositary in each case what steps it wishes to take in relation to each such instrument — whether by confirmation of termination, confirmation of succession or accession. During the period of examination the Government of Brunei Darussalam will on a basis of reciprocity accept all treaty rights and obligations accruing and arising under all multilateral trea-

BRUNEI (Cont'd)

ties which were prior to independence validly applied or extended to Brunei Darussalam.''

AVIATION

Air transport agreement, with annexes. Signed at Washington June 20, 1997; entered into force June 20, 1997.
TIAS

COMMERCE

Treaty of peace, friendship, commerce and navigation. Signed at Brunei June 23, 1850; entered into force July 11, 1853.
10 Stat. 909; TS 33; 5 Bevans 1080.

CONSULS

Consular convention between the United States and the United Kingdom. Signed at Washington June 6, 1951; entered into force September 7, 1952.
3 UST 3426; TIAS 2494; 165 UNTS 121.

COPYRIGHT (See APPENDIX)

ECONOMIC AND TECHNICAL COOPERATION

Economic cooperation agreement between the United States and the United Kingdom. Signed at London July 6, 1948; applicable to Brunei October 26, 1949.
62 Stat. 2596; TIAS 1795; 12 Bevans 874; 22 UNTS 263.

Amendments:
January 3, 1950 (1 UST 184; TIAS 2036; 86 UNTS 304).
May 25, 1951 (2 UST 1292; TIAS 2277; 99 UNTS 308).
February 25, 1953 (4 UST 1528; TIAS 2815; 172 UNTS 332).

POSTAL MATTERS

International express mail agreement, with detailed regulations. Signed at Bandar Seri Begawan and Washington December 15, 1990 and January 8, 1991; entered into force February 18, 1991.
TIAS 11785.

TRADE-MARKS

Declaration by the United States and the United Kingdom affording reciprocal protection to trade-marks. Signed at London October 24, 1877; entered into force October 24, 1877.
20 Stat. 703; TS 138; 12 Bevans 198.

BULGARIA

ATOMIC ENERGY

Agreement for cooperation in the field of peaceful uses of nuclear energy, with annex and agreed minute. Signed at Sofia June 21, 1994; entered into force March 29, 1996.
TIAS 12549.

AVIATION

Civil aviation security agreement. Signed at Sofia April 24, 1991; entered into force April 24, 1991.
TIAS 11984.

CONSULS

Consular convention, with agreed memorandum and exchange of letters. Signed at Sofia April 15, 1974; entered into force May 29, 1975.
26 UST 687; TIAS 8067.

COPYRIGHT (See APPENDIX)

CULTURAL RELATIONS

Agreement on exchanges and cooperation in cultural, scientific, educational, technological and other fields. Signed at Washington June 13, 1977; entered into force March 23, 1978.
29 UST 3419; TIAS 9020; 1123 UNTS 91.

DEFENSE

Agreement concerning the provision of training related to defense articles under the United States International Military Education and Training (IMET) Program. Exchange of notes at Sofia February 11 and April 7, 1992; entered into force April 7, 1992.
NP

Agreement regarding grants under the Foreign Assistance Act of 1961, as amended, and the furnishing of defense articles, related training and other defense services from the United States to Bulgaria. Exchange of notes at Sofia

May 4 and December 5, 1994; entered into force December 5, 1994.
TIAS 12279.

Agreement concerning the protection of classified military information. Signed at Sofia February 1, 1995; entered into force February 1, 1995.
TIAS 12280.

EMPLOYMENT

Agreement relating to the employment of dependents of official government employees. Exchange of notes at Sofia October 8 and 29, 1991; entered into force October 29, 1991.
TIAS 11983.

ENVIRONMENTAL COOPERATION

Agreement for cooperation in the Global Learning and Observations to Benefit the Environment (GLOBE) Program, with appendices. Signed at Sofia September 8, 1998; entered into force September 8, 1998.
TIAS

EXTRADITION

Extradition treaty. Signed at Sofia March 19, 1924; entered into force June 24, 1924.
43 Stat. 1886; TS 687; 5 Bevans 1086; 26 LNTS 27.

Supplementary extradition treaty. Signed at Washington June 8, 1934; entered into force August 15, 1935.
49 Stat. 3250; TS 894; 5 Bevans 1103; 161 LNTS 409.

ENVIRONMENTAL COOPERATION

Agreement for cooperation in the Global Learning and Observations to Benefit the Environment (GLOBE) Program, with appendices. Signed at Yaounde November 6, 1998; entered into force November 6, 1998.
TIAS

FINANCE

Investment incentive agreement. Signed at Sofia June 7, 1991; entered into force September 30, 1991.
TIAS 11500.

BULGARIA (Cont'd)

INVESTMENT

Treaty concerning the encouragement and reciprocal protection of investment, with annex, protocol and exchange of letters. Signed at Washington September 23, 1992; entered into force June 2, 1994.
TIAS

MAPPING

Basic exchange and cooperative agreement for topographic mapping, nautical and aeronautical charting, safety to flight and sea navigation information, geodesy and gravimetrics, digital data, and related global geospatial information and services. Signed at Washington May 13, 1998; entered into force May 13, 1998.
NP

MARITIME MATTERS

Agreement on maritime transport, with exchanges of letters. Signed at Sofia February 19, 1981; entered into force February 19, 1981.
33 UST 1116; TIAS 10098; 1281 UNTS 9.

Extension and amendment:
February 7 and 13, 1984 (TIAS 10942).

NATIONALITY

Naturalization treaty. Signed at Sofia November 23, 1923; entered into force April 5, 1924.
43 Stat. 1759; TS 684; 5 Bevans 1083; 25 LNTS 238.

PACIFIC SETTLEMENT OF DISPUTES

Treaty of arbitration. Signed at Washington January 21, 1929; entered into force July 22, 1929.
46 Stat. 2332; TS 792; 5 Bevans 1094; 93 LNTS 337.

Treaty of conciliation. Signed at Washington January 21, 1929; entered into force July 22, 1929.
46 Stat. 2334; TS 793; 5 Bevans 1097; 93 LNTS 331.

PEACE CORPS

Agreement concerning the establishment of a Peace Corps program in Bulgaria. Signed at

Washington September 27, 1990; entered into force September 27, 1990.
TIAS 11498.

POSTAL MATTERS

Convention for the exchange of postal money orders. Signed at Washington April 3, 1922; operative October 1, 1923.
NP

Protocol modifying the convention for the exchange of money orders. Signed at Washington September 6, 1923; operative October 1, 1923.
NP

Parcel post convention. Signed at Sofia August 2, 1922, and at Washington August 26, 1922; operative November 11, 1919.
42 Stat. 2205; Post Office Department print.

Memorandum of understanding concerning the operation of the INTELPOST service, with details of implementation. Signed at Sofia and Washington April 20 and June 13, 1990; entered into force June 25, 1990.
TIAS 11763.

International express mail agreement, with detailed regulations. Signed at Sofia and Washington April 5 and May 20, 1991; entered into force June 17, 1991.
TIAS 11811.

SCIENTIFIC COOPERATION

Agreement on scientific and technological cooperation, with annexes. Signed at Washington February 9, 1978; entered into force February 9, 1978.
TIAS

TRADE AND COMMERCE

Agreement for the reciprocal waiving of legalization on certificates of origin accompanying merchandise. Exchange of notes at Sofia January 5, 1938; entered into force January 5, 1938.
52 Stat. 1509; EAS 124; 5 Bevans 1105; 191 LNTS 207.

Agreement on trade relations, with exchanges of letters. Signed at Washington April 22, 1991; entered into force November 22, 1991.
TIAS

Agreement relating to trade in textiles and textile products, with annexes. Exchange of notes at Sofia December 2 and 23, 1993; entered into force December 23, 1993; effective January 1, 1993.
NP

Amendment and extension:
April 22 and May 2, 1996 (NP).

BURKINA FASO

AVIATION

Air transport agreement, with annexes. Signed at Washington July 27, 2000; entered into force July 27, 2000.
TIAS

COPYRIGHT (See APPENDIX)

DEFENSE

Agreement concerning the provision of training related to defense articles under the United States International Military Education and Training (IMET) Program. Exchange of notes at Ouagadougou February 20 and August 26, 1986; entered into force August 26, 1986.
TIAS 11282.

ECONOMIC AND TECHNICAL COOPERATION

Agreement providing for the furnishing of economic, technical and related assistance. Exchange of notes at Ouagadougou June 1, 1961; entered into force June 1, 1961.
12 UST 867; TIAS 4787; 410 UNTS 223.

Agency for International Development:
June 30 and July 1, 1977 (29 UST 5363; TIAS 9117).
September 9, 1977 (29 UST 5279; TIAS 9105).
June 8, 1978 (30 UST 3185; TIAS 9388).

FINANCE

Agreement relating to investment guaranties. Exchange of notes at Ouagadougou June 18, 1965; entered into force June 18, 1965.
16 UST 1068; TIAS 5847; 549 UNTS 133.

GEODETIC SURVEY

Arrangement relating to a geodetic survey along the 12th parallel arc. Exchange of notes at Ouagadougou June 28 and August 21, 1967; entered into force August 21, 1967.
18 UST 2848; TIAS 6374; 700 UNTS 297.

PEACE CORPS

Agreement on general conditions for the employment of Peace Corps volunteers. Signed at

BURKINA FASO (Cont'd)

Ouagadougou February 6, 1975; entered into force February 6, 1975.
26 UST 2681; TIAS 8183; 1052 UNTS 221.

POSTAL MATTERS

International express mail agreement, with detailed regulations. Signed at Ouagadougou and Washington October 12 and November 5, 1987; entered into force December 5, 1987.
TIAS 11567.

Postal money order agreement. Signed at Ouagadougou and Washington April 25 and August 17, 1994; entered into force September 1, 1994.
NP

BURMA

On January 4, 1948 Burma became a fully independent sovereign state. The treaty between the Government of the United Kingdom and the Provisional Government of Burma, signed at London October 17, 1947, provides in article 2 that "All obligations and responsibilities heretofore devolving on the Government of the United Kingdom which arise from any valid international instrument shall henceforth, insofar as such instrument may be held to have application to Burma, devolve upon the Provisional Government of Burma. The rights and benefits heretofore enjoyed by the Government of the United Kingdom in virtue of the application of any such international instrument to Burma shall henceforth be enjoyed by the Provisional Government of Burma."

AGRICULTURAL COMMODITIES

Agricultural commodities agreement with exchange of notes. Signed at Rangoon November 9, 1962; entered into force November 9, 1962.
13 UST 2299; TIAS 5198; 461 UNTS 113.

AVIATION

Air transport agreement. Signed at Rangoon September 28, 1949; entered into force September 28, 1949.
63 Stat. 2716; TIAS 1983; 5 Bevans 1121; 55 UNTS 3.

CONSULS

Convention to regulate commerce (article IV) between the United States and the United Kingdom. Signed at London July 3, 1815; entered into force July 3, 1815.
8 Stat. 228; TS 110; 12 Bevans 49.

COPYRIGHT (See APPENDIX)

DEFENSE

Agreement concerning the provision of training related to defense articles under the United States International Military Education and Training (IMET) Program. Exchange of notes at Rangoon April 8 and May 27, 1980; entered into force May 27, 1980.
32 UST 968; TIAS 9745; 1222 UNTS 337.

ECONOMIC AND TECHNICAL COOPERATION

Economic cooperation agreement. Signed at Rangoon March 21, 1957; entered into force October 9, 1957.
8 UST 1862; TIAS 3931; 300 UNTS 11.

Amendments:
September 12, 1959 (10 UST 1733; TIAS 4326; 358 UNTS 352).
June 29, 1960 (11 UST 2249; TIAS 4601; 394 UNTS 284).

Agreement providing special assistance to Burma on a grant basis to finance preliminary engineering and architectural surveys for two proposed construction projects. Exchange of notes at Rangoon June 24, 1959; entered into force June 24, 1959.
10 UST 1730; TIAS 4325; 358 UNTS 91.

EDUCATION

Agreement providing for the United States Educational Foundation. Signed at Rangoon December 22, 1947; entered into force December 22, 1947.
62 Stat. 1814; TIAS 1685; 5 Bevans 1108; 25 UNTS 27.

Amendments:
December 18, 1948 and May 12, 1949 (63 Stat. 2704; TIAS 1976; 5 Bevans 1119; 80 UNTS 312).
August 29, 1961 (12 UST 1195; TIAS 4834; 418 UNTS 326).

EXTRADITION

Extradition treaty between the United States and the United Kingdom. Signed at London December 22, 1931; applicable to Burma from November 1, 1941.
47 Stat. 2122; TS 849; 12 Bevans 482; 163 LNTS 59.

FINANCE

Agreement on the use of kyats accrued under Title I of the Agricultural Trade Development and Assistance Act of 1954, as amended. Signed at Rangoon June 1, 1966; entered into force June 1, 1966.
17 UST 788; TIAS 6034; 580 UNTS 253.

INFORMATIONAL MEDIA GUARANTIES

Agreement relating to an informational media guaranty program in Burma. Exchange of notes at Rangoon October 8 and 23, 1956; entered into force October 23, 1956.
7 UST 3165; TIAS 3695; 282 UNTS 37.

NARCOTIC DRUGS

Agreement relating to the provision of helicopters and related assistance by the United States to help Burma in suppressing illegal narcotic drug production and traffic. Exchange of notes at Rangoon June 29, 1974; entered into force June 29, 1974.
25 UST 1518; TIAS 7887.

PROPERTY

Convention between the United States and the United Kingdom relating to tenure and disposition of real and personal property. Signed at Washington March 2, 1899.[1]
31 Stat. 1939; TS 146; 12 Bevans 246.

Supplementary convention between the United States and the United Kingdom extending the time within which notifications may be given of the accession of British colonies or foreign possessions to the convention of March 2, 1899. Signed at Washington January 13, 1902.[1]
32 Stat. 1914; TS 402; 12 Bevans 261.

NOTE:
[1] Convention considered to remain applicable to Burma after separation from India on April 1, 1937.

PUBLICATIONS

Agreement for the exchange of official publications. Exchange of notes at Rangoon January 26 and April 5, 1948; entered into force April 5, 1948.
62 Stat. 1892; TIAS 1744; 5 Bevans 1116; 73 UNTS 73.

BURMA (Cont'd)

TRADE

Agreement concerning trade in certain textile products, with annexes. Exchange of notes at Rangoon August 25 and September 16, 1987; entered into force September 16, 1987; effective January 1, 1987.
NP

Amendment:
November 17 and December 13, 1988 (NP).

TRADE-MARKS

Declaration by the United States and the United Kingdom affording reciprocal protection to trade-marks. Signed at London October 24, 1877; entered into force October 24, 1877.
20 Stat. 703; TS 138; 12 Bevans 198.

BURUNDI

COPYRIGHT (See APPENDIX)

DEFENSE

Agreement concerning the provision of training related to defense articles under the United States International Military Education and Training (IMET) Program. Exchange of notes at Bujumbura September 21 and October 8, 1982; entered into force October 8, 1982.
TIAS 10577; 1871 UNTS 315.

ECONOMIC AND TECHNICAL COOPERATION

General agreement for special development assistance. Exchange of notes at Bujumbura February 13 and 18, 1970; entered into force February 18, 1970.
21 UST 589; TIAS 6843; 740 UNTS 233.

FINANCE

Agreement relating to investment guaranties. Exchange of notes at Bujumbura May 6, 1969; entered into force May 6, 1969.
21 UST 829; TIAS 6852; 753 UNTS 35.

PEACE CORPS

Agreement relating to the establishment of a Peace Corps program in Burundi. Exchange of notes at Bujumbura August 31, 1982; entered into force August 31, 1982.
TIAS 10465; 1751 UNTS 105.

POSTAL MATTERS

International express mail agreement, with detailed regulations. Signed at Bujumbura and Washington November 10 and December 13, 1989; entered into force January 15, 1990.
TIAS 11895.

CAMBODIA

AGRICULTURAL COMMODITIES

Agricultural commodities agreement with annex. Signed at Phnom Penh March 2, 1971; entered into force March 2, 1971.
22 UST 441; TIAS 7079; 792 UNTS 123.

Amendments:
September 7, 1971 (22 UST 1583; TIAS 7184; 807 UNTS 364).
November 4, 1971 (22 UST 1755; TIAS 7209).
December 21, 1971 (22 UST 2058; TIAS 7241).

Related agreements:
January 13, 1972 (23 UST 14; TIAS 7269).
June 23, 1972 (23 UST 1238; TIAS 7394).
October 2, 1972 (23 UST 3128; TIAS 7487).
October 20, 1972 (23 UST 3131; TIAS 7487).
November 24, 1972 (23 UST 3693; TIAS 7515).
February 2, 1973 (24 UST 445; TIAS 7560).
July 25, 1973 (24 UST 1947; TIAS 7703).
August 2, 1973 (24 UST 1950; TIAS 7703).
August 9, 1973 (24 UST 1952; TIAS 7703).
August 13, 1973 (24 UST 1954; TIAS 7703).
October 8, 1973 (24 UST 2518; TIAS 7767).
October 18, 1973 (24 UST 2521; TIAS 7767).
November 10, 1973 (24 UST 2522; TIAS 7767).
November 15, 1973 (24 UST 2524; TIAS 7767).
December 14, 1973 (24 UST 2526; TIAS 7767).
April 8, 1974 (25 UST 1773; TIAS 7909).
May 16, 1974 (25 UST 1777; TIAS 7909).
May 24, 1974 (25 UST 1778; TIAS 7909).

Agricultural commodities agreement. Signed at Phnom Penh August 10, 1974; entered into force August 10, 1974.
26 UST 45; TIAS 8008; 991 UNTS 330.

Amendments:
September 17, 1974 (26 UST 66; TIAS 8008; 991 UNTS 342).
October 25, 1974 (26 UST 69; TIAS 8008; 991 UNTS 344).
January 14, 1975 (26 UST 72; TIAS 8008; 991 UNTS 346).

AVIATION

Memorandum of understanding for airfield upgrading at Ream, Pochentong and Battambang. Signed at Phnom Penh August 12, 1972; entered into force August 12, 1972.
23 UST 3144; TIAS 7491; 898 UNTS 161.

CLAIMS

Agreement concerning the settlement of certain property claims. Signed at Washington October 6, 1994; entered into force October 6, 1994.
TIAS 12193.

COPYRIGHT (See APPENDIX)

DEFENSE

Agreement relating to the provision of defense articles to Cambodia. Exchange of notes at Phnom Penh August 20, 1970; entered into force August 20, 1970.
21 UST 2178; TIAS 6965; 764 UNTS 233.

Agreement concerning payment to the United States of net proceeds from the sale of defense articles furnished under the military assistance program. Exchange of notes at Phnom Penh May 14 and June 19, 1974; entered into force July 1, 1974.
25 UST 1668; TIAS 7902.

Agreement regarding the status of United States military personnel and civilian employees of the Department of Defense who may be temporarily present in Cambodia in connection with military assistance activities and other official duties. Exchange of notes at Phnom Penh October 12, 1995 and January 22, 1996; entered into force January 22, 1996.
NP

ECONOMIC AND TECHNICAL COOPERATION

Economic, technical and related assistance agreement. Signed at Phnom Penh October 25, 1994; entered into force October 25, 1994.
TIAS 12573.

MAPPING

Agreement relating to mutual mapping assistance between the Khmer Geographic Service and the American Mapping Service. Signed at Phnom Penh October 17, 1957; entered into force October 17, 1957.
8 UST 1761; TIAS 3929; 299 UNTS 203.

CAMBODIA (Cont'd)

PEACE CORPS

Agreement concerning the program of the Peace Corps in Cambodia. Signed at Washington October 3, 1994; entered into force October 3, 1994.
TIAS 12569.

POSTAL MATTERS

International express mail agreement, with detailed regulations. Signed at Phnom Penh and Washington April 27 and October 28, 1994; entered into force January 1, 1995.
NP

PUBLICATIONS

Agreement relating to the exchange of official publications. Exchange of notes at Phnom Penh July 15, 1960; entered into force July 15, 1960.
11 UST 1923; TIAS 4540; 380 UNTS 129.

TRADE

Agreement on trade relations and intellectual property rights protection, with exchanges of notes. Signed at Washington October 4, 1996; entered into force October 25, 1996.
TIAS

Agreement relating to trade in cotton, wool, man-made fiber, non-cotton vegetable fiber and silk blend textiles and textile products, with annexes. Signed at Phnom Penh January 20, 1999; entered into force January 20, 1999; effective January 1, 1999.
NP

CAMEROON

COPYRIGHT (See APPENDIX)

DEFENSE

Agreement concerning the provision of training related to defense articles under the United States International Military Education and Training (IMET) Program. Exchange of notes at Yaounde March 3 and June 19, 1980; entered into force June 19, 1980.
32 UST 2606; TIAS 9862; 1274 UNTS 103.

ECONOMIC AND TECHNICAL COOPERATION

Agreement providing for the furnishing of economic, technical and related assistance. Exchange of notes at Yaounde May 26, 1961; entered into force May 26, 1961.
12 UST 967; TIAS 4801; 413 UNTS 195.

Amendment:
December 8, 1961 (13 UST 282; TIAS 4973; 445 UNTS 367).

Agency for International Development:
May 18, 1978 (30 UST 4547; TIAS 9477).
August 30, 1978 (30 UST 5031; TIAS 9497).

EMPLOYMENT

Agreement relating to the employment of dependents of official government employees. Exchange of notes at Washington May 7, 1992 and January 15, 1993; entered into force January 15, 1993.
TIAS 11916.

ENVIRONMENTAL COOPERATION

Agreement for cooperation in the Global Learning and Observations to Benefit the Environment (GLOBE) Program, with appendices. Signed at Yaounde November 6, 1998; entered into force November 6, 1998.
TIAS

FINANCE

Agreement relating to investment guaranties. Exchange of notes at Washington March 7, 1967; entered into force March 7, 1967.
18 UST 292; TIAS 6231; 688 UNTS 315.

Agreement regarding the consolidation and rescheduling of certain debts owed to, guaranteed by, or insured by the United States Government and its agencies, with annexes. Signed at Yaounde January 3, 1990; entered into force February 12, 1990.
NP

Agreement regarding the phased discharge of certain debts owed to the Government of the United States, with annexes. Signed at Yaounde January 3, 1990; entered into force January 3, 1990.
NP

Agreement regarding the consolidation and rescheduling or refinancing of certain debts owed to, guaranteed by or insured by the United States Government and its agencies, with annexes. Signed at Yaounde August 19, 1992; entered into force October 12, 1992.
NP

Agreement regarding the consolidation and rescheduling or refinancing of certain debts owed to, guaranteed by or insured by the United States Government and its agencies, with annexes. Signed at Yaounde September 12, 1994; entered into force December 5, 1994.
NP

Agreement regarding the consolidation and rescheduling of certain debts owed to, guaranteed by, or insured by the United States Government and its agencies, with annexes. Signed at Yaounde May 6, 1996; entered into force July 31, 1996.
NP

Agreement regarding the consolidation, reduction and rescheduling of certain debts owed to, guaranteed by, or insured by the United States Government and its agencies, with annexes. Signed at Yaounde July 29, 1998; entered into force September 10, 1998.
NP

INVESTMENT

Treaty concerning the reciprocal encouragement and protection of investment. Signed at Washington February 26, 1986; entered into force April 6, 1989.
TIAS

PEACE CORPS

Agreement relating to the establishment of a Peace Corps program in Cameroon. Exchange of notes at Yaounde July 23 and September 10, 1962; entered into force September 10, 1962.
13 UST 2114; TIAS 5171; 461 UNTS 177.

POSTAL MATTERS

International express mail agreement, with detailed regulations. Signed at Yaounde and Washington April 25 and June 22, 1990; entered into force August 1, 1990.
TIAS 11762.

CANADA

AMITY

Treaty of amity, commerce and navigation between the United States and Great Britain (Jay Treaty).[1] Signed at London November 19, 1794; entered into force October 28, 1795.
8 Stat. 116; TS 105; 12 Bevans 13.

Explanatory article to article 3 of the November 19, 1794 treaty of amity, commerce and navigation between the United States and Great Britain.[1] Signed at Philadelphia May 4, 1796; entered into force October 6, 1796.
8 Stat. 130; TS 106; 12 Bevans 34.

CANADA (Cont'd)

Treaty of peace and amity between the United States and Great Britain. Signed at Ghent December 24, 1814; entered into force February 17, 1815.
8 Stat. 218; TS 109; 12 Bevans 41.

Treaty for an amicable settlement of all causes of differences between the United States and Great Britain (Treaty of Washington).[2] Washington May 8, 1871; entered into force June 17, 1871.
17 Stat. 863; TS 133; 12 Bevans 170.

NOTES:
[1] Only article 3 so far as it relates to the right of Indians to pass across the border, and articles 9 and 10 appear to remain in force. But see *Akins v. U.S.,* 551 F.2d 1222 (1977).
[2] Articles I-XVII and XXXIV-XLII have been executed; articles XVIII-XXV, XXX, and XXXII terminated July 1, 1885; articles XXVIII and XXIX not considered in force.

ARCTIC

Agreement on Arctic cooperation. Signed at Ottawa January 11, 1988; entered into force January 11, 1988.
TIAS 11565.

ATOMIC ENERGY

Agreement for cooperation on civil uses of atomic energy. Signed at Washington June 15, 1955; entered into force July 21, 1955.
6 UST 2595; TIAS 3304; 235 UNTS 175.

Extension and amendments:[1]
June 26, 1956 (8 UST 275; TIAS 3771; 279 UNTS 318).
June 11, 1960 (11 UST 1780; TIAS 4518; 377 UNTS 412).
May 25, 1962 (13 UST 1400; TIAS 5102; 453 UNTS 362).
June 23, 1999.

Agreement for cooperation regarding atomic information for mutual defense purposes. Signed at Washington June 15, 1955; entered into force July 22, 1955.
6 UST 2607; TIAS 3305; 235 UNTS 201.

Agreement for cooperation on uses of atomic energy for mutual defense purposes. Signed at Washington May 22, 1959; entered into force July 27, 1959.
10 UST 1293; TIAS 4271; 354 UNTS 63.

Agreement respecting cooperation in radioactive waste management. Signed at Ottawa August 25, 1982; entered into force August 25, 1982.
TIAS 10456; 1751 UNTS 23.

Agreement regarding participation in the international piping integrity research group.

Signed at Ottawa and Bethesda April 28 and May 20, 1987; entered into force May 20, 1987.
TIAS 12227.

Administrative arrangement concerning cooperation and the exchange of information in nuclear regulatory matters, with appendices. Signed at Washington June 21, 1989; entered into force June 21, 1989.
TIAS 12242.

Agreement concerning cooperation on the application of non-proliferation assurances to Canadian uranium to be transferred from Canada to the U.S. for enrichment and fabrication into fuel and retransferred to Taiwan for use in nuclear reactors, with annex. Exchange of letters at Washington February 24 and March 5, 1993; entered into force March 5, 1993.
TIAS 12490; 1914 UNTS 209.

Administrative arrangement for cooperation and the exchange of information in nuclear regulatory matters, with appendices. Signed at Ottawa August 15, 1996; entered into force August 15, 1996.
TIAS

Agreement relating to participation in the USNRC program of severe accident research. Signed at Ottawa and Rockville September 5 and October 20, 1997; entered into force October 20, 1997.
TIAS

NOTE:
[1] See also agreement of May 22, 1959 for cooperation on uses of atomic energy for mutual defense purposes (10 UST 1293; TIAS 4271).

AVIATION

Arrangement relating to the issuance of certificates of competency or licenses for the piloting of civil aircraft. Exchange of notes at Washington July 28, 1938; entered into force August 1, 1938.
53 Stat. 1937; EAS 130; 6 Bevans 108; 192 LNTS 115.

Agreement relating to cooperation between the United States and Canada in air search and rescue operations along the common boundary. Exchange of notes at Washington January 24 and 31, 1949; entered into force January 31, 1949.
63 Stat. 2328; TIAS 1882; 6 Bevans 478; 43 UNTS 119.

Agreement relating to the use by civil aircraft of Stephenville and Argentia military air bases in Newfoundland. Exchange of notes at Ottawa June 4, 1949; entered into force June 4, 1949.
63 Stat. 2486; TIAS 1933; 6 Bevans 488; 200 UNTS 201.

Agreement concerning air traffic control. Exchange of notes at Ottawa December 20 and

27, 1963; entered into force December 27, 1963.
14 UST 1737; TIAS 5480; 494 UNTS 21.

Agreement on air transport preclearance, with annexes. Signed at Ottawa May 8, 1974; entered into force May 8, 1974.
25 UST 763; TIAS 7825.

Related agreement:
August 23 and October 15, 1979 (31 UST 5606; TIAS 9677).

Memorandum of agreement relating to the provision of flight inspection services. Signed at Washington and Koblenz March 10 and April 1, 1978; entered into force April 1, 1978.
30 UST 278; TIAS 9198.

Amendment:
February 4 and 24, 1982 (TIAS 10565; 1871 UNTS 516).

Agreement concerning the airworthiness and environmental certification of imported civil aeronautical products. Exchange of letters at Ottawa August 31, 1984; entered into force August 31, 1984.
TIAS 11023; 1469 UNTS 339.

Air transport agreement, with annexes. Signed at Ottawa February 24, 1995; entered into force February 24, 1995.
TIAS

Related agreement:
January 20 and June 12, 2000.

Memorandum of cooperation for mutual cooperation in the area of civil aviation research, engineering and development, with annex. Signed at Washington and Ottawa May 6 and July 9, 1996; entered into force July 9, 1996.
TIAS

Agreement for promotion of aviation safety. Signed at Toronto June 12, 2000; entered into force June 12, 2000.
TIAS

BOUNDARIES (See also AMITY)

Convention respecting fisheries, boundary and the restoration of slaves. Signed at London October 20, 1818; entered into force January 30, 1819.
8 Stat. 248; TS 112; 12 Bevans 57.

Treaty to settle and define the boundaries between the territories of the United States and the possessions of Her Britannic Majesty in North America; for the final suppression of the African slave trade, and for the giving up of criminals, fugitive from justice, in certain cases (Webster-Ashburton Treaty).[1] Washington August 9, 1842; entered into force October 13, 1842.
8 Stat. 572; TS 119; 12 Bevans 82.

Treaty establishing the boundary in the territory on the northwest coast of America lying westward of the Rocky Mountains (Oregon

CANADA (Cont'd)

Treaty). Signed at Washington June 15, 1846; entered into force July 17, 1846.
9 Stat. 869; TS 120; 12 Bevans 95.

Declaration adopting maps of boundary prepared by the Joint Commission of the Northwest Boundary for surveying and marking the boundaries between the United States and British possessions on the forty-ninth parallel of north latitude, under the first article of the treaty of June 15, 1846 between the United States and the United Kingdom. Signed at Washington February 24, 1870; entered into force February 24, 1870.
TS 129; 12 Bevans 157.

Protocol of a conference respecting the northwest water boundary. Signed at Washington March 10, 1873; entered into force March 10, 1873.
18 Stat. 369; TS 135; 12 Bevans 190.

Convention providing for the settlement of questions between the United States and the United Kingdom with respect to the boundary line between the territory of Alaska and the British possessions in North America.[2] Signed at Washington January 24, 1903; entered into force March 3, 1903.
32 Stat. 1961; TS 419; 12 Bevans 263.

Acceptance of the report of the commissioners to complete the award under the convention of January 24, 1903 respecting the boundary line between Alaska and the British North American possessions. Exchange of notes at Washington March 25, 1905; entered into force March 25, 1905.
TS 476; 12 Bevans 269.

Convention providing for the surveying and marking out upon the ground of the 141st degree of west longitude where said meridian forms the boundary line between Alaska and the British possessions in North America.[3] Signed at Washington April 21, 1906; entered into force August 16, 1906.
34 Stat. 2948; TS 452; 12 Bevans 276.

Treaty concerning the Canadian international boundary. Signed at Washington April 11, 1908; entered into force June 4, 1908.
35 Stat. 2003; TS 497; 12 Bevans 297.

Treaty concerning the boundary line in Passamaquoddy Bay. Signed at Washington May 21, 1910; entered into force August 20, 1910.
36 Stat. 2477; TS 551; 12 Bevans 341.

Treaty in regard to the boundary between the United States and Canada. Signed at Washington February 24, 1925; entered into force July 17, 1925.
44 Stat. 2102; TS 720; 6 Bevans 7; 43 LNTS 239.

Treaty to submit to binding dispute settlement the delimitation of the maritime boundary in the Gulf of Maine Area, with annexed agreements, as amended. Signed at Washington

March 29, 1979; entered into force November 20, 1981.[4]
33 UST 2797; TIAS 10204; 1288 UNTS 27.

NOTES:
[1] Article 10 supplemented by convention of July 12, 1889 (See under CANADA—EXTRADITION).
[2] Obsolete except for first paragraph of article VI.
[3] Obsolete except for article II.
[4] For the subsequent judgment of the International Court of Justice of October 12, 1984, see Case concerning Delimitation of the Maritime Boundary in the Gulf of Maine Area. 1984 I.C.J. Reports 246.
With the implementation of the special agreement to submit the dispute to a chamber of the I.C.J., the agreement for possible submission to a court of arbitration never entered into force.

BOUNDARY WATERS (See also AMITY, BOUNDARIES, MARITIME MATTERS and POLLUTION)

Treaty relating to the boundary waters and questions arising along the boundary between the United States and Canada.[1] Signed at Washington January 11, 1909; entered into force May 5, 1910.
36 Stat. 2448; TS 548; 12 Bevans 319.

Convention to regulate the level of the Lake of the Woods, with an accompanying protocol and an agreement. Signed at Washington February 24, 1925; entered into force July 17, 1925.
44 Stat. 2108; TS 721; 6 Bevans 14; 43 LNTS 251.

Amendment:
February 21 and June 19, 1979 (30 UST 5998; TIAS 9534; 1180 UNTS 77).

Arrangement relating to the level of Lake Memphremagog. Exchange of notes at Ottawa September 20 and November 6, 1935; entered into force November 6, 1935.
Foreign Relations, 1935, Vol. II, p. 53; 6 Bevans 71.

Convention providing for emergency regulation of the level of Rainy Lake and of certain other boundary waters. Signed at Ottawa September 15, 1938; entered into force October 3, 1940.
54 Stat. 1800; TS 961; 6 Bevans 115; 203 LNTS 207.

Arrangement relating to the early development of certain portions of the Great Lakes-St. Lawrence Basin project (Long Lac-Ogoki Works). Exchange of notes at Washington October 14 and 31 and November 7, 1940; entered into force November 7, 1940.
54 Stat. 2426; EAS 187; 6 Bevans 199; 203 LNTS 267.

Agreement relating to the temporary raising of level of Lake St. Francis during low-water pe-

riods. Exchange of notes at Washington November 10, 1941; entered into force November 10, 1941.
56 Stat. 1832; EAS 291; 6 Bevans 236; 23 UNTS 280.

Extension:
August 31 and September 7, 1944 (58 Stat. 1437; EAS 424; 105 UNTS 310).

Agreement relating to the Upper Columbia River Basin. Exchange of notes at Ottawa February 25 and March 3, 1944; entered into force March 3, 1944.
58 Stat. 1236; EAS 399; 6 Bevans 342; 109 UNTS 191.

Treaty relating to uses of waters of the Niagara River. Signed at Washington February 27, 1950; entered into force October 10, 1950.
1 UST 694; TIAS 2130; 132 UNTS 223.

Related agreements:
September 13, 1954 (5 UST 1979; TIAS 3064; 236 UNTS 382).
April 17, 1973 (24 UST 895; TIAS 7599).

Agreement relating to the St. Lawrence seaway project for the construction of certain navigation facilities. Exchange of notes at Washington June 30, 1952; entered into force June 30, 1952.
5 UST 1788; TIAS 3053; 234 UNTS 199.

Agreement establishing the St. Lawrence River Joint Board of Engineers. Exchange of notes at Washington November 12, 1953; entered into force November 12, 1953.
5 UST 2538; TIAS 3116; 234 UNTS 97.

Agreement relating to the St. Lawrence seaway project for the construction of certain navigation facilities. Exchange of notes at Ottawa August 17, 1954; entered into force August 17, 1954.
5 UST 1784; TIAS 3053; 234 UNTS 210.

Related agreements:
October 24, 1956 (7 UST 2865; TIAS 3668; 281 UNTS 281).
November 7 and December 4, 1956 (7 UST 3271; TIAS 3708).
July 23 and October 26, 1956 and February 26, 1957 (8 UST 279; TIAS 3772; 279 UNTS 179).
November 30, 1956 and April 8 and 9, 1957 (8 UST 637; TIAS 3814; 283 UNTS 217).
May 19, 1955 and February 27, 1959 (10 UST 383; TIAS 4199; 341 UNTS 3).
October 17, 1961 (12 UST 1284; TIAS 4851; 426 UNTS 201).
June 8, 1959 and October 17, 1961 (12 UST 1669; TIAS 4883; 424 UNTS 101).

Agreement governing tolls on the St. Lawrence Seaway. Exchange of notes at Ottawa March 9, 1959; entered into force March 9, 1959.
10 UST 323; TIAS 4192; 340 UNTS 295.

Amendments:
March 20, 1978 (29 UST 3165; TIAS 9003).
November 13 and 16, 1984 (TIAS 11061).
May 3, 1985 (TIAS 11309; 1466 UNTS 436).
March 30 and August 1, 1989 (TIAS 11966).

CANADA (Cont'd)

April 26 and May 1, 1991 (TIAS 11885).
December 12 and 20, 1991 (TIAS 11866).
June 15 and 30, 1992 (TIAS 11866).
June 10 and July 12, 1994 (TIAS 12697).
August 9 and October 18, 1995 (TIAS 12697).

Treaty relating to cooperative development of the water resources of the Columbia River Basin. Signed at Washington January 17, 1961; entered into force September 16, 1964, with related agreements effected by exchanges of notes at Washington January 22, 1964, and at Ottawa September 16, 1964.
15 UST 1555; TIAS 5638; 542 UNTS 244.

Related agreement:
October 4, 1965 (16 UST 1263; TIAS 5877; 592 UNTS 272).

Agreement governing the operation of pilotage on the Great Lakes. Exchange of notes at Ottawa August 23, 1978 and March 29, 1979; entered into force March 29, 1979; effective January 18, 1977.
30 UST 4027; TIAS 9445; 1171 UNTS 45.

Amendments:
February 12, 1991 (TIAS 11813; 1853 UNTS 431).
October 15, 1992 and June 17, 1993 (TIAS 12154).

Treaty relating to the Skagit River and Ross Lake, and the Seven Mile Reservoir on the Pend d'Oreille River, with annex. Signed at Washington April 2, 1984; entered into force December 14, 1984.
TIAS 11088; 1469 UNTS 309.

Agreement concerning cooperation in flood control, with construction plan. Exchange of notes at Ottawa and Washington August 29 and 30, 1988; entered into force August 30, 1988.
TIAS 11641.

Agreement for water supply and flood control in the Souris River Basin, with annexes. Signed at Washington October 26, 1989; entered into force October 26, 1989.
TIAS 11731.

Amendment:
December 20 and 22, 2000.

Agreement for the sale of Canada's entitlement to downstream power benefits within the United States, with attachment. Exchange of notes at Washington March 31, 1999; entered into force March 31, 1999.
TIAS

NOTE:
[1] Paragraphs 3, 4, and 5 of article V terminated October 10, 1950 upon the entry into force of the treaty relating to uses of waters of the Niagara River, signed February 27, 1950 (1 UST 694; TIAS 2130; 132 UNTS 223).

CAMPOBELLO

Agreement relating to the establishment of the Roosevelt Campobello International Park. Signed at Washington January 22, 1964; entered into force August 14, 1964.
15 UST 1504; TIAS 5631; 530 UNTS 89.

CIVIL EMERGENCY PLANNING

Agreement on cooperation in comprehensive civil emergency planning and management, with annex. Signed at Ottawa April 28, 1986; entered into force April 28, 1986.
TIAS 11404.

CLAIMS

Convention for the establishment of a tribunal to decide questions of indemnity arising from the operation of the smelter at Trail, British Columbia. Signed at Ottawa April 15, 1935; entered into force August 3, 1935.
49 Stat. 3245; TS 893; 6 Bevans 60; 162 LNTS 73.

Agreement supplementary to the convention signed April 15, 1935 for the establishment of a tribunal to decide questions of indemnity and future regime arising from the operation of the smelter at Trail, British Columbia. Exchange of notes at Washington November 17, 1949 and January 24, 1950; entered into force January 24, 1950.
3 UST 539; TIAS 2412; 151 UNTS 171.

Agreement relating to claims arising out of traffic accidents involving vehicles of the armed forces of the United States and Canada. Exchange of notes at Ottawa March 1 and 23, 1944; entered into force March 23, 1944.
60 Stat. 1948; TIAS 1581; 6 Bevans 345; 125 UNTS 345.

Agreement relating to waiver of certain claims involving government vessels. Exchange of notes at Washington September 28 and November 13 and 15, 1946; entered into force November 15, 1946.
61 Stat. 2520; TIAS 1582; 6 Bevans 422; 7 UNTS 141.

Agreement relating to the settlement of certain war accounts and claims. Exchange of notes at Washington March 14, 1949; entered into force March 14, 1949.
63 Stat. 2432; TIAS 1925; 6 Bevans 482; 82 UNTS 3.

COMMERCE (See AMITY)

CONSERVATION

Convention for the protection of migratory birds in the United States and Canada. Signed at Washington August 16, 1916; entered into force December 7, 1916.
39 Stat. 1702; TS 628; 12 Bevans 375.

Amendment:
December 14, 1995.

Arrangement prohibiting the importation of raccoon dogs. Exchange of letters at Ottawa and Washington September 1 and 4, 1981; entered into force September 4, 1981.
33 UST 3764; TIAS 10259; 1541 UNTS 129.

Agreement on the conservation of the Porcupine Caribou Herd, with annex. Signed at Ottawa July 17, 1987; entered into force July 17, 1987.
TIAS 11259.

CONSULS

Convention to regulate commerce (article IV) between the United States and the United Kingdom. Signed at London July 3, 1815; effective July 3, 1815.
8 Stat. 228; TS 110; 12 Bevans 49.

Arrangement relating to visits of consular officers to citizens of their own country serving sentences in penal institutions. Exchange of notes at Ottawa July 29 and September 19, 1935; entered into force September 19, 1935.
Foreign Relations, 1935, Vol. II, p. 57; 6 Bevans 65.

COPYRIGHT (See APPENDIX)

CULTURAL PROPERTY

Agreement concerning the imposition of import restrictions on certain categories of archaeological and ethnological material, with appendix. Signed at Washington April 10, 1997; entered into force April 10, 1997.
TIAS

CUSTOMS

Agreement relating to importation privileges for government officials and employees. Exchanges of notes at Ottawa July 21, October 29 and November 9, 1942; entered into force November 9, 1942.
57 Stat. 1379; EAS 383; 6 Bevans 289; 101 UNTS 233.

Agreement regarding mutual assistance and cooperation between customs administrations. Signed at Quebec June 20, 1984; entered into force January 8, 1985.
TIAS 11253; 1469 UNTS 319.

CANADA (Cont'd)

DEFENSE

Declaration by the Prime Minister of Canada and the President of the United States of America regarding the establishing of a Permanent Joint Board on Defense. Made at Ogdensburg, New York, August 18, 1940.
Department of State *Bulletin*, Vol. III, No. 61, August 24, 1940, p. 154; 6 Bevans 189; Canada Treaty Series, 1940, No. 14.

Arrangement relating to naval and air bases. Exchange of notes at Washington September 2, 1940; entered into force September 2, 1940.
54 Stat. 2405; EAS 181; 12 Bevans 551; 203 LNTS 201.

Agreement regarding leased naval and air bases, and exchanges of notes. Signed at London March 27, 1941; entered into force March 27, 1941.
55 Stat. 1560; EAS 235; 12 Bevans 560; 204 LNTS 15.

Amendment:
May 22, 1985.

Protocol concerning the defense of Newfoundland. Signed at London March 27, 1941; entered into force March 27, 1941.
55 Stat. 1599; EAS 235; 12 Bevans 560; 204 LNTS 70.

Hyde Park agreement. Announcement made at Hyde Park April 20, 1941 by the President of the United States of America and the Prime Minister of Canada.
Department of State *Bulletin*, Vol. IV, No. 96, April 26, 1941, p. 494; 6 Bevans 216.

Arrangement relating to visits in uniform by members of defense forces. Exchange of notes at Ottawa August 28 and September 4, 1941; entered into force September 11, 1941.
55 Stat. 1551; EAS 233; 6 Bevans 231; 119 UNTS 285.

Agreement relating to payment for certain defense installations in Canada and at Goose Bay, Labrador. Exchange of notes at Washington June 23 and 27, 1944; entered into force June 27, 1944.
58 Stat. 1290; EAS 405; 6 Bevans 360; 101 UNTS 273.

Agreement relating to reconversion of industry. Exchange of notes at Ottawa May 7 and 15, 1945; entered into force May 15, 1945.
61 Stat. 3958; TIAS 1752; 6 Bevans 397; 125 UNTS 353.

United States-Canadian Permanent Joint Board on Defense to continue collaboration for security purposes. Announced in Ottawa and in Washington February 12, 1947.
Department of State *Bulletin*, Vol. XVI, No. 399, February 23, 1947, p. 361; 6 Bevans 430; Canada Treaty Series, 1947, No. 43.

Agreement relating to the leased naval base at Argentia, Newfoundland. Exchange of notes at London August 13 and October 23, 1947; entered into force October 23, 1947.
61 Stat. 4065; TIAS 1809; 12 Bevans 827; 66 UNTS 277.

Amendment:
May 22, 1985.

Agreement establishing a Joint Industrial Mobilization Committee. Exchange of notes at Ottawa April 12, 1949; entered into force April 12, 1949.
63 Stat. 2331; TIAS 1889; 6 Bevans 486; 206 UNTS 241.

Agreement relating to a final settlement for all war surplus property disposed of pursuant to the agreements effected by exchanges of notes of November 22 and December 20, 1944; March 30, 1946; and July 11 and 15, 1946. Exchange of notes at Ottawa June 17 and 18, 1949; entered into force June 18, 1949.
2 UST 2272; TIAS 2352; 200 UNTS 258.

Agreement relating to economic cooperation for defense. Exchange of notes at Washington October 26, 1950; entered into force October 26, 1950.
1 UST 716; TIAS 2136; 132 UNTS 247.

Agreement relating to the extension and coordination of the continental radar defense system.[1] Exchange of notes at Washington August 1, 1951; entered into force August 1, 1951.
5 UST 1721; TIAS 3049; 233 UNTS 109.

Related agreements:
May 25, 1964 (15 UST 665; TIAS 5587; 526 UNTS 251).
September 30, 1966 (17 UST 1416; TIAS 6102; 616 UNTS 193).
June 30, 1971 (22 UST 1449; TIAS 7154; 797 UNTS 303).
March 22, 1974 (25 UST 283; TIAS 7799; 944 UNTS 173).

Agreement modifying the leased bases agreement of March 27, 1941 with the United Kingdom concerning bases in Canada. Exchange of notes at Washington February 13 and March 19, 1952; entered into force March 19, 1952.
3 UST 4271; TIAS 2572; 174 UNTS 267.

Agreement relating to the application of the NATO status of forces agreement to U.S. forces in Canada, including those at the leased bases in Newfoundland and Goose Bay, Labrador except for certain arrangements under the leased bases agreement. Exchange of notes at Washington April 28 and 30, 1952; entered into force September 27, 1953.
5 UST 2139; TIAS 3074; 235 UNTS 269.

Agreement on the establishment and operation of a distant early warning system between the United States and Canada. Exchange of notes, with annex, at Washington May 5, 1955; entered into force May 5, 1955.[2]
6 UST 763; TIAS 3218; 241 UNTS 179.

Agreement relating to the establishment and operation of certain radar stations in the Newfoundland-Labrador area. Exchange of notes at Ottawa June 13, 1955; entered into force June 13, 1955.
6 UST 6045; TIAS 3452; 268 UNTS 87.

Agreement relating to the construction and operation of certain radar stations in British Columbia, Ontario, and Nova Scotia.[1] Exchange of notes at Ottawa June 15, 1955; entered into force June 15, 1955.
6 UST 6051; TIAS 3453; 268 UNTS 101.

Agreement relating to the construction of a petroleum products pipeline between the United States Air Force dock at St. John's, Newfoundland, and Pepperrell Air Force Base, Newfoundland, with annex. Exchange of notes at Ottawa September 22, 1955; entered into force September 22, 1955.
6 UST 3899; TIAS 3392; 256 UNTS 227.

Agreement providing for the establishment of a Canada-United States Committee on Joint Defense. Exchange of notes at Ottawa August 29 and September 2, 1958; entered into force September 2, 1958.
9 UST 1159; TIAS 4098; 335 UNTS 249.

Agreement relating to communications facilities at Cape Dyer, Baffin Island to support the Greenland extension of the distant early warning system. Exchange of notes at Ottawa April 13, 1959; entered into force April 13, 1959, operative January 15, 1959.
10 UST 739; TIAS 4208; 342 UNTS 43.

Agreement relating to the establishment, maintenance and operation of short range tactical air navigation (TACAN) facilities in Canada, with annex. Exchange of notes at Ottawa May 1, 1959; entered into force May 1, 1959.
10 UST 790; TIAS 4218; 343 UNTS 27.

Amendment:
September 19 and 23, 1961 (12 UST 1357; TIAS 4856; 421 UNTS 79).

Agreement relating to the establishment of a ballistic missile early warning system. Exchange of notes at Ottawa July 13, 1959; entered into force July 13, 1959.
10 UST 1260; TIAS 4264; 353 UNTS 237.

Agreement relating to the extension and strengthening of the continental air defense system (CADIN). Exchange of notes at Ottawa September 27, 1961; entered into force September 27, 1961.
12 UST 1375; TIAS 4859; 421 UNTS 85.

Amendments:
May 6, 1964 (15 UST 427; TIAS 5574; 524 UNTS 324).
November 24, 1965 (16 UST 1768; TIAS 5907; 573 UNTS 330).

Agreement concerning the establishment, operation and maintenance of certain ground-to-air communications facilities in northern Canada, with annex. Exchange of notes at Ottawa December 1, 1965; entered into force December 1, 1965.
16 UST 1789; TIAS 5911; 574 UNTS 37.

Agreement relating to the establishment of a ferry service between North Sydney, Nova

CANADA (Cont'd)

Scotia and Argentia, Newfoundland, with annex. Exchange of notes at Washington June 6 and 10, 1966; entered into force June 10, 1966.
17 UST 792; TIAS 6035; 639 UNTS 13.

Agreement relating to the winter maintenance of the Haines Road. Exchange of notes at Ottawa May 10 and June 23, 1967; entered into force June 23, 1967.
18 UST 1244; TIAS 6274; 685 UNTS 410.

Agreement relating to the use of certain facilities at the United States Air Force Pinetree radar site at Hopedale, Labrador. Exchange of notes at Ottawa June 11, September 19, 1969 and February 24, 1970; entered into force February 24, 1970.
21 UST 596; TIAS 6844; 740 UNTS 241.

Agreement relating to the transfer of the Redcliff site to Canada. Exchange of notes at Ottawa May 10, 1971; entered into force May 10, 1971.
22 UST 1778; TIAS 7217.

Agreement relating to new financial arrangements to govern the operation and maintenance of Pinetree radar stations in Canada with annex. Exchange of notes at Ottawa August 16, 1971; entered into force August 16, 1971; operative August 1, 1971.
22 UST 1529; TIAS 7173; 807 UNTS 19.

Lease of three radar sets (AN/PPS-15) to Canada, with general provisions. Signed at Washington November 18, 1975; entered into force November 18, 1975.
27 UST 2375; TIAS 8317; 1054 UNTS 319.

Agreement relating to the installation, operation, and maintenance of a circuit for narrative record traffic between the defense agencies. Signed at Ottawa and at Washington January 7 and 19, 1976; entered into force January 19, 1976.
27 UST 1971; TIAS 8293.

Agreement relating to the continued operation and maintenance of the torpedo test range in the Strait of Georgia and the installation and utilization of an advanced underwater acoustic measurement system at Jervis Inlet, with annex. Exchange of notes at Ottawa January 13 and April 14, 1976; entered into force April 14, 1976.
27 UST 3723; TIAS 8386.

Extension:
June 3 and 17, 1986 (TIAS 11368).

Agreement relating to the purchase by Canada of eighteen Lockheed P-3 long-range patrol aircraft, with related notes. Exchange of letters at Washington July 6 and 7, 1976; entered into force July 7, 1976.
27 UST 3732; TIAS 8388.

Agreement relating to the continued use of facilities at Goose Bay airport by the United States, with annex. Exchange of notes at Ottawa November 10 and 24, 1976; entered into force November 24, 1976; effective October 1, 1976.
27 UST 4322; TIAS 8454.

Memorandum of understanding concerning region operations control center. Signed at Ottawa and Washington March 5 and April 11, 1977; entered into force April 11, 1977.
29 UST 1075; TIAS 8869.

Agreement relating to performance evaluation of a variable depth sonar system in conjunction with a high speed surface vessel, with annexes (Project Hytow). Signed at Washington and Ottawa September 12 and October 12, 1977; entered into force October 12, 1977.
29 UST 5561; TIAS 9129.

Undertaking relating to the examination and audit of certain subcontracts awarded to Pratt and Whitney of Canada, with memorandum of understanding. Exchange of notes at Washington October 13 and 28, 1977; entered into force October 28, 1977.
29 UST 2852; TIAS 8980.

Memorandum of understanding concerning NAVSTAR global positioning system, with annex. Signed at Washington and Ottawa August 7 and October 5, 1978; entered into force October 5, 1978.
31 UST 5857; TIAS 9689; 1221 UNTS 23.

Memorandum of understanding pertaining to coordination of cooperative research and development. Signed February 1, 1979; entered into force February 1, 1979.
30 UST 3595; TIAS 9414; 1230 UNTS 349.

Agreement regarding continued cooperation in the North American Aerospace Defense Command. Exchange of notes at Ottawa March 11, 1981; entered into force March 11, 1981, effective May 12, 1981.
33 UST 1277; TIAS 10111; 1285 UNTS 49.

Extension:
April 30, 1991 (TIAS 12261; 1853 UNTS 441).

Letter of agreement concerning narrative record telecommunication interface arrangements, with appendices. Signed at Ottawa and Washington September 15 and October 22, 1981; entered into force October 22, 1981.
33 UST 3852; TIAS 10265; 1543 UNTS 125.

Agreement concerning the test and evaluation of United States defense weapons systems in Canada. Exchange of notes at Washington February 10, 1983; entered into force February 10, 1983.
TIAS 10659; 1469 UNTS 275.

Mutual logistical support agreement, with annexes. Signed at Stuttgart February 11, 1983; entered into force February 11, 1983.
TIAS 10658.

Memorandum of understanding on the exchange of service personnel between the United States Marine Corps and Canadian Forces. Signed at Washington September 19, 1984; entered into force September 19, 1984.
TIAS 11135.

Agreement regarding modernization of the North American Air Defense System, with memorandum of understanding. Exchange of notes at Quebec March 18, 1985; entered into force March 18, 1985.
TIAS 12260.

Memorandum of understanding on reciprocal training of reserve officers between the Canadian Land Forces Command and Staff College and the U.S. Marine Corps Command and Staff College. Signed November 4, 1985; entered into force November 4, 1985.
TIAS 11321.

Agreement concerning the exchange of fuel for naval ships and aircraft, with enclosure. Signed at Ottawa and Washington May 5 and June 27, 1986; entered into force June 27, 1986.
TIAS 11380.

Memorandum of understanding on aviation cooperation. Signed at Washington and Ottawa March 20 and April 9, 1987; entered into force April 9, 1987.
TIAS 11294.

Memorandum of understanding concerning the personnel exchange program between the United States Navy and the Canadian Forces, with appendix. Signed at Washington May 27 and June 9, 1988; entered into force June 9, 1988.
NP

Memorandum of understanding concerning mutual logistical support, with annexes. Signed at Ottawa June 6, 1989; entered into force June 6, 1989.
TIAS 11974.

Agreement concerning cooperative testing and evaluation of defense systems. Exchange of notes at Washington February 10, 1993; entered into force February 10, 1993.
TIAS 12262; 1914 UNTS 193.

Memorandum of understanding concerning defense communications service, with annex and appendices. Signed at Ottawa and Arlington September 9 and October 13, 1993; entered into force October 13, 1993.
TIAS 12263.

Agreement concerning the establishment of certain mutual defense commitments. Exchange of notes at Washington and Ottawa March 4 and August 19, 1994; entered into force August 19, 1994.
TIAS 12526.

Memorandum of understanding concerning the measures to be taken for the transfer, security and safeguarding of technical information and equipment to the Department of National Defence for use in the Canadian arctic subsurface surveillance system. Signed at Washington and Ottawa May 31 and September 23, 1994; entered into force September 23, 1994.
TIAS 12264.

CANADA (Cont'd)

Memorandum of understanding concerning counterterrorism research and development, with annex. Signed at Washington and Ottawa June 12 and 23, 1995; entered into force June 23, 1995.
TIAS

Agreement regarding the organization and operations of the North American Aerospace Defense Command (NORAD). Exchange of notes at Washington March 28, 1996; entered into force March 28, 1996; effective May 12, 1996.
TIAS

Memorandum of understanding for technology research and development projects, with annex. Signed at Washington and Ottawa July 18 and August 29, 1996; entered into force August 29, 1996.
TIAS

Agreement on a full and final settlement of all claims for costs of environmental clean-up at former U.S. military installations in Canada. Exchange of notes at Washington October 7 and 9, 1996; entered into force October 9, 1996.
TIAS

Agreement extending the agreement of May 12, 1958, as amended and extended, concerning the organization and the operation of the North American Aerospace Defense Command (NORAD). Exchange of notes at Washington June 16, 2000; entered into force June 16, 2000; effective May 12, 2001.
TIAS

NOTES:
[1] Provisions are terminated to the extent that they are inconsistent with the agreement of August 16, 1971 (TIAS 7173). See also agreements of June 13, 1955 (TIAS 3452), June 15, 1955 (TIAS 3453) and September 27, 1961 (TIAS 4859).
[2] See also agreements of April 13, 1959 (TIAS 4208) and July 13, 1959 (TIAS 4264).

ECONOMIC AND TECHNICAL COOPERATION

Agreement relating to post-war economic settlements. Exchange of notes at Washington November 30, 1942; entered into force November 30, 1942.
56 Stat. 1815; EAS 287; 6 Bevans 292; 119 UNTS 305.

EDUCATION

Agreement for the establishment of a binational educational exchange foundation. Signed at Ottawa February 13, 1990; entered into force February 13, 1990.
TIAS

EMBASSY SITES

Agreement concerning construction of new chanceries in Washington and Ottawa. Exchange of notes at Washington May 13 and October 2, 1985; entered into force October 2, 1985.
TIAS 11328.

EMPLOYMENT (See also LABOR; SOCIAL SECURITY)

Arrangement relating to the employment of dependents of government employees. Exchange of notes at Washington June 4 and 12, 1980; entered into force June 12, 1980.
TIAS 10693.

Amendment:
October 3 and November 13, 1997.

ENERGY

Implementing arrangement on collaboration in joint planning and exchange of information and personnel in energy research and development. Signed at Ottawa December 24, 1986; entered into force December 24, 1986.[1]
TIAS

Memorandum of understanding for cooperation in the field of magnetic fusion energy. Signed at Washington November 19, 1987; entered into force November 19, 1987.
TIAS

Implementing arrangement in the area of natural gas hydrates research and development. Signed at Ottawa and Washington December 11, 1987 and February 16, 1988; entered into force February 16, 1988.[1]
TIAS

Arrangement in the area of coal/heavy oil co-processing. Signed at Washington and Ottawa January 19 and February 14, 1989; entered into force February 14, 1989.[1]
TIAS

NOTE:
[1] Implements memorandum of understanding of December 4, 1986 which by its terms is not legally binding.

EXTRADITION

Treaty on extradition, as amended by exchange of notes of June 28 and July 9, 1974.[1] Signed at Washington December 3, 1971; entered into force March 22, 1976.
27 UST 983; TIAS 8237.

Amendment:
January 11, 1988 (1853 UNTS 407).

NOTE:
[1] Applicable to all territories.

FINANCE

Agreement relating to exemptions from exchange control measures. Exchange of notes at Ottawa June 18, 1940; entered into force June 18, 1940.
54 Stat. 2317; EAS 174; 6 Bevans 182; 203 LNTS 41.

FIRE PROTECTION

Agreement relating to the participation of the Provinces of New Brunswick and Quebec in the northeastern interstate forest fire protection compact. Exchange of notes at Washington January 29, 1970; entered into force January 29, 1970.
21 UST 415; TIAS 6825; 753 UNTS 43.

Agreement concerning cooperation in the detection and suppression of forest fires along the boundary between the Yukon Territory and Alaska with memorandum of agreement. Exchange of notes at Washington June 1, 1971; entered into force June 1, 1971.
22 UST 721; TIAS 7132; 793 UNTS 77.

Arrangement on mutual assistance in fighting forest fires. Exchange of notes at Ottawa May 4 and 7, 1982; entered into force May 7, 1982.
TIAS 10436.

FISHERIES

Agreement adopting, with certain modifications, the rules and method of procedure recommended in the award of September 7, 1910, of the North Atlantic Coast Fisheries Arbitration. Signed at Washington July 20, 1912; entered into force November 15, 1912.
37 Stat. 1634; TS 572; 12 Bevans 357.

Convention for the extension to halibut fishing vessels of port privileges on the Pacific Coasts of the United States of America and Canada. Signed at Ottawa March 24, 1950; entered into force July 13, 1950.
1 UST 536; TIAS 2096; 200 UNTS 211.

Convention for the preservation of the halibut fishery of the Northern Pacific Ocean and Bering Sea. Signed at Ottawa March 2, 1953; entered into force October 28, 1953.
5 UST 5; TIAS 2900; 222 UNTS 77.

Amendment:
March 29, 1979 (32 UST 2483; TIAS 9855).

Convention on Great Lakes fisheries. Signed at Washington September 10, 1954; entered into force October 11, 1955.
6 UST 2836; TIAS 3326; 238 UNTS 97.

Amendment:
April 5, 1966 and May 19, 1967 (18 UST 1402; TIAS 6297).

Treaty on Pacific Coast albacore tuna vessels and port privileges, with annexes. Signed at

CANADA (Cont'd)

Washington May 26, 1981; entered into force July 29, 1981.
33 UST 615; TIAS 10057; 1274 UNTS 247.

Amendment:
October 3 and 9, 1997.

Treaty concerning Pacific salmon, with annexes and memorandum of understanding. Signed at Ottawa January 28, 1985; entered into force March 18, 1985.
TIAS 11091; 1469 UNTS 357.

Amendments:
July 24 and August 12, 1998.
June 30, 1999.

Agreement on fisheries enforcement. Signed at Ottawa September 26, 1990; entered into force December 16, 1991.
TIAS 11753.

Agreement on the establishment of a mediation procedure regarding the Pacific Salmon Treaty. Signed at Montreal Sepember 11, 1995; entered into force September 11, 1995.
TIAS 12689.

FORESTRY

Memorandum of understanding on cooperation in the field of forestry-related programs. Signed at Washington May 17, 1990; entered into force May 17, 1990.
TIAS 11723.

HEALTH AND SANITATION

Arrangement concerning quarantine inspection of vessels entering Puget Sound and waters adjacent thereto or the Great Lakes via the St. Lawrence River. Exchange of notes at Ottawa October 10 and 23, 1929; entered into force October 23, 1929.
47 Stat. 2573; EAS 1; 6 Bevans 35; 96 LNTS 167.

Memorandum of understanding on the monitoring of food, beverage and sanitary services provided on common carriers operating between the United States and Canada. Signed at Ottawa and at Washington August 20 and September 8, 1975; entered into force September 8, 1975.
28 UST 884; TIAS 8485.

HIGHWAYS

Agreement providing for the construction of a military highway to Alaska. Exchange of notes at Ottawa March 17 and 18, 1942; entered into force March 18, 1942.
56 Stat. 1458; EAS 246; 6 Bevans 261; 101 UNTS 205.

Agreement relating to the southern terminus of the Alaska Highway. Exchange of notes at Ottawa May 4 and 9, 1942; entered into force May 9, 1942.
57 Stat. 1373; EAS 380; 6 Bevans 274; 101 UNTS 215.

Agreement relating to the construction of flight strips along the Alaska Highway. Exchange of notes at Ottawa August 26 and September 10, 1942; entered into force September 10, 1942.
57 Stat. 1375; EAS 381; 6 Bevans 282; 101 UNTS 221.

Agreement relating to the construction of the Haines-Champagne section of the Alaska Highway. Exchange of notes at Ottawa November 28 and December 7, 1942; entered into force December 7, 1942.
57 Stat. 1377; EAS 382; 6 Bevans 295; 101 UNTS 227.

Agreement relating to access to the Alaska Highway. Exchange of notes at Ottawa April 10, 1943; entered into force April 10, 1943.
57 Stat. 1274; EAS 362; 6 Bevans 319; 21 UNTS 237.

Agreement relating to the designation of the highway from Dawson Creek, British Columbia, to Fairbanks, Alaska, as the "Alaska Highway". Exchange of notes at Washington July 19, 1943; entered into force July 19, 1943.
57 Stat. 1023; EAS 331; 6 Bevans 324; 29 UNTS 289.

Agreement relating to cooperation in reconstruction of Canadian portions of the Alaska Highway. Exchange of notes at Ottawa January 11 and February 11, 1977; entered into force February 11, 1977.
28 UST 5303; TIAS 8631; 1087 UNTS 3.

HOUSING

Memorandum of understanding on cooperation in the field of housing and urban affairs. Signed at Ottawa June 28, 1977; entered into force June 28, 1977.
29 UST 2363; TIAS 8942.

JUDICIAL PROCEDURE

Arrangement relating to the admission to practice before patent offices. Exchange of notes at Washington December 3 and 28, 1937, and January 24, 1938; operative January 1, 1938.
52 Stat. 1475; EAS 118; 6 Bevans 97; 187 LNTS 27.

Procedures for mutual assistance in the administration of justice in connection with the Boeing Company matter. Signed at Washington March 15, 1977; entered into force March 15, 1977.
28 UST 2463; TIAS 8567.

Treaty on mutual legal assistance in criminal matters, with annex. Signed at Quebec March 18, 1985; entered into force January 24, 1990.
TIAS

Agreement regarding the sharing of forfeited assets and equivalent funds. Signed at Ottawa March 22, 1995; entered into force March 22, 1995.
TIAS 12618.

LABOR

Agreement relating to unemployment insurance benefits. Exchange of notes at Ottawa March 6 and 12, 1942; entered into force April 12, 1942.
56 Stat. 1451; EAS 244; 6 Bevans 257; 119 UNTS 295.

Amendments:
July 31 and September 11, 1951 (3 UST 2812; TIAS 2452; 206 UNTS 311).
October 29, 1984 and June 21, 1985 (TIAS 11334).

Agreement relating to workmen's compensation and unemployment insurance in connection with construction projects in Canada. Exchange of notes at Ottawa November 2 and 4, 1942; entered into force November 4, 1942.
56 Stat. 1770; EAS 279; 6 Bevans 284; 24 UNTS 217.

Agreement relating to the extension of the Canadian Unemployment Insurance Act to Canadian employees of the United States Armed Services in Canada. Exchange of notes at Washington December 20, 1955 and April 23, 1956; entered into force April 23, 1956.
8 UST 1879; TIAS 3933; 300 UNTS 29.

MAPPING

Agreement on mapping, charting and geodesy, with annexes. Signed at Ottawa August 24, 1976; entered into force August 24, 1976.
28 UST 3663; TIAS 8594.

Memorandum of understanding concerning global geospatial information and services cooperation. Signed at Ottawa and Bethesda January 11 and 19, 2000; entered into force January 19, 2000.
NP

MARITIME MATTERS (See also NAVAL VESSELS)

Treaty providing for reciprocal rights for United States and Canada in matters of conveyance of prisoners and wrecking and salvage. Signed at Washington May 18, 1908; entered into force June 30, 1908.
35 Stat. 2035; TS 502; 12 Bevans 314.

CANADA (Cont'd)

Load line convention. Signed at Washington December 9, 1933; entered into force July 26, 1934.
49 Stat. 2685; TS 869; 6 Bevans 54; 152 LNTS 39.

Agreement relating to reciprocal recognition of load line regulations for vessels engaged in international voyages on the Great Lakes. Exchanges of notes at Ottawa April 29, August 24, and October 22, 1938, September 2 and October 18, 1939, and January 10 and March 4, 1940; entered into force March 4, 1940.
54 Stat. 2300; EAS 172; 6 Bevans 171; 202 LNTS 429.

Search and rescue agreement, with attachment. Signed at Ottawa and Washington September 12 and October 25, 1974; entered into force October 25, 1974.
TIAS 11963.

Memorandum of understanding concerning reciprocal recognition of Great Lakes load lines. Signed at Ottawa November 21, 1977; entered into force November 21, 1977.
29 UST 4948; TIAS 9088; 1230 UNTS 345.

Agreement for a cooperative vessel traffic management system for the Juan de Fuca region, with annex. Exchange of notes at Ottawa December 19, 1979; entered into force December 19, 1979.
32 UST 377; TIAS 9706; 1221 UNTS 67.

Memorandum of understanding concerning cooperation in marine transportation technology and systems research and development. Signed at Ottawa June 18, 1981; entered into force June 18, 1981.
33 UST 2082; TIAS 10172; 1529 UNTS 483.

METEOROLOGICAL RESEARCH

Agreement relating to the establishment of a cooperative meteorological rocket project at Cold Lake, Alberta. Exchange of notes at Ottawa September 29 and October 6, 1966; entered into force October 6, 1966.
17 UST 1832; TIAS 6128; 675 UNTS 63.

Amendment:
February 13 and April 24, 1969 (20 UST 720; TIAS 6682; 714 UNTS 326).

NAVAL VESSELS (See also MARITIME MATTERS)

Agreement relating to naval forces on the American Lakes (Rush-Bagot Agreement). Exchange of notes at Washington April 28 and 29, 1817; entered into force April 29, 1817.
8 Stat. 231; TS 110 1/2; 12 Bevans 54.

Agreement relating to the construction of naval vessels on the Great Lakes (interpretation of the Rush-Bagot Agreement). Exchange of notes at Ottawa June 9 and 10, 1939; entered into force June 10, 1939.
61 Stat. 4069; TIAS 1836; 6 Bevans 149; 149 UNTS 332.

Agreement relating to the armament of naval vessels to be incapable of immediate use (interpretation of the Rush-Bagot Agreement). Exchange of notes at Ottawa October 30 and November 2, 1940; entered into force November 2, 1940.
61 Stat. 4077; TIAS 1836; 6 Bevans 196; 149 UNTS 350.

Agreement relating to naval vessels for training naval reserve personnel (interpretation of the Rush-Bagot Agreement). Exchange of notes at Washington November 18 and December 6, 1946; entered into force December 6, 1946.
61 Stat. 4082; TIAS 1836; 6 Bevans 426; 149 UNTS 3.

NAVIGATION

Agreement relating to the transfer to Canada of Loran stations at Port aux Basques, Battle Harbour, and Bonavista. Exchange of notes at Ottawa June 26 and 30, 1953; entered into force June 30, 1953.
4 UST 2174; TIAS 2865; 215 UNTS 103.

Agreement relating to the construction and operation of a Loran station at Cape Christian, Baffin Island. Exchange of notes at Ottawa May 1 and 3, 1954; entered into force May 3, 1954.
5 UST 1459; TIAS 3019; 221 UNTS 339.

Agreement relating to the loan of certain equipment for use in Canadian Loran-A stations. Exchange of notes at Ottawa June 7 and 8, 1965; entered into force June 8, 1965.
16 UST 824; TIAS 5817; 546 UNTS 201.

Amendments:
April 19 and July 28, 1966 (17 UST 1140; TIAS 6072; 601 UNTS 366).
July 27 and October 25, 1967 (18 UST 2933; TIAS 6386; 701 UNTS 117).

Agreement relating to the establishment of a Loran-A station at Gray Point, British Columbia. Exchange of notes at Ottawa April 8, 1971; entered into force April 8, 1971.
22 UST 531; TIAS 7095; 792 UNTS 315.

Agreement relating to the construction, operation and maintenance of a Loran-C station in the vicinity of Williams Lake, British Columbia, with annex. Exchange of notes at Ottawa May 28 and June 3, 1976; entered into force June 3, 1976.
27 UST 2611; TIAS 8331; 1054 UNTS 327.

Amendment:
May 3 and 8, 1991 (TIAS 11836; 1853 UNTS 417).

Agreement relating to the establishment of an experimental Loran-C power chain, with annex. Exchange of notes at Washington March 29, 1977; entered into force March 29, 1977; effective August 1, 1975.
28 UST 2431; TIAS 8560.

Extension:
October 23 and December 5, 1980 (32 UST 4229; TIAS 9944; 1265 UNTS 386).

Agreement regarding two data link transmitters as part of an electronic aid to navigation subsystem, with annex. Exchange of notes at Ottawa September 29 and October 16, 1978; entered into force October 16, 1978; effective September 1, 1977.
30 UST 2199; TIAS 9327; 1171 UNTS 27.

Agreement concerning four OMEGA navigation system monitoring stations in Canada. Exchange of notes at Ottawa July 26 and December 20, 1978; entered into force December 20, 1978.
30 UST 2840; TIAS 9365; 1180 UNTS 69.

Agreement relating to the construction, operation and maintenance of a Loran-C station in British Columbia. Exchange of notes at Ottawa March 19 and 29, 1979; entered into force March 29, 1979.
30 UST 4049; TIAS 9446; 1171 UNTS 35.

Agreement relating to coordination between the United States and Canadian Coast Guards of icebreaking operations in the Great Lakes and St. Lawrence Seaway system. Exchange of notes at Ottawa October 28 and December 5, 1980; entered into force December 5, 1980.
32 UST 4334; TIAS 9950; 1266 UNTS 87.

Extension:
December 4, 1990 (TIAS 11786).

Agreement for the establishment, operation and maintenance of two Loran-C chains for the Canadian east coast and the Labrador sea, with annex. Exchange of notes at Ottawa March 30 and May 3, 1984; entered into force May 3, 1984.
TIAS 11146; 1469 UNTS 291.

PACIFIC SETTLEMENT OF DISPUTES (See also BOUNDARIES)

Treaty amending in their application to Canada certain provisions of the treaty for the advancement of peace between the United States and the United Kingdom signed at Washington September 15, 1914. Signed at Washington September 6, 1940; entered into force August 13, 1941.
55 Stat. 1214; TS 975; 6 Bevans 190.

PATENTS

Agreement relating to the mutual interchange of patent rights in connection with RDX and

CANADA (Cont'd)

other explosives. Exchange of notes at Washington September 3 and 27, 1946; entered into force September 27, 1946.
61 Stat. 2949; TIAS 1628; 6 Bevans 419; 21 UNTS 3.

PIPELINES

Agreement concerning transit pipelines. Signed at Washington January 28, 1977; entered into force October 1, 1977.
28 UST 7449; TIAS 8720.

Agreement on principles applicable to a northern natural gas pipeline, with annexes. Signed at Ottawa September 20, 1977; entered into force September 20, 1977 with respect to certain provisions; July 24, 1978 with respect to remaining provisions.
29 UST 3581; TIAS 9030; 1230 UNTS 311.

Amendment:
June 6, 1978 (29 UST 3621; TIAS 9030; 1230 UNTS 340).

POLLUTION

Agreement relating to the establishment of a Canada-United States committee on water quality in the St. John River and its tributary rivers and streams which cross the Canada-United States boundary, with annex. Exchange of notes at Ottawa September 21, 1972; entered into force September 21, 1972.
23 UST 2813; TIAS 7470.

Amendment:
February 22, 1984 (TIAS 10947).

Agreement relating to the establishment of joint pollution contingency plans for spills of oil and other noxious substances. Exchange of notes at Ottawa June 19, 1974; entered into force June 19, 1974.
25 UST 1280; TIAS 7861.

Agreement on Great Lakes water quality, 1978, with annexes and terms of reference. Signed at Ottawa November 22, 1978; entered into force November 22, 1978.
30 UST 1383; TIAS 9257; 1153 UNTS 187.

Amendments:
October 16, 1983 (TIAS 10798).
November 18, 1987 (TIAS 11551).

Memorandum of intent concerning transboundary air pollution, with annex. Signed at Washington August 5, 1980; entered into force August 5, 1980.
32 UST 2521; TIAS 9856; 1274 UNTS 235.

Memorandum of understanding regarding accidental and unauthorized discharges of pollutants along the inland boundary, with appendix.

Signed at Ottawa October 17, 1985; entered into force October 17, 1985.
TIAS 11170.

Agreement concerning the transboundary movement of hazardous waste. Signed at Ottawa October 28, 1986; entered into force November 8, 1986.
TIAS 11099.

Amendment:
November 4 and 25, 1992.

Agreement on air quality, with annexes. Signed at Ottawa March 13, 1991; entered into force March 13, 1991.
TIAS

Amendment:
December 7, 2000.

POSTAL MATTERS

Money order agreement. Signed at Washington September 30 and at Ottawa October 3, 1901; operative July 1, 1901.
NP

International express mail agreement, with detailed regulations. Signed at Ottawa and Washington July 18, 23 and August 14, 1979; entered into force August 14, 1979; effective August 1, 1979.
31 UST 5745; TIAS 9684; 1221 UNTS 43.

Postal convention, with detailed regulations. Signed at Ottawa and Washington September 10 and 14, 1981; entered into force January 1, 1982.
33 UST 3810; TIAS 10263; 1541 UNTS 135.

PRISONER TRANSFER (See also under MARITIME MATTERS)

Treaty on the execution of penal sentences. Signed at Washington March 2, 1977; entered into force July 19, 1978.
30 UST 6263; TIAS 9552.

PRIVILEGES AND IMMUNITIES

Agreement concerning the privileges and immunities of members of the administrative and technical staffs of the Embassy of Canada in the United States and the Embassy of the United States in Canada. Exchange of notes at Ottawa August 26 and September 2, 1993; entered into force September 21, 1993.
TIAS 12506.

PROPERTY (See also SURPLUS PROPERTY)

Convention between the United States and the United Kingdom relating to tenure and disposi-

tion of real and personal property. Signed at Washington March 2, 1899; applicable to Canada June 17, 1922.
31 Stat. 1939; TS 146; 12 Bevans 246.

Supplementary convention providing for the accession of the Dominion of Canada to the real and personal property convention of March 2, 1899. Signed at Washington October 21, 1921; entered into force June 17, 1922.
42 Stat. 2147; TS 663; 12 Bevans 390; 12 LNTS 425.

REMOTE SENSING

Agreement on cooperation in the Boreal Ecosystem-Atmosphere Study (BOREAS). Signed at Washington April 18, 1994; entered into force April 18, 1994.
TIAS 12538.

Agreement concerning the operation of commercial remote sensing satellite systems, with annexes. Signed at Washington June 16, 2000; entered into force June 16, 2000.
TIAS

SANCTIONS

Agreement confirming acceptance by Canada of the terms of the memorandum of understanding of August 1, 1994, for a multinational observer group to monitor and advise on Haiti. Exchange of notes at Washington August 29, 1994; entered into force August 29, 1994.
TIAS

SATELLITES

Agreement on cooperation in inter-continental testing in connection with experimental communications satellites. Exchange of notes at Washington August 13 and 23, 1963; entered into force August 23, 1963.
14 UST 1701; TIAS 5474; 494 UNTS 13.

Agreement regarding an experimental communications technology satellite project with memorandum of understanding. Exchange of notes at Washington April 21 and 27, 1971; entered into force April 27, 1971.
22 UST 713; TIAS 7131.

Agreement concerning cooperation on the RADARSAT Project. Exchange of notes at Washington November 12, 1991; entered into force November 12, 1991.
TIAS 12206; 1883 UNTS 467.

Amendment:
October 24, 2000.

SCIENTIFIC COOPERATION

Memorandum of understanding concerning the furnishing of balloon launching and associated

CANADA (Cont'd)

services. Signed at Washington and Ottawa August 26 and September 9, 1983; entered into force September 9, 1983.
TIAS 10800.

Agreement regarding allocation of intellectual property rights, interests and royalties for intellectual property created or furnished under certain scientific and technological cooperative research activities, with attachment. Exchange of notes at Ottawa February 4, 1997; entered into force February 4, 1997.
TIAS

SEABEDS

Agreement relating to the agreement of August 14, 1987 on the resolution of practical problems with respect to deep seabed mining areas.[1] Exchange of notes at Ottawa August 14, 1987; entered into force August 14, 1987.
TIAS 11438.

NOTE:
[1] Parties to the multilateral agreement of August 14, 1987 are Belgium, Canada, Italy, Netherlands and Union of Soviet Socialist Republics.

SEWAGE DISPOSAL SYSTEM

Agreement relating to the construction of a sewage line from Dunseith, North Dakota to Boissevain, Manitoba. Exchange of notes at Ottawa January 13, April 22 and June 9, 1966; entered into force June 9, 1966.
17 UST 810; TIAS 6037; 580 UNTS 263.

SHELLFISH

Agreement providing for cooperative efforts to be directed toward sanitary control of the shellfish industry. Exchange of notes at Washington March 4 and April 30, 1948; entered into force April 30, 1948.
62 Stat. 1898; TIAS 1747; 6 Bevans 472; 77 UNTS 191.

SMUGGLING

Convention to suppress smuggling. Signed at Washington June 6, 1924; entered into force July 27, 1925.
44 Stat. 2097; TS 718; 6 Bevans 1; 43 LNTS 225.

SOCIAL SECURITY

Agreement relating to Canada Pension Plan. Signed at Ottawa May 5, 1967; entered into force May 5, 1967; effective January 1, 1967.
18 UST 486; TIAS 6254; 685 UNTS 245.

Amendment:
October 12 and December 19, 1983 (TIAS 10864).

Agreement with respect to social security.[1] Signed at Ottawa March 11, 1981; entered into force August 1, 1984.
TIAS 10863; 1469 UNTS 249.

Administrative arrangement for the implementation of the agreement of March 11, 1981 with respect to social security. Signed at Washington May 22, 1981; entered into force August 1, 1984.
TIAS 10863.

Supplementary agreement amending the agreement of March 11, 1981 and the administrative arrangement of May 22, 1981 with respect to social security. Signed at Ottawa May 10, 1983; entered into force August 1, 1984.
TIAS 10863; 1469 UNTS 271.

Second supplementary agreement amending the agreement of March 11, 1981, as amended, with respect to social security. Signed at Ottawa May 28, 1996; entered into force October 1, 1997.
TIAS

NOTE:
[1] See also understanding and administrative arrangement of March 30, 1983, with the Government of Quebec (TIAS 10863).

SPACE COOPERATION

Agreement relating to a cooperative program concerning the development and procurement of a space shuttle attached remote manipulator system. Exchange of notes at Washington June 23, 1976; entered into force June 23, 1976.
27 UST 3801; TIAS 8400; 1059 UNTS 81.

Memorandum of understanding for a cooperative program concerning design (Phase B) of a permanently manned space station. Signed at Ottawa April 16, 1985; entered into force April 16, 1985.
TIAS 11180.

Memorandum of understanding concerning cooperation in the flight of the Canadian measurements of pollution in the troposphere (MOPITT) instrument on the NASA polar orbiting platform and related support for an international earth observing system, with appendix. Signed at Washington November 15, 1994; entered into force November 15, 1994.
TIAS

Memorandum of understanding on the Orbiter Space Vision System. Signed at Washington and St. Hubert November 9, 1995 and February 23, 1996; entered into force February 23, 1996.
TIAS

Agreement concerning the training of mission specialists for space shuttle flights, with implementing agreement. Exchange of notes at Ottawa August 31, 1995 and May 17, 1996; entered into force May 17, 1996.
TIAS

Agreement concerning cooperation on the Canadian Microgravity Isolation Mount, with attachment. Exchange of notes at Ottawa July 31, 1997; entered into force July 31, 1997.
TIAS

SURPLUS PROPERTY

Agreement relating to the disposal of government-owned surplus property. Exchange of notes at Ottawa January 9, 1947; entered into force January 9, 1947.
61 Stat. 2738; TIAS 1603; 6 Bevans 428; 11 UNTS 341.

Agreement relating to the disposal of surplus United States property in Canada. Exchange of notes at Ottawa August 28 and September 1, 1961; entered into force September 1, 1961.
12 UST 1228; TIAS 4841; 421 UNTS 199.

Amendment:
December 21, 1983 and March 14, 1984 (TIAS 11063; 1466 UNTS 443).

TAXATION

Agreement relating to provincial and municipal taxation of United States defense projects in Canada. Exchange of notes at Ottawa August 6 and 9, 1943; entered into force August 9, 1943.
57 Stat. 1065; EAS 339; 6 Bevans 326; 29 UNTS 295.

Agreement concerning the administration of income tax in Canada affecting employees within Canada of the United States Government who are subject to such tax. Exchange of notes at Ottawa August 1 and September 17, 1973; entered into force September 17, 1973.
28 UST 1134; TIAS 8499.

Convention with respect to taxes on income and capital, with exchange of notes. Signed at Washington September 26, 1980; entered into force August 16, 1984.[1]
TIAS 11087; 1469 UNTS 189.

Protocol amending the convention of September 26, 1980, with respect to taxes on income and on capital, with exchange of letters. Signed at Ottawa June 14, 1983; entered into force August 16, 1984.
TIAS 11087.

Second protocol amending the convention of September 26, 1980, with respect to taxes on income and on capital, as amended by the pro-

CANADA (Cont'd)

tocol of June 14, 1983. Signed at Washington March 28, 1984; entered into force August 16, 1984.
TIAS 11087.

Protocol amending the convention with respect to taxes on income and on capital of September 26, 1980, as amended by protocols of June 14, 1983 and March 28, 1984. Signed at Washington March 17, 1995; entered into force November 9, 1995.
TIAS

Protocol amending the convention with respect to taxes on income and on capital of September 26, 1980, as amended. Signed at Ottawa July 29, 1997; entered into force December 16, 1997.
TIAS

NOTE:
[1] With respect to estates of persons deceased prior to January 1, 1985, the convention of February 17, 1961 for the avoidance of double taxation and the prevention of fiscal evasion with respect to taxes on estates of deceased persons (13 UST 382; TIAS 4995; 445 UNTS 143) shall continue to have effect.
See also Article XXX of the 1980 convention for the continued effect of the convention and protocol of March 4, 1942 for the avoidance of double taxation and prevention of fiscal evasion in the case of income taxes (56 Stat. 1399; TS 983; 6 Bevans 244; 124 UNTS 271).

TECHNICAL COOPERATION

Memorandum of understanding concerning a program of cooperation in areas of statistics. Signed at Washington March 27, 1986; entered into force March 27, 1986.
TIAS 11400.

TELECOMMUNICATION

Arrangement governing radio communications between private experimental stations. Exchanges of notes at Washington October 2 and December 29, 1928 and January 12, 1929; operative January 1, 1929.
TS 767-A; 6 Bevans 26; 102 LNTS 143.

Extension:
April 23 and May 2 and 4, 1934 (48 Stat. 1876; EAS 62; 147 LNTS 338).

Agreement providing for the allocation of channels in the radio frequency band 88 to 108 megacycles for frequency modulation broadcasting. Exchange of notes at Washington January 8 and October 15, 1947; entered into force October 15, 1947.
61 Stat. 3800; TIAS 1726; 6 Bevans 447; 82 UNTS 53.

Convention relating to the operation by citizens of either country of certain radio equipment or stations in the other country. Signed at Ottawa February 8, 1951; entered into force May 15, 1952.
3 UST 3787; TIAS 2508; 207 UNTS 17.

Agreement concerning the coordination and use of radio frequencies above thirty megacycles per second, with annex. Exchange of notes at Ottawa October 24, 1962; entered into force October 24, 1962.
13 UST 2418; TIAS 5205; 462 UNTS 68.

Amendments:
June 16 and 24, 1965 (16 UST 923; TIAS 5833; 549 UNTS 300).
February 26 and April 7, 1982 (TIAS 10646).
November 2, 1993 and January 4, 1994 (TIAS 12529).

Agreement for promotion of safety on the Great Lakes by means of radio, with technical regulations and exchange of notes of May 6, 1974. Signed at Ottawa February 26, 1973; entered into force May 6, 1975.
25 UST 935; TIAS 7837.

Amendments:
December 29, 1978 (30 UST 2523; TIAS 9352; 1170 UNTS 339).
December 22, 1987, August 10 and October 24, 1988.

Agreement relating to the AM broadcasting service in the medium frequency band, with annexes. Signed at Ottawa January 17, 1984; entered into force January 17, 1984.
TIAS 11263.

TELEVISION

Agreement concerning the allotment and assignment of television broadcasting channels in areas adjacent to the border of the United States and Canada, with working arrangement. Exchange of notes at Washington November 3, 1993 and January 5, 1994; entered into force January 5, 1994.
TIAS 12530.

TERRITORIAL ACQUISITION

Protocol of the cession of Horseshoe Reef. Signed at London December 9, 1850; entered into force December 9, 1850.
18 Stat. 325; 12 Bevans 109.

TRADE AND COMMERCE (See also AMITY)

Agreement supplementary to the general agreement on tariffs and trade, with exchange of notes.[1] Signed at Geneva October 30, 1947;

entered into force October 30, 1947; operative January 1, 1948.
61 Stat. 3695; TIAS 1702; 6 Bevans 451; 27 UNTS 19.

Agreement relating to the establishment of a Joint United States-Canadian Committee on Trade and Economic Affairs. Exchange of notes at Washington November 12, 1953; entered into force November 12, 1953.
5 UST 314; TIAS 2922; 223 UNTS 139.

Amendments:
October 2, 1961 (14 UST 1496; TIAS 5448; 470 UNTS 394).
September 17, 1963 (14 UST 1496; TIAS 5448).

Agreement relating to tariff duty on certain fish and fish products. Signed at Geneva June 8, 1955; entered into force July 24, 1955.
6 UST 6231; TIAS 3474; 247 UNTS 163.

Agreement concerning automotive products. Signed at Johnson City, Texas January 16, 1965; entered into force provisionally January 16, 1965 and definitively September 16, 1966.
17 UST 1372; TIAS 6093.

Interim agreement relating to the renegotiation of schedule XX (United States) to the general agreement on tariffs and trade. Signed at Washington December 17, 1965; entered into force December 17, 1965.
16 UST 1789; TIAS 5912; 574 UNTS 49.

Amendment:
June 30, 1967 (18 UST 1749; TIAS 6316; 693 UNTS 362).

Arrangement regarding levels of Canadian oil exports and the proposed looping of the Interprovincial Pipeline via Chicago. Exchange of notes at Washington September 25, 1967; entered into force September 25, 1967.
20 UST 4108; TIAS 6806; 730 UNTS 317.

Agreement within the context of the multilateral trade negotiations relating to provincial liquor marketing practices and related letters of February 4 and March 20, 1980. Exchange of letters at Geneva April 12, 1979; entered into force September 1, 1981.
TIAS

Arrangement within the context of the multilateral trade negotiations concerning cheeses and related letters of February 4 and March 20, 1980. Signed at Geneva June 15, 1979; entered into force January 1, 1980.
32 UST 5292; TIAS 9980; 1266 UNTS 59.

Agreement within the context of the multilateral trade negotiations concerning canned turkey and related letters of February 4 and March 20, 1980. Signed at Geneva July 10, 1979; entered into force September 1, 1981.
TIAS

Memorandum of understanding within the context of the multilateral trade negotiations regarding the staging of certain tariff reductions. Signed at Washington September 17 and 21, 1979; entered into force September 21, 1979.
32 UST 5273; TIAS 9978; 1266 UNTS 69.

CANADA (Cont'd)

Amendment:
October 9, 1979 (32 UST 5273; TIAS 9978; 1266 UNTS 77).

Understanding on safeguards relating to procedures under Article XIX of the general agreement on tariffs and trade, with related letter. Exchange of letters at Washington February 17, 1984; entered into force February 17, 1984. TIAS 10958.

Agreement concerning trade in certain softwood lumber products with memorandum of understanding and related letters. Exchange of notes at Washington December 30, 1986; entered into force December 30, 1986. TIAS

Memorandum of understanding on the exchange of import data, with annexes. Signed at Montreal July 29, 1987; entered into force July 29, 1987. TIAS

Free-trade agreement, with exchanges of letters.[2] Signed at Ottawa, Washington and Palm Springs December 22 and 23, 1987 and January 2, 1988; entered into force January 1, 1989. TIAS

Agreement regarding the application of their competition and deceptive marketing practices laws. Signed at Washington and Ottawa August 1 and 3, 1995; entered into force August 3, 1995. TIAS

NOTES:
[1] This agreement rendered inoperative, for such time as the United States and Canada are both contracting parties to the general agreement on tariffs and trade, the trade agreement of November 17, 1938 (53 Stat. 2348; EAS 149; 6 Bevans 117; 199 LNTS 91) and related agreement of March 18, 1947 (61 Stat. 3054; TIAS 1638; 6 Bevans 439; 117 UNTS 79).
[2] This agreement is suspended, subject to certain transition arrangements with respect to dispute settlement proceedings under Chapters 18 and 19, for such time as the United States and Canada are parties to the North American Free Trade Agreement signed at Washington, Ottawa, and Mexico City December 8, 11, 14, and 17, 1992.

WEATHER MODIFICATION

Agreement relating to the exchange of information on weather modification activities. Signed at Washington March 26, 1975; entered into force March 26, 1975. 26 UST 540; TIAS 8056.

CAPE VERDE

AVIATION

Agreement relating to the provision of site test, commissioning and/or periodic flight checks of air navigation aids by the Federal Aviation Administration. Signed at Washington and Praia October 13 and November 19, 1976; entered into force November 19, 1976. 28 UST 8086; TIAS 8742; 1087 UNTS 111.

Extensions and amendments:
August 17 and October 18, 1977 (29 UST 5893; TIAS 9158).
March 10 and April 4, 1978 (29 UST 5895; TIAS 9158).

Civil aviation security agreement. Signed at Washington October 11, 1989; entered into force October 11, 1989. TIAS 11705.

COPYRIGHT (See APPENDIX)

DEFENSE

Agreement concerning the provision of training related to defense articles under the United States International Military Education and Training (IMET) Program. Exchange of notes at Praia December 9 and 16, 1987; entered into force December 16, 1987. NP

ECONOMIC AND TECHNICAL COOPERATION

Agency for International Development:
June 30, 1975 (28 UST 959; TIAS 8487).
June 30, 1975 (28 UST 2903; TIAS 8573).
November 3, 1975 (28 UST 970; TIAS 8487).
March 3 and 23, 1976 (28 UST 2921; TIAS 8573).
May 21, 1977 (29 UST 335; TIAS 8819).
May 22, 1978 (30 UST 3128; TIAS 9382; 1178 UNTS 289).

ENVIRONMENTAL COOPERATION

Agreement for cooperation in the Global Learning and Observations to Benefit the Environment (GLOBE) Program, with appendices. Signed at Praia August 9, 2000; entered into force August 9, 2000. TIAS

POSTAL MATTERS

Postal money order agreement. Signed at Washington and Praia April 17 and June 17, 1991; entered into force August 26, 1991. TIAS 11818.

International express mail agreement, with detailed regulations. Signed at Praia and Washington December 27, 1991 and February 25, 1992; entered into force March 7, 1992. TIAS 11855.

CARIBBEAN COMMUNITY SECRETARIAT

ECONOMIC AND TECHNICAL COOPERATION

Agency for International Development:
August 30, 1978 (30 UST 5054; TIAS 9498; 1234 UNTS 29).

CENTRAL AFRICAN REPUBLIC

COPYRIGHT (See APPENDIX)

DEFENSE

Agreement concerning the provision of training related to the defense articles under the United States International Military Education and Training (IMET) Program. Exchange of notes at Bangui August 31 and September 7, 1982; entered into force September 7, 1982. TIAS 10709; 1607 UNTS 107.

ECONOMIC AND TECHNICAL COOPERATION

Agreement relating to economic, technical and related assistance. Exchange of notes at Bangui February 10, 1963; entered into force February 10, 1963. 14 UST 185; TIAS 5294; 473 UNTS 83.

FINANCE

Agreement relating to investment guaranties. Exchange of notes at Bangui December 31, 1964; entered into force January 1, 1965. 15 UST 2556; TIAS 5747; 542 UNTS 29.

Agreement regarding the consolidation and rescheduling of certain debts owed to, or guaranteed by the United States Government through the Export-Import Bank, with annexes. Signed

CENTRAL AFRICAN REPUBLIC (Cont'd)

at Washington April 29, 1983; entered into force June 13, 1983.
TIAS 10721; 1578 UNTS 55.

Agreement regarding the consolidation and rescheduling of certain debts owed to, or guaranteed by the United States Government through the Export-Import Bank, with annexes. Signed at Bangui February 16, 1984; entered into force April 16, 1984.
TIAS 10967.

Agreement regarding the consolidation and rescheduling of certain debts owed to or guaranteed by the United States Government through the Export-Import Bank of the United States. Signed at Washington May 23, 1986; entered into force August 1, 1986.
NP

Agreement regarding the consolidation and rescheduling of certain debts owed to, guaranteed by or insured by the United States Government and its agencies, with annexes. Signed at Bangui March 22, 1990; entered into force May 3, 1990.
NP

Agreement regarding the consolidation, reduction and rescheduling of certain debts owed to, guaranteed by or insured by the United States Government and its agencies, with annexes. Signed at Bangui September 6, 1994; entered into force October 11, 1994.
NP

Agreement regarding the consolidation, reduction and rescheduling of certain debts owed to, guaranteed by, or insured by the United States Government and its Agency, with annexes. Signed at Bangui September 1, 1999; entered into force December 15, 1999.
NP

PEACE CORPS

Agreement relating to the establishment of a Peace Corps program in the Central African Republic. Exchange of notes at Bangui September 9 and November 24, 1966; entered into force November 24, 1966.
17 UST 2205; TIAS 6157; 681 UNTS 21.

POSTAL MATTERS

International express mail agreement, with detailed regulations. Signed at Bangui and Washington June 22 and September 21, 1988; entered into force November 1, 1988.
TIAS 11636.

CENTRAL AMERICAN BANK FOR ECONOMIC INTEGRATION

ECONOMIC AND TECHNICAL COOPERATION

Agency for International Development:
February 2, 1977 (29 UST 921; TIAS 8855).

CENTRO REGIONAL DE SISMOLOGIA PARA AMERICA DEL SUR (CERESIS)

SCIENTIFIC COOPERATION

Memorandum of understanding concerning scientific and technical cooperation in the earth sciences, with annexes. Signed at Reston, Santiago and Lima October 6, November 17 and December 3, 1998; entered into force December 3, 1998.
TIAS

CHAD

COPYRIGHT (See APPENDIX)

DEFENSE

Agreement concerning the provision of training related to defense articles under the United States International Military Education and Training (IMET) Program. Exchange of notes at N'Djamena February 22 and April 22, 1983; entered into force April 22, 1983.
TIAS 10822.

Mutual defense assistance agreement. Exchange of notes at N'Djamena July 19 and 20, 1983; entered into force July 20, 1983.
TIAS 10748.

Agreement concerning the status of U.S. military personnel in Chad. Exchange of notes at N'Djamena September 22 and 23, 1987; entered into force September 23, 1987.
NP

Agreement regarding the status of United States military personnel and civilian employees of the United States Department of Defense who may be temporarily present in Chad in connection with their official duties relating to humanitarian demining activities. Exchange of notes at N'Djamena January 27 and February 23, 1998; entered into force February 23, 1998.
TIAS

ECONOMIC AND TECHNICAL COOPERATION

Agreement on economic, technical and related assistance. Signed at N'Djamena September 22, 1986; entered into force September 22, 1986.
TIAS

Agency for International Development:
August 30, 1976 (29 UST 1139; TIAS 8871).
January 25, 1977 (29 UST 2581; TIAS 8959).
June 10, 1977 (29 UST 5741; TIAS 9146).
August 25, 1977 (30 UST 7393; TIAS 9594).
August 30, 1977 (29 UST 2596; TIAS 8959).
September 28, 1977 (29 UST 2613; TIAS 8959).
February 28, 1978 (30 UST 7393; TIAS 9594).
June 2, 1978 (30 UST 3132; TIAS 9383).

EMPLOYMENT

Agreement relating to the employment of dependents of official government employees. Exchange of notes at N'Djamena April 19, 1991 and June 23, 1992; entered into force June 23, 1992.
TIAS

ENVIRONMENTAL COOPERATION

Agreement for cooperation in the Global Learning and Observations to Benefit the Environment (GLOBE) Program, with appendices. Signed at N'Djamena and Washington September 27 and November 28, 1995; entered into force November 28, 1995.
TIAS

FINANCE

Agreement relating to investment guaranties. Exchange of notes at Fort Lamy May 12, 1965; entered into force May 12, 1965.
16 UST 789; TIAS 5812; 546 UNTS 183.

PEACE CORPS

Agreement for the establishment of a Peace Corps program in Chad. Exchange of notes at Fort Lamy August 31, 1966; entered into force August 31, 1966.
17 UST 1384; TIAS 6094.

POSTAL MATTERS

International express mail agreement, with detailed regulations. Signed at N'Djamena and Washington July 19 and 23 and August 6, 1987; entered into force August 17, 1987.
TIAS 11553.

CHILE

AGRICULTURAL COMMODITIES[1]

Agricultural commodities agreement. Signed at Santiago November 8, 1960; entered into force November 8, 1960.
11 UST 2668; TIAS 4663; 405 UNTS 85.

Agricultural commodities agreement with exchanges of notes. Signed at Santiago August 7, 1962; entered into force August 7, 1962.
13 UST 2269; TIAS 5195; 461 UNTS 61.

Amendments:
August 29 and September 10, 1962 (13 UST 2269; TIAS 5195; 461 UNTS 70).
November 29, 1962 (13 UST 2878; TIAS 5252; 469 UNTS 440).
February 14, 1963 (14 UST 245; TIAS 5304; 474 UNTS 376).
June 30, 1964 (15 UST 1428; TIAS 5616; 530 UNTS 374).
November 17, 1964 (15 UST 2176; TIAS 5702; 531 UNTS 392).

Agreement setting forth certain understandings concerning the agricultural commodities agreement of August 7, 1962, as amended. Exchange of notes at Santiago October 3 and 4, 1962; entered into force October 4, 1962.
13 UST 2269; TIAS 5195; 461 UNTS 74.

Amendment:
March 1 and 27, 1963 (14 UST 468; TIAS 5342; 476 UNTS 354).

Agricultural commodities agreement with exchange of notes. Signed at Santiago July 27, 1965; entered into force September 23, 1965.
16 UST 1725; TIAS 5898; 574 UNTS 83.

Amendment:
February 8, 1966 (17 UST 251; TIAS 5974; 579 UNTS 349).

Agricultural commodities agreement with agreement and annex. Exchange of notes at Santiago December 29, 1967; entered into force December 29, 1967.
18 UST 3106; TIAS 6403; 697 UNTS 63.

Amendment:
December 17, 1968 (20 UST 388; TIAS 6641; 715 UNTS 382).

Related agreement:
April 29, 1969 (20 UST 704; TIAS 6679; 715 UNTS 3).

Agricultural commodities agreement, with related notes. Signed at Santiago October 25, 1974; entered into force October 25, 1974.
25 UST 3395; TIAS 7993.

Amendments:
November 22, 1974 (25 UST 3427; TIAS 7993).
April 1, 1975 (26 UST 259; TIAS 8030; 992 UNTS 409).
May 22, 1975 (26 UST 962; TIAS 8083).

Related agreements:
July 31, 1975 (26 UST 2718; TIAS 8188).
April 19, 1976 (27 UST 1551; TIAS 8262; 1052 UNTS 283).
October 29, 1976 (27 UST 3871; TIAS 8405; 1059 UNTS 169).

AGRICULTURE

Memorandum of understanding for scientific and technical cooperation in agricultural research and development. Signed at Santiago August 28, 1981; entered into force August 28, 1981.
33 UST 3742; TIAS 10256; 1541 UNTS 113.

AMITY

Treaty of peace, amity, commerce, and navigation, with additional and explanatory convention signed at Santiago September 1, 1833.[1] Signed at Santiago May 16, 1832; entered into force April 29, 1834.
8 Stat. 434; TS 40; 6 Bevans 518.

NOTE:
[1] Articles relating to commerce and navigation terminated January 20, 1850.

ATOMIC ENERGY

Agreement providing for a grant for the acquisition of certain nuclear research and training equipment and materials. Exchange of notes at Santiago July 23, 1959 and February 19, 1960; entered into force February 19, 1960.
11 UST 395; TIAS 4457; 371 UNTS 255.

AVIATION

Air transport agreement with exchanges of notes. Signed at Santiago May 10, 1947; entered into force December 30, 1948.
62 Stat. 3755; TIAS 1905; 6 Bevans 626; 55 UNTS 21.

Agreement for cooperation in the promotion and development of civil aviation, with annex. Signed at Washington and Santiago July 11, 1997; entered into force July 11, 1997.
TIAS

COMMERCE

Provisional commercial agreement. Exchange of notes at Santiago January 6 and February 1, 1938; entered into force January 5, 1940.
52 Stat. 1479; EAS 119; 6 Bevans 584; 190 LNTS 9.

COPYRIGHT (See APPENDIX)

CUSTOMS

Reciprocal agreement relating to free importation privileges for consular officers. Exchange of notes at Washington March 12, April 16, and May 12, 1952; entered into force May 12, 1952.
3 UST 4293; TIAS 2577; 177 UNTS 103.

DEFENSE

Military assistance agreement. Signed at Santiago April 9, 1952; entered into force July 11, 1952.
3 UST 5123; TIAS 2703; 186 UNTS 53.

Agreement for disposition of equipment and materials furnished by the United States under the military assistance agreement of April 9, 1952, and no longer required by Chile. Exchange of notes at Santiago November 30 and December 28, 1956; entered into force December 28, 1956.
8 UST 13; TIAS 3730; 266 UNTS 421.

Agreement relating to the deposit by Chile of ten percent of the value of grant military assistance and excess defense articles. Exchange of notes at Santiago March 28 and April 11, 1972; entered into force April 11, 1972; effective February 7, 1972.
23 UST 930; TIAS 7361.

Memorandum of understanding on the exchange of officers between the U.S. Marine Corps and the Chilean Navy's Marine Corps. Signed at Washington October 30, 1989; entered into force October 30, 1989.
NP

Memorandum of understanding on the exchange of staff noncommissioned officers between the U.S. Marine Corps and the Chilean Navy's Marine Corps. Signed at Washington and Santiago February 7 and 26, 1992; entered into force February 26, 1992.
NP

Agreement governing the protection of classified military information or material. Exchange of notes at Santiago August 13 and September 1, 1992; entered into force September 1, 1992.
TIAS 12281.

Acquisition and cross-servicing agreement, with annexes. Signed at Manaus October 17, 2000; entered into force October 17, 2000.
TIAS

CHILE (Cont'd)

ECONOMIC AND TECHNICAL COOPERATION

Basic agreement for technical cooperation. Signed at Santiago January 16, 1951; entered into force July 27, 1951.
3 UST 390; TIAS 2403; 151 UNTS 147.

Amendments:
January 8, 1952 (3 UST 4697; TIAS 2627; 179 UNTS 265).
October 17, 1952 (3 UST 5136; TIAS 2704; 184 UNTS 376).

Agreement providing for a loan to Chile for reconstruction and rehabilitation as a consequence of the May 1960 earthquakes. Exchange of notes at Santiago August 3, 1961; entered into force August 3, 1961.
12 UST 1390; TIAS 4862; 433 UNTS 21.

Agreement concerning the establishment of an Americas Fund and Administering Board. Signed at Santiago June 30, 1993; entered into force June 30, 1993.
TIAS 12504.

Agency for International Development:
January 26, 1976 (28 UST 5038; TIAS 8611).

EDUCATION

Agreement for educational cooperation. Signed at Washington February 26, 1997; entered into force November 9, 1998.
TIAS

ENVIRONMENTAL COOPERATION

Agreement for cooperation in the Global Learning and Observations to Benefit the Environment (GLOBE) Program, with appendices. Signed at Santiago April 16, 1998; entered into force April 16, 1998.
TIAS

EXTRADITION

Treaty providing for the extradition of fugitives from justice. Signed at Santiago April 17, 1900; entered into force June 26, 1902.
32 Stat. 1850; TS 407; 6 Bevans 543.

FINANCE

Agreement regarding the consolidation and rescheduling of certain debts owed to, guaranteed or insured by the United States Government and its agencies, with annexes. Signed at Washington February 6, 1974; entered into force February 6, 1974.
25 UST 1712; TIAS 7908.

Memorandum of understanding regarding the consolidation and rescheduling of certain Chilean debts owed to, guaranteed or insured by the United States Government and its agencies. Signed at Washington June 17, 1974; entered into force June 17, 1974; effective May 15, 1974.
25 UST 2683; TIAS 7940.

Agreement regarding the consolidation and rescheduling of certain debts owed to the Agency for International Development pursuant to certain loan agreements, with schedules. Signed at Washington July 1, 1974; entered into force July 1, 1974.
25 UST 2691; TIAS 7940.

Agreement regarding the consolidation and rescheduling of payments under PL-480 Title I agricultural commodity agreements, with annexes. Signed at Washington October 22, 1974; entered into force October 22, 1974.
25 UST 2704; TIAS 7940.

Agreement regarding the consolidation and rescheduling of certain debts owed to, guaranteed or insured by the United States Government and its agencies, with annexes and statement. Signed at Washington July 3, 1975; entered into force September 8, 1975.
28 UST 5587; TIAS 8649.

Agreement regarding the consolidation and rescheduling of payments under PL 480 Title I agricultural commodity agreements. Signed at Washington April 5, 1976; entered into force April 5, 1976.
28 UST 5587; TIAS 8649.

Agreement regarding the consolidation and rescheduling of certain debts owed to the Agency for International Development pursuant to certain loan agreements, with schedules. Signed at Washington May 26, 1976; entered into force May 26, 1976.
28 UST 5609; TIAS 8649.

Investment incentive agreement. Exchange of notes at Santiago September 22, 1983; entered into force February 14, 1984.
TIAS 10832.

Agreement regarding the consolidation and rescheduling of certain debts owed to, guaranteed by or insured by the United States Government and its agencies, with annexes. Signed at Washington February 6, 1986; entered into force March 17, 1986.
NP

Agreement regarding the consolidation and rescheduling or refinancing of certain debts owed to, guaranteed by or insured by the United States Government and its agencies, with annexes. Signed at Washington August 13, 1987; entered into force September 21, 1987.
NP

Agreement regarding the reduction of certain debts owed to the United States Government and its agencies, with appendices. Signed at Washington June 27, 1991; entered into force August 8, 1991.
NP

Agreement regarding the reduction of certain debts related to foreign assistance owed to the Government of the United States and its agencies, with appendices. Signed at Washington and Santiago December 11 and 15, 1992; entered into force January 14, 1993.
NP

HEALTH

Memorandum of understanding regarding cooperation in establishing and implementing emergency procedures to ensure the safety of fresh fruit exported to the United States from Chile. Signed at Washington October 27, 1989; entered into force October 27, 1989.
TIAS 11894.

INFORMATIONAL MEDIA GUARANTIES

Agreement relating to an informational media guaranty program in Chile. Exchange of notes at Santiago January 14, 1955; entered into force January 14, 1955.
6 UST 41; TIAS 3166; 238 UNTS 191.

MARITIME MATTERS

Agreement relating to the transfer to Chile of certain United States naval vessels. Exchange of notes at Washington January 4, 1951, with memorandum of understanding dated January 9, 1951; entered into force January 4, 1951.
3 UST 2741; TIAS 2444; 165 UNTS 105.

Agreement for the loan of a submarine to Chile. Exchange of notes at Santiago June 28 and July 16, 1960; entered into force July 16, 1960.
11 UST 2197; TIAS 4589; 393 UNTS 271.

Extension and amendment:
December 2 and 7, 1960 (11 UST 2527; TIAS 4638; 401 UNTS 364).
May 13 and 17, 1968 (19 UST 5368; TIAS 6519; 706 UNTS 317).

NARCOTIC DRUGS

Agreement concerning cooperation to suppress the processing, trafficking, consumption and export of narcotic drugs. Signed at Santiago August 5, 1994; entered into force August 5, 1994.
TIAS 12561.

CHILE (Cont'd)

NAVIGATION

Agreement for the establishment and operation of an OMEGA navigation system signal monitor. Signed at Washington and Santiago August 23 and September 5, 1984; entered into force September 5, 1984.
TIAS 11201.

PACIFIC SETTLEMENT OF DISPUTES

Treaty for the settlement of disputes that may occur between the United States of America and Chile. Signed at Washington July 24, 1914; entered into force January 19, 1916.
39 Stat. 1645; TS 621; 6 Bevans 550.

POSTAL MATTERS

Money order convention. Signed at Washington August 12, 1897; entered into force January 1, 1898.
NP

International express mail agreement with detailed regulations. Signed at Montevideo September 8, 1986; entered into force September 26, 1986.
TIAS 11392.

PUBLICATIONS

Agreement relating to the exchange of official publications. Exchange of notes at Santiago October 22 and 27, 1937; entered into force October 27, 1937.
51 Stat. 331; EAS 112; 6 Bevans 566.

RELIEF SUPPLIES AND PACKAGES

Agreement granting duty-free entry, exemption from internal taxation, and free transportation within Chile to ultimate beneficiary for certain relief supplies and equipment for U.S. rehabilitation and relief agencies. Exchange of notes at Santiago April 5, 1955; entered into force April 5, 1955.
6 UST 717; TIAS 3210; 250 UNTS 253.

SCIENTIFIC COOPERATION

Memorandum of understanding for scientific cooperation in the earth sciences. Signed at Reston and Santiago August 2 and 26, 1982; entered into force August 26, 1982.
TIAS 10457; 1751 UNTS 47.

Amendment and extension:
April 30 and August 27, 1993 (TIAS 12161).

Agreement regarding the marine scientific research activities of the research vessel Hero. Signed at Santiago June 1, 1983; entered into force June 1, 1983.
TIAS 10825.

Basic agreement relating to scientific and technological cooperation, with annexes. Signed at Washington May 14, 1992; entered into force January 19, 1994.
TIAS 12453; 1792 UNTS 321.

Extension:
May 5 and June 22, 1999.

Memorandum of understanding concerning scientific and technical cooperation in the earth sciences, with annexes. Signed at Reston and Santiago September 30 and November 17, 1994; entered into force November 17, 1994.
TIAS

Agreement for the establishment of a cooperative biomedical research program. Signed at Washington and Santiago April 30 and May 5, 1997; entered into force May 5, 1997.
TIAS

SMUGGLING

Convention for the prevention of smuggling of alcoholic beverages. Signed at Washington May 27, 1930; entered into force November 25, 1930.
46 Stat. 2852; TS 829; 6 Bevans 558; 133 LNTS 141.

SPACE COOPERATION

Agreement concerning the use of Mataveri Airport, Isla de Pascua, as a space shuttle emergency landing and rescue site. Signed at Santiago August 2, 1985; entered into force November 6, 1985.
TIAS 11248.

TAXATION

Agreement concerning the reciprocal exemption from income tax of income derived from the international operation of aircraft. Exchange of notes at Washington and Santiago August 6 and December 4, 1990; entered into force December 4, 1990.
TIAS 11764.

TELECOMMUNICATION

Agreement relating to radio communications between amateur stations on behalf of third parties. Exchange of notes at Santiago August

2 and 17, 1934; entered into force August 17, 1934.
49 Stat. 3667; EAS 72; 6 Bevans 564; 157 LNTS 15.

Agreement relating to the reciprocal granting of authorizations to permit licensed amateur radio operators of either country to operate their stations in the other country. Exchange of notes at Washington November 30, 1967; entered into force December 30, 1967.
18 UST 2882; TIAS 6380; 701 UNTS 175.

TRACKING STATIONS

Agreement concerning a cooperative program for tracking and receiving radio signals from earth satellites and space vehicles. Exchange of notes at Santiago February 16 and 19, 1959; entered into force February 19, 1959; operative from December 31, 1958.
10 UST 783; TIAS 4216; 343 UNTS 17.

VISAS

Agreement relating to passport visas for non-immigrants. Exchange of notes at Santiago August 29, 1950; effective September 1, 1950.
1 UST 719; TIAS 2137; 122 UNTS 43.

WEATHER STATIONS

Agreement relating to a cooperative meteorological observation program in Chile. Exchange of notes at Santiago February 23, June 2 and September 7, 1977; entered into force February 15, 1978; effective January 1, 1977.
29 UST 1969; TIAS 8912.

CHINA [1]

NOTE:
[1] See also note under CHINA (Taiwan) at end of the bilateral section.

In connection with Hong Kong, the People's Republic of China submitted to the Secretary General of the United Nations a note, dated June 20, 1997, which reads in pertinent part as follows:

"In accordance with the Joint Declaration of the Government of the United Kingdom of Great Britain and North Ireland and the Government of the People's Republic of China on the Question of Hong Kong signed on 19 December 1984 (hereinafter referred to as the Joint Declaration), the People's Republic of China will resume the exercise of sovereignty over Hong Kong with effect from 1 July 1997. Hong Kong will, with effect from that date, become a Special Administrative Region of the People's Republic of China.

It is provided in Section I of Annex I to the Joint Declaration, "Elaboration by the Govern-

CHINA [1] (Cont'd)

ment of the People's Republic of China of its Basic Policies Regarding Hong Kong'', and in Articles 12, 13 and 14 of the Basic Law of the Hong Kong Special Administrative Region of the People's Republic of China, which was adopted on 4 April 1990 by the National People's Congress of the People's Republic of China (hereinafter referred to as the Basic law), that the Hong Kong Special Administrative Region will enjoy a high degree of autonomy, except in foreign and defence affairs which are the responsibility of the Central People's Government of the People's Republic of China. Furthermore, it is provided both in Section XI of Annex I to the Joint Declaration and Article 153 of the Basic Law that international agreements to which the People's Republic of China is not a party but which are implemented in Hong Kong may continue to be implemented in the Hong Kong Special Administrative Region.

In this connection, on behalf of the Government of the People's Republic of China, I would like to inform Your Excellency as follows:

I. The treaties listed in Annex I [not printed herein] to this Note, to which the People's Republic of China is a party, will be applied to the Hong Kong Special Administrative Region with effect from 1 July 1997 as they:

(i) are applied to Hong Kong before 1 July 1997; or

(ii) fall within the category of foreign affairs or defence or, owing to their nature and provisions, must apply to the entire territory of a State; or

(iii) are not applied to Hong Kong before 1 July 1997 but with respect to which it has been decided to apply them to the Hong Kong Special Administrative Region with effect from that date (denoted by an asterisk in Annex I.)

II. The treaties listed in Annex II [not printed herein] to this Note, to which the People's Republic of China is not yet a party and which apply to Hong Kong before 1 July 1997, will continue to apply to the Hong Kong Special Administrative Region with effect from 1 July 1997.

The provisions of the International Covenant on Civil and Political Rights and the International Covenant on Economic, Social and Cultural Rights as applied to Hong Kong shall remain in force beginning from 1 July 1997. . . .

III. The Government of the People's Republic of China has already carried out separately the formalities required for the application of the treaties listed in the aforesaid Annexes, including all the related amendments, protocols, reservations and declarations, to the Hong Kong Special Administrative Region with effect from 1 July 1997.

IV. With respect to any other treaty not listed in the Annexes to this Note, to which the People's Republic of China is or will become a party, in the event that it is decided to apply such treaty to the Hong Kong Special Administrative Region, the Government of the People's Republic of China will carry out separately the formalities for such application. For the avoidance of doubt, no separate formalities will need to be carried out by the Government of the People's Republic of China with respect to treaties which fall within the category of foreign affairs or defence or which, owing to their nature and provisions, must apply to the entire territory of a State.''

In connection with Macao, the People's Republic of China submitted to the Secretary General of the United Nations a note, dated December 13, 1999, which reads in pertinent part as follows:

''In accordance with the Joint Declaration of the Government of the People's Republic of China and the Government of the Republic of Portugal on the Question of Macao signed on 13 April 1987 (hereinafter referred to as the Joint Declaration), the Government of the People's Republic of China will resume the exercise of sovereignty over Macao with effect from 20 December 1999. Macao will, from that date, become a Special Administrative Region of the People's Republic of China.

It is provided in Section I of Elaboration by the Government of the People's Republic of China of its Basic Policies Regarding Macao, which is Annex I to the Joint Declaration, and in Article 12, 13 and 14 of the Basic Law of the Macao Special Administrative Region of the People's Republic of China (hereinafter referred to as the Basic Law), which was adopted by the National People's Congress of the People's Republic of China on 31 March 1993, that the Macao Special Administrative Region will enjoy a high degree of autonomy, except in foreign and defence affairs which are the responsibilities of the Central People's Government of the People's Republic of China. Furthermore, it is provided both in Section VIII of Annex I to the Joint Declaration and Article 138 of the Basic Law that international agreements to which the People's Republic of China is not a party but which are implemented in Macao may continue to be implemented in the Macao Special Administrative Region.

In this connection, on behalf of the Government of the People's Republic of China, I have the honour to inform your Excellency that:

I. The Treaties listed in Annex I [not printed herein] to this Note, to which the People's Republic of China is a Party, will be applied to the Macao Special Administrative Region with effect from 20 December 1999 so long as they are one of the following categories:

(i) Treaties that apply to Macao before 20 December 1999;

(ii) Treaties that must apply to the entire territory of a state as they concern foreign affairs or defence or their nature or provisions so require.

II. The Treaties listed in Annex II [not printed herein] to this Note, to which the People's Republic of China is not yet a Party and which apply to Macao before 20 December 1999, will continue to apply to the Macao Special Administrative Region with effect from 20 December 1999.

III. The Government of the People's Republic of China has notified the treaty depositories concerned of the application of the treaties including their amendments and protocols as lised in the aforesaid Annexes as well as reservations and declarations made thereto by the Chinese Government to the Macao Special Administrative Region with effect from 20 December 1999.

IV. With respect to other treaties that are not listed in the Annexes to this Note, to which the People's Republic of China is or will become a Party, the Government of the People's Republic of China will go through separately the necessary formalities for their application to the Macao Special Administrative Region if it is so decided.''

Listings and annotations in ''Part 2: Multilateral Treaties and Other Agreements'', to the effect that Hong Kong and Macao are parties to treaties or other agreements, are based on the above notes, annexes and notifications from depositaries.

ATOMIC ENERGY

Agreement for cooperation concerning peaceful uses of nuclear energy, with annexes and agreed minute. Signed at Washington July 23, 1985; entered into force December 30, 1985. TIAS 12027.

Agreement on cooperation concerning peaceful uses of nuclear technologies, with annex. Signed at Beijing June 29, 1998; entered into force June 29, 1998. TIAS

Protocol on cooperation in nuclear safety matters. Signed at Vienna September 24, 1998; entered into force September 24, 1998. TIAS

AVIATION

Agreement relating to civil air transport, with annexes and exchanges of letters. Signed at Washington September 17, 1980; entered into force September 17, 1980. 33 UST 4559; TIAS 10326.

Amendments:
February 10, 1992 (TIAS 12448).
February 16 and March 27, 1996.
April 8, 1999.

CHINA [1] (Cont'd)

Memorandum of agreement for technical cooperation in the field of civil aviation, with annex. Signed at Washington March 14, 1986; entered into force March 14, 1986.
TIAS 12006.

Agreement concerning the airworthiness certification of imported civil aeronautical products. Exchange of notes at Beijing October 8 and 14, 1991; entered into force October 14, 1991.
TIAS 12437.

CLAIMS

Agreement concerning the settlement of claims. Signed at Beijing May 11, 1979; entered into force May 11, 1979.
30 UST 1957; TIAS 9306; 1153 UNTS 289.

Amendment:
September 28, 1979 (31 UST 5596; TIAS 9675).

Memorandum of understanding concerning settlement of claims relating to deaths, injuries or losses suffered by Chinese personnel as a result of the U.S. bombing of the Chinese Embassy in the Federal Republic of Yugoslavia, with annex. Signed at Beijing July 30, 1999; entered into force July 30, 1999.
TIAS

CONSULS

Agreement on the mutual establishment of consular relations and the opening of consulates general, with annex. Signed at Washington January 31, 1979; entered into force January 31, 1979.
30 UST 17; TIAS 9177.

Consular convention, with exchange of notes. Signed at Washington September 17, 1980; entered into force February 19, 1982.
33 UST 2973; TIAS 10209; 1529 UNTS 199.

Agreement modifying the consular convention of September 17, 1980. Exchange of notes at Beijing January 17, 1981; entered into force February 19, 1982.
33 UST 3048; TIAS 10209.

Agreement concerning the establishment of additional consulates general. Exchange of notes at Washington September 17, 1980; entered into force September 17, 1980.
TIAS 12007.

Agreement concerning the establishment of additional consulates general, with annex and related letter. Exchange of notes at Beijing June 16, 1981; entered into force June 16, 1981.
TIAS 12007.

Agreement concerning the enlargement of existing consular districts. Exchange of notes at June 16, 1981; entered into force June 16, 1981.
TIAS

Agreement regarding the maintenance of the U.S. consulate general in the Hong Kong Special Administrative Region. Signed at Beijing March 25, 1997; entered into force July 1, 1997.
TIAS

COPYRIGHT (See APPENDIX)

CULTURAL RELATIONS

Cultural agreement. Signed at Washington January 31, 1979, entered into force January 31, 1979.
30 UST 26; TIAS 9178.

EDUCATION

Agreement for cooperation in educational exchanges. Signed at Beijing March 28, 2000; entered into force March 28, 2000.
TIAS

EMBASSY SITES

Agreement concerning the mutual provision of properties for use of the two countries, with appendices. Signed at Beijing March 23, 1991; entered into force April 22, 1991.
TIAS

Memorandum of understanding concerning the provision of properties in Washington, D.C., Beijing, and Guangzhou. Signed at Beijing November 1, 2000; entered into force November 1, 2000.
TIAS

ENVIRONMENTAL COOPERATION

Agreement for cooperation in the Global Learning and Observations to Benefit the Environment (GLOBE) Program, with appendices. Signed at Beijing October 18, 1995; entered into force October 18, 1995.
TIAS 12698.

FINANCE

Agreement relating to investment guaranties, with related notes and statement. Exchange of notes at Beijing October 30, 1980; entered into force October 30, 1980.
32 UST 4010; TIAS 9924; 1267 UNTS 315.

FISHERIES

Agreement concerning fisheries off the coasts of the United States, with annexes and agreed minutes. Signed at Washington July 23, 1985; entered into force November 19, 1985.
TIAS 12002; 1443 UNTS 151.

Amendments and extensions:
March 14 and 22, 1990 (TIAS 11893).
May 12 and July 6, 1992 (TIAS 11907).
June 6 and July 1, 1996.

Memorandum of understanding on effective cooperation and implementation of United Nations General Assembly Resolution 46/215 of December 20, 1991. Signed at Washington December 3, 1993; entered into force December 3, 1993.
TIAS

Extension:
October 22 and December 27, 1996.

INDUSTRIAL AND TECHNOLOGICAL COOPERATION

Accord on industrial and technological cooperation. Signed at Washington January 12, 1984; entered into force January 12, 1984.
TIAS 10920.

INTELLECTUAL PROPERTY

Memorandum of understanding on the protection of intellectual property. Signed at Washington January 17, 1992; entered into force January 17, 1992.
TIAS 12036.

LABOR

Memorandum of understanding on prohibiting import and export trade in prison labor products. Signed at Washington August 7, 1992; entered into force August 7, 1992.
TIAS

Statement of cooperation on the implementation of the memorandum of understanding on prohibiting import and export trade in prison labor products. Signed at Beijing March 13, 1994; entered into force March 13, 1994.
TIAS

MARITIME MATTERS

Agreement concerning maritime search and rescue cooperation. Signed at Washington January 20, 1987; entered into force January 20, 1987.
TIAS 12013.

CHINA ¹ (Cont'd)

Agreement on establishing a consultation mechanism to strengthen military maritime safety. Signed at Beijing January 19, 1998; entered into force January 19, 1998.
TIAS

PEACE CORPS

Agreement concerning the United States volunteer program in China. Signed at Beijing June 29, 1998; entered into force June 29, 1998.
TIAS

POSTAL MATTERS

Parcel post agreement, with detailed regulations. Signed at Washington October 9, 1980; entered into force November 8, 1980.
32 UST 2919; TIAS 9887.

International express mail agreement, with detailed regulations. Signed at Washington October 9, 1980; entered into force October 9, 1980.
32 UST 4441; TIAS 9959; 1267 UNTS 253.

Memorandum of understanding concerning the operation of the INTELPOST field trial, with details of implementation. Signed at Beijing and Washington January 17 and February 5, 1987; entered into force March 1, 1987.
NP

Postal money order agreement. Signed at Washington and Beijing June 19 and 27, 1992; entered into force July 1, 1992.
NP

PRIVILEGES AND IMMUNITIES

Agreement relating to privileges and immunities for the respective diplomatic missions in Washington and Beijing. Exchange of notes at Washington January 5, 1981; entered into force January 5, 1981.
TIAS

REMOTE SENSING

Memorandum of understanding relating to establishment and operation of a Landsat system, with annex. Signed at Washington and Beijing July 2 and 8, 1985; entered into force July 8, 1985.
TIAS 11128.

SATELLITES

Memorandum of agreement on liability for satellite launches. Signed at Washington December 17, 1988; entered into force March 16, 1989.
TIAS

SCIENTIFIC COOPERATION

Agreement on cooperation in science and technology, with exchange of letters. Signed at Washington January 31, 1979; entered into force January 31, 1979.
30 UST 35; TIAS 9179; 1150 UNTS 349.

Amendment and extensions:
May 22, 1991.
August 6 and 28, 1996.

TAXATION

Agreement with respect to mutual exemption from taxation of transportation income of shipping and air transport enterprises. Signed at Beijing March 5, 1982; entered into force September 23, 1983; effective January 1, 1981.
TIAS 10884.

Agreement for the avoidance of double taxation and the prevention of tax evasion with respect to taxes on income, with protocol and exchange of notes. Signed at Beijing April 30, 1984; entered into force November 21, 1986.
TIAS 12065.

Protocol concerning the interpretation of paragraph 7 of the protocol to the agreement for the avoidance of double taxation and the prevention of tax evasion with respect to taxes on income of April 30, 1984. Signed at Beijing May 10, 1986; entered into force November 21, 1986.
TIAS 12065.

TECHNOLOGY TRANSFER

Memorandum of agreement on satellite technology safeguards. Signed at Beijing February 11, 1993; entered into force February 11, 1993.
TIAS 12486.

TELECOMMUNICATION

Agreement on the establishment of the direct secure telephone link. Signed at Beijing April 29, 1998; entered into force April 29, 1998.
TIAS

TOURISM

Memorandum of understanding on the development of bilateral tourism relations. Signed at Beijing August 5, 1982; entered into force August 5, 1982.
TIAS 10426.

TRADE AND COMMERCE

Agreement on trade exhibitions. Signed at Beijing May 10, 1979; entered into force May 10, 1979.
30 UST 4472; TIAS 9470; 1171 UNTS 305.

Agreement on trade relations. Signed at Beijing July 7, 1979; entered into force February 1, 1980.
31 UST 4651; TIAS 9630; 1202 UNTS 179.

Arrangement relating to a visa system for exports to the United States of cotton, wool and manmade fiber textiles and textile products. Exchange of letters at Washington February 16, 1984; entered into force February 16, 1984.
TIAS 10945.

Agreement for orderly trade in ammonium paratungstate and tungstic acid, with annexes. Signed at Washington September 28, 1987; entered into force September 28, 1987; effective October 1, 1987.
TIAS

Agreement concerning trade in textiles and textile products, with annexes. Exchange of letters at Beijing February 2, 1988; entered into force February 2, 1988; effective January 1, 1988.
NP

Amendments and extension:
May 24 and 26, 1988 (NP).
August 26 and September 7, 1988 (NP).
November 7, 1988 and January 24, 1989 (NP).
April 28 and May 1, 1989 (NP).
April 23 and 24, 1991 (NP).

Memorandum of agreement regarding international trade in commercial launch services, with annexes. Signed at Beijing March 13, 1995; entered into force March 13, 1995; effective January 1, 1995.
TIAS

Amendment:
October 27, 1997.

Agreement concerning trade in textile and apparel products, with annexes. Exchange of notes at Beijing March 29 and June 8, 1995; entered into force June 8, 1995; effective January 1, 1994.
NP

VISAS

Agreement relating to the reciprocal issuance of visas to crew members of aircraft and vessels. Exchange of notes at Beijing January 7, 1981; entered into force January 7, 1981.
32 UST 4533; TIAS 9965; 1267 UNTS 335.

CHINA [1] (Cont'd)

Agreement relating to reciprocal facilitation of visa issuance. Exchange of notes at Beijing December 2, 1985; entered into force January 2, 1986.
TIAS

Agreement relating to the reciprocal facilitation of visa issuance. Exchange of notes at Beijing April 14, 1993; entered into force May 14, 1993.
TIAS 12495.

HONG KONG

AVIATION

Agreement concerning air services, with annex. Signed at Hong Kong April 7, 1997; entered into force April 7, 1997.
TIAS

COPYRIGHT (See APPENDIX)

EXTRADITION

Agreement for the surrender of fugitive offenders. Signed at Hong Kong December 20, 1996; entered into force January 21, 1998.
TIAS

JUDICIAL ASSISTANCE

Agreement on mutual legal assistance in criminal matters, with annex. Signed at Hong Kong April 15, 1997; entered into force January 21, 2000.
TIAS

POSTAL MATTERS

Parcel post agreement and regulations of execution. Signed at Hong Kong January 18 and at Washington February 2, 1961; entered into force July 1, 1961.
12 UST 328; TIAS 4721.

International express mail agreement, with detailed regulations. Signed at Hong Kong and Washington January 2 and February 6, 1979; entered into force March 15, 1979; effective February 1, 1979.
30 UST 3427; TIAS 9398; 1180 UNTS 25.

PRISONER TRANSFER

Agreement for the transfer of sentenced persons. Signed at Hong Kong April 15, 1997; entered into force April 18, 1999.
TIAS

TAXATION

Agreement for the reciprocal exemption with respect to taxes on income from the international operation of ships. Exchange of notes at Hong Kong August 1, 1989; entered into force August 1, 1989.
TIAS 11892; 1549 UNTS 91.

TRADE AND COMMERCE

Agreement relating to trade in certain textiles and textile products, with annexes. Exchange of letters at Hong Kong August 4, 1986; entered into force August 4, 1986; effective January 1, 1986.
NP

Amendments:
August 5 and 12, 1987 (NP).
August 5 and 12, 1987 (NP).
March 2 and 7, 1988 (NP).
July 15 and 20, 1988 (NP).
November 4 and 7, 1988 (NP).
December 20 and 21, 1989 and January 5, 1990 (NP).

Agreement concerning trade in textiles and textile products, with annexes. Exchange of notes at Hong Kong October 9, 1991; entered into force October 9, 1991; effective January 1, 1992.
NP

Amendments:
March 2 and 11, 1993 (NP).
February 3 and April 27, 1993 (NP).

MACAO

AVIATION

Air transport agreement, with annexes. Signed at Macao July 3, 1996; entered into force July 3, 1996.
TIAS

COPYRIGHT (See APPENDIX)

POSTAL MATTERS

Parcel post agreement with detailed regulations for execution. Signed at Macao February 23 and at Washington June 8, 1973; entered into force August 1, 1974.
25 UST 2982; TIAS 7961.

International express mail agreement, with detailed regulations. Signed at Macao and Washington May 3 and June 14, 1983; entered into force October 1, 1983.
TIAS 10736.

Memorandum of understanding concerning the operation of the INTELPOST field trial, with details of implementation. Signed at Macao and Washington April 29 and May 21, 1985; entered into force May 21, 1985.
TIAS 11246.

TRADE AND COMMERCE

Administrative arrangement relating to a visa system. Exchange of letters at Washington and Macao August 21, 1981; entered into force August 21, 1981.
TIAS

Amendment:
November 2 and December 12, 1988.

Agreement relating to trade in cotton, wool, and man-made fiber textiles and textile products, with annexes. Exchange of letters at Hong Kong and Macao December 28, 1983 and January 9, 1984; entered into force January 9, 1984; effective January 1, 1984.
TIAS 10917.

Amendments and extension:
February 26 and 28, 1986 (NP).
November 10 and 27, 1986 (NP).
April 14 and 28, 1987 (NP).
January 8 and 12, 1988 (NP).
November 7 and December 30, 1988 (NP).
February 10 and March 3, 1989 (NP).
November 1, 1991, January 21 and 27, 1992 (NP).

Agreement relating to trade in textiles and textile products, with annexes. Exchange of notes at Hong Kong and Macao March 29 and May 21, 1994; entered into force May 21, 1994; effective January 1, 1991.
NP

COLOMBIA

AGRICULTURAL COMMODITIES

Agricultural commodities agreement with memorandum of understanding. Exchange of notes at Bogota October 6, 1959; entered into force October 6, 1959.
10 UST 1799; TIAS 4337; 358 UNTS 145.

Amendments:
April 26, 1961 (12 UST 516; TIAS 4747; 407 UNTS 285).
September 6 and 8, 1961 (13 UST 204; TIAS 4962; 442 UNTS 334).
November 9 and 20, 1961 (12 UST 3124; TIAS 4911; 433 UNTS 377).

COLOMBIA (Cont'd)

January 31 and February 14, 1962 (13 UST 262; TIAS 4970; 445 UNTS 362).
June 20, 1962 (13 UST 1323; TIAS 5088; 458 UNTS 344).

Agricultural commodities agreement with exchange of notes of March 29 and April 15, 1963. Signed at Bogota March 27, 1963; entered into force March 27, 1963.
14 UST 1502; TIAS 5450; 489 UNTS 289.

Amendment:
October 11 and 25, 1963 (15 UST 146; TIAS 5531; 511 UNTS 313).

Agricultural commodities agreement with exchange of notes of October 8, 1964 and February 11, 1965. Signed at Bogota October 8, 1964; entered into force October 8, 1964.
16 UST 683; TIAS 5797; 579 UNTS 3.

Agricultural commodities agreement with exchange of notes. Signed at Bogota March 10, 1966; entered into force March 10, 1966.
17 UST 1965; TIAS 6138; 674 UNTS 139.

Agricultural commodities agreement with annex. Signed at Bogota May 31, 1968; entered into force May 31, 1968.
19 UST 6031; TIAS 6563; 702 UNTS 3.

Agricultural commodities agreement with annex. Signed at Bogota March 4, 1970; entered into force March 4, 1970.
22 UST 1618; TIAS 7189; 806 UNTS 255.

Amendment:
April 19, May 4 and 12, 1971 (24 UST 412; TIAS 7553; 898 UNTS 335).

Related agreements:
April 24, 1973 (24 UST 1056; TIAS 7623).
May 11, 1973 (24 UST 1633; TIAS 7667).
December 11, 1973 (25 UST 180; TIAS 7781).
April 22, 1974 (25 UST 627; TIAS 7812).

Agricultural commodities agreement with annex. Signed at Bogota June 26, 1972; entered into force June 26, 1972.
24 UST 751; TIAS 7580.

Amendments:
June 26 and 28, 1972 (24 UST 761; TIAS 7580).
August 16 and September 1, 1972 (24 UST 764; TIAS 7580).

AGRICULTURE

Agreement for the eradication of foot-and-mouth disease in the areas adjacent to the Colombian-Panamanian border, with annex. Signed at Bogota August 8, 1979; entered into force October 10, 1979.
33 UST 1643; TIAS 10138.

AMITY (See also COMMERCE)

Treaty for the settlement of differences arising out of the events which took place on the Isthmus of Panama in November 1903. Signed at Bogota April 6, 1914; entered into force March 1, 1922.
42 Stat. 2122; TS 661; 6 Bevans 900; 9 LNTS 301.

ATOMIC ENERGY

Agreement providing for a grant for the acquisition of nuclear training and research equipment and materials. Exchange of notes at Bogota July 31, 1959 and January 11, 1960; entered into force January 11, 1960.
11 UST 138; TIAS 4421; 371 UNTS 37.

Agreement for cooperation concerning civil uses of nuclear energy, with annex and exchange of notes. Signed at Bogota January 8, 1981; entered into force September 7, 1983.
TIAS 10722; 1607 UNTS 33.

AVIATION

Air transport agreement and exchanges of notes. Signed at Bogota October 24, 1956; entered into force provisionally January 1, 1957.
14 UST 429; TIAS 5338; 476 UNTS 77.

Amendments:
October 23, 1968 (19 UST 7501; TIAS 6593; 701 UNTS 386).
October 16 and 22, 1981 and April 21, 1982 (34 UST 1152; TIAS 10404).
August 11, October 11 and November 22, 2000.

Agreement relating to the sale of six C-47 aircraft to Colombia for civilian cargo and passenger service. Signed at Bogota April 21, 1976; entered into force April 21, 1976.
27 UST 4317; TIAS 8453; 1071 UNTS 73.

COMMERCE

Treaty of peace, amity, navigation, and commerce, with additional article.[1] Signed at Bogota December 12, 1846; entered into force June 10, 1848.
9 Stat. 881; TS 54; 6 Bevans 868.

NOTE:
[1] Article 33 terminated by the United States effective July 1, 1916, in accordance with the Seamen's Act (38 Stat. 1164).

CONSULS (See also COMMERCE)

Consular convention.[1] Signed at Washington May 4, 1850; entered into force October 30, 1851.
10 Stat. 900; TS 55; 6 Bevans 882.

NOTE:
[1] Article III, paragraphs 8 and 11, terminated by the United States as of July 1, 1916 in accordance with the Seamen's Act (38 Stat. 1164).

COPYRIGHT (See APPENDIX)

CUSTOMS

Agreement relating to reciprocal customs privileges for consular officers. Exchange of notes at Washington May 9 and 10, 1968; entered into force May 10, 1968.
19 UST 4864; TIAS 6491; 698 UNTS 237.

Agreement regarding mutual assistance. Signed at Miami September 21, 1999; entered into force September 21, 1999.
TIAS

DEFENSE

Agreement relating to the procurement of strategic materials. Exchange of notes at Bogota March 29, 1943; entered into force March 29, 1943.
58 Stat. 1546; EAS 442; 6 Bevans 954; 124 UNTS 139.

Military assistance agreement. Exchange of notes at Bogota April 17, 1952; entered into force April 17, 1952.
3 UST 3690; TIAS 2496; 174 UNTS 15.

Agreement for performance by members of Army, Navy, and Air Force missions of duties of military assistance advisory group specified in article V of military assistance agreement of April 17, 1952. Exchange of notes at Bogota July 13 and September 16, 1955; entered into force September 20, 1955.
6 UST 3904; TIAS 3393; 256 UNTS 221.

Agreement providing for disposition of equipment and materials furnished by the United States under the military assistance agreement of April 17, 1952. Exchange of notes at Bogota February 22 and March 14, 1956; entered into force March 14, 1956.
7 UST 475; TIAS 3531; 270 UNTS 392.

Agreement relating to the furnishing of military equipment, materials, and services. Exchange of notes at Bogota April 3, 1961; entered into force April 3, 1961.
12 UST 492; TIAS 4740; 407 UNTS 3.

COLOMBIA (Cont'd)

Agreement relating to the deposit of ten percent of the grants of military assistance and excess defense articles given by the United States with related aide memoire. Exchange of notes at Bogota August 25, 1972; entered into force August 25, 1972; effective February 7, 1972.
23 UST 3149; TIAS 7492; 898 UNTS 171.

Agreement concerning general security of military information. Exchange of notes at Bogota December 16, 1981; entered into force December 16, 1981.
33 UST 4444; TIAS 10315.

Memorandum of agreement on the exchange of naval personnel. Signed at Bogota and Washington March 8 and April 30, 1985; entered into force April 30, 1985.
TIAS 11255.

Memorandum of understanding concerning Colombian integration into the Caribbean Basin Radar Network (CBRN). Signed at Bogota February 22, 1989; entered into force February 22, 1989.
TIAS 12282.

ECONOMIC AND TECHNICAL COOPERATION

Agreement for a cooperative program of agriculture and natural resources in Colombia. Exchange of notes at Bogota May 25 and June 9, 1953; entered into force June 9, 1953.
4 UST 1601; TIAS 2827; 213 UNTS 3.

Agreement for interchange of technical knowledge and skills and related activities for development of Cauca Valley region. Exchange of notes at Bogota July 29 and November 15 and 28, 1955; entered into force November 28, 1955.
6 UST 6035; TIAS 3451; 241 UNTS 39.

General agreement for economic, technical and related assistance. Signed at Bogota July 23, 1962; entered into force July 23, 1962.
13 UST 1778; TIAS 5123; 458 UNTS 123.

Agreement concerning the establishment of an Americas Account and Administering Council. Signed at Bogota June 18, 1993; entered into force June 18, 1993.
TIAS 12502.

Agency for International Development:
December 24, 1975 (28 UST 179; TIAS 8467; 1071 UNTS 31).
March 12, 1976 (28 UST 1419; TIAS 8515).
April 22, 1976 (28 UST 1438; TIAS 8516; 1071 UNTS 79).
June 14, 1976 (28 UST 1515; TIAS 8519; 1071 UNTS 155).
October 19, 1976 (28 UST 8273; TIAS 8760).
October 19, 1976 (28 UST 8291; TIAS 8761).

November 29, 1976 (28 UST 8709; TIAS 8768).
November 29, 1976 (28 UST 8748; TIAS 8769; 1095 UNTS 3).

EDUCATION

Agreement for financing certain educational exchange programs. Exchange of notes at Bogota June 12, 1967 and March 8, 1971; entered into force March 11, 1971.
22 UST 1705; TIAS 7198; 808 UNTS 368.

EMPLOYMENT

Agreement relating to the employment of dependents of official government employees. Exchange of notes at Bogota March 30 and May 25, 1982; entered into force May 25, 1982.
TIAS 10729; 1607 UNTS 95.

ENVIRONMENTAL COOPERATION

Agreement for cooperation in the Global Learning and Observations to Benefit the Environment (GLOBE) Program, with appendices. Signed at Washington October 28, 1998; entered into force October 28, 1998.
TIAS

EXTRADITION

Extradition treaty, with annex. Signed at Washington September 14, 1979; entered into force March 4, 1982.
TIAS

FINANCE

Agreement relating to investment guaranties. Exchange of letters at Bogota October 5, 1962; entered into force October 5, 1962.
13 UST 2465; TIAS 5210; 459 UNTS 191.

Investment incentive agreement. Exchange of notes at Washington April 3, 1985; entered into force April 3, 1985.
TIAS 12043.

Amendment:
July 18 and August 19, 1985 (TIAS 12043).

Agreement regarding the reduction of certain debts related to foreign assistance owed to the Government of the United States and its agencies, with appendices. Signed at Washington December 15, 1992; entered into force January 14, 1993.
NP

Amendments:
June 1 and 30, 1993 (NP).
July 2 and 19, 1993 (NP).

FISHERIES

Agreement on certain fishing rights in implementation of the treaty and exchange of notes of September 8, 1972 (TIAS 10120). Exchange of notes at Bogota October 24 and December 6, 1983; entered into force December 6, 1983; effective March 1, 1984.
TIAS 10842.

HIGHWAYS

Agreement for cooperation in the construction of the Colombia segment of the Darien Gap Highway. Signed at Washington May 6, 1971; entered into force May 6, 1971.
22 UST 617; TIAS 7112; 793 UNTS 3.

JUDICIAL ASSISTANCE

Procedures for mutual assistance in the administration of justice in connection with the Lockheed Aircraft Corporation matter. Signed at Washington April 22, 1976; entered into force April 22, 1976.
27 UST 1059; TIAS 8244.

Related agreements:
July 7 and 15, 1980 (32 UST 1921; TIAS 9809; 1234 UNTS 423).
August 28 and September 10, 1980 (32 UST 2599; TIAS 9860; 1274 UNTS 261).

MAPPING

Arrangement covering the accomplishment of aerial photographic coverage of Colombia with annexes. Signed at Bogota July 4, 1975; entered into force July 4, 1975.
28 UST 1063; TIAS 8493.

Cooperative arrangement for the production of topographic maps of Colombia, with annexes. Signed at Washington and Bogota April 21 and 28, 1986; entered into force April 28, 1986.
NP

MISSIONS, MILITARY

Agreement concerning an army mission, a naval mission, and an air force mission of the United States armed forces in Colombia. Signed at Bogota October 7, 1974; entered into force April 16, 1975.
29 UST 2901; TIAS 8986; 1148 UNTS 75.

COLOMBIA (Cont'd)

NARCOTIC DRUGS

Agreement relating to cooperation to curb the illegal traffic in narcotics. Exchange of notes at Bogota July 21 and August 6, 1980; entered into force August 6, 1980.
32 UST 2301; TIAS 9838; 1274 UNTS 255.

Memorandum of understanding concerning cooperation in the seizure and forfeiture of property and proceeds of illicit trafficking in narcotic drugs. Signed at Bogota July 24, 1990; entered into force July 24, 1990.
TIAS 12417.

Mutual cooperation agreement to combat, prevent and control money laundering arising from illicit activities. Signed at San Antonio February 27, 1992; entered into force February 27, 1992.
TIAS 12450.

Agreement to suppress illicit traffic by sea. Signed at Bogota February 20, 1997; entered into force February 20, 1997.
TIAS

Supplemental memorandum through which mechanisms are established for implementing the July 24, 1990 memorandum of understanding concerning the transfer of forfeited assets. Signed at Washington October 28, 1998; entered into force October 28, 1998.
TIAS

PEACE CORPS

Agreement for using volunteers to carry out social and economic development projects in Colombia. Signed at Bogota April 2, 1963; entered into force July 12, 1963.
26 UST 1764; TIAS 8134; 1006 UNTS 7.

POSTAL MATTERS

Agreement relating to the exchange of money orders. Exchange of letters at Bogota and Washington July 27, August 15 and 24, September 7, November 26 and December 7 and 20, 1935, and January 11, 1936; operative January 1, 1936.
169 LNTS 79.

Parcel post agreement. Signed at Bogota January 31 and at Washington February 7, 1939; operative April 1, 1939.
53 Stat. 2136; Post Office Department print; 196 LNTS 53.

International express mail agreement, with detailed regulations. Signed at Washington and Bogota June 13 and July 7, 1983; entered into force September 3, 1983.
TIAS 10738.

PUBLICATIONS

Agreement relating to the exchange of official publications. Exchange of notes at Washington July 15 and 26, 1949; entered into force July 26, 1949.
63 Stat. 2799; TIAS 2048; 6 Bevans 998; 73 UNTS 105.

SCIENTIFIC COOPERATION

Memorandum of understanding for scientific and technical cooperation in the earth sciences. Signed at Bogota June 22, 1984; entered into force June 22, 1984.
TIAS 11206.

TAXATION

Agreement for relief from double taxation on earnings from operations of ships and aircraft. Exchange of notes at Washington August 1, 1961; entered into force December 11, 1961.
12 UST 3141; TIAS 4916; 433 UNTS 123.

Amendment:
October 16, 1987 (TIAS 11563).

TELECOMMUNICATION

Agreement relating to radio communications between amateur stations on behalf of third parties. Exchange of notes at Bogota November 16 and 29, 1963; entered into force December 29, 1963.
14 UST 1754; TIAS 5483; 494 UNTS 49.

Agreement relating to the reciprocal granting of authorizations to permit licensed amateur radio operators of either country to operate their stations in the other country. Exchange of notes at Bogota October 19 and 28, 1965; entered into force November 28, 1965.
16 UST 1742; TIAS 5899; 574 UNTS 109.

TERRITORIAL STATUS (See also FISHERIES)

Treaty concerning the status of Quita Sueño, Roncador and Serrana, with exchange of notes. Signed at Bogota September 8, 1972; entered into force September 17, 1981.[1]
33 UST 1405; TIAS 10120; 1307 UNTS 379.

NOTE:
[1] With understanding.

TRADE (See also COMMERCE)

Memorandum of understanding setting forth mutual trade concessions and contributions to the multilateral trade negotiations, and related letters of January 28 and June 30, 1980.

Signed at Bogota April 23, 1979; entered into force October 3, 1981.
33 UST 4459; TIAS 10316.

Agreement relating to trade in cotton textiles. Signed at Washington April 3, 1992; entered into force April 3, 1992; effective January 1, 1992.
NP

VISAS

Agreement relating to the extension of the validity of nonimmigrant visas. Exchange of notes at Bogota June 13 and 26, 1956 and May 22, 1957; entered into force June 21, 1957.
10 UST 1250; TIAS 4263; 354 UNTS 21.

Amendment:
June 5 and 11, 1957 (10 UST 1250; TIAS 4263; 354 UNTS 29).

WEATHER STATIONS

Agreement relating to the re-establishment, operation, and maintenance of the rawinsonde observation stations at Bogota and on San Andres Island, with memorandum of arrangement. Exchange of letters at Bogota April 28 and September 8, 1981; entered into force September 8, 1981.
TIAS 12377.

COMMISSION OF THE CARTAGENA AGREEMENT (ANDEAN GROUP) [1]

NOTE:
[1] Representatives of Bolivia, Colombia, Ecuador, Peru, and Venezuela signed for the Commission.

ECONOMIC AND TECHNICAL COOPERATION

Memorandum of understanding concerning trade, financing, science and technology, development of industry, agriculture and infrastructure. Signed at Washington November 21, 1979; entered into force November 21, 1979.
32 UST 4399; TIAS 9953; 1266 UNTS 293.

SCIENTIFIC COOPERATION

Memorandum of understanding on science and technology cooperation. Signed at Washington November 21, 1979; entered into force November 21, 1979.
32 UST 4327; TIAS 9949; 1266 UNTS 285.

COMMISSION OF THE CARTAGENA AGREEMENT (ANDEAN GROUP) (Cont'd)

TRADE

Agreement within the context of the multilateral trade negotiations and related note of April 14, 1980. Signed at Lima December 14, 1979; entered into force January 1, 1980.
32 UST 5283; TIAS 9979; 1266 UNTS 301.

COMOROS

DEFENSE

Agreement concerning the provision of training related to defense articles under the United States International Military Education and Training (IMET) Program. Exchange of notes at Moroni August 5, 1986 and September 22, 1987; entered into force September 22, 1987.
TIAS 11403.

PEACE CORPS

Agreement relating to the establishment of a Peace Corps program in the Comoros. Exchange of notes at Moroni December 22, 1987; entered into force December 22, 1987.
TIAS 12070.

TELECOMMUNICATION

Agreement relating to radio communications between amateur stations on behalf of third parties. Exchange of notes at Moroni March 8 and September 8, 1989; entered into force October 8, 1989.
TIAS 11699.

CONGO

AGRICULTURAL COMMODITIES

Agricultural commodities agreement. Signed at Brazzaville August 16, 1982; entered into force August 16, 1982.
TIAS 11055.

Agricultural commodities agreement. Signed at Washington February 14, 1990; entered into force February 14, 1990.
NP

AVIATION

Air transport services agreement between the United States and France. Signed at Paris March 27, 1946; entered into force March 27, 1946.
61 Stat. 3445; TIAS 1679; 7 Bevans 1109; 139 UNTS 114.

Extensions and amendments:
June 23 and July 11, 1950 (1 UST 593; TIAS 2106; 139 UNTS 142).
March 19, 1951 (2 UST 1033; TIAS 2257; 139 UNTS 151).
March 19, 1951 (2 UST 1037; TIAS 2258; 139 UNTS 146).
August 27, 1959 (10 UST 1791; TIAS 4336; 358 UNTS 277).

COPYRIGHT (See APPENDIX)

EMPLOYMENT

Agreement relating to the employment of dependents of official government employees. Exchange of notes at Washington April 11 and May 23, 1997; entered into force May 23, 1997.
TIAS

EXTRADITION

Extradition convention between the United States and France. Signed at Paris January 6, 1909; entered into force July 27, 1911.
37 Stat. 1526; TS 561; 7 Bevans 872.

Supplementary extradition convention between the United States and France. Signed at Paris January 15, 1929; entered into force May 19, 1929.
46 Stat. 2276; TS 787; 7 Bevans 972; 92 LNTS 259.

Supplementary extradition convention between the United States and France. Signed at Paris April 23, 1936; entered into force September 24, 1936.
50 Stat. 1117; TS 909; 7 Bevans 995; 172 LNTS 197.

FINANCE

Agreement relating to investment guaranties. Exchange of notes at Brazzaville July 26 and September 1, 1962; entered into force September 1, 1962.
13 UST 2185; TIAS 5183; 459 UNTS 117.

Agreement regarding the consolidation and rescheduling of certain debts owed to, guaranteed by or insured by the United States Government and its agencies, with annexes. Signed at Brazzaville June 26, 1987; entered into force August 7, 1987.
NP

Agreement regarding the consolidation and rescheduling or refinancing of certain debts owed to, guaranteed by, or insured by the United States Government and its agency, with annexes. Signed at Brazzaville May 6, 1994; entered into force June 30, 1994.
NP

Agreement regarding the consolidation and rescheduling or refinancing of certain debts owed to, guaranteed by or insured by the United States Government and its agency, with annexes. Signed at Brazzaville November 21, 1994; entered into force January 19, 1995.
NP

INVESTMENT

Treaty concerning the reciprocal encouragement and protection of investment, with annex. Signed at Washington February 12, 1990; entered into force August 13, 1994.
TIAS

PEACE CORPS

Agreement concerning the establishment of a Peace Corps program in the Congo. Exchange of notes at Brazzaville April 21, 1990; entered into force April 21, 1990.
TIAS

POSTAL MATTERS

International express mail agreement, with detailed regulations. Signed at Brazzaville and Washington July 15 and August 12, 1988; entered into force September 15, 1988.
TIAS 11659.

Memorandum of understanding concerning the operation of the INTELPOST service, with details of implementation. Signed at Brazzaville and Washington March 20, 1990 and May 13, 1991; entered into force May 28, 1991.
TIAS 11835.

TREATY OBLIGATIONS

Treaty obligations assumed by the Congo upon its independence. Exchange of notes at Brazzaville May 12 and August 5, 1961; entered into force August 5, 1961.
13 UST 2065; TIAS 5161; 603 UNTS 19.

VISAS

Reciprocal agreement between the United States and France relating to visa fees for non-

CONGO (Cont'd)

immigrants. Exchanges of notes at Washington August 19 and September 4, 5, and 16, 1947; entered into force September 16, 1947; operative October 1, 1947.
61 Stat. 3776; TIAS 1721; 7 Bevans 1210; 84 UNTS 19.

CONGO, DEMOCRATIC REPUBLIC OF THE

AGRICULTURAL COMMODITIES

Agricultural commodities agreement, with exchange of letters. Signed at Leopoldville November 18, 1961; entered into force November 18, 1961.
12 UST 3202; TIAS 4925; 433 UNTS 207.

Amendments:
May 4 and 11, 1962 (13 UST 1241; TIAS 5069; 456 UNTS 514).
May 23 and June 8, 1962 (13 UST 2019; TIAS 5159; 460 UNTS 330).
July 27, 1962 (13 UST 2079; TIAS 5164; 462 UNTS 366).
August 31, 1962 (13 UST 2181; TIAS 5182; 460 UNTS 333).
November 2, 1962 (13 UST 2559; TIAS 5221; 460 UNTS 337).
August 28 and September 4, 1964 (15 UST 1803; TIAS 5653; 531 UNTS 378).

Agricultural commodities agreement, with exchange of notes and aide-memoire. Signed at Leopoldville February 23, 1963; entered into force February 23, 1963.
14 UST 1562; TIAS 5460; 493 UNTS 3.

Amendment:
August 28 and September 4, 1964 (15 UST 1803; TIAS 5653; 531 UNTS 378).

Agricultural commodities agreement, with exchange of notes and aide-memoire. Signed at Leopoldville February 23, 1963; entered into force February 23, 1963.
14 UST 1573; TIAS 5461; 493 UNTS 17.

Amendments:
December 18 and 19, 1963 (14 UST 1758; TIAS 5484; 505 UNTS 339).
August 28 and September 4, 1964 (15 UST 1803; TIAS 5653; 531 UNTS 378).
December 9, 1964 (15 UST 2235; TIAS 5711; 531 UNTS 413).

Agricultural commodities agreement with exchange of notes. Signed at Leopoldville April 28, 1964; entered into force April 28, 1964.
15 UST 358; TIAS 5565; 526 UNTS 55.

Amendments:
August 25, 1964 (15 UST 1884; TIAS 5662; 531 UNTS 426).
December 9, 1964 (15 UST 2235; TIAS 5711; 531 UNTS 413).

April 29, 1965 (16 UST 667; TIAS 5794; 546 UNTS 393).
September 21 and 28, 1965 (16 UST 1268; TIAS 5878; 579 UNTS 282).

Agricultural commodities agreement with exchange of notes. Signed at Leopoldville December 9, 1964; entered into force December 9, 1964.
15 UST 2214; TIAS 5708; 531 UNTS 249.

Agricultural commodities agreement, with exchange of notes. Signed at Leopoldville July 19, 1965; entered into force July 19, 1965.
16 UST 2001; TIAS 5935; 593 UNTS 215.

Amendment:
April 22 and 25, 1966 (17 UST 835; TIAS 6042; 593 UNTS 233).

Agricultural commodities agreement with exchange of notes. Signed at Kinshasa October 3, 1966; entered into force October 3, 1966.
17 UST 2258; TIAS 6166; 680 UNTS 241.

Agricultural commodities agreement with annex. Signed at Kinshasa and Lubumbashi March 15, 1967; entered into force March 15, 1967.
18 UST 1826; TIAS 6329; 692 UNTS 120.

Amendments:
April 6, 1967 (18 UST 1826; TIAS 6329; 692 UNTS 144).
June 16 and 26, 1967 (18 UST 1826; TIAS 6329; 692 UNTS 148).
December 15 and 21, 1967 (18 UST 3138; TIAS 6404; 692 UNTS 151).

Related agreements:
December 11, 1967 (18 UST 3065; TIAS 6396; 701 UNTS 183).
August 12, 1968 (19 UST 5911; TIAS 6545; 707 UNTS 137).
May 14, 1969 (20 UST 762; TIAS 6687; 715 UNTS 23).
October 21, 1969 (20 UST 2401; TIAS 6712; 726 UNTS 223).
March 24 and July 7, 1970 (21 UST 1577; TIAS 6921).
October 7, 1971 (22 UST 1784; TIAS 7219).

Agricultural commodities agreement. Signed at Kinshasa March 25, 1976; entered into force March 25, 1976.
27 UST 3841; TIAS 8403; 1059 UNTS 35.

Amendments:
April 28, 1976 (27 UST 3863; TIAS 8403; 1059 UNTS 55).
August 23 and December 7, 1976 (28 UST 1269; TIAS 8507).

Related agreements:
May 24, 1977 (29 UST 287; TIAS 8813).
August 15 and 19, 1977 (29 UST 292; TIAS 8813).
September 19 and 20, 1977 (29 UST 294; TIAS 8813).
July 7, 1978 (30 UST 1535; TIAS 9262; 1148 UNTS 445).
August 25, 1978 (30 UST 1521; TIAS 9261; 1150 UNTS 194).
December 27, 1978 and January 3, 1979 (30 UST 1532; TIAS 9261; 1150 UNTS 209).

July 27, 1979 (NP).
August 29 and 30, 1979 (NP).

Agricultural commodities agreement, with memorandum of understanding. Signed at Kinshasa May 30, 1980; entered into force May 30, 1980.
NP

Amendment:
October 10 and 31, 1980 (NP).

Related agreements:
May 7, 1981 (NP).
April 3, 1982 (NP).
June 21 and July 7, 1982 (NP).
November 27, 1982 (NP).
December 10, 1983 (NP).
August 20 and 28, 1984 (NP).
December 22, 1984 (NP).
July 1 and 3, 1985 (NP).
August 6 and 19, 1985 (NP).

Agricultural commodities agreement. Signed at Kinshasa November 27, 1985; entered into force November 27, 1985.
NP

Amendment:
January 22, 1987 (NP).
July 2, 1987 (NP).

Agricultural commodities agreement. Signed at Kinshasa February 24, 1988; entered into force February 24, 1988.
NP

Amendments:
August 13, 1988 (NP).
October 4 and 5, 1988 (NP).

Related agreements:
May 2, 1989 (NP).
July 29, 1989 (NP).
November 2 and 21, 1989 (NP).

Agricultural commodities agreement. Signed at Kinshasa February 7, 1990; entered into force February 7, 1990.
NP

Amendment:
August 3 and 15, 1990 (NP).

AVIATION

Air transport agreement. Signed at New York August 14, 1970; entered into force August 14, 1970.
21 UST 1932; TIAS 6935; 763 UNTS 71.

COPYRIGHT (See APPENDIX)

DEFENSE

Agreement relating to military assistance and provision for a military mission to Congo (Leopoldville). Exchange of notes at Leopold-

CONGO, DEMOCRATIC REPUBLIC OF THE (Cont'd)

ville June 24 and July 19, 1963; entered into force July 19, 1963.
15 UST 142; TIAS 5530; 511 UNTS 47.

Agreement relating to the deposit by Zaire of ten percent of the value of grant military assistance and excess defense articles furnished by the United States. Exchange of notes at Kinshasa April 18 and May 16, 1972; entered into force May 16, 1972; effective February 7, 1972.
23 UST 1442; TIAS 7422.

Agreement concerning the provision of training related to defense articles under the United States International Military Education and Training (IMET) Program. Exchange of notes at Kinshasa December 22, 1983 and June 16, 1984; entered into force June 16, 1984.
TIAS 10985.

Agreement regarding the status of U.S. military personnel and civilian employees of the Department of Defense who may be present in Zaire in connection with humanitarian efforts. Exchange of notes at Kinshasa July 21 and 22, 1994; entered into force July 22, 1994.
NP

ECONOMIC AND TECHNICAL COOPERATION

Economic cooperation agreement between the United States and Belgium.[1] Signed at Brussels July 2, 1948; entered into force July 29, 1948.
62 Stat. 2173; TIAS 1781; 5 Bevans 678; 19 UNTS 127.

Agency for International Development:
June 29, 1976 (28 UST 4501; TIAS 8604).

NOTE:
[1] Only article III is applicable to Congo (Leopoldville).

ENERGY

Agreement for technical assistance for the maintenance of the extra high voltage DC intertie Inga-Shaba project. Signed at Kinshasa April 14, 1984; entered into force April 14, 1984.
TIAS 11518.

Amendment and extension:
July 3, 1986 (TIAS 11518).

FINANCE

Agreement relating to investment guaranties with related notes. Exchange of notes at Leopoldville October 25 and November 17, 1962; entered into force November 17, 1962.
14 UST 285; TIAS 5308; 474 UNTS 41.

Agreement regarding the consolidation and rescheduling of certain debts owed to, guaranteed or insured by the United States government and its agencies. Signed at Washington June 17, 1977; entered into force August 30, 1977.
28 UST 7593; TIAS 8731.

Agreement regarding the consolidation and rescheduling of payments due under PL 480 Title I agricultural commodity agreements, with annexes. Signed at Washington July 19, 1978; entered into force July 19, 1978.
30 UST 3511; TIAS 9405; 1179 UNTS 37.

Agreement regarding the consolidation and rescheduling of certain debts owed to, guaranteed or insured by the United States Government and its agencies, with annexes. Signed at Washington February 7, 1979; entered into force April 4, 1979.
30 UST 3601; TIAS 9416; 1171 UNTS 135.

Agreement regarding the consolidation and rescheduling of payments due under PL 480 Title I agricultural commodities agreements, with annexes. Signed at Washington August 1, 1979; entered into force August 1, 1979.
30 UST 6279; TIAS 9553; 1179 UNTS 49.

Agreement regarding the consolidation and rescheduling of certain debts owed to, guaranteed or insured by the United States Government and its agencies, with annexes. Signed at Kinshasa July 28, 1980; entered into force October 20, 1980.
32 UST 3631; TIAS 9907.

Agreement regarding the consolidation and rescheduling of payments due under PL 480 Title I agricultural commodity agreements, with annexes. Signed at Kinshasa March 10, 1981; entered into force March 10, 1981.
33 UST 1249; TIAS 10108; 1285 UNTS 3.

Implementation agreement regarding the consolidation and rescheduling of repayments due under Agency for International Development loans. Signed at Kinshasa April 8, 1981; entered into force April 8, 1981.
33 UST 1725; TIAS 10141.

Agreement regarding the consolidation and rescheduling of certain debts owed to, guaranteed or insured by the United States Government and its agencies, with annexes. Signed at Kinshasa July 23, 1982; entered into force August 30, 1982.
NP

Agreement regarding the consolidation and rescheduling of certain debts owed to, guaranteed or insured by the United States Government and its agencies. Signed at

Kinshasa May 3, 1984; entered into force June 11, 1984.
NP

Agreement regarding the consolidation and rescheduling of certain debts owed to, guaranteed by or insured by the United States Government and its agencies, with annexes. Signed at Kinshasa December 3, 1985; entered into force January 9, 1986.
NP

Agreement regarding the consolidation and rescheduling of certain debts owed to, guaranteed by or insured by the United States Government and its agencies, with annexes. Signed at Kinshasa April 9, 1987; entered into force May 18, 1987.
NP

Agreement regarding the consolidation and rescheduling of certain debts owed to, guaranteed by or insured by the United States Government and its agencies, with annexes. Signed at Kinshasa February 20, 1988; entered into force April 18, 1988.
NP

Agreement regarding the consolidation and rescheduling of certain debts owed to, guaranteed by, or insured by the United States Government and its agencies, with annexes. Signed at Kinshasa December 23, 1989; entered into force February 5, 1990.
NP

INVESTMENT

Treaty concerning the reciprocal encouragement and protection of investment, with protocol. Signed at Washington August 3, 1984; entered into force July 28, 1989.
TIAS

PEACE CORPS

Agreement relating to the establishment of a Peace Corps program in the Democratic Republic of the Congo. Exchange of notes at Kinshasa May 8 and October 12, 1970; entered into force October 12, 1970.
23 UST 268; TIAS 7304.

POSTAL MATTERS

International express mail agreement, with detailed regulations. Signed at Kinshasa and Washington June 29 and July 20, 1990; entered into force August 30, 1990.
TIAS 11736.

COOK ISLANDS

BOUNDARIES

Treaty on friendship and delimitation of the maritime boundary between the United States and the Cook Islands. Signed at Rarotonga June 11, 1980; entered into force September 8, 1983.
TIAS 10774; 1676 UNTS 223.

FINANCE

Investment incentive agreement. Exchange of notes at Wellington and Rarotonga September 2 and October 10, 1983; entered into force April 16, 1984.
TIAS 10843; 1676 UNTS 235.

PEACE CORPS

Agreement relating to the establishment of a Peace Corps program in the Cook Islands. Exchange of notes at Wellington and Rarotonga April 28, 1981; entered into force April 28, 1981.
33 UST 1080; TIAS 10093; 1285 UNTS 113.

COSTA RICA

AGRICULTURAL COMMODITIES

Agricultural commodities agreement, with memorandum of understanding. Signed at San Jose March 25, 1982; entered into force April 28, 1982.
TIAS 11035.

Related agreements:
October 30, 1982 (TIAS 11035).
April 26, 1983 (TIAS 11035).

Agricultural commodities agreement, with memorandum of understanding. Signed at San Jose November 22, 1983; entered into force January 19, 1984.
TIAS 11036.

Amendment:
July 3 and 27, 1984 (TIAS 11036).

Agricultural commodities agreement. Signed at San Jose November 19, 1984; entered into force January 2, 1985.
TIAS 11037.

Agricultural commodities agreement. Signed at San Jose November 29, 1985; entered into force January 2, 1986.
NP

Agricultural commodities agreement. Signed at San Jose January 14, 1987; entered into force April 29, 1987.
NP

Amendment:
July 2 and 7, 1987 (NP).

Agricultural commodities agreement. Signed at San Jose March 3, 1988; entered into force September 20, 1988.
NP

Amendment:
October 17, 1988 (NP).

AGRICULTURE

Agreement relating to cooperative rubber investigations in Costa Rica. Exchange of notes at San Jose April 19 and June 16, 1941; entered into force June 16, 1941.
55 Stat. 1368; EAS 222; 6 Bevans 1056; 103 LNTS 173.

Extensions and amendments:
April 3, 1943 (57 Stat. 944; EAS 318; 6 Bevans 1074; 13 UNTS 463).
June 21 and July 1, 1943 (57 Stat. 1048; EAS 335).

Agreement confirming the cooperative agreement for the prevention of foot-and-mouth disease and rinderpest in Costa Rica. Exchange of notes at San Jose April 5 and June 6, 1972; entered into force June 6, 1972.
23 UST 1122; TIAS 7372.

AVIATION

Agreement relating to the free movement of the military aircraft of each country into and through the airspace of the other. Exchange of notes at San Jose February 19 and 25, 1952; entered into force February 25, 1952.
3 UST 3882; TIAS 2518; 174 UNTS 233.

Agreement concerning air transport. Exchange of notes at San Jose October 20 and November 23, 1983; entered into force November 23, 1983.
TIAS 10894.

Air transport agreement, with annexes. Signed at San Jose May 8, 1997; entered into force October 15, 1999.
TIAS

COMMERCE

Treaty of friendship, commerce and navigation. Signed at Washington July 10, 1851; entered into force May 26, 1852.
10 Stat. 916; TS 62; 6 Bevans 1013.

CONSULS (See also COMMERCE)

Consular convention.[1] Signed at San Jose January 12, 1948; entered into force March 19, 1950.
1 UST 247; TIAS 2045; 70 UNTS 27.

NOTE:
[1] Applicable to all areas of land and water subject to the sovereignty or authority of either state.

COPYRIGHT (See APPENDIX)

CULTURAL HERITAGE

Memorandum of understanding on cooperation in management and protection of national parks and other protected natural and cultural heritage sites. Signed at Vail, Colorado October 8, 1991; entered into force October 8, 1991.
TIAS 11793.

DEFENSE

Agreement relating to the furnishing of defense articles and services to Costa Rica for the purpose of contributing to its internal security. Exchange of notes at San Jose May 21 and June 18, 1962; entered into force June 18, 1962.
13 UST 2094; TIAS 5167; 461 UNTS 155.

Agreement relating to privileges and immunities for United States personnel providing assistance to the drought stricken provinces in northern Costa Rica. Exchange of notes at San Jose March 30, 1983; entered into force March 30, 1983.
NP

Memorandum of understanding establishing a Caribbean Basin Radar Network (CBRN) in Costa Rica. Signed at San Jose August 17, 1990; entered into force August 17, 1990.
TIAS 12283.

Agreement concerning a Medical Readiness Training Exercise (MD 50701), with annexes. Exchange of notes at San Jose December 21, 1994 and January 3, 1995; entered into force January 3, 1995.
NP

ECONOMIC AND TECHNICAL COOPERATION

General agreement for economic, technical and related assistance. Signed at San Jose December 22, 1961; entered into force September 7, 1962.
13 UST 1978; TIAS 5155; 460 UNTS 277.

COSTA RICA (Cont'd)

Agency for International Development:
April 26, 1976 (28 UST 8929; TIAS 8777).
August 30, 1978 (30 UST 4993; TIAS 9496;
  1179 UNTS 207).

EMPLOYMENT

Agreement relating to the employment of dependents of official government employees. Exchange of notes at San Jose June 8, 1992; entered into force June 8, 1992.
TIAS 12455.

ENVIRONMENTAL COOPERATION

Agreement for cooperation in the Global Learning and Observations to Benefit the Environment (GLOBE) Program, with appendices. Signed at San Jose April 22, 1996; entered into force April 22, 1996.
TIAS

EXTRADITION

Extradition treaty, with exchange of notes. Signed at San Jose December 4, 1982; entered into force October 11, 1991.
TIAS

FINANCE

Agreement relating to investment guaranties. Signed at San Jose November 22, 1968; entered into force October 24, 1969.
20 UST 3001; TIAS 6776; 726 UNTS 157.

Agreement regarding the consolidation and rescheduling of certain debts owed to, guaranteed or insured by the United States Government and its agencies, with annexes. Signed at Washington May 18, 1984; entered into force June 22, 1984.
NP

Agreement regarding the consolidation and rescheduling of certain debts owed to, guaranteed by or insured by the United States Government and its agencies, with annexes. Signed at San Jose December 16, 1985; entered into force January 29, 1986.
NP

Agreement regarding the consolidation and rescheduling of certain debts owed to, guaranteed by or insured by the United States Government and its agencies. Signed at San Jose February 22, 1990; entered into force April 9, 1990.
NP

Swap agreement among the United States Treasury and the Central Bank of Costa Rica/ Government of Costa Rica. Signed at Washington and San Jose May 18, 1990; entered into force May 18, 1990.
TIAS

Agreement regarding the consolidation and rescheduling or refinancing of certain debts owed to, guaranteed by, or insured by the United States Government and its agencies, with annexes. Signed at San Jose February 19, 1992; entered into force April 20, 1992.
NP

Agreement regarding the consolidation and rescheduling or refinancing of certain debts owed to, guaranteed by or insured by the United States Government and its agencies, with annexes. Signed at San Jose November 22, 1993; entered into force August 10, 1994.
NP

HIGHWAYS

Agreement relating to the construction of the inter-American highway within the borders of Costa Rica. Exchange of notes at Washington January 16, 1942; entered into force January 16, 1942.
56 Stat. 1840; EAS 293; 6 Bevans 1068; 23 UNTS 285.

Amendment:
January 13 and 17, 1951 (2 UST 1844; TIAS 2319; 134 UNTS 215).

MAPPING

Agreement relating to photomapping project. Exchange of notes at San Jose August 6 and October 2, 1946; entered into force October 2, 1946.
NP

Amendment:
December 3 and 7, 1953 (NP).

Cooperative arrangement for the production of topographic maps of Costa Rica, with annexes. Signed at San Jose and Washington June 4 and 18, 1986; entered into force June 18, 1986.
TIAS 11373.

Basic exchange and cooperative agreement for topographic mapping, nautical and aeronautical charting and information, geodesy and geophysics, digital data and related mapping, charting and geodesy materials, with glossary. Signed at San Jose and Fairfax June 14 and July 2, 1996; entered into force July 2, 1996.
NP

NARCOTIC DRUGS

Agreement relating to the provision of assistance to curb the production and traffic in illegal narcotics. Exchange of notes at San Jose

May 29 and June 2, 1975; entered into force June 2, 1975.
26 UST 3868; TIAS 8220; 1045 UNTS 17.

Agreement relating to the provision of additional assistance to support cooperative efforts to curb illegal narcotics production and traffic. Exchange of notes at San Jose June 21 and 24, 1976; entered into force June 24, 1976.
28 UST 2924; TIAS 8574; 1068 UNTS 189.

Agreement concerning cooperation to suppress illicit traffic. Signed at San Jose December 1, 1998; entered into force November 19, 1999.
TIAS

Amendment:
July 2, 1999.

PEACE CORPS

Agreement relating to the establishment of a Peace Corps program in Costa Rica. Exchange of notes at San Jose November 21 and 23, 1962; entered into force August 11, 1964.
15 UST 2317; TIAS 5719; 541 UNTS 67.

POLLUTION

Agreement concerning the transboundary movement of hazardous wastes from Costa Rica to the United States. Exchange of notes at San Jose September 30 and November 17, 1997; entered into force November 17, 1997.
TIAS

POSTAL MATTERS

Money order convention. Signed at Washington June 6 and at San Jose June 26, 1903; entered into force July 20, 1903.
33 Stat. 2175.

International express mail agreement, with detailed regulations. Signed at San Jose and Washington August 19 and September 14, 1989; entered into force September 15, 1989.
TIAS 11690.

Postal money order agreement. Signed at Mexico August 16, 1991; entered into force October 1, 1991.
TIAS 11799.

PUBLICATIONS

Agreement relating to the exchange of official publications. Exchange of notes at San Jose November 30 and December 2, 1950; entered into force December 2, 1950.
2 UST 405; TIAS 2180; 133 UNTS 61.

COSTA RICA (Cont'd)

TAXATION

Agreement for the exchange of information with respect to taxes, with exchange of notes. Signed at San Jose March 15, 1989; entered into force February 12, 1991.
TIAS 12059.

TELECOMMUNICATION

Agreement relating to radio communications between amateur stations on behalf of third parties. Exchange of notes at Washington August 13 and October 19, 1956; entered into force October 19, 1956.
7 UST 2839; TIAS 3665; 278 UNTS 65.

Agreement relating to the reciprocal granting of authorizations to permit licensed amateur radio operators of either country to operate their stations in the other country. Exchange of notes at San Jose August 17 and 24, 1964; entered into force August 24, 1964.
15 UST 1787; TIAS 5649; 531 UNTS 107.

Agreement concerning the establishment and operation of a Voice of America radio broadcast station in Costa Rica. Exchange of notes at San Jose July 17 and August 7, 1984; entered into force August 7, 1984.
TIAS 11236.

TRADE (See also COMMERCE)

Convention concerning commercial travelers and protocol. Signed at San Jose March 31, 1924; entered into force June 24, 1924.
43 Stat. 1765; TS 688; 6 Bevans 1041.

Agreement on a consultative mechanism relating to trade in cotton, wool, and man-made fiber textiles and textile products, with annex. Exchange of notes at San Jose February 7, 1984; entered into force February 7, 1984; effective January 1, 1984.
TIAS 10956.

Agreement relating to trade in cotton, wool and man-made fiber textiles and textile products, with annexes. Signed at Washington March 20, 1992; entered into force March 20, 1992; effective January 1, 1992.
NP

Amendment and extension:
May 5 and October 20, 1994 (NP).

VISAS

Agreement for the waiver of passport visa fees for nonimmigrants. Exchange of notes at San Jose June 29, 1925; operative July 25, 1925.
6 Bevans 1046.

WEATHER STATIONS

Agreement relating to the operation and maintenance of a rawinsonde observation station at San Jose, with memorandum of arrangement. Exchange of notes at San Jose April 29 and June 8, 1976; entered into force June 8, 1976; effective January 1, 1976.
28 UST 6075; TIAS 8669.

COTE D'IVOIRE

AGRICULTURAL COMMODITIES

Agricultural commodities agreement with exchange of notes. Signed at Abidjan March 10, 1964; entered into force March 10, 1964.
15 UST 273; TIAS 5552; 526 UNTS 285.

Agricultural commodities agreement, with exchange of notes. Signed at Abidjan April 5, 1965; entered into force April 5, 1965.
16 UST 624; TIAS 5784; 546 UNTS 143.

Amendment:
June 1, 1966 (17 UST 768; TIAS 6030; 580 UNTS 318).

Agricultural commodities agreement. Signed at Abidjan June 21, 1989; entered into force June 21, 1989.
NP

Agricultural commodities agreement. Signed at Abidjan May 16, 1990; entered into force May 16, 1990.
NP

AVIATION

Air transport agreement, with memorandum of understanding and exchange of notes. Signed at Abidjan February 24, 1978; entered into force provisionally February 24, 1978; definitively June 3, 1980.
32 UST 1165; TIAS 9766; 1220 UNTS 243.

COPYRIGHT (See APPENDIX)

DEFENSE

Agreement concerning the provision of training related to defense articles under the United States International Military Education and Training (IMET) Program. Exchange of notes at Abidjan March 21 and April 21, 1983; entered into force April 21, 1983.
TIAS 10700.

ECONOMIC AND TECHNICAL COOPERATION

Agreement providing for economic, technical and related assistance. Exchange of notes at Abidjan May 17, 1961; entered into force May 17, 1961.
12 UST 652; TIAS 4765; 409 UNTS 241.

FINANCE

Agreement relating to investment guaranties. Exchange of notes at Abidjan December 1, 1961; entered into force December 1, 1961.
13 UST 2711; TIAS 5242; 462 UNTS 221.

Agreement regarding the consolidation and rescheduling of certain debts owed to, guaranteed by or insured by the United States Government and its agencies, with annexes. Signed at Abidjan February 27, 1985; entered into force April 10, 1985.
NP

Agreement regarding the consolidation and rescheduling of certain debts owed to, guaranteed by or insured by the United States Government and its agencies, with annexes. Signed at Abidjan January 31, 1986; entered into force March 10, 1986.
NP

Agreement regarding the consolidation and rescheduling of certain debts owed to, guaranteed by or insured by the United States Government and its agencies, with annexes. Signed at Abidjan March 31, 1987; entered into force May 21, 1987.
NP

Agreement regarding the consolidation and rescheduling of certain debts owed to, guaranteed by or insured by the United States Government and its agencies, with annexes. Signed at Abidjan July 14, 1988; entered into force August 26, 1988.
NP

Agreement regarding the consolidation and rescheduling of certain debts owed to, guaranteed by or insured by the United States Government and its agencies, with annexes. Signed at Abidjan September 29, 1990; entered into force November 16, 1990.
NP

Agreement regarding the consolidation and rescheduling or refinancing of certain debts owed to, guaranteed by, or insured by the United States Government and its agencies, with annexes. Signed at Abidjan May 29, 1992; entered into force July 20, 1992.
NP

Agreement regarding the consolidation and rescheduling or refinancing of certain debts owed to, guaranteed by or insured by the United States Government and its agencies, with annexes. Signed at Abidjan August 26, 1994; entered into force October 7, 1994.
NP

COTE D'IVOIRE (Cont'd)

Agreement regarding the consolidation, reduction and rescheduling of certain debts owed to, guaranteed by, or insured by the United States Government and its Agencies, with annexes. Signed at Washington July 29, 1998; entered into force September 10, 1998.
NP

HEALTH

Agreement concerning a cooperative project to study AIDS in Cote d'Ivoire. Signed at Abidjan March 13, 1990; entered into force March 13, 1990.
TIAS 12705.

Extension:
August 23, October 24 and December 2, 1995 (TIAS 12705).

PEACE CORPS

Agreement relating to the establishment of a Peace Corps program in Ivory Coast. Exchange of notes at Abidjan April 5 and 21, 1962; entered into force April 21, 1962.
15 UST 345; TIAS 5561; 526 UNTS 39.

POSTAL MATTERS

International express mail agreement, with detailed regulations. Signed at Abidjan and Washington May 5 and 27, 1987; entered into force June 15, 1987.
NP

Postal money order agreement. Signed at Abidjan and Washington January 5 and 25, 1994; entered into force March 1, 1994.
NP

CROATIA

For agreements prior to the independence of Croatia, see YUGOSLAVIA.

COPYRIGHT (See APPENDIX)

DEFENSE

Agreement regarding the status of military and civilian personnel of the United States Department of Defense who may be temporarily present in Croatia in connection with the joint U.S.-Croatian military exercise "Croatian Slunj MTA 00" and related activities. Ex-

change of notes at Zagreb November 6 and 9, 2000; entered into force November 9, 2000.
NP

Extension:
November 30 and December 2, 2000.

ECONOMIC AND TECHNICAL COOPERATION

Agreement concerning economic, technical and related assistance. Signed at Zagreb May 6, 1994; entered into force May 1, 1995.
TIAS

EMPLOYMENT

Agreement relating to the employment of dependents of official government employees. Exchange of notes at Washington May 24 and June 20, 1995; entered into force June 20, 1995.
TIAS 12669.

ENVIRONMENTAL COOPERATION

Agreement for cooperation in the Global Learning and Observations to Benefit the Environment (GLOBE) Program, with appendices. Signed at Zagreb April 12, 1995; entered into force April 12, 1995.
TIAS 12628.

FINANCE

Investment incentive agreement. Signed at Washington January 15, 1993; entered into force January 15, 1993.
TIAS 12141.

Agreement regarding the consolidation and rescheduling of certain debts owed to, guaranteed by or insured by the United States Government and its agencies, with annexes. Signed at Zagreb February 1, 1996; entered into force July 23, 1996.
NP

POSTAL MATTERS

International express mail agreement. Signed at Zagreb and Washington September 14 and 30, 1992; entered into force December 14, 1992.
TIAS 11908.

Postal money order agreement. Signed at Zagreb and Washington January 19 and February 10, 1994; entered into force April 1, 1994.
NP

SCIENTIFIC COOPERATION

Agreement for scientific and technological cooperation, with annexes. Signed at Washington March 18, 1994; entered into force May 18, 2000.
TIAS

CUBA

AVIATION

Agreement to facilitate notification of private flights between Cuba and the United States. Exchange of notes at Habana January 19 and February 26, 1953; entered into force February 26, 1953.
4 UST 210; TIAS 2779; 205 UNTS 213.

Air transport agreement. Signed at Habana May 26, 1953; entered into force June 30, 1953.
4 UST 2837; TIAS 2892; 224 UNTS 75.

Amendment:
May 21 and July 30, 1957 (8 UST 1407; TIAS 3891; 289 UNTS 322).

BOUNDARIES

Maritime boundary agreement. Signed at Washington December 16, 1977; entered into force provisionally January 1, 1978.
TIAS

CONSULS

Consular convention. Signed at Habana April 22, 1926; entered into force December 1, 1926.
44 Stat. 2471; TS 75; 6 Bevans 1149; 60 LNTS 371.

COPYRIGHT (See APPENDIX)

CUSTOMS

Agreement relating to free-entry privileges for noncommissioned personnel. Exchange of notes at Habana March 23 and May 16, 1932; entered into force May 16, 1932.
5 UST 1638; TIAS 3040; 234 UNTS 283.

DEFENSE

Agreement for the lease to the United States of lands in Cuba for coaling and naval stations. Signed at Habana February 16, 1903, and at Washington February 23, 1903; entered into force February 23, 1903.
TS 418; 6 Bevans 1113.

CUBA (Cont'd)

Agreement providing conditions for the lease of coaling or naval stations. Signed at Habana July 2, 1903; entered into force October 6, 1903.
TS 426; 6 Bevans 1120.

Agreement relating to the control of electromagnetic radiations in the event of attack. Exchange of notes at Habana December 10 and 18, 1951; entered into force December 18, 1951.
3 UST 2860; TIAS 2459; 165 UNTS 3.

Military assistance agreement. Signed at Habana March 7, 1952; entered into force March 7, 1952.
3 UST 2901; TIAS 2467; 165 UNTS 11.

Agreement providing for disposition of equipment and materials furnished by the United States under the agreement of March 7, 1952. Exchange of notes at Habana March 18 and May 3, 1955; entered into force May 3, 1955.
6 UST 2059; TIAS 3272; 258 UNTS 408.

Agreement providing for performance by members of Army, Navy, and Air Force missions of duties of military assistance advisory group specified in article V of the military assistance agreement of March 7, 1952. Exchange of notes at Habana June 24 and August 3, 1955; entered into force August 10, 1955.
6 UST 2955; TIAS 3343; 265 UNTS 41.

ECONOMIC AND TECHNICAL COOPERATION

General agreement for technical cooperation. Signed at Habana June 20, 1951; entered into force June 20, 1951.
2 UST 1231; TIAS 2272; 148 UNTS 3.

Amendment:
January 7 and 8, 1952 (3 UST 4704; TIAS 2629; 179 UNTS 254).

EXTRADITION

Treaty providing for the mutual extradition of fugitives from justice. Signed at Washington April 6, 1904; entered into force March 2, 1905.[1]
33 Stat. 2265; TS 440; 6 Bevans 1128.

Additional extradition treaty. Signed at Habana January 14, 1926; entered into force June 18, 1926.
44 Stat. 2392; TS 737; 6 Bevans 1136; 61 LNTS 363.

NOTE:
[1] For amendment to the Spanish text, see 33 Stat. 2273; TS 441; 6 Bevans 1134.

FINANCE

Agreement relating to investment guaranties under section 413 (b)(4) of the Mutual Security Act of 1954 as amended. Exchange of notes at Habana February 4, 1957; entered into force November 29, 1957.
8 UST 2375; TIAS 3953; 302 UNTS 273.

GENERAL RELATIONS

Treaty for the adjustment of title to the ownership of the Isle of Pines. Signed at Washington March 2, 1904; entered into force March 23, 1925.
44 Stat. 1997; TS 709; 6 Bevans 1124; 127 LNTS 143.

Treaty of relations. Signed at Washington May 29, 1934; entered into force June 9, 1934.
48 Stat. 1682; TS 866; 6 Bevans 1161.

INTERESTS SECTIONS

Agreement relating to the establishment of interests sections of the United States and Cuba in the Embassy of Switzerland in Havana and the Embassy of Czechoslovakia in Washington, respectively. Exchange of notes at New York May 30, 1977; entered into force May 30, 1977.
30 UST 2101; TIAS 9313.

Amendment:
February 15 and 25, 1991.

MARITIME MATTERS

Agreement providing for the informal visits of warships. Exchange of notes at Habana February 11 and 21, 1949; entered into force March 4, 1949.
5 UST 762; TIAS 2965; 231 UNTS 108.

Extension and amendments:
February 13 and 28 and March 3, 1950 (5 UST 762; TIAS 2965; 231 UNTS 113).
November 23, 1953 and January 20, 1954 (5 UST 778; TIAS 2965; 231 UNTS 127).

Arrangement relating to the reciprocal exemption of the pleasure yachts of the two countries from navigation dues and from usual requirements of entry and clearance. Exchange of notes at Washington December 12 and 17, 1951; entered into force December 17, 1951.
3 UST 52; TIAS 2391; 152 UNTS 87.

Agreement concerning financial arrangements for the furnishing of certain supplies and services to naval vessels of both countries. Signed at Habana January 10, 1956; entered into force April 9, 1956.
7 UST 63; TIAS 3479; 240 UNTS 101.

MIGRATION

Joint communique on immigration matters, with minute on implementation. Signed at New York December 14, 1984; entered into force December 14, 1984.
TIAS 11057.

Joint communique concerning normalizing migration procedures. Signed at New York September 9, 1994; entered into force September 9, 1994.
TIAS

Joint statement further normalizing migration procedures. Signed at Washington May 2, 1995; entered into force May 2, 1995.
TIAS

MISSIONS, MILITARY

Agreement providing for the services of a United States Air Force mission to Cuba. Signed at Washington December 22, 1950; entered into force December 22, 1950.
1 UST 887; TIAS 2166; 122 UNTS 97.

Extension:
May 3 and 17, 1955 (6 UST 2266; TIAS 3295; 264 UNTS 351).

Agreement providing for the services of a United States Army mission to Cuba. Signed at Washington August 28, 1951; entered into force August 28, 1951.
2 UST 1677; TIAS 2309; 134 UNTS 225.

Extension:
May 3 and 17, 1955 (6 UST 2263; TIAS 3294; 264 UNTS 355).

Agreement providing for the services of a United States Naval mission to Cuba. Signed at Washington August 28, 1951; entered into force August 28, 1951.
2 UST 1689; TIAS 2310; 140 UNTS 239.

Extension:
May 3 and 17, 1955 (6 UST 784; TIAS 3222; 253 UNTS 360).

NARCOTIC DRUGS (See also SMUGGLING)

Arrangement for the direct exchange of certain information regarding the traffic in narcotic drugs. Exchange of notes at Habana February 12 and March 7, 1930; entered into force March 7, 1930.
6 Bevans 1157.

POSTAL MATTERS

Postal money order convention. Signed at Washington June 29, 1908; operative July 1, 1908.
NP

CUBA (Cont'd)

Parcel post convention. Signed at Washington July 24, 1930; entered into force September 1, 1930.
46 Stat. 2844; Post Office Department print.

PUBLICATIONS

Agreement for the exchange of official publications. Exchange of notes at Habana May 4 and 12, 1938; entered into force May 12, 1938.
52 Stat. 1497; EAS 123; 6 Bevans 1173; 191 LNTS 19.

REFUGEES

Memorandum of understanding between the Embassy of Switzerland in Habana representing the interests of the United States in Cuba and the Foreign Ministry of the Government of Cuba concerning the movement to the United States of Cubans wishing to live in the United States, with related notes. Exchange of notes at Habana November 6, 1965; entered into force November 6, 1965.
17 UST 1045; TIAS 6063; 601 UNTS 81.

SMUGGLING (See also NARCOTIC DRUGS)

Convention between the United States of America and the Republic of Cuba for the suppression of smuggling operations between their respective territories. Signed at Habana March 11, 1926; entered into force June 28, 1926.
44 Stat. 2402; TS 739; 6 Bevans 1144; 61 LNTS 383.

TELECOMMUNICATION

Agreement relating to the exchange of third-party messages between radio amateurs. Exchange of notes at Habana September 17, 1951 and February 27, 1952; entered into force February 27, 1952.
3 UST 3892; TIAS 2520; 168 UNTS 3.

TRADE AND COMMERCE

Exclusive agreement supplementary to the general agreement on tariffs and trade, exchanges of notes and memoranda, and supplementary exchange of notes signed at Washington December 19 and 22, 1947. Signed at Geneva October 30, 1947; entered into force October 30, 1947; operative January 1, 1948.
61 Stat. 3699; TIAS 1703; 6 Bevans 1229; 119 UNTS 163.

CUSTOMS COOPERATION COUNCIL

TAXATION

Tax reimbursement agreement, with annex. Signed at Brussels January 26, 1990; entered into force January 26, 1990.
TIAS 11711.

CYPRUS

A treaty concerning the establishment of the Republic of Cyprus was signed August 16, 1960 by the Governments of the United Kingdom, Greece, Turkey and Cyprus (British Treaty Series No. 4 (1691)). Article 8 of the treaty provides that the Republic of Cyprus assumes, from August 16, 1960, all international obligations and responsibilities of the United Kingdom in so far as they may be held to have application to the Republic of Cyprus. Also, the international rights and benefits enjoyed by the Government of the United Kingdom by virtue of their application to the territory of the Republic of Cyprus are from August 16, 1960 enjoyed by the Government of the Republic of Cyprus.

AGRICULTURAL COMMODITIES

Memorandum of understanding regarding the grant, delivery and free distribution of 12,000 metric tons of wheat and 10,000 metric tons of barley. Signed at Nicosia December 8, 1960; entered into force December 8, 1960.
11 UST 2687; TIAS 4666; 405 UNTS 145.

Memorandum of understanding regarding the grant, sale and use of proceeds from the sale of 28,000 metric tons of wheat. Signed at Nicosia December 8, 1960; entered into force December 8, 1960.
11 UST 2693; TIAS 4667; 405 UNTS 158.

Memorandum of understanding regarding the grant, sale and use of proceeds from the sale of 40,000 metric tons of wheat. Signed at Nicosia January 15, 1962; entered into force January 15, 1962.
13 UST 113; TIAS 4945; 435 UNTS 15.

Memorandum of understanding regarding the grant to Cyprus of agricultural commodities for an expanded school lunch program. Signed at Nicosia March 2, 1962; entered into force March 2, 1962.
13 UST 291; TIAS 4975; 445 UNTS 189.

Agricultural commodities agreement with exchange of notes. Signed at Nicosia June 18, 1963; entered into force June 18, 1963.
14 UST 936; TIAS 5382; 479 UNTS 191.

AVIATION

Arrangement between the United States and the United Kingdom relating to pilot licenses to operate civil aircraft. Exchange of notes at Washington March 28 and April 5, 1935; entered into force May 5, 1935.
49 Stat. 3731; EAS 77; 12 Bevans 501; 162 LNTS 59.

Agreement between the United States and the United Kingdom relating to air services. Signed at Bermuda February 11, 1946; entered into force February 11, 1946.
60 Stat. 1499; TIAS 1507; 12 Bevans 726; 3 UNTS 253.

CONSULS

Consular convention between the United States and the United Kingdom. Signed at Washington June 6, 1951; entered into force September 7, 1952.
3 UST 3426; TIAS 2494; 165 UNTS 121.

COPYRIGHT (See APPENDIX)

CUSTOMS

Agreement regarding mutual assistance between customs services. Signed at Washington June 2, 1987; entered into force August 21, 1987.
TIAS 12113.

ECONOMIC AND TECHNICAL COOPERATION

Economic cooperation agreement between the United States and the United Kingdom. Signed at London July 6, 1948; applicable to Cyprus July 6, 1948.
62 Stat. 2596; TIAS 1795; 12 Bevans 874; 22 UNTS 263.

Amendments:
January 3, 1950 (1 UST 184; TIAS 2036; 86 UNTS 304).
May 25, 1951 (2 UST 1292; TIAS 2277; 99 UNTS 308).
February 25, 1953 (4 UST 1528; TIAS 2815; 172 UNTS 332).

General agreement for technical cooperation. Signed at Nicosia June 29, 1961; entered into force June 29, 1961.
12 UST 890; TIAS 4792; 411 UNTS 55.

CYPRUS (Cont'd)

EDUCATION

Agreement for financing certain educational exchange programs. Signed at Nicosia January 18, 1962; entered into force January 18, 1962.
13 UST 92; TIAS 4943; 435 UNTS 3.

Amendment:
August 12 and September 7, 1968 (19 UST 6292; TIAS 6579; 701 UNTS 376).

ENVIRONMENTAL COOPERATION

Agreement for cooperation in the Global Learning and Observations to Benefit the Environment (GLOBE) Program, with appendices. Signed at Nicosia November 24, 1998; entered into force November 24, 1998.
TIAS

EXTRADITION

Extradition treaty. Signed at Washington June 17, 1996; entered into force September 14, 1999.
TIAS

FINANCE

Agreement relating to investment guaranties. Exchange of notes at Nicosia May 29, 1963; entered into force May 29, 1963.
14 UST 843; TIAS 5364; 487 UNTS 283.

MUTUAL SECURITY

Agreement between the United States and the United Kingdom relating to the assurances required under the Mutual Security Act of 1951. Exchange of notes at London January 8, 1952; applicable to Cyprus January 8, 1952.
3 UST 4665; TIAS 2622; 126 UNTS 307.

PEACE CORPS

Agreement relating to the establishment of a Peace Corps program in Cyprus. Exchange of notes at Nicosia August 23, 1962; entered into force August 23, 1962.
13 UST 2089; TIAS 5166; 461 UNTS 147.

POSTAL MATTERS

Parcel post agreement with detailed regulations for execution. Signed at Nicosia May 7 and at Washington June 8, 1973; entered into force September 1, 1974.
25 UST 3015; TIAS 7962.

International express mail/datapost special express memorandum of understanding, with detailed regulations. Signed at Nicosia and Washington September 13 and October 18, 1985; entered into force November 1, 1985.
TIAS 11159.

Memorandum of understanding concerning the operation of the INTELPOST service, with details of implementation. Signed at Nicosia and Washington March 12 and April 3, 1987; entered into force May 6, 1987.
TIAS 11298.

PROPERTY

Convention between the United States and the United Kingdom relating to the tenure and disposition of real and personal property. Signed at Washington March 2, 1899; applicable to Cyprus February 9, 1901.
31 Stat. 1939; TS 146; 12 Bevans 246.

SHIPPING

Agreement relating to jurisdiction over vessels utilizing the Louisiana Offshore Oil Port. Exchange of notes at Nicosia August 3 and September 7, 1983; entered into force September 7, 1983.
TIAS 10782.

Agreement for scientific and technological cooperation, with annexes. Signed at Prague June 11, 1998; entered into force September 30, 1998.
TIAS

TAXATION

Convention for the avoidance of double taxation and the prevention of fiscal evasion with respect to taxes on income, with related notes. Signed at Nicosia March 19, 1984; entered into force December 31, 1985.
TIAS 10965.

Agreement concerning reciprocal exemption from income tax of income derived from the international operation of ships and aircraft. Exchange of notes at Nicosia June 21 and July 8, 1988; entered into force July 8, 1988.
TIAS 11595.

TELECOMMUNICATION

Agreement relating to the reciprocal granting of authorizations to permit licensed amateur radio operators of either country to operate their stations in the other country. Exchange of notes at Nicosia March 4 and 10, 1987; entered into force March 10, 1987.
TIAS 11521.

TRADE-MARKS

Declaration by the United States and the United Kingdom relating to reciprocal protection to trade-marks. Signed at London October 24, 1877; entered into force October 24, 1877.
20 Stat. 703; TS 138; 12 Bevans 198.

VISAS

Agreement relating to the reciprocal waiver of fingerprinting requirements for nonimmigrants. Exchange of notes at Nicosia July 11, 1962 and January 11, 1963; entered into force January 11, 1963.
14 UST 6; TIAS 5271; 471 UNTS 127.

CZECH REPUBLIC

For agreements prior to the independence of the Czech Republic, see CZECHOSLOVAKIA.

ATOMIC ENERGY

Arrangement for the exchange of technical information and cooperation in nuclear safety matters, with addenda. Signed at Rockville November 10, 1994; entered into force November 10, 1994.
TIAS 12579.

Arrangement for the exchange of technical information and cooperation in nuclear safety matters, with addenda. Signed at Vienna September 20, 2000; entered into force September 20, 2000.
TIAS

AVIATION

Air transport agreement, with annexes. Signed at Prague September 10, 1996; entered into force September 10, 1996.
TIAS

COPYRIGHT (See APPENDIX)

DEFENSE

Security agreement concerning security measures for the protection of classified military information. Signed at Prague September 19, 1995; entered into force September 19, 1995.
TIAS 12245.

CZECH REPUBLIC
(Cont'd)

Agreement concerning exchange of scientific and technical information, with appendix. Signed at Washington March 1, 1996; entered into force March 1, 1996.
TIAS

Acquisition and cross-servicing agreement, with annex and implementing arrangement. Signed at Prague November 19, 1996; entered into force November 19, 1996.
TIAS

EMPLOYMENT

Agreement relating to the employment of dependents of official government employees. Exchange of notes at Prague February 18 and October 1, 1993; entered into force October 1, 1993.
TIAS

ENVIRONMENTAL COOPERATION

Agreement for cooperation in the Global Learning and Observations to Benefit the Environment (GLOBE) Program, with appendices. Signed at Prague April 20, 1995; entered into force April 20, 1995.
TIAS 12632.

JUDICIAL ASSISTANCE

Treaty on mutual legal assistance in criminal matters. Signed at Washington February 4, 1998; entered into force May 7, 2000.
TIAS

POSTAL MATTERS

International express mail agreement, with detailed regulations. Signed at Prague and Washington June 29 and September 1, 1993; entered into force September 1, 1993.
NP

SCIENTIFIC COOPERATION

Memorandum of understanding on science and engineering cooperation, with annexes. Signed at Prague July 13, 1994; entered into force July 13, 1994.
TIAS 12556.

Agreement for scientific and technological cooperation, with annexes. Sighed at Prague June

11, 1998; entered into force September 30, 1998.
TIAS

Memorandum of understanding concerning scientific and technical cooperation in the earth sciences. Signed at Reston and Prague April 10 and June 15, 2000; entered into force June 15, 2000.
TIAS

TAXATION

Convention for the avoidance of double taxation and the prevention of fiscal evasion with respect to taxes on income and capital. Signed at Prague September 16, 1993; entered into force December 23, 1993.
TIAS

TRADE

Agreement amending and extending the agreement of June 25, July 3 and 22, 1986, as amended and extended (U.S.–Czechoslovakia), concerning trade in textiles and textile products. Exchange of notes at Prague August 11, 1993 and April 11, 1994; entered into force April 11, 1994.
NP

CZECHOSLOVAKIA

On December 31, 1992, at midnight, Czechoslovakia ceased to exist and was succeeded by two separate and independent states, the Czech Republic and the Slovak Republic.

The status of the agreements listed below is under review.

ARMS LIMITATION

Agreement regarding inspections on the territory of the Czechoslovak Socialist Republic provided for by the U.S.-U.S.S.R. treaty of December 8, 1987 on the elimination of their intermediate-range and shorter-range missiles. Exchange of notes at Prague December 18, 1987 and January 4, 1988; entered into force June 1, 1988.
TIAS

ATOMIC ENERGY

Arrangement concerning the exchange of technical information and cooperation in nuclear safety matters, with addenda and exchange of letters. Signed at Rockville April 14, 1989; entered into force April 14, 1989.
TIAS

Agreement on cooperation in peaceful uses of nuclear energy, with annex and agreed minute. Signed at Vienna June 13, 1991; entered into force February 13, 1992.
TIAS

AVIATION

Agreement for the reciprocal acceptance of certificates of airworthiness for imported aircraft. Exchange of notes at Prague October 1 and 21, 1970; entered into force October 21, 1970.
21 UST 2468; TIAS 6987; 776 UNTS 67.

Air transport agreement, with schedule and annex. Signed at Prague June 29, 1987; entered into force June 29, 1987.
TIAS 11162.

Amendments and extension:
March 21 and May 27, 1991 (TIAS 11838).
December 31, 1992 (TIAS 11915).

CLAIMS

Agreement regarding settlement for certain war accounts and claims incident to the operations of the United States Army in Europe, and accompanying notes. Signed at Praha July 25, 1947; entered into force July 25, 1947.
61 Stat. 3410; TIAS 1675; 6 Bevans 1320; 90 UNTS 19.

Agreement on the settlement of certain outstanding claims and financial issues, with annexes and related exchange of letters. Signed at Prague January 29, 1982; entered into force February 2, 1982.
TIAS 11264.

Amendments:
February 2, 1982 (TIAS 11264).
February 12, 1982 (TIAS 11264).

COMMERCE

Agreement relating to commercial policy. Exchange of notes at Washington November 14, 1946; entered into force November 14, 1946.
61 Stat. 2431; TIAS 1569; 6 Bevans 1314; 7 UNTS 119.

Agreement relating to the establishment of a New York branch of the commercial section of the Czechoslovak Embassy. Exchange of notes at Washington August 8 and 28, 1967; entered into force August 28, 1967.
20 UST 2979; TIAS 6771; 726 UNTS 139.

CONSULS

Consular convention, with agreed memorandum and related notes. Signed at Prague

CZECHOSLOVAKIA
(Cont'd)

July 9, 1973; entered into force November 6, 1987.
TIAS 11083.

COPYRIGHT (See APPENDIX)

CULTURAL PROPERTY

Agreement for the protection and preservation of cultural properties, with annex. Signed at Washington March 17, 1992; entered into force March 17, 1992.
TIAS 11399.

CULTURAL RELATIONS

Agreement on cooperation in culture, education, science, technology and other fields, with annex. Signed at Prague April 15, 1986; entered into force April 15, 1986.
TIAS

EXTRADITION

Treaty concerning the mutual extradition of fugitive criminals. Signed at Prague July 2, 1925; entered into force March 29, 1926.
44 Stat. 2367; TS 734; 6 Bevans 1247; 50 LNTS 143.

Supplementary extradition treaty. Signed at Washington April 29, 1935; entered into force August 28, 1935.
49 Stat. 3253; TS 895; 6 Bevans 1283; 162 LNTS 83.

FINANCE

Agreement relating to the funding of the indebtedness of Czechoslovakia to the United States. Signed at Washington October 13, 1925; operative June 15, 1925.
Treasury Department print; 6 Bevans 1253.

Agreement modifying the debt funding agreement of October 13, 1925. Signed at Washington June 10, 1932; operative July 1, 1931.
Treasury Department print; 6 Bevans 1277.

Investment incentive agreement. Signed at Prague October 18, 1990; entered into force October 18, 1990.
TIAS

INVESTMENT

Treaty concerning the reciprocal encouragement and protection of investment, with annex, protocol and exchanges of letters. Signed at Washington October 22, 1991; entered into force December 19, 1992.
TIAS

LEND-LEASE

Preliminary agreement regarding principles applying to mutual aid in the prosecution of the war against aggression. Signed at Washington July 11, 1942; entered into force July 11, 1942.
56 Stat. 1562; EAS 261; 6 Bevans 1300; 90 UNTS 257.

Agreement on settlement for lend-lease and certain claims. Signed at Praha September 16, 1948; entered into force September 16, 1948.
62 Stat. 2850; TIAS 1818; 6 Bevans 1326; 90 UNTS 35.

MAPPING

Basic exchange and cooperative agreement for topographic mapping, nautical and aeronautical charting, geodesy and geophysics, digital data and related MC & G materials. Signed at Prague December 10, 1991; entered into force December 10, 1991.
NP

NARCOTIC DRUGS

Arrangement for the direct exchange of certain information regarding the traffic in narcotic drugs. Exchange of notes at Prague February 9 and June 15, 1928; entered into force June 15, 1928.
6 Bevans 1263.

PACIFIC SETTLEMENT OF DISPUTES

Treaty of arbitration. Signed at Washington August 16, 1928; entered into force April 11, 1929.
46 Stat. 2254; TS 781; 6 Bevans 1268; 89 LNTS 225.

Treaty of conciliation. Signed at Washington August 16, 1928; entered into force April 11, 1929.
46 Stat. 2257; TS 782; 6 Bevans 1271; 89 LNTS 219.

PEACE CORPS

Agreement on the program of the United States Peace Corps in Czechoslovakia. Signed at Prague June 25, 1990; entered into force June 25, 1990.
TIAS 12076.

POSTAL MATTERS

Money order convention. Signed at Washington June 30 and at Prague July 20, 1924; entered into force August 1, 1924.
NP

Agreement concerning exchange of parcel post, and regulations of execution. Signed at Washington September 15, and at Praha September 29, 1950; entered into force October 1, 1950.
8 UST 997; TIAS 3865; 290 UNTS 3.

International express mail agreement, with detailed regulations. Signed at Prague and Washington July 25 and August 17, 1988; entered into force September 30, 1988.
TIAS 11645.

SCIENTIFIC COOPERATION

Agreement for scientific and technological cooperation, with annexes. Signed at Washington October 22, 1991; entered into force June 3, 1992.
TIAS 11971.

Memorandum of understanding concerning scientific and technical cooperation in the earth sciences, with annex. Signed at Prague April 10, 1992; entered into force April 10, 1992.
TIAS 11972.

TRADE (See also COMMERCE)

Agreement providing for consultations should textile or apparel exports from Czechoslovakia cause market disruptions in the United States. Exchange of notes at Prague March 22 and 28, 1977; entered into force March 28, 1977.
28 UST 5463; TIAS 8645; 1087 UNTS 283.

Agreement concerning exports of certain textile products to the United States. Exchange of notes at Prague June 25, July 3 and 22, 1986; entered into force July 22, 1986; effective June 1, 1986.
NP

Amendments and extensions:
December 21, 1987, April 15 and May 4, 1988 (NP).
June 12 and August 10, 1989 (NP).

Agreement on trade relations, with related exchanges of letters. Signed at Washington April 12, 1990; entered into force November 17, 1990.
TIAS

CZECHOSLOVAKIA
(Cont'd)

Amendment:
February 25 and May 12, 1992.

VISAS

Agreement relating to multiple entry visas for diplomatic personnel. Exchange of notes at Prague December 18 and 21, 1962; entered into force December 21, 1962.
13 UST 3842; TIAS 5258; 469 UNTS 115.

Agreement relating to issuance of non-immigrant visas on a facilitated basis to certain holders of diplomatic or official passports. Exchange of notes at Prague June 20, 1978; entered into force June 20, 1978; effective July 1, 1978.
30 UST 1593; TIAS 9266; 1150 UNTS 107.

DENMARK

AUTOMOTIVE TRAFFIC

Agreement relating to reciprocal treatment of passenger motor vehicles. Exchange of notes at Bar Harbor, Maine, September 4, 1928, and at Washington October 27, 1928, and February 2, 1929; entered into force February 2, 1929; operative February 1, 1929.
48 Stat. 1871; EAS 61; 7 Bevans 83.

AVIATION

Arrangement relating to pilot licenses to operate civil aircraft. Exchange of notes at Copenhagen March 14 and 24, 1934; entered into force April 16, 1934.
48 Stat. 1865; EAS 59; 7 Bevans 99; 149 LNTS 485.

Agreement relating to air transport services. Exchange of notes at Washington December 16, 1944; entered into force provisionally January 1, 1945; definitively September 29, 1945.
58 Stat. 1458; EAS 430; 7 Bevans 114; 10 UNTS 213.

Amendments:
August 6, 1954 (5 UST 1422; TIAS 3014; 222 UNTS 366).
June 16, 1995 (TIAS 12663).

Air service agreement relating to facilities at Kastrup Airport in Denmark. Exchange of notes at Copenhagen September 26 and October 1, 1946; entered into force October 1, 1946.
61 Stat. 3851; TIAS 1734; 7 Bevans 125; 42 UNTS 219.

Agreement concerning establishment and operation of certain aeronautical facilities and services in Greenland and Appendix. Signed at Copenhagen July 7, 1960; entered into force July 7, 1960.
11 UST 1861; TIAS 4531; 380 UNTS 39.

Amendment:
March 26 and September 6, 1976 (28 UST 3654; TIAS 8593).

Agreement relating to the reciprocal acceptance of airworthiness certifications. Exchange of notes at Washington January 6, 1982; entered into force January 6, 1982.
34 UST 27; TIAS 10335.

Agreement for promotion of aviation safety. Signed at Copenhagen November 6, 1998; entered into force November 6, 1998.
TIAS

COMMERCE

General convention of friendship, commerce, and navigation.[1] Signed at Washington April 26, 1826; entered into force August 10, 1826; operative April 26, 1826.
8 Stat. 340; TS 65; 7 Bevans 1.

Treaty of friendship, commerce and navigation, with protocol and minutes of interpretation.[2] Signed at Copenhagen October 1, 1951; entered into force July 30, 1961.
12 UST 908; TIAS 4797; 421 UNTS 105.

NOTES:
[1] Does not apply to Greenland and Iceland (article 6). This convention was abrogated April 15, 1856 and renewed, with the exception of article 5, by the convention of April 11, 1857 (TS 67), and terminated, with the exception of articles 8, 9 and 10 relating to consular matters, by the treaty of October 1, 1951 (TIAS 4797).
[2] Applicable to all Danish territories except Greenland, and to all territories over which the United States has jurisdiction or international responsibility except the Trust Territory of the Pacific Islands.

CONSULS (See COMMERCE)

COPYRIGHT (See APPENDIX)

DEFENSE (See also MUTUAL SECURITY)

Mutual defense assistance agreement. Signed at Washington January 27, 1950; entered into force January 27, 1950.
1 UST 19; TIAS 2011; 48 UNTS 115.

Agreement concerning the defense of Greenland. Signed at Copenhagen April 27, 1951; entered into force June 8, 1951.
2 UST 1485; TIAS 2292; 94 UNTS 35.

Related agreements:
December 2, 1960 (11 UST 2642; TIAS 4657; 402 UNTS 245).
September 30, 1986 (TIAS 12284).

Agreement relating to the disposition of equipment and material no longer required by Denmark in the furtherance of its mutual defense assistance program. Exchange of notes at Copenhagen November 16, 1951 and April 28, 1952; entered into force April 28, 1952.
3 UST 5278; TIAS 2726; 180 UNTS 275.

Amendment:
September 12, 1960 (11 UST 2116; TIAS 4570; 388 UNTS 356).

Agreement relating to the offshore procurement program in Denmark with model contract attached. Exchange of notes at Copenhagen June 8, 1954; entered into force June 8, 1954.
9 UST 141; TIAS 3987; 307 UNTS 133.

Agreement relating to the status of the personnel of the U.S. Military Assistance Advisory Group and of the personnel of the offshore procurement program. Exchange of notes at Copenhagen December 12, 1956; entered into force December 12, 1956.
9 UST 271; TIAS 4002; 304 UNTS 311.

Agreement relating to a weapons production program. Exchange of notes at Copenhagen April 12, 1960; entered into force April 12, 1960.[1]
11 UST 1440; TIAS 4484.

Memorandum of understanding concerning the principles governing mutual cooperation in the research, development, production, procurement and logistic support of defense equipment. Signed at Copenhagen and Washington January 2 and 30, 1980; entered into force January 30, 1980.
33 UST 3128; TIAS 10216.

Agreement on general security of military information. Exchange of notes at Copenhagen January 23 and February 27, 1981; entered into force February 27, 1981.
33 UST 1264; TIAS 10109; 1264 UNTS 475.

Mutual logistical support agreement, with annex. Signed at Vedbaek and Stuttgart-Vaihingen June 1 and 14, 1982; entered into force June 14, 1982.
TIAS 10411.

Memorandum of understanding concerning use of Sondrestrom Aviation Facility, Kulusuk Airfield and other matters related to U.S. military activities in Greenland. Signed at Copenhagen March 13, 1991; entered into force March 13, 1991.
TIAS 12285; 1653 UNTS 389.

Acquisition and cross-servicing agreement, with annexes. Signed at Vedbaek, Denmark

DENMARK (Cont'd)

and Patch Barracks, Germany January 5 and 8, 1998; entered into force January 8, 1998.
TIAS

Agreement regarding the exchange of administrative and professional personnel, with annexes. Signed at Washington July 7, 1998; entered into force July 7, 1998.
NP

NOTE:
[1] For amendment of paragraph 4.a.(4) of the agreement, see exchange of letters of May 11 and 18, 1960 (11 UST 1447; TIAS 4484).

ECONOMIC AND TECHNICAL COOPERATION

Economic cooperation agreement.[1] Signed at Copenhagen June 29, 1948; entered into force July 2, 1948.
62 Stat. 2199; TIAS 1782; 7 Bevans 141; 22 UNTS 217.

Amendments:
November 4 and 18, 1948 (62 Stat. 3753; TIAS 1904; 7 Bevans 157; 55 UNTS 322).
February 7, 1950 (1 UST 148; TIAS 2022; 79 UNTS 294).
February 2 and 9, 1951 (2 UST 647; TIAS 2218; 132 UNTS 380).
November 24, 1952 (3 UST 5181; TIAS 2713; 184 UNTS 327).

NOTE:
[1] Applicable to Greenland.

EDUCATION

Agreement for financing certain educational exchange programs. Exchange of notes at Copenhagen May 28, 1962; entered into force May 28, 1962.
13 UST 1154; TIAS 5060; 450 UNTS 215.

Amendments:
February 18 and 25, 1965 (16 UST 154; TIAS 5775; 542 UNTS 386).
November 2, 1971 and April 27, 1972 (23 UST 2683; TIAS 7462).

EMPLOYMENT

Agreement relating to the employment of dependents of official government employees, with addendum. Exchange of notes at Washington May 16 and 20, 1983; entered into force May 20, 1983.
TIAS 10694.

EXTRADITION

Treaty on extradition.[1] Signed at Copenhagen June 22, 1972; entered into force July 31, 1974.
25 UST 1293; TIAS 7864.

NOTE:
[1] Applicable to all territories.

FINANCE

Agreement relating to guaranties authorized under section 111(b)(3) of the Economic Cooperation Act of 1948, as amended. Exchange of notes at Washington July 30 and August 8, 1952; entered into force August 9, 1952.
3 UST 5056; TIAS 2689; 181 UNTS 249.

INDUSTRIAL PROPERTY (See also TRADE-MARKS)

Agreement with respect to the protection of industrial designs or models. Exchange of notes at Washington and Bar Harbor, Maine, June 22 and 26, 1906; entered into force June 26, 1906.
TS 483; 7 Bevans 45.

MAPPING

Basic exchange and cooperative agreement concerning mapping, charting and geodesy cooperation, with glossary. Signed at Fairfax and Vedbaek December 20, 1995 and February 7, 1996; entered into force February 7, 1996.
NP

MARITIME MATTERS

Agreement for mutual exemption of vessels from readmeasurement in the ports of their respective countries. Signed at Washington February 26, 1886; entered into force April 1, 1886.
TS 70; 7 Bevans 27.

Amendment:
October 2 and 28, 1895 (7 Bevans 32).

Agreement relating to a shipbuilding program in Denmark. Exchange of notes at Copenhagen May 8, 1959; entered into force May 8, 1959.
10 UST 939; TIAS 4226; 344 UNTS 185.

Amendment:
May 17, 1961 (12 UST 625; TIAS 4761; 410 UNTS 348).

MUTUAL SECURITY

Agreement relating to the assurances required by the Mutual Security Act of 1951. Exchange

of notes at Copenhagen January 8, 1952; entered into force January 8, 1952.
3 UST 4554; TIAS 2605; 179 UNTS 65.

NARCOTIC DRUGS

Arrangement for the direct exchange of certain information regarding the traffic in narcotic drugs. Exchange of notes at Copenhagen February 3 and April 23, 1928; entered into force April 23, 1928.
7 Bevans 78.

NAVIGATION

Agreement concerning the closure of the long-range radio aid to navigation transmitting station at Angissoq, Greenland, with annex. Signed at Copenhagen December 12, 1994; entered into force December 12, 1994.
TIAS

Agreement for the transfer of ownership of long-range radio aid to navigation transmitting station at Ejde, Faroe Islands, Denmark, with annex. Signed at Copenhagen December 12, 1994; entered into force December 12, 1994.
TIAS

PACIFIC SETTLEMENT OF DISPUTES

Treaty for the advancement of peace. Signed at Washington April 17, 1914; entered into force January 19, 1915.
38 Stat. 1883; TS 608; 7 Bevans 53.

Arbitration treaty. Signed at Washington June 14, 1928; entered into force April 17, 1929.
46 Stat. 2265; TS 784; 7 Bevans 80; 88 LNTS 173.

PATENTS

Agreement to facilitate the interchange of patent rights and technical information for defense purposes. Signed at Copenhagen February 19, 1960; entered into force February 19, 1960.
11 UST 148; TIAS 4423; 354 UNTS 151.

Agreement approving the procedures for the reciprocal filing of classified patent applications in the United States and Denmark. Exchange of notes at Copenhagen June 13 and 20, 1960; entered into force June 20, 1960.
11 UST 1788; TIAS 4521; 378 UNTS 400.

POSTAL MATTERS

Money order convention. Signed at Washington November 11 and at Copenhagen November 29, 1887; operative January 1, 1888.
NP

DENMARK (Cont'd)

Agreement concerning the exchange of parcel post, and detailed regulations of execution.[1] Signed at Copenhagen December 9 and at Washington December 28, 1932; entered into force provisionally July 1, 1932 and definitively August 18, 1933.
47 Stat. 2402; Post Office Department print; 140 LNTS 453.

Agreement for collect-on-delivery service.[1] Signed at Copenhagen October 13, and at Washington November 11, 1933; operative November 1, 1933.
48 Stat. 1671; Post Office Department print; 145 LNTS 113.

International express mail agreement, with detailed regulations. Signed at Copenhagen and Washington October 19 and November 19, 1984; entered into force January 2, 1985.
TIAS 11011.

NOTE:
[1] Applicable to Puerto Rico, the Virgin Islands, Guam, Samoa, Faroe Islands and Greenland.

PUBLICATIONS

Agreement for the exchange of official publications. Exchange of notes at Copenhagen July 27 and August 1, 1949; entered into force August 1, 1949.
63 Stat. 2680; TIAS 1971; 7 Bevans 159; 79 UNTS 147.

SCIENTIFIC COOPERATION

Memorandum of understanding concerning the furnishing of balloon launching and associated services. Signed at Copenhagen and Washington September 14 and 20, 1983; entered into force September 20, 1983.
TIAS 10801.

SHIPPING

Agreement relating to jurisdiction over vessels utilizing the Louisiana Offshore Oil Port. Exchange of notes at Washington August 17 and 22, 1978; entered into force August 22, 1978.
30 UST 1702; TIAS 9278; 1153 UNTS 139.

SMUGGLING

Convention for prevention of smuggling of intoxicating liquors. Signed at Washington May 29, 1924; entered into force July 25, 1924.
43 Stat. 1809; TS 693; 7 Bevans 72; 27 LNTS 361.

TAXATION

Agreement relating to relief from double income tax on shipping profits. Exchanges of notes at Washington May 22, August 9 and 18, October 24, 25, and 28, and December 5 and 6, 1922; entered into force December 6, 1922; operative January 1, 1921.
47 Stat. 2612; EAS 14; 7 Bevans 65; 113 LNTS 381.

Amendment:
July 6, 1987 (TIAS 11278).

Convention for the avoidance of double taxation and the prevention of fiscal evasion with respect to taxes on income. Signed at Washington May 6, 1948; entered into force December 1, 1948; operative January 1, 1948 for U.S. tax and April 1, 1948 for Danish tax.
62 Stat. 1730; TIAS 1854; 7 Bevans 131; 26 UNTS 55.

Agreement relating to relief from taxation of United States expenditures in Denmark for common defense. Exchange of notes at Copenhagen April 7 and 9, 1952; entered into force April 9, 1952; operative April 7, 1952.
3 UST 4041; TIAS 2546; 177 UNTS 257.

Convention for the avoidance of double taxation and the prevention of fiscal evasion with respect to taxes on estates. Signed at Washington April 27, 1983; entered into force November 7, 1984.
TIAS 11089.

Convention for the avoidance of double taxation and the prevention of fiscal evasion with respect to taxes on income, with protocol. Signed at Washington August 19, 1999; entered into force March 31, 2000.
TIAS

TECHNOLOGICAL COOPERATION

Agreement concerning a Danish-American Fund for the exchange of technology, with appendix. Signed at Copenhagen March 25, 1985; entered into force March 25, 1985.
TIAS 11179.

Amendment:
May 2, 1988 (TIAS 11580).

TELECOMMUNICATION

Agreement relating to the registration with the International Telecommunication Union of frequencies used by United States authorities in Greenland. Exchange of notes at Washington March 25 and April 4, 1952; entered into force April 4, 1952.
3 UST 4047; TIAS 2548; 177 UNTS 13.

Agreement relating to the reciprocal granting of authorizations to permit licensed amateur radio operators of either country to operate their stations in the other country. Exchange of notes at Copenhagen October 11, 1973; entered into force October 11, 1973.
24 UST 2156; TIAS 7730; 938 UNTS 327.

TERRITORIAL ACQUISITION

Convention for the cession to the United States of the Danish West Indies, and declaration by the United States. Signed at New York August 4, 1916; entered into force January 17, 1917.
39 Stat. 1706; TS 629; 7 Bevans 56.

TRADE (See also COMMERCE)

Convention for discontinuance of the sound dues. Signed at Washington April 11, 1857; entered into force January 12, 1858.
11 Stat. 719; TS 67; 7 Bevans 11.

Agreement providing compensatory concessions under the general agreement on tariffs and trade for certain tariff actions taken by the United States. Exchange of notes at Geneva January 26 and February 12, 1962; entered into force February 12, 1962.
13 UST 936; TIAS 5032.

TRADE-MARKS

Convention for the reciprocal protection of trade-marks and trade labels. Signed at Copenhagen June 15, 1892; entered into force September 28, 1892.
27 Stat. 963; TS 72; 7 Bevans 30.

Understanding granting persons domiciled in the United States engaged in gainful occupation the access by registration to the exclusive right of utilization of trade-marks in Denmark. Exchange of notes at Washington June 26 and October 15, 1953; entered into force October 15, 1953.
4 UST 2040; TIAS 2860; 215 UNTS 111.

VISAS

Arrangement relating to the waiver of passport visa fees for nonimmigrants. Exchange of notes at Copenhagen July 2 and September 29, 1925; operative August 6, 1925.
7 Bevans 76.

Agreement for the waiver of visa requirements for American citizens entering Denmark for a temporary period, and the granting of gratis visas valid for twenty-four months to Danish subjects coming to the United States for temporary visits. Exchanges of notes at Copenhagen June 9 and 21 and July 7 and 8, 1947; entered into force July 8, 1947.
62 Stat. 4068; TIAS 2110; 7 Bevans 128; 132 UNTS 145.

Amendment:
April 30 and May 1, 1958.

DJIBOUTI

COPYRIGHT (See APPENDIX)

DEFENSE

Agreement concerning the provision of training related to defense articles under the United States International Military Education and Training (IMET) Program. Exchange of notes at Djibouti October 9, 1983 and June 3, 1984; entered into force June 3, 1984.
TIAS 10983.

Agreement regarding grants under the Foreign Assistance Act of 1961, as amended, and the furnishing of defense articles, related training and other defense services from the United States to Djibouti. Exchange of notes at Djibouti June 3 and 13, 1992; entered into force June 13, 1992.
TIAS 12286.

ECONOMIC AND TECHNICAL COOPERATION

Agency for International Development:
January 9, 1978 (29 UST 5764; TIAS 9150).

EMPLOYMENT

Agreement relating to the employment of dependents of official government employees. Exchange of notes at Djibouti November 21 and December 24, 1991; entered into force December 24, 1991.
TIAS 11843.

FINANCE

Investment incentive agreement. Exchange of notes at Djibouti May 11, 1983; entered into force May 11, 1983.
TIAS

POSTAL MATTERS

International express mail agreement, with detailed regulations. Signed at Djibouti and Washington June 25, July 28 and August 11, 1987; entered into force August 17, 1987.
TIAS 11554.

SCIENTIFIC COOPERATION

Memorandum of understanding concerning scientific and technical cooperation in the earth sciences, with annexes. Signed at Reston and Djibouti April 29 and December 9, 1993; entered into force December 9, 1993.
TIAS 12520.

DOMINICA

On November 8, 1978 Dominica became an independent state. In a note dated December 23, 1982 to the Secretary-General of the United Nations, the Prime Minister made a statement reading in part as follows:

"The Government of the Commonwealth of Dominica hereby declares that, with regard to multilateral treaties applied or extended to the former British associated state of Dominica, it will continue to apply the terms of each such treaty provisionally and on the basis of reciprocity until such time as it notifies the depository authority of its decision in respect thereof.

"As regards bilateral treaties applied or extended to, or entered into on behalf of the former British associated state of Dominica, the Government of the Commonwealth of Dominica declares that it will examine each such treaty and communicate its views to the other state party concerned. In the mean-time, the Government of the Commonwealth of Dominica will continue to observe the terms of each such treaty, which validly so applies and is not inconsistent with its independent sovereign status, provisionally and on the basis of reciprocity."

AVIATION

Agreement between the United States and the United Kingdom concerning air services, with annexes and exchange of letters. Signed at Bermuda July 23, 1977; entered into force July 23, 1977.
28 UST 5367; TIAS 8641.

Amendment:
April 25, 1978 (29 UST 2680; TIAS 8965).

CONSULS

Consular convention between the United States and the United Kingdom. Signed at Washington June 6, 1951; entered into force September 7, 1952.
3 UST 3426; TIAS 2494; 165 UNTS 121.

COPYRIGHT (See APPENDIX)

DEFENSE

Agreement concerning the provision of training related to defense articles under the United States International Military Education and Training (IMET) Program. Exchange of notes at Bridgetown and Roseau December 11, 1980 and February 4, 1981; entered into force February 4, 1981.
33 UST 856; TIAS 10069; 1267 UNTS 95.

ECONOMIC AND TECHNICAL COOPERATION

General agreement for economic, technical, and related assistance. Signed at Dominica September 16, 1983; entered into force September 16, 1983.
TIAS 10830.

EXTRADITION

Treaty on extradition. Signed at Roseau October 10, 1996; entered into force May 25, 2000.
TIAS

FINANCE

Agreement relating to investment guaranties. Signed at Roseau October 11, 1968; entered into force October 11, 1968.
19 UST 6063; TIAS 6568; 702 UNTS 263.

JUDICIAL ASSISTANCE

Treaty on mutual legal assistance in criminal matters. Signed at Roseau October 10, 1996; entered into force May 25, 2000.
TIAS

NARCOTIC DRUGS

Agreement concerning maritime counter-drug operations. Signed at Roseau April 19, 1995; entered into force April 19, 1995.
TIAS 12630.

PEACE CORPS

Agreement relating to the establishment of a Peace Corps program in Dominica. Exchange of letters at Bridgetown and Roseau May 15 and 22, 1980; entered into force May 22, 1980.
32 UST 5811; TIAS 10016; 1267 UNTS 87.

PEACEKEEPING

Agreement for the furnishing of commodities and services in connection with the peacekeeping force for Grenada. Exchange of notes at Bridgetown and Roseau November 25, 1983 and January 13, 1984; entered into force January 13, 1984.
TIAS 10923.

DOMINICA (Cont'd)

POSTAL MATTERS

International express mail agreement. Signed at Roseau and Washington September 24, 1997 and December 30, 1999; entered into force February 15, 2000.
NP

PRIVILEGES AND IMMUNITIES

Agreement relating to privileges and immunities for Department of Defense engineering personnel temporarily in Dominica for the purpose of emergency repairs. Exchange of letters at Bridgetown and Roseau September 17, 1979; entered into force September 17, 1979.
31 UST 5056; TIAS 9655.

REFUGEES

Memorandum of understanding for the establishment within the territory of Dominica of facilities to provide temporary protection under the auspices of the United Nations High Commissioner for Refugees for nationals of Haiti fleeing their country, with related letter. Signed at Dominica July 10, 1994; entered into force July 10, 1994.
TIAS

TAXATION

Agreement for the exchange of information with respect to taxes. Signed at Washington October 1, 1987; entered into force May 9, 1988.
TIAS 11543.

TELECOMMUNICATION

Agreement between the United States and the United Kingdom relating to the reciprocal granting of authorizations to permit licensed amateur radio operators of either country to operate their stations in the other country. Exchange of notes at London November 26, 1965; applicable to Dominica December 11, 1969.
16 UST 2047; TIAS 5941; 561 UNTS 193.

Agreement between the United States and the United Kingdom extending to certain territories the application of the agreement of November 26, 1965 relating to the reciprocal granting of authorizations to permit licensed amateur radio operators of either country to operate their stations in the other country. Exchange of notes at London December 11, 1969; entered into force December 11, 1969.
20 UST 4089; TIAS 6800; 732 UNTS 334.

Agreement relating to radio communications between amateur stations on behalf of third parties. Exchange of telexes at Bridgetown and Roseau December 8, 1983 and February 9, 1984; entered into force March 10, 1984.
TIAS 11145.

TRADE-MARKS

Declaration by the United States and the United Kingdom affording reciprocal protection to trade-marks. Signed at London October 24, 1877; entered into force October 24, 1877.
20 Stat. 703; TS 138; 12 Bevans 198.

DOMINICAN REPUBLIC

AGRICULTURAL COMMODITIES

Agricultural commodities agreement with exchange of notes. Signed at Santo Domingo November 30, 1962; entered into force November 30, 1962.
13 UST 3863; TIAS 5261; 471 UNTS 25.

Amendment:
September 14, 1963 (14 UST 1531; TIAS 5453; 505 UNTS 332).

Agricultural commodity agreement. Signed at Washington August 13, 1963; entered into force August 13, 1963.
14 UST 1027; TIAS 5398; 492 UNTS 327.

Agricultural commodities agreement, with exchange of notes. Signed at Santo Domingo March 18, 1965; entered into force March 18, 1965.
16 UST 168; TIAS 5778; 542 UNTS 215.

Agricultural commodities agreement with annex. Signed at Santo Domingo April 1, 1968; entered into force April 1, 1968.
20 UST 817; TIAS 6696; 713 UNTS 241.

Amendment:
May 9 and 10, 1968 (20 UST 837; TIAS 6696; 713 UNTS 266).

Related agreements:
May 10, 1968 (20 UST 2739; TIAS 6739; 719 UNTS 87).
June 11, 1968 (20 UST 839; TIAS 6697; 713 UNTS 285).

Agricultural commodities agreement with annex. Signed at Santo Domingo March 28, 1969; entered into force March 28, 1969.
20 UST 735; TIAS 6685; 713 UNTS 295.

Amendments:
April 15, 1969 (20 UST 756; TIAS 6685; 713 UNTS 295).
June 23, 1969 and June 24, 1970 (21 UST 1738; TIAS 6929; 756 UNTS 330).

Agricultural commodities agreement with annex. Signed at Santo Domingo March 31, 1970; entered into force March 31, 1970.
21 UST 1069; TIAS 6863; 741 UNTS 15.

Amendment:
May 14 and June 24, 1970 (21 UST 1741; TIAS 6930).

Related agreements:
April 1, 1971 (22 UST 562; TIAS 7100; 792 UNTS 273).
February 14, 1972 (23 UST 149; TIAS 7285; 829 UNTS 259).
March 30 and April 14, 1972 (23 UST 603; TIAS 7320).
May 4 and 17, 1972 (23 UST 779; TIAS 7340).
June 12, 1973 (26 UST 3839; TIAS 8215).

Agricultural commodities agreement. Signed at Santo Domingo September 28, 1977; entered into force September 28, 1977.
29 UST 2377; TIAS 8944.

Amendment:
December 13 and 20, 1977 (29 UST 2416; TIAS 8944).

Related agreements:
January 11, 1979 (30 UST 6567; TIAS 9568; 1182 UNTS 121).
January 3, 1980 (32 UST 792; TIAS 9730; 1222 UNTS 95).
April 9 and 11, 1980 (32 UST 1029; TIAS 9753; 1222 UNTS 107).
June 13 and July 22, 1980 (TIAS 10494).
February 20, 1981 (33 UST 1707; TIAS 10139).
May 21, 1982 (34 UST 1047; TIAS 10391).
August 2 and 26, 1982 (TIAS 10487).
December 11, 1982 (TIAS 10629).
August 22, 1983 (TIAS 10769).
January 13, 1984 (NP).
May 21, 1984 (NP).
August 30, 1984 (NP).
October 23 and 30, 1984 (NP).

Agricultural commodities agreement. Signed at Santo Domingo May 15, 1985; entered into force July 3, 1985.
NP

Amendments:
August 1, 1985 (NP).
August 19, 1985 (NP).
August 18, 1986 (NP).

Agricultural commodities agreement, with memorandum of understanding. Signed at Santo Domingo June 30, 1987; entered into force June 1, 1988.
NP

Amendment:
April 29, 1988 (NP).

Related agreements:
August 24, 1989 (NP).
September 27, 1989 (NP).

DOMINICAN REPUBLIC (Cont'd)

AVIATION

Air transport agreement and exchange of notes. Signed at Ciudad Trujillo July 19, 1949; entered into force July 19, 1949.
63 Stat. 2615; TIAS 1955; 7 Bevans 289; 51 UNTS 145.

Amendment:
October 19, 1971 (22 UST 1732; TIAS 7202).

Agreement relating to the transit of military aircraft. Exchange of notes at Ciudad Trujillo August 11, 1950; entered into force August 11, 1950.
1 UST 747; TIAS 2143; 92 UNTS 329.

Memorandum of agreement relating to the provision of flight inspection services. Signed at Washington and Santo Domingo August 16, 1978 and June 22, 1979; entered into force June 22, 1979; effective October 1, 1978.
TIAS

Amendment:
May 19 and July 13, 1998.

Memorandum of agreement concerning assistance in developing and modernizing the Dominican Republic's civil aviation system, with annex. Signed at Santo Domingo March 11 and 17, 1988; entered into force March 17, 1988.
TIAS 11777.

COPYRIGHT (See APPENDIX)

CUSTOMS

Agreement providing free entry upon arrival for Embassy employees, and certain duty-free importations, including new and used automobiles, for six months thereafter. Exchange of notes at Washington January 12 and 23, 1950; entered into force January 23, 1950.
5 UST 1064; TIAS 2989; 236 UNTS 3.

DEFENSE

Military assistance agreement.[1] Signed at Washington March 6, 1953; entered into force June 10, 1953.
4 UST 184; TIAS 2777; 199 UNTS 267.

Agreement providing for disposition of equipment and materials furnished by the United States under the military assistance agreement of March 6, 1953. Exchange of notes at Ciudad Trujillo March 23 and April 22, 1955; entered into force April 22, 1955.
6 UST 1185; TIAS 3263; 239 UNTS 325.

Military assistance agreement. Signed at Santo Domingo March 8, 1962; entered into force June 10, 1964.
15 UST 699; TIAS 5590; 527 UNTS 29.

Agreement relating to the deposit by the Dominican Republic of ten percent of the value of military grant assistance and excess defense articles furnished by the United States. Exchange of notes at Santo Domingo March 23 and April 17, 1972; entered into force April 17, 1972; effective February 7, 1972.
23 UST 1094; TIAS 7366; 852 UNTS 235.

Agreement concerning payment to the United States of net proceeds from the sale of defense articles furnished under the military assistance program. Exchange of notes at Santo Domingo May 30 and August 8, 1974; entered into force August 8, 1974; effective July 1, 1974.
25 UST 2433; TIAS 7924.

Agreement concerning the status of United States Government personnel temporarily present in the Dominican Republic in connection with their official duties. Exchange of notes at Santo Domingo July 20 and August 4, 1988; entered into force August 4, 1988.
NP

NOTE:
[1] Terminated June 20, 1961 except that the provisions of paragraphs 2, 3, 4, 5 and 6 of article 1 continue in force.

ECONOMIC AND TECHNICAL COOPERATION

General agreement for economic, technical and related assistance. Signed at Santo Domingo January 11, 1962; entered into force January 11, 1962.
13 UST 60; TIAS 4936; 433 UNTS 133.

Agency for International Development:
October 16, 1974 (27 UST 2835; TIAS 8353; 1068 UNTS 49).
October 1, 1975 (27 UST 2387; TIAS 8319; 1054 UNTS 235).
February 25, 1976 (28 UST 2125; TIAS 8537; 1068 UNTS 74).
September 30, 1976 (28 UST 3007; TIAS 8579).
April 7, 1977 (29 UST 1683; TIAS 8901).

EVACUATION

Convention entered into in accordance with the "modus operandi" of evacuation, signed June 30, 1922, for the purpose of rectifying certain orders, resolutions, and contracts. Signed at Santo Domingo June 12, 1924; entered into force December 4, 1925.
44 Stat. 2193; TS 729; 7 Bevans 206; 48 LNTS 91.

EXTRADITION

Convention for the mutual extradition of fugitives from justice. Signed at Santo Domingo June 19, 1909; entered into force August 2, 1910.
36 Stat. 2468; TS 550; 7 Bevans 200.

FINANCE

Agreement relating to investment guaranties. Signed at Washington May 2, 1962; entered into force May 2, 1962.
13 UST 440; TIAS 5005; 442 UNTS 99.

Agreement regarding the consolidation and rescheduling of certain debts owed to, guaranteed by or insured by the United States Government and its agencies, with annexes. Signed at Santo Domingo March 6, 1986; entered into force September 9, 1986.
NP

Agreement regarding the consolidation and rescheduling or refinancing of certain debts owed to, guaranteed by, or insured by the United States Government and its agencies, with annexes. Signed at Santo Domingo October 30, 1992; entered into force November 9, 1993.
NP

LABOR

Agreement relating to workmen's compensation in connection with certain projects under construction or operation in the Dominican Republic. Exchange of notes at Ciudad Trujillo October 14 and 19, 1943; entered into force October 19, 1943.
57 Stat. 1180; EAS 353; 7 Bevans 268; 21 UNTS 295.

MAPPING

Basic exchange and cooperative agreement for topographic mapping, nautical and aeronautical charting and information, geodesy and geophysics, digital data and related mapping, charting and geodesy materials, with glossary. Signed at Santo Domingo and Fairfax September 18 and 25, 1995; entered into force September 25, 1995.
NP

MARITIME MATTERS

Maritime search and rescue agreement. Signed at Santo Domingo March 20, 1992; entered into force March 20, 1992.
TIAS 11875.

DOMINICAN REPUBLIC (Cont'd)

NARCOTIC DRUGS

Agreement on international narcotics control cooperation. Signed at Santo Domingo November 18, 1985; entered into force November 18, 1985.
TIAS 11350.

Agreement concerning maritime counter-drug operations. Signed at Santo Domingo March 23, 1995; entered into force March 23, 1995.
TIAS 12620.

PEACE CORPS

Agreement relating to the establishment of a Peace Corps program in the Dominican Republic. Signed at Washington May 2, 1962; entered into force May 2, 1962.
13 UST 447; TIAS 5007; 442 UNTS 107.

POSTAL MATTERS

International express mail agreement, with detailed regulations. Signed at Santo Domingo and Washington December 3, 1990 and January 8, 1991; entered into force February 18, 1991.
TIAS 11782.

Postal money order agreement. Signed at Washington and Santo Domingo August 6 and 14, 1995; entered into force September 1, 1995.
NP

PUBLICATIONS

Agreement relating to the exchange of official publications. Exchange of notes at Ciudad Trujillo December 9 and 10, 1942; entered into force December 10, 1942.
56 Stat. 1851; EAS 297; 7 Bevans 248; 24 UNTS 257.

SANCTIONS

Memorandum of understanding for a multinational observer group to monitor and advise on Haiti sanctions enforcement. Signed at Santo Domingo August 1, 1994; entered into force August 1, 1994.
TIAS

SCIENTIFIC COOPERATION

Memorandum of understanding concerning co-operation in geological sciences. Signed at Santo Domingo January 23, 1984; entered into force January 23, 1984.
TIAS 10932.

TAXATION

Agreement for the exchange of information with respect to taxes. Signed at Santo Domingo August 7, 1989; entered into force October 12, 1989.
TIAS 11694.

TELECOMMUNICATION

Agreement relating to radio communications between amateur stations on behalf of third parties. Exchange of notes at Santo Domingo April 18 and 22, 1963; entered into force May 22, 1963.
14 UST 817; TIAS 5360; 487 UNTS 169.

Agreement relating to the reciprocal granting of authorizations to permit licensed amateur radio operators of either country to operate their stations in the other country. Exchange of notes at Santo Domingo January 28 and February 2, 1965; entered into force February 2, 1965.
16 UST 93; TIAS 5766; 542 UNTS 117.

TRADE AND COMMERCE

Agreement relating to the multilateral trade negotiations. Exchange of letters at Santo Domingo December 21, 1979 and January 2, 1980; entered into force January 2, 1980.
32 UST 5301; TIAS 9981; 1266 UNTS 311.

Agreement relating to trade in cotton, wool and man-made fiber textiles and textile products, with annexes. Exchange of notes at Santo Domingo June 11 and September 23, 1992; entered into force September 23, 1992; effective June 1, 1991.
NP

Amendments and extension:
February 16 and March 12, 1993 (NP).
April 13 and August 11, 1994 (NP).

VISAS

Agreement concerning period of validity of and fees for nonimmigrant visas. Exchange of notes at Ciudad Trujillo December 14 and 16, 1955; entered into force February 1, 1956.
7 UST 135; TIAS 3484; 241 UNTS 101.

WEATHER STATIONS

Agreement for the continuation of a cooperative program for meteorological observations. Exchange of notes at Santo Domingo April 7 and 11, 1969; entered into force April 11, 1969; effective July 1, 1968.
20 UST 647; TIAS 6670; 707 UNTS 243.

EAST AFRICAN COMMON SERVICES ORGANIZATION

AGRICULTURAL COMMODITIES

Agricultural commodities agreement between the United States, and Kenya, Tanzania, Uganda, and the East African Common Services Organization with memorandum of understanding. Signed at Dar-es-Salaam February 18, 1966, and at Nairobi February 19 and 22 and March 4, 1966; entered into force March 4, 1966.
17 UST 628; TIAS 6010; 578 UNTS 57.

ECUADOR

AGRICULTURAL COMMODITIES

Agricultural commodities agreement with memorandum of understanding and exchange of notes. Signed at Quito September 27, 1960; entered into force September 27, 1960.
11 UST 2427; TIAS 4626; 401 UNTS 115.

Agricultural commodities agreement with exchanges of notes. Signed at Quito April 3, 1961; entered into force April 3, 1961.
12 UST 671; TIAS 4768; 409 UNTS 139.

Agricultural commodities agreement with exchange of notes. Signed at Quito April 5, 1963; entered into force April 5, 1963.
14 UST 775; TIAS 5356; 477 UNTS 135.

Amendment:
October 6, 1964 (15 UST 1967; TIAS 5673; 531 UNTS 400).

Agricultural commodities agreement, with exchange of notes. Signed at Quito June 25, 1965; entered into force June 25, 1965.
16 UST 960; TIAS 5835; 549 UNTS 23.

Amendment:
October 24, 1966 (17 UST 2275; TIAS 6168; 680 UNTS 400).

Agricultural commodities agreement. Signed at Quito June 30, 1969; entered into force June 30, 1969.
21 UST 1107; TIAS 6867; 745 UNTS 90.

ECUADOR (Cont'd)

Amendments:
September 29 and October 1, 1969 (21 UST 1134; TIAS 6867; 745 UNTS 116).
March 4 and April 6, 1970 (21 UST 1137; TIAS 6867; 745 UNTS 120).
May 18 and June 23, 1972 (23 UST 1216; TIAS 7388; 852 UNTS 307).

Related agreements:
June 30, 1971 (22 UST 1561; TIAS 7179; 806 UNTS 355).
October 7 and November 4, 1971 (22 UST 1757; TIAS 7210).
December 20 and 22, 1971 (22 UST 2071; TIAS 7247).
May 18 and June 23, 1972 (23 UST 1216; TIAS 7388; 852 UNTS 307).
July 31, 1972 (23 UST 2449; TIAS 7436).
January 19, 1973 (24 UST 442; TIAS 7559).

Agricultural commodities agreement. Signed at Quito May 17, 1985; entered into force May 17, 1985.
NP

Amendment:
June 20, 1986 (NP).

AMITY

Treaty of peace, friendship, navigation and commerce.[1] Signed at Quito June 13, 1839; entered into force April 9, 1842.
8 Stat. 534; TS 76; 7 Bevans 296.

NOTE:
[1] Articles with respect to commerce and navigation terminated August 25, 1892.

AVIATION

Agreement relating to transit and technical stop rights for U.S. military planes in Ecuador. Exchange of notes at Quito June 7 and 11, 1946; entered into force June 11, 1946.
3 UST 536; TIAS 2411; 167 UNTS 135.

Commercial air transport services agreement. Signed at Quito January 8, 1947; entered into force April 24, 1947.
61 Stat. 2773; TIAS 1606; 7 Bevans 409; 22 UNTS 119.

Amendment:
January 3 and 10, 1951 (2 UST 482; TIAS 2196; 133 UNTS 312).

Agreement relating to a civil aviation mission to Ecuador. Exchange of notes at Quito October 24 and 27, 1947; entered into force October 27, 1947.
61 Stat. 4013; TIAS 1774; 7 Bevans 422; 44 UNTS 45.

Amendment:
June 30 and October 13, 1949 (7 Bevans 460).

Memorandum of agreement concerning assistance in developing and modernizing Ecuador's civil aviation system. Signed at Washington and Quito October 9 and November 6, 1985; entered into force November 6, 1985.
TIAS 11313.

Memorandum of agreement concerning assistance in developing and modernizing Ecuador's civil aviation infrastructure. Signed at Washington and Quito March 5 and 23, 1998; entered into force March 23, 1998.
TIAS

COMMERCE (See AMITY)

COPYRIGHT (See APPENDIX)

CULTURAL PROPERTY

Agreement for the recovery and return of stolen archaeological, historical and cultural properties. Signed at Washington November 17, 1983; entered into force January 14, 1987.
TIAS 11075.

CUSTOMS

Agreement providing for certain customs courtesies and free entry privileges for consular officers and administrative personnel on a reciprocal basis. Exchange of notes at Quito October 22 and November 6, 1957, and related note of November 11, 1957; entered into force November 6, 1957.
8 UST 2469; TIAS 3967; 307 UNTS 49.

DEFENSE

Agreement for the return of equipment and materials furnished Ecuador under the military assistance agreement. Exchange of notes at Quito June 20 and July 19, 1956; entered into force July 19, 1956.
11 UST 246; TIAS 4439; 372 UNTS 149.

Agreement relating to eligibility for United States military assistance and training pursuant to the International Security Assistance and Arms Export Control Act of 1976. Exchange of notes at Quito August 17 and September 3, 1976; entered into force September 3, 1976.
27 UST 4009; TIAS 8420; 1059 UNTS 143.

General security of military information agreement. Exchange of notes at Quito July 12, 1985; entered into force July 12, 1985.
TIAS 11257.

Agreement regarding the furnishing of defense articles and services on a grant basis to Ecuador from the United States. Exchange of notes at Quito January 30 and March 4, 1992; entered into force March 4, 1992.
TIAS

Agreement regarding the status of United States military personnel and civilian employees of the Department of Defense who may be present in Ecuador in connection with their official duties. Exchange of notes at Quito October 8, 1997; entered into force October 8, 1997.
TIAS

Acquisition and cross-servicing agreement, with annexes. Signed at Manaus October 18, 2000; entered into force October 18, 2000.
TIAS

Agreement concerning joint military training exercises, with attachment. Exchange of notes at Quito October 16 and 31, 2000; entered into force October 31, 2000; effective October 1, 2000.
TIAS

ECONOMIC AND TECHNICAL COOPERATION

General agreement for economic, technical and related assistance. Signed at Quito April 17, 1962; entered into force April 17, 1962.
13 UST 425; TIAS 5003; 442 UNTS 69.

EDUCATION

Agreement for financing certain educational exchange programs. Signed at Quito September 20, 1963; entered into force September 20, 1963.
14 UST 1418; TIAS 5439; 488 UNTS 147.

ENVIRONMENTAL COOPERATION

Agreement for cooperation in the Global Learning and Observations to Benefit the Environment (GLOBE) Program, with appendices. Signed at Quito April 22, 1996; entered into force April 22, 1996.
TIAS

EXTRADITION

Extradition treaty. Signed at Quito June 28, 1872; entered into force November 12, 1873.
18 Stat. 199; TS 79; 7 Bevans 321.

Supplementary extradition treaty. Signed at Quito September 22, 1939; entered into force May 29, 1941.
55 Stat. 1196; TS 972; 7 Bevans 346.

ECUADOR (Cont'd)

FINANCE

Agreement relating to investment guaranties under section 413(b)(4) of the Mutual Security Act of 1954. Exchange of notes at Washington March 28 and 29, 1955; entered into force March 29, 1955.
6 UST 843; TIAS 3230; 261 UNTS 343.

Amendments:
September 4, 1963 (14 UST 1251; TIAS 5426; 488 UNTS 262).
July 9, 1993 (TIAS 12156).

Related agreement:
November 28, 1984 (TIAS 11001).

Agreement regarding the consolidation and rescheduling of debts owed to, guaranteed by or insured by the United States Government and its agencies, with annexes. Signed at Quito March 19, 1984; entered into force May 4, 1984.
TIAS 10966.

Agreement regarding the consolidation and rescheduling of certain debts owed to, guaranteed by or insured by the United States Government and its agencies, with annexes. Signed at Washington January 14, 1986; entered into force March 10, 1986.
NP

Swap agreement between the United States Treasury and the Central Bank of Ecuador/Republic of Ecuador, with related letter. Signed at Washington and Quito December 3, 1987; entered into force December 3, 1987.
TIAS

Agreement regarding the consolidation and rescheduling of certain debts owed to, guaranteed by or insured by the United States Government and its agencies, with annexes. Signed at Quito July 8, 1988; entered into force August 22, 1988.
NP

Agreement regarding the consolidation and rescheduling or refinancing of certain debts owed to, guaranteed by or insured by the United States Government and its agencies, with annexes. Signed at Washington July 30, 1990; entered into force September 12, 1990.
NP

Agreement regarding the consolidation and rescheduling or refinancing of certain debts owed to, guaranteed by, or insured by the United States Government and its agencies, with annexes. Signed at Quito July 30, 1992; entered into force September 11, 1992.
NP

Agreement regarding the consolidation and rescheduling or refinancing of certain debts owed to, guaranteed by or insured by the United States Government and its agencies,

with annexes. Signed at Washington January 19, 1995; entered into force March 1, 1995.
NP

INTELLECTUAL PROPERTY

Agreement concerning the protection and enforcement of intellectual property rights. Signed at Washington October 15, 1993; entered into force October 15, 1993.
TIAS 12679.

Amendment:
July 28, 1995 (TIAS 12679).

INVESTMENT

Treaty concerning the encouragement and reciprocal protection of investment, with protocol. Signed at Washington August 27, 1993; entered into force May 11, 1997.
TIAS

MAPPING

Agreement on mapping, charting and geodesy. Signed at Quito February 29, 1976; entered into force February 29, 1976.
27 UST 1943; TIAS 8290.

Cooperative arrangement for the production of topographic maps of Ecuador, with annexes. Signed at Washington and Quito April 21 and June 12, 1986; entered into force June 12, 1986.
TIAS 11374.

MARITIME MATTERS

Agreement concerning financial arrangements for the furnishing of certain supplies and services to naval vessels of both countries. Signed at Quito July 8, 1955; entered into force October 6, 1955.
6 UST 2959; TIAS 3344; 265 UNTS 49.

NARCOTIC DRUGS

Agreement concerning cooperation in the control of the illicit traffic in narcotic drugs. Exchange of notes at Quito November 5 and 20, 1971; entered into force November 10, 1971.
22 UST 2109; TIAS 7255.

Memorandum of understanding on measures to prevent the diversion of chemical substances. Signed at Quito June 17, 1991; entered into force June 17, 1991.
TIAS 12129.

Agreement for the prevention and control of narcotic related money laundering. Signed at

Quito August 7, 1992; entered into force February 4, 1993.
TIAS 12471.

Agreement to implement the United Nations convention against illicit trafficking in narcotic drugs and psychotropic substances of December 20, 1988, as it relates to the transfer of confiscated property, securities and instrumentalities. Signed at Quito June 27, 1994; entered into force July 15, 1994.
TIAS

Interim agreement concerning the use of facilities in Ecuador to increase aerial detection and control of illegal narcotics trafficking operations. Exchange of notes at Quito March 31 and April 1, 1999; entered into force April 1, 1999.
TIAS

Extension:
September 29, 1999.

Agreement of cooperation concerning United States access to and use of installations at the Ecuadorian Air Force Base in Manta for aerial counter-narcotics activities, with implementing arrangement. Signed at Quito November 12, 1999; entered into force November 17, 1999.
TIAS

OCEANOGRAPHY

Cooperative scientific and technical project for joint oceanographic research. Exchange of notes at Quito March 17, 1983; entered into force March 17, 1983.
TIAS 10674.

PACIFIC SETTLEMENT OF DISPUTES

Arbitration convention. Signed at Washington January 7, 1909; entered into force June 22, 1910.
36 Stat. 2456; TS 549; 7 Bevans 328.

Treaty for the advancement of peace. Signed at Washington October 13, 1914; entered into force January 22, 1916.
39 Stat. 1650; TS 622; 7 Bevans 330.

PEACE CORPS

Agreement relating to the establishment of a Peace Corps program in Ecuador. Exchange of notes at Quito August 3, 1962; entered into force August 3, 1962.
13 UST 1903; TIAS 5145; 460 UNTS 133.

POSTAL MATTERS

Agreement for the exchange of registered and insured parcel post packages. Signed at Quito

ECUADOR (Cont'd)

July 11 and at Washington August 6, 1929; operative July 1, 1929.
46 Stat. 2378; Post Office Department print.

International express mail agreement, with detailed regulations. Signed at Quito and Washington March 20 and April 11, 1990; entered into force March 30, 1990.
TIAS 11900.

Postal money order agreement. Signed at Quito and Washington August 1 and 8, 1990; entered into force October 15, 1990.
TIAS 11741.

PRIVILEGES AND IMMUNITIES

Agreement on immunities and privileges for the United States Inter-American Geodetic Survey mission. Signed at Quito November 23, 1973; entered into force November 23, 1973.
24 UST 2304; TIAS 7755; 938 UNTS 403.

PUBLICATIONS

Agreement relating to the exchange of official publications. Exchange of notes at Quito October 21 and 29, 1947; entered into force October 29, 1947.
61 Stat. 3322; TIAS 1668; 7 Bevans 427; 21 UNTS 21.

RELIEF SUPPLIES AND PACKAGES

Agreement granting duty-free entry, exemption from internal taxation, and free transportation within Ecuador to ultimate beneficiary for certain relief supplies and equipment for American voluntary relief and rehabilitation agencies. Exchange of notes at Quito September 6, 1955; entered into force September 6, 1955.
6 UST 3871; TIAS 3388; 256 UNTS 185.

Amendment:
August 3, 1970 (21 UST 2502; TIAS 6992; 772 UNTS 450).

SCIENTIFIC COOPERATION

Memorandum of understanding concerning scientific and technical cooperation in the earth sciences, with annexes. Signed at Reston and Quito April 3 and July 15, 1997; entered into force July 15, 1997.
TIAS

TELECOMMUNICATION

Agreement relating to radio communications between amateur stations on behalf of third parties. Exchange of notes at Quito March 16 and 17, 1950; entered into force March 17, 1950.
3 UST 2672; TIAS 2433; 177 UNTS 115.

Agreement relating to the reciprocal granting of authorizations to permit licensed amateur radio operators of either country to operate their stations in the other country. Exchange of notes at Quito March 26, 1965; entered into force March 26, 1965.
16 UST 181; TIAS 5779; 542 UNTS 237.

VISAS

Agreement relating to the reciprocal issuance of nonimmigrant visas. Exchange of notes at Quito December 11, 1962 and January 7, 1963; entered into force January 7, 1963; operative February 7, 1963.
14 UST 757; TIAS 5354; 477 UNTS 101.

EGYPT

AGRICULTURAL COMMODITIES

Agricultural commodities agreement with exchanges of notes. Signed at Cairo September 2, 1961; entered into force September 2, 1961.
12 UST 1240; TIAS 4844; 421 UNTS 251.

Amendments:
October 7, 1961 (12 UST 1434; TIAS 4868; 433 UNTS 406).
November 11, 1961 (12 UST 1661; TIAS 4881; 424 UNTS 394).
March 28, 1962 (13 UST 318; TIAS 4982; 445 UNTS 374).

Agricultural commodities agreement with exchange of notes. Signed at Cairo February 10, 1962; entered into force February 10, 1962.
13 UST 121; TIAS 4947; 435 UNTS 107.

Amendments:
April 23, 1962 (13 UST 369; TIAS 4991; 445 UNTS 394).
May 21, 1962 (13 UST 1244; TIAS 5070; 459 UNTS 324).
September 1, 1962 (13 UST 1921; TIAS 5149; 460 UNTS 340).

Agricultural commodities agreement with exchange of notes. Signed at Washington October 8, 1962; entered into force October 8, 1962.
13 UST 2166; TIAS 5179; 462 UNTS 39.

Amendments:
June 15, 1963 (14 UST 1426; TIAS 5440; 488 UNTS 322).
October 7, 1963 (14 UST 1426; TIAS 5440; 488 UNTS 326).

April 20, 1964 (15 UST 527; TIAS 5579; 524 UNTS 330).
June 30, 1964 (15 UST 1437; TIAS 5617; 530 UNTS 386).
July 20, 1964 (15 UST 1676; TIAS 5640; 531 UNTS 396).

Agricultural commodities agreement with exchange of notes. Signed at Cairo January 3, 1966; entered into force January 3, 1966.
17 UST 17; TIAS 5951; 579 UNTS 83.

Agricultural commodities agreement with exchange of notes. Signed at Cairo January 3, 1966; entered into force January 3, 1966.
17 UST 6; TIAS 5950; 579 UNTS 63.

Agricultural commodities agreement. Signed at Cairo June 7, 1974; entered into force June 7, 1974.
25 UST 1245; TIAS 7855.

Amendments:
September 11 and 12, 1974 (25 UST 2482; TIAS 7930).
November 10, 1974 (26 UST 863; TIAS 8070).
April 1, 1975 (26 UST 865; TIAS 8070).
May 2 and 6, 1975 (26 UST 867; TIAS 8070).
June 30, 1975 (26 UST 1915; TIAS 8147; 1021 UNTS 470).
December 30, 1986 (NP).
August 26 and 27, 1987 (NP).

Related agreements:
October 28, 1975 (26 UST 2928; TIAS 8201).
March 6, 1976 (27 UST 1505; TIAS 8259; 1049 UNTS 369).
May 4, 1976 (27 UST 1509; TIAS 8259; 1049 UNTS 371).
June 14, 1976 (27 UST 1512; TIAS 8259; 1049 UNTS 373).
September 28 and 29, 1976 (28 UST 5693; TIAS 8654).
October 26, 1976 (27 UST 3877; TIAS 8406; 1059 UNTS 161).
February 14, 1977 (28 UST 2449; TIAS 8564).
April 18, 1977 (29 UST 332; TIAS 8818).
August 4, 1977 (29 UST 496; TIAS 8828).
December 7, 1977 (29 UST 3856; TIAS 9040; 1124 UNTS 77).
April 20, 1978 (29 UST 3870; TIAS 9040; 1124 UNTS 85).
August 3, 1978 (29 UST 3872; TIAS 9040; 1124 UNTS 85).
November 8, 1978 (30 UST 966; TIAS 9230; 1150 UNTS 337).
March 20, 1979 (30 UST 3974; TIAS 9437; 1171 UNTS 380).
July 10, 1979 (30 UST 3976; TIAS 9437; 1171 UNTS 380).
October 4, 1979 (32 UST 1664; TIAS 9793).
May 22, 1980 (32 UST 1644; TIAS 9793).
June 30, 1980 (33 UST 1033; TIAS 10089; 1279 UNTS 332).
July 31, 1980 (32 UST 1664; TIAS 9793).
August 27, 1980 (32 UST 2347; TIAS 9843).
December 14, 1980 (33 UST 695; TIAS 10060).
April 21, 1981 (33 UST 995; TIAS 10083).
December 21, 1981 (33 UST 4658; TIAS 10328).
February 5, 1982 (33 UST 4658; TIAS 10328).
August 11, 1982 (34 UST 1091; TIAS 10393).
November 23, 1982 (TIAS 10613).

EGYPT (Cont'd)

August 18, 1983 (TIAS 10762).
January 23, 1984 (TIAS 11044).
April 19 and May 3, 1984 (TIAS 11044).
August 2, 1984 (TIAS 11044).
December 16, 1984 (TIAS 11047).
November 12, 1985 (NP).
September 21, 1986 (NP).
December 30, 1986 (NP).
March 21, 1988 (NP).
October 13, 1988 (NP).

Agricultural commodities agreement, with annexes. Signed at Cairo March 20, 1979; entered into force March 20, 1979.
31 UST 5714; TIAS 9683; 1221 UNTS 121.

Amendments:
June 30, 1980 (33 UST 1033; TIAS 10089).
June 28, 1981 (33 UST 1033; TIAS 10089).
May 24, 1982 (TIAS 10427; 1736 UNTS 392).
August 17 and 18, 1983 (TIAS 10763).

Agricultural commodities agreement. Signed at Cairo March 20, 1989; entered into force March 20, 1989.
NP

Amendment:
July 26, 1989 (NP).

Related agreements:
January 28, 1990 (NP).
August 26, 1990 (NP).

ATOMIC ENERGY

Agreement for cooperation concerning peaceful uses of nuclear energy, with annex and agreed minute. Signed at Washington June 29, 1981; entered into force December 29, 1981.
33 UST 2915; TIAS 10208; 1529 UNTS 143.

AVIATION

Agreement relating to the use of Payne Field for international civil air traffic. Exchange of notes at Cairo June 15, 1946; entered into force June 15, 1946.
3 UST 363; TIAS 2397; 151 UNTS 135.

Air transport agreement. Signed at Cairo May 5, 1964; entered into force provisionally May 5, 1964; definitively April 7, 1965.
15 UST 2202; TIAS 5706; 531 UNTS 229.

Agreement concerning assistance in evaluating Egypt's civil aviation infrastructure. Signed at Cairo July 24, 1995; entered into force July 24, 1995.
TIAS

Memorandum of agreement concerning the provision of civil aviation assistance. Signed at Washington and Cairo September 12 and 14, 1997; entered into force September 14, 1997.
TIAS

CANALS

Arrangement relating to assistance by the United States in the salvage and/or removal from the Suez Canal of sunken vessels and certain other hazards to navigation, with annex. Exchange of notes at Cairo June 11, 1974; entered into force June 11, 1974.
25 UST 1273; TIAS 7859.

CLAIMS

Agreement concerning claims of nationals of the United States, with agreed minute and related notes. Signed at Cairo May 1, 1976; entered into force October 27, 1976.
27 UST 4214; TIAS 8446.

Agreement concerning United States Government and other claims, with exchange of notes. Signed at Cairo May 19, 1979; entered into force November 5, 1979.
30 UST 7303; TIAS 9589; 1182 UNTS 51.

COPYRIGHT (See APPENDIX)

CULTURAL RELATIONS

Cultural agreement. Signed at Cairo May 21, 1962; entered into force May 21, 1962.
13 UST 1253; TIAS 5072; 458 UNTS 197.

CUSTOMS

Arrangement providing for reciprocal privileges for consular officers to import articles for their personal use free of duty. Exchange of notes at Washington March 16 and April 7, 1932; entered into force April 7, 1932.
11 Bevans 1337.

DEFENSE

Agreement relating to mutual defense assistance. Exchange of notes at Cairo April 29, 1952; entered into force April 29, 1952.
7 UST 841; TIAS 3564; 241 UNTS 3.

Amendment:
December 9 and 10, 1952 (7 UST 844; TIAS 3565; 241 UNTS 8).

Agreement concerning privileges and immunities of United States military and related personnel in Egypt, with related letter and agreed minute. Exchange of notes at Cairo July 26, 1981; entered into force December 5, 1981.
33 UST 3353; TIAS 10238.

General security of military information agreement. Signed at Cairo February 10, 1982; entered into force February 10, 1982.
34 UST 203; TIAS 10349.

Memorandum of understanding concerning the principles governing scientist and engineer exchange and mutual cooperation in research and development, procurement and logistic support of defense equipment, with annex. Signed at Washington March 23, 1988; entered into force March 23, 1988.
TIAS 11572.

Memorandum of understanding relating to the coproduction of the M1A1 tank in Egypt, with annexes. Signed at Cairo November 1, 1988; entered into force November 1, 1988.
TIAS 12287.

Amendment:
April 11 and August 7, 1989.

Memorandum of understanding concerning a cooperative project for the development of a display subprogram for the E-2C L-304 mission computer. Signed at Washington and Cairo May 6 and 15, 1991; entered into force May 15, 1991.
TIAS 11837.

Agreement for technology research and development projects. Signed at Cairo and Washington February 24 and 27, 1998; entered into force February 27, 1998.
TIAS

ECONOMIC AND TECHNICAL COOPERATION

Economic, technical, and related assistance agreement, with exchanges of notes. Signed at Cairo August 16, 1978; entered into force October 15, 1978.
30 UST 4609; TIAS 9481; 1169 UNTS 271.

Statement relating to greater support to economic progress in Egypt. Released at Washington February 4, 1982; entered into force February 4, 1982.
34 UST 165; TIAS 10346; 1556 UNTS 327.

Agency for International Development:
February 13, 1975 (26 UST 371; TIAS 8039; 992 UNTS 181).
December 18, 1975 (27 UST 4081; TIAS 8427).
May 22, 1976 (28 UST 2956; TIAS 8577).
May 30, 1976 (27 UST 2636; TIAS 8335; 1055 UNTS 57).
May 30, 1976 (27 UST 2649; TIAS 8336; 1055 UNTS 79).
June 30, 1976 (28 UST 1441; TIAS 8517).
July 22, 1976 (28 UST 2969; TIAS 8577).
July 29, 1976 (28 UST 2231; TIAS 8541).
July 29, 1976 (28 UST 2349; TIAS 8548).
July 29, 1976 (28 UST 6971; TIAS 8699).
July 31, 1976 (28 UST 2930; TIAS 8575).
July 31, 1976 (28 UST 6989; TIAS 8700).
July 31, 1976 (28 UST 7017; TIAS 8702).
September 4, 1976 (28 UST 2971; TIAS 8578).
September 30, 1976 (28 UST 2932; TIAS 8575).
September 30, 1976 (28 UST 6197; TIAS 8679).

EGYPT (Cont'd)

September 30, 1976 (28 UST 8419; TIAS 8764).

September 30, 1976 (28 UST 8877; TIAS 8775).

September 30, 1976 (28 UST 8064; TIAS 8741).

January 22, 1977 (29 UST 1039; TIAS 8866).

March 6, 1977 (29 UST 304; TIAS 8815).

March 29, 1977 (29 UST 501; TIAS 8830).

June 2, 1977 (30 UST 6551; TIAS 9567).

July 10, 1977 (30 UST 6565; TIAS 9567).

August 11, 1977 (30 UST 2282; TIAS 9336; 1169 UNTS 11).

August 31, 1977 (30 UST 2288; TIAS 9336; 1169 UNTS 18).

September 20, 1977 (30 UST 2226; TIAS 9330; 1171 UNTS 352).

September 27, 1977 (30 UST 4265; TIAS 9458; 1169 UNTS 31).

September 27, 1977 (30 UST 4462; TIAS 9469; 1169 UNTS 61).

September 28, 1977 (30 UST 2230; TIAS 9331; 1169 UNTS 111).

September 28, 1977 (30 UST 4388; TIAS 9464; 1169 UNTS 93).

September 29, 1977 (30 UST 2258; TIAS 9334; 1169 UNTS 165).

September 29, 1977 (30 UST 2271; TIAS 9335; 1169 UNTS 147).

September 29, 1977 (30 UST 4401; TIAS 9465; 1169 UNTS 185).

September 29, 1977 (30 UST 4424; TIAS 9466; 1169 UNTS 205).

September 29, 1977 (30 UST 4699; TIAS 9486; 1169 UNTS 127).

September 30, 1977 (29 UST 5628; TIAS 9136; 1152 UNTS 453).

September 30, 1977 (29 UST 5631; TIAS 9137; 1152 UNTS 439).

September 30, 1977 (30 UST 2240; TIAS 9332; 1169 UNTS 223).

September 30, 1977 (30 UST 4491; TIAS 9473; 1178 UNTS 75).

December 29, 1977 (29 UST 5621; TIAS 9134).

December 29, 1977 (29 UST 5624; TIAS 9135; 1152 UNTS 443).

February 27, 1978 (30 UST 4577; TIAS 9479; 1169 UNTS 247).

March 7, 1978 (30 UST 4711; TIAS 9486; 1169 UNTS 136).

March 29, 1978 (30 UST 4515; TIAS 9473; 1178 UNTS 84).

March 29, 1978 (30 UST 4569; TIAS 9478).

May 18, 1978 (30 UST 2289; TIAS 9336; 1169 UNTS 19).

June 1, 1978 (30 UST 2891; TIAS 9370; 1177 UNTS 401).

August 15, 1978 (30 UST 2290; TIAS 9336; 1169 UNTS 20).

August 17, 1978 (30 UST 4626; TIAS 9483).

August 28, 1978 (30 UST 6661; TIAS 9575; 1181 UNTS 279).

August 31, 1978 (30 UST 2269; TIAS 9334; 1169 UNTS 174).

August 31, 1978 (30 UST 6059; TIAS 9538).

September 28, 1978 (30 UST 6225; TIAS 9550; 1178 UNTS 157).

September 30, 1978 (30 UST 6338; TIAS 9558; 1178 UNTS 177).

September 30, 1978 (30 UST 6579; TIAS 9569; 1182 UNTS 3).

August 29, 1979 (31 UST 872; TIAS 9624; 1202 UNTS 233).

September 22, 1979 (32 UST 42; TIAS 9699).

October 19, 1979 (32 UST 426; TIAS 9709).

June 30, 1980 (32 UST 1834; TIAS 9802).

June 30, 1980 (32 UST 1857; TIAS 9803).

June 30, 1980 (32 UST 1889; TIAS 9806; 1274 UNTS 131).

September 28, 1980 (32 UST 2696; TIAS 9872; 1274 UNTS 420).

June 28, 1981 (33 UST 2463; TIAS 10191; 1529 UNTS 103).

June 28, 1981 (33 UST 2487; TIAS 10192; 1529 UNTS 123).

August 27, 1981 (33 UST 3718; TIAS 10254).

August 29, 1981 (33 UST 3664; TIAS 10247; 1541 UNTS 438).

September 22, 1981 (33 UST 3981; TIAS 10277).

September 27, 1981 (33 UST 4010; TIAS 10279).

September 27, 1981 (33 UST 4028; TIAS 10280).

September 27, 1981 (33 UST 4052; TIAS 10281).

February 5, 1982 (34 UST 171; TIAS 10347; 1556 UNTS 333).

April 12, 1982 (34 UST 582; TIAS 10377).

August 16, 1982 (TIAS 10471).

August 31, 1982 (TIAS 10473; 1751 UNTS 524).

June 30, 1983 (TIAS 10728).

July 25, 1983 (TIAS 10764).

July 25, 1983 (TIAS 10806).

August 9, 1983 (TIAS 10770).

September 12, 1983.

September 28, 1983.

November 10, 1983 (TIAS 10895).

November 10, 1983.

May 14, 1984 (TIAS 11065).

May 14, 1984 (NP).

July 31, 1984 (NP).

August 8, 1984 (NP).

September 26, 1984 (NP).

March 12, 1985 (NP).

March 12, 1985 (NP).

March 13, 1985 (NP).

March 31, 1985 (NP).

May 13, 1985 (NP).

August 15, 1985 (NP).

September 12, 1985 (NP).

September 12, 1985 (NP).

September 24, 1985 (NP).

September 26, 1985 (NP).

December 31, 1985 (NP).

December 31,1985 (NP).

December 31,1985 (NP).

March 31, 1986 (NP).

June 19, 1986 (NP).

August 21, 1986 (NP).

August 21, 1986 (NP).

August 27, 1986 (NP).

August 28, 1986 (NP).

September 29, 1986 (NP).

September 30, 1986 (NP).

March 8, 1987 (NP).

May 18, 1987 (NP).

June 25, 1987 (NP).

June 25, 1987 (NP).

July 30, 1987 (NP).

September 21, 1987 (NP).

September 21, 1987 (NP).

September 24, 1987 (NP).

February 9, 1988 (NP).

June 22, 1988 (NP).

June 23, 1988 (NP).

September 27, 1988 (NP).

September 30, 1988 (NP).

June 14, 1989 (NP).

June 21, 1989 (NP).

August 17, 1989 (NP).

September 27, 1989 (NP).

July 9, 1990 (NP).

August 21, 1990 (NP).

August 21, 1990 (NP).

August 21, 1990 (NP).

August 31, 1990 (NP).

September 30, 1990 (NP).

September 30, 1990 (NP).

May 30, 1991 (NP).

September 9, 1991 (NP).

September 9, 1991 (NP).

February 12, 1992 (NP).

August 24, 1992 (NP).

September 14, 1992 (NP).

September 13, 1993 (NP).

September 23, 1993 (NP).

September 29, 1994 (NP).

May 18, 1995 (NP).

August 12, 1995 (NP).

September 30, 1995 (NP).

August 25, 1997 (NP).

September 28, 1997 (NP).

September 28, 1997 (NP).

September 29, 1997 (NP).

September 29, 1997 (NP).

September 29, 1997 (NP).

September 29, 1997 (NP).

August 31, 1998 (NP).

August 31, 1998 (NP).

August 31, 1998 (NP).

August 31, 1998 (NP).

September 3, 1998 (NP).

September 6, 1998 (NP).

September 17, 1998 (NP).

September 17, 1998 (NP).

September 17, 1998 (NP).

September 23, 1998 (NP).

September 23, 1998 (NP).

September 23, 1998 (NP).

September 29, 1998 (NP).

September 29, 1998 (NP).

September 30, 1998 (NP).

September 30, 1998 (NP).

EDUCATION

Agreement for financing certain educational exchange programs. Exchange of notes at Cairo January 5 and February 21, 1967; entered into force February 21, 1967.
18 UST 307; TIAS 6234; 688 UNTS 229.

ENVIRONMENTAL COOPERATION

Agreement for cooperation in the Global Learning and Observations to Benefit the Environment (GLOBE) Program, with appendices. Signed at Cairo March 20, 1995; entered into force March 20, 1995.
TIAS 12616.

EGYPT (Cont'd)

EXTRADITION

Convention between the United States and the Ottoman Empire relating to extradition. Signed at Constantinople August 11, 1874; entered into force April 22, 1875.
19 Stat. 572; TS 270; 10 Bevans 642.

FINANCE

Agreement regarding the consolidation and rescheduling of past due debts owed to United States Government agencies with annexes. Signed at Cairo December 6, 1971; entered into force August 28, 1972.
23 UST 1457; TIAS 7424; 852 UNTS 3.

Agreement regarding the consolidation and rescheduling of certain debts owed to, guaranteed by, or insured by the United States Government and its agencies, with annexes and related letter. Signed at Cairo November 14, 1987; entered into force February 22, 1988.
NP

Agreement regarding the reorganization of certain debts owed to, guaranteed by, or insured by the United States Government and its agencies, with annexes. Signed at Washington July 18, 1991; entered into force September 3, 1991.
NP

Investment incentive agreement. Signed at Washington July 1, 1999; entered into force July 1, 1999.
TIAS

GENERAL RELATIONS

Agreement concerning principles of relations and cooperation. Signed at Cairo June 14, 1974; entered into force June 14, 1974.
25 UST 2359; TIAS 7913.

HEALTH

Agreement on cooperation in health, with annex. Signed at Geneva May 9, 1989; entered into force May 9, 1989.
TIAS 12031.

INFORMATIONAL MEDIA GUARANTIES

Agreement relating to an informational media guaranty program. Exchange of notes at Washington March 3 and 7, 1955; entered into force March 7, 1955.
6 UST 691; TIAS 3206; 252 UNTS 159.

INVESTMENT

Treaty concerning the reciprocal encouragement and protection of investments, with annex and protocol. Signed at Washington September 29, 1982; entered into force June 27, 1992.
TIAS

Related agreements:
March 11, 1985.
March 11, 1986.

JUDICIAL ASSISTANCE

Agreement on procedures for mutual assistance in connection with matters relating to the Westinghouse Electric Corporation. Signed at Washington November 29, 1978; entered into force November 29, 1978.
30 UST 3996; TIAS 9441; 1169 UNTS 328.

Related agreements:
December 21, 1978 and January 3, 1979 (30 UST 4005; TIAS 9442; 1169 UNTS 335).
March 19 and April 17, 1979 (30 UST 4007; TIAS 9443; 1169 UNTS 337).

Agreement on procedures for mutual assistance in connection with matters relating to the General Electric Company. Signed at Washington September 17, 1993; entered into force September 17, 1993.
NP

Amendment:
November 18, 1994 (NP).

MAPPING

Mapping, charting and geodesy cooperative and exchange agreement, with annexes. Signed at Washington June 25, 1981; entered into force June 25, 1981.
NP

NARCOTIC DRUGS

Arrangement for the direct exchange of certain information regarding the traffic in narcotic drugs. Exchange of notes at Alexandria June 20, 1930 and Cairo August 26, 1930; entered into force August 26, 1930.
11 Bevans 1331.

Agreement regarding the transfer of forfeited assets. Signed at Cairo May 20, 1993; entered into force May 20, 1993.
TIAS 12499.

NAVIGATION

Agreement for the establishment and operation of an OMEGA navigation system monitoring station. Signed at Alexandria June 14, 1980; entered into force June 14, 1980.
TIAS 12375.

PACIFIC SETTLEMENT OF DISPUTES

Treaty of arbitration. Signed at Washington August 27, 1929; entered into force August 24, 1932.
47 Stat. 2130; TS 850; 11 Bevans 1325; 142 LNTS 323.

Treaty of conciliation. Signed at Washington August 27, 1929; entered into force August 24, 1932.
47 Stat. 2132; TS 851; 11 Bevans 1327; 142 LNTS 317.

PEACEKEEPING

Agreement relating to implementation of the Egyptian-Israeli peace treaty of March 26, 1979.[1] Letter signed at Washington March 26, 1979; entered into force March 26, 1979.
32 UST 2148; TIAS 9827.

Agreement to transfer title of the United States Field Mission base camp at Umm Khusheib from the United States Sinai Support Mission to the Government of the Arab Republic of Egypt. Signed at Umm Khusheib April 22, 1982; entered into force April 22, 1982.
TIAS 10410.

NOTE:
[1] See also MULTINATIONAL FORCE AND OBSERVERS in bilateral section and PEACEKEEPING in multilateral section.

POSTAL MATTERS

Agreement for the exchange of international money orders. Signed at Cairo October 6, 1958 and at Washington October 31, 1958; entered into force July 1, 1959.
10 UST 1351; TIAS 4279; 355 UNTS 355.

Agreement concerning the exchange of parcel post and regulations of execution. Signed at Cairo December 30, 1958 and at Washington January 13, 1959; entered into force October 1, 1959.
10 UST 1664; TIAS 4315; 358 UNTS 3.

International express mail agreement with detailed regulations. Signed at Cairo and Washington December 3 and 22, 1983; entered into force February 1, 1984.
TIAS 10854.

Memorandum of understanding concerning the operation of the INTELPOST field trial, with details of implementation. Signed at Cairo and Washington August 18 and September 13, 1985; entered into force September 13, 1985.
TIAS 11157.

EGYPT (Cont'd)

RELIEF SUPPLIES AND PACKAGES

Agreement relating to duty-free entry and defrayment of inland transportation charges on relief supplies and packages. Exchange of notes at Cairo October 30, 1954; entered into force October 30, 1954.
5 UST 2551; TIAS 3119; 234 UNTS 139.

TAXATION

Convention for the avoidance of double taxation and the prevention of fiscal evasion with respect to taxes on income.[1] Signed at Cairo August 24, 1980; entered into force December 31, 1981.
33 UST 1809; TIAS 10149; 1529 UNTS 41.

NOTE:
[1] With an understanding and a reservation.

TOURISM

Agreement on the development and facilitation of tourism. Signed at Cairo February 21, 1983; entered into force August 16, 1983.
TIAS 10680.

TRADE AND COMMERCE

Provisional commercial agreement relating to most-favored-nation treatment in customs matters. Exchange of notes at Cairo May 24, 1930; entered into force May 24, 1930.
47 Stat. 2582; EAS 5; 11 Bevans 1329; 117 LNTS 419.

Agreement relating to trade in textiles and textile products. Exchange of notes at Cairo December 7 and 28, 1977; entered into force December 28, 1977; effective January 1, 1978.
29 UST 2774; TIAS 8973.

Amendments and extension:
June 21 and 25, 1984 (NP).
March 7 and 14, 1988 (NP).
January 16 and February 26, 1990 (NP).
March 15 and June 9, 1992 (NP).

VISAS

Agreement providing for the abolition of non-immigrant visa fees. Exchange of notes at Cairo June 3 and August 1, 1963; entered into force August 1, 1963; operative September 1, 1963.
14 UST 1191; TIAS 5416; 488 UNTS 189.

EL SALVADOR

AGRICULTURAL COMMODITIES

Agricultural commodities agreement, with exchange of notes. Signed at San Salvador August 21, 1961; entered into force August 21, 1961.
12 UST 1210; TIAS 4838; 418 UNTS 35.

Agricultural commodity agreement. Signed at Washington May 7, 1963; entered into force May 7, 1963.
14 UST 418; TIAS 5335; 476 UNTS 35.

Amendments:
June 16, 1981 (TIAS 11050).
June 19, 1981 (TIAS 11050).
August 31 and September 2, 1981 (TIAS 11050).

Related agreements:
September 1, 1982 (TIAS 11051).
May 18, 1983 (TIAS 11052).
August 6, 1983 (TIAS 11052).
July 13, 1984 (TIAS 11053).
August 20, 1984 (TIAS 11053).
January 29, 1985 (NP).
August 8, 1985 (NP).

Amendment:
June 27, 1986 (NP).

Amendment:
September 29, 1987 (NP).

Agricultural commodities agreement. Signed at San Salvador March 10, 1988; entered into force September 11, 1988.
NP

Amendments:
July 20, 1988 (NP).
September 7, 1988 (NP).

Related agreements:
July 20, 1989 (NP).

Agricultural commodities agreement. Signed at San Salvador January 19, 1990; entered into force March 6, 1990.
NP

Amendment:
August 2, 1990 (NP).

Agricultural commodities agreement. Signed at San Salvador December 12, 1990; entered into force May 24, 1991.
NP

AGRICULTURE

Agreement confirming the cooperative agreement for the prevention of foot-and-mouth disease and rinderpest in El Salvador. Exchange of notes at San Salvador February 28 and March 2, 1973; entered into force March 2, 1973.
24 UST 1931; TIAS 7701.

AVIATION

Air transport agreement, with annexes. Signed at San Jose May 8, 1997; entered into force January 3, 2000.
TIAS

COPYRIGHT (See APPENDIX)

CULTURAL PROPERTY

Memorandum of understanding concerning the imposition of import restrictions on certain categories of archaeological material from the prehispanic cultures of the Republic of El Salvador, with appendix. Signed at Washington March 8, 1995; entered into force March 8, 1995.
TIAS 12609.

Amendment and extension:
March 7, 2000.

CUSTOMS

Agreement granting reciprocal customs privileges for Foreign Service personnel. Exchange of notes at Washington March 18 and May 9, 1958; entered into force May 9, 1958.
9 UST 617; TIAS 4043; 316 UNTS 29.

DEFENSE

Agreement relating to the furnishing of defense articles and services to El Salvador for the purpose of contributing to its internal security. Exchange of notes at San Salvador April 10 and 13, 1962; entered into force April 13, 1962.
13 UST 985; TIAS 5040; 451 UNTS 307.

Agreement relating to the deposit by El Salvador of ten percent of the value of grant military assistance and excess defense articles furnished by the United States. Exchange of notes at San Salvador April 25 and June 15, 1972; entered into force June 15, 1972; effective February 1, 1972.
23 UST 1331; TIAS 7416.

Agreement concerning payment to the United States of net proceeds from the sale of defense articles furnished under the military assistance program. Exchange of notes at San Salvador October 24 and December 6, 1974; entered into force December 6, 1974; effective July 1, 1974.
25 UST 3155; TIAS 7979.

EL SALVADOR (Cont'd)

ECONOMIC AND TECHNICAL COOPERATION

General agreement for economic, technical and related assistance. Signed at San Salvador December 19, 1961; entered into force January 16, 1962.
13 UST 266; TIAS 4971; 445 UNTS 175.

Agreement concerning the establishment of an Americas Fund and Administering Commission. Signed at Washington June 18, 1993; entered into force July 5, 1994.
TIAS

Agency for International Development:
August 28, 1987 (NP).
February 1, 1988 (NP).
June 30, 1988 (NP).

EMPLOYMENT

Agreement relating to employment of dependents of official government employees. Exchange of notes at San Salvador January 19 and March 11, 1983; entered into force March 11, 1983.
TIAS 12380.

EXTRADITION

Treaty of extradition. Signed at San Salvador April 18, 1911; entered into force July 10, 1911.
37 Stat. 1516; TS 560; 7 Bevans 507.

FINANCE

Agreement relating to the guaranty of private investments. Signed at San Salvador January 29, 1960; entered into force April 8, 1960.
11 UST 405; TIAS 4459; 372 UNTS 3.

Agreement regarding the consolidation and rescheduling or refinancing of certain debts owed to, guaranteed by, or insured by the United States Government and its agencies, with annexes. Signed at Washington November 13, 1990; entered into force January 4, 1991.
NP

Agreement regarding the reduction of certain debts related to agriculture owed to the Government of the United States and its agencies, with appendices. Signed at San Salvador December 15, 1992; entered into force January 14, 1993.
NP

Agreement regarding the reduction of certain debts related to foreign assistance owed to the Government of the United States and its agencies, with appendices. Signed at San Salvador December 15, 1992; entered into force January 14, 1993.
NP

HIGHWAYS

Agreement relating to the construction of the inter-American highway. Exchange of notes at Washington January 30 and February 13, 1942; entered into force February 13, 1942.
56 Stat. 1842; EAS 294; 7 Bevans 558; 23 UNTS 293.

Amendment:
February 19 and March 19, 1951 (2 UST 1840; TIAS 2318; 134 UNTS 245).

LABOR

Arrangement relating to workmen's compensation and unemployment insurance for American citizens employed on projects in El Salvador. Exchange of notes at San Salvador September 24, 28, and 29, 1943; entered into force September 29, 1943.
7 Bevans 586.

MAPPING

Basic exchange and cooperative agreement for topographic mapping, nautical and aeronautical charting and information, geodesy and geophysics, digital data and related mapping, charting and geodesy materials, with glossary. Signed at Delgado (San Salvador) and Fairfax May 10 and 22, 1996; entered into force May 22, 1996.
NP

MISSIONS, MILITARY

Agreement providing for a United States Army mission to El Salvador. Signed at San Salvador September 23, 1954; entered into force November 17, 1954.
5 UST 2870; TIAS 3144; 237 UNTS 91.

Extensions and amendments:
March 16 and 31, 1959 (10 UST 730; TIAS 4206; 342 UNTS 351).
March 27 and May 3, 1963 (14 UST 484; TIAS 5345; 476 UNTS 333).

Air Force mission agreement. Signed at San Salvador November 21, 1957; entered into force November 21, 1957.
8 UST 2356; TIAS 3951; 303 UNTS 19.

Extension and amendments:
March 16 and 31, 1959 (10 UST 730; TIAS 4206; 342 UNTS 361).
January 15 and 22, 1960 (11 UST 76; TIAS 4410; 371 UNTS 324).

NARCOTIC DRUGS

Agreement of cooperation concerning United States access to and use of facilities at the International Airport of El Salvador for aerial counter-narcotics activities. Signed at San Salvador March 31, 2000; entered into force August 23, 2000.
TIAS

PEACE CORPS

Agreement relating to the establishment of a Peace Corps program in El Salvador. Exchange of notes at San Salvador August 11, November 13 and 20, 1961; entered into force November 13, 1961.
12 UST 2983; TIAS 4899; 433 UNTS 221.

POSTAL MATTERS

International express mail agreement, with detailed regulations. Signed at San Salvador and Washington August 29 and October 6, 1989; entered into force October 30, 1989.
TIAS 11689.

Postal money order agreement. Signed at Mexico August 16, 1991; entered into force October 1, 1991.
TIAS 11800.

PUBLICATIONS

Agreement relating to the exchange of official publications. Exchange of notes at San Salvador November 21 and 27, 1941; entered into force November 27, 1941.
55 Stat. 1478; EAS 230; 7 Bevans 551; 120 UNTS 161.

SCIENTIFIC COOPERATION

Memorandum of understanding covering cooperative investigations in earthquake research. Signed at Reston and San Salvador April 16 and 24, 1984; entered into force April 24, 1984.
TIAS 11183.

TAXATION

Agreement concerning relief from double taxation on income derived from operation of aircraft. Exchange of notes at San Salvador December 17, 1987; entered into force December 17, 1987.
TIAS 11557.

EL SALVADOR (Cont'd)

TELECOMMUNICATION

Arrangement relating to radio communications between amateur stations on behalf of third parties. Exchange of notes at San Salvador April 5, 1962; entered into force May 5, 1962.
13 UST 411; TIAS 5001; 442 UNTS 41.

Agreement relating to the granting of authorizations to permit licensed amateur radio operators of either country to operate their stations in the other country. Exchange of notes at San Salvador May 24 and June 5, 1967; entered into force June 5, 1967.
18 UST 1661; TIAS 6309; 692 UNTS 221.

TRADE AND COMMERCE

Convention facilitating the work of traveling salesmen. Signed at Washington January 28, 1919; entered into force January 18, 1921.
41 Stat. 1725; TS 651; 7 Bevans 514.

Trade agreement. Signed at San Salvador February 19, 1937; entered into force May 31, 1937.
50 Stat. 1564; EAS 101; 7 Bevans 536; 179 LNTS 219.

Agreement terminating certain provisions of the reciprocal trade agreement of February 19, 1937. Exchange of notes at San Salvador June 29, 1962; entered into force June 29, 1962.
13 UST 1358; TIAS 5095.

Agreement relating to trade in cotton textiles. Exchange of notes at San Salvador March 2 and April 30, 1987; entered into force April 30, 1987.
NP

Amendments and extension:
November 23, 1988 and April 26, 1989 (NP).
December 18 and 27, 1989 (NP).

VISAS

Agreement providing for the reciprocal abolishment of certain visa fees and tourist and immigration charges. Exchange of notes at San Salvador December 7 and 15, 1953; entered into force January 14, 1954.
5 UST 859; TIAS 2977; 236 UNTS 25.

EQUATORIAL GUINEA

COPYRIGHT (See APPENDIX)

DEFENSE

Agreement concerning the provision of training related to defense articles under the United States International Military Education and Training (IMET) Program. Exchange of notes at Malabo March 9 and 30, 1983; entered into force March 30, 1983.
TIAS 10891.

FINANCE

Investment incentive agreement. Signed at Washington June 11, 1998; entered into force June 11, 1998.
TIAS

PEACE CORPS

Agreement relating to the establishment of a Peace Corps program in Equatorial Guinea. Exchange of notes at Malabo November 18, 1987; entered into force November 18, 1987.
TIAS

POSTAL MATTERS

International express mail agreement, with detailed regulations. Signed at Malabo and Washington April 9 and May 21, 1991; entered into force July 1, 1991.
TIAS 11810.

ERITREA

For agreements prior to the independence of Eritrea, see ETHIOPIA.

DEFENSE

Agreement concerning the provision of training under the United States International Military Education and Training (IMET) Program. Exchange of notes at Asmara December 28 and 31, 1993; entered into force December 31, 1993.
NP

Agreement regarding grants under the Foreign Assistance Act of 1961, as amended, and the furnishing of defense articles, related training and other services from the United States to Eritrea. Exchange of notes at Asmara August 31 and September 30, 1995; entered into force September 30, 1995.
TIAS

FINANCE

Investment incentive agreement. Signed at Washington May 4, 1994; entered into force July 7, 1994.
TIAS 12179.

PEACE CORPS

Agreement relating to the establishment of a Peace Corps Program in Eritrea. Exchange of notes at Asmara May 20, 1994; entered into force May 20, 1994.
TIAS 12103.

POSTAL MATTERS

International express mail agreement, with detailed regulations. Signed at Asmara and Washington July 4 and 18, 1994; entered into force November 1, 1994.
NP

ESTONIA

COMMERCE

Treaty of friendship, commerce, and consular rights, and protocol. Signed at Washington December 23, 1925; entered into force May 22, 1926.
44 Stat. 2379; TS 736; 7 Bevans 620; 50 LNTS 13.

CONSULS (See COMMERCE)

COPYRIGHT (See APPENDIX)

DEFENSE

Agreement concerning the provision of training related to defense articles under the United States International Military, Education and Training (IMET) Program. Exchange of notes at Tallinn May 18 and 25, 1992; entered into force May 25, 1992.
NP

Agreement regarding grants under the Foreign Assistance Act of 1961, as amended, and the furnishing of defense articles, related training or other defense services from the United States to the Republic of Estonia. Exchange of

ESTONIA (Cont'd)

notes at Tallinn February 11 and 12, 1993; entered into force February 12, 1993.
TIAS 12288.

Acquisition and cross-servicing agreement, with annex. Signed at Tallinn and Stuttgart September 9 and October 21, 1998; entered into force October 21, 1998.
TIAS

Agreement concerning security measures for the protection of classified military information. Signed at Tallinn February 23, 2000; entered into force February 23, 2000.
TIAS

DIPLOMATIC RELATIONS

Memorandum of understanding concerning diplomatic relations. Signed at Tallinn September 4, 1991; entered into force September 4, 1991.
TIAS 12131.

EMPLOYMENT

Agreement concerning the employment on a reciprocal basis of dependents of official government employees. Exchange of notes at Tallinn September 25 and October 20, 2000; entered into force November 22, 2000.
TIAS

EXTRADITION

Treaty for extradition of fugitives from justice. Signed at Tallinn November 8, 1923; entered into force November 15, 1924.
43 Stat. 1849; TS 703; 7 Bevans 602; 43 LNTS 277.

Supplementary extradition treaty. Signed at Washington October 10, 1934; entered into force May 7, 1935.
49 Stat. 3190; TS 888; 7 Bevans 645; 159 LNTS 149.

FINANCE

Debt funding agreement. Signed at Washington October 28, 1925; operative December 15, 1922.
Treasury Department print; 7 Bevans 613.

Agreement modifying the debt funding agreement of October 28, 1925. Signed at Washington June 11, 1932; operative July 1, 1931.
Treasury Department print; 7 Bevans 642.

Investment incentive agreement. Signed at Indianapolis October 28, 1991; entered into force October 28, 1991.
TIAS 12099.

FISHERIES

Agreement concerning fisheries off the coasts of the United States, with annex. Signed at Washington June 1, 1992; entered into force December 22, 1992.
TIAS

INVESTMENT

Treaty for the encouragement and reciprocal protection of investment, with annex. Signed at Washington April 19, 1994; entered into force February 16, 1997.
TIAS

JUDICIAL ASSISTANCE

Treaty on mutual legal assistance in criminal matters. Signed at Washington April 2, 1998; entered into force October 20, 2000.
TIAS

MAPPING

Basic exchange and cooperative agreement for topographic mapping, nautical and aeronautical charting, geodesy and geophysics, digital data and related mapping, charting and geodesy materials. Signed at Tallinn December 7, 1993; entered into force December 7, 1993.
NP

MARITIME MATTERS

Agreement relating to mutual recognition of ship measurement certificates. Exchange of notes at Washington August 21, 1926 and at New York November 30, 1926; entered into force November 30, 1926.
47 Stat. 2597; EAS 9; 7 Bevans 635; 62 LNTS 313.

NORTH ATLANTIC TREATY

Agreement to treat the agreement of June 19, 1995, among the States Parties to the North Atlantic Treaty and other States participating in the Partnership for Peace regarding the status of their forces as binding between the United States and Estonia. Exchange of notes at Tallinn July 14 and 18, 1995; entered into force July 18, 1995.
TIAS

PACIFIC SETTLEMENT OF DISPUTES

Treaty of arbitration. Signed at Tallinn August 27, 1929; entered into force June 18, 1930.
46 Stat. 2757; TS 816; 7 Bevans 637; 102 LNTS 233.

Treaty of conciliation. Signed at Tallinn August 27, 1929; entered into force June 18, 1930.
46 Stat. 2760; TS 817; 7 Bevans 639; 102 LNTS 239.

PEACE CORPS

Agreement concerning the program of the Peace Corps of the United States in Estonia. Signed at Tallinn February 6, 1992; entered into force February 6, 1992.
TIAS

POSTAL MATTERS

International express mail agreement, with detailed regulations. Signed at Tallinn and Washington December 31, 1991 and February 10, 1992; entered into force March 7, 1992.
TIAS 11852.

Postal money order agreement. Signed at Tallinn and Washington March 9 and 22, 1993; entered into force June 1, 1993.
TIAS 11920.

PUBLICATIONS

Agreement relating to the exchange of official publications. Exchange of notes at Tallinn December 6, 1938; entered into force July 15, 1939.
53 Stat. 2059; EAS 138; 7 Bevans 647.

TAXATION

Convention for the avoidance of double taxation and the prevention of fiscal evasion with respect to taxes on income. Signed at Washington January 25, 1998; entered into force December 30, 1999.
TIAS

TRADE (See also COMMERCE)

Agreement according mutual unconditional most-favored-nation treatment in customs matters. Exchange of notes at Washington March 2, 1925; entered into force August 1, 1925.
TS 722; 7 Bevans 608; 43 LNTS 289.

ETHIOPIA

Eritrea announced its independence from Ethiopia April 27, 1993.

The status of the agreements listed below is under review.

AGRICULTURAL COMMODITIES

Agricultural commodities agreement, with exchange of notes. Signed at Addis Ababa August 13, 1962; entered into force August 13, 1962.
13 UST 1833; TIAS 5132; 459 UNTS 31.

Agricultural commodities agreement, with exchange of notes. Signed at Addis Ababa June 11, 1963; entered into force June 11, 1963.
14 UST 836; TIAS 5363; 487 UNTS 269.

Agricultural commodities agreement, with exchange of notes. Signed at Addis Ababa August 17, 1965; entered into force August 17, 1965.
16 UST 1119; TIAS 5854; 564 UNTS 119.

Agricultural commodities agreement with exchange of notes. Signed at Addis Ababa December 14, 1965; entered into force December 14, 1965.
16 UST 2019; TIAS 5937; 574 UNTS 115.

Agricultural commodities agreement. Signed at Addis Ababa June 15, 1976; entered into force June 15, 1976.
28 UST 7344; TIAS 8715.

AVIATION

Agreement on civil aviation safety and security. Exchange of notes at Addis Ababa May 29 and June 2, 1998; entered into force June 2, 1998.
TIAS

CLAIMS

Compensation agreement, with agreed minutes. Signed at Addis Ababa December 19, 1985; entered into force December 19, 1985.
TIAS 11193.

COMMERCE

Treaty of amity and economic relations, and related notes. Signed at Addis Ababa September 7, 1951; entered into force October 8, 1953.
4 UST 2134; TIAS 2864; 206 UNTS 41.

Agreement amending the treaty of amity and economic relations of September 7, 1951, to terminate notes concerning administration of justice. Exchange of notes at Addis Ababa September 16, 1965 and October 20, 1972; entered into force May 3, 1973.
24 UST 2136; TIAS 7726.

CONSULS (See COMMERCE)

DEFENSE

Agreement relating to mutual defense assistance. Exchange of notes at Addis Ababa June 12 and 13, 1952; entered into force June 13, 1952.
3 UST 5498; TIAS 2751; 205 UNTS 17.

Agreement relating to a special program of facilities assistance. Exchange of notes at Addis Ababa December 26, 1957; entered into force December 26, 1957.
8 UST 2483; TIAS 3969; 307 UNTS 71.

Agreement relating to the disposition of equipment and materials no longer needed in the furtherance of the mutual defense assistance program. Exchange of notes at Addis Ababa January 2 and 6, 1958; entered into force January 6, 1958.
9 UST 339; TIAS 4013; 303 UNTS 342.

Agreement concerning payment to the United States of net proceeds from the sale of defense articles furnished under the military assistance program. Exchange of notes at Addis Ababa May 13 and June 26, 1974; entered into force July 1, 1974.
25 UST 1437; TIAS 7872.

Agreement regarding the status of U.S. military personnel and civilian employees of the Department of Defense present in Ethiopia. Exchange of notes at Addis Ababa May 27 and 31, 1994; entered into force May 31, 1994.
NP

Agreement regarding the furnishing of commodities, services and related training to assist Ethiopia's forces participating in the African Crisis Response Initiative, with attachment. Exchange of notes at Addis Ababa February 2 and 6, 1998; entered into force February 6, 1998.
TIAS

ECONOMIC AND TECHNICAL COOPERATION

Agreement for economic and technical cooperation. Signed at Addis Ababa November 15, 1993; entered into force November 15, 1993.
TIAS 12167.

EDUCATION

Agreement for financing certain educational programs, with exchange of notes. Signed at Addis Ababa December 6, 1961; entered into force December 6, 1961.
12 UST 3057; TIAS 4905; 433 UNTS 231.

EMPLOYMENT

Agreement relating to the employment of dependents of official government employees. Exchange of notes at Addis Ababa August 31 and September 2, 1999; entered into force September 2, 1999.
TIAS

FINANCE

Agreement relating to investment guaranties. Exchange of notes at Addis Ababa August 3, 1962; entered into force August 3, 1962.
13 UST 1856; TIAS 5134; 459 UNTS 79.

Amendment:
March 17, 1967 and March 8, 1968 (19 UST 4725; TIAS 6469; 697 UNTS 280).

Agreement regarding the consolidation and rescheduling or refinancing of certain debts owed to, guaranteed by or insured by the United States Government and its agencies, with annexes. Signed at Washington May 3, 1993; entered into force June 18, 1993.
NP

Agreement regarding the consolidation and rescheduling of certain debts owed to the United States Government and its Agency, with annexes. Signed at Addis Ababa October 9, 1997; entered into force December 3, 1997.
NP

LEND-LEASE

Agreement on the principles applying to mutual aid in the prosecution of the war against aggression, and exchange of notes. Signed at Washington August 9, 1943; entered into force August 9, 1943.
57 Stat. 1043; EAS 334; 7 Bevans 668; 29 UNTS 303.

Agreement on lend-lease settlement. Signed at Addis Ababa May 20, 1949; entered into force May 20, 1949.
63 Stat. 2446; TIAS 1931; 7 Bevans 678; 89 UNTS 99.

ETHIOPIA (Cont'd)

PACIFIC SETTLEMENT OF DISPUTES

Treaty of arbitration. Signed at Addis Ababa January 26, 1929; entered into force August 5, 1929.
46 Stat. 2357; TS 799; 7 Bevans 662; 101 LNTS 517.

Treaty of conciliation. Signed at Addis Ababa January 26, 1929; entered into force August 5, 1929.
46 Stat. 2368; TS 800; 7 Bevans 665; 101 LNTS 529.

PEACE CORPS

Agreement relating to the establishment of a Peace Corps program in Ethiopia. Exchange of notes at Addis Ababa May 23, 1962; entered into force May 23, 1962.
13 UST 1227; TIAS 5067; 456 UNTS 293.

POSTAL MATTERS

Parcel post agreement, with regulations of execution. Signed at Addis Ababa and Washington June 3 and 15, 1967; entered into force September 1, 1967.
18 UST 1622; TIAS 6305; 692 UNTS 263.

International express mail agreement, with detailed regulations. Signed at Addis Ababa and Washington August 3 and September 1, 1989; entered into force September 15, 1989.
TIAS 11954.

Memorandum of understanding concerning the operation of the INTELPOST service, with details of implementation. Signed at Addis Ababa and Washington March 26 and July 16, 1990; entered into force August 15, 1990.
TIAS 11955.

PUBLICATIONS

Agreement relating to the exchange of official publications. Exchange of notes at Addis Ababa November 25, 1964; entered into force November 25, 1964.
15 UST 2150; TIAS 5698; 532 UNTS 125.

TAXATION

Agreement to exempt from income tax, on a reciprocal basis, income derived from the international operation of aircraft and ships. Exchange of notes at Addis Ababa October 30 and November 12, 1998; entered into force November 12, 1998; effective January 1, 1998.
TIAS

EUROPEAN ATOMIC ENERGY COMMUNITY (EURATOM)

ATOMIC ENERGY

Agreement in the field of nuclear material safeguards research and development, with annex. Signed at Brussels January 28, 1982; entered into force January 28, 1982.
34 UST 49; TIAS 10338.

Agreement for exchange of information concerning a cooperative program in the field of management of radioactive wastes. Signed at Brussels October 6, 1982; entered into force October 6, 1982.
TIAS 10521; 1777 UNTS 375.

Extension:
May 29, 1987 and February 23, 1988 (TIAS 11570).

Arrangement in the field of nuclear safety research, with addenda. Signed at Brussels September 20, 1984; entered into force September 20, 1984.
TIAS 11116.

Memorandum of understanding concerning research on the health and environmental effects of radiation, with annex. Signed at Brussels July 7, 1986; entered into force July 7, 1986.
TIAS 12146.

Agreement for cooperation in the field of controlled thermonuclear fusion. Signed at Brussels December 15, 1986; entered into force December 15, 1986.
TIAS 11412.

Agreement in the field of nuclear material safeguards research and development, with annexes. Signed at Brussels and Washington January 6, 1995; entered into force January 6, 1995.
TIAS 12596.

Agreement for cooperation in the peaceful uses of nuclear energy, with annexes, agreed minute and declaration. Signed at Brussels November 7, 1995 and March 29, 1996; entered into force April 12, 1996.
TIAS

Technical exchange and cooperation arrangement in the field of nuclear safety research, with annexes. Signed at Rockville October 29, 1999; entered into force October 29, 1999.
TIAS

EUROPEAN COMMUNITY

ATOMIC ENERGY

Technical exchange arrangement on severe accident research related to molten fuel-coolant interactions, with annex. Signed at Rockville

and Rome March 3 and 23, 1995; entered into force March 23, 1995.
TIAS

COPYRIGHT (See APPENDIX)

CUSTOMS

Agreement on customs cooperation and mutual assistance in customs matters. Done at The Hague May 28, 1997; entered into force August 1, 1997.
TIAS

LIQUOR

Agreement on the mutual recognition of certain distilled spirits/spirit drinks, with related exchange of letters. Exchange of letters at Brussels and Washington March 15 and 25, 1994; entered into force March 25, 1994.
TIAS

METROLOGY

Implementing arrangement for cooperation in the fields of metrology and measurement standards. Signed at Brussels October 5, 1999; entered into force October 5, 1999.
TIAS

NARCOTIC DRUGS

Agreement on precursors and chemical substances frequently used in the illicit manufacture of narcotic drugs or psychotropic substances, with annexes and exchange of letters. Signed at The Hague May 28, 1997; entered into force July 1, 1997.
TIAS

SCIENTIFIC COOPERATION

Agreement for scientific and technological cooperation, with annex. Signed at Washington December 5, 1997; entered into force October 14, 1998.
TIAS

TRADE AND COMMERCE

Joint declaration on commercial relations. Signed at Geneva March 7, 1962; entered into force March 7, 1962.
13 UST 958; TIAS 5033; 445 UNTS 195.

Agreement suspending the agreements of March 7, 1962 (TIAS 5034 and 5035), relating to quality wheat and other grains. Exchange of

EUROPEAN COMMUNITY (Cont'd)

notes at Geneva June 30, 1967; entered into force January 5, 1968; effective July 1, 1967. 20 UST 2864; TIAS 6761; 723 UNTS 411.

Agreement regulating certain trade in cheese. Exchange of letters at Brussels December 20, 1974 and January 14, 1975; entered into force January 14, 1975. 26 UST 1773; TIAS 8135; 1006 UNTS 85.

Agreement within the context of the multilateral trade negotiations regarding trade in certain agricultural products, and related letter of October 28, 1980. Done at Geneva April 12, 1979; entered into force January 1, 1980. 32 UST 5309; TIAS 9982; 1265 UNTS 249.

Agreement within the context of the multilateral trade negotiations concerning tariff concessions for table grapes, and related letter of October 28, 1980. Letter signed at Brussels July 27, 1979; entered into force January 1, 1980. 32 UST 5322; TIAS 9983; 1265 UNTS 281.

Agreement within the context of the multilateral trade negotiations concerning beer containers and beer, and related letter of October 28, 1980. Signed October 31, 1979; entered into force January 1, 1980. 32 UST 5328; TIAS 9984; 1265 UNTS 265.

Agreement relating to certain chemicals in United States schedule XX to the general agreement on tariffs and trade. Signed December 21, 1979; entered into force December 21, 1979. 32 UST 5332; TIAS 9985; 1265 UNTS 269.

Agreement relating to staging of a chemical concession in United States schedule XX to the general agreement on tariffs and trade. Signed at Brussels December 27, 1979; entered into force December 27, 1979. 32 UST 5335; TIAS 9986; 1265 UNTS 273.

Agreement relating to modification of United States schedule XX to the general agreement on tariffs and trade, pursuant to article XXVIII. Signed January 2, 1980; entered into force January 2, 1980. 32 UST 5337; TIAS 9987; 1265 UNTS 277.

Agreement for the conclusion of negotiations under GATT article XXIV:6, with annexes and related letter. Signed at Washington and Brussels January 30, 1987; entered into force January 30, 1987. TIAS

Agreement concerning exports of pasta, with settlement, annex and related letter. Exchange of letters at Brussels and Washington August 12 and September 15, 1987; entered into force September 15, 1987. TIAS

Agreement on steel trade liberalization, with appendices. Exchange of letters at Washington

and Brussels November 20, 1989; entered into force November 20, 1989. TIAS

Agreement regarding the application of competition laws. Signed at Washington September 23, 1991; entered into force September 23, 1991. TIAS

Agreement concerning the application of the GATT agreement on trade in civil aircraft of April 12, 1979 on trade in large civil aircraft, with annexes. Signed at Washington and Brussels July 17, 1992; entered into force July 17, 1992. TIAS

Agreement for the conclusion of negotiations between the European Community and the United States under Article XXIV:6, with annexes and exchanges of letters. Signed at Geneva July 22, 1996; entered into force July 22, 1996; effective December 30, 1995. TIAS

Agreement on mutual recognition, with annexes. Signed at London May 18, 1998; entered into force December 1, 1998. TIAS

Agreement on the application of positive comity principles in the enforcement of their competition laws. Signed at Brussels and Washington June 3 and 4, 1998; entered into force June 4, 1998. TIAS

Agreement on sanitary measures to protect public and animal health in trade in live animals and animal products. Signed at Brussels July 20, 1999; entered into force August 1, 1999. TIAS

EUROPEAN ORGANIZATION FOR THE EXPLOITATION OF METEOROLOGICAL SATELLITES (EUMETSAT)

SATELLITES

Agreement on an initial joint polar-orbiting operational satellite system, with annex. Signed at Washington November 19, 1998; entered into force November 19, 1998. TIAS

Agreement on access to images and meteorological data distribution material from the EUMETSAT geostationary meteorological satellites. Signed at Darmstadt July 19, 2000; entered into force July 19, 2000. TIAS

EUROPEAN ORGANIZATION FOR NUCLEAR RESEARCH (CERN)

ATOMIC ENERGY

Agreement concerning scientific and technical cooperation on Large Hadron Collider activities. Signed at Washington December 8, 1997; entered into force December 8, 1997. TIAS

Experiments Protocol relating to the agreement of December 8, 1997, concerning scientific and technical cooperation on Large Hadron Collider activities. Signed at Geneva December 19, 1997; entered into force December 19, 1997. TIAS

Accelerator Protocol relating to the agreement of December 8, 1997, concerning scientific and technical cooperation on Large Hadron Collider activities. Signed at Geneva December 19, 1997; entered into force December 19, 1997. TIAS

EUROPEAN SPACE AGENCY

SPACE COOPERATION

Memorandum of understanding for a cooperative program concerning design (Phase B) of a permanently manned space station. Signed at Paris June 3, 1985; entered into force June 3, 1985. TIAS 11351.

Memorandum of understanding concerning the Solar Terrestrial Science Program, with related exchange of letters. Signed at Washington November 30, 1989; entered into force November 30, 1989. TIAS 12216.

Memorandum of understanding concerning space shuttle flight activities in the launch and retrieval of the European Retrieval Carrier Spacecraft. Signed at Paris October 3, 1991; entered into force October 3, 1991. TIAS 12217.

Memorandum of understanding enabling early utilization opportunities of the international space station. Signed at Washington and Paris March 11 and 18, 1997; entered into force March 18, 1997. TIAS

FIJI

On October 10, 1970 Fiji became an independent state. In a note dated October 10, 1970 to the Secretary-General of the United Nations, the Prime Minister of Fiji made a statement reading in part as follows: "[M]any treaty rights and obligations of the Government of the United Kingdom in respect to Fiji were succeeded to by Fiji upon independence by virtue of customary international law. . . . It is desired that it be presumed that each treaty has been legally succeeded to by Fiji and that action be based on this presumption until a decision is reached that it should be regarded as having lapsed. Should the Government of Fiji be of the opinion that it has legally succeeded to a treaty, and wishes to terminate the operation of the treaty, it will in due course give notice of termination in the terms thereof."

AVIATION

Air transport agreement. Signed at Suva October 1, 1979; entered into force provisionally October 1, 1979; definitively October 11, 1979.
32 UST 3747; TIAS 9917.

Amendments:
October 25, 1985 (TIAS 11143).
July 10 and August 19, 1996.

CONSULS

Consular convention between the United States and the United Kingdom. Signed at Washington June 6, 1951; entered into force September 7, 1952.
3 UST 3426; TIAS 2494; 165 UNTS 121.

Agreement continuing in force between the United States and Fiji the consular convention of June 6, 1951 (3 UST 3426) between the United States and the United Kingdom. Exchange of notes at Suva and Washington October 16 and December 12, 1972; entered into force December 12, 1972.
23 UST 3770; TIAS 7525.

COPYRIGHT (See APPENDIX)

DEFENSE

Agreement concerning the provision of training related to defense articles under the United States International Military Education and Training (IMET) Program. Exchange of notes at Suva November 18, 1985 and February 14, 1986; entered into force February 14, 1986.
TIAS 11105.

Acquisition and cross-servicing agreement, with annexes. Signed at Suva April 14, 1998; entered into force April 14, 1998.
TIAS

ENVIRONMENTAL COOPERATION

Agreement for cooperation in the Global Learning and Observations to Benefit the Environment (GLOBE) Program, with appendices. Signed at Suva January 28, 1997; entered into force January 28, 1997.
TIAS

EXTRADITION

Extradition treaty between the United States and the United Kingdom. Signed at London December 22, 1931; entered into force June 24, 1935.
47 Stat. 2122; TS 849; 12 Bevans 482; 163 LNTS 59.

Agreement continuing in force between the United States and Fiji the extradition treaty of December 22, 1931 (47 Stat. 2122) between the United States and the United Kingdom. Exchange of notes at Suva and Washington July 14, 1972 and August 17, 1973; entered into force August 17, 1973.
24 UST 1965; TIAS 7707.

FINANCE

Agreement relating to investment guaranties. Exchange of notes at Suva December 30, 1975 and January 9, 1976; entered into force January 9, 1976.
27 UST 1826; TIAS 8281.

PEACE CORPS

Agreement relating to the establishment of a Peace Corps program in Fiji. Exchange of notes at Suva June 25, 1968; entered into force June 25, 1968.
19 UST 5208; TIAS 6515; 648 UNTS 65.

Agreement continuing in force the agreement of June 25, 1968 relating to the establishment of a Peace Corps program in Fiji. Exchange of notes at Suva and Washington April 25 and June 27, 1972; entered into force June 27, 1972.
23 UST 1156; TIAS 7377.

POSTAL MATTERS

Parcel post agreement, with detailed regulations of execution. Signed at Washington November 15, 1938, and at Suva January 10, 1939; operative January 2, 1939.
53 Stat. 2031; Post Office Department print; 196 LNTS 185.

Agreement providing for parcel post insurance. Signed at Suva April 12 and at Washington April 22, 1965; entered into force July 1, 1965.
16 UST 850; TIAS 5822; 685 UNTS 23.

International express mail agreement, with detailed regulations. Signed at Suva and Washington September 13 and October 10, 1991; entered into force November 16, 1991.
TIAS 11791.

PROPERTY

Convention between the United States and the United Kingdom relating to tenure and disposition of real and personal property. Signed at Washington March 2, 1899; entered into force August 7, 1900; applicable to Fiji February 9, 1901.
31 Stat. 1939; TS 146; 12 Bevans 246.

Supplementary convention relating to the tenure and disposition of real and personal property of March 2, 1899. Signed at Washington May 27, 1936; entered into force March 10, 1941.
55 Stat. 1101; TS 964; 5 Bevans 140; 203 LNTS 367.

Agreement continuing in force between the United States and Fiji the conventions of March 2, 1899 and May 27, 1936 between the United States and the United Kingdom relating to tenure and disposition of real and personal property. Exchange of notes at Suva and at Washington November 2 and December 9, 1971; entered into force December 9, 1971.
22 UST 1806; TIAS 7222.

TAXATION

Agreement for the reciprocal exemption with respect to taxes on income from the international operation of ships and aircraft. Exchange of notes at Suva June 19 and August 12, 1996; entered into force August 12, 1996; effective January 1, 1996.
TIAS

TELECOMMUNICATION

Agreement relating to the reciprocal granting of authorizations to permit licensed amateur radio operators of either country to operate their stations in the other country. Exchange of notes at London November 26, 1965; entered into force November 26, 1965; applicable to Fiji December 11, 1969.
16 UST 2047; TIAS 5941; 561 UNTS 193.

Agreement extending to certain territories the application of the agreement of November 26, 1965 relating to the reciprocal granting of au-

FIJI (Cont'd)

thorizations to permit licensed amateur radio operators of either country to operate their stations in the other country. Exchange of notes at London December 11, 1969; entered into force December 11, 1969.
20 UST 4089; TIAS 6800; 732 UNTS 334.

Agreement continuing in force between the United States and Fiji the agreement of November 25, 1965 between the United States and the United Kingdom relating to the reciprocal granting of authorizations to permit licensed amateur radio operators of either country to operate their stations in the other country. Exchange of notes at Suva and Washington July 10 and August 14, 1972; entered into force August 14, 1972.
23 UST 1334; TIAS 7417.

TRADE AND COMMERCE

Agreement concerning trade in cotton and man-made fiber textiles and textile products, with annexes. Exchange of notes at Suva May 24 and August 20, 1991; entered into force August 20, 1991; effective January 1, 1990.
NP

Agreement concerning trade in textiles and textile products, with annexes. Exchange of notes at Suva August 27, 1993 and February 18, 1994; entered into force February 18, 1994; effective January 1, 1993.
NP

Amendments and extensions:
October 11 and November 10, 1994 (NP).
October 26 and December 29, 1995 (NP).

TRADE-MARKS

Declaration affording reciprocal protection to trade-marks. Signed at London October 24, 1877; entered into force October 24, 1877.
20 Stat. 703; TS 138; 12 Bevans 198.

Agreement continuing in force between the United States and Fiji the declaration affording reciprocal protection to trademarks of October 24, 1877 (20 Stat. 703) by the United States and the United Kingdom. Exchange of notes at Suva and at Washington August 30 and November 4, 1971; entered into force November 4, 1971.
22 UST 1891; TIAS 7232.

FINLAND

ATOMIC ENERGY

Agreement for cooperation concerning peaceful uses of nuclear energy, with annexes and

agreed minute. Signed at Washington May 2, 1985; entered into force March 27, 1992.
TIAS 12384; 1678 UNTS 127.

Arrangement for the exchange of technical information and cooperation in nuclear safety matters. Signed at Vienna September 25, 1985; entered into force September 25, 1985.
TIAS 11121.

Agreement relating to participation in the USNRC program of severe accident research, with addendum. Signed at Rockville and Espoo July 6 and August 5, 1994; entered into force August 5, 1994; effective January 1, 1994.
TIAS

Arrangement for the exchange of technical information and cooperation in nuclear safety matters, with addenda. Signed at Washington April 9, 1996; entered into force April 9, 1996.
TIAS

Agreement relating to participation in the USNRC Program of severe accident research, with addendum. Signed at Rockville and Espoo October 29 and November 12, 1998; entered into force November 12, 1998.
TIAS

AVIATION

Air transport agreement. Signed at Helsinki March 29, 1949; entered into force April 28, 1949.
63 Stat. 2550; TIAS 1945; 7 Bevans 752; 55 UNTS 59.

Amendment:
June 9, 1995 (TIAS 12657).

Related agreement:
May 12, 1980 (32 UST 2368; TIAS 9845).

Agreement relating to the reciprocal acceptance of certificates of airworthiness for imported civil glider aircraft and civil aircraft appliances. Exchange of notes at Washington March 7, 1974; entered into force March 7, 1974.
25 UST 262; TIAS 7795; 944 UNTS 165.

COMMERCE

Treaty of friendship, commerce, and consular rights, and protocol. Signed at Washington February 13, 1934; entered into force August 10, 1934.
49 Stat. 2659; TS 868; 7 Bevans 718; 152 LNTS 45.

Protocol modifying article IV of the treaty of friendship, commerce, and consular rights of February 13, 1934. Signed at Washington December 4, 1952; entered into force September 24, 1953.
4 UST 2047; TIAS 2861; 205 UNTS 149.

Protocol to the treaty of friendship, commerce and consular rights of February 13, 1934, as

modified. Signed at Washington July 1, 1991; entered into force December 1, 1992.
TIAS

CONSULS (See COMMERCE)

COPYRIGHT (See APPENDIX)

CUSTOMS

Agreement regarding mutual assistance in customs matters. Signed at Washington January 5, 1988; entered into force July 13, 1989.
TIAS 12116.

DEFENSE

General security of military information agreement, with exchange of letters. Exchange of notes at Helsinki October 11, 1991; entered into force October 11, 1991.
TIAS 12238; 1676 UNTS 193.

Agreement concerning exchange of research and development information, with appendix. Signed at Washington and Helsinki September 11 and October 5, 1995; entered into force October 5, 1995.
TIAS 12289.

Acquisition and cross-servicing agreement, with annex. Signed at Helsinki and Stuttgart June 25 and July 25, 1998; entered into force July 25, 1998.
TIAS

EDUCATION

Agreement for financing certain educational exchange programs. Signed at Helsinki July 2, 1952; entered into force July 2, 1952.
3 UST 4126; TIAS 2555; 165 UNTS 203.

Amendments:
November 30, 1956 (7 UST 3255; TIAS 3704; 263 UNTS 418).
May 30, 1959 (10 UST 1043; TIAS 4241; 346 UNTS 334).
November 14, 1960 (11 UST 2351; TIAS 4614; 400 UNTS 382).
October 29, 1975 (26 UST 2898; TIAS 8196).

EMPLOYMENT

Agreement relating to the employment of dependents of official government employees. Exchange of notes at Helsinki March 1 and 12, 1996; entered into force April 11, 1996.
TIAS

FINLAND (Cont'd)

ENERGY

Memorandum of understanding for cooperation in energy research and development. Signed at Washington November 6, 1980; entered into force November 6, 1980.
32 UST 4143; TIAS 9932; 1267 UNTS 23.

Extension:
January 3, 1986 (TIAS 12124).

Memorandum of understanding for cooperation in energy research and development. Signed at Washington October 23, 1990; entered into force October 23, 1990.
TIAS 12125.

ENVIRONMENTAL COOPERATION

Agreement for cooperation in the Global Learning and Observations to Benefit the Environment (GLOBE) Program, with appendices. Signed at Helsinki March 23, 1995; entered into force March 23, 1995.
TIAS 12621.

EXTRADITION

Extradition treaty. Signed at Helsinki June 11, 1976; entered into force May 11, 1980.
31 UST 944; TIAS 9626; 1203 UNTS 165.

FINANCE

Debt funding agreement. Signed at Washington May 1, 1923; operative December 15, 1922.
Treasury Department print; 7 Bevans 689.

Agreement modifying the debt funding agreement of May 1, 1923. Signed at Washington May 23, 1932; operative July 1, 1931.
Treasury Department print; 7 Bevans 716.

Agreement relating to investment guaranties under section 413(b)(4) of the Mutual Security Act of 1954, as amended. Exchange of notes at Helsinki July 22, 1959; entered into force July 22, 1959.
10 UST 1317; TIAS 4275; 354 UNTS 39.

MAPPING

Basic exchange and cooperative agreement concerning geospatial information and services cooperation. Signed at Helsinki August 30, 2000; entered into force August 30, 2000.
NP

NATIONALITY

Convention regulating military obligations of persons having dual nationality. Signed at Helsinki January 27, 1939; entered into force October 3, 1939.
54 Stat. 1712; TS 953; 7 Bevans 747; 201 LNTS 197.

PACIFIC SETTLEMENT OF DISPUTES

Treaty of arbitration. Signed at Washington June 7, 1928; entered into force January 14, 1929.
45 Stat. 2724; TS 768; 7 Bevans 711; 87 LNTS 9.

Treaty of conciliation. Signed at Washington June 7, 1928; entered into force January 14, 1929.
45 Stat. 2726; TS 769; 7 Bevans 713; 87 LNTS 15.

POSTAL MATTERS

Money order convention. Signed at Washington March 17 and at Helsingfors June 26, 1924; operative October 1, 1924.
NP

Parcel post convention. Signed at Helsingfors September 1 and at Washington September 23, 1932; operative August 1, 1932.
47 Stat. 2169; Post Office Department print.

International express mail agreement, with detailed regulations. Signed at Washington November 19, 1984; entered into force February 7, 1985.
TIAS 11010.

Memorandum of understanding concerning the operation of the INTELPOST field trial, with details of implementation. Signed at Helsinki and Washington August 23 and September 23, 1985; entered into force September 23, 1985.
TIAS 11158.

PUBLICATIONS

Agreement relating to the exchange of official publications. Exchange of notes at Washington December 28 and 30, 1938; entered into force December 30, 1938; operative January 1, 1939.
53 Stat. 2071; EAS 139; 7 Bevans 744; 195 LNTS 419.

SCIENTIFIC COOPERATION

Memorandum of understanding on cooperation in the fields of mining, mineral processing, materials science and related environmental

technology. Signed at Washington June 3, 1993; entered into force June 3, 1993.
TIAS 12153.

Agreement relating to scientific and technological cooperation, with annexes. Signed at Washington May 16, 1995; entered into force August 27, 1995.
TIAS 12647; 1890 UNTS 195.

Memorandum of understanding concerning scientific and technical cooperation in the earth sciences. Signed at Reston and Espoo March 30 and May 3, 2000; entered into force May 3, 2000.
TIAS

SHIPPING

Agreement relating to jurisdiction over vessels utilizing the Louisiana Offshore Oil Port. Exchange of notes at Washington December 1, 1982; entered into force December 1, 1982.
TIAS 10615.

SOCIAL SECURITY

Agreement on social security, with administrative arrangement. Signed at Helsinki June 3, 1991; entered into force November 1, 1992.
TIAS 12105; 1705 UNTS 153.

TAXATION

Convention for the avoidance of double taxation and the prevention of fiscal evasion with respect to taxes on estates and inheritances. Signed at Washington March 3, 1952; entered into force December 18, 1952.
3 UST 4464; TIAS 2595; 177 UNTS 141.

Agreement for relief from double taxation on earnings from operation of ships and aircraft. Exchange of notes at Helsinki April 8 and 22, 1988; entered into force April 22, 1988.
TIAS 11576.

Convention for the avoidance of double taxation and the prevention of fiscal evasion with respect to taxes on income and on capital.[1] Signed at Helsinki September 21, 1989; entered into force December 30, 1990.
TIAS 12101.

NOTE:
[1] With an understanding.

TELECOMMUNICATION

Agreement relating to the reciprocal granting of authorizations to permit licensed amateur radio operators of either country to operate their stations in the other country. Exchange of notes at Helsinki December 15 and 27, 1967; entered into force December 27, 1967.
18 UST 3153; TIAS 6406; 697 UNTS 55.

FINLAND (Cont'd)

TRADE (See also COMMERCE)

Letter and arrangement within the context of the multilateral trade negotiations concerning cheeses, and related letter of January 30, 1980. Done at Geneva April 12, 1979; entered into force January 1, 1980.
32 UST 5340; TIAS 9988; 1267 UNTS 3.

Agreement relating to article XII of the general agreement on tariffs and trade, and related letter of January 30, 1980. Letter signed at Geneva April 12, 1979; entered into force March 13, 1980.
32 UST 5348; TIAS 9989; 1267 UNTS 19.

Agreement within the context of the multilateral trade negotiations regarding alcoholic beverages, and related letter of January 30, 1980. Letters signed at Geneva and Washington April 12 and December 4, 1979; entered into force March 13, 1980.
32 UST 5351; TIAS 9990; 1267 UNTS 13.

Agreement on removal of trade distorting practices in steel, with appendix and related exchange of letters. Exchange of letters at Washington and Helsinki February 28 and March 23, 1990; entered into force March 23, 1990.
TIAS   ; 1591 UNTS 427.

TRANSPORTATION

Memorandum of understanding concerning cooperation in the field of transportation. Signed at Washington July 23, 1981; entered into force July 23, 1981.
33 UST 3258; TIAS 10222.

Project agreement for cooperation in the field of icebreaking technology. Signed at Washington July 23, 1981; entered into force July 23, 1981.
33 UST 3261; TIAS 10223.

Extension:
May 9 and June 13, 1983 (TIAS 10731; 1607 UNTS 540).

Memorandum of understanding on highway transportation technology exchange. Signed at Madrid May 19, 1993; entered into force May 19, 1993.
TIAS 12498.

VISAS

Agreement relating to the maximum validity of visas for four years and the abolition of visa fees for certain classes of nonimmigrant visas. Exchange of notes at Helsinki July 7, August 26 and December 14, 1955; entered into force December 14, 1955; operative January 1, 1956.
9 UST 1175; TIAS 4102; 335 UNTS 263.

Amendment:
February 15 and 20, 1956 (9 UST 1179; TIAS 4102; 335 UNTS 272).

Agreement relating to the waiver of visa requirements for nonimmigrants. Exchange of notes at Washington August 15, 1958; entered into force August 15, 1958, operative September 15, 1958.
9 UST 1183; TIAS 4103; 314 UNTS 43.

FOOD AND AGRICULTURE ORGANIZATION

ECONOMIC AND TECHNICAL COOPERATION

Agreement relating to a Fund-in-Trust grant to the FAO to supplement activities under the Off-Shore Fishery Development Project for Viet-Nam. Exchange of notes at Washington and Rome May 26, 1967; entered into force May 26, 1967.
18 UST 1618; TIAS 6304.

PEACE CORPS

Agreement concerning the Peace Corps. Exchange of notes at Rome March 23 and 29, 1962; entered into force March 29, 1962.
13 UST 1391; TIAS 5101; 454 UNTS 13.

FORMER YUGOSLAV REPUBLIC OF MACEDONIA

For agreements prior to the independence of the Former Yugoslav Republic of Macedonia, see YUGOSLAVIA.

COPYRIGHT (See APPENDIX)

DEFENSE

Acquisition and cross-servicing agreement, with attachment. Exchange of notes at Skopje July 27 and September 23, 1998; entered into force September 23, 1998.
TIAS

EMPLOYMENT

Agreement concerning the reciprocal employment of dependents of official government employees, with attachment. Exchange of notes at Washington December 10, 1998; entered into force December 10, 1998.
TIAS

FINANCE

Investment incentive agreement, with attachment. Exchange of notes at Skopje April 5, 1996; entered into force April 5, 1996.
TIAS

Agreement on the consolidation of the debt of the borrower, with attachment. Exchange of letters at Skopje September 17, 1997; entered into force December 3, 1997.
NP

NORTH ATLANTIC TREATY

Agreement to treat as binding the agreement of June 19, 1995, among the States Parties to the North Atlantic Treaty and the other States participating in the Partnership for Peace regarding the status of their forces between the United States and Macedonia. Exchange of notes at Skopje June 3, 1996; entered into force June 3, 1996.
TIAS

SCIENTIFIC COOPERATION

Agreement on scientific and technical cooperation, with attachment. Exchange of notes at Skopje October 10, 1995; entered into force October 10, 1995.
TIAS

TRADE

Agreement and visa arrangement relating to trade in cotton, wool, man-made fiber, non-cotton vegetable fiber and silk-blend textiles and textile products, with attachment. Exchange of notes at Skopje November 7, 1997; entered into force November 7, 1997.
NP

FRANCE

AGRICULTURE

Memorandum of understanding on cooperation in agricultural science and technology. Signed at Washington March 15, 1982; entered into force March 15, 1982.
TIAS 10508; 1777 UNTS 323.

Extension:
March 3, 1987 (TIAS 11522).

FRANCE (Cont'd)

ATOMIC ENERGY

Agreement for cooperation on uses of atomic energy for mutual defense purposes. Signed at Washington May 7, 1959; entered into force July 20, 1959.
10 UST 1279; TIAS 4268; 354 UNTS 83.

Agreement for cooperation in the operation of atomic weapons systems for mutual defense purposes. Signed at Paris July 27, 1961; entered into force October 9, 1961.
12 UST 1423; TIAS 4867; 433 UNTS 29.

Amendment:
July 22, 1985 (TIAS 11208).

Agreement in the field of liquid metal-cooled fast breeder reactors, with related letters. Signed at Paris January 18, 1977; entered into force January 18, 1977.
29 UST 605; TIAS 8839.

Agreement concerning the retransfer of nuclear power light water reactor technology, with annexes and exchange of notes. Signed at Washington January 22, 1981; entered into force March 13, 1981.
33 UST 968; TIAS 10080.

Technical exchange and cooperation arrangement in the field of fast breeder reactor safety research, with appendix. Signed at Paris and Washington June 7 and 21, 1983; entered into force June 21, 1983.
TIAS 10741.

Technical exchange and cooperation arrangement in the field of safety of radioactive waste management. Signed at Washington and Paris January 3 and 10, 1984; entered into force January 10, 1984.
TIAS 10918.

Agreement in the field of (energy) remote systems technology, with appendix. Signed at Paris September 13, 1985; entered into force September 13, 1985.
TIAS 11532.

Technical exchange and cooperation arrangement in the field of light water reactor safety research, with appendices. Signed at Paris and Washington November 28 and December 31, 1986; entered into force December 31, 1986.
TIAS 11523.

Agreement regarding participation in the USNRC international piping integrity research group, with appendices. Signed at Fontenay-aux-Roses and Bethesda February 20 and March 5, 1987; entered into force March 5, 1987.
TIAS 12220.

Agreement for the exchange of technical information and cooperation in the regulation of nuclear safety, with patent addendum. Signed at

Paris September 4, 1990; entered into force September 4, 1990.
TIAS

Agreement concerning cooperation on the application of non-proliferation assurances to material, nuclear material, equipment and facilities transferred from France to Taiwan for use in Taiwan's nuclear research and light water nuclear power reactor programs, with annex and related exchanges of notes. Exchange of notes at Washington January 19, 1993; entered into force January 19, 1993.
TIAS

Technical exchange and cooperation arrangement in the field of light water reactor safety research, with appendices and annex. Signed at Rockville and Fontenay-aux-Roses April 25 and May 22, 1995; entered into force May 22, 1995.
TIAS 12654.

AVIATION

Agreement relating to air service facilities in French territory. Exchange of notes at Paris June 18, 1946; entered into force June 18, 1946.
61 Stat. 4088; TIAS 1852; 7 Bevans 1172; 42 UNTS 183.

Amendment:
May 8 and 17, 1947 (61 Stat. 4095; TIAS 1853; 7 Bevans 1208; 42 UNTS 194).

Agreement relating to the reciprocal acceptance of airworthiness certifications. Exchange of notes at Paris August 29 and September 26, 1973; entered into force September 26, 1973.
24 UST 2142; TIAS 7728.

Agreement relating to cooperation with respect to research and development activities in the field of civil aviation. Signed at Washington and Paris July 10, 1980; entered into force July 10, 1980.
32 UST 2873; TIAS 9881; 1274 UNTS 201.

Agreement for promotion of aviation safety. Signed at Paris May 14, 1996; entered into force May 14, 1996.
TIAS

Air transport agreement, with annexes. Signed at Washington June 18, 1998; entered into force June 18, 1998.
TIAS

Amendment:
October 10, 2000.

NOTES:
[1] Applicable to all territories.

[2] A compromis of arbitration was signed at Paris January 22, 1963 (14 UST 120; TIAS 5280; 473 UNTS 3). The arbitral decision was rendered December 22, 1963 (16 *R. Int'l Arb. Awards* 11, 3 *Int'l Legal Materials* 668 (1964)). A decision interpreting this award was rendered June 28, 1964. Another compromis of arbitration concerning a different dispute was signed at Washington July 11, 1978 (30 UST 1659; TIAS 9274). The arbitral decision was rendered December 9, 1978.

CLAIMS (See also LEND-LEASE)

Agreement relating to the procedure for the settlement of claims of French nationals who were prisoners of war of United States forces during World War II. Exchange of notes at Paris June 4, October 15 and December 6, 1951; and January 17 and February 2, 1952; entered into force February 2, 1952.
5 UST 622; TIAS 2951; 247 UNTS 223.

COMMERCE

Convention of navigation and commerce, with separate article.[1] Signed at Washington June 24, 1822; entered into force February 12, 1823; operative October 1, 1822.
8 Stat. 278; TS 87; 7 Bevans 822.

Agreement modifying the provisions of article VII of the convention of navigation and commerce of June 24, 1822. Signed at Washington July 17, 1919; entered into force January 10, 1921.
41 Stat. 1723; TS 650; 7 Bevans 899.

Convention of establishment, protocol, and declaration.[2] Signed at Paris November 25, 1959; entered into force December 21, 1960.
11 UST 2398; TIAS 4625; 401 UNTS 75.

NOTES:
[1] Article VI terminated by the United States July 1, 1916 in accordance with the Seamen's Act (38 Stat. 1164).
[2] Applicable to Martinique, Guadeloupe, French Guiana and Reunion.

CONSULS

Consular convention, with protocol and exchange of notes. Signed at Paris July 18, 1966; entered into force January 7, 1968.
18 UST 2939; TIAS 6389; 700 UNTS 257.

COPYRIGHT (See APPENDIX)

CULTURAL RELATIONS

Agreement to establish an artist fellowship exchange program. Signed at Washington No-

FRANCE (Cont'd)

vember 30, 1984; entered into force November 30, 1984.
TIAS 11189.

CUSTOMS

Agreement relating to the suppression of customs frauds. Exchange of notes at Paris December 10 and 12, 1936; entered into force December 12, 1936; operative December 15, 1936.
50 Stat. 1468; EAS 99; 7 Bevans 1014; 176 LNTS 403.

Agreement for cooperation with respect to the operation of distribution license systems. Exchange of notes at Paris September 5, 1986; entered into force September 5, 1986.
TIAS 12389.

DEFENSE (See also MUTUAL SECURITY)

Mutual defense assistance agreement. Signed at Washington January 27, 1950; entered into force January 27, 1950.
1 UST 34; TIAS 2012; 80 UNTS 171.

Agreement regarding the establishment of an air depot at Deols-La Martinerie. Signed at Paris February 27, 1951; entered into force February 27, 1951.
17 UST 1865; TIAS 6130; 674 UNTS 55.

Agreement regarding certain air bases and facilities in Metropolitan France placed at the disposition of the United States Air Force. Signed at Paris October 4, 1952; entered into force October 4, 1952.
17 UST 1873; TIAS 6131; 674 UNTS 65.

Agreement relating to the transfer to Paris of the headquarters of the Deputy Commander of the Allied Forces in Europe. Exchange of notes at Paris June 17, 1953; entered into force June 17, 1953.
17 UST 1906; TIAS 6134; 674 UNTS 83.

Agreement relating to the disposition of equipment and material no longer required in the furtherance of the mutual defense assistance program, and related notes. Exchange of notes at Paris September 23, 1955; entered into force September 23, 1955.
6 UST 5971; TIAS 3440; 270 UNTS 341.

Memorandum of understanding relating to sales to France of military equipment, materials, and services under the mutual defense assistance agreement of January 27, 1950, and exchange of letters. Signed at Washington January 30, 1958; entered into force January 30, 1958.
9 UST 71; TIAS 3980; 304 UNTS 349.

Agreement for the transfer of special tools to France under the mutual defense assistance agreement of January 27, 1950. Exchange of notes at Paris October 28, 1958; entered into force October 28, 1958.
9 UST 1450; TIAS 4140; 337 UNTS 397.

Agreement concerning system of communications and depots. Signed at Paris December 8, 1958; entered into force December 8, 1958.
17 UST 1890; TIAS 6132; 674 UNTS 99.

Agreement relating to a weapons production program. Exchange of notes at Paris September 19, 1960; entered into force September 19, 1960.
11 UST 2333; TIAS 4611; 400 UNTS 21.

Memorandum of understanding relating to military procurement, with an exchange of letters. Signed at Washington December 20, 1961; entered into force December 20, 1961.
12 UST 3132; TIAS 4914; 433 UNTS 340.

Agreement regarding the operation, maintenance and security of the Donges-Metz pipeline system, with protocol and exchange of letters. Signed at Paris March 24, 1967; entered into force April 1, 1967.
18 UST 352; TIAS 6242; 688 UNTS 357.

Memorandum of understanding relating to a cooperative research project in titanium alloys, with annex. Signed at Washington and Paris June 23 and August 26, 1977; entered into force August 26, 1977.
TIAS 12290.

General security of information agreement. Signed at Paris September 7, 1977; entered into force September 7, 1977.
29 UST 1985; TIAS 8914.

Memorandum of understanding regarding the exchange of scientists and engineers. Signed at Paris and Washington January 24 and February 14, 1985; entered into force February 14, 1985.
TIAS 11160.

Memorandum of agreement concerning the use of Diane Range, Solenzara, Corsica. Signed at Paris March 27, 1986; entered into force March 27, 1986.
TIAS 11402.

Agreement on mutual logistic support, with annexes. Signed at Casteau February 23, 1987; entered into force February 23, 1987.
TIAS 12293.

Amendments:
October 15, 1987 (TIAS 12293).
August 19 and September 11, 1991 (TIAS 12293).

Memorandum of understanding for a cooperative deep submergence rescue system program, with annexes. Signed at Washington and Paris January 27 and February 21, 1989; entered into force February 21, 1989.
TIAS 12291.

Memorandum of agreement concerning a cooperative program of information exchange and development of cooperative research projects on free electron laser technology. Signed at Paris January 31, 1990; entered into force January 31, 1990.
TIAS 12292.

Agreement concerning air defense simulation. Signed at Washington and Paris January 13 and July 19, 1993; entered into force July 19, 1993.
TIAS 12294.

Agreement concerning technology research and development projects, with annex. Signed at Paris and Washington December 9, 1993 and January 10, 1994; entered into force January 10, 1994.
TIAS 12295.

Agreement regarding the exchange of scientists and engineers, with annexes. Signed at Washington and Paris January 14 and 28, 1994; entered into force January 28, 1994.
NP

Agreement regarding the continuous processing of composite propellants, with annexes. Signed at Paris and Washington April 5 and May 16, 1994; entered into force May 16, 1994.
TIAS 12316.

Agreement for cooperative research in the field of helicopter aeromechanics, with annex. Signed at Paris October 27, 1994; entered into force October 27, 1994.
TIAS 12528.

Agreement concerning cooperation on the image/information reformatter for reconnaissance system interoperability, with annex. Signed at Paris and Washington January 18 and 30, 1995; entered into force January 30, 1995.
TIAS 12318.

Agreement for the adaptation and testing of a dry/low emissions upgrade for the intercooled recuperated (ICR) gas turbine engine, with annexes. Signed at Washington and Paris June 13 and August 30, 1995; entered into force August 30, 1995.
TIAS 12687.

Amendment:
July 11 and September 22, 2000.

ECONOMIC AND TECHNICAL COOPERATION (See also INDUSTRIAL COOPERATION)

Economic cooperation agreement.[1] Signed at Paris June 28, 1948; entered into force July 10, 1948.
62 Stat. 2223; TIAS 1783; 7 Bevans 1257; 19 UNTS 9.

Amendments:
September 21 and October 8, 1948 (62 Stat. 3720; TIAS 1897; 7 Bevans 1278; 34 UNTS 418).
November 17 and 20, 1948 (62 Stat. 3720; TIAS 1897; 7 Bevans 1288; 34 UNTS 421).

FRANCE (Cont'd)

January 9, 1950 (1 UST 151; TIAS 2023; 79 UNTS 270).
May 22, 1951 (2 UST 1173; TIAS 2264; 141 UNTS 358).
September 25 and 27, 1951 (2 UST 2376; TIAS 2359; 174 UNTS 284).
September 11, 1953 (4 UST 2036; TIAS 2859; 214 UNTS 350).

NOTE:
[1] Applicable to Reunion, New Caledonia, Tuamotu Archipelago, including Society Islands, Austral Islands, Marquesas Archipelago, St. Pierre and Miquelon, Martinique, Guadeloupe, French Guiana.

EDUCATION

Agreement relating to certain academic and cultural exchanges and programs in the field of education. Signed at Paris May 7, 1965; entered into force May 28, 1965.
16 UST 1659; TIAS 5889; 573 UNTS 183.

ENERGY

Memorandum of understanding for the exchange of energy information. Signed at Washington July 20 and 22, 1987; entered into force July 22, 1987.
TIAS 11546.

Memorandum of understanding concerning an exchange of energy-related information in the area of enhanced oil recovery. Signed at Washington and Paris January 27 and February 16, 1988; entered into force February 16, 1988.
TIAS

Agreement for cooperation in high energy laser-matter interaction physics research and development. Signed at Washington and Paris December 12 and 19, 1988; entered into force December 19, 1988.
TIAS

Extension:
November 6 and December 6, 1990.

EXTRADITION

Extradition convention.[1] Signed at Paris January 6, 1909; entered into force July 27, 1911.
37 Stat. 1526; TS 561; 7 Bevans 872.

Supplementary extradition convention with exchanges of letters.[1] Signed at Paris February 12, 1970; entered into force April 3, 1971.
22 UST 407; TIAS 7075; 791 UNTS 273.

NOTE:
[1] Applicable to all territories.

FINANCE

Debt funding agreement. Signed at Washington April 29, 1926; operative June 15, 1925.
100 LNTS 27; Treasury Department print; 7 Bevans 949.

Agreement modifying the debt funding agreement of April 29, 1926. Signed at Washington June 10, 1932; operative July 1, 1931.
Treasury Department print; 7 Bevans 987.

Agreement relating to the allocation of the proceeds of German assets to be received from Sweden as a result of Swedish-Allied negotiations of July 18, 1946. Exchange of notes at Washington July 18, 1946; entered into force July 18, 1946.
61 Stat. 3840; TIAS 1731; 7 Bevans 1176; 125 UNTS 165.

Agreement relating to guaranties authorized by section 111(b)(3) of the Economic Cooperation Act of 1948, as amended. Exchange of notes at Washington July 9 and 22, 1952; entered into force July 24, 1952.
3 UST 5048; TIAS 2687; 181 UNTS 319.

FISHERIES

Agreement on matters relating to fishing in the economic zones of the French overseas territories of New Caledonia and Wallis and Futuna Islands. Signed at Washington March 1, 1991; entered into force November 1, 1991.
TIAS 11781.

INDUSTRIAL COOPERATION

Memorandum of understanding relating to the development of technology-based joint ventures between small United States and French companies. Signed at Washington and Paris February 21 and 25, 1986; entered into force February 25, 1986.
TIAS 12044.

INDUSTRIAL PROPERTY

Agreement relating to industrial property rights affected by World War II. Signed at Washington April 4, 1947; entered into force November 10, 1947.
61 Stat. 3316; TIAS 1667; 7 Bevans 1202; 24 UNTS 133.

Amendment:
October 28, 1947 (62 Stat. 1876; TIAS 1725; 7 Bevans 1222; 77 UNTS 348).

LEND-LEASE

Agreement relating to principles applying to mutual aid in the prosecution of the war against aggression. Signed at Washington February 28, 1945; entered into force February 28, 1945.
59 Stat. 1304; EAS 455; 7 Bevans 1075; 76 UNTS 193.

Agreement relating to supplies and services. Signed at Washington February 28, 1945; entered into force February 28, 1945.
59 Stat. 1307; EAS 455; 7 Bevans 1081; 76 UNTS 223.

Agreement, with accompanying memorandum and exchanges of letters, relating to principles applying to the provision of aid to the armed forces of the United States. Exchange of notes at Washington February 28, 1945; entered into force February 28, 1945; operative June 6, 1944.
59 Stat. 1313; EAS 455; 7 Bevans 1078; 76 UNTS 213.

Understanding relating to article VII of the lend-lease agreement signed February 28, 1945. Exchange of notes at Washington November 8, 1945; entered into force November 8, 1945.
7 Bevans 1098; 76 UNTS 151.

LEND-LEASE SETTLEMENT

Memorandum of understanding regarding settlement for lend-lease, reciprocal aid, surplus war property, and claims, with related documents. Signed at Washington May 28, 1946; entered into force May 28, 1946.
61 Stat. 4175; TIAS 1928; 7 Bevans 1126; 84 UNTS 59.

Agreement relating to the transfer of surplus United States property and installations in France and certain French overseas territories, with related documents. Signed at Washington May 28, 1946; entered into force May 28, 1946.
61 Stat. 4179; TIAS 1928; 7 Bevans 1130; 84 UNTS 80.

Memorandum of agreement regarding expenditures of the United States armed forces in France and French overseas territories, with related documents. Signed at Washington May 28, 1946; entered into force May 28, 1946.
61 Stat. 4206; TIAS 1928; 7 Bevans 1155; 84 UNTS 141.

Agreement relating to expenditures of the United States armed forces in France and French overseas territories, implementing the agreement of May 28, 1946. Exchange of notes at Washington February 27, 1948; entered into force February 27, 1948.
62 Stat. 3826; TIAS 1930; 7 Bevans 1245; 84 UNTS 207.

Agreement respecting maritime claims and litigation. Signed at Washington March 14, 1949; entered into force March 14, 1949.
63 Stat. 2499; TIAS 1935; 7 Bevans 1300; 84 UNTS 225.

Agreement regarding settlement of certain residual financial claims and accounts. Signed at

FRANCE (Cont'd)

Washington March 14, 1949; entered into force March 14, 1949.
63 Stat. 2507; TIAS 1936; 7 Bevans 1304; 84 UNTS 237.

Agreement on postponement of installations pursuant to paragraph 3 of the lend-lease agreement of May 28, 1946, and paragraph 2 of the surplus property agreement of December 6, 1947. Signed at Washington January 30, 1958; entered into force January 30, 1958.
9 UST 67; TIAS 3979; 304 UNTS 9.

LIQUOR

Agreement providing for the recognition and protection by France of the appellation of origin of bourbon whiskey and continued protection by the United States of appellations of origin of the French brandies, cognac, armagnac and calvados. Exchange of notes at Paris December 2, 1970 and January 18, 1971; entered into force March 20, 1971.
22 UST 36; TIAS 7041; 777 UNTS 77.

MAPPING

Agreement for the mapping of certain French territories in the Pacific. Exchange of notes at Paris November 27, 1948; entered into force November 27, 1948.
3 UST 491; TIAS 2407; 168 UNTS 119.

Agreement concerning mapping, charting and geodesy cooperation, with annex. Signed at Paris January 20, 1993; entered into force January 20, 1993.
NP

MARITIME MATTERS

Agreement concerning the wreck of the CSS *Alabama*. Signed at Paris October 3, 1989; entered into force October 3, 1989.
TIAS 11687.

MILITARY CEMETERIES AND MONUMENTS

Agreement concerning the interment in France and in territories of the French Union, or removal to the United States, of the bodies of American soldiers killed in the war of 1939-1945. Signed at Paris October 1, 1947; entered into force October 1, 1947.
61 Stat. 3767; TIAS 1720; 7 Bevans 1215; 148 UNTS 303.

Agreement regarding the transport, burial, and embalming of bodies of members of United States forces dying in France. Signed at Paris July 1, 1955; entered into force July 1, 1955.
6 UST 3787; TIAS 3380; 270 UNTS 19.

Agreement relating to the grant of plots of land located in France for the creation of permanent military cemeteries or the construction of war memorials, with annexes. Signed at Paris March 19, 1956; entered into force March 19, 1956.
7 UST 561; TIAS 3537; 275 UNTS 37.

MUTUAL SECURITY

Agreement relating to the assurances required by the Mutual Security Act of 1951. Exchange of notes at Paris January 5, 1952; entered into force January 5, 1952.
3 UST 4559; TIAS 2606; 181 UNTS 177.

NARCOTIC DRUGS

Arrangement for the direct exchange of certain information regarding the traffic in narcotic drugs. Exchange of notes at Paris December 27, 1927, and January 30, 1928; entered into force January 30, 1928.
7 Bevans 966.

Agreement for the co-ordination of preventive and repressive action against the illicit narcotic and dangerous drug traffic. Signed at Paris February 26, 1971; entered into force February 26, 1971.
28 UST 8045; TIAS 8739.

Extension and amendment:
September 11, 1974 (28 UST 8056; TIAS 8739).
January 28, 1981 (TIAS 10538).

NATIONALITY

Agreement relating to the fulfillment of military obligations during the wars of 1914-1918 and 1939-1945 by persons with dual nationality. Exchange of notes at Paris December 22, 1948; entered into force December 22, 1948.
62 Stat. 3621; TIAS 1876; 7 Bevans 1294; 67 UNTS 38.

Extension:
November 18 and December 31, 1952 (3 UST 5345; TIAS 2741; 185 UNTS 396).

NAVIGATION

Memorandum of understanding concerning the operation and maintenance of OMEGA station Le Reunion, with appendices. Signed at Washington June 24, 1981; entered into force June 24, 1981.
33 UST 2109; TIAS 10176; 1530 UNTS 13.

OCEANOGRAPHY

Memorandum of understanding on the participation of France in the ocean drilling program, with annex. Signed at Paris October 23, 1984; entered into force October 23, 1984.
TIAS 11219.

Memorandum of understanding on the participation of France in the ocean drilling program as a regular member, with annexes. Signed at Washington and Paris July 22 and August 2, 1993; entered into force August 2, 1993; effective October 1, 1993.
TIAS

PACIFIC SETTLEMENT OF DISPUTES

Treaty to facilitate the settlement of disputes. Signed at Washington September 15, 1914; entered into force January 22, 1915.
38 Stat. 1887; TS 609; 7 Bevans 883.

Treaty of arbitration and exchange of notes dated March 1 and 5, 1928. Signed at Washington February 6, 1928; entered into force April 22, 1929.
46 Stat. 2269; TS 785; 7 Bevans 968; 91 LNTS 323.

PATENTS

Agreement to facilitate interchange of patent rights and technical information for defense purposes. Signed at Paris March 12, 1957; entered into force March 12, 1957.
8 UST 353; TIAS 3782; 279 UNTS 275.

Agreement approving the procedures for reciprocal filing of classified patent application in the United States and France. Exchange of notes at Paris May 28 and July 10, 1959; entered into force July 10, 1959.
10 UST 2151; TIAS 4386; 367 UNTS 336.

POSTAL MATTERS

Postal money order convention. Signed at Washington August 19, 1931; operative February 1, 1932.
NP

Convention relative to the exchange of parcel post. Signed at Paris December 7 and at Washington December 30, 1935; operative August 1, 1935.
49 Stat. 3322; Post Office Department print; 171 LNTS 117.

International express mail agreement, with detailed regulations. Signed at Washington and Paris March 17 and April 13, 1981; entered into force May 18, 1981.
33 UST 1305; TIAS 10113; 1285 UNTS 75.

FRANCE (Cont'd)

PRISONER TRANSFER

Convention on the transfer of sentenced persons. Signed at Washington January 25, 1983; entered into force February 1, 1985.
TIAS 10823.

PUBLICATIONS

Agreement relating to exchange of official publications. Exchange of notes at Paris August 14, 1945; entered into force January 1, 1946.
60 Stat. 1944; TIAS 1579; 7 Bevans 1095; 73 UNTS 237.

RELIEF SUPPLIES AND PACKAGES

Agreement for free entry and free inland transportation of relief supplies and packages. Signed at Paris December 23, 1948; entered into force Decmeber 23, 1948.
62 Stat. 3587; TIAS 1873; 7 Bevans 1296; 67 UNTS 171.

Amendments:
January 31, 1950 (1 UST 224; TIAS 2043; 67 UNTS 171).
August 3, 1950 (1 UST 597; TIAS 2107; 93 UNTS 367).
July 2 and August 5, 1952 (3 UST 5039; TIAS 2684; 181 UNTS 345).

SATELLITES

Agreement on cooperation in intercontinental testing in connection with experimental communications satellites. Exchange of notes at Paris March 31, 1961; entered into force March 31, 1961.
12 UST 483; TIAS 4738; 409 UNTS 135.

Agreement concerning development of satellite and balloon techniques and instrumentation for the study of meteorological phenomena (Project EOLE). Exchange of notes at Washington June 16 and 17, 1966; entered into force June 17, 1966.
17 UST 1123; TIAS 6069; 601 UNTS 113.

Memorandum of understanding for joint development of the TOPEX/POSEIDON (oceanographic satellite) project. Signed at Washington March 23, 1987; entered into force March 23, 1987.
TIAS 12207.

SCIENTIFIC COOPERATION

Memorandum of understanding concerning the furnishing of balloon launching and associated services. Signed at Washington and Paris August 26 and November 11, 1983; entered into force November 11, 1983.
TIAS 10803.

Agreement incorporating an intellectual property annex into cooperative agreements between scientific and technical agencies of the United States and France. Exchange of notes at Paris July 27, 1994 and June 6, 1997; entered into force June 6, 1997.
TIAS

SHIPPING

Agreement relating to jurisdiction over vessels utilizing the Louisiana Offshore Oil Port, with annex. Exchange of notes at Washington March 24 and April 6, 1983; entered into force April 6, 1983.
TIAS 10682.

SMUGGLING

Convention for prevention of smuggling of intoxicating liquors. Signed at Washington June 30, 1924; entered into force March 12, 1927.
45 Stat. 2403; TS 755; 7 Bevans 938; 61 LNTS 415.

SOCIAL SECURITY

Agreement on social security. Signed at Paris March 2, 1987; entered into force July 1, 1988.
TIAS 12106.

Administrative arrangement concerning the application of the agreement on social security of March 2, 1987. Signed at Washington October 21, 1987; entered into force July 1, 1988.
TIAS 12106.

SPACE COOPERATION

Agreement concerning emergency use of the Combined Forces Base at Hao, French Polynesia, by the U.S. space shuttle. Signed at Paris September 6, 1984; entered into force September 6, 1984.
TIAS 11163.

Memorandum of understanding for cooperation in the Jason program. Signed at Washington and Paris December 14 and 20, 1996; entered into force December 20, 1996.
TIAS

TAXATION

Agreement relating to relief from taxation of United States Government expenditures in France in the interests of common defense. Exchange of notes at Paris June 13, 1952; entered into force June 13, 1952.
3 UST 4828; TIAS 2655; 181 UNTS 3.

Amendment:
November 27, 1956 (7 UST 3405; TIAS 3712; 265 UNTS 356).

Agreement relating to the payment by the United States of taxes on electricity provided the surplus commodity housing units in France. Exchange of notes at Paris August 1, 1963; entered into force August 1, 1963.
15 UST 727; TIAS 5595; 527 UNTS 89.

Convention for the avoidance of double taxation and the prevention of fiscal evasion with respect to taxes on estates, inheritances and gifts. Signed at Washington November 24, 1978; entered into force October 1, 1980.
32 UST 1935; TIAS 9812; 1234 UNTS 187.

Convention for the avoidance of double taxation and the prevention of fiscal evasion with respect to taxes on income and capital, with exchanges of notes. Signed at Paris August 31, 1994; entered into force December 30, 1995.
TIAS

TELECOMMUNICATION

Agreement relating to the reciprocal granting of authorizations to permit licensed amateur radio operators of either country to operate their stations in the other country.[1] Exchange of notes at Paris May 5, 1966; entered into force July 1, 1966.
17 UST 719; TIAS 6022; 593 UNTS 279.

Amendment:
October 3, 1969 (20 UST 2398; TIAS 6711).

NOTE:
[1] Applicable to all territories.

TERRITORIAL ACQUISITION

Treaty for the cession of Louisiana. Signed at Paris April 30, 1803; entered into force October 21, 1803.
8 Stat. 200; TS 86; 7 Bevans 812.

TRADE AND COMMERCE (See COMMERCE)

VISAS

Reciprocal agreement relating to visa fees for nonimmigrants.[1] Exchanges of notes at Washington August 19 and September 4, 5, and 16,

FRANCE (Cont'd)

1947; entered into force September 16, 1947; operative October 1, 1947.
61 Stat. 3776; TIAS 1721; 7 Bevans 1210; 84 UNTS 19.

Arrangement for the waiver by France of visa requirements for United States citizens visiting Metropolitan France and certain French territories, and for the granting by the United States of gratis passport visas to French citizens as nonimmigrants. Exchange of notes at Paris March 16 and 31, 1949; entered into force March 31, 1949.
63 Stat. 2737; TIAS 1987; 7 Bevans 1311; 84 UNTS 283.

Agreement relating to the reciprocal issuance of nonimmigrant visas for treaty traders and treaty investors. Exchange of notes at Paris September 1 and 21, 1961; entered into force September 21, 1961; operative October 21, 1961.
12 UST 3197; TIAS 4924; 433 UNTS 243.

NOTE:
[1] Applicable to all territories.

FRENCH GUIANA

POSTAL MATTERS

Parcel post convention. Signed at Washington August 21, 1914; operative November 1, 1914.
38 Stat. 1829; Post Office Department print.

FRENCH POLYNESIA

POSTAL MATTERS

International express mail agreement, with detailed regulations. Signed at Papeete and Washington November 30, 1995 and April 5, 1996; entered into force June 15, 1996.
NP

GUADELOUPE

POSTAL MATTERS

Parcel post convention. Signed at Washington February 20, 1913; operative April 1, 1913.
38 Stat. 1633; Post Office Department print.

MARTINIQUE

POSTAL MATTERS

Money order agreement. Signed at Washington November 16, 1911; operative January 1, 1912.
NP

Parcel post convention. Signed at Washington February 20, 1913; operative April 1, 1913.
38 Stat. 1623; Post Office Department print.

SOCIETY ISLANDS

POSTAL MATTERS

Parcel post convention. Signed at Washington April 30, 1918; operative June 1, 1918.
41 Stat. 1645; Post Office Department print.

GABON

COPYRIGHT (See APPENDIX)

DEFENSE

Agreement concerning the provision of training related to defense articles under the United States International Military Education and Training (IMET) Program. Exchange of notes at Libreville March 21, 1983 and July 5, 1984; entered into force July 5, 1984.
TIAS 10986.

Agreement regarding the status of United States military and civilian personnel of the U.S. Department of Defense temporarily present in Gabon in connection with "Gabon 2000" and other activities. Exchange of notes at Libreville November 26 and December 1, 1999; entered into force December 1, 1999.
NP

ECONOMIC AND TECHNICAL COOPERATION

Agency for International Development:
February 21, 1976 (28 UST 5041; TIAS 8612).

FINANCE

Agreement relating to investment guaranties. Exchange of notes at Libreville April 10, 1963; entered into force April 10, 1963.
14 UST 380; TIAS 5328; 474 UNTS 113.

Agreement regarding the consolidation and rescheduling of certain debts owed to, guaranteed by or insured by the United States Government and its agencies, with annexes. Signed at Libreville February 11, 1988; entered into force March 21, 1988.
NP

Agreement regarding the consolidation and rescheduling of certain debts owed to, guaranteed by or insured by the United States Government and its agencies, with annexes. Signed at Libreville February 16, 1989; entered into force March 30, 1989.
NP

Agreement regarding the consolidation and rescheduling or refinancing of certain debts owed to, guaranteed by or insured by the United States Government and its agencies, with annexes. Signed at Libreville March 5, 1990; entered into force April 9, 1990.
NP

Agreement regarding the consolidation and rescheduling or refinancing of certain debts owed to, guaranteed by or insured by the United States Government and its agencies, with annexes. Signed at Libreville September 2, 1994; entered into force November 28, 1994.
NP

Agreement regarding the consolidation and rescheduling of certain debts owed to, guaranteed by or insured by the United States Government and its agencies, with annexes. Signed at Libreville June 17, 1996; entered into force August 12, 1996.
NP

POSTAL MATTERS

International express mail agreement, with detailed regulations. Signed at Libreville and Washington January 23 and March 8, 1989; entered into force April 17, 1989.
TIAS 11616.

SCIENTIFIC COOPERATION

Memorandum of understanding concerning scientific and technical cooperation in the earth sciences, with annexes. Signed at Libreville December 14, 22 and 29, 1995 and January 11, 1996; entered into force January 11, 1996.
TIAS

SHIPPING

Agreement relating to jurisdiction over vessels utilizing the Louisiana Offshore Oil Port. Exchange of notes at Libreville July 25 and August 2, 1984; entered into force August 2, 1984.
TIAS 11215.

SOCIAL SECURITY

Agreement to provide certain social security benefits for certain employees of the United States in Gabon. Signed at Libreville August 25, 1970; entered into force August 25, 1970; effective January 1, 1968.
21 UST 2570; TIAS 6999; 175 UNTS 205.

THE GAMBIA

On February 18, 1965 The Gambia became an independent state. By an exchange of letters on June 20, 1966 between the High Commissioner for the United Kingdom in The Gambia and the Prime Minister of The Gambia, the Government of The Gambia agreed "that all obligations and responsibilities of the Government of the United Kingdom which arose from any valid international instrument applying to The Gambia immediately before the 18th of February, 1965 continued to apply to The Gambia and were assumed by the Government of The Gambia as from that date; and (ii) that the rights and benefits enjoyed by the Government of the United Kingdom by virtue of the application of any such international instrument to The Gambia continued to be enjoyed by the Government of The Gambia."

AVIATION

Arrangement between the United States and the United Kingdom relating to pilot licenses to operate civil aircraft. Exchange of notes at Washington March 28 and April 5, 1935; entered into force May 5, 1935.
49 Stat. 3731; EAS 77; 12 Bevans 513; 162 UNTS 59.

Agreement between the United States and the United Kingdom relating to air services. Signed at Bermuda February 11, 1946; entered into force February 11, 1946.
60 Stat. 1499; TIAS 1507; 12 Bevans 726; 3 UNTS 253.

Amendment:
May 27, 1966 (17 UST 683; TIAS 6019; 573 UNTS 274).

Agreement on aviation security. Exchange of notes at Banjul September 14 and 15, 1992; entered into force September 15, 1992.
TIAS 11910.

CONSULS

Consular convention between the United States and the United Kingdom. Signed at Washington June 6, 1951; entered into force September 7, 1952.
3 UST 3426; TIAS 2494; 165 UNTS 121.

COPYRIGHT (See APPENDIX)

DEFENSE

Agreement concerning the provision of training related to defense articles under the United States International Military Education and Training (IMET) Program. Exchange of notes

at Banjul December 27, 1983 and January 5, 1984; entered into force January 5, 1984.
TIAS 10916.

ECONOMIC AND TECHNICAL COOPERATION

Economic cooperation agreement between the United States and the United Kingdom. Signed at London July 6, 1948; applicable to The Gambia July 6, 1948.
62 Stat. 2596; TIAS 1795; 12 Bevans 874; 22 UNTS 263.

Amendments:
January 3, 1950 (1 UST 184; TIAS 2036; 86 UNTS 304).
May 25, 1951 (2 UST 1292; TIAS 2277; 99 UNTS 308).
February 25, 1953 (4 UST 1528; TIAS 2815; 172 UNTS 332).
June 26 and August 20, 1959 (11 UST 2680; TIAS 4664; 405 UNTS 288).

Agency for International Development:
October 26 and 28, 1977 (29 UST 5753; TIAS 9148).
January 12 and February 20, 1978 (29 UST 5772; TIAS 9152).

EXTRADITION

Extradition treaty between the United States and the United Kingdom. Signed at London December 22, 1931; entered into force June 24, 1935.
47 Stat. 2122; TS 849; 12 Bevans 482; 163 LNTS 59.

FINANCE

Agreement relating to investment guaranties. Exchange of notes at Bathurst July 24 and November 4, 1967; entered into force November 4, 1967.
18 UST 2997; TIAS 6392; 701 UNTS 139.

MUTUAL SECURITY

Agreement between the United States and the United Kingdom relating to the assurances required under the Mutual Security Act of 1951. Exchange of notes at London January 8, 1952; entered into force January 8, 1952.
3 UST 4665; TIAS 2622; 126 UNTS 307.

PEACE CORPS

Agreement relating to the establishment of a Peace Corps program in The Gambia. Exchange of notes at Bathurst November 26 and

December 5, 1966; entered into force December 5, 1966.
17 UST 2346; TIAS 6181; 681 UNTS 49.

PROPERTY

Convention between the United States and the United Kingdom relating to the tenure and disposition of real and personal property. Signed at Washington March 2, 1899; applicable to The Gambia February 9, 1901.
31 Stat. 1939; TS 146; 12 Bevans 246.

Supplementary convention relating to the tenure and disposition of real and personal property. Signed at Washington May 27, 1936; entered into force March 10, 1941.
55 Stat. 1101; TS 964; 5 Bevans 140; 203 LNTS 367.

SPACE COOPERATION

Agreement concerning the use of Banjul International Airport as a space shuttle emergency landing site. Signed at Banjul March 7, 1988; entered into force March 7, 1988.
TIAS 12148.

TELECOMMUNICATION

Agreement relating to radio communications between amateur stations on behalf of third parties. Exchange of notes at Banjul March 17, 1981; entered into force April 16, 1981.
33 UST 1401; TIAS 10119.

TRADE-MARKS

Declaration by the United States and the United Kingdom affording reciprocal protection to trade-marks. Signed at London October 24, 1877; entered into force October 24, 1877.
20 Stat. 703; TS 138; 12 Bevans 198.

GEORGIA

For agreements prior to December 31, 1991, see UNION OF SOVIET SOCIALIST REPUBLICS.

COPYRIGHT (See APPENDIX)

DEFENSE

Agreement concerning the provision of training under the United States International Military Education and Training (IMET) Program. Ex-

GEORGIA (Cont'd)

change of notes at Tbilisi December 30, 1993; entered into force December 30, 1993.
NP

Agreement regarding grants under the Foreign Assistance Act of 1961, as amended, and the furnishing of defense articles, related training, and other defense services from the United States of America to the Government of Georgia. Exchange of notes at Tbilisi June 4 and July 15, 1999; entered into force July 15, 1999.
TIAS

ECONOMIC AND TECHNICAL COOPERATION

Agreement regarding cooperation to facilitate humanitarian and technical economic assistance. Signed at Tbilisi July 31, 1992; entered into force July 31, 1992.
TIAS 12468.

EMPLOYMENT

Agreement relating to the employment of dependents of official government employees. Exchange of notes at Washington December 5, 1994 and June 20, 1995; entered into force June 20, 1995.
TIAS 12667.

ENVIRONMENTAL COOPERATION

Agreement concerning the Regional Environmental Centre for the Caucasus. Signed November 8, 2000; entered into force November 8, 2000.
TIAS

FINANCE

Investment incentive agreement. Signed at Tbilisi June 27, 1992; entered into force June 27, 1992.
TIAS 12463.

INVESTMENT

Treaty concerning the encouragement and reciprocal protection of investment, with annex. Signed at Washington March 7, 1994; entered into force August 17, 1997.
TIAS

POSTAL MATTERS

Express mail agreement, with detailed regulations. Signed at Tbilisi and Washington August 16 and September 3, 1996; entered into force November 1, 1996.
NP

TRADE

Agreement on trade relations, with exchanges of letters. Signed at Tbilisi March 1, 1993; entered into force August 13, 1993.
TIAS 12489.

WEAPONS

Agreement concerning cooperation in the area of the prevention of proliferation of weapons of mass destruction and the promotion of defense and military relations. Signed at Washington July 17, 1997; entered into force November 10, 1997.
TIAS

GERMANY, FEDERAL REPUBLIC OF

The Federal Republic of Germany provided a note to the Department dated October 15, 1990, which reads in pertinent part as follows:

"The Embassy of the Federal Republic of Germany presents its compliments to the Department of State and has the honor to inform the Department that, with regard to the continued application of treaties of the Federal Republic of Germany and the treatment of treaties of the German Democratic Republic following its accession to the Federal Republic of Germany with effect from 3 October 1990, the Treaty of 31 August 1990 between the Federal Republic of Germany and the German Democratic Republic on the Establishment of German Unity (Unification Treaty) contains the following relevant provisions.

1. Article 11

Treaties of the Federal Republic of Germany

The Contracting Parties proceed on the understanding that international treaties and agreements to which the Federal Republic of Germany is a Contracting Party, including treaties establishing its membership of international organizations or institutions, shall retain their validity and that the rights and obligations arising therefrom, with the exception of the treaties named in Annex I (not included herein), shall also relate to the territory specified in Article 3. Where adjustments become necessary in individual cases, the all-German Government shall consult with the respective Contracting Parties.

.   .   .   .

2. Article 12

Treaties of the German Democratic Republic

(1) The Contracting Parties are agreed that, in connection with the establishment of German unity, international treaties of the German Democratic Republic shall be discussed with the Contracting Parties concerned with a view to regulating or confirming their continued application, adjustment or expiry, taking into account protection of confidence, the interests of the states concerned, the treaty obligations of the Federal Republic of Germany as well as the principles of a free, democratic basic order governed by the rule of law, and respecting the competence of the European Communities.

(2) The United Germany shall determine its position with regard to the adoption of international treaties of the German Democratic Republic following consultations with the respective Contracting Parties and with the European Communities where the latter's competence is affected.

.   .   .   .

The Federal Republic of Germany will proceed in accordance with these provisions."

AGRICULTURAL COMMODITIES

Agreement for the sale of feed grain and the purchase of building materials for United States defense purposes. Signed at Washington February 18, 1955; entered into force February 18, 1955.
6 UST 655; TIAS 3199; 247 UNTS 257.

AGRICULTURE

Agreement on cooperation in the field of agricultural science and technology. Signed at Bonn June 1, 1981; entered into force June 1, 1981.
34 UST 958; TIAS 10381; 1560 UNTS 423.

ARMS LIMITATION

Agreement regarding inspections on the territory of the German Democratic Republic provided for by the U.S.-U.S.S.R. treaty of December 8, 1987 on the elimination of their intermediate-range and shorter-range missiles. Exchange of notes at Berlin December 23, 1987; entered into force June 1, 1988.[1]
TIAS

NOTE:
[1] Agreement concluded with the German Democratic Republic.

GERMANY, FEDERAL REPUBLIC OF (Cont'd)

ATOMIC ENERGY

Agreement for cooperation on uses of atomic energy for mutual defense purposes. Signed at Bonn May 5, 1959; entered into force July 27, 1959.
10 UST 1322; TIAS 4276; 355 UNTS 307.

Technical exchange and cooperative arrangement in the field of management of radioactive wastes, with patent addendum and appendix. Signed at Bonn December 20, 1974; entered into force December 20, 1974.
29 UST 4544; TIAS 9067; 1148 UNTS 91.

Agreement for research and development in the field of liquid metal-cooled breeder reactors. Signed at Bonn June 8, 1976; entered into force June 8, 1976.
28 UST 5741; TIAS 8657.

Agreement for cooperation in the field of nuclear materials safeguards and physical security research and development, with annex. Exchange of notes at Bonn and Washington September 29, 1977; entered into force September 29, 1977.
29 UST 4709; TIAS 9076.

Extension:
April 23 and July 22, 1985 (TIAS 12386).

Arrangement for the exchange of technical information and cooperation in nuclear safety matters, with patent addendum and exchange of letters. Signed at Washington July 6, 1981; entered into force July 6, 1981.
TIAS

Extension:
July 17, 1986.

Agreement for the exchange of classified information, with related exchange of letters. Signed at Washington July 6, 1981; entered into force July 6, 1981.
TIAS 10872.

Agreement concerning the listing of reactors supplied from the Federal Republic of Germany to the Taiwan Power Company on the inventory of the IAEA safeguards agreement of December 6, 1971 (TIAS 7228). Exchange of letters at Washington November 5, 1981; entered into force November 5, 1981.
33 UST 4505; TIAS 10321.

Agreement in the field of remote systems technology, with appendix. Signed at Washington April 24, 1987; entered into force April 24, 1987.
TIAS 12143.

Arrangement for the exchange of information and cooperation in nuclear safety matters, with annexes. Signed at Berlin October 19, 1995; entered into force October 19, 1995.
TIAS 12699.

Technical exchange and cooperative arrangement in the field of reactor safety research and development, with annexes. Signed at Washington December 13, 1995; entered into force December 13, 1995.
TIAS

AVIATION

Air transport agreement and exchanges of notes. Signed at Washington July 7, 1955; entered into force April 16, 1956.
7 UST 527; TIAS 3536; 275 UNTS 3.

Amendments:
November 1, 1978 (30 UST 7323; TIAS 9591; 1203 UNTS 280).
April 25, 1989 (TIAS 11942).

Agreement relating to the reciprocal acceptance of airworthiness certifications. Exchange of notes at Bonn-Bad Godesberg and Bonn March 12 and May 31, 1974; entered into force May 31, 1974.
25 UST 3056; TIAS 7965.

Agreement for application to Land Berlin of agreement of March 12 and May 31, 1974 relating to the reciprocal acceptance of airworthiness certifications. Exchange of notes at Bonn and Bonn-Bad Godesberg November 3, 1976 and March 18, 1980; entered into force March 18, 1980.
32 UST 538; TIAS 9724; 1220 UNTS 353.

Memorandum of understanding relating to cooperation in the development of national airspace systems, with annex. Signed at Washington and Bonn October 3 and November 6, 1984; entered into force November 6, 1984.
TIAS 11025.

Memorandum of understanding concerning air navigation services in Berlin, with related exchange of letters. Signed at Bonn October 23, 1990; entered into force October 23, 1990.
TIAS 11746.

Agreement for promotion of aviation safety. Signed at Milwaukee May 23, 1996; entered into force July 18, 1997.
TIAS

CLAIMS

Agreement regarding the settlement of the claim of the United States for postwar economic assistance (other than surplus property) to Germany. Signed at London February 27, 1953; entered into force September 16, 1953.
4 UST 893; TIAS 2795; 224 UNTS 13.

Agreement relating to the indebtedness of Germany for awards made by the Mixed Claims Commission, United States and Germany. Signed at London February 27, 1953; entered into force September 16, 1953.
4 UST 908; TIAS 2796; 224 UNTS 31.

Agreement concerning the settlement of claims against United States forces and authorities which arose during the period of August 1, 1945 to June 30, 1947. Exchange of letters at Bonn March 24 and 30, 1953; entered into force March 30, 1953.
5 UST 2149; TIAS 3076; 235 UNTS 285.

Agreement relating to an advance payment by Germany on its indebtedness to the United States for postwar economic assistance. Exchange of notes at Bonn March 20, 1959; entered into force March 20, 1959.
10 UST 401; TIAS 4200; 341 UNTS 15.

Agreement relating to partial settlement of German postwar debt to the United States resulting from postwar economic assistance (other than surplus property). Exchange of notes at Bonn April 25, 1961; entered into force April 25, 1961.
12 UST 477; TIAS 4737; 410 UNTS 340.

Agreement concerning the settlement of claims which have arisen through the non-duty use of private motor vehicles of members of the United States Forces insured by the Brandaris insurance company.[1] Exchange of letters at Bonn February 28 and March 14, 1963; entered into force March 14, 1963.
14 UST 342; TIAS 5318; 474 UNTS 71.

Agreement relating to prepayment of the remaining German debt to the United States resulting from postwar economic assistance (excluding surplus property). Exchange of notes at Bonn December 29, 1966; entered into force December 29, 1966.
18 UST 101; TIAS 6204; 688 UNTS 63.

Agreement concerning the settlement of certain property claims, with annex. Signed at Bonn May 13, 1992; entered into force December 28, 1992.
TIAS 11959; 1911 UNTS 27.

Agreement concerning final benefits to certain United States nationals who were victims of National Socialist measures of persecution, with exchange of notes. Signed at Bonn September 19, 1995; entered into force September 19, 1995.
TIAS

Supplementary agreement to the agreement of September 19, 1995 concerning final benefits to certain United States nationals who were victims of National Socialist measures of persecution. Exchange of notes at Bonn January 25, 1999; entered into force January 25, 1999.
TIAS

Agreement concerning the Foundation "Remembrance, Responsibility and the Future", with annexes. Signed at Berlin July 17, 2000; entered into force October 19, 2000.
TIAS

NOTE:
[1] Applicable also in respect of incidents which occurred in West Berlin.

GERMANY, FEDERAL REPUBLIC OF (Cont'd)

COMMERCE

Treaty of friendship, commerce, and consular rights.[1] Signed at Washington December 8, 1923; entered into force October 14, 1925. 44 Stat. 2132; TS 725; 8 Bevans 153; 52 LNTS 133.

Agreement concerning the treaty of friendship, commerce, and consular rights of December 8, 1923, as amended.[1] Signed at Bonn June 3, 1953; entered into force October 22, 1954. 5 UST 1939; TIAS 3062; 253 UNTS 89.

Treaty of friendship, commerce and navigation with protocol and exchanges of notes. Signed at Washington October 29, 1954; entered into force July 14, 1956. 7 UST 1839; TIAS 3593; 273 UNTS 3.

NOTE:
[1] Articles I-V, VII-XVI, and XXIX-XXXII of the 1923 treaty as amended and as applied by the agreement of June 3, 1953 (TIAS 3062) were replaced and terminated by the treaty of October 29, 1954 (TIAS 3593). Article VI of the 1923 treaty terminated June 2, 1954 (see 5 UST 827; TIAS 2972).

CONSULS (See COMMERCE)

COPYRIGHT (See also APPENDIX)

Copyright agreement. Signed at Washington January 15, 1892; entered into force May 6, 1892. TS 100; 8 Bevans 129.

Agreement relating to the extension of time for fulfilling the conditions and formalities of the copyright laws of the United States. Exchange of notes at Washington November 20, 1964 and July 12, 1967; entered into force July 12, 1967. 18 UST 2366; TIAS 6341; 692 UNTS 331.

CULTURAL RELATIONS

Agreement concerning cultural relations. Exchange of notes at Washington April 9, 1953; entered into force April 9, 1953. 4 UST 939; TIAS 2798; 204 UNTS 79.

Agreement with respect to the transfer of certain works of art seized in Germany by the United States Army at the end of World War II, with annex. Exchange of notes at Washington January 28, 1986; entered into force January 28, 1986. TIAS 11977.

CUSTOMS

Agreement regarding mutual assistance between the customs services of the United States and the Federal Republic of Germany. Signed at Washington August 23, 1973; entered into force June 13, 1975. 26 UST 1092; TIAS 8098.

DEFENSE (See also MUTUAL SECURITY)

Agreement relating to the purchase by the Federal Republic of Germany from the United States of certain equipment for police use. Exchange of notes at Washington November 23, 1953; entered into force November 23, 1953. 5 UST 170; TIAS 2911; 224 UNTS 107.

Agreement relating to offshore procurement. Signed at Bonn April 4, 1955; entered into force February 7, 1957. 8 UST 157; TIAS 3755; 279 UNTS 73.

Agreement on the model contract containing standard contract clauses referred to in article 16 of the agreement of April 4, 1955 relating to offshore procurement. Exchange of notes at Bonn April 4, 1955; entered into force February 7, 1957. 8 UST 497; TIAS 3804; 289 UNTS 326.

Mutual defense assistance agreement. Signed at Bonn June 30, 1955; entered into force December 27, 1955. 6 UST 5999; TIAS 3443; 240 UNTS 47.

Agreement for the return of equipment pursuant to the mutual defense assistance agreement. Exchange of notes at Bonn June 30, 1955; entered into force December 27, 1955. 6 UST 6005; TIAS 3444; 240 UNTS 69.

Amendment:
March 9, 1961 (12 UST 243; TIAS 4703; 405 UNTS 323).

Agreement relating to the sale to the Federal Republic of certain military equipment, materials, and services pursuant to sec. 106 of the Mutual Security Act of 1954, as amended. Exchange of notes at Washington October 8, 1956; entered into force October 8, 1956. 7 UST 2787; TIAS 3660; 278 UNTS 9.

Extensions and amendments:
June 15 and October 24, 1960 (11 UST 2242; TIAS 4599; 393 UNTS 332).
November 24, 1961 (12 UST 3045; TIAS 4903; 434 UNTS 328).

Agreement relating to the training of German army personnel pursuant to the mutual defense assistance agreement. Exchange of notes at Bonn December 12, 1956; entered into force December 12, 1956. 8 UST 149; TIAS 3753; 280 UNTS 63.

Agreement relating to the training of German navy personnel pursuant to the mutual defense assistance agreement. Exchange of notes at

Bonn December 12, 1956; entered into force December 12, 1956. 8 UST 153; TIAS 3754; 280 UNTS 71.

Agreement relating to the disbandment of the German element of the Civilian Service Organization maintained by American Forces in Germany under the Forces Convention. Exchange of notes at Bonn April 11, 1957; entered into force April 11, 1957. 8 UST 645; TIAS 3815; 283 UNTS 233.

Amendment:
April 11, 1957 (8 UST 645; TIAS 3815; 283 UNTS 237).

Agreement relating to the training of German air force and the transfer to the Federal Republic of the air bases at Landsberg, Kaufbeuren and Fuerstenfeldbruck and the air depot at Erding. Exchange of notes at Bonn December 10, 1957; entered into force December 10, 1957. 8 UST 2475; TIAS 3968; 307 UNTS 59.

Agreements implementing the NATO status of forces agreement of August 3, 1959 (TIAS 5351). Signed at Bonn August 3, 1959; entered into force July 1, 1963. 14 UST 689; TIAS 5352; 490 UNTS 30.

Agreement relating to the use of the International Airport Frankfurt/Main and related papers. Exchange of letters at Bonn November 10 and 18, 1959; entered into force November 18, 1959; effective April 1, 1959. TIAS

Agreement relating to a weapons production program. Exchange of notes at Bonn May 27, 1960; entered into force May 27, 1960. 11 UST 1606; TIAS 4504; 377 UNTS 45.

Agreement relating to the disposition of equipment and materials furnished to the Federal Republic on a grant basis under the mutual defense assistance agreement of June 30, 1955. Exchange of notes at Bonn May 25, 1962; entered into force May 25, 1962. 13 UST 1341; TIAS 5092; 458 UNTS 259.

Agreement to support personnel from the Federal Republic of Germany stationed in the United States during emergencies. Signed at Bonn October 21, and at Washington December 18, 1965; entered into force December 18, 1965. 16 UST 1912; TIAS 5922; 579 UNTS 193.

Agreement relating to the AIM-9L Sidewinder air-to-air missile. Signed at Washington February 14, 1975; entered into force February 14, 1975. 29 UST 2924; TIAS 8987; 1120 UNTS 23.

Memorandum of understanding relating to cooperative tests for the ROLAND 2 all weather short range air defense system, with annexes. Signed at Bonn and Washington February 18 and 28, 1975; entered into force February 28, 1975. 31 UST 4754; TIAS 9636.

Agreement concerning the transfer of the U.S. bridge and ferry equipment to the Federal Re-

GERMANY, FEDERAL REPUBLIC OF (Cont'd)

public of Germany, with annex. Signed at Heidelberg and Bonn May 26 and June 1, 1976; entered into force June 1, 1976.
29 UST 1497; TIAS 8893; 1115 UNTS 45.

Memorandum of understanding concerning cooperative development of an advanced surface-to-air missile system. Signed at Washington and Bonn July 16 and 22, 1976; entered into force July 22, 1976.
28 UST 5771; TIAS 8658.

Agreement on the release and testing of strebo submunitions and on the exchange of information. Signed at Washington and Bonn August 4 and November 4, 1976; entered into force November 4, 1976.
TIAS 12298.

Agreement relating to the security of information on the JT-10D aircraft engine. Exchange of notes at Washington February 24 and March 18, 1977; entered into force March 18, 1977.
28 UST 7146; TIAS 8708.

Agreement on the provision of United States Army training to the German Air Force in the United States, with annexes. Signed at Bonn and Washington May 24 and July 6, 1977; entered into force July 6, 1977.
29 UST 4859; TIAS 9081; 1148 UNTS 107.

Agreement on the stationing of training components of the Federal Minister of Defense in the United States, with annexes. Signed at Bonn and Washington May 24 and July 6, 1977; entered into force July 6, 1977.
30 UST 2671; TIAS 9358.

Memorandum of understanding for coproduction and sale of the sidewinder AIM-9L missile system. Signed at Washington October 7, 1977; entered into force October 14, 1977.
30 UST 298; TIAS 9202; 1148 UNTS 117.

Amendment:
March 17 and April 21, 1978 (30 UST 315; TIAS 9202; 1148 UNTS 125).

Memorandum of understanding for coproduction and sale of modular thermal imaging systems (MOD FLIR) and their components, with annexes.[1] Signed at Washington and Bonn February 27 and March 3, 1978; entered into force April 20, 1978.
TIAS 10876.

Related agreement:
March 26, 1979 (TIAS 10876).

Memorandum of understanding concerning the principles governing mutual cooperation in the research and development, production, procurement and logistic support of defense equipment. Signed at Schwanewede October 17, 1978; entered into force October 17, 1978.
TIAS 12297.

Administrative agreement relating to addition of an educational program under paragraph 4, article 71 of the supplementary agreement of August 3, 1959 (TIAS 5351). Exchange of notes at Bonn November 23 and December 28, 1979; entered into force January 1, 1980.
32 UST 783; TIAS 9729; 1220 UNTS 307.

Memorandum of understanding for cooperation within the area of army tactical data systems for the purpose of standardization and interoperability. Signed at Washington and Bonn January 6 and April 14, 1980; entered into force April 14, 1980.
32 UST 1003; TIAS 9751; 1221 UNTS 3.

Agreement concerning the support of USAFE A-10 aircraft at forward operating locations (FOLS) in the territory of the Federal Republic of Germany, with related letter. Signed at Bonn and Ramstein November 5 and 9, 1981; entered into force November 9, 1981; effective October 1, 1979.
33 UST 4170; TIAS 10293.

Agreement concerning host nation support during crisis or war, with annexes. Signed at Bonn April 15, 1982; entered into force April 15, 1982.
34 UST 557; TIAS 10376.

Agreement concerning mutual support in Europe and adjacent waters, with annex. Signed at Bonn January 21, 1983; entered into force January 21, 1983.
TIAS 12299.

Amendments:
December 21, 1987 (TIAS 12299).
January 21 and 26, 1994 (TIAS 12299).

Memorandum of understanding for the dual production and sale of the stinger weapon system, with agreed minute and annexes. Signed at Washington April 27, 1983; entered into force April 27, 1983.
TIAS

Amendments:
March 20 and 26, 1986.
March 23 and April 24, 1995.
April 24 and May 14, 1996.
July 10 and August 22, 1996.

Memorandum of understanding concerning a cooperative project of research in the field of powder metallurgy of titanium alloys. Signed at Washington January 8, 1985; entered into force January 8, 1985.
TIAS 11140.

Memorandum of understanding concerning the exchange of Air Force officers. Signed at Bonn and Washington January 15 and February 20, 1986; entered into force February 20, 1986.
NP

Memorandum of understanding for a cooperative software development and implementation for the EIFEL system, with annex. Signed at Bonn and Washington March 10 and June 13, 1986; entered into force June 13, 1986.
TIAS

Memorandum of understanding concerning cooperative production of the EX-31 guided missile weapon system, with annexes. Signed at Washington August 3, 1987; entered into force September 17, 1987.
TIAS 12300.

Memorandum of understanding concerning German support of the joint U.S. services program for testing and evaluation of the IFFN system, with annexes. Signed at Bonn and Washington July 14 and August 3, 1988; entered into force August 3, 1988.
TIAS 12301.

Memorandum of understanding concerning a cooperative program for harmonization, development, production and support of a maritime patrol aircraft, with annexes. Signed at Bonn and Washington February 17 and April 5, 1989; entered into force April 5, 1989.
TIAS 12302.

Memorandum of understanding for cooperative projects of research and development in the field of high energy laser technology, with annex. Signed at Bonn April 14, 1989; entered into force April 14, 1989.
TIAS 12303.

Amendment and extension:
April 7 and May 26, 1994 (TIAS 12303).

Memorandum of agreement concerning a cooperative program for extended air defense, with attachment and annex. Signed at Washington and Bonn April 28 and May 17, 1989; entered into force May 17, 1989.
TIAS 11702.

Memorandum of understanding concerning the joint research, development and demonstration of advanced armor protection systems (AAPS), with annexes. Signed at Washington and Bonn January 4 and 11, 1990; entered into force January 11, 1990.
TIAS 12304.

Memorandum of understanding on the mutual exchange of documents. Signed at Bonn and Washington January 18, 1989 and February 9, 1990; entered into force February 9, 1990.
TIAS 12305.

Memorandum of understanding concerning the SAXON-FPN synthetic aperture radar experiment, with annexes. Signed at Washington and Bonn May 25 and June 1, 1990; entered into force June 1, 1990.
TIAS 12306.

Memorandum of understanding for cooperative projects of research and development in the field of modular avionics, with supplement. Signed at Bonn and Washington June 26 and July 3, 1990; entered into force July 3, 1990.
TIAS 12307.

Memorandum of understanding for cooperation within the area of short range air defense (SHORAD) command and control systems for the purpose of standardization and interoperability. Signed at Alexandria and Bonn June 14

GERMANY, FEDERAL REPUBLIC OF (Cont'd)

and December 20, 1991; entered into force December 20, 1991.
TIAS 12308.

Memorandum of agreement concerning a joint enhanced maneuverable fighter aircraft research, development and flight test program, with annexes. Signed at Arlington and Bonn March 25 and June 11, 1992; entered into force June 11, 1992.
TIAS 12309.

Memorandum of understanding concerning a cooperative program on biological effects of ionizing radiation. Signed at Bonn and Washington August 2 and 23, 1993; entered into force August 23, 1993.
TIAS 12310.

Memorandum of understanding for cooperative research in the field of helicopter aeromechanics, with annex. Signed at Alexandria and Bonn September 2 and 16, 1994; entered into force September 16, 1994.
TIAS 12311.

Memorandum of agreement concerning German participation in the George C. Marshall European Center for Security Studies at Garmisch-Partenkirchen, with annexes. Signed at Stuttgart December 2, 1994; entered into force December 2, 1994.
TIAS 12312.

Memorandum of understanding for research and technology projects, with annex. Signed at Bonn and Washington March 9 and 17, 1995; entered into force March 17, 1995.
TIAS 12313.

Memorandum of agreement for the acquisition and co-production of air-to-air STINGER (ATAS) subsystem components, with annex. Signed at Bonn and Washington January 24 and March 27, 1995; entered into force March 27, 1995.
TIAS 12314.

Amendment:
August 20 and November 23, 1999.

Agreement concerning collaborative logistics support measures for the Nuclear, Biological, Chemical Reconnaissance System (NBCRS). Signed at Alexandria and Bonn March 30 and April 18, 1995; entered into force April 18, 1995.
TIAS 12629.

Agreement concerning cooperative engineering and manufacturing development of the RAM Block I Upgrade to the MK–31 Guided Missile Weapon System (GMWS), with annexes. Signed at Bonn and Washington March 14 and 27, 1996; entered into force March 27, 1996.
TIAS

Arrangement relating to the status of troop care enterprises and their employees under Article 72, paragraph 4 of the Supplementary Agreement of August 3, 1959 to the NATO Status of Forces Agreement, with related letters. Exchange of notes at Bonn March 27, 1998; entered into force March 27, 1998.
TIAS

Arrangement regarding the application of Article 73 of the Supplementary Agreement of August 3, 1959 to the NATO Status of Forces Agreement. Exchange of notes at Bonn March 27, 1998; entered into force March 27, 1998.
TIAS

Agreement for participation in the German Geoscience Space Mission CHAMP. Signed at Washington and Bonn January 28 and February 12, 1999; entered into force February 12, 1999.
TIAS

Memorandum of agreement for the Vectoring Extremely Short Take Off and Landing (ESTOL) Control Tailless Operation Research (VECTOR) technology demonstration project, with annex. Signed at Bonn and Washington April 6 and 15, 1999; entered into force April 15, 1999.
TIAS

Agreement regarding the exchange of military personnel, with annexes. Signed at Bonn March 15, 2000; entered into force March 15, 2000.
NP

NOTE:
[1] Articles IE, VIIIA, and XII superseded by agreement of February 12, May 21, and December 22, 1981; see NORTH ATLANTIC TREATY ORGANIZATION—COOPERATIVE AGREEMENTS in multilateral section.

ECONOMIC AND TECHNICAL COOPERATION

Economic cooperation agreement. Signed at Bonn December 15, 1949; entered into force provisionally December 29, 1949; definitively February 6, 1950.
64 Stat. (3) B81; TIAS 2024; 8 Bevans 268; 92 UNTS 269.

Amendments:
February 27 and March 28, 1951 (2 UST 1295; TIAS 2278; 141 UNTS 390).
November 14 and December 30, 1952 (3 UST 5323; TIAS 2736; 212 UNTS 329).

EDUCATION

Agreement for conducting certain educational exchange programs. Signed at Bonn November 20, 1962; entered into force January 24, 1964.
15 UST 78; TIAS 5518; 505 UNTS 263.

Amendment:
January 11, 1974 (25 UST 169; TIAS 7778).

ENERGY

Memorandum of understanding for an exchange of energy-related information. Signed at Washington November 20, 1987; entered into force November 20, 1987.
TIAS

Agreement on cooperation in energy research, science and technology, and development. Signed at Washington February 20, 1998; entered into force February 20, 1998.
TIAS

ENVIRONMENTAL COOPERATION

Agreement on cooperation in environmental affairs. Signed at Bonn May 9, 1974; entered into force March 26, 1975.
26 UST 840; TIAS 8069.

Amendment and extension:
March 22, 1985 (TIAS 11251).

EXTRADITION

Extradition treaty, with protocol. Signed at Bonn June 20, 1978; entered into force August 29, 1980.
32 UST 1485; TIAS 9785; 1220 UNTS 269.

Supplementary treaty to the treaty concerning extradition of June 20, 1978. Signed at Washington October 21, 1986; entered into force March 11, 1993.
TIAS

FINANCE

Agreement regarding the validation of dollar bonds of German issue. Signed at Bonn February 27, 1953; entered into force February 27, 1953.
4 UST 797; TIAS 2793; 223 UNTS 167.

Agreement regarding certain matters arising from the validation of German dollar bonds. Signed at Bonn April 1, 1953; entered into force September 16, 1953.
4 UST 885; TIAS 2794; 224 UNTS 3.

Confirmation of effectiveness in Berlin of agreements relating to the validation of certain German dollar bonds (TIAS 2793 and 2794). Exchange of notes at Washington February 25 and April 9, 1954.
5 UST 1; 223 UNTS 167.

Second agreement regarding certain matters arising from the validation of certain German dollar bonds. Signed at Bonn August 16, 1960; entered into force June 30, 1961.
12 UST 943; TIAS 4798; 418 UNTS 235.

GERMANY, FEDERAL REPUBLIC OF (Cont'd)

Investment incentive agreement. Signed at Berlin September 14, 1990; entered into force August 9, 1991.
TIAS 12130.

Agreement relating to and bringing into force the investment incentive agreement of September 14, 1990. Exchange of notes at Washington August 9, 1991; entered into force August 9, 1991.
TIAS 12130.

GENERAL RELATIONS

Treaty establishing friendly relations. Signed at Berlin August 25, 1921; entered into force November 11, 1921.
42 Stat. 1939; TS 658; 8 Bevans 145; 12 LNTS 192.

HEALTH

Agreement on cooperation in the field of biomedical research and technology. Signed at Bonn September 22, 1976; entered into force September 22, 1976.
27 UST 4358; TIAS 8457; 1066 UNTS 223.

Extension:
October 23 and December 10, 1986.

JUDICIAL ASSISTANCE

Agreement relating to the taking of evidence. Exchange of notes at Bad Godesberg and Bonn February 11, 1955, January 13 and October 8, 1956; entered into force October 8, 1956.
32 UST 4181; TIAS 9938; 1265 UNTS 41.

Agreement relating to reciprocal legal assistance in penal matters and information from penal register. Exchange of notes at Bonn November 7 and December 28, 1960, and January 3, 1961; entered into force January 3, 1961.
12 UST 1156; TIAS 4826; 416 UNTS 93.

Agreement concerning mutual assistance in the administration of justice in connection with the Lockheed Aircraft Corporation matter, with agreed minutes. Signed at Washington September 24, 1976; entered into force September 24, 1976.
27 UST 3429; TIAS 8373.

Related agreement:
January 10 and February 1, 1979 (30 UST 3533; TIAS 9407; 1169 UNTS 3).

Agreement relating to the taking of evidence. Exchange of notes at Bonn October 17, 1979

and February 1, 1980; entered into force February 1, 1980.
32 UST 4189; TIAS 9938; 1265 UNTS 46.

MAPPING

Basic exchange and cooperative agreement concerning mapping, charting and geodesy cooperation, with annex. Signed at Euskirchen and Fairfax October 17 and 26, 1994; entered into force October 26, 1994.
NP

MARITIME MATTERS

Agreement relating to the return to the Federal Republic of Germany of Tripartite Naval Commission vessels. Signed at Bonn August 20, 1953; entered into force August 20, 1953.
4 UST 2815; TIAS 2891; 224 UNTS 49.

Agreement relating to the transfer of title of the United States destroyer, *U.S.S. Charles Ausburne,* to the Federal Republic. Exchange of notes at Bonn February 27, 1968; entered into force February 27, 1968.
19 UST 5015; TIAS 6502; 706 UNTS 251.

MUTUAL SECURITY

Agreement relating to the assurances required under the Mutual Security Act of 1951. Exchange of letters at Bonn December 19 and 28, 1951; entered into force December 28, 1951.
3 UST 4564; TIAS 2607; 181 UNTS 45.

NARCOTIC DRUGS

Arrangement concerning the exchange of information relating to the illicit traffic in narcotics. Exchange of notes at Washington January 17 and August 24, 1955, and March 7, 1956; entered into force March 7, 1956.
7 UST 371; TIAS 3514; 271 UNTS 361.

Agreement concerning cooperation in the field of control of drug and narcotics abuse. Exchange of notes at Bonn and Bonn-Bad Godesberg June 9, 1978; entered into force June 9, 1978.
30 UST 4434; TIAS 9467; 1177 UNTS 317.

OCEANOGRAPHY

Memorandum of understanding on the participation of the Federal Republic of Germany in the ocean drilling program, with annex. Signed at Bonn and Washington March 2 and 5, 1984; entered into force March 5, 1984.
TIAS 10960.

Memorandum of understanding on the participation of the Federal Republic of Germany in

the ocean drilling program as a regular member, with annex. Signed at Washington and Bonn March 5 and 31, 1993; entered into force March 31, 1993; effective October 1, 1993.
TIAS

PACIFIC SETTLEMENT OF DISPUTES

Treaty of arbitration. Signed at Washington May 5, 1928; entered into force February 25, 1929.
45 Stat. 2744; TS 774; 8 Bevans 192; 90 LNTS 177.

Treaty of conciliation. Signed at Washington May 5, 1928; entered into force February 25, 1929.
45 Stat. 2748; TS 775; 8 Bevans 194; 90 LNTS 171.

PATENTS

Patent agreement. Signed at Washington February 23, 1909; entered into force August 1, 1909.
36 Stat. 2178; TS 531; 8 Bevans 143.

Agreement to facilitate interchange of patent rights and technical information for defense purposes, and exchange of notes. Signed at Bonn January 4, 1956; entered into force January 4, 1956.
7 UST 45; TIAS 3478; 268 UNTS 143.

Agreement approving the procedures for reciprocal filing of classified patent applications in the United States and the Federal Republic of Germany. Exchange of notes at Bonn March 9 and May 23, 1959, and related note of July 31, 1959; entered into force May 26, 1959.
10 UST 2001; TIAS 4369; 361 UNTS 337.

Amendment:
January 14 and May 28, 1964 (15 UST 765; TIAS 5601; 529 UNTS 350).

POSTAL MATTERS

Agreement concerning the exchange of parcel post together with regulations of execution. Signed at Berlin February 6 and at Washington March 16, 1939; entered into force March 16, 1939; operative from January 2, 1939.
53 Stat. 2183; Post Office Department print; 198 LNTS 237.

International express mail/datapost agreement, with detailed regulation. Signed at Bonn and Washington December 15, 1978 and January 22, 1979; entered into force August 8, 1979; effective February 1, 1979.
30 UST 3789; TIAS 9426.

GERMANY, FEDERAL REPUBLIC OF (Cont'd)

PROPERTY TRANSFER

Agreement concerning the transfer of the Berlin Document Center to the Federal Republic of Germany, with exchanges of notes. Signed at Berlin October 18, 1993; entered into force October 18, 1993.
TIAS

Agreement concerning real property exchange, with attachments. Signed at Bonn September 23, 1994; entered into force September 23, 1994.
TIAS

PUBLICATIONS

Agreement relating to the exchange of official publications. Exchange of notes at Washington October 27, 1954; entered into force October 27, 1954.
5 UST 2563; TIAS 3121; 234 UNTS 131.

RELIEF SUPPLIES AND PACKAGES

Agreement relating to duty-free entry into the Federal Republic of Germany of relief shipments and the defrayment of transportation costs of such shipments, with memorandum attached. Exchange of notes at Bonn April 10, May 25, and June 7, 1951; entered into force May 29, 1951; operative December 29, 1949.
5 UST 2820; TIAS 3135; 238 UNTS 161.

Extension and amendment:
July 8 and September 6, 1952 (5 UST 2835; TIAS 3137; 238 UNTS 167).

SATELLITES

Agreement on cooperation in intercontinental testing in connection with experimental communications satellites. Exchange of notes at Bonn September 5 and 29, 1961; entered into force September 29, 1961.
12 UST 1682; TIAS 4885; 424 UNTS 113.

Memorandum of understanding on the Roentgensatellit program. Signed at Vienna August 8, 1982; entered into force August 8, 1982.
TIAS 10669.

SCIENTIFIC COOPERATION

Agreement on cooperation in research toward an improved understanding of the continental crust by scientific drilling, with annexes.

Signed at Washington June 3, 1988; entered into force June 3, 1988.
TIAS 11677.

Agreement incorporating an intellectual property annex into cooperative agreements between US-FRG scientific and technical agencies. Exchange of notes at Washington March 4 and 7, 1994; entered into force March 7, 1994.
TIAS 12176.

Agreement on cooperation in research in the geosciences, with annex. Signed at Bonn March 7, 1994; entered into force March 7, 1994.
TIAS 12535.

SHIPPING

Agreement relating to jurisdiction over vessels utilizing the Louisiana Offshore Oil Port. Exchange of notes at Washington July 2, September 4 and 15, 1981; entered into force September 15, 1981.
33 UST 3278; TIAS 10225.

SOCIAL SECURITY

Agreement on the pension insurance of certain employees of the United States Army. Signed at Bonn September 11, 1970; entered into force June 1, 1972; effective November 1, 1950.
23 UST 638; TIAS 7326.

Agreement on social security, with final protocol. Signed at Washington January 7, 1976; entered into force December 1, 1979.
30 UST 6099; TIAS 9542; 1177 UNTS 257.

Administrative agreement for the implementation of the agreement on social security of January 7, 1976. Signed at Washington June 21, 1978; entered into force October 30, 1979; effective December 1, 1979.
30 UST 6150; TIAS 9542; 1177 UNTS 270.

Amendments:
October 2, 1986 (TIAS 12115).
March 6, 1995.

SPACE COOPERATION

Memorandum of understanding on the project of active magnetospheric particle tracer explorers. Signed at Washington October 15, 1981; entered into force October 15, 1981.
33 UST 4088; TIAS 10286; 1549 UNTS 339.

Memorandum of understanding for cooperative flights of spaceborne imaging radar. Signed at Bonn October 6, 1987; entered into force October 6, 1987.
TIAS

Amendments:
February 18 and March 25, 1994.
September 26 and 30, 1997.

Memorandum of understanding for the Stratospheric Observatory for Infrared Astronomy Program. Signed at Washington and Bonn December 16 and 20, 1996; entered into force December 20, 1996.
TIAS

Memorandum of understanding for participation in the German Geoscience Challenging Mini-Satellite Payload for Geoscientific Research and Applications (CHAMP) program. Signed at Washington July 31, 1997; entered into force July 31, 1997.
TIAS

SURPLUS PROPERTY

Agreement regarding the settlement of the obligations of the Federal Republic of Germany to the United States for surplus property furnished Germany. Signed at London February 27, 1953; entered into force September 16, 1953.
4 UST 923; TIAS 2797; 205 UNTS 103.

Agreement relating to the deduction of $2,350,000 from the indebtedness of the Federal Republic to the United States for certain claims pursuant to articles I and VII of the surplus property payments agreement of February 27, 1953. Exchange of notes at Washington May 17 and August 17, 1954; entered into force August 18, 1954.
5 UST 1476; TIAS 3021; 233 UNTS 31.

Agreement for the final disposition of certain claims to be paid from the amount deducted from the indebtedness of the Federal Republic pursuant to article I of the surplus property payments agreement of February 27, 1953. Exchange of notes at Washington March 11 and April 14, 1955; entered into force April 19, 1955.
6 UST 1065; TIAS 3245; 263 UNTS 351.

TAXATION

Agreement concerning tax relief to be accorded by the Federal Republic of Germany to United States expenditures in interest of the common defense, with annex and exchange of letters. Signed at Bonn October 15, 1954; entered into force November 8, 1955.
6 UST 3081; TIAS 3360; 239 UNTS 135.

Convention for the avoidance of double taxation with respect to taxes on estates. Signed at Bonn December 3, 1980; entered into force June 27, 1986.
TIAS 11082.

Convention for the avoidance of double taxation and the prevention of fiscal evasion with respect to taxes on income and capital and to certain other taxes, with a related protocol, exchanges of notes and memorandum of under-

GERMANY, FEDERAL REPUBLIC OF (Cont'd)

standing.[1] Signed at Bonn August 29, 1989; entered into force August 21, 1991.
TIAS   ; 1708 UNTS 3.

Protocol amending the convention of December 3, 1980 for the avoidance of double taxation with respect to taxes on estates, inheritances and gifts. Signed at Washington December 14, 1998; entered into force December 14, 2000.
TIAS

NOTE:
[1] With an understanding.

TELECOMMUNICATION

Agreement regarding the operation of certain radio installations from within the Federal Republic. Signed at Bonn June 11, 1952; entered into force May 5, 1955.
7 UST 789; TIAS 3559; 273 UNTS 105.

Agreement relating to the return of the Emden-Cherbourg-Horta submarine telegraph cable to German ownership.[1] Exchange of notes at Washington November 4, 1959 and March 16, 1960; entered into force March 16, 1960.
11 UST 254; TIAS 4441; 371 UNTS 101.

Agreement relating to the reciprocal granting of authorizations to permit licensed amateur radio operators of either country to operate their station in the other country. Exchange of notes at Bonn June 23 and 30, 1966; entered into force June 30, 1966.
17 UST 1120; TIAS 6068; 601 UNTS 107.

Agreement regarding operation of the radio installation at Erching. Signed at Bonn January 22 and 26, 1979; entered into force January 26, 1979.
30 UST 3540; TIAS 9408.

NOTE:
[1] The U.S. signed in its own behalf and in behalf of the United Kingdom and France.

TRADE (See also COMMERCE)

Agreement regarding the importation of foreign films into and the screen time quota for exhibition in the Federal Republic of Germany. Signed at Bonn April 26, 1956; entered into force August 17, 1957.
8 UST 735; TIAS 3829; 283 UNTS 267.

Agreement providing compensatory concessions under the general agreement on tariffs and trade for certain tariff actions taken by the United States. Exchange of notes at Geneva January 29, 1962; entered into force January 29, 1962.
13 UST 939; TIAS 5032.

Agreement relating to mutual cooperation regarding restrictive business practices. Signed at Bonn June 23, 1976; entered into force September 11, 1976.
27 UST 1956; TIAS 8291.

TRANSPORTATION

Memorandum of understanding regarding cooperation on the development of advanced ground transportation. Signed at Bonn June 12, 1973; entered into force June 12, 1973.
27 UST 3831; TIAS 8402; 1059 UNTS 3.

Extension and amendments:
March 23 and June 9 and 15, 1976 (27 UST 3836; TIAS 8402; 1059 UNTS 8).
July 12 and August 30, 1978 (30 UST 4100; TIAS 9449; 1228 UNTS 472).

Memorandum of understanding concerning cooperation in the field of transportation. Signed at Washington September 3, 1975; entered into force September 3, 1975.
28 UST 8024; TIAS 8736.

GHANA

On March 6, 1957 Ghana became an independent state. In an exchange of letters dated November 25, 1957 between the Government of the United Kingdom and the Government of Ghana it was agreed that all obligations and responsibilities of the Government of the United Kingdom which arise from any valid international instrument shall henceforth in so far as such instrument may be held to have application to Ghana be assumed by the Government of Ghana. The rights and benefits heretofore enjoyed by the Government of the United Kingdom by virtue of the application of any such international instrument to the Gold Coast shall as from March 6, 1957 be enjoyed by the Government of Ghana.

AGRICULTURAL COMMODITIES

Agricultural commodities agreement with exchange of notes. Signed at Accra April 1, 1966; entered into force April 1, 1966.
17 UST 484; TIAS 5991; 579 UNTS 157.

Agricultural commodities agreement with annex. Signed at Accra March 3, 1967; entered into force March 3, 1967.
18 UST 369; TIAS 6245; 688 UNTS 283.

Amendments:
April 6, 1967 (18 UST 369; TIAS 6245; 688 UNTS 310).
December 18, 1967 (18 UST 3071; TIAS 6397; 702 UNTS 404).

Related agreements:
October 27, 1967 (18 UST 2824; TIAS 6370).

January 3, 1968 (19 UST 4645; TIAS 6453; 697 UNTS 3).
February 9 and 21, 1968 (19 UST 4653; TIAS 6454).
July 16 and 18, 1968 (19 UST 5906; TIAS 6544; 706 UNTS 330).
August 2 and 8, 1968 (19 UST 5906; TIAS 6544; 706 UNTS 334).
December 10, 1968 (19 UST 7848; TIAS 6621; 714 UNTS 3).
June 9, 1969 (20 UST 813; TIAS 6695; 714 UNTS 13).
June 22, 1970 (21 UST 1352; TIAS 6891; 752 UNTS 67).
November 12, 1971 (22 UST 1760; TIAS 7211).
August 2 and December 12, 1971 (23 UST 68; TIAS 7272).

Agricultural commodities agreement, with agreed minutes. Signed at Accra February 9, 1979; entered into force February 9, 1979.
30 UST 3555; TIAS 9411; 1171 UNTS 147.

Agricultural commodities agreement, with related letter and agreed minutes. Signed at Accra April 14, 1980; entered into force April 14, 1980.
32 UST 909; TIAS 9738; 1222 UNTS 247.

Related agreements:
March 31, 1981 (33 UST 1521; TIAS 10127).
August 19, 1982 (TIAS 10496).

Agricultural commodities agreement. Signed at Accra July 31, 1985; entered into force July 31, 1985.
NP

Agricultural commodities agreement. Signed at Accra July 14, 1986; entered into force July 14, 1986.
NP

Agricultural commodities agreement. Signed at Accra June 15, 1987; entered into force June 15, 1987.
NP

Related agreements:
September 23, 1988 (NP).
March 28 and 31, 1989 (NP).

Agricultural commodities agreement. Signed at Accra February 8, 1990; entered into force February 8, 1990.
NP

AVIATION

Arrangement between the United States and the United Kingdom relating to pilot licenses to operate civil aircraft. Exchange of notes at Washington March 28 and April 5, 1935; entered into force May 5, 1935.
49 Stat. 3731; EAS 77; 12 Bevans 513; 162 LNTS 59.

Agreement between the United States and the United Kingdom relating to air services.

GHANA (Cont'd)

Signed at Bermuda February 11, 1946; entered into force February 11, 1946.
60 Stat. 1499; TIAS 1507; 12 Bevans 726; 3 UNTS 253.

Amendment:
September 26 and October 13, 1994 (TIAS 12571).

CONSULS

Consular convention and protocol of signature between the United States and the United Kingdom.[1] Signed at Washington June 6, 1951; entered into force September 7, 1952.
3 UST 3426; TIAS 2494; 165 UNTS 121.

NOTE:
[1] Paragraph 1 of article 7 not in force for Ghana.

COPYRIGHT (See APPENDIX)

DEFENSE

Mutual defense assistance agreement between the United States and the United Kingdom. Signed at Washington January 27, 1950; made applicable to the Gold Coast July 19, 1952.[1]
1 UST 126; TIAS 2017; 80 UNTS 261.

Agreement relating to the deposit by Ghana of ten percent of the value of grant military assistance furnished by the United States. Exchange of notes at Accra April 13 and May 29, 1972; entered into force May 29, 1972; effective February 7, 1972.
23 UST 1310; TIAS 7410.

Agreement concerning the provision of training related to defense articles under the United States International Military Education and Training (IMET) Program. Exchange of notes at Accra December 4, 1985 and February 28, 1986; entered into force February 28, 1986.
TIAS 11102.

Agreement concerning assistance under the Foreign Assistance Act of 1961, as amended, and the furnishing of defense articles, related training and other defense services from the United States to Ghana. Exchange of notes at Accra March 2 and 7, 1995; entered into force March 7, 1995.
TIAS

Agreement regarding the provision of commodities, services and associated military education and training to Ghanaian forces participating in ECOMOG peacekeeping operations. Exchange of notes at Accra October 28 and November 19, 1996; entered into force November 19, 1996.
TIAS

Agreement regarding the provision of commodities, services and related training to assist the Republic of Ghana's forces participating in the African Crisis Response Initiative. Exchange of notes at Accra November 24, 1997 and January 8, 1998; entered into force January 8, 1998.
TIAS

Agreement regarding the status of U.S. military personnel and civilian employees of the U.S. Department of Defense temporarily present in Ghana in connection with the African Crisis Response Initiative and other activities. Exchange of notes at Accra November 24, 1997 and February 24, 1998; entered into force February 24, 1998.
TIAS

Agreement regarding the status of U.S. military and civilian personnel of the U.S. Department of Defense temporarily present in Ghana in connection with humanitarian relief operations in Southern Africa. Exchange of notes at Accra March 22 and April 7, 2000; entered into force April 7, 2000.
NP

NOTE:
[1] Only article IV is applicable to Ghana.

ECONOMIC AND TECHNICAL COOPERATION

Economic cooperation agreement between the United States and the United Kingdom. Signed at London July 6, 1948; applicable to the Gold Coast July 6, 1948.
62 Stat. 2596; TIAS 1795; 12 Bevans 874; 22 UNTS 263.

Amendments:
January 3, 1950 (1 UST 184; TIAS 2036; 86 UNTS 304).
May 25, 1951 (2 UST 1292; TIAS 2277; 99 UNTS 308).
February 25, 1953 (4 UST 1528; TIAS 2815; 172 UNTS 332).

General agreement for technical cooperation. Signed at Accra June 3, 1957; entered into force June 3, 1957.
8 UST 793; TIAS 3838; 284 UNTS 63.

Agency for International Development:
September 29, 1976 (29 UST 173; TIAS 8804).
May 24, 1977 (29 UST 342; TIAS 8820).
March 31, 1978 (30 UST 4534; TIAS 9476).

EDUCATION

Agreement for financing certain educational exchange programs. Signed at Accra January 24, 1962; entered into force January 24, 1962.
13 UST 87; TIAS 4942; 435 UNTS 23.

EMPLOYMENT

Agreement relating to the employment of dependents of official government employees. Exchange of notes at Accra July 28, 1989 and April 17, 1991; entered into force April 17, 1991.
TIAS

ENVIRONMENTAL COOPERATION

Agreement for cooperation in the Global Learning and Observations to Benefit the Environment (GLOBE) Program, with appendices. Signed at Accra March 20, 1998; entered into force March 20, 1998.
TIAS

EXTRADITION

Extradition treaty between the United States and the United Kingdom. Signed at London December 22, 1931; applicable to the Gold Coast June 24, 1935.
47 Stat. 2122; TS 849; 12 Bevans 482; 163 LNTS 59.

FINANCE

Agreement relating to investment guaranties under section 413(b)(4) of the Mutual Security Act of 1954, as amended. Exchange of notes at Accra September 30, 1958; entered into force September 30, 1958.
9 UST 1321; TIAS 4121; 336 UNTS 169.

Amendment:
March 3, 1967 (18 UST 231; TIAS 6222; 688 UNTS 376).

PEACE CORPS

Agreement relating to the establishment and operation of a Peace Corps program in Ghana. Exchange of notes at Accra July 19, 1961; entered into force July 19, 1961.
12 UST 1066; TIAS 4811; 416 UNTS 167.

POSTAL MATTERS

Parcel post agreement and detailed regulations. Signed at Accra June 3 and at Washington June 14, 1951; entered into force August 1, 1951.
2 UST 1859; TIAS 2322; 137 UNTS 81.

International express mail agreement, with detailed regulations. Signed at Accra and Washington February 9 and March 1, 1990; entered into force April 16, 1990.
TIAS 11714.

GHANA (Cont'd)

PROPERTY

Convention between the United States and the United Kingdom relating to tenure and disposition of real and personal property. Signed at Washington March 2, 1899; applicable to the Gold Coast July 6, 1901.
31 Stat. 1939; TS 146; 12 Bevans 246.

RELIEF SUPPLIES AND PACKAGES

Agreement providing for duty-free entry into Ghana and exemption from internal taxation of relief supplies and packages. Exchange of notes at Accra April 9, 1959; entered into force April 9, 1959.
10 UST 720; TIAS 4203; 342 UNTS 21.

Amendment:
April 8 and May 3, 1971 (22 UST 575; TIAS 7104; 791 UNTS 376).

SOCIAL SECURITY

Agreement concerning United States participation on a voluntary, limited basis in the Ghanaian social security system. Exchange of notes at Accra May 16, September 10 and October 30, 1973; entered into force October 30, 1973.
24 UST 2202; TIAS 7734; 938 UNTS 353.

TELECOMMUNICATION

Agreement relating to radio communications between amateur stations on behalf of third parties. Exchange of notes at Accra October 13 and 27, 1977; entered into force November 26, 1977.
29 UST 2787; TIAS 8975.

TRADE-MARKS

Declaration by the United States and the United Kingdom relating to reciprocal protection to trade-marks. Signed at London October 24, 1877; entered into force October 24, 1877.
20 Stat. 703; TS 138; 12 Bevans 198.

TREATY OBLIGATIONS

Agreement relating to treaty rights and obligations assumed by Ghana upon its independence. Exchange of notes at Accra September 4 and December 21, 1957, and February 12, 1958; entered into force February 12, 1958.
13 UST 240; TIAS 4966; 442 UNTS 175.

GREECE

ATOMIC ENERGY

Agreement for cooperation on the uses of atomic energy for mutual defense purposes. Exchange of notes at Athens May 6, 1959; entered into force August 11, 1959.
10 UST 1429; TIAS 4292; 357 UNTS 163.

Arrangement for the exchange of technical information and cooperation in nuclear safety matters, with addendum. Signed at Athens and Washington October 17, 1983 and December 16, 1983 and February 24, 1984; entered into force February 24, 1984; effective October 17, 1983.
TIAS 10950.

Arrangement for the exchange of technical information and cooperation in nuclear safety matters, with addenda. Signed at Vienna September 22, 1998; entered into force September 22, 1998.
TIAS

AVIATION

Air service agreement. Exchange of notes at Athens March 11 and June 16 and 25, 1952; entered into force June 25, 1952.
3 UST 4856; TIAS 2658; 181 UNTS 53.

Air transport agreement, with annex. Signed at Athens July 31, 1991; entered into force May 15, 1992.
TIAS

Extension:
July 19 and 25, 2000.

COMMERCE

Agreement regarding commercial relations. Exchange of notes at Washington January 2 and 11, 1946; entered into force January 11, 1946.
60 Stat. 1483; TIAS 1505; 8 Bevans 396; 3 UNTS 203.

Treaty of friendship, commerce, and navigation. Signed at Athens August 3, 1951; entered into force October 13, 1954.
5 UST 1829; TIAS 3057; 224 UNTS 279.

CONSULS

Convention concerning the rights and privileges of consuls,[1] and protocol of amendment signed March 5 and 18, 1903. Signed at Athens November 19 and December 2, 1902; entered into force July 9, 1903.
33 Stat. 2122; TS 424; 8 Bevans 313.

NOTE:
[1] Notice of termination was given by the United States of articles XII and XIII, effective July 1, 1916, in accordance with the Seamen's Act (38 Stat. 1164). The notice was accepted by the Greek Government with the understanding that only such provisions of these articles as were in conflict with the Act should be abrogated, and all other provisions, especially those concerning the arrest, detention, and imprisonment of deserters from war vessels, should continue in force.

COPYRIGHT (See APPENDIX)

CUSTOMS

Agreement regarding reciprocal free entry privileges of consular officers and clerks. Exchange of notes at Athens October 10, 1940; entered into force October 10, 1940.
8 Bevans 373.

Agreement relating to the importation of goods by American personnel in Greece under the military facilities agreement. Exchange of notes at Athens June 27, 1955; entered into force June 27, 1955.
6 UST 3711; TIAS 3368.

Agreement regarding mutual assistance between customs administrations. Signed at Athens July 31, 1991; entered into force January 17, 1993.
TIAS 12078.

DEFENSE (See also MUTUAL SECURITY)

Agreement relating to the use of certain Greek Islands for training exercises by Marine units of the United States fleet in the Mediterranean. Exchange of notes at Athens February 11 and 21, 1949; entered into force February 21, 1949.
63 Stat. 2683; TIAS 1972; 8 Bevans 455; 88 UNTS 29.

Agreement relating to the disposition of equipment and material furnished by the United States under the Act to Provide Assistance to Greece and Turkey, as amended, found surplus to the needs of the armed forces of Greece. Exchange of notes at Athens December 21, 1951, and January 7, 1952; entered into force January 7, 1952.
3 UST 3997; TIAS 2537; 177 UNTS 249.

Amendment:
April 17 and 18, 1961 (12 UST 496; TIAS 4741; 407 UNTS 238).

Agreement concerning the inspection and acceptance testing, security, and storage of military items produced by Greek industries under the offshore procurement program, with memoranda of understanding. Exchange of notes at

GREECE (Cont'd)

Athens December 17 and 24, 1952; entered into force December 24, 1952.
3 UST 5330; TIAS 2738; 185 UNTS 193.

Agreement concerning military facilities.[1] Signed at Athens October 12, 1953; entered into force October 12, 1953.
4 UST 2189; TIAS 2868; 191 UNTS 319.

Agreement concerning the status of United States forces in Greece. Signed at Athens September 7, 1956; entered into force September 7, 1956.
7 UST 2555; TIAS 3649; 278 UNTS 141.

Agreement relating to the deposit by Greece of ten percent of the value of grant military assistance and excess defense articles furnished by the United States. Exchange of notes at Athens January 11 and 12, 1973; entered into force January 12, 1973; effective February 7, 1972.
24 UST 225; TIAS 7543; 938 UNTS 155.

Agreement relating to payment to the United States of net proceeds from the sale of defense articles and eligibility for United States military assistance and training under the military assistance program. Exchange of notes at Athens August 31, 1976; entered into force August 31, 1976.
27 UST 3999; TIAS 8418; 1059 UNTS 137.

Agreement concerning the grant of defense articles and services under the military assistance program. Exchange of notes at Athens August 30, 1979; entered into force August 30, 1979.
30 UST 7267; TIAS 9583; 1182 UNTS 147.

Amendment:
August 13 and 26, 1982 (TIAS 10464; 1751 UNTS 498).

Agreement on defense and economic cooperation, with annex. Signed at Athens September 8, 1983; entered into force December 20, 1983.
TIAS 10814; 1590 UNTS 117.

Amendment:
February 27, 1990.

General security of military information agreement, with annex on industrial security procedures. Exchange of notes at Athens January 7, 1986; entered into force January 7, 1986.
TIAS 11980.

Defense industrial cooperation agreement, with annexes and exchange of letters. Signed at Athens November 10, 1986; entered into force November 10, 1986.
TIAS 12320.

Amendment:
March 17 and April 4, 1997.

Mutual defense cooperation agreement, with annex. Signed at Athens July 8, 1990; entered into force November 6, 1990.
TIAS 12321.

Extension:
April 20 and May 5, 2000.

Memorandum of understanding concerning the joint use of Hellenic Air Force bases by United States Air Force operational units, with annex. Signed at Athens and Ramstein AB May 6 and June 8, 1992; entered into force June 8, 1992.
TIAS 12322.

Memorandum of agreement concerning the exchange of engineers and scientists, with annexes. Signed at Athens October 12, 1992; entered into force October 12, 1992.
NP

Agreement concerning the transfer of U.S. Government-origin defense articles or related training or other defense services to the Government of the Hellenic Republic. Exchange of notes at Athens January 22 and 27, 1993; entered into force January 27, 1993.
TIAS 12323.

Agreement concerning mutual logistic support, with annexes. Signed at Papagos Camp (Greece) and Patch Barracks (Germany) June 28 and August 5, 1996; entered into force August 5, 1996.
TIAS

Amendment and extension:
December 10, 1999 and January 31, 2000.

NOTE:
[1] Article III, Paragraph 1, abrogated by agreement of September 7, 1956 (TIAS 3649), except for reference to memorandum of understanding of Feb. 4, 1953 (TIAS 2775) which continues in effect.

ECONOMIC AND TECHNICAL COOPERATION

Agreement on aid to Greece, and exchanges of notes of May 26 and June 15 and 18, 1947. Signed at Athens June 20, 1947; entered into force June 20, 1947.
61 Stat. 2907; TIAS 1625; 8 Bevans 403; 7 UNTS 267.

Economic cooperation agreement. Signed at Athens July 2, 1948; entered into force July 3, 1948.
62 Stat. 2293; TIAS 1786; 8 Bevans 431; 23 UNTS 43.

Amendments:
December 15 and 24, 1949 (64 Stat. B104; TIAS 2025; 8 Bevans 459; 79 UNTS 298).
March 6 and 30, 1951 (2 UST 843; TIAS 2238; 132 UNTS 384).
October 14, 1952 and December 2, 1953 (5 UST 2844; TIAS 3139; 225 UNTS 250).
April 19, 1963 (14 UST 397; TIAS 5331; 476 UNTS 250).

Agreement for cooperation in the economic, scientific, technological, and educational and cultural fields. Signed at Athens April 22, 1980; entered into force April 22, 1980.
32 UST 1034; TIAS 9754; 1234 UNTS 327.

EDUCATION

Agreement for financing educational exchange programs. Signed at Athens December 13, 1963; entered into force December 13, 1963.
14 UST 1770; TIAS 5486; 494 UNTS 55.

EMPLOYMENT

Agreement relating to employment of dependents of official government employees. Exchange of notes at Athens January 30 and February 17, 1995; entered into force July 7, 1995.
TIAS 12605.

ENVIRONMENTAL COOPERATION

Agreement for cooperation in the Global Learning and Observations to Benefit the Environment (GLOBE) Program, with appendices. Signed at Athens December 12, 1995; entered into force December 12, 1995.
TIAS 12709.

EXTRADITION

Treaty of extradition, and exchange of notes. Signed at Athens May 6, 1931; entered into force November 1, 1932.
47 Stat. 2185; TS 855; 8 Bevans 353; 138 LNTS 293.

Protocol interpreting article I of the treaty of extradition signed at Athens May 6, 1931. Signed at Athens September 2, 1937; entered into force September 2, 1937.
51 Stat. 357; EAS 114; 8 Bevans 366; 185 LNTS 408.

FINANCE

Debt funding agreement. Signed at Washington May 10, 1929; operative January 1, 1928.
Treasury Department print; 8 Bevans 333.

Agreement modifying the debt funding agreement of May 10, 1929. Signed at Washington May 24, 1932; operative July 1, 1931.
Treasury Department print; 8 Bevans 361.

Agreement relating to guaranties authorized by section 111(b)(3) of the Economic Cooperation Act of 1948, as amended. Exchange of notes at Washington April 21 and 23, 1952; entered into force April 29, 1952.
3 UST 4250; TIAS 2568; 177 UNTS 283.

GREECE (Cont'd)

Amendment:
April 19, 1963 (14 UST 397; TIAS 5331; 476 UNTS 250).

Agreement concerning the uses of the drachmae deposited under the agricultural commodities agreement of January 7, 1960. Exchange of notes at Athens April 20 and 29, 1961; entered into force April 29, 1961.
12 UST 499; TIAS 4742; 407 UNTS 290.

Agreement providing for the refunding of certain indebtedness due from Greece to the United States and amortization schedule. Signed at Athens May 28, 1964; entered into force November 5, 1966.
17 UST 2331; TIAS 6178; 680 UNTS 143.

INDUSTRIAL COOPERATION (See under DEFENSE)

JUDICIAL ASSISTANCE

Procedures for mutual assistance in the administration of justice in connection with the Lockheed Aircraft Corporation matter. Signed at Washington May 20, 1976; entered into force May 20, 1976.
27 UST 2006; TIAS 8300; 1052 UNTS 349.

LEND-LEASE

Preliminary agreement regarding principles applying to mutual aid in the prosecution of the war against aggression. Signed at Washington July 10, 1942; entered into force July 10, 1942.
56 Stat. 1559; EAS 260; 8 Bevans 381; 103 UNTS 289.

MAPPING

Basic exchange and cooperative agreement for topographic mapping, nautical and aeronautical charting, digital data, goedesy and geophysics and related materials. Signed at Athens May 25, 1993; entered into force May 25, 1993.
NP

MUTUAL SECURITY

Agreement relating to the assurances required under the Mutual Security Act of 1951. Exchange of notes at Athens December 21, 1951, and January 7, 1952; entered into force January 7, 1952.
3 UST 4569; TIAS 2608; 180 UNTS 171.

NARCOTIC DRUGS

Arrangement for the direct exchange of certain information regarding the traffic in narcotic drugs. Exchange of notes at Athens February 7 and October 15, 1928; entered into force October 15, 1928.
8 Bevans 331.

PACIFIC SETTLEMENT OF DISPUTES

Treaty of arbitration. Signed at Washington June 19, 1930; entered into force September 23, 1932.
47 Stat. 2161; TS 853; 8 Bevans 349; 136 LNTS 393.

Treaty of conciliation. Signed at Washington June 19, 1930; entered into force September 23, 1932.
47 Stat. 2165; TS 854; 8 Bevans 351; 136 LNTS 399.

PATENTS

Agreement to facilitate interchange of patent rights and technical information for defense purposes. Signed at Athens June 16, 1955; entered into force June 16, 1955.
6 UST 2173; TIAS 3286; 262 UNTS 137.

Agreement approving the procedures for the reciprocal filing of classified patent applications. Exchange of notes at Athens April 26, 1960; entered into force April 26, 1960.
11 UST 1389; TIAS 4476; 372 UNTS 299.

POSTAL MATTERS

Money order convention. Signed at Athens November 9 and at Washington December 8, 1923; operative April 1, 1927.
NP

Agreement concerning the exchange of parcel post, and regulations of execution. Signed at Athens July 14 and at Washington August 1, 1933; operative June 1, 1933.
48 Stat. 1594; Post Office Department print.

International express mail agreement, with detailed regulations. Signed at Athens and Washington June 5 and 21, 1985; entered into force July 1, 1985.
TIAS 11152.

Memorandum of understanding concerning the operation of the INTELPOST field trial, with details of implementation. Signed at Athens and Washington July 25 and August 15, 1985; entered into force August 19, 1985.
TIAS 11247.

PUBLICATIONS

Agreement relating to the exchange of official publications. Exchange of notes at Athens September 26 and October 24, 1950; entered into force October 24, 1950.
2 UST 473; TIAS 2193; 133 UNTS 41.

RELIEF SUPPLIES AND PACKAGES

Agreement relating to duty-free entry and free inland transportation of relief supplies and packages. Signed at Athens February 9, 1949; entered into force February 9, 1949.
63 Stat. 2359; TIAS 1898; 8 Bevans 450; 79 UNTS 95.

Amendments:
December 19, 1951 and May 7, 1952 (3 UST 4282; TIAS 2574; 179 UNTS 216).
July 18 and December 22, 1952 (3 UST 5327; TIAS 2737; 185 UNTS 400).

SHIPPING

Agreement relating to jurisdiction over vessels utilizing the Louisiana Offshore Oil Port. Exchange of notes at Athens May 7 and 12, 1982; entered into force May 12, 1982.
TIAS 10453.

SMUGGLING

Convention for prevention of smuggling of alcoholic beverages. Signed at Washington April 25, 1928; entered into force February 18, 1929.
45 Stat. 2736; TS 772; 8 Bevans 327; 91 LNTS 231.

SOCIAL SECURITY

Agreement on social security, with administrative arrangement. Signed at Athens June 22, 1993; entered into force September 1, 1994.
TIAS

TAXATION

Convention and protocol for the avoidance of double taxation and the prevention of fiscal evasion with respect to taxes on the estates of deceased persons.[1] Signed at Athens February 20, 1950; protocol signed at Athens July 18, 1953; entered into force December 30, 1953.
5 UST 12; TIAS 2901; 196 UNTS 269.

Protocol modifying and supplementing the convention of February 20, 1950, for the avoidance of double taxation and the prevention of fiscal evasion with respect to taxes on the estates of deceased persons. Signed at Ath-

GREECE (Cont'd)

ens February 12, 1964; entered into force October 27, 1967.
18 UST 2853; TIAS 6375; 632 UNTS 315.

Convention and protocol for the avoidance of double taxation and prevention of fiscal evasion with respect to taxes on income.[2] Signed at Athens February 20, 1950; protocol signed at Athens April 20, 1953; entered into force December 30, 1953.
5 UST 47; TIAS 2902; 196 UNTS 291.

Agreement regarding privileges, immunities, and exemptions from taxes or other levies and charges accorded by Greece in implementation of the common defense program and any and all foreign aid programs of the United States. Exchange of notes at Athens February 4, 1953; entered into force February 4, 1953.
4 UST 166; TIAS 2775; 189 UNTS 3.

Agreement concerning relief from double taxation on earnings derived from the operation of ships and aircraft. Exchange of notes at Washington June 10, 1988; entered into force June 10, 1988.
TIAS 11585.

NOTES:
[1] For understanding regarding certain errors in the English text, see exchange of notes of August 3 and 19, 1954 (5 UST 1543; TIAS 3032; 222 UNTS 423).
[2] For understanding regarding certain errors in the Greek text, see exchange of notes of November 29 and December 19, 1961 (13 UST 151; TIAS 4951; 435 UNTS 334).

TELECOMMUNICATION

Agreement concerning the transfer of community radios to the Government of Greece, with three schedules attached. Signed at Athens August 18, 1954; entered into force August 18, 1954.
5 UST 1725; TIAS 3050; 234 UNTS 161.

Agreement relating to the reciprocal granting of authorizations to permit licensed amateur radio operators of either country to operate their stations in the other country. Exchanges of notes at Athens June 20 and July 5, 1978; entered into force July 5, 1978.
30 UST 1648; TIAS 9272; 1153 UNTS 81.

Agreement for the operation of [Voice of America] re-broadcasting stations in Greece, with annexes. Signed at Washington May 20, 1996; entered into force March 17, 1997.
TIAS

TERMINATION

Agreement concerning termination of certain bilateral agreements. Exchange of notes at Ath-

ens January 17 and February 22, 1995; entered into force February 22, 1995.
TIAS 12606.

TRADE (See also COMMERCE)

Protocol relating to compensatory tariff concessions made by Greece to the United States under the general agreement on tariffs and trade with exchange of letters. Signed at Athens May 31, 1971; entered into force May 31, 1971.
22 UST 787; TIAS 7138; 797 UNTS 241.

Agreement providing for consultations should cotton textile or cotton textile product exports from Greece cause market disruption in the United States. Exchange of notes at Athens December 29, 1975 and January 5, 1976; entered into force January 5, 1976.
27 UST 1632; TIAS 8273.

VISAS

Arrangement for the reciprocal reduction of nonimmigrant passport visa fees. Exchange of notes at Athens January 7 and 29, 1949; entered into force January 29, 1949.
63 Stat. 2905; TIAS 2144; 8 Bevans 447; 88 UNTS 35.

Agreement concerning the reciprocal waiver of visas for non-immigrants. Exchange of notes at Athens December 28, 1999 and January 24, 2000; entered into force January 24, 2000.
TIAS

GRENADA

On February 7, 1974 Grenada became an independent state. In a note dated August 19, 1974 to the Secretary-General of the United Nations, the Prime Minister made a statement reading in part as follows:

"I have the honour to inform you that the Government of Grenada, having attained Independence on the 7th February, 1974, and being conscious of the desirability of continuing and maintaining existing International Agreements which applied before Independence and being willing to accept its obligations under International Law to honour its treaty commitments, acknowledges that the many treaty rights and obligations entered into by the Government of the United Kingdom in respect of the Government of Grenada, were succeeded to by the Government of Grenada upon the attainment of Independence and in accordance with customary International Law and Practice.

"2. It is desirous, therefore, that it be accepted that each treaty has been legally succeeded to by the Government of Grenada and that actions relating to all treaties be based on this succession until a decision is otherwise taken and due notification communicated to the

United Nations and to the states signatories thereto in respect of any such particular treaty.

"3. The Government of Grenada reserves the right to terminate the operation of any such treaty succeeded to if it is desirable to do so. In such circumstances due notice will be given of any such termination and in the terms thereof."

AVIATION

Agreement between the United States and the United Kingdom relating to air services. Signed at Bermuda February 11, 1946; entered into force February 11, 1946.
60 Stat. 1499; TIAS 1507; 3 UNTS 253.

Amendment:
May 27, 1966 (17 UST 683; TIAS 6019; 573 UNTS 274).

Agreement modifying the agreement of February 11, 1946, as amended, as applied to air services between the United States and Grenada. Exchange of notes at St. George's March 19 and May 11, 1987; entered into force May 11, 1987.
TIAS 11279.

CONSULS

Consular convention between the United States and the United Kingdom. Signed at Washington June 6, 1951; entered into force September 7, 1972.
3 UST 3426; TIAS 2494; 165 UNTS 121.

COPYRIGHT (See APPENDIX)

DEFENSE

Agreement concerning the status of United States forces in Grenada. Exchange of notes at St. George's March 12 and 13, 1984; entered into force March 13, 1984.
TIAS

Agreement concerning the provision of training related to defense articles under the United States International Military Education and Training (IMET) Program. Exchange of notes at St. George's May 18 and 24, 1984; entered into force May 24, 1984.
NP

Agreement concerning the status of United States Armed Forces personnel in Grenada. Exchange of notes at St. George's December 7, 1992 and October 11, 1993; entered into force October 11, 1993.
TIAS

GRENADA (Cont'd)

ECONOMIC AND TECHNICAL COOPERATION

General agreement for economic, technical and related assistance. Signed at Grenada May 7, 1984; entered into force May 7, 1984.
TIAS 11132.

EMPLOYMENT

Agreement relating to employment of dependents of official government employees, with addendum. Exchange of notes at St. George's September 14 and 15, 1987; entered into force September 15, 1987.
TIAS 11539.

EXTRADITION

Extradition treaty. Done at St. George's May 30, 1996; entered into force September 14, 1999.
TIAS

FINANCE

Agreement relating to investment guaranties. Signed at St. Georges June 27, 1968; entered into force June 27, 1968.
19 UST 5211; TIAS 6516; 730 UNTS 217.

INVESTMENT

Treaty concerning the reciprocal encouragement and protection of investment. Signed at Washington May 2, 1986; entered into force March 3, 1989.
TIAS

JUDICIAL ASSISTANCE

Treaty on mutual legal assistance in criminal matters, with forms. Done at St. George's May 30, 1996; entered into force September 14, 1999.
TIAS

NARCOTIC DRUGS

Agreement concerning maritime counter-drug operations. Signed at St. George's May 16, 1995; entered into force May 16, 1995.
TIAS 12648.

Agreement regarding the provision of articles, services and associated military education and training by the United States Government for anti-narcotics purposes. Exchange of notes at St. George's December 23, 1996 and March 14, 1997; entered into force March 14, 1997.
TIAS

PEACE CORPS

Agreement relating to the establishment of a Peace Corps program in Grenada. Exchange of notes at Bridgetown and Grenada December 19, 1966 and December 16, 1967; entered into force December 16, 1967.
18 UST 3073; TIAS 6398; 701 UNTS 277.

POSTAL MATTERS

Money order agreement. Signed at Washington July 29 and at Grenada August 29, 1904; operative October 1, 1904.
NP

Agreement for the direct exchange of parcels by parcel post. Signed at Grenada May 20 and at Washington June 21, 1935; operative July 1, 1935.
49 Stat. 3229; Post Office Department print; 162 LNTS 157.

International express mail agreement. Signed at St. George's and Washington January 4 and April 4, 1995; entered into force May 1, 1995.
NP

PROPERTY

Convention between the United States and the United Kingdom relating to tenure and disposition of real and personal property. Signed at Washington March 2, 1899; applicable to Grenada February 9, 1901.
31 Stat. 1939; TS 146; 12 Bevans 246.

Supplementary convention relating to the tenure and disposition of real and personal property. Signed at Washington May 27, 1936; entered into force March 10, 1941.
55 Stat. 1101; TS 964; 203 LNTS 367.

TAXATION

Agreement for the exchange of information with respect to taxes. Signed at Washington December 18, 1986; entered into force July 13, 1987.
TIAS 11410.

TELECOMMUNICATION

Agreement relating to the reciprocal granting of authorizations to permit licensed amateur radio operators of either country to operate their stations in the other country. Exchange of notes at London November 26, 1965; applicable to Grenada December 11, 1979.
16 UST 2047; TIAS 5941; 561 UNTS 193.

Agreement between the United States and the United Kingdom extending to certain territories the application of the agreement of November 26, 1965 relating to the reciprocal granting of authorizations to permit licensed amateur radio operators of either country to operate their stations in the other country. Exchange of notes at London December 11, 1969; entered into force December 11, 1969.
20 UST 4089; TIAS 6800; 732 UNTS 334.

Arrangement relating to radio communications between amateur stations on behalf of third parties. Exchange of notes at St. George's December 5 and 8, 1983; entered into force December 8, 1983.
TIAS 10855.

Agreement concerning establishment of a radio relay station of the United States Information Agency (VOA) on the Island of Grenada. Signed at St. George's September 29, 1987; entered into force March 23, 1988.
TIAS 12394.

TRADE-MARKS

Declaration by the United States and the United Kingdom affording reciprocal protection to trade-marks. Signed at London October 24, 1877; entered into force October 24, 1877.
20 Stat. 703; TS 138; 12 Bevans 198.

GUATEMALA

AGRICULTURAL COMMODITIES

Agricultural commodities agreement, with memorandum of understanding. Signed at Guatemala August 1, 1984; entered into force September 28, 1984.
TIAS 11043.

Agricultural commodities agreement, with memorandum of understanding. Signed at Guatemala June 6, 1985; entered into force August 7, 1985.
NP

Amendments:
August 9, 1985 (NP).
July 2, 1986 (NP).
August 29, 1986 (NP).

Agricultural commodities agreement. Signed at Guatemala May 26, 1987; entered into force November 5, 1987.
NP

Amendment:
September 22, 1987 (NP).

GUATEMALA (Cont'd)

Agricultural commodities agreement. Signed at Guatemala June 16, 1988; entered into force June 26, 1989.
NP

Agricultural commodities agreement. Signed at Guatemala October 28, 1988; entered into force June 27, 1989.
NP

AGRICULTURE

Memorandum of understanding relating to co-operative efforts to protect crops from pest damage and diseases. Signed at Guatemala February 21, 1977; entered into force February 21, 1977.
29 UST 228; TIAS 8807.

Agreement relating to a cooperative program for the prevention of foot-and-mouth disease, rinderpest, and other exotic diseases in Guatemala. Signed at Guatemala March 3, 1977; entered into force March 3, 1977.
29 UST 242; TIAS 8808.

Cooperative agreement to assist the Government of Guatemala in execution of an eradication program of the Mediterranean fruit fly (MEDFLY). Signed at Guatemala October 22, 1981; entered into force October 22, 1981.
33 UST 4123; TIAS 10288; 1549 UNTS 361.

Extension:
September 17, 1985 (TIAS 11930).

AMITY

Treaty of peace, amity, commerce, and navigation.[1] Signed at Guatemala March 3, 1849; entered into force May 13, 1852.
10 Stat. 875; TS 149; 8 Bevans 461.

NOTE:
[1] Articles relating to commerce and navigation terminated November 4, 1874.

ATOMIC ENERGY

Agreement providing for a grant to assist in the acquisition of certain nuclear research and training equipment and materials. Exchange of notes at Guatemala April 7 and 23, 1960; entered into force April 23, 1960.
11 UST 1449; TIAS 4485.

AVIATION

Military air transit agreement. Exchange of notes at Guatemala December 20, 1949; entered into force December 20, 1949.
64 Stat. B122; TIAS 2042; 8 Bevans 610; 70 UNTS 71.

Memorandum of cooperation for mutual cooperation in the promotion and development of civil aviation. Signed at Washington and Guatemala May 26 and June 11, 1999; entered into force June 11, 1999.
TIAS

COMMERCE (See also AMITY)

Convention for the development of commerce and to increase the exchange of commodities by facilitating the work of traveling salesmen. Signed at Washington December 3, 1918; entered into force August 25, 1919.
41 Stat. 1669; TS 642; 8 Bevans 498.

COPYRIGHT (See APPENDIX)

CULTURAL PROPERTY

Agreement for the recovery and return of stolen archaeological, historical and cultural properties. Signed at Washington May 21, 1984; entered into force August 22, 1984.
TIAS 11077.

Memorandum of understanding concerning the imposition of import restrictions on archaeological objects and materials from the pre-Columbian cultures of Guatemala, with appendix. Signed at Washington September 29, 1997; entered into force September 29, 1997.
TIAS

DEFENSE

Agreement providing for the transfer of equipment and material to the Government of Guatemala subject to certain understandings. Exchange of notes at Guatemala July 27 and 30, 1954; entered into force July 30, 1954.
5 UST 1926; TIAS 3059; 234 UNTS 235.

Military assistance agreement. Signed at Guatemala June 18, 1955; entered into force June 18, 1955.
6 UST 2107; TIAS 3283; 262 UNTS 105.

Agreement relating to the disposition of equipment and materials no longer required in furtherance of the mutual defense assistance program. Exchange of notes at Guatemala December 16, 1957; entered into force December 16, 1957.
8 UST 2463; TIAS 3966; 307 UNTS 306.

Agreement relating to the furnishing of defense articles and services to Guatemala for the purpose of contributing to its internal security. Exchange of notes at Guatemala May 25 and August 2, 1962; entered into force August 2, 1962.
13 UST 2128; TIAS 5173; 461 UNTS 199.

Agreement concerning payment to the United States of net proceeds from the sale of defense articles furnished under the military assistance program. Exchange of notes at Guatemala September 20 and 27, 1974; entered into force September 27, 1974; effective July 1, 1974.
25 UST 2489; TIAS 7932.

Agreement concerning security assistance matters and the provision of articles, services and associated military education and training by the United States Government for anti-narcotics purposes. Exchange of notes at Guatemala January 12 and February 1, 1999; entered into force February 1, 1999.
TIAS

ECONOMIC AND TECHNICAL COOPERATION

General agreement for technical cooperation. Signed at Guatemala September 1, 1954; entered into force September 1, 1954.
5 UST 2010; TIAS 3068; 199 UNTS 51.

Development assistance agreement. Signed at Washington December 13, 1954; entered into force December 13, 1954.
5 UST 2972; TIAS 3155; 237 UNTS 169.

Agency for International Development:
November 3, 1975 (27 UST 4267; TIAS 8450).
April 8, 1976 (28 UST 1581; TIAS 8521).
September 20, 1976 (28 UST 7213; TIAS 8713).
September 14, 1977 (29 UST 3337; TIAS 9015; 1123 UNTS 191).
May 18, 1978 (30 UST 2699; TIAS 9360; 1231 UNTS 329).
April 13, 1987 (NP).
September 24, 1987 (NP).
June 27, 1988 (NP).
July 7, 1989 (NP).
January 13, 1997 (NP).
July 24, 1997 (NP).
September 16, 1997 (NP).
April 21, 1998 (NP).
June 3, 1998 (NP).

EMPLOYMENT

Agreement relating to the employment of dependents of official government employees, with agreement and addendum. Exchange of notes at Washington March 22 and 23, 1990; entered into force March 23, 1990.
TIAS

GUATEMALA (Cont'd)

ENVIRONMENTAL COOPERATION

Agreement for cooperation in the Global Learning and Observations to Benefit the Environment (GLOBE) Program, with appendices. Signed at Guatemala December 5, 1997; entered into force December 5, 1997.
TIAS

EXTRADITION

Treaty for the mutual extradition of fugitives from justice. Signed at Washington February 27, 1903; entered into force August 15, 1903.
33 Stat. 2147; TS 425; 8 Bevans 482.

Supplementary extradition convention. Signed at Guatemala February 20, 1940; entered into force March 13, 1941.
55 Stat. 1097; TS 963; 8 Bevans 528.

FINANCE

Agreement relating to investment guaranties.[1] Exchange of notes at Guatemala August 9, 1960; entered into force August 29, 1962.
13 UST 2008; TIAS 5158; 461 UNTS 15.

NOTE:
[1] For corrections in the Spanish text, see exchange of notes of August 23 and 27, 1962 (13 UST 2008; TIAS 5158; 461 UNTS 15).

HIGHWAYS

Agreement relating to the construction of the inter-American highway. Exchange of notes at Guatemala May 19, 1943; entered into force May 19, 1943.
57 Stat. 1111; EAS 345; 8 Bevans 545; 28 UNTS 377.

Amendments:
May 18, 1948 (62 Stat. 3923; TIAS 2001; 8 Bevans 596; 67 UNTS 161).
July 28 and August 28, 1954 (5 UST 2244; TIAS 3084; 237 UNTS 294).

Agreement providing for cooperation in the construction of the inter-American Highway in Guatemala. Exchange of notes at Guatemala September 25 and October 3, 1963; entered into force October 3, 1963.
14 UST 1591; TIAS 5463; 493 UNTS 45.

MAPPING

Agreement governing cooperation in mapping, charting and geodesy. Signed at Washington and Guatemala February 14 and 27, 1986; entered into force February 27, 1986.
TIAS 11211.

Basic exchange and cooperative agreement for topographic mapping, nautical and aeronautical charting and information, geodesy and geophysics, digital data and related mapping, charting and geodesy materials, with glossary. Signed at Guatemala and Fairfax June 7 and July 2, 1996; entered into force July 2, 1996.
NP

MISSIONS, MILITARY

Agreement relating to the status of the Army and Air Force missions to Guatemala. Exchange of notes at Guatemala April 29 and May 4, 1965; entered into force May 4, 1965.
16 UST 742; TIAS 5802; 545 UNTS 163.

PATENTS

Convention for the reciprocal protection of patents. Signed at Guatemala November 10, 1906; entered into force July 9, 1907.
35 Stat. 1878; TS 463; 8 Bevans 489.

PEACE CORPS

Agreement relating to the establishment of a Peace Corps program in Guatemala. Exchange of notes at Guatemala City December 28 and 29, 1962; entered into force December 29, 1962.
14 UST 280; TIAS 5307; 474 UNTS 31.

POSTAL MATTERS

Parcel post agreement. Signed at Guatemala October 25, and at Washington November 30, 1945; operative August 1, 1945.
59 Stat. 1827; EAS 499; 139 UNTS 45.

International express mail agreement, with detailed regulations. Signed at Guatemala and Washington November 7 and December 19, 1989; entered into force February 15, 1990.
TIAS 11717.

PROPERTY

Convention relating to tenure and disposition of real and personal property. Signed at Guatemala August 27, 1901; entered into force September 26, 1902.
32 Stat. 1944; TS 412; 8 Bevans 480.

PUBLICATIONS

Agreement relating to the exchange of official publications. Exchange of notes at Guatemala March 23 and April 13, 1944; entered into force March 23, 1944.
58 Stat. 1362; EAS 412; 8 Bevans 555; 106 UNTS 213.

SCIENTIFIC COOPERATION

Memorandum of cooperation on research collaboration in the area of human infectious diseases, with annex. Signed at Barcenas May 13, 1999; entered into force September 7, 2000.
TIAS

TELECOMMUNICATION

Agreement relating to the reciprocal granting of authorizations to permit licensed amateur radio operators of either country to operate their stations in the other country. Exchange of notes at Guatemala November 30 and December 11, 1967; entered into force October 2, 1969.
20 UST 2883; TIAS 6766; 726 UNTS 147.

Arrangement relating to radio communications between amateur stations on behalf of third parties. Exchange of notes at Guatemala October 21 and November 19, 1971; entered into force May 26, 1973.
24 UST 1120; TIAS 7636.

TRADE-MARKS

Convention for the reciprocal protection of trade-marks and trade labels. Signed at Guatemala April 15, 1901; entered into force April 7, 1902.
32 Stat. 1866; TS 404; 8 Bevans 478.

VISAS

Agreement providing reciprocally for gratis nonimmigrant visas valid for multiple entries. Exchange of notes at Guatemala May 30, 1956; entered into force May 30, 1956.
7 UST 1075; TIAS 3589; 275 UNTS 271.

GUINEA

AGRICULTURAL COMMODITIES

Agricultural commodities agreement, with exchanges of notes. Signed at Conakry February 2, 1962; entered into force February 2, 1962.
13 UST 131; TIAS 4948; 435 UNTS 35.

GUINEA (Cont'd)

Amendments:
May 3, 1962 (13 UST 1114; TIAS 5057; 451 UNTS 341).
June 29, 1962 (13 UST 1800; TIAS 5126; 458 UNTS 364).

Agricultural commodities agreement with exchange of notes. Signed at Conakry May 22, 1963; entered into force May 22, 1963.
14 UST 1003; TIAS 5394; 487 UNTS 251.

Amendments:
November 2, 1963 (14 UST 1784; TIAS 5487; 494 UNTS 362).
July 1 and 11, 1964 (15 UST 2169; TIAS 5700; 531 UNTS 408).
September 18, 1965 (16 UST 1671; TIAS 5890; 574 UNTS 256).

Agricultural commodities agreement with exchange of notes. Signed at Conakry June 13, 1964; entered into force June 13, 1964.
15 UST 1926; TIAS 5668; 531 UNTS 263.

Amendments:
October 7, 1964 (15 UST 2172; TIAS 5701; 531 UNTS 280).
December 21, 1964 (15 UST 2238; TIAS 5712; 531 UNTS 284).

Agricultural commodities agreement, with exchange of notes. Signed at Conakry February 4, 1966; entered into force February 4, 1966.
17 UST 109; TIAS 5966; 579 UNTS 213.

Agricultural commodities agreement, with annex. Signed at Conakry October 18, 1967; entered into force October 18, 1967.
18 UST 2887; TIAS 6381; 701 UNTS 65.

Related agreements:
February 3, 1969 (20 UST 380; TIAS 6640; 714 UNTS 157).
October 23 and 28, 1969 (20 UST 3045; TIAS 6782; 727 UNTS 436).
August 8, 1970 (21 UST 2208; TIAS 6971; 764 UNTS 211).
March 12, 1971 (22 UST 1035; TIAS 7147; 796 UNTS 317).
June 17, 1971 (22 UST 1574; TIAS 7182; 806 UNTS 347).
May 15 and 23, 1972 (23 UST 1296; TIAS 7406).
March 15, 1973 (25 UST 2729; TIAS 7942; 1279 UNTS 271).
March 30 and April 11, 1973 (25 UST 2747; TIAS 7942; 1279 UNTS 283).
May 8, 1974 (25 UST 917; TIAS 7835).
May 24, 1974 (25 UST 924; TIAS 7835).
June 13 and 14, 1974 (25 UST 1277; TIAS 7860).

Agricultural commodities agreement. Signed at Conakry May 8, 1975; entered into force May 8, 1975.
27 UST 1474; TIAS 8258; 1049 UNTS 87.

Agricultural commodities agreement. Signed at Conakry April 21, 1976; entered into force April 21, 1976.
27 UST 3467; TIAS 8378.

Related agreements:
September 22, 1976 (28 UST 3269; TIAS 8585; 1087 UNTS 27).
June 13 and 15, 1977 (29 UST 1028; TIAS 8864; 1115 UNTS 363).
December 10, 1977 (TIAS 10726).
May 29, 1979 (34 UST 529; TIAS 10375).
May 22, 1980 (32 UST 1375; TIAS 9779; 1274 UNTS 51).
May 9, 1981 (TIAS 10726).
June 7, 1982 (TIAS 10726).
June 4, 1983 (TIAS 10726).
June 11, 1984 (TIAS 11039).

Agricultural commodities agreement. Signed at Conakry June 14, 1985; entered into force June 14, 1985.
NP

Agricultural commodities agreement. Signed at Conakry January 3, 1986; entered into force January 3, 1986.
NP

Related agreement:
May 18, 1987 (NP).

Agricultural commodities agreement under food for progress, with attachments. Signed at Conakry September 15, 1986; entered into force September 15, 1986.
NP

COPYRIGHT (See APPENDIX)

CULTURAL RELATIONS

Cultural relations agreement. Exchange of notes at Washington October 28, 1959; entered into force October 28, 1959.
10 UST 1829; TIAS 4342; 358 UNTS 169.

DEFENSE

Agreement relating to military assistance. Exchange of notes at Conakry June 29, 1965; entered into force June 29, 1965.
16 UST 1073; TIAS 5848; 549 UNTS 139.

Agreement concerning the provision of training related to defense articles under the United States International Military Education and Training (IMET) Program. Exchange of notes at Conakry March 29, 1983 and February 13, 1984; entered into force February 13, 1984.
TIAS 10944.

Agreement regarding grants under the Foreign Assistance Act of 1961, as amended, and the furnishing of defense articles, related training, and other defense services from the United States of America to the Government of the Republic of Guinea. Exchange of notes at Conakry July 13 and December 22, 2000; entered into force December 22, 2000.
TIAS

ECONOMIC AND TECHNICAL COOPERATION

Agreement providing for the furnishing of economic, technical and related assistance. Exchange of notes at Conakry September 30, 1960; entered into force September 30, 1960.
11 UST 2258; TIAS 4603; 394 UNTS 103.

Agency for International Development:
September 27, 1977 (29 UST 5043; TIAS 9091).
March 31, 1978 (29 UST 5098; TIAS 9091).
April 14 and June 5, 1978 (29 UST 5756; TIAS 9149).

ENVIRONMENTAL COOPERATION

Agreement for cooperation in the Global Learning and Observations to Benefit the Environment (GLOBE) Program, with appendices. Signed at Conakry May 14, 1998; entered into force May 14, 1998.
TIAS

FINANCE

Agreement relating to investment guaranties. Exchange of notes at Washington May 9, 1962; entered into force May 9, 1962.
13 UST 1091; TIAS 5052; 451 UNTS 197.

Agreement regarding the consolidation and rescheduling of certain debts owed to or guaranteed by the United States Government and its agencies, with annexes. Signed at Conakry February 27, 1987; entered into force April 8, 1987.
NP

Agreement regarding the consolidation and rescheduling of certain debts owed to, guaranteed by or insured by the United States Government and its agencies, with annexes. Signed at Conakry November 22, 1989; entered into force January 22, 1990.
NP

Agreement regarding the consolidation and rescheduling or refinancing of certain debts owed to, guaranteed by or insured by the United States Government and its agencies, with annexes. Signed at Conakry June 24, 1993; entered into force September 13, 1993.
NP

Agreement regarding the consolidation, reduction and rescheduling of certain debts owed to, guaranteed by, or insured by the United States Government and its agencies. Signed at Conakry November 18, 1996; entered into force April 9, 1997.
NP

Agreement regarding the consolidation, reduction and rescheduling of certain debts owed to, guaranteed by, or insured by the United States Government and its agencies, with annexes.

GUINEA (Cont'd)

Signed at Conakry October 29, 1997; entered
into force December 17, 1997.
NP

INFORMATIONAL MEDIA GUARANTIES

Agreement relating to an informational media
guaranty program in Guinea. Exchange of
notes at Conakry October 31 and November 3,
1962; entered into force November 3, 1962.
13 UST 2508; TIAS 5217; 459 UNTS 259.

PEACE CORPS

Agreement relating to the establishment of a
Peace Corps program in Guinea. Exchange of
notes at Conakry December 11 and 14, 1962;
entered into force December 14, 1962.
13 UST 2729; TIAS 5246; 462 UNTS 247.

POSTAL MATTERS

International express mail agreement, with detailed regulations. Signed at Conakry and
Washington December 31, 1987 and February
2, 1988; entered into force March 15, 1988.
TIAS 11562.

TELECOMMUNICATION

Agreement relating to radio communication facilities at or near Embassy sites for transmission of official messages. Exchange of
notes at Conakry February 19 and April 23,
1963; entered into force April 23, 1963.
14 UST 847; TIAS 5365; 487 UNTS 291.

GUINEA-BISSAU

COPYRIGHT (See APPENDIX)

DEFENSE

Agreement concerning the provision of training
related to defense articles under the United
States International Military Education and
Training (IMET) Program. Exchange of notes
at Bissau September 10 and October 16, 1986;
entered into force October 16, 1986.
TIAS 11378.

ECONOMIC AND TECHNICAL COOPERATION

Agency for International Development:
November 10, 1977 (29 UST 5289; TIAS
    9107).
January 8, 1978 (29 UST 5768; TIAS 9151).

EMPLOYMENT

Agreement relating to the employment of de-
pendents of official government employees.
Exchange of notes at Bissau July 23, 1997 and
February 16, 1998; entered into force February
16, 1998.
TIAS

FINANCE

Investment incentive agreement. Exchange of
notes at Bissau August 14 and 15, 1985; entered into force August 20, 1986.
TIAS 12088.

PEACE CORPS

Agreement relating to the establishment of a
Peace Corps program in Guinea-Bissau. Exchange of notes at Bissau January 12 and 15,
1988; entered into force January 15, 1988.
TIAS 12104.

POSTAL MATTERS

International express mail agreement, with detailed regulations. Signed at Bissau and Washington July 17 and August 28, 1991; entered
into force September 30, 1991.
TIAS 11797.

GULF COOPERATION COUNCIL

METROLOGY

Memorandum of understanding concerning
technical cooperation on standards, with annex.
Signed at Bahrain March 10, 1996; entered
into force March 10, 1996.
TIAS

GUYANA

On May 26, 1966, Guyana (former British
Guiana) became an independent state. In a letter dated June 30, 1966 to the Secretary General of the United Nations, the Prime Minister
of Guyana made a statement reading in part as
follows:

"I have the honour to inform you that the
Government of Guyana, conscious of the desirability of maintaining existing legal relationships, and conscious of its obligations under
international law to honour its treaty commitments, acknowledges that many treaty rights
and obligations of the Government of the
United Kingdom in respect to British Guiana
were succeeded to by Guyana upon independence by virtue of customary international law.

"2. Since, however, it is likely that by virtue
of customary international law certain treaties
may have lapsed at the date of independence
of Guyana, it seems essential that each treaty
should be subjected to legal examination. It is
proposed after this examination has been completed, to indicate which, if any, of the treaties
which may have lapsed by customary international law the Government of Guyana wishes to treat as having lapsed.

"3. As a result, the manner in which British
Guiana was acquired by the British Crown,
and its history previous to that date, consideration will have to be given to the question
which, if any, treaties contracted previous to
1804 remain in force by virtue of customary
international law.

"4. It is desired that it be presumed that each
treaty has been legally succeeded to by Guyana and that action be based on this presumption until a decision is reached that it should
be regarded as having lapsed. Should the Government of Guyana be of the opinion that it
has legally succeeded to a treaty and wishes to
terminate the operation of the treaty, it will in
due course give notice of termination in the
terms thereof."

AGRICULTURAL COMMODITIES

Agricultural commodities agreement with
annex. Signed at Georgetown September 17,
1968; entered into force September 17, 1968.
19 UST 6692; TIAS 6585; 702 UNTS 183.

Related agreements:
October 14, 1970 (21 UST 2201; TIAS 6969;
    776 UNTS 57).
June 8, 1972 (23 UST 922; TIAS 7359).

Agricultural commodities agreement. Signed at
Georgetown January 27, 1978; entered into
force January 27, 1978.
29 UST 5725; TIAS 9145.

Amendment:
May 16 and 29, 1978 (29 UST 5739; TIAS
    9145).

Related agreements:
June 1, 1979 (30 UST 5936; TIAS 9527; 1180
    UNTS 407).
April 23, 1980 (32 UST 1046; TIAS 9755;
    1222 UNTS 287).
July 12 and 14, 1980 (32 UST 2063; TIAS
    9818).

GUYANA (Cont'd)

Agricultural commodities agreement. Signed at Georgetown August 7, 1986; entered into force August 7, 1986.
NP

Amendment:
September 25 and 30, 1986 (NP).

Agricultural commodities agreement. Signed at Georgetown May 2, 1987; entered into force May 2, 1987.
NP

Amendment:
August 18, 1987 (NP).

Related agreements:
November 25, 1987 (NP).
July 28, 1988 (NP).
February 22, 1989 (NP).
July 31, 1989 (NP).
January 9, 1990 (NP).
July 19 and 23, 1990 (NP).
October 3 and 23, 1990 (NP).
November 9, 1990 (NP).

AVIATION

Arrangement between the United States and the United Kingdom relating to pilot licenses to operate civil aircraft. Exchange of notes at Washington March 28, and April 5, 1935; entered into force May 5, 1935.
49 Stat. 3731; EAS 77; 12 Bevans 513; 162 LNTS 59.

Agreement between the United States and the United Kingdom relating to air services. Signed at Bermuda February 11, 1946; entered into force February 11, 1946.
60 Stat. 1499; TIAS 1507; 12 Bevans 726; 3 UNTS 253.

CONSULS

Consular convention between the United States and the United Kingdom. Signed at Washington June 6, 1951; entered into force September 7, 1952.
3 UST 3426; TIAS 2494; 165 UNTS 121.

COPYRIGHT (See APPENDIX)

DEFENSE (See also MUTUAL SECURITY)

Agreement concerning the provision of training related to defense articles under the United States International Military Education and Training (IMET) Program. Exchange of notes at Georgetown January 13 and 22, 1981; entered into force January 22, 1981.
33 UST 850; TIAS 10068.

Agreement regarding grants under the Foreign Assistance Act of 1961, as amended, and the furnishing of defense articles, related training and other defense services from the United States to Guyana. Exchange of notes at Georgetown March 31 and June 8, 1994; entered into force June 8, 1994.
TIAS 12253.

Agreement regarding the status of military and civilian personnel of the United States Department of Defense temporarily present in Guyana in connection with military exercises and training, counter-drug related activities, United States security assistance programs, or other agreed purposes. Exchange of notes at Georgetown December 28 and 29, 2000; entered into force December 29, 2000.
NP

ECONOMIC AND TECHNICAL COOPERATION

General agreement for economic, technical and related assistance. Signed at Georgetown November 8, 1979; entered into force November 8, 1979.
31 UST 4826; TIAS 9644.

Agency for International Development:
November 9, 1971 (28 UST 1019; TIAS 8491).
September 14, 1972 (28 UST 1043; TIAS 8492).
November 6, 1975 (28 UST 1038; TIAS 8491).
November 6, 1975 (28 UST 1060; TIAS 8492).
June 6 and July 6, 1977 (29 UST 4881; TIAS 9083; 1134 UNTS 217).
July 13, 1977 (29 UST 2623; TIAS 8962; 1123 UNTS 111).

EXTRADITION

Extradition treaty between the United States and the United Kingdom. Signed at London December 22, 1931; entered into force June 24, 1935.
47 Stat. 2122; TS 849; 12 Bevans 482; 163 LNTS 59.

FINANCE

Agreement relating to investment guaranties. Signed at Georgetown May 29, 1965; entered into force August 18, 1965.
16 UST 2050; TIAS 5942; 605 UNTS 87.

Agreement regarding the consolidation and rescheduling or refinancing of certain debts owed to, guaranteed by, or insured by the United States Government and its agencies, with annexes. Signed at Georgetown September 8, 1989; entered into force October 13, 1989.
NP

Swap agreement among the United States Treasury and the Bank of Guyana/Republic of Guyana, with memorandum of understanding. Signed at Georgetown and Washington June 19 and 20, 1990; entered into force June 20, 1990.
TIAS

Agreement regarding the consolidation and rescheduling of certain debts owed to, guaranteed by, or insured by the United States Government and its agencies, with annexes. Signed at Georgetown March 28, 1991; entered into force May 13, 1991.
NP

Agreement regarding the discharge of certain debts owed to the Government of the United States, with annex. Signed at Georgetown September 30, 1991; entered into force September 30, 1991.
NP

Agreement regarding the consolidation and rescheduling or refinancing of certain debts owed to, guaranteed by or insured by the United States Government and its agencies, with annexes. Signed at Washington April 5, 1994; entered into force May 23, 1994.
NP

Agreement regarding the reduction and reorganization of certain debts owed to, guaranteed by, or insured by the United States Government and its agencies, with annexes. Signed at Georgetown March 27, 1997; entered into force June 6, 1997.
NP

PEACE CORPS

Agreement relating to the establishment of a Peace Corps program in Guyana. Exchange of notes at Georgetown May 31 and June 7, 1967; entered into force June 7, 1967.
18 UST 1259; TIAS 6277; 686 UNTS 25.

POSTAL MATTERS

Parcel post agreement with detailed regulations of execution. Signed at Georgetown August 13 and at Washington September 6, 1938; entered into force October 1, 1938.
53 Stat. 1989; Post Office Department print; 193 LNTS 117.

International express mail agreement with detailed regulations. Signed at Georgetown and Washington February 25 and March 31, 1986; entered into force July 1, 1986.
TIAS 11406.

Postal money order agreement. Signed at Georgetown and Washington September 23

GUYANA (Cont'd)

and October 10, 1991; entered into force November 15, 1991.
TIAS 11792.

International express mail agreement, with detailed regulations. Signed at Georgetown and Washington June 22 and July 16, 1994; entered into force November 1, 1994.
NP

PROPERTY

Convention between the United States and the United Kingdom relating to the tenure and disposition of real and personal property. Signed at Washington March 2, 1899; applicable to British Guiana June 17, 1901.
31 Stat. 1939; TS 146; 12 Bevans 246.

Supplementary convention relating to the tenure and disposition of real and personal property of March 2, 1899. Signed at Washington May 27, 1936; entered into force March 10, 1941.
55 Stat. 1101; TS 964; 5 Bevans 140; 203 UNTS 367.

SCIENTIFIC COOPERATION

Memorandum of understanding concerning scientific and technical cooperation in the earth and mapping sciences, with annexes. Signed at Georgetown July 21, 1993; entered into force July 21, 1993.
TIAS 12158.

TAXATION

Agreement for the exchange of information with respect to taxes. Signed at Georgetown July 22, 1992; entered into force August 27, 1992.
TIAS 12137.

TELECOMMUNICATION

Agreement relating to the reciprocal granting of authorizations to permit licensed amateur radio operators of either country to operate their stations in the other country. Exchange of notes at Georgetown May 6 and 13, 1968; entered into force May 13, 1968.
19 UST 4892; TIAS 6494; 698 UNTS 243.

Arrangement relating to radio communications between the amateur stations on behalf of third parties. Exchange of notes at Georgetown May 30 and June 6, 1972; entered into force July 6, 1972.
23 UST 906; TIAS 7355.

TRADE-MARKS

Declaration by the United States and the United Kingdom affording reciprocal protection to trade-marks. Signed at London October 24, 1877; entered into force October 24, 1877.
20 Stat. 703; TS 138; 12 Bevans 198.

VISAS

Agreement relating to extended validity of passports issued by Guyana. Exchange of notes at Georgetown May 20 and July 18, 1970; entered into force January 18, 1971.
22 UST 233; TIAS 7056; 781 UNTS 159.

HAGUE CONFERENCE ON PRIVATE INTERNATIONAL LAW

TAXATION

Tax reimbursement agreement, with annex. Signed at The Hague January 27, 1993; entered into force January 27, 1993.
TIAS 12142.

HAITI

AGRICULTURAL COMMODITIES

Agricultural commodities agreement. Signed at Port-au-Prince March 20, 1975; entered into force March 20, 1975.
28 UST 4462; TIAS 8600.

Related agreements:
March 22, 1976 (28 UST 4483; TIAS 8601).
May 14 and 17, 1976 (28 UST 4490; TIAS 8601).
November 30, 1976 (NP).
April 13, 1977 (NP).
June 23, 1978 (NP).

Agricultural commodities agreement, with memorandum of understanding. Signed at Port-au-Prince June 8, 1979; entered into force June 8, 1979.
NP

Related agreements:
June 24, 1980 (NP).
May 25, 1981 (NP).
May 28, 1982 (NP).
August 17 and 18, 1982 (NP).
June 8, 1983 (NP).
June 12, 1984 (NP).

Agricultural commodities agreement, with annexes and memorandum of understanding. Signed at Port-au-Prince May 30, 1985; entered into force May 30, 1985.
NP

Amendments:
June 2 and 5, 1986 (NP).
June 19, 1987 (NP).

AVIATION

Memorandum of agreement [NAT–I–3448] concerning the provision of civil aviation assistance. Signed at Washington and Port Au Prince August 27 and September 3, 1997; entered into force September 3, 1997.
TIAS

COPYRIGHT (See APPENDIX)

CUSTOMS

Agreement relating to reciprocal customs privileges for consular officers and clerks. Exchange of notes at Port-au-Prince August 14 and 24, 1945; entered into force August 24, 1945.
59 Stat. 1868; EAS 503; 8 Bevans 791; 139 UNTS 311.

DEFENSE

Military assistance agreement. Signed at Washington January 28, 1955; entered into force September 12, 1955.
6 UST 3847; TIAS 3386; 270 UNTS 83.

Agreement for disposition of equipment and materials furnished by the United States under the military assistance agreement of January 28, 1955 and no longer required by Haiti. Exchange of notes at Port-au-Prince March 21 and April 5, 1955; entered into force April 5, 1955.
6 UST 3867; TIAS 3387; 270 UNTS 97.

Agreement relating to the transfer of military equipment, materials and services to Haiti. Exchange of notes at Port-au-Prince September 1, 1960; entered into force September 1, 1960.
11 UST 2097; TIAS 4567; 388 UNTS 249.

Agreement between the governments participating in the multinational force (MNF) authorized pursuant to security council resolution 940 and the Republic of Haiti on the status of MNF forces in Haiti, with related letter. Signed at Miami and Washington December 8 and 22, 1994; entered into force December 22, 1994.
NP

Agreement regarding the status of U.S. military personnel and civilian employees of the Department of Defense temporarily in Haiti in connection with their official duties. Exchange of notes at Port-au-Prince May 10 and 11, 1995; entered into force May 11, 1995.
NP

HAITI (Cont'd)

ECONOMIC AND TECHNICAL COOPERATION

General agreement for technical cooperation. Exchange of notes at Port-au-Prince May 2, 1951; entered into force May 2, 1951.
3 UST 545; TIAS 2414; 151 UNTS 191.

Amendment:
December 15, 1951 and January 8, 1952 (3 UST 4731; TIAS 2635; 180 UNTS 372).

Agreement providing for emergency assistance to Haiti in connection with hurricane disaster. Exchange of notes at Port-au-Prince March 22 and April 1, 1955; entered into force April 1, 1955; operative October 15, 1954.
6 UST 855; TIAS 3232; 261 UNTS 361.

Agency for International Development:
June 29, 1976 (29 UST 1525; TIAS 8897; 1115 UNTS 183).
September 28 and 30, 1976 (29 UST 67; TIAS 8790; 1115 UNTS 219).
April 27, 1977 (29 UST 1249; TIAS 8877; 1115 UNTS 233).
August 30, 1977 (29 UST 5159; TIAS 9094).

EXTRADITION

Treaty for the mutual extradition of fugitives from justice. Signed at Washington August 9, 1904; entered into force June 28, 1905.
34 Stat. 2858; TS 447; 8 Bevans 653.

FINANCE

Agreement relating to guaranties authorized by section 111(b)(3) of the Economic Cooperation Act of 1948, as amended. Exchange of notes at Washington March 13 and April 2, 1953; entered into force April 2, 1953.
4 UST 1546; TIAS 2818; 212 UNTS 143.

Amendments:
November 25 and December 1, 1970 (21 UST 2651; TIAS 7006; 776 UNTS 331).
October 7 and 14, 1975 (29 UST 3387; TIAS 9018).

Agreement regarding the consolidation, reduction and rescheduling of certain debts owed to, guaranteed by or insured by the United States Government and its agencies, with annexes. Signed at Port au Prince August 7, 1995; entered into force September 7, 1995.
NP

Investment incentive agreement. Signed at Port au Prince June 29, 1998; entered into force June 29, 1998.
TIAS

JUDICIAL ASSISTANCE

Agreement on procedures for mutual assistance in law enforcement matters. Signed at Port-au-Prince August 15, 1986; entered into force August 15, 1986.
TIAS 11389.

MARITIME MATTERS

Agreement for the loan of a US Navy net tender to Haiti. Exchange of notes at Port-au-Prince July 8, 1960; entered into force July 8, 1960.
11 UST 1881; TIAS 4534; 380 UNTS 135.

METEOROLOGICAL COOPERATION

Hurricane warning agreement, with memorandum of arrangement. Exchange of notes at Port-au-Prince December 22, 1981; entered into force December 22, 1981.
TIAS

NARCOTIC DRUGS

Agreement for the interdiction of narcotics trafficking. Signed at Port–au–Prince August 31, 1988; entered into force August 31, 1988.
TIAS

PACIFIC SETTLEMENT OF DISPUTES

Arbitration convention. Signed at Washington January 7, 1909; entered into force November 15, 1909.
36 Stat. 2193; TS 535; 8 Bevans 658.

PEACE CORPS

Agreement relating to the establishment of a Peace Corps program in Haiti. Exchange of notes at Port-au-Prince August 12 and 13, 1982; entered into force August 13, 1982.
TIAS 10445.

POSTAL MATTERS

International express mail agreement, with detailed regulations. Signed at Port au Prince and Washington January 22 and and March 13, 1997; entered into force July 1, 1997.
NP

PROPERTY

Agreement relating to exchange of lands in Haiti. Signed at Port-au-Prince October 19, 1942; entered into force October 19, 1942.
56 Stat. 1784; EAS 283; 8 Bevans 764; 120 LNTS 171.

PUBLICATIONS

Agreement relating to the exchange of official publications. Exchange of notes at Port-au-Prince May 29, and June 5, 1941; entered into force May 29, 1941.
55 Stat. 1278; EAS 210; 8 Bevans 734; 101 LNTS 125.

RELIEF SUPPLIES AND PACKAGES

Agreement providing for duty-free entry into Haiti and exemption from internal taxation of relief supplies and packages. Exchange of notes at Port-au-Prince September 8 and 9, 1958; entered into force September 9, 1958.
9 UST 1170; TIAS 4101; 335 UNTS 257.

TECHNICAL ASSISTANCE

Agreement for the furnishing of commodities to Haiti on a reimbursable basis, with annex. Signed at Washington September 28, 1993; entered into force September 28, 1993.
TIAS

Amendment and extension:
October 7, 1994.

TELECOMMUNICATION

Agreement for the exchange of third party messages between radio amateurs of the United States and Haiti. Exchange of notes at Port-au-Prince January 4 and 6, 1960; entered into force February 5, 1960.
11 UST 1; TIAS 4399; 367 UNTS 75.

Agreement relating to the reciprocal granting of authorizations to permit licensed amateur radio operators of either country to operate their stations in the other country. Exchange of notes at Port-au-Prince April 17 and May 17, 1979; entered into force May 17, 1979.
30 UST 4245; TIAS 9456.

Agreement regarding terms of reference for the operation of the Radio Democracy project. Exchange of letters at Washington July 1 and 7, 1994; entered into force July 7, 1994.
TIAS 12555.

HAITI (Cont'd)

TRADE AND COMMERCE

Agreement relating to trade in cotton, wool and man-made fiber textiles and textile products, with annexes. Exchange of letters at Port-au-Prince September 26 and 30, 1986; entered into force September 30, 1986; effective January 1, 1987.
NP

Amendments and extension:
June 9 and 23, 1987 (NP).
July 18, November 19 and 28, 1990 (NP).

HONDURAS

AGRICULTURAL COMMODITIES

Agricultural commodities agreement. Signed at Tegucigalpa March 5, 1975; entered into force March 5, 1975.
26 UST 318; TIAS 8037.

Amendment:
April 18, 1975 (26 UST 1068; TIAS 8094).

Related agreement:
June 9, 1976 (27 UST 2353; TIAS 8313; 1055 UNTS 93).

Agricultural commodities agreement, with annexes and minutes. Signed at Tegucigalpa February 27, 1979; entered into force February 27, 1979.
30 UST 5695; TIAS 9521; 1178 UNTS 29.

Amendments:
July 18, 1980 (32 UST 3256; TIAS 9894).
May 22, 1981 (33 UST 1965; TIAS 10160).

Agricultural commodities agreement, with annexes. Signed at Tegucigalpa June 11, 1982; entered into force June 11, 1982.
NP

Amendments:
August 30, 1982 (NP).
December 3, 1982 (NP).

Related agreements:
June 27, 1983 (NP).
June 21, 1985 (NP).

Agreement for sales of agricultural commodities. Signed at Tegucigalpa December 16, 1983; entered into force December 16, 1983.
NP

Amendments:
February 24, 1984 (NP).
June 19, 1984 (NP).
July 26, 1984 (NP).

Related agreements:
March 11, 1985 (NP).
June 21, 1985 (NP).

Agricultural commodities agreement. Signed at Tegucigalpa March 15, 1986; entered into force March 15, 1986.
NP

Agricultural commodities agreement. Signed at Tegucigalpa March 11, 1987; entered into force March 11, 1987.
NP

Related agreements:
March 7, 1988 (NP).
February 9, 1989 (NP).
July 24, 1989 (NP).
March 29, 1990 (NP).

AGRICULTURE

Agreement continuing in force the agreement of February 28, 1941 relating to plantation rubber investigations in Honduras. Exchange of notes at Tegucigalpa June 18 and 28, 1943; entered into force July 1, 1943.
57 Stat. 1220; EAS 358; 8 Bevans 948; 117 UNTS 220.

Agreement confirming the cooperative agreement for the prevention of foot-and-mouth disease and rinderpest in Honduras. Exchange of notes at Tegucigalpa November 17 and December 20, 1972; entered into force December 20, 1972.
24 UST 942; TIAS 7604; 938 UNTS 139.

Memorandum of understanding relating to cooperative efforts to protect crops from plant pest damage and plant diseases. Signed at Washington and Tegucigalpa March 4 and April 18, 1977; entered into force April 18, 1977.
29 UST 319; TIAS 8816.

AVIATION

Military air transit agreement. Exchange of notes at Tegucigalpa January 22, March 20, and April 23, 1952; entered into force April 23, 1952.
3 UST 3734; TIAS 2502; 198 UNTS 251.

Civil aviation security agreement. Signed at Tegucigalpa August 5, 1991; entered into force August 5, 1991.
TIAS 11804.

Memorandum of agreement concerning assistance in developing and modernizing Honduras' civil aviation infrastructure. Signed at Washington and Tegucigalpa July 24 and August 23, 1996; entered into force August 23, 1996.
TIAS

COMMERCE

Treaty of friendship, commerce and consular rights.[1] Signed at Tegucigalpa December 7, 1927; entered into force July 19, 1928.
45 Stat. 2618; TS 764; 8 Bevans 905; 87 LNTS 421.

NOTE:
[1] Provisions which are inconsistent with the trade agreement of December 18, 1935 (49 Stat. 3851; EAS 86) are replaced by that agreement.

CONSULS (See COMMERCE)

COPYRIGHT (See APPENDIX)

DEFENSE

Military assistance agreement. Signed at Tegucigalpa May 20, 1954; entered into force May 20, 1954.[1]
5 UST 843; TIAS 2975; 222 UNTS 87.

Agreement for performance by members of Army and Air Force missions of duties of military assistance advisory group specified in article V of military assistance agreement. Exchange of notes at Tegucigalpa April 17 and 25, 1956; entered into force April 26, 1956.
7 UST 929; TIAS 3576; 269 UNTS 25.

Agreement relating to the disposition of equipment and materials furnished by the United States under the military assistance agreement of May 20, 1954. Exchange of notes at Tegucigalpa May 20 and 24, 1954; entered into force May 24, 1954.
13 UST 78; TIAS 4940; 433 UNTS 155.

Agreement relating to military assistance. Exchange of notes at Tegucigalpa October 24, 1962; entered into force October 24, 1962.
13 UST 2474; TIAS 5213; 459 UNTS 211.

Agreement relating to the deposit by Honduras of ten percent of the value of grant military assistance and excess defense articles furnished by the United States. Exchange of notes at Tegucigalpa April 4 and June 26, 1972; entered into force June 26, 1972; effective February 7, 1972.
23 UST 1235; TIAS 7393.

Agreement concerning payment to the United States of net proceeds from the sale of defense articles furnished under the military assistance program. Exchange of notes at Tegucigalpa May 9, 1974 and May 15, 1975; entered into force May 15, 1975; effective July 1, 1974.
26 UST 893; TIAS 8073.

Agreement relating to the military assistance agreement of May 20, 1954, concerning the use of certain facilities in Honduras by the United States, with annex. Exchange of notes

HONDURAS (Cont'd)

at Tegucigalpa May 6 and 7, 1982; entered into force May 7, 1982.
TIAS 10578; 1871 UNTS 456.

Agreement relating to privileges and immunities for U.S. armed forces personnel participating in combined military exercises in Honduras. Exchange of notes at Tegucigalpa December 8, 1982; entered into force December 8, 1982.
TIAS 10890.

Protocol I to the military assistance agreement of May 20, 1954 concerning the exercise of criminal jurisdiction over United States personnel present in Honduras, with annex. Signed at Washington May 20, 1985; entered into force April 9, 1987.
TIAS 11256.

Protocol II to the military assistance agreement of May 20, 1954, concerning the conduct of combined military exercises and maneuvers, with annex. Signed at Tegucigalpa November 14, 1988; entered into force May 10, 1989.
TIAS 12254.

Agreement concerning security assistance matters and the provision of articles, services and associated military education and training by the United States Government for anti-narcotics purposes. Exchange of notes at Tegucigalpa October 16 and 22, 1998; entered into force October 22, 1998.
TIAS

NOTE:
[1] See also agreements of May 6 and 7, 1982 and May 20, 1985 (TIAS 11202).

ECONOMIC AND TECHNICAL COOPERATION

General agreement for economic and technical cooperation. Signed at Tegucigalpa April 12, 1961; entered into force May 27, 1961.
12 UST 959; TIAS 4800; 413 UNTS 181.

Agency for International Development:
February 19, 1975 (27 UST 3311; TIAS 8366; 1068 UNTS 221).
November 28, 1977 (30 UST 90; TIAS 9181).
September 24, 1982 (TIAS 10505; 1777 UNTS 357).
March 25, 1985 (NP).
May 21, 1985 (NP).
July 25, 1985 (NP).
June 19, 1986 (NP).
June 19, 1987 (NP).
August 28, 1987 (NP).
August 20, 1988 (NP).
March 29, 1990 (NP).
June 5, 1991 (NP).
September 10, 1992 (NP).
June 9, 1999.
July 30, 1999.

EMPLOYMENT

Agreement relating to the employment of dependents of official government employees. Exchange of notes at Tegucigalpa June 11 and November 27, 1985; entered into force November 27, 1985.
TIAS 11340.

ENVIRONMENTAL COOPERATION

Agreement for cooperation in the Global Learning and Observations to Benefit the Environment (GLOBE) Program, with appendices. Signed at Tegucigalpa November 13, 1997; entered into force November 13, 1997.
TIAS

EXTRADITION

Treaty for the extradition of fugitives from justice. Signed at Washington January 15, 1909; entered into force July 10, 1912.
37 Stat. 1616; TS 569; 8 Bevans 892.

Supplementary extradition convention. Signed at Tegucigalpa February 21, 1927; entered into force June 5, 1928.
45 Stat. 2489; TS 761; 8 Bevans 903; 85 LNTS 491.

FINANCE

Agreement relating to investment guaranties under section 413(b)(4) of the Mutual Security Act of 1954. Exchange of notes at Tegucigalpa April 22 and June 10, 1955; entered into force June 10, 1955.
6 UST 2049; TIAS 3270; 258 UNTS 51.

Amendment:
February 24 and April 30, 1966 (17 UST 665; TIAS 6015; 578 UNTS 274).

Swap agreement among the United States Treasury and the Central Bank of Honduras/ Government of Honduras, with memorandum of understanding. Signed at Tegucigalpa and Washington June 27 and 28, 1990; entered into force June 28, 1990.
TIAS

Amendment and extension:
November 30 and December 13, 1990.

Agreement regarding the consolidation and rescheduling or refinancing of certain debts owed to, guaranteed by, or insured by the United States Government and its agencies, with annexes. Signed at Tegucigalpa December 20, 1990; entered into force February 1, 1991.
NP

Amendment:
February 25 and 28, 1992 (NP).

Agreement regarding the discharge of certain debts owed to the Government of the United States, with annex. Signed at Washington September 26, 1991; entered into force September 26, 1991.
NP

Agreement regarding the consolidation and rescheduling or refinancing of certain debts owed to, guaranteed by or insured by the United States Government and its agencies, with annexes. Signed at Tegucigalpa February 2, 1993; entered into force March 29, 1993.
NP

Agreement regarding the consolidation, reduction and rescheduling of certain debts owed to, guaranteed by, or insured by the United States Government and its agencies. Signed at Tegucigalpa December 4, 1996; entered into force April 10, 1997.
NP

Agreement regarding the reduction, consolidation, and rescheduling of certain debts owed to, guaranteed by, or insured by the United States Government and its agencies, with annexes. Signed at Tegucigalpa August 23, 1999; entered into force September 27, 1999.
NP

HIGHWAYS

Agreement relating to the inter-American highway. Exchange of notes at Washington September 9 and October 26, 1942; entered into force October 26, 1942.
56 Stat. 1848; EAS 296; 8 Bevans 945; 24 UNTS 209.

Amendment:
May 10 and 12, 1955 (6 UST 3763; TIAS 3376; 270 UNTS 3).

MAPPING

Arrangement for hydrographic and nautical cartography. Signed at Tegucigalpa August 30, 1976; entered into force August 30, 1976.
30 UST 3453; TIAS 9399; 1178 UNTS 5.

Basic exchange and cooperative agreement for topographic mapping, nautical and aeronautical charting and information, geodesy and geophysics, digital data and related mapping, charting and geodesy materials, with glossary. Signed at Comayaguela and Fairfax August 24 and September 5, 1995; entered into force September 5, 1995.
NP

MISSIONS, MILITARY

Agreement establishing a United States Air Force mission to the Republic of Honduras. Signed at Washington March 6, 1950; entered into force March 6, 1950.
1 UST 199; TIAS 2040; 80 UNTS 51.

HONDURAS (Cont'd)

Extension and amendment:
April 22 and May 20, 1960 (11 UST 1507;
    TIAS 4494; 376 UNTS 408).

Agreement establishing a United States Army
mission to the Republic of Honduras. Signed at
Washington March 6, 1950; entered into force
March 6, 1950.
1 UST 212; TIAS 2041; 80 UNTS 71.

Extension and amendment:
April 22 and May 20, 1960 (11 UST 1507;
    TIAS 4494; 376 UNTS 408).

NARCOTIC DRUGS

Agreement on mutual cooperation to combat
the production of and illicit trafficking in
drugs. Signed at Tegucigalpa November 14,
1988; entered into force May 15, 1989.
TIAS 11632.

PEACE CORPS

Agreement relating to the establishment of a
Peace Corps program in Honduras. Exchange
of notes at Tegucigalpa July 16 and 20, 1962;
entered into force July 20, 1962.
13 UST 1892; TIAS 5142; 460 UNTS 125.

POSTAL MATTERS

Money order convention. Signed at Washington June 25 and at Tegucigalpa July 16,
1896; operative October 1, 1896.
30 Stat. 1607.

International express mail agreement, with detailed regulations. Signed at Buenos Aires September 11, 1990; entered into force November
15, 1990.
TIAS 11748.

Postal money order agreement. Signed at Mon-
tevideo March 14, 1991; entered into force
May 1, 1991.
TIAS 11926.

PUBLICATIONS

Agreement relating to the exchange of official
publications. Exchange of notes at Tegucigalpa
March 1 and 24, 1950; entered into force
March 24, 1950.
1 UST 391; TIAS 2057; 93 UNTS 11.

RELIEF SUPPLIES AND PACKAGES

Agreement providing duty-free entry into Honduras, exemption from internal taxation and
transportation within Honduras to ultimate beneficiary, for certain relief supplies and equipment. Exchange of notes at Tegucigalpa March
21, 1955; entered into force March 21, 1955.
6 UST 795; TIAS 3225; 253 UNTS 3.

SCIENTIFIC COOPERATION

Memorandum of understanding concerning scientific, technical and policy cooperation in the
earth and mapping sciences, with annexes.
Signed at Tegucigalpa June 10, 1991; entered
into force June 10, 1991.
TIAS 12432.

TAXATION

Agreement for the exchange of information
with respect to taxes. Signed at Washington
September 27, 1990; entered into force October 11, 1991.
TIAS 11745.

TELECOMMUNICATION

Agreement relating to radio communications
between amateur radio stations on behalf of
third parties. Exchange of notes at Tegucigalpa
October 26, 1959, and February 17, 1960, and
related note of February 19, 1960; entered into
force March 17, 1960.
11 UST 257; TIAS 4442; 371 UNTS 109.

Agreement relating to the reciprocal granting
of authorizations to permit licensed amateur
radio operators of either country to operate
their stations in the other country. Exchange of
notes at Tegucigalpa December 29, 1966, January 24 and April 17, 1967; entered into force
April 17, 1967.
18 UST 525; TIAS 6259; 685 UNTS 165.

TERRITORIAL SOVEREIGNTY

Treaty on the Swan Islands with related notes.
Signed at San Pedro Sula November 22, 1971;
entered into force September 1, 1972.
23 UST 2630; TIAS 7453.

TRADE (See also COMMERCE)

Trade agreement.[1] Signed at Tegucigalpa December 18, 1935; entered into force March 2,
1936.
49 Stat. 3851; EAS 86; 8 Bevans 919; 167
    LNTS 313.

NOTES:
[1] The schedules, articles I, II, IV and V, together with references to article V contained in
article XVI, terminated February 28, 1961 (12
UST 84; TIAS 4677; 402 UNTS 169).

HUNGARY

AGRICULTURE

Joint statement on the development of agricultural trade and cooperation. Signed at Washington May 13, 1981; entered into force May
13, 1981.
33 UST 1186; TIAS 10103; 1285 UNTS 121.

ATOMIC ENERGY

Arrangement for the exchange of technical information and cooperation in nuclear safety
matters, with patent addendum. Signed at Budapest September 24, 1990; entered into force
September 24, 1990.
TIAS 12226.

Agreement for cooperation concerning peaceful
uses of nuclear energy, with annex and agreed
minute. Signed at Vienna June 10, 1991; entered into force February 13, 1992.
TIAS 12433.

Arrangement for the exchange of technical information and cooperation in nuclear safety
matters, with addenda. Signed at Vienna September 16, 1996; entered into force September
16, 1996.
TIAS

Agreement relating to participation in the U.S.
Nuclear Regulatory Commission program of
severe accident research, with addendum.
Signed at Rockville and Budapest January 27
and February 2, 1999; entered into force February 2, 1999; effective January 1, 1998.
TIAS

AVIATION

Air transport agreement, with annex and
memorandum of understanding. Signed at Budapest July 12, 1989; entered into force definitively February 8, 1990.
TIAS 11260.

Extension:
June 22 and July 6, 2000.

CLAIMS

Agreement regarding the settlement of claims,
with exchanges of letters and negotiating
records. Signed at Washington March 6, 1973;
entered into force March 6, 1973.
24 UST 522; TIAS 7569; 938 UNTS 167.

HUNGARY (Cont'd)

CONSULS

Consular convention. Signed at Budapest July 7, 1972; entered into force July 6, 1973.
24 UST 1141; TIAS 7641.

COPYRIGHT (See also APPENDIX)

Copyright convention. Signed at Budapest January 30, 1912; entered into force October 16, 1912.
37 Stat. 1631; TS 571; 5 Bevans 444.

CULTURAL RELATIONS

Agreement on cooperation in culture, education, science and technology. Signed at Budapest April 6, 1977; entered into force May 21, 1979.
30 UST 1502; TIAS 9259.

DEFENSE

Agreement concerning exchange of scientific and technical information, with attachment (Master Data Exchange Agreement). Signed at Washington May 16, 1995; entered into force May 16, 1995.
TIAS 12319.

Agreement concerning security measures for the protection of classified military information. Signed at Washington May 16, 1995; entered into force June 4, 1996.
TIAS 12649.

Mutual logistic support agreement, with annex and implementing arrangement. Signed at Budapest December 9, 1996; entered into force December 9, 1996.
TIAS

Agreement concerning the activities of United States Forces in the territory of the Republic of Hungary. Signed at Budapest May 14, 1997; entered into force June 23, 1997.
TIAS

ECONOMIC AND TECHNICAL COOPERATION

Agreement concerning economic, technical and related assistance, with related letter. Signed at Budapest December 22, 1995; entered into force December 22, 1995.
TIAS

EDUCATION

Agreement for the establishment of the Hungarian-American commission for educational exchange, with memorandum of understanding. Signed at Washington December 6, 1990; entered into force December 6, 1990.
TIAS 12034.

Agreement regarding the status of the American International School of Budapest. Exchange of notes at Budapest November 30, 1998; entered into force November 30, 1998.
TIAS

EMBASSY SITES

Agreement regarding new chancery facilities in Budapest, with associated agreement on purchase of lots. Signed at Budapest September 29, 1989; entered into force September 29, 1989.
TIAS

EMPLOYMENT

Agreement relating to employment of dependents of official government employees. Exchange of notes at Budapest November 18, 1991 and January 16, 1992; entered into force January 16, 1992.
TIAS 11841.

ENVIRONMENTAL COOPERATION

Agreement for cooperation in the Global Learning and Observations to Benefit the Environment (GLOBE) Program, with appendices. Signed at Washington March 10, 1999; entered into force March 10, 1999.
TIAS

EXTRADITION

Treaty on extradition. Signed at Budapest December 1, 1994; entered into force March 18, 1997.
TIAS

FINANCE

Debt funding agreement. Signed at Washington April 25, 1924; operative December 15, 1923.
Treasury Department print; 8 Bevans 1108.

Agreement modifying the debt funding agreement of April 25, 1924. Signed at Washington May 27, 1932; operative July 1, 1931.
Treasury Department print; 8 Bevans 1140.

Investment guaranty agreement. Signed at Budapest October 9, 1989; entered into force December 27, 1989.
TIAS 12040.

Swap agreement among the United States Treasury and the National Bank of Hungary/ Government of Hungary, with memorandum of understanding. Signed at Washington and Budapest June 19, 1990; entered into force June 19, 1990.
TIAS

GENERAL RELATIONS

Treaty establishing friendly relations. Signed at Budapest August 29, 1921; entered into force December 17, 1921.
42 Stat. 1951; TS 660; 8 Bevans 982; 48 LNTS 191.

INTELLECTUAL PROPERTY

Agreement on intellectual property, with protocol and exchanges of letters. Signed at Washington September 24, 1993; entered into force November 9, 1994.
TIAS 12138.

JUDICIAL ASSISTANCE

Agreement on establishing an International Law Enforcement Academy, with implementing agreement. Signed at Budapest April 24, 1995; entered into force November 3, 1995.
TIAS 12637.

Treaty on mutual legal assistance in criminal matters, with attachments. Signed at Budapest December 1, 1994; entered into force March 18, 1997.
TIAS

MAPPING

Exchange and cooperative agreement for military, topographic mapping, aeronautical charting, digital data and related MC & G materials. Signed at Budapest December 9, 1991; entered into force December 9, 1991.
NP

MILITARY CEMETERIES AND MONUMENTS

Agreement relating to interment of American military personnel in Hungary. Exchange of notes at Budapest June 18, July 15, and August 9, 1946; entered into force August 9, 1946.
61 Stat. 3898; TIAS 1748; 8 Bevans 1145; 148 UNTS 313.

HUNGARY (Cont'd)

NORTH ATLANTIC TREATY

Agreement to treat the agreement of June 19, 1995, among the States Parties to the North Atlantic Treaty and other States participating in the Partnership for Peace regarding the status of their forces as legally binding between the United States and Hungary. Exchange of notes at Budapest July 6, 1995; entered into force July 6, 1995.
TIAS

PACIFIC SETTLEMENT OF DISPUTES

Arbitration treaty. Signed at Washington January 26, 1929; entered into force July 24, 1929.
46 Stat. 2349; TS 797; 8 Bevans 1134; 96 LNTS 173.

Conciliation treaty. Signed at Washington January 26, 1929; entered into force July 24, 1929.
46 Stat. 2353; TS 798; 8 Bevans 1137; 96 LNTS 207.

PEACE CORPS

Agreement concerning the operation of the United States Peace Corps in Hungary. Signed at Budapest February 14, 1990; entered into force July 12, 1990.
TIAS 12072.

POSTAL MATTERS

Convention for the exchange of money orders. Signed at Washington April 3 and at Budapest May 6, 1922; entered into force June 15, 1922.
NP

Agreement for collect-on-delivery service. Signed at Budapest December 15, 1930 and at Washington January 15, 1931; operative February 1, 1931.
46 Stat. 2894; Post Office Department print.

Parcel post agreement, with detailed regulations. Signed at Washington May 11, 1979; entered into force provisionally May 11, 1979; definitively August 8, 1979.
32 UST 1695; TIAS 9797; 1734 UNTS 165.

International express mail agreement, with detailed regulations. Signed at Budapest and Washington June 24 and July 10, 1987; entered into force September 1, 1987.
TIAS 11306.

SCIENTIFIC COOPERATION

Memorandum of understanding for scientific and technical cooperation in earth sciences. Signed at Reston and Budapest January 6 and 20, 1984; entered into force January 20, 1984.
TIAS 11388.

Extensions:
March 17 and April 21, 1986 (TIAS 11388).
January 26 and February 9, 1988 (TIAS 11575).

Agreement on scientific and technical cooperation, with annexes. Signed at Washington March 23, 1987; entered into force March 23, 1987.
TIAS 11520.

Agreement for scientific and technological cooperation, with annexes. Signed at Washington March 15, 2000; entered into force May 11, 2000.
TIAS

Memorandum of understanding concerning scientific and technical cooperation in the earth sciences. Signed at Budapest and Reston November 22, 2000; entered into force November 22, 2000.
TIAS

TAXATION

Convention for the avoidance of double taxation and the prevention of fiscal evasion with respect to taxes on income, with exchange of notes. Signed at Washington February 12, 1979; entered into force September 18, 1979.
30 UST 6357; TIAS 9560; 1180 UNTS 205.

TRADE AND COMMERCE

Agreement relating to the establishment in New York of a branch office of the commercial section of the Hungarian Embassy. Exchange of notes at Washington September 19, 1969; entered into force September 19, 1969.
20 UST 2982; TIAS 6772; 726 UNTS 177.

Agreement providing for consultations should exports of cotton, wool, and man-made fiber textiles and apparel products from Hungary cause market disruption in the United States. Exchange of notes at Budapest February 12 and 18, 1976; entered into force February 18, 1976.
27 UST 1619; TIAS 8270.

Agreement on trade relations. Signed at Budapest March 17, 1978; entered into force July 7, 1978.
29 UST 2711; TIAS 8967.

Agreement within the context of the multilateral trade negotiations on nontariff matters, and related letters of May 30, 1980. Letters done at Geneva August 31 and December 27, 1978

and January 10, 1979; entered into force January 1, 1980.
32 UST 5357; TIAS 9991.

Agreement within the context of the multilateral trade negotiations on tariff matters, with annexes and exchange of letters. Signed at Budapest November 18, 1978; entered into force January 1, 1980.
32 UST 5371; TIAS 9992; 1265 UNTS 86.

Amendments:
June 13, 1979 and May 30, 1980 (32 UST 5371; TIAS 9992; 1265 UNTS 115).
September 4 and 18, 1980 (32 UST 5371; TIAS 9992; 1265 UNTS 117).

Agreement relating to trade in wool textiles products. [1] Exchange of letters at Budapest February 15 and 25, 1983; entered into force February 25, 1983; effective October 1, 1982.
TIAS 10666.

Amendments and extensions:
February 13 and 24, 1984 (NP).
January 18 and February 6, 1985 (NP).
August 15 and 21, 1986 (NP).
December 30, 1986 and January 6, 1987 (NP).
July 20 and 29, 1987 (NP).
April 8 and 15, 1988 (NP).
May 25 and June 17, 1988 (NP).
June 23 and August 1, 1988 (NP).
November 29 and December 13, 1988 (NP).
April 7 and July 28, 1994 (NP).

Arrangement relating to a visa system for exports to the United States of wool textiles and textile products. Exchange of letters at Washington February 2 and 3, 1984; entered into force February 3, 1984.
TIAS 10937.

Amendment:
October 27 and 31, 1988 (NP).

NOTE:
[1] The title of the Agreement was changed to Agreement relating to trade in cotton, wool and man-made fiber textiles and textile products by amendment of April 8 and 15, 1988.

TRANSPORTATION

Understanding concerning research cooperation in the field of transportation. Signed at Budapest October 11, 1978; entered into force October 11, 1978.
30 UST 743; TIAS 9216.

VISAS

Agreement relating to issuance of nonimmigrant visas on a facilitated basis to certain holders of diplomatic or official passports. Exchange of notes at Budapest March 29 and April 7, 1976; entered into force April 7, 1976.
28 UST 1311; TIAS 8513.

Agreement relating to reciprocal facilitation of visas for diplomatic and official passport hold-

HUNGARY (Cont'd)

ers. Exchange of notes at Budapest February 10, 1978; entered into force February 10, 1978.
30 UST 248; TIAS 9193.

Agreement relating to reciprocal facilitation of transit or temporary duty visas for diplomatic and official passport holders. Exchange of notes at Budapest February 10, 1978; entered into force April 11, 1978.
30 UST 255; TIAS 9194.

ICELAND

AVIATION

Air transport agreement, with annexes. Signed at Washington June 14, 1995; entered into force October 12, 1995.
TIAS 12661.

Memorandum of agreement relating to the loan of aviation-related equipment to the Civil Aviation Administration of Iceland. Signed at Washington December 8, 1997; entered into force December 8, 1997.
TIAS

COPYRIGHT (See APPENDIX)

DEFENSE (See also MUTUAL SECURITY)

Defense agreement pursuant to the North Atlantic Treaty. Signed at Reykjavik May 5, 1951; entered into force May 5, 1951.
2 UST 1195; TIAS 2266; 205 UNTS 173.

Annex on the status of United States personnel and property. Signed at Reykjavik May 8, 1951; entered into force May 8, 1951.
2 UST 1533; TIAS 2295; 205 UNTS 180.

Agreement concerning the sale to Iceland of certain military equipment, materials, and services. Exchange of notes at Reykjavik October 4 and December 10, 1954; entered into force December 10, 1954.
5 UST 2991; TIAS 3157; 237 UNTS 191.

Agreement relating to the presence of defense forces in Iceland, discontinuing the discussions for revision of the 1951 defense agreement and setting up an Iceland Defense Standing Group. Exchanges of notes at Reykjavik December 6, 1956; entered into force December 6, 1956.
7 UST 3437; TIAS 3716; 265 UNTS 261.

Agreement relating to the continuation of the defense agreement of May 5, 1951, with memorandum of understanding and agreed minute. Exchange of notes at Reykjavik Octo-

ber 22, 1974; entered into force October 22, 1974.
25 UST 3079; TIAS 7969.

Agreement concerning the provision of training related to defense articles under the United States International Military Education and Training (IMET) Program. Exchange of notes at Reykjavik January 7 and February 12, 1986; entered into force February 12, 1986.
TIAS 11107.

Treaty to facilitate defense relationship, with related memorandum of understandings. Signed at New York September 24, 1986; entered into force October 31, 1986.
TIAS 11098.

Memorandum of understanding regarding the resolution of certain groundwater contamination. Signed at Reykjavik July 17, 1989; entered into force July 17, 1989.
TIAS 12315.

ECONOMIC AND TECHNICAL COOPERATION

Economic cooperation agreement. Signed at Reykjavik July 3, 1948; entered into force July 3, 1948.
62 Stat. 2363; TIAS 1787; 8 Bevans 1193; 20 UNTS 141.

Amendments:
February 7, 1950 (1 UST 154; TIAS 2026; 79 UNTS 280).
February 23, 1951 (2 UST 1317; TIAS 2284; 148 UNTS 398).
October 9, 1952 and October 1, 1953 (5 UST 166; TIAS 2910; 223 UNTS 316).

Agreement concerning special economic assistance to Iceland on a loan basis. Exchange of notes at Reykjavik June 23, 1959; entered into force June 23, 1959.
10 UST 1237; TIAS 4260; 354 UNTS 3.

Agreement providing for an assistance grant in support of Iceland's economic stabilization program. Exchange of notes at Washington December 30, 1960; entered into force December 30, 1960.
11 UST 2574; TIAS 4647; 401 UNTS 43.

EDUCATION

Agreement for financing certain educational exchange programs. Signed at Reykjavik February 13, 1964; entered into force February 13, 1964.
15 UST 226; TIAS 5542; 524 UNTS 235.

EXTRADITION

Conventions between the United States and Denmark applicable to Iceland:

Treaty for the extradition of fugitives from justice. Signed at Washington January 6, 1902 (32 Stat. 1096; TS 405; 7 Bevans 38). Supplementary treaty for the extradition of criminals. Signed at Washington November 6, 1905 (34 Stat. 2887; TS 449; 7 Bevans 43); entered into force for Iceland February 19, 1906.

LEND-LEASE

Agreement relating to aid for defense, with note. Signed at Washington November 21, 1941; entered into force November 21, 1941.
58 Stat. 1455; EAS 429; 8 Bevans 1163; 124 UNTS 179.

MAPPING

Basic exchange and cooperative agreement concerning global geospatial information and services cooperation, with annexes. Signed at Bethesda and Reykjavik June 7 and July 1, 1999; entered into force July 1, 1999.
NP

MUTUAL SECURITY

Agreement relating to the assurances required under the Mutual Security Act of 1951. Exchange of notes at Reykjavik January 7 and 8, 1952; entered into force January 8, 1952.
3 UST 4577; TIAS 2609; 180 UNTS 183.

PACIFIC SETTLEMENT OF DISPUTES

Treaty between the United States and Denmark looking to the advancement of the cause of general peace. Signed at Washington April 17, 1914; entered into force January 19, 1915.
38 Stat. 1883; TS 608; 7 Bevans 53.

Treaty of arbitration. Signed at Washington May 15, 1930; entered into force October 2, 1930.
46 Stat. 2841; TS 828; 8 Bevans 1154; 108 LNTS 109.

POSTAL MATTERS

Money order convention. Signed at Washington June 23 and at Reykjavik July 5, 1928, operative October 1, 1928.
NP

Agreement concerning the exchange of parcel post and detailed regulations of execution. Signed at Reykjavik October 11 and at Washington October 31, 1938; operative September 1, 1938.
53 Stat. 2006; Post Office Department print.

ICELAND (Cont'd)

International express mail agreement, with detailed regulations. Signed at Reykjavik and Washington July 10 and August 8, 1985; entered into force November 7, 1985.
TIAS 11155.

Memorandum of understanding concerning the operation of the INTELPOST service, with details of implementation. Signed at Reykjavik and Washington March 5 and April 3, 1987; entered into force May 6, 1987.
TIAS 11299.

PUBLICATIONS

Agreement relating to the exchange of official publications. Exchange of notes at Reykjavik August 17, 1942; entered into force August 17, 1942.
56 Stat. 1600; EAS 269; 8 Bevans 1166; 24 UNTS 163.

SCIENTIFIC COOPERATION

Memorandum of understanding for scientific and technical cooperation in earth sciences. Signed at Reykjavik and Reston January 28 and April 9, 1982; entered into force April 9, 1982.
TIAS 10409.

Amendments and extensions:
March 5 and August 9, 1991 (TIAS 11801).
June 9 and July 8, 1999.

Memorandum of understanding on cooperation in science and engineering research, with annexes. Signed at Reykjavik September 30, 2000; entered into force September 30, 2000.
TIAS

SHELLFISH

Memorandum of understanding concerning cooperation to assure the sanitary quality of bivalve mollusca exported to the United States. Signed at Reykjavik and Washington October 25 and December 28, 1978; entered into force December 28, 1978.
30 UST 2873; TIAS 9368; 1180 UNTS 89.

TAXATION

Agreement relating to relief from taxation of United States expenditures in Iceland for common defense. Exchange of notes at Reykjavik March 5 and 18, 1952; entered into force March 18, 1952.
3 UST 4150; TIAS 2557; 177 UNTS 263.

Convention for the avoidance of double taxation and the prevention of fiscal evasion with respect to taxes on income and capital. Signed at Reykjavik May 7, 1975; entered into force December 26, 1975.
26 UST 2004; TIAS 8151.

TELECOMMUNICATION

Agreement relating to the registration with the International Frequency Registration Board of radio frequencies for the use of the Iceland defense force. Exchange of notes at Reykjavik July 11 and 20, 1955; entered into force July 20, 1955.
6 UST 3910; TIAS 3395; 256 UNTS 245.

Agreement relating to the reciprocal granting of authorizations to permit licensed amateur radio operators of either country to operate their stations in the other country. Exchange of notes at Reykjavik April 26, 1978; entered into force April 26, 1978.
30 UST 1516; TIAS 9260; 1150 UNTS 41.

TRADE AND COMMERCE

Agreement within the context of the multilateral trade negotiations concerning cheese and other agricultural products, and related letter of January 30, 1980. Exchanges of letters at Washington May 16 and 25, June 12, [undated], September 18 and October 15, 1979; entered into force January 1, 1980.
32 UST 5428; TIAS 9993; 1267 UNTS 37.

VISAS

Arrangement relating to the waiver of passport visa fees for nonimmigrants. Exchange of notes at Copenhagen November 3 and December 21, 1925; and June 11, 19, and 21, 1926; entered into force June 21, 1926; operative August 6, 1925.
8 Bevans 1150.

Agreement relating to the reciprocal extension of the validity period of visas for certain nonimmigrants. Exchange of notes at Reykjavik June 4, 1956; entered into force June 4, 1956; operative August 1, 1956.
7 UST 1017; TIAS 3584; 275 UNTS 189.

WHALING

Agreement concerning Icelandic whaling for scientific purposes, with summary of discussions. Exchange of letters at Washington September 14 and 15, 1987; entered into force September 15, 1987.
TIAS 11541.

INDIA

The Schedule to the Indian Independence (International Arrangements) Order, 1947, provides that (1) membership of all international organizations together with the rights and obligations attached to such membership devolves solely upon India; (2) rights and obligations under all international agreements to which India is a party immediately before the appointed day [August 15, 1947] devolve upon India and Pakistan and will, if necessary, be apportioned between them, except that rights and obligations under international agreements having an exclusive application to an area comprised in the Dominion of India devolve upon it.

The Dominion of India, which came into being August 15, 1947, became the Republic of India on January 26, 1950, but remains a member of the British Commonwealth of Nations. This change is understood not to have affected any agreements listed below in their application between the United States and India.

AGRICULTURAL COMMODITIES

Agricultural commodities agreement with exchange of notes. Signed at Washington May 4, 1960; entered into force May 4, 1960.
11 UST 1544; TIAS 4499; 376 UNTS 279.

Amendments:
July 29, 1960 (11 UST 1941; TIAS 4543; 384 UNTS 386).
September 23, 1960 (11 UST 2132; TIAS 4574; 389 UNTS 336).
March 9, 1961 (12 UST 177; TIAS 4691; 406 UNTS 346).

Agricultural commodities agreement with exchange of notes. Signed at New Delhi May 1, 1962; entered into force May 1, 1962.
13 UST 1080; TIAS 5051; 451 UNTS 179.

Amendment:
May 17, 1962 (13 UST 1080; TIAS 5051; 451 UNTS 179).

Agricultural commodities agreement, with exchange of notes. Signed at New Delhi November 26, 1962; entered into force November 26, 1962.
13 UST 2589; TIAS 5225; 460 UNTS 203.

Amendments:
April 1, 1963 (14 UST 340; TIAS 5317; 474 UNTS 372).
September 4, 1963 (14 UST 1246; TIAS 5424; 488 UNTS 314).
April 17, 1964 (15 UST 349; TIAS 5562; 526 UNTS 326).

Agricultural commodities agreement with exchange of notes. Signed at Washington November 30, 1962; entered into force November 30, 1962.
13 UST 2492; TIAS 5215; 459 UNTS 231.

INDIA (Cont'd)

Agricultural commodity agreement. Signed at Washington May 9, 1963; entered into force May 9, 1963.
14 UST 422; TIAS 5336; 476 UNTS 43.

Agricultural commodities agreement. Signed at Washington June 27, 1963; entered into force June 27, 1963.
14 UST 950; TIAS 5384; 479 UNTS 215.

Amendment:
December 9 and 20, 1963 (14 UST 1787; TIAS 5488; 494 UNTS 358).

Agricultural commodities agreement with exchange of notes. Signed at New Delhi September 30, 1964; entered into force September 30, 1964.
15 UST 1941; TIAS 5669; 532 UNTS 321.

Amendments:
December 31, 1964 (15 UST 2393; TIAS 5729; 532 UNTS 340).
April 21, 1965 (16 UST 664; TIAS 5793; 546 UNTS 412).
July 26, 1965 (16 UST 1064; TIAS 5846; 579 UNTS 324).
September 29, 1965 (16 UST 1257; TIAS 5875; 579 UNTS 330).
November 4, 1965 (16 UST 1707; TIAS 5895; 574 UNTS 280).
December 10, 1965 (16 UST 1833; TIAS 5913; 574 UNTS 284).
February 5, 1966 (17 UST 106; TIAS 5965; 579 UNTS 334).
May 27, 1966 (17 UST 778; TIAS 6032; 593 UNTS 324).
October 14, 1966 (17 UST 1564; TIAS 6113; 607 UNTS 348).
November 21, 1966 (17 UST 2057; TIAS 6146; 676 UNTS 380).
December 23, 1966 (18 UST 73; TIAS 6198; 680 UNTS 378).

Agricultural commodities agreement with annex. Signed at New Delhi February 20, 1967; entered into force February 20, 1967.
18 UST 217; TIAS 6221; 688 UNTS 197.

Related agreements:
June 24, 1967 (18 UST 2351; TIAS 6338; 692 UNTS 309).
September 12, 1967 (18 UST 2372; TIAS 6342; 693 UNTS 77).
December 30, 1967 (18 UST 3182; TIAS 6414; 697 UNTS 107).
December 23, 1968 (20 UST 394; TIAS 6642; 714 UNTS 69).
April 25, 1969 (20 UST 758; TIAS 6686; 714 UNTS 117).
May 29, 1969 (20 UST 776; TIAS 6691; 714 UNTS 78).
October 13, 1969 (20 UST 3038; TIAS 6781; 726 UNTS 211).
March 17, 1970 (21 UST 851; TIAS 6855).
June 26, 1970 (21 UST 1519; TIAS 6914; 753 UNTS 424).
April 1, 1971 (22 UST 638; TIAS 7115; 792 UNTS 283).

May 7, 1971 (22 UST 644; TIAS 7115; 792 UNTS 296).
May 20, 1971 (22 UST 646; TIAS 7115; 792 UNTS 300).

Agricultural commodities agreement. Signed at Washington March 20, 1975; entered into force March 20, 1975.
26 UST 195; TIAS 8026; 992 UNTS 117.

Agricultural commodities agreement, with agreed minutes. Signed at New Delhi May 3, 1976; entered into force May 3, 1976.
27 UST 2331; TIAS 8312; 1055 UNTS 21.

Agricultural commodities agreement, with agreed minutes. Signed at New Delhi February 3, 1977; entered into force February 3, 1977.
28 UST 6027; TIAS 8668; 1087 UNTS 159.

Agricultural commodities agreement with agreed minutes. Signed at New Delhi January 27, 1978; entered into force January 27, 1978.
29 UST 5663; TIAS 9142.

ATOMIC ENERGY

Agreement providing for a grant of nuclear research equipment in the field of agriculture. Exchange of notes at New Delhi April 22 and June 13, 1960; entered into force June 13, 1960.
11 UST 1619; TIAS 4505; 377 UNTS 37.

Agreement providing for a grant for assistance in obtaining materials and equipment for establishing a Radiation Medicine Centre at Tata Memorial Hospital, Bombay. Exchange of notes at New Delhi January 4 and February 1, 1963; entered into force February 1, 1963.
14 UST 156; TIAS 5288; 473 UNTS 37.

AVIATION

Agreement relating to transit privileges for military aircraft. Exchange of notes at New Delhi July 2 and 4, 1949; entered into force July 5, 1949.
3 UST 575; TIAS 2417; 200 UNTS 181.

Amendments:
June 9 and 15, 1955 (14 UST 1449; TIAS 5442; 488 UNTS 242).
March 5 and July 22, 1963 (14 UST 1449; TIAS 5442; 488 UNTS 246).
March 5 and August 29, 1963 (14 UST 1449; TIAS 5442; 488 UNTS 250).

Air transport agreement. Signed at New Delhi February 3, 1956; entered into force February 3, 1956.
7 UST 275; TIAS 3504; 272 UNTS 75.

Amendment:
May 4, 1989 (TIAS 11775).

Agreement amending and implementing the air transport agreement of February 3, 1956, and replacing the notes relating thereto exchanged the same date. Exchange of notes at New

Delhi October 26, 1964; entered into force October 26, 1964.
15 UST 2031; TIAS 5682; 533 UNTS 334.

COMMERCE

Convention to regulate commerce (article III) between the United States and the United Kingdom. Signed at London July 3, 1815; entered into force July 3, 1815.
8 Stat. 228; TS 110; 12 Bevans 49.

CONSULS

Convention to regulate commerce (article IV) between the United States and the United Kingdom. Signed at London July 3, 1815; effective July 3, 1815.
8 Stat. 228; TS 110; 12 Bevans 49.

COPYRIGHT (See also APPENDIX)

Agreement relating to copyright relations. Exchange of notes at Washington October 21, 1954; entered into force October 21, 1954; operative August 15, 1947.
5 UST 2525; TIAS 3114; 234 UNTS 119.

CULTURAL HERITAGE

Memorandum of understanding on the planning, conservation and management of natural and cultural heritage sites. Signed at New Delhi May 18, 1989; entered into force May 18, 1989.
TIAS

DEFENSE

Agreement relating to the transfer by the Government of the United States to the Government of India of certain military supplies and equipment (military sales agreement). Exchange of notes at Washington March 7 and 16, 1951; entered into force March 16, 1951.
2 UST 872; TIAS 2241; 14 UNTS 47.

Understanding that the assurances contained in the agreement of March 7 and 16, 1951 are applicable to equipment, materials, information, and services furnished under the Mutual Security Act of 1954, as amended, and such other applicable U.S. laws as may come into effect. Exchange of notes at New Delhi April 16 and December 17, 1958; entered into force December 17, 1958.
10 UST 1713; TIAS 4322; 358 UNTS 77.

Agreement supplementing the 1951 military sales agreement. Exchange of notes at Wash-

INDIA (Cont'd)

ington November 14, 1962; entered into force November 14, 1962.
13 UST 2449; TIAS 5206; 461 UNTS 224.

Agreement relating to military assistance. Exchange of notes at New Delhi January 13, 1965; entered into force January 13, 1965.
16 UST 33; TIAS 5753; 541 UNTS 107.

ECONOMIC AND TECHNICAL COOPERATION

General agreement for technical cooperation. Signed at New Delhi December 28, 1950; entered into force December 28, 1950.
2 UST 425; TIAS 2185; 99 UNTS 39.

Agreement relating to the technical cooperation program. Signed at New Delhi January 5, 1952; entered into force January 5, 1952.
3 UST 2921; TIAS 2470; 157 UNTS 39.

Extension:
June 29, 1957 (8 UST 732; TIAS 3828; 288 UNTS 368).

Agreement to establish a Joint Commission on Economic, Commercial, Scientific, Technological, Educational and Cultural Cooperation. Signed at New Delhi October 28, 1974; entered into force October 28, 1974.
25 UST 2807; TIAS 7947.

Agreed minutes of the second session of the United States-India Joint Commission on Economic, Commercial, Scientific, Technological, Educational and Cultural Cooperation. Signed at Washington October 7, 1975; entered into force October 7, 1975.
26 UST 2590; TIAS 8176; 1028 UNTS 23.

Agency for International Development:
August 26, 1978 (30 UST 4749; TIAS 9488; 1170 UNTS 231).
August 26, 1978 (30 UST 4789; TIAS 9489; 1233 UNTS 269).
May 27, 1980 (32 UST 5941; TIAS 10022).
June 30, 1980 (32 UST 5969; TIAS 10023).
December 15, 1980 (32 UST 5941; TIAS 10022).
December 15, 1980 (32 UST 5969; TIAS 10023).
July 30, 1983 (TIAS 10765).
July 30, 1983 (TIAS 10766).
March 9, 1984 (TIAS 10765).
July 31, 1984 (NP).
July 31, 1984 (NP).
September 29, 1984 (NP).
June 26, 1985 (NP).
August 19, 1998 (NP).
August 24, 1998 (NP).
September 25, 1998 (NP).

EDUCATION

Agreement for financing certain educational exchange programs. Signed at New Delhi June 19, 1963; entered into force June 19, 1963.
14 UST 918; TIAS 5379; 479 UNTS 175.

EMPLOYMENT

Arrangement on employment for family members of a diplomatic mission or consular post. Signed at New Delhi April 10, 2000; entered into force April 10, 2000.
TIAS

ENERGY

Memorandum of understanding for cooperation in enhanced oil recovery and underground coal gasification technologies. Signed at Washington August 31, 1987; entered into force August 31, 1987.
TIAS

ENVIRONMENTAL COOPERATION

Agreement for cooperation in the Global Learning and Observations to Benefit the Environment (GLOBE) Program, with appendices. Signed at New Delhi August 25, 2000; entered into force August 25, 2000.
TIAS

EXTRADITION

Extradition treaty, with exchange of letters. Signed at Washington June 25, 1997; entered into force July 21, 1999.
TIAS

FINANCE

Agreement regarding the consolidation and rescheduling of certain debts owed to the United States Government and its agencies, with annexes. Signed at Washington March 30, 1973; entered into force March 30, 1973.
24 UST 907; TIAS 7601.

Agreement on Public Law 480 and other funds, with annexes. Signed at New Delhi February 18, 1974; entered into force February 18, 1974.
25 UST 866; TIAS 7831.

Agreements regarding the consolidation and rescheduling of certain debts owed to the United States Government and its agencies, with annexes. Signed at Washington June 7, 1974; entered into force June 7, 1974.
25 UST 1547; TIAS 7890.

Agreement regarding the consolidation and rescheduling of certain debts owed to the United States Government and its agencies, with annexes. Signed at Washington May 2, 1975; entered into force June 13, 1975.
26 UST 951; TIAS 8082.

Investment incentive agreement. Signed at New Delhi November 19, 1997; entered into force April 16, 1998.
TIAS

JUDICIAL ASSISTANCE

Agreement on procedures for mutual assistance in connection with matters relating to the Boeing Company. Signed at Washington August 19, 1977; entered into force August 19, 1977.
28 UST 7497; TIAS 8726; 1087 UNTS 209.

Related agreements:
March 28 and April 17, 1979 (TIAS 10878).
November 18 and December 10, 1981 (TIAS 10878).

LEND-LEASE

Agreement on settlement for lend-lease, reciprocal aid, surplus war property, and claims. Signed at Washington May 16, 1946; entered into force May 16, 1946.
60 Stat. 1753; TIAS 1532; 8 Bevans 1226; 4 UNTS 183.

Amendment:
June 24 and 26, 1946 (8 Bevans 1233).

METEOROLOGY

Agreement on cooperation in the conduct of the monsoon experiment (MONEX-79), with annexes. Signed at New Delhi May 24, 1979; entered into force May 24, 1979.
30 UST 5877; TIAS 9524; 1180 UNTS 355.

NARCOTIC DRUGS

Mutual cooperation agreement for reducing demand, preventing illicit use of and traffic in drugs, and for matters relating to licit trade in opiates. Signed at New Delhi March 29, 1990; entered into force March 29, 1990.
TIAS 12412.

PEACE CORPS

Agreement relating to the establishment of a Peace Corps program in India. Exchange of notes at New Delhi November 13 and 21, 1962; entered into force November 21, 1962; operative December 20, 1961.
13 UST 2735; TIAS 5247; 462 UNTS 255.

INDIA (Cont'd)

POSTAL MATTERS

Parcel post agreement with detailed regulations. Signed at New Delhi July 29 and at Washington September 17, 1954; entered into force January 1, 1955.
6 UST 819; TIAS 3229; 239 UNTS 69.

International express mail agreement, with detailed regulations. Signed at New Delhi and Washington November 20 and December 11, 1986; entered into force January 17, 1987.
TIAS 11415.

PROPERTY

Convention between the United States and the United Kingdom applicable to India from June 30, 1902:

Convention relating to tenure and disposition of real and personal property. Signed at Washington March 2, 1899 (31 Stat. 1939; TS 146; 12 Bevans 246).

Supplementary convention extending the time within which notifications may be given of the accession of British colonies or foreign possessions to the convention of March 2, 1899. Signed at Washington January 13, 1901 (32 Stat. 1914; TS 402; 12 Bevans 261).

PUBLICATIONS

Agreement for the exchange of official publications. Exchange of notes at New Delhi November 8, 1950 and January 11, 1951; entered into force January 11, 1951.
2 UST 1563; TIAS 2297; 148 UNTS 49.

RELIEF SUPPLIES AND PACKAGES

Agreement for duty-free entry and defrayment of inland transportation charges of voluntary agency supplies and equipment. Signed at New Delhi December 5, 1968; entered into force December 5, 1968.
19 UST 7836; TIAS 6617; 713 UNTS 351.

SCIENTIFIC COOPERATION

Agreement on the Indo-U.S. Science and Technology Forum. Signed at New Delhi March 21, 2000; entered into force March 21, 2000.
TIAS

SURPLUS PROPERTY

Agreement concerning fulfillment of India's obligations under the agreement of May 16, 1946, as amended, on settlement for lend-lease, reciprocal aid, surplus war property, and claims. Exchange of letters at New Delhi January 24, 1975; entered into force January 24, 1975.
26 UST 305; TIAS 8035; 992 UNTS 111.

TAXATION

Agreement concerning the reciprocal exemption from income tax of income derived from the international operation of ships and aircraft. Exchange of notes at New Delhi April 12, 1989; entered into force April 12, 1989.
TIAS 11771.

Convention for the avoidance of double taxation and the prevention of fiscal evasion with respect to taxes on income. Signed at New Delhi September 12, 1989; entered into force December 18, 1990.
TIAS

TELECOMMUNICATION

Agreement relating to the reciprocal granting of authorizations to permit licensed amateur radio operators of either country to operate their stations in the other country. Exchange of notes at New Delhi May 16 and 25, 1966; entered into force May 25, 1966.
17 UST 813; TIAS 6038; 593 UNTS 157.

TRADE (See also COMMERCE)

Memorandum of understanding setting forth mutual trade concessions and contributions to the multilateral trade negotiations, and related letters of September 4 and October 30, 1980. Signed at Geneva March 24, 1979; entered into force April 24, 1980.
32 UST 5436; TIAS 9994; 1265 UNTS 197.

Agreement relating to trade in textiles and textile products, with annexes. Exchange of notes at Washington February 6, 1987; entered into force February 6, 1987; effective January 1, 1987.
NP

Amendments:
March 4 and 10, 1987 (NP).
September 15 and October 2 and 16, 1987 (NP).
April 21 and May 30, 1988 (NP).
May 24, June 23, August 26 and September 12, 1988 (NP).
December 6 and 21, 1989 (NP).

TRADE-MARKS

Declaration by the United States and the United Kingdom affording reciprocal protection to trade-marks. Signed at London October 24, 1877; entered into force October 24, 1877.
20 Stat. 703; TS 138; 12 Bevans 198.

VISAS

Arrangement for the continuance, on a reciprocal basis, of the existing practice of levying a fee of $2.00 for a nonimmigrant visa. Exchange of notes at New Delhi July 19 and August 11, 1948; entered into force August 11, 1948.
5 UST 193; TIAS 2913; 224 UNTS 115.

INDONESIA

Sovereignty over Indonesia was transferred on December 27, 1949, by the Kingdom of the Netherlands to the Republic of Indonesia in accordance with the Charter of the Transfer of Sovereignty signed on that date.

The Agreement on Transitional Measures adopted by the Round Table Conference at The Hague on November 2, 1949, provides that the treaty obligations of the Republic of Indonesia arising out of treaties and other international agreements concluded by the Netherlands are considered ''as the rights and obligations of the Republic of the United States of Indonesia only where and inasmuch as such treaties and agreements are applicable to the jurisdiction of the Republic of the United States of Indonesia and with the exception of rights and duties arising out of treaties and agreements to which the Republic of the United States of Indonesia cannot become a party on the ground of the provisions of such treaties and agreements.''

AGRICULTURAL COMMODITIES

Agricultural commodities agreement with exchange of notes. Signed at Djakarta October 26, 1961; entered into force October 26, 1961.
12 UST 2955; TIAS 4897; 433 UNTS 249.

Amendment:
November 17, 1961 (12 UST 2955; TIAS 4897; 433 UNTS 249).

Agricultural commodities agreement, with exchange of notes. Signed at Djakarta February 19, 1962; entered into force February 19, 1962.
13 UST 154; TIAS 4952; 435 UNTS 137.

Amendments:
May 15, 1962 (13 UST 1100; TIAS 5054; 451 UNTS 346).
July 11, 1962 (13 UST 1765; TIAS 5118; 460 UNTS 344).

INDONESIA (Cont'd)

December 10, 1962 (13 UST 3824; TIAS 5254; 469 UNTS 436).
June 28, 1963 (14 UST 929; TIAS 5381; 479 UNTS 394).
August 13, 1964 (15 UST 1508; TIAS 5632; 530 UNTS 370).

Agricultural commodities agreement with exchange of notes. Signed at Djakarta April 18, 1966; entered into force April 18, 1966.
17 UST 669; TIAS 6016; 578 UNTS 107.

Amendment:
June 6, 1966 (17 UST 786; TIAS 6033; 593 UNTS 339).

Agricultural commodities agreement with exchange of notes. Signed at Washington June 28, 1966; entered into force June 28, 1966.
17 UST 841; TIAS 6044; 593 UNTS 201.

Agricultural commodities agreement with exchange of notes. Signed at Washington September 30, 1966; entered into force September 30, 1966.
17 UST 1515; TIAS 6107; 616 UNTS 199.

Agricultural commodities agreement with annex. Signed at Djakarta September 15, 1967; entered into force September 15, 1967.
18 UST 2393; TIAS 6346; 693 UNTS 87.

Amendment:
November 6, 1967 (18 UST 3100; TIAS 6401).

Related agreements:
November 1, 1967 (18 UST 2921; TIAS 6382; 701 UNTS 133).
November 22, 1967 (18 UST 3156; TIAS 6407; 697 UNTS 19).
February 15, 1968 (19 UST 4757; TIAS 6473; 697 UNTS 27).
August 5, 1968 (19 UST 5987; TIAS 6551; 702 UNTS 125).
August 16, 1968 (19 UST 6006; TIAS 6556; 702 UNTS 135).
September 5, 1968 (19 UST 6009; TIAS 6557; 702 UNTS 143).
April 23, 1969 (20 UST 2698; TIAS 6731; 720 UNTS 334).
November 17, 1969 (20 UST 4084; TIAS 6799; 726 UNTS 249).
April 10, 1970 (21 UST 1509; TIAS 6911; 753 UNTS 251).
June 17, 1970 (21 UST 2638; TIAS 7003; 775 UNTS 89).
October 2, 1970 (21 UST 2641; TIAS 7004; 772 UNTS 157).
December 17, 1970 (22 UST 369; TIAS 7067; 792 UNTS 416).
December 23, 1970 (22 UST 10; TIAS 7036; 775 UNTS 99).
March 17, 1971 (22 UST 477; TIAS 7085; 792 UNTS 187).
August 7, 1971 (22 UST 1571; TIAS 7181; 807 UNTS 9).
November 10, 1971 (22 UST 1831; TIAS 7225).
November 18, 1971 (22 UST 1833; TIAS 7226).

December 21, 1971 (22 UST 2100; TIAS 7251).
December 23, 1971 (22 UST 2102; TIAS 7252).
December 30, 1971 (22 UST 2104; TIAS 7253).
January 5, 1972 (23 UST 4; TIAS 7266).
May 26, 1972 (23 UST 919; TIAS 7358).
August 28, 1972 (23 UST 2624; TIAS 7451).
October 27, 1972 (23 UST 3225; TIAS 7501).
November 3, 1972 (23 UST 3724; TIAS 7520).
November 13, 1972 (23 UST 3724; TIAS 7520).
November 13, 1972 (23 UST 3724; TIAS 7520).
December 11, 1972 (23 UST 4317; TIAS 7538).
December 12, 1972 (23 UST 4317; TIAS 7538).
December 13, 1972 (23 UST 4317; TIAS 7538).
January 22, 1973 (24 UST 452; TIAS 7562).
February 14, 1973 (24 UST 858; TIAS 7589).
December 31, 1973 (24 UST 2516; TIAS 7766).

Agricultural commodities agreement, with agreed minutes. Signed at Jakarta May 30, 1975; entered into force May 30, 1975.
26 UST 1748; TIAS 8133; 1006 UNTS 211.

Agricultural commodities agreement. Signed at Jakarta April 19, 1976; entered into force April 19, 1976.
27 UST 2279; TIAS 8308; 1052 UNTS 233.

Amendments:
May 26 and 28, 1976 (27 UST 2296; TIAS 8308; 1052 UNTS 245).
June 14 and 15, 1976 (27 UST 2298; TIAS 8308; 1052 UNTS 247).
September 8 and 11, 1976 (27 UST 3534; TIAS 8379; 1059 UNTS 466).
October 15, 1976 (27 UST 3866; TIAS 8404; 1059 UNTS 468).
October 18 and 19, 1976 (27 UST 3869; TIAS 8404; 1059 UNTS 470).
November 15 and 17, 1976 (27 UST 4095; TIAS 8428).

Agricultural commodities agreement, with agreed minutes. Signed at Jakarta May 17, 1977; entered into force May 17, 1977.
28 UST 6172; TIAS 8677.

Amendments:
September 9, 1977 (29 UST 1982; TIAS 8913; 1115 UNTS 361).
December 16, 1977 (29 UST 2877; TIAS 8984; 1115 UNTS 361).
February 23, 1978 (29 UST 6059; TIAS 9169).
July 13, 1978 (29 UST 6065; TIAS 9169).
December 6, 1978 (29 UST 6070; TIAS 9169).
July 19, 1979 (30 UST 5941; TIAS 9528; 1177 UNTS 395).
October 2, 1979 (31 UST 5506; TIAS 9665; 1221 UNTS 355).

Agricultural commodities agreement, with agreed minutes. Signed at Jakarta March 6, 1980; entered into force March 6, 1980.
32 UST 851; TIAS 9734; 1221 UNTS 247.

Agricultural commodities agreement, with agreed minutes. Signed at Jakarta December 2, 1980; entered into force December 2, 1980.
33 UST 805; TIAS 10063; 1268 UNTS 3.

Amendment:
June 2, 1986 (NP).

Related agreements:
March 20, 1982 (34 UST 153; TIAS 10345).
April 16, 1983 (TIAS 10716; 1578 UNTS 39).
August 12, 1983 (TIAS 10716; 1578 UNTS 46).
December 9, 1983 (NP).
March 22, 1984 (NP).
August 31, 1984 (NP).
February 13, 1985 (NP).
June 2, 1986 (NP).
September 18 and 22, 1986 (NP).

Agricultural commodities agreement. Signed at Jakarta June 16, 1987; entered into force June 16, 1987.
NP

Amendment:
September 2 and 3, 1987 (NP).

Agricultural commodities agreement. Signed at Jakarta June 3, 1988; entered into force June 3, 1988.
NP

Amendment:
July 28, 1988 (NP).

Related agreements:
October 22, 1988 (NP).
February 11 and 13, 1989 (NP).

ATOMIC ENERGY

Agreement for cooperation concerning peaceful uses of atomic energy with annex and agreed minute. Signed at Washington June 30, 1980; entered into force December 30, 1981.
33 UST 3194; TIAS 10219.

Arrangement for the exchange of technical information and cooperation in nuclear safety matters, with addenda. Signed at Vienna September 23, 1998; entered into force September 23, 1998.
TIAS

AVIATION

Air transport agreement with schedule. Signed at Djakarta January 15, 1968; entered into force January 15, 1968.
19 UST 4496; TIAS 6441; 697 UNTS 209.

Amendments:
May 2, 1986 (TIAS 11371).
April 12 and June 19, 1990 (TIAS 11760).

Agreement concerning the airworthiness and environmental certification of imported civil aeronautical products. Exchange of notes at Ja-

INDONESIA (Cont'd)

karta January 23, 1987; entered into force January 23, 1987.
TIAS 11320.

Memorandum of agreement concerning assistance in developing and modernizing the Indonesian civil aviation infrastructure, with annexes. Signed at Washington and Jakarta August 23 and October 19, 1990; entered into force October 19, 1990.
TIAS 11749.

Memorandum of agreement concerning assistance in the development of Indonesia's civil aeronautics and air commerce, with annex. Signed at Washington and Jakarta April 3 and May 3, 1996; entered into force May 3, 1996.
TIAS

COPYRIGHT (See also APPENDIX)

Agreement on copyright protection. Signed at Washington March 22, 1989; entered into force August 1, 1989.
TIAS 11608.

CUSTOMS

Agreement granting reciprocal customs privileges to diplomatic and consular officers and personnel. Exchange of notes at Washington March 23 and 31, 1961; entered into force March 31, 1961.
12 UST 251; TIAS 4706; 405 UNTS 119.

DEFENSE

Agreement for a program of military assistance in the form of constabulary equipment to be supplied by the United States to the Republic of Indonesia. Exchange of notes at Djakarta August 15, 1950; entered into force August 15, 1950.
2 UST 1619; TIAS 2306; 134 UNTS 255.

Agreement for the transfer from a grant to an aid on a reimbursable basis of the undelivered balance of constabulary equipment authorized under the agreement of August 15, 1950. Exchange of notes at Washington January 5, and at Djakarta January 12, 1953; entered into force January 12, 1953.
4 UST 113; TIAS 2768; 198 UNTS 400.

Agreement relating to the sale to Indonesia of military equipment, materials, and services. Exchange of notes at Djakarta August 13, 1958; entered into force August 13, 1958.
9 UST 1149; TIAS 4095; 335 UNTS 187.

Agreement relating to the furnishing of military equipment, materials, and services for a program of civic action. Exchange of notes at Djakarta April 14, 1967; entered into force April 14, 1967.
18 UST 384; TIAS 6247; 689 UNTS 3.

Agreement relating to the provision by the United States of basic pilot training aircraft. Exchange of notes at Djakarta April 9 and 17, 1969; entered into force April 17, 1969.
20 UST 702; TIAS 6678; 719 UNTS 121.

Agreement relating to the furnishing of combat equipment to Indonesia as additional military assistance. Exchange of notes at Djakarta August 18 and 19, 1970; entered into force August 19, 1970.
21 UST 2140; TIAS 6959; 764 UNTS 219.

Agreement concerning payment to the United States of net proceeds from the sale of defense articles furnished under the military assistance program. Exchange of notes at Jakarta June 12 and 29, 1974; entered into force July 1, 1974.
25 UST 2609; TIAS 7938.

Agreement relating to eligibility for United States military assistance and training pursuant to the International Security Assistance and Arms Export Control Act of 1976. Exchange of notes at Jakarta August 3 and 24, 1976; entered into force August 24, 1976.
27 UST 4006; TIAS 8419; 1059 UNTS 131.

ECONOMIC AND TECHNICAL COOPERATION

Economic cooperation agreement. Signed at Djakarta October 16, 1950; entered into force provisionally October 16, 1950 (recognized by the Republic of Indonesia as a binding obligation pending Parliamentary action).
7 UST 2241; TIAS 3624; 281 UNTS 105.

Agreement relating to continuation of economic and technical cooperation under the agreement of October 16, 1950. Exchange of notes at Washington January 5 and at Djakarta January 12, 1953; entered into force January 12, 1953.
4 UST 18, TIAS 2762; 215 UNTS 121.

Agreement relating to the assumption by Indonesia of all responsibilities and obligations of the Netherlands incurred under the economic cooperation agreements of July 2, 1948, as amended, and April 26, 1949, as amended, and the loan agreements of October 28, 1948 and December 22, 1949; and memorandum of understanding. Signed at Washington February 11, 1952 by the United States, Indonesia, and the Netherlands; entered into force February 11, 1952.
3 UST 2989; TIAS 2484; 165 UNTS 77.

Agency for International Development:
June 30, 1975 (28 UST 3227; TIAS 8584).
July 28, 1976 (29 UST 5107; TIAS 9092).
October 28, 1976 (28 UST 3265; TIAS 8584).
October 28, 1976 (28 UST 8201; TIAS 8755; 1095 UNTS 33).
October 28, 1976 (28 UST 8245; TIAS 8759).

October 28, 1976 (28 UST 8389; TIAS 8763; 1095 UNTS 63).
January 24, 1977 (29 UST 685; TIAS 8848).
January 24, 1977 (29 UST 711; TIAS 8849).
July 27, 1977 (29 UST 5124; TIAS 9092).
January 3, 1978 (29 UST 2156; TIAS 8931).
March 30, 1978 (30 UST 1831; TIAS 9294).
April 12, 1978 (29 UST 5126; TIAS 9092).
April 12, 1978 (30 UST 1988; TIAS 9308; 1152 UNTS 333).
April 12, 1978 (30 UST 2030; TIAS 9310).
April 12, 1978 (30 UST 2123; TIAS 9317).
April 12, 1978 (30 UST 2354; TIAS 9342).
April 12, 1978 (30 UST 2379; TIAS 9343).
May 6, 1978 (30 UST 2643; TIAS 9357).
July 13, 1978 (30 UST 3339; TIAS 9394).
August 31, 1978 (30 UST 5509; TIAS 9514).
August 31, 1987 (NP).
August 31, 1988 (NP).
March 21, 1990 (NP).
September 28, 1992 (NP).
August 31, 1993 (NP).
March 3, 1994 (NP).
March 21, 1995 (NP).
June 11, 1996 (NP).
August 6, 1996 (NP).
August 30, 1996 (NP).
May 7, 1997 (NP).
August 1, 1997 (NP).
August 12, 1998 (NP).
September 17, 1998 (NP).
August 6, 1999 (NP).

EDUCATION

Educational and cultural agreement. Signed at Jakarta July 15, 1992; entered into force July 15, 1992.
TIAS 12466.

FINANCE

Agreement relating to investment guaranties. Exchange of notes at Djakarta January 7, 1967; entered into force August 22, 1967.
18 UST 1850; TIAS 6330; 692 UNTS 109.

Memorandum of agreement regarding debt rescheduling under the agricultural commodities agreement of June 28, 1966, with annexes. Signed at Djakarta December 30, 1967; entered into force December 30, 1967.
20 UST 501; TIAS 6656; 724 UNTS 364.

Memorandum of agreement regarding debt rescheduling under the agricultural commodities agreement of April 18, 1966, as amended, with annexes. Signed at Djakarta December 30, 1967; entered into force December 30, 1967.
20 UST 494; TIAS 6655; 724 UNTS 350.

Memorandum of agreement regarding debt rescheduling under the agricultural commodities agreement of April 18, 1966, as amended, with annexes. Signed at Djakarta December 20, 1968; entered into force December 20, 1968.
20 UST 494; TIAS 6655; 724 UNTS 356.

Memorandum of agreement regarding debt rescheduling under the agricultural commodities

INDONESIA (Cont'd)

agreement of June 28, 1966, with annexes. Signed at Djakarta December 20, 1968; entered into force December 20, 1968.
20 UST 501; TIAS 6656; 724 UNTS 370.

Memorandum of agreement regarding debt rescheduling under the agricultural commodities agreement of April 18, 1966, as amended, with annexes. Signed at Djakarta February 6, 1970; entered into force February 6, 1970.
21 UST 437; TIAS 6830; 740 UNTS 424.

Memorandum of agreement regarding debt rescheduling under the agricultural commodities agreement of June 28, 1966, with annexes. Signed at Djakarta February 6, 1970; entered into force February 6, 1970.
21 UST 442; TIAS 6831; 740 UNTS 442.

Memorandum of agreement regarding the rescheduling of payments under the agricultural commodities agreements of April 18, 1966, as amended, and June 28, 1966, as amended; the surplus property agreement of May 28, 1947, as amended and certain loan and credit agreements. Signed at Djakarta March 16, 1971; entered into force March 16, 1971.
22 UST 514; TIAS 7092; 792 UNTS 170.

Agreement regarding the consolidation and rescheduling of certain debts owed to, guaranteed by, or insured by the United States Government and its agencies, with annexes. Signed at Washington September 1, 1999; entered into force October 22, 1999.
NP

HEALTH

Agreement concerning the establishment of a United States naval medical research unit in Indonesia. Signed at Djakarta January 16, 1970; entered into force January 16, 1970.
21 UST 1; TIAS 6813; 240 UNTS 143.

INFORMATIONAL MEDIA GUARANTIES

Agreement relating to an informational media guaranty program pursuant to section 1011 of the U.S. Information and Educational Exchange Act of 1948, as amended. Exchange of notes at Djakarta September 15, 1955; entered into force September 15, 1955.
6 UST 3957; TIAS 3406; 256 UNTS 293.

MAPPING

Memorandum of understanding concerning mapping, charting, and geodesy cooperation. Signed at Jakarta October 21, 1977; entered into force October 21, 1977.
29 UST 4810; TIAS 9079; 1134 UNTS 339.

MARITIME MATTERS

Agreement on maritime search and rescue. Signed at Jakarta July 5, 1988; entered into force July 5, 1988.
TIAS 11655.

NARCOTIC DRUGS

Understandings concerning the assignment of a Drug Enforcement Administration representative to the American Embassy in Jakarta to advance the U.S.-Indonesian common interest in preventing illegal traffic in narcotic drugs, with annex. Exchange of letters at Jakarta April 1, 1975; entered into force April 1, 1975.
27 UST 2001; TIAS 8299; 1052 UNTS 227.

PEACE CORPS

Agreement relating to the establishment of a Peace Corps program in Indonesia. Exchange of notes at Djakarta March 8 and 14, 1963; entered into force March 14, 1963.
14 UST 1789; TIAS 5489; 505 UNTS 79.

POSTAL MATTERS

Agreement concerning the exchange of parcel post, and detailed regulations of execution. Signed at Bandoeng June 14 and at Washington October 4, 1934; operative October 4, 1933.
49 Stat. 2967; Post Office Department print; 158 LNTS 395.

International express mail agreement, with detailed regulations. Signed at Jakarta and Washington January 23 and February 26, 1987; entered into force April 1, 1987.
TIAS 11300.

Postal money order agreement. Signed at Jakarta and Washington September 21 and November 1, 1993; entered into force December 1, 1993.
NP

PUBLICATIONS

Agreement relating to the exchange of official publications. Exchange of notes at Djakarta May 17 and June 7, 1950; entered into force June 7, 1950.
1 UST 649; TIAS 2122; 98 UNTS 167.

SATELLITES

Agreement concerning the furnishing of launching and associated services by the National Aeronautics and Space Administration for Indonesian satellites, with annexes. Ex-change of notes at Washington March 26, 1975; entered into force March 26, 1975.
26 UST 524; TIAS 8054; 992 UNTS 308.

Agreement concerning the furnishing of launching and associated services for Palapa-B spacecraft. Exchange of notes at Washington April 11, 1979; entered into force April 11, 1979.
30 UST 4253; TIAS 9457; 1171 UNTS 255.

SCIENTIFIC COOPERATION

Agreement for cooperation in scientific research and technological development. Signed at Jakarta January 15, 1992; entered into force July 10, 1992.
TIAS

Extension:
July 3, 1997.

Memorandum of understanding concerning cooperation on standards, metrology and conformance. Signed at Jakarta November 16, 1994; entered into force November 16, 1994.
TIAS 12581.

Memorandum of understanding concerning technological development cooperation in the earth sciences. Signed at Jakarta May 3, 1995; entered into force May 3, 1995.
TIAS 12641.

SURPLUS PROPERTY

Agreement regarding a line of credit for the purchase of United States surplus property. (Part of U.S.-Netherlands lend-lease settlement). Signed at Washington May 28, 1947 by the United States, Netherlands Indies, and the Netherlands; entered into force May 28, 1947.
61 Stat. 3947; TIAS 1750; 8 Bevans 1250; 17 UNTS 29.

Agreement relating to the release of the Netherlands from its obligations as guarantor for Indonesia under the surplus property agreement of May 28, 1947. Exchange of notes at The Hague September 17, 1952, at Djakarta October 15, 1952, and at Washington April 8, 1953; entered into force April 8, 1953.
4 UST 1557; TIAS 2820; 205 UNTS 324.

Memorandum of agreement regarding the rescheduling of payments under the surplus property agreement of May 28, 1947. Signed at Djakarta December 30, 1967; entered into force December 30, 1967.
18 UST 3261; TIAS 6419; 697 UNTS 119.

Memorandum of agreement regarding the second rescheduling of payments under the surplus property agreement of May 28, 1947, with annexes. Signed at Djakarta December 20, 1968; entered into force December 20, 1968.
19 UST 7838; TIAS 6618; 723 UNTS 432.

Memorandum of agreement regarding the third rescheduling of payments under the surplus

INDONESIA (Cont'd)

property agreement of May 28, 1947, with annexes. Signed at Djakarta February 6, 1970; entered into force February 6, 1970.
21 UST 447; TIAS 6832; 740 UNTS 464.

TAXATION

Convention for the avoidance of double taxation and the prevention of fiscal evasion with respect to taxes on income, with protocol and exchange of notes. Signed at Jakarta July 11, 1988; entered into force December 30, 1990.
TIAS 11593.

Protocol amending the convention of July 11, 1988, for the avoidance of double taxation and the prevention of fiscal evasion with respect to taxes on income. Signed at Jakarta July 24, 1996; entered into force December 23, 1996.
TIAS

TELECOMMUNICATION

Agreement relating to the reciprocal granting of authorizations to permit licensed amateur radio operators of either country to operate their stations in the other country. Exchange of notes at Djakarta December 10, 1968; entered into force December 10, 1968.
20 UST 490; TIAS 6654; 707 UNTS 149.

TRADE AND COMMERCE

Memorandum of understanding setting forth mutual trade concessions and contributions to the multilateral trade negotiations, with exchange of letters, and related letter of February 21, 1980. Signed at Jakarta November 29, December 20 and 27, 1979; entered into force January 1, 1980.
TIAS 10569.

Arrangement relating to a visa system for exports of apparel and non apparel of cotton, wool and man-made fiber manufactured in Indonesia. Exchange of notes at Jakarta June 1 and 14, 1984; entered into force June 14, 1984.
NP

Agreement relating to subsidization of exports in the context of the agreement on interpretation and application of articles VI, XVI and XXIII (subsidies code) of the General Agreement on Tariffs and Trade (TIAS 9619). Exchange of letters at Washington February 28, 1985; entered into force February 28, 1985.
TIAS 11325.

Amendment:
April 10, 1986.

Administrative arrangement relating to visa and certification procedures for exports of textiles and textile products from Indonesia. Ex-

change of letters at Washington March 25, 1987; entered into force March 25, 1987; effective July 1, 1987.
NP

Amendment:
December 1 and 3, 1988 (NP).

Agreement concerning trade in textiles and textile products, with annexes. Signed at Jakarta May 8, 1992; entered into force May 8, 1992; effective July 1, 1992.
NP

Amendment:
June 16 and July 21, 1993 (NP).

INTER-AMERICAN DEVELOPMENT BANK

FINANCE

Social progress trust fund agreement with exchange of letters. Signed at Washington June 19, 1961; entered into force June 19, 1961.
12 UST 632; TIAS 4763; 410 UNTS 33.

Related agreements:
February 17, 1964 (15 UST 104; TIAS 5522; 511 UNTS 296).
September 7, 1966 (17 UST 1200; TIAS 6081).
April 28, 1972 (23 UST 1497; TIAS 7430).
October 3, 1975 (27 UST 2627; TIAS 8333; 1054 UNTS 338).

INTER–AMERICAN INSTITUTE FOR COOPERATION ON AGRICULTURE

TAXATION

Tax reimbursement agreement. Signed at Washington December 30, 1994; entered into force December 30, 1994.
TIAS 12594.

INTERNATIONAL ATOMIC ENERGY AGENCY

ATOMIC ENERGY [1]

Agreement for cooperation in the civil uses of atomic energy. Signed at Vienna May 11, 1959; entered into force August 7, 1959.
10 UST 1424; TIAS 4291; 339 UNTS 359.

Extension and amendments:
February 12, 1974 (25 UST 1199; TIAS 7852).
January 14, 1980 (32 UST 1143; TIAS 9762; 1220 UNTS 316).

Agreement for the application of safeguards in the United States, with protocol. Done at Vienna November 18, 1977; entered into force December 9, 1980.
32 UST 3059; TIAS 9889.

Agreement relating to provision by the United States Nuclear Regulatory Commission to the International Atomic Energy Agency of experts in the various fields of the peaceful applications of atomic energy. Signed at Vienna and Bethesda May 29 and September 16, 1981; entered into force September 16, 1981.
33 UST 3849; TIAS 10264; 1543 UNTS 111.

Agreement for the application of safeguards in connection with the treaty of February 14, 1967, for the prohibition of nuclear weapons in Latin America, with protocol. Signed at Vienna February 17, 1989; entered into force April 6, 1989.
TIAS 12398.

NOTE:
[1] For agreements between the IAEA, the United States, and other countries, see under ATOMIC ENERGY in multilateral section.

TAXATION

Tax reimbursement agreement, with annex. Signed at Vienna April 5, 1989; entered into force April 5, 1989.
TIAS 11774.

INTERNATIONAL CENTRE FOR THE STUDY OF THE PRESERVATION AND THE RESTORATION OF CULTURAL PROPERTY (ICCROM)

TAXATION

Agreement relating to a procedure for United States income tax reimbursement. Exchange of letters at Rome April 1 and May 4, 1981; entered into force May 4, 1981; effective January 1981.
33 UST 1922; TIAS 10155.

INTERNATIONAL CIVIL AVIATION ORGANIZATION

TAXATION

Tax reimbursement agreement, with annex. Signed at Montreal July 14, 1992; entered into force July 14, 1992.
TIAS 12465.

INTERNATIONAL COTTON ADVISORY COMMITTEE

TAXATION

Agreement relating to a procedure for United States income tax reimbursement. Exchange of notes at Washington November 17 and 19, 1981; entered into force January 1, 1982.
33 UST 4242; TIAS 10299.

INTERNATIONAL HYDROGRAPHIC BUREAU

TAXATION

Agreement relating to a procedure for United States income tax reimbursement. Exchange of letters at Marseilles December 7 and 13, 1982; entered into force January 1, 1983.
TIAS 12058.

INTERNATIONAL LABOR ORGANIZATION

PEACE CORPS

Agreement concerning the Peace Corps program. Exchange of notes at Geneva February 21 and 22, 1963; entered into force February 22, 1963.
14 UST 1554; TIAS 5458; 489 UNTS 347.

TAXATION

Agreement relating to a procedure for United States income tax reimbursement, with annex. Signed at Washington May 18, 1984; entered into force May 18, 1984, effective January 1, 1984.
TIAS 11076.

INTERNATIONAL MARITIME ORGANIZATION

TAXATION

Tax reimbursement agreement, with annex. Signed at London January 12, 1995; entered into force January 12, 1995.
TIAS 12597.

INTERNATIONAL MONETARY FUND

FINANCE

Agreement relating to provision of financing by the United States in connection with the establishment of the Supplementary Financing Facility. Exchange of letters at Washington January 5 and 12, 1979; entered into force January 16, 1979.
30 UST 3526; TIAS 9406; 1180 UNTS 131.

INTERNATIONAL NATURAL RUBBER ORGANIZATION

TAXATION

Tax reimbursement agreement, with annex. Signed at Kuala Lumpur October 5, 1988; entered into force October 5, 1988.
TIAS 11627.

INTERNATIONAL ORGANIZATION FOR MIGRATION

TAXATION

Tax reimbursement agreement, with annex. Signed at Washington September 17, 1997; entered into force September 17, 1997.
TIAS

INTERNATIONAL TELECOMMUNICATION UNION

CONFERENCES

Arrangements relating to the holding, organization and financing of the 1998 Plenipotentiary

Conference of the International Telecommunication Union at Minneapolis, with annexes and exchange of letters. Signed at Geneva November 28, 1997; entered into force November 28, 1997.
TIAS

TAXATION

Tax reimbursement agreement, with annex. Signed at Geneva January 19, 1990; entered into force January 19, 1990.
TIAS 11710.

TELECOMMUNICATION

Special arrangement permitting third party exchanges between the International Telecommunications Union amateur radio station and amateur radio stations under United States jurisdiction. Exchange of letters at Geneva and Washington April 28 and June 7, 1976; entered into force June 7, 1976.
28 UST 5019; TIAS 8608.

INTERNATIONAL TELECOMMUNICATIONS SATELLITE ORGANIZATION

HEADQUARTERS

Headquarters agreement. Signed at Washington November 22 and 24, 1976; entered into force November 24, 1976.
28 UST 2248; TIAS 8542.

SATELLITES

Memorandum of agreement with respect to the Pan American Satellite Corporation consultation, with related letter. Signed at Washington November 10, 1986; entered into force November 10, 1986.
TIAS 12390.

INTERNATIONAL TRIBUNAL FOR THE PROSECUTION OF PERSONS RESPONSIBLE FOR GENOCIDE AND OTHER SERIOUS VIOLATIONS OF INTERNATIONAL HUMANITARIAN LAW COMMITTED IN THE TERRITORY OF RWANDA

WAR CRIMES

Agreement on surrender of persons, with statement of understanding. Signed at The Hague January 24, 1995; entered into force February 14, 1996.
TIAS 12601.

INTERNATIONAL TRIBUNAL FOR THE PROSECUTION OF PERSONS RESPONSIBLE FOR SERIOUS VIOLATIONS OF INTERNATIONAL HUMANITARIAN LAW IN THE TERRITORY OF THE FORMER YUGOSLAVIA

WAR CRIMES

Agreement on surrender of persons. Signed at The Hague October 5, 1994; entered into force February 14, 1996.
TIAS 12570; 1911 UNTS 223.

INTERNATIONAL TROPICAL TIMBER ORGANIZATION

TAXATION

Tax reimbursement agreement, with annex. Signed at Tokyo December 27, 1988; entered into force December 27, 1988.
TIAS 11629.

INTER-PARLIAMENTARY UNION

TAXATION

Agreement relating to a procedure for United States income tax reimbursement. Exchange of notes at Geneva September 17 and October 27, 1981; entered into force October 27, 1981; effective January 1, 1981.
33 UST 4142; TIAS 10290; 1549 UNTS 383.

IRAN

AGRICULTURAL COMMODITIES

Agricultural commodities agreement with exchanges of notes of July 26 and 28, 1960. Signed at Tehran July 26, 1960; entered into force July 26, 1960.
11 UST 1944; TIAS 4544; 384 UNTS 141.

Amendments:
September 26, 1960 (11 UST 2208; TIAS 4592; 394 UNTS 318).
October 20, 1960 (11 UST 2239; TIAS 4598; 394 UNTS 324).
April 10 and 17, 1961 (12 UST 321; TIAS 4719; 405 UNTS 370).
May 18 and June 1, 1961 (12 UST 855; TIAS 4785; 410 UNTS 355).

Agreement concerning the closeout of the collection account of the agricultural commodities agreement of February 20, 1956. Exchange of notes at Tehran March 29 and July 2, 1961; entered into force July 2, 1961.
12 UST 3221; TIAS 4928; 434 UNTS 321.

Agricultural commodities agreement, with exchange of notes of January 29 and February 8, 1962. Signed at Tehran January 29, 1962; entered into force January 29, 1962.
13 UST 174; TIAS 4956; 435 UNTS 53.

Amendments:
February 17 and 20, 1962 (13 UST 174; TIAS 4956; 435 UNTS 53).
February 10 and September 1, 1964 (15 UST 1955; TIAS 5671; 531 UNTS 382).

Agricultural commodities agreement with exchanges of notes of October 15 and December 30, 1962 and February 3, 1963. Signed at Tehran October 15, 1962; entered into force October 15, 1962.
14 UST 215; TIAS 5300; 473 UNTS 291.

Agricultural commodities agreement, with exchange of notes of November 18, 1963 and June 11, 1964. Signed at Tehran November 17, 1963; entered into force November 17, 1963.
15 UST 755; TIAS 5600; 530 UNTS 41.

Agricultural commodities agreement, with exchange of notes. Signed at Tehran September 29, 1964; entered into force September 29, 1964.
15 UST 1958; TIAS 5672; 531 UNTS 163.

Agricultural commodities agreement with exchange of notes. Signed at Tehran November 16, 1964; entered into force November 16, 1964.
15 UST 2140; TIAS 5696; 532 UNTS 213.

Amendments:
December 15, 1964 (15 UST 2327; TIAS 5721; 532 UNTS 213).
April 28, 1965 (16 UST 662; TIAS 5792; 546 UNTS 408).
October 13, 1965 (16 UST 1870; TIAS 5918; 574 UNTS 276).

Agricultural commodities agreement with exchange of notes. Signed at Tehran December 20, 1966; entered into force December 20, 1966.
17 UST 2372; TIAS 6183; 681 UNTS 101.

AVIATION

Air transport agreement, with exchange of notes. Signed at Tehran February 1, 1973; entered into force January 9, 1974.
26 UST 1929; TIAS 8149; 1027 UNTS 129.

Memorandum of agreement relating to the provision of technical assistance to the Iranian Civil Aviation Organization, with annex. Signed at Washington and Tehran May 12 and June 9, 1977; entered into force June 9, 1977.
29 UST 5319; TIAS 9111.

CLAIMS

Declarations of the Government of the Democratic and Popular Republic of Algeria concerning commitments and settlement of claims by the United States and Iran with respect to resolution of the crisis arising out of the detention of 52 United States nationals in Iran, with Undertakings and Escrow Agreement.[1] Initialed at Algiers January 19, 1981; entered into force January 19, 1981.
TIAS

Settlement agreement regarding certain claims before the Iran-U.S. Claims Tribunal, with annex. Signed at The Hague February 9, 1996; entered into force February 9, 1996.
TIAS

Settlement agreement on the case concerning the aerial incident of July 3, 1988 before the International Court of Justice, with annexes. Signed at The Hague February 9, 1996; entered into force February 9, 1996.
TIAS

General agreement on the settlement of certain I.C.J. and Tribunal cases, with related statement. Signed at The Hague February 9, 1996; entered into force February 9, 1996.
TIAS

IRAN (Cont'd)

NOTE:
[1] For technical agreements concerning the security account, see NETHERLANDS—CLAIMS.

COMMERCE

Treaty of amity, economic relations, and consular rights. Signed at Tehran August 15, 1955; entered into force June 16, 1957.
8 UST 899; TIAS 3853; 284 UNTS 93.

CONSULS (See COMMERCE)

DEFENSE

Mutual defense assistance agreement. Exchange of notes at Washington May 23, 1950; entered into force May 23, 1950.
1 UST 420; TIAS 2071; 81 UNTS 3.

Agreement relating to the continuation of military assistance to Iran. Exchange of notes at Tehran April 24, 1952; entered into force April 24, 1952.
5 UST 788; TIAS 2967.

Agreement relating to the disposition of equipment and materials no longer required in the furtherance of the mutual defense assistance program. Exchange of notes at Tehran July 12 and October 31, 1957; entered into force October 31, 1957.
8 UST 2369; TIAS 3952; 303 UNTS 320.

Agreement relating to the safeguarding of classified information, with annex. Exchange of notes at Tehran May 28 and June 6, 1974; entered into force June 6, 1974.
25 UST 1266; TIAS 7857.

Agreement relating to the furnishing of certain federal catalog data and cataloging services to Iran. Signed at Washington December 5, 1974 and at Tehran January 25, 1975; entered into force January 25, 1975.
26 UST 302; TIAS 8034; 991 UNTS 401.

Agreement concerning management, disposal, and utilization of funds derived from the sale of military assistance program property. Signed at Tehran October 6, 1975; entered into force October 6, 1975.
TIAS

Agreement concerning management, disposal, and utilization of funds derived from sale of military assistance program property. Signed at Tehran October 19, 1976; entered into force October 19, 1976.
TIAS

Memorandum of understanding concerning revisions of Foreign Military Sales letters of offer and acceptance in force between the United States and Iran. Signed at Tehran February 3, 1979; entered into force February 3, 1979.
30 UST 3597; TIAS 9415.

DISASTER ASSISTANCE

Memorandum of understanding relating to the provision of advisory technical assistance to Iran in organizing its civil emergency preparedness capability. Signed January 26, 1977; entered into force January 26, 1977.
30 UST 4354; TIAS 9461.

ECONOMIC AND TECHNICAL COOPERATION

General agreement for economic cooperation. Signed at Tehran December 21, 1961; entered into force December 21, 1961.
12 UST 3229; TIAS 4930; 433 UNTS 269.

Joint communique concerning United States-Iran relations and establishment of a Joint Commission for cooperation in various fields. Issued at Tehran November 2, 1974; entered into force November 2, 1974.
25 UST 3073; TIAS 7967.

Agreed minutes of the Joint Commission:
March 4, 1975 (26 UST 420; TIAS 8042).
August 7, 1976 (27 UST 4329; TIAS 8455).
February 28, 1978 (30 UST 1027; TIAS 9238; 1152 UNTS 103).

EDUCATION

Agreement for financing certain educational exchange programs. Signed at Tehran October 24, 1963; entered into force October 24, 1963.
14 UST 1510; TIAS 5451; 489 UNTS 303.

FINANCE

Agreement relating to investment guaranties under section 413(b)(4) of the Mutual Security Act of 1954, as amended. Exchange of notes at Tehran September 17 and 21, 1957; entered into force September 24, 1957.
8 UST 1599; TIAS 3913; 293 UNTS 287.

Agreement supplementing the agreement of September 17 and 21, 1957 relating to investment guaranties. Exchange of notes at Tehran March 12, 1970; entered into force March 12, 1970.
22 UST 1030; TIAS 7146; 797 UNTS 396.

HOSTAGES (See CLAIMS)

JUDICIAL ASSISTANCE

Agreement on procedures for mutual assistance in connection with matters relating to the Lockheed Aircraft Corporation, Grumman Corporation and Northrop Corporation. Signed at Washington June 14, 1977; entered into force June 14, 1977.
28 UST 5205; TIAS 8621.

METEOROLOGY

Agreement relating to a cooperative program to improve and modernize the Iranian meteorological services, with annexes. Signed at Tehran November 26, 1977; entered into force November 26, 1977.
29 UST 5546; TIAS 9127; 1134 UNTS 359.

MISSIONS, MILITARY

Agreement relating to the privileges and immunities granted American military and non-military technicians assisting in the modernization program of the Imperial Iranian Armed Forces. Exchange of notes at Tehran May 24 and 30, 1973; entered into force May 30, 1973.
25 UST 3048; TIAS 7963.

PEACE CORPS

Agreement relating to the establishment of a Peace Corps program in Iran. Exchange of notes at Tehran September 5 and 16, 1962; entered into force September 16, 1962.
22 UST 434; TIAS 7078; 791 UNTS 19.

POSTAL MATTERS

Parcel post agreement with detailed regulations for execution. Signed at Tehran July 15 and at Washington August 28, 1969; entered into force January 1, 1971.
21 UST 2605; TIAS 7002; 775 UNTS 17.

PUBLICATIONS

Agreement relating to the exchange of official publications. Exchange of notes at Tehran August 21, 1943; entered into force August 21, 1943.
57 Stat. 1133; EAS 349; 8 Bevans 1280; 101 UNTS 189.

IRAN (Cont'd)

RELIEF SUPPLIES AND PACKAGES

Agreement relating to duty-free entry and defrayment of inland transportation charges for relief supplies to Iran. Exchange of notes at Tehran September 22 and October 5 and 13, 1953; entered into force October 13, 1953.
4 UST 2809; TIAS 2890; 222 UNTS 67.

TRADE (See also COMMERCE)

Agreement terminating the reciprocal trade agreement of April 8, 1943, as amended. Exchange of notes at Tehran July 27, 1960; entered into force July 27, 1960.
11 UST 2163; TIAS 4581; 393 UNTS 338.

VISAS

Agreement relating to the reciprocal waiver of passport visa fees for nonimmigrants. Exchange of notes at Tehran March 27 and April 20 and 21, 1926; entered into force April 21, 1926; operative May 15, 1926.
8 Bevans 1260.

Agreement relating to the reciprocal issuance of multiple-entry nonimmigrant visas. Exchange of letters at Tehran December 13 and 16, 1976; entered into force December 16, 1976; effective January 1, 1977.
28 UST 8161; TIAS 8751.

IRAQ

CLAIMS

Agreement concerning claims resulting from attack on the U.S.S. *Stark*. Exchange of notes at Baghdad March 27 and 28, 1989; entered into force March 28, 1989.
TIAS 12030.

COMMERCE (See also ECONOMIC AND TECHNICAL COOPERATION)

Treaty of commerce and navigation. Signed at Baghdad December 3, 1938; entered into force June 19, 1940.
54 Stat. 1790; TS 960; 9 Bevans 7; 203 LNTS 107.

CULTURAL RELATIONS

Cultural agreement. Signed at Baghdad January 23, 1961; entered into force August 13, 1963.
14 UST 1168; TIAS 5411; 488 UNTS 163.

CUSTOMS

Agreement relating to the privilege, on a reciprocal basis, of free entry to all articles imported for the personal use of consular officers. Exchange of notes at Washington March 14, May 15, June 19, and August 8, 1951; entered into force August 8, 1951.
5 UST 657; TIAS 2956; 229 UNTS 185.

DEFENSE

Agreement confirming understanding of Iraq that paragraphs 1 and 4 of the military assistance agreement of April 21, 1954 apply to equipment or materials transferred by the United States to Iraq on a reimbursable basis. Exchange of notes at Baghdad December 3, 1955; entered into force December 3, 1955.
6 UST 6014; TIAS 3447; 241 UNTS 19.

Agreement terminating the military assistance agreement of April 21, 1954 (TIAS 3108), the agreement of July 25, 1955 relating to the disposition of military equipment and materials (TIAS 3289), and the economic assistance agreement of May 18 and 22, 1957 (TIAS 3835). Exchange of notes at Baghdad May 30 and July 7, 1959; entered into force July 21, 1959.
10 UST 1415; TIAS 4289; 357 UNTS 153.

ECONOMIC AND TECHNICAL COOPERATION

General agreement for technical cooperation. Signed at Baghdad April 10, 1951; entered into force June 2, 1951.
3 UST 541; TIAS 2413; 151 UNTS 179.

Amendment:
December 18, 1951 and February 21, 1952 (3 UST 4748; TIAS 2638; 198 UNTS 225).

Commercial, economic and technical cooperation agreement. Signed at Washington August 26, 1987; entered into force October 27, 1987.
TIAS 12020.

EDUCATION

Agreement providing for the United States education foundation in Iraq. Signed at Baghdad August 16, 1951; entered into force August 16, 1951.
2 UST 1908; TIAS 2327; 147 UNTS 65.

EXTRADITION

Extradition treaty. Signed at Baghdad June 7, 1934; entered into force April 23, 1936.
49 Stat. 3380; TS 907; 9 Bevans 1; 170 LNTS 267.

LEND-LEASE

Agreement on the principles applying to aid for defense, and exchange of notes. Signed at Washington July 31, 1945; entered into force July 31, 1945.
59 Stat. 1535; EAS 470; 9 Bevans 22; 121 UNTS 239.

POSTAL MATTERS

International express mail agreement, with detailed regulations. Signed at Baghdad and Washington April 6 and May 5, 1989; entered into force June 15, 1989.
TIAS 11609.

PUBLICATIONS

Agreement relating to the exchange of official publications. Exchange of notes at Baghdad February 16, 1944; entered into force February 16, 1944.
58 Stat. 1253; EAS 403; 9 Bevans 14; 109 UNTS 223.

VISAS

Agreement for the reciprocal reduction of passport visa fees for nonimmigrants. Exchange of notes at Baghdad February 27, 1939; entered into force February 27, 1939; operative March 20, 1939.
9 Bevans 12.

Agreement relating to the reciprocal issuance of nonimmigrant passport visas. Exchange of notes at Baghdad June 6, 1956; entered into force June 6, 1956.
7 UST 1067; TIAS 3587; 275 UNTS 265.

IRELAND

ATOMIC ENERGY

Agreement providing for a grant to assist in the acquisition of certain nuclear research and training equipment and materials. Exchange of notes at Dublin March 24, 1960; entered into force April 7, 1960.
11 UST 376; TIAS 4453; 371 UNTS 237.

IRELAND (Cont'd)

AVIATION

Arrangement relating to air navigation. Exchange of notes at Dublin September 29 and November 4, 1937; entered into force November 4, 1937; operative December 4, 1937.
51 Stat. 319; EAS 110; 9 Bevans 36; 185 LNTS 71.

Agreement relating to air transport services. Exchange of notes at Washington February 3, 1945; entered into force February 3, 1945; operative February 15, 1945.
59 Stat. 1402; EAS 460; 9 Bevans 43; 122 UNTS 305.

Amendments:
January 25, 1988 and September 29, 1989 (TIAS 11692).
July 25 and September 6, 1990 (TIAS 11739).

Memorandum of agreement relating to flight inspection services. Signed at Washington and Dublin March 10 and August 4, 1978; entered into force August 4, 1978; effective September 1, 1978.
30 UST 230; TIAS 9190; 1150 UNTS 141.

Agreement on preinspection of aircraft passengers and crew at Shannon airport. Signed at Dublin June 25, 1986; entered into force June 25, 1986.
TIAS 11379.

Related agreement:
March 31, 1988 (TIAS 11379).

Agreement for promotion of aviation safety. Signed at Dublin February 5, 1997; entered into force February 5, 1997.
TIAS

Agreement on technical cooperation in civil aviation matters. Signed at Dublin June 11, 1999; entered into force June 11, 1999.
TIAS

COMMERCE

Treaty of friendship, commerce and navigation, with protocol. Signed at Dublin January 21, 1950; entered into force September 14, 1950.
1 UST 785; TIAS 2155; 206 UNTS 269.

Protocol to the treaty of friendship, commerce and navigation of January 21, 1950. Signed at Washington June 24, 1992; entered into force November 18, 1992.
TIAS

CONSULS

Consular convention.[1] Signed at Dublin May 1, 1950; entered into force June 12, 1954.
5 UST 949; TIAS 2984; 222 UNTS 107.

Supplementary protocol to the consular convention of May 1, 1950. Signed at Dublin March 3, 1952; entered into force June 12, 1954.
5 UST 949; TIAS 2984; 222 UNTS 107.

NOTE:
[1] Applicable to all territories.

COPYRIGHT (See APPENDIX)

CUSTOMS

Agreement regarding mutual assistance between their customs administrations. Signed at Dublin September 16, 1996; entered into force May 21, 1998.
TIAS

EDUCATION

Agreement for a program of educational exchange. Signed at Dublin October 27, 1988; entered into force February 3, 1992.
TIAS   ; 1732 UNTS 141.

EMPLOYMENT

Agreement relating to the employment of dependents of official government employees. Exchange of notes at Washington September 17, 1996 and August 1, 1997; entered into force August 1, 1997.
TIAS

ENVIRONMENTAL COOPERATION

Agreement for cooperation in the Global Learning and Observations to Benefit the Environment (GLOBE) Program, with appendices. Signed at Dublin June 12, 1995; entered into force June 12, 1995.
TIAS 12659.

EXTRADITION

Treaty on extradition. Signed at Washington July 13, 1983; entered into force December 15, 1984.
TIAS 10813.

FINANCE [1]

NOTE:
[1] For international fund for Ireland, see under FINANCE in multilateral section.

Agreement relating to investment guaranties under section 413(b)(4) of the Mutual Security Act of 1954, as amended. Exchange of notes at Dublin October 5, 1955; entered into force October 5, 1955.
6 UST 3953; TIAS 3405; 256 UNTS 285.

POSTAL MATTERS

Convention for the exchange of postal money orders. Signed at Washington December 14 and at Dublin December 31, 1923; operative January 1, 1924.
56 LNTS 303.

Parcel post convention. Signed at Dublin April 23 and at Washington May 6, 1926; operative May 1, 1926.
44 Stat. 2412; Post Office Department print; 56 LNTS 433.

International express mail agreement with detailed regulations. Signed at Dublin and Washington February 29 and March 20, 1984; entered into force May 19, 1984.
TIAS 10971; 1566 UNTS 169.

PROPERTY

Convention between the United States and the United Kingdom relating to tenure and disposition of real and personal property.[1] Signed at Washington March 2, 1899; entered into force August 7, 1900.
31 Stat. 1939; TS 146; 12 Bevans 246.

NOTE:
[1] Only article III is in force for Ireland.

SOCIAL SECURITY

Agreement on social security, with administrative arrangement. Signed at Washington April 14, 1992; entered into force September 1, 1993.
TIAS 12117.

TAXATION

Convention for the avoidance of double taxation and the prevention of fiscal evasion with respect to taxes on the estates of deceased persons. Signed at Dublin September 13, 1949; entered into force December 20, 1951.
2 UST 2294; TIAS 2355; 127 UNTS 119.

Convention for the avoidance of double taxation and the prevention of fiscal evasion with respect to taxes on income and capital gains, with protocol and related agreement.[1] Signed at Dublin July 28, 1997; entered into force December 17, 1997.
TIAS

Amendment:
September 24, 1999.

IRELAND (Cont'd)

NOTE:
[1] With understanding.

TELECOMMUNICATION

Agreement relating to the reciprocal granting of authorizations to permit licensed amateur radio operators of either country to operate their stations in the other country. Exchange of notes at Dublin October 10, 1968; entered into force October 10, 1968.
19 UST 6057; TIAS 6566; 694 UNTS 103.

VISAS

Agreement relating to the relaxation of visa requirements for American citizens entering Ireland and the granting of gratis nonimmigrant passport visas to Irish citizens entering the United States. Exchange of notes at Dublin August 1, 1949; entered into force August 1, 1949.
63 Stat. 2807; TIAS 2050; 9 Bevans 66; 82 UNTS 37.

ISRAEL

AGRICULTURAL COMMODITIES

Agricultural commodities agreement, with memorandum of understanding. Signed at Washington May 3, 1962; entered into force May 3, 1962.
13 UST 432; TIAS 5004; 442 UNTS 83.

Amendments:
October 12 and 16, 1962 (13 UST 2176; TIAS 5180; 460 UNTS 348).
January 26 and February 1, 1963 (14 UST 200; TIAS 5296; 473 UNTS 368).

Agreement relating to the closeout of the collection accounts of the agricultural commodities agreements of April 29, 1955, November 10, 1955, September 11, 1956, and November 7, 1957. Exchange of notes at Tel Aviv June 14 and Jerusalem August 28, 1962; entered into force August 28, 1962.
13 UST 2068; TIAS 5162; 448 UNTS 317.

Agricultural commodities agreement, with memorandum of understanding. Signed at Washington December 6, 1962; entered into force December 6, 1962.
13 UST 2550; TIAS 5220; 460 UNTS 151.

Amendments:
December 24 and 30, 1963 (14 UST 1794; TIAS 5490; 494 UNTS 334).
April 27, 1964 (15 UST 314; TIAS 5557; 515 UNTS 310).

June 23, 1964 (15 UST 730; TIAS 5596; 515 UNTS 314).
July 6, 1964 (15 UST 1396; TIAS 5610; 515 UNTS 318).
May 26 and 27, 1965 (16 UST 770; TIAS 5808; 545 UNTS 352).
June 22, 1965 (16 UST 770; TIAS 5808; 545 UNTS 356).

Agreement providing agricultural commodities for the improvement and expansion of the school feeding program in Israel, with annex. Exchange of notes at Tel Aviv and Jerusalem February 28 and March 21, 1963; entered into force March 21, 1963.
14 UST 471; TIAS 5344; 476 UNTS 131.

Agricultural commodities agreement, with exchange of notes. Signed at Washington December 22, 1964; entered into force December 22, 1964.
15 UST 2329; TIAS 5722; 532 UNTS 231.

Agricultural commodities agreement with exchange of notes. Signed at Washington June 6, 1966; entered into force June 6, 1966.
17 UST 727; TIAS 6023; 578 UNTS 143.

Agricultural commodities agreement with exchange of notes. Signed at Washington June 6, 1966; entered into force June 6, 1966.
17 UST 817; TIAS 6039; 593 UNTS 165.

Agricultural commodities agreement with annexes. Signed at Washington August 4, 1967; entered into force August 4, 1967.
18 UST 1684; TIAS 6314; 653 UNTS 81.

Related agreements:
March 29, 1968 (19 UST 4716; TIAS 6466; 653 UNTS 113).
August 19, 1968 (19 UST 5924; TIAS 6547; 653 UNTS 121).
January 17, 1969 (20 UST 1; TIAS 6625; 714 UNTS 129).
May 7, 1970 (21 UST 1115; TIAS 6871; 745 UNTS 209).
August 27, 1970 (21 UST 1965; TIAS 6938).
October 5, 1970 (21 UST 2152; TIAS 6962).
February 9, 1971 (22 UST 216; TIAS 7052; 792 UNTS 99).
June 4, 1971 (22 UST 676; TIAS 7123; 792 UNTS 108).
August 4, 1971 (22 UST 1471; TIAS 7161; 792 UNTS 112).
January 13, 1972 (23 UST 11; TIAS 7268; 829 UNTS 203).
July 18, 1972 (23 UST 1241; TIAS 7395).
October 13, 1972 (23 UST 2823; TIAS 7472).
November 19, 1973 (24 UST 2255; TIAS 7745).

Agricultural commodities agreement. Signed at Washington December 16, 1974; entered into force December 16, 1974.
25 UST 3140; TIAS 7978; 991 UNTS 413.

Amendment:
October 17, 1975 (26 UST 2926; TIAS 8200; 1021 UNTS 479).

Related agreements:
September 30, 1976 (27 UST 3543; TIAS 8382).
October 12, 1976 (27 UST 3545; TIAS 8382).

December 10, 1976 (27 UST 4173; TIAS 8443).
December 21, 1977 (29 UST 3281; TIAS 9012; 1124 UNTS 69).
January 16, 1979 (30 UST 2896; TIAS 9371; 1179 UNTS 377).
July 23, 1980 (32 UST 2571; TIAS 9858; 1274 UNTS 217).

AGRICULTURE

Agreement to establish the United States-Israel Agricultural Research and Development Fund, with appendix. Signed at Jerusalem October 25, 1977; entered into force November 6, 1978.
29 UST 5582; TIAS 9131.

ATOMIC ENERGY

Agreement providing for a grant to assist in the acquisition of certain nuclear research and training equipment and materials. Exchange of notes at Tel Aviv October 19 and at Jerusalem December 19, 1960; entered into force December 19, 1960.
11 UST 2631; TIAS 4655; 401 UNTS 195.

Agreement continuing in effect safeguards and guarantee provisions of the agreement of July 12, 1955 (6 UST 2641; TIAS 3311), as amended, for cooperation concerning civil uses of atomic energy. Exchange of notes at Washington April 7 and 8, 1977; entered into force April 8, 1977.
28 UST 2407; TIAS 8557.

Arrangement for the exchange of technical information and cooperation in nuclear safety matters, with addenda. Signed at Washington April 11, 1983; entered into force April 11, 1983.
TIAS 10689.

Arrangement for the exchange of technical information and cooperation in nuclear safety matters, with addenda. Signed at Rockville July 11, 1988; entered into force July 11, 1988.
TIAS 12225.

Arrangement for the exchange of technical information and cooperation in nuclear safety and research matters, with addenda. Signed at Vienna September 23, 1998; entered into force September 23, 1998.
TIAS

AVIATION

Air transport agreement. Signed at Tel Aviv June 13, 1950; entered into force June 13, 1950.[1]
3 UST 4582; TIAS 2610; 212 UNTS 93.

ISRAEL (Cont'd)

Amendments:
August 16, 1978 (29 UST 3144; TIAS 9002;
    1123 UNTS 321).
December 16, 1986 and January 5, 1987
    (TIAS 11524).

Agreement relating to the reciprocal acceptance of certificates of airworthiness for imported aircraft. Exchange of notes at Washington July 23, 1968; entered into force July
23, 1968.
19 UST 5459; TIAS 6530; 653 UNTS 159.

Amendment:
September 4, 1974 (25 UST 2445; TIAS
    7926).

Memorandum of agreement relating to technical assistance in developing and improving
air traffic operation in the Ben Gurion Airport.
Signed at Washington January 27, 1983; entered into force January 27, 1983.
TIAS 10838; 1590 UNTS 73.

Memorandum of cooperation concerning technical cooperation in civil aviation security with
annex. Signed at Washington and Tel Aviv
July 6 and September 30, 1990; entered into
force September 30, 1990.
TIAS 11970.

Agreement for promotion of aviation safety.
Signed December 19, 2000; entered into force
December 19, 2000.
TIAS

NOTE:
   [1] For correction of Hebrew text, see exchange of notes of February 21, 1951 (3 UST
4610; TIAS 2610).

CLAIMS

Agreement concerning claims arising from
damage to the United States ship ''Liberty''.
Exchange of notes at Washington December
15 and 17, 1980; entered into force December
17, 1980.
32 UST 4434; TIAS 9957; 1268 UNTS 33.

COMMERCE

Treaty of friendship, commerce, and navigation, with protocol and exchange of notes.
Signed at Washington August 23, 1951; entered into force April 3, 1954.
5 UST 550; TIAS 2948; 219 UNTS 237.

COPYRIGHT (See also
APPENDIX)

Agreement relating to reciprocal copyright relations. Exchange of notes at Washington May

4, 1950; entered into force May 4, 1950; operative May 15, 1948.
1 UST 645; TIAS 2121; 132 UNTS 189.

CUSTOMS

Agreement regarding mutual assistance in customs matters. Signed at Washington May 16,
1996; entered into force September 24, 1997.
TIAS

DEFENSE (See also MUTUAL
SECURITY)

Agreement relating to mutual defense assistance. Exchange of notes at Tel Aviv July 1
and 23, 1952; entered into force July 23, 1952.
3 UST 4985; TIAS 2675; 179 UNTS 139.

Agreement relating to general procurement arrangements for goods and services. Exchange
of notes at Washington July 15 and 20, 1965;
entered into force July 20, 1965.
16 UST 983; TIAS 5839; 549 UNTS 55.

Agreement relating to the purchase of various
goods from Israel for sale in United States
Navy ships stores overseas. Exchange of notes
at Washington July 20 and 26, 1965; entered
into force July 26, 1965.
16 UST 981; TIAS 5838; 549 UNTS 49.

Agreement regarding payment for tooling costs
of accelerated production of M-60A1 tanks.
Signed at Washington and New York August
22 and October 23, 1975; entered into force
October 23, 1975.
TIAS 12324.

Agreement concerning construction of airbase
facilities. Signed at Tel Aviv April 6, 1979;
entered into force April 6, 1979.
30 UST 4107; TIAS 9450; 1171 UNTS 233.

Agreement concerning funding of airbase construction. Signed at Tel Aviv April 6, 1979;
entered into force April 6, 1979.
30 UST 4134; TIAS 9451; 1171 UNTS 251.

General security of information agreement. Exchange of notes at Tel Aviv and Jerusalem
July 30 and December 10, 1982; entered into
force December 10, 1982.
TIAS 10617.

Memorandum of agreement concerning the
principles governing mutual cooperation in research and development, scientist and engineer
exchange, and procurement and logistic support of defense equipment, with annexes and
attachment. Signed at Washington December
14, 1987; entered into force December 14,
1987.
TIAS

Amendment:
December 19, 1997 and January 8, 1998.

Mutual logistic support agreement, with annexes. Signed at Stuttgart-Vaihingen and Tel

Aviv May 10 and 24, 1988; entered into force
May 24, 1988.
TIAS 12325.

Amendment:
June 22, 1990 and October 9, 1991 (TIAS
    12325).

Agreement on the status of United States personnel, with annexes and related letter. Signed
at Jerusalem January 22, 1991; entered into
force January 12, 1994.
TIAS

Agreement on the status of Israeli personnel.
Signed at Jerusalem January 22, 1991; entered
into force January 12, 1994.
TIAS

Memorandum of understanding for a loan of a
multi-sensor integrated system for the purpose
of test and evaluation. Signed at Tel Aviv and
Washington September 13 and October 18,
1991; entered into force October 18, 1991.
TIAS 12326.

Memorandum of agreement concerning the tactical high energy laser (THEL) advanced concept technology demonstration (ACTD).
Signed at Washington and Tel Aviv July 12
and 18, 1996; entered into force July 18, 1996.
TIAS

Amendments:
April 20 and May 2, 1997.
December 3 and 12, 1997.

Agreement for technology research and development projects, with annex. Signed at Washington and Tel Aviv August 22 and September
3, 1996; entered into force September 3, 1996.
TIAS

Acquisition and cross-servicing agreement,
with annexes. Signed at Washington and Stuttgart February 9 and 10, 1998; entered into
force February 10, 1998.
TIAS

Agreement amending and extending the memorandum of agreement of March 30, 1989, as
amended and extended, concerning cooperative
research on development and implementation
of a theater ballistic missile defense test bed.
Signed at Washington and New York March
29, 1999; entered into force March 29, 1999.
TIAS

Agreement for the loan of Python-4 infrared
air-to-air missiles for the purpose of testing,
evaluation and analysis. Signed at Tel Aviv
March 29, 2000; entered into force March 29,
2000.
TIAS

ECONOMIC AND TECHNICAL
COOPERATION

General agreement for technical cooperation.
Signed at Tel Aviv February 26, 1951; entered
into force February 26, 1951.
3 UST 379; TIAS 2401; 137 UNTS 57.

ISRAEL (Cont'd)

Amendment:
June 21, 1954 (5 UST 1401; TIAS 3010; 219
UNTS 348).

Agreement relating to emergency economic assistance. Exchange of notes at Washington
May 1, 1952; entered into force May 1, 1952.
3 UST 4266; TIAS 2571; 177 UNTS 89.

Agreement relating to economic assistance.
Signed at Tel Aviv May 9, 1952; entered into
force May 9, 1952.
3 UST 4174; TIAS 2561; 177 UNTS 269.

Agreement relating to special economic assistance. Exchange of notes at Tel Aviv and Jerusalem November 25, 1953; entered into force
November 25, 1953.
4 UST 2308; TIAS 2884; 219 UNTS 205.

Amendment:
January 31, 1955 (6 UST 561; TIAS 3189; 241
UNTS 520).

Joint statement of the U.S.-Israel Joint Committee for Investment and Trade relating to expansion of economic cooperation. Signed at
Washington May 13, 1975; entered into force
May 13, 1975.
26 UST 1674; TIAS 8127; 1006 UNTS 153.

Agreement establishing the Israel-United States
Binational Industrial Research and Development Foundation, with annexes. Signed at Jerusalem March 3, 1976; entered into force May
18, 1977.
28 UST 5129; TIAS 8615.

Agency for International Development:
June 27, 1975 (26 UST 1873; TIAS 8144).
September 22, 1976 (28 UST 3179; TIAS
8581).
November 23, 1976 (28 UST 5813; TIAS
8660).
December 5, 1977 (29 UST 3559; TIAS 9028;
1124 UNTS 49).
December 5, 1977 (29 UST 5213; TIAS 9097).
December 5, 1977 (29 UST 5231; TIAS 9098).
November 15, 1979 (31 UST 4794; TIAS
9639).
December 12, 1979 (31 UST 5545; TIAS
9670).
December 3, 1980 (32 UST 4204; TIAS 9941;
1268 UNTS 27).
March 27, 1981 (33 UST 1952; TIAS 10158).
July 1, 1981 (33 UST 1956; TIAS 10158).
December 31, 1981 (33 UST 4064; TIAS
10283).
March 31, 1982 (34 UST 1096; TIAS 10394).
May 18, 1982 (34 UST 1100; TIAS 10394).
December 16, 1982 (TIAS 10630).
December 30, 1982 (TIAS 10630).
March 31, 1983 (TIAS 10685).
December 29, 1983 (TIAS 10912).
October 31, 1984 (NP).
September 11, 1985 (NP).
October 30, 1985 (NP).
May 15, 1986 (NP).
September 29, 1986 (NP).
November 17, 1986 (NP).

EDUCATION

Agreement for financing certain educational
exchange programs, with memorandum of understanding. Exchange of notes at Tel Aviv
and Jerusalem June 18 and 22, 1962; entered
into force June 22, 1962.
13 UST 1364; TIAS 5097; 448 UNTS 273.

Amendments:
March 21 and 23, 1967 (18 UST 346; TIAS
6240; 630 UNTS 404).
January 10 and 30, 1985 (TIAS 11223).

EMBASSY SITES

Land lease and purchase agreement for construction of diplomatic facilities, with annexes.
Signed at Jerusalem January 18, 1989; entered
into force January 18, 1989.
TIAS

Amendments:
March 21 and April 10, 1989.
July 14 and 23, 1989.
January 22 and 30, 1990.
January 21 and March 8, 1992 (TIAS 11858).

EMPLOYMENT

Agreement relating to the employment of de-
pendents of official government employees.
Exchange of notes at Tel Aviv and Jerusalem
September 23 and October 3, 1985; entered
into force October 3, 1985.
TIAS 11171.

ENERGY

Memorandum of arrangement concerning an
oil supply arrangement, with annex. Signed at
Washington March 26, 1979; entered into force
March 26, 1979.
30 UST 5989; TIAS 9533; 1234 UNTS 221.

Memorandum of agreement concerning an oil
supply arrangement, with related understanding. Signed at Washington June 22, 1979;
entered into force November 25, 1979.
30 UST 5994; TIAS 9533; 1234 UNTS 224.

Amendment and extension:
October 19 and November 13, 1994 (TIAS
12580).

Contingency implementing arrangements for
the memorandum of agreement of June 22,
1979, concerning an oil supply arrangement,
with related letter. Signed at Washington October 17, 1980; entered into force October 17,
1980.
32 UST 3667; TIAS 9908; 1266 UNTS 370.

Amendment:
June 21 and 27, 1995 (TIAS 12670).

Agreement on cooperation in energy research
and development, with annex. Signed at Jerusalem June 3, 1984; entered into force June 3,
1984.
TIAS 11133.

Extension:
May 18 and June 11, 1990.

Agreement in basic energy sciences, with
annex. Signed at Jerusalem May 27, 1987; entered into force May 27, 1987.
TIAS

ENVIRONMENTAL COOPERATION

Memorandum of understanding concerning cooperation in the field of environmental protection, with annexes. Signed at Jerusalem February 20, 1991; entered into force February 20,
1991.
TIAS 11832.

Agreement for cooperation in the Global
Learning and Observations to Benefit the Envi-
ronment (GLOBE) Program, with appendices.
Signed at Jerusalem March 24, 1995; entered
into force March 24, 1995.
TIAS 12622.

EXTRADITION

Convention relating to extradition. Signed at
Washington December 10, 1962; entered into
force December 5, 1963.[1]
14 UST 1707; TIAS 5476; 484 UNTS 283.

NOTE:
[1] For understanding regarding certain errors
in the translation of the Hebrew text, see exchange of notes of April 4 and 11, 1967 (18
UST 382; TIAS 6246).

FINANCE

Agreement relating to the industrial investment
guaranty program pursuant to section 111(b)(3)
of the Economic Cooperation Act of 1948, as
amended. Exchange of notes at Tel Aviv August 7 and 8, 1952; entered into force August
8, 1952.
3 UST 5045; TIAS 2686; 181 UNTS 37.

Amendments:
July 31 and August 11, 1957 (8 UST 1410;
TIAS 3892; 289 UNTS 318).
February 5 and 20, 1963 (14 UST 337; TIAS
5316; 474 UNTS 332).

Agreement on encouragement of investment.
Signed at Washington September 12, 1994; en-
tered into force September 12, 1994.
TIAS 12190.

ISRAEL (Cont'd)

HEALTH

Agreement for cooperation in the field of health. Signed at Geneva May 6, 1985; entered into force May 6, 1985.
TIAS 11213.

Amendment and extension:
January 7, 1990 (TIAS 11709).

INFORMATIONAL MEDIA GUARANTIES

Agreement relating to the informational media guaranty program pursuant to section 111(b)(3) of the Economic Cooperation Act of 1948, as amended. Exchange of notes at Tel Aviv June 9, 1952; entered into force June 9, 1952.
3 UST 4398; TIAS 2588; 178 UNTS 297.

JUDICIAL ASSISTANCE

Treaty on mutual legal assistance in criminal matters, with related exchange of notes. Signed at Jerusalem January 26, 1998; entered into force May 25, 1999.
TIAS

LABOR

Memorandum of understanding for cooperation in the field of labor. Signed at Washington and Jerusalem November 6, 1986; entered into force November 6, 1986.
TIAS 11856.

Extension:
February 7 and March 3, 1992 (TIAS 11856).

MUTUAL SECURITY

Agreement relating to assurances and economic assistance as authorized in the Mutual Security Act of 1951. Exchange of notes at Washington December 7, 1951; entered into force December 7, 1951.
3 UST 2874; TIAS 2462; 157 UNTS 53.

PEACEKEEPING

Memorandum of agreement concerning assurances, consultations, and United States policy on matters related to Middle East peace. Initialed at Jerusalem September 1, 1975; signed at Washington and Jerusalem February 27, 1976; entered into force February 27, 1976.[1]
32 UST 2150; TIAS 9828.

Memorandum of agreement concerning the United States role at any future Geneva peace conference. Initialed at Jerusalem September 1, 1975; signed at Washington and Jerusalem February 27, 1976; entered into force February 27, 1976.[1]
32 UST 2160; TIAS 9829.

Memorandum of agreement relating to assurances concerning Middle East peace. Signed at Washington March 26, 1979; entered into force March 26, 1979.
32 UST 2141; TIAS 9825; 1252 UNTS 77.

Agreement relating to implementation of the Egyptian-Israeli peace treaty of March 26, 1979.[2] Letter signed at Washington March 26, 1979; entered into force March 26, 1979.
32 UST 2146; TIAS 9826.

Agreement relating to privileges and immunities for United States military members and civilian observers of the Multinational Force and Observers on leave in Israel. Exchange of notes at Jerusalem and Tel Aviv September 28 and October 1, 1982; entered into force October 1, 1982.
TIAS 10558; 1871 UNTS 323.

Memorandum of agreement concerning ballistic missile threats. Signed at Washington and Jerusalem October 31, 1998; entered into force October 31, 1998.
TIAS

NOTES:
   [1] Some provisions are no longer in force.
   [2] See also MULTINATIONAL FORCE AND OBSERVERS in bilateral section and PEACEKEEPING in multilateral section.

POSTAL MATTERS

International express mail agreement, with detailed regulations. Signed at Washington and Jerusalem September 8 and October 24, 1982; entered into force January 24, 1983.
TIAS 10548; 1777 UNTS 397.

Memorandum of understanding concerning the operation of the INTELPOST service, with details of implementation. Signed at Jerusalem and Washington July 20 and November 5, 1987; entered into force November 5, 1987; effective September 1, 1987.
TIAS 11568.

Postal money order agreement. Signed at Jerusalem and Washington December 15, 1988 and January 9, 1989; entered into force March 1, 1989.
TIAS 11613.

PUBLICATIONS

Agreement relating to the exchange of official publications. Exchange of notes at Tel Aviv February 13 and 19, 1950; entered into force February 19, 1950.
1 UST 912; TIAS 2169; 122 UNTS 117.

RELATIONS

Memorandum of agreement regarding joint political, security and economic cooperation. Signed at Washington and Jerusalem April 21 and 28, 1988; entered into force April 21, 1988.
TIAS 11578.

SCIENTIFIC COOPERATION

Agreement on the United States-Israel binational science foundation with exchange of letters. Signed at New York September 27, 1972; entered into force September 27, 1972.
23 UST 2669; TIAS 7460.

Memorandum of understanding covering marine and freshwater scientific and technical cooperation, with annexes. Signed at Jerusalem June 5, 1989; entered into force June 5, 1989.
TIAS 11673.

Memorandum of understanding on scientific and technical cooperation in the field of water resources development, with annexes. Signed at Washington and Haifa January 26 and February 8, 1990; entered into force February 8, 1990.
TIAS 11708.

Memorandum of understanding for cooperation in scientific exchanges and workshops, with annexes. Signed at Washington and Jerusalem April 30 and June 26, 1991; entered into force June 26, 1991.
TIAS 11823.

SEISMIC OBSERVATIONS

Memorandum of understanding concerning the installation, operation and maintenance of a seismic station. Signed at Tel Aviv May 1, 1985; entered into force May 1, 1985.
TIAS 11176.

TAXATION

Convention with respect to taxes on income.[1] Signed at Washington November 20, 1975; entered into force December 30, 1994.
TIAS

Amendments:
May 30, 1980.[1]
January 26, 1993.[2]

NOTES:
   [1] With understanding.
   [2] With understanding and declaration.

TELECOMMUNICATION

Agreement relating to radio communication facilities at or near Embassy sites for trans-

ISRAEL (Cont'd)

mission of official messages. Exchange of notes at Tel Aviv and Jerusalem May 10 and 21, 1963; entered into force May 21, 1963.
14 UST 866; TIAS 5367; 487 UNTS 319.

Agreement relating to radio communications between amateur stations on behalf of third parties. Exchange of notes at Washington July 7, 1965; entered into force August 6, 1965.
16 UST 883; TIAS 5827; 549 UNTS 281.

Agreement relating to the reciprocal granting of authorizations to permit licensed amateur radio operators of either country to operate their stations in the other country. Exchange of notes at Washington June 15, 1966; entered into force June 15, 1966.
17 UST 760; TIAS 6028; 578 UNTS 159.

Agreement terminating the agreement of June 18, 1987, for the establishment and operation of a radio relay station in Israel. Exchange of notes at Tel Aviv and Jerusalem November 3, 1994; entered into force November 3, 1994.
TIAS

TERRORISM

Counterterrorism cooperation accord. Signed at Washington April 30, 1996; entered into force July 29, 1996.
TIAS   ; 1966 UNTS 3.

TRADE (See also COMMERCE)

Agreement on the establishment of a free trade area, with annexes, exchange of letters and related letter. Signed at Washington April 22, 1985; entered into force August 19, 1985.
TIAS

VISAS

Agreement relating to the issue of visas to authorized crew members of aircraft operated by air carriers designated by Israel and the United States. Exchange of notes at Tel Aviv March 27 and June 1, 1951; entered into force June 1, 1951.
3 UST 4796; TIAS 2650; 212 UNTS 129.

Agreement providing for the reciprocal waiver of nonimmigrant passport visa fees. Exchanges of notes at Jerusalem and Tel Aviv February 14 and 28 and March 2, 1955; entered into force March 2, 1955.
7 UST 2125; TIAS 3614; 220 UNTS 113.

WEATHER STATIONS

Agreement relating to a cooperative meteorological program in support of the rawinsonde observation station at Bet Dagan. Exchange of notes at Tel Aviv and Jerusalem April 29 and May 22, 1968; entered into force May 22, 1968; effective January 1, 1968.
19 UST 5180; TIAS 6510; 653 UNTS 143.

ITALY

AGRICULTURAL COMMODITIES

Agreement relating to the use of lira equivalent for the purchase of agricultural commodities allocated to Italy pursuant to the Mutual Security Act of 1951, as amended. Exchange of letters at Rome May 19, 1955; entered into force May 19, 1955.
6 UST 3718; TIAS 3369; 269 UNTS 83.

ATOMIC ENERGY

Agreement for cooperation on uses of atomic energy for mutual defense purposes. Signed at Rome December 3, 1960; entered into force May 24, 1961.
12 UST 641; TIAS 4764; 410 UNTS 3.

General administrative agreement relating to participation in the USNRC program of severe accident, source term and containment research. Signed at Rome and Bethesda May 11 and June 5, 1987; entered into force June 5, 1987.
TIAS

Arrangement for the exchange of technical information and cooperation in nuclear safety matters, with addendum. Signed at Vienna September 28, 1999; entered into force September 28, 1999.
TIAS

AVIATION

Air navigation arrangement.[1] Exchange of notes at Washington October 13 and 14, 1931; entered into force October 31, 1931.
47 Stat. 2668; EAS 24; 9 Bevans 167; 137 LNTS 209.

Agreement relating to air service facilities in Italy with annex. Exchange of notes at Rome June 9, 1947; entered into force June 9, 1947.
62 Stat. 4074; TIAS 2127; 9 Bevans 200; 104 UNTS 157.

Air transport agreement with memorandum and exchange of notes. Signed at Rome June 22, 1970; entered into force provisionally June 22, 1970; definitively August 9, 1973.
21 UST 2096; TIAS 6957; 764 UNTS 161.

Amendments:
October 25, 1988 (TIAS 11634).
December 30, 1998 and February 2, 1999.

Memorandum of understanding relating to the air transport services agreement of June 22, 1970, as amended, with related exchange of letters. Signed at Rome September 27, 1990; entered into force September 27, 1990.[2]
TIAS 11767.

Agreement amending and supplementing the air transport services agreement of June 22, 1970, as amended, and amending the memorandum of understanding of September 27, 1990, with memorandum of understanding. Exchange of notes at Rome November 22 and December 23, 1991; entered into force December 23, 1991.
TIAS 11845.

Agreement relating to reciprocal acceptance of airworthiness certifications. Exchange of notes at Rome June 30 and August 3, 1973; entered into force August 3, 1973.
25 UST 1565; TIAS 7895.

Agreement for promotion of aviation safety. Signed at Rome October 27, 1999; entered into force October 27, 1999.
TIAS

NOTES:
[1] Article 9 terminated January 26, 1955 (see 6 UST 25; TIAS 3164).
[2] Amendment to Article 10 not yet in force.

CLAIMS

Memorandum of understanding regarding settlement of certain wartime claims and related matters; memorandum of understanding regarding Italian assets in the United States and certain claims of United States nationals, and supplementary exchanges of notes. Signed at Washington August 14, 1947; entered into force August 14, 1947.[1]
61 Stat. 3962; TIAS 1757; 9 Bevans 215; 36 UNTS 53.

Agreement relating to procedure for final settlement of claims of Italian prisoners of war. Exchange of letters at Rome February 14, 1948; entered into force February 14, 1948.
62 Stat. 3853; TIAS 1948; 9 Bevans 299; 67 UNTS 115.

Amendment:
January 14, 1949 (63 Stat. 2602; TIAS 1950; 9 Bevans 338; 67 UNTS 115).

Memorandum of understanding regarding war damage claims. Signed at Rome March 29, 1957; entered into force October 22, 1957.
8 UST 1725; TIAS 3924; 299 UNTS 157.

Agreement supplementing the memorandum of understanding of March 29, 1957 regarding war damage claims. Exchange of notes at Rome July 12, 1960; entered into force June 15, 1961.
12 UST 904; TIAS 4796; 411 UNTS 312.

ITALY (Cont'd)

NOTE:

[1] For agreed interpretation of the agreement signed August 14, 1947, see exchange of notes verbales of February 24, 1949 (63 Stat. 2415; TIAS 1919; 9 Bevans 342; 80 UNTS 319).

COMMERCE

Agreement relating to the resumption of normal commercial relations. Exchange of notes at Washington December 6, 1945; entered into force December 6, 1945.
59 Stat. 1731; EAS 492; 9 Bevans 190; 3 UNTS 131.

Treaty of friendship, commerce, and navigation, protocol, additional protocol, and exchange of notes. Signed at Rome February 2, 1948; entered into force July 26, 1949.
63 Stat. 2255; TIAS 1965; 9 Bevans 261; 79 UNTS 171.

Agreement supplementing the treaty of friendship, commerce and navigation of February 2, 1948. Signed at Washington September 26, 1951; entered into force March 2, 1961.
12 UST 131; TIAS 4685; 404 UNTS 326.

CONSULS

Consular convention.[1] Signed at Washington May 8, 1878; entered into force September 18, 1878.
20 Stat. 725; TS 178; 9 Bevans 91.

NOTE:

[1] Article XI replaced by convention of February 24, 1881 (22 Stat. 831; TS 179); articles XI and XIII abrogated by the United States, effective July 1, 1916, in accordance with the Seamen's Act (38 Stat. 1164).

COPYRIGHT (See also APPENDIX)

Reciprocal copyright arrangement. Exchange of notes at Washington October 28, 1892; entered into force October 28, 1892.
9 Bevans 104.

Reciprocal copyright arrangement. Exchanges of notes at Manchester, Massachusetts, September 2, 1914; and at Washington February 12 and March 4 and 11, 1915; entered into force March 11, 1915; operative May 1, 1915.
9 Bevans 129.

DEFENSE (See also MUTUAL SECURITY)

Mutual defense assistance agreement. Exchange of notes at Washington January 27, 1950; entered into force January 27, 1950.
1 UST 50; TIAS 2013; 80 UNTS 145.

Agreement relating to the disposition of equipment and material furnished Italy and no longer required in the furtherance of its mutual defense assistance program. Exchange of notes at Rome November 20 and December 14, 1951; entered into force December 14, 1951.
5 UST 2829; TIAS 3136; 238 UNTS 310.

Amendment:
September 7, 1960 (11 UST 2129; TIAS 4573; 389 UNTS 307).

Agreement relating to offshore procurement program with memorandum of understanding and model contract attached. Exchange of notes at Rome March 31, 1954; entered into force March 31, 1954.
5 UST 2185; TIAS 3083; 235 UNTS 293.

Agreement concerning facilities for overhaul and repair of jet engines in Torino, Italy. Signed at Rome July 8, 1955; entered into force July 8, 1955.
6 UST 3797; TIAS 3381; 270 UNTS 29.

Agreement relating to a weapons production program. Exchange of notes at Rome July 7, 1960; entered into force July 7, 1960.
11 UST 1912; TIAS 4538; 380 UNTS 143.

Agreement relating to the safeguarding of classified information with annex. Exchange of notes at Washington August 4, 1964; entered into force August 4, 1964.
15 UST 1494; TIAS 5629; 529 UNTS 205.

Amendment:
April 15 and September 2, 1982 (TIAS 10632).

Memorandum of understanding concerning the principles governing mutual cooperation in the research, development, production and procurement of defense equipment. Signed at Washington September 11, 1978; entered into force September 11, 1978.
TIAS 12356.

Mutual logistical support agreement, with annexes. Signed at Stuttgart February 23, 1983; entered into force February 23, 1983.
TIAS 11165.

Memorandum of understanding on the exchange of officers between the United States Air Force and the Italian Air Force. Signed at Rome and Washington May 30 and August 12, 1988; entered into force August 12, 1988.
NP

Technical arrangement concerning the installation and maintenance of a U.S. interface with the Italian MRCS-403 radar at Capo Frasca, Sardinia. Signed at Rome and Ramstein AB

August 1 and 23, 1988; entered into force August 23, 1988.
TIAS 12343.

Memorandum of agreement on the exchange of officers between the United States Marine Corps and the Italian Navy. Signed at Rome and Washington June 7 and July 26, 1993; entered into force July 26, 1993.
NP

Memorandum of understanding concerning use of installations/infrastructure by U.S. forces in Italy, with annexes. Signed at Rome February 2, 1995; entered into force February 2, 1995.
TIAS 12317.

Memorandum of understanding for the Project Ulysses, with annexes. Signed at Washington and Rome April 23 and August 1, 1997; entered into force August 1, 1997.
TIAS

DISASTER ASSISTANCE

Agreement relating to the provision of assistance to earthquake victims of Italy. Exchange of notes at Rome June 9, 1976; entered into force June 9, 1976.
27 UST 3988; TIAS 8416; 1059 UNTS 73.

ECONOMIC AND TECHNICAL COOPERATION

Economic cooperation agreement. Signed at Rome June 28, 1948; entered into force June 28, 1948.
62 Stat. 2421; TIAS 1789; 9 Bevans 306; 20 UNTS 43.

Amendments:
September 28 and October 2, 1948 (62 Stat. 3815; TIAS 1917; 9 Bevans 326; 55 UNTS 318).
February 7, 1950 (1 UST 160; TIAS 2028; 79 UNTS 274).
May 21, 1951 (2 UST 1169; TIAS 2263; 141 UNTS 362).
January 13, 1953 (4 UST 116; TIAS 2769; 200 UNTS 264).

Agreement relating to the use of counterpart funds derived from United States economic aid to Trieste. Exchange of notes at Rome February 11, 1955; entered into force February 11, 1955.
6 UST 593; TIAS 3195; 241 UNTS 91.

EDUCATION

Agreement for exchanges in the fields of education and culture. Signed at Rome December 15, 1975; entered into force July 28, 1980.
32 UST 1981; TIAS 9813; 1228 UNTS 145.

Memorandum of understanding relating to exchanges and cooperation in the field of edu-

ITALY (Cont'd)

cation, with annex. Signed at Rome May 4, 1978; entered into force May 4, 1978.
30 UST 116; TIAS 9182; 1150 UNTS 67.

EMPLOYMENT

Agreement relating to the employment of dependents of diplomatic agents, consular personnel and administrative and technical staff. Exchange of notes at Rome June 9, 1997; entered into force April 30, 1999.
TIAS

ENERGY

Memorandum of understanding concerning energy research and development cooperation, with annex. Signed at Rome December 5, 1985; entered into force December 5, 1985.
TIAS 11515.

Extension:
May 28, 1991.

ENVIRONMENTAL COOPERATION

Memorandum of understanding concerning cooperation in the field of environmental protection. Signed at Rome March 3, 1987; entered into force March 3, 1987.
TIAS 11283.

EXTRADITION

Extradition treaty. Signed at Rome October 13, 1983; entered into force September 24, 1984.
TIAS 10837; 1590 UNTS 161.

FINANCE

Agreement relating to the funding of the indebtedness of Italy to the United States. Signed at Washington November 14, 1925; operative June 15, 1925.
Treasury Department print; 9 Bevans 145.

Agreement modifying the agreement of November 14, 1925. Signed at Washington June 3, 1932; operative July 1, 1931.
Treasury Department print; 9 Bevans 176.

Agreement relating to the disposal of currencies, securities and articles of value taken in Italy from the German forces. Exchange of notes at Rome May 16, 1951; entered into force May 16, 1951.
3 UST 2950; TIAS 2476; 206 UNTS 325.

Agreement relating to guaranties authorized by section 111(b)(3) of the Economic Cooperation Act of 1948, as amended. Exchange of notes at Rome December 28, 1951; entered into force December 28, 1951.
3 UST 2877; TIAS 2463; 157 UNTS 63.

Amendment:
October 18, 1957 (8 UST 1881; TIAS 3934; 291 UNTS 309).

Agreement relating to the establishment of a revolving industrial loan fund for Southern Italy. Exchange of notes at Rome June 16, 1954; entered into force June 16, 1954.
5 UST 2116; TIAS 3073; 236 UNTS 149.

FISHERIES

Agreement concerning large-scale driftnet fishing on the high seas. Exchange of notes at Washington July 22 and 26, 1996; entered into force July 26, 1996.
TIAS

HEALTH

Memorandum of understanding for cooperation in the field of health and medicine, with annex. Signed at Rome November 21, 1977; entered into force November 21, 1977.
29 UST 5897; TIAS 9159.

JUDICIAL ASSISTANCE

Procedures for mutual assistance in the administration of justice in connection with the Lockheed Aircraft Corporation matter. Signed at Washington March 29, 1976; entered into force April 12, 1976.
27 UST 3437; TIAS 8374.

Treaty on mutual assistance in criminal matters, with memorandum of understanding. Signed at Rome November 9, 1982; entered into force November 13, 1985.[1]
TIAS

NOTE:
[1] Except for the application of Article 18, paragraph 2.

MAPPING

Memorandum of understanding relating to cooperation in mapping and geodesy. Signed at Washington July 18, 1985; entered into force July 18, 1985.
TIAS 11258.

Basic exchange and cooperative agreement for topographic mapping, nautical and aeronautical charting and information, geodesy and geophysics, digital data and related materials, with

annexes. Signed at Rome September 11, 1992; entered into force September 11, 1992.
NP

MARRIAGE

Agreement relating to documentary requirements for marriage of American citizens in Italy. Exchange of notes at Rome July 29 and August 18, 1964; entered into force March 26, 1966.
18 UST 342; TIAS 6239; 688 UNTS 37.

MILITARY CEMETERIES AND MONUMENTS

Agreement relating to interment of American military personnel in Italy. Exchange of notes verbales at Rome September 13 and 24, 1946; entered into force September 24, 1946.
61 Stat. 3750; TIAS 1713; 9 Bevans 194; 148 UNTS 323.

Amendment:
December 18, 1947, January 21, March 24, and April 19, 1948 (62 Stat. 1889; TIAS 1743; 9 Bevans 258, 304; 148 UNTS 332).

MUTUAL SECURITY

Agreement relating to the assurances required by the Mutual Security Act of 1951. Exchange of notes at Rome January 7, 1952; entered into force January 7, 1952.
3 UST 4613; TIAS 2611; 179 UNTS 165.

NARCOTIC DRUGS

Arrangement for the direct exchange of certain information regarding the traffic in narcotic drugs. Exchange of notes at Rome January 5 and April 27, 1928; entered into force April 27, 1928.
9 Bevans 156.

NAVIGATION

Memorandum of understanding concerning the installation and management of U.S. navigational aids. Signed at Rome and Ramstein October 8 and 11, 1985; entered into force October 11, 1985.
TIAS 11191.

Agreement for the transfer of ownership of the long-range radio aid to navigation transmitting and monitoring stations at Lampedusa, Sellia Marina and Crotone, Italy. Signed at Rome November 17, 1994; entered into force February 4, 1997.
TIAS

ITALY (Cont'd)

PACIFIC SETTLEMENT OF DISPUTES

Treaty for the advancement of peace. Signed at Washington May 5, 1914; entered into force March 19, 1915.
39 Stat. 1618; TS 615; 9 Bevans 126.

Treaty modifying the terms of article II of the treaty for the advancement of peace. Signed at Washington September 23, 1931; entered into force July 30, 1932.
47 Stat. 2102; TS 848; 9 Bevans 164; 134 LNTS 191.

Treaty of arbitration. Signed at Washington April 19, 1928; entered into force January 20, 1931.
46 Stat. 2890; TS 831; 9 Bevans 153; 113 LNTS 183.

PATENTS

Agreement on arrangements respecting patents and technical information in defense programs. Signed at Rome October 3, 1952; entered into force provisionally October 3, 1952; definitively December 16, 1960.
12 UST 189; TIAS 4693.

Agreement approving the procedures for reciprocal filing of classified patent applications in the United States and Italy. Exchange of notes at Rome March 9 and October 27, 1959; entered into force provisionally October 27, 1959; definitively December 16, 1960.
12 UST 189; TIAS 4693.

Amendment:
April 29 and August 2, 1960 (12 UST 208; TIAS 4693).

PEACE TREATIES

Agreement concerning the designation of a permanent third member of the United States-Italian Conciliation Commission established pursuant to article 83 of the treaty of peace with Italy (TIAS 1648; 4 Bevans 311; 49 and 50 UNTS). Exchange of notes at Rome February 12 and 13, 1951; entered into force February 13, 1951.
2 UST 807; TIAS 2232; 148 UNTS 57.

Agreement regarding the release of Italy from certain of its obligations to the United States under the treaty of peace with Italy (TIAS 1648; 4 Bevans 311; 49 and 50 UNTS). Exchange of notes at Washington December 8 and 21, 1951; entered into force December 21, 1951.
3 UST 2869; TIAS 2461; 167 UNTS 163.

POSTAL MATTERS

Convention relating to exchange of money orders. Signed at Washington March 31 and at Florence April 20, 1877; operative July 2, 1877.
20 Stat. 683.

Additional convention to the convention of March 31 and April 20, 1877 relating to exchange of money orders. Signed at Rome August 9 and at Washington August 24, 1880; operative October 1, 1880.
21 Stat. 788.

Parcel post convention. Signed at Washington October 11, 1929; entered into force December 1, 1929.
46 Stat. 2397; Post Office Department print.

International express mail agreement with detailed regulations. Signed at Rome and Washington November 21 and December 9, 1983; entered into force February 18, 1984.
TIAS 10848.

RELIEF SUPPLIES AND PACKAGES

Agreement providing for duty-free entry of relief supplies and packages and for the payment of transportation charges. Exchange of notes at Rome November 26, 1948; entered into force November 26, 1948.
62 Stat. 3809; TIAS 1914; 9 Bevans 328; 79 UNTS 71.

Amendments:
November 26, 1948 (62 Stat. 3809; TIAS 1914; 9 Bevans 331; 79 UNTS 71).
July 19, 1952 (3 UST 5078; TIAS 2694; 181 UNTS 353).

SATELLITES

Agreement concerning cooperation in a scientific experiment for the purpose of launching a scientific satellite into an equatorial orbit. Exchange of notes at Rome September 5, 1962; entered into force September 5, 1962.
13 UST 2120; TIAS 5172; 461 UNTS 185.

Agreement confirming a memorandum of understanding regarding the launching of NASA satellites from the San Marco Range. Exchange of notes at Rome April 30 and June 12, 1969; entered into force June 12, 1969.
20 UST 4119; TIAS 6809; 732 UNTS 3.

Extension:
November 25 and 26, 1974 (25 UST 3110; TIAS 7972).

Agreement confirming a memorandum of understanding concerning the furnishing of certain services by NASA for Italian satellites. Exchange of notes at Rome June 15 and 20, 1970; entered into force June 20, 1970.
21 UST 1465; TIAS 6903; 753 UNTS 259.

Memorandum of understanding concerning furnishing of launch and associated services for ITALSAT program. Signed at Washington and Rome September 29 and October 10, 1983; entered into force March 5, 1984.
TIAS 10840.

Agreement concerning development of the Tethered Satellite System (TSS), with memorandum of understanding. Exchange of notes at Rome June 6 and 27, 1984; entered into force June 6, 1986.
TIAS 12205.

Amendment:
February 9 and 12, 1996.

Agreement concerning development and launch of the Laser Geodynamics Satellite-2 (Lageos-2), with memorandum of understanding. Exchange of notes at Rome April 22 and July 30, 1985; entered into force February 13, 1989.
TIAS

SCIENTIFIC COOPERATION

Memorandum of understanding concerning the furnishing of balloon launching and associated services. Signed at Washington and Rome September 2 and 30, 1983; entered into force September 30, 1983.
TIAS 10794.

Agreement for scientific and technological cooperation. Signed at Rome April 1, 1988; entered into force April 1, 1988.
TIAS 11574.

Amendment and extension:
October 4, 1993 (TIAS 12165).

SEABEDS

Agreement relating to the agreement of August 14, 1987 on the resolution of practical problems with respect to deep seabed mining areas.[1] Exchange of notes at Rome August 14, 1987; entered into force August 14, 1987.
TIAS 11438.

NOTE:
[1] Parties to the multilateral agreement of August 14, 1987 are Belgium, Canada, Italy, Netherlands and Union of Soviet Socialist Republics.

SHIPPING

Agreement relating to jurisdiction over vessels utilizing the Louisiana Offshore Oil Port. Exchange of notes at Washington January 12 and 19, 1982; entered into force January 19, 1982.
TIAS 10598; 1871 UNTS 195.

ITALY (Cont'd)

SOCIAL SECURITY

Agreement on social security, with administrative protocol. Signed at Washington May 23, 1973; entered into force November 1, 1978.
29 UST 4263; TIAS 9058; 1228 UNTS 81.

Supplemental agreement to the agreement of May 23, 1973 on the matter of social security. Signed at Rome April 17, 1984; entered into force January 1, 1986.
TIAS 11173.

SPACE COOPERATION

Agreement for the design, development, operation and utilization of two mini pressurized logistics modules and a mini laboratory for Space Station Freedom, with memorandum of understanding. Exchange of notes at Rome January 29 and June 1, 1992; entered into force June 1, 1992.
TIAS

SURPLUS PROPERTY

Agreement for the sale in Italy of waste material and scrap and of usable property in excess of the requirements of the United States military authorities. Signed at Rome June 22, 1957; entered into force June 22, 1957.
8 UST 881; TIAS 3850; 284 UNTS 51.

TAXATION

Agreement relating to relief from taxation of United States expenditures in Italy for the common defense. Exchange of notes at Rome March 5, 1952; entered into force March 5, 1952.
3 UST 4234; TIAS 2566; 179 UNTS 3.

Convention for the avoidance of double taxation and the prevention of fiscal evasion with respect to taxes on estates and inheritances. Signed at Washington March 30, 1955; entered into force October 26, 1956.
7 UST 2977; TIAS 3678; 257 UNTS 199.

Agreement concerning taxation of income of some U.S. Navy employees in Italy. Exchange of notes at Rome July 24, 1982; entered into force September 28, 1984; effective January 1, 1982.
TIAS 11499.

Convention with protocol for the avoidance of double taxation with respect to taxes on income and the prevention of fraud or fiscal evasion, with exchange of notes.[1] Signed at Rome April 17, 1984; entered into force December 30, 1985; effective with respect to certain pro-

visions February 1, 1986, with respect to others January 1, 1985.
TIAS 11064.

NOTE:
[1] With understanding.

TELECOMMUNICATION

Agreement relating to the reciprocal granting of authorizations to permit licensed amateur radio operators of either country to operate their stations in the other country. Exchange of notes at Rome July 28 and August 28, 1981; entered into force August 28, 1981.
33 UST 4393; TIAS 10308; 1549 UNTS 309.

TRADE (See also COMMERCE)

Agreement providing compensatory concessions under the general agreement on tariffs and trade for certain tariff actions taken by the United States. Exchange of notes at Geneva December 8 and 9, 1961, and March 7, 1962; entered into force March 7, 1962.
13 UST 942; TIAS 5032.

TRADE-MARKS

Declaration for the reciprocal protection of marks of manufacture and trade. Signed at Washington June 1, 1882; entered into force June 1, 1882.
23 Stat. 726; TS 180; 9 Bevans 101.

VISAS

Agreement relating to the waiver of passport visa fees for nonimmigrants. Exchange of notes at Rome February 11, 21, and 26, 1929; operative March 1, 1929.
9 Bevans 158.

Arrangement relating to the waiver of passport visas and passport visa fees. Exchange of notes verbales dated at Rome September 28 and 29, 1948; entered into force September 29, 1948; operative November 1, 1948.
62 Stat. 3480; TIAS 1867; 9 Bevans 323; 84 UNTS 43.

JAMAICA

On August 6, 1962 Jamaica attained fully responsible status within the British Commonwealth. By an exchange of notes on August 7, 1962 between the High Commissioner for the United Kingdom in Jamaica and the Prime Minister and Minister of External Affairs and Defense of Jamaica, the Government of Jamaica agreed to assume, from August 6, 1962, all obligations and responsibilities of the United Kingdom which arise from any valid

instrument (including any instrument made by the Government of the Federation of The West Indies by virtue of the authority entrusted by the Government of the United Kingdom). The rights and benefits heretofore enjoyed by the Government of the United Kingdom by virtue of application of any such international instrument to Jamaica are from August 6, 1962 enjoyed by the Government of Jamaica.

AGRICULTURAL COMMODITIES

Agricultural commodities agreement with annex. Signed at Kingston October 11, 1973; entered into force October 11, 1973.
24 UST 2211; TIAS 7737.

Agricultural commodities agreement with annex. Signed at Kingston April 16, 1975; entered into force April 16, 1975.
26 UST 1705; TIAS 8130.

Amendments:
June 9, 1975 (26 UST 1722; TIAS 8130).
December 3 and 15, 1976 (28 UST 2388; TIAS 8551).

Related agreement:
September 30, 1976 (28 UST 2385; TIAS 8550).

Agricultural commodities agreement. Signed at Kingston August 8 1977; entered into force August 8, 1977.
29 UST 373; TIAS 8824.

Amendment:
December 2 and 21, 1977 (29 UST 373; TIAS 8824).

Related agreements:
August 2, 1978 (30 UST 213; TIAS 9188; 1148 UNTS 328).
September 5, 1978 (30 UST 217; TIAS 9188; 1148 UNTS 333).
October 13 and 25, 1978 (30 UST 221; TIAS 9188; 1148 UNTS 336).
March 7 and 29, 1979 (30 UST 3979; TIAS 9438).
May 2, 1979 (30 UST 3983; TIAS 9438).
July 5, 1979 (30 UST 3987; TIAS 9438).
February 8, 1980 (32 UST 1819; TIAS 9799).
February 6, 1981 (33 UST 1497; TIAS 10124; 1284 UNTS 275).
August 5, 1981 (33 UST 1501; TIAS 10124; 1284 UNTS 279).

Agricultural commodities agreement, with memorandum of understanding. Signed at Kingston April 30, 1982; entered into force April 30, 1982.
TIAS 10495.

Related agreements:
February 24, 1983 (TIAS 10665).
May 30, 1984 (NP).
December 17, 1984 (NP).
March 19 and 28, 1985 (NP).
July 25 and 30, 1985 (NP).

JAMAICA (Cont'd)

Agricultural commodities agreement. Signed at Kingston January 15, 1986; entered into force January 15, 1986.
NP

Amendments:
May 29 and June 4, 1986 (NP).
August 18 and 27, 1986 (NP).
September 24 and October 8, 1986 (NP).
October 30 and 31, 1986 (NP).

Agricultural commodities agreement, with agreed minutes. Signed at Kingston January 15, 1987; entered into force January 15, 1987.
NP

Amendments:
June 25 and July 1, 1987 (NP).
September 29 and October 2, 1987 (NP).
November 9, 1987 (NP).
January 5 and 6, 1988 (NP).
April 29 and May 2, 1988 (NP).
June 27 and 28, 1988 (NP).
August 10, 1988 (NP).
September 8 and 27, 1988 (NP).

Related agreements:
September 22, 1988 (NP).
February 21, 1989 (NP).
August 18 and September 12, 1989 (NP).
November 24, 1989 (NP).
February 14 and March 1, 1990 (NP).
June 6, 1990 (NP).
July 20 and 23, 1990 (NP).
October 12, 1990 (NP).
March 8 and 14, 1991 (NP).

AVIATION

Arrangement between the United States and the United Kingdom relating to pilot licenses to operate civil aircraft. Exchange of notes at Washington March 28 and April 5, 1935; entered into force May 5, 1935.
49 Stat. 3731; EAS 77; 12 Bevans 513; 162 UNTS 59.

Air transport agreement with exchange of notes. Signed at Kingston October 2, 1969; entered into force October 2, 1969.
20 UST 2962; TIAS 6770; 726 UNTS 183.

Amendments:
April 4, 1979 (31 UST 308; TIAS 9613; 1220 UNTS 333).
June 6 and December 13, 1994 (TIAS 12586).

Agreement concerning conversion and remittance of Jamaica dollar earnings by U.S. airlines. Exchange of notes at Kingston March 22 and 30, 1984; entered into force March 30, 1984.
TIAS 10975; 1658 UNTS 309.

CONSULS

Consular convention between the United States and the United Kingdom. Signed at Washington June 6, 1951; entered into force September 7, 1952.
3 UST 3426; TIAS 2494; 165 UNTS 121.

COPYRIGHT (See APPENDIX)

DEFENSE

Agreement relating to the furnishing of defense articles and services to Jamaica. Exchange of notes at Kingston June 6, 1963; entered into force June 6, 1963.
14 UST 821; TIAS 5361; 477 UNTS 29.

Agreement concerning the provision of training related to defense articles under the United States International Military Education and Training (IMET) Program. Exchange of notes at Kingston November 13, 1980 and February 17, 1981; entered into force February 17, 1981.
TIAS 10536; 1777 UNTS 319.

ECONOMIC AND TECHNICAL COOPERATION

General agreement for economic, technical and related assistance. Signed at Kingston October 24, 1963; entered into force October 24, 1963.
14 UST 1550; TIAS 5457; 489 UNTS 337.

Agency for International Development:
November 13, 1975 (29 UST 5905; TIAS 9160; 1148 UNTS 275).
November 25, 1977 (29 UST 5932; TIAS 9160; 1148 UNTS 294).
December 15, 1977 (29 UST 4049; TIAS 9048; 1135 UNTS 43).
March 23, 1978 (30 UST 4518; TIAS 9474; 1170 UNTS 49).
January 19, 1981 (33 UST 1560; TIAS 10133; 1529 UNTS 347).
December 29, 1981 (33 UST 4071; TIAS 10284).
December 17, 1982 (TIAS 10644; 1647 UNTS 51).

EMPLOYMENT

Agreement relating to the employment of dependents of official government employees. Exchange of notes at Kingston May 3 and October 11, 1982; entered into force October 11, 1982.
TIAS 10886; 1577 UNTS 417.

ENVIRONMENTAL COOPERATION

Agreement concerning the establishment of an Enterprise for the Americas Environmental Foundation. Signed at Washington November 26, 1991; entered into force November 26, 1991.
TIAS 11848.

EXTRADITION

Extradition treaty. Signed at Kingston June 14, 1983; entered into force July 7, 1991.
TIAS

FINANCE

Agreement relating to investment guaranties. Exchange of notes at Kingston December 11, 1962 and January 4, 1963; entered into force January 4, 1963.
14 UST 1; TIAS 5270; 471 UNTS 119.

Agreement regarding the consolidation and rescheduling of certain debts owed to, guaranteed or insured by the United States Government and its agencies, with annexes. Signed at Washington November 8, 1984; entered into force December 13, 1984.
TIAS 10999.

Agreement regarding the consolidation and rescheduling of certain debts owed to, guaranteed by or insured by the United States Government and its agencies, with annexes. Signed at Washington September 26, 1985; entered into force November 18, 1985.
NP

Agreement regarding the consolidation and rescheduling of certain debts owed to, guaranteed by, or insured by the United States Government and its agencies, with annexes. Signed at Kingston November 12, 1987; entered into force January 7, 1988.
NP

Amendment:
February 2 and March 15, 1989 (NP).

Agreement regarding the consolidation and rescheduling of certain debts owed to, guaranteed by, or insured by the United States Government and its agencies, with annexes. Signed at Kingston July 6, 1989; entered into force August 24, 1989.
NP

Amendment:
November 27, 1989 and January 18, 1990 (NP).

Agreement regarding the consolidation and rescheduling or refinancing of certain debts owed to, guaranteed by, or insured by the United States Government and its agencies,

JAMAICA (Cont'd)

with annexes. Signed at Kingston December 20, 1990; entered into force February 8, 1991.
NP

Agreement regarding the consolidation and rescheduling or refinancing of certain debts owed to, guaranteed by, or insured by the United States Government and its agencies, with annexes. Signed at Kingston January 14, 1992; entered into force March 2, 1992.
NP

Amendment:
August 28 and September 11, 1992 (NP).

Agreement regarding the reduction of certain debts related to foreign assistance owed to the Government of the United States and its agencies, with appendices. Signed at Washington and Kingston January 13 and 15, 1993; entered into force February 14, 1993.
NP

Agreement regarding the consolidation and rescheduling or refinancing of certain debts owed to, guaranteed by or insured by the United States Government and its agencies, with annexes. Signed at Kingston October 22, 1993; entered into force January 3, 1994.
NP

INVESTMENT

Treaty concerning the reciprocal encouragement and protection of investment, with annex and protocol. Signed at Washington February 4, 1994; entered into force March 7, 1997.
TIAS

JUDICIAL ASSISTANCE

Procedures for mutual assistance in connection with matters relating to the Jamaica Nutrition Holdings Ltd., its holding company, State Trading Corporation and its associated companies. Signed at Washington March 30, 1979; entered into force March 30, 1979.
30 UST 3868; TIAS 9430; 1170 UNTS 59.

Treaty on mutual legal assistance in criminal matters, with attachments. Signed at Kingston July 7, 1989; entered into force July 25, 1995.
TIAS

NARCOTIC DRUGS

Agreement relating to the provision of helicopters and related assistance to Jamaica in connection with a program to interdict the illicit narcotics traffic between Jamaica and the United States (Operation Buccaneer). Exchange of notes at Kingston August 9 and 21

and September 23, 1974; entered into force September 23, 1974.
25 UST 3068; TIAS 7966.

Agreement concerning cooperation in suppressing illicit maritime drug trafficking. Signed at Kingston May 6, 1997; entered into force March 10, 1998.
TIAS

PEACE CORPS

Agreement relating to the establishment of a Peace Corps program in Jamaica. Exchange of notes at Kingston February 15 and 22, 1962; entered into force February 22, 1962.
13 UST 166; TIAS 4954; 435 UNTS 127.

PEACEKEEPING

Agreement for the furnishing of commodities and services in connection with the peacekeeping force for Grenada. Exchange of notes at Kingston November 29 and December 6, 1983; entered into force December 6, 1983.
TIAS 10849.

Agreement concerning the disposition of commodities and services furnished in connection with peacekeeping operations for Grenada. Exchange of notes at Kingston February 2 and April 21, 1987; entered into force April 21, 1987.
TIAS 11270.

POSTAL MATTERS

Postal convention. Signed at Washington July 22 and at Kingston September 3, 1887; operative October 1, 1887.
25 Stat. 1393.

Money order agreement. Signed at Washington September 20 and at Kingston October 6, 1922; operative November 1, 1922.

International express mail agreement, with detailed regulations. Signed at Kingston and Washington January 9 and February 11, 1991; entered into force March 18, 1991.
TIAS 11812.

PROPERTY

Convention between the United States and the United Kingdom relating to the tenure and disposition of real and personal property. Signed at Washington March 2, 1899; applicable to Jamaica February 9, 1901.
31 Stat. 1939; TS 146; 12 Bevans 246.

Supplementary convention relating to the tenure and disposition of real and personal prop-

erty. Signed at Washington May 27, 1936; applicable to Jamaica March 10, 1941.
55 Stat. 1101; TS 964; 5 Bevans 140; 203 LNTS 367.

PUBLICATIONS

Agreement for the exchange of official publications. Exchange of notes at Kingston December 20, 1966; entered into force December 20, 1966.
17 UST 2409; TIAS 6187; 681 UNTS 115.

REFUGEES

Memorandum of understanding for the establishment within the Jamaican territorial sea and internal waters of a facility to process nationals of Haiti seeking refuge within or entry to the United States of America. Signed at Kingston June 2, 1994; entered into force June 2, 1994.
TIAS

TAXATION

Convention for the avoidance of double taxation and the prevention of fiscal evasion with respect to taxes on income, with exchange of notes.[1] Signed at Kingston May 21, 1980; entered into force December 29, 1981.
33 UST 2865; TIAS 10206.

Protocol amending the convention for the avoidance of double taxation and the prevention of fiscal evasion with respect to taxes on income, with exchange of notes.[1] Signed at Kingston July 17, 1981; entered into force December 29, 1981.
33 UST 2903; TIAS 10207.

Agreement concerning administration of income tax affecting Jamaican citizens employed by the U.S. Government. Exchange of notes at Kingston April 3 and May 1, 1986; entered into force May 1, 1986.
TIAS 11362.

Agreement for the exchange of information with respect to taxes. Signed at Washington December 18, 1986; entered into force December 18, 1986.
TIAS 11411.

NOTE:
[1] With reservation and understanding.

TELECOMMUNICATION

Agreement relating to the reciprocal granting of authorizations to permit licensed amateur radio operators of either country to operate their stations in the other country. Exchange of notes at Kingston March 4 and April 28, 1971; entered into force April 28, 1971.
22 UST 694; TIAS 7127; 792 UNTS 337.

JAMAICA (Cont'd)

Agreement relating to radio communications between amateur stations on behalf of third parties. Exchange of notes at Kingston February 24 and May 12, 1977; entered into force June 11, 1977.
29 UST 1888; TIAS 8908.

TRADE AND COMMERCE

Agreement relating to trade in textiles, with annexes. Exchange of letters at Washington August 27, 1986; entered into force August 27, 1986; effective September 1, 1986.
NP

Amendments and extension:
January 29 and February 4, 1987 (NP).
March 3 and 30 and April 7, 1987 (NP).
August 7, 10 and 18, 1987 (NP).
September 2 and October 1 and 20, 1987 (NP).
December 17, 1987 and February 1, 1988 (NP).
April 5 and 14, 1988 (NP).
October 26 and November 1, 1988 (NP).
November 9 and 30, 1988 (NP).
September 14 and December 19, 1988 (NP).
October 29 and 31, 1990 (NP).
November 27 and December 10, 1992 (NP).
May 10 and June 22, 1993 (NP).

Administrative arrangement relating to visa and certification procedures for exports of textile products from Jamaica. Exchange of letters at Washington August 27, 1986; entered into force August 27, 1986; effective September 1, 1986.
NP

Amendments:
March 3 and 30 and April 7, 1987 (NP).
September 14 and December 19, 1988 (NP).
May 10 and June 22, 1993 (NP).

TRADE-MARKS

Declaration by the United States and the United Kingdom affording reciprocal protection to trade-marks. Signed at London October 24, 1877; entered into force October 24, 1877.
20 Stat. 703; TS 138; 12 Bevans 198.

WEATHER STATIONS

Agreement for a cooperative meteorological program in Jamaica, with memorandum of arrangement. Exchange of notes at Kingston August 27 and 29, 1985; entered into force August 29, 1985.
TIAS 11324.

JAPAN

AMAMI ISLANDS

Agreement concerning the Amami Islands, and exchange of notes. Signed at Tokyo December 24, 1953; entered into force December 25, 1953.
4 UST 2912; TIAS 2895; 222 UNTS 193.

ATOMIC ENERGY

Agreement in the field of liquid metal-cooled fast breeder reactors. Signed at Tokyo January 31, 1979; entered into force January 31, 1979.
32 UST 1997; TIAS 9814; 1252 UNTS 83.

Extension:
January 27, 1989.

Agreement on cooperation in fast-reactor safety research. Signed at Washington and Tokyo August 22 and September 20, 1983; entered into force September 20, 1983.
TIAS

Memorandum of agreement for cooperation in breeder reactor projects. Signed at Tokyo September 30, 1983; entered into force September 30, 1983.
TIAS 10796.

Agreement concerning severe nuclear accident research. Signed at Tokyo and Washington September 27 and October 1, 1984; entered into force October 1, 1984.
TIAS

Technical exchange arrangement in the field of nuclear regulatory matters and nuclear safety research. Signed at Tokyo and Washington December 28 and 31, 1985; entered into force December 31, 1985.
TIAS

Agreement in the area of radioactive waste management. Signed at Washington December 3, 1986; entered into force December 3, 1986.
TIAS

Agreement on decommissioning nuclear facilities. Signed at Washington and Tokyo June 11 and July 2, 1987; entered into force July 2, 1987.
TIAS 12144.

Agreement for cooperation concerning peaceful uses of nuclear energy, with annexes, agreed minutes, implementing agreement and exchanges of notes. Signed at Tokyo November 4, 1987; entered into force July 17, 1988.
TIAS   ; 1574 UNTS 287.

Agreement in the field of liquid metal-cooled fast breeder reactors. Signed at Washington January 11, 1991; entered into force January 11, 1991; effective July 31, 1990.
TIAS 12210.

AVIATION

Civil air transport agreement and exchange of notes relating to provisional application. Signed at Tokyo August 11, 1952; entered into force provisionally August 11, 1952; definitively September 15, 1953.
4 UST 1948; TIAS 2854; 212 UNTS 27.

Amendments:
May 9, 1972 (23 UST 677; TIAS 7333).
July 26, 1977 (29 UST 1375; TIAS 8882).
August 21, 1996.
April 20, 1998.

Agreement relating to acceptance of air-worthiness certification. Exchange of notes at Washington November 29, 1977; entered into force November 29, 1977.
29 UST 2167; TIAS 8934.

Interim agreement relating to the civil air transport agreement of August 11, 1952, as amended (TIAS 2854, 7333, 8882), with record of consultations, memorandum of understanding and exchange of letters. Exchange of letters at Washington September 7, 1982; entered into force September 7, 1982.[1]
TIAS 10434; 1736 UNTS 284.

Interim agreement relating to the civil air transport agreement of August 11, 1952, as amended, with memorandum of understanding, exchange of letters and related letter. Exchange of notes at Bonn May 1, 1985; entered into force May 1, 1985.
TIAS 11999.

Implementing arrangement on cooperation in the field of national air traffic control service system, with annex. Signed at Tokyo May 13, 1985; entered into force May 13, 1985.
TIAS 11141.

Interim agreement relating to the civil air transport agreement of August 11, 1952, as amended, with memorandum of understanding. Exchange of notes at Washington December 27, 1989; entered into force December 27, 1989.
TIAS 12406.

Interim arrangement relating to the civil air transport agreement of August 11, 1952, as amended, with attachment. Exchange of notes at Washington February 26, 1996; entered into force February 26, 1996.
TIAS

NOTE:
[1] Provisions relating to Guam, Saipan and Micronesia have been superseded by the 1985 memorandum of understanding.

BONIN ISLANDS

Agreement concerning Nanpo Shoto and other islands with exchange of notes. Signed at Tokyo April 5, 1968; entered into force June 26, 1968.
19 UST 4895; TIAS 6495; 683 UNTS 285.

JAPAN (Cont'd)

CANALS

Agreement concerning Japanese participation in the commission for the study of alternatives to the Panama Canal, with attachments. Exchange of notes at New York September 26, 1985; entered into force September 26, 1985.[1]
TIAS

Extension:
September 25, 1990.

NOTE:
[1] Similar notes were exchanged on the same date between Japan and Panama.

CLAIMS

Agreement for settlement for the AWA MARU claim. Signed at Tokyo April 14, 1949; entered into force April 14, 1949.
63 Stat. 2397; TIAS 1911; 9 Bevans 467; 89 UNTS 141.

Agreement relating to compensation for personal and property damage as a result of nuclear tests in the Marshall (Bikini) Islands. Exchange of notes at Tokyo January 4, 1955; entered into force January 4, 1955.
6 UST 1; TIAS 3160; 237 UNTS 197.

Agreement relating to settlement of claims of Japanese nationals formerly resident in certain Japanese Islands arising from measures taken by the United States in connection with the exercise of its rights under article 3 of the peace treaty. Exchange of notes at Tokyo June 8, 1961; entered into force June 8, 1961.
12 UST 830; TIAS 4781; 410 UNTS 183.

COMMERCE

Treaty of friendship, commerce, and navigation, protocol, and exchange of notes of August 29, 1953.[1] Signed at Tokyo April 2, 1953; entered into force October 30, 1953.
4 UST 2063; TIAS 2863; 206 UNTS 143.

NOTE:
[1] Applicable to Bonin Is. and Ryukyu Is.

CONSERVATION

Convention for the protection of migratory birds and birds in danger of extinction, and their environment, with annex. Signed at Tokyo March 4, 1972; entered into force September 19, 1974.
25 UST 3329; TIAS 7990.

Amendment:
September 19, 1974 (25 UST 3329; TIAS 7990).

CONSULS

Consular convention and protocol. Signed at Tokyo March 22, 1963; entered into force August 1, 1964.
15 UST 768; TIAS 5602; 518 UNTS 179.

COPYRIGHT (See APPENDIX)

CULTURAL AND EDUCATIONAL RELATIONS

Agreement establishing the Joint Committee on United States-Japan Cultural and Educational Cooperation. Exchange of notes at Tokyo November 8, 1968; entered into force November 8, 1968.
19 UST 7549; TIAS 6597; 702 UNTS 277.

Amendment:
February 25, 1977 (28 UST 5326; TIAS 8635).

Agreement on educational exchange programs. Signed at Tokyo February 15, 1979; entered into force December 24, 1979.
31 UST 381; TIAS 9615; 1202 UNTS 149.

Agreement concerning the Mike Mansfield Fellowship Program. Exchange of notes at Tokyo August 21, 1996; entered into force August 21, 1996.
TIAS

CUSTOMS

Agreement regarding mutual assistance between customs administrations, with exchange of notes. Signed at Washington June 17, 1997; entered into force June 17, 1997.
TIAS

DEFENSE

Mutual defense assistance agreement, with annexes.[1] Signed at Tokyo March 8, 1954; entered into force May 1, 1954.
5 UST 661; TIAS 2957; 232 UNTS 169.

Agreement for return of equipment under article I of the mutual defense assistance agreement. Signed at Tokyo March 8, 1954; entered into force May 1, 1954.
5 UST 708; TIAS 2958; 232 UNTS 215.

Agreement relating to the transfer of military equipment and supplies to Japan. Exchange of notes at Tokyo November 19, 1954; entered into force November 19, 1954.
5 UST 2404; TIAS 3101; 238 UNTS 207.

Arrangement relating to the furnishing of military equipment pursuant to article I of the mutual defense assistance agreement.[2] Exchange

of notes at Tokyo January 7, 1955; entered into force January 7, 1955.
6 UST 9; TIAS 3161; 251 UNTS 404.

Agreement relating to a program of aircraft assembly or manufacture in Japan. Exchange of notes at Tokyo June 3, 1955; entered into force June 3, 1955.
6 UST 3817; TIAS 3383; 270 UNTS 51.

Agreement setting forth understandings with respect to the program of aircraft assembly or manufacture in Japan pursuant to the agreement of June 3, 1955. Exchange of notes at Tokyo April 13, 1956; entered into force April 13, 1956.
7 UST 649; TIAS 3547; 273 UNTS 223.

Agreement relating to a cost-sharing program for the production and development in Japan of P2V anti-submarine and sea patrol aircraft. Exchange of notes at Tokyo January 25, 1958; entered into force January 25, 1958.
9 UST 124; TIAS 3984; 304 UNTS 81.

Treaty of mutual cooperation and security, with agreed minute and exchanges of notes. Signed at Washington January 19, 1960; entered into force June 23, 1960.
11 UST 1632; TIAS 4509; 373 UNTS 186.

Amendment:
December 26, 1990 (TIAS 12335).

Agreement under article VI of the treaty of mutual cooperation and security regarding facilities and areas and the status of United States armed forces in Japan, with agreed minutes and exchange of notes.[3] Signed at Washington January 19, 1960; entered into force June 23, 1960.
11 UST 1652; TIAS 4510; 373 UNTS 248.

Understanding revising references to the mutual security treaty (TIAS 4509) and the administrative agreement in the mutual defense assistance agreement of March 8, 1954 (TIAS 2957). Exchange of notes at Washington January 19, 1960; entered into force June 23, 1960.
11 UST 1758; TIAS 4511.

Agreement relating to a program for the assembly and manufacture in Japan of F-104 type aircraft by Japanese industry. Exchange of notes at Tokyo April 15, 1960; entered into force April 15, 1960.
11 UST 1361; TIAS 4471; 372 UNTS 267.

Agreement relating to cost-sharing of United States furnished equipment for one NIKE and two HAWK surface-to-air missile battalions with annex. Exchange of notes at Tokyo April 26, 1963; entered into force April 26, 1963.
14 UST 490; TIAS 5347; 477 UNTS 37.

Agreement relating to a joint cost-sharing program for the production of equipment and the providing of technical assistance for the base air defense ground environment (BADGE) system. Exchange of notes at Tokyo December 4, 1964; entered into force December 4, 1964.
15 UST 2339; TIAS 5724; 532 UNTS 249.

JAPAN (Cont'd)

Related agreement:
June 18, 1965 (16 UST 861; TIAS 5823; 550
UNTS 415).

Agreement relating to a production program in
Japan of the Hawk and Nike Hercules missile
system. Exchange of notes at Tokyo October
13, 1967; entered into force October 13, 1967.
18 UST 2804; TIAS 6365; 701 UNTS 33.

Related agreements:
December 22, 1972 (24 UST 434; TIAS 7558).
July 12, 1977 (29 UST 1892; TIAS 8909).

Agreement relating to a program for the acquisition and production in Japan of the F-4EJ
aircraft and related equipment and material.
Exchange of notes at Tokyo April 4, 1969; entered into force April 4, 1969.
20 UST 545; TIAS 6664; 707 UNTS 207.

Related agreements:
November 21, 1972 (23 UST 3794; TIAS
    7529).
July 12, 1977 (29 UST 1901; TIAS 8910).

Agreement relating to the change in designation of organization of its personnel from Military Assistance Advisory Group to the Mutual
Defense Assistance Office pursuant to the mutual defense assistance agreement of March 8,
1954 (TIAS 2957). Exchange of notes at
Tokyo July 4, 1969; entered into force July 4,
1969.
20 UST 2525; TIAS 6715; 719 UNTS 294.

Agreement relating to the production and acquisition in Japan of the Sparrow missile for
ship-to-air application. Exchange of notes at
Tokyo July 12, 1977; entered into force October 7, 1977.
29 UST 1513; TIAS 8896.

Agreement relating to acquisition and production in Japan of F-15 aircraft and related
equipment and materials. Exchange of notes at
Tokyo June 20, 1978; entered into force June
20, 1978.
30 UST 1599; TIAS 9267.

Related agreements:
December 28, 1984 (TIAS 11978).
February 14, 1989 (TIAS 12331).
March 31, 1992 (TIAS 12331).

Agreement relating to acquisition and production in Japan of P-3C aircraft and related
equipment and materials. Exchange of notes at
Tokyo June 20, 1978; entered into force June
20, 1978.
30 UST 1608; TIAS 9268; 1150 UNTS 123.

Related agreements:
September 10, 1985 (TIAS 12017).
March 24, 1989 (TIAS 12017).
March 24, 1995 (TIAS 12341).

Agreement for the transfer of defense-related
technologies, with annex. Exchange of notes at

Tokyo November 8, 1983; entered into force
November 8, 1983.
TIAS 10835.

Amendments:
January 8, 1988 (TIAS 12329).
December 22, 1994 (TIAS 12329).
February 6, 1998.

Agreement relating to the acquisition and production in Japan of the patriot weapon system.
Exchange of notes at Tokyo October 4, 1985;
entered into force October 4, 1985.
TIAS 11979.

Agreement relating to the furnishing of assistance in the field of training for defense services personnel and defense-related civilian personnel. Exchange of notes at Tokyo January
21, 1986; entered into force January 21, 1986.
TIAS 12005.

Agreement relating to a program for the development of the XSH-60J weapon system. Exchange of notes at Tokyo January 20, 1987;
entered into force January 20, 1987.
TIAS 12014.

Agreement concerning special measures relating to article XXIV of the agreement under article VI (TIAS 4510) of the treaty of mutual
cooperation and security regarding facilities
and areas and the status of United States forces
in Japan, with agreed minutes. Signed at
Tokyo January 30, 1987; entered into force
June 1, 1987.
TIAS 12328; 1574 UNTS 267.

Amendment:
March 2, 1988 (TIAS 12328; 1574 UNTS
    281).

Agreement concerning Japanese participation
in research in the strategic defense initiative.
Signed at Washington July 21, 1987; entered
into force July 21, 1987.
TIAS

Agreement concerning the acquisition and production of the EP-3 aircraft in Japan. Exchange
of notes at Tokyo March 29, 1988; entered
into force March 29, 1988.
TIAS

Amendments:
March 31, 1992.
March 26, 1993.
March 29, 1994.
March 31, 1995.
March 29, 1996.
March 28, 1997.
March 27, 1998.

Agreement on cooperation in the development
of the support fighter (FS-X) weapon system.
Exchange of notes at Tokyo November 29,
1988; entered into force November 29, 1988.
TIAS 12330.

Agreement concerning the acquisition and production in Japan of the HYDRA 70 Rocket
System. Exchange of notes at Tokyo March
31, 1989; entered into force March 31, 1989.
TIAS 12332.

Agreement concerning the acquisition and production in Japan of the SH-60J and UH-60J
aircraft. Exchange of notes at Tokyo March
31, 1989; entered into force March 31, 1989.
TIAS

Amendments:
March 30, 1990.
March 29, 1991.
March 31, 1992.
January 8, 1993.
March 22, 1994.
March 10, 1995.
March 29, 1996.
March 28, 1997.
March 27, 1998.
March 23, 1999.

Agreement concerning the acquisition and production in Japan of the Sparrow Missile System (AIM-7M). Exchange of notes at Tokyo
March 27, 1990; entered into force March 27,
1990.
TIAS 12333.

Amendment:
March 29, 1991 (TIAS 12333).

Agreement concerning Japan's financial contribution for U.S. administrative and related
expenses for the Japanese fiscal year 1990 pursuant to the mutual defense assistance agreement of March 8, 1954. Exchange of notes at
Tokyo August 28, 1990; entered into force August 28, 1990.
TIAS 12334.

Agreement concerning new special measures
relating to Article XXIV of the agreement of
January 19, 1960, under Article VI of the treaty of mutual cooperation and security regarding facilities and areas and the status of United
States armed forces in Japan, with agreed minutes and exchange of notes. Signed at Washington January 14, 1991; entered into force
April 17, 1991.
TIAS   ; 1853 UNTS 87.

Agreement concerning Japan's financial contribution for U.S. administrative and related
expenses for the Japanese fiscal year 1991 pursuant to the mutual defense assistance agreement of March 8, 1954. Exchange of notes at
Tokyo September 27, 1991; entered into force
September 27, 1991.
TIAS 12336.

Agreement amending the agreement of December 17, 1982, as amended, for the acquisition
and production in Japan of the AH-1S helicopter system. Exchange of notes at Tokyo
March 31, 1992; entered into force March 31,
1992.
TIAS

Agreement concerning Japan's financial contribution for U.S. administrative and related
expenses for the Japanese fiscal year 1992 pursuant to the mutual defense assistance agreement of March 8, 1954, with related exchange
of letters. Exchange of notes at Tokyo September 25, 1992; entered into force September
25, 1992.
TIAS 12337.

JAPAN (Cont'd)

Agreement concerning the acquisition and production in Japan of the Multiple Launch Rocket System and related equipment and materials. Exchange of notes at Tokyo January 8, 1993; entered into force January 8, 1993.
TIAS

Amendment:
January 28, 1997.

Agreement for the assembly and repair in Japan of the AN/ALQ-131 System (Electronic Countermeasures Pod) and related equipment and materials, with exchange of letters. Exchange of notes at Tokyo March 12, 1993; entered into force March 12, 1993.
TIAS 12338.

Agreement concerning Japan's financial contribution for U.S. administrative and related expenses for the Japanese fiscal year 1993 pursuant to the mutual defense assistance agreement of March 8, 1954. Exchange of notes at Tokyo February 1, 1994; entered into force February 1, 1994.
TIAS 12339.

Agreement concerning Japan's financial contribution for U.S. administrative and related expenses for the Japanese fiscal year 1994 pursuant to the mutual defense assistance agreement of March 8, 1954. Exchange of notes at Tokyo December 6, 1994; entered into force December 6, 1994.
TIAS 12340.

Agreement concerning new special measures relating to Article XXIV of the agreement of January 19, 1960, under Article VI of the treaty of mutual cooperation and security regarding facilities and areas and the status of United States armed forces in Japan, with agreed minutes and exchange of notes. Signed at New York September 27, 1995; entered into force April 1, 1996.
TIAS 12693.

Agreement concerning Japan's financial contribution for U.S. administrative and related expenses for Japanese fiscal year 1995 pursuant to the mutual defense assistance agreement of March 8, 1954. Exchange of notes at Tokyo October 13, 1995; entered into force October 13, 1995.
TIAS 12342.

Agreement concerning cooperative research of fighting vehicle propulsion technology using ceramic materials. Exchange of notes at Tokyo October 31, 1995; entered into force October 31, 1995.
TIAS 12701.

Agreement concerning cooperative research of advanced steel technology. Exchange of notes at Tokyo October 31, 1995; entered into force October 31, 1995.
TIAS 12344.

Agreement concerning the furnishing of information from the Government of the United States to the Government of Japan which will be necessary for the effective conduct of the studies on ballistic missile defense by the Government of Japan. Exchange of notes at Tokyo February 23, 1996; entered into force February 23, 1996.
TIAS

Agreement concerning reciprocal provision of logistic support, supplies and services between the Armed Forces of the United States of America and the Self-Defense Forces of Japan, with annex. Signed at Tokyo April 15, 1996; entered into force October 22, 1996.
TIAS

Amendment:
April 28, 1998.

Agreement relating to the production of the Support Fighter (F-2) Weapon system. Exchange of notes at Tokyo July 30, 1996; entered into force July 30, 1996.
TIAS

Agreement concerning a program for the cooperative research of eyesafe laser radar. Exchange of notes at Washington September 20, 1996; entered into force September 20, 1996.
TIAS

Agreement concerning a cash contribution by Japan for administrative and related expenses arising from implementation of the mutual defense agreement. Exchange of notes at Tokyo December 17, 1996; entered into force December 17, 1996.
TIAS

Agreement concerning a cash contribution by Japan for administrative and related expenses arising from implementation of the mutual defense agreement. Exchange of notes at Tokyo October 17, 1997; entered into force October 17, 1997.
TIAS

Agreement concerning a cooperative modification program for the ACES II Ejection Seat. Exchange of notes at Tokyo March 27, 1998; entered into force March 27, 1998.
TIAS

Agreement concerning a program for the cooperative research of Advanced Hybrid Propulsion Technologies. Exchange of notes at Tokyo May 26, 1998; entered into force May 26, 1998.
TIAS

Agreement concerning a cash contribution by Japan for administrative and related expenses arising from implementation of the mutual defense agreement. Exchange of notes at Tokyo May 29, 1998; entered into force May 29, 1998.
TIAS

Agreement concerning a program for the cooperative research of Shallow Water Acoustic Technology (SWAT). Exchange of notes at

Tokyo June 18, 1999; entered into force June 18, 1999.
TIAS

Agreement concerning a cash contribution by Japan for administrative and related expenses arising from implementation of the mutual defense agreement. Exchange of notes at Tokyo June 29, 1999; entered into force June 29, 1999.
TIAS

Agreement concerning a program for the cooperative research on ballistic missile defense technologies. Exchange of notes at Tokyo August 16, 1999; entered into force August 16, 1999.
TIAS

Agreement concerning the acquisition and production in Japan of the UH-60J and UH-60JA aircraft and related equipment and material. Exchange of notes at Tokyo March 10, 2000; entered into force March 10, 2000.
TIAS

Agreement concerning a program for the cooperative research of Low Vulnerability Gun Propellant for Artillery. Exchange of notes at Tokyo March 24, 2000; entered into force March 24, 2000.
TIAS

Agreement concerning a cash contribution by Japan for administrative and related expenses arising from implementation of the mutual defense assistance agreement of March 8, 1954. Exchange of notes at Tokyo June 2, 2000; entered into force June 2, 2000.
TIAS

NOTES:
[1] For the revision of references in the agreement consequent to the mutual security treaty (TIAS 4509), see exchange of notes of January 19, 1960 (11 UST 1758; TIAS 4511). See also agreement of July 4, 1969 (TIAS 6715).
[2] For agreement on the clarification of terms, see exchange of notes of November 25, 1957 (8 UST 2413; TIAS 3958; 303 UNTS 348).
[3] For the understanding concerning the application of the agreement to small maritime claims, see exchange of notes of August 22, 1960 (11 UST 2160; TIAS 4580; 394 UNTS 310). For special measures under Article XXIV, see agreement of January 30, 1987.

ECONOMIC AND TECHNICAL COOPERATION

Productivity agreement. Signed at Tokyo April 7, 1955; entered into force April 7, 1955.
6 UST 1007; TIAS 3241; 263 UNTS 285.

Agreement providing for a third-country technical assistance training program in Japan. Exchange of notes at Tokyo March 23, 1960; entered into force March 23, 1960.
11 UST 1382; TIAS 4475; 372 UNTS 289.

JAPAN (Cont'd)

EDUCATION (See CULTURAL AND EDUCATIONAL RELATIONS)

ENERGY

Agreement on cooperation in research and development in energy and related fields, with exchange of notes. Signed at Washington May 2, 1979; entered into force May 2, 1979.
30 UST 4365; TIAS 9463; 1171 UNTS 283.

Related agreements:
May 7, 1982 (TIAS 10458; 1751 UNTS 471).
January 24, 1983 (TIAS 10656; 1647 UNTS 67).

Amendment and extensions:
February 1, 1990 (TIAS 12599).
January 13, 1995 (TIAS 12599).
January 28, 2000.
April 18, 2000.

ENVIRONMENTAL COOPERATION

Agreement on cooperation in the field of environmental protection, with agreed minutes. Signed at Washington August 5, 1975; entered into force August 5, 1975.
26 UST 2534; TIAS 8172; 1027 UNTS 371.

Extensions and amendment:
August 5, 1980 (32 UST 2468; TIAS 9853; 1274 UNTS 336).
July 31, 1985 (TIAS 12387).

Agreement concerning cooperation in the Global Learning and Observations to Benefit the Environment (GLOBE) Program. Exchange of notes at Washington August 29, 1995; entered into force August 29, 1995.
TIAS 12686.

EXTRADITION

Treaty on extradition, with exchange of notes. Signed at Tokyo March 3, 1978; entered into force March 26, 1980.
31 UST 892; TIAS 9625; 1203 UNTS 225.

FINANCE

Agreement regarding guaranty of investments in Japan, with a related exchange of notes. Signed at Tokyo March 8, 1954; entered into force May 1, 1954.
5 UST 791; TIAS 2968; 232 UNTS 251.

Agreement concerning payments from Japanese utility companies for uranium enrichment services. Exchange of notes at Washington September 1, 1978; entered into force September 1, 1978.
30 UST 1850; TIAS 9295; 1153 UNTS 151.

HEALTH

Agreement relating to the establishment of the Radiation Effects Research Foundation. Exchange of notes at Tokyo December 27, 1974; entered into force December 27, 1974.
26 UST 7; TIAS 8001.

JUDICIAL ASSISTANCE

Procedures for mutual assistance in the administration of justice in connection with the Lockheed Aircraft Corporation matter. Signed at Washington March 23, 1976; entered into force March 23, 1976.
27 UST 946; TIAS 8233.

Related agreement:
January 20 and 22, 1979 (30 UST 3473; TIAS 9400; 1180 UNTS 157).

MARITIME MATTERS

Agreement on maritime search and rescue. Signed at Tokyo December 12, 1986; entered into force December 12, 1986.
TIAS 11413.

Amendment:
September 30, 1998.

METROLOGY

Implementing arrangement for cooperation in the fields of metrology and measurement standards. Signed at Tokyo November 2, 1999; entered into force November 2, 1999.
TIAS

MISSIONS, TECHNICAL

Agreement relating to the sending of technical missions by Japan to the United States to study the production of defense equipment and supplies. Exchange of notes at Washington January 21, 1954; entered into force January 21, 1954.
5 UST 317; TIAS 2923; 223 UNTS 145.

NARCOTIC DRUGS

Arrangement for the direct exchange of certain information regarding the traffic in narcotic drugs. Exchange of notes at Tokyo February 16 and July 6, 1928; entered into force July 6, 1928.
9 Bevans 452.

Arrangement for the exchange of information relating to the seizure of illicit narcotic drugs and to persons engaged in the illicit traffic. Exchange of notes at Tokyo April 23 and September 6, 1929; entered into force September 6, 1929.
9 Bevans 455.

NAVIGATION

Agreement relating to the establishment, operation, and maintenance of an OMEGA navigational aid station in Japan. Exchange of notes at Tokyo August 15, 1972; entered into force August 15, 1972.
23 UST 1480; TIAS 7428; 898 UNTS 55.

OCEANOGRAPHY

Memorandum of understanding on the participation of Japan in the ocean drilling program, with annex. Signed at Washington June 5, 1985; entered into force June 5, 1985.
TIAS 12385.

Memorandum of understanding on the participation of Japan in the ocean drilling program as a regular member, with annex. Signed at Washington and Tokyo September 21, 1993; entered into force September 21, 1993; effective October 1, 1993.
TIAS

PATENTS

Agreement to facilitate the interchange of patent rights and technical information for purposes of defense, and protocol. Signed at Tokyo March 22, 1956; entered into force June 6, 1956.
7 UST 1021; TIAS 3585; 275 UNTS 195.

Agreement implementing the agreement of March 22, 1956, to facilitate interchange of patent rights and technical information for purposes of defense, with memorandum of understanding, procedures, related notes and letters. Exchange of notes at Tokyo April 12, 1988; entered into force April 12, 1988.
TIAS

POSTAL MATTERS

Memorandum of understanding relating to the initiation of accelerated mail service. Signed at Tokyo and Washington May 8 and 27, 1975; entered into force May 27, 1975; effective June 16, 1975.
29 UST 90; TIAS 8794.

JAPAN (Cont'd)

PROPERTY

Arrangement relating to perpetual leaseholds. Exchange of notes at Tokyo March 25, 1937; entered into force March 25, 1937.
50 Stat. 1611; EAS 104; 9 Bevans 464; 181 LNTS 217.

Agreement relating to the payment of damages caused by United States aircraft to property of Japanese nationals. Exchange of notes at Tokyo August 24, 1955; entered into force August 24, 1955.
6 UST 4064; TIAS 3418; 257 UNTS 297.

PUBLICATIONS

Agreement relating to the exchange of official publications. Exchange of notes at Tokyo September 5, 1956; entered into force September 5, 1956.
7 UST 2497; TIAS 3638; 277 UNTS 267.

REMOTE SENSING

Memorandum of understanding relating to the operation of the Landsat system, with annex. Signed at Washington and Tokyo July 5 and August 11, 1983; entered into force August 11, 1983.
TIAS 10784; 1581 UNTS 143.

Agreement concerning the acquisition by the Government of Japan of remote sensing parts and components and related information for the indigenous development of an Information Gathering Satellite System. Exchange of notes of Tokyo September 29, 1999; entered into force September 29, 1999.
TIAS

RYUKYU ISLANDS

Agreement concerning the Ryukyu Islands and the Daito Islands with related arrangements. Signed at Washington and Tokyo June 17, 1971; entered into force May 15, 1972.
23 UST 446; TIAS 7314.

SATELLITES

Agreement providing for a program of cooperation in the testing of experimental communications satellites. Exchange of notes at Tokyo November 6, 1962; entered into force November 6, 1962.
13 UST 2470; TIAS 5212; 459 UNTS 203.

Agreement concerning the furnishing of launching and associated services by NASA for Japanese satellites, with memorandum of

understanding. Exchange of notes at Washington May 23, 1975; entered into force May 23, 1975.
26 UST 1029; TIAS 8090.

Agreement concerning cooperation regarding the Geotail Scientific Satellite Program. Exchange of notes at Tokyo September 25, 1989; entered into force September 25, 1989.
TIAS 12203.

Memorandum of understanding for cooperation in the Advanced Earth Observing Satellite Program, with appendix and exchange of notes. Signed at Washington and Tokyo October 14 and 25, 1994; entered into force October 25, 1994.
TIAS 12202.

Amendment:
June 4 and 10, 1996.

Agreement concerning cooperation on the Advanced Earth Observation Satellite–II (ADEOS–II) Program, with memorandum of understanding. Exchange of notes at Washington March 14, 1997; entered into force March 14, 1997.
TIAS

SCIENTIFIC COOPERATION

Memorandum of understanding regarding cooperation in the field of geological sciences. Signed at Reston and Tsukuba, Ibaraki February 8 and 25, 1985; entered into force February 25, 1985.
TIAS 11178.

Agreement on cooperation in research and development in science and technology, with annexes and exchanges of letters. Signed at Toronto June 20, 1988; entered into force June 20, 1988.
TIAS 12025.

Amendment and extension:
July 16, 1999.

Memorandum of understanding covering cooperation in the field of earth sciences. Signed at Tsukuba and Reston October 13 and 28, 1988; entered into force October 28, 1988.
TIAS

Amendment and extension:
May 14 and June 24, 1993.

Memorandum of understanding concerning cooperation in the field of hydrology, water resources and global climate change, with addendum. Signed at Reston and Tsukuba January 3 and February 3, 1992; entered into force February 3, 1992.
TIAS 11851.

Extension:
January 26 and February 1, 1995.

Agreement concerning cooperation in joint scientific balloon launchings, with memorandum of understanding. Exchange of notes at Wash-

ington June 2, 1993; entered into force June 2, 1993.
TIAS

Implementing arrangement in the field of basic science and technology, with annex. Signed at Washington May 3, 1996; entered into force May 3, 1996.
TIAS

SHELLFISH

Agreement providing for cooperative efforts to be directed toward sanitary control of the shellfish industry. Exchange of notes at Washington October 24, 1962; entered into force October 24, 1962.
13 UST 2452; TIAS 5207; 462 UNTS 119.

SMUGGLING

Convention for prevention of smuggling of intoxicating liquors. Signed at Washington May 31, 1928; entered into force January 16, 1930.
46 Stat. 2446; TS 807; 9 Bevans 446; 101 LNTS 63.

SOCIAL SECURITY

Agreement concerning enrollment of Japanese employees of the Okinawa office of the Voice of America in the employment insurance scheme of Japan. Exchange of notes at Tokyo September 30 and October 15, 1976; entered into force October 15, 1976; effective April 1, 1976.
27 UST 4312; TIAS 8452; 1066 UNTS 291.

SPACE COOPERATION

Agreement concerning cooperation in space activities for peaceful purposes. Exchange of notes at Tokyo July 31, 1969; entered into force July 31, 1969.
20 UST 2720; TIAS 6735; 720 UNTS 79.

Agreement relating to space launch assistance, with exchange of letters. Exchange of notes at Washington December 3, 1980; entered into force December 3, 1980.
32 UST 4197; TIAS 9940; 1266 UNTS 143.

Agreement relating to space shuttle contingency landing sites. Exchange of notes at Tokyo January 24, 1985; entered into force January 24, 1985.
TIAS 12382.

Agreement concerning the furnishing of launch and associated services for the Spacelab mission, with memorandum of understanding. Exchange of notes at Washington March 29, 1985; entered into force March 29, 1985.
TIAS 11938.

JAPAN (Cont'd)

Memorandum of understanding for a cooperative program concerning design (Phase B) of a permanently manned space station. Signed at Tokyo May 9, 1985; entered into force May 9, 1985.
TIAS 11327.

Agreement concerning collaboration in the Space Flyer Unit (SFU) program. Exchange of notes at Washington February 4, 1994; entered into force February 4, 1994.
TIAS

Agreement concerning cross-waiver of liability for cooperation in the exploration and use of space for peaceful purposes, with annex and exchanges of notes. Signed at Washington April 24, 1995; entered into force July 20, 1995.
TIAS 12638.

Memorandum of understanding for joint development of the Tropical Rainfall Measuring Mission, with appendix. Signed at Washington October 20, 1995; entered into force October 20, 1995.
TIAS

Amendment:
May 30, 1997.

Agreement concerning cooperation on the Balloon-Borne Superconducting Magnet Spectrometer Program. Exchange of notes at Washington August 1, 1996; entered into force August 1, 1996.
TIAS

Agreement concerning cooperation on the Advanced Spaceborne Thermal Emission and Reflection Radiometer Program. Exchange of notes at Washington October 24, 1996; entered into force October 24, 1996.
TIAS

Agreement concerning cooperation on the Very Long Baseline Interferometer Space Observatory Program, with memorandum of understanding. Exchange of notes at Washington February 7, 1997; entered into force February 7, 1997.
TIAS

Agreement concerning cooperation on the Mars Exploration PLANET-B Program, with memorandum of understanding. Exchange of notes at Washington June 29, 1998; entered into force June 29, 1998.
TIAS

Agreement extending the agreement of December 12, 1994, as amended and extended, on the Astronaut Training Program, with attachment. Exchange of notes at Washington December 8, 2000; entered into force December 12, 2000.
TIAS

TAXATION

Agreement relating to tax relief for expenditures made by the United States in Japan under mutual security programs. Exchange of notes at Tokyo July 14 and 25, 1952; entered into force July 25, 1952.
3 UST 2955; TIAS 2477; 198 UNTS 281.

Convention for the avoidance of double taxation and the prevention of fiscal evasion with respect to taxes on estates, inheritances, and gifts. Signed at Washington April 16, 1954; entered into force April 1, 1955.
6 UST 113; TIAS 3175; 238 UNTS 3.

Convention for the avoidance of double taxation and prevention of fiscal evasion with respect to taxes on income with related notes. Signed at Tokyo March 8, 1971; entered into force July 9, 1972.
23 UST 967; TIAS 7365.

Agreement concerning reciprocal exemption from taxation of income accruing from the business of shipping. Exchange of notes at Washington August 29, 1989; entered into force August 29, 1989.
TIAS 11697.

TELECOMMUNICATION

Agreement relating to the reciprocal granting of authorizations to permit licensed amateur radio operators of either country to operate their stations in the other country. Exchange of notes at Tokyo August 8, 1985; entered into force September 7, 1985.
TIAS 12004.

TRACKING STATIONS

Agreement relating to the establishment by Japan of a satellite tracking station in Okinawa. Exchange of notes at Tokyo September 2, 1968; entered into force September 2, 1968.
19 UST 6011; TIAS 6558; 702 UNTS 151.

Amendment:
September 25, 1969 (20 UST 3017; TIAS 6778; 727 UNTS 429).

TRADE (See also COMMERCE)

Agreement for the establishment of a Joint United States-Japan Committee on Trade and Economic Affairs. Exchange of notes at Washington June 22, 1961; entered into force June 22, 1961.
12 UST 731; TIAS 4776; 410 UNTS 53.

Agreement providing compensatory concessions under the general agreement on tariffs and trade for certain tariff actions taken by the United States. Exchange of notes at Geneva February 9, 1962; entered into force February 9, 1962.
13 UST 948; TIAS 5032.

Agreement supplementary to the general agreement on tariffs and trade to provide compensatory concessions for increases in certain import duties. Signed at Geneva December 31, 1962; entered into force December 31, 1962.
13 UST 3906; TIAS 5267; 471 UNTS 83.

Interim agreement relating to the renegotiation of Schedule XX (United States) to the general agreement on tariffs and trade. Signed at Geneva September 6, 1966; entered into force September 6, 1966.
17 UST 1485; TIAS 6106; 616 UNTS 215.

Amendment:
June 30, 1967 (18 UST 1751; TIAS 6317; 693 UNTS 376).

Agreement within the context of the multilateral trade negotiations concerning Japanese importation of peas and beans. Exchange of letters at Geneva July 11, 1979; entered into force April 25, 1980.
32 UST 5450; TIAS 9995; 1266 UNTS 95.

Agreement within the context of the multilateral trade negotiations relating to agricultural and wood products, with annex. Exchange of letters at Geneva July 11, 1979; entered into force April 25, 1980.
32 UST 5453; TIAS 9996; 1266 UNTS 101.

Agreement to accelerate tariff reductions. Exchange of letters at Washington September 30, 1981; entered into force September 30, 1981.
33 UST 4490; TIAS 10318.

Agreement continuing in effect agreement of December 19, 1980 (TIAS 9961) relating to government procurement in the field of telecommunications, with related letters. Exchange of letters at Washington January 30, 1984; entered into force January 30, 1984; effective January 1, 1984.
TIAS 10935.

Extension:
December 23, 1986.

Agreement concerning trade in certain steel products, with arrangement, agreed minutes and related letter. Exchange of letters at Washington May 14, 1985; entered into force May 14, 1985; effective October 1, 1984.
TIAS

Agreement concerning trade in cotton, wool and man-made fiber textiles with visa arrangement and related exchanges of notes with record of understanding. Exchange of notes at Washington February 6, 1987; entered into force February 6, 1987.
NP

Amendment:
July 20, 1989 (NP).

Agreement concerning market access for beef, fresh oranges, orange juice and other products,

JAPAN (Cont'd)

with annex. Exchange of letters at Washington July 5, 1988; entered into force July 5, 1988.
TIAS

Agreement concerning market access for various agricultural products, with annexes. Exchange of letters at Washington August 2, 1988; entered into force August 2, 1988.

Framework on steel trade liberalization, with appendix. Signed at Washington February 14, 1990; entered into force February 14, 1990.
TIAS

Agreement concerning trade in semiconductor products, with arrangement. Exchange of letters at Washington June 11, 1991; entered into force June 11, 1991; effective August 1, 1991.
TIAS

Agreement concerning trade in certain machine tools, with arrangement, agreed minutes, exchanges of notes and related letters. Exchange of letters at Washington June 30, 1992; entered into force June 30, 1992.
TIAS

Agreement concerning cooperation on anti-competitive activities. Signed at Washington October 7, 1999; entered into force October 7, 1999.
TIAS

TRUST TERRITORY OF THE PACIFIC ISLANDS

Agreement concerning the trust territory of the Pacific Islands with exchanges of notes. Signed at Tokyo April 18, 1969; entered into force July 7, 1969.
20 UST 2654; TIAS 6724; 719 UNTS 127.

Agreement implementing the agreement of April 18, 1969 concerning the trust territory of the Pacific Islands. Exchange of notes at Washington March 13, 1973; entered into force March 13, 1973.
24 UST 767; TIAS 7581.

Agreement relating to the use of interest accrued in connection with payments made under the agreement of April 18, 1969 concerning the trust territory of the Pacific Islands. Exchange of notes at Tokyo April 18, 1975; entered into force April 18, 1975.
26 UST 671; TIAS 8064; 992 UNTS 340.

Agreement extending the period for provision of products and services by Japan under the agreement of April 18, 1969 concerning the trust territory of the Pacific Islands. Exchange of notes at Tokyo April 18, 1975; entered into force April 18, 1975.
26 UST 666; TIAS 8063; 992 UNTS 336.

VISAS

Agreement relating to the reciprocal waiver of nonimmigrant visa fees. Exchange of notes at Tokyo May 21, August 12 and 26, and September 18, 1952; entered into force September 18, 1952; operative October 1, 1952.
5 UST 363; TIAS 2930; 227 UNTS 85.

Agreement relating to the reciprocal issuance of nonimmigrant visas. Exchange of notes at Tokyo August 9 and 23, 1966; entered into force September 22, 1966.
17 UST 1228; TIAS 6087.

WHALING

Agreement concerning commercial sperm whaling in the western division stock of the North Pacific, with summary of discussions. Exchange of letters at Washington November 13, 1984; entered into force November 13, 1984.
TIAS 11070.

JORDAN

AGRICULTURAL COMMODITIES

Agricultural commodities agreement with exchange of notes. Signed at Amman April 5, 1966; entered into force April 5, 1966.
17 UST 361; TIAS 5985; 593 UNTS 239.

Amendment:
August 25, 1966 (17 UST 361; TIAS 5985; 593 UNTS 254).

Agricultural commodities agreement with exchange of notes. Signed at Amman August 25, 1966; entered into force August 25, 1966.
17 UST 1215; TIAS 6085.

Agricultural commodities agreement with annex. Signed at Amman April 4, 1968; entered into force April 4, 1968.
19 UST 4764; TIAS 6475; 698 UNTS 177.

Related agreements:
April 21, 1969 (20 UST 694; TIAS 6675; 707 UNTS 253).
August 20, 1970 (21 UST 2051; TIAS 6949; 763 UNTS 95).
February 17, 1972 (23 UST 87; TIAS 7276;).
May 20, 1973 (24 UST 2019; TIAS 7716; 938 UNTS 206).
July 25, 1973 (24 UST 2031; TIAS 7716; 938 UNTS 218).
August 2, 1973 (24 UST 2033; TIAS 7716; 938 UNTS 220).
September 25 and 29, 1973 (24 UST 2363; TIAS 7760; 938 UNTS 222).
March 12, 1974 (25 UST 280; TIAS 7798; 944 UNTS 396).

Agricultural commodities agreement. Signed at Amman November 27, 1974; entered into force November 27, 1974.
25 UST 3438; TIAS 7995.

Amendment:
March 20, 1975 (26 UST 481; TIAS 8050; 992 UNTS 410).

Related agreements:
October 14, 1975 (26 UST 2905; TIAS 8197).
March 4, 1976 (27 UST 1465; TIAS 8257; 1049 UNTS 381).
April 27, 1976 (27 UST 1471; TIAS 8257; 1049 UNTS 384).
June 23, 1976 (27 UST 2362; TIAS 8314; 1054 UNTS 372).
November 29, 1976 (28 UST 1292; TIAS 8511).
August 10, 1977 (29 UST 365; TIAS 8822).
January 10, 1978 (29 UST 4243; TIAS 9057; 1134 UNTS 41).
April 15, 1978 (29 UST 4260; TIAS 9057; 1134 UNTS 49).
January 17, 1979 (30 UST 2913; TIAS 9373; 1180 UNTS 141).
June 29, 1980 (32 UST 2258; TIAS 9834).

AVIATION

Agreement relating to the provision of technical assistance and services to the Civil Aviation Department of Jordan. Signed at Amman and Washington April 1 and May 3, 1980; entered into force June 1, 1980.
32 UST 1360; TIAS 9777; 1267 UNTS 77.

Extension:
May 31 and June 25, 1990 (TIAS 11738).

Air transport agreement, with annexes. Signed at Amman November 10, 1996; entered into force November 10, 1996.
TIAS

COPYRIGHT (See APPENDIX)

DEFENSE

Agreement concerning payment to the United States of net proceeds from the sale of defense articles furnished under the military assistance program. Exchange of letters at Amman May 20 and August 24, 1974; entered into force August 24, 1974; effective July 1, 1974.
25 UST 2422; TIAS 7921.

Agreement relating to the furnishing of defense articles and services to Jordan. Exchange of notes at Amman October 20, 1976 and February 23, 1977; entered into force February 23, 1977.
28 UST 4494; TIAS 8602.

Agreement concerning the grant of defense articles and services under the military assistance

JORDAN (Cont'd)

program. Exchange of notes at Amman August 27, 1979; entered into force August 28, 1979.
30 UST 7537; TIAS 9597; 1205 UNTS 9.

Amendment:
August 18 and September 20, 1982 (TIAS 10501).

Agreement concerning the grant of defense articles and services under the military assistance program. Exchange of notes at Amman August 14 and 30, 1980; entered into force August 30, 1980; effective August 28, 1980.
32 UST 2412; TIAS 9850.

Amendment:
August 18 and September 20, 1982 (TIAS 10501).

Mutual support agreement with annexes. Signed at Amman October 30, 1988; entered into force October 30, 1988.
TIAS 12345.

Amendment:
February 16 and 29, 2000.

Agreement concerning the transfer of United States Government granted or sold defense articles or related training or other defense services to the Government of Jordan. Exchange of notes at Amman August 13 and 27, 2000; entered into force August 27, 2000.
TIAS

ECONOMIC AND TECHNICAL COOPERATION

Agreement relating to economic assistance. Exchange of notes at Amman June 29, 1957; entered into force June 29, 1957.
8 UST 1069; TIAS 3869; 288 UNTS 263.

General agreement providing for economic, technical, and related assistance to Jordan. Exchange of notes at Amman June 25 and 27, 1957; entered into force July 1, 1957.
8 UST 1073; TIAS 3870; 288 UNTS 269.

Agency for International Development:
June 9, 1977 (29 UST 4922; TIAS 9085; 1134 UNTS 19).
September 1, 1993 (NP).
June 26, 1997 (NP).
August 26, 1997 (NP).
August 26, 1997 (NP).
February 5, 1998 (NP).
June 9, 1998 (NP).
August 10, 1998 (NP).
August 10, 1998 (NP).

EDUCATION

Agreement for the establishment of the American-Jordanian Commission for Educational Exchange, with attachment. Signed at Amman

May 12, 1993; entered into force May 12, 1993.
TIAS 12497.

ENVIRONMENTAL COOPERATION

Agreement for cooperation in the Global Learning and Observations to Benefit the Environment (GLOBE) Program, with appendices. Signed at Amman October 31, 1996; entered into force October 31, 1996.
TIAS

EXTRADITION

Extradition treaty. Signed at Washington March 28, 1995; entered into force July 29, 1995.
TIAS

FINANCE

Agreement relating to investment guaranties under section 413(b)(4) of the Mutual Security Act of 1954. Exchange of notes at Amman July 10 and September 24, 1956; entered into force September 24, 1956.
7 UST 2829; TIAS 3663; 278 UNTS 51.

Amendments:
November 20, 1957 and February 22, 1958 (9 UST 335; TIAS 4012; 303 UNTS 377).
June 25, 1963 (14 UST 1017; TIAS 5395; 487 UNTS 356).

Agreement regarding the consolidation and rescheduling or refinancing of certain debts owed to, guaranteed by, or insured by the United States Government and its agencies, with annexes. Signed at Amman October 31, 1989; entered into force December 6, 1989.
NP

Agreement regarding the consolidation and rescheduling or refinancing of certain debts owed to, guaranteed by, or insured by the United States Government and its agencies, with annexes. Signed at Amman May 10, 1992; entered into force June 22, 1992.
NP

Amendment:
October 7 and November 1, 1993 (NP).

Agreement regarding the consolidation and rescheduling or refinancing of certain debts owed to, guaranteed by or insured by the United States Government and its agencies, with annexes. Signed at Amman August 18, 1994; entered into force September 19, 1994.
NP

Agreement regarding the reduction of certain debts related to foreign assistance owed to the Government of the United States, with an-

nexes. Signed at Amman September 29, 1994; entered into force September 29, 1994.
NP

Agreement regarding the reduction of certain debts owed to, guaranteed by or insured by the Government of the United States and its agencies, with annexes. Signed at Amman September 25, 1995; entered into force September 30, 1995.
NP

Agreement regarding the consolidation and rescheduling of certain debts owed to, guaranteed by, or insured by the United States Government and its agencies, with annexes. Signed at Amman August 25, 1997; entered into force September 25, 1997.
NP

Agreement regarding the reduction of certain debts owed to the Government of the United States, with annex. Signed at Amman September 25, 1997; entered into force September 25, 1997.
NP

Agreement regarding the consolidation and rescheduling of certain debts owed to, guaranteed by, or insured by the United States Government and its agencies, with annexes. Signed at Amman October 17, 1999; entered into force December 13, 1999.
NP

MAPPING

Arrangement concerning cooperation in mapping, charting and geodesy, with annexes. Signed at Amman December 1, 1986; entered into force December 1, 1986.
NP

PEACE CORPS

Agreement concerning the program of the Peace Corps in Jordan. Signed at Amman October 28, 1996; entered into force October 28, 1996.
TIAS

POSTAL MATTERS

International express mail agreement, with detailed regulations. Signed at Amman and Washington December 31, 1986 and January 30, 1987; entered into force March 27, 1987.
TIAS 11308.

RELATIONS

Joint statement on United States-Jordan relations. Issued at Amman June 18, 1974; entered into force June 18, 1974.
25 UST 1510; TIAS 7885.

JORDAN (Cont'd)

RELIEF SUPPLIES AND PACKAGES

Agreement relating to duty-free entry and defrayment of inland transportation charges for relief supplies of United States voluntary agencies. Exchange of notes at Amman May 1 and June 29, 1954; entered into force June 29, 1954.
5 UST 2896; TIAS 3145; 237 UNTS 111.

Amendment:
July 6, September 28, and October 15, 1955 (8 UST 369; TIAS 3784; 279 UNTS 324).

SCIENTIFIC COOPERATION

Memorandum of understanding concerning scientific and technical cooperation in mineral sciences and technology, with annexes. Signed at Washington and Amman November 13 and December 10, 1990; entered into force December 10, 1990.
TIAS 11949.

TAXATION

Agreement concerning the reciprocal exemption from income tax of income derived from the international operation of ships and aircraft. Exchange of notes at Amman April 7, 1988; entered into force April 7, 1988.
TIAS 11888.

TELECOMMUNICATION

Agreement relating to radio communications between amateur stations on behalf of third parties. Exchange of notes at Washington November 13 and 30, 1972; entered into force December 30, 1972.
23 UST 3492; TIAS 7508.

Agreement relating to the reciprocal granting of authorizations to permit licensed amateur radio operators of either country to operate their stations in the other country. Exchange of letters at Amman February 6 and March 11, 1979; entered into force March 11, 1979.
30 UST 3783; TIAS 9425; 1170 UNTS 9.

KAZAKHSTAN

For agreements prior to December 31, 1991, see UNION OF SOVIET SOCIALIST REPUBLICS.

ATOMIC ENERGY

Arrangement for the exchange of technical information and cooperation in nuclear safety matters, with addendum. Signed at Washington February 14, 1994; entered into force February 14, 1994.
TIAS 12532.

Agreement for cooperation concerning peaceful uses of nuclear energy, with annex and agreed minute. Signed at Washington November 18, 1997; entered into force November 5, 1999.
TIAS

Implementing arrangement concerning the decommissioning of the BN-350 Reactor. Signed at Washington December 19, 1999; entered into force December 19, 1999.
TIAS

COPYRIGHT (See APPENDIX)

DEFENSE

Agreement concerning the conversion of military technologies and capabilities into civilian activities. Signed at Almaty March 19, 1994; entered into force March 19, 1994.
TIAS

Agreement concerning the establishment and operation of nuclear test seismic monitoring stations in Kazakhstan. Signed at Washington November 18, 1997; entered into force November 18, 1997.
TIAS

ECONOMIC AND TECHNICAL COOPERATION

Agreement regarding cooperation to facilitate the provision of assistance. Signed at Washington May 20, 1992; entered into force May 20, 1992.
TIAS 11474.

Agency for International Development:
July 28 and August 5, 1997 (NP).

EMPLOYMENT

Agreement relating to the employment of dependents of official government employees. Exchange of notes at Washington May 23 and June 3, 1996; entered into force June 3, 1996.
TIAS 11496.

ENVIRONMENTAL COOPERATION

Agreement on cooperation in the fields of protection of the environment and natural resources, with annex. Signed at Washington March 27, 1995; entered into force March 27, 1995.
TIAS 12623.

Agreement for cooperation in the Global Learning and Observations to Benefit the Environment (GLOBE) Program, with appendices. Signed at Washington March 27, 1995; entered into force March 27, 1995.
TIAS 12624.

FINANCE

Investment incentive agreement. Signed at Washington May 19, 1992; entered into force May 19, 1992.
TIAS

INVESTMENT

Treaty concerning the reciprocal encouragement and protection of investment, with annex. Signed at Washington May 19, 1992; entered into force January 12, 1994.
TIAS

NARCOTIC DRUGS

Agreement concerning the elimination of the illicit production, processing, trafficking and consumption of narcotics within Kazakhstan, with annex. Signed at Almaty May 6, 1997; entered into force May 6, 1997.
TIAS

NORTH ATLANTIC TREATY

Agreement to treat the agreement of June 19, 1995, among the States Parties to the North Atlantic Treaty and other States participating in the Partnership for Peace regarding the status of their forces as binding between the United States and Kazakhstan. Exchange of notes at Almaty March 21 and 28, 1997; entered into force March 28, 1997.
TIAS

PEACE CORPS

Agreement concerning the activity of the Peace Corps of the United States in the Republic of Kazakhstan. Signed at Washington December 22, 1992; entered into force December 22, 1992.
TIAS 12084.

KAZAKHSTAN (Cont'd)

SEISMIC OBSERVATIONS

Agreement concerning the establishment and operation of nuclear test seismic monitoring stations in Kazakhstan. Signed at Washington November 18, 1997; entered into force November 18, 1997.
TIAS

TAXATION

Convention for the avoidance of double taxation and the prevention of fiscal evasion with respect to taxes on income and capital, with protocol. Signed at Almaty October 24, 1993; entered into force December 30, 1996.
TIAS

Agreement concerning the relationship between the taxation convention of October 24, 1993 and the General Agreement on Trade in Services with regard to the consultation, most-favored-nation and national treatment provisions. Exchange of notes at Washington July 10, 1995; entered into force December 30, 1996.
TIAS

TELECOMMUNICATION

Agreement for the establishment of a government-to-government communications link, with annexes. Signed at Almaty December 13, 1993; entered into force December 13, 1993.
TIAS

Amendment:
June 30, 1995.

TRADE AND COMMERCE

Agreement on trade relations, with related exchanges of letters. Signed at Washington May 19, 1992; entered into force February 18, 1993.
TIAS

WEAPONS

Agreement concerning control, accounting and physical protection of nuclear material to promote the prevention of nuclear weapons proliferation. Signed at Almaty December 13, 1993; entered into force December 13, 1993.
TIAS

Amendments:
June 30, 1995.
November 17, 1997.

Agreement concerning the provision of assistance to the Republic of Kazakhstan related to the establishment of export control systems to prevent the proliferation of weapons of mass destruction. Signed at Almaty December 13, 1993; entered into force December 13, 1993.
TIAS

Amendment:
June 30, 1995.

Agreement concerning the destruction of silo launchers of intercontinental ballistic missiles, emergency response and the prevention of proliferation of nuclear weapons. Signed at Almaty December 13, 1993; entered into force December 13, 1993.
TIAS

Extension:
December 1 and 5, 2000.

Agreement concerning the provision to Kazakhstan of emergency response equipment and related training in connection with the removal of nuclear warheads from Kazakhstan for destruction and the removal of intercontinental ballistic missiles and the destruction of their silo launchers, with annex. Signed at Almaty December 13, 1993; entered into force December 13, 1993.
TIAS

Extension:
November 17, 1997.

Agreement concerning the provision of material, services and related training to Kazakhstan in connection with the destruction of silo launchers of intercontinental ballistic missiles and associated equipment and components. Signed at Almaty December 13, 1993; entered into force December 13, 1993.
TIAS

Amendment:
July 1, 1995.

Agreement concerning the elimination of nuclear weapons infrastructure. Signed at Almaty September 22 and October 3, 1995; entered into force October 3, 1995.
TIAS

Amendments:
June 10, 1996.
September 9, 1998.
December 17, 1999.
July 29, 2000.

Agreement concerning cooperation in the area of the prevention of proliferation of weapons of mass destruction. Signed at Washington November 18, 1997; entered into force November 18, 1997.
TIAS

Implementing arrangements concerning long-term disposition of BN–350 nuclear material. Signed at Washington November 18, 1997; entered into force November 18, 1997.
TIAS

KENYA

AGRICULTURAL COMMODITIES

Agricultural commodities agreement with exchange of notes. Signed at Nairobi December 7, 1964; entered into force December 7, 1964.
15 UST 2348; TIAS 5725; 532 UNTS 263.

Amendments:
February 15, 1965 (16 UST 122; TIAS 5769; 542 UNTS 398).
September 1, 1965 (16 UST 1216; TIAS 5870; 579 UNTS 318).
December 1, 1965 (16 UST 1873; TIAS 5919).
February 28, 1966 (17 UST 81; TIAS 5963).
March 14 and April 25, 1967 (18 UST 397; TIAS 6249; 688 UNTS 422).

Agricultural commodities agreement, with minutes of negotiation. Signed at Nairobi March 6, 1980; entered into force March 6, 1980.
32 UST 869; TIAS 9735; 1222 UNTS 127.

Amendment:
May 15, 1980 (32 UST 2027; TIAS 9815).

Agricultural commodities agreement. Signed at Nairobi December 31, 1980 and January 7, 1981; entered into force December 31, 1980.
32 UST 4555; TIAS 9969; 1268 UNTS 47.

Amendment:
May 4 and 22, 1981 (33 UST 3136; TIAS 10217).

Related agreements:
June 3, 1982 (TIAS 10468).
October 29, 1982 (TIAS 10554; 1871 UNTS 391).
August 24, 1984 (TIAS 11045).

Agricultural commodities agreement. Signed at Nairobi July 16, 1985; entered into force July 16, 1985.
NP

Agricultural commodities agreement. Signed at Nairobi July 16, 1986; entered into force July 16, 1986.
NP

Agricultural commodities agreement. Signed at Nairobi June 29, 1987; entered into force June 29, 1987.
NP

Agricultural commodities agreement. Signed at Nairobi February 26, 1988; entered into force February 26, 1988.
NP

Amendment:
July 15 and 20, 1988 (NP).

Agricultural commodities agreement. Signed at Nairobi October 17, 1988; entered into force October 17, 1988.
NP

KENYA (Cont'd)

COPYRIGHT (See APPENDIX)

DEFENSE

Agreement relating to eligibility for United States military assistance and training pursuant to the International Security Assistance and Arms Export Control Act of 1976. Exchange of notes at Nairobi August 10 and 24, 1976; entered into force August 24, 1976.
28 UST 2468; TIAS 8568.

Agreement regarding Kenya's participation in the African Crisis Response Initiative and the furnishing of commodities, services, and related training by the Government of the United States of America for peacekeeping and humanitarian response purposes. Exchange of notes at Nairobi March 10 and August 23, 2000; entered into force August 23, 2000.
TIAS

Agreement regarding grants under the Foreign Assistance Act of 1961, as amended, and the furnishing of defense articles, related training, and other defense services from the United States of America to the Government of Kenya. Exchange of notes at Nairobi July 28 and August 23, 2000; entered into force August 23, 2000.
TIAS

ECONOMIC AND TECHNICAL COOPERATION

Economic cooperation agreement between the United States and the United Kingdom. Signed at London July 6, 1948; applicable to Kenya July 6, 1948.
62 Stat. 2596; TIAS 1795; 22 UNTS 263.

Amendments:
January 3, 1950 (1 UST 184; TIAS 2036; 86 UNTS 304).
May 25, 1951 (2 UST 1292; TIAS 2277; 99 UNTS 308).
February 25, 1953 (4 UST 1528; TIAS 2815; 172 UNTS 332).

Agreement between the United States and the United Kingdom for technical cooperation in respect of the territories for the international relations of which the Government of the United Kingdom are responsible. Signed at London July 13, 1951; applicable to Kenya July 14, 1961.
2 UST 1307; TIAS 2281; 105 UNTS 71.

Agency for International Development:
September 11, 1974 (28 UST 5617; TIAS 8650).
November 10, 1975 (28 UST 265; TIAS 8470).
June 30, 1976 (28 UST 1562; TIAS 8520).

July 1, 1977 (29 UST 2509; TIAS 8954).
July 20, 1977 (28 UST 5661; TIAS 8650).

ENVIRONMENTAL COOPERATION

Agreement for cooperation in the Global Learning and Observations to Benefit the Environment (GLOBE) Program. Signed at Nairobi June 9, 1997; entered into force June 9, 1997.
TIAS

EXTRADITION

Extradition treaty between the United States and the United Kingdom. Signed at London December 22, 1931; applicable to Kenya June 24, 1935.
47 Stat. 2122; TS 849; 12 Bevans 482; 163 LNTS 59.

Agreement to continue in force between the United States and Kenya the extradition treaty of December 22, 1931 between the United States and the United Kingdom. Exchange of notes at Nairobi May 14 and August 19, 1965; entered into force August 19, 1965.
16 UST 1866; TIAS 5916; 574 UNTS 153.

FINANCE

Agreement regarding the consolidation and rescheduling of certain debts owed to, guaranteed by or insured by the United States Government and its agency, with annexes. Signed at Nairobi July 1, 1994; entered into force August 26, 1994.
NP

Investment incentive agreement. Signed at Nairobi December 3, 1998; entered into force December 3, 1998.
TIAS

PEACE CORPS

Agreement relating to the establishment of a peace corps program in Kenya. Exchange of notes at Nairobi August 26, 1964; entered into force August 26, 1964.
15 UST 1906; TIAS 5666; 531 UNTS 51.

POSTAL MATTERS

International express mail agreement. Signed at Washington December 11, 1989; entered into force January 30, 1990.
NP

SOCIAL SECURITY

Agreement concerning United States participation on a limited voluntary basis in the National Social Security Fund of Kenya. Exchange of notes at Nairobi January 31 and March 21, 1977; entered into force March 25, 1977.
29 UST 678; TIAS 8847.

TRADE AND COMMERCE

Agreement concerning trade in textiles and textile products, with attachment. Exchange of notes at Nairobi August 26 and October 25, 1994; entered into force October 25, 1994; effective January 1, 1994.
NP

KIRIBATI

On July 12, 1979, the Gilbert Islands became the independent state of Kiribati. Referring to the status of conventions, treaties and other international instruments applied to, or entered into on behalf of the Gilbert Islands by the United Kingdom prior to independence, the Beretitenti (President) of Kiribati, in a note dated September 11, 1979, to the Secretary-General of the United Nations, made a statement reading in part as follows:

"The Government of the Republic of Kiribati desires that questions of succession to such conventions, treaties and other international instruments be governed by accepted rules of international law and by the relevant principles contained in the Convention on Succession of States in respect of Treaties, done at Vienna on 23 August 1978. Accordingly, the Government of the Republic of Kiribati declares that, with regard to multilateral treaties applied or extended to the former Gilbert Islands it will continue to apply the terms of each such treaty provisionally and on the basis of reciprocity until such time as it notifies the depositary authority of its decision with respect thereto. With regard to bilateral treaties applied or extended to, or entered into on behalf of, the former Gilbert Islands, the Government of the Republic of Kiribati declares that it will examine each such treaty and communicate its views to the other State Party concerned. In the meantime the Government of the Republic of Kiribati will continue to observe the terms of each such treaty, which validly so applies and is not inconsistent with its advent to independence, provisionally and on a basis of reciprocity."

AVIATION

Agreement between the United States and the United Kingdom concerning air services, with annexes and exchange of letters. Signed at

KIRIBATI (Cont'd)

Bermuda July 23, 1977; entered into force July 23, 1977.
28 UST 5367; TIAS 8641.

Amendment:
April 25, 1978 (29 UST 2680; TIAS 8965).

CONSULS

Consular convention between the United States and the United Kingdom. Signed at Washington June 6, 1951; entered into force September 7, 1952.
3 UST 3426; TIAS 2494; 165 UNTS 121.

EXTRADITION

Extradition treaty between the United States and the United Kingdom with protocol of signature and exchange of notes. Signed at London June 8, 1972; entered into force January 21, 1977.
28 UST 227; TIAS 8468.

FINANCE

Investment incentive agreement. Exchange of notes at Suva and Tarawa January 22, 1990; entered into force January 22, 1990.
TIAS 12095.

FRIENDSHIP

Treaty of friendship, with agreed minute. Signed at Tarawa September 20, 1979; entered into force September 23, 1983.
TIAS 10777.

PEACE CORPS

Agreement relating to the establishment of a Peace Corps program in the Gilbert and Ellice Islands. Exchange of notes at Suva and Tarawa November 12 and 20, 1974; entered into force November 20, 1974.
25 UST 3383; TIAS 7991.

TELECOMMUNICATION

Agreement between the United States and the United Kingdom relating to the reciprocal granting of authorizations to permit licensed amateur radio operators of either country to operate their stations in the other country. Exchange of notes at London November 26, 1965; applicable to Kiribati December 11, 1969.
16 UST 2047; TIAS 5941; 561 UNTS 193.

Agreement between the United States and the United Kingdom extending to certain territories the application of the agreement of November 26, 1965 relating to the reciprocal granting of authorizations to permit licensed amateur radio operators of either country to operate their stations in the other country. Exchange of notes at London December 11, 1969; entered into force December 11, 1969.
20 UST 4089; TIAS 6800; 732 UNTS 334.

TERRITORIAL SOVEREIGNTY
(See FRIENDSHIP)

TRADE-MARKS

Declaration by the United States and the United Kingdom affording reciprocal protection to trade-marks. Signed at London October 24, 1877; entered into force October 24, 1877.
20 Stat. 703; TS 138; 12 Bevans 198.

KOREA

AGRICULTURAL COMMODITIES

Agricultural commodities agreement, with exchange of notes. Signed at Seoul March 2, 1962; entered into force March 2, 1962.
13 UST 254; TIAS 4969; 442 UNTS 185.

Amendment:
June 12, 1962 (13 UST 1297; TIAS 5082; 459 UNTS 342).

Agricultural commodities agreement with exchange of notes. Signed at Seoul November 7, 1962; entered into force November 7, 1962.
13 UST 2455; TIAS 5208; 462 UNTS 129.

Amendments:
June 17, 1963 (14 UST 903; TIAS 5375; 479 UNTS 416).
July 5, 1963 (14 UST 983; TIAS 5388; 479 UNTS 420).
August 16, 1963 (14 UST 1050; TIAS 5403; 487 UNTS 386).

Agricultural commodities agreement with exchanges of notes. Signed at Seoul March 18, 1964; entered into force March 18, 1964.
15 UST 250; TIAS 5547; 524 UNTS 263.

Amendment:
June 15, 1964 (15 UST 732; TIAS 5597; 526 UNTS 372).

Agricultural commodities agreement with exchange of notes. Signed at Seoul December 31, 1964; entered into force December 31, 1964.
15 UST 2396; TIAS 5730; 535 UNTS 315.

Agricultural commodities agreement with exchange of notes. Signed at Seoul March 7, 1966; entered into force March 7, 1966.
17 UST 239; TIAS 5973; 579 UNTS 137.

Amendment:
December 5, 1966 (18 UST 98; TIAS 6203; 688 UNTS 438).

Agricultural commodities agreement with annex. Signed at Seoul March 25, 1967; entered into force March 25, 1967.
18 UST 1228; TIAS 6272; 685 UNTS 101.

Amendment:
February 24, 1968 (19 UST 4656; TIAS 6455; 697 UNTS 344).

Related agreements:
May 10, 1968 (19 UST 5495; TIAS 6536; 707 UNTS 21).
October 23, 1968 (19 UST 7541; TIAS 6595; 707 UNTS 31).
February 26, 1969 (20 UST 522; TIAS 6661; 707 UNTS 41).
April 8, 1969 (20 UST 644; TIAS 6669; 707 UNTS 53).
March 7, 1970 (21 UST 600; TIAS 6845).
March 20, 1970 (21 UST 1057; TIAS 6859; 741 UNTS 3).
January 27, 1971 (22 UST 236; TIAS 7057).
January 28, 1971 (22 UST 238; TIAS 7058; 781 UNTS 350).
January 29, 1971 (22 UST 241; TIAS 7059; 781 UNTS 187).
April 12, 1971 (22 UST 1685; TIAS 7193; 806 UNTS 287).
April 12, 1971 (22 UST 1689; TIAS 7194; 806 UNTS 297).
May 6, 1971 (22 UST 632; TIAS 7113; 792 UNTS 394).
December 17, 1971 (22 UST 2069; TIAS 7246).
February 14, 1972 (23 UST 70; TIAS 7273).
May 19, 1972 (23 UST 782; TIAS 7341).
October 20, 1972 (23 UST 3138; TIAS 7489).
November 17, 1972 (23 UST 3806; TIAS 7531).
November 24, 1972 (23 UST 3806; TIAS 7531).
December 7, 1972 (23 UST 3806; TIAS 7531).
February 21, 1973 (24 UST 735; TIAS 7578).
April 12, 1973 (24 UST 987; TIAS 7610).
May 29, 1973 (24 UST 1129; TIAS 7638).
December 7, 1974 (25 UST 3128; TIAS 7976).
February 26, 1975 (26 UST 177; TIAS 8023; 992 UNTS 361).
March 13, 1975 (26 UST 182; TIAS 8023; 992 UNTS 363).
May 27, 1975 (26 UST 1857; TIAS 8142; 1021 UNTS 449).
July 1, 1975 (26 UST 1861; TIAS 8142; 1021 UNTS 451).

Agricultural commodities agreement. Signed at Seoul February 18, 1976; entered into force February 18, 1976.
27 UST 1527; TIAS 8261; 1049 UNTS 109).

Amendments:
April 9, 1976 (27 UST 1527; TIAS 8261; 1049 UNTS 118).
August 9, 1976 (27 UST 3536; TIAS 8380).

KOREA (Cont'd)

December 22, 1976 (28 UST 1272; TIAS 8508).
December 7, 1977 (29 UST 2768; TIAS 8971).

Agricultural commodities agreement. Signed at Seoul July 21, 1977; entered into force July 21, 1977.
29 UST 345; TIAS 8821.

Amendment:
July 18, 1978 (30 UST 193; TIAS 9186; 1148 UNTS 441).

Agricultural commodities agreement. Signed at Seoul June 7, 1979; entered into force June 7, 1979.
30 UST 6471; TIAS 9562.

Amendment:
January 25, 1980 (32 UST 845; TIAS 9733).

Related agreement:
May 18, 1981 (33 UST 1894; TIAS 10151; 1529 UNTS 365).

ATOMIC ENERGY

Agreement providing for a grant to the Government of Korea to assist in the acquisition of certain nuclear research and training equipment and materials. Exchange of notes at Seoul October 14 and November 18, 1960; entered into force November 18, 1960.
11 UST 2364; TIAS 4617; 400 UNTS 49.

Agreement for cooperation concerning civil uses of atomic energy with appendix. Signed at Washington November 24, 1972; entered into force March 19, 1973.
24 UST 775; TIAS 7583.

Extension and amendment:
May 15, 1974 (25 UST 1102; TIAS 7842).

Arrangement concerning research and development in nuclear material control, accountancy, verification, physical protection and advanced containment and surveillance technologies for international safeguards applications, with annex. Signed at Vienna September 19, 1994; entered into force September 19, 1994.
TIAS

Agreement relating to participation in the USNRC program of severe accident research, with addendum. Signed at Rockville and Taejon March 7, 27 and 29, 2000; entered into force March 29, 2000.
TIAS

Arrangement for the exchange of technical information and cooperation in regulatory and safety research matters, with annexes. Signed at Vienna September 19, 2000; entered into force September 19, 2000.
TIAS

AVIATION

Air transport agreement, with annexes. Signed at Washington June 9, 1998; entered into force June 9, 1998.
TIAS

CLAIMS

Utilities claims settlement agreement between the Unified Command and Korea. Signed at Seoul December 18, 1958; entered into force December 18, 1958.
10 UST 41; TIAS 4168; 325 UNTS 233.

COMMERCE

Treaty of friendship, commerce, and navigation, with protocol. Signed at Seoul November 28, 1956; entered into force November 7, 1957.
8 UST 2217; TIAS 3947; 302 UNTS 281.

CONSULS

Consular convention.[1] Signed at Seoul January 8, 1963; entered into force December 19, 1963.
14 UST 1637; TIAS 5469; 493 UNTS 105.

NOTE:
[1] Applicable to all areas of land and water subject to the sovereignty or authority of either state.

COPYRIGHT (See APPENDIX)

CULTURAL RELATIONS

Agreement establishing the Korean-American Cultural Exchange Committee. Exchange of notes at Seoul April 17, 1981; entered into force April 17, 1981.
33 UST 1773; TIAS 10145; 1529 UNTS 359.

CUSTOMS

Agreement on mutual customs service assistance. Signed at Washington November 3, 1986; entered into force March 10, 1987.
TIAS 12010.

DEFENSE (See also MUTUAL SECURITY)

Arrangement relating to the transfer of authority to the Government of the Republic of Korea and the withdrawal of United States occupation forces. Exchange of letters at Seoul August 9 and 11, 1948; entered into force August 11, 1948.

Agreement concerning interim military and security matters during the transitional period. Signed at Seoul August 24, 1948; entered into force August 24, 1948.
62 Stat. 3817; TIAS 1918; 9 Bevans 477; 79 UNTS 57.

Mutual defense assistance agreement. Signed at Seoul January 26, 1950; entered into force January 26, 1950.
1 UST 137; TIAS 2019; 80 UNTS 205.

Mutual defense treaty. Signed at Washington October 1, 1953; entered into force November 17, 1954.
5 UST 2368; TIAS 3097; 238 UNTS 199.

Agreed minute relating to continued cooperation in economic and military matters. Initialed at Seoul November 17, 1954; entered into force November 17, 1954.
6 UST 3913; TIAS 3396; 256 UNTS 251.

Amendment:
January 30, 1962 (13 UST 244; TIAS 4967; 442 UNTS 323).

Agreement relating to the establishment of minimum facilities for an arsenal and the reworking of ammunition. Exchange of notes at Seoul May 29, 1955; entered into force May 29, 1955.
6 UST 3919; TIAS 3397; 256 UNTS 263.

Agreement providing for the disposition of equipment and materials furnished to Korea under the mutual defense assistance agreement. Exchange of notes at Seoul May 28 and July 2, 1956; entered into force July 2, 1956.
7 UST 2174; TIAS 3616; 281 UNTS 41.

Agreement under article IV of the mutual defense treaty of October 1, 1953, regarding facilities and areas and the status of United States armed forces in Korea, with agreed minutes and exchange of notes. Signed at Seoul July 9, 1966; entered into force February 9, 1967.
17 UST 1677; TIAS 6127; 674 UNTS 163.

Agreement regarding the status of the Korean Service Corps with agreed understandings. Signed at Seoul February 23, 1967; entered into force March 10, 1967.
18 UST 249; TIAS 6226; 688 UNTS 245.

Memorandum of understanding relating to the establishment of an M-16 rifle production program in Korea, with annexes. Signed at Seoul and Washington March 31 and April 22, 1971; entered into force April 22, 1971.
29 UST 3537; TIAS 9026.

Amendments:
July 30, 1976 (29 UST 3547; TIAS 9026).
October 14, 1977 (29 UST 3550; TIAS 9026).

Agreement concerning payment to the United States of net proceeds from the sale of defense articles furnished under the military assistance

KOREA (Cont'd)

program. Exchange of notes at Seoul June 25 and 27, 1974; entered into force July 1, 1974. 25 UST 1434; TIAS 7871.

Memorandum of agreement concerning conventional ammunition logistics, with protocol. Signed at Seoul November 25, 1974; entered into force November 25, 1974. 27 UST 2817; TIAS 8351.

Agreement relating to eligibility for United States military assistance and training pursuant to the International Security Assistance and Arms Export Control Act of 1976. Exchange of notes at Seoul February 14 and 25, 1977; entered into force February 25, 1977. TIAS 10559; 1577 UNTS 289.

Memorandum of agreement regarding the construction of facilities at 2nd ID USA to improve combined defense capabilities. Signed at Seoul February 2, 1982; entered into force February 2, 1982. 34 UST 125; TIAS 10343.

Memorandum of understanding for fuel exchange between the United States Navy and the Korean Air Force, with appendix. Signed at Seoul October 31, 1986; entered into force October 31, 1986. TIAS

Memorandum of understanding concerning the operation of USAF aircraft at Taegu. Signed at Osan March 26 and April 9, 1987; entered into force April 9, 1987. TIAS 12019.

Mutual logistics support agreement, with annexes. Signed at Seoul June 8, 1988; entered into force June 8, 1988. TIAS 12024.

Amendment: February 5, 1991.

Memorandum of understanding on defense technological and industrial cooperation. Signed at Seoul June 8, 1988; entered into force June 8, 1988. TIAS

Memorandum of understanding on royalty fees for U.S. origin defense articles. Signed at Washington July 18, 1989; entered into force July 18, 1989. TIAS 12032.

Amendment: August 2, 1993 (TIAS 12505).

Memorandum of understanding for a cooperative technology project concerning coastal/harbor defense, with annex. Signed at Washington and Taejon November 13 and 26, 1990; entered into force November 26, 1990. TIAS

Agreement for the establishment of the Joint United States Military Affairs Group to the

Republic of Korea. Signed at Seoul January 25, 1991; entered into force February 27, 1991. TIAS 12035.

Agreement terminating the agreed understandings and exchange of letters related to the agreement of July 9, 1966 under Article IV of the mutual defense treaty regarding facilities and areas and the status of United States Armed Forces in Korea. Exchange of letters at Seoul February 1, 1991; entered into force February 1, 1991. TIAS

Memorandum of agreement for a cooperative research and development program for new underground ammunition storage technologies, with annex. Signed at Alexandria and Seoul July 3 and August 12, 1991; entered into force August 12, 1991. TIAS

Agreement concerning wartime host nation support, with annexes and agreed minute. Signed at Seoul November 21, 1991; entered into force December 23, 1992. TIAS   ; 1738 UNTS 265.

Memorandum of understanding for the co-assembly and coproduction of M9 armored combat earthmover (ACE). Signed at Washington and Seoul April 23 and May 30, 1992; entered into force May 30, 1992. TIAS

Amendment: July 30 and August 14, 1996.

Agreement concerning special measures relating to article V of the agreement under article IV of the mutual defense treaty regarding facilities and areas and the status of United States Armed Forces in the Republic of Korea. Signed at Seoul November 24, 1995; entered into force January 1, 1996. TIAS

Memorandum of understanding concerning technology research and development projects, with annex. Signed at Washington and Seoul May 29, 1996; entered into force May 29, 1996. TIAS

Memorandum of agreement concerning construction, operation and maintenance of a munitions demilitarization facility (DEFAC) in the Republic of Korea. Signed at Seoul April 21, 1999; entered into force April 21, 1999. TIAS

Agreement regarding the exchange of engineers and scientists, with annexes. Sigend at Washington June 30, 2000; entered into force June 30, 2000. NP

ECONOMIC AND TECHNICAL COOPERATION

Agreement on economic coordination between the Republic of Korea and the United States

acting as the Unified Command, with exchange of notes and minutes.[1] Signed at Pusan May 24, 1952; entered into force May 24, 1952. 3 UST 4420; TIAS 2593; 179 UNTS 23.

Agreement providing for economic, technical and related assistance, with agreed minute and related exchange of notes. Exchange of notes at Seoul February 8, 1961; entered into force February 28, 1961. 12 UST 268; TIAS 4710; 405 UNTS 37.

Agreements relating to exemptions from Korean income and social security taxes in connection with economic and technical programs in Korea. Exchanges of notes at Seoul February 8, 1961; entered into force February 8, 1961. 12 UST 976; TIAS 4802; 413 UNTS 392.

Agreement concerning supplemental economic assistance. Letter of October 16, 1971; entered into force October 16, 1971. 28 UST 7591; TIAS 8730.

Agency for International Development:
September 11, 1974 (28 UST 555; TIAS 8476).
April 30, 1975 (28 UST 569; TIAS 8476).
September 13, 1975 (28 UST 572; TIAS 8476).
September 13, 1975 (28 UST 860; TIAS 8484).
September 13, 1975 (28 UST 311; TIAS 8471).
September 19, 1975 (28 UST 827; TIAS 8483).
July 1, 1976 (28 UST 2382; TIAS 8549).
July 26, 1976 (28 UST 2325; TIAS 8546).
January 19, 1977 (29 UST 2017; TIAS 8921).

NOTE:
[1] Superseded February 28, 1961 with exception of paragraph 13, article III, by agreement of February 8, 1961 (TIAS 4710).

EDUCATION

Agreement for financing certain educational exchange programs. Signed at Seoul June 18, 1963; entered into force June 18, 1963. 14 UST 850; TIAS 5366; 487 UNTS 297.

Amendments:
June 10 and November 2, 1965 (17 UST 71; TIAS 5960; 586 UNTS 282).
September 24 and November 26, 1971 (22 UST 2056; TIAS 7240).
June 1 and July 10, 1972 (23 UST 1328; TIAS 7415; 852 UNTS 282).

Memorandum of understanding on education, with annex. Signed at Seoul October 28, 1981; entered into force October 28, 1981. 33 UST 1993; TIAS 10163.

ENERGY

Memorandum of understanding providing for a cooperative laboratory relationship in advanc-

KOREA (Cont'd)

ing development of coal technology. Signed at Washington November 6, 1981; entered into force November 6, 1981.
TIAS

Extension:
October 7 and November 5, 1986.

Memorandum of understanding providing for a cooperative laboratory relationship in areas of energy conservation. Signed at Washington November 6, 1981; entered into force November 6, 1981.
TIAS

Extension:
October 7 and November 5, 1986.

Memorandum of understanding providing for a cooperative laboratory relationship in advancing development and use of solar energy. Signed at Washington November 6, 1981; entered into force November 6, 1981.
TIAS

Extension:
October 7 and November 5, 1986.

ENVIRONMENTAL COOPERATION

Agreement for cooperation in the Global Learning and Observations to Benefit the Environment (GLOBE) Program, with appendices. Signed at Seoul April 21, 1995; entered into force April 21, 1995.
TIAS 12635.

EXTRADITION

Extradition treaty. Signed at Washington June 9, 1998; entered into force December 20, 1999.
TIAS

FINANCE

Initial financial and property settlement.[1] Signed at Seoul September 11, 1948; entered into force September 20, 1948.
62 Stat. 3422; TIAS 1851; 9 Bevans 481; 89 UNTS 155.

Amendment:
September 11, 1948 (62 Stat. 3443; TIAS 1851; 9 Bevans 489; 89 UNTS 186).

Electric power agreement. Signed at Seoul June 13, 1949; entered into force December 28, 1949.
9 UST 509; TIAS 4026; 316 UNTS 278.

Agreement regarding expenditures by forces under command of the Commanding General of the Armed Forces of Member States of the United Nations, and exchange of notes of September 5 and 6, 1950. Signed at Taegu July 28, 1950; entered into force July 28, 1950.
1 UST 705; TIAS 2135; 140 UNTS 57.

Agreement relating to investment guaranties under section 413(b)(4) of the Mutual Security Act of 1954, as amended. Exchange of notes at Seoul February 19, 1960; entered into force February 19, 1960.
11 UST 202; TIAS 4431; 372 UNTS 109.

Amendment:
April 16, 1965 (16 UST 655; TIAS 5790; 546 UNTS 372).

Investment incentive agreement. Signed at Washington July 30, 1998; entered into force July 30, 1998.
TIAS

NOTE:
[1] Article VII superseded by electric power agreement of June 13, 1949 (9 UST 509; TIAS 4026; 316 UNTS 278). Agreement superseded in part by article II of agreement on facilities and areas and the status of United States armed forces in Korea of July 9, 1966 (17 UST 1677; TIAS 6127).

FISHERIES

Agreement regarding the collection and exchange of data on fisheries harvests in the international waters of the Bering Sea. Exchange of notes at Washington April 25 and July 14, 1988; entered into force July 14, 1988.
TIAS 11596.

HEALTH

Agreement relating to the provision of medical treatment to Korean veterans of the Korean and Vietnam conflicts in Veterans Administration hospitals in the United States. Exchange of notes at Seoul February 3, 1978; entered into force February 3, 1978.
30 UST 4479; TIAS 9471; 1170 UNTS 17.

Memorandum of understanding concerning the sanitary control of fresh frozen molluscan shellfish destined for exportation from Korea to the United States, with annex. Signed at Rockville and Washington October 28, 1998; entered into force October 28, 1998.
TIAS

INFORMATIONAL MEDIA GUARANTIES

Agreement for an informational media guaranty program. Exchange of notes at Seoul April 4, 1958 and September 25, 1959; entered into force September 25, 1959.
10 UST 1826; TIAS 4341; 358 UNTS 163.

INTELLECTUAL PROPERTY

Record of understanding on intellectual property rights, with related letter. Signed at Washington August 28, 1986; entered into force August 28, 1986.
TIAS 11948.

JUDICIAL ASSISTANCE

Treaty on mutual legal assistance in criminal matters, with annex and exchange of notes. Signed at Washington November 23, 1993; entered into force May 23, 1997.
TIAS

MAPPING

Arrangement concerning cooperation in mapping, charting, and geodesy, with annexes. Signed at Washington July 20, 1976; entered into force July 20, 1976.
NP

Amendment:
July 19, 1985 (NP).

METROLOGY

Memorandum of understanding for cooperation relating to standardization, conformity assessment and legal metrology. Signed at Washington May 9, 2000; entered into force May 9, 2000.
TIAS

MISSIONS, MILITARY

Agreement for the establishment of the United States military advisory group to the Republic of Korea. Signed at Seoul January 26, 1950; entered into force January 26, 1950; operative July 1, 1949.
3 UST 2696; TIAS 2436; 178 UNTS 97.

Amendment:
October 21, 1960 (11 UST 2348; TIAS 4613; 400 UNTS 386).

MUTUAL SECURITY

Agreement relating to the assurances required by the Mutual Security Act of 1951. Exchange of notes at Pusan January 4 and 7, 1952; entered into force January 7, 1952.
3 UST 4619; TIAS 2612; 179 UNTS 105.

PATENTS

Agreement relating to the reciprocal granting and protection of the right of priority on pat-

KOREA (Cont'd)

ents. Exchange of notes at Seoul October 30, 1978; entered into force October 30, 1978.
30 UST 2183; TIAS 9324; 1170 UNTS 23.

Agreement for the safeguarding of secrecy of inventions relating to defense and for which applications for patents have been made. Signed at Seoul January 6, 1992; entered into force July 29, 1993.
TIAS 12445; 1751 UNTS 153.

PETROLEUM

Petroleum agreement of 1964, with agreed minutes. Signed at Seoul May 12, 1964; entered into force September 3, 1964.
15 UST 1412; TIAS 5614; 529 UNTS 299.

POSTAL MATTERS

Parcel post agreement and detailed regulations. Signed at Seoul February 17, 1949; entered into force December 1, 1949.
64 Stat. (3) B46; TIAS 2002; 9 Bevans 500; 74 UNTS 167.

Insured parcel post agreement. Signed at Seoul July 15 and at Washington August 17, 1960; entered into force January 1, 1961.
11 UST 2456; TIAS 4630; 400 UNTS 339.

International express mail agreement, with detailed regulations. Signed at Seoul and Washington December 27, 1979 and January 14, 1980; entered into force March 1, 1980.
32 UST 4343; TIAS 9951; 1274 UNTS 3.

Memorandum of understanding concerning the operation of the INTELPOST field trial, with details of implementation. Signed at Seoul and Washington February 19 and March 4, 1985; entered into force March 4, 1985.
TIAS 11244.

PRISONER TRANSFER

Memorandum of agreement on the transfer of prisoners of war/civilian internees. Signed at Seoul February 12, 1982; entered into force February 12, 1982.
TIAS 10406; 1734 UNTS 295.

PUBLICATIONS

Agreement for the exchange of official publications. Exchange of notes at Seoul April 18 and September 24, 1966; entered into force September 24, 1966.
17 UST 1552; TIAS 6110; 607 UNTS 157.

RELIEF SUPPLIES AND PACKAGES

Agreement relating to duty-free entry and defrayment of inland transportation charges on relief supplies and packages, with memorandum of interpretation. Exchange of notes at Seoul April 22 and May 2, 1955; entered into force May 2, 1955.
6 UST 1189; TIAS 3264; 258 UNTS 3.

Amendments:
November 9 and December 28, 1962 (13 UST 3838; TIAS 5257; 469 UNTS 428).
May 19, 1971 (22 UST 698; TIAS 7128; 791 UNTS 360).

SCIENTIFIC COOPERATION

Memorandum of understanding concerning technical cooperation in chemistry, physics and engineering measurement sciences. Signed at Gaithersburg September 12, 1994; entered into force September 12, 1994.
TIAS 12563.

Amendment and extension:
March 22 and April 1, 2000.

Agreement relating to scientific and technical cooperation, with annexes. Signed at Washingon July 2, 1999; entered into force July 2, 1999; effective April 29, 1999.
TIAS

Memorandum of understanding concerning cooperation in science and technology. Signed at Arlington September 21, 2000; entered into force September 21, 2000.
TIAS

SHELLFISH

Agreement concerning the improvement and standardization of shellfish sanitation practices and exchanges of information on sanitary controls applied to the production and handling of fresh or frozen oysters, clams and mussels, with related notes. Exchange of notes at Washington November 24, 1972; entered into force November 24, 1972.
23 UST 3696; TIAS 7516; 898 UNTS 91.

SURPLUS PROPERTY

Agreement on disposal of United States excess property located in Korea, with memorandum of interpretation.[1] Signed at Seoul October 1, 1959; entered into force October 1, 1959.
10 UST 1747; TIAS 4328; 358 UNTS 115.

NOTES:
[1] For waiver of restriction in paragraph 4 of the memorandum, see exchange of notes of February 1, 1963 (14 UST 212; TIAS 5299; 473 UNTS 354).

TAXATION

Convention for the avoidance of double taxation and the prevention of fiscal evasion with respect to taxes on income and the encouragement of international trade and investment, with related notes. Signed at Seoul June 4, 1976; entered into force October 20, 1979.
30 UST 5253; TIAS 9506; 1178 UNTS 3.

TRADE (See also COMMERCE)

Agreement on tariff and non-tariff measures within the context of the multilateral trade negotiations with related letters of May 30 and June 12, 1980. Exchange of letters at Seoul December 27, 1979; entered into force January 6, 1981.
TIAS

Agreement on access of United States firms to Korea's insurance markets. Exchange of letters at Washington August 28, 1986; entered into force August 28, 1986.
TIAS

Related agreement:
September 10, 1987.

Agreement concerning trade in certain textiles and textile products, with annexes. Exchange of letters at Washington November 21 and December 4, 1986; entered into force December 4, 1986; effective January 1, 1986.
NP

Amendments:
December 18 and 23, 1986 (NP).
January 20 and February 11, 1987 (NP).
February 2 and 11, 1987 (NP).
March 4 and 20, 1987 (NP).
September 14, 1990 (NP).
September 14, 1990 (NP).
November 30 and December 3, 1990 (NP).

Agreement relating to limitation of imports of specialty steel from Korea, with annexes and agreed minutes. Exchange of letters at Washington October 20, 1987; entered into force October 20, 1987.
TIAS

Record of understanding concerning market access for cigarettes. Signed at Washington May 27, 1988; entered into force May 27, 1988.
TIAS

Agreement concerning the importation and distribution of foreign motion pictures in the Republic of Korea. Exchange of notes at Washington December 30, 1988; entered into force December 30, 1988.
TIAS

Agreement concerning market access for wine and wine products in Korea, with annexes. Exchange of letters at Washington January 18, 1989; entered into force January 18, 1989.
TIAS

Arrangement concerning trade in certain steel products, with appendices. Exchange of letters

KOREA (Cont'd)

at Washington April 20, 1990; entered into force April 20, 1990; effective October 1, 1989.
TIAS

Framework agreement for agreements on steel trade liberalization, with appendices and exchange of letters. Signed at Washington April 20, 1990; entered into force April 20, 1990.
TIAS

Agreement relating to trade in textiles and textile products, with attachment. Exchange of notes at Washington September 14, 1990; entered into force September 14, 1990; effective January 1, 1990.
NP

Amendments and extension:
January 24 and February 1, 1991 (NP).
November 8 and 30, 1993 (NP).
April 2 and 8, 1997 (NP).

Visa arrangement concerning trade in textiles and textile products, with annexes. Exchange of letters at Washington April 8 and 10, 1991; entered into force April 10, 1991.
NP

VISAS

Agreement relating to the issuance of nonimmigrant visas and the reciprocal waiver of fees. Exchange of notes at Seoul March 28, 1968; entered into force April 27, 1968.
19 UST 4789; TIAS 6479; 693 UNTS 199.

KUWAIT

AVIATION

Agreement on aviation security. Exchange of notes at Kuwait November 22, 1987 and January 11, 1988; entered into force July 5, 1988.
TIAS 12023.

CONSULS

Consular convention between the United States and the United Kingdom. Signed at Washington June 6, 1951; entered into force September 7, 1952.
3 UST 3426; TIAS 2494; 165 UNTS 121.

COPYRIGHT (See APPENDIX)

DEFENSE

Agreement concerning the procurement of defense articles and defense services by Kuwait and the establishment of a U.S. Liaison Office in Kuwait. Exchange of notes at Kuwait February 24 and April 15, 1975; entered into force April 15, 1975.
26 UST 682; TIAS 8066; 992 UNTS 199.

Technical security arrangement. Signed at Kuwait January 18, 1976; entered into force January 18, 1976.
27 UST 4177; TIAS 8444; 1071 UNTS 377.

Amendment:
June 26, 1977 (29 UST 1874; TIAS 8905).

FINANCE

Agreement on investment guaranties. Signed at Kuwait April 24, 1989; entered into force October 24, 1989.
TIAS 12071.

HEALTH

Memorandum of agreement for technical cooperation in the field of health. Signed at Geneva May 7, 1986; entered into force May 7, 1986.
TIAS 11370.

JUDICIAL ASSISTANCE

Agreement on procedures for mutual assistance in connection with matters relating to the Boeing Company. Signed at Washington October 6, 1978; entered into force October 6, 1978.
NP

Related agreement:
December 21, 1978 and January 2, 1979 (NP).

MAPPING

Basic exchange and cooperative agreement for geospatial information and services. Signed at Washington and Kuwait August 7, 1998; entered into force August 7, 1998.
NP

POSTAL MATTERS

Agreement concerning the exchange of parcel post and regulations of execution. Signed at Kuwait October 9, 1963 and at Washington October 21, 1963; entered into force September 16, 1964.
15 UST 1841; TIAS 5658; 530 UNTS 281.

International express mail agreement with detailed regulations. Signed at Kuwait and Washington February 28 and March 11, 1981; entered into force April 1, 1981.
33 UST 1353; TIAS 10114; 1285 UNTS 29.

SCIENTIFIC COOPERATION

Memorandum of understanding concerning scientific and technical cooperation in the earth sciences, with annexes. Signed at Reston June 8, 1998; entered into force June 8, 1998.
TIAS

TELECOMMUNICATION

Agreement relating to the reciprocal granting of authorizations to permit licensed amateur radio operators of either country to operate their stations in the other country. Exchange of notes at Kuwait July 19 and 24, 1966; entered into force July 19, 1966.
17 UST 1039; TIAS 6061; 593 UNTS 289.

Agreement for the establishment and operation of a United States radio relay station in the State of Kuwait. Signed at Kuwait August 2, 1992; entered into force August 29, 1992.
TIAS 12469.

VISAS

Agreement relating to the reciprocal granting of nonimmigrant passport visas. Exchange of notes at Kuwait December 11 and 27, 1960; entered into force December 27, 1960; operative January 26, 1961.
11 UST 2650; TIAS 4659; 401 UNTS 185.

KYRGYZ REPUBLIC

For agreements prior to December 31, 1991, see UNION OF SOVIET SOCIALIST REPUBLICS.

AVIATION

Agreement extending the annexes to the US-USSR civil air transport agreement of June 1, 1990. Exchange of notes at Bishkek April 6 and 13, 1993; entered into force April 6, 1993.
TIAS 12494.

KYRGYZ REPUBLIC
(Cont'd)

COPYRIGHT (See APPENDIX)

DEFENSE

Agreement concerning the provision of training related to defense articles under the United States International Military Education and Training (IMET) Program. Exchange of notes at Bishkek February 7 and 25, 1994; entered into force February 25, 1994.
NP

ECONOMIC AND TECHNICAL COOPERATION

Agreement regarding cooperation to facilitate the provision of assistance. Signed at Washington May 19, 1993; entered into force May 19, 1993.
TIAS 12152.

Agreement to establish a joint commission for agribusiness and rural development, with annexes. Signed at Bishkek December 13, 1993; entered into force December 13, 1993.
TIAS 12521.

EMPLOYMENT

Agreement relating to the employment of dependents of official government employees. Exchange of notes at Washington December 6 and 22, 1993; entered into force December 22, 1993.
TIAS 12170.

ENVIRONMENTAL COOPERATION

Agreement for cooperation in the Global Learning and Observations to Benefit the Environment (GLOBE) Program, with appendices. Signed at Washington June 9, 1995; entered into force June 9, 1995.
TIAS 12658.

FINANCE

Investment incentive agreement. Signed at Washington May 8, 1992; entered into force May 8, 1992.
TIAS 12452.

INVESTMENT

Treaty concerning the encouragement and reciprocal protection of investment, with annex. Signed at Washington January 19, 1993; entered into force January 12, 1994.
TIAS

PEACE CORPS

Agreement concerning the activity of the Peace Corps in Kyrgyzstan. Signed at Washington November 5, 1992; entered into force November 5, 1992.
TIAS 11502.

TRADE AND COMMERCE

Agreement on trade relations, with related exchanges of letters. Signed at Washington May 8, 1992; entered into force August 21, 1992.
TIAS

LAKE CHAD BASIN COMMISSION

ECONOMIC AND TECHNICAL COOPERATION

Agency for International Development:
June 25, 1976 (28 UST 6098; TIAS 8671).

LAOS

COPYRIGHT (See APPENDIX)

DEFENSE

Memorandum of understanding concerning payment to the United States of the net proceeds from the sale of defense articles furnished under the military assistance program. Signed at Vientiane May 31, 1974; entered into force May 31, 1974; effective July 1, 1974.
27 UST 2989; TIAS 8357; 1066 UNTS 115.

Agreement regarding the furnishing of defense articles, related training and other defense services from the United States to Laos. Exchange of notes at Vientiane December 7, 1992 and September 29, 1993; entered into force September 29, 1993.
TIAS 12346.

ECONOMIC AND TECHNICAL COOPERATION

Economic cooperation agreement, with annex and exchange of notes. Signed at Vientiane September 9, 1951; entered into force September 9, 1951.
2 UST 2177; TIAS 2344; 174 UNTS 141.

Agreement providing for additional direct economic assistance. Exchange of notes at Vientiane July 6 and 8, 1955; entered into force July 8, 1955; operative from January 1, 1955.
7 UST 2833; TIAS 3664; 278 UNTS 59.

FINANCE

Investment incentive agreement. Signed at Washington March 8, 1996; entered into force March 26, 1996.
TIAS

MUTUAL SECURITY

Agreement relating to the assurances required by the Mutual Security Act of 1951. Exchange of notes at Vientiane December 18 and 31, 1951; entered into force December 31, 1951.
3 UST 4622; TIAS 2613; 198 UNTS 243.

NARCOTIC DRUGS

Memorandum of understanding concerning cooperation on narcotics issues. Signed at Vientiane January 9, 1990; entered into force January 9, 1990.
TIAS 12407.

POSTAL MATTERS

International express mail agreement. Signed at Vientiane and Washington September 10 and October 16, 1991; entered into force November 16, 1991.
NP

TECHNICAL ASSISTANCE

Memorandum of understanding concerning prosthetics and rehabilitation assistance. Signed at Vientiane May 15, 1990; entered into force May 15, 1990.
TIAS 11721.

TRADE

Agreement relating to trade in textiles and textile products, with annexes. Signed at Wash-

LAOS (Cont'd)

ington September 15, 1994; entered into force September 15, 1994.
NP

Amendment and extension:
June 23 and August 4, 2000.

LATVIA

COMMERCE

Provisional commercial agreement according mutual unconditional most-favored-nation treatment in customs matters. Signed at Riga February 1, 1926; entered into force April 30, 1926.
TS 740; 9 Bevans 528; 55 LNTS 33.

Treaty of friendship, commerce, and consular rights. Signed at Riga April 20, 1928; entered into force July 25, 1928.
45 Stat. 2641; TS 765; 9 Bevans 531; 80 LNTS 35.

CONSULS (See COMMERCE)

COPYRIGHT (See APPENDIX)

CUSTOMS

Agreement regarding mutual assistance between their customs administrations. Signed at Washington April 17, 1998; entered into force July 23, 1999.
TIAS

DEFENSE

Agreement concerning the provision of training related to defense articles under the United States International Military Education and Training (IMET) Program. Exchange of notes at Riga February 21 and March 4, 1992.
NP

Agreement concerning security measures for the protection of classified military information. Signed at Washington January 15, 1998; entered into force January 15, 1998.
TIAS

Acquisition and cross-servicing agreement, with annexes. Signed at Riga and Patch Barracks March 28 and 30, 1998; entered into force March 30, 1998.

DIPLOMATIC RELATIONS

Memorandum of understanding concerning diplomatic relations. Signed at Riga September 5, 1991; entered into force September 5, 1991.
TIAS 12132.

ECONOMIC AND TECHNICAL ASSISTANCE

Agreement concerning economic, technical and related assistance. Signed at Riga December 20, 1995; entered into force February 7, 1996.
TIAS

EMPLOYMENT

Agreement relating to the employment of dependents of official government employees. Exchange of notes at Riga April 24 and July 16, 1996; entered into force July 16, 1996.
TIAS

ENVIRONMENTAL COOPERATION

Agreement for cooperation in the Global Learning and Observations to Benefit the Environment (GLOBE) Program, with appendices. Signed at Riga January 27, 1999; entered into force January 27, 1999.
TIAS

EXTRADITION

Treaty of extradition. Signed at Riga October 16, 1923; entered into force March 1, 1924.
43 Stat. 1738; TS 677; 9 Bevans 515; 27 LNTS 371.

Supplementary extradition treaty. Signed at Washington October 10, 1934; entered into force March 29, 1935.
49 Stat. 3131; TS 884; 9 Bevans 554; 158 LNTS 263.

FINANCE

Agreement relating to the funding of the indebtedness of Latvia to the United States. Signed at Washington September 24, 1925; operative December 15, 1922.
Treasury Department print; 9 Bevans 521.

Agreement modifying the debt funding agreement of September 24, 1925. Signed at Washington June 11, 1932; operative July 1, 1931.
Treasury Department print; 9 Bevans 551.

Investment incentive agreement. Signed at Indianapolis October 28, 1991; entered into force October 28, 1991.
TIAS 12440.

FISHERIES

Agreement concerning fisheries off the coasts of the United States, with annex. Signed at Washington April 8, 1993; entered into force October 29, 1993.
TIAS 12150.

Extension:
February 13 and May 23, 1997.

INVESTMENT

Treaty concerning the encouragement and reciprocal protection of investment, with annex and protocol. Signed at Washington January 13, 1995; entered into force December 26, 1996.
TIAS

JUDICIAL ASSISTANCE

Memorandum of understanding concerning cooperation in the pursuit of Nazi war criminals. Signed at Riga September 11, 1992; entered into force September 11, 1992.
TIAS 12477.

Treaty on mutual legal assistance in criminal matters, with exchange of notes. Signed at Washington June 13, 1997; entered into force September 17, 1999.
TIAS

MAPPING

Basic exchange and cooperative agreement for topographic mapping, nautical and aeronautical charting, geodesy and geophysics, digital data and related mapping, charting and geodesy materials, with attachment. Signed at Riga August 24, 1993; entered into force August 24, 1993.
NP

PACIFIC SETTLEMENT OF DISPUTES

Treaty of arbitration. Signed at Riga January 14, 1930; entered into force July 10, 1930.
46 Stat. 2763; TS 818; 9 Bevans 546; 105 LNTS 307.

Treaty of conciliation. Signed at Riga January 14, 1930; entered into force July 10, 1930.
46 Stat. 2766; TS 819; 9 Bevans 548; 105 LNTS 301.

LATVIA (Cont'd)

PEACE CORPS

Agreement concerning the program of the Peace Corps of the United States in Latvia. Signed at Riga February 6, 1992; entered into force February 6, 1992.
TIAS 12081.

POSTAL MATTERS

International express mail agreement, with detailed regulations. Signed at Washington April 17, 1992; entered into force April 17, 1992.
TIAS 11860.

Postal money order agreement. Signed at Washington and Riga August 16 and September 8, 1993; entered into force December 1, 1993.
NP

TAXATION

Convention for the avoidance of double taxation and the prevention of fiscal evasion with respect to taxes on income. Signed at Washington January 15, 1998; entered into force December 30, 1999.
TIAS

TRADE

Agreement on trade relations and intellectual property rights protection. Signed at Riga July 6, 1994; entered into force January 20, 1995.
TIAS

VISAS

Agreement for the reciprocal waiver of passport visa fees for nonimmigrants. Exchange of notes at Riga February 18 and March 27, 1935; entered into force March 27, 1935; operative April 1, 1935.
9 Bevans 556.

WEAPONS

Agreement concerning technical assistance related to the elimination of conventional weapons systems and facilities formerly controlled by the Russian Federation Armed Forces stationed in the territory of the Republic of Latvia. Signed at Riga August 12, 1994; entered into force August 12, 1994.
TIAS

Agreement concerning the provision of assistance related to the dismantlement of the unfin-

ished Skrunda LPAR Facility formerly controlled by the Russian Federation Armed Forces stationed in the territory of the Republic of Latvia. Signed at Riga August 12, 1994; entered into force August 12, 1994.
TIAS

LEBANON

AGRICULTURAL COMMODITIES

Agricultural commodities agreement with annex. Signed at Beirut June 11, 1970; entered into force June 11, 1970.
21 UST 2039; TIAS 6948; 763 UNTS 15.

Related agreements:
August 31, 1971 (22 UST 1568; TIAS 7180; 807 UNTS 41).
October 7 and 25, 1971 (22 UST 1764; TIAS 7212).
April 28 and May 4, 1972 (23 UST 668; TIAS 7331).

Agricultural commodities agreement. Signed at Beirut April 25, 1977; entered into force June 21, 1977.
28 UST 6153; TIAS 8676.

Related agreements:
March 23, 1978 (30 UST 1934; TIAS 9303; 1152 UNTS 176).
May 17 and June 23, 1978 (30 UST 1941; TIAS 9304; 1152 UNTS 182).
September 26 and October 6, 1978 (30 UST 1948; TIAS 9304; 1152 UNTS 186).
November 24, 1978 (30 UST 1950; TIAS 9304; 1152 UNTS 188).

ATOMIC ENERGY

Agreement providing for a grant to the Government of Lebanon to assist in the acquisition of nuclear research and training equipment and supplies. Exchange of notes at Beirut September 16, 1959; entered into force September 16, 1959.
10 UST 1834; TIAS 4343; 358 UNTS 175.

AVIATION

Air transport agreement with exchange of notes. Signed at Beirut September 1, 1972; entered into force provisionally September 1, 1972; definitively June 5, 1974.
24 UST 245; TIAS 7546.

Agreement relating to air transport route rights. Exchange of notes at Beirut September 24 and October 13, 1977; entered into force October 13, 1977.
28 UST 7479; TIAS 8722; 1087 UNTS 313.

Agreement relating to air transport route rights. Exchange of notes at Washington December

22, 1982; entered into force December 22, 1982.
TIAS 10489; 1751 UNTS 17.

Amendment:
April 29, 1983 (TIAS 10701).

COPYRIGHT (See APPENDIX)

CUSTOMS

Agreement between the United States and France relating to customs privileges for educational, religious, and philanthropic institutions in Syria and Lebanon. Exchange of notes at Paris February 18, 1937; entered into force February 18, 1937.
51 Stat. 279; EAS 107; 7 Bevans 1017; 184 LNTS 479.

DEFENSE

Agreement relating to reimbursable military aid. Exchange of notes at Beirut March 6 and 23, 1953; entered into force March 23, 1953.
5 UST 2908; TIAS 3147; 239 UNTS 45.

Military assistance agreement. Exchange of notes at Beirut June 3 and 6, 1957; entered into force June 6, 1957.
8 UST 943; TIAS 3855; 284 UNTS 155.

Amendment:
June 9 and 12, 1958 (9 UST 927; TIAS 4055; 317 UNTS 350).

Agreement relating to the deposit by Lebanon of ten percent of the value of grant military assistance furnished by the United States. Exchange of notes at Beirut April 12 and May 8, 1972; entered into force May 8, 1972; effective February 7, 1972.
23 UST 687; TIAS 7334.

Agreement regarding grants under the Foreign Assistance Act of 1961, as amended, and the furnishing of defense articles, related training and other defense services from the United States to Lebanon. Exchange of notes at Beirut June 21 and July 18, 1994; entered into force July 18, 1994.
TIAS 12347.

ECONOMIC AND TECHNICAL COOPERATION

General agreement for technical cooperation. Signed at Beirut May 29, 1951; entered into force December 13, 1951.
3 UST 2843; TIAS 2457; 160 UNTS 49.

Agreement relating to the assurances required under section 511(b) of the Mutual Security Act of 1951. Exchange of notes at Beirut De-

LEBANON (Cont'd)

cember 26, 1951 and January 5, 1952; entered into force January 5, 1952.
3 UST 4751; TIAS 2639; 180 UNTS 199.

Technical cooperation program agreement. Signed at Beirut June 26, 1952; entered into force June 26, 1952.
3 UST 4860; TIAS 2659; 181 UNTS 187.

Amendments:
April 14, 1953 (4 UST 1563; TIAS 2821; 212 UNTS 360).
April 30, 1954 (5 UST 1078; TIAS 2991; 247 UNTS 442).

Agreement relating to special economic assistance. Exchange of notes at Beirut June 11 and 18, 1954; entered into force June 18, 1954.
5 UST 1392; TIAS 3009; 233 UNTS 177.

Agreement granting special assistance to Lebanon for budgetary support. Exchange of notes at Beirut September 2 and 3, 1958; entered into force September 3, 1958.
9 UST 1260; TIAS 4113; 336 UNTS 91.

Agency for International Development:
March 21, 1978 (30 UST 1710; TIAS 9280; 1152 UNTS 163).

ENVIRONMENTAL COOPERATION

Agreement for cooperation in the Global Learning and Observations to Benefit the Environment (GLOBE) Program, with appendices. Signed at Antelias December 23, 1998; entered into force December 23, 1998.
TIAS

FINANCE

Investment incentive agreement. Exchange of notes at Beirut September 17, 1980 and February 10, 1981; entered into force April 30, 1981.
33 UST 861; TIAS 10070; 1280 UNTS 471.

GENERAL RELATIONS

Convention between the United States and France relating to rights in Syria and Lebanon. Signed at Paris April 4, 1924; entered into force July 13, 1924.
43 Stat. 1821; TS 695; 7 Bevans 925.

Agreement relating to rights of American nationals. Exchange of notes at Beirut September 7 and 8, 1944; entered into force September 8, 1944.
58 Stat. 1493; EAS 435; 9 Bevans 562; 124 UNTS 187.

NARCOTIC DRUGS

Grant agreement for a cooperative program to curtail illicit traffic in narcotics and dangerous drugs. Signed at Beirut June 29, 1973; entered into force June 29, 1973.
24 UST 1672; TIAS 7673.

PEACEKEEPING

Agreement on United States participation in a multinational force in Beirut. Exchange of notes at Beirut August 18 and 20, 1982; entered into force August 20, 1982.
TIAS 10463; 1751 UNTS 3.

Agreement on United States participation in a multinational force in Beirut. Exchange of notes at Beirut September 25, 1982; entered into force September 25, 1982.
TIAS 10509; 1777 UNTS 363.

POSTAL MATTERS

Convention for the exchange of postal money orders. Signed at Washington January 21, 1946 and at Beirut March 15, 1947; entered into force July 1, 1947.
61 Stat. 4251; TIAS 1984; 9 Bevans 571; 140 UNTS 73.

LESOTHO

In a note dated September 7, 1971 to the Secretary General of the United Nations, the Minister of Foreign Affairs of Lesotho made a Declaration reading in part as follows:

"Reference is made to the Declarations of the Government of the Kingdom of Lesotho in relation to its treaty relationships dated 22 March 1967 and 5 March 1969.

"As regards bilateral treaties validly concluded by the Government of the United Kingdom on behalf of the country formerly known as Basutoland, or validly applied or extended by the said Government to the country known as Basutoland, the Government of the Kingdom of Lesotho, it will be recalled, willingly undertook to apply within its territory, on a basis of reciprocity, the terms of all such treaties from the date of Independence until October 4, 1970, unless abrogated or modified earlier by mutual consent. That time has now expired before it has been possible to evaluate all the treaties.

"The Government of the Kingdom of Lesotho, mindful of the desirability of the continuity of treaty relationships consistent with its independent status, and desirous of continuing negotiations with the various States concerned in relation to the possible continuation, modification or termination of such treaties, has decided that the period during which it will apply, on a basis of reciprocity, the terms of

such bilateral treaties shall be extended without limit of time, pending the reaching of a satisfactory accord with each State concerned.

"Nothing in this Declaration shall, however, be held to constitute a succession to treaties which are not consistent with the accession to full sovereign status by the Kingdom of Lesotho, nor shall it be held to constitute an extension or renewal of treaties which, by virtue of their termination clauses, have already expired or have been terminated before the date of this Declaration.

"Under the terms of the Declaration of the Government of the Kingdom of Lesotho of 22 March 1967 it is not necessary to extend the period in relation to multilateral treaties. As represented in that Declaration, the Government of the Kingdom of Lesotho will review each of the multilateral treaties which has been applied or extended to the country formerly known as Basutoland and indicate to the depositary concerned what steps it desires to take in relation to such instrument.

"During this period of review, as stated in the Declaration of 22 March 1967, any party to a multilateral treaty which has, prior to independence, been applied or extended to the country known as Basutoland, may, on a basis of reciprocity, rely as against Lesotho on the terms of such treaty, the Government of the Kingdom of Lesotho wishes it to be understood, as stated in its Declaration of 5 March 1969, that this is merely a transitional arrangement. Under no circumstances should it be implied that by these Declarations of Lesotho has either acceded to any particular treaty or indicated continuity of any particular treaty by way of succession."

COPYRIGHT (See APPENDIX)

ECONOMIC AND TECHNICAL COOPERATION

Agreement for economic, technical and related assistance. Signed at Maseru October 17, 1984; entered into force October 17, 1984.
TIAS 11167.

EXTRADITION

Extradition treaty between the United States and the United Kingdom. Signed at London December 22, 1931; entered into force June 24, 1935.
47 Stat. 2122; TS 849; 12 Bevans 482; 163 LNTS 59.

LESOTHO (Cont'd)

FINANCE

Agreement relating to investment guaranties. Signed at Maseru February 24, 1967; entered into force March 7, 1967.
18 UST 273; TIAS 6227; 688 UNTS 275.

PEACE CORPS

Agreement relating to the establishment of a Peace Corps program in Lesotho. Exchange of notes at Washington September 22, 1967; entered into force September 22, 1967.
18 UST 2357; TIAS 6339; 693 UNTS 141.

POSTAL MATTERS

International express mail agreement, with detailed regulations. Signed at Maseru and Washington June 19 and July 20, 1990; entered into force August 30, 1990.
TIAS 11737.

PROPERTY

Convention between the United States and the United Kingdom relating to the tenure and disposition of real and personal property. Signed at Washington March 2, 1899; applicable to Basutoland July 24, 1902.
31 Stat. 1939; TS 146; 12 Bevans 246.

Supplementary convention relating to the tenure and disposition of real and personal property of March 2, 1899. Signed at Washington May 27, 1936; entered into force March 10, 1941.
55 Stat. 1101; TS 964; 5 Bevans 140; 203 LNTS 367.

TRADE

Agreement concerning trade in textiles and textile products, with annexes. Exchange of notes at Maseru March 2 and May 25, 1994; entered into force May 25, 1994; effective December 1, 1992.
NP

TRADE-MARKS

Declaration by the United States and the United Kingdom affording reciprocal protection to trade-marks. Signed at London October 24, 1877; entered into force October 24, 1877.
20 Stat. 703; TS 138; 12 Bevans 198.

LIBERIA

AGRICULTURAL COMMODITIES

Agricultural commodities agreement with exchange of notes. Signed at Monrovia April 12, 1962; entered into force April 12, 1962.
13 UST 391; TIAS 4996; 445 UNTS 213.

Agricultural commodities agreement with exchange of notes. Signed at Monrovia January 6, 1966; entered into force January 6, 1966.
17 UST 543; TIAS 6001; 592 UNTS 101.

Agricultural commodities agreement, with annex. Signed at Monrovia October 23, 1967; entered into force October 23, 1967.
18 UST 2777; TIAS 6363; 701 UNTS 91.

Related agreements:
June 24, 1970 (21 UST 1967; TIAS 6939; 763 UNTS 43).
April 26, 1972 (23 UST 1275; TIAS 7401).

Agricultural commodities agreement. Signed at Monrovia August 13, 1980; entered into force August 13, 1980.
32 UST 2319; TIAS 9841.

Related agreements:
January 8, 1981 (TIAS 10618).
June 12 and July 3, 1981 (TIAS 10810).
August 25 and 28, 1981 (TIAS 10810).
April 6, 1982 (TIAS 10820).
November 19 and December 8, 1982 (TIAS 10820).
December 17, 1982 (TIAS 10911).
December 15, 1983 (TIAS 10911).

Agricultural commodities agreement. Signed at Monrovia July 22, 1985; entered into force July 22, 1985.
NP

Related agreement:
April 28, 1986 (NP).

Agricultural commodities agreement. Signed at Monrovia June 22, 1987; entered into force June 22, 1987.
NP

AVIATION

Air navigation agreement. Exchange of notes at Monrovia June 14, 1939; entered into force June 15, 1939.
54 Stat. 2018; EAS 166; 9 Bevans 615; 202 LNTS 93.

Air transport agreement, with memorandum of understanding. Signed at Monrovia March 30, 1978; entered into force March 30, 1978.
29 UST 3063; TIAS 8997; 1124 UNTS 193.

COMMERCE

Treaty of friendship, commerce and navigation. Signed at Monrovia August 8, 1938; entered into force November 21, 1939.
54 Stat. 1739; TS 956; 9 Bevans 595; 201 LNTS 163.

CONSULS

Consular convention. Signed at Monrovia October 7, 1938; entered into force December 21, 1939.
54 Stat. 1751; TS 957; 9 Bevans 607; 201 LNTS 183.

COPYRIGHT (See APPENDIX)

CUSTOMS

Agreement relating to privileges, on a reciprocal basis, of free entry to all articles imported for the personal use of diplomatic and consular personnel. Exchange of notes at Washington May 2 and July 22, 1949; entered into force July 22, 1949.
5 UST 734; TIAS 2961; 232 UNTS 283.

DEFENSE

Agreement relating to mutual defense assistance. Exchange of notes at Washington November 16 and 19, 1951; entered into force November 19, 1951.
3 UST 2805; TIAS 2450; 167 UNTS 141.

Understanding that the assurances contained in the agreement of November 16 and 19, 1951 are applicable to equipment, materials, information, and services furnished under the Mutual Security Act of 1954, as amended, and such other applicable U.S. laws as may come into effect. Exchange of notes at Monrovia April 10 and July 19, 1958; entered into force July 19, 1958.
10 UST 1995; TIAS 4367; 361 UNTS 316.

Agreement relating to the transfer to Liberia of certain property located at Roberts Field, Liberia. Exchange of notes at Washington April 19, 1955, and August 21 and September 22, 1956; entered into force January 4, 1957.
8 UST 141; TIAS 3751; 278 UNTS 109.

Agreement of cooperation. Signed at Washington July 8, 1959; entered into force July 8, 1959.
10 UST 1598; TIAS 4303; 357 UNTS 93.

Agreement concerning the furnishing of military equipment and materials to Liberia. Exchange of notes at Monrovia May 23 and June 17, 1961; entered into force June 17, 1961.
12 UST 876; TIAS 4788; 410 UNTS 233.

LIBERIA (Cont'd)

Amendment:
January 18 and 23, 1962 (13 UST 58; TIAS 4935; 433 UNTS 390).

Agreement relating to the transfer of the Port of Monrovia to Liberia. Exchange of notes at Monrovia April 13 and 14, 1964; entered into force April 14, 1964.
15 UST 641; TIAS 5583; 526 UNTS 221.

Agreement relating to the deposit by Liberia of ten percent of the value of grant military assistance and excess defense articles furnished by the United States. Exchange of notes at Monrovia April 27 and May 10, 1972; entered into force May 10, 1972; effective February 7, 1972.
23 UST 886; TIAS 7350.

Agreement on construction of additional facilities at Roberts International Airport. Signed at Monrovia February 3, 1983; entered into force February 3, 1983.
TIAS 10677.

Amendment:
March 25 and April 4, 1983 (TIAS 10677).

Agreement concerning the provision of training related to defense articles under the United States International Military Education and Training (IMET) Program. Exchange of notes at Monrovia February 23 and September 7, 1983; entered into force September 7, 1983.
TIAS 10783.

ECONOMIC AND TECHNICAL COOPERATION

Memorandum of understanding on the Joint Liberian-United States Commission for Economic Development. Signed at Monrovia October 6, 1955; entered into force October 6, 1955; operative February 3, 1956.
7 UST 600; TIAS 3541; 275 UNTS 87.

General agreement for technical assistance and cooperation. Signed at Monrovia October 6, 1955; entered into force February 3, 1956.
7 UST 603; TIAS 3542; 275 UNTS 93.

Agency for International Development;
August 12, 1977 (29 UST 978; TIAS 8857).
August 12, 1977 (29 UST 2663; TIAS 8963).

EDUCATION

Agreement for financing certain educational exchange programs. Signed at Monrovia May 8, 1964; entered into force May 8, 1964.
15 UST 660; TIAS 5586; 526 UNTS 239.

EMPLOYMENT

Agreement relating to the employment of dependents of official government employees. Exchange of notes at Washington October 2 and 16, 1984; entered into force October 16, 1984.
TIAS

EXTRADITION

Treaty of extradition. Signed at Monrovia November 1, 1937; entered into force November 21, 1939.
54 Stat. 1733; TS 955; 9 Bevans 589; 201 LNTS 151.

FINANCE

Agreement relating to investment guaranties under section 413(b)(4) of the Mutual Security Act of 1954, as amended.[1] Exchange of notes at Monrovia September 6 and 12, 1960; entered into force September 12, 1960.
11 UST 2119; TIAS 4571; 389 UNTS 245.

Amendment:
September 26 and 29, 1964 (15 UST 2064; TIAS 5686; 533 UNTS 348).

Agreement regarding the consolidation and rescheduling of certain debts owed to, or guaranteed by the United States Government and its agencies, with annexes. Signed at Monrovia May 7, 1981; entered into force June 29, 1981.
33 UST 1929; TIAS 10156.

Agreement regarding the consolidation and rescheduling of payments due under P. L. 480 Title I agricultural commodity agreement, with annexes. Signed at Monrovia October 15, 1981; entered into force October 15, 1981.
33 UST 1945; TIAS 10157.

Agreements regarding the consolidation and rescheduling of certain debts owed to, or guaranteed by the United States Government and its agencies, with annexes. Signed at Monrovia October 19 and November 1, 1982; entered into force December 22, 1982.
TIAS 10528; 1777 UNTS 393.

Agreement regarding the consolidation and rescheduling of certain debts owed to or guaranteed by the United States Government and its agencies, with annexes and implementing agreement regarding payments due under P. L. 480 agricultural commodity agreements, with annexes. Signed at Monrovia June 22, 1984; entered into force July 27, 1984.
TIAS 10995.

Agreement regarding the consolidation and rescheduling of certain debts owed to, guaranteed by or insured by the United States Government and its agencies, with annexes and implementing agreement regarding payments due under P.L. 480 agricultural commodity agree-

ments. Signed at Monrovia May 3, 1985; entered into force June 24, 1985.
NP

NOTE:
[1] Subparagraphs (d) and (e) of paragraph 3 terminated September 29, 1964.

LEND-LEASE

Preliminary agreement regarding principles applying to mutual aid for defense and exchange of notes. Signed at New York June 8, 1943; entered into force June 8, 1943.
57 Stat. 978; EAS 324; 9 Bevans 630; 117 UNTS 241.

MISSIONS, MILITARY

Agreement relating to a military mission. Signed at Washington January 11, 1951; entered into force January 11, 1951.
2 UST 1; TIAS 2171; 122 UNTS 125.

Extensions and amendments:
March 27 and 31, 1959 (11 UST 2655; TIAS 4660; 405 UNTS 310).
December 17, 1963 and April 24, 1964 (15 UST 708; TIAS 5591; 526 UNTS 320).
April 22 and May 5, 1987 (TIAS 11538).

PACIFIC SETTLEMENT OF DISPUTES

Arbitration convention with exchange of notes. Signed at Monrovia February 10, 1926; entered into force September 27, 1926.
44 Stat. 2438; TS 747; 9 Bevans 585; 88 LNTS 346.

Treaty of conciliation. Signed at Monrovia August 21, 1939; entered into force March 13, 1941.
55 Stat. 1137; TS 968; 9 Bevans 618; 204 LNTS 165.

PEACE CORPS

Agreement relating to the establishment of a Peace Corps program in Liberia. Exchange of notes at Monrovia March 5 and 8, 1962; entered into force March 12, 1962.
13 UST 308; TIAS 4980; 445 UNTS 41.

POSTAL MATTERS

Agreement concerning the exchange of parcel post, and regulations of execution. Signed at Monrovia March 16, and at Washington May 9, 1957; entered into force August 1, 1957.
8 UST 1035; TIAS 3866; 290 UNTS 59.

LIBERIA (Cont'd)

International express mail agreement, with detailed regulations. Signed at Monrovia and Washington November 15, 1988 and January 6, 1989; entered into force January 30, 1989.
TIAS 11620.

PUBLICATIONS

Agreement relating to the exchange of official publications. Exchange of notes at Monrovia January 15, 1942; entered into force January 15, 1942.
56 Stat. 1419; EAS 239; 9 Bevans 621; 117 UNTS 227.

SCIENTIFIC COOPERATION

Memorandum of understanding for scientific and technical cooperation in the earth sciences. Signed at Reston and Monrovia February 24 and March 20, 1986; entered into force March 20, 1986.
TIAS 11393.

SHIPPING

Agreement relating to jurisdiction over vessels utilizing the Louisiana Offshore Oil Port. Exchange of notes at Washington October 27, 1978 and January 15, 1979; entered into force January 15, 1979.
30 UST 1706; TIAS 9279; 1153 UNTS 283.

TAXATION

Agreement for reciprocal relief from double taxation on earnings from operation of ships and aircraft. Exchange of notes at Monrovia July 1 and August 11, 1982; entered into force August 11, 1982.
TIAS 10435.

Amendment:
October 7 and 23, 1987 (TIAS 11921).

TELECOMMUNICATION

Agreement relating to radio communications between amateur stations on behalf of third parties. Exchange of notes at Monrovia November 9, 1950 and January 8, 9, and 10, 1951; entered into force January 11, 1951.
2 UST 683; TIAS 2223; 132 UNTS 255.

Agreement providing for radio relay facilities to be used by the Voice of America. Signed at Monrovia August 13, 1959; entered into force August 13, 1959.
10 UST 1444; TIAS 4293; 357 UNTS 181.

Agreement supplementing articles III and VII of the agreement of August 13, 1959 relating to radio relay facilities in Liberia. Exchange of notes at Monrovia August 8 and 15, 1960; entered into force August 15, 1960.
12 UST 1367; TIAS 4858; 421 UNTS 332.

Amendment:
July 11 and 24, 1961 (12 UST 1367; TIAS 4858; 421 UNTS 340).

Agreement relating to the reciprocal granting of authorizations to permit licensed amateur radio operators of either country to operate their stations in the other country. Exchange of notes at Monrovia March 20, 1974 and July 22, 1977; entered into force July 22, 1977.
29 UST 1494; TIAS 8892.

VISAS

Agreement relating to the waiver of passport visa fees for nonimmigrants. Signed at Monrovia August 31, 1925; entered into force August 31, 1925; operative September 1, 1925.
9 Bevans 584.

Arrangement relating to the period of validity of temporary visitors' visas. Exchange of notes at Monrovia October 27 and 28, 1947; entered into force October 28, 1947; operative December 1, 1947.
62 Stat. 3930; TIAS 2021; 9 Bevans 641; 82 UNTS 23.

LIBYA

COPYRIGHT (See APPENDIX)

DEFENSE

Military assistance agreement.[1] Signed at Tripoli June 30, 1957; entered into force June 30, 1957.
8 UST 957; TIAS 3857; 284 UNTS 177.

Arrangement for return of equipment and material no longer needed in the furtherance of the mutual defense assistance program. Signed at Tripoli June 30, 1957; entered into force June 30, 1957.
8 UST 963; TIAS 3858; 284 UNTS 188.

Agreement relating to the termination of outstanding agreements with Libya. Exchange of notes at Tripoli February 5, 1972; entered into force February 5, 1972.
23 UST 82; TIAS 7275.

NOTE:
[1] Terminated February 5, 1972 except that article I paragraphs 2 and 4, arrangements under article I, paragraphs 3, 5, and 7, and under article II remain in force.

LIECHTENSTEIN

COPYRIGHT (See APPENDIX)

EMPLOYMENT

Agreement relating to employment of dependents of official government employees. Exchange of notes at Bern and Vaduz September 18 and November 14, 1997; entered into force November 14, 1997.
TIAS

EXTRADITION

Extradition treaty. Signed at Bern May 20, 1936; entered into force June 28, 1937.
50 Stat. 1337; TS 915; 9 Bevans 648; 183 LNTS 181.

SOCIAL SECURITY

Agreement concerning reciprocity of payment of certain social security benefits. Exchange of notes at Bern April 13, 1972; entered into force April 13, 1972; effective July 1, 1968.
23 UST 2896; TIAS 7476.

VISAS

Arrangement for the waiver of passport visa fees for nonimmigrants. Exchange of notes at Bern April 22 and June 18 and 30, 1926; entered into force June 30, 1926; operative June 1, 1925.
9 Bevans 644.

Arrangement relating to the waiver of passport visa fees for nonimmigrants. Exchanges of notes at Washington October 22 and 31 and November 4 and 13, 1947; entered into force November 13, 1947.
6 UST 93; TIAS 3172; 251 UNTS 79.

LITHUANIA

ATOMIC ENERGY

Arrangement for the exchange of technical information and cooperation in nuclear safety matters, with addendum. Signed at Vienna September 22, 2000; entered into force September 22, 2000.
TIAS

LITHUANIA (Cont'd)

COPYRIGHT (See APPENDIX)

CUSTOMS

Arrangement regarding reciprocal privileges for consular officers to import articles free of duty for their personal use. Exchanges of notes at Washington July 28, September 17 and 19, and October 4, 1934; entered into force October 4, 1934; operative October 15, 1934.
9 Bevans 685.

DEFENSE

Agreement concerning the provision of training related to defense articles under the United States International Military Education and Training (IMET) Program. Exchange of notes at Vilnius March 31 and June 10, 1992; entered into force June 10, 1992.
NP

Agreement regarding grants under the Foreign Assistance Act of 1961, as amended, and the furnishing of defense articles, related training or other defense services from the United States to Lithuania. Exchange of notes at Vilnius February 11 and March 26, 1993; entered into force March 26, 1993.
TIAS 12348.

Security agreement concerning security measures for the protection of classified military information. Signed at Vilnius November 21, 1995; entered into force November 21, 1995.
TIAS 12243.

Acquisition and cross-servicing agreement, with annexes. Signed at Vilnius and Patch Barracks (Germany) March 29 and April 30, 1996; entered into force April 30, 1996.
TIAS

Agreement concerning exchange of research and development information, with appendix. Signed at Washington October 16, 1997; entered into force October 16, 1997.
TIAS

DIPLOMATIC RELATIONS

Memorandum of understanding concerning diplomatic relations. Signed at Vilnius September 6, 1991; entered into force September 6, 1991.
TIAS 12133.

EMPLOYMENT

Agreement relating to the employment of dependents of official government employees.

Exchange of notes at Washington November 21 and December 8, 1994; entered into force December 8, 1994.
TIAS 12197.

EXTRADITION

Treaty of extradition. Signed at Kaunas April 9, 1924; entered into force August 23, 1924.
43 Stat. 1835; TS 699; 9 Bevans 655; 51 LNTS 191.

Supplementary extradition treaty. Signed at Washington May 17, 1934; entered into force January 8, 1935.
49 Stat. 3077; TS 879; 9 Bevans 683; 157 LNTS 441.

FINANCE

Agreement for the funding of the debt of Lithuania to the United States. Signed at Washington September 22, 1924; operative June 15, 1924.
Treasury Department print; 9 Bevans 661.

Amendment:
June 9, 1932 (Treasury Department print; 9 Bevans 681).

Investment incentive agreement. Signed at Indianapolis October 28, 1991; entered into force February 7, 1992.
TIAS 12640; 1775 UNTS 291.

FISHERIES

Agreement concerning fisheries off the coasts of the United States, with annex. Signed at Washington November 12, 1992; entered into force July 28, 1993.
TIAS 12139.

Extension:
June 5 and October 15, 1996.

JUDICIAL ASSISTANCE

Memorandum of understanding concerning cooperation in the pursuit of war criminals, with related note. Signed at Vilnius August 3, 1992; entered into force August 3, 1992.
TIAS 12470.

Treaty on mutual legal assistance in criminal matters. Signed at Washington January 16, 1998; entered into force August 26, 1999.
TIAS

MAPPING

Basic exchange and cooperative agreement for topographic mapping, nautical and aeronautical

charting, geodesy and geophysics, digital data and related mapping, charting and geodesy materials. Signed at Vilnius January 21, 1994; entered into force February 15, 1994.
NP

Basic exchange and cooperative agreement concerning global geospatial information and services cooperation, with annexes. Signed at Vilnius June 11, 1999; entered into force June 11, 1999.
NP

PACIFIC SETTLEMENT OF DISPUTES

Arbitration treaty. Signed at Washington November 14, 1928; entered into force January 20, 1930.
46 Stat. 2457; TS 809; 9 Bevans 671; 100 LNTS 111.

Treaty of conciliation. Signed at Washington November 14, 1928; entered into force January 20, 1930.
46 Stat. 2459; TS 810; 9 Bevans 673; 100 LNTS 117.

PEACE CORPS

Agreement concerning the program of the Peace Corps of the United States in Lithuania. Signed at Vilnius February 7, 1992; entered into force February 7, 1992.
TIAS 12447.

POSTAL MATTERS

Convention for the exchange of money orders. Signed at Washington April 10 and at Kaunas July 30, 1923; operative October 15, 1923.
NP

Amendments:
May 26 and June 13, 1934 (NP).
June 11 and 28, 1934 (NP).

Parcel post agreement. Signed at Kaunas December 4 and at Washington December 28, 1939; operative February 1, 1940.
54 Stat. 2021; Post Office Department print; 202 LNTS 381.

International express mail agreement, with detailed regulations. Signed at Vilnius and Washington September 21 and October 29, 1992; entered into force December 14, 1992.
TIAS 11905.

Postal money order agreement. Signed at Vilnius and Washington January 26 and February 5, 1993; entered into force June 1, 1993.
NP

LITHUANIA (Cont'd)

TAXATION

Convention for the avoidance of double taxation and the prevention of fiscal evasion with respect to taxes on income. Signed at Washington January 15, 1998; entered into force December 30, 1999.
TIAS

TRADE AND COMMERCE

Agreement according mutual unconditional most-favored-nation treatment in customs matters. Exchange of notes at Washington December 23, 1925; entered into force July 10, 1926.
TS 742; 9 Bevans 668; 54 LNTS 377.

TRADE-MARKS

Agreement relating to the registration of trade-marks. Exchange of notes at Riga September 14, 1929 and at Kaunas October 11, 1929; entered into force October 11, 1929.
9 Bevans 675.

VISAS

Arrangement for the reciprocal waiver of passport visa fees for nonimmigrants. Exchange of notes at Washington April 17, 1937; entered into force April 17, 1937; operative May 1, 1937.
9 Bevans 688.

LUXEMBOURG

AVIATION

Air transport agreement, with annex. Signed at Luxembourg August 19, 1986; entered into force August 3, 1988.
TIAS 11249.

Amendment:
June 6, 1995 (TIAS 12656).

CLAIMS

Memorandum of understanding regarding claims between the two Governments arising out of the conduct of the war. Signed at Luxembourg September 12, 1946; entered into force September 12, 1946.
62 Stat. 4006; TIAS 2067; 9 Bevans 721; 149 UNTS 19.

Agreement relating to war damage to private property. Exchange of notes at Luxembourg June 15, 1955; entered into force June 15, 1955.
6 UST 2577; TIAS 3302; 264 UNTS 279.

COMMERCE

Treaty of friendship, establishment and navigation, and protocol. Signed at Luxembourg February 23, 1962; entered into force March 28, 1963.
14 UST 251; TIAS 5306; 474 UNTS 3.

COPYRIGHT (See APPENDIX)

DEFENSE (See also MUTUAL SECURITY)

Mutual defense assistance agreement. Signed at Washington January 27, 1950; entered into force March 28, 1950.
1 UST 69; TIAS 2014; 80 UNTS 187.

Agreement relating to the offshore procurement program. Signed at Luxembourg April 17, 1954; entered into force September 30, 1955.
6 UST 3989; TIAS 3415; 257 UNTS 255.

Agreement approving the offshore procurement contract with Luxembourg. Exchange of notes at Luxembourg April 17, 1954; entered into force September 30, 1955.
6 UST 4009; TIAS 3416; 257 UNTS 270.

Amendment:
May 10 and July 16, 1954 (6 UST 4009; TIAS 3416; 257 UNTS 292).

Memorandum of understanding relating to the disposal of redistributable and excess property furnished in connection with the mutual defense assistance program, with related notes. Signed at Luxembourg July 7, 1954; entered into force July 7, 1954.
5 UST 1524; TIAS 3029; 233 UNTS 23.

Amendment:
March 4 and June 10, 1960 (11 UST 2169; TIAS 4583; 393 UNTS 328).

Agreement concerning general security of military information. Signed at Luxembourg September 17, 1981; entered into force September 17, 1981.
33 UST 3922; TIAS 10270; 1543 UNTS 117.

Memorandum of understanding on reciprocal defense procurement, with annex. Signed at Luxembourg December 2, 1982; entered into force December 2, 1982.
TIAS

Mutual logistics support agreement, with annexes. Signed at Luxembourg December 15, 1983; entered into force December 15, 1983.
TIAS 10859.

Amendment:
July 21, 1992 (TIAS 12524).

Agreement concerning NATO civil air augmentation. Signed at Scott AFB and Luxembourg March 11 and May 17, 1985; entered into force May 17, 1985.
TIAS 11108.

ECONOMIC AND TECHNICAL COOPERATION

Economic cooperation agreement. Signed at Luxembourg July 3, 1948; entered into force July 3, 1948.
62 Stat. 2451; TIAS 1790; 9 Bevans 722; 24 UNTS 35.

Amendments:
November 17 and December 22, 1948 (62 Stat. 3750; TIAS 1903; 9 Bevans 740; 55 UNTS 324).
January 17 and 19, 1950 (1 UST 163; TIAS 2030; 79 UNTS 306).
August 30 and October 17, 1951 (2 UST 2149; TIAS 2342; 137 UNTS 280).
December 31, 1952 and February 26, 1953 (4 UST 226; TIAS 2780; 212 UNTS 286).

EDUCATION

Agreement for the financing of certain academic and cultural exchanges and programs in the field of education. Signed at Brussels December 12, 1968; entered into force May 13, 1971.
22 UST 1538; TIAS 7175; 806 UNTS 231.

ENVIRONMENTAL COOPERATION

Agreement concerning cooperation in the Global Learning and Observations to Benefit the Environment (GLOBE) Program, with appendices. Signed at Luxembourg October 10, 1996; entered into force October 10, 1996.
TIAS

EXTRADITION

Treaty of extradition. Signed at Berlin October 29, 1883; entered into force August 13, 1884.
23 Stat. 808; TS 196; 9 Bevans 694.

Supplementary extradition convention. Signed at Luxembourg April 24, 1935; entered into force March 3, 1936.
49 Stat. 3355; TS 904; 9 Bevans 707; 168 LNTS 129.

LUXEMBOURG (Cont'd)

FINANCE

Agreement relating to investment guaranties under section 413(b)(4) of the Mutual Security Act of 1954, as amended. Exchange of notes at Luxembourg November 26 and December 7, 1956; entered into force December 7, 1956.
7 UST 3432; TIAS 3715; 265 UNTS 255.

LEND-LEASE

Mutual aid settlement. Exchange of memorandums at Luxembourg August 29, 1946; entered into force August 29, 1946.
62 Stat. 4003; TIAS 2065; 9 Bevans 718; 140 UNTS 101.

MILITARY CEMETERIES AND MONUMENTS

Agreement concerning the establishment of a permanent World War II cemetery in Luxembourg with exchange of notes. Signed at Luxembourg March 20, 1951; entered into force June 11, 1952.
3 UST 2745; TIAS 2445; 180 UNTS 283.

Agreement concerning concessions granted to United States in establishing a permanent World War II cemetery in Luxembourg. Exchange of notes at Luxembourg March 20, 1951; entered into force March 20, 1951.
3 UST 2750; TIAS 2446; 180 UNTS 289.

MUTUAL SECURITY

Agreement relating to the assurances required under the Mutual Security Act of 1951. Exchange of notes at Luxembourg January 8, 1952; entered into force January 8, 1952.
3 UST 4627; TIAS 2614; 180 UNTS 191.

PACIFIC SETTLEMENT OF DISPUTES

Treaty of arbitration. Signed at Luxembourg April 6, 1929; entered into force September 2, 1930.
46 Stat. 2809; TS 825; 9 Bevans 701; 106 LNTS 475.

Treaty of conciliation. Signed at Luxembourg April 6, 1929; entered into force September 2, 1930.
46 Stat. 2813; TS 826; 9 Bevans 704; 106 LNTS 469.

POSTAL MATTERS

Money order convention. Signed at Washington June 2 and at Luxembourg April 24, 1930; effective July 1, 1930.
NP

International express mail agreement, with detailed regulations. Signed at Luxembourg and Washington April 21 and June 14, 1983; entered into force October 1, 1983.
TIAS 10737.

Memorandum of understanding concerning the operation of the INTELPOST field trial, with details of implementation. Signed at Luxembourg and Washington April 29 and May 28, 1985; entered into force June 3, 1985.
TIAS 11245.

SOCIAL SECURITY

Agreement on social security, with administrative arrangement. Signed at Luxembourg February 12, 1992; entered into force November 1, 1993.
TIAS 12119.

TAXATION

Agreement relating to relief from taxation of United States expenditures in Luxembourg for common defense. Exchange of notes at Luxembourg March 10 and 13, 1952; entered into force March 13, 1952.
3 UST 4001; TIAS 2538; 168 UNTS 57.

Convention with respect to taxes on income and property. Signed at Washington December 18, 1962; entered into force December 22, 1964; effective January 1, 1964.
15 UST 2355; TIAS 5726; 532 UNTS 277.

Agreement concerning the reciprocal exemption from income tax of income derived from the international operation of ships and aircraft. Exchange of notes at Luxembourg April 11 and June 22, 1989; entered into force January 8, 1993.
TIAS 12056.

Convention for the avoidance of double taxation and the prevention of fiscal evasion with respect to taxes on income and capital, with related exchange of notes. Signed at Luxembourg April 3, 1996; entered into force December 20, 2000.
TIAS

TELECOMMUNICATION

Agreement relating to the establishment of a radio range station in Luxembourg. Exchange of notes at Luxembourg July 22 and August 17, 1953; entered into force August 17, 1953.
5 UST 1823; TIAS 3056; 234 UNTS 219.

Agreement relating to reciprocal granting of authorizations to permit licensed amateur radio operators of either country to operate their stations in the other country. Exchange of notes at Luxembourg July 7 and 29, 1965; entered into force July 29, 1965.
16 UST 1746; TIAS 5900; 573 UNTS 197.

TRADE AND COMMERCE (See COMMERCE. See also BENELUX)

VISAS

Agreement relating to the waiver of visas and visa fees for nonimmigrants. Exchange of notes at Luxembourg April 25 and May 22 and 26, 1936; entered into force May 26, 1936; operative June 15, 1936.
9 Bevans 710.

MADAGASCAR

By a note dated December 4, 1962, the Minister of Foreign Affairs of the Malagasy Republic informed the American Ambassador of the following (translation): ''No official act specifies, in the agreements with the French Republic, the juridical position of the Malagasy Republic with regard to the rights and obligations contracted for Madagascar in the treaties, agreements, and conventions signed by France prior to Madagascar's accession to international sovereignty. In accordance with usage, the Malagasy Republic considers itself implicitly bound by such texts unless it explicitly denounces them. The Ministry of Foreign Affairs informs the Embassy of the United States of America that, in order to avoid any ambiguity, the Malagasy Republic transmits, as soon as it is in a position to reach an affirmative decision on each of the texts in question, a formal declaration in which it declares itself bound by the Treaty, the Agreement or the Convention under consideration.''

AGRICULTURAL COMMODITIES

Agricultural commodities agreement, with minutes of negotiation. Signed at Antananarivo August 19, 1981; entered into force August 19, 1981.
33 UST 3139; TIAS 10218.

Related agreements:
August 12, 1982 (TIAS 10479).
December 28, 1982 (TIAS 10627; 1581 UNTS 97).
July 13, 1983 (TIAS 10744).
March 7, 1984 (TIAS 11046).
December 12, 1984 (TIAS 11046).

MADAGASCAR (Cont'd)

Agricultural commodities agreement. Signed at Antananarivo September 27, 1985; entered into force September 27, 1985.
NP

Amendments:
October 28 and November 7, 1985 (NP).
July 2 and August 8, 1986 (NP).

Related agreements:
June 10, 1987 (NP).
October 23 and 30, 1987 (NP).

Agricultural commodities agreement under food for progress, with attachments. Signed at Antananarivo August 13, 1986; entered into force August 13, 1986.
NP

AVIATION

Air transport services agreement between the United States and France. Signed at Paris March 27, 1946; entered into force March 27, 1946.
61 Stat. 3445; TIAS 1679; 7 Bevans 1109; 139 UNTS 114.

Extensions and amendments:
June 23 and July 11, 1950 (1 UST 593; TIAS 2106; 139 UNTS 142).
March 19, 1951 (2 UST 1033; TIAS 2257; 139 UNTS 151).
March 19, 1951 (2 UST 1037; TIAS 2258; 139 UNTS 146).
August 27, 1959 (10 UST 1791; TIAS 4336; 358 UNTS 277).

COMMERCE

Convention of navigation and commerce between the United States and France, with separate article.[1] Signed at Washington June 24, 1822; extended to Madagascar in 1896.
8 Stat. 278; TS 87; 7 Bevans 822.

Agreement modifying the provisions of article VII of the convention of navigation and commerce of June 24, 1822. Signed at Washington July 17, 1919; entered into force January 10, 1921.
41 Stat. 1723; TS 650; 7 Bevans 899.

NOTE:
[1] Article VI abrogated by the United States July 1, 1916 in accordance with the Seamen's Act (38 Stat. 1164).

COPYRIGHT (See APPENDIX)

DEFENSE

Agreement concerning the provision of training related to defense articles under the United States International Military Education and Training (IMET) Program. Exchange of notes at Antananarivo February 25, 1983 and May 3, 1984; entered into force May 3, 1984.
TIAS 10982.

Agreement relating to the status of United States military and civilian personnel of the United States Department of Defense temporarily present in Madagascar in connection with humanitarian relief operations. Exchange of notes at Antananarivo March 11 and 13, 2000; entered into force March 13, 2000.
NP

ECONOMIC AND TECHNICAL COOPERATION

Agreement providing for the furnishing of economic, technical and related assistance. Exchange of notes at Tananarive June 22, 1961; entered into force June 22, 1961.
12 UST 1049; TIAS 4808; 413 UNTS 219.

Agency for International Development:
July 25, 1973 (24 UST 2159; TIAS 7731; 938 UNTS 257).

FINANCE

Agreement regarding the consolidation and rescheduling of certain debts owed to, guaranteed by or insured by the United States Government, with annexes. Signed at Washington September 28, 1984; entered into force November 19, 1984.
TIAS 10998.

Agreement regarding the consolidation and rescheduling of certain debts owed to, guaranteed by or insured by the United States Government and its agencies, with annex. Signed at Antananarivo October 8, 1985; entered into force November 12, 1985.
NP

Agreement regarding the consolidation and rescheduling of certain debts owed to, guaranteed by or insured by the United States Government and its agencies, with annexes. Signed at Antananarivo May 7, 1987; entered into force June 15, 1987.
NP

Agreement regarding the consolidation and rescheduling of certain debts owed to, guaranteed by, or insured by the United States Government and its agencies, with annexes. Signed at Antananarivo August 9, 1989; entered into force September 14, 1989.
NP

Amendment:
March 23 and May 2, 1990 (NP).

Agreement regarding the consolidation and rescheduling of certain debts owed to, guaranteed by, or insured by the United States Government and its agencies, with annexes. Signed at Antananarivo June 19, 1991; entered into force August 9, 1991.
NP

Agreement regarding the consolidation, reduction and rescheduling of certain debts owed to, guaranteed by, or insured by the United States Government and its Agency, with annexes. Signed at Washington December 16, 1997; entered into force March 4, 1998.
NP

Investment incentive agreement. Signed at Washington March 31, 1998; entered into force February 7, 2000.
TIAS

PEACE CORPS

Agreement relating to the establishment of a Peace Corps program in Madagascar. Exchange of notes at Antananarivo June 11, 1992; entered into force June 11, 1992.
TIAS 12107.

POSTAL MATTERS

International express mail agreement, with detailed regulations. Signed at Antananarivo and Washington April 28 and May 26, 1988; entered into force July 15, 1988.
TIAS 11597.

VISAS

Reciprocal agreement between the United States and France relating to visa fees for nonimmigrants. Exchanges of notes at Washington August 19 and September 4, 5, and 16, 1947; entered into force September 16, 1947; operative October 1, 1947.
61 Stat. 3776; TIAS 1721; 7 Bevans 1210; 84 UNTS 19.

MALAWI

AGRICULTURAL COMMODITIES

Agricultural commodities agreement, with agreed minutes. Signed at Blantyre December 30, 1980; entered into force December 30, 1980.
33 UST 1571; TIAS 10134; 1529 UNTS 317.

MALAWI (Cont'd)

Amendment:
May 22, 1981 (33 UST 1599; TIAS 10134; 1529 UNTS 331).

COPYRIGHT (See APPENDIX)

DEFENSE

Agreement concerning the provision of training related to defense articles under the United States International Military Education and Training (IMET) Program. Exchange of notes at Lilongwe March 20 and May 1, 1980; entered into force May 1, 1980.
32 UST 965; TIAS 9744; 1222 UNTS 331.

Agreement regarding grants under the Foreign Assistance Act of 1961, as amended, and the furnishing of defense articles, related training and other defense services from the United States to Malawi. Exchange of notes at Lilongwe May 28 and July 24, 1992; entered into force July 24, 1992.
TIAS 12525.

Agreement regarding the provision of commodities, services and associated military education and training to assist the Republic of Malawi's forces participating in the African Crisis Response Initiative. Exchange of notes at Lilongwe July 28 and August 27, 1997; entered into force August 27, 1997.
TIAS

ECONOMIC AND TECHNICAL COOPERATION

Agency for International Development:
April 29, 1976 (29 UST 5245; TIAS 9099).

EMPLOYMENT

Agreement concerning the employment of dependents of official government employees. Exchange of notes at Washington October 29, 1998 and April 16, 1999; entered into force April 16, 1999.
TIAS

EXTRADITION

Extradition treaty between the United States and the United Kingdom. Signed at London December 22, 1931; applicable to Nyasaland June 24, 1935.
47 Stat. 2122; TS 849; 12 Bevans 482; 163 LNTS 59.

Agreement continuing in force between the United States and Malawi the extradition treaty and the double taxation convention [1] between the United States and the United Kingdom. Exchange of notes at Zomba and Blantyre December 17, 1966, January 6 and April 4, 1967; entered into force April 4, 1967.
18 UST 1822; TIAS 6328; 692 UNTS 191.

NOTE:
[1] Notification of termination of the 1945 taxation convention as applicable to Malawi given by the United States June 28, 1983, effective January 1, 1984.

FINANCE

Agreement relating to investment guaranties. Exchange of notes at Blantyre May 1 and July 21, 1967; entered into force July 21, 1967.
18 UST 2335; TIAS 6334; 693 UNTS 3.

Agreement regarding the consolidation and rescheduling of certain debts owed to, guaranteed or insured by the United States Government and its agencies, with annexes. Signed at Lilongwe March 10, 1983; entered into force May 16, 1983.
TIAS 10684.

Agreement regarding the consolidation and rescheduling of certain debts owed to, guaranteed or insured by the United States Government and its agencies with annexes and implementing agreement regarding repayments due under A.I.D. loans, with annexes. Signed at Lilongwe April 30, 1984; entered into force June 11, 1984.
TIAS 10993.

Agreement regarding the consolidation and rescheduling of certain debts owed to, guaranteed by or insured by the United States Government and its agencies, with annexes. Signed at Lilongwe February 21, 1989; entered into force April 6, 1989.
NP

PEACE CORPS

Agreement relating to the establishment of a Peace Corps program in Malawi. Exchange of notes at Blantyre and Zomba September 14, 1971; entered into force September 14, 1971.
22 UST 1633; TIAS 7191.

POSTAL MATTERS

International express mail agreement, with detailed regulations. Signed at Lilongwe and Washington April 26 and June 21, 1988; entered into force July 15, 1988.
TIAS 11582.

MALAYSIA

On August 31, 1957 the Federation of Malaya attained fully responsible status within the British Commonwealth (Federation of Malaya Independence Act, 1957). By an exchange of notes dated September 12, 1957 between the United Kingdom and the Federation of Malaya there were formally transferred to the Federation, as of August 31, 1957, the rights and obligations of treaties and agreements entered into between the United Kingdom and any other government in so far as such instruments may be held to have application to or in respect of the Federation of Malaya. The British Colonies of North Borneo and Sarawak and the State of Singapore were federated with the existing States of the Federation of Malaya under the provisions of a general agreement between them and the United Kingdom, signed at London July 9, 1963. On September 16, 1963 the Federation of Malaya changed its name to Malaysia. The Constitution of the Federation of Malaya was amended by the Malaysia Act of 1963 to provide for the Government of Malaysia's assumption of rights and obligations of treaties and agreements entered into between the United Kingdom and any other government on behalf of the Borneo States and Singapore. On August 9, 1965 Singapore became an independent and sovereign state.

AVIATION

Arrangement between the United States and the United Kingdom relating to pilot licenses to operate civil aircraft. Exchange of notes at Washington March 28 and April 5, 1935; entered into force May 5, 1935.
49 Stat. 3731; EAS 77; 12 Bevans 513; 162 LNTS 59.

Agreement concerning assistance in developing and modernizing Malaysia's civil aviation infrastructure. Signed at Washington and Kuala Lumpur July 22 and August 6, 1994; entered into force August 6, 1994.
TIAS

Agreement for promotion of aviation safety. Signed at Kuala Lumpur May 28, 1996; entered into force May 28, 1996.
TIAS

Air transport agreement, with annexes. Signed at San Francisco June 21, 1997; entered into force June 21, 1997.
TIAS

CONSULS

Consular convention and protocol of signature between the United States and the United Kingdom. Signed at Washington June 6, 1951; entered into force September 7, 1952.
3 UST 3426; TIAS 2494; 165 UNTS 121.

MALAYSIA (Cont'd)

COPYRIGHT (See APPENDIX)

DEFENSE

Agreement relating to the purchase by Malaya of military equipment, materials, and services from the United States. Exchange of notes at Washington June 30 and July 9, 1958; entered into force July 9, 1958.
9 UST 1235; TIAS 4108; 336 UNTS 79.

Agreement relating to the deposit by Malaysia of ten percent of the value of grant military assistance furnished by the United States. Exchange of notes at Kuala Lumpur March 8 and April 4, 1972; entered into force April 4, 1972; effective February 7, 1972.
23 UST 294; TIAS 7309.

Agreement relating to eligibility for United States military assistance and training pursuant to the International Security Assistance and Arms Export Control Act of 1976. Exchange of notes at Kuala Lumpur February 11 and March 14, 1977; entered into force March 14, 1977.
29 UST 663; TIAS 8845.

Agreement concerning a military education exchange program. Exchange of letters at Washington and Kuala Lumpur May 16 and 29, 1991; entered into force May 29, 1991.
NP

Acquisition and cross-servicing agreement, with annexes. Signed at Kuala Lumpur March 18, 1994; entered into force March 18, 1994.
TIAS 12349.

ECONOMIC AND TECHNICAL COOPERATION

Economic cooperation agreement between the United States and the United Kingdom. Signed at London July 6, 1948; applicable to the Federation of Malaya July 20, 1948.
62 Stat. 2596; TIAS 1795; 12 Bevans 874; 22 UNTS 263.

Amendments:
January 3, 1950 (1 UST 184; TIAS 2036; 86 UNTS 304).
May 25, 1951 (2 UST 1292; TIAS 2277; 99 UNTS 308).
February 25, 1953 (4 UST 1528; TIAS 2815; 172 UNTS 332).

EDUCATION

Agreement concerning the establishment of the Malaysian-American Commission on Educational Exchange. Signed at Kuala Lumpur

August 3, 1995; entered into force August 3, 1995.
TIAS 12681.

EXTRADITION

Extradition treaty, with exchange of notes. Signed at Kuala Lumpur August 3, 1995; entered into force June 2, 1997.
TIAS

FINANCE

Agreement relating to investment guaranties under section 413(b)(4) of the Mutual Security Act of 1954, as amended. Exchange of notes at Kuala Lumpur April 21, 1959; entered into force April 21, 1959.
10 UST 776; TIAS 4214; 343 UNTS 3.

Amendment:
June 24, 1965 (16 UST 1086; TIAS 5850; 564 UNTS 230).

NARCOTIC DRUGS

Agreement relating to a cooperative program to combat the spread of heroin addiction and other forms of drug abuse in Malaysia. Exchange of notes at Kuala Lumpur November 16 and December 8, 1978; entered into force December 8, 1978.
30 UST 7183; TIAS 9577; 1182 UNTS 101.

Amendment:
April 9 and May 18, 1979 (30 UST 7192; TIAS 9577; 1182 UNTS 105).

Memorandum of understanding for reducing demand, preventing illicit use and combatting illicit production and traffic of drugs, including precursor chemicals. Signed at Kuala Lumpur April 20, 1989; entered into force April 20, 1989.
TIAS 12399.

PEACE CORPS

Agreement relating to the establishment of a Peace Corps program in the Federation of Malaya. Exchange of notes at Kuala Lumpur September 4, 1961; entered into force September 4, 1961.
12 UST 1236; TIAS 4843; 421 UNTS 215.

Agreement between the United States and the United Kingdom relating to the establishment of a Peace Corps program in North Borneo. Exchange of notes at London October 25, 1962; entered into force October 25, 1962.
13 UST 2389; TIAS 5201; 457 UNTS 137.

Agreement between the United States and the United Kingdom relating to the establishment of a Peace Corps program in Sarawak. Ex-

change of notes at London October 25, 1962; entered into force October 25, 1962.
13 UST 2394; TIAS 5202; 457 UNTS 129.

POLLUTION

Agreement concerning the transboundary movement of hazardous wastes from Malaysia to the United States. Signed at Kuala Lumpur March 10, 1995; entered into force March 10, 1995.
TIAS 12612.

POSTAL MATTERS

Parcel post convention. Signed at Kuala Lumpur January 21 and at Washington March 22, 1935; entered into force April 1, 1935.
49 Stat. 3133; Post Office Department print; 161 LNTS 41.

International express mail agreement, with detailed regulations. Signed at Washington and Kuala Lumpur February 14 and March 14, 1983; entered into force June 1, 1983.
TIAS 10671.

Postal money order agreement. Signed at Washington and Kuala Lumpur June 20 and July 7, 1995; entered into force August 1, 1995.
NP

PROPERTY

Convention between the United States and the United Kingdom relating to tenure and disposition of real and personal property.[1] Signed at Washington March 2, 1899.
31 Stat. 1939; TS 146; 12 Bevans 246.

NOTE:
[1] Notification given on February 9, 1901 of application to the Straits Settlements.

TAXATION

Agreement concerning reciprocal exemption with respect to taxes on income of shipping and air transport enterprises. Signed at Kuala Lumpur April 18, 1989; entered into force March 12, 1990.
TIAS 11618.

TRADE AND COMMERCE

Agreement relating to trade in cotton, wool and man-made fiber textiles and textile products, with annexes. Exchange of notes at Kuala Lumpur July 1 and 11, 1985; entered into force July 11, 1985.
NP

MALAYSIA (Cont'd)

Amendments and extension:
September 9 and 15, 1987 (NP).
March 29 and April 19, 1988 (NP).
November 10 and 21, 1988 (NP).
February 6 and May 20, 1992 (NP).

TRADE-MARKS

Declaration by the United States and the United Kingdom relating to reciprocal protection to trade-marks. Signed at London October 24, 1877; entered into force October 24, 1877.
20 Stat. 703; TS 138; 12 Bevans 198.

VISAS

Agreement between the United States and the United Kingdom relating to visas. Exchange of notes at London October 15 and 22, 1954.

Agreement continuing in force the 1954 agreement with respect to the Federation of Malaya. Exchange of letters at Kuala Lumpur March 5 and 12, 1958.

MALDIVES

AGRICULTURAL COMMODITIES

Agricultural commodities agreement. Signed at Colombo July 13, 1985; entered into force July 13, 1985.
NP

Amendment:
August 25, 1986 (NP).

Agricultural commodities agreement. Signed at Male August 18, 1987; entered into force August 18, 1987.
NP

AVIATION

Memorandum of agreement concerning assistance in developing and modernizing Maldives's civil aviation infrastructure, with annex. Signed at Washington and Male February 12 and 17, 1997; entered into force February 17, 1997.
TIAS

COPYRIGHT (See APPENDIX)

DEFENSE

Agreement concerning the provision of training related to defense articles under the United States International Military Education and Training (IMET) Program. Exchange of notes and telex at Colombo and Male March 4 and April 9, 1983; entered into force April 9, 1983.
TIAS 10851.

POSTAL MATTERS

International express mail agreement, with detailed regulations. Signed at Male and Washington October 20 and November 8, 1990; entered into force December 5, 1990.
TIAS 11766.

TRADE AND COMMERCE

Arrangement relating to a visa system for exports of cotton, wool and man-made fiber apparel products from the Republic of Maldives. Exchange of letters at Colombo and Male December 29, 1981 and March 22, 1982; entered into force March 22, 1982; effective October 1, 1982.
TIAS 10442.

Agreement relating to trade in wool sweaters, with annex. Exchange of notes at Colombo and Male September 7 and 19, 1984; entered into force September 19, 1984; effective September 29, 1982.
NP

Amendments and extension:
January 6 and 14, 1986 (NP).
July 16 and October 13, 1986 (NP).
December 18, 1987 and February 17, 1988 (NP).

MALI

AGRICULTURAL COMMODITIES

Agricultural commodities agreement, with exchange of notes. Signed at Washington July 14, 1965; entered into force July 14, 1965.
16 UST 1099; TIAS 5852; 564 UNTS 101.

Amendment:
December 8 and 15, 1965 (16 UST 1765; TIAS 5906).

AVIATION

Civil aviation security agreement. Signed at Bamako June 25, 1993; entered into force June 25, 1993.
TIAS 12155.

COPYRIGHT (See APPENDIX)

CULTURAL PROPERTY

Agreement concerning the imposition of import restrictions on archaeological material from the region of the Niger River Valley and the Bandiagara Escarpment (Cliff), with appendix. Signed at Washington September 19, 1997; entered into force September 19, 1997.
TIAS

DEFENSE

Military assistance agreement. Exchange of notes at Bamako May 20, 1961; entered into force May 20, 1961.
12 UST 1030; TIAS 4805; 413 UNTS 205.

Understanding regarding delivery of two C-47 aircraft and related articles and services. Exchange of notes at Bamako January 5, 1967; entered into force January 5, 1967.
18 UST 338; TIAS 6238.

Agreement relating to the deposit by Mali of ten percent of the value of grant military assistance and excess defense articles furnished by the United States. Exchange of notes at Bamako April 18 and June 6, 1972; entered into force June 6, 1972; effective February 7, 1972.
23 UST 1106; TIAS 7368.

Agreement concerning the provision of training related to defense articles under the United States International Military Education and Training (IMET) Program. Exchange of notes at Bamako November 4, 1983 and March 23, 1984; entered into force March 23, 1984.
NP

Agreement regarding the status of U.S. military personnel and civilian employees of the Department of Defense who may be temporarily present in Mali in connection with the African Crisis Response Initiative. Exchange of notes at Bamako July 30 and September 30, 1997; entered into force September 30, 1997.
NP

ECONOMIC AND TECHNICAL COOPERATION

Agreement providing for the furnishing of economic, technical and related assistance. Ex-

MALI (Cont'd)

change of notes at Bamako January 4, 1961; entered into force January 4, 1961.
12 UST 1; TIAS 4668; 405 UNTS 165.

Agency for International Development:
January 28, 1974 (28 UST 1; TIAS 8461; 1066 UNTS 172).
January 28, 1975 (28 UST 17; TIAS 8461; 1066 UNTS 181).
November 6, 1974 and May 7, 1975 (29 UST 5746; TIAS 9147).
May 29, 1975 (29 UST 5749; TIAS 9147).
June 30, 1975 (28 UST 19; TIAS 8461; 1066 UNTS 182).
August 22, 1975 (28 UST 21; TIAS 8461; 1066 UNTS 183).
January 11 and February 2, 1977 (29 UST 5751; TIAS 9147).
May 13, 1977 (29 UST 2305; TIAS 8940).
May 13, 1977 (29 UST 5129; TIAS 9093).

EMPLOYMENT

Agreement relating to the employment of dependents of official government employees. Exchange of notes at Washington March 6 and June 20, 1995; entered into force June 20, 1995.
TIAS 12668.

ENVIRONMENTAL COOPERATION

Agreement for cooperation in the Global Learning and Observations to Benefit the Environment (GLOBE) Program, with appendices. Signed at Washington November 19, 1997; entered into force November 19, 1997.
TIAS

FINANCE

Agreement relating to investment guaranties. Exchange of notes at Bamako June 4 and 9, 1964; entered into force June 9, 1964.
15 UST 1533; TIAS 5636; 530 UNTS 133.

Agreement regarding the consolidation and rescheduling of certain debts owed to, guaranteed by, or insured by the United States Government and its agencies, with annexes. Signed at Bamako June 3, 1989; entered into force July 21, 1989.
NP

GEODETIC SURVEY

Geodetic survey agreement. Signed at Bamako January 17, 1968; entered into force January 17, 1968.
19 UST 4568; TIAS 6446; 697 UNTS 231.

PEACE CORPS

Agreement relating to the establishment of a Peace Corps program in Mali. Exchange of notes at Bamako December 23, 1969 and April 17, 1971; entered into force April 17, 1971.
26 UST 2611; TIAS 8178; 1027 UNTS 121.

POSTAL MATTERS

International express mail agreement, with detailed regulations. Signed at Bamako and Washington April 2 and 16, 1987; entered into force June 1, 1987.
TIAS 11304.

Postal money order agreement. Signed at Bamako and Washington February 10 and April 7, 1994; entered into force May 1, 1994.
NP

SCIENTIFIC COOPERATION

Memorandum of understanding concerning scientific and technical cooperation in the earth sciences, with annexes. Signed at Bamako April 23, 1996; entered into force April 23, 1996.
TIAS

SOCIAL SECURITY

Agreement to provide social security benefits for certain employees of the United States in Mali. Signed at Bamako December 2, 1969; entered into force January 1, 1970.
21 UST 2145; TIAS 6961; 764 UNTS 151.

MALTA

On September 21, 1964 Malta attained fully responsible status within the British Commonwealth (Malta Independence Act, 1964). By an exchange of letters dated December 31, 1964 between the Government of the United Kingdom and the Government of Malta, it was agreed that all obligations and responsibilities of the Government of the United Kingdom which arise from any valid international instrument shall, as from September 21, 1964, be assumed by the Government of Malta insofar as such instruments may be held to have application to Malta. Also, rights and benefits heretofore enjoyed by the Government of the United Kingdom in virtue of the application of any such international instrument to Malta shall, as from September 21, 1964, be enjoyed by the Government of Malta.

AVIATION

Arrangement between the United States and the United Kingdom relating to pilot licenses to operate civil aircraft. Exchange of notes at Washington March 28 and April 5, 1935; applicable to Malta May 5, 1935.
49 Stat. 3731; EAS 77; 12 Bevans 513; 162 LNTS 59.

Air transport agreement, with annexes. Signed at Washington October 12, 2000; entered into force October 12, 2000.
TIAS

COMMERCE

Convention to regulate the commerce between the United States and the United Kingdom.[1] Signed at London July 3, 1815; entered into force July 3, 1815.
8 Stat. 228; TS 110; 12 Bevans 49.

Convention continuing in force indefinitely the convention of July 3, 1815 between the United States and the United Kingdom. Signed at London August 6, 1827; entered into force April 2, 1828.
8 Stat. 361; TS 117; 12 Bevans 76.

NOTE:
[1] Article IV superseded from September 7, 1952 by consular convention of June 6, 1951 (3 UST 3426; TIAS 2494).

CONSULS

Consular convention between the United States and the United Kingdom. Signed at Washington June 6, 1951; entered into force September 7, 1952.
3 UST 3426; TIAS 2494; 165 UNTS 121.

COPYRIGHT (See APPENDIX)

DEFENSE

Agreement concerning the provision of training related to defense articles under the United States International Military Education and Training (IMET) Program. Exchange of notes at Floriana February 6 and 13, 1989; entered into force February 13, 1989.
NP

ECONOMIC AND TECHNICAL COOPERATION

Economic cooperation agreement between the United States and the United Kingdom. Signed at London July 6, 1948; applicable to Malta July 6, 1948.
62 Stat. 2596; TIAS 1795; 12 Bevans 874; 22 UNTS 263.

MALTA (Cont'd)

Amendments:
January 3, 1950 (1 UST 184; TIAS 2036; 86 UNTS 304).
May 25, 1951 (2 UST 1292; TIAS 2277; 99 UNTS 308).
February 25, 1953 (4 UST 1528; TIAS 2815; 172 UNTS 332).

Agency for International Development:
June 15, 1973 (24 UST 1914; TIAS 7699).

EDUCATION

Memorandum of understanding on the Fulbright Exchange Program. Signed at Valletta May 29, 1997; entered into force May 29, 1997.
TIAS

EMPLOYMENT

Agreement relating to employment of dependents of official government employees. Exchange of notes at Floriana September 25 and October 3, 1991; entered into force October 3, 1991.
TIAS 11795.

EXTRADITION

Extradition treaty between the United States and the United Kingdom. Signed at London December 22, 1931; applicable to Malta June 24, 1935.
47 Stat. 2122; TS 849; 12 Bevans 482; 163 UNTS 59.

FINANCE

Agreement relating to investment guaranties. Signed at Washington November 16, 1966; entered into force January 26, 1967.
18 UST 106; TIAS 6205; 688 UNTS 45.

PEACE CORPS

Agreement relating to the establishment of a Peace Corps program in Malta. Exchange of notes at Valletta April 29 and June 24, 1970; entered into force June 24, 1970.
21 UST 1486; TIAS 6907; 753 UNTS 281.

POSTAL MATTERS

International express mail agreement. Signed at Valletta August 20 and October 29, 1991; entered into force December 2, 1991.
TIAS 11789.

PROPERTY

Convention between the United States and the United Kingdom relating to the tenure and disposition of real and personal property. Signed at Washington March 2, 1899; applicable to Malta May 29, 1947.
31 Stat. 1939; TS 146; 12 Bevans 246.

Supplementary convention between the United States and the United Kingdom relating to the tenure and disposition of real and personal property. Signed at Washington May 27, 1936; applicable to Malta May 29, 1947.
55 Stat. 1101; TS 964; 5 Bevans 140; 203 LNTS 367.

TAXATION

Agreement on reciprocal exemption from taxes on earnings derived from the operation of ships and aircraft. Exchange of notes at Washington December 26, 1996 and March 11, 1997; entered into force March 11, 1997.
TIAS

TRADE (See also COMMERCE)

Agreement providing for consultations on problems of market disruption caused by cotton textile or cotton textile product exports from Malta. Exchange of notes at Floriana and Valletta September 17 and 22, 1975; entered into force September 22, 1975.
26 UST 2747; TIAS 8192; 1045 UNTS 107.

TRADE-MARKS

Declaration by the United States and the United Kingdom affording reciprocal protection to trade-marks. Signed at London October 24, 1877; entered into force October 24, 1877.
20 Stat. 703; TS 138; 12 Bevans 198.

VISAS

Arrangement between the United States and the United Kingdom providing for waiver of the visa requirement for United States citizens visiting Malta and for waiver of visa fees for British subjects residents of Malta visiting the United States. Exchange of notes at Washington October 31 and December 12, 1949; entered into force December 12, 1949; operative December 1, 1949.
64 Stat. B137; TIAS 2069; 12 Bevans 950; 92 UNTS 191.

MARSHALL ISLANDS

Agreement for the implementation of the Compact of Free Association between the Government of the United States and the Government of the Republic of the Marshall Islands (Title II, PL 99-239), with related agreements. Signed at Majuro October 10, 1986; entered into force October 15, 1986; effective October 21, 1986.
TIAS

Amendments:
October 20, 1986.
March 18, 1988 (TIAS 11661).

AVIATION

Memorandum of agreement concerning assistance in developing and modernizing the Marshall Island's civil aviation system. Signed at Washington and Majuro May 23 and June 15, 1989; entered into force June 15, 1989.
TIAS 11665.

DEFENSE

Agreement regarding the provision of services of a military civic action team to the Marshall Islands. Signed at Honolulu July 26, 1988; entered into force October 24, 1988.
TIAS 11657.

Supplementary agreement regarding the military use and operating rights of the Government of the United States in the Marshall Islands, with annex and agreed minute. Signed at Majuro June 12, 1989; entered into force July 1, 1989.
TIAS 11671.

EDUCATION

Agreement regarding augmentation of educational assistance. Signed at Washington September 7, 1988; entered into force September 7, 1988.
TIAS 11639.

ENVIRONMENTAL COOPERATION

Agreement for cooperation in the Global Learning and Observations to Benefit the Environment (GLOBE) Program, with appendices. Signed at Majuro October 17, 1996; entered into force October 17, 1996.
TIAS

MARSHALL ISLANDS (Cont'd)

FINANCE

Investment incentive agreement. Exchange of notes at Majuro January 20, 1988 and January 25, 1989; entered into force January 25, 1989.
TIAS 12092.

RELATIONS

Agreement relating to diplomatic relations, with related notes. Exchange of notes at Washington August 23 and September 6, 1989; entered into force September 6, 1989.
TIAS 11890.

TAXATION

Agreement concerning the reciprocal exemption from income tax of income derived from the international operation of ships and aircraft. Exchange of notes at Majuro December 5, 1989; entered into force December 5, 1989.
TIAS 11728.

Agreement for the exchange of information with respect to taxes, with attachment and exchange of notes. Signed at Majuro March 14, 1991; entered into force March 14, 1991.
TIAS 11830.

TELECOMMUNICATION

Agreement relating to radio communications between amateur radio stations on behalf of third parties. Exchange of notes at Majuro October 8 and 15, 1991; entered into force November 14, 1991.
TIAS 12439.

Agreement relating to the reciprocal granting of authorizations to permit licensed amateur radio operators of either country to operate their stations in the other country. Exchange of notes at Majuro October 15 and 18, 1993; entered into force October 18, 1993.
TIAS 12512.

MAURITANIA

AGRICULTURAL COMMODITIES

Agreement relating to the transfer of agricultural commodities to Mauritania to assist in alleviating the shortage caused by prolonged drought. Signed at Nouakchott May 28, 1976; entered into force May 28, 1976.
29 UST 5775; TIAS 9153; 1146 UNTS 227.

Agreement for the transfer of food grain (sorghum). Signed at Nouakchott April 18, 1978; entered into force April 18, 1978.
30 UST 3067; TIAS 9379; 1178 UNTS 269.

Amendment:
April 18, 1978 (30 UST 3073; TIAS 9379; 1178 UNTS 273).

COPYRIGHT (See APPENDIX)

DEFENSE

Agreement concerning the provision of training related to defense articles under the United States International Military Education and Training (IMET) Program. Exchange of notes at Nouakchott May 21, 1982 and August 26, 1984; entered into force August 26, 1984.
TIAS 10987.

ECONOMIC AND TECHNICAL COOPERATION

General agreement for special development assistance. Signed at Nouakchott March 23, 1971; entered into force March 23, 1971.
22 UST 667; TIAS 7121; 792 UNTS 205.

Agency for International Development:
February 26, 1974 (26 UST 3894; TIAS 8224; 1045 UNTS 3).

FINANCE

Agreement relating to investment guaranties. Exchange of notes at Nouakchott May 4 and July 3, 1964; entered into force July 3, 1964.
15 UST 2385; TIAS 5727; 532 UNTS 307.

Agreement regarding the consolidation and rescheduling of certain debts owed to, guaranteed by or insured by the United States Government and its agencies, with annex. Signed at Washington August 14, 1985; entered into force September 23, 1985.
NP

Agreement regarding the consolidation and rescheduling of certain debts owed to, guaranteed by, or insured by the United States Government and its agency, with annexes. Signed at Nouakchott February 4, 1990; entered into force March 12, 1990.
NP

Agreement regarding the consolidation and rescheduling of certain debts owed to, guaranteed by or insured by the United States Government and its agencies, with annexes. Signed at Washington July 29, 1993; entered into force September 13, 1993.
NP

PEACE CORPS

Agreement relating to the establishment of a Peace Corps program in Mauritania. Exchange of notes at Nouakchott September 19 and October 17, 1966; entered into force October 17, 1966.
17 UST 2046; TIAS 6143; 676 UNTS 3.

POSTAL MATTERS

International express mail agreement, with detailed regulations. Signed at Nouakchott and Washington June 28 and July 17, 1992; entered into force September 21, 1992.
TIAS 11872.

SCIENTIFIC COOPERATION

Agreement for scientific and technical cooperation in the earth sciences. Signed at Reston and Nouakchott September 9, 1986 and January 11, 1987; entered into force January 11, 1987.
TIAS 11284.

MAURITIUS

On March 12, 1968 Mauritius became an independent state. In a note dated March 12, 1968 to the Secretary-General of the United Nations, the Prime Minister and Minister of External Affairs made a statement reading in part as follows:

"I have the honour to inform you that the Government of Mauritius, conscious of the desirability of maintaining existing legal relationships, and conscious of its obligation under international law to honour its treaty commitments, acknowledges that many treaty rights and obligations of the Government of the United Kingdom in respect of Mauritius were succeeded to by Mauritius upon independence by virtue of customary international law.

"Since, however, it is likely that by virtue of customary international law certain treaties may have lapsed at the date of independence of Mauritius, it seems essential that each treaty should be subjected to legal examination. It is proposed after this examination has been completed, to indicate which, if any, of the treaties which may have lapsed by customary international law the Government of Mauritius wish to treat as having lapsed.

"It is desired that it be presumed that each treaty has been legally succeeded to by Mauritius and that action be based upon this presumption until a decision is reached that it should be regarded as having lapsed. Should the Government of Mauritius be of the opinion that they have legally succeeded to a treaty but subsequently wish to terminate its operation, they will in due course give notice of termination in the terms thereof."

MAURITIUS (Cont'd)

AGRICULTURAL COMMODITIES

Agricultural commodities agreement, with agreed minutes. Signed at Port Louis June 29, 1979; entered into force June 29, 1979.
30 UST 6079; TIAS 9541; 1180 UNTS 421.

Related agreements:
July 11, 1980 (32 UST 1927; TIAS 9811; 1234 UNTS 411).
May 27, 1981 (33 UST 3249; TIAS 10221).
June 25, 1981 (TIAS 10477).
April 8, 1982 (34 UST 471; TIAS 10372).
December 30, 1982 (TIAS 10628; 1581 UNTS 109).
March 29 and July 4, 1984 (TIAS 11041).

AVIATION

Agreement between the United States and the United Kingdom relating to air services. Signed at Bermuda February 11, 1946; entered into force February 11, 1946.
60 Stat. 1499; TIAS 1507; 12 Bevans 726; 3 UNTS 253.

Amendment:
May 27, 1966 (17 UST 683; TIAS 6019).

Agreement relating to the installation, operation and use of distance measuring equipment at Plaisance Airfield. Exchange of notes at Port Louis November 4 and December 29, 1969; entered into force December 29, 1969.
21 UST 434; TIAS 6829; 740 UNTS 135.

CONSULS

Consular convention between the United States and the United Kingdom. Signed at Washington June 6, 1951; entered into force September 7, 1952.
3 UST 3426; TIAS 2494; 165 UNTS 121.

COPYRIGHT (See APPENDIX)

DEFENSE

Agreement regarding the status of U.S. military personnel and civilian employees of the Department of Defense who may be temporarily present in Mauritius in connection with their official duties. Exchange of notes at Port Louis April 10 and May 7 and 8, 1998; entered into force May 8, 1998.
NP

ECONOMIC AND TECHNICAL COOPERATION

Economic cooperation agreement between the United States and the United Kingdom. Signed at London July 6, 1948; applicable to Mauritius July 6, 1948.
62 Stat. 2596; TIAS 1795; 12 Bevans 874; 22 UNTS 263.

Amendments:
January 3, 1950 (1 UST 184; TIAS 2036; 86 UNTS 304).
May 25, 1951 (2 UST 1292; TIAS 2277; 99 UNTS 308).
February 25, 1953 (4 UST 1528; TIAS 2815; 172 UNTS 332).

EMPLOYMENT

Agreement relating to the employment of dependents of official government employees. Exchange of notes at Port Louis March 17 and June 13, 1997; entered into force June 13, 1997.
TIAS

EXTRADITION

Extradition treaty between the United States and the United Kingdom. Signed at London December 22, 1931; entered into force June 24, 1935.
47 Stat. 2122; TS 849; 12 Bevans 482; 163 LNTS 59.

FINANCE

Investment incentive agreement. Signed at Port Louis December 15, 1997; entered into force May 26, 1998.
TIAS

PEACE CORPS

Agreement relating to the establishment of a Peace Corps program in Mauritius. Exchange of notes at Port Louis March 18, 1971; entered into force March 18, 1971.
22 UST 453; TIAS 7080; 792 UNTS 197.

POSTAL MATTERS

International express mail agreement. Signed at Port Louis and Washington September 9 and October 2, 1992; entered into force December 14, 1992.
TIAS 11909.

PROPERTY

Convention between the United States and the United Kingdom relating to the tenure and disposition of real and personal property. Signed at Washington March 2, 1899; applicable to Mauritius June 10, 1901.
31 Stat. 1939; TS 146; 12 Bevans 246.

Supplementary convention relating to the tenure and disposition of real and personal property of March 2, 1899. Signed at Washington May 27, 1936; entered into force March 10, 1941.
55 Stat. 1101; TS 964; 5 Bevans 140; 203 LNTS 367.

TRADE AND COMMERCE

Agreement concerning trade in cotton, wool and man-made fiber textiles and apparel, with annex. Exchange of notes at Port Louis June 3 and 4, 1985; entered into force June 4, 1985.
NP

Amendments and extensions:
September 29 and October 7, 1986 (NP).
March 23, 1987 (NP).
March 31 and April 13, 1987 (NP).
December 8, 1987 and January 12, 1988 (NP).
December 14, 1988 and January 25, 1989 (NP).
January 15 and February 5, 1991 (NP).
July 7 and 21 and August 12, 1992 (NP).

Agreement relating to trade in textiles and textile products, with annexes. Exchange of notes at Port Louis March 17, July 1 and 29, 1994; entered into force July 29, 1994.
NP

TRADE-MARKS

Declaration by the United States and the United Kingdom relating to reciprocal protection to trade-marks. Signed at London October 24, 1877; entered into force October 24, 1877.
20 Stat. 703; TS 138; 12 Bevans 198.

MEXICO

AGRICULTURAL COMMODITIES

Agreement concerning the closeout of the collection accounts of the agricultural commodities agreement of October 23, 1957, as amended (TIAS 3935, 4070, 4129, and 4178). Exchange of notes at Mexico July 6, 1961 and August 9, 1962; entered into force August 9, 1962.
13 UST 1953; TIAS 5153; 461 UNTS 325.

MEXICO (Cont'd)

AGRICULTURE

Convention safeguarding livestock interests through the prevention of infectious and contagious diseases. Signed at Washington March 16, 1928; entered into force January 18, 1930.
46 Stat. 2451; TS 808; 9 Bevans 959; 106 LNTS 481.

Agreement relating to plantation rubber investigations. Exchange of notes at Mexico July 10 and September 20, 1943; entered into force July 1, 1943.
57 Stat. 1278; EAS 364; 117 UNTS 323.

Agreement relating to the establishment of an agricultural commission. Exchange of notes at Mexico January 6 and 27, 1944; entered into force January 27, 1944.
58 Stat. 1425; EAS 421; 9 Bevans 1162; 106 UNTS 275.

Agreement establishing the Mexican-United States Commission for the Prevention of Foot-and-Mouth Disease. Exchange of notes at Washington August 26, 1952; entered into force August 26, 1952.
6 UST 2543; TIAS 3300; 264 UNTS 269.

Amendment:
December 12, 1953 and July 30, 1954 (7 UST 937; TIAS 3578).

Agreement confirming an agreement to eradicate screw-worms. Exchange of notes at Mexico August 28, 1972; entered into force August 28, 1972.
23 UST 2465; TIAS 7438.

Amendment:
October 19 and December 7, 1990 (TIAS 12427).

Memorandum of understanding concerning cooperative efforts to protect crops from plant pest damage and diseases. Signed at Mexico February 8, 1973; entered into force February 8, 1973.
28 UST 7004; TIAS 8701.

Amendments:
September 10 and October 9, 1973 (28 UST 7013; TIAS 8701).
July 15 and 24, 1976 (28 UST 7015; TIAS 8701).

Cooperative agreement relating to provision of services to assist in eradication of the Mediterranean fruit fly (MEDFLY). Signed at Guatemala October 22, 1981; entered into force October 22, 1981.
34 UST 481; TIAS 10373.

Extension:
September 30, 1985 (TIAS 11934).

Memorandum of understanding regarding mutual cooperation in the regulation of raw agricultural products involved in commerce between Mexico and the United States, with annex. Signed at Mexico November 28, 1988; entered into force November 28, 1988.
TIAS

ATOMIC ENERGY

Agreement in the area of nuclear reactor safety research. Signed at Bethesda and Mexico May 27 and June 2, 1987; entered into force June 2, 1987.
TIAS 12234.

Arrangement for the exchange of technical information and cooperation in nuclear safety and research matters. Signed at Mexico March 5, 1997; entered into force March 5, 1997.
TIAS

NOTE:
[1] Implementing procedures replaced by implementing procedures signed at Rockville and Mexico September 8 and October 6, 1989.

AVIATION

Agreement to facilitate the reciprocal transit of military aircraft. Signed at Washington April 1, 1941; entered into force April 25, 1941.
55 Stat. 1191; TS 971; 9 Bevans 1049.

Agreement to facilitate flight notifications on non-scheduled, private, commercial or industrial flights between Mexico and the United States in both directions across the border. Exchange of notes at Washington July 15, 1952; entered into force August 1, 1952.
3 UST 4943; TIAS 2667; 181 UNTS 263.

Air transport agreement. Signed at Mexico August 15, 1960; entered into force provisionally August 15, 1960 and definitively January 17, 1961.
12 UST 60; TIAS 4675; 402 UNTS 177.

Extensions and amendments:
July 31, 1970 (22 UST 1492; TIAS 7167; 800 UNTS 356).
September 23, 1988.
November 21, 1991 (TIAS 11950).
September 25 and December 4, 1997.
February 15, 1999.

Agreement for acceptance by the United States of certificates of airworthiness for aircraft manufactured by Lockheed Azcarate, S.A. Exchange of notes at Washington June 26 and July 19, 1961; entered into force July 19, 1961.
12 UST 1384; TIAS 4861; 433 UNTS 43.

Amendment:
January 19 and 30, 1962 (13 UST 199; TIAS 4961; 442 UNTS 343).

Memorandum of agreement relating to technical assistance in reviewing air traffic operations in Mexico City terminal area. Signed at Washington February 19, 1981; entered into force February 19, 1981.
TIAS 10870; 1577 UNTS 345.

Agreement on reduced air fares. Exchange of letters at Mexico September 23, 1988; entered into force September 23, 1988.
TIAS

Memorandum of understanding on additional services (double designation), with annex. Signed at Mexico September 23, 1988; entered into force September 23, 1988.
TIAS

Agreement concerning assistance in developing and modernizing Mexico's civil aviation infrastructure in the managerial, operational and technical areas, with annex. Signed at Washington and Mexico June 4 and July 4, 1991; entered into force July 4, 1991.
TIAS

Memorandum of cooperation for Research and Development of the Global Navigation Satellite System (GNSS). Signed at Mexico July 11, 1996; entered into force July 11, 1996.
TIAS

Memorandum of cooperation in the promotion and development of civil aviation, with letter of understanding. Signed at Washington and Mexico September 17, October 14 and 16, 1997; entered into force October 16, 1997.
TIAS

Memorandum of agreement for the provision of assistance in developing and modernizing Mexico's civil aviation infrastructure. Signed at Mexico City and Washington October 14 and 20, 1997; entered into force October 20, 1997.
TIAS

BOUNDARIES

Treaty relating to the boundary line, transit of persons, etc., across the Isthmus of Tehuantepec (Gadsden Treaty).[1] Signed at Mexico December 30, 1853; entered into force June 30, 1854.
10 Stat. 1031; TS 208; 9 Bevans 812.

Treaty terminating article VIII of the boundary treaty of December 30, 1853. Signed at Washington April 13, 1937; entered into force December 21, 1937.
52 Stat. 1457; TS 932; 9 Bevans 1023.

Convention for the solution of the problem of the Chamizal. Signed at Mexico August 29, 1963; entered into force January 14, 1964.
15 UST 21; TIAS 5515; 505 UNTS 185.

Act approving minute no. 228 of the International Boundary and Water Commission concerning demarcation of new international boundary between the United States and Mexico. Signed at Washington October 27, 1967; entered into force October 28, 1967.
18 UST 2836; TIAS 6372; 724 UNTS 308.

Treaty to resolve pending boundary differences and maintain the Rio Grande and Colorado River as the international boundary between the United States and Mexico, with maps.

MEXICO (Cont'd)

Signed at Mexico November 23, 1970; entered into force April 18, 1972.
23 UST 371; TIAS 7313.

Act approving Minute 257 of the International Boundary and Water Commission confirming relocation of the channel of the Rio Grande. Signed at Washington May 26, 1977; entered into force May 26, 1977.
28 UST 5256; TIAS 8625.

Treaty on maritime boundaries. Signed at Mexico City May 4, 1978; entered into force November 13, 1997.
TIAS

NOTE:
[1] Article VIII terminated December 21, 1937.

BOUNDARY WATERS

Convention to avoid the difficulties occasioned by reason of the changes which take place in the beds of the Rio Grande and Colorado River.[1] Signed at Washington March 1, 1889; entered into force December 24, 1890.
26 Stat. 1512; TS 232; 9 Bevans 877.

Convention providing for the equitable distribution of the waters of the Rio Grande for irrigation purposes. Signed at Washington May 21, 1906; entered into force January 16, 1907.
34 Stat. 2953; TS 455; 9 Bevans 924.

Convention for the rectification of the Rio Grande (Rio Bravo del Norte) in the El Paso-Juarez Valley, and exchanges of notes of February 1 and September 8, 1933. Signed at Mexico February 1, 1933; entered into force November 10, 1933.
48 Stat. 1621; TS 864; 9 Bevans 976.

Treaty relating to the utilization of waters of the Colorado and Tijuana Rivers and of the Rio Grande, and supplementary protocol signed November 14, 1944. Signed at Washington February 3, 1944; entered into force November 8, 1945.
59 Stat. 1219; TS 994; 9 Bevans 1166; 3 UNTS 313.

Agreement to proceed with the construction of Amistad Dam on the Rio Grande to form part of the system of international storage dams provided for by the water treaty of February 3, 1944. Signed at Ciudad Acuna October 24, 1960; entered into force October 24, 1960.
11 UST 2396; TIAS 4624; 401 UNTS 137.

Agreement approving Minute 242 of the International Boundary and Water Commission setting forth a permanent and definitive solution to the international problem of the salinity of the Colorado River. Exchange of notes at Mexico August 30, 1973; entered into force August 30, 1973.
24 UST 1968; TIAS 7708.

Minute 261 of the International Boundary and Water Commission concerning recommendations for the solution to the border sanitation problems. Signed at El Paso September 24, 1979; entered into force October 2, 1979.
31 UST 5099; TIAS 9658; 1221 UNTS 189.

Minute 264 of the International Boundary and Water Commission: Recommendations for solution of the New River border sanitation problem at Calexico, California Mexicali, Baja California Norte. Signed at Ciudad Juarez August 26, 1980; entered into force December 4, 1980.
32 UST 3764; TIAS 9918; 1267 UNTS 163.

Minute 270 of the International Boundary and Water Commission: Recommendations concerning border sanitation problem at San Diego, California-Tijuana, Baja California. Signed at Ciudad Juarez April 30, 1985; entered into force July 16, 1985.
TIAS 11267.

Minute 273 of the International Boundary and Water Commission: Recommendations for the solution of the border sanitation problem at Naco, Arizona-Naco, Sonora. Signed at El Paso March 19, 1987; entered into force April 15, 1987.
TIAS 11292.

Amendment:
September 19, 1996.

Minute 274 of the International Boundary and Water Commission: Joint project for improvement of the quality of waters of the New River at Calexico, California-Mexicali, Baja California, with joint report. Signed at Ciudad Juarez April 15, 1987; entered into force May 13, 1987.
TIAS 11316.

Agreement concerning rediversion of Rio Grande waters allocated to Mexico under the convention of 1906. Exchange of notes at Mexico June 24 and November 10, 1987; entered into force November 10, 1987.
TIAS 11549.

Minute 276 of the International Boundary and Water Commission: Conveyance, treatment and disposal of sewage from Nogales, Arizona and Nogales, Sonora exceeding the capacities allocated to the United States and Mexico at the Nogales international sewage treatment plant under Minute 227, with joint report. Signed at Ciudad Juarez July 26, 1988; entered into force August 19, 1988.
TIAS 12396.

Minute 279 of the International Boundary and Water Commission: Joint measures to improve the quality of the waters of the Rio Grande at Laredo, Texas/Nuevo Laredo, Tamaulipas, with joint report. Signed at Laredo and Nuevo Laredo August 28, 1989; entered into force August 28, 1989.
TIAS 11701.

Minute 283 of the International Boundary and Water Commission: Conceptual plan for the international solution to the border sanitation problem in San Diego, California/Tijuana, Baja

California. Signed at El Paso July 2, 1990; entered into force August 8, 1990.
TIAS 11735.

Minute 290 of the International Boundary and Water Commission: Replacement of the International Cordova-Bridge of the Americas over the Rio Grande at El Paso, Texas-Ciudad Juarez, Chihuahua, Mexico. Signed at Ciudad Juarez September 21, 1993; entered into force September 24, 1993.
TIAS

Minute 291 of the International Boundary and Water Commission: Improvements to the conveying capacity of the international boundary segment of the Colorado River. Signed at San Diego July 16, 1994; entered into force August 16, 1994.
TIAS

Minute 298 of the International Boundary and Water Commission: Recommendations for construction of works parallel to the city of Tijuana, B.C. wastewater pumping and disposal system and rehabilitation of the San Antonio de los Buenos treatment plant. Signed at El Paso December 2, 1997; entered into force January 23, 1998.
TIAS

Minute 306 of the International Boundary and Water Commission: Conceptual framework for United States-Mexico studies for future recommendations concerning the riparian and estuarine ecology of the limitrophe section of the Colorado River and its associated delta. Signed at El Paso December 12, 2000; entered into force December 13, 2000.
TIAS

NOTE:
[1] Extended indefinitely by article 2 of treaty signed February 3, 1944 (59 Stat. 1219; TS 994). This convention established the International Boundary Commission, subsequently the International Boundary and Water Commission.

CHAMIZAL (See BOUNDARIES)

CLAIMS

Convention for the adjustment and settlement of certain outstanding claims. Signed at Washington November 19, 1941; entered into force April 2, 1942.
56 Stat. 1347; TS 980; 9 Bevans 1059; 125 UNTS 287.

CONSERVATION

Convention for the protection of migratory birds and game mammals. Signed at Mexico February 7, 1936; entered into force March 15, 1937.
50 Stat. 1311; TS 912; 9 Bevans 1017; 178 LNTS 309.

MEXICO (Cont'd)

Amendment:
May 5, 1997.

Agreement supplementing the convention of February 7, 1936 for the protection of migratory birds and game mammals. Exchange of notes at Mexico and Tlatelolco March 10, 1972; entered into force March 10, 1972.
23 UST 260; TIAS 7302.

Memorandum of understanding on cooperation in management and protection of national parks and other protected natural and cultural heritage sites, with annex. Signed at Mexico and Washington November 30, 1988 and January 24, 1989; entered into force January 24, 1989.
TIAS 11599.

Extension:
March 16, 1994.

Memorandum of understanding on cooperation in the identification, conservation, management and research in cultural heritage sites. Signed at Washington June 10, 1998; entered into force June 10, 1998.
TIAS

Memorandum of understanding concerning biodiversity conservation cooperation particularly in forest resources. Signed at Washington June 10, 1998; entered into force June 10, 1998.
TIAS

CONSULS

Consular convention. Signed at Mexico August 12, 1942; entered into force July 1, 1943. Exchanges of notes dated August 12 and December 11 and 12, 1942.
57 Stat. 800; TS 985; 9 Bevans 1076; 125 UNTS 301.

COPYRIGHT (See APPENDIX)

CULTURAL PROPERTY

Treaty of cooperation providing for the recovery and return of stolen archaeological, historical and cultural properties. Signed at Mexico July 17, 1970; entered into force March 24, 1971.
22 UST 494; TIAS 7088; 791 UNTS 313.

CULTURAL RELATIONS

Agreement establishing a United States-Mexican Commission on Cultural Cooperation. Exchange of notes at Mexico December 28, 1948 and August 30, 1949; entered into force August 30, 1949.
63 Stat. 2842; TIAS 2086; 9 Bevans 1264; 98 UNTS 183.

Amendments:
June 15, 1972 (23 UST 925; TIAS 7360).
October 30, 1978 and January 23, 1979 (30 UST 2932; TIAS 9374; 1177 UNTS 338).

CUSTOMS

Agreement relating to the opening of a border inspection station for the international traffic of persons and goods between the United States and Mexico. Exchange of notes at Washington July 31 and August 5, 1959; entered into force August 5, 1959.
10 UST 1398; TIAS 4285; 356 UNTS 3.

Agreement regarding mutual assistance between their customs administrations. Signed at Washington June 20, 2000; entered into force June 20, 2000.
TIAS

DEFENSE

Agreement relating to the deposit by Mexico of ten percent of the value of military training scholarships provided by the United States. Exchange of notes at Mexico April 4 and July 12, 1972; entered into force July 12, 1972; effective February 7, 1972.
23 UST 2809; TIAS 7469.

Agreement concerning the provision of training related to defense articles under the United States International Military Education and Training (IMET) Program. Exchange of notes at Mexico August 21 and September 24, 1987; entered into force September 24, 1987.
NP

DISASTER ASSISTANCE

Agreement on cooperation in cases of natural disasters. Signed at Mexico January 15, 1980; entered into force provisionally January 15, 1980; definitively March 18, 1981.
32 UST 5714; TIAS 10013; 1241 UNTS 207.

DRIVER'S LICENSES

Memorandum of understanding relating to the recognition and validity of commercial driver's licenses and licencias federales de conductor, with annex. Signed at Washington November 21, 1991; entered into force November 21, 1991.
TIAS 12442.

ECONOMIC AND TECHNICAL COOPERATION

General agreement for technical cooperation. Exchange of notes at Mexico June 27, 1951; entered into force June 27, 1951.
2 UST 1243; TIAS 2273; 141 UNTS 211.

Amendments:
January 21 and 22, 1952 (3 UST 4781; TIAS 2646; 200 UNTS 312).
April 13, 1954 (5 UST 1373; TIAS 3006; 233 UNTS 306).

Agreement relating to a program of industrial productivity in Mexico. Exchange of notes at Mexico February 21 and November 15, 1961; entered into force November 15, 1961.
13 UST 1882; TIAS 5140; 460 UNTS 113.

Agreement providing for the designation of officials to maintain contact between Mexico and the United States in matters relating to economic and social development of the border area. Exchange of notes at Mexico June 23, 1970; entered into force June 23, 1970.
21 UST 1475; TIAS 6905; 753 UNTS 275.

EDUCATION

Agreement relating to creation of a joint commission to review operation of the Abraham Lincoln and Benito Juarez scholarship funds. Exchange of notes at Mexico September 30 and October 25, 1966; entered into force October 25, 1966.
17 UST 2023; TIAS 6140; 676 UNTS 11.

Agreement for the establishment of the U.S.-Mexico commission for educational and cultural exchange, with memorandum of understanding. Signed at Monterrey November 27, 1990; entered into force November 27, 1990.
TIAS 11769.

Amendments and extension:
March 30 and May 10, 1995.
May 5, 1997.
May 18, 2000.

ENERGY

Agreement on natural gas. Announced September 21, 1979; entered into force September 21, 1979.
31 UST 5097; TIAS 9657; 1221 UNTS 185.

Agreement for energy cooperation, with annex. Signed at Mexico May 7, 1996; entered into force May 7, 1996.
TIAS

MEXICO (Cont'd)

ENVIRONMENTAL COOPERATION (See also BOUNDARY WATERS; POLLUTION)

Agreement on cooperation for the protection and improvement of the environment in the border area. Signed at La Paz August 14, 1983; entered into force February 16, 1984.
TIAS 10827; 1352 UNTS 67.

Annexes:
Agreement of cooperation for solution of the border sanitation problem at San Diego, California-Tijuana, Baja California. Signed at San Diego July 18, 1985; entered into force July 18, 1985.
TIAS 11269.
Agreement of cooperation regarding pollution of the environment along the inland international boundary by discharges of hazardous substances, with appendices. Signed at San Diego July 18, 1985; entered into force November 29, 1985.
TIAS 11269.
Agreement of cooperation regarding the transboundary shipments of hazardous wastes and hazardous substances. Signed at Washington November 12, 1986; entered into force January 29, 1987.
TIAS 11269.
Agreement of cooperation regarding transboundary air pollution caused by copper smelters along their common border. Signed at Washington January 29, 1987; entered into force January 29, 1987.
TIAS 11269.
Agreement of cooperation regarding international transport of urban air pollution, with appendix. Signed at Washington October 3, 1989; entered into force August 22, 1990.
TIAS 11269.

Amendments:
May 7, 1996.
June 4, 1999.

Agreement on cooperation for the protection and improvement of the environment in the metropolitan area of Mexico City. Signed at Washington October 3, 1989; entered into force August 22, 1990.
TIAS 11688.

Agreement concerning the establishment of a border environment cooperation commission and a North American development bank, with annex. Signed at Washington and Mexico November 16 and 18, 1993; entered into force January 1, 1994.
TIAS 12516.

Agreement for cooperation in the Global Learning and Observations to Benefit the Environment (GLOBE) Program, with appendices. Signed at Mexico November 15, 1996; entered into force November 15, 1996.
TIAS

EXTRADITION

Extradition treaty, with appendix. Signed at Mexico May 4, 1978; entered into force January 25, 1980.
31 UST 5059; TIAS 9656.

FINANCE

Agreement regarding the consolidation and rescheduling of certain debts owed to, guaranteed or insured by the United States through the Export-Import Bank of the United States. Signed at Mexico March 7, 1984; entered into force May 2, 1984.
TIAS 10961.

Agreement regarding the consolidation and rescheduling of certain debts owed to, guaranteed by, or insured by the United States Government and its agencies, with annexes. Signed at Washington April 9, 1987; entered into force May 21, 1987.
NP

Swap agreement between the United States Treasury and the Banco de Mexico/Government of Mexico, with memorandum of understanding. Signed at Washington and Mexico September 14, 1989; entered into force September 14, 1989.
TIAS

Agreement regarding the consolidation and rescheduling or refinancing of certain debts owed to, guaranteed by, or insured by the United States Government and its agencies, with annexes. Signed at Mexico March 14, 1990; entered into force April 23, 1990.
NP

Swap agreement among the United States Treasury and the Banco de Mexico/Government of Mexico, with memorandum of understanding. Signed at Washington and Mexico March 23, 1990; entered into force March 23, 1990.
TIAS

Exchange stabilization agreement between the United States Treasury and the Banco de Mexico/Government of Mexico. Signed at Washington and Mexico April 26, 1994; entered into force April 26, 1994.
TIAS

FIRE PROTECTION

Wildfire protection agreement for the common border. Signed at Mexico City June 4, 1999; entered into force June 4, 1999.
TIAS

FORESTRY

Memorandum of understanding on cooperation in forestry and natural resources. Signed at

Mexico May 5, 1997; entered into force May 5, 1997.
TIAS

HEALTH

Memorandum of understanding concerning exchange of information on, and control of, products involved in commerce between the United States and Mexico which are regulated on behalf of the United States by the Food and Drug Administration. Signed at Mazatlan August 13, 1974; entered into force August 13, 1974.
28 UST 1622; TIAS 8522.

Agreement for scientific cooperation on alcohol-related problems. Signed at Washington March 11, 1982; entered into force March 11, 1982.
TIAS 10491.

Memorandum of understanding regarding cooperation in the scientific and regulatory fields of health. Signed at Mexico February 22, 1988; entered into force February 22, 1988.
TIAS 11651.

Memorandum of understanding regarding cooperation in ensuring the safety and wholesomeness of fresh and fresh frozen oysters, clams and mussels exported to the United States from Mexico. Signed at Acapulco November 12, 1988; entered into force November 12, 1988.
TIAS

Memorandum of understanding regarding mutual cooperation in the regulation of raw agricultural products involved in commerce between Mexico and the United States, with annex. Signed at Mexico November 28, 1988; entered into force November 28, 1988.
TIAS

HOUSING

Agreement for cooperation in the field of housing and urban development. Signed at Mexico February 16, 1979; entered into force February 16, 1979.
30 UST 5865; TIAS 9523; 1180 UNTS 255.

JUDICIAL ASSISTANCE

Procedures for mutual assistance in the administration of justice in connection with the General Tire and Rubber Company and the Firestone Tire and Rubber Company matters. Signed at Washington June 23, 1976; entered into force June 23, 1976.
28 UST 2083; TIAS 8533.

Related agreements:
February 23 and March 6, 1978 (29 UST 2153; TIAS 8930).
May 31 and June 1, 1978 (29 UST 3200; TIAS 9005; 1124 UNTS 433).

MEXICO (Cont'd)

November 17 and December 5, 1978 (30 UST 2177; TIAS 9322).
August 25 and November 9, 1981 (33 UST 4353; TIAS 10305).
November 10 and 25, 1981 (33 UST 4353; TIAS 10305).

Treaty on cooperation for mutual legal assistance. Signed at Mexico December 9, 1987; entered into force May 3, 1991.
TIAS

Mutual cooperation agreement for the exchange of information in respect to transactions in currency through financial institutions in order to combat illicit activities. Signed at Washington October 28, 1994; entered into force February 3, 1995.
TIAS

Memorandum of understanding on procedures for cooperation regarding law enforcement activities. Signed at Merida February 15, 1999; entered into force February 15, 1999.
TIAS

MAPPING

Memorandum concerning cooperation and mutual assistance in mapping, charting and geodesy. Signed at Mexico July 25, 1975; entered into force July 25, 1975.
27 UST 1083; TIAS 8248.

MARITIME MATTERS

Treaty for the sending of vessels for purposes of assistance and salvage. Signed at Mexico June 13, 1935; entered into force March 7, 1936.
49 Stat. 3359; TS 905; 9 Bevans 1015; 168 LNTS 135.

Agreement on maritime search and rescue. Signed at Mexico August 7, 1989; entered into force June 25, 1990.
TIAS 11700; 1580 UNTS 385.

MIGRATORY WORKERS

Joint statement relating to the problem of illegal entry into the United States by Mexican migratory workers, with annexes. Signed at Washington July 18, 1973; entered into force July 18, 1973.
26 UST 1724; TIAS 8131; 1006 UNTS 25.

NARCOTIC DRUGS

Arrangement for the direct exchange of certain information regarding the traffic in narcotic drugs. Exchange of notes at Mexico August 5 and October 2, 1930; entered into force October 2, 1930.
9 Bevans 967.

Agreement concerning a grant to Mexico of reference books in the field of narcotics abuse. Exchange of letters at Mexico June 26 and 27, 1973; entered into force June 27, 1973.
24 UST 1805; TIAS 7694.

Agreement relating to the provision by the United States of communications equipment to combat contraband and especially the illegal flow of narcotics across the border. Exchange of notes at Mexico and Tlatelolco August 31, 1973; entered into force August 31, 1973.
24 UST 1978; TIAS 7709.

Agreement relating to the provision by the United States of technical assistance in an epidemiological study of drug abuse in Mexico. Exchange of notes at Mexico October 26 and November 7, 1973; entered into force November 7, 1973.
24 UST 2245; TIAS 7742; 938 UNTS 367.

Agreement concerning the provision of four helicopters and related assistance by the United States to help Mexico in curbing traffic in illegal narcotics. Exchange of letters at Mexico December 3, 1973; entered into force December 3, 1973.
25 UST 1694; TIAS 7906.

Amendments:
December 21, 1973 (25 UST 1698; TIAS 7906).
June 24, 1974 (25 UST 1700; TIAS 7906).

Agreement providing additional helicopters and related assistance to Mexico in support of its efforts to curb production and traffic in illegal narcotics. Exchange of letters at Mexico February 1, 1974; entered into force February 1, 1974.
25 UST 1704; TIAS 7907.

Amendments:
June 24, 1974 (25 UST 1708; TIAS 7907).
December 4, 1974 (25 UST 3172; TIAS 7983).

Agreement relating to the provision of support by the United States for a multi-spectral aerial photographic system capable of detecting opium poppy cultivation, with annexes. Exchange of letters at Mexico June 10 and 24, 1974; entered into force June 24, 1974.
25 UST 1286; TIAS 7863.

Amendment:
September 19, 1974 (25 UST 2963; TIAS 7956).

Agreement providing additional helicopters and related assistance to Mexico in support of its efforts to curb illegal production and traffic in narcotics. Exchange of letters at Mexico November 1, 1974; entered into force November 1, 1974.
25 UST 2956; TIAS 7955.

Agreement relating to a training program for Mexican helicopter pilots and mechanics as part of U.S.-Mexican cooperative efforts to reduce traffic in illegal narcotics. Exchange of letters at Mexico September 30, 1974; entered into force September 30, 1974.
25 UST 3166; TIAS 7982; 991 UNTS 367.

Agreement relating to the provision of assistance to Mexico in narcotics enforcement training activities. Exchange of letters at Mexico December 4, 1974; entered into force December 4, 1974.
25 UST 3176; TIAS 7984; 991 UNTS 373.

Agreement relating to cooperative arrangements to support Mexican efforts to curb the illegal traffic in narcotics. Exchange of letters at Mexico December 11, 1974; entered into force December 11, 1974.
26 UST 1274; TIAS 8108.

Amendments:
February 24, 1975 (26 UST 1285; TIAS 8108).
March 20, 1975 (26 UST 1289; TIAS 8108).
May 18, 1976 (27 UST 1977; TIAS 8295).

Agreement concerning the provision by the United States of four mobile interdiction systems for use in curbing the illicit flow of narcotic substances through Mexico. Exchange of letters at Mexico February 24, 1975; entered into force February 24, 1975.
26 UST 414; TIAS 8041; 991 UNTS 379.

Agreement relating to the provision of equipment and training by the United States to support U.S.-Mexican efforts to curb illegal narcotics traffic. Exchange of letters at Mexico May 29, 1975; entered into force May 29, 1975.
26 UST 1633; TIAS 8123; 1006 UNTS 37.

Agreement relating to the provision of equipment and training by the United States to support U.S.-Mexican efforts to curb illegal narcotics traffic. Exchange of letters at Mexico June 25, 1975; entered into force June 25, 1975.
26 UST 1659; TIAS 8125; 1006 UNTS 43.

Agreement to indemnify and safeguard the United States Government, its personnel and contractors for liability arising out of aircraft operations training in support of the cooperative program to curb illegal narcotics traffic. Exchange of letters at Mexico September 12, 1975; entered into force September 12, 1975.
27 UST 1985; TIAS 8296.

Amendment:
August 13, 1976 (28 UST 8241; TIAS 8758).

Agreement relating to the provision of two helicopters by the United States to support U.S.-Mexican efforts to curb the production and traffic in illegal narcotics. Exchange of letters at Mexico October 24 and 29, 1975; entered into force October 29, 1975.
27 UST 1996; TIAS 8298.

Agreement relating to the provision of aircraft by the United States to support U.S.-Mexican efforts to curb the illegal production and traffic in narcotics. Exchange of letters at Mexico January 29, 1976; entered into force January 29, 1976.
27 UST 4261; TIAS 8449.

MEXICO (Cont'd)

Agreement relating to the provision of supplies, equipment, and services by the United States to support U.S.-Mexican efforts to curb the illegal production and traffic in narcotics. Exchange of letters at Mexico February 4, 1976; entered into force February 4, 1976.
27 UST 1973; TIAS 8294.

Amendment:
May 18, 1976 (27 UST 1977; TIAS 8295).

Agreement relating to additional cooperative arrangements to curb illegal traffic in narcotics. Exchange of letters at Mexico June 30, 1976; entered into force June 30, 1976.
27 UST 1990; TIAS 8297.

Agreement relating to the provision of additional equipment, material and technical support by the United States to curb illegal traffic in narcotics. Exchange of letters at Mexico August 9, 1976; entered into force August 9, 1976.
27 UST 3937; TIAS 8411; 1059 UNTS 123.

Agreement relating to the provision of additional assistance by the United States to curb illegal traffic in narcotics and amending the agreements of August 9, 1976 and May 18, 1976. Exchange of letters at Mexico September 30, 1976; entered into force September 30, 1976.
27 UST 4306; TIAS 8451.

Agreement relating to additional cooperative arrangements to curb the illegal production and traffic in narcotics. Exchange of letters at Mexico November 22, 1976; entered into force November 22, 1976.
28 UST 8157; TIAS 8750.

Agreement relating to additional cooperative arrangements to curb the illegal production and traffic in narcotics. Exchange of letters at Mexico February 16, 1977; entered into force February 16, 1977.
29 UST 5334; TIAS 9113; 1148 UNTS 2.

Extension and amendments:
July 28, 1977 (29 UST 5334; TIAS 9113; 1148 UNTS 8).
December 19, 1977 (29 UST 5347; TIAS 9114; 1148 UNTS 11).
January 3, 1978 (29 UST 5352; TIAS 9115; 1148 UNTS 14).

Agreement relating to additional cooperative arrangements to curb the illegal traffic in narcotics. Exchange of letters at Mexico March 8, 1977; entered into force March 8, 1977.
29 UST 268; TIAS 8810.

Agreement relating to additional cooperative arrangements to curb the illegal traffic in narcotics, with annexes. Exchange of notes at Mexico June 2, 1977; entered into force June 2, 1977.
29 UST 2483; TIAS 8952.

Amendments:
September 28, 1977 (29 UST 2496; TIAS 8952).
July 20 and 26, 1978 (30 UST 1285; TIAS 9251; 1153 UNTS 454).
August 24, 1978 (30 UST 1289; TIAS 9251; 1153 UNTS 457).
January 15, 1979 (30 UST 1294; TIAS 9251; 1153 UNTS 460).
September 27 and 28, 1979 (31 UST 4760; TIAS 9637; 1202 UNTS 416).
December 5, 1979 (31 UST 5913; TIAS 9695; 1221 UNTS 376).
April 11, 1980 (32 UST 992; TIAS 9749; 1221 UNTS 379).
November 6, 1980 (32 UST 4157; TIAS 9933; 1266 UNTS 326).
January 2, 1981 (32 UST 4525; TIAS 9963; 1266 UNTS 329).
August 19, 1981 (33 UST 3683; TIAS 10249; 1541 UNTS 433).
October 14, 1981 (33 UST 4081; TIAS 10285; 1549 UNTS 463).
December 4, 1981 (33 UST 4406; TIAS 10310; 1549 UNTS 466).
January 6 and 8, 1982 (34 UST 35; TIAS 10336).
March 15 and 17, 1982 (34 UST 350; TIAS 10360; 1556 UNTS 386).
August 6, 1982 (TIAS 10430; 1736 UNTS 365).
November 8, 1982 (TIAS 10582; 1871 UNTS 502).
February 9, 1983 (TIAS 10657).
May 12 and 27, 1983 (TIAS 10657).
November 10, 1983 (TIAS 10907).
January 4, 1984 (TIAS 11124).
May 29, 1984 (TIAS 11124).
October 29, 1984 (TIAS 11124).
February 4, 1985.
April 3, 1985.
September 13 and 25, 1985.
November 13 and 29, 1985.
November 29 and December 2, 1985.
January 13 and March 12, 1986 (TIAS 11517).
March 14 and April 7, 1986 (TIAS 11517).
June 3 and July 1, 1986 (TIAS 11517).
November 3 and December 18, 1986 (TIAS 11517).
July 14 and 28, 1987 (TIAS 11561).
August 7 and 28, 1987 (TIAS 11561).
August 10 and 28, 1987 (TIAS 11561).
December 22, 1987 and February 11, 1988 (TIAS 11652).

Agreement relating to additional cooperative arrangements to curb the illegal traffic in narcotics. Exchange of letters at Mexico July 29, 1977; entered into force July 29, 1977.
29 UST 1509; TIAS 8895.

Agreement relating to additional cooperative arrangements to curb the illegal traffic in narcotics. Exchange of letters at Mexico August 5, 1977; entered into force August 5, 1977.
29 UST 2500; TIAS 8953.

Amendment:
September 29, 1977 (29 UST 2505; TIAS 8953).

Agreement relating to computerization of information in support of programs against illegal narcotics production and traffic. Exchange of letters at Mexico September 6, 1977; entered into force September 6, 1977.
29 UST 2551; TIAS 8955.

Agreement relating to the development of telecommunications capability to support the narcotics control effort. Exchange of letters at Mexico September 7, 1977; entered into force September 7, 1977.
29 UST 1994; TIAS 8915.

Agreement concerning training for helicopter pilots as part of the cooperative effort to reduce illegal narcotics traffic. Exchange of letters at Mexico April 3, 1978; entered into force April 3, 1978.
30 UST 1007; TIAS 9234; 1152 UNTS 235.

Agreement relating to additional cooperative arrangements to curb the illegal production and traffic in narcotics. Exchange of letters at Mexico May 15, 1978; entered into force May 15, 1978.
30 UST 1270; TIAS 9250; 1152 UNTS 241.

Amendments:
January 5, 1979 (30 UST 1276; TIAS 9250; 1152 UNTS 245).
February 7, 1979 (30 UST 1280; TIAS 9250; 1152 UNTS 248).
July 23, 1979 (30 UST 6186; TIAS 9544; 1179 UNTS 414).

Agreement relating to additional cooperative arrangements to curb the illegal traffic in narcotics. Exchange of letters at Mexico May 16, 1978; entered into force May 16, 1978.
30 UST 1299; TIAS 9252; 1152 UNTS 257.

Amendments:
January 8, 1979 (30 UST 1305; TIAS 9252; 1152 UNTS 261).
July 24, 1979 (30 UST 6197; TIAS 9546; 1179 UNTS 419).

Agreement concerning an illicit crop detection system to be used in curbing the illegal traffic in narcotics. Exchange of letters at Mexico May 22, 1978; entered into force May 22, 1978.
30 UST 1237; TIAS 9248; 1152 UNTS 269.

Amendments:
September 26, 1978 (30 UST 1247; TIAS 9248; 1152 UNTS 275).
January 12, 1979 (30 UST 1251; TIAS 9248; 1152 UNTS 278).
December 6, 1979 (31 UST 5904; TIAS 9693; 1221 UNTS 449).
January 27, 1981 (33 UST 990; TIAS 10082; 1274 UNTS 411).

Agreement relating to additional cooperative arrangements to curb the illegal traffic in narcotics. Exchange of letters at Mexico May 23, 1978; entered into force May 23, 1978.
30 UST 1255; TIAS 9249; 1152 UNTS 289.

Amendments:
July 11 and 13, 1978 (30 UST 1262; TIAS 9249; 1152 UNTS 293).
January 11, 1979 (30 UST 1266; TIAS 9249; 1152 UNTS 296).

MEXICO (Cont'd)

Agreement relating to additional cooperative arrangements to curb the illegal traffic in narcotics. Exchange of letters at Mexico May 24, 1978; entered into force May 24, 1978.
30 UST 1488; TIAS 9258; 1148 UNTS 26.

Amendments:
January 9, 1979 (30 UST 1494; TIAS 9258; 1148 UNTS 31).
April 20, 1979 (30 UST 1498; TIAS 9258; 1148 UNTS 34).

Agreement relating to the provision and utilization of aircraft to curb the illegal traffic in narcotics. Exchange of letters at Mexico August 23, 1978; entered into force August 23, 1978.
30 UST 1319; TIAS 9254; 1152 UNTS 305.

Amendment:
July 26, 1979 (30 UST 6191; TIAS 9545; 1179 UNTS 424).

Agreement relating to computerization of information in support of programs against illegal narcotics production and traffic. Exchange of letters at Mexico August 25, 1978; entered into force August 25, 1978.
30 UST 1309; TIAS 9253; 1152 UNTS 311.

Amendment:
January 10, 1979 (30 UST 1315; TIAS 9253; 1152 UNTS 315).

Agreement concerning the provision of additional technical assistance to curb the illegal traffic in narcotics. Exchange of letters at Mexico September 28, 1978; entered into force September 28, 1978.
30 UST 1729; TIAS 9282; 1152 UNTS 323.

Agreement relating to salary supplements to personnel dedicated to opium poppy eradication and narcotics interdiction. Exchange of letters at Mexico December 3, 1979; entered into force December 3, 1979.
31 UST 5918; TIAS 9696; 1221 UNTS 199.

Amendments:
April 25, 1980 (32 UST 1324; TIAS 9772; 1221 UNTS 203).
October 10, 1980 (32 UST 2901; TIAS 9884; 1274 UNTS 436).
December 29, 1981 (33 UST 4679; TIAS 10329).

Agreement relating to additional cooperative arrangements to curb the illegal traffic in narcotics. Exchange of letters at Mexico April 7, 1980; entered into force April 7, 1980.
32 UST 997; TIAS 9750.

Agreement relating to additional cooperative arrangements to curb the illegal traffic in narcotics. Exchange of letters at Mexico July 25, 1980; entered into force July 25, 1980.
32 UST 2105; TIAS 9822.

Amendments:
December 2, 1980 (33 UST 1217; TIAS 10106; 1285 UNTS 347).

March 31, 1981 (33 UST 1535; TIAS 10129).
April 2, 1982 (TIAS 10519).
May 17, 1984 (TIAS 11122).
September 25 and October 10, 1984 (TIAS 11122).
April 2, 1985 (TIAS 11346).
July 24 and August 20, 1985 (TIAS 11347).

Agreement relating to additional cooperative arrangements to curb the illegal traffic in narcotics. Exchange of letters at Mexico January 3, 1981; entered into force January 3, 1981.
33 UST 823; TIAS 10064; 1267 UNTS 181.

Agreement relating to additional cooperative arrangements to curb the illegal traffic in narcotics. Exchange of letters at Mexico April 8, 1981; entered into force April 8, 1981.
33 UST 1757; TIAS 10142.

Agreement relating to additional cooperative arrangements to curb the illegal traffic in narcotics. Exchange of letters at Mexico March 29, 1983; entered into force March 29, 1983.
TIAS 10675.

Amendments:
April 25, 1985 (TIAS 11348).
November 25 and 29, 1985 (TIAS 11349).
January 29 and March 12, 1986 (TIAS 11348).
August 25 and September 29, 1986 (TIAS 11349).
September 27 and 30, 1986 (TIAS 12090).
March 16 and April 14, 1987 (TIAS 11548).

Agreement relating to additional cooperative arrangements to curb the illegal traffic in narcotics. Exchange of letters at Mexico November 5, 1984; entered into force November 5, 1984.
TIAS 11125.

Agreement on cooperation in combatting narcotics trafficking and drug dependency. Signed at Mexico February 23, 1989; entered into force July 30, 1990.
TIAS 11604.

PEACE TREATIES

Treaty of peace, friendship, limits, and settlement.[1] Signed at Guadalupe Hidalgo February 2, 1848; entered into force May 30, 1848.
9 Stat. 922; TS 207; 9 Bevans 791.

NOTE:
[1] Articles V, VI and VII were amended and article XI was abrogated by the Gadsden treaty, signed December 30, 1853 (10 Stat. 1031; TS 208). Articles II-IV, XII-XV, and XVII-XX have been executed.

POLICE EQUIPMENT

Agreement relating to the transfer of equipment for the use of the national police force of Mexico. Exchange of notes at Washington June 26, 1961; entered into force June 26, 1961.
12 UST 1063; TIAS 4810; 413 UNTS 229.

POLLUTION (See also BOUNDARY WATERS; ENVIRONMENTAL COOPERATION)

Agreement of cooperation regarding pollution of the marine environment by discharges of hydrocarbons and other hazardous substances, with annexes. Signed at Mexico July 24, 1980; entered into force provisionally July 24, 1980; definitively March 30, 1981.
32 UST 5899; TIAS 10021; 1241 UNTS 225.

Memorandum of understanding for the exchange of technical information and for cooperation in the field of air quality research. Signed at Washington July 19, 1990; entered into force July 19, 1990.
TIAS 11756.

POSTAL MATTERS

International express mail agreement, with detailed regulations, as amended by declaration of July 28, 1987. Signed at Mexico February 13, 1981; entered into force September 1, 1987.
TIAS 11005.

Postal money order agreement. Signed at Mexico and Washington May 31 and June 17, 1988; entered into force August 1, 1988.
TIAS 11584.

PRISONER TRANSFER

Treaty on the execution of penal sentences. Signed at Mexico November 25, 1976; entered into force November 30, 1977.
28 UST 7399; TIAS 8718.

PUBLICATIONS

Agreement relating to the exchange of official journals and parliamentary papers. Exchange of notes at Mexico September 9 and 24, 1937; entered into force September 24, 1937.
51 Stat. 311; EAS 108; 9 Bevans 1025; 185 LNTS 23.

Agreement relating to the exchange of official publications. Exchange of notes at Washington June 3 and August 29, 1938; entered into force September 1, 1938.
53 Stat. 1977; EAS 134; 9 Bevans 1028; 195 LNTS 359.

SATELLITES

Agreement concerning the transmission and reception of signals from satellites for the provision of satellite services to users in the United

MEXICO (Cont'd)

States and Mexico. Signed at Mexico April 28, 1996; entered into force November 6, 1996.
TIAS

Protocol concerning the transmission and reception of signals from satellites for the provision of direct-to-home satellite services in the United States and Mexico, with exchange of letters. Signed at Washington November 8, 1996; entered into force November 11, 1996.
TIAS

SCIENTIFIC COOPERATION

Agreement for scientific and technical cooperation. Exchange of notes at Washington June 15, 1972; entered into force June 15, 1972.
23 UST 934; TIAS 7362.

Amendment:
August 10 and September 22, 1994 (TIAS 12566).

Memorandum of understanding on scientific and technical cooperation in the mapping and earth sciences, with annex. Signed at Washington August 12, 1992; entered into force August 12, 1992.
TIAS 11961.

Memorandum of understanding concerning scientific and technical cooperation in the earth and mapping sciences, with annexes. Signed at Mexico May 9, 1994; entered into force May 9, 1994.
TIAS 12180.

Memorandum of understanding concerning scientific and technical cooperation in the earth and mapping sciences. Signed at Mexico November 29, 1994; entered into force November 29, 1994.
TIAS 12583.

Memorandum of understanding concerning scientific and technical cooperation on biological data and information, with annex. Signed at Washington May 16, 1995; entered into force May 16, 1995.
TIAS 12650.

Memorandum of understanding concerning scientific and technical cooperation in the earth and mapping sciences, with annex. Signed at Mexico May 7, 1996; entered into force May 7, 1996.
TIAS

Memorandum of cooperation in epidemiology. Signed at Mexico City June 4, 1999; entered into force June 4, 1999.
TIAS

SOCIAL SECURITY

Agreement relating to the payment of social security benefits. Exchange of notes at Mexico and Tlatelolco March 27, 1968; entered into force March 27, 1968.
24 UST 1045; TIAS 7620.

SPACE

Agreement for participation by Mexican scientists in certain programs of space research by the National Aeronautics and Space Administration. Exchange of notes at Mexico February 27, 1965; entered into force February 27, 1965.
16 UST 620; TIAS 5783; 546 UNTS 135.

STOLEN PROPERTY (See also CULTURAL PROPERTY)

Convention for the recovery and return of stolen or embezzled vehicles and aircraft. Signed at Washington January 15, 1981; entered into force June 28, 1983.
TIAS 10653.

TAXATION

Agreement for the exchange of information with respect to taxes. Signed at Washington November 9, 1989; entered into force January 18, 1990.
TIAS 12404.

Convention for the avoidance of double taxation and the prevention of fiscal evasion with respect to taxes on income, with protocol.[1] Signed at Washington September 18, 1992; entered into force December 28, 1993.
TIAS

Additional protocol that modifies the convention of September 18, 1992, for the avoidance of double taxation and the prevention of fiscal evasion with respect to taxes on income. Signed at Mexico September 8, 1994; entered into force October 26, 1995.
TIAS

Protocol that modifies the agreement of November 9, 1989, for the exchange of information with respect to taxes. Signed at Mexico September 8, 1994; entered into force October 26, 1995.
TIAS 12404.

NOTE:
[1] With understandings.

TELECOMMUNICATION

Arrangement for radio communications between amateur stations on behalf of third parties. Exchange of notes at Mexico July 31, 1959; entered into force August 30, 1959.
10 UST 1449; TIAS 4295; 357 UNTS 187.

Agreement relating to the assignment and use of television channels along the United States-Mexican border. Exchange of notes at Mexico April 18, 1962; entered into force April 18, 1962.
13 UST 997; TIAS 5043; 452 UNTS 3.

Amendments:
August 20, 1975 (26 UST 2700; TIAS 8185; 1052 UNTS 374).
August 23 and September 4, 1979 (31 UST 4810; TIAS 9641).
January 22 and April 7, 1980 (32 UST 975; TIAS 9746; 1220 UNTS 327).
December 22, 1981 and August 17, 1982 (TIAS 10447; 1736 UNTS 316).
October 12, November 13, 1984, April 8 and 25, 1985.
September 14 and 26, 1988 (1540 UNTS 404).

Agreement concerning frequency modulation broadcasting in the 88 to 108 MHz band with annexes and related notes. Signed at Washington November 9, 1972; entered into force August 9, 1973.
24 UST 1815; TIAS 7697.

Amendments:
March 20 and November 9, 1978 (30 UST 3927; TIAS 9436; 1169 UNTS 368).
February 2 and April 24, 1979 (30 UST 3967; TIAS 9436; 1169 UNTS 382).
June 4 and August 1, 1979 (31 UST 4841; TIAS 9647).
October 2 and 11, 1979 (31 UST 4841; TIAS 9647).
September 5, 1979 and January 23, 1980 (31 UST 4841; TIAS 9647).
February 18 and May 20, 1981 (33 UST 1959; TIAS 10159).
March 3 and May 21, 1981 (33 UST 3330; TIAS 10234).
May 22 and August 4, 1981 (33 UST 3333; TIAS 10234).
August 19 and October 26, 1981 (33 UST 3336; TIAS 10234).
October 7 and December 9, 1981 (33 UST 3339; TIAS 10234).
March 18 and July 2, 1982 (TIAS 10466; 1751 UNTS 428).
August 11 and September 8, 1982 (TIAS 10466; 1751 UNTS 433).
February 14 and April 8, 1983 (TIAS 10688).
October 13, 1982 and June 7, 1983.
February 25 and June 7, 1983.
July 21 and September 22, 1983 (TIAS 10792).
June 24, 1983, January 10, February 6, February 27, April 11, and June 12, 1984.
July 6 and September 10, 1984 (TIAS 11231).
November 6 and December 7, 1984 (TIAS 11231).
December 21, 1984 and March 18, 1985 (TIAS 11268).
September 7, 1984, February 28, March 21 and May 14, 1985 (TIAS 11344).

Agreement relating to assignments and usage of television broadcasting channels in the frequency range 470-806 MHz (channels 14-69) along the United States-Mexico border. Signed

MEXICO (Cont'd)

at Mexico June 18, 1982; entered into force January 17, 1983.
TIAS 10535.

Amendments:
October 31, 1984 and April 8, 1985 (TIAS 11237).
June 22 and October 19, 1988 (TIAS 12426).

Agreement relating to the AM broadcasting service in the medium frequency band, with annexes. Signed at Mexico August 28, 1986; entered into force April 27, 1987.
TIAS

Agreement regarding an earth station coordination procedure, with annex. Signed at Chestertown July 2, 1991; entered into force February 25, 1993.
TIAS 12434.

Administrative arrangement concerning frequencies used by the International Water and Boundary Commission, with annex. Signed at Queretaro August 11, 1992; entered into force August 11, 1992.
TIAS 12472.

Agreement relating to the FM broadcasting service in the band 88–108 MHz, with annexes. Signed at Queretaro August 11, 1992; entered into force June 2, 1995.
TIAS 12474.

Agreement for the use of the band 1605 to 1705 KHz in the AM broadcasting service, with annexes. Signed at Queretaro August 11, 1992; entered into force May 30, 1995.
TIAS 12473.

Agreement on the use of the 17.7–17.8 GHz band. Signed at Washington June 21, 1993; entered into force March 8, 1994.
TIAS   ; 1792 UNTS 303.

Agreement concerning the allocation and use of frequency bands by terrestrial non-broadcasting radiocommunication services along the common border, with annexes. Signed at Williamsburg June 16, 1994; entered into force June 2, 1995.
TIAS 12548.

Protocol concerning the allocation and use of the bands 901–902 MHz, 930–931 MHz and 940–941 MHz bands for personal communications services along the common border, with appendices. Signed at Washington May 16, 1995; entered into force May 16, 1995.
TIAS 12651.

Protocol concerning the use of the band 1850–1990 MHz for personal communications services along the common border. Signed at Washington May 16, 1995; entered into force May 16, 1995.
TIAS 12652.

Protocol concerning the use of channels in the 932.5–935 MHz and the 941.5–944 MHz bands for fixed point-to-point services along the common border, with appendices. Signed at Morelia, Michoacan April 26, 1996; entered into force April 26, 1996.
TIAS

Protocol concerning the use of bands allocated to the aeronautical radionavigation and aeronautical communications services along the common border, with appendices. Signed at Morelia, Michoacan April 26, 1996; entered into force April 26, 1996.
TIAS

Protocol concerning use of the 929–930 MHz and 931–932 MHz bands for paging services along the common border, with appendices and letter of understanding. Signed at Washington February 27, 1997; entered into force February 27, 1997.
TIAS

Memorandum of understanding for the use of radio frequencies, coordination and cooperation for emergency purposes, with annexes. Signed at Washington and Mexico City December 9, 1998; entered into force December 9, 1998.
TIAS

Protocol concerning the transmission and reception of signals from satellites for the provision of mobile-satellite services and associated feeder links in the United States of America and the United Mexican States, with appendix. Signed at Mexico City December 21, 1998; entered into force December 21, 1998.
TIAS

TOURISM

Agreement on the development and facilitation of tourism. Signed at Washington October 3, 1989; entered into force August 22, 1990.
TIAS 12403.

TRADE AND COMMERCE

Agreement relating to tariff concessions on certain lead products. Exchange of letters at Mexico October 31 and November 8, 1979; entered into force November 8, 1979; effective January 1, 1980.
TIAS 10568; 1871 UNTS 61.

Related agreement:
August 5, 1980 (TIAS 10568; 1871 UNTS 61).

Understanding regarding subsidies and countervailing duties. Signed at Washington April 23, 1985; entered into force April 23, 1985.
TIAS

Understanding concerning a framework of principles and procedures for consultations regarding trade and investment relations, with agenda. Signed at Mexico November 6, 1987; entered into force November 6, 1987.
TIAS 12395.

Agreement concerning trade in cotton, wool, and man-made fiber textiles and textile products, with annexes. Signed at Mazatlan February 13, 1988; entered into force February 13, 1988; effective January 1, 1988.
NP

Amendments and extension:
August 26 and September 7, 1988 (NP).
October 25 and November 17, 1988 (NP).
November 17 and 23, 1988 (NP).
November 7, 1988 and January 3, 1989 (NP).
October 2 and November 1, 1989 (NP).
April 20, July 25 and August 1, 1990 (NP).
July 19 and August 3, 1990 (NP).
October 31 and November 13, 19 and 21, 1991 (NP).

Agreement on steel trade liberalization, with appendices. Signed at Washington October 3, 1989; entered into force October 3, 1989.
TIAS

TRANSPORTATION

Memorandum of understanding concerning research cooperation in the field of transportation. Signed at Merida November 16, 1972; entered into force November 16, 1972.
30 UST 823; TIAS 9221.

VISAS

Agreement on documentation for nonimmigrants traveling between the United States and Mexico. Exchange of notes at Mexico October 28 and November 10 and 12, 1953; entered into force November 12, 1953.
5 UST 174; TIAS 2912; 224 UNTS 187.

Amendment:
May 29, 1974 (25 UST 1172; TIAS 7847).

WEATHER STATIONS

Agreement for a cooperative meteorological observation program in Mexico, with memorandum of understanding. Exchange of notes at Mexico and Tlatelolco July 31, 1970; entered into force August 1, 1970.
21 UST 1978; TIAS 6941; 756 UNTS 117.

Amendment and extensions:
September 3, 1974 (25 UST 2450; TIAS 7927).

MICRONESIA

A letter of November 2, 1995, from the Government of the Federated States of Micronesia to the Secretary-General of the United Nations refers to a letter of May 22, 1992, ". . . containing a declaration setting out the position of the Government of the Federated States of Micronesia (FSM) with regard to international agreements entered into by the United States of America and made applicable to the FSM pursuant to the United Nations Trusteeship

MICRONESIA (Cont'd)

Agreement for the former Japanese Mandated Islands.''

''The Declaration stated that as to bilateral treaties validly concluded by the United States on behalf of the FSM, or validly applied or extended by the former to the latter before 3 November 1986, the Government of the FSM would examine each such treaty and communicate its views to the other State Party concerned. The Declaration also stated that the Government of the FSM would continue to observe the terms of each treaty which validly so applied and was not inconsistent with the letter or the spirit of the Constitution of the FSM, provisionally and on a basis of reciprocity. The period of examination was to extend until 3 November 1995, except in the case of any treaty in respect of which an earlier statement of views was or had been made. At the expiration of this period, the Government of the FSM would consider such of these treaties that could not by the application of the rules of customary international law be regarded as otherwise surviving, as having terminated.''

The letter of November 2, 1995, extends ''. . . the period of examination of the bilateral treaties indicated above for two additional years, or until 3 November 1997.''

''With regard to multilateral treaties previously applied, the Declaration of 22 May 1992 stated that the Government of the FSM intends to review each of them individually and to communicate to the depositary in each case what steps it would take, whether by way of confirmation of termination or confirmation of succession or accession. During such period of review, any party to a multilateral treaty that had been validly applied or extended to the Federated States of Micronesia prior to 3 November 1986, and was not inconsistent with the letter or spirit of the Constitution of the FSM, may, on the basis of reciprocity, rely as against the FSM on the terms of such treaty.''

Agreement for the implementation of the Compact of Free Association between the Government of the United States and the Government of the Federated States of Micronesia (Title II, PL 99-239), with related agreements. Signed at Washington October 24, 1986; entered into force October 24, 1986; effective November 3, 1986.
TIAS

Amendment:
March 9, 1988 (TIAS 11660).

AGRICULTURE

Agreement concerning technical assistance in soil and water conservation. Signed at Palikir April 20, 1990; entered into force April 20, 1990.
TIAS 12221.

AVIATION

Memorandum of agreement concerning assistance in developing and modernizing Micronesia's civil aviation infrastructure. Signed at Washington and Kolonia October 30, 1989 and January 10, 1990; entered into force January 10, 1990.
TIAS 12408.

DEFENSE

Agreement concerning certain technical assistance to be provided by the Department of the Army. Signed at Honolulu September 21, 1989; entered into force September 21, 1989.
TIAS 11889.

EDUCATION

Agreement regarding augmentation of educational assistance. Signed at Washington August 19, 1987; entered into force August 19, 1987.
TIAS 11277.

ENVIRONMENTAL COOPERATION

Agreement for cooperation in the Global Learning and Observations to Benefit the Environment (GLOBE) Program, with appendices. Signed at Kolonia November 7, 1997; entered into force November 7, 1997.
TIAS

FINANCE

Agreement relating to investment guaranties. Exchange of notes at Kolonia February 13 and March 3, 1988; entered into force March 3, 1988.
TIAS 12047.

MARITIME MATTERS

Maritime search and rescue agreement. Signed at Honolulu June 10, 1988; entered into force June 10, 1988.
TIAS 11586.

RELATIONS

Agreement relating to diplomatic relations, with related notes. Exchange of notes at Washington August 23 and 24, 1989; entered into force August 24, 1989.
TIAS 11891.

TELECOMMUNICATION

Agreement relating to radio communications between amateur stations on behalf of third parties. Exchange of notes at Kolonia April 4 and September 12, 1989; entered into force October 12, 1989.
TIAS 12401.

Agreement terminating the agreement of June 25, 1983, regarding the provision of telecommunication services. Exchange of notes at Kolonia and Palikir May 28 and June 7, 1993; entered into force June 7, 1993.
TIAS 12501.

MOLDOVA

For agreements prior to December 31, 1991, see UNION OF SOVIET SOCIALIST REPUBLICS.

COPYRIGHT (See APPENDIX)

DEFENSE

Agreement regarding grants under the Foreign Assistance Act of 1961, as amended, and the furnishing of defense articles, related training and other defense services from the United States to Moldova. Exchange of notes at Chisinau October 9 and 10, 1997; entered into force October 10, 1997.
TIAS

ECONOMIC AND TECHNICAL COOPERATION

Agreement regarding cooperation to facilitate the provision of assistance. Signed at Chisinau March 21, 1994; entered into force March 21, 1994.
TIAS

EMPLOYMENT

Agreement relating to the employment of dependents of official government employees, with attachment. Exchange of notes at Chisinau September 8 and 13, 1994; entered into force September 13, 1994.
TIAS 12191.

ENVIRONMENTAL COOPERATION

Agreement for cooperation in the Global Learning and Observations to Benefit the Environment (GLOBE) Program, with appendices.

MOLDOVA (Cont'd)

Signed at Washington January 30, 1995; entered into force January 30, 1995.
TIAS 12603.

FINANCE

Investment incentive agreement. Signed at Washington June 19, 1992; entered into force December 2, 1992.
TIAS 12459.

INVESTMENT

Treaty concerning the encouragement and reciprocal protection of investment, with annex, protocol and exchange of letters. Signed at Washington April 21, 1993; entered into force November 25, 1994.
TIAS

NORTH ATLANTIC TREATY

Agreement to treat the agreement of June 19, 1995, among the States Parties to the North Atlantic Treaty and the other States participating in the Partnership for Peace regarding the status of their forces as binding between the United States and Moldova. Exchange of notes at Chisinau August 1, 1996; entered into force August 1, 1996.
TIAS

PEACE CORPS

Agreement concerning the program of the Peace Corps of the United States in the Republic of Moldova. Signed at Chisinau February 2, 1993; entered into force February 2, 1993.
TIAS 12485.

TRADE

Agreement on trade relations, with exchanges of letters. Signed at Washington June 19, 1992; entered into force July 2, 1992.
TIAS

WEAPONS

Agreement concerning cooperation in the area of the prevention of proliferation of weapons of mass destruction and the promotion of defense and military relations. Signed at Chisinau June 23, 1997; entered into force June 23, 1997.

MONACO

COPYRIGHT (See also APPENDIX)

Agreement relating to reciprocal copyright relations. Exchange of notes at Monaco and Nice September 24, 1952; entered into force September 24, 1952; operative October 15, 1952.
3 UST 5112; TIAS 2702; 186 UNTS 43.

EXTRADITION

Extradition treaty. Signed at Monaco February 15, 1939; entered into force March 28, 1940.
54 Stat. 1780; TS 959; 9 Bevans 1272; 202 LNTS 61.

TELECOMMUNICATION

Agreement relating to the reciprocal granting of authorizations to permit licensed amateur radio operators of either country to operate their stations in the other country. Exchange of notes at Monaco March 29 and at Paris October 16, 1968; entered into force December 1, 1968.
19 UST 7852; TIAS 6622; 719 UNTS 115.

VISAS

Agreement relating to the reciprocal waiver of passport visa fees for nonimmigrants. Exchange of notes at Monaco and Nice March 31, 1952; entered into force March 31, 1952; operative May 1, 1952.
3 UST 3942; TIAS 2528; 177 UNTS 195.

MONGOLIA

COPYRIGHT (See APPENDIX)

CULTURAL RELATIONS

Agreement for cooperation in cultural and educational exchange. Signed at New York September 29, 1989; entered into force September 29, 1989.
TIAS 11478.

CUSTOMS

Agreement regarding cooperation and mutual assistance in customs matters. Signed at Hong Kong June 19, 1996; entered into force June 19, 1996.
TIAS

ECONOMIC AND TECHNICAL COOPERATION

Agreement concerning economic, technical and related assistance with protocol and memorandum of understanding. Signed at Ulaanbaatar September 8, 1992; entered into force September 8, 1992.
TIAS 12476.

EMBASSY SITES

Memorandum of understanding concerning facilitation of the work of diplomatic missions, with attachments. Signed at Washington March 27, 1992; entered into force March 27, 1992.
TIAS

EMPLOYMENT

Agreement concerning the employment of dependents of official government employees. Exchange of notes at Ulaanbaatar March 24 and April 5, 1999; entered into force April 5, 1999.
TIAS

ENVIRONMENTAL COOPERATION

Agreement for cooperation in the Global Learning and Observations to Benefit the Environment (GLOBE) Program, with appendices. Signed at Ulaanbaatar May 6, 1997; entered into force May 6, 1997.
TIAS

FINANCE

Investment incentive agreement. Signed at New York September 29, 1990; entered into force January 4, 1991.
TIAS 11501.

INVESTMENT

Treaty concerning the encouragement and reciprocal protection of investment, with annex and protocol. Signed at Washington October 6, 1994; entered into force January 1, 1997.
TIAS

PEACE CORPS

Agreement on cooperation through the United States Peace Corps in Mongolia. Signed at Ulaanbaatar August 2, 1990; entered into force August 2, 1990.
TIAS 11505.

MONGOLIA (Cont'd)

POSTAL MATTERS

Express mail agreement, with detailed regulations. Signed at Ulaanbaatar and Washington June 5 and July 1, 1996; entered into force September 1, 1996.
NP

RELATIONS

Memorandum of understanding concerning facilitation of the work of diplomatic missions. Signed at Washington January 27, 1987; entered into force January 27, 1987.
TIAS 11457.

REMOTE SENSING

Memorandum of understanding on cooperation in the collection of the 1 kilometer advanced very high resolution radiometer image data. Signed at Ulaanbaatar March 9, 1993; entered into force March 9, 1993.
TIAS 12708.

Extension:
December 7, 1995 (TIAS 12708).

SCIENTIFIC COOPERATION

Agreement relating to scientific and technical cooperation, with annex. Signed at Washington January 23, 1991; entered into force January 23, 1991.
TIAS 11495.

Extension:
January 20 and 22, 1996 (TIAS 11495).

Memorandum of understanding concerning scientific and technical cooperation in the earth sciences. Signed at Reston November 9, 1992; entered into force November 9, 1992.
TIAS 11911.

Memorandum of understanding concerning scientific and technical cooperation in the earth sciences. Signed at Reston November 16, 1999 and January 25, 2000; entered into force January 25, 2000.
TIAS

TRADE AND COMMERCE

Agreement on trade relations, with exchange of letters. Signed at Washington January 23, 1991; entered into force November 27, 1991.
TIAS

VISAS

Agreement concerning the reciprocal issuance of visas to government officials. Exchange of notes at Ulaanbaatar August 2, 1990; entered into force August 2, 1990.
TIAS 12418.

MONTENEGRO

FINANCE

Investment incentive agreement. Signed at Washington and Brussels March 23 and 29, 2000; entered into force March 29, 2000.
TIAS

MOROCCO

The independence of Morocco was recognized in a joint declaration signed March 2, 1956 on behalf of the Government of France and the Sultan of Morocco.

A diplomatic agreement on general relations between France and Morocco signed at Paris May 28, 1956, provided *inter alia* (1) that none of the provisions of that agreement must be interpreted as affecting the obligations which result either from the Charter of the United Nations or from agreements, treaties, or conventions in force between one of the High Contracting Parties and third powers (article 6), and (2) that Morocco assumes the obligations resulting from international treaties passed by France in the name of Morocco as well as those resulting from international acts relating to Morocco which have not been subject to observations on its part (article 11).

AGRICULTURAL COMMODITIES

Agricultural commodities agreement with exchange of notes. Exchange of notes at Rabat February 9, 1962; entered into force February 9, 1962.
13 UST 210; TIAS 4964; 442 UNTS 135.

Agricultural commodities agreement with exchange of notes. Exchange of notes at Rabat September 11, 1962; entered into force September 11, 1962.
13 UST 2698; TIAS 5241; 462 UNTS 207.

Agricultural commodities agreement with related notes. Exchange of notes at Rabat December 29, 1964; entered into force December 29, 1964.
17 UST 847; TIAS 6045; 593 UNTS 185.

Agricultural commodities agreement, with related notes. Exchange of notes at Rabat April 23, 1965; entered into force April 23, 1965.
17 UST 873; TIAS 6049; 594 UNTS 4.

Amendments:
October 8, 1965 (17 UST 873; TIAS 6049; 594 UNTS 20).
April 21, 1966 (17 UST 873; TIAS 6049; 594 UNTS 24).
August 12, 1966 (17 UST 1644; TIAS 6122; 676 UNTS 388).
October 25, 1966 (17 UST 2026; TIAS 6141; 676 UNTS 392).

Agricultural commodities agreement with related notes. Exchange of notes at Rabat April 21, 1966; entered into force April 21, 1966.
17 UST 2288; TIAS 6172; 680 UNTS 201.

Agricultural commodities agreement with exchange of notes. Signed at Rabat August 12, 1966; entered into force August 12, 1966.
17 UST 2029; TIAS 6142; 675 UNTS 293.

Amendment:
October 25, 1966 (17 UST 2029; TIAS 6142; 675 UNTS 308).

Agricultural commodities agreement with annexes. Signed at Rabat April 20, 1967; entered into force April 20, 1967.
18 UST 496; TIAS 6256; 685 UNTS 177.

Related agreements:
October 27, 1967 (18 UST 2925; TIAS 6384; 701 UNTS 123).
May 2, 1968 (19 UST 4845; TIAS 6488; 698 UNTS 209).
February 25, 1969 (20 UST 464; TIAS 6648; 714 UNTS 193).
September 13, 1969 (20 UST 4060; TIAS 6793; 727 UNTS 440).
September 4, 1970 (21 UST 2142; TIAS 6960; 764 UNTS 239).
January 21, 1971 (22 UST 220; TIAS 7053; 792 UNTS 75).
April 21 and May 4, 1971 (22 UST 651; TIAS 7117; 792 UNTS 82).
August 18, 1971 (22 UST 1552; TIAS 7176; 807 UNTS 31).
March 2, 1972 (23 UST 163; TIAS 7288).
April 19, 1973 (24 UST 2274; TIAS 7749; 938 UNTS 195).
May 11, 1973 (24 UST 2277; TIAS 7749; 938 UNTS 202).

Agricultural commodities agreement. Signed at Rabat May 17, 1976; entered into force May 17, 1976.
27 UST 2301; TIAS 8309; 1052 UNTS 329.

Related agreements:
July 26, 1977 (29 UST 5867; TIAS 9156).
February 3, 1978 (29 UST 5954; TIAS 9162).
August 28, 1979 (31 UST 1009; TIAS 9628; 1202 UNTS 203).
May 21, 1980 (33 UST 1093; TIAS 10094; 1284 UNTS 247).
July 3, 1981 (33 UST 2688; TIAS 10197).
August 18 and 19, 1981 (33 UST 2693; TIAS 10197).
January 19, 1982 (34 UST 356; TIAS 10361).
August 13 and 18, 1982 (TIAS 10750).
July 15, 1983 (TIAS 10768).
August 26, 1983 (TIAS 10768).
February 2, 1984 (TIAS 11042).
July 5, 1984 (TIAS 11042).

MOROCCO (Cont'd)

Agricultural commodities agreement. Signed at Rabat February 19, 1985; entered into force February 19, 1985.
NP

Amendment:
May 27, 1986 (NP).

Related agreements:
February 19, 1985 (NP).
April 26, 1985 (NP).
July 24, 1985 (NP).
May 27, 1986 (NP).
July 24, 1986 (NP).
January 22, 1987 (NP).

Agricultural commodities agreement with memorandum of understanding. Signed at Rabat June 25, 1987; entered into force June 25, 1987.
NP

Amendments:
March 25, 1988 (NP).
August 31 and September 2, 1988 (NP).

Related agreements:
October 20, 1988 (NP).
April 24, 1990 (NP).

ATOMIC ENERGY

Agreement for cooperation concerning peaceful uses of nuclear energy, with annex and agreed minute. Signed at Washington May 30, 1980; entered into force May 16, 1981.
32 UST 5823; TIAS 10018; 1267 UNTS 101.

AVIATION

Air transport agreement with exchange of notes. Signed at Rabat February 9, 1970; entered into force February 9, 1970.
21 UST 1180; TIAS 6877; 756 UNTS 37.

Memorandum of agreement on technical assistance with the Federal Aviation Administration, with annex. Signed at Rabat April 18, 1983; entered into force April 18, 1983.
TIAS 10702.

COMMERCE (See PEACE TREATIES)

CONSULS (See PEACE TREATIES)

COPYRIGHT (See APPENDIX)

CULTURAL RELATIONS

Cultural agreement. Signed at Washington February 10, 1967; entered into force February 10, 1967.
18 UST 174; TIAS 6215; 688 UNTS 149.

DEFENSE

Agreement concerning the use of certain facilities in Morocco by the United States. Exchange of notes at Washington May 27, 1982; entered into force May 27, 1982.
34 UST 1127; TIAS 10399; 1566 UNTS 139.

ECONOMIC AND TECHNICAL COOPERATION

Agreement providing for economic, technical, and related assistance. Exchange of notes at Rabat April 2, 1957; entered into force April 2, 1957.
8 UST 459; TIAS 3799; 288 UNTS 157.

Amendment:
May 19, 1958 (9 UST 923; TIAS 4054; 317 UNTS 354).

Agreement to establish the U.S.-Moroccan Joint Committee for Economic Relations. Signed at Washington September 25, 1980; entered into force September 25, 1980.
32 UST 2677; TIAS 9870; 1275 UNTS 63.

Agency for International Development:
November 7, 1975 (28 UST 57; TIAS 8464).
June 14, 1976 (28 UST 1479; TIAS 8518).

EDUCATION

Agreement establishing a Binational Commission for Educational and Cultural Exchange. Signed at Marrakech February 12, 1982; entered into force May 20, 1982.
TIAS 10407.

EMPLOYMENT

Agreement relating to the employment of dependents of official government employees.

Exchange of notes at Rabat February 27 and April 2, 1992; entered into force April 2, 1992.
TIAS

ENVIRONMENTAL COOPERATION

Agreement for cooperation in the Global Learning and Observations to Benefit the Environment (GLOBE) Program, with appendices. Signed at Rabat March 27, 1996; entered into force March 27, 1996.
TIAS

FINANCE

Agreement relating to investment guaranties under section 413 (b)(4) of the Mutual Security Act of 1954, as amended. Exchange of notes at Rabat March 31, 1961; entered into force March 31, 1961.
12 UST 386; TIAS 4728; 406 UNTS 249.

Amendments:
October 2, 1963 (14 UST 1547; TIAS 5456; 489 UNTS 399).
September 21 and November 30, 1992 (TIAS 12140).

Agreement regarding the consolidation and rescheduling of certain debts owed to, guaranteed by or insured by the United States Government and its agencies, with annexes. Signed at Rabat December 30, 1983; entered into force February 10, 1984.
TIAS 11015.

Agreement regarding the consolidation and rescheduling of certain debts owed to, guaranteed by or insured by the United States Government and its agencies, with annexes. Signed at Rabat December 23, 1985 and February 13, 1986; entered into force January 21, 1986.
NP

Agreement regarding the consolidation and rescheduling of certain debts owed to, guaranteed by, or insured by the United States Government and its agencies, with annexes. Signed at Rabat March 1, 1988; entered into force April 11, 1988.
NP

Agreement regarding the consolidation and rescheduling of certain debts owed to, guaranteed by, or insured by the United States Government and its agencies, with annexes. Signed at Rabat August 21, 1989; entered into force September 25, 1989.
NP

Agreement regarding the consolidation and rescheduling or refinancing of certain debts owed to, guaranteed by, or insured by the United States Government and its agencies, with annexes. Signed at Rabat February 14, 1991; entered into force March 29, 1991.
NP

MOROCCO (Cont'd)

Agreement regarding the consolidation and rescheduling or refinancing of certain debts owed to, guaranteed by, or insured by the United States Government and its agencies, with annexes. Signed at Rabat August 24, 1992; entered into force October 12, 1992.
NP

INVESTMENT

Treaty concerning the encouragement and reciprocal protection of investments, with protocol. Signed at Washington July 22, 1985; entered into force May 29, 1991.
TIAS

JUDICIAL ASSISTANCE

Convention on mutual assistance in criminal matters. Signed at Rabat October 17, 1983; entered into force June 23, 1993.
TIAS

MAPPING

Agreement concerning mapping, charting and geodesy cooperation. Signed at Rabat April 29, 1982; entered into force April 29, 1982.
34 UST 987; TIAS 10386.

Memorandum of agreement concerning hydrographic surveys and nautical charting. Signed at Rabat November 20, 1985; entered into force November 20, 1985.
TIAS 11210.

NARCOTIC DRUGS

Agreement regarding joint cooperation in fighting against international terrorism, organized crime, and the illicit production, trafficking and abuse of narcotics. Signed at Rabat February 10, 1989; entered into force February 10, 1989.
TIAS 12029.

PEACE CORPS

Agreement relating to the establishment of a Peace Corps program in Morocco. Exchange of notes at Rabat February 8 and 9, 1963; entered into force February 9, 1963.
23 UST 209; TIAS 7297.

Amendment:
March 10, 1972 (23 UST 209; TIAS 7297).

PEACE TREATIES

Treaty of peace.[1] Signed at Meccanez September 16, 1836; entered into force January 28, 1837.
8 Stat. 484; TS 244-2; 9 Bevans 1286.

NOTE:
[1] Extraterritorial jurisdiction in Morocco relinquished by the United States October 6, 1956.

POSTAL MATTERS

Agreement for the exchange of international money orders. Signed at Rabat October 31 and at Washington November 30, 1961; entered into force April 2, 1962.
13 UST 1102; TIAS 5055; 451 UNTS 167.

International express mail agreement, with detailed regulations. Signed at Rabat and Washington March 18 and May 11, 1988; entered into force June 1, 1988.
TIAS 11588.

SCIENTIFIC COOPERATION

Memorandum of understanding concerning scientific and technical cooperation in the earth sciences, with annexes. Signed at Reston and Rabat August 27 and October 11, 1993; entered into force October 11, 1993.
TIAS 12166.

Memorandum of understanding concerning scientific and technical cooperation in the earth sciences, with annexes. Signed at Reston and Rabat January 13 and March 9, 2000; entered into force March 9, 2000.
TIAS

SPACE COOPERATION

Agreement concerning the use of Ben Guerir Air Base as a space shuttle emergency landing site. Signed at Rabat and Washington January 21 and 28, 1987; entered into force January 28, 1987.
TIAS 12209.

TAXATION

Convention for the avoidance of double taxation and the prevention of fiscal evasion with respect to taxes on income, with related notes.[1] Signed at Rabat August 1, 1977; entered into force December 30, 1981.
33 UST 2545; TIAS 10194.

Agreement interpreting certain articles of the convention of August 1, 1977 (TIAS 10194). Signed at Washington and Rabat October 25,

1979 and at Rabat April 17, 1981; entered into force December 30, 1981.
33 UST 2672; TIAS 10195.

NOTE:
[1] With reservation and understanding.

TOURISM

Agreement on the development and facilitation of tourism. Signed at Washington July 22, 1985; entered into force July 22, 1985.
TIAS 12001.

VISAS

Arrangement between the United States and France for the waiver by France of visa requirements for United States citizens visiting Metropolitan France and certain French territories, and for the granting by the United States of gratis passport visas to French citizens resident in those territories who enter the United States as nonimmigrants. Exchange of notes at Paris March 16 and 31, 1949; entered into force March 31, 1949.
63 Stat. 2737; TIAS 1987; 7 Bevans 1311; 84 UNTS 283.

MOZAMBIQUE

AGRICULTURAL COMMODITIES

Agricultural commodities agreement, with agreed minutes. Signed at Maputo June 28, 1979; entered into force June 28, 1979.
31 UST 4711; TIAS 9635.

Related agreements:
June 23, 1980 (32 UST 2548; TIAS 9857; 1274 UNTS 109).
July 24, 1980 (32 UST 2548; TIAS 9857; 1274 UNTS 119).
February 23, 1981 (33 UST 1143; TIAS 10100; 1281 UNTS 25).

Agricultural commodities agreement. Signed at Maputo January 11, 1985; entered into force January 11, 1985.
NP

Amendments:
January 17 and 18, 1985 (NP).
May 23, 1985 (NP).

Related agreements:
April 11, 1986 (NP).
July 9, 1986 (NP).
August 22, 1986 (NP).

MOZAMBIQUE (Cont'd)

COPYRIGHT (See APPENDIX)

DEFENSE

Agreement concerning the provision of training related to defense articles under the United States International Military Education and Training (IMET) Program. Exchange of notes at Maputo November 7, 1984 and April 12, 1985; entered into force April 12, 1985.
TIAS 11338.

Agreement regarding grants under the Foreign Assistance Act of 1961, as amended, and the furnishing of defense articles, related training and other defense services from the United States to Mozambique. Exchange of notes at Maputo March 30 and May 13, 1994; entered into force May 13, 1994.
TIAS

Agreement concerning the status of United States military and civilian personnel of the U.S. Department of Defense temporarily present in Mozambique in connection with humanitarian relief operations. Exchange of notes at Maputo March 3 and 7, 2000; entered into force March 7, 2000.
NP

ECONOMIC AND TECHNICAL COOPERATION

Agency for International Development:
September 14, 1976 (28 UST 7165; TIAS 8711; 1087 UNTS 19).
December 2, 1977 (29 UST 5294; TIAS 9108; 1134 UNTS 375).

EMPLOYMENT

Agreement relating to the employment of dependents of official government employees. Exchange of notes at Washington June 29 and July 14, 1998; entered into force July 14, 1998.
TIAS

FINANCE

Agreement regarding the consolidation and rescheduling of certain debts owed to, guaranteed by or insured by the United States Government and its agencies, with annex. Signed at Maputo February 12, 1987; entered into force March 27, 1987.
NP

Agreement regarding the consolidation and rescheduling of certain debts owed to, guaranteed by, or insured by the United States Gov-

ernment and its agencies, with annexes. Signed at Maputo March 6, 1990; entered into force April 23, 1990.
NP

Agreement regarding the consolidation and rescheduling of certain debts owed to, guaranteed by, or insured by the United States Government and its agencies, with annexes. Signed at Maputo August 27, 1991; entered into force September 30, 1991.
NP

Agreement regarding the consolidation and rescheduling of certain debts owed to, guaranteed by or insured by the United States Government and its agency, with annexes. Signed at Maputo August 13, 1993; entered into force September 27, 1993.
NP

Amendment:
July 13 and August 31, 1995 (NP).

Agreement regarding the consolidation, reduction and rescheduling of certain debts owed to, guaranteed by, or insured by the United States Government and its agency, with annexes. Signed at Maputo August 13, 1997; entered into force September 29, 1997.
TIAS

Amendment:
September 30 and October 27, 1998.

Investment incentive agreement. Signed at Maputo September 23, 1999; entered into force September 23, 1999.
TIAS

PEACE CORPS

Agreement concerning the program of the Peace Corps in Mozambique. Signed at Maputo December 27, 1991; entered into force December 27, 1991.
TIAS

POSTAL MATTERS

International express mail agreement, with detailed regulations. Signed at Maputo and Washington July 9 and 23, 1990; entered into force August 30, 1990.
TIAS 11758.

SCIENTIFIC COOPERATION

Memorandum of understanding for scientific and technical cooperation in the earth sciences. Signed at Reston April 10, 1986; entered into force April 10, 1986.
TIAS 11958.

MULTINATIONAL FORCE AND OBSERVERS

CLAIMS

Agreement concerning the settlement of claims by the United States against the Multinational Force and Observers (MFO). Exchange of notes at Rome May 3, 1990; entered into force May 3, 1990.
TIAS 11899.

PEACEKEEPING

Agreement relating to participation of United States military and civilian personnel in the Multinational Force and Observers established by Egypt and Israel, with annexes and agreed minute, and related exchange of letters.[1] Exchange of letters at Washington March 26, 1982; entered into force March 26, 1982.
TIAS 10557.

NOTE:
[1] See also PEACEKEEPING in multilateral section and in bilateral section under EGYPT and ISRAEL.

MUTUAL AID AND LOAN GUARANTY FUND OF THE COUNCIL OF THE ENTENTE STATES

ECONOMIC AND TECHNICAL COOPERATION

Agency for International Development:
August 31, 1976 (28 UST 8807; TIAS 8773).
August 31 and September 29, 1976 (28 UST 8637; TIAS 8766).

NAMIBIA

COPYRIGHT (See APPENDIX)

DEFENSE

Agreement regarding grants under the Foreign Assistance Act of 1961, as amended, and the furnishing of defense articles, related training and other defense services from the United States Government to the Republic of Namibia. Exchange of notes at Windhoek May 21, 1992 and February 19, 1998; entered into force February 19, 1998.
TIAS

NAMIBIA (Cont'd)

ECONOMIC AND TECHNICAL COOPERATION

General agreement for special development assistance. Signed at New York September 28, 1990; entered into force September 28, 1990. TIAS 11901.

Agreement for special development assistance. Signed at Windhoek May 27, 1992; entered into force May 27, 1992. TIAS 11863.

EMPLOYMENT

Agreement relating to the employment of dependents of official government employees. Exchange of notes at Windhoek January 24 and June 8, 1994; entered into force June 8, 1994. TIAS 12184.

ENVIRONMENTAL COOPERATION

Agreement for cooperation in the Global Learning and Observations to Benefit the Environment (GLOBE) Program, with appendices. Signed at Windhoek October 8, 1997; entered into force October 8, 1997. TIAS

FINANCE

Investment incentive agreement. Signed at Washington June 20, 1990; entered into force June 5, 1991. TIAS 12096.

POSTAL MATTERS

International express mail agreement, with detailed regulations. Signed at Windhoek and Washington September 30 and October 24, 1994; entered into force December 1, 1994. NP

SCIENTIFIC COOPERATION

Memorandum of understanding concerning scientific and technical cooperation in the earth sciences, with annexes. Signed at Reston and Windhoek July 27 and August 23, 1995; entered into force August 23, 1995. TIAS 12683.

NAURU

On January 31, 1968 Nauru became an independent state. In a note dated May 28, 1968 to the Secretary-General of the United Nations, the Chief Secretary made a statement reading in part as follows:

"Prior to Nauru attaining independence on 31st January, 1968, treaty relationships were entered into, on its behalf, by the Government of the Commonwealth of Australia. The Government of Nauru now wishes to make clear its position in regard to obligations arising from those treaties entered into prior to 31st January, 1968 by the Government of the Commonwealth of Australia, and accordingly makes the following declarations.

"In respect of all bilateral treaties validly concluded by Australia on behalf of Nauru, or validly applied or extended by Australia to Nauru, before 31st January, 1968, the Government of Nauru will continue, on a basis of reciprocity, to apply the terms of such treaties for a period of twenty-four months unless such treaties are abrogated or modified earlier by agreement with the other contracting parties. At the expiration of this period the Government of Nauru will regard each such treaty as having terminated unless it has earlier agreed with the other contracting party to continue that treaty in existence.

"It is the earnest hope of the Government of Nauru that during the aforementioned period of twenty-four months, the normal processes of diplomatic negotiations will enable it to reach satisfactory accord with the States concerned upon the possibility of the continuance or modification or termination of such treaties. In respect of multilateral treaties, the Government of Nauru intends to review each of them individually and to indicate to the depositary in each case what steps it wishes to take, whether by way of confirmation of succession, confirmation of termination or accession, in relation to each such instrument. During such period of review, any party to a multilateral treaty which was, prior to independence, validly applied or extended to Nauru may, on a basis of reciprocity, rely as against Nauru on the terms of the treaty." In subsequent notes to the Secretary-General of the United Nations this period of review has been extended indefinitely.

EXTRADITION

Extradition treaty between the United States and the United Kingdom, signed at London December 22, 1931; applicable to Australia (including Papua, Norfolk Island, and the mandated territories of New Guinea and Nauru), in accordance with article 14, from August 30, 1935. 47 Stat. 2122; TS 849; 12 Bevans 482; 163 LNTS 59.

POSTAL MATTERS

International express mail agreement, with detailed regulations. Signed at Washington and Nauru October 8, 1993 and January 17, 1994; entered into force April 4, 1994. NP

WEATHER STATIONS

Agreement providing for the construction and operation of a weather station on Nauru Island. Exchange of notes at Canberra February 19 and 25, 1958; entered into force February 25, 1958. 9 UST 266; TIAS 4001; 317 UNTS 153.

NEPAL

COMMERCE

Agreement relating to friendship and commerce. Exchange of notes at Kathmandu April 25, 1947; entered into force April 25, 1947. 61 Stat. 2566; TIAS 1585; 10 Bevans 1; 16 UNTS 97.

CONSULS (See COMMERCE)

DEFENSE

Agreement regarding military assistance under the Foreign Assistance Act of 1961, as amended, and the furnishing of defense articles, related training and other defense services from the United States to Nepal. Exchange of notes at Kathmandu September 19, 1994 and January 25, 1995; entered into force January 25, 1995. TIAS 12350.

Agreement concerning the status of United States military and civilian personnel of the U.S. Department of Defense temporarily present in the Kingdom of Nepal in connection with the Multi-Platoon Training Event. Exchange of notes at Kathmandu January 12 and 13, 2000; entered into force January 13, 2000. NP

ECONOMIC AND TECHNICAL COOPERATION

General agreement for technical cooperation. Signed at New Delhi January 23, 1951; entered into force January 23, 1951. 2 UST 489; TIAS 2198; 184 UNTS 65.

Amendment:
January 2 and 8, 1952 (3 UST 4760; TIAS 2642; 184 UNTS 74).

NEPAL (Cont'd)

Agency for International Development:
June 5, 1975 (29 UST 137; TIAS 8801).
July 21, 1975 (29 UST 2473; TIAS 8949).
January 13, 1976 (28 UST 1950; TIAS 8531; 1071 UNTS 353).
February 4, 1976 (28 UST 2934; TIAS 8576).
June 30, 1976 (29 UST 114; TIAS 8799).
September 21, 1976 (29 UST 137; TIAS 8801).
August 4, 1977 (29 UST 561; TIAS 8832).
August 4, 1977 (29 UST 2458; TIAS 8948).

EDUCATION

Agreement for financing certain educational exchange programs. Signed at Kathmandu June 9, 1961; entered into force June 9, 1961.
12 UST 1253; TIAS 4845; 421 UNTS 223.

Amendment:
July 10 and December 13, 1974 and May 18, 1975 (27 UST 2831; TIAS 8352).

EMPLOYMENT

Agreement relating to the employment of dependents of official government employees. Exchange of notes at Washington December 19, 1996 and May 13, 1997; entered into force May 13, 1997.
TIAS

ENVIRONMENTAL COOPERATION

Agreement for cooperation in the Global Learning and Observations to Benefit the Environment (GLOBE) Program, with appendices. Signed at Kathmandu March 3, 2000; entered into force March 3, 2000.
TIAS

FINANCE

Agreement relating to investment guaranties authorized by section 413 (b)(4) of the Mutual Security Act of 1954, as amended. Exchange of notes at Washington May 17, 1960; entered into force May 17, 1960.
11 UST 1396; TIAS 4477; 372 UNTS 313.

Amendment:
June 4, 1963 (14 UST 994; TIAS 5391; 487 UNTS 376).

JUDICIAL ASSISTANCE

Procedures for mutual assistance in connection with matters relating to the Boeing Company.

Signed at Washington January 5, 1979; entered into force January 5, 1979.
30 UST 2495; TIAS 9347; 1171 UNTS 111.

PEACE CORPS

Agreement relating to the establishment of a Peace Corps program in Nepal. Exchange of notes at Kathmandu August 24, 1962; entered into force August 24, 1962.
13 UST 1909; TIAS 5146; 460 UNTS 143.

POSTAL MATTERS

Express mail agreement, with detailed regulations. Signed at Nepal and Washington July 9 and October 25, 1996; entered into force January 1, 1997.
NP

TRADE (See also COMMERCE)

Agreement relating to trade in cotton textiles, with annexes. Exchange of notes at Kathmandu May 30 and June 1, 1986; entered into force June 1, 1986.
NP

Amendments and extensions:
November 17 and December 4, 1988 (NP).
December 21, 1989 and January 10, 1990 (NP).
November 19 and 28, 1990 (NP).
December 2, 1993 and July 22, 1994 (NP).
April 18 and 30, 1996 (NP).

Administrative arrangement relating to a visa system for exports of Nepalese textile products. Exchange of notes at Kathmandu July 28 and August 18, 1986; entered into force August 18, 1986; effective October 1, 1986.
NP

Amendment:
November 19 and 28, 1990 (NP).

NETHERLANDS

ATOMIC ENERGY

Agreement for cooperation on uses of atomic energy for mutual defense purposes. Signed at The Hague May 6, 1959; entered into force July 27, 1959.
10 UST 1334; TIAS 4277; 355 UNTS 327.

Agreement in the area of nuclear reactor safety research. Signed at Bethesda and The Hague May 27 and September 1, 1987; entered into force September 1, 1987.
TIAS 12223.

Arrangement for the exchange of technical information and cooperation in regulatory and safety research matters, with appendices and

patent addendum. Signed at Vienna September 23, 1987; entered into force September 23, 1987.
TIAS 12222.

Arrangement for the exchange of technical information and cooperation in regulatory and safety research matters. Signed at Vienna October 2, 1997; entered into force October 2, 1997.
TIAS

AVIATION

Agreement providing for nonassertion of sovereign immunity from suit of air transport enterprises.[1] Exchange of notes at Washington June 19, 1953; entered into force June 19, 1953.
4 UST 1610; TIAS 2828; 212 UNTS 249.

Air transport agreement.[1] Signed at Washington April 3, 1957; entered into force provisionally April 3, 1957; definitively May 31, 1957.
12 UST 837; TIAS 4782; 410 UNTS 193.

Amendments:
March 31, 1978 (29 UST 3088; TIAS 8998; 1123 UNTS 345).[2]
June 11, 1986 (TIAS 11365).
October 13 and December 22, 1987 (TIAS 11927).
January 29 and March 13, 1992 (TIAS 11929).
October 14, 1992 (TIAS 11976).

Agreement relating to the reciprocal acceptance of airworthiness certifications.[1] Exchange of notes at The Hague January 16, 1974; entered into force August 1, 1974.
25 UST 1422; TIAS 7869.

Memorandum of agreement relating to the provision of flight inspection services. Signed at Washington and The Hague March 10 and June 15, 1978; entered into force June 15, 1978; effective April 1, 1978.
30 UST 283; TIAS 9199.

Amendment:
February 19 and May 4, 1982 (TIAS 10546).
TIAS

Agreement for the promotion of aviation safety. Signed at The Hague September 13, 1995; entered into force December 1, 1996.
TIAS 12691.

Agreement relating to air transportation between the United States and Aruba, with annexes. Signed at Washington September 18, 1997; entered into force June 11, 1998.
TIAS

NOTES:
[1] Applicable to all territories, except Aruba.
[2] Articles 3, 4, 6 and 9 have been superseded by subsequent amendments.

NETHERLANDS (Cont'd)

CLAIMS

Memorandum of understanding regarding claims by the Netherlands to looted securities, with annex and related note. Signed at Washington January 19, 1951; entered into force January 19, 1951.
2 UST 1262; TIAS 2275; 141 UNTS 221.

Agreement relating to selection of De Nederlandsche Bank of Amsterdam by the United States, Iran, and Algeria as the mutually agreeable central bank to manage the depositary of funds in the security account established by the January 19, 1981 Declaration of the Government of the Democratic and Popular Republic of Algeria,[1] with related technical agreements signed August 17, 1981. Exchange of notes at The Hague July 10, 1981; entered into force July 10, 1981.
TIAS

NOTE:
[1] See IRAN—CLAIMS.

COMMERCE

Agreement relating to commercial policy. Exchange of notes at Washington November 21, 1946; entered into force November 21, 1946.
61 Stat. 2424; TIAS 1564; 10 Bevans 181; 12 UNTS 173.

Treaty of friendship, commerce and navigation, with protocol and exchange of notes.[1] Signed at The Hague March 27, 1956; entered into force December 5, 1957.
8 UST 2043; TIAS 3942; 285 UNTS 231.

NOTES:
[1] Applicable to Aruba and Netherlands Antilles, and to all territories over which the United States has jurisdiction or international responsibility except the Trust Territory of Pacific Islands.

COPYRIGHT (See APPENDIX)

CUSTOMS

Arrangement regarding reciprocal free entry privileges for consular officers. Exchange of notes at The Hague and at Washington April 7, June 17, August 20, and September 19, 1930; entered into force September 19, 1930.
Foreign Relations, 1931, Vol. II, p. 771; 10 Bevans 105.

Amendment:
February 1, 1947 and August 20, 1948.

Reciprocal arrangement providing that trade commissioners may import, free of duty, articles for their personal use during their official residence. Exchange of notes at The Hague July 2 and November 10, 1936; entered into force November 10, 1936.

Agreement on mutual administrative assistance for the proper application of customs law and for the prevention, investigation and combating of customs offences, with annex. Signed at Washington October 28, 1996; entered into force May 1, 1998.
TIAS

DEFENSE (See also MUTUAL SECURITY)

Mutual defense assistance agreement. Signed at Washington January 27, 1950; entered into force January 27, 1950.
1 UST 88; TIAS 2015; 80 UNTS 219.

Agreement concerning the participation of the Netherlands forces in the United Nations operations in Korea. Signed at Washington May 15, 1952; entered into force May 15, 1952.
3 UST 3987; TIAS 2534; 177 UNTS 233.

Agreement relating to the disposition of equipment and materials furnished by the United States under the mutual defense assistance agreement and no longer required for the purposes for which originally made available. Exchange of notes at The Hague November 12 and 26, 1953; entered into force November 26, 1953.
11 UST 2017; TIAS 4556; 388 UNTS 303.

Amendment:
August 10 and 13, 1960 (11 UST 2017; TIAS 4556; 388 UNTS 303).

Agreement relating to a memorandum of understanding and a model contract for the offshore procurement program. Exchange of notes at The Hague April 15 and May 7, 1954; entered into force July 30, 1954.
5 UST 2027; TIAS 3069; 213 UNTS 325.

Agreement relating to the stationing of United States armed forces in the Netherlands, with annex. Exchange of notes at The Hague August 13, 1954; entered into force November 16, 1954.
6 UST 103; TIAS 3174; 251 UNTS 91.

Agreement establishing an air defense technical center with cost reimbursement contract attached. Exchange of notes at The Hague December 14, 1954; entered into force December 14, 1954.
6 UST 915; TIAS 3236; 262 UNTS 35.

Agreement relating to a weapons production program. Exchange of notes at The Hague March 24, 1960; entered into force provisionally March 24, 1960; definitively January 2, 1962.
12 UST 180; TIAS 4692; 406 UNTS 165.

Administrative arrangements pertaining to prefinanced NATO common infrastructure projects. Exchange of letters at The Hague and

Heidelberg May 30 and July 24, 1975; entered into force July 24, 1975.
30 UST 2885; TIAS 9369; 1177 UNTS 247.

General arrangement relating to the cooperative production of the M109 vehicle and its components. Signed at The Hague May 3, 1966; entered into force May 3, 1966.
29 UST 5713; TIAS 9144.

Amendments:
March 17, 1969 (29 UST 5721; TIAS 9144).
December 30, 1974 and June 5, 1975 (29 UST 5722; TIAS 9144).
March 2 and April 14, 1979 (TIAS 10641).
January 31, 1983 (TIAS 10641).

Memorandum of understanding concerning principles governing mutual cooperation in research and development, production and procurement of conventional defense equipment. Signed at Washington and The Hague July 25 and August 24, 1978; entered into force August 24, 1978.
33 UST 3105; TIAS 10214.

Agreement relating to storage of prepositioned war readiness materials by United States forces. Exchange of notes at The Hague January 15, 1981; entered into force August 20, 1981.
33 UST 891; TIAS 10073; 1268 UNTS 77.

Agreement establishing a television transmitter at Soesterberg Airfield. Exchange of notes at The Hague December 7, 1981 and March 4, 1982; entered into force July 19, 1983.
TIAS 10883; 1359 UNTS 249.

Mutual logistical support agreement, with annexes. Signed at Stuttgart February 22, 1983; entered into force February 22, 1983.
TIAS 10663; 1359 UNTS 257.

Amendment:
February 27 and March 20, 1992 (TIAS 12353).

Memorandum of understanding regarding the exchange of Air Force officers. Signed at The Hague and Washington May 22, 1984 and May 7, 1985; entered into force May 7, 1985.
TIAS 11233.

Agreement on termination of agreement of November 4, 1985 concerning the stationing, support and operation of the Ground Launched Cruise Missile (GLCM) system in the territory of the Netherlands. Exchange of notes at The Hague December 18, 1987; entered into force June 1, 1988.
TIAS

Memorandum of understanding between the United States Air Forces in Europe and the Royal Netherlands Air Force concerning the logistical support/services for the Soviet inspection(s) under the INF Treaty at Woensdrecht AB, Netherlands, with annexes. Signed at Royal Netherlands Air Force Headquarters and Ramstein Air Base, Germany, July 13 and August 10, 1989; entered into force August 10, 1989.
TIAS 12351.

NETHERLANDS (Cont'd)

Memorandum of understanding regarding the joint training of Royal Netherlands Air Force and United States Air Force aircrews on the F-16 weapons system in the United States. Signed at The Hague October 30, 1989; entered into force October 30, 1989.
NP

Memorandum of understanding concerning the residual value of the U.S. funded facilities for the Ground Launched Cruise Missile (GLCM) at Woensdrecht Air Base, the Netherlands, with annexes. Signed at The Hague December 6, 1989; entered into force December 6, 1989.
TIAS 12352.

Memorandum of understanding concerning measures to be taken for the transfer, security and safeguarding of technical information, software and equipment to the Ministry of Defense to enable industry to establish North Sea ACMI range display and debriefing system facilities in the Netherlands. Signed at Washington July 6, 1992; entered into force July 6, 1992.
TIAS 12354.

Memorandum of understanding for the dynamic behavior of composite ship structures (DYCOSS) project, with annexes. Signed at The Hague and Washington July 18 and August 11, 1994; entered into force August 11, 1994.
TIAS 12355.

Memorandum of understanding for the tip vortex cavitation project, with annexes. Signed at Washington and The Hague April 25 and July 15, 1996; entered into force July 15, 1996.
TIAS

Agreement concerning a cooperative project for the measurement and analysis of the infrared celestial background. Signed at Washington and The Hague June 24 and September 16, 1996; entered into force September 16, 1996.
TIAS

Memorandumm of understanding concerning technology research and development projects, with annex. Signed at Washington May 14, 1998; entered into force May 14, 1998.
TIAS

ECONOMIC AND TECHNICAL COOPERATION

Economic cooperation agreement. Signed at The Hague July 2, 1948; entered into force July 2, 1948.
62 Stat. 2477; TIAS 1791; 10 Bevans 240; 20 UNTS 91.

Amendments:
January 16 and February 2, 1950 (1 UST 665; TIAS 2126; 93 UNTS 361).
March 7 and April 3, 1951 (2 UST 1319; TIAS 2285; 141 UNTS 368).

November 28, 1952 (3 UST 5260; TIAS 2721; 173 UNTS 382).

Agreement relating to the assumption by Indonesia of all responsibilities and obligations of the Netherlands incurred under the economic cooperation agreements of July 2, 1948, as amended, and April 26, 1949, as amended, and the loan agreements of October 28, 1948, and December 22, 1949, and memorandum of understanding. Signed at Washington February 11, 1952, by the United States, Indonesia, and the Netherlands; entered into force February 11, 1952.
3 UST 2989; TIAS 2484; 165 UNTS 77.

General agreement for technical cooperation for Suriname and Netherlands Antilles.[1] Signed at The Hague January 22, 1954; entered into force April 21, 1954.
5 UST 919; TIAS 2982; 190 UNTS 207.

NOTE:
[1] Also applicable to Aruba.

EDUCATION

Agreement for the financing of certain education exchange programs. Signed at The Hague October 16, 1972; entered into force August 8, 1973.
24 UST 1924; TIAS 7700.

EMPLOYMENT

Agreement relating to the employment of dependents of official government employees. Exchange of notes at The Hague June 23, 1986; entered into force May 13, 1987.
TIAS 11359.

ENERGY

Memorandum of understanding concerning the exchange of energy information. Signed at Washington and The Hague June 1 and 29, 1982; entered into force June 29, 1982.
TIAS 10873; 1577 UNTS 409.

Extension:
June 9 and 25, 1987 (TIAS 11536).

ENVIRONMENTAL COOPERATION

Memorandum of understanding concerning cooperation in the field of environmental protection. Signed at Paris June 17, 1985; entered into force June 17, 1985.
TIAS 11161.

Memorandum of understanding for cooperation in the GLOBE program. Signed at Washington

February 28, 1995; entered into force February 28, 1995.
TIAS 12607.

EXTRADITION

Extradition treaty, with appendix.[1] Signed at The Hague June 24, 1980; entered into force September 15, 1983.
TIAS 10733.

NOTE:
[1] Applicable to Aruba and Netherlands Antilles.

FINANCE

Agreement relating to the guaranties authorized by section 111 (b)(3) of the Economic Cooperation Act of 1948, as amended. Exchange of notes at Washington September 24 and October 7, 1952; entered into force October 8, 1952.
3 UST 5060; TIAS 2690; 173 UNTS 378.

JUDICIAL ASSISTANCE

Procedures for mutual assistance in the administration of justice in connection with the Lockheed Aircraft Corporation matter. Signed at Washington March 29, 1976; entered into force March 29, 1976.
27 UST 1064; TIAS 8245.

Related agreement:
March 21, 1979 (30 UST 2500; TIAS 9348; 1171 UNTS 215).

Treaty on mutual assistance in criminal matters, with exchange of notes.[1] Signed at The Hague June 12, 1981; entered into force September 15, 1983.
TIAS 10734; 1359 UNTS 209.

Agreement on mutual administrative assistance in the exchange of information in securities matters. Signed at The Hague December 11, 1989; entered into force July 1, 1992.
TIAS 12405.

Agreement regarding mutual cooperation in the tracing, freezing, seizure and forfeiture of proceeds and instrumentalities of crime and the sharing of forfeited assets. Signed at Washington November 20, 1992; entered into force August 4, 1994.
TIAS 12482.

Agreement on mutual administrative assistance in the exchange of information in futures matters. Signed at Washington April 29, 1993; entered into force February 1, 1994.
TIAS 12151.

NOTE:
[1] Not applicable to requests for assistance relating to fiscal offenses addressed to Aruba or the Netherlands Antilles.

NETHERLANDS (Cont'd)

LEND-LEASE

Preliminary agreement regarding principles applying to mutual aid in the prosecution of the war against aggression, and exchange of notes. Signed at Washington July 8, 1942; entered into force July 8, 1942.
56 Stat. 1554; EAS 259; 10 Bevans 142; 103 UNTS 277.

Mutual aid agreement relating to supplies and services, with accompanying memorandum and exchange of notes. Signed at Washington April 30, 1945; entered into force April 30, 1945.
59 Stat. 1627; EAS 480; 10 Bevans 158; 139 UNTS 341.

Agreement relating to principles applying to the provision of aid to the armed forces of the United States, and exchange of notes. Exchange of notes at Washington April 30, 1945; operative from July 8, 1942.
59 Stat. 1635; EAS 480; 10 Bevans 167; 139 UNTS 319.

LEND-LEASE SETTLEMENT

Agreement regarding settlement for lend-lease, reciprocal aid, surplus property, military relief, and claims, and exchanges of notes with memorandum of arrangement between the United States, the United Kingdom, and the Netherlands. Signed at Washington May 28, 1947; entered into force May 28, 1947.
61 Stat. 3924; TIAS 1750; 8 Bevans 1250; 10 Bevans 188 and 213; 17 UNTS 29.

Amendment:
June 1 and 8, 1950 (1 UST 638; TIAS 2119; 81 UNTS 320).

MAPPING

Basic exchange and cooperative agreement concerning mapping, charting and geodesy cooperation, with glossary. Signed at Fairfax April 26, 1995; entered into force April 26, 1995.
NP

MILITARY CEMETERIES AND MONUMENTS

Agreement concerning American military cemeteries with annex. Signed at The Hague May 4, 1970; entered into force November 18, 1970.
21 UST 2416; TIAS 6978; 775 UNTS 77.

MUTUAL SECURITY

Agreement relating to the assurances required by the Mutual Security Act of 1951. Exchange of notes at The Hague January 8, 1952; entered into force January 8, 1952.
3 UST 4633; TIAS 2615; 173 UNTS 372.

NARCOTIC DRUGS

Agreement concerning the use of facilities in the Netherlands Antilles and Aruba for the purpose of conducting counternarcotics detection and monitoring and interdiction missions. Exchange of notes at The Hague April 9 and 13, 1999; entered into force April 13, 1999.
TIAS

NAVIGATION

Arrangement concerning the installation and support of a USAFE Loran C/D transmitter site, with annex. Signed at Ramstein and The Hague May 17 and July 12, 1982; entered into force July 12, 1982.
TIAS 12379.

PACIFIC SETTLEMENT OF DISPUTES

Treaty for the advancement of peace. Signed at Washington December 18, 1913; entered into force March 10, 1928. Declaration interpretative of article I, signed at Washington February 13, 1928, entered into force February 27, 1928.
45 Stat. 2462; TS 760; 10 Bevans 64.

Treaty of arbitration. Signed at Washington January 13, 1930; entered into force July 17, 1930.
46 Stat. 2769; TS 820; 10 Bevans 100; 107 LNTS 69.

PATENTS

Agreement to facilitate the interchange of patent rights and technical information for defense purposes with exchange of notes. Signed at The Hague April 29, 1955; entered into force provisionally April 29, 1955; definitively July 13, 1955.
6 UST 2187; TIAS 3287; 219 UNTS 105.

Agreement approving the procedures for reciprocal filing of classified patent applications in the United States and the Netherlands. Exchange of notes at The Hague October 8, 1959; entered into force October 8, 1959.
10 UST 1774; TIAS 4332; 358 UNTS 286.

POSTAL MATTERS

Money order convention. Signed at Washington November 30 and at The Hague December 21, 1886; entered into force April 1, 1887.
NP

Parcel post agreement and detailed regulations. Signed at Washington September 5 and at The Hague September 20, 1937; entered into force November 1, 1937.
51 Stat. 295; Post Office Department print; 184 LNTS 319.

International express mail agreement, with detailed regulations. Signed at The Hague and Washington May 19 and June 10, 1980; entered into force September 1, 1980.
32 UST 2033; TIAS 9816; 1252 UNTS 153.

International express mail agreement, with detailed regulations. Signed at Oranjestad and Washington August 15 and September 14, 1989; entered into force October 16, 1989.
TIAS 11695.

RELIEF SUPPLIES AND PACKAGES

Agreement relating to duty-free entry of relief goods, relief packages, and standard packs and to the defrayment of transportation charges thereon. Exchange of notes at The Hague January 17, 1949; entered into force January 17, 1949.
63 Stat. 2322; TIAS 1881; 10 Bevans 259; 32 UNTS 241.

SEABEDS

Agreement relating to the agreement of August 14, 1987 on the resolution of practical problems with respect to deep seabed mining areas.[1] Exchange of notes at The Hague August 14, 1987; entered into force October 19, 1988.
TIAS 11438; 1649 UNTS 117.

NOTE:
[1] Parties to the multilateral agreement of August 14, 1987 are Belgium, Canada, Italy, Netherlands and Union of Soviet Socialist Republics.

SHIPPING

Agreement relating to jurisdiction over vessels utilizing the Louisiana Offshore Oil Port. Exchange of notes at Washington March 9 and 16, 1981; entered into force November 2, 1981.
33 UST 1555; TIAS 10132; 1307 UNTS 409.

NETHERLANDS (Cont'd)

SMUGGLING

Convention for the prevention of smuggling of alcoholic liquors. Signed at Washington August 21, 1924; entered into force April 8, 1925.
44 Stat. 2013; TS 712; 10 Bevans 76; 33 LNTS 434.

SOCIAL SECURITY

Agreement on social security, with administrative arrangement. Signed at The Hague December 8, 1987; entered into force November 1, 1990.
TIAS

Protocol to the agreement on social security and administrative arrangement of December 8, 1987. Signed at The Hague December 7, 1989; entered into force November 1, 1990.
TIAS

SURPLUS PROPERTY

Agreement relating to the release of the Netherlands from its obligations as guarantor for Indonesia under the surplus property agreement of May 28, 1947. Exchange of notes at The Hague September 17, 1952, at Djakarta October 15, 1952, and at Washington April 8, 1953; entered into force April 8, 1953.
4 UST 1557; TIAS 2820; 205 UNTS 324.

TAXATION

Convention with respect to taxes on income and certain other taxes.[1] Signed at Washington April 29, 1948; entered into force December 1, 1948.
62 Stat. 1757; TIAS 1855; 10 Bevans 225; 32 UNTS 167.

Convention modifying and supplementing the convention of April 29, 1948, as amended, for avoidance of double taxation with respect to taxes on income and certain other taxes. Signed at Washington December 30, 1965; entered into force July 8, 1966.
17 UST 896; TIAS 6051; 577 UNTS 295.

Agreement relating to relief from taxation on United States Government expenditures in the Netherlands for the common defense. Exchange of notes, with memorandum attached, at The Hague March 7, 1952; entered into force March 7, 1952.
3 UST 4183; TIAS 2563; 135 UNTS 199.

Agreement concerning the tax relief techniques and procedures pursuant to the agreement of March 7, 1952. Exchange of notes at The Hague May 29 and June 22, 1953; entered into force June 22, 1953.
5 UST 2556; TIAS 3120; 234 UNTS 320.

Convention for the avoidance of double taxation and the prevention of fiscal evasion with respect to taxes on estates and inheritances with protocol. Signed at Washington July 15, 1969; entered into force February 3, 1971.
22 UST 247; TIAS 7061; 791 UNTS 201.

Convention for the avoidance of double taxation and the prevention of fiscal evasion with respect to taxes on income with understanding and exchange of notes. Signed at Washington December 18, 1992; entered into force December 31, 1993.
TIAS

Protocol amending the convention of December 18, 1992, for the avoidance of double taxation and the prevention of fiscal evasion with respect to taxes on income, with exchange of notes. Signed at Washington October 13, 1993; entered into force December 30, 1993.
TIAS

Protocol amending Article VIII of the convention of April 29, 1948, with respect to taxes on income and certain other taxes as applicable to the Netherlands Antilles. Signed at Washington October 10, 1995; entered into force December 30, 1996.
TIAS

NOTE:
[1] The convention was supplemented by a protocol, signed at Washington June 15, 1955, for the purpose of facilitating the extension of the convention to the Netherlands Antilles (6 UST 3696; TIAS 3366; 239 UNTS 342). This was effectuated in accordance with exchanges of notes at Washington June 24 and August 7, 1952 and September 15 and November 4 and 10, 1955 (6 UST 3703; TIAS 3367; 239 UNTS 346). A further protocol modifying and supplementing the extension of the convention to the Netherlands Antilles was signed at The Hague October 23, 1963 (15 UST 1900; TIAS 5665; 521 UNTS 377). The convention became applicable to Aruba as a separate entity as of January 1, 1986.

In accordance with notifications given by the United States on June 29 and July 10, 1987, the convention ceased to apply to Aruba and the Netherlands Antilles, as of January 1, 1988, with the exception of Article VIII of the convention and such ancillary provisions as apply to effectuate, modify, or limit that article.

TELECOMMUNICATION

Agreement relating to the reciprocal granting of authorizations to permit licensed amateur radio operators of either country to operate their stations in the other country.[1] Exchange of notes at The Hague June 22, 1966; entered into force December 21, 1966.
17 UST 2426; TIAS 6189; 590 UNTS 109.

NOTE:
[1] Applicable to Aruba and Netherlands Antilles.

TRADE AND COMMERCE (See COMMERCE. See also BENELUX)

TRANSPORTATION

Memorandum of understanding concerning cooperation in the field of transportation. Signed at Washington and The Hague September 28 and October 6, 1977; entered into force October 6, 1977.
29 UST 3577; TIAS 9029; 1134 UNTS 327.

VISAS

Agreement relating to the reciprocal waiver of passport visa fees for nonimmigrants.[1] Exchanges of notes at The Hague January 21, February 11, and March 5 and 13, 1946; entered into force April 15, 1946.
61 Stat. 3834; TIAS 1728; 10 Bevans 178; 84 UNTS 3.

Agreement relating to visa requirements. Exchange of notes at The Hague July 30 and August 20, 1947; entered into force August 20, 1947.
61 Stat. 3838; TIAS 1729; 10 Bevans 220; 84 UNTS 11.

NOTE:
[1] Applicable to Aruba and Netherlands Antilles.

WEATHER STATIONS

Agreement providing for lending ultra high frequency radio equipment for installation on Netherlands ocean weather ships stationed along the North Atlantic route. Exchange of notes at Washington March 16 and 21, 1955; entered into force March 21, 1955.
9 UST 1302; TIAS 4119; 289 UNTS 129.

Agreement relating to continuation of the cooperative meteorological observation program in the Netherlands Antilles.[1] Exchange of notes at The Hague June 15, 1970; entered into force provisionally June 15, 1970; definitively December 11, 1970.
21 UST 2643; TIAS 7005; 772 UNTS 147.

Agreement relating to cooperation regarding a hurricane monitoring and forecasting program for the Caribbean, with memorandum of arrangement. Exchange of notes at The Hague July 26, 1979; entered into force May 8, 1980.
32 UST 414; TIAS 9708; 1221 UNTS 175.

NOTE:
[1] Also applicable to Aruba.

NETHERLANDS (Cont'd)

NETHERLANDS ANTILLES

AVIATION

Memorandum of agreement concerning assistance in developing and modernizing the Netherlands Antilles civil aviation infrastructure. Signed at Washington and Willemstad March 28 and August 6, 1991; entered into force August 6, 1991.
TIAS 11803.

Agreement relating to air transport between the Netherlands Antilles and the United States of America, with annexes. Signed at Washington July 14, 1998; entered into force February 16, 1999.
TIAS

POSTAL MATTERS

Parcel post agreement and detailed regulations for execution. Signed at Willemstad May 10 and at Washington May 17, 1951; operative February 1, 1951.
2 UST 1509; TIAS 2294.

Agreement for the exchange of international money orders. Signed at Willemstad December 20, 1960 and at Washington January 11, 1961; entered into force May 1, 1961.
12 UST 664; TIAS 4767.

International express mail agreement, with detailed regulations. Signed at Willemstad and Washington June 10 and 22, 1987; entered into force August 3, 1987.
TIAS 11305.

NEW CALEDONIA

POSTAL MATTERS

International express mail agreement, with detailed regulations. Signed at Noumea and Washington April 9 and May 28, 1991; entered into force July 1, 1991.
TIAS 11809.

NEW ZEALAND

AEROSPACE DISTURBANCES

Agreement concerning a program of research on aerospace disturbances, with memorandum of understanding. Exchange of notes at Wellington May 15, 1963; entered into force May 15, 1963.
14 UST 524; TIAS 5350; 477 UNTS 55.

ANTARCTICA

Agreement relating to cooperation in scientific and logistical operations in Antarctica, with memorandum of understanding. Exchange of notes at Wellington December 24, 1958; entered into force December 24, 1958.
9 UST 1502; TIAS 4151; 324 UNTS 111.

Extension:
October 18, 1960 (11 UST 2205; TIAS 4591; 447 UNTS 356).

ATOMIC ENERGY

Agreement providing for a grant to assist in the acquisition of nuclear research and training equipment and materials. Exchange of notes at Wellington March 23, 1960; entered into force March 23, 1960.
11 UST 277; TIAS 4445; 371 UNTS 147.

AVIATION

Agreement concerning the acceptance of certificates of airworthiness for imported aircraft. Exchange of notes at Washington March 20, 1970; entered into force March 20, 1970.
21 UST 1040; TIAS 6857; 740 UNTS 313.

Amendment:
March 16 and 30, 1979 (30 UST 3993; TIAS 9440; 1203 UNTS 351).

Air transport agreement, with annexes. Signed at Washington June 18, 1997; entered into force June 18, 1997.
TIAS

BOUNDARIES

Treaty on the delimitation of the maritime boundary between Tokelau and the United States of America. Signed at Atafu December 2, 1980; entered into force September 3, 1983.
TIAS 10775.

CONSULS

Convention to regulate commerce (article IV) between the United States and the United Kingdom. Signed at London July 3, 1815; entered into force July 3, 1815.
8 Stat. 228; TS 110; 12 Bevans 49.

COPYRIGHT (See APPENDIX)

CUSTOMS

Agreement regarding mutual assistance between their customs services. Signed at Hong Kong June 13, 1996; entered into force June 13, 1996.
TIAS   ; 1950 UNTS 3.

DEFENSE

Agreement relating to mutual defense assistance. Exchange of notes at Washington June 19, 1952; entered into force June 19, 1952.
3 UST 4408; TIAS 2590; 178 UNTS 315.

Understanding that the assurances contained in the mutual defense assistance agreement of June 19, 1952 are applicable to equipment, materials, information and services furnished under the Mutual Security Act of 1954, as amended, and such other applicable United States laws as may come into effect. Exchange of notes at Wellington March 25, 1960; entered into force March 25, 1960.
11 UST 315; TIAS 4450; 380 UNTS 424.

Agreement relating to a reciprocal arrangement under which, in certain circumstances, either of the respective armed forces would advance funds to units or personnel of the other for their temporary support, with annex. Exchange of notes at Wellington September 3, 1969; entered into force September 3, 1969.
20 UST 2839; TIAS 6755; 723 UNTS 233.

Agreement concerning defense communications services, with annexes. Signed at Wellington and Arlington August 12 and November 18, 1992; entered into force November 18, 1992.
TIAS 12357.

Memorandum of agreement concerning the Navstar Global Positioning System, with annex. Signed at Washington September 2, 1994; entered into force September 2, 1994.
TIAS 12358.

Agreement concerning certain mutual defense commitments. Exchange of notes at Washington July 16, 1996; entered into force July 16, 1996.
TIAS   ; 1950 UNTS 15.

EDUCATION

Agreement for the financing of certain educational and cultural exchange programs. Signed at Wellington February 3, 1970; entered into force March 3, 1970.
21 UST 421; TIAS 6827; 240 UNTS 217.

EMPLOYMENT

Agreement relating to the employment of dependents of official government employees. Exchange of notes at Washington May 18 and 21, 1999; entered into force May 21, 1999.
TIAS

NEW ZEALAND (Cont'd)

EXTRADITION

Treaty on extradition.[1] Signed at Washington January 12, 1970; entered into force December 8, 1970.
22 UST 1; TIAS 7035; 791 UNTS 253.

NOTE:
[1] Applicable to all territories.

HEALTH

Memorandum of understanding relative to exporting dry milk products to the United States. Signed at Wellington and at Washington October 23 and November 11, 1975; entered into force November 11, 1975.
28 UST 345; TIAS 8472.

LEND-LEASE

Agreement relating to the principles applying to the provision of aid in the prosecution of war. Exchange of notes at Washington September 3, 1942; entered into force September 3, 1942.
56 Stat. 1611; EAS 272; 10 Bevans 285; 24 UNTS 185.

Agreement on settlement for lend-lease and reciprocal aid, surplus war property, and claims. Signed at Washington July 10, 1946; entered into force July 10, 1946.
60 Stat. 1791; TIAS 1536; 10 Bevans 296; 6 UNTS 341.

MAPPING

Agreement relating to an aerial photographic survey of the New Zealand coastline. Exchange of notes at Washington October 30, 1959; entered into force October 30, 1959.
10 UST 1983; TIAS 4364; 361 UNTS 21.

NAVIGATION

Agreement for the establishment and operation of an OMEGA navigation system monitoring facility. Exchange of notes at Wellington March 3, 1983; entered into force March 3, 1983.
TIAS 10668; 1675 UNTS 265.

OCEANOGRAPHY

Agreement concerning the installation, operation and maintenance in New Zealand of Global Sea Level Data Collection (GSL) Stations, with arrangements. Exchange of notes at

Wellington November 18, 1992; entered into force November 18, 1992.
TIAS 11973.

PACIFIC SETTLEMENT OF DISPUTES

Treaty amending in their application to New Zealand certain provisions of the treaty for the advancement of peace between the United States and the United Kingdom signed at Washington September 15, 1914. Signed at Washington September 6, 1940; entered into force August 13, 1941.
55 Stat. 1217; TS 976; 10 Bevans 282.

POSTAL MATTERS

Money order convention. Signed at Wellington October 8 and at Washington December 6, 1881; operative January 1, 1882.
NP

Agreement concerning the exchange of parcel post. Signed at Wellington March 3 and at Washington April 24, 1933; operative October 1, 1932.
48 Stat. 1491; Post Office Department print.

Memorandum of understanding concerning international express mail service, with detailed regulations. Signed at Wellington and Washington August 1 and 20, 1984; entered into force October 28, 1984.
TIAS 11003.

Memorandum of understanding concerning the operation of the INTELPOST service, with details of implementation. Signed at Berne April 28, 1989; entered into force May 1, 1989.
TIAS 11610.

PROPERTY

Convention between the United States and the United Kingdom relating to tenure and disposition of real and personal property. Signed at Washington March 2, 1899; entered into force for New Zealand June 10, 1901.
31 Stat. 1939; TS 146; I Malloy 774.

Supplementary convention relating to the tenure and disposition of real and personal property. Signed at Washington May 27, 1936, by the United States, United Kingdom, Australia, and New Zealand; entered into force March 10, 1941.
55 Stat. 1101; TS 964; 5 Bevans 140; 203 LNTS 367.

SCIENTIFIC COOPERATION

Agreement concerning the establishment of an astronomical observatory at Blackbirch Ridge, with memorandum of understandings and

agreed minute. Exchange of notes at Wellington November 11, 1982; entered into force November 11, 1982.
TIAS 10604; 1675 UNTS 247.

Agreement for scientific and technological cooperation, with annex and exchange of letters. Signed at Washington May 21, 1991; entered into force May 21, 1991.
TIAS 11829.

SHELLFISH

Memorandum of understanding concerning cooperation to assure the sanitary quality of bivalve mulluscs exported to the United States. Signed at Washington and Wellington October 14 and 30, 1980; entered into force October 30, 1980.
32 UST 4545; TIAS 9968; 1266 UNTS 35.

TAXATION

Convention for the avoidance of double taxation and the prevention of fiscal evasion with respect to taxes on income, with protocol.[1] Signed at Wellington July 23, 1982; entered into force November 2, 1983.
TIAS 10772.

NOTE:
[1] Does not include Tokelau or the Associated Self Governing States of the Cook Is. and Niue.

TELECOMMUNICATION

Agreement relating to the reciprocal granting of authorizations to permit licensed amateur radio operators of either country to operate their stations in the other country. Exchange of notes at Wellington June 21, 1967; entered into force June 21, 1967.
18 UST 1272; TIAS 6281; 644 UNTS 77.

TRACKING STATIONS

Agreement for a space vehicle tracking program. Exchange of notes at Wellington July 9, 1968; entered into force July 9, 1968.
19 UST 5836; TIAS 6539; 644 UNTS 99.

TRADE AND COMMERCE

Agreement relating to the multilateral trade negotiations, and related letter of February 4, 1980. Signed at Geneva May 21, 1979; entered into force January 1, 1980.
32 UST 5868; TIAS 10019; 1266 UNTS 23.

NEW ZEALAND (Cont'd)

VISAS

Agreement relating to the reciprocal reduction of nonimmigrant passport visa fees and the extension of validity of temporary visitors' visas.[1] Exchange of notes at Wellington March 14, 1949; entered into force March 14, 1949; operative April 1, 1949.
63 Stat. 2538; TIAS 1940; 10 Bevans 331; 32 UNTS 369.

Agreement relating to the abolition of visa fees and the extension of the period of validity for certain types of nonimmigrant visas. Exchange of notes at Wellington December 16, 1957, and May 2 and 5, 1958; entered into force May 5, 1958; operative June 1, 1958.
9 UST 913; TIAS 4053; 317 UNTS 59.

Amendment:
May 13, 1958 (9 UST 919; TIAS 4053; 317 UNTS 70).

NOTE:
[1] Applicable to all territories.

NICARAGUA

AGRICULTURAL COMMODITIES

Agricultural commodities agreement. Signed at Managua August 31, 1979; entered into force August 31, 1979.
32 UST 1615; TIAS 9790; 1234 UNTS 230.

Amendments:
February 11 and 13, 1980 (32 UST 1628; TIAS 9790; 1234 UNTS 241).
March 20 and 25, 1980 (32 UST 1632; TIAS 9790; 1234 UNTS 244).
June 19, 1980 (32 UST 1814; TIAS 9798; 1234 UNTS 247).

AGRICULTURE

Agreement continuing in force an agreement of January 11, 1941, relating to plantation rubber investigations in Nicaragua. Exchange of notes at Managua June 23 and 26, 1943; entered into force July 1, 1943.
57 Stat. 1212; EAS 357; 10 Bevans 436; 117 UNTS 253.

Agreement confirming the cooperative agreement for the prevention of foot-and-mouth disease and rinderpest in Nicaragua. Exchange of notes at Managua March 24 and April 13, 1972; entered into force April 13, 1972.
23 UST 1228; TIAS 7392; 852 UNTS 201.

Cooperative agreement for the eradication of screwworms. Signed at Washington November 26, 1991; entered into force January 11, 1993.
TIAS 12444.

AVIATION

Air transport agreement, with annexes. Signed at San Jose May 8, 1997; entered into force December 5, 1997.
TIAS

Memorandum of agreement for the provision of assistance in developing and modernizing Nicaragua's civil aviation infrastructure. Signed at Washington and Managua April 29 and August 30, 1999; entered into force August 30, 1999.
TIAS

COPYRIGHT (See APPENDIX)

CULTURAL PROPERTY

Agreement concerning the imposition of import restrictions on archaeological material from the pre-Hispanic cultures of the Republic of Nicaragua. Signed at Managua June 16, 1999; entered into force October 20, 2000.
TIAS

CUSTOMS

Interim agreement relating to customs exemptions of diplomatic and consular officials. Exchange of notes at Washington December 3, 1951, and October 9, 1952; entered into force October 9, 1952.
3 UST 5154; TIAS 2708; 184 UNTS 105.

DEFENSE

Military assistance agreement. Signed at Managua April 23, 1954; entered into force April 23, 1954.
5 UST 453; TIAS 2940; 229 UNTS 37.

Agreement relating to the disposition of equipment and materials furnished by the United States under the military assistance agreement of April 23, 1954. Exchange of notes at Managua April 23, 1954; entered into force April 23, 1954.
13 UST 116; TIAS 4946; 435 UNTS 340.

Agreement for performance by members of army and air force missions of duties of military assistance advisory group specified in article V of military assistance agreement. Exchange of notes at Managua January 17 and February 9, 1957; entered into force February 9, 1957.
8 UST 285; TIAS 3773; 279 UNTS 191.

Agreement relating to deposit by Nicaragua of ten percent of the value of grant military assistance and excess defense articles furnished by the United States. Exchange of notes at Managua March 6 and April 10, 1972; entered into force April 10, 1972; effective February 7, 1972.
23 UST 671; TIAS 7332.

Agreement concerning payment to the United States of net proceeds from the sale of defense articles furnished under the military assistance program. Exchange of notes at Managua May 15 and June 28, 1974; entered into force July 1, 1974.
25 UST 1450; TIAS 7876.

Agreement regarding the status of U.S. military and civilian personnel of the Department of Defense present in Nicaragua in connection with the disaster relief/assistance effort and mutually agreed follow-on activities. Exchange of notes at Managua November 7 and 25, 1998; entered into force November 25, 1998.
NP

ECONOMIC AND TECHNICAL COOPERATION

General agreement for economic, technical and related assistance. Exchange of notes at Managua March 30, 1962; entered into force May 14, 1962.
13 UST 1208; TIAS 5065; 456 UNTS 241.

Agency for International Development:
August 30, 1978 (30 UST 5157; TIAS 9502).
May 31, 1990 (NP).
September 26, 1990 (NP).
May 8, 1991 (NP).
December 5, 1992 (NP).
January 19, 1994 (NP).

EMPLOYMENT

Agreement relating to the employment of dependents of official government employees. Exchange of notes at Managua January 26 and February 2, 1994; entered into force February 2, 1994.
TIAS 12173.

EXTRADITION

Treaty on extradition. Signed at Washington March 1, 1905; entered into force July 14, 1907.
35 Stat. 1869; TS 462; 10 Bevans 356.

FINANCE

Agreement relating to investment guaranties under section 413(b)(4) of the Mutual Security Act of 1954, as amended. Exchange of notes

NICARAGUA (Cont'd)

at Managua April 14, 1959; entered into force April 14, 1959.
10 UST 846; TIAS 4222; 343 UNTS 119.

Agreement relating to extended risk investment guaranties. Exchange of notes at Managua May 9, 1966; entered into force September 21, 1968.
19 UST 6192; TIAS 6572; 700 UNTS 245.

Agreement regarding the discharge of certain debts owed to the Government of the United States, with annex. Signed at Managua September 25, 1991; entered into force September 25, 1991.
NP

Agreement regarding the consolidation and re-scheduling or refinancing of certain debts owed to, guaranteed by, or insured by the United States Government and its agencies, with annexes. Signed at Managua May 13, 1992; entered into force July 10, 1992.
NP

Amendment:
July 21 and September 26, 1997 (NP).

Agreement among the United States and the Government of Nicaragua/Central American Business Administration Institute regarding the assumption, payment and discharge of certain debts. Exchange of notes at Managua August 28, 1995; entered into force August 28, 1995.
NP

Agreement regarding the consolidation and re-scheduling of certain debts owed to, guaranteed by or insured by the United States Government and its agencies, with annexes. Signed at Managua August 28, 1995; entered into force November 1, 1995.
NP

Agreement regarding the consolidation, reduction and rescheduling of certain debts owed to, guaranteed by, or insured by the United States Government and its agencies, with annexes. Signed at Managua October 20, 1998; entered into force December 21, 1998.
NP

Amendment:
April 9 and May 19, 1999 (NP).

HIGHWAYS

Agreement relating to the construction of the inter-American highway. Exchange of notes at Washington April 8, 1942; entered into force April 8, 1942.
56 Stat. 1845; EAS 295; 10 Bevans 424; 24 UNTS 145.

Amendment:
April 4 and 20, 1951 (2 UST 1848; TIAS 2320; 138 UNTS 57).

Agreement relating to the construction of the Rama Road. Exchange of notes at Washington April 8 and 18, 1942; entered into force April 18, 1942.
2 UST 722; TIAS 2229; 132 UNTS 343.

Amendments:
September 2, 1953 (4 UST 1944; TIAS 2853; 215 UNTS 69).
March 13 and August 2, 1956 (7 UST 2237; TIAS 3623; 281 UNTS 99).

MAPPING

Basic exchange and cooperative agreement for topographic mapping, nautical and aeronautical charting and information, geodesy and geo-physics, digital data and related mapping, charting and geodesy materials. Signed at Managua and Fairfax November 28 and December 1, 1994; entered into force December 1, 1994.
NP

MISSIONS, MILITARY [1]

Agreement relating to an air force mission to Nicaragua. Signed at Managua November 19, 1952; entered into force November 19, 1952.
3 UST 5027; TIAS 2683; 186 UNTS 2.

Extensions and amendments:
August 21 and 27, 1956 (7 UST 2465; TIAS 3634; 277 UNTS 352).
March 25 and May 22, 1959 (10 UST 1446; TIAS 4294; 357 UNTS 369).

Agreement providing for a United States Army mission to Nicaragua. Signed at Managua November 19, 1953; entered into force November 19, 1953.
4 UST 2238; TIAS 2876; 206 UNTS 117.

Amendment:
March 25 and May 22, 1959 (10 UST 1446; TIAS 4294; 357 UNTS 369).

NOTE:
[1] The Air Force and Army missions were consolidated September 10, 1965.

PEACE CORPS

Agreement relating to the establishment of a Peace Corps program in Nicaragua. Exchange of notes at Managua May 23 and 25, 1968; entered into force May 25, 1968.
19 UST 5073; TIAS 6507; 707 UNTS 61.

POSTAL MATTERS

Agreement for parcel post service. Signed at Managua March 19 and at Washington April 4, 1956; entered into force July 1, 1956.
7 UST 1051; TIAS 3586; 275 UNTS 231.

International express mail agreement, with detailed regulations. Signed at Managua and Washington July 24 and August 16, 1991; entered into force September 30, 1991.
TIAS 11798.

PUBLICATIONS

Agreement relating to the exchange of official publications. Exchange of notes at Managua February 14 and 19, 1940; entered into force February 14, 1940.
54 Stat. 2294; EAS 171; 10 Bevans 411; 203 LNTS 47.

RELATIONS

Agreement of friendship and cooperation. Signed at Managua January 6, 1992; entered into force January 6, 1992.
TIAS 11844.

SCIENTIFIC COOPERATION

Memorandum of understanding concerning sci-entific cooperation in the earth and mapping sciences, with annexes. Signed at Reston and Managua March 4 and 10, 1999; entered into force March 10, 1999.
TIAS

TELECOMMUNICATION

Agreement relating to radio communications between amateur stations on behalf of third parties. Exchange of notes at Managua October 8 and 16, 1956; entered into force October 16, 1956.
7 UST 3159; TIAS 3694; 282 UNTS 29.

Agreement relating to the reciprocal granting of authorizations to permit licensed amateur radio operators of either country to operate their stations in the other country. Exchange of notes at Managua September 3 and 20, 1966; entered into force September 20, 1966.
17 UST 1560; TIAS 6112; 607 UNTS 167.

TRADE

Agreement terminating the agreement of September 5, 1972 relating to trade in cotton textiles and providing for consultations on problems of market disruption as defined in the arrangement regarding international trade in textiles of December 20, 1973. Exchange of notes at Managua December 26, 1974 and January 3, 1975; entered into force January 3, 1975.
26 UST 41; TIAS 8007.

NICARAGUA (Cont'd)

VISAS

Agreement relating to the reciprocal granting of nonimmigrant visas, without fee, for maximum validity for four years. Exchange of notes at Managua July 6, September 30 and October 22, 1955; entered into force October 22, 1955.
10 UST 1696; TIAS 4319; 358 UNTS 51.

NIGER

COPYRIGHT (See APPENDIX)

DEFENSE

Agreement relating to the furnishing of military equipment, materials and services to Niger to help assure its security and independence. Exchange of notes at Niamey May 22 and June 14, 1962; entered into force June 14, 1962.
13 UST 1301; TIAS 5083; 458 UNTS 233.

Agreement concerning the provision of training related to defense articles under the United States International Military Education and Training (IMET) Program. Exchange of notes at Niamey March 11 and June 9, 1980; entered into force June 9, 1980.
33 UST 576; TIAS 10049; 1267 UNTS 123.

Agreement regarding the terms and conditions relating to the furnishing of defense articles and services on a grant basis to the Government of Niger by the United States. Exchange of notes at Niamey July 18 and September 24, 1992; entered into force September 24, 1992.
TIAS 12359.

ECONOMIC AND TECHNICAL COOPERATION

Agreement providing for the furnishing of economic, technical and related assistance. Exchange of notes at Niamey May 26, 1961; entered into force May 26, 1961.
12 UST 858; TIAS 4786; 410 UNTS 213.

Agency for International Development:
September 17, 1975 (29 UST 5377; TIAS 9118; 1148 UNTS 227).
June 9, 1976 (29 UST 5708; TIAS 9143).
July 1, 1977 (29 UST 5711; TIAS 9143).
July 23, 1977 (29 UST 5377; TIAS 9118; 1148 UNTS 243).
September 26, 1977 (29 UST 4737; TIAS 9078).
April 25, 1978 (30 UST 3077; TIAS 9380; 1178 UNTS 281).
June 10, 1987 (NP).

FINANCE

Agreement relating to investment guaranties. Exchange of notes at Niamey February 28 and April 26, 1962; entered into force April 26, 1962.
13 UST 2203; TIAS 5187; 459 UNTS 129.

Agreement regarding the consolidation and rescheduling of certain debts owed to, guaranteed by or insured by the United States Government and its agencies, with annexes. Signed at Niamey June 11, 1984; entered into force July 24, 1984.
TIAS 10994.

Agreement regarding the consolidation and rescheduling of certain debts owed to, guaranteed by or insured by the United States Government and its agencies, with annexes. Signed at Niamey April 9, 1985; entered into force May 28, 1985.
NP

Agreement regarding the consolidation and rescheduling of certain debts owed to, guaranteed by, or insured by the United States Government and its agencies, with annexes. Signed at Niamey April 11, 1986; entered into force May 19, 1986.
NP

Agreement regarding the consolidation and rescheduling of certain debts owed to, guaranteed by or insured by the United States Government and its agencies, with annexes. Signed at Niamey February 10, 1988; entered into force March 17, 1988.
NP

Agreement regarding the consolidation and rescheduling of certain debts owed to, guaranteed by or insured by the United States Government and its agencies, with annexes. Signed at Niamey February 21, 1989; entered into force March 30, 1989.
NP

Agreement regarding the consolidation and rescheduling of certain debts owed to, guaranteed by, or insured by the United States Government and its agencies, with annexes. Signed at Washington June 29, 1989; entered into force August 24, 1989.
NP

Agreement regarding the consolidation and rescheduling of certain debts owed to, guaranteed by, or insured by the United States Government and its agencies, with annexes. Signed at Washington February 12, 1991; entered into force March 28, 1991.
NP

Agreement regarding the consolidation, reduction and rescheduling of certain debts owed to, guaranteed by or insured by the United States Government and its agencies, with annexes. Signed at Niamey July 29, 1994; entered into force August 29, 1994.
NP

Agreement regarding the consolidation, reduction and rescheduling of certain debts owed to,

guaranteed by, or insured by the United States Government and its Agencies, with annexes. Signed at Niamey January 14, 1998; entered into force March 27, 1998.
NP

PEACE CORPS

Agreement relating to the establishment of a Peace Corps program in Niger. Exchange of notes at Niamey July 23, 1962; entered into force July 23, 1962.
14 UST 868; TIAS 5368; 487 UNTS 325.

POSTAL MATTERS

International express mail agreement, with detailed regulations. Signed at Niamey and Washington May 6 and 29, 1987; entered into force June 15, 1987.
TIAS 11302.

SOCIAL SECURITY

Agreement to provide certain social security benefits for certain employees of the United States in Niger. Signed at Niamey July 21, 1975; entered into force July 21, 1975; effective January 1, 1974.
26 UST 2758; TIAS 8194; 1045 UNTS 65.

NIGERIA

On October 1, 1960 the territories formerly comprising the British Colony and Protectorate of Nigeria attained fully responsible status within the British Commonwealth under the name of the Federation of Nigeria (Federation of Nigeria Independence Act, 1960). By an exchange of notes, dated October 1, 1960, between the High Commissioner for the United Kingdom in the Federation of Nigeria and the Prime Minister of the Federation of Nigeria, Nigeria agreed to assume, from October 1, 1960, all obligations and responsibilities of the United Kingdom which arise from any valid international instrument insofar as such instruments may be held to have application to or in respect of Nigeria are from October 1, 1960 enjoyed by the Federation of Nigeria.

AGRICULTURE

Agreement for the provision of technical services in the preparation of a comprehensive soil survey of Nigeria. Signed at Lagos September 22, 1980; entered into force August 1, 1981.
33 UST 798; TIAS 10062; 1267 UNTS 225.

NIGERIA (Cont'd)

AVIATION

Arrangement between the United States and the United Kingdom relating to pilot licenses to operate civil aircraft. Exchange of notes at Washington March 28 and April 5, 1935; entered into force May 5, 1935.
49 Stat. 3731; EAS 77; 12 Bevans 513; 162 LNTS 59.

Air transport agreement, with memorandum of understanding. Signed at Lagos April 27, 1978; entered into force provisionally April 27, 1978; definitively June 16, 1978.
29 UST 3102; TIAS 8999; 1124 UNTS 255.

CONSULS

Consular convention between the United States and the United Kingdom. Signed at Washington June 6, 1951; entered into force September 7, 1952.
3 UST 3426; TIAS 2494; 165 UNTS 121.

COPYRIGHT (See APPENDIX)

DEFENSE (See also MUTUAL SECURITY)

Agreement relating to the deposit by Nigeria of ten percent of the value of grant military assistance furnished by the United States. Exchange of notes at Lagos April 12 and 20, 1972; entered into force April 20, 1972; effective February 7, 1972.
23 UST 773; TIAS 7338.

Agreement concerning the provision of training related to defense articles under the United States International Military Education and Training (IMET) Program. Exchange of notes at Lagos November 19, 1985 and February 26, 1986; entered into force February 26, 1986.
TIAS 11106.

Agreement regarding the provision of commodities and services to Nigerian forces participating in ECOMOG peacekeeping operations. Exchange of notes at Abuja November 9, 1996; entered into force November 9, 1996.
TIAS

Agreement regarding grants under the Foreign Assistance Act of 1961, as amended, and the furnishing of defense articles, related training, and other defense services from the United States of America to the Government of the Federal Republic of Nigeria. Exchange of notes at Abuja July 27 and August 17, 2000; entered into force August 17, 2000.
TIAS

Agreement concerning the status of United States military and civilian personnel of the U.S. Department of Defense temporarily present in Nigeria in connection with military training and other activities as may be agreed upon by the two governments. Exchange of notes at Abuja August 24 and September 7, 2000; entered into force September 7, 2000.
NP

ECONOMIC AND TECHNICAL COOPERATION

Economic cooperation agreement between the United States and the United Kingdom. Signed at London July 6, 1948; applicable to Nigeria July 6, 1948.
62 Stat. 2596; TIAS 1795; 12 Bevans 874; 22 UNTS 263.

Amendments:
January 3, 1950 (1 UST 184; TIAS 2036; 86 UNTS 304).
May 25, 1951 (2 UST 1292; TIAS 2277; 99 UNTS 308).
February 25, 1953 (4 UST 1528; TIAS 2815; 172 UNTS 332).

EDUCATION

Agreement on the training of Nigerian technical educators, with annexes. Signed at Washington September 9, 1981; entered into force September 9, 1981.
33 UST 3783; TIAS 10261; 1541 UNTS 181.

EXTRADITION

Extradition treaty between the United States and the United Kingdom. Signed at London December 22, 1931; applicable to Nigeria June 24, 1935.
47 Stat. 2122; TS 849; 12 Bevans 482; 163 LNTS 59.

FINANCE

Investment guarantee agreement, with agreed minute. Signed at Lagos August 3, 1974; entered into force February 10, 1975.
26 UST 102; TIAS 8012; 991 UNTS 323.

Agreement regarding the consolidation and rescheduling of certain debts owed to, guaranteed by or insured by the United States Government and its agencies, with annexes. Signed at Lagos December 23, 1987; entered into force February 16, 1988.
NP

Agreement regarding the consolidation and rescheduling of certain debts owed to, guaranteed by, or insured by the United States Government and its agencies. Signed at Lagos De-

cember 4, 1989; entered into force January 22, 1990.
NP

Agreement regarding the consolidation and rescheduling or refinancing of certain debts owed to, guaranteed by, or insured by the United States Government and its agencies, with annexes. Signed at Lagos August 2, 1991; entered into force September 18, 1991.
NP

JUDICIAL ASSISTANCE

Procedures for mutual assistance in the administration of justice in connection with the Lockheed Aircraft Corporation matter. Signed at Washington April 20, 1976; entered into force April 20, 1976.
27 UST 1054; TIAS 8243.

Related agreement:
March 8 and 26, 1979 (NP).

Agreement on procedures for mutual assistance in law enforcement matters. Signed at Washington November 2, 1987; entered into force November 2, 1987.
TIAS 11540.

MUTUAL SECURITY

Agreement between the United States and the United Kingdom relating to the assurances required under the Mutual Security Act of 1951. Exchange of notes at London January 8, 1952; applicable to Nigeria January 8, 1952.
3 UST 4665; TIAS 2622; 126 UNTS 307.

NARCOTIC DRUGS

Mutual cooperation agreement for reducing demand, preventing illicit use and combatting illicit production and trafficking in drugs. Exchange of notes at Lagos January 13 and 24, 1989; entered into force January 24, 1989.
TIAS 11598.

PEACE CORPS

Agreement establishing a Peace Corps program in Nigeria. Exchange of notes at Lagos August 19 and 22, 1991; entered into force August 22, 1991.
TIAS 12108.

POSTAL MATTERS

International express mail agreement, with detailed regulations. Signed at Lagos and Washington March 7 and April 21, 1986; entered into force July 1, 1986.
TIAS 11407.

NIGERIA (Cont'd)

Postal money order agreement, with attachments. Signed at Lagos and Washington June 14 and 28, 1990; entered into force September 1, 1990.
TIAS 11759.

PROPERTY

Convention between the United States and the United Kingdom relating to the tenure and disposition of real and personal property.[1] Signed at Washington March 2, 1899.
31 Stat. 1939; TS 146; 12 Bevans 246.

NOTE:
[1] Notification given on July 22, 1901 of application to Northern Nigeria, and on July 27, 1901 of application to Southern Nigeria.

TELECOMMUNICATION

Agreement relating to the installation and operation of a radio transmitter by the Embassy of Nigeria. Exchange of notes at Washington November 19 and 22, 1974 and June 4, 1975; entered into force June 4, 1975.
27 UST 3297; TIAS 8364; 1068 UNTS 457.

TRADE

Agreement concerning trade in textiles and textile products, with annexes. Signed at Lagos July 30, 1992; entered into force July 30, 1992; effective January 1, 1990.
NP

TRADE-MARKS

Declaration by the United States and the United Kingdom relating to reciprocal protection to trade-marks. Signed at London October 24, 1877; entered into force October 24, 1877.
20 Stat. 703; TS 138; 12 Bevans 198.

NIUE

PEACE CORPS

Agreement concerning the program of the Peace Corps in Niue. Signed at Alofi September 23, 1994; entered into force September 23, 1994.
TIAS 12109.

NORTH ATLANTIC TREATY ORGANIZATION (NATO)

DEFENSE

Agreement regarding U.S. approval for retransfer of U.S. defense articles and services to NATO for purposes of supporting the NATO-led Implementation Force (IFOR). Exchange of letters at Brussels December 18, 1995; entered into force December 18, 1995.
TIAS

EMPLOYMENT

Arrangement concerning the employment by the North Atlantic Treaty Organization of United States nationals. Signed at London September 29, 1951; entered into force September 29, 1951.
5 UST 1112; TIAS 2992.

Agreement concerning the employment by the International Military Headquarters of United States nationals. Signed at Paris February 25, 1953; entered into force February 25, 1953.
5 UST 890; TIAS 2978.

Supplemental arrangement concerning the employment by NATO bodies of United States nationals. Signed at Brussels June 3, 1983; entered into force June 3, 1983.
TIAS 10695.

HEADQUARTERS

Agreement between the United States and the Headquarters of the Supreme Allied Commander Atlantic regarding the headquarters, with exchange of letters. Signed at Washington October 22, 1954; entered into force October 22, 1954; operative April 10, 1954.
5 UST 2519; TIAS 3113; 249 UNTS 175.

PRIVILEGES AND IMMUNITIES

Agreement concerning the application of part IV of the agreement on the status of the North Atlantic Treaty Organization, national representatives and international staff, September 20, 1951 (TIAS 2992) to the officials of NATO civilian bodies located on the territory of the United States of America. Signed at Brussels March 3, 1981; entered into force March 3, 1981.
33 UST 1272; TIAS 10110; 1307 UNTS 423.

SATELLITE COMMUNICATIONS

Agreement concerning the North Atlantic Treaty Organization satellite communications earth terminal in the United States. Signed at Washington July 10 and at Mons, Belgium August 20, 1970; entered into force August 20, 1970.
21 UST 2089; TIAS 6955; 764 UNTS 225.

TAXATION

Tax reimbursement agreement, with annex. Signed at Brussels July 18, 1990; entered into force July 18, 1990.
TIAS 11947.

TELECOMMUNICATION

Memorandum of understanding concerning the interconnection of the NICS TARE and the US AUTODIN network, with annex. Signed at Brussels and Washington April 26 and May 31, 1991; entered into force May 31, 1991.
TIAS

Memorandum of agreement concerning the interconnection of the Initial Voice Switched Network (IVSN) of the NATO Integrated Communications System and the Defense Switched Network (DSN) of the U.S. Defense Information Infrastructure, with annex. Signed at Brussels and Arlington February 16 and April 21, 1995; entered into force April 21, 1995.
TIAS 12633.

NORTH ATLANTIC TREATY ORGANIZATION AEW&C PROGRAMME MANAGEMENT ORGANIZATION (NAPMO)

DEFENSE

Memorandum of agreement concerning the cooperative production of radar system improvements for the E-3 aircraft. Signed at Hanscom AFB and Washington August 3 and 11, 1995; entered into force August 11, 1995.
TIAS 12682.

Memorandum of agreement concerning cooperative projects for the E-3 aircraft, with annex. Signed at Washington and Brunssum August 10 and 30, 1999; entered into force August 30, 1999.
TIAS

NORTH ATLANTIC TREATY ORGANIZATION MAINTENANCE AND SUPPLY ORGANIZATION (NAMSO)

SUPPLIES

Agreement for credit sales of military equipment, materials, and services. Signed at Paris June 22, 1959; entered into force June 22, 1959.
10 UST 1156; TIAS 4252.

Basic agreement on mutual support, with annex. Signed at Stuttgart-Vaihingen February 2, 1982; entered into force February 2, 1982.
34 UST 118; TIAS 10342; 1556 UNTS 315.

Amendment:
April 30 and May 7, 1990 (TIAS 12414).

Agreement regarding consolidated procurement of munitions. Signed at Washington and Capellen April 5 and 12, 1988; entered into force April 12, 1988.
TIAS

Agreement regarding the transfer of USG-origin spare parts and components maintained and serviced by NAMSO. Exchange of notes at Brussels and Capellen November 16, 1992 and March 5, 1993; entered into force March 5, 1993.
TIAS

NORWAY

ATOMIC ENERGY

Revised agreement for cooperation concerning civil uses of atomic energy, with annex and agreed minute. Signed at Oslo January 12, 1984; entered into force July 2, 1984.
TIAS 10979.

AVIATION

Arrangement relating to pilot licenses to operate civil aircraft. Exchange of notes at Washington October 16, 1933; entered into force November 15, 1933.
48 Stat. 1818; EAS 51; 10 Bevans 514; 145 LNTS 31.

Agreement relating to air transport services. Exchange of notes at Washington October 6, 1945; entered into force October 6, 1945; operative October 15, 1945.
59 Stat. 1658; EAS 482; 10 Bevans 553; 122 UNTS 319.

Amendments:
August 6, 1954 (5 UST 1433; TIAS 3015; 222 UNTS 269).
June 16, 1995 (TIAS 12664).

Agreement relating to air service facilities at Gardermoen Airfield. Signed at Oslo November 12, 1946; entered into force November 12, 1946.
61 Stat. 3861; TIAS 1737; 10 Bevans 560; 42 UNTS 227.

Agreement relating to certificates of airworthiness for imported aircraft. Exchange of notes at Oslo February 5, 1957; entered into force February 5, 1957.
8 UST 265; TIAS 3769; 279 UNTS 169.

Amendment:
January 24, 1978 (29 UST 5660; TIAS 9141).

CLAIMS

Memorandum of understanding on conflicting claims to enemy property. Signed at Washington June 21, 1952; entered into force April 27, 1954.
5 UST 907; TIAS 2980; 236 UNTS 9.

COMMERCE

Treaty of commerce and navigation, with separate article.[1] Signed at Stockholm July 4, 1827; entered into force January 18, 1828.
8 Stat. 346; TS 348; 11 Bevans 876.

Treaty of friendship, commerce, and consular right with exchange of notes and additional article signed February 25, 1929. Signed at Washington June 5, 1928; entered into force September 13, 1932.
47 Stat. 2135; TS 852; 10 Bevans 481; 134 LNTS 81.

NOTE:
[1] Articles 13 and 14 were abrogated effective July 1, 1916; the entire treaty, with the exception of that part of article 1 concerning entry and residence of nationals of one country in territories of the other for purposes of trade, was terminated September 13, 1932, by the treaty of friendship, commerce, and consular rights signed June 5, 1928, and the additional article thereto signed February 25, 1929 (TS 852).

CONSULS (See COMMERCE)

COPYRIGHT (See APPENDIX)

CUSTOMS

Arrangement relating to customs treatment of importations for consular offices and officers.

Exchange of notes at Washington January 20, 1932; entered into force January 20, 1932; operative February 1, 1932.
47 Stat. 2698; EAS 32; 10 Bevans 505; 126 LNTS 393.

Agreement regarding mutual assistance between customs authorities. Signed at Oslo May 17, 1989; entered into force August 30, 1989.
TIAS 12118.

DEFENSE (See also MUTUAL SECURITY)

Mutual defense assistance agreement. Signed at Washington January 27, 1950; entered into force February 24, 1950.
1 UST 106; TIAS 2016; 80 UNTS 241.

Agreement relating to the disposition of excess equipment and materials furnished by the United States under the mutual defense assistance agreement. Exchange of notes at Oslo December 12 and 28, 1950; entered into force December 28, 1950.
6 UST 6151; TIAS 3467; 240 UNTS 391.

Agreement relating to the disposition of equipment and materials furnished by the United States under the mutual defense assistance agreement and found surplus to the needs of the armed forces of Norway. Exchange of notes at Oslo May 15 and June 26, 1953; entered into force June 26, 1953.
6 UST 6153; TIAS 3468; 240 UNTS 396.

Amendment:
September 1, 1960 and January 14, 1961 (12 UST 214; TIAS 4695; 406 UNTS 312).

Agreement concerning participation of a Norwegian mobile surgical hospital in the United Nations operations in Korea. Signed at Washington September 17, 1951; entered into force September 17, 1951.
2 UST 1903; TIAS 2325; 140 UNTS 313.

Agreement concerning the status of military assistance advisory group under article I, paragraph 1(a) of the NATO status of forces agreement (TIAS 2846). Exchange of notes at Oslo April 13, 1954; entered into force April 13, 1954.
5 UST 619; TIAS 2950; 229 UNTS 223.

Agreement relating to a weapons production program. Exchange of notes at Oslo February 13, 1960; entered into force February 13, 1960.
11 UST 2105; TIAS 4569; 388 UNTS 255.

Amendment:
April 26 and September 16, 1960 (11 UST 2105; TIAS 4569; 388 UNTS 255).

Agreement relating to a shipbuilding program for the Norwegian Navy. Exchange of notes at Oslo July 6, 1960; entered into force July 6, 1960.
11 UST 1796; TIAS 4522; 378 UNTS 25.

Agreement relating to a shipbuilding program of the Norwegian Navy. Exchange of notes at

NORWAY (Cont'd)

Oslo November 29, 1960; entered into force January 31, 1961.
12 UST 101; TIAS 4681; 404 UNTS 251.

Agreement relating to the safeguarding of classified information with annex. Exchange of notes at Oslo February 26, 1970; entered into force February 26, 1970.
21 UST 462; TIAS 6836; 240 UNTS 251.

Amendment:
September 27, 1984 (TIAS 11136).

Agreement relating to the coproduction of the M109G vehicles. Signed at Oslo December 30, 1966; entered into force December 30, 1966.
TIAS 12360.

Amendment:
February 6, 1976 (TIAS 12360).

Memorandum of understanding concerning the principles governing mutual cooperation in the research and development, production and procurement of defense equipment, with annexes. Signed May 19, 1978; entered into force May 19, 1978.
33 UST 3111; TIAS 10215.

Memorandum of understanding governing prestockage and reinforcement of Norway. Signed at Washington January 16, 1981; entered into force January 16, 1981.
32 UST 4538; TIAS 9966; 1266 UNTS 17.

Mutual logistical support agreement, with annex. Signed at Stuttgart-Vaihingen and Oslo January 29 and August 20, 1982; entered into force August 20, 1982.
TIAS 10449.

Amendment:
November 14, 1992 and January 15, 1993 (TIAS 12361).

Memorandum of understanding on the exchange of officers between the United States and Royal Norwegian Air Forces. Signed at Oslo and Washington November 14, 1983 and January 5, 1984; entered into force January 5, 1984.
TIAS 10915.

Memorandum of understanding regarding the exchange of scientists and engineers, with annexes. Signed at Washington February 11, 1985; entered into force February 11, 1985.
TIAS 11150.

Memorandum of understanding on the exchange of officers between the United States Marine Corps and the Norwegian Army. Signed at Oslo and Washington May 21 and July 3, 1986; entered into force July 3, 1986.
NP

Memorandum of understanding concerning the provision of United States hospital prepositioned storage to support Allied Forces during operations in the Norwegian Sea and in Norway. Signed at London and Oslo February 17 and April 10, 1987; entered into force April 10, 1987.
TIAS 11662.

Memorandum of understanding concerning a cooperative project on investigation of the ocean using radar, with annexes. Signed at Oslo and Arlington June 19 and July 18, 1989; entered into force July 18, 1989.
TIAS

Memorandum of agreement concerning the exchange of engineers and scientists, with annexes. Signed at Washington and Oslo September 2 and 24, 1992; entered into force September 24, 1992.
NP

Agreement concerning the transfer of U.S. Government-origin defense articles or related training or other defense services to the Government of Norway. Exchange of notes at Oslo September 18 and October 1, 1992; entered into force October 1, 1992.
TIAS 12362.

Agreement regarding cooperation on environmental protection in defense matters. Signed at Baltimore May 19, 1994; entered into force May 19, 1994.
TIAS 12363.

Memorandum of understanding for the dynamic analysis support system project, with annexes. Signed at Washington and Haakonsvern August 12 and November 14, 1994; entered into force November 14, 1994.
TIAS 12364.

Memorandum of understanding for the composite hull embedded sensor system (CHESS), with annex. Signed at Washington and Kjeller June 6 and 24, 1996; entered into force June 24, 1996.
TIAS

Agreement regarding the exchange of engineers and scientists, with annexes. Signed at Oslo and Washington January 11 and April 15, 1999; entered into force April 15, 1999.
NP

ECONOMIC AND TECHNICAL COOPERATION

Economic cooperation agreement. Signed at Oslo July 3, 1948; entered into force July 3, 1948.
62 Stat. 2514; TIAS 1792; 10 Bevans 580; 20 UNTS 185.

Amendments:
January 17, 1950 (1 UST 166; TIAS 2032; 79 UNTS 284).
July 5, 1951 (2 UST 1289; TIAS 2276; 148 UNTS 402).
January 8, 1953 (4 UST 109; TIAS 2767; 198 UNTS 366).

EDUCATION

Agreement relating to the United States Educational Foundation in Norway, and exchange of notes. Signed at Oslo May 25, 1949; entered into force May 25, 1949.
63 Stat. 2764; TIAS 2000; 10 Bevans 598; 32 UNTS 345.

Amendments:
August 12 and October 30, 1954 (5 UST 2545; TIAS 3118; 234 UNTS 298).
June 15, 1955 (6 UST 2103; TIAS 3282; 261 UNTS 380).
June 21, 1960 (11 UST 1602; TIAS 4503; 377 UNTS 390).
March 16, 1964 (15 UST 241; TIAS 5545; 524 UNTS 294).

EMPLOYMENT

Agreement relating to the employment of dependents of official government employees. Exchange of notes at Oslo April 15 and July 21, 1981; entered into force July 21, 1981.
TIAS 10882.

ENERGY

Agreement concerning cooperation in the field of fossil energy research and development. Signed at Washington and Oslo March 19 and April 22, 1987; entered into force April 22, 1987.
TIAS 12127.

ENVIRONMENTAL COOPERATION

Agreement for cooperation in the Global Learning and Observations to Benefit the Environment (GLOBE) Program. Signed at Washington April 5, 1995; entered into force April 5, 1995.
TIAS 12627.

EXTRADITION

Extradition treaty. Signed at Oslo June 9, 1977; entered into force March 7, 1980.
31 UST 5619; TIAS 9679; 1220 UNTS 221.

FINANCE

Agreement relating to guaranties authorized by section 111 (b)(3) of the Economic Cooperation Act of 1948, as amended. Exchange of notes at Washington March 28 and April 1, 1952; entered into force April 1, 1952.
3 UST 4246; TIAS 2567; 177 UNTS 291.

NORWAY (Cont'd)

LEND-LEASE

Preliminary agreement regarding principles applying to mutual aid in the prosecution of the war against aggression, and exchange of notes. Signed at Washington July 11, 1942; entered into force July 11, 1942.
56 Stat. 1565; EAS 262; 10 Bevans 531.

Agreement regarding settlement for lend-lease, military relief, and claims, and exchanges of notes. Signed at Washington February 24, 1948; entered into force February 24, 1948.
62 Stat. 1848; TIAS 1716; 10 Bevans 566; 34 UNTS 155.

MAPPING

Basic exchange and cooperative agreement concerning geospatial information and services cooperation. Signed at Oslo July 8, 1998; entered into force July 8, 1998.
NP

MUTUAL SECURITY

Agreement relating to the assurances required under the Mutual Security Act of 1951. Exchange of notes at Oslo January 8, 1952; entered into force January 8, 1952.
3 UST 4639; TIAS 2616; 179 UNTS 185.

NATIONALITY

Treaty relating to exemption from military service or other act of allegiance of persons having dual nationality. Signed at Oslo November 1, 1930; entered into force February 11, 1931.
46 Stat. 2904; TS 832; 10 Bevans 503; 112 LNTS 399.

NAVIGATION

Agreement for the transfer of ownership of the long-range radio aid to navigation transmitting stations at Bo and Jan Mayen Island, Norway, with annex. Signed at Oslo December 15, 1994; entered into force December 15, 1994.
TIAS

PACIFIC SETTLEMENT OF DISPUTES

Treaty for the advancement of peace. Signed at Washington June 24, 1914; entered into force October 21, 1914.
38 Stat. 1843; TS 599; 10 Bevans 456.

Treaty of arbitration. Signed at Washington February 20, 1929; entered into force June 7, 1929.
46 Stat. 2278; TS 788; 10 Bevans 498; 91 LNTS 413.

PATENTS

Agreement to facilitate interchange of patent rights and technical information for defense purposes, with agreed minutes. Signed at Oslo April 6, 1955; entered into force April 6, 1955.
6 UST 799; TIAS 3226; 269 UNTS 65.

Agreement approving procedures for reciprocal filing of classified patent applications in the United States and Norway. Exchange of notes at Oslo December 5, 1958 and January 6 and 17, 1959; entered into force January 17, 1959.
10 UST 302; TIAS 4187; 341 UNTS 410.

Amendment:
April 25 and August 12, 1960 (11 UST 2002; TIAS 4552; 388 UNTS 374).

POSTAL MATTERS

Money order convention. Signed at Washington November 30, 1886 and at Christiania on February 5, 1887; operative April 1, 1887.
NP

Parcel post convention. Signed at Oslo October 6 and at Washington November 9, 1934; operative November 1, 1934.
49 Stat. 3042; Post Office Department print; 156 LNTS 33.

International express mail agreement, with detailed regulations. Signed at Oslo and Washington July 5 and August 10, 1984; entered into force October 15, 1984.
TIAS 11007.

Memorandum of understanding concerning the operation of the INTELPOST field trial, with details of implementation. Signed at Oslo and Washington July 9 and 25, 1985; entered into force July 25, 1985.
TIAS 11154.

PUBLICATIONS

Agreement for the exchange of official publications. Exchange of notes at Oslo June 20, 1947 and March 15, 1948; entered into force March 15, 1948.
62 Stat. 1954; TIAS 1758; 10 Bevans 577; 73 UNTS 81.

Amendment:
August 10 and 11, 1964 (15 UST 1502; TIAS 5630; 530 UNTS 334).

RELIEF SUPPLIES AND PACKAGES

Agreement for free entry and free inland transportation of relief supplies and packages. Exchange of notes at Oslo October 31, 1949; entered into force October 31, 1949.
64 Stat. (3) B71; TIAS 2006; 10 Bevans 607; 68 UNTS 3.

SCIENTIFIC COOPERATION

Memorandum of understanding on cooperation in geological sciences. Signed at Reston and Trondheim December 9, 1987 and February 4, 1988; entered into force February 4, 1988.
TIAS 11646.

Memorandum of understanding concerning scientific and technical cooperation in the earth sciences, with annexes. Signed at Reston and Trondheim September 14 and October 12, 1989; entered into force October 12, 1989.
TIAS 11706.

SEISMOLOGICAL RESEARCH

Agreement relating to the installation, operation and management of a seismic array facility in Norway. Exchange of notes at Oslo June 15, 1968; entered into force June 15, 1968.
19 UST 5439; TIAS 6526; 707 UNTS 79.

SHIPPING

Agreement relating to jurisdiction over vessels utilizing the Louisiana Offshore Oil Port. Exchange of notes at Washington July 11, 1978; entered into force July 11, 1978.
30 UST 1671; TIAS 9275; 1153 UNTS 89.

SMUGGLING

Convention for prevention of smuggling of intoxicating liquors. Signed at Washington May 24, 1924; entered into force July 2, 1924.
43 Stat. 1772; TS 689; 10 Bevans 473; 26 LNTS 44.

SOCIAL SECURITY

Agreement on social security, with final protocol and administrative agreement. Signed at Washington January 13, 1983; entered into force July 1, 1984.
TIAS 10818.

NORWAY (Cont'd)

TAXATION

Convention for the avoidance of double taxation and the prevention of fiscal evasion with respect to taxes on estates and inheritances. Signed at Washington June 13, 1949; entered into force December 11, 1951.
2 UST 2353; TIAS 2358; 127 UNTS 163.

Agreement relating to relief from taxation of United States Government expenditures in Norway for common defense. Exchange of notes at Oslo June 27, 1952; entered into force June 27, 1952.
3 UST 5253; TIAS 2720; 184 UNTS 271.

Convention for the avoidance of double taxation and the prevention of fiscal evasion with respect to taxes on income and property with related notes. Signed at Oslo December 3, 1971; entered into force November 29, 1972.
23 UST 2832; TIAS 7474.

Protocol amending the convention of December 3, 1971 (TIAS 7474) for the avoidance of double taxation and the prevention of fiscal evasion with respect to taxes on income and property.[1] Signed at Oslo September 19, 1980; entered into force December 15, 1981.
33 UST 2828; TIAS 10205.

Agreement concerning the reciprocal exemption from income tax of income derived from the international operation of ships and aircraft. Exchange of notes at Washington May 24, 1990; entered into force May 24, 1990.
TIAS 11715.

NOTE:
[1] With understanding.

TELECOMMUNICATION

Agreement relating to the reciprocal granting of authorizations to permit licensed amateur radio operators of either country to operate their stations in the other country. Exchange of notes at Oslo May 27 and June 1, 1967; entered into force June 1, 1967.
18 UST 1241; TIAS 6273; 631 UNTS 119.

TRADE (See also COMMERCE)

Arrangement within the context of the multilateral trade negotiations concerning cheeses, and related letter of January 30, 1980. Signed at Geneva May 17, 1979; entered into force January 1, 1980.
32 UST 5460; TIAS 9997; 1266 UNTS 3.

Agreement within the context of the multilateral trade negotiations regarding turkey rolls, and related letter of January 30, 1980. Letter done at Geneva June 28, 1979; entered into force January 1, 1980.
32 UST 5468; TIAS 9998; 1266 UNTS 11.

VISAS

Agreement for the waiver by Norway of visa requirements for United States citizens entering continental Norway and of the visa fee for United States citizens entering Norwegian territory outside continental Norway, and for the waiver by the United States of the visa fee for Norwegian citizens entering the United States and possessions as nonimmigrants. Exchange of notes at Washington July 7 and 29, 1947; entered into force July 29, 1947; operative August 1, 1947.
61 Stat. 3101; TIAS 1644; 10 Bevans 563; 87 UNTS 343.

Amendment:
April 25, 1958.

Agreement relating to the waiver of visas for American citizens proceeding to Svalbard (Spitzbergen) and the temporary suspension of visa requirements for American citizens proceeding to certain Norwegian possessions. Exchange of notes at Washington September 10 and October 19, 1948; entered into force October 19, 1948.
62 Stat. 3649; TIAS 1884; 10 Bevans 596; 87 UNTS 348.

OMAN

AVIATION

Agreement on aviation security. Exchange of notes at Muscat June 28 and 30, 1994; entered into force June 30, 1994.
TIAS 12554.

COMMERCE

Treaty of amity, economic relations and consular rights and protocol. Signed at Salalah December 20, 1958; entered into force June 11, 1960.
11 UST 1835; TIAS 4530; 380 UNTS 181.

CONSULS (See COMMERCE)

COPYRIGHT (See APPENDIX)

DEFENSE

Agreement concerning the provision of training related to defense articles under the United States International Military Education and Training (IMET) Program. Exchange of notes at Muscat January 4 and April 28, 1986; entered into force April 28, 1986.
TIAS 11981.

Memorandum of understanding concerning storage facilities for United States prepositioned war reserve petroleum products, with annexes. Signed at Shaw AFB and Seeb September 18, 1986; entered into force September 18, 1986.
TIAS 11506.

Related agreement:
February 2 and March 11, 1987 (TIAS 11291).

Agreement regarding grants under the Foreign Assistance Act of 1961, as amended, and the furnishing of defense articles, related training and other defense services from the United States to Oman. Exchange of notes at Muscat May 5 and June 1, 1992; entered into force June 1, 1992.
TIAS

ECONOMIC AND MILITARY COOPERATION

Agreement concerning the use of certain facilities in Oman by the United States. Exchange of notes at Muscat June 4, 1980; entered into force June 4, 1980.
32 UST 1636; TIAS 9791; 1234 UNTS 353.

ECONOMIC AND TECHNICAL COOPERATION

Agreement to establish a joint commission on economic and technical cooperation. Signed at Muscat August 19, 1980; entered into force August 19, 1980.
33 UST 2428; TIAS 10189; 1529 UNTS 13.

Amendment and extension:
December 1, 1990.

Agreement on economic and technical cooperation. Signed at Muscat December 1, 1990; entered into force December 1, 1990.
TIAS

FINANCE

Agreement relating to investment guaranties. Exchange of notes at Muscat September 9, 1976; entered into force September 9, 1976.
28 UST 5670; TIAS 8651; 1087 UNTS 11.

PEACE CORPS

Agreement relating to the establishment of a Peace Corps program in Oman. Exchange of notes at Muscat November 15 and 28, 1972; entered into force November 28, 1972.
24 UST 1013; TIAS 7614.

Amendment:
May 4 and August 25, 1977 (29 UST 5358; TIAS 9116; 1148 UNTS 366).

OMAN (Cont'd)

POSTAL MATTERS

International express mail agreement. Signed at Muscat and Washington February 12 and March 27, 1986; entered into force May 1, 1986.
NP

TRADE

Agreement relating to trade in textiles and textile products, with attachment. Exchange of notes at Muscat December 13, 1993 and January 15, 1994; entered into force January 15, 1994.
NP

Amendment and extension:
September 30 and November 6, 1995.

ORGANIZATION FOR THE DEVELOPMENT OF THE SENEGAL RIVER

ECONOMIC AND TECHNICAL COOPERATION

Agency for International Development:
February 25, 1976 (28 UST 5081; TIAS 8613).
August 31, 1976 (28 UST 8985; TIAS 8779).

ORGANIZATION FOR ECONOMIC COOPERATION AND DEVELOPMENT (OECD)

ATOMIC ENERGY

Cooperative arrangement with the Nuclear Energy Agency of OECD in the field of nuclear data and computer programs. Signed at Paris December 16, 1985; entered into force December 16, 1985.
TIAS

TAXATION

Tax reimbursement agreement, with annex. Signed at Paris October 15, 1987; entered into force October 15, 1987.
TIAS

ORGANIZATION FOR THE PROHIBITION OF CHEMICAL WEAPONS

TAXATION

Tax reimbursement agreement, with annex. Signed at The Hague February 25, 1999; entered into force February 25, 1999.
TIAS

ORGANIZATION OF AMERICAN STATES

ECONOMIC AND TECHNICAL COOPERATION

Understanding relating to the establishment and operation of training centers and other services under the program of technical cooperation of the Organization of American States. Exchange of notes at Washington February 12 and March 3, 1952; entered into force March 3, 1952.
3 UST 2995; TIAS 2485; 165 UNTS 67.

Agreement between the United States and the Pan American Union (General Secretariat of the Organization of American States) concerning certain funds to be made available under the Alliance of Progress. Signed at Washington November 29, 1961; entered into force November 29, 1961.
12 UST 1690; TIAS 4887; 424 UNTS 119.

Related agreement:
February 17, 1964 (15 UST 105; TIAS 5523; 511 UNTS 298).

HEADQUARTERS

Headquarters agreement, with annexes. Signed at Washington May 14, 1992; entered into force November 17, 1994.
TIAS

Amendment:
May 24 and 29, 1996.

PRIVILEGES AND IMMUNITIES

Agreement relating to privileges and immunities. Signed at Washington March 20, 1975; entered into force March 20, 1975.
26 UST 1025; TIAS 8089.

TAXATION

Agreement relating to a procedure for United States income tax reimbursement, with ad-

denda. Signed at Washington January 10, 1984; entered into force January 10, 1984; effective January 1, 1984.
TIAS 10919.

PAKISTAN

The Schedule to the Independence (International Arrangements) Order, 1947, provides that rights and obligations under all international agreements to which India is a party immediately before the appointed day [August 15, 1947] devolve upon India and Pakistan and will, if necessary, be apportioned between them; except that (1) Pakistan will take such steps as may be necessary to apply for membership of such international organizations as it chooses to join, and (2) rights and obligations under international agreements having an exclusive application to an area comprised in the Dominion of Pakistan will devolve upon it.

AGRICULTURAL COMMODITIES

Agreement for additional emergency assistance in agricultural commodities. Exchange of notes at Karachi January 18, 1955; entered into force January 18, 1955.
6 UST 557; TIAS 3188; 241 UNTS 53.

Agreement relating to the sale of certain surplus agricultural commodities and providing for the use of proceeds for urgent relief requirements of Pakistan. Signed at Karachi September 29, 1955; entered into force September 29, 1955.
6 UST 6145; TIAS 3466; 268 UNTS 374.

Agricultural commodities agreement with exchange of notes. Signed at Karachi October 14, 1961; entered into force October 14, 1961.
12 UST 1287; TIAS 4852; 426 UNTS 237.

Amendments:
December 3, 1962 (13 UST 2613; TIAS 5228; 460 UNTS 326).
May 31, 1963 (14 UST 1187; TIAS 5415; 488 UNTS 304).
February 10, 1964 (15 UST 108; TIAS 5524; 511 UNTS 304).
November 28, 1964 (15 UST 2211; TIAS 5707; 531 UNTS 374).
March 30, 1966 (17 UST 642; TIAS 6012; 578 UNTS 281).

Agricultural commodities agreement with exchange of notes. Signed at Karachi May 26, 1966; entered into force May 26, 1966.
17 UST 925; TIAS 6052; 594 UNTS 27.

Amendments:
August 10, 1966 (17 UST 1167; TIAS 6074; 603 UNTS 348).
October 6, 1966 (17 UST 1654; TIAS 6125; 674 UNTS 394).
October 25, 1966 (17 UST 1654; TIAS 6125; 674 UNTS 398).

PAKISTAN (Cont'd)

December 28, 1966 (18 UST 22; TIAS 6194; 681 UNTS 386).
June 28, 1967 (18 UST 1307; TIAS 6286).

Agricultural commodities agreement with annex. Signed at Islamabad May 11, 1967; entered into force May 11, 1967.
18 UST 512; TIAS 6258; 685 UNTS 291.

Related agreements:
August 3, 1967 (18 UST 1757; TIAS 6320; 693 UNTS 21).
December 26, 1967 (18 UST 3275; TIAS 6422; 697 UNTS 43).
May 16, 1968 (19 UST 4915; TIAS 6496; 697 UNTS 137).
May 16 and June 13, 1969 (20 UST 2696; TIAS 6730; 720 UNTS 330).
July 3, 1969 (20 UST 2878; TIAS 6765; 726 UNTS 167).
October 3, 1969 (20 UST 4111; TIAS 6807; 732 UNTS 47).
January 10, 1970 (21 UST 375; TIAS 6821; 732 UNTS 59).
November 25, 1970 (22 UST 484; TIAS 7087; 792 UNTS 3).
March 25, 1971 (22 UST 492; TIAS 7087; 792 UNTS 22).
July 27, 1971 (22 UST 1517; TIAS 7170; 792 UNTS 26).
August 6, 1971 (22 UST 1893; TIAS 7233).
March 9, 1972 (23 UST 257; TIAS 7301).
March 18, 1972 (23 UST 912; TIAS 7357).
April 6, 1972 (23 UST 912; TIAS 7357).
May 3, 1972 (23 UST 912; TIAS 7357).
May 11, 1972 (23 UST 776; TIAS 7339).
July 21, 1972 (23 UST 1474; TIAS 7426).
September 1, 1972 (23 UST 2658; TIAS 7457).
September 21, 1972 (23 UST 2802; TIAS 7466).
October 12, 1972 (23 UST 3142; TIAS 7490).
November 15, 1972 (23 UST 3730; TIAS 7521).
January 31, 1973 (24 UST 454; TIAS 7563).
March 19, 1973 (24 UST 882; TIAS 7595).
June 20, 1973 (24 UST 1655; TIAS 7670).
September 10, 1973 (24 UST 2009; TIAS 7714).
November 2, 1973 (24 UST 2242; TIAS 7741).
November 12, 1973 (24 UST 2249; TIAS 7743).
July 5, 1974 (25 UST 1444; TIAS 7874).

Agricultural commodities agreement. Signed at Islamabad November 23, 1974; entered into force November 23, 1974.
25 UST 3090; TIAS 7971; 1052 UNTS 160.

Amendments:
March 3, 1975 (26 UST 185; TIAS 8024; 1052 UNTS 173).
May 27, 1975 (26 UST 678; TIAS 8065; 1052 UNTS 176).

Related agreements:
August 7, 1975 (26 UST 2725; TIAS 8189; 1052 UNTS 195).
February 5, 1976 (27 UST 1555; TIAS 8263; 1052 UNTS 203).

August 10, 1976 (27 UST 3820; TIAS 8401).
August 20, 1976 (27 UST 3826; TIAS 8401).
December 29, 1976 (28 UST 1277; TIAS 8509).
December 22, 1977 (29 UST 3654; TIAS 9035; 1124 UNTS 107).
April 10, 1978 (29 UST 3673; TIAS 9035; 1124 UNTS 117).
January 24, 1979 (30 UST 2903; TIAS 9372; 1180 UNTS 185).

Agricultural commodities agreement, with minutes. Signed at Islamabad March 25, 1980; entered into force March 25, 1980.
32 UST 1434; TIAS 9782; 1222 UNTS 183.

Amendment:
July 2, 1980 (32 UST 1885; TIAS 9805).

Related agreements:
June 4, 1981 (33 UST 3937; TIAS 10273).
April 15, 1982 (34 UST 968; TIAS 10382).
May 15, 1983 (TIAS 10715; 1578 UNTS 79).
March 20, 1984 (TIAS 10970).

Agricultural commodities agreement. Signed at Islamabad April 28, 1985; entered into force April 28, 1985.
NP

Related agreement:
May 19, 1986 (NP).

Agricultural commodities agreement. Signed at Islamabad June 25, 1987; entered into force June 25, 1987.
NP

Related agreements:
March 24, 1988 (NP).
September 22, 1988 (NP).
March 15, 1990 (NP).

AVIATION

Understanding that the air services agreement between the United States and India, signed November 14, 1946 (61 Stat. 2573; TIAS 1586), is deemed to have been concluded between Pakistan and the United States, and that United States airlines may carry traffic between points in India and Pakistan subject to the terms of that agreement. Exchange of notes at Karachi June 1 and 16, 1948.
5 UST 2164; TIAS 3078; 235 UNTS 29.

Agreement revising that route annex to the air transport agreement of November 14, 1946. Exchange of notes at Karachi March 28 and April 18, 1961; entered into force April 18, 1961.
12 UST 846; TIAS 4783; 410 UNTS 300.

Air transport agreement, with annexes. Signed at Rawalpindi April 10, 1997; entered into force April 10, 1997.
TIAS

Amendment:
April 12 and 29, 1999.

COMMERCE

Treaty of friendship and commerce, and protocol. Signed at Washington November 12, 1959; entered into force February 12, 1961.
12 UST 110; TIAS 4683; 404 UNTS 259.

CONSULS

Convention to regulate commerce (article IV) between the United States and the United Kingdom. Signed at London July 3, 1815; effective July 3, 1815.
8 Stat. 228; TS 110; 12 Bevans 49.

COPYRIGHT (See APPENDIX)

CUSTOMS

Arrangement relating to reciprocal concessions and privileges accorded to diplomatic and consular officers. Exchange of notes at Washington October 27, 1948, and February 4, 1949; entered into force February 4, 1949.
10 Bevans 646.

DEFENSE

Agreement relating to transfer of military supplies and equipment to Pakistan. Exchange of notes at Washington November 29 and December 15, 1950.
1 UST 884; TIAS 2165; 122 UNTS 89.

Mutual defense assistance agreement. Signed at Karachi May 19, 1954; entered into force May 19, 1954.
5 UST 852; TIAS 2976; 202 UNTS 301.

Defense support assistance agreement. Signed at Karachi January 11, 1955; entered into force January 11, 1955.
6 UST 501; TIAS 3183; 251 UNTS 111.

Amendment:
March 11, 1961 (12 UST 226; TIAS 4698; 406 UNTS 318).

Agreement providing for the disposition of equipment and materials furnished to Pakistan under the mutual defense assistance agreement of May 19, 1954. Signed at Karachi March 15 and May 15, 1956; entered into force May 15, 1956.
7 UST 2389; TIAS 3627; 280 UNTS 368.

Construction agreement pursuant to article I, paragraph 1, of the mutual defense assistance agreement of May 19, 1954. Signed at Karachi May 28, 1956; entered into force May 28, 1956.
7 UST 923; TIAS 3575.

PAKISTAN (Cont'd)

Agreement of cooperation. Signed at Ankara March 5, 1959; entered into force March 5, 1959.
10 UST 317; TIAS 4190; 327 UNTS 285.

Agreement concerning general security of military information. Exchange of notes at Islamabad April 6, June 21 and 24, 1982; entered into force June 24, 1982.
TIAS 10455.

Agreement concerning the provision of training related to defense articles under the United States International Military Education and Training (IMET) Program. Exchange of notes at Islamabad December 10, 1985 and July 30, 1986; entered into force July 30, 1986.
NP

Memorandum of understanding on coassembly and coproduction of AN/UAS-12A night sight equipment, with appendix. Signed at Rawalpindi January 27, 1990; entered into force January 27, 1990.
TIAS 12365.

ECONOMIC AND TECHNICAL COOPERATION

Agreement for technical cooperation. Signed at Karachi February 9, 1951; entered into force February 9, 1951.
2 UST 1008; TIAS 2254; 100 UNTS 67.

Amendment:
January 8, 1952 (3 UST 2616; TIAS 2427; 157 UNTS 370).

Supplementary agreement for technical cooperation. Signed at Karachi February 2, 1952; entered into force February 2, 1952.
3 UST 3767; TIAS 2506; 131 UNTS 346.

Amendments:
March 27, 1953 (4 UST 1478; TIAS 2811; 172 UNTS 350).
December 28, 1953 (4 UST 2805; TIAS 2889; 222 UNTS 410).
June 24, 1954 (5 UST 1361; TIAS 3004; 233 UNTS 302).
January 18, 1955 (6 UST 511; TIAS 3185; 239 UNTS 358).

Agreement relating to emergency flood assistance for East Pakistan. Exchange of notes at Washington August 23, 1954; entered into force August 23, 1954.
5 UST 1779; TIAS 3052; 234 UNTS 243.

Amendment:
November 29 and December 16, 1954 (5 UST 2182; TIAS 3082; 234 UNTS 250).

Agreement relating to the commitment of $500 million by the United States to the Pakistan second five-year plan. Exchange of notes at

Karachi July 25, 1962; entered into force July 25, 1962.
13 UST 1864; TIAS 5136; 459 UNTS 87.

Joint Commission on Economic, Commercial, Scientific, Technological, Educational, and Cultural Cooperation. Signed at Washington December 6, 1982; entered into force December 6, 1982.
TIAS 10623.

Agency for International Development:
October 10, 1975 (28 UST 123; TIAS 8466).
March 9, 1976 (28 UST 2328; TIAS 8547).
April 8, 1976 (28 UST 3615; TIAS 8588).
September 9, 1976 (28 UST 7160; TIAS 8710).
September 22, 1976 (28 UST 7419; TIAS 8719).
October 27, 1976 (28 UST 8105; TIAS 8747).
January 18, 1977 (28 UST 2345; TIAS 8547).
April 1, 1977 (29 UST 1577; TIAS 8899; 1115 UNTS 103).
April 2, 1977 (29 UST 1623; TIAS 8900; 1115 UNTS 135).
January 12, 1978 (29 UST 2161; TIAS 8932).
November 8, 1978 (30 UST 7541; TIAS 9598; 1181 UNTS 364).
April 13, 1982 (34 UST 597; TIAS 10378).
May 23, 1983 (TIAS 10724).
July 25, 1983 (TIAS 10867).
December 19, 1983 (NP).
June 25, 1985 (NP).
July 8, 1986 (NP).
July 15, 1986 (NP).
September 25, 1986 (NP).
July 31, 1987 (NP).
September 24, 1987 (NP).
September 29, 1987 (NP).
August 4, 1988 (NP).
August 4, 1988 (NP).
August 29, 1988 (NP).
August 29, 1988 (NP).
September 22, 1988 (NP).
September 29, 1988 (NP).
September 29, 1988 (NP).
September 27, 1989 (NP).
August 9, 1990 (NP).

EDUCATION

Agreement for financing certain educational exchange programs. Signed at Islamabad October 18, 1972; entered into force October 18, 1972.
23 UST 3115; TIAS 7483; 938 UNTS 11.

ENVIRONMENTAL COOPERATION

Agreement for co-operation in the Global Learning and Observations to Benefit the Environment (GLOBE) Program, with appendices. Signed at Islamabad November 18, 1997; entered into force November 18, 1997.
TIAS

EXTRADITION

Extradition treaty between the United States and the United Kingdom, signed at London December 22, 1931, made applicable to India, in accordance with the provisions of article 14, from March 9, 1942.
47 Stat. 2122; TS 849; 12 Bevans 482; 163 LNTS 59.

FINANCE

Agreements regarding the consolidation and rescheduling of certain debts owed to the United States Government and its agencies with annexes and related letter. Signed at Washington September 20, 1972; entered into force September 20, 1972.
23 UST 2601; TIAS 7449.

Agreement regarding the consolidation and rescheduling of certain debts owed to the United States Government, with annexes. Signed at Washington March 4, 1976; entered into force May 12, 1976.
27 UST 4231; TIAS 8447.

Amendment:
April 13 and June 5, 1979 (30 UST 5985; TIAS 9532; 1177 UNTS 391).

Agreement regarding the consolidation and rescheduling of certain debts owed to the United States Government and the Agency for International Development, with annexes. Signed at Islamabad May 10, 1981; entered into force July 13, 1981.
33 UST 3628; TIAS 10246; 1541 UNTS 3.

Implementing agreement regarding the consolidation and rescheduling of certain debts owed to the Agency for International Development. Signed at Islamabad August 18, 1981; entered into force September 7, 1981.
33 UST 3628; TIAS 10246; 1541 UNTS 21.

Agreement regarding the consolidation and rescheduling of payments due under P.L. 480 Title I agricultural commodity agreements, with annexes. Signed at Islamabad September 27, 1981; entered into force September 27, 1981.
33 UST 3628; TIAS 10246.

Investment incentive agreement. Signed at Islamabad November 18, 1997; entered into force January 28, 1998.
TIAS

Agreement regarding the consolidation and rescheduling of certain debts owed to, guaranteed by, or insured by the United States Government and its agencies, with annexes. Signed at Islamabad November 26, 1999; entered into force February 23, 2000.
NP

PAKISTAN (Cont'd)

INFORMATIONAL MEDIA GUARANTIES

Agreement relating to an informational media guaranty program pursuant to section 111 (b)(3) of the Economic Cooperation Act of 1948, as amended. Exchange of notes at Karachi February 12 and May 1, 1954; entered into force May 1, 1954.
5 UST 2272; TIAS 3088; 237 UNTS 231.

Amendments:
January 1 and 8, 1957 (8 UST 1757; TIAS 3928; 299 UNTS 420).
August 10, 1962 and April 15, 1963 (15 UST 167; TIAS 5535; 510 UNTS 318).

JUDICIAL ASSISTANCE

Agreement on procedures for mutual assistance in connection with matters relating to the Lockheed Aircraft Corporation and the Boeing Company. Signed at Washington September 9, 1977; entered into force September 9, 1977.
28 UST 7488; TIAS 8724.

Related agreement:
January 6 and 10, 1978 (29 UST 492; TIAS 8827; 1115 UNTS 177).

LEND-LEASE

In a note of June 12, 1948, to the American Ambassador at Karachi, the Minister of Foreign Affairs gave assurance that: "the terms of the United States Settlement Agreement with India of May 16, 1946 [60 Stat. 1753; TIAS 1532], would continue to devolve on the Government of Pakistan to the extent to which they are applicable and have to be fulfilled in Pakistan."

MARITIME MATTERS

Agreement concerning financial arrangements for the furnishing of certain supplies and services to naval vessels. Signed at Karachi September 10, 1956; entered into force December 9, 1956.
7 UST 2493; TIAS 3637; 277 UNTS 259.

PEACE CORPS

Agreement relating to the establishment of a Peace Corps program in Pakistan. Exchange of notes at Karachi May 31, 1962; entered into force May 31, 1962; operative from October 28, 1961.
13 UST 1563; TIAS 5113; 460 UNTS 75.

POSTAL MATTERS

Agreement for the exchange of parcels by parcel post, and detailed regulations of execution. Signed at Karachi July 20 and at Washington October 7, 1955; entered into force January 1, 1956.
7 UST 1; TIAS 3475; 241 UNTS 255.

International express mail agreement, with detailed regulations. Signed at Islamabad and Washington March 11 and 30, 1987; entered into force May 1, 1987.
TIAS 11315.

INTELPOST memorandum of understanding, with detailed regulations. Signed at Islamabad and Washington February 23 and March 11, 1993; entered into force March 15, 1993.
TIAS 11917.

PROPERTY

Convention between the United States and the United Kingdom applicable to Pakistan:
Convention relating to tenure and disposition of real and personal property. Signed at Washington March 2, 1899 (31 Stat. 1939; TS 146; 12 Bevans 246). %Loc 31 in 5300

Supplementary convention extending the time within which notifications may be given of the accession of British colonies or foreign possessions to the convention of March 2, 1899. Signed at Washington January 13, 1902 (32 Stat. 1914; TS 402; 12 Bevans 261).

PUBLICATIONS

Agreement for the exchange of official publications. Exchange of notes at Karachi April 25 and May 23, 1951; entered into force May 23, 1951.
2 UST 1701; TIAS 2311; 134 UNTS 265.

Amendment:
April 22 and December 29, 1953 (5 UST 2850; TIAS 3141; 237 UNTS 312).

REFUGEE RELIEF

Agreement for assistance in the transport of relief commodities to Afghan refugee camps in Pakistan. Signed at Islamabad September 30, 1981; entered into force September 30, 1981.
33 UST 3932; TIAS 10272.

RELIEF SUPPLIES AND PACKAGES

Agreement relating to duty-free entry and defrayment of inland transportation charges on relief supplies and packages for Pakistan. Exchange of notes at Karachi June 18, 1953, and

October 2, 1954; entered into force October 2, 1954.
5 UST 1983; TIAS 3065; 236 UNTS 187.

SCIENTIFIC COOPERATION

Memorandum of understanding relating to scientific and technical cooperation. Signed at Washington March 2, 1981; entered into force March 2, 1981.
33 UST 1388; TIAS 10116.

Extension:
July 27, 1987.

TAXATION

Convention for the avoidance of double taxation and the prevention of fiscal evasion with respect to taxes on income. Signed at Washington July 1, 1957; entered into force May 21, 1959.
10 UST 984; TIAS 4232; 344 UNTS 203.

Agreement for the reciprocal exemption with respect to taxes on income from the international operation of ships. Exchange of notes at Islamabad July 26 and 27, 1989; entered into force July 27, 1989.
TIAS 11679.

TRADE (See also COMMERCE)

Memorandum of understanding relating to concessions and contributions to be made to the multilateral trade negotiations, with related letters, and related letter of January 28, 1980. Done at Geneva April 2 and 11, and August 2 and 30, 1979; entered into force August 30, 1979.
32 UST 5471; TIAS 9999; 1265 UNTS 213.

Agreement concerning trade in textiles and textile products, with annexes and exchange of letters. Exchange of notes at Washington May 20 and June 11, 1987; entered into force June 11, 1987.
NP

Amendments and extension:
July 20 and 31, 1987 (NP).
April 24 and May 30, 1988 (NP).
October 14 and 17, 1988 (NP).
March 4 and 10, July 17, September 15 and November 13, 1988 (NP).
November 30 and December 20, 1990 (NP).
January 23 and March 12, 1992 (NP).

TRADE-MARKS

Declaration by the United States and the United Kingdom affording reciprocal protection to trade-marks. Signed at London October 24, 1877; entered into force October 24, 1877.
20 Stat. 703; TS 138; I Malloy 737.

PAKISTAN (Cont'd)

VISAS

Agreement relating to the reciprocal reduction of visa fees. Exchange of notes at Karachi October 10 and 18, 1949; entered into force October 18, 1949; operative November 15, 1949.
3 UST 365; TIAS 2398; 141 UNTS 333.

Amendments:
August 16, October 11, November 19, and December 16 and 29, 1952, and March 19 and April 8, 1953 (4 UST 11; TIAS 2761; 204 UNTS 378).
August 4, October 20, and November 25 and 29, 1955 (6 UST 6107; TIAS 3463; 240 UNTS 438).

Agreement relating to the reciprocal issuance of nonimmigrant visas, and related notes of July 28, 1959, September 6 and 29, 1961. Exchange of notes at Karachi March 16 and June 27, 1959; entered into force June 27, 1959; operative August 1, 1959.
12 UST 1685; TIAS 4886; 360 UNTS 327.

PALAU

Agreement for the implementation of the Compact of Free Association between the Government of the United States and the Government of Palau. Signed January 10, 1986; entered into force October 1, 1994.
TIAS

AVIATION

Memorandum of agreement concerning assistance in developing and modernizing Palau's civil aviation infrastructure. Signed at Washington and Koror December 11, 1995 and January 17 and February 8, 1996; entered into force February 8, 1996.
TIAS

ENVIRONMENTAL COOPERATION

Agreement concerning cooperation in the Global Learning and Observations to Benefit the Environment (GLOBE) Program, with appendices. Signed at Koror January 30, 1997; entered into force January 30, 1997.
TIAS

PEACE CORPS

Agreement concerning the program of the Peace Corps in Palau. Signed at Koror March 8, 1995; entered into force March 8, 1995.
TIAS 12610.

RELATIONS

Agreement concerning relations under the Vienna convention on diplomatic relations. Signed at Washington December 14, 1994; entered into force March 2, 1995.
TIAS 12587.

PALESTINE LIBERATION ORGANIZATION

FINANCE

Agreement on encouragement of investment. Signed at Gaza and Washington August 11 and September 12, 1994; entered into force September 12, 1994.
TIAS 12564.

PANAMA

AGRICULTURE

Agreement confirming the cooperative agreement for the prevention of foot-and-mouth disease and rinderpest in Panama. Exchange of notes at Panama June 21 and October 5, 1972; entered into force October 5, 1972.
23 UST 3108; TIAS 7482.

Amendment:
May 28 and June 12, 1974 (25 UST 1522; TIAS 7888).

AVIATION

Agreement concerning the regulation of commercial aviation in the Republic of Panama. Exchange of notes at Panama April 22, 1929; entered into force April 22, 1929.
Foreign Relations, 1929, Vol. III, p. 729; 10 Bevans 729.

Agreement relating to the establishment of headquarters in Panama for a civil aviation technical assistance group for the Latin American area. Exchange of notes at Panama August 8, 1952; entered into force August 8, 1952.
3 UST 5064; TIAS 2691; 181 UNTS 257.

Agreement relating to the furnishing by the Federal Aviation Agency of certain services and materials for air navigation aids. Exchange of notes at Panama December 5, 1967 and February 22, 1968; entered into force February 22, 1968.
19 UST 4731; TIAS 6471; 698 UNTS 79.

Memorandum of agreement relating to the provision of flight inspection services. Signed at Washington and Panama August 16 and September 1, 1978; entered into force September 1, 1978; effective October 1, 1978.
30 UST 268; TIAS 9196; 1150 UNTS 231.

Memorandum of agreement concerning assistance in developing and modernizing Panama's civil aviation infrastructure, with annexes. Signed at Panama and Washington January 24 and February 15, 1990; entered into force February 15, 1990.
TIAS 11707.

Air transport agreement, with annexes. Signed at Panama May 8, 1997; entered into force December 28, 1998.
TIAS

Amendment:
May 27 and June 10, 1998.

Memorandum of cooperation for the promotion and development of civil aviation. Signed at Washington and Panama February 17 and March 3, 1998; entered into force March 3, 1998.
TIAS

CANALS

Agreement for enlargement and use by Canal Zone of sewerage facilities in Colon Free Zone Area. Exchange of notes at Panama March 8 and 25, 1954; entered into force March 25, 1954.
5 UST 782; TIAS 2966; 232 UNTS 289.

Treaty concerning the permanent neutrality and operation of the Panama Canal, with annexes and protocol.[1] Signed at Washington September 7, 1977; entered into force October 1, 1979, subject to amendments, conditions, reservations, and understandings.
33 UST 1; TIAS 10029; 1161 UNTS 177.

NOTE:
[1] Parties to the Protocol:

Argentina	Korea
Barbados	Liberia
Belize	Malawi
Bolivia	Netherlands
Chile	Nicaragua
China(Taiwan)	Norway
Costa Rica	Philippines
Denmark	St. Vincent & the
Dominican Rep.	Grenadines
Ecuador	Saudi Arabia
Egypt	Spain
El Salvador	Sweden
Equatorial Guinea	Tunisia
Finland	Union of Soviet
Germany, Fed. Rep.	Socialist Reps.
Guatemala	United Kingdom
Honduras	Uruguay
Israel	Venezuela
Jamaica	Vietnam, Soc. Rep.

Agreement concerning creation of a preparatory committee to study alternatives to the Panama Canal. Exchange of notes at Washington September 30, 1982; entered into force September 30, 1982.
TIAS

Agreement concerning establishment of the commission for the study of alternatives to the Panama Canal, with annex and related notes.

PANAMA (Cont'd)

Exchange of notes at New York September 26, 1985; entered into force September 26, 1985.[1] TIAS 11935.

Extension:
September 25, 1990.

Agreement concerning enforcement of alimony and child support obligations of Panama Canal Commission employees, with annexes. Exchange of notes at Panama February 22, 1988; entered into force February 22, 1988.
TIAS

NOTE:
[1] See also exchanges of notes of the same date concerning Japanese participation.

CEMETERIES

Agreement authorizing the United States to construct a custodian's house in the Corozal Cemetery. Exchange of notes at Panama September 29 and 30, 1982; entered into force September 29, 1982.
TIAS 10518; 1777 UNTS 343.

Agreement concerning the use of Corozal Cemetery. Signed at Panama City June 11, 1999; entered into force June 27, 2000.
TIAS

CONSERVATION

Agreement pursuant to article VI of the convention on nature protection and wildlife preservation in the Western Hemisphere of October 12, 1940 (56 Stat. 1354; TS 981), with related notes. Signed at Washington September 7, 1977; entered into force October 1, 1979.
33 UST 446; TIAS 10035; 1280 UNTS 311.

Agreement relating to custodianship of the Barro Colorado Nature Monument by the Smithsonian Tropical Research Institute. Exchange of notes signed at Washington September 7, 1977; entered into force October 1, 1979.
33 UST 457; TIAS 10036; 1280 UNTS 319.

COPYRIGHT (See APPENDIX)

CUSTOMS

Declaration permitting consuls to take note in person, or by authorized representatives, of declarations of values of exports made by shippers before customs officers. Exchange of notes at Washington April 17, 1913; entered into force June 1, 1913.
TS 578; 10 Bevans 699.

Agreement relating to customs privileges for consular officers. Exchange of notes at Panama January 7 and 31, 1935; entered into force January 31, 1935.
5 UST 1520; TIAS 3028; 234 UNTS 277.

DEFENSE

Agreement relating to the sale of military equipment, materials, and services to Panama. Exchange of notes at Panama May 20, 1959; entered into force May 20, 1959; operative from April 27, 1959.
10 UST 1000; TIAS 4234; 346 UNTS 235.

Agreement relating to the furnishing of defense articles and services to Panama for the purpose of contributing to its internal security. Exchange of notes at Panama March 26 and May 23, 1962; entered into force May 23, 1962.
13 UST 1294; TIAS 5081; 458 UNTS 225.

Agreement relating to the deposit by Panama of ten percent of the value of grant military assistance and excess defense articles furnished by the United States. Exchange of notes at Panama April 4 and May 9, 1972; entered into force May 9, 1972; effective February 7, 1972.
23 UST 897; TIAS 7353.

Agreement concerning payment to the United States of net proceeds from the sale of defense articles furnished under the military assistance program. Exchange of notes at Panama May 20 and December 6, 1974; entered into force December 6, 1974; effective July 1, 1974.
25 UST 3135; TIAS 7977; 991 UNTS 317.

Agreement concerning general security of military information. Signed at Panama August 17, 1984; entered into force August 17, 1984.
TIAS 11196.

ECONOMIC AND MILITARY COOPERATION

Agreement relating to economic and military cooperation. Exchange of notes at Panama September 7, 1978; entered into force September 7, 1978.
30 UST 1825; TIAS 9293; 1153 UNTS 157.

ECONOMIC AND TECHNICAL COOPERATION

General agreement for technical and economic cooperation. Signed at Panama December 11, 1961; entered into force March 5, 1962.
13 UST 274; TIAS 4972; 445 UNTS 161.

Agency for International Development:
May 6, 1969 (28 UST 5711; TIAS 8656).
September 30, 1971 (28 UST 5732; TIAS 8656).
September 10, 1975 (28 UST 353; TIAS 8473).

November 19, 1975 (28 UST 5471; TIAS 8647).
November 28, 1975 (29 UST 2037; TIAS 8925).
June 2, 1976 (28 UST 5739; TIAS 8656).
October 14, 1976 (28 UST 8295; TIAS 8762).
December 30, 1976 (28 UST 2258; TIAS 8543).
December 30, 1976 (28 UST 2276; TIAS 8544).
November 25, 1977 (29 UST 5781; TIAS 9154; 1231 UNTS 83).
December 21, 1977 (29 UST 5599; TIAS 9133; 1148 UNTS 414).
August 23, 1978 (30 UST 4827; TIAS 9490; 1233 UNTS 205).
December 24, 1984 (NP).

EMPLOYMENT

Agreement relating to the employment of dependents of official government employees. Exchange of notes at Panama November 26, 1993; entered into force November 26, 1993.
TIAS 12517.

ENERGY

Agreement relating to electric power. Exchange of notes at Panama October 1, 1979; entered into force October 1, 1979.
TIAS 10600; 1581 UNTS 3.

EXTRADITION

Treaty providing for the extradition of criminals. Signed at Panama May 25, 1904; entered into force May 8, 1905.
34 Stat. 2851; TS 445; 10 Bevans 673.

FINANCE

Agreement relating to legal tender and fractional silver coinage by Panama. Exchange of notes at Washington and New York June 20, 1904; entered into force June 20, 1904.
10 Bevans 681.

Amendments:
March 26 and April 2, 1930 (10 Bevans 731).
May 28 and June 6, 1931 (10 Bevans 734).
March 2, 1936 (53 Stat. 1807; TS 945).
June 17, 1946 (10 Bevans 834).
May 9 and 24, 1950.
September 11 and October 22, 1953.
August 23 and October 25, 1961.
September 26 and October 23, 1962.

Agreement relating to payment to be made by Panama to the Panama Canal Company and the Canal Zone Government for goods and services, with agreed minute. Exchange of notes at Panama March 25, 1980; entered into force March 25, 1980.
TIAS 10601; 1590 UNTS 3.

PANAMA (Cont'd)

Agreement relating to payments to be made by the Panama Canal Commission to Panama pursuant to articles III(5) and XIII(4) of the Panama Canal Treaty, with agreed minute. Exchange of notes at Panama March 25, 1980; entered into force March 25, 1980.
TIAS 10601; 1590 UNTS 17.

Understanding relating to Article X of the treaty concerning the treatment and protection of investments of October 27, 1982. Exchange of notes at Panama July 1 and 12, 1985; entered into force May 30, 1991.
TIAS

Agreement regarding the consolidation and rescheduling of certain debts owed to, guaranteed by or insured by the United States Government and its agencies, with annexes. Signed at Washington July 2, 1986; entered into force August 18, 1986.
NP

Swap agreement among the United States Treasury and the Government of Panama/Banco Nacional de Panama, with letter of understandings. Signed at Washington and Panama January 29 and 30, 1992; entered into force January 30, 1992.
TIAS

Investment incentive agreement. Signed at Panama City April 19, 2000; entered into force July 12, 2000.
TIAS

HIGHWAYS

Agreement relating to the construction of the inter-American highway. Exchange of notes at Panama May 15 and June 7, 1943; entered into force June 7, 1943.
57 Stat. 1298; EAS 365; 10 Bevans 826; 21 UNTS 269.

Amendment:
January 16 and 26, 1951 (2 UST 1852; TIAS 2321; 137 UNTS 69).

Agreement for cooperation in the construction of the Panama segment of the Darien Gap highway. Signed at Washington May 6, 1971; entered into force May 6, 1971.
22 UST 602; TIAS 7111; 793 UNTS 31.

Amendments:
May 15, 1974 (33 UST 3622; TIAS 10245; 1540 UNTS 420).
September 13, 1979 (33 UST 3622; TIAS 10245; 1540 UNTS 421).
July 18, 1980 (33 UST 3622; TIAS 10245; 1540 UNTS 422).

HOUSING

Agreement regarding housing civilian and military personnel of U.S. Forces stationed in Panama. Exchange of notes November 29, 1984; effective October 1, 1984.
TIAS

INVESTMENT

Treaty concerning the treatment and protection of investments, with annex and agreed minutes. Signed at Washington October 27, 1982; entered into force May 30, 1991.
TIAS

JUDICIAL ASSISTANCE

Informal arrangement relating to cooperation between the American Embassy, or Consulate, and Panamanian authorities when American merchant seamen or tourists are brought before a magistrate's court. Exchange of notes at Panama September 18 and October 15, 1947; effective October 15, 1947.
10 Bevans 841.

Arrangement concerning assistance in the development of civilian law enforcement institutions. Signed at Panama December 28, 1990; entered into force December 28, 1990.
TIAS 12425.

Treaty on mutual assistance in criminal matters, with annex and appendix. Signed at Panama April 11, 1991; entered into force September 6, 1995.
TIAS

MAPPING

Cooperative arrangement for the production of topographic maps of Panama, with annexes. Signed at Washington and Panama January 29, 1986; entered into force January 29, 1986.
TIAS 11212.

MARITIME MATTERS

Agreement relating to the mutual recognition of ship measurement certificates. Exchange of notes at Washington August 17, 1937; entered into force August 17, 1937.
50 Stat. 1626; EAS 106; 10 Bevans 781; 182 LNTS 159.

METEOROLOGY

Agreement relating to the Port Meteorological Office. Exchange of notes at Panama October 1, 1979; entered into force October 1, 1979.
TIAS 10599; 1871 UNTS 33.

MISSIONS, MILITARY

Agreement relating to the detail of a military officer to serve as adviser to the Minister of Foreign Affairs of Panama. Signed at Washington July 7, 1942; entered into force July 7, 1942.
56 Stat. 1545; EAS 258; 10 Bevans 817; 9 UNTS 289.

Extension and amendments:
February 17, March 23, September 22, and November 6, 1959 (12 UST 718; TIAS 4773; 409 UNTS 307).
March 26 and July 6, 1962 (13 UST 2598; TIAS 5226; 460 UNTS 360).
September 20 and October 8, 1962 (13 UST 2600; TIAS 5226; 460 UNTS 362).

NARCOTIC DRUGS

Mutual cooperation for reducing demand, preventing illicit use and combatting illicit production and traffic of drugs. Signed at Panama January 10, 1990; entered into force January 10, 1990.
TIAS 12409.

Arrangement for support and assistance from the United States Coast Guard for the National Maritime Service of the Ministry of Government and Justice. Signed at Panama March 18, 1991; entered into force March 18, 1991.
TIAS 11833.

Memorandum of understanding concerning the provision of helicopters for the purpose of more effectively combatting the illicit production and trafficking of drugs and other international criminal activities, with general provisions. Signed at Washington September 6, 1995; entered into force September 6, 1995.
TIAS 12688.

PEACE CORPS

Agreement relating to the establishment of a Peace Corps program in Panama. Exchange of notes at Washington May 1, 1990; entered into force November 23, 1990.
TIAS

POSTAL MATTERS

International express mail agreement, with detailed regulations. Signed at Panama and Washington March 29 and May 21, 1985; entered into force July 1, 1985.
TIAS 11151.

Postal money order agreement. Signed at Montevideo March 15, 1991; entered into force May 1, 1991.
TIAS 11821.

PANAMA (Cont'd)

PRISONER TRANSFER

Treaty on the execution of penal sentences. Signed at Panama January 11, 1979; entered into force June 27, 1980.
32 UST 1565; TIAS 9787; 1280 UNTS 363.

PROPERTY TRANSFER

Agreement relating to the status of the Cardenas (FAA housing) area under the agreement in implementation of Article III of the Panama Canal Treaty. Signed at Panama August 29, 1980; entered into force August 29, 1980.
33 UST 570; TIAS 10048; 1280 UNTS 415.

Agreement concerning the transfer of the Gamboa Penitentiary from the United States to Panama. Exchange of notes at Panama December 30, 1980; entered into force December 30, 1980.
TIAS 10602.

Agreement concerning disposition of the Mount Hope warehouse and transportation areas. Exchange of notes at Panama February 12 and May 7, 1982; entered into force May 7, 1982.
TIAS 10474.

Agreement concerning transfer of the Ancon District Court (Building 310) from the United States to Panama. Exchange of notes at Panama July 13, 1982; entered into force July 13, 1982.
TIAS 10544; 1777 UNTS 333.

Agreement concerning transfer of Mindi and Coco Solo housing units from the United States to Panama. Exchange of notes at Panama August 9 and 11, 1982; entered into force August 11, 1982.
TIAS

PUBLICATIONS

Agreement relating to the exchange of official publications. Exchange of notes at Panama November 27, 1941, and March 7, 1942; entered into force November 27, 1941.
56 Stat. 1444; EAS 243; 10 Bevans 805; 101 UNTS 157.

SCIENTIFIC COOPERATION

Agreement relating to the operation in Panama of the Smithsonian Tropical Research Institute, with annex. Exchange of notes at Washington September 7, 1977; entered into force September 7, 1977; effective October 1, 1979.
33 UST 465; TIAS 10037; 1280 UNTS 327.

SHIPPING

Agreement relating to jurisdiction over vessels utilizing the Louisiana Offshore Oil Port. Exchange of notes at Washington August 15 and October 10, 1980; entered into force October 10, 1980.
32 UST 2906; TIAS 9885; 1275 UNTS 97.

SMUGGLING

Convention for prevention of smuggling of intoxicating liquors. Signed at Washington June 6, 1924; entered into force January 19, 1925.
43 Stat. 1875; TS 707; 10 Bevans 717; 138 LNTS 397.

SOCIAL SECURITY

Agreement concerning participation by members of the Panama Canal Commission and United States forces in the Panamanian social security system. Exchange of notes at Panama March 9, 1982; entered into force March 9, 1982.
TIAS 10492.

TAXATION

Arrangement providing for relief from double income tax on shipping profits. Exchange of notes at Washington January 15, February 8, and March 28, 1941; entered into force March 28, 1941; operative January 1, 1936.
55 Stat. 1363; EAS 221; 10 Bevans 801; 103 UNTS 163.

Amendment:
July 30 and December 30, 1987 (TIAS 11555).

Agreement for withholding of Panamanian income tax from compensation paid to Panamanians employed within Canal Zone by the canal, railroad, or auxiliary works. Exchange of notes at Panama August 12 and 30, 1963; entered into force August 30, 1963.
14 UST 1478; TIAS 5445; 488 UNTS 11.

Agreement relating to the withholding of contributions for educational insurance from salaries paid to certain Canal Zone employees. Exchange of notes at Panama September 8 and October 13, 1972; entered into force October 13, 1972.
23 UST 3495; TIAS 7509; 898 UNTS 189.

Agreement relating to the agreements in implementation of articles III and IV of the Panama Canal Treaty with respect to tax on moveable property. Exchange of notes at Panama October 1, 1979; entered into force October 1, 1979.
33 UST 565; TIAS 10047; 1280 UNTS 409.

Agreement concerning taxation of income of United States contractors and subcontractors of the Panama Canal Commission or United

States Forces, with attachments and related note. Exchange of notes at Panama September 11, 1986; entered into force September 11, 1986.
TIAS

TELECOMMUNICATION

Agreement for radio communications between amateur stations on behalf of third parties. Exchange of notes at Panama July 19 and August 1, 1956; entered into force September 1, 1956.
7 UST 2179; TIAS 3617; 281 UNTS 49.

Agreement relating to the granting of reciprocal authorizations to permit licensed amateur radio operators of either country to operate their stations in the other country. Exchange of notes at Panama November 16, 1966; entered into force November 16, 1966.
17 UST 2215; TIAS 6159; 680 UNTS 303.

TRADE AND COMMERCE

Convention facilitating the work of traveling salesmen. Signed at Washington February 8, 1919; entered into force December 8, 1919.
41 Stat. 1696; TS 646; 10 Bevans 714.

Agreement relating to trade in cotton, wool and man-made fiber textiles and textile products, with annexes. Exchange of notes at Panama November 22 and 29, 1991; entered into force November 29, 1991.
NP

Amendment:
March 16 and April 10, 1992 (NP).

VISAS

Reciprocal agreement for gratis nonimmigrant visas. Exchange of notes at Panama March 27 and May 22 and 25, 1956; entered into force June 1, 1956.
7 UST 905; TIAS 3573; 268 UNTS 333.

Agreement modifying the agreement of March 27 and May 22 and 25, 1956 for gratis nonimmigrant visas. Exchange of notes at Panama June 14 and 17, 1971; entered into force June 17, 1971.
22 UST 815; TIAS 7142; 796 UNTS 353.

PAN AMERICAN UNION

(See ORGANIZATION OF AMERICAN STATES)

PAPUA NEW GUINEA

On September 16, 1975 Papua New Guinea became an independent state. In a note dated

PAPUA NEW GUINEA
(Cont'd)

September 16, 1975 to the Secretary-General of the United Nations, the Governor-General made a statement reading in part as follows:

"1. The Government of Papua New Guinea will make an examination of all treaties applying to its territory before independence, both bilateral and multilateral, with a view to making a statement of intention in respect of each of them. The statement will declare the Government's view as to whether the treaty continues or should be continued in force (on the basis of either succession or mutual consent, and with or without modification), or should be treated as having lapsed, or should be terminated. The statement will be forwarded to the other party or parties or to the depository, as may be appropriate.

"2. During the period of examination, the Government will, on a basis of reciprocity, accept all treaty rights and obligations accruing and arising under treaties previously applicable. The period of examination will extend for five years from the date of Independence, that is, until 15th September, 1980, except in the case of any treaty in respect of which an earlier statement of intention is made."

CONSULS

Convention to regulate commerce (article IV) between the United States and the United Kingdom. Signed at London July 3, 1815; entered into force July 3, 1815.
8 Stat. 228; TS 110; 12 Bevans 49.

COPYRIGHT (See APPENDIX)

DEFENSE

Status of forces agreement. Signed at Port Moresby February 28, 1989; entered into force February 28, 1989.
TIAS 11612.

Memorandum of understanding concerning an exchange of officers. Signed at Port Moresby and Honolulu May 17 and June 13, 1989; entered into force June 13, 1989.
TIAS 11667.

Memorandum of understanding concerning joint and combined military activities by Papua New Guinea defense forces and United States military forces in independent Papua New Guinea, with appendices. Signed at Port Moresby March 26, 1990; entered into force March 26, 1990.
TIAS 12366.

ECONOMIC AND TECHNICAL COOPERATION

Development cooperation agreement. Signed at Port Moresby May 7, 1990; entered into force May 7, 1990.
TIAS 11722.

EXTRADITION

Extradition treaty between the United States and the United Kingdom. Signed at London December 22, 1931, applicable to Australia (including Papua, Norfolk Island, and the mandated territories of New Guinea and Nauru), in accordance with article 14, from August 30, 1935.
47 Stat. 2122; TS 849; 12 Bevans 482; 163 LNTS 59.

Agreement continuing in force between the United States and Papua New Guinea the extradition treaty of December 22, 1931, between the United States and the United Kingdom, with enclosures. Exchange of notes at Port Moresby and Waigani February 2 and 23, 1988; entered into force February 23, 1988.
TIAS

FINANCE

Agreement relating to investment guaranties. Exchange of notes at Port Moresby and Waigani November 28, 1977 and April 4, 1978; entered into force April 13, 1978.
29 UST 3190; TIAS 9004; 1124 UNTS 237.

FISHERIES

Agreement concerning fishing by United States vessels in Papua New Guinea's archipelagic waters pursuant to the treaty on fisheries between the United States and certain Pacific Island states. Exchange of notes at Waigani and Port Moresby March 4, 5 and 25, 1987; entered into force March 25, 1987.
TIAS 11290.

PEACE CORPS

Agreement relating to the establishment of a Peace Corps program in Papua New Guinea, with related note. Exchange of notes at Washington October 6, 1980; entered into force October 6, 1980.
32 UST 2984; TIAS 9882; 1275 UNTS 89.

POSTAL MATTERS

Agreement for exchange of postal parcels between the United States and the Territory of Papua and the Trust Territory of New Guinea,

and detailed regulations of execution. Signed at Canberra May 22 and at Washington June 20, 1958; entered into force October 1, 1958.
9 UST 1266; TIAS 4115; 336 UNTS 97.

Memorandum of understanding concerning the operation of the INTELPOST field trial, with details of implementation. Signed at Boroko and Washington June 30 and November 23, 1987; entered into force January 1, 1988.
TIAS 11301.

International express mail agreement with detailed regulations. Signed at Boroko and Washington August 4 and 19, 1988; entered into force September 30, 1988.
TIAS 11644.

TELECOMMUNICATION

Agreement relating to the reciprocal granting of authorizations to permit licensed amateur radio operators of either country to operate their stations in the other country. Exchange of notes at Port Moresby and Waigani August 17, 1989 and April 26, 1990; entered into force April 26, 1990.
TIAS

PARAGUAY

AGRICULTURAL COMMODITIES

Agricultural commodities agreement with exchanges of notes. Signed at Asuncion July 7, 1961; entered into force July 7, 1961.
12 UST 1397; TIAS 4864; 433 UNTS 53.

Agricultural commodities agreement with exchanges of notes. Signed at Asuncion November 24, 1962; entered into force November 24, 1962.
13 UST 3874; TIAS 5263; 471 UNTS 49.

Agricultural commodities agreement with exchange of notes. Signed at Asuncion September 16, 1963; entered into force September 16, 1963.
14 UST 1807; TIAS 5493; 494 UNTS 101.

Agricultural commodities agreement with exchange of notes. Signed at Asuncion November 14, 1963; entered into force November 14, 1963.
14 UST 1818; TIAS 5494; 505 UNTS 87.

Agricultural commodities agreement with exchange of notes. Signed at Asuncion September 5, 1964; entered into force September 5, 1964.
15 UST 1807; TIAS 5654; 530 UNTS 225.

Agricultural commodities agreement with exchange of notes. Signed at Asuncion April 27, 1966; entered into force April 27, 1966.
17 UST 699; TIAS 6020; 578 UNTS 121.

PARAGUAY (Cont'd)

Agricultural commodities agreement with annex. Signed at Asuncion December 22, 1967; entered into force December 22, 1967.
20 UST 668; TIAS 6674; 706 UNTS 217.

Agricultural commodities agreement with annex. Signed at Asuncion June 7, 1969; entered into force June 7, 1969.
20 UST 854; TIAS 6701; 719 UNTS 161.

Agricultural commodities agreement with annex. Signed at Asuncion July 14, 1970; entered into force July 14, 1970.
21 UST 2226; TIAS 6974; 775 UNTS 155.

Agricultural commodities agreement with annex. Signed at Asuncion March 22, 1971; entered into force March 22, 1971.
23 UST 97; TIAS 7279.

AVIATION

Air transport agreement. Signed at Asuncion February 28, 1947; entered into force February 16, 1948.
62 Stat. 1940; TIAS 1753; 10 Bevans 948; 44 UNTS 25.

Agreement amending the air transport agreement of February 28, 1947, and relating to charter air services. Exchange of notes at Asuncion March 8 and 9, 1978; entered into force March 9, 1978.
29 UST 2697; TIAS 8966.

Memorandum of agreement concerning assistance in developing and modernizing the Paraguay civil aviation infrastructure, with annex. Signed at Washington May 27, 1992; entered into force May 27, 1992.
TIAS 11862.

COMMERCE

Treaty of friendship, commerce, and navigation. Signed at Asuncion February 4, 1859; entered into force March 7, 1860.
12 Stat. 1091; TS 272; 10 Bevans 888.

CONSULS (See COMMERCE)

COPYRIGHT (See APPENDIX)

CUSTOMS

Agreement for reciprocal import privileges for non-diplomatic personnel. Exchange of notes at Asuncion May 9 and 11, 1956; entered into force May 11, 1956.
7 UST 933; TIAS 3577.

DEFENSE

Agreement concerning the furnishing of assistance to Paraguay for the purpose of increasing the air transport capability of the Paraguayan Air Force. Exchange of notes at Asuncion August 25, 1962; entered into force August 25, 1962.
13 UST 2132; TIAS 5174; 461 UNTS 207.

Agreement providing for assistance to increase the road construction and maintenance capability of the Paraguayan Army. Exchange of notes at Asuncion February 10, 1964; entered into force February 10, 1964.
15 UST 149; TIAS 5532; 511 UNTS 53.

Agreement relating to the furnishing of additional military assistance to Paraguay. Exchange of notes at Asuncion April 11, 1966; entered into force April 11, 1966.
17 UST 661; TIAS 6014; 578 UNTS 99.

Agreement concerning payment to the United States of net proceeds from the sale of defense articles furnished under the military assistance program. Exchange of notes at Asuncion June 27, 1974; entered into force July 1, 1974.
25 UST 1440; TIAS 7873.

Agreement concerning United States Armed Forces technical personnel deployments to Paraguay. Exchange of notes at Asuncion February 28, 1995; entered into force February 28, 1995.
NP

ECONOMIC AND TECHNICAL COOPERATION

General agreement for economic, technical and related assistance. Signed at Asuncion September 26, 1961; entered into force September 26, 1961.
13 UST 2287; TIAS 5196; 461 UNTS 91.

Agency for International Development:
June 30, 1975 (28 UST 5867; TIAS 8665).
December 7, 1976 (28 UST 5923; TIAS 8665).
August 15, 1977 (29 UST 2940; TIAS 8990; 1120 UNTS 31).

EDUCATION

Agreement for financing certain educational exchange programs. Signed at Asuncion August 20, 1963; entered into force October 1, 1964.
15 UST 1982; TIAS 5675; 531 UNTS 197.

ENVIRONMENTAL COOPERATION

Agreement for cooperation in the Global Learning and Observations to Benefit the Environment Program, with appendices. Signed at Asuncion October 27, 2000; entered into force October 27, 2000.
TIAS

EXTRADITION

Treaty on extradition. Signed at Asuncion May 24, 1973; entered into force May 7, 1974.
25 UST 967; TIAS 7838.

FINANCE

Investment incentive agreement. Signed at Asuncion September 24, 1992; entered into force May 19, 1993.
TIAS 12478.

MAPPING

Cooperative mapping agreement. Signed at Asuncion January 16, 1962; entered into force January 16, 1962.
13 UST 52; TIAS 4934; 433 UNTS 169.

NARCOTIC DRUGS

Agreement on the control of the unlawful use of and illicit trafficking in narcotics and other dangerous drugs. Signed at Asuncion October 26, 1972; entered into force provisionally October 26, 1972; definitively January 11, 1973.
24 UST 1008; TIAS 7613.

Mutual cooperation agreement for reducing demand, illicit production and traffic of drugs. Signed at Asuncion September 22, 1988; entered into force September 22, 1988.
TIAS 12397.

PACIFIC SETTLEMENT OF DISPUTES

Treaty for the advancement of peace. Signed at Asuncion August 29, 1914; entered into force March 9, 1915.
39 Stat. 1615; TS 614; 10 Bevans 902.

PEACE CORPS

Agreement relating to the establishment of a Peace Corps program in Paraguay. Exchange of notes at Asuncion November 4, 1966; entered into force November 4, 1966.
17 UST 2050; TIAS 6144; 676 UNTS 17.

PARAGUAY (Cont'd)

POSTAL MATTERS

International express mail agreement, with detailed regulations. Signed at Asuncion and Washington July 13 and August 22, 1988; entered into force September 30, 1988.
TIAS 11643.

Postal money order agreement. Signed at Asuncion and Washington October 5 and 21, 1994; entered into force December 1, 1994.
NP

PUBLICATIONS

Agreement relating to the exchange of official publications. Exchange of notes at Asuncion November 26 and 28, 1942; entered into force November 28, 1942; operative August 5, 1942.
56 Stat. 1868; EAS 301; 10 Bevans 916; 101 UNTS 173.

RELIEF SUPPLIES AND PACKAGES

Agreement providing for duty-free entry into Paraguay and exemption from internal taxation of relief supplies and packages. Signed at Asuncion April 4, 1957; entered into force April 4, 1957.
8 UST 617; TIAS 3811; 283 UNTS 193.

Amendments:
December 27, 1960 and March 7, 1961 (12 UST 240; TIAS 4702; 405 UNTS 328).
September 25 and October 26, 1970 (21 UST 2507; TIAS 6993; 772 UNTS 462).

SEISMIC OBSERVATIONS

Memorandum of understanding concerning the operation of a seismic monitoring station in Paraguay. Signed at Asuncion September 13, 1999; entered into force September 13, 1999.
TIAS

TELECOMMUNICATION

Agreement relating to radio communications between amateur stations on behalf of third parties. Exchange of notes at Asuncion August 31 and October 6, 1960; entered into force November 5, 1960.
11 UST 2229; TIAS 4596; 393 UNTS 281.

Agreement relating to the reciprocal granting of authorizations to permit licensed amateur radio operators of either country to operate their stations in the other country. Exchange of notes at Asuncion March 18, 1966; entered into force March 18, 1966.
17 UST 328; TIAS 5978; 586 UNTS 189.

Agreement relating to establishing and maintaining monitoring premises and installations of the Foreign Broadcast Information Service (FBIS). Exchange of notes at Asuncion May 24, 1973; entered into force May 24, 1973.
24 UST 1132; TIAS 7639.

TRADE (See also COMMERCE)

Convention facilitating the work of traveling salesmen. Signed at Washington October 20, 1919; entered into force March 22, 1922.
42 Stat. 2128; TS 662; 10 Bevans 906.

Reciprocal trade agreement and supplemental exchanges of notes. Signed at Asuncion September 12, 1946; entered into force April 9, 1947.
61 Stat. 2688; TIAS 1601; 10 Bevans 933; 125 UNTS 179.

Related agreement:
April 2, 1962 (13 UST 407; TIAS 5000; 442 UNTS 315).

Agreement terminating parts and amending and continuing parts of the agreement of September 12, 1946. Exchange of notes at Asuncion June 26, 1963; entered into force June 26, 1963.
14 UST 1021; TIAS 5396; 487 UNTS 334.

PERU

AGRICULTURAL COMMODITIES

Agricultural commodities agreement for drought assistance. Exchange of notes at Lima April 17 and May 4 and 8, 1956; entered into force May 8, 1956.
7 UST 2529; TIAS 3645; 278 UNTS 117.

Agricultural commodities agreement for drought assistance. Exchange of notes at Washington July 16 and 19, 1957; entered into force July 19, 1957.
8 UST 970; TIAS 3860; 289 UNTS 271.

Agricultural commodities agreement with exchanges of notes. Signed at Lima February 12, 1960; entered into force February 12, 1960.
11 UST 186; TIAS 4430; 372 UNTS 83.

Amendments:
October 25 and November 24, 1960 (11 UST 2621; TIAS 4652; 402 UNTS 360).
October 4 and December 27, 1960 (12 UST 259; TIAS 4708; 405 UNTS 354).
April 25 and July 31, 1961 (12 UST 1178; TIAS 4831; 418 UNTS 412).
June 4 and 18, 1962 (13 UST 1346; TIAS 5093; 458 UNTS 349).

Agricultural commodities agreement with exchange of notes. Signed at Lima March 20, 1962; entered into force March 20, 1962.
13 UST 326; TIAS 4984; 445 UNTS 61.

Agricultural commodity agreement. Signed at Washington September 23, 1963; entered into force September 23, 1963.
14 UST 1260; TIAS 5428; 488 UNTS 91.

Agricultural commodities agreement with exchange of notes. Signed at Lima February 13, 1964; entered into force February 13, 1964.
15 UST 187; TIAS 5539; 511 UNTS 119.

Agricultural commodities agreement. Signed at Lima April 26, 1978; entered into force April 26, 1978.
30 UST 7662; TIAS 9604.

Amendments:
October 27, 1978 (30 UST 7691; TIAS 9604).
February 7, 1979 (30 UST 7695; TIAS 9604).
June 22, 1979 (30 UST 7699; TIAS 9604).

Related agreements:
February 14, 1980 (32 UST 2700; TIAS 9873).
February 5, 1981 (33 UST 4297; TIAS 10301).
April 5, 1982 (TIAS 10448).
March 29, 1983 (TIAS 10679).
July 18, 1983 (TIAS 10679).

Agricultural commodities agreement. Signed at Lima May 11, 1984; entered into force May 11, 1984.
TIAS 11040.

Agricultural commodities agreement, with memorandum of understanding. Signed at Lima April 17, 1985; entered into force April 17, 1985.
NP

Related agreement:
August 11, 1986 (NP).

Agricultural commodities agreement. Signed at Lima July 10, 1987; entered into force July 10, 1987.
NP

Agricultural commodities agreement. Signed at Lima June 28, 1988; entered into force June 28, 1988.
NP

Amendment:
August 12, 1988 (NP).

Related agreements:
May 3, 1989 (NP).
August 31, 1990 (NP).

AGRICULTURE

Memorandum of understanding relating to cooperative efforts to protect crops from plant pest damage and plant diseases. Signed at Lima November 30, 1981; entered into force November 30, 1981.
33 UST 4360; TIAS 10306.

PERU (Cont'd)

ATOMIC ENERGY

Agreement providing for a grant to the Government of Peru to assist in the acquisition of nuclear research and training equipment and materials. Exchange of notes at Lima July 12 and August 22, 1959; entered into force August 22, 1959.
10 UST 1600; TIAS 4304; 357 UNTS 99.

Agreement for cooperation concerning peaceful uses of nuclear energy, with annex and agreed minute. Signed at Washington June 26, 1980; entered into force April 15, 1982.
33 UST 4246; TIAS 10300.

AVIATION

Memorandum of agreement concerning the provision of assistance in developing and modernizing Peru's civil aviation infrastructure. Signed at Washington and Lima August 17 and 23, 1995; entered into force August 23, 1995.
TIAS

Air transport agreement, with annexes. Signed at Lima June 10, 1998; entered into force February 8, 1999.
TIAS

Memorandum of cooperation concerning mutual cooperation in the promotion and development of civil aviation. Signed at Washington and Lima March 16 and 27, 2000; entered into force March 27, 2000.
TIAS

COPYRIGHT (See APPENDIX)

CULTURAL PROPERTY

Agreement for the recovery and return of stolen archaeological, historical and cultural properties. Signed at Lima September 15, 1981; entered into force September 15, 1981.
33 UST 1607; TIAS 10136.

Memorandum of understanding concerning the imposition of import restrictions on archaeological material from the prehispanic cultures and certain ethnological material from the colonial period of Peru. Signed at Washington June 9, 1997; entered into force June 9, 1997.
TIAS

CUSTOMS

Agreement granting reciprocal customs privileges to diplomatic and consular officers and personnel. Exchange of notes at Lima Novem-

ber 7 and December 28, 1960, and February 4 and 13, 1961; entered into force February 13, 1961.
12 UST 217; TIAS 4696; 406 UNTS 177.

DEFENSE

Military assistance agreement. Signed at Lima February 22, 1952; entered into force April 26, 1952.
3 UST 2890; TIAS 2466; 165 UNTS 31.

Agreement providing for disposition of equipment and materials furnished by the United States under the military assistance agreement of February 22, 1952. Exchange of notes at Lima March 22 and April 30, 1955; entered into force April 30, 1955.
6 UST 2064; TIAS 3273; 258 UNTS 415.

Agreement for performance by members of Army, Navy, and military aviation missions of duties specified in article V of the military assistance agreement of February 22, 1952. Exchanges of notes at Lima June 28, July 18, and October 20 and 28, 1955; entered into force October 26, 1955.
6 UST 3771; TIAS 3377; 239 UNTS 181.

Agreement relating to the furnishing of defense articles and services to Peru. Exchange of notes at Lima December 17 and 20, 1962; entered into force December 20, 1962.
13 UST 3896; TIAS 5265; 471 UNTS 75.

Agreement relating to the deposit by Peru of ten percent of the value of grant military assistance furnished by the United States. Exchange of notes at Lima May 3, 1972; entered into force May 3, 1972; effective February 7, 1972.
23 UST 877; TIAS 7348.

Memorandum of understanding on exchange of officers between United States and Peruvian Marine Corps. Signed at Lima and Washington August 20 and September 22, 1986; entered into force September 22, 1986.
TIAS 11383.

Agreement concerning the status of certain United States military personnel who may serve for a period of less than ninety days at the ground-based radar site at Yurimaguas, and at other locations as agreed by the Peruvian Air Force. Exchange of notes at Lima November 7, 1995; entered into force November 7, 1995.
NP

Agreement concerning security assistance matters and the provision of articles, services and associated military educational training by the United States Government for antinarcotics purposes. Exchange of notes at Lima October 14, 1999 and January 14, 2000; entered into force January 14, 2000.
TIAS

ECONOMIC AND TECHNICAL COOPERATION

General agreement for technical cooperation. Signed at Lima January 25, 1951; entered into force January 15, 1953.
4 UST 132; TIAS 2772.

Amendments:
January 7, 1952 (4 UST 139; TIAS 2772).
February 21 and 28, 1952 (4 UST 143; TIAS 2772).
January 15, 1953 (4 UST 146; TIAS 2772).

Agreement concerning the establishment of an Americas Fund and Administering Board. Signed at Lima December 24, 1997; entered into force December 24, 1997.
TIAS

Agency for International Development:
September 29, 1976 (28 UST 6235; TIAS 8681).
September 29, 1976 (28 UST 6313; TIAS 8682).
May 31, 1978 (30 UST 2793; TIAS 9363; 1233 UNTS 37).
June 30, 1978 (30 UST 3303; TIAS 9393; 1233 UNTS 87).
July 19, 1978 (30 UST 3141; TIAS 9385; 1179 UNTS 21).
July 19, 1978 (30 UST 3147; TIAS 9385; 1179 UNTS 27).
July 20, 1983 (TIAS 10977).
September 30, 1983 (TIAS 10977).
October 17, 1983 (TIAS 10977).
March 30, 1984 (TIAS 10977).
May 11, 1984 (NP).
September 27, 1984 (NP).
September 25, 1987 (NP).
September 30, 1991 (NP).
May 12, 1995 (NP).
September 26, 1996 (NP).
August 18, 1997 (NP).

EDUCATION

Agreement for financing certain educational exchange programs. Signed at Lima January 28, 1965; entered into force August 25, 1965.
16 UST 1149; TIAS 5858; 587 UNTS 273.

Amendment:
November 23, 1981 and January 19, 1982 (34 UST 15; TIAS 10332).

EMPLOYMENT

Agreement relating to employment of dependents of official government employees. Exchange of notes at Lima August 27, 1987 and February 17, 1988; entered into force February 17, 1988.
TIAS 11650.

PERU (Cont'd)

ENVIRONMENTAL COOPERATION

Agreement for cooperation in the Global Learning and Observations to Benefit the Environment (GLOBE) Program, with appendices. Signed at Lima July 10, 1997; entered into force July 10, 1997.
TIAS

EXTRADITION

Treaty on extradition. Signed at Lima November 28, 1899; entered into force February 22, 1901.
31 Stat. 1921; TS 288; 10 Bevans 1074.

Related agreement:
February 15, 1990 (TIAS 12410).

FINANCE

Agreement relating to investment guaranties under section 413 (b)(4)(B)(i) of the Mutual Security Act of 1954. Exchange of notes at Lima March 14 and 16, 1955; entered into force March 16, 1955.
6 UST 678; TIAS 3203; 252 UNTS 151.

Agreement regarding the consolidation and rescheduling of certain debts owed to, guaranteed or insured by the United States Government and its agencies, with annexes. Signed at Lima July 5, 1979; entered into force August 22, 1979.
32 UST 1; TIAS 9698; 1221 UNTS 159.

Agreement regarding the consolidation and rescheduling of certain debts owed to, guaranteed by or insured by the United States Government and its agencies, with implementing agreement. Signed at Lima November 29, 1983; entered into force March 9, 1984.
TIAS 10978.

Agreement regarding the consolidation and rescheduling or refinancing of certain debts owed to, guaranteed by, or insured by the United States Government and its agencies, with annexes. Signed at Washington August 27, 1992; entered into force September 30, 1992.
NP

Investment incentive and financial agreement. Signed at Washington December 16, 1992; entered into force December 16, 1992.
TIAS 12542.

SWAP agreement between the United States Treasury and the Government of Peru/Central Bank of Peru, with memorandum of understanding. Signed at Washington March 9, 1993; entered into force March 9, 1993.
TIAS

Agreement regarding the consolidation and rescheduling or refinancing of certain debts owed to, guaranteed by or insured by the United States Government and its agencies, with annexes. Signed at Washington August 30, 1993; entered into force September 30, 1993.
NP

Agreement supplementing the investment incentive and financial agreement of December 16, 1992, relating to the Export-Import Bank. Signed at Washington May 20, 1994; entered into force May 20, 1994.
TIAS 12542.

Agreement regarding the rescheduling and reorganization of certain debts owed to or guaranteed by the United States Government and its agencies. Signed at Lima December 31, 1996; entered into force February 18, 1997.
NP

HEALTH

Agreement for the establishment and operation of the Naval Medical Research Institute (NAMRID) in Lima. Signed at Lima October 21, 1983; entered into force October 21, 1983.
TIAS 10836.

JUDICIAL ASSISTANCE

Procedures for mutual assistance in connection with matters relating to the Lockheed Aircraft Corporation. Signed at Washington August 8, 1979; entered into force August 8, 1979.
NP

MAPPING

Agreement relating to the making of aeronautical charts for air navigation. Exchange of notes at Lima March 7 and April 23, 1942; entered into force April 23, 1942.
10 Bevans 1138.

Agreement relating to a program of aerial and topographic cartography of Peru and exchanges of notes. Signed at Lima February 5, 1948; entered into force February 5, 1948.
10 Bevans 1269.

Cooperative arrangement for the production of topographic maps of Peru. Signed at Washington and Lima April 25 and May 22, 1986; entered into force May 22, 1986.
TIAS 11372.

MARITIME MATTERS

Agreement concerning financial arrangements for the furnishing of certain supplies and services to naval vessels of both countries. Signed

at Lima January 7, 1955; entered into force April 7, 1955.
6 UST 806; TIAS 3227; 261 UNTS 321.

Agreement relating to the loan of a floating dry dock to Peru. Exchange of notes at Washington June 15, 1959; entered into force June 15, 1959.
10 UST 1053; TIAS 4244; 346 UNTS 279.

Memorandum of understanding on maritime trade. Signed at Washington May 1, 1987; entered into force May 1, 1987.
TIAS 11273.

NARCOTICS

Agreement regarding cooperation in the prevention and control of money laundering arising from illicit trafficking in narcotic drugs and psychotropic substances, with attachment. Signed at Lima October 14, 1991; entered into force October 14, 1991.
TIAS 12438.

PACIFIC SETTLEMENT OF DISPUTES

Arbitration convention. Signed at Washington December 5, 1908; entered into force June 29, 1909.
36 Stat. 2169; TS 528; 10 Bevans 1081.

Treaty for the advancement of peace. Signed at Lima July 14, 1914; entered into force March 4, 1915.
39 Stat. 1611; TS 613; 10 Bevans 1083.

POSTAL MATTERS

International express mail agreement, with detailed regulations. Signed at Lima and Washington October 29 and November 30, 1990; entered into force January 14, 1991.
TIAS 11787.

Agreement for the transmission and payment of postal money orders. Signed at Washington and Lima August 21 and September 8, 1995; entered into force December 1, 1995.
NP

PRISONER TRANSFER

Treaty on the execution of penal sentences. Signed at Washington July 6, 1979; entered into force July 21, 1980.
32 UST 1471; TIAS 9784; 1233 UNTS 139.

PUBLICATIONS

Agreement relating to the exchange of official publications. Exchange of notes at Lima Octo-

PERU (Cont'd)

ber 16 and 20, 1936; entered into force October 20, 1936.
50 Stat. 1601; EAS 103; 10 Bevans 1106; 181 LNTS 161.

RELIEF SUPPLIES AND PACKAGES

Agreement granting duty-free entry, exemption from internal taxation, and free transportation within Peru for supplies for U.S. rehabilitation and relief agencies distributing surplus agricultural food products in Peru. Exchange of notes at Lima October 21 and 25, 1954; entered into force October 29, 1954.
5 UST 2725; TIAS 3128; 238 UNTS 247.

Amendment:
June 23 and August 3, 1955 (7 UST 781; TIAS 3557; 273 UNTS 295).

RULES OF WARFARE

Convention regarding the rights of neutrals at sea. Signed at Lima July 22, 1856; entered into force October 31, 1857.
11 Stat. 695; TS 277; 10 Bevans 1019.

SCIENTIFIC COOPERATION

Agreement concerning scientific and technical cooperation in the earth and mapping sciences, with annexes. Signed at Lima July 19, 1990; entered into force July 19, 1990.
TIAS 12416.

TAXATION

Agreement concerning the reciprocal exemption from income tax of income derived from the international operation of ships. Exchange of notes at Lima December 15, 1988; entered into force December 15, 1988.
TIAS 11621.

Agreement for the exchange of tax information. Signed at Cartagena February 15, 1990; entered into force March 31, 1993.
TIAS 12060.

TELECOMMUNICATION

Arrangement concerning radio communications between amateur stations on behalf of third parties. Exchange of notes at Lima February 16 and May 23, 1934; entered into force May 23, 1934.
49 Stat. 3555; EAS 66; 10 Bevans 1103.

Agreement relating to the reciprocal granting of authorizations to permit licensed amateur radio operators of either country to operate their stations in the other country. Exchange of notes at Lima June 28 and August 11, 1965; entered into force August 11, 1965.
16 UST 1160; TIAS 5860; 564 UNTS 135.

TRADE AND COMMERCE

Convention concerning commercial travelers, and protocol. Signed at Lima January 19, 1923; entered into force July 8, 1924.
43 Stat. 1802; TS 692; 10 Bevans 1091.

Agreement terminating the agreement of November 23, 1971 relating to trade in cotton textiles and providing for consultation on problems of market disruption caused by exports of textiles or textile products from Peru. Exchange of notes at Lima June 13 and September 10, 1975; entered into force September 10, 1975.
26 UST 2125; TIAS 8153.

Memorandum of understanding within the context of the multilateral trade negotiations concerning concessions and contributions, with related letters of January 24 and 29, 1980. Signed at Geneva and Lima March 8 and June 28, 1979; entered into force February 8, 1980.
TIAS 10732.

Agreement relating to trade in cotton, wool and man-made fiber textiles and textile products, with annexes. Exchange of notes at Lima January 3, 1985; entered into force January 3, 1985.
NP

Extensions and amendments:
July 17 and September 26, 1985 (NP).
October 24, 1985 and January 23, 1986 (NP).
March 19 and April 8, 1987 (NP).
November 27, 1987 and January 6, February 3, March 18 and June 2 and 10, 1988 (NP).
July 26, 1989 (NP).
July 11 and October 4, 1990 (NP).

Visa arrangement regarding trade in textiles, with annex. Exchange of letters at Washington July 17 and August 22, 1985; entered into force August 22, 1985; effective September 1, 1985.
NP

Amendment:
February 19 and 28, 1991 (NP).

VISAS

Agreement relating to the waiver of nonimmigrant passport visas and visa fees. Exchange of notes at Lima April 6 and September 26, and related note of October 9, 1956; entered into force September 26, 1956; operative January 1, 1957.
8 UST 468; TIAS 3800; 288 UNTS 165.

Amendment:
January 4 and 7, 1957 (8 UST 468; TIAS 3800; 288 UNTS 170).

Agreement relating to the reciprocal liberalization of nonimmigrant visa regulations. Exchange of notes at Lima March 18 and April 23, 1970; entered into force April 23, 1970.
21 UST 1317; TIAS 6885; 751 UNTS 355.

WEATHER STATIONS

Agreement for the continuation of the cooperative meteorological program in Peru. Exchange of notes at Lima July 7, 1964; entered into force July 7, 1964; operative January 1, 1963.
15 UST 1523; TIAS 5634; 530 UNTS 113.

PHILIPPINES

AGRICULTURAL COMMODITIES

Agricultural commodities agreement with exchanges of notes. Signed at Manila November 24, 1961; entered into force November 24, 1961.
12 UST 3036; TIAS 4902; 433 UNTS 315.

Agreement relating to the deposit rate for pesos under the agricultural commodities agreement of November 24, 1961. Exchange of notes at Manila August 14 and September 5, 1962; entered into force September 5, 1962.
14 UST 128; TIAS 5281; 473 UNTS 364.

Agricultural commodities agreement with exchange of notes. Signed at Manila May 14, 1964; entered into force May 14, 1964.
15 UST 531; TIAS 5580; 526 UNTS 113.

Agricultural commodities agreement, with exchange of notes. Signed at Manila April 23, 1965; entered into force April 23, 1965.
16 UST 632; TIAS 5785; 546 UNTS 157.

Agricultural commodities agreement with exchange of notes. Signed at Manila December 22, 1966; entered into force December 22, 1966.
18 UST 89; TIAS 6202; 591 UNTS 219.

Agricultural commodities agreement with annex. Signed at Manila March 24, 1970; entered into force March 24, 1970.
21 UST 1046; TIAS 6858; 745 UNTS 151.

Amendment:
May 21 and 28, 1970 (21 UST 1315; TIAS 6884; 752 UNTS 415).

Related agreements:
April 16, 1971 (22 UST 544; TIAS 7097; 792 UNTS 321).
November 22, 1971 (22 UST 1835; TIAS 7227).
May 4, 1972 (23 UST 627; TIAS 7324).
August 16, 1972 (23 UST 1499; TIAS 7431).

PHILIPPINES (Cont'd)

October 27 and 31, 1972 (23 UST 3487; TIAS 7506).
March 9, 1973 (24 UST 1089; TIAS 7629).
April 30, 1974 (25 UST 723; TIAS 7822).

Agricultural commodities agreement. Signed at Manila May 12, 1977; entered into force May 12, 1977.
28 UST 6708; TIAS 8684.

Agricultural commodities agreement. Signed at Manila August 24, 1978; entered into force August 24, 1978.
30 UST 198; TIAS 9187; 1150 UNTS 149.

Related agreement:
August 6, 1979 (30 UST 6301; TIAS 9555; 1181 UNTS 3).

Agricultural commodities agreement. Signed at Manila July 8, 1985; entered into force July 8, 1985.
NP

Amendment:
April 14, 1988 (NP).

Agricultural commodities agreement. Signed at Manila June 20, 1986; entered into force June 20, 1986.
NP

Agricultural commodities agreement. Signed at Manila April 19, 1988; entered into force April 19, 1988.
NP

Amendments:
May 23, 1988 (NP).
July 31, 1990 (NP).

AGRICULTURE

Memorandum of understanding on cooperation in the field of agricultural science and technology. Signed at Manila February 10, 1988; entered into force February 10, 1988.
TIAS 11925.

ATOMIC ENERGY

Agreement for cooperation concerning civil uses of atomic energy. Signed at Washington June 13, 1968; entered into force July 19, 1968.
19 UST 5389; TIAS 6522; 706 UNTS 183.

Arrangement for the exchange of technical information and cooperation in nuclear safety matters, with addenda. Signed at Bethesda and Manila May 24 and June 18, 1985; entered into force June 18, 1985.
TIAS 11343.

AVIATION

Agreement, with memorandum of consultation, concerning air transport services, with exchanges of letters. Exchange of notes at Washington September 16, 1982; entered into force September 16, 1982.
TIAS 10443.

Amendments:
May 29, 1987 and January 13, 1988 (TIAS 11564).
November 20, 1995 (TIAS 12702).

CLAIMS

Agreement relating to settlement of claims for damages arising from maneuvers at Laur Training Area. Exchange of aide memoire at Manila February 6, 1957; entered into force February 6, 1957.
9 UST 313; TIAS 4009; 303 UNTS 237.

Agreement relating to settlement of claims for damages arising from SEATO maneuvers and ground field training exercises. Exchange of aide memoire at Manila November 1, 1957; entered into force November 1, 1957.
8 UST 2456; TIAS 3965; 307 UNTS 39.

Agreement relating to settlement of claims for damages arising from maneuvers in Laur-Dingalan Bay area. Exchange of aide memoire at Manila February 20, 1958; entered into force February 20, 1958.
9 UST 327; TIAS 4011; 303 UNTS 261.

Agreement relating to settlement of claims arising from maneuvers at Laur Training Area during January and February 1959. Exchange of aide memoire at Manila January 21, 1959; entered into force January 21, 1959.
10 UST 204; TIAS 4184; 341 UNTS 255.

Agreement on the settlement of claims for pay and allowances of recognized Philippine guerillas not previously paid in full and for erroneous deductions of advanced salary from the backpay of eligible Philippine veterans. Signed at Manila June 29, 1967; entered into force June 29, 1967.
18 UST 1392; TIAS 6295; 686 UNTS 71.

CONSULS (See also GENERAL RELATIONS)

Consular convention. Signed at Manila March 14, 1947; entered into force November 18, 1948.
62 Stat. 1593; TIAS 1741; 11 Bevans 74; 45 UNTS 23.

COPYRIGHT (See also APPENDIX)

Arrangement relating to reciprocal copyright relations between the United States and the

Philippines. Exchange of notes at Washington October 21, 1948; entered into force October 21, 1948.
62 Stat. 2996; TIAS 1840; 11 Bevans 160; 77 UNTS 197.

CUSTOMS

Agreement relating to extension of free-entry privileges to dependents of United States Government employees newly assigned to South Viet-Nam who elect to reside in the Philippines. Exchange of notes at Manila May 14 and 28, 1965; entered into force May 28, 1965.
19 UST 7807; TIAS 6612; 713 UNTS 235.

Agreement concerning matters of customs administration with annexes. Signed at Washington January 4, 1967; entered into force January 4, 1967.
18 UST 148; TIAS 6212; 590 UNTS 51.

Agreement relating to customs regulations governing cargo consigned to United States military authorities or armed forces personnel, with annexes. Exchange of notes at Manila April 24, 1969; entered into force May 4, 1969.
20 UST 2816; TIAS 6752; 723 UNTS 185.

DEFENSE (See also MUTUAL SECURITY)

Mutual defense treaty. Signed at Washington August 30, 1951; entered into force August 27, 1952.
3 UST 3947; TIAS 2529; 177 UNTS 133.

Agreement relating to military assistance. Exchange of notes at Manila June 26, 1953; entered into force July 5, 1953.
4 UST 1682; TIAS 2834; 213 UNTS 77.

Agreement relating to military assistance. Exchange of notes at Manila April 27, 1955; entered into force April 27, 1955.
6 UST 847; TIAS 3231; 261 UNTS 351.

Amendments:
April 20, 1956 (7 UST 727; TIAS 3551; 273 UNTS 316).
June 14, 1957 (8 UST 859; TIAS 3845; 291 UNTS 342).
April 14, 1958 (9 UST 397; TIAS 4019; 308 UNTS 324).

Related agreements:
August 23 and 30, 1979 (30 UST 7275; TIAS 9584; 1182 UNTS 153).
August 12 and 22, 1980 (32 UST 2393; TIAS 9847; 1274 UNTS 287).
August 19 and 30, 1981 (33 UST 3347; TIAS 10236).
August 16 and September 30, 1982 (TIAS 10504).

Agreement relating to the administration by the Philippine Department of Education of public schools within the United States Naval Reservation, Subic Bay. Exchange of notes at Ma-

PHILIPPINES (Cont'd)

nila October 28, 1955; entered into force October 28, 1955; operative December 1, 1955.
6 UST 3109; TIAS 3361; 239 UNTS 165.

Agreement providing for disposition of equipment and material furnished by the United States. Exchange of notes at Manila July 27, 1953 and March 3, 1956; entered into force March 3, 1956.
7 UST 425; TIAS 3523; 270 UNTS 400.

Interim arrangement to permit the exploitation of mineral resources located on specific sites within the U.S. Military Reservation, Fort Stotsenberg, Tarlac. Exchange of notes at Manila April 8, 1957; entered into force April 8, 1957.
9 UST 309; TIAS 4008; 303 UNTS 227.

Agreement for the establishment of a Mutual Defense Board and the assignment of Philippine military liaison officers to United States military bases in the Philippines. Exchange of notes at Manila May 15, 1958; entered into force May 15, 1958.
9 UST 547; TIAS 4033; 316 UNTS 163.

Agreement relating to the relocation of the Air Post Office from the Manila Air Station to the chancery grounds of the Embassy. Exchange of notes at Manila March 27 and July 17, 1958; entered into force July 17, 1958.
9 UST 1073; TIAS 4082; 335 UNTS 199.

Agreement relating to the establishment of a United States communications facility at Mt. Cabuyao. Exchange of notes at Manila March 16, 1965; entered into force March 16, 1965.
16 UST 158; TIAS 5776; 542 UNTS 199.

Agreement relating to the revision of Article XIII of the military base agreement of March 14, 1947, as amended, on criminal jurisdiction arrangements, with annex, agreed minutes and implementing arrangements. Exchange of notes at Manila August 10, 1965; entered into force August 10, 1965.
16 UST 1090; TIAS 5851; 564 UNTS 208.

Agreement relating to the installation of a submarine cable with a terminal facility at San Miguel Communications Station. Exchange of notes at Manila August 12, 1965; entered into force August 12, 1965.
16 UST 1127; TIAS 5855; 579 UNTS 47.

Agreement relating to the establishment of commercial banking facilities at the United States naval base at Subic Bay. Exchange of notes at Manila November 3 and 15, 1965; entered into force November 15, 1965.
16 UST 1948; TIAS 5931; 574 UNTS 205.

Agreement relating to the installation and operation of a petroleum products pipeline from Subic Bay Naval Reservation through Basa Air Base to Clark Air Base. Exchange of notes at Manila August 26, 1966; entered into force August 26, 1966.
17 UST 1206; TIAS 6083.

Agreement relating to the exploitation of natural resources within United States bases in the Philippines. Exchange of notes at Manila August 24, 1967; entered into force August 24, 1967.
18 UST 2340; TIAS 6335; 693 UNTS 53.

Agreement relating to the expansion of banking facilities at Clark Air Base and Sangley Point Navy Base. Exchange of notes at Manila January 17 and 23, 1968; entered into force January 23, 1968.
19 UST 4513; TIAS 6443; 698 UNTS 37.

Agreement relating to the employment of Philippine nationals in the United States military bases in the Philippines. Signed at Manila May 27, 1968; entered into force May 27, 1968.
19 UST 5892; TIAS 6542; 658 UNTS 347.

Amendments:
September 5, 1985.
July 19, 1989.

Agreement relating to the recruitment and employment of Filipino citizens by the United States military forces and contractors of military and civilian agencies of the United States in certain areas of the Pacific and Southeast Asia. Signed at Manila December 28, 1968; entered into force December 28, 1968.
19 UST 7560; TIAS 6598; 658 UNTS 365.

Agreement relating to the installation of a submarine cable from Southern Taiwan to the United States Navy Communications Station, San Miguel, Zambales, Philippines. Exchange of notes at Manila December 21, 1970 and January 6, 1971; entered into force January 6, 1971.
22 UST 363; TIAS 7065; 792 UNTS 37.

Agreement concerning payment to the United States of net proceeds from the sale of defense articles furnished under the military assistance program. Exchange of notes at Manila May 16 and July 16, 1974; entered into force July 16, 1974; effective July 1, 1974.
25 UST 1447; TIAS 7875.

Agreement amending the agreement of March 14, 1947, as amended, concerning military bases, with implementing arrangements, exchanges of notes, and related letters.[1] Exchange of notes at Manila January 7, 1979; entered into force January 7, 1979.
30 UST 863; TIAS 9224.

Memorandum of understanding for the exchange of individual personnel between the United States Army Western Command and the Armed Forces of the Philippines. Signed at Manila March 25, 1981; entered into force March 25, 1981.
TIAS 10871; 1577 UNTS 355.

Administrative arrangements, implementing the agreement of January 7, 1979 (TIAS 9224), for the performance of customs, immigration and quarantine functions at United States facilities at Clark Air Base and Subic Naval Base in the Republic of the Philippines, with annex and exchanges of notes. Signed at Manila Decem-

ber 8, 1982; entered into force December 8, 1982.
TIAS 10585; 1871 UNTS 433.

Agreement regarding the relinquishment of certain areas at the San Miguel Naval Communications Station, Province of Zambales and the U.S. Navy transmitter site at Capas, Province of Tarlac, with maps. Exchange of notes at Manila January 31 and May 13, 1991; entered into force May 13, 1991.
TIAS

Agreement regarding the relinquishment of the U.S. Facility at Wallace Air Station, the Crow Valley Weapons Range and the U.S. Air Force Transmitter site at O'Donnell. Exchange of notes at Manila September 11 and 16, 1991; entered into force September 16, 1991.
TIAS

Agreement modifying the agreement of May 15, 1958, for the establishment of a Mutual Defense Board and the assignment of Philippine military liaison officers to U.S. military bases in the Philippines. Exchange of notes at Manila April 2 and May 10, 1993; entered into force May 10, 1993.
TIAS 12496.

Agreement regarding the status of U.S. military and civilian personnel. Exchange of notes at Manila April 2, June 11 and 21, 1993; entered into force June 21, 1993.
TIAS

Extensions:
September 19, 1994.
April 28, 1995.
November 29, December 1 and 8, 1995.

Agreement regarding the treatment of United States armed forces visiting the Philippines. Signed at Manila February 10, 1998; entered into force June 1, 1999.
TIAS

Agreement regarding the treatment of Republic of Philippines personnel visiting the United States of America. Signed at Manila October 9, 1998; entered into force June 1, 1999.
TIAS

NOTE:
[1] See also administrative arrangement of December 8, 1982 (TIAS 10585).

ECONOMIC AND TECHNICAL COOPERATION

Economic and technical cooperation agreement. Signed at Manila April 27, 1951; entered into force May 21, 1951.
3 UST 3707; TIAS 2498; 174 UNTS 251.

Agency for International Development:
December 23, 1975 (28 UST 975; TIAS 8489).
March 11, 1976 (28 UST 2296; TIAS 8545).
April 28, 1976 (28 UST 5955; TIAS 8666).
August 6, 1976 (28 UST 7035; TIAS 8703; 1087 UNTS 349).
August 6, 1976 (28 UST 7073; TIAS 8704).

PHILIPPINES (Cont'd)

February 7, 1977 (28 UST 7070; TIAS 8703; 1087 UNTS 349).
June 27, 1977 (29 UST 1911; TIAS 8911).
August 31, 1977 (29 UST 5477; TIAS 9124).
January 13, 1978 (29 UST 4383; TIAS 9059).
January 13, 1978 (29 UST 4383; TIAS 9060; 1230 UNTS 3).
January 13, 1978 (29 UST 4415; TIAS 9061).
March 6, 1978 (29 UST 5534; TIAS 9125).
April 19, 1978 (30 UST 2403; TIAS 9344; 1230 UNTS 43).
May 3, 1978 (30 UST 2545; TIAS 9353; 1230 UNTS 93).
May 3, 1978 (30 UST 2577; TIAS 9354; 1230 UNTS 127).
May 3, 1978 (30 UST 2601; TIAS 9355; 1230 UNTS 159).
May 3, 1978 (30 UST 2622; TIAS 9356; 1230 UNTS 179).
May 19, 1978 (30 UST 2763; TIAS 9362; 1230 UNTS 199).
June 2, 1978 (30 UST 3153; TIAS 9387).
August 18, 1978 (30 UST 4645; TIAS 9484; 1230 UNTS 261).
May 28, 1987 (NP).
September 28, 1987 (NP).
September 28, 1988 (NP).
August 1, 1989 (NP).
August 28, 1989 (NP).
May 10, 1990 (NP).
September 28, 1990 (NP).
September 28, 1990 (NP).
September 28, 1990 (NP).
August 30, 1991 (NP).
September 30, 1996 (NP).
June 19, 1997 (NP).
June 23, 1997 (NP).
August 6, 1997 (NP).
August 29, 1997 (NP).
August 29, 1997 (NP).
August 29, 1997 (NP).
April 7, 1998 (NP).
May 4, 1998 (NP).
May 8, 1998 (NP).
June 11, 1998 (NP).
June 11, 1998 (NP).
July 2, 1998 (NP).
July 2, 1998 (NP).
September 30, 1998 (NP).

EDUCATION

Agreement for financing certain educational exchange programs. Signed at Manila March 23, 1963; entered into force March 23, 1963.
14 UST 352; TIAS 5321; 474 UNTS 81.

Amendment:
December 11, 1968, January 31 and March 19, 1969 (20 UST 508; TIAS 6657; 719 UNTS 354).

Agreement concerning the Special Fund for Education. Exchange of notes at Manila April 26, 1966; entered into force April 26, 1966.[1]
19 UST 5079; TIAS 6508; 706 UNTS 110.

NOTE:
[1] For implementing agreements, see 19 UST 5082; TIAS 6508; 706 UNTS 57 (May 18, 1967, June 26, 1967, August 11, 1967 and June 11, 1968); 20 UST 2845; TIAS 6756; 723 UNTS 243 (September 5, 1969); 22 UST 501; TIAS 7089; 792 UNTS 261 (March 30, 1971); 23 UST 251; TIAS 7300 (March 21, 1972).

EMPLOYMENT

Agreement relating to the employment of dependents of official government employees. Exchange of notes at Washington September 20 and October 20, 1983; entered into force October 20, 1983.
TIAS 10805.

ENVIRONMENTAL COOPERATION

Agreement for cooperation in the Global Learning and Observations to Benefit the Environment (GLOBE) Program, with appendices. Signed at Manila January 14, 1999; entered into force January 14, 1999.
TIAS

EXTRADITION

Extradition treaty. Signed at Manila November 13, 1994; entered into force November 22, 1996.
TIAS

FINANCE

Agreement establishing a joint American-Philippine financial commission. Exchange of notes at Manila September 13 and 17, 1946; entered into force September 17, 1946.
61 Stat. 2840; TIAS 1612; 11 Bevans 34; 15 UNTS 249.

Agreement relating to the repayment of funds advanced to the National Defense Forces, Republic of the Philippines, by the United States Philippines-Ryukyus Command. Signed at Washington November 6, 1950; entered into force November 6, 1950.
1 UST 765; TIAS 2151; 122 UNTS 63.

Agreement for adjustment of the amount and final settlement of obligations under the agreement of November 6, 1950 relating to the repayment of funds advanced to Philippine National Defense Forces. Exchange of notes at Washington March 27, 1961; entered into force March 27, 1961.
12 UST 297; TIAS 4715; 405 UNTS 304.

Agreement regarding the consolidation and rescheduling of certain debts owed to, guaranteed by or insured by the United States Government and its agencies, with annexes. Signed at Manila July 29, 1985; entered into force August 30, 1985.
NP

Agreement regarding the consolidation and rescheduling of certain debts owed to, guaranteed by, or insured by the United States Government and its agencies, with annexes. Signed at Manila May 16, 1988; entered into force June 17, 1988.
NP

Amendment:
April 25, 1989 (NP).

Agreement regarding the consolidation and rescheduling or refinancing of certain debts owed to, guaranteed by, or insured by the United States Government and its agencies, with annexes. Signed at Manila November 3, 1989; entered into force December 13, 1989.
NP

Agreement regarding the consolidation and rescheduling or refinancing of certain debts owed to, guaranteed by, or insured by the United States Government and its agencies with annexes. Signed at Washington December 11, 1991; entered into force March 2, 1992.
NP

Amendment:
March 4 and 9, 1993 (NP).

Agreement relating to investments supported by the Overseas Private Investment Corporation. Signed at Manila October 22, 1998; entered into force February 15, 2000.
TIAS

GENERAL RELATIONS

Provisional agreement concerning friendly relations and diplomatic and consular representation. Signed at Manila July 4, 1946; entered into force July 4, 1946.
60 Stat. 1800; TIAS 1539; 11 Bevans 1; 6 UNTS 335.

Treaty of general relations, and protocol. Signed at Manila July 4, 1946; entered into force October 22, 1946.
61 Stat. 1174; TIAS 1568; 11 Bevans 3; 7 UNTS 3.

HEALTH

Agreement permanently locating the United States Naval Medical Research Unit-Two (NAMRU-2) in the Philippines. Exchange of notes at Manila February 26, 1979 and June 5, 1981; entered into force June 5, 1981.
33 UST 2093; TIAS 10174; 1529 UNTS 469.

Agreement on employees' compensation and medical care programs [for Philippine employees of U.S. Forces], with annex. Signed at Manila March 10, 1982; entered into force March 10, 1982.
34 UST 312; TIAS 10358.

PHILIPPINES (Cont'd)

Amendment:
July 19, 1989.

Agreement continuing the operations of the United States Veterans Administration in the Philippines. Signed at Manila May 19, 1987; entered into force May 19, 1987; effective October 1, 1986.
TIAS 11280.

Agreement continuing the operations of the United States Department of Veterans Affairs in the Philippines. Signed at Manila May 3, 1990; entered into force May 3, 1990; effective October 1, 1989.
TIAS 11725.

INFORMATIONAL MEDIA GUARANTIES

Agreement relating to an informational media guaranty program. Exchange of notes at Manila October 14, 1954 and January 19, 1955; entered into force January 19, 1955.
6 UST 549; TIAS 3187; 241 UNTS 514.

Amendment:
December 12, 1955 and February 10, 1958 (9 UST 274; TIAS 4003; 303 UNTS 336).

JUDICIAL ASSISTANCE

Agreement concerning the provision of documents to Government of the Republic of the Philippines. Exchange of notes at Washington March 15, 1986; entered into force March 15, 1986.
NP

Agreement on procedures for mutual legal assistance. Signed at Manila March 31, 1987; entered into force March 31, 1987.
NP

Treaty on mutual legal assistance in criminal matters, with attachments. Signed at Manila November 13, 1994; entered into force November 22, 1996.
TIAS

MAPPING

Agreement concerning mapping, charting and geodesy cooperation, with annexes. Signed at Makati and Fairfax June 27 and September 9, 1991; entered into force September 9, 1991.
NP

MARITIME MATTERS

Agreement relating to naval charter for lease of vessels to the Philippines. Exchanges of notes at Manila September 26 and December 9, 1947, and May 6 and June 7, 1948; entered into force June 7, 1948.
62 Stat. 3870; TIAS 1954; 11 Bevans 137; 70 UNTS 280.

Agreement relating to the loan of a floating dry dock to the Republic of the Philippines. Exchange of notes at Manila September 28 and October 4, 1961; entered into force October 4, 1961.
12 UST 1415; TIAS 4865; 433 UNTS 83.

Extension and amendment:
November 4, 1966 (17 UST 1963; TIAS 6137; 674 UNTS 382).

MILITARY CEMETERIES AND MONUMENTS

Agreement relating to cooperation in consecrating Corregidor Island as a World War II memorial site, with annex. Exchange of notes at Manila December 22, 1965; entered into force December 22, 1965.
16 UST 1925; TIAS 5925; 579 UNTS 203.

MUTUAL SECURITY

Agreement relating to the assurances required under the Mutual Security Act of 1951. Exchange of notes at Manila January 4 and 7, 1952; entered into force January 7, 1952.
3 UST 4644; TIAS 2617; 179 UNTS 193.

PATENTS

Agreement relating to the reciprocal application of certain rights of priority in the filing of patent applications. Exchange of notes at Washington February 12 and August 4 and 23, 1948; entered into force August 23, 1948.
62 Stat. 3461; TIAS 1861; 11 Bevans 149; 82 UNTS 11.

PEACE CORPS

Agreement relating to the establishment of a Peace Corps program in the Republic of the Philippines. Exchange of notes at Manila October 11 and 31, 1961; entered into force October 31, 1961.
12 UST 1699; TIAS 4889; 424 UNTS 129.

POSTAL MATTERS

Convention for the exchange of money orders. Signed at Washington January 29, and at Manila March 12, 1951; entered into force April 1, 1951.
8 UST 1083; TIAS 3871; 288 UNTS 285.

Parcel post convention. Signed at Manila September 21 and at Washington November 12, 1964; entered into force November 1, 1965.
16 UST 1680; TIAS 5893; 574 UNTS 159.

International express mail agreement, with detailed regulations. Signed at Manila and Washington April 21 and May 22, 1992; entered into force September 21, 1992.
TIAS 11861.

PUBLICATIONS

Agreement relating to the exchange of official publications. Exchange of notes at Manila April 12 and June 7, 1948; entered into force June 7, 1948.
62 Stat. 2024; TIAS 1767; 11 Bevans 134; 73 UNTS 89.

Amendment:
December 2 and 20, 1965 (16 UST 1909; TIAS 5921; 578 UNTS 196).

RELIEF SUPPLIES AND PACKAGES

Agreement providing for duty-free entry into the Philippines and exemption from internal taxation of relief supplies and packages. Exchange of notes at Manila April 29, 1954 and October 18, 1956; entered into force October 18, 1956.
8 UST 144; TIAS 3752; 280 UNTS 55.

Amendment:
August 6 and September 19, 1970 (21 UST 2510; TIAS 6994; 772 UNTS 458).

SOCIAL SECURITY

Agreement providing for social security coverage for non-United States citizen employees of the United States armed forces in the Philippines. Exchange of notes at Manila April 23, 1962 and August 30, 1963; entered into force August 30, 1963.
14 UST 1523; TIAS 5452; 489 UNTS 323.

Agreement providing for social security coverage for non-United States citizen employees of the United States Employees Association, JUSMAG Officers Club, JUSMAG NCO Club, and the AID Employees' Recreation Association in the Philippines. Exchange of notes at Manila August 30 and October 8, 1963; entered into force October 8, 1963.
14 UST 1523; TIAS 5452; 489 UNTS 332.

Agreement providing for social security coverage for Philippine citizen civilian employees of the Agency for International Development Mission to the Philippines, with annex. Ex-

PHILIPPINES (Cont'd)

change of notes at Manila November 12, 1964 and March 10, 1965; entered into force March 10, 1965.
20 UST 536; TIAS 6663; 706 UNTS 41.

Agreement providing for social security coverage for Philippine citizen civilian employees of the Peace Corps and United States Joint Military Advisory Group (JUSMAG), with annex. Exchange of notes at Manila April 5 and July 15, 1965; entered into force July 15, 1965.
20 UST 540; TIAS 6663; 706 UNTS 49.

TAXATION

Convention with respect to taxes on income.[1] Signed at Manila October 1, 1976; entered into force October 16, 1982.
TIAS 10417.

NOTE:
[1] With reservations and understandings.

TELECOMMUNICATION

Agreement regarding radio broadcasting facilities with protocol and exchange of notes. Signed at Manila May 6, 1963; entered into force May 6, 1963.
14 UST 741; TIAS 5353; 477 UNTS 67.

Amendment:
September 10, 1965 (16 UST 1186; TIAS 5865; 595 UNTS 368).

Agreement relating to the transfer to the Philippines of radio broadcasting facilities at Malolos, Bulacan Province pursuant to the agreement of May 6, 1963, as amended. Exchange of notes at Manila July 13, 1966; entered into force July 13, 1966.
17 UST 1028; TIAS 6060; 595 UNTS 374.

Agreement relating to the reciprocal granting of authorizations to permit licensed amateur radio operators of either country to operate their stations in the other country. Exchange of notes at Manila October 25, 1976; entered into force October 25, 1976.
27 UST 3985; TIAS 8415; 1059 UNTS 67.

Agreement relating to radio communications between amateur stations on behalf of third parties, with attachment. Exchange of notes at Manila February 13 and June 4, 1991; entered into force June 4, 1991.
TIAS 12431.

TOURISM

Agreement on the development and facilitation of reciprocal tourism. Signed at Washington September 17, 1982; entered into force September 17, 1982.
TIAS 10498.

TRADE AND COMMERCE

Agreement relating to entry of nationals of either country into the territories of the other for purposes of trade, investment, and related activities. Exchange of notes at Washington September 6, 1955; entered into force September 6, 1955.
6 UST 3030; TIAS 3349; 238 UNTS 109.

Agreement on trade concessions and contributions within the framework of the multilateral trade negotiations, and related letters of January 28 and February 4, 1980. Signed at Manila October 30, 1979; entered into force October 30, 1979.
33 UST 4468; TIAS 10317; 1156 UNTS 105.

Agreement relating to subsidization of exports in the context of the agreement on interpretation and application of articles VI, XVI and XXIII (subsidies code) of the General Agreement on Tariffs and Trade (TIAS 9619). Exchange of letters at Manila and Washington March 14 and 15, 1985; entered into force March 15, 1985.
TIAS 11333.

Agreement relating to trade in textiles and textile products, with annexes. Exchange of letters at Washington March 4, 1987; entered into force March 4, 1987.
NP

Amendments and extensions:
December 28, 1990 and February 26, 1991 (NP).
July 12, 1991 (NP).
March 6, 1992 (NP).
July 7 and 29, 1994 (NP).

VISAS

Agreement relating to waiver of nonimmigrant passport visa fees. Exchange of notes at Manila November 24, 1952; entered into force November 24, 1952; operative December 24, 1952.
3 UST 5196; TIAS 2715; 181 UNTS 155.

POLAND

AGRICULTURAL COMMODITIES

Agricultural commodities agreement with exchange of notes. Signed at Washington June 7, 1957; entered into force June 7, 1957.
8 UST 799; TIAS 3839; 291 UNTS 41.

Amendments:
August 14, 1957 (8 UST 1289; TIAS 3878; 291 UNTS 52).

January 8, 1958 (9 UST 1; TIAS 3973; 307 UNTS 330).
May 26 and 29, 1959 (10 UST 1049; TIAS 4243; 346 UNTS 350).
July 21, 1960 (11 UST 1871; TIAS 4532; 380 UNTS 464).
April 10 and 11, 1967 (19 UST 7788; TIAS 6610; 723 UNTS 296).

Agricultural commodities agreement and exchange of notes. Signed at Washington February 15, 1958; entered into force February 15, 1958.
9 UST 199; TIAS 3991; 307 UNTS 217.

Amendments:
June 6, 1958 (9 UST 707; TIAS 4046; 317 UNTS 376).
May 26 and 29, 1959 (10 UST 1049; TIAS 4243; 346 UNTS 350).
July 21, 1960 (11 UST 1871; TIAS 4532; 380 UNTS 469).
April 10 and 11, 1967 (19 UST 7788; TIAS 6610; 723 UNTS 296).

Agricultural commodities agreement with exchange of notes. Signed at Washington June 10, 1959; entered into force June 10, 1959.
10 UST 1058; TIAS 4245; 347 UNTS 41.

Amendments:
November 10, 1959 (10 UST 1410; TIAS 4288; 357 UNTS 396).
February 11, 1960 (11 UST 99; TIAS 4415; 371 UNTS 364).
July 21, 1960 (11 UST 1871; TIAS 4532; 380 UNTS 474).
April 10 and 11, 1967 (19 UST 7788; TIAS 6610; 723 UNTS 296).

Agricultural commodities agreement with exchanges of notes. Signed at Washington July 21, 1960; entered into force July 21, 1960.
11 UST 1887; TIAS 4535; 380 UNTS 157.

Amendment:
April 10 and 11, 1967 (19 UST 7788; TIAS 6610; 723 UNTS 296).

Agricultural commodities agreement with exchanges of notes. Signed at Washington December 15, 1961; entered into force December 15, 1961.
12 UST 3065; TIAS 4907; 434 UNTS 3.

Amendments:
April 19, 1962 (13 UST 401; TIAS 4998; 445 UNTS 383).
April 10 and 11, 1967 (19 UST 7788; TIAS 6610; 723 UNTS 296).

Agricultural commodities agreement with exchanges of notes. Signed at Washington February 1, 1963; entered into force February 1, 1963.
14 UST 803; TIAS 5359; 487 UNTS 143.

Amendment:
April 10 and 11, 1967 (19 UST 7788; TIAS 6610; 723 UNTS 296).

Agricultural commodities agreement with exchanges of notes. Signed at Washington Feb-

POLAND (Cont'd)

ruary 3, 1964; entered into force February 3, 1964.
15 UST 40; TIAS 5516; 505 UNTS 215.

Amendment:
April 10 and 11, 1967 (19 UST 7788; TIAS 6610; 723 UNTS 296).

Agricultural commodities agreement with exchanges of notes. Signed at Washington February 3, 1964; entered into force February 3, 1964.
15 UST 59; TIAS 5517; 505 UNTS 245.

Related agreements:
April 10, 1967 (19 UST 7788; TIAS 6610; 724 UNTS 324).
April 10 and 11, 1967 (19 UST 7788; TIAS 6610; 723 UNTS 296).

Agricultural commodities agreement, with agreed minute. Signed at Warsaw August 28, 1981; entered into force August 28, 1981.
34 UST 1134; TIAS 10400.

Agricultural commodities agreement. Signed at Warsaw November 30, 1989; entered into force November 30, 1989.
NP

Amendment:
March 16 and 28, 1990 (NP).

ATOMIC ENERGY

Agreement for cooperation concerning peaceful uses of nuclear energy, with annex and agreed minute. Signed at Vienna September 18, 1991; entered into force September 3, 1992.
TIAS 12435.

AVIATION

Agreement relating to the acceptance of airworthiness certifications, with annex. Exchange of notes at Washington November 8, 1976; entered into force November 8, 1976.
27 UST 3882; TIAS 8407; 1059 UNTS 179.

Amendment:
January 28, 1980 (32 UST 529; TIAS 9723; 1221 UNTS 342).

Air transport agreement, with schedule and annex. Signed at Warsaw February 1, 1988; entered into force October 11, 1988; effective January 1, 1988.
TIAS 12424.

Amendments and extension:
December 4 and 28, 1990 (TIAS 12424).
June 4, 1996 and April 24, 1997.

Memorandum of agreement concerning assistance in developing and modernizing Poland's civil aviation infrastructure. Signed at Wash-

ington and Warsaw January 5 and 14, 1998; entered into force January 14, 1998.
TIAS

CLAIMS

Agreement relating to settlement of claims of nationals of the United States against Poland and exchange of notes. Signed at Washington July 16, 1960; entered into force July 16, 1960.
11 UST 1953; TIAS 4545; 384 UNTS 169.

Protocol to the claims settlement agreement of July 16, 1960. Signed at Warsaw November 29, 1960; entered into force November 29, 1960.
11 UST 2450; TIAS 4629; 401 UNTS 338.

CONSULS

Consular convention, with protocols and exchanges of notes. Signed at Warsaw May 31, 1972; entered into force July 6, 1973.
24 UST 1231; TIAS 7642.

COPYRIGHT (See APPENDIX)

CULTURAL RELATIONS

Agreement concerning the reciprocal establishment of cultural and information centers. Signed at Warsaw July 10, 1989; entered into force July 10, 1989.
TIAS

CUSTOMS

Agreement relating to reciprocal customs privileges for foreign service personnel. Exchange of notes at Warsaw October 5 and 30, 1945; entered into force October 30, 1945.
61 Stat. 2297; TIAS 1544; 11 Bevans 283; 15 UNTS 225.

Agreement regarding cooperation and mutual assistance between customs services. Signed at Warsaw August 8, 1990; entered into force May 15, 1991.
TIAS 12077.

DEFENSE

Agreement concerning provision of training related to defense articles under the United States International Military Education Training (IMET) Program. Exchange of notes at Warsaw April 25 and June 6, 1991; entered into force June 6, 1991.
NP

Agreement concerning security measures for the protection of classified military information. Signed at Washington February 17, 1995; entered into force February 17, 1995.
TIAS 12247.

Agreement concerning exchange of research and development information, with appendix (Master Information Exchange Agreement). Signed at Warsaw June 9, 1995; entered into force June 9, 1995.
TIAS 12367.

Acquisition and cross-servicing agreement, with annexes. Signed at Warsaw November 22, 1996; entered into force November 22, 1996.
TIAS

ECONOMIC AND TECHNICAL COOPERATION

Agreement to establish a joint commission on humanitarian assistance, with annexes. Signed at Warsaw July 17, 1989; entered into force July 17, 1989.
TIAS

EDUCATION

Agreement for the establishment of an office for U.S.-Polish educational exchanges. Signed at Washington March 22, 1990; entered into force March 22, 1990.
TIAS

EMPLOYMENT

Agreement relating to the employment of dependents of official government employees, with annex. Exchange of notes at Warsaw April 30 and May 16, 1991; entered into force May 16, 1991.
TIAS 12430.

ENERGY

Agreement for collaboration to demonstrate an emerging retrofit of clean coal technology at a powerplant in Cracow, Poland, with annexes. Signed at Washington March 15, 1990; entered into force March 15, 1990.
TIAS

ENVIRONMENTAL COOPERATION

Memorandum of understanding concerning cooperation in the field of environmental protection. Signed at Washington May 15, 1995; entered into force May 15, 1995.
TIAS 12646.

POLAND (Cont'd)

Agreement for cooperation in the Global Learning and Observations to Benefit the Environment (GLOBE) Program, with appendices. Signed at Warsaw April 22, 1997; entered into force April 22, 1997.
TIAS

EXTRADITION

Extradition treaty. Signed at Washington July 10, 1996; entered into force September 17, 1999.
TIAS

FINANCE

Agreement relating to the funding of the indebtedness of Poland to the United States. Signed at Washington November 14, 1924; operative December 15, 1922.
Treasury Department print; 11 Bevans 195; 58 LNTS 97.

Agreement modifying the debt funding agreement of November 14, 1924. Signed at Washington June 10, 1932; operative July 1, 1931.
Treasury Department print; 11 Bevans 260.

Agreement establishing a procedure for funding international travel and transportation and other travel-related expenses from U.S.-owned zlotys in Poland. Exchange of notes at Washington October 7, 1972; entered into force October 7, 1972; effective January 1, 1973.
24 UST 426; TIAS 7557.

Agreement deferring purchase by the United States, scheduled for January 2, 1973, of dollar exchange for zlotys accrued under certain agricultural commodities agreements. Exchange of notes at Washington December 29, 1972; entered into force December 29, 1972.
24 UST 424; TIAS 7557.

Agreement deferring purchase by the United States of dollar exchange for zlotys accrued under certain agricultural commodities agreements. Exchange of notes at Washington February 5, 1973; entered into force February 5, 1973.
24 UST 431; TIAS 7557.

Agreement deferring purchase by the United States of dollar exchange for zlotys accrued under certain agricultural commodities agreements and terminating the agreement of August 6, 1968 (TIAS 7473) relating to United States Government pensions, with schedule. Exchange of notes at Washington May 15, 1975; entered into force May 15, 1975.
26 UST 2398; TIAS 8164; 1027 UNTS 323.

Agreement regarding the consolidation and rescheduling of certain debts owed to, guaranteed by or assured by the United States Government and its agencies, with annexes. Signed at Warsaw August 27, 1981; entered into force October 20, 1981.
33 UST 3727; TIAS 10255; 1541 UNTS 85.

Agreement regarding the consolidation and rescheduling of certain debts owed to, guaranteed by or insured by the United States Government and its agencies. Signed at Warsaw July 29, 1986; entered into force September 8, 1986.
NP

Agreement regarding the consolidation and rescheduling of certain debts for 1985, owed to, guaranteed by, or insured by the United States Government and its agencies, with annexes. Signed at Warsaw July 10, 1989; entered into force September 6, 1989.
NP

Agreement regarding the consolidation and rescheduling of certain debts for 1987, owed to, guaranteed by, or insured by the United States Government and its agencies, with annexes. Signed at Warsaw July 10, 1989; entered into force September 6, 1989.
NP

Investment guaranty agreement. Signed at Warsaw October 13, 1989; entered into force February 21, 1990.
TIAS 12039.

Swap agreement among the United States Treasury and the Narodowy Bank Polski/Government of Poland, with memorandum of understanding. Signed at Washington and Poland December 22, 1989; entered into force December 22, 1989.
TIAS

Agreement between the United States and the Narodowy Bank Polski/Government of Poland concerning the contribution by the United States to the Polish Stabilization Fund, with memorandum of understanding. Signed at Washington December 29, 1989; entered into force December 29, 1989.
TIAS

Amendment and extension:
December 6 and 18, 1991.

Agreement regarding the consolidation and rescheduling of certain debts owed to, guaranteed by, or insured by the United States Government and its agencies, with annexes. Signed at Warsaw August 24, 1990; entered into force October 22, 1990.
NP

Agreement regarding the reduction and reorganization of certain debts owed to, guaranteed by, or insured by the Government of the United States and its agencies, with annexes. Signed at Warsaw July 17, 1991; entered into force September 3, 1991.
NP

Agreement between the United States and the Government of Poland/Narodowy Bank Polski concerning the Polish Bank Privatization Fund Account, with memorandum of understanding.

Signed at Washington December 28, 1992; entered into force December 28, 1992.
TIAS

HEALTH

Agreement on cooperation in the field of health. Signed at Washington October 8, 1974; entered into force October 8, 1974.
25 UST 2750; TIAS 7943.

INFORMATIONAL MEDIA GUARANTIES

Agreement providing for an informational media guaranty program. Exchange of notes at Warsaw February 12, 1958; entered into force February 12, 1958.
9 UST 253; TIAS 3999; 304 UNTS 287.

INVESTMENT

Treaty concerning business and economic relations, with annex, protocol and related exchanges of letters. Signed at Washington March 21, 1990; entered into force August 6, 1994.
TIAS

JUDICIAL ASSISTANCE

Treaty on mutual legal assistance in criminal matters, with forms. Done at Washington July 10, 1996; entered into force September 17, 1999.
TIAS

LEND-LEASE

Preliminary agreement regarding principles applying to mutual aid in the prosecution of the war against aggression. Signed at Washington July 1, 1942; entered into force July 1, 1942.
56 Stat. 1542; EAS 257; 11 Bevans 274; 103 UNTS 267.

Agreement on the settlement for lend-lease and certain claims. Signed at Washington June 28, 1956; entered into force June 28, 1956.
7 UST 1930; TIAS 3594; 273 UNTS 79.

MAPPING

Basic exchange and cooperative agreement for military topographic mapping, nautical and aeronautical charting, geodesy and geophysics, digital data and related MC&G materials. Signed at Washington November 10, 1992; entered into force November 10, 1992.
NP

POLAND (Cont'd)

MARITIME MATTERS

Agreement relating to the mutual recognition of ship measurement certificates. Exchanges of notes at Washington January 17, March 14, and April 22, 1930, and October 5, 1934; operative April 22, 1930.
49 Stat. 3663; EAS 71; 11 Bevans 229; 156 LNTS 91.

NARCOTIC DRUGS

Arrangement for the direct exchange of certain information regarding the traffic in narcotic drugs. Exchange of notes at Warsaw August 17 and September 17, 1931; entered into force September 17, 1931.
11 Bevans 257.

PACIFIC SETTLEMENT OF DISPUTES

Treaty of arbitration. Signed at Washington August 16, 1928; entered into force February 3, 1930.
46 Stat. 2438; TS 805; 11 Bevans 218; 99 LNTS 409.

Treaty of conciliation. Signed at Washington August 16, 1928; entered into force February 3, 1930.
46 Stat. 2442; TS 806; 11 Bevans 221; 99 LNTS 403.

PEACE CORPS

Agreement concerning the program of the United States Peace Corps in Poland. Signed at Warsaw February 23, 1990; entered into force February 23, 1990.
TIAS 12073.

POSTAL MATTERS

Money order convention. Signed at Washington August 22, 1922, and at Warsaw July 14, 1923; entered into force September 1, 1923.
NP

Convention concerning the exchange of parcel post. Signed at Warsaw February 19 and at Washington April 26, 1923; entered into force April 1, 1923.
43 Stat. 1640; Post Office Department print.

International express mail agreement, with detailed regulations. Signed at Washington December 11, 1989; entered into force February 1, 1990.
TIAS 11720.

PUBLICATIONS

Agreement relating to the distribution in Poland of a Polish-language magazine on life in the United States. Exchange of notes at Warsaw May 30, 1958; entered into force May 30, 1958.
9 UST 601; TIAS 4040; 315 UNTS 231.

SCIENTIFIC COOPERATION

Agreement on cooperation in science and technology, with annexes. Signed at Warsaw September 4, 1992; entered into force December 8, 1992.
TIAS

Memorandum of understanding on science and engineering cooperation, with annex. Signed at Washington October 26, 1994; entered into force October 26, 1994.
TIAS 12576.

SHIPPING

Agreement relating to jurisdiction over vessels utilizing the Louisiana Offshore Oil Port. Exchange of notes at Washington March 30 and April 10, 1984; entered into force April 10, 1984.
TIAS

SMUGGLING

Convention to aid in the prevention of smuggling of alcoholic beverages into the United States. Signed at Washington June 19, 1930; entered into force August 2, 1930.
46 Stat. 2773; TS 821; 11 Bevans 233; 108 LNTS 323.

SOCIAL SECURITY

Agreement concerning the United States Government participation in the Polish social insurance system for Polish national employees of the United States Government in Poland. Exchange of notes at Warsaw June 15 and September 30, 1971; entered into force September 30, 1971.
22 UST 1725; TIAS 7200.

SURPLUS PROPERTY

Credit arrangement for the purchase of American surplus property abroad. Signed at Washington April 22, 1946; entered into force April 22, 1946.
12 UST 368; TIAS 4725; 406 UNTS 214.

Extensions and amendments:
September 17, 1947 (12 UST 368; TIAS 4725; 406 UNTS 219).
December 10, 1947 (12 UST 368; TIAS 4725; 406 UNTS 221).

Agreement relating to the payment of arrearages on the surplus property agreement of April 22, 1946. Exchange of notes at Warsaw March 20, 1961; entered into force March 20, 1961.
12 UST 368; TIAS 4725; 406 UNTS 222.

TAXATION

Convention for the avoidance of double taxation and the prevention of fiscal evasion with respect to taxes on income, with related notes. Signed at Washington October 8, 1974; entered into force July 22, 1976.
28 UST 891; TIAS 8486.

TRADE AND COMMERCE

Agreement relating to economic and financial cooperation. Exchange of notes at Washington April 24, 1946; entered into force April 24, 1946.
60 Stat. 1609; TIAS 1516; 11 Bevans 286; 4 UNTS 155.

Joint statement on the development of agricultural trade. Signed at Washington October 8, 1974; entered into force October 8, 1974.
25 UST 2763; TIAS 7944.

Agreement relating to tariff and nontariff matters within the framework of the multilateral trade negotiations, and related letters of June 27 and October 20, 1980. Exchange of letters at Geneva February 28, 1979; entered into force January 1, 1980.
32 UST 5498; TIAS 10001; 1265 UNTS 187.

Agreement concerning trade in textiles and textile products, with annexes. Exchange of notes at Washington December 30 and 31, 1991; entered into force December 31, 1991; effective January 1, 1992.
NP

Amendment and extension:
December 6 and 31, 1993 (NP).

TRANSPORTATION

Memorandum of understanding concerning research cooperation in the field of transportation. Signed at Warsaw November 3, 1971; entered into force November 3, 1971.
29 UST 5642; TIAS 9139; 1152 UNTS 19.

Extension and amendments:
October 16, 1978 (29 UST 5649; TIAS 9139; 1152 UNTS 22).
February 28 and June 22, 1979 (30 UST 7287; TIAS 9586; 1182 UNTS 401).

POLAND (Cont'd)

VISAS

Agreement relating to the reciprocal waiver of visa fees for performing artists. Exchange of notes at Warsaw December 17, 1962 and January 21, 1963; entered into force January 21, 1963; operative February 1, 1963.
14 UST 118; TIAS 5279; 471 UNTS 151.

PORTUGAL

On December 13, 1999, Portugal submitted to the United Nations a note explaining that as of December 20, 1999, the Portuguese Republic would cease to be responsible for the international rights and obligations arising from the application of treaties to Macao. Bilateral agreements between the United States and Macao are listed after bilateral treaties under CHINA. The applicability of multilateral treaties to Macao is indicated in "Part 2: Multilateral Treaties and Other Agreements." See also note under CHINA.

AVIATION

Agreement relating to air transport services, and exchange of notes. Signed at Lisbon December 6, 1945; entered into force December 6, 1945.
59 Stat. 1846; EAS 500; 11 Bevans 351; 3 UNTS 139.

Amendments:
June 28, 1947 (61 Stat. 3185; TIAS 1656; 11 Bevans 362; 24 UNTS 300).
November 11, 1952 (3 UST 5263; TIAS 2722; 184 UNTS 322).
May 30, 1970 (21 UST 2027; TIAS 6946; 763 UNTS 292).

Memorandum of agreement concerning provision of site test and commissioning and/or periodic flight checks of Portuguese Civil Aviation Administration air navigation aids. Signed at Washington and Lisbon March 10 and April 13, 1978; entered into force April 13, 1978; effective April 1, 1978.
30 UST 293; TIAS 9201.

Memorandum of agreement concerning the provision of assistance in developing and modernizing Portugal's civil aviation infrastructure. Signed at Washington and Lisbon July 30, 1998; entered into force July 30, 1998.
TIAS

COPYRIGHT (See APPENDIX)

CULTURAL RELATIONS

Protocol relating to exchanges in the field of physical education and sports. Signed at Lisbon December 22, 1976; entered into force December 22, 1976.
28 UST 5342; TIAS 8637.

CUSTOMS

Agreement regarding mutual assistance between customs services. Signed at Washington September 15, 1994; entered into force June 20, 1996.
TIAS 12565.

DEFENSE (See also MUTUAL SECURITY)

Mutual defense assistance agreement. Signed at Lisbon January 5, 1951; entered into force January 5, 1951.
2 UST 438; TIAS 2187; 133 UNTS 75.

Defense agreement regarding use of facilities in the Azores. Signed at Lisbon September 6, 1951; entered into force September 6, 1951.
5 UST 2263; TIAS 3087; 237 UNTS 217.

Extensions and amendments:[1]
November 15, 1957 (8 UST 2353; TIAS 3950; 303 UNTS 354).
December 9, 1971 (22 UST 2106; TIAS 7254; 851 UNTS 274).
June 18, 1979 (33 UST 580; TIAS 10050; 1265 UNTS 288).
December 13, 1983 (TIAS 10938).

Agreement relating to the disposition of equipment and material furnished by the United States under the mutual defense assistance agreement of January 5, 1951, found surplus to the needs of the armed forces of Portugal. Exchange of notes at Lisbon June 16 and July 9, 1952; entered into force July 9, 1952.
3 UST 4979; TIAS 2674; 180 UNTS 251.

Amendment:
September 15, 1960 (11 UST 2202; TIAS 4590; 393 UNTS 315).

Agreement relating to a weapons production program. Exchange of notes at Lisbon September 26, 1960; entered into force September 26, 1960.
11 UST 2218; TIAS 4594; 393 UNTS 257.

Agreement relating to the deposit by Portugal of ten percent of the value of grant military assistance and excess defense articles furnished by the United States. Exchange of notes at Lisbon March 16 and May 2, 1972; entered into force May 2, 1972; effective February 7, 1972.
23 UST 881; TIAS 7349.

Agreement relating to payment to the United States of net proceeds from the sale of defense articles furnished under the military assistance program. Exchange of notes at Lisbon May 30, 1974 and June 30, 1975; entered into force June 30, 1975; effective July 1, 1974.
26 UST 1004; TIAS 8087.

Memorandum of understanding concerning the principles governing mutual cooperation in the research, development, production, procurement and logistic support of defense equipment. Signed at Lisbon and Washington December 18, 1978 and March 28, 1979; entered into force March 28, 1979.
30 UST 3892; TIAS 9433; 1171 UNTS 221.

Agreement concerning the grant of defense articles and services under the military assistance program. Exchange of notes at Lisbon August 14 and 27, 1979; entered into force August 27, 1979.
30 UST 7555; TIAS 9599; 1205 UNTS 3.

Amendment:
August 16 and September 29, 1982 (TIAS 10503).

Agreement concerning the grant of defense articles and services under the military assistance program. Exchange of notes at Lisbon August 12 and 28, 1980; entered into force August 28, 1980.
32 UST 2388; TIAS 9846; 1275 UNTS 3.

Amendment:
August 16 and September 29, 1982 (TIAS 10503).

Agreement concerning the grant of defense articles and services under the military assistance program. Exchange of notes at Lisbon August 24 and 28, 1981; entered into force August 28, 1981.
33 UST 3702; TIAS 10252; 1541 UNTS 105.

Amendment:
August 16 and September 29, 1982 (TIAS 10503).

Agreement concerning general security of military information. Exchange of notes at Lisbon August 19 and September 10, 1982; entered into force September 10, 1982.
TIAS 11060.

Agreement concerning the installation in Portugal of a ground-based electro-optical deep space surveillance (GEODSS) station. Exchange of notes at Lisbon March 27, 1984; entered into force March 27, 1984.
TIAS 10973.

Technical agreement in implementation of the defense agreement of September 6, 1951, as amended (TIAS 3087, 3950, 7254, 10050), with annexes and related notes. Signed at Lisbon May 18, 1984; entered into force December 23, 1985.
TIAS 12368.

Agreement relating to the employment of Portuguese nationals by the United States Forces, Azores. Signed at Lisbon and Washington Oc-

PORTUGAL (Cont'd)

tober 9 and 16, 1984; entered into force October 16, 1984.
TIAS 12051.

Agreement on cooperation and defense, with supplemental technical and labor agreements and exchange of notes. Signed at Lisbon June 1, 1995; entered into force November 21, 1995.
TIAS

Acquisition and cross-servicing agreement, with annexes. Signed at Lisbon January 14, 1998; entered into force January 14, 1998.
TIAS

NOTE:
[1] See also technical agreement of May 18, 1984 and employment agreement of October 9 and 16, 1984.

ECONOMIC AND MILITARY COOPERATION

Agreement relating to economic and military assistance. Exchange of notes at Lisbon December 13, 1983; entered into force February 4, 1984.
TIAS 10939.

ECONOMIC AND TECHNICAL COOPERATION

Economic cooperation agreement.[1] Signed at Lisbon September 28, 1948; entered into force September 28, 1948.
62 Stat. 2856; TIAS 1819; 11 Bevans 370; 29 UNTS 213.

Amendments:
February 14, 1950 (1 UST 169; TIAS 2033; 79 UNTS 310).
May 17, 1951 (2 UST 1298; TIAS 2279; 134 UNTS 370).
March 9 and 18, 1953 (4 UST 1437; TIAS 2801; 207 UNTS 320).

Agreement relating to the provision of economic assistance to Portugal, with related letter. Exchange of letters at Brussels December 9, 1971; entered into force December 9, 1971.
23 UST 264; TIAS 7303.

Agency for International Development:
February 28, 1975 (26 UST 238; TIAS 8028; 992 UNTS 239).
February 28, 1975 (26 UST 348; TIAS 8038; 992 UNTS 251).
June 30, 1975 (26 UST 1072; TIAS 8095; 1006 UNTS 279).
November 3, 1975 (28 UST 1123; TIAS 8496).
August 13, 1976 (28 UST 5991; TIAS 8667).
August 13, 1976 (30 UST 647; TIAS 9209).

August 13, 1976 (32 UST 5991; TIAS 10025; 1274 UNTS 329).
March 4, 1977 (30 UST 757; TIAS 9218).
September 30, 1977 (29 UST 3927; TIAS 9044).
September 30, 1977 (32 UST 5991; TIAS 10025; 1274 UNTS 331).
September 30, 1977 (32 UST 6001; TIAS 10026).
September 30, 1977 (32 UST 6025; TIAS 10027).
September 30, 1977 (32 UST 6051; TIAS 10028).
March 1, 1978 (30 UST 1761; TIAS 9286; 1152 UNTS 149).
December 30, 1986 (NP).

NOTE:
[1] Applicable to all Portuguese territories.

EDUCATION

Agreement for financing certain educational exchange programs. Signed at Lisbon March 19, 1960; entered into force March 19, 1960.
11 UST 268; TIAS 4444; 371 UNTS 131.

Amendments:
June 3 and December 4, 1963 (15 UST 171; TIAS 5536; 511 UNTS 288).
July 6, August 16 and September 3, 1982 (TIAS 10438; 1736 UNTS 304).

EXTRADITION

Extradition convention and exchange of notes concerning the death penalty.[1] Signed at Washington May 7, 1908; entered into force November 14, 1908.
35 Stat. 2071; TS 512; 11 Bevans 314.

NOTE:
[1] Applicable to all territories.

FINANCE

Agreement relating to guaranties authorized under section 111 (b)(3) of the Economic Cooperation Act of 1948, as amended. Exchange of notes at Washington May 22 and 25, 1953; entered into force May 26, 1953.
4 UST 1596; TIAS 2826; 212 UNTS 290.

Agreement relating to resumption of the investment guaranty program and interpretation of the agreement of May 22 and 25, 1953. Exchange of notes at Lisbon October 31 and November 10, 1977; entered into force November 10, 1977.
29 UST 2792; TIAS 8977.

MAPPING

Basic exchange and cooperative agreement concerning mapping, charting and geodesy cooperation, with annexes. Signed at Fairfax and

Lisbon July 30, 1997; entered into force July 30, 1997.
NP

MUTUAL SECURITY

Agreement relating to the assurances required by the Mutual Security Act of 1951. Exchange of notes at Lisbon January 8, 1952; entered into force January 8, 1952.
3 UST 4648; TIAS 2618; 207 UNTS 51.

NARCOTIC DRUGS

Arrangement for the direct exchange of certain information regarding the traffic in narcotic drugs. Exchange of notes at Lisbon February 11, 1928, and February 22, 1929; entered into force February 22, 1929.
11 Bevans 341.

PACIFIC SETTLEMENT OF DISPUTES

Treaty for the advancement of peace. Signed at Lisbon February 4, 1914; entered into force October 24, 1914.
38 Stat. 1847; TS 600; 11 Bevans 331.

Arbitration treaty. Signed at Washington March 1, 1929; entered into force October 31, 1929.
46 Stat. 2421; TS 803; 11 Bevans 344; 99 LNTS 375.

PATENTS

Agreement to facilitate interchange of patent rights and technical information for defense purposes. Signed at Lisbon October 31, 1960; entered into force October 31, 1960.
11 UST 2314; TIAS 4608; 394 UNTS 127.

POSTAL MATTERS

Parcel post agreement and regulations of execution.[1] Signed at Lisbon January 12, 1959 and at Washington February 27, 1959; entered into force May 1, 1959.
10 UST 801; TIAS 4220; 343 UNTS 49.

International express mail agreement, with detailed regulations. Signed at Washington and Lisbon November 20 and December 21, 1984; entered into force January 15, 1985.
TIAS 11013.

Memorandum of understanding concerning the operation of the INTELPOST field trial, with details of implementation. Signed at Lisbon and Washington April 15 and July 3, 1985; entered into force August 1, 1985.
TIAS 11243.

PORTUGAL (Cont'd)

NOTE:
[1] Applicable to Puerto Rico, the Virgin Islands, Guam, Samoa, the Azores and Madeira Archipelagoes.

SCIENTIFIC COOPERATION

Memorandum of understanding for a cooperative program in earth science studies. Signed at Reston and Lisbon April 28 and May 18, 1987; entered into force May 18, 1987.
TIAS 11274.

SHIPPING

Agreement relating to jurisdiction over vessels utilizing the Louisiana Offshore Oil Port. Exchange of notes at Washington June 22 and July 11, 1979; entered into force July 11, 1979.
30 UST 5931; TIAS 9526; 1179 UNTS 125.

SOCIAL SECURITY

Agreement on social security, with administrative arrangement. Signed at Lisbon March 30, 1988; entered into force August 1, 1989.
TIAS 12121.

TAXATION

Agreement relating to relief from taxation of United States expenditures in Portugal for the common defense. Exchange of notes at Lisbon April 1, 1953; entered into force April 1, 1953.
4 UST 361; TIAS 2784; 205 UNTS 41.

Convention for the avoidance of double taxation and the prevention of fiscal evasion with respect to taxes on income, with protocol. Signed at Washington September 6, 1994; entered into force December 18, 1995.
TIAS

TELECOMMUNICATION

Agreement relating to the reciprocal granting of authorizations to permit licensed amateur radio operators of either country to operate their stations in the other country. Exchange of notes at Lisbon May 17 and 26, 1965; entered into force May 26, 1965.
16 UST 817; TIAS 5815; 546 UNTS 189.

Agreement relating to the continuation of international broadcast activities carried out in Portugal by RARET. Exchange of notes at Lisbon February 15, 1977; entered into force February 15, 1977.
29 UST 660; TIAS 8844.

TRADE AND COMMERCE

Commercial arrangement. Exchange of notes at Washington June 28, 1910; entered into force June 28, 1910.
TS 514 1/2; 11 Bevans 324.

Agreement terminating the agreement of November 17, 1970 (TIAS 6980), relating to trade in cotton textiles and providing for consultations on problems of market disruption from exports of cotton, wool and man-made fiber textiles and apparel products from Portugal. Exchange of notes at Washington August 20, 1975; entered into force August 20, 1975.
26 UST 2713; TIAS 8187; 1052 UNTS 291.

Agreement relating to beef and cheese within the context of the multilateral trade negotiations, and related letters of February 4 and 12, 1980. Exchanges of letters at Washington June 12 and 18 and November 5 and 7, 1979; entered into force January 1, 1980.
32 UST 5504; TIAS 10002; 1266 UNTS 213.

VISAS

Agreement relating to reciprocal facilitation of visa issuance. Exchange of notes at Lisbon June 7, 1983; entered into force July 7, 1983.
TIAS 10723; 1607 UNTS 139.

PREPARATORY COMMISSION FOR THE COMPREHENSIVE NUCLEAR-TEST-BAN TREATY ORGANIZATION

TAXATION

Tax reimbursement agreement, with annex. Signed at Washington October 21, 1998; entered into force October 21, 1998.
TIAS

QATAR

AVIATION

Agreement on the security of civil aviation. Signed at Doha June 27, 1994; entered into force June 30, 1994.
TIAS

COPYRIGHT (See APPENDIX)

FINANCE

Investment incentive agreement. Exchange of notes at Doha March 28, 1987; entered into force April 1, 1987.
TIAS

POSTAL MATTERS

International express mail agreement, with detailed regulations. Signed at Doha and Washington January 19 and February 14, 1983; entered into force June 1, 1983.
TIAS 10661.

Memorandum of understanding concerning the operation of the INTELPOST field trial, with details of implementation. Signed at Doha and Washington August 12 and September 13, 1985; entered into force September 13, 1985.
TIAS 11156.

TRADE

Agreement concerning trade in textiles and textile products, with annexes. Exchange of notes at Doha February 11 and May 30, 1995; entered into force May 30, 1995; effective January 1, 1994.
NP

ROMANIA

AGRICULTURAL COMMODITIES

Agricultural commodities agreement. Signed at Bucharest March 13, 1990; entered into force March 13, 1990.
NP

AGRICULTURE

Protocol on cooperation in agriculture. Signed at Washington September 11, 1975; entered into force September 11, 1975.
26 UST 2486; TIAS 8166; 1028 UNTS 3.

ATOMIC ENERGY

Agreement clarifying certain understandings relating to the supply of enriched uranium to Romania for the TRIGA reactor. Exchange of notes at Washington February 13, 1978; entered into force February 13, 1978.
29 UST 2961; TIAS 8992; 1120 UNTS 97.

ROMANIA (Cont'd)

Agreement for cooperation concerning peaceful uses of nuclear energy, with annex and agreed minute. Signed at Washington July 15, 1998; entered into force August 25, 1999.
TIAS

AVIATION

Agreement relating to the reciprocal acceptance of airworthiness certifications. Exchange of notes at Washington December 7, 1976; entered into force December 7, 1976.
27 UST 4138; TIAS 8440.

Air transport agreement, with annexes. Signed at Washington July 15, 1998; entered into force August 19, 1999.
TIAS

CONSULS

Consular convention with protocol. Signed at Bucharest July 5, 1972; entered into force July 6, 1973.
24 UST 1317; TIAS 7643.

COPYRIGHT (See APPENDIX)

CULTURAL PROPERTY

Agreement for the protection and preservation of certain cultural properties. Signed at Bucharest July 8, 1992; entered into force provisionally, July 8, 1992; definitively, July 29, 1993.
TIAS 12136.

CULTURAL RELATIONS

Understanding regarding the establishment and operation in the United States and Romania of an American and a Romanian library, respectively. Signed at Bucharest August 3, 1969; entered into force August 3, 1969.
20 UST 2712; TIAS 6733; 720 UNTS 91.

Agreement on cooperation and exchanges in the cultural, educational, scientific and technological fields. Signed at Bucharest December 13, 1974; entered into force January 1, 1975.
26 UST 31; TIAS 8006.

CUSTOMS

Agreement regarding mutual assistance between their customs administrations. Signed at

Washington July 16, 1998; entered into force June 1, 1999.
TIAS

DEFENSE

Agreement concerning the provision of training related to defense articles under the United States International Military Education and Training (IMET) program. Exchange of notes at Bucharest November 23 and December 7, 1992; entered into force December 7, 1992.
NP

Agreement concerning military assistance under the United States Foreign Assistance Act of 1961, as amended, and the furnishing of defense articles, related training, and other defense services from the United States to Romania. Exchange of notes at Bucharest October 3, 1994 and March 31, 1995; entered into force March 31, 1995.
TIAS

ECONOMIC AND TECHNICAL COOPERATION

Joint statement on economic, industrial and technological cooperation. Issued at Washington December 5, 1973.
26 UST 2342; TIAS 8159.

Long term agreement on economic, industrial and technical cooperation, with annexes. Signed at Bucharest November 21, 1976; entered into force May 5, 1977.
28 UST 5228; TIAS 8624; 1087 UNTS 119.

EDUCATION

Agreement for the establishment of an Office for U.S.–Romanian Educational and Scholarly Exchanges, with annex. Signed at Bucharest July 30, 1992; entered into force July 30, 1992.
TIAS 12467.

EMPLOYMENT

Agreement relating to the employment of dependents of official government employees. Exchange of notes at Washington July 1 and 28, 1993; entered into force July 28, 1993.
TIAS 12159.

ENVIRONMENTAL COOPERATION

Agreement for cooperation in the Global Learning and Observations to Benefit the Environment (GLOBE) Program, with appendices. Signed at Bucharest and Washington April 11

and May 22, 1995; entered into force May 22, 1995.
TIAS 12653.

EXTRADITION

Extradition treaty. Signed at Bucharest July 23, 1924; entered into force April 7, 1925.
44 Stat. 2020; TS 713; 11 Bevans 391.

Supplementary extradition treaty. Signed at Bucharest November 10, 1936; entered into force July 27, 1937.
50 Stat. 1349; TS 916; 11 Bevans 423; 181 LNTS 177.

FINANCE

Agreement relating to the funding of the debt of Romania to the United States. Signed at Washington December 4, 1925; operative June 15, 1925.
Treasury Department print; 11 Bevans 398.

Agreement modifying the debt funding agreement of December 4, 1925. Signed at Washington June 11, 1932; operative July 1, 1931.
Treasury Department print; 11 Bevans 420.

Agreement relating to investment guaranties. Exchange of notes at Bucharest April 28, 1973; entered into force April 28, 1973.
24 UST 1073; TIAS 7627.

Agreement regarding the consolidation and rescheduling of certain debts owed to, guaranteed or insured by the United States Government and its agencies, with annexes. Signed at Bucharest March 10, 1983; entered into force April 22, 1983.
TIAS 10683.

Agreement regarding the consolidation and rescheduling of certain debts owed to, guaranteed or insured by the United States Government and its agencies, with annexes. Signed at Bucharest February 15, 1984; entered into force April 16, 1984.
TIAS 10957.

Swap agreement among the United States Treasury, the National Bank of Romania/Government of Romania, with memorandum of understanding. Signed at Washington and Bucharest March 6, 1991; entered into force March 6, 1991.
TIAS

Investment incentive agreement. Signed at Bucharest June 30, 1992; entered into force December 4, 1992.
TIAS 12464.

INVESTMENT

Treaty concerning the reciprocal encouragement and protection of investment, with annex, protocol and related letter. Signed at Bucharest

ROMANIA (Cont'd)

May 28, 1992; entered into force January 15, 1994.
TIAS

MILITARY CEMETERIES AND MONUMENTS

Agreement relating to war graves registration and associated matters. Exchange of notes at Bucharest June 19 and 28, 1946; entered into force June 28, 1946.
61 Stat. 4042; TIAS 1796; 11 Bevans 428; 148 UNTS 355.

NARCOTIC DRUGS

Arrangement for the direct exchange of certain information regarding the traffic in narcotic drugs. Exchange of notes at Bucharest February 4, 1928, and April 17, 1929; entered into force April 17, 1929.
11 Bevans 414.

PACIFIC SETTLEMENT OF DISPUTES

Treaty of arbitration. Signed at Washington March 21, 1929; entered into force July 22, 1929.
46 Stat. 2336; TS 794; 11 Bevans 408; 105 LNTS 79.

Treaty of conciliation. Signed at Washington March 21, 1929; entered into force July 22, 1929.
46 Stat. 2339; TS 795; 11 Bevans 411; 105 LNTS 85.

PEACE CORPS

Agreement concerning the program of the United States Peace Corps in Romania. Signed at Washington January 24, 1992; entered into force January 24, 1992.
TIAS 12080.

POSTAL MATTERS

Convention for the exchange of money orders. Signed at Washington October 18 and at Bucharest November 17, 1932; entered into force January 1, 1933.
NP

Agreement concerning the exchange of parcel post, and regulations of execution. Signed at Washington August 10, 1937, and at Bucharest March 12, 1937; entered into force September 1, 1937.
50 Stat. 1630; Post Office Department print; 183 LNTS 7.

Parcel post agreement, with detailed regulations. Signed at Washington June 19, 1981; entered into force July 19, 1981.
NP

International express mail agreement, with detailed regulations. Signed at Washington December 14, 1989; entered into force February 15, 1990.
TIAS 11718.

RELATIONS

Joint statement concerning relations between the United States and Romania. Signed at Washington December 5, 1973; entered into force December 5, 1973.
24 UST 2257; TIAS 7746; 938 UNTS 457.

SCIENTIFIC COOPERATION

Agreement on cooperation in science and technology, with annexes. Signed at Washington July 15, 1998; entered into force April 5, 2000.
TIAS

TAXATION

Convention with respect to taxes on income. Signed at Washington December 4, 1973; entered into force February 26, 1976; effective January 1, 1974.
27 UST 165; TIAS 8228.

TRADE AND COMMERCE

Agreement on trade relations. Signed at Bucharest April 2, 1975; entered into force August 3, 1975.
26 UST 2305; TIAS 8159.

Protocol on development of agricultural trade. Signed at Washington September 11, 1975; entered into force September 11, 1975.
26 UST 2500; TIAS 8167; 1028 UNTS 13.

Agreement relating to tariff and nontariff matters within the framework of the multilateral trade negotiations, and related letters of September 30, 1980. Letters done at Bucharest and Washington March 2 and November 8, 1979; entered into force January 1, 1980.
32 UST 5489; TIAS 10000; 1266 UNTS 253.

Agreement relating to trade in cotton textiles, with annex. Exchange of notes at Bucharest January 28 and March 31, 1983; entered into force March 31, 1983; effective January 1, 1983.
NP

Amendments and extensions:
December 5 and 12, 1984 (NP).
May 8 and June 15, 1985 (NP).
June 16 and 30, 1987 (NP).
December 30 and 31, 1987 (NP).
November 28, 1988 and January 12, 1989 (NP).
December 28, 1988 and May 27, 1989 (NP).
May 7, June 10 and August 15, 1991 (NP).
February 17 and 24, 1993 (NP).
December 9, 1993 and January 5, 1994 (NP).

Administrative arrangement concerning a visa system relating to trade in certain textile products. Exchange of letters at Bucharest October 13, 1982 and August 25, 1983; entered into force August 25, 1983.
NP

Amendment:
September 16, 1988 and January 18 and 31, 1989 (NP).

Agreement relating to trade in wool and man-made fiber textiles and textile products. Exchange of notes at Bucharest November 7 and 16, 1984; entered into force November 16, 1984; effective January 1, 1985.
NP

Amendments and extensions:
December 30 and 31, 1987 (NP).
November 28, 1988 and January 12, 1989 (NP).
December 28, 1988 and May 27, 1989 (NP).
March 18, 1988 and May 29, 1989 (NP).
February 26 and March 13, 1992 (NP).
December 9, 1993 and January 5, 1994 (NP).
June 6 and July 25, 1994 (NP).

Agreement suspending mutual application of most-favored-nation tariff treatment under the trade agreement of April 2, 1975. Signed at Bucharest June 22, 1988; entered into force June 22, 1988; effective July 3, 1988.
TIAS

Agreement on trade relations, with related exchanges of letters. Signed at Bucharest April 3, 1992; entered into force November 8, 1993.
TIAS

Agreement relating to trade in textiles and textile products, with annexes. Signed at Washington December 20, 1994; entered into force December 20, 1994; effective January 1, 1994.
NP

Amendment and extension:
February 1 and 7, 1996 (NP).

TRADE-MARKS

Convention for the reciprocal protection of trade-marks. Signed at Bucharest March 18/31, 1906; entered into force June 25, 1906.
34 Stat. 2901; TS 451; 11 Bevans 389.

ROMANIA (Cont'd)

VISAS

Agreement relating to the issuance of visas to diplomatic and non-diplomatic personnel. Exchange of notes at Bucharest April 20, May 14 and 26, 1962; entered into force May 26, 1962; operative June 1, 1962.
13 UST 1192; TIAS 5063; 456 UNTS 265.

Amendment:
May 31 and June 17, 1967 (18 UST 1266; TIAS 6279; 685 UNTS 404).

Agreement relating to reciprocal simplification of procedures for issuance of diplomatic and official visas. Exchange of notes at Bucharest September 12 and October 10, 1977; entered into force October 10, 1977.
29 UST 2765; TIAS 8970.

Agreement relating to reciprocal facilitation of visa issuance. Exchange of notes at Bucharest September 1 and October 10, 1977; entered into force October 10, 1977.
29 UST 4705; TIAS 9075; 1134 UNTS 209.

RUSSIAN FEDERATION

For agreements prior to December 31, 1991, see UNION OF SOVIET SOCIALIST REPUBLICS.

ATOMIC ENERGY

Agreement concerning the disposition of highly enriched uranium extracted from nuclear weapons. Signed at Washington February 18, 1993; entered into force February 18, 1993.
TIAS

Memorandum of understanding relating to transparency and additional arrangements concerning the agreement of February 18, 1993 concerning the disposition of highly enriched uranium extracted from nuclear weapons. Signed at Washington September 1, 1993; entered into force September 1, 1993.
TIAS

Agreement concerning operational safety enhancements, risk reduction measures and nuclear safety regulations for civil nuclear facilities in the Russian Federation. Signed at Moscow December 16, 1993; entered into force December 16, 1993.
TIAS 11488.

Agreement on cooperation in research on radiation effects for the purpose of minimizing the consequences of radioactive contamination on health and the environment, with annex. Signed at Moscow January 14, 1994; entered into force January 14, 1994.
TIAS 11481.

Amendment and extension:
March 10, 2000.

Protocol on highly enriched uranium (HEU) transparency arrangements in furtherance of the memorandum of understanding of September 1, 1993. Signed at Washington March 18, 1994; entered into force March 18, 1994.
TIAS

Agreement for cooperation on enhancing the safety of Russian nuclear fuel cycle facilities and research reactors. Signed at Moscow June 30, 1995; entered into force June 30, 1995.
TIAS 12672.

Memorandum of cooperation in the field of research on fundamental properties of matter. Signed at Washington February 7, 1997; entered into force February 7, 1997.
TIAS

Agreement concerning cooperation regarding plutonium production reactors, with annexes. Signed at Moscow September 23, 1997; entered into force September 23, 1997.
TIAS

Agreement concerning the modification of the operating Seversk (Tomsk Region) and Zheleznogorsk (Krasnoyarsk Region) plutonium production reactors, with related letter. Signed at Moscow September 23, 1997; entered into force September 23, 1997.
TIAS

Amendment:
October 20, 1999 and January 21, 2000.

Memorandum of understanding concerning cooperation regarding plutonium production reactors. Signed at Moscow September 23, 1997; entered into force September 23, 1997.
TIAS

Agreement regarding assurances concerning the source material transferred from the United States to the Russian Federation, with annex. Exchange of notes at Washington March 24, 1999; entered into force March 24, 1999.
TIAS

Agreement concerning the transfer of source material to the Russian Federation, with annex and administrative arrangement. Signed at Washinton March 24, 1999; entered into force March 24, 1999.
TIAS

AVIATION

Memorandum of understanding on air navigation, airspace use and air traffic control. Signed at Washington June 17, 1992; entered into force June 17, 1992.
TIAS 11477.

Air transport agreement, with annexes. Signed at Moscow January 14, 1994; entered into force January 14, 1994.
TIAS

Amendment:
April 5, 1999.

Memorandum of understanding on technical cooperation towards a bilateral airworthiness agreement. Signed at Moscow June 30, 1995; entered into force June 30, 1995.
TIAS 12673.

Agreement for promotion of aviation safety. Signed at Moscow September 2, 1998; entered into force September 2, 1998.
TIAS

Memorandum of understanding on cooperation in the field of civil aircraft accident/incident investigation and prevention. Signed at Moscow September 2, 1998; entered into force September 2, 1998.
TIAS

Memorandum of cooperation concerning cooperation in the promotion and development of civil aviation. Signed at Washington and Moscow February 19 and March 22, 1999; entered into force March 22, 1999.
TIAS

COPYRIGHT (See APPENDIX)

CUSTOMS

Agreement on cooperation and mutual assistance in customs matters. Signed at Washington September 28, 1994; entered into force December 15, 1994.
TIAS

Agreement concerning the procedure for the customs documentation and duty-free entry of goods transported within the framework of US-Russian cooperation in the exploration and use of space for peaceful purposes. Signed at Moscow December 16, 1994; entered into force August 26, 1996.
TIAS 12588.

DEFENSE

Agreement concerning the provision of training related to defense articles under the United States International Military Education and Training (IMET) Program. Exchange of notes at Moscow and Washington April 22 and June 17, 1992; entered into force June 17, 1992.
NP

Memorandum on cooperation in the field of defense conversion. Signed at Moscow December 16, 1993; entered into force December 16, 1993.
TIAS

Protocol on cooperation in the implementation of certain defense conversion projects. Signed at Moscow December 16, 1993; entered into force December 16, 1993.
TIAS

RUSSIAN FEDERATION (Cont'd)

Amendment and extension:
March 18, 1994.
January 21 and March 1, 2000.

Agreement for cooperation in installing and operating seismic stations for monitoring nuclear weapons tests. Signed at Washington and Moscow October 15 and 19, 1996; entered into force October 19, 1996.
TIAS

ECONOMIC AND TECHNICAL COOPERATION

Agreement regarding cooperation to facilitate the provision of assistance. Signed at Moscow April 4, 1992; entered into force April 4, 1992.
TIAS 11464.

Grant agreement for an energy efficiency and environment commodity import program. Signed at Moscow December 16, 1993; entered into force December 16, 1993.
TIAS 11483.

Agreement to establish a joint commission for agribusiness and rural development, with annexes. Signed at Moscow March 11, 1994; entered into force March 11, 1994.
TIAS

Memorandum of understanding for the establishment of the Russian-American oil and gas technology center in Tyumen City, with annex. Signed at Washington and Tyumen City June 23 and July 26, 1994; entered into force July 26, 1994.
TIAS 12558.

EMBASSY SITES

Memorandum of mutual understanding on settlement of the problem of the new embassy administrative buildings in Washington and Moscow. Signed at Washington June 17, 1992; entered into force June 17, 1992.
TIAS

Amendment:
December 15, 1992.

EMERGENCY PREPAREDNESS

Memorandum of understanding on cooperation in natural and man-made technological emergency prevention and response. Signed at Moscow July 16, 1996; entered into force July 16, 1996.
TIAS

ENVIRONMENTAL COOPERATION

Agreement on cooperation in the field of protection of the environment and natural resources, with annex. Signed at Washington June 23, 1994; entered into force June 23, 1994.
TIAS 12550.

Agreement on cooperation in the prevention of pollution of the environment in the Arctic. Signed at Moscow December 16, 1994; entered into force December 16, 1994.
TIAS 12589.

Agreement for cooperation in the Global Learning and Observations to Benefit the Environment (GLOBE) Program, with appendices. Signed at Moscow December 16, 1994; entered into force December 16, 1994.
TIAS 12590.

FINANCE

Investment incentive agreement. Signed at Washington April 3, 1992; entered into force June 17, 1992.
TIAS 11471.

Agreement regarding the consolidation and rescheduling of certain debts owed to or guaranteed by the United States Government, with annexes. Signed at Washington September 30, 1993; entered into force November 4, 1993.
NP

Agreement regarding the consolidation and rescheduling of certain debts owed to or guaranteed by the United States Government, with annexes. Signed at Moscow October 25, 1994; entered into force December 19, 1994.
NP

Agreement regarding the rescheduling of certain debts owed to or guaranteed by the United States Government, with annexes. Signed at Washington October 9, 1995; entered into force November 29, 1995.
NP

Amendment:
November 28 and December 1, 1995 (NP).

Agreement regarding the rescheduling of certain debts owed to or guaranteed by the United States Government, with annexes. Signed at Washington February 6, 1997; entered into force May 7, 1997.
NP

Agreement regarding the rescheduling of certain debts owed to or guaranteed by the United States Government, with annexes. Signed at Moscow May 26, 2000; entered into force June 29, 2000.
NP

FISHERIES

Agreement concerning Pacific salmon fishing within the respective 200-nautical mile zones of the United States and Russia. Exchange of notes at Washington August 27 and September 3, 1992; entered into force September 3, 1992.
TIAS 11449.

Agreement amending and extending the agreement of May 31, 1988, on mutual fisheries relations, with annex. Exchange of notes at Washington March 11 and September 15, 1993; entered into force April 4, 1994.
TIAS 12172.

Agreement on the conservation of straddling fish stocks in the central part of the Sea of Okhotsk. Signed at Moscow June 13, 1996; entered into force June 13, 1996.
TIAS

Agreement extending the agreement of May 31, 1988 on mutual fisheries relations, as amended and extended. Exchange of notes at Moscow July 28 and November 23, 1998; entered into force June 18, 1999; effective December 31, 1998.
TIAS

FORESTRY

Memorandum of understanding on cooperation in the field of forestry, with annex. Signed at Washington May 13, 1994; entered into force May 13, 1994.
TIAS 12541.

FUELS AND ENERGY

Agreement on scientific and technical cooperation in the field of fuels and energy, with annex. Signed at Washington June 17, 1992; entered into force June 17, 1992.
TIAS

HEALTH

Agreement on cooperation in the fields of public health and biomedical research. Signed at Moscow January 14, 1994; entered into force January 14, 1994.
TIAS 11473.

Memorandum of understanding on cooperation in the field of basic biomedical research. Signed at Washington June 23, 1994; entered into force June 23, 1994.
TIAS

RUSSIAN FEDERATION (Cont'd)

JUDICIAL ASSISTANCE

Agreement on cooperation in criminal law matters, with annex. Signed at Moscow June 30, 1995; entered into force February 5, 1996. TIAS 12674.

MARITIME MATTERS

Agreement amending the agreement of May 25, 1972 on the prevention of incidents on and over the high seas. Exchange of notes at Moscow October 12, 1997 and May 28, 1998; entered into force May 28, 1998. TIAS

NUCLEAR MATERIAL

Agreement to cooperate on national protection, control and accounting of nuclear materials. Signed at Moscow June 30, 1995; entered into force June 30, 1995. TIAS

Agreement on scientific and technical cooperation in the management of plutonium that has been withdrawn from nuclear military programs, with annex. Signed at Moscow July 24, 1998; entered into force July 24, 1998. TIAS

NUCLEAR RISK REDUCTION

Agreement on the Nuclear Cities Initiative, with annex. Signed at Vienna September 22, 1998; entered into force September 22, 1998. TIAS

Memorandum of agreement on the establishment of a joint center for the exchange of data from early warning systems and notifications of missile launches, with appendices. Signed at Moscow June 4, 2000; entered into force June 4, 2000. TIAS

Memorandum of understanding on notifications of missile launches, with appendices and joint statement. Signed at Brussels December 16, 2000; entered into force December 16, 2000. TIAS

SCIENTIFIC COOPERATION

Agreement on science and technology cooperation, with annexes. Signed at Moscow December 16, 1993; entered into force December 16, 1993. TIAS 12527.

Memorandum of understanding on cooperation in geoscience, with annexes. Signed at Washington June 23, 1994; entered into force June 23, 1994. TIAS 12552.

Memorandum of understanding on basic scientific research cooperation, with annexes. Signed at Washington June 23, 1994; entered into force June 23, 1994. TIAS 12551.

Memorandum of understanding for scientific and technical cooperation in the physical, chemical and engineering sciences. Signed at Moscow July 16, 1996; entered into force July 16, 1996. TIAS

Memorandum of understanding on cooperation in high performance scientific computing. Signed at Washington February 7, 1997; entered into force February 7, 1997. TIAS

Memorandum of understanding on basis scientific research cooperation, with annexes. Signed at Washington February 7, 1997; entered into force February 7, 1997. TIAS

Memorandum of understanding on cooperation in seismology and geodynamics, with appendix. Signed at Washington March 24, 1999; entered into force March 24, 1999. TIAS

SPACE COOPERATION

Agreement concerning cooperation in the exploration and use of outer space for peaceful purposes, with annex. Signed at Washington June 17, 1992; entered into force June 17, 1992. TIAS 12457.

Implementing agreement on human space flight cooperation, with annexes. Signed at Moscow October 5, 1992; entered into force April 29, 1993. TIAS 12481.

Protocol to the implementing agreement of October 5, 1992 on human space flight cooperation. Signed at Moscow December 16, 1993; entered into force December 16, 1993. TIAS 12522.

Interim agreement for the conduct of activities leading to Russian partnership in the detailed design, development, operation and utilization of the permanently manned civil space station. Signed at Washington June 23, 1994; entered into force June 30, 1995. TIAS

Implementing agreement on the flight of a U.S. stratospheric aerosol and gas experiment (SAGE) III and a total ozone mapping spectrometer (TOMS) aboard Russian meteor–3M spacecraft, with annexes. Signed at Moscow

December 16, 1994; entered into force February 22, 1995. TIAS 12592.

Memorandum of understanding on cooperation relating to the Space Biomedical Center for Training and Research in the Russian Federation, with annex. Signed at Moscow June 30, 1995; entered into force June 30, 1995. TIAS 12675.

TAXATION

Convention for the avoidance of double taxation and the prevention of fiscal evasion with respect to taxes on income and capital, with protocol. Signed at Washington June 17, 1992; entered into force December 16, 1993. TIAS

TRADE

Agreement on trade relations, with related exchanges of letters. Signed at Washington June 1, 1990; entered into force June 17, 1992. TIAS

Amendment:
September 26 and October 31, 1990.

Agreement regarding international trade in commercial space launch services. Signed at Washington September 2, 1993; entered into force September 2, 1993. TIAS

Amendment:
January 30, 1996.

Agreement on the exports of firearms and ammunition from the Russian Federation to the United States, with annexes. Signed at Washington April 3, 1996; entered into force April 3, 1996. TIAS

WEAPONS

Agreement concerning the safe and secure transportation, storage and destruction of weapons and the prevention of weapons proliferation, with implementing agreements. Signed at Washington June 17, 1992; entered into force June 17, 1992. TIAS

Agreement concerning the safe, secure and ecologically sound destruction of chemical weapons. Signed at Washington July 30, 1992; entered into force July 30, 1992. TIAS

RUSSIAN FEDERATION (Cont'd)

Amendments:
March 18, 1994.
May 28, 1996.
April 10, 1997.
December 29, 1997.
November 6, 1998 and January 14, 1999.
November 9 and 14, 2000.

Agreement concerning technical assistance for design of a safe, secure and ecologically sound storage facility for fissile material derived from the destruction of nuclear weapons. Signed at Washington October 6, 1992; entered into force October 6, 1992.
TIAS

Protocol to the agreement of June 17, 1992 concerning the safe and secure transportation and storage of nuclear weapons through the provision of emergency response equipment and related training. Signed at Moscow March 26, 1993; entered into force March 26, 1993.
TIAS

Amendment and extensions:
March 23, 1994.
May 25, 1994.
May 28, 1996.
February 6 and April 1, 1998.

Agreement concerning cooperation in the elimination of strategic offensive arms, with annexes. Signed at Moscow August 26, 1993; entered into force August 26, 1993.
TIAS

Amendments:
April 3, 1995.
June 19, 1995.
May 27, 1996.
April 11, 1997.
February 11, 1998.
June 9, 1998.
August 16, 1999.
July 26 and August 8, 2000.

Agreement concerning the provision of material, services and training relating to the construction of a sàfe, secure and ecologically sound storage facility for fissile material derived from the destruction of nuclear weapons. Signed at Washington September 2, 1993; entered into force September 2, 1993.
TIAS

Amendments and extension:
June 20, 1995.
September 6, 1996.
April 9, 1997.
January 27, 1999.
May 21 and 26, 1999.
September 15, 1999.
August 8 and 21, 2000.

Agreement concerning control, accounting and physical protection of nuclear material. Signed at Washington September 2, 1993; entered into force September 2, 1993.
TIAS

Amendment:
January 20, 1995.

Agreement concerning cooperation in nuclear weapons storage security through provision of material, services and related training. Signed at Moscow April 3, 1995; entered into force April 3, 1995.
TIAS

Amendments and extensions:
June 21, 1995.
May 27, 1996.
April 8, 1997.
December 14, 1998 and January 14, 1999.
December 14, 1998 and January 14, 1999.
November 1, 1999.
August 9, 1999 and January 25, 2000.
June 1 and 12, 2000.

Agreement concerning cooperation in nuclear weapons transportation security through provision of material, services and related training. Signed at Moscow April 3, 1995; entered into force April 3, 1995.
TIAS

Amendments and extension:
June 21, 1995.
May 27, 1996.
December 14, 1998 and January 14, 1999.
August 9, 1999 and January 25, 2000.
June 1 and 12, 2000.

RWANDA

COPYRIGHT (See APPENDIX)

DEFENSE

Agreement concerning the provision of training related to defense articles under the United States International Military Education and Training (IMET) Program. Exchange of notes at Kigali March 6 and 11, 1980; entered into force March 11, 1980.
33 UST 3064; TIAS 10211; 1529 UNTS 7.

Agreement regarding grants under the Foreign Assistance Act of 1961, as amended, and the furnishing of defense articles, related training and other defense services from the United States to Rwanda. Exchange of notes at Kigali January 26 and February 6, 1998; entered into force February 6, 1998.
TIAS

ECONOMIC AND TECHNICAL COOPERATION

Economic and technical cooperation agreement. Signed at Kigali June 7, 1989; entered into force January 17, 1992.
TIAS 12063.

Agency for International Development:
April 26 and 29, 1977 (29 UST 5269; TIAS 9102; 1134 UNTS 157).

EMPLOYMENT

Agreement relating to the employment of dependents of official government employees, with related note. Exchange of notes at Washington July 15 and October 22, 1992; entered into force October 22, 1992.
TIAS 11904.

FINANCE

Agreement relating to investment guaranties. Exchange of notes at Kigali July 6 and August 9, 1965; entered into force April 27, 1967.
18 UST 2346; TIAS 6337; 692 UNTS 101.

Agreement regarding the consolidation, reduction, and rescheduling of certain debts owed to the United States Government and its Agency, with annexes. Signed at Kigali October 26, 1999; entered into force December 13, 1999.
NP

PEACE CORPS

Agreement relating to the establishment of a Peace Corps program in Rwanda. Exchange of notes at Kigali December 20, 1974; entered into force December 20, 1974.
25 UST 3387; TIAS 7992.

POSTAL MATTERS

International express mail agreement with detailed regulations. Signed at Kigali and Washington January 15 and February 8, 1988; entered into force March 15, 1988.
TIAS 11648.

SAINT KITTS and NEVIS

On September 19, 1983 Saint Christopher and Nevis became an independent state. In a note dated November 2, 1983 to the Secretary-General of the United Nations, the Prime Minister and Minister of Foreign Affairs made a statement reading in part as follows:

"I have the honour to refer to the attainment of independence by the former British Associated State of St. Christopher and Nevis on 19th September, 1983, as Saint Christopher and Nevis or Saint Kitts and Nevis, and to the question of status of conventions, treaties and other international instruments applied to, or entered into on behalf of Saint Christopher and Nevis by the United Kingdom Government prior to independence.

SAINT KITTS and NEVIS (Cont'd)

"The Government of Saint Christopher and Nevis considers that questions of succession to such conventions, treaties and other international instruments should be governed by the accepted rules of international law and by the relevant principles contained in the Convention on Succession of States in respect of Treaties done at Vienna on 23rd August, 1978.

"The Government of Saint Christopher and Nevis hereby declares that, with regard to multilateral treaties applied or extended to the former British Associated State of Saint Christopher and Nevis, it will continue to apply the terms of each treaty provisionally and on the basis of reciprocity until such time as it notifies the depositary authority of its decision in respect thereof.

"As regards bilateral treaties applied or extended to, or entered into on behalf of the former British Associated State of Saint Christopher and Nevis, the Government of Saint Christopher and Nevis declares that it will examine each such treaty and communicate its views to the other State Party concerned. In the meantime, the Government of Saint Christopher and Nevis will continue to observe the terms of each treaty, which validly so applies and is not inconsistent with its independent sovereign status, provisionally and on basis of reciprocity."

AVIATION

Agreement between the United States and the United Kingdom concerning air services, with annexes and exchange of letters. Signed at Bermuda July 23, 1977; entered into force July 23, 1977.
28 UST 5367; TIAS 8641.

Amendments:
April 25, 1978 (29 UST 2680; TIAS 8965).
December 29, 1979 (32 UST 524; TIAS 9722).
December 4, 1980 (33 UST 655; TIAS 10059).
August 11 and November 30, 1987 (TIAS 11545).

CONSULS

Consular convention between the United States and the United Kingdom. Signed at Washington June 6, 1951; entered into force September 7, 1952.
3 UST 3426; TIAS 2494; 165 UNTS 121.

COPYRIGHT (See APPENDIX)

DEFENSE

Agreement concerning the provision of training related to defense articles under the United States International Military Education and Training (IMET) Program. Exchange of notes at St. John's and Basseterre March 19 and 20, 1984; entered into force March 20, 1984.
TIAS 10972.

Agreement concerning the status of United States Armed Forces personnel present in St. Christopher and Nevis. Exchange of notes at St. John's and Basseterre March 2 and June 9, 1987; entered into force June 9, 1987.
TIAS

ECONOMIC AND TECHNICAL COOPERATION

General agreement for economic, technical and related assistance. Signed at Basseterre April 24, 1986; entered into force April 24, 1986.
TIAS 11514.

EXTRADITION

Extradition treaty. Signed at Basseterre September 18, 1996; entered into force February 23, 2000.
TIAS

FINANCE

Agreement relating to investment guaranties. Signed at Basseterre November 21, 1968; entered into force November 21, 1968.
19 UST 7546; TIAS 6596; 702 UNTS 311.

JUDICIAL ASSISTANCE

Treaty on mutual legal assistance in criminal matters, with related exchange of notes. Signed at Basseterre September 18, 1997; entered into force February 23, 2000.
TIAS

NARCOTIC DRUGS

Agreement concerning maritime counter-drug operations. Signed at Basseterre April 13, 1995; entered into force April 13, 1995.
TIAS

Amendment:
June 27, 1996.

PEACE CORPS

Agreement relating to the establishment of a Peace Corps program in St. Kitts/Nevis. Exchange of letters at Bridgetown and Basseterre May 15, 1980 and January 13, 1981; entered into force January 13, 1981.
33 UST 846; TIAS 10067; 1275 UNTS 131.

PEACEKEEPING

Agreement for the furnishing of commodities and services in connection with the peacekeeping force for Grenada. Exchange of notes at St. John's and Basseterre January 19 and 20, 1984; entered into force January 20, 1984.
TIAS 10929.

POSTAL MATTERS

Convention for the exchange of postal money orders with the British Colony of Saint Christopher, Nevis and Anguilla. Signed at Basseterre, St. Kitts, June 27 and at Washington September 14, 1959; entered into force February 1, 1960.
11 UST 1433; TIAS 4483.

International express mail agreement, with detailed regulations. Signed at St. Kitts and Washington June 16 and August 21, 1997; entered into force October 1, 1997.
NP

PROPERTY

Convention between the United States and the United Kingdom relating to tenure and disposition of real and personal property. Signed at Washington March 2, 1899; applicable to St. Christopher-Nevis June 17, 1901.
31 Stat. 1939; TS 146; 12 Bevans 246.

Supplementary convention relating to the tenure and disposition of real and personal property. Signed at Washington May 27, 1936; entered into force March 10, 1941.
55 Stat. 1101; TS 964; 5 Bevans 140; 203 LNTS 367.

TELECOMMUNICATION

Agreement relating to radio communications between amateur stations on behalf of third parties. Exchange of notes at St. John's and St. Kitts July 6 and 9, 1984; entered into force August 8, 1984.
TIAS 11147.

TRADE-MARKS

Declaration by the United States and the United Kingdom affording reciprocal protec-

SAINT KITTS and NEVIS (Cont'd)

tion to trade-marks. Signed at London October 24, 1877; entered into force October 24, 1877.
20 Stat. 703; TS 138; 12 Bevans 198.

SAINT LUCIA

On February 22, 1979, Saint Lucia became an independent state. In a note dated March 14, 1979, to the Secretary-General of the United Nations, the Prime Minister made a statement reading in part as follows: "Saint Lucia . . . is now ready to participate with other nations in fulfilling obligations under international law with respect to treaties to which this Government succeeded upon Independence. However, it is necessary to examine in depth such treaties to ascertain whether or not under customary international law any may have lapsed. Until this has been done the Government of Saint Lucia wish:

(a) that it be presumed that each treaty has been legally succeeded to by Saint Lucia; and

(b) that future action be based on the presumption in (a) above.

You will be notified in due course of those treaties this Government regards as having lapsed and those treaties which this Government wishes to terminate."

AVIATION

Agreement between the United States and the United Kingdom concerning the opening of certain military air bases in the Caribbean area and Bermuda to use by civil aircraft and exchange of notes. Signed at Washington February 24, 1948; entered into force February 24, 1948.
62 Stat. 1860; TIAS 1717; 12 Bevans 850; 73 UNTS 143.

Agreement between the United States and the United Kingdom relating to the future status and use of Beane Field, St. Lucia. Exchange of notes at London August 20, 1964; entered into force August 20, 1964.
15 UST 1685; TIAS 5642; 531 UNTS 85.

Agreement between the United States and the United Kingdom concerning air services, with annexes and exchange of letters. Signed at Bermuda July 23, 1977; entered into force July 23, 1977.
28 UST 5367; TIAS 8641.

Amendment:
April 25, 1978 (29 UST 2680; TIAS 8965).

CONSULS

Consular convention between the United States and the United Kingdom. Signed at Washington June 6, 1951; entered into force September 7, 1952.
3 UST 3426; TIAS 2494; 165 UNTS 121.

COPYRIGHT (See APPENDIX)

DEFENSE

Agreement concerning the provision of training related to defense articles under the United States International Military Education and Training (IMET) Program. Exchange of notes at Bridgetown and Castries December 11, 1980 and January 27, 1981; entered into force January 27, 1981.
33 UST 983; TIAS 10081; 1275 UNTS 185.

ECONOMIC AND TECHNICAL COOPERATION

General agreement for economic, technical and related assistance. Signed at Castries October 20, 1983; entered into force October 20, 1983.
TIAS 10831.

EXTRADITION

Extradition treaty. Signed at Castries April 18, 1996; entered into force February 2, 2000.
TIAS

FINANCE

Agreement relating to investment guaranties. Signed at Castries August 9, 1968; entered into force August 9, 1968.
19 UST 5921; TIAS 6546; 730 UNTS 225.

JUDICIAL ASSISTANCE

Treaty on mutual legal assistance in criminal matters, with forms. Signed at Castries April 18, 1996; entered into force February 2, 2000.
TIAS

NARCOTIC DRUGS

Agreement concerning maritime counter-drug operations. Signed at Castries April 20, 1995; entered into force April 20, 1995.
TIAS

Amendment:
June 5, 1996.

PEACE CORPS

Agreement relating to the establishment of a Peace Corps program in St. Lucia. Exchange of letters at Bridgetown and Castries May 15 and July 8, 1980; entered into force July 8, 1980.
32 UST 4408; TIAS 9954; 1267 UNTS 137.

PEACEKEEPING

Agreement for the furnishing of commodities and services in connection with the peacekeeping force for Grenada. Exchange of notes at Bridgetown and Castries November 25, 1983 and January 13, 1984; entered into force January 13, 1984.
TIAS 10924.

POSTAL MATTERS

Money order agreement. Signed at Washington July 29 and at Grenada August 29, 1904; operative October 1, 1904.
NP

Agreement for the direct exchange of parcels by parcel post. Signed at Grenada May 20 and at Washington June 21, 1935; operative July 1, 1935.
49 Stat. 3229; 162 LNTS 157.

International express mail agreement with detailed regulations. Signed at Castries and Washington August 11 and September 14, 1989; entered into force September 15, 1989.
TIAS 11953.

INTELPOST memorandum of understanding, with detailed regulations. Signed at Castries and Washington September 22 and October 29, 1992; entered into force November 23, 1992.
TIAS 11902.

PROPERTY

Convention between the United States and the United Kingdom relating to tenure and disposition of real and personal property. Signed at Washington March 2, 1899; applicable to St. Lucia February 9, 1901.
31 Stat. 1939; TS 146; 12 Bevans 246.

Supplementary convention relating to the tenure and disposition of real and personal property. Signed at Washington May 27, 1936; entered into force March 10, 1941.
55 Stat. 1101; TS 964; 5 Bevans 140; 203 LNTS 367.

REFUGEES

Memorandum of understanding for the establishment within the territory of St. Lucia of facilities to provide temporary protection under

SAINT LUCIA (Cont'd)

the auspices of the United Nations High Commissioner for Refugees for nationals of Haiti fleeing their country. Signed at St. Lucia July 15, 1994; entered into force July 15, 1994.
TIAS

TAXATION

Agreement for the exchange of information with respect to taxes, with annex. Signed at Washington January 30, 1987; entered into force April 22, 1991.
TIAS 12057.

TELECOMMUNICATIONS

Agreement between the United States and the United Kingdom relating to the reciprocal granting of authorizations to permit licensed amateur radio operators of either country to operate their stations in the other country. Exchange of notes at London November 26, 1965; applicable to St. Lucia December 11, 1969.
16 UST 2047; TIAS 5941; 561 UNTS 193.

Agreement between the United States and the United Kingdom extending to certain territories the application of the agreement of November 26, 1965 relating to the reciprocal granting of authorizations to permit licensed amateur radio operators of either country to operate their stations in the other country. Exchange of notes at London December 11, 1969; entered into force December 11, 1969.
20 UST 4089; TIAS 6800; 732 UNTS 334.

Arrangement relating to radio communications between amateur stations on behalf of third parties. Exchange of notes at Bridgetown and Castries August 10, 1981 and February 17, 1982; entered into force March 19, 1982.
34 UST 287; TIAS 10354.

TRADE-MARKS

Declaration by the United States and the United Kingdom affording reciprocal protection to trade-marks. Signed at London October 24, 1877; entered into force October 24, 1877.
20 Stat. 703; TS 138; 12 Bevans 198.

SAINT VINCENT and THE GRENADINES

On October 27, 1979 Saint Vincent and the Grenadines became an independent state. In a note dated September 30, 1983, to the Secretary-General of the United Nations, the Prime Minister and Minister of Finance made a statement reading in part as follows:

"I have the honour to refer to the attainment of independence by the former British Associated State of St. Vincent on 27th October, 1979, as the State of St. Vincent and the Grenadines, and to the question of status of convention, treaties and other international instruments applied to or entered into on behalf of St. Vincent by the United Kingdom Government prior to independence.

"The Government of the State of St. Vincent and the Grenadines considers that questions of succession to such conventions, treaties and other international instruments should be governed by the accepted rules of international law and by the relevant principles contained in the Convention on Succession of States in respect of treaties done at Vienna on 23rd August, 1978.

"The Government of the State of St. Vincent and the Grenadines hereby declares that, with regard to multilateral treaties applied or extended to the former British Associated State of St. Vincent, it will continue to apply the terms of each such treaty provisionally and on the basis of reciprocity until such time as it notifies the depository authority of its decision in respect thereof.

"As regards bilateral treaties applied or extended to, or entered into on behalf of the former British Associated State of St. Vincent, the Government of the State of St. Vincent and the Grenadines declares that it will examine each such treaty and communicate its views to the other State Party concerned. In the meantime, the Government of the State of St. Vincent and the Grenadines will continue to observe the terms of each such treaty, which validly so applies and is not inconsistent with its independent sovereign status, provisionally and on basis of reciprocity."

AVIATION

Agreement between the United States and the United Kingdom concerning air services, with annexes and exchange of letters. Signed at Bermuda July 23, 1977; entered into force July 23, 1977.
28 UST 5367; TIAS 8641.

Amendment:
April 25, 1978 (29 UST 2680; TIAS 8965).

CONSULS

Consular convention between the United States and the United Kingdom. Signed at Washington June 6, 1951; entered into force September 7, 1952.
3 UST 3426; TIAS 2494; 165 UNTS 121.

COPYRIGHT (See APPENDIX)

DEFENSE

Agreement concerning the provision of training related to defense articles under the United States International Military Education and Training (IMET) Program. Exchange of notes at Bridgetown and Kingstown December 11, 1980 and January 20, 1981; entered into force January 20, 1981.
33 UST 912; TIAS 10076; 1275 UNTS 149.

ECONOMIC AND TECHNICAL COOPERATION

General agreement for economic, technical and related assistance. Signed at Kingstown September 30, 1983; entered into force September 30, 1983.
TIAS 10833.

EXTRADITION

Extradition treaty. Signed at Kingstown August 15, 1996; entered into force September 8, 1999.
TIAS

FINANCE

Agreement relating to investment guaranties. Exchange of notes at Bridgetown and St. Vincent May 15 and June 14, 1972; entered into force June 14, 1972.
23 UST 3802; TIAS 7530.

JUDICIAL ASSISTANCE

Treaty on mutual legal assistance in criminal matters, with a related protocol. Signed at Kingstown January 8, 1998; entered into force September 8, 1999.
TIAS

NARCOTIC DRUGS

Agreement concerning maritime counter-drug operations. Signed at Kingstown and Bridgetown June 29 and July 4, 1995; entered into force July 4, 1995.
TIAS 12676.

PEACE CORPS

Agreement relating to the establishment of a Peace Corps program in St. Vincent. Exchange of letters at Bridgetown and St. Vin-

SAINT VINCENT and THE GRENADINES (Cont'd)

cent May 15 and June 26, 1980; entered into force June 26, 1980.
32 UST 5815; TIAS 10017; 1267 UNTS 129.

PEACEKEEPING

Agreement for the furnishing of commodities and services in connection with the peacekeeping force for Grenada. Exchange of notes at Bridgetown and St. Vincent November 25, 1983 and January 13, 1984; entered into force January 13, 1984.
TIAS 10925.

POSTAL MATTERS

Money order agreement. Signed at Washington July 29 and at Grenada August 29, 1904; operative October 1, 1904.
NP

Agreement for the direct exchange of parcels by parcel post. Signed at Grenada May 20 and at Washington June 21, 1935; operative July 1, 1935.
49 Stat. 3229; Post Office Department print; 162 LNTS 157.

International express mail agreement, with detailed regulations. Signed at Kingston and Washington January 27 and February 25, 1992; entered into force March 7, 1992.
TIAS 11854.

PROPERTY

Convention between the United States and the United Kingdom relating to tenure and disposition of real and personal property. Signed at Washington March 2, 1899; applicable to St. Vincent February 9, 1901.
31 Stat. 1939; TS 146; 12 Bevans 246.

Supplementary convention relating to the tenure and disposition of real and personal property. Signed at Washington May 27, 1936; entered into force March 10, 1941.
55 Stat. 1101; TS 964; 5 Bevans 140; 203 LNTS 367.

TAXATION

Agreement concerning reciprocal exemption from income tax of income derived from the international operation of ships and aircraft. Exchange of notes at Bridgetown and Kingston October 11, 1988 and February 15, 1989; entered into force February 15, 1989.
TIAS 11601.

TELECOMMUNICATION

Agreement between the United States and the United Kingdom relating to the reciprocal granting of authorizations to permit licensed amateur radio operators of either country to operate their stations in the other country. Exchange of notes at London November 26, 1965; applicable to St. Vincent December 11, 1969.
16 UST 2047; TIAS 5941; 561 UNTS 193.

Agreement between the United States and the United Kingdom extending to certain territories the application of the agreement of November 26, 1965 relating to the reciprocal granting of authorizations to permit licensed amateur radio operators of either country to operate their stations in the other country. Exchange of notes at London December 11, 1969; entered into force December 11, 1969.
20 UST 4089; TIAS 6800; 732 UNTS 334.

Agreement relating to radio communications between amateur stations on behalf of third parties. Exchange of notes at Bridgetown and St. Vincent April 22 and September 27, 1982; entered into force September 27, 1982; effective October 27, 1982.
TIAS 10885.

TRADE-MARKS

Declaration by the United States and the United Kingdom affording reciprocal protection to trade-marks. Signed at London October 24, 1877; entered into force October 24, 1877.
20 Stat. 703; TS 138; 12 Bevans 198.

SAN MARINO

EXTRADITION

Treaty for the mutual extradition of fugitive criminals. Signed at Rome January 10, 1906; entered into force July 8, 1908.
35 Stat. 1971; TS 495; 11 Bevans 440.

Supplementary extradition convention. Signed at Washington October 10, 1934; entered into force June 28, 1935.
49 Stat. 3198; TS 891; 11 Bevans 446; 161 LNTS 149.

SAO TOME AND PRINCIPE

DEFENSE

Agreement concerning the provision of training related to defense articles under the United States International Military Education and Training (IMET) Program. Exchange of notes at Libreville and Sao Tome April 2, 1985 and

February 26, 1986; entered into force February 26, 1986.
NP

FINANCE

Investment incentive agreement. Signed at Washington September 10, 1998; entered into force September 10, 1998.
TIAS

TELECOMMUNICATION

Agreement for the operation of radio transmission facilities. Signed at Sao Tome May 22, 1992; entered into force June 21, 1992.
TIAS

SAUDI ARABIA

AVIATION

Memorandum of arrangement relating to technical assistance in developing and modernizing Saudi Arabia's civil aviation system, with annex. Signed at Washington and Riyadh May 16 and August 3, 1985; entered into force August 3, 1985.
TIAS 11397.

Air transport agreement, with annexes. Signed at Jeddah October 2, 1993; entered into force October 2, 1993.
TIAS 12508.

COMMERCE

Provisional agreement in regard to diplomatic and consular representation, juridical protection, commerce, and navigation. Signed at London November 7, 1933; entered into force November 7, 1933.
48 Stat. 1826; EAS 53; 11 Bevans 456; 142 LNTS 329.

CONSULS (See COMMERCE)

COPYRIGHT (See APPENDIX)

CULTURAL RELATIONS

Agreement for cultural exchange. Signed at Jidda July 25, 1968; entered into force July 25, 1968.
20 UST 2804; TIAS 6749; 723 UNTS 141.

SAUDI ARABIA (Cont'd)

DEFENSE [1]

Agreement relating to the extending of procurement assistance to Saudi Arabia for the transfer of military supplies and equipment. Exchange of notes at Jidda June 18, 1951; entered into force June 18, 1951.
2 UST 1460; TIAS 2289; 141 UNTS 67.

Agreement providing for a military assistance advisory group.[2] Exchange of notes at Jidda June 27, 1953; entered into force June 27, 1953.
4 UST 1482; TIAS 2812; 212 UNTS 335.

Agreement for the loan of F-86 aircraft to Saudi Arabia.[3] Exchange of notes at Jidda November 10 and 13, 1962; entered into force November 13, 1962.
14 UST 1181; TIAS 5414; 488 UNTS 175.

Amendment:
May 1 and 22, 1963 (14 UST 1184; TIAS 5414; 488 UNTS 180).

Agreement relating to the construction of certain military facilities in Saudi Arabia. Exchange of notes at Jidda May 24 and June 5, 1965; entered into force June 5, 1965; operative May 24, 1965.
16 UST 890; TIAS 5830; 548 UNTS 285.

Extensions:
June 25 and July 8, 1985.
February 13 and 14, 1989.

Agreement relating to the transfer of F-86 aircraft to Saudi Arabia. Exchange of notes at Jidda May 16 and November 11, 1965; entered into force November 11, 1965.
17 UST 1390; TIAS 6095.

Agreement on privileges and immunities for United States personnel engaged in the training program for the maintenance and operation of F-5 aircraft in Saudi Arabia. Exchange of notes at Jidda April 4 and July 5, 1972; entered into force July 5, 1972.
23 UST 1469; TIAS 7425.

Agreement relating to the deposit by Saudi Arabia of ten percent of the value of grant military assistance provided by the United States. Exchange of notes at Jidda April 11, 19 and May 15, 1972; entered into force May 15, 1972.
23 UST 2664; TIAS 7459.

Memorandum of understanding concerning the Saudi Arabian National Guard modernization program. Signed at Jidda March 19, 1973; entered into force March 19, 1973.
24 UST 1106; TIAS 7634.

NOTES:
[1] See also agreement on cooperation in the field of economics, technology, industry and defense (TIAS 7974) under ECONOMIC AND TECHNICAL COOPERATION.

[2] Terminated February 27, 1977, except that the provisions of paragraph 7 remain in force in respect of activities under the agreement of February 8 and 27, 1977 (28 UST 2409; TIAS 8558). See MISSIONS, MILITARY.
[3] Paragraph 1, first sentence of paragraph 5 and paragraphs 7 and 8 terminated by agreement of May 16 and November 11, 1965 (17 UST 1390; TIAS 6095).

ECONOMIC AND TECHNICAL COOPERATION

Economic assistance agreement for the expansion of the Port of Damman. Exchange of notes at Jidda March 1 and at Riyadh May 1, 1958; entered into force May 1, 1958.
9 UST 589; TIAS 4038; 315 UNTS 221.

Agreement on cooperation in the fields of economics, technology, industry and defense. Signed at Washington June 8, 1974; entered into force June 8, 1974.
25 UST 3115; TIAS 7974.

Joint communique on the first session of the U.S.-Saudi Arabian Joint Commission on Economic Cooperation. Done at Washington February 27, 1975; entered into force February 27, 1975.
26 UST 1689; TIAS 8128; 1006 UNTS 121.

Project agreement for technical cooperation in agriculture and water. Signed at Riyadh November 23, 1975; entered into force January 27, 1976.
28 UST 1103; TIAS 8494.

Project agreement for technical cooperation in science and technology, with appendices. Signed at Riyadh February 29, 1976; entered into force August 7, 1978.
29 UST 3393; TIAS 9019; 1123 UNTS 3.

Project agreement for technical cooperation in upgrading and improving the scientific and technical capability of the consumer protection department in the Saudi Arabian Ministry of Commerce. Signed at Washington May 3, 1977; entered into force August 8, 1977.
29 UST 1240; TIAS 8876.

Project agreement for technical cooperation in establishing an information center. Signed at Washington May 3, 1977; entered into force August 10, 1977.
29 UST 1232; TIAS 8875.

Agreement for technical cooperation in desalination, with appendices. Signed at Washington May 3, 1977; entered into force August 30, 1977.
29 UST 1323; TIAS 8878.

Project agreement for technical cooperation in audit administration and training, with annexes. Signed at Riyadh May 16, 1978; entered into force May 25, 1978.
30 UST 1205; TIAS 9246; 1152 UNTS 353.

Project agreement for technical cooperation in customs administration and training. Signed at

Riyadh and Washington June 11 and 22, 1978; entered into force August 10, 1978.
30 UST 2165; TIAS 9321; 1170 UNTS 121.

Project agreement for technical cooperation in supply management development, with attachments. Signed at Riyadh July 13, 1978; entered into force August 10, 1978.
30 UST 1719; TIAS 9281; 1152 UNTS 409.

Project agreement for technical cooperation in executive management development. Signed at Jeddah November 18, 1978; entered into force March 4, 1979.
30 UST 2161; TIAS 9320; 1170 UNTS 135.

FINANCE

Agreement on guaranteed private investment. Signed at Washington February 27, 1975; entered into force April 26, 1975.
26 UST 459; TIAS 8045; 992 UNTS 231.

MISSIONS, MILITARY

Agreement relating to a United States military training mission in Saudi Arabia. Exchange of notes at Jidda February 8 and 27, 1977; entered into force February 27, 1977.
28 UST 2409; TIAS 8558.

POSTAL MATTERS

Memorandum of understanding for the exchange of international express mail, with details of implementation. Signed at Washington November 2, 1984; entered into force February 1, 1985.
TIAS 11009.

SHIPPING

Agreement relating to jurisdiction over vessels utilizing the Louisiana Offshore Oil Port. Exchange of notes at Jidda March 1, 1981 and October 20, 1982; entered into force October 20, 1982.
TIAS 10552; 1871 UNTS 165.

TAXATION

Agreement for reciprocal exemption of taxes on income from the international operation of a ship or ships or aircraft. Signed at Riyadh December 11, 1999; entered into force January 31, 2000.
TIAS

SENEGAL

AGRICULTURAL COMMODITIES

Agricultural commodities agreement with exchange of notes. Signed at Dakar July 3, 1963; entered into force July 3, 1963.
15 UST 738; TIAS 5599; 527 UNTS 95.

Amendment:
January 24, 1964 (15 UST 738; TIAS 5599; 527 UNTS 95).

Agricultural commodities agreement, with annexes and memorandum of understanding. Signed at Dakar May 16, 1980; entered into force May 16, 1980.
33 UST 3385; TIAS 10239.

Amendments:
December 23, 1980 (33 UST 3471; TIAS 10239).
July 14 and 16, 1982 (TIAS 10647).
July 22 and 28, 1983 (TIAS 10752).
March 22 and April 3, 1984 (TIAS 10752).

Agricultural commodities agreement, with memorandum of understanding and related letter. Signed at Dakar December 17, 1985; entered into force December 17, 1985.
NP

Amendment:
July 3, 1986 (NP).

Agricultural commodities agreement. Signed at Dakar June 1, 1987; entered into force June 1, 1987.
NP

Amendment:
July 24, 1987 (NP).

Agricultural commodities agreement, with memorandum of understanding. Signed at Dakar August 3, 1988; entered into force August 3, 1988.
NP

Agricultural commodities agreement. Signed at Dakar April 11, 1989; entered into force April 11, 1989.
NP

Agricultural commodities agreement. Signed at Dakar March 9, 1990; entered into force March 9, 1990.
NP

AVIATION

Air transport services agreement, with memorandum of understanding. Signed at Dakar March 28, 1979; entered into force provisionally March 28, 1979; definitively August 17, 1984.
TIAS 11261.

Amendment:
April 1, 1998.

COPYRIGHT (See APPENDIX)

DEFENSE

Agreement relating to the furnishing of military equipment, materials and services to Senegal for the purpose of assuring its security and supporting its development. Exchange of notes at Dakar July 20, 1962; entered into force July 20, 1962.
13 UST 1803; TIAS 5127; 458 UNTS 137.

Agreement concerning the provision of training related to defense articles under the United States International Military Education and Training (IMET) Program. Exchange of notes at Dakar February 25 and July 15, 1983; entered into force July 15, 1983.
TIAS 10839.

Agreement regarding the provision of commodities, services and associated military education and training to assist Senegalese forces participating in the African Crisis Response Initiative. Exchange of notes at Dakar July 24 and August 29, 1997; entered into force August 29, 1997.
TIAS

ECONOMIC AND TECHNICAL COOPERATION

Agreement providing for economic, financial, technical and related assistance. Signed at Washington May 13, 1961; entered into force May 13, 1961.
12 UST 566; TIAS 4754; 409 UNTS 231.

Agency for International Development:
March 23, 1974 (27 UST 2672; TIAS 8339; 1066 UNTS 231).
November 6, 1974 and May 28, 1975 (29 UST 1006; TIAS 8862).
August 5 and 7, 1975 (27 UST 2688; TIAS 8339; 1066 UNTS 239).
March 2 and May 28, 1976 (29 UST 1009; TIAS 8862).
February 21, 1978 (30 UST 3052; TIAS 9377; 1178 UNTS 209).
March 29, 1978 (30 UST 3058; TIAS 9377; 1178 UNTS 213).

EMPLOYMENT

Agreement relating to employment of dependents of staff members of diplomatic and consular missions. Signed at Dakar April 28, 1998; entered into force April 28, 1998.
TIAS

ENVIRONMENTAL COOPERATION

Agreement for cooperation in the Global Learning and Observations to Benefit the Environment (GLOBE) Program, with appendices. Signed at Dakar March 17, 1995; entered into force March 17, 1995.
TIAS

FINANCE

Agreement relating to investment guaranties. Signed at Dakar June 12, 1963; entered into force provisionally June 12, 1963; definitively March 27, 1970.
18 UST 3197; TIAS 6417.

Agreement regarding the consolidation and rescheduling of certain debts owed to or guaranteed by the United States Government and its agencies, with annexes. Signed at Dakar August 26, 1982; entered into force October 25, 1982.
TIAS 10475; 1751 UNTS 55.

Agreement regarding the consolidation and rescheduling of certain debts owed to or guaranteed by the United States Government and its agencies, with annexes. Signed at Washington August 11, 1983; entered into force September 13, 1983.
TIAS 10808.

Agreement regarding the consolidation and rescheduling of certain debts owed to, guaranteed or insured by the United States Government and its agencies, with annexes. Signed at Dakar August 22, 1984; entered into force September 24, 1984.
NP

Agreement regarding the consolidation and rescheduling of certain debts owed to, guaranteed by or insured by the United States Government and its agencies, with annexes. Signed at Dakar June 5, 1985; entered into force July 15, 1985.
NP

Agreement regarding the consolidation and rescheduling of certain debts owed to, guaranteed by or insured by the United States Government and its agencies, with annexes. Signed at Washington April 10, 1987; entered into force May 18, 1987.
NP

Agreement regarding the consolidation and rescheduling of certain debts owed to, guaranteed by or insured by the United States Government and its agencies, with annexes. Signed at Dakar June 10, 1988; entered into force July 28, 1988.
NP

Agreement regarding the consolidation and rescheduling of certain debts owed to, guaranteed by, or insured by the United States Government and its agencies, with annexes. Signed

SENEGAL (Cont'd)

at Dakar July 14, 1989; entered into force August 24, 1989.
NP

Agreement regarding the consolidation and rescheduling of certain debts owed to, guaranteed by, or insured by the United States Government and its agencies, with annexes. Signed at Dakar July 13, 1990; entered into force September 5, 1990.
NP

Agreement regarding the consolidation and rescheduling of certain debts owed to, guaranteed by, or insured by the United States Government and its agencies, with annexes. Signed at Dakar November 26, 1991; entered into force February 10, 1992.
NP

Agreement regarding the consolidation, reduction and rescheduling of certain debts owed to, guaranteed by or insured by the United States Government and its agencies, with annexes. Signed at Dakar July 28, 1994; entered into force August 29, 1994.
NP

Agreement regarding the consolidation, reduction and rescheduling of certain debts owed to, guaranteed by or insured by the United States Government and its agencies, with annexes. Signed at Dakar August 28, 1995; entered into force November 1, 1995.
NP

Amendment:
November 17, 1997 and May 28, 1998 (NP).

Agreement regarding the reduction and reorganization of certain debts owed to, guaranteed by, or insured by the United States Government and its agencies, with annexes. Signed at Dakar December 17, 1998; entered into force March 17, 1999.
NP

INVESTMENT

Treaty concerning the reciprocal encouragement and protection of investment, with annex and protocol. Signed at Washington December 6, 1983; entered into force October 25, 1990.
TIAS

PEACE CORPS

Agreement relating to the establishment of a Peace Corps program in Senegal. Exchange of notes at Dakar January 10 and 17, 1963; entered into force January 17, 1963.
14 UST 1622; TIAS 5467.

POSTAL MATTERS

International express mail agreement, with detailed regulations. Signed at Dakar and Washington June 5 and July 3, 1986; entered into force September 1, 1986.
TIAS 11519.

Postal money order agreement. Signed at Dakar and Washington January 31 and March 20, 1995; entered into force May 1, 1995.
NP

TRACKING STATIONS

Agreement regarding the establishment and operation of a space vehicle tracking and communication facility in connection with the space shuttle. Exchange of notes at Dakar January 30 and February 5, 1981; entered into force February 5, 1981.
33 UST 1028; TIAS 10088; 1295 UNTS 161.

Amendments and extensions:
November 30 and December 22, 1981 (33 UST 4550; TIAS 10325).

SEYCHELLES

On June 28, 1976 Seychelles became an independent state. By an exchange of notes dated June 29, 1976 between the Government of the United Kingdom and the Government of Seychelles, it was agreed that all obligations and responsibilities of the Government of the United Kingdom which arise from any valid international instrument shall, as from the 29th of June 1976, be assumed by the Government of Seychelles insofar as such instruments may be held to have application to Seychelles. Also, rights and benefits heretofore enjoyed by the Government of the United Kingdom in virtue of the application of any such international instrument to Seychelles shall, as from the 29th of June 1976, be enjoyed by the Government of Seychelles.

CONSULS

Consular convention between the United States and the United Kingdom. Signed at Washington June 6, 1951; entered into force September 7, 1952.
3 UST 3426; TIAS 2494; 165 UNTS 121.

DEFENSE

Agreement concerning the provision of training related to defense articles under the United States International Military Education and Training (IMET) Program. Exchange of notes at Victoria November 14, 1985 and February 21, 1986; entered into force February 21, 1986.
TIAS 11104.

ECONOMIC AND TECHNICAL COOPERATION

Economic cooperation agreement between the United States and the United Kingdom. Signed at London July 6, 1948; applicable to Seychelles July 6, 1948.
62 Stat. 2596; TIAS 1795; 12 Bevans 874; 22 UNTS 263.

Amendments:
January 3, 1950 (1 UST 184; TIAS 2036; 86 UNTS 304).
May 25, 1951 (2 UST 1292; TIAS 2277; 99 UNTS 308).
February 25, 1953 (4 UST 1528; TIAS 2815; 172 UNTS 332).

EXTRADITION

Extradition treaty between the United States and the United Kingdom. Signed at London December 22, 1931; entered into force June 24, 1935.
47 Stat. 2122; TS 849; 12 Bevans 482; 163 LNTS 59.

MUTUAL SECURITY

Agreement between the United States and the United Kingdom relating to the assurances required under the Mutual Security Act of 1951. Exchange of notes at London January 8, 1952; entered into force January 8, 1952.
3 UST 4665; TIAS 2622; 126 UNTS 307.

PEACE CORPS

Agreement relating to the establishment of a Peace Corps program in the Seychelles. Exchange of notes at Victoria May 31 and June 9, 1978; entered into force June 9, 1978.
30 UST 1916; TIAS 9300; 1153 UNTS 41.

POSTAL MATTERS

International express mail agreement, with detailed regulations. Signed at Victoria and Washington May 13 and June 15, 1992; entered into force September 21, 1992.
TIAS 11871.

TELECOMMUNICATION

Agreement between the United States and the United Kingdom relating to the reciprocal granting of authorizations to permit licensed amateur radio operators of either country to operate their stations in the other country. Exchange of notes at London November 26, 1965; applicable to Seychelles December 11, 1969.
16 UST 2047; TIAS 5941; 561 UNTS 193.

SEYCHELLES (Cont'd)

Agreement between the United States and the United Kingdom extending to certain territories the application of the agreement of November 26, 1965 relating to the reciprocal granting of authorizations to permit licensed amateur radio operators of either country to operate their stations in the other country. Exchange of notes at London December 11, 1969; entered into force December 11, 1969.
20 UST 4089; TIAS 6800; 732 UNTS 334.

TRADE-MARKS

Declaration by the United States and the United Kingdom affording reciprocal protection to trade-marks. Signed at London October 24, 1877; entered into force October 24, 1877.
20 Stat. 703; TS 138; 12 Bevans 198.

SIERRA LEONE

On April 27, 1961 Sierra Leone attained fully responsible status within the British Commonwealth (Sierra Leone Independence Act, 1961). By an exchange of letters, dated May 5, 1961, between the High Commissioner for the United Kingdom in Sierra Leone and the Minister of External Affairs of Sierra Leone, the Government of Sierra Leone agreed to assume, from April 27, 1961, all obligations and responsibilities of the United Kingdom which arise from any valid international instrument insofar as such instrument may be held to have application to Sierra Leone. Also, rights and benefits enjoyed by the Government of the United Kingdom by virtue of the application of any such international instrument to Sierra Leone are from April 27, 1961 enjoyed by the Government of Sierra Leone.

AGRICULTURAL COMMODITIES

Agricultural commodities agreement with exchange of notes. Signed at Freetown, January 29, 1965; entered into force January 29, 1965.
16 UST 71; TIAS 5762; 542 UNTS 87.

Amendments:
May 5, 1965 (16 UST 908; TIAS 5831; 549 UNTS 346).
March 10, 1966 (17 UST 187; TIAS 5970; 579 UNTS 338).
June 2, 1966 (17 UST 833; TIAS 6041; 593 UNTS 334).

Agricultural commodities agreement with annex. Signed at Freetown January 23, 1968; entered into force January 23, 1968.
19 UST 4516; TIAS 6444; 698 UNTS 43.

Related agreements:
April 8, 1969 (20 UST 664; TIAS 6673; 707 UNTS 233).
April 30, 1971 (22 UST 599; TIAS 7110; 792 UNTS 351).
November 30, 1971 (22 UST 1781; TIAS 7218).

Agricultural commodities agreement. Signed at Freetown August 18, 1977; entered into force August 18, 1977.
29 UST 1482; TIAS 8891.

Agricultural commodities agreement. Signed at Freetown August 31, 1978; entered into force August 31, 1978.
30 UST 672; TIAS 9210; 1150 UNTS 211.

Related agreements:
August 23, 1979 (31 UST 496; TIAS 9617).
September 5 and 6, 1979 (31 UST 503; TIAS 9617).
August 8, 1980 (32 UST 2310; TIAS 9840).
September 29, 1980 (32 UST 4194; TIAS 9939).
March 25, 1981 (33 UST 1505; TIAS 10125; 1307 UNTS 429).
August 17 and 18, 1981 (33 UST 1515; TIAS 10125; 1307 UNTS 437).
July 28, 1982 (TIAS 10516).
April 29, 1983 (TIAS 10968).
February 23, 1984 (TIAS 10968).

Agricultural commodities agreement. Signed at Freetown May 9, 1985; entered into force May 9, 1985.
NP

Agricultural commodities agreement. Signed at Freetown May 5, 1986; entered into force May 5, 1986.
NP

Amendment:
August 1, 1986 (NP).

Agricultural commodities agreement. Signed at Freetown June 10, 1987; entered into force June 10, 1987.
NP

Amendments:
August 18, 1987 (NP).
June 16, 1988 (NP).
September 27, 1988 (NP).

Agricultural commodities agreement. Signed at Freetown June 8, 1990; entered into force June 8, 1990.
NP

AVIATION

Arrangement between the United States and the United Kingdom relating to pilot licenses to operate civil aircraft. Exchange of notes at Washington March 28 and April 5, 1935; entered into force May 5, 1935.
49 Stat. 3731; EAS 77; 12 Bevans 513; 162 LNTS 59.

Agreement between the United States and the United Kingdom relating to air services. Signed at Bermuda February 11, 1946; entered into force February 11, 1946.
60 Stat. 1499; TIAS 1507; 12 Bevans 726; 3 UNTS 253.

CONSULS

Consular convention between the United States and the United Kingdom. Signed at Washington June 6, 1951; entered into force September 7, 1952.
3 UST 3426; TIAS 2494; 165 UNTS 121.

COPYRIGHT (See APPENDIX)

DEFENSE

Agreement concerning the provision of training related to defense articles under the United States International Military Education and Training (IMET) Program. Exchange of notes at Freetown April 1 and May 26, 1982; entered into force May 26, 1982.
34 UST 1115; TIAS 10397; 1566 UNTS 125.

Agreement regarding grants under the Foreign Assistance Act of 1961, as amended, and the furnishing of defense articles, related training and other defense services to the Government of Sierra Leone. Exchange of notes at Freetown May 3 and 19, 1999; entered into force May 19, 1999.
TIAS

ECONOMIC AND TECHNICAL COOPERATION

General agreement for a program of economic, technical and related assistance. Signed at Freetown May 5, 1961; entered into force May 5, 1961.
12 UST 547; TIAS 4752; 409 UNTS 193.

EMPLOYMENT

Agreement relating to the enmployment of dependents of official government employees. Exchange of notes at Freetown January 17 and February 24, 1997; entered into force February 24, 1997.
TIAS

EXTRADITION

Extradition treaty between the United States and the United Kingdom. Signed at London

SIERRA LEONE (Cont'd)

December 22, 1931; entered into force June 24, 1935.
47 Stat. 2122; TS 849; 12 Bevans 482; 163 LNTS 59.

FINANCE

Agreement relating to investment guaranties under section 413 (b)(4) of the Mutual Security Act of 1954, as amended. Exchange of notes at Freetown May 16 and 19, 1961; entered into force May 19, 1961.
12 UST 619; TIAS 4759; 409 UNTS 251.

Amendment:
December 28, 1962 and November 13, 1963 (14 UST 1667; TIAS 5470; 494 UNTS 324).

Agreement regarding the consolidation and rescheduling of certain debts owed to, guaranteed by or insured by the United States Government and its agencies, with annex. Signed at Freetown August 28, 1985; entered into force October 23, 1985.
NP

Agreement regarding the consolidation and rescheduling of certain debts owed to, guaranteed by or insured by the United States Government and its agencies, with annexes. Signed at Freetown August 21, 1987; entered into force November 5, 1987.
NP

Agreement regarding the consolidation and rescheduling or refinancing of certain debts owed to, guaranteed by, or insured by the United States Government and its agencies, with annexes. Signed at Freetown April 19, 1993; entered into force June 18, 1993.
NP

Agreement regarding the consolidation and rescheduling of certain debts owed to, guaranteed by or insured by the United States Government, with annexes. Signed at Freetown January 11, 1995; entered into force March 1, 1995.
NP

Agreement regarding the consolidation and rescheduling of certain debts owed to, guaranteed by or insured by the United States Government, with annexes. Signed at Freetown August 7, 1996; entered into force October 16, 1996.
NP

JUDICIAL PROCEDURE

Agreement to facilitate the conduct of litigation with international aspects in either country. Exchange of notes at Freetown March 31

and May 6, 1966; entered into force May 6, 1966.
17 UST 944; TIAS 6056; 594 UNTS 47.

PEACE CORPS

Agreement relating to the establishment of a Peace Corps program in Sierra Leone. Exchange of notes at Freetown December 29, 1961; entered into force December 29, 1961.
12 UST 3181; TIAS 4922; 434 UNTS 43.

POSTAL MATTERS

Parcel post convention. Signed at Freetown February 27 and at Washington April 16, 1930; operative May 1, 1930.
46 Stat. 2736; Post Office Department print; 109 LNTS 9.

International express mail agreement, with detailed regulations. Signed at Freetown and Washington May 31 and July 26, 1988; entered into force August 15, 1988.
TIAS 11591.

Postal money order agreement. Signed at Freetown and Washington March 29 and July 18, 1989; entered into force September 18, 1989.
TIAS 11683.

INTELPOST memorandum of understanding, with detailed regulations. Signed at Freetown and Washington June 5 and 19, 1995; entered into force August 1, 1995.
NP

PROPERTY

Convention between the United States and the United Kingdom relating to the tenure and disposition of real and personal property. Signed at Washington March 2, 1899; applicable to Sierra Leone February 9, 1901.
31 Stat. 1939; TS 146; 12 Bevans 246.

TELECOMMUNICATION

Agreement relating to the reciprocal granting of authorizations to permit licensed amateur radio operators of either country to operate their stations in the other country. Exchange of notes at Freetown August 14 and 16, 1965; entered into force August 16, 1965.
16 UST 1131; TIAS 5856; 579 UNTS 55.

Agreement relating to radio communications between amateur stations on behalf of third parties. Exchange of notes at Freetown October 23, 1985 and June 18, 1986; entered into force July 18, 1986.
TIAS 11358.

TRADE-MARKS

Declaration by the United States and the United Kingdom relating to reciprocal protection to trade-marks. Signed at London October 24, 1877; entered into force October 24, 1877.
20 Stat. 703; TS 138; 12 Bevans 198.

SINGAPORE

On August 9, 1965 Singapore became an independent and sovereign state. Article 13 of the Constitution and Malaysia (Singapore Amendment) Act, 1965 annexed to the Independence of Singapore agreement, 1965 reads in part as follows: "Any treaty, agreement or convention entered into before Singapore Day between the Yang di-Pertuan Agong or the Government of Malaysia and another country or countries, including those deemed to be so by Article 169 of the Constitution of Malaysia shall insofar as such instruments have application to Singapore, be deemed to be a treaty, agreement or convention between Singapore and that country or countries, and any decision taken by an international organization and accepted before Singapore Day by the Government of Malaysia shall insofar as that decision has application to Singapore be deemed to be a decision of an international organization of which Singapore is a member."

AVIATION

Arrangement between the United States and the United Kingdom relating to pilot licenses to operate civil aircraft. Exchange of notes at Washington March 28, and April 5, 1935; entered into force May 5, 1935.
49 Stat. 3731; EAS 77; 12 Bevans 513; 162 LNTS 59.

Memorandum of agreement relating to the provision of flight inspection services. Signed at Washington and Singapore August 16 and October 25, 1978; entered into force October 25, 1978; effective October 1, 1978.
30 UST 263; TIAS 9195; 1150 UNTS 263.

Agreement relating to the reciprocal acceptance of airworthiness certifications. Exchange of notes at Singapore August 21, 1981; entered into force August 21, 1981.
33 UST 2788; TIAS 10203; 1530 UNTS 3.

Air transport agreement, with annexes. Signed at Singapore April 8, 1997; entered into force April 8, 1997.
TIAS

CONSULS

Consular convention between the United States and the United Kingdom. Signed at Washington June 6, 1951; entered into force September 7, 1952.
3 UST 3426; TIAS 2494; 165 UNTS 121.

SINGAPORE (Cont'd)

COPYRIGHT (See also APPENDIX)

Agreement regarding the establishment of copyright relations, with enclosures. Exchange of letters at Washington April 16 and 27, 1987; entered into force April 27, 1987; effective May 18, 1987.
TIAS 11928.

DEFENSE

Agreement relating to the purchase by Malaya of military equipment, materials, and services from the United States. Exchange of notes at Washington June 30 and July 9, 1958; entered into force July 9, 1958.
9 UST 1235; TIAS 4108; 336 UNTS 79.

Agreement relating to the establishment of a United States Air Force management training assistance team in Singapore, with appendices. Exchange of letters at Singapore February 23 and 24, 1977; entered into force February 24, 1977.
29 UST 1474; TIAS 8889.

Memorandum of understanding for the exchange of individual personnel between the United States Army Western Command and the Republic of Singapore Armed Forces. Signed at Singapore January 5, 1981; entered into force January 5, 1981.
NP

Agreement concerning the provision of training related to defense articles under the United States International Military Education and Training (IMET) Program. Exchange of notes at Singapore May 12 and June 23, 1981; entered into force June 23, 1981.
33 UST 2034; TIAS 10166; 1529 UNTS 491.

Memorandum of understanding concerning exchange of service personnel between the United States Navy and Republic of Singapore Air Force. Signed at Singapore and Washington July 19 and September 1, 1982; entered into force September 1, 1982.
TIAS 10482; 1751 UNTS 115.

Agreement concerning general security of military information. Exchange of notes at Singapore June 25, 1982 and March 9, 1983; entered into force March 9, 1983.
TIAS 10819; 1590 UNTS 85.

Memorandum of understanding concerning configuration management of tactical command, control and communications standards, with annexes. Signed at Camp Smith, Hawaii February 22, 1991; entered into force February 22, 1991.
TIAS 12369.

Agreement on the status of Singapore personnel in the United States, with agreed minutes. Signed at Singapore December 3, 1993; entered into force December 3, 1993.
TIAS 12519.

Agreement concerning exchange of research and development information, with appendix. Signed at Washington December 4, 1995; entered into force December 4, 1995.
TIAS 12370.

Agreement concerning technology research and development projects, with annex. Signed at Washington May 2, 1998; entered into force May 2, 1998.
TIAS

ECONOMIC AND TECHNICAL COOPERATION

Economic cooperation agreement between the United States and the United Kingdom. Signed at London July 6, 1948; applicable to Singapore July 6, 1948.
62 Stat. 2596; TIAS 1795; 12 Bevans 874; 22 UNTS 263.

Amendments:
January 3, 1950 (1 UST 184; TIAS 2036; 86 UNTS 304).
May 25, 1951 (2 UST 1292; TIAS 2277; 99 UNTS 308).
February 25, 1953 (4 UST 1528; TIAS 2815; 172 UNTS 332).

EXTRADITION

Extradition treaty between the United States and the United Kingdom. Signed at London December 22, 1931; entered into force June 24, 1935.
47 Stat. 2122; TS 849; 12 Bevans 482; 163 LNTS 59.

Agreement confirming the continuance in force between the United States and Singapore of the December 22, 1931 extradition treaty between the United States and the United Kingdom. Exchange of notes at Singapore April 23 and June 10, 1969; entered into force June 10, 1969.
20 UST 2764; TIAS 6744; 723 UNTS 201.

FINANCE

Agreement relating to investment guaranties. Exchange of notes at Singapore March 25, 1966; entered into force March 25, 1966.
17 UST 534; TIAS 5999; 580 UNTS 221.

POSTAL MATTERS

Parcel post convention. Signed at Kuala Lumpur January 21 and at Washington March 22, 1935; entered into force April 1, 1935.
49 Stat. 3133; Post Office Department print; 161 LNTS 41.

International express mail agreement, with detailed regulations. Signed at Singapore and Washington January 5 and 10, 1979; entered into force February 9, 1979; effective January 1, 1979.
30 UST 3383; TIAS 9396; 1180 UNTS 109.

Memorandum of understanding concerning the operation of the INTELPOST field trial, with details of implementation. Signed at Singapore and Washington November 26, 1986 and February 5, 1987; entered into force February 5, 1987; effective December 1, 1986.
TIAS 11307.

PROPERTY

Convention between the United States and the United Kingdom relating to tenure and disposition of real and personal property.[1] Signed at Washington March 2, 1899; entered into force August 7, 1900.
31 Stat. 1939; TS 146; 12 Bevans 246.

NOTE:
[1] Notification given on February 9, 1901 of application to the Straits Settlements.

SHIPPING

Agreement relating to jurisdiction over vessels utilizing the Louisiana Offshore Oil Port. Exchange of notes at Singapore September 1, 1983 and January 16, 1984; entered into force January 17, 1984.
TIAS 10926.

SOCIAL SECURITY

Agreement concerning United States participation on a limited voluntary basis in the Central Provident Fund Act for certain employees of the United States Government in Singapore. Exchange of notes at Singapore September 8 and 9, 1975; entered into force September 9, 1975.
26 UST 2734; TIAS 8190; 1052 UNTS 297.

TAXATION

Agreement concerning reciprocal exemption from income tax of income derived from the international operation of ships and aircraft. Exchange of notes at Singapore July 5 and 28, 1988; entered into force July 28, 1988.
TIAS 11658.

SINGAPORE (Cont'd)

TRADE AND COMMERCE

Agreement relating to trade in cotton, wool and man-made fiber textiles and textile products, with annexes. Exchange of notes at Singapore May 30 and June 5, 1986; entered into force June 5, 1986; effective January 1, 1986.
NP

Amendment and extension:
March 6, April 1 and July 22, 1991 (NP).

TRADE-MARKS

Declaration by the United States and the United Kingdom relating to reciprocal protection to trade-marks. Signed at London October 24, 1877; entered into force October 24, 1877. 20 Stat. 703; TS 138; 12 Bevans 198.

VISAS

Agreement relating to visas. Exchange of notes at London October 15 and 22, 1954.

Agreement continuing in force the 1954 agreement with respect to the Federation of Malaya. Exchange of letters at Kuala Lumpur March 5 and 12, 1958.

SLOVAK REPUBLIC

For agreements prior to the independence of the Slovak Republic, see CZECHO-SLOVAKIA.

ATOMIC ENERGY

Renewal arrangement for the exchange of technical information and cooperation in nuclear safety matters, with addenda. Signed at Vienna September 21, 2000; entered into force September 21, 2000.
TIAS

COPYRIGHT (See APPENDIX)

DEFENSE

Agreement concerning security measures for the protection of classified military information. Signed at Washington April 11, 1995; entered into force April 11, 1995.
TIAS 12246.

Acquisition and cross-servicing agreement, with annex. Signed at Bratislava December 15, 1998; entered into force December 15, 1998.

EDUCATION

Agreement for the establishment of the J. William Fulbright Commission for Educational Exchange in the Slovak Republic, with memorandum of understanding. Signed at Bratislava September 22, 1994; entered into force September 22, 1994.
TIAS 12567.

EMPLOYMENT

Agreement relating to the employment of dependents of official government employees. Exchange of notes at Bratislava April 8, 1994, February 17 and July 12, 1995; entered into force July 12, 1995.
TIAS 12677.

NORTH ATLANTIC TREATY

Agreement to treat the agreement of June 19, 1995, among the States Parties to the North Atlantic Treaty and other States participating in the Partnership for Peace regarding the status of their forces as binding between the United States and Slovakia. Exchange of notes at Bratislava August 2 and 4, 1995; entered into force August 4, 1995.
TIAS

POSTAL MATTERS

International express mail agreement, with detailed regulations. Signed at Bratislava and Washington June 24 and 27, 1994; entered into force August 1, 1994.
NP

SCIENTIFIC COOPERATION

Memorandum of understanding on science and engineering cooperation, with annexes. Signed at Bratislava July 14, 1994; entered into force July 14, 1994.
TIAS 12557.

TAXATION

Convention for the avoidance of double taxation and the prevention of fiscal evasion with respect to taxes on income and capital.[1] Signed at Bratislava October 8, 1993; entered into force December 30, 1993.
TIAS

NOTE:
[1] With understanding.

TRADE AND COMMERCE

Agreement relating to trade in textiles and textile products, with attachment. Exchange of notes at Bratislava August 6 and October 6, 1993; entered into force October 6, 1993; effective June 1, 1993.
NP

Amendment:
April 6 and 29, 1994 (NP).

SLOVENIA

For agreements prior to the independence of Slovenia, see YUGOSLAVIA.

COPYRIGHT (See APPENDIX)

CULTURAL PROPERTY

Agreement on the protection and preservation of certain cultural properties. Signed at Washington May 8, 1996; entered into force June 23, 1997.
TIAS

DEFENSE

Agreement concerning the provision of training related to defense articles under the United States International Military Education and Training (IMET) Program. Exchange of notes at Ljubljana July 29 and August 6, 1993; entered into force August 6, 1993.
NP

Security agreement concerning security measures for the protection of classified military information. Signed at Washington May 8, 1996; entered into force June 27, 1997.
TIAS

EDUCATION

Memorandum of understanding concerning the exchange of graduate students, post-doctoral researchers and lecturers under the auspices of the Fulbright Program. Signed at Ljubljana December 8, 1993; entered into force January 20, 1999.
TIAS

SLOVENIA (Cont'd)

EMPLOYMENT

Agreement relating to the employment of dependents of official government employees. Exchange of notes at Ljubljana April 30 and May 8, 1998; entered into force June 10, 1998. TIAS

FINANCE

Investment incentive agreement. Signed at Washington April 26, 1994; entered into force September 8, 1994. TIAS 12178.

POSTAL MATTERS

International express mail agreement, with detailed regulations. Signed at Ljubljana and Washington January 27 and March 22, 1993; entered into force May 1, 1993. TIAS 11918.

Postal money order agreement. Signed at Washington and Ljubljana September 1 and 21, 1995; entered into force February 1, 1996. NP .

SCIENTIFIC COOPERATION

Agreement for scientific and technological cooperation, with annexes. Signed at Ljubljana June 21, 1999; entered into force December 17, 1999. TIAS

WEAPONS

Agreement concerning cooperation in the prevention of the proliferation of weapons of mass destruction. Signed at Ljubljana June 21, 1999; entered into force June 26, 2000. TIAS

SOLOMON ISLANDS

On July 7, 1978, Solomon Islands became an independent state. In a note dated July 7, 1978 to the Secretary General of the United Nations, the Prime Minister made a statement reading in part as follows:

"I have the honour to inform you that Solomon Islands is now an independent nation ready to participate with other nations in fulfilling obligations under international law with respect to treaties to which this Government succeeded upon Independence. However, it is necessary to examine in depth such treaties to ascertain whether or not under customary international law any may have lapsed. Until this has been done the Government of Solomon Islands wish—

(a) that it be presumed that each treaty has been legally succeeded to by Solomon Islands; and

(b) that future action be based on the presumption in (a) above.

"You will be notified in due course of those treaties this Government regards as having lapsed and those treaties which this Government wishes to terminate. Notice of lapse or termination in an appropriate form will also be given to the country or countries that is or are party to those treaties."

COPYRIGHT (See APPENDIX)

DEFENSE

Agreement concerning the provision of training related to defense articles under the United States International Military Education and Training (IMET) Program. Exchange of notes at Port Moresby and Honiara June 7 and August 18, 1983; entered into force August 18, 1983. TIAS 10759.

Agreement concerning the status of members of the United States Forces in Solomon Islands. Signed at Honiara July 3, 1991; entered into force July 3, 1991. TIAS

ECONOMIC AND TECHNICAL COOPERATION

Economic cooperation agreement between the United States and the United Kingdom. Signed at London July 6, 1948; applicable to Solomon Islands July 6, 1948. 62 Stat. 2596; TIAS 1795; 12 Bevans 874; 22 UNTS 263.

Amendments:
January 3, 1950 (1 UST 184; TIAS 2036; 86 UNTS 304).
May 25, 1951 (2 UST 1292; TIAS 2277; 99 UNTS 308).
February 25, 1953 (4 UST 1528; TIAS 2815; 172 UNTS 332).

EXTRADITION

Extradition treaty between the United States and the United Kingdom, with protocol of signature and exchange of notes. Signed at London June 8, 1972; entered into force January 21, 1977. 28 UST 277; TIAS 8468.

MUTUAL SECURITY

Agreement between the United States and the United Kingdom relating to the assurances required under the Mutual Security Act of 1951. Exchange of notes at London January 8, 1952; applicable to Solomon Islands January 8, 1952. 3 UST 4665; TIAS 2622; 126 UNTS 307.

PEACE CORPS

Agreement concerning the program of the Peace Corps in the Solomon Islands. Signed at Honiara November 6, 1998; entered into force November 6, 1998. TIAS

POSTAL MATTERS

International express mail agreement, with detailed regulations. Signed at Honiara and Washington April 19 and June 27, 1991; entered into force August 1, 1991. TIAS 11808.

TELECOMMUNICATION

Agreement between the United States and the United Kingdom relating to the reciprocal granting of authorizations to permit licensed amateur radio operators of either country to operate their stations in the other country. Exchange of notes at London November 26, 1965; applicable to the Solomon Islands December 11, 1969. 16 UST 2047; TIAS 5941; 561 UNTS 193.

Agreement between the United States and the United Kingdom extending to certain territories the application of the agreement relating to the reciprocal granting of authorizations to permit licensed amateur radio operators of either country to operate their stations in the other country. Exchange of notes at London December 11, 1969; entered into force December 11, 1969. 20 UST 4089; TIAS 6800; 732 UNTS 334.

SOMALIA

AGRICULTURAL COMMODITIES

Agricultural commodities agreement with annex. Signed at Washington March 15, 1968; entered into force March 15, 1968. 19 UST 4698; TIAS 6465; 698 UNTS 95.

Agricultural commodities agreement. Signed at Mogadiscio March 20, 1978; entered into force March 20, 1978. 30 UST 827; TIAS 9222.

SOMALIA (Cont'd)

Amendment:
July 18 and August 10, 1978 (30 UST 2351; TIAS 9341; 1171 UNTS 370).

Related agreements:
July 11, 1979 (TIAS 10454).
June 25, 1980 (32 UST 2245; TIAS 9833).
August 14 and 17, 1980 (32 UST 2245; TIAS 9833).
January 12, 1981 (33 UST 828; TIAS 10065; 1268 UNTS 65).
June 17, 1982 (TIAS 10429).
January 30, 1983 (TIAS 10637; 1578 UNTS 29).
February 29, 1984 (TIAS 10969).

Agricultural commodities agreement. Signed at Mogadishu March 24, 1985; entered into force March 24, 1985.
NP

Related agreements:
February 27, 1986 (NP).
August 9, 1987 (NP).

DEFENSE

Agreement concerning the furnishing of defense articles and services to Somalia. Exchange of notes at Mogadiscio March 22 and 23 and April 19 and 29, 1978; entered into force April 29, 1978.
32 UST 1683; TIAS 9794.

Agreement concerning the provision of training related to defense articles under the United States International Military Education and Training (IMET) Program. Exchange of notes at Mogadishu April 5 and June 6, 1981; entered into force June 6, 1981.
33 UST 2041; TIAS 10167; 1529 UNTS 477.

ECONOMIC AND TECHNICAL COOPERATION

Agreement on economic and technical cooperation. Exchange of notes at Mogadishu June 14, October 12 and 13, 1981; entered into force October 13, 1981.
33 UST 3975; TIAS 10276; 1549 UNTS 325.

Agency for International Development:
June 7, 1976 (29 UST 998; TIAS 8859; 1115 UNTS 59).
December 18, 1977 (29 UST 5297; TIAS 9109).

FINANCE

Agreement relating to investment guaranties. Exchange of notes at Mogadiscio November 27, 1962 and January 8, 1964; entered into force January 8, 1964.
15 UST 6; TIAS 5512; 505 UNTS 165.

Agreement regarding the consolidation and rescheduling of certain debts owed to, guaranteed by or insured by the United States Government and its agencies, with annexes. Signed at Washington May 9, 1985; entered into force June 12, 1985.
NP

Agreement regarding the consolidation and rescheduling of certain debts owed to, guaranteed by or insured by the United States Government and its agencies, with annexes. Signed at Mogadishu January 25, 1988; entered into force February 26, 1988.
NP

MAPPING

Agreement concerning mapping, charting and geodesy cooperation, with annex. Signed at Washington and Mogadishu December 31, 1984; entered into force December 31, 1984.
TIAS 11224.

PEACE CORPS

Agreement relating to the establishment of a Peace Corps program in the Somali Republic. Exchange of notes at Mogadiscio March 29 and April 17, 1962; entered into force April 17, 1962.
13 UST 499; TIAS 5016; 436 UNTS 107.

POSTAL MATTERS

International express mail agreement, with detailed regulations. Signed at Mogadishu and Washington June 28 and July 26, 1988; entered into force August 15, 1988.
TIAS 11592.

SOUTH AFRICA

ATOMIC ENERGY

Agreement for cooperation concerning peaceful uses of nuclear energy, with annex and agreed minute. Signed at Pretoria August 25, 1995; entered into force December 4, 1997.
TIAS 12685.

Arrangement for the exchange of technical information and cooperation in nuclear safety matters, with addenda. Signed at Rockville March 30, 2000; entered into force March 30, 2000.
TIAS

AVIATION

Air navigation arrangement. Exchange of notes at Pretoria March 17 and September 20, 1933; entered into force September 20, 1933.
48 Stat. 1828; EAS 54; 11 Bevans 462; 148 LNTS 189.

Arrangement relating to pilot licenses to operate civil aircraft. Exchange of notes at Pretoria March 17 and September 20, 1933; entered into force September 20, 1933.
48 Stat. 1837; EAS 55; 11 Bevans 469; 148 LNTS 203.

Arrangement relating to certificates of airworthiness for imported aircraft. Exchange of notes at Pretoria October 29, 1954, and February 22, 1955; entered into force February 22, 1955.
6 UST 657; TIAS 3200; 247 UNTS 247.

Amendment:
June 7 and October 8, 1984 (TIAS 11024).

Agreement on aviation security. Exchanges of notes at Pretoria August 19, October 3, 11 and 30, 1991; entered into force October 30, 1991.
TIAS 11788.

Air transport agreement, with annex. Signed at Washington July 23, 1996; entered into force July 23, 1996.
TIAS

Memorandum of understanding concerning charter air transportation. Signed at Washington July 23, 1996; entered into force July 23, 1996.
TIAS

Memorandum of cooperation concerning mutual cooperation in the area of air navigation and air traffic control. Signed at Washington and Pretoria May 15 and 20, 1998; entered into force May 20, 1998.
TIAS

CONSERVATION

Terms of reference of the Conservation, Environment and Water Committee of the South Africa-United States Binational Commission. Signed at Pretoria December 5, 1995; entered into force December 5, 1995.
TIAS 12706.

CONSULS

Convention to regulate commerce (article IV) between the United States and the United Kingdom. Signed at London July 3, 1815; effective July 3, 1815.
8 Stat. 228; TS 110; 12 Bevans 49.

SOUTH AFRICA (Cont'd)

COPYRIGHT (See APPENDIX)

DEFENSE

Agreement relating to mutual defense assistance. Exchange of notes at Washington November 9, 1951; entered into force November 9, 1951.
3 UST 2565; TIAS 2424; 160 UNTS 41.

Agreement concerning the provision of training under the United States International Military Education and Training (IMET) Program. Exchange of notes at Pretoria June 14 and July 11, 1994; entered into force July 11, 1994.
NP

Agreement regarding grants under the Foreign Assistance Act of 1961, as amended, and the furnishing of defense articles, related training and other defense services from the United States to South Africa. Exchange of notes at Pretoria November 8, 1994 and October 24, 1995; entered into force October 24, 1995.
TIAS

Agreement concerning cooperation on defense trade controls. Signed at Pretoria January 24, 1997; entered into force January 24, 1997.
TIAS

Agreement concerning security measures for the protection of classified military information. Signed at Pretoria November 20, 1998; entered into force November 20, 1998.
TIAS

Agreement regarding the status of military personnel and civilian employees of the U.S. Department of Defense who may be present in the Republic of South Africa in connection with mutually agreed exercises and activities. Exchange of notes at Pretoria April 9 and June 10, 1999; entered into force June 10, 1999.
NP

ECONOMIC AND TECHNICAL COOPERATION

Economic, technical and related assistance agreement. Signed at Pretoria December 5, 1995; entered into force December 5, 1995.
TIAS 12707.

Agency for International Development:
September 26, 1995 (NP).
September 28, 1995 (NP).
September 27, 1996 (NP).
September 27, 1996 (NP).
July 31, 1997 (NP).
July 31, 1997 (NP).
July 31 and August 22, 1997 (NP).
September 29, 1997 (NP).
September 30, 1998 (NP).
September 30, 1998 (NP).

EDUCATION

Agreement concerning the establishment of the South African-United States commission for educational exchange. Signed at Cape Town February 17, 1997; entered into force February 17, 1997.
TIAS

ENVIRONMENTAL COOPERATION

Agreement for cooperation in the Global Learning and Observations to Benefit the Environment (GLOBE) Program, with annexes. Signed at Cape Town February 17, 1997; entered into force February 17, 1997.
TIAS

EXTRADITION

Treaty relating to the reciprocal extradition of criminals.[1] Signed at Washington December 18, 1947; entered into force April 30, 1951.
2 UST 884; TIAS 2243; 148 UNTS 85.

NOTE:
   [1] Applicable to all territories.

FINANCE

Investment incentive agreement. Signed at Cape Town November 30, 1993; entered into force February 10, 1994.
TIAS 12169.

HEALTH

Memorandum of understanding for cooperation in the fields of public health and biomedical research. Signed at Washington May 23, 2000; entered into force May 23, 2000.
TIAS

LEND-LEASE

Agreement placing all forms of mutual aid reciprocally on a cash basis. Exchange of notes at Washington April 17, 1945; entered into force April 17, 1945.
60 Stat. 1576; TIAS 1511; 11 Bevans 486; 90 UNTS 267.

Agreement relating to settlement for lend-lease, reciprocal aid, surplus war property and claims. Exchange of notes at Washington March 21, 1947; entered into force March 21, 1947.
61 Stat. 2640; TIAS 1593; 11 Bevans 493; 16 UNTS 47.

PACIFIC SETTLEMENT OF DISPUTES

Treaty to amend in their application to the Union of South Africa certain provisions of the treaty for the advancement of peace between the United States and the United Kingdom signed September 15, 1914. Signed at Washington April 2, 1940; entered into force March 11, 1941.
55 Stat. 1130; TS 966; 11 Bevans 476.

POSTAL MATTERS

Parcel post convention. Signed at Cape Town April 17 and at Washington June 20, 1919; entered into force April 12, 1919.
41 Stat. 1656; Post Office Department print.

International express mail agreement, with detailed regulations. Signed at Pretoria and Washington May 25 and June 29, 1981; entered into force July 1, 1981.
33 UST 2434; TIAS 10190; 1530 UNTS 31.

Insured postal parcels agreement. Signed at Pretoria and Washington June 19 and August 5, 1992; entered into force October 1, 1992.
TIAS 11869.

PROPERTY

The following conventions between the United States and the United Kingdom may be considered in force with respect to the Republic of South Africa by virtue of the adherence by the United Kingdom for the Cape Colony on February 9, 1901, and for the Orange River Colony and the Transvaal on July 24, 1902, except for Natal and Namibia:

Convention relating to tenure and disposition of real and personal property. Signed at Washington March 2, 1899.
31 Stat. 1939; TS 146; 12 Bevans 246.

Supplementary convention extending the time within which notifications may be given of the accession of British colonies or foreign possessions to the convention of March 2, 1899. Signed at Washington January 13, 1902.
32 Stat. 1914; TS 402; 12 Bevans 261.

PUBLICATIONS

Agreement relating to the exchange of official publications. Exchange of notes at Pretoria November 16, 1949; entered into force November 16, 1949.
64 Stat. (3) B109; TIAS 2038; 11 Bevans 513; 73 UNTS 97.

SOUTH AFRICA (Cont'd)

REMOTE SENSING

Memorandum of understanding relating to the operation of the Landsat system, with annex. Signed at Washington and Pretoria September 19 and October 19, 1983; entered into force October 19, 1983.
TIAS 10797.

SEISMIC OBSERVATIONS

Agreement for cooperation regarding an integrated, real-time global seismic data acquisition system. Signed at Pretoria December 1, 1987; entered into force December 1, 1987.
TIAS 11560.

TAXATION

Convention with respect to taxes on the estates of deceased persons. Signed at Cape Town April 10, 1947; entered into force July 15, 1952.
3 UST 3792; TIAS 2509; 167 UNTS 211.

Protocol supplementing the estate tax convention of April 10, 1947. Signed at Pretoria July 14, 1950; entered into force July 15, 1952.
3 UST 3792; TIAS 2509; 167 UNTS 228.

Convention for the avoidance of double taxation and the prevention of fiscal evasion with respect to taxes on income and capital gains. Signed at Cape Town February 17, 1997; entered into force December 28, 1997.
TIAS

TELECOMMUNICATION

Agreement relating to the reciprocal granting of authorizations to permit licensed amateur radio operators of either country to operate their stations in the other country. Exchange of notes at Pretoria March 28 and May 1, 1985; entered into force May 1, 1985.
TIAS 11332.

Arrangement relating to radio communications between amateur stations on behalf of third parties. Exchange of notes at Pretoria September 13 and October 4, 1993; entered into force October 4, 1993.
TIAS 12509.

TRADE AND COMMERCE

Agreement relating to postwar economic settlements. Exchange of notes at Washington April 17, 1945; entered into force April 17, 1945.
60 Stat. 1579; TIAS 1512; 11 Bevans 489; 90 UNTS 275.

VISAS

Agreement relating to the reciprocal issuance of passport visas to nonimmigrants.[1] Exchange of notes at Cape Town March 28 and April 3, 1956; entered into force May 1, 1956.
7 UST 631; TIAS 3544; 249 UNTS 395.

Amendment:
March 31, 1958 (9 UST 1023; TIAS 4076; 300 UNTS 382).

NOTE:
[1] Applied to Namibia.

SOUTH PACIFIC COMMISSION

TAXATION

Agreement relating to a procedure for United States income tax reimbursement. Exchange of notes at Suva and Noumea December 21, 1981 and April 28, 1982; entered into force April 28, 1982; effective January 1, 1982.
34 UST 979; TIAS 10384.

SOUTH PACIFIC FORUM FISHERIES AGENCY

ECONOMIC AND TECHNICAL COOPERATION

Agreement concerning the economic development of the South Pacific region. Signed at Port Moresby April 2, 1987; entered into force June 15, 1988.
TIAS 11296.

SPAIN

ATOMIC ENERGY

Arrangement for the exchange of technical information and cooperation in nuclear safety matters, with patent addendum. Signed at Vienna September 27, 1989; entered into force September 27, 1989.
TIAS 12233.

Agreement in the field of radioactive waste management. Signed at Madrid December 16, 1992; entered into force December 16, 1992.
TIAS

Arrangement for the exchange of technical information and cooperation in nuclear safety matters, with addenda. Signed at Rockville May 11, 1995; entered into force May 11, 1995.
TIAS 12644.

Arrangement for the exchange of technical information and cooperation in nuclear safety matters, with addenda. Signed at Vienna September 19, 2000; entered into force September 19, 2000.
TIAS

AVIATION

Arrangement relating to certificates of airworthiness for imported aircraft. Exchange of notes at Madrid September 23, 1957; entered into force September 23, 1957.
8 UST 1549; TIAS 3906; 290 UNTS 261.

Amendment:
September 18 and October 13, 1978 (30 UST 750; TIAS 9217).

Air transport agreement. Signed at Madrid February 20, 1973; entered into force provisionally February 20, 1973; definitively August 3, 1973.
24 UST 2102; TIAS 7725.

Amendments:
May 31, 1989 (TIAS 11672; 1597 UNTS 466).
November 27, 1991 (TIAS 11946; 1722 UNTS 304).

Related agreement:
February 20, March 31 and April 7, 1987 (TIAS 11297).

Memorandum of agreement relating to technical assistance to Spain in civil aviation activities. Signed at Washington and Madrid June 30 and July 22, 1982; entered into force July 22, 1982.
TIAS 10547.

Agreement for the promotion of aviation safety. Signed at Washington September 23, 1999; entered into force September 23, 1999.
TIAS

CLAIMS

Arrangement relating to claims. Exchange of notes at Washington August 24, 1927, and May 13 and June 20, 1929; entered into force June 20, 1929.
47 Stat. 2641; EAS 18; 11 Bevans 697; 120 LNTS 401.

Agreement regarding claims arising from Exercise CRISEX. Signed at Madrid November 13, 1979; entered into force November 13, 1979.
31 UST 5876; TIAS 9690.

COMMERCE

Treaty of friendship and general relations.[1][2] Signed at Madrid July 3, 1902; entered into force April 14, 1903.
33 Stat. 2105; TS 422; 11 Bevans 628.

SPAIN (Cont'd)

NOTES:

[1] Applicable to all territories.

[2] Notice of termination was given by the United States of articles XXIII and XXIV, effective July 1, 1916, in accordance with the Seamen's Act (38 Stat. 1164). The notice was accepted by the Spanish Government with the understanding that only such provisions of these articles as were in conflict with the act should be terminated, and all other provisions, especially those concerning the arrest, detention, and imprisonment of deserters from war vessels, should continue in force; also on the understanding that United States consuls in Spain should not exercise the powers of which Spanish consuls in the United States were deprived by the provisions of the Act.

CONSULS (See COMMERCE)

COPYRIGHT (See also APPENDIX)

Copyright agreement.[1] Exchange of notes at Washington July 6 and 15, 1895; entered into force July 10, 1895.
TS 342-A; 11 Bevans 597.

Agreement relating to the restoration of the copyright agreement of July 6 and 15, 1895. Exchange of notes at Madrid January 29 and November 18 and 26, 1902; entered into force November 26, 1902.
TS 474; 11 Bevans 639.

NOTE:

[1] Applicable to all Spanish territories.

CUSTOMS

Agreement regarding mutual assistance between customs services. Signed at Madrid July 3, 1990; entered into force February 28, 1993.
TIAS 12120; 1717 UNTS 223.

DEFENSE

Mutual defense assistance agreement with tax relief annex and interpretative note in regard to tax relief annex. Signed at Madrid September 26, 1953; entered into force September 26, 1953.
4 UST 1876; TIAS 2849; 207 UNTS 61.

Agreement confirming the bilateral arrangements for a facilities assistance program pursuant to the mutual defense assistance agreement of September 26, 1953. Exchange of notes at Madrid April 9 and May 11 and 19, 1954; entered into force May 19, 1954.
5 UST 2377; TIAS 3098; 235 UNTS 87.

Supplementary agreements:
May 25, 1955 (6 UST 1155; TIAS 3257; 251 UNTS 416).
September 17, 1956 (7 UST 2777; TIAS 3658; 278 UNTS 283).

Agreement relating to offshore procurement in Spain, with memorandum of understanding and standard contract attached. Exchange of notes at San Sebastian July 30, 1954; entered into force July 30, 1954.
5 UST 2328; TIAS 3094; 235 UNTS 45.

Amendments:
October 26, 1954 (5 UST 2357; TIAS 3094; 235 UNTS 66).
October 29 and November 11, 1958 (10 UST 344; TIAS 4196; 341 UNTS 400).

Agreement relating to the disposition of military equipment and materials furnished by the United States under the mutual defense assistance agreement. Exchange of notes at Madrid November 27, 1956; entered into force November 27, 1956.
7 UST 3392; TIAS 3710; 265 UNTS 374.

Agreement concerning the grant of defense articles and services under the military assistance program. Exchange of notes at Madrid August 30, 1979; entered into force August 30, 1979.
30 UST 7238; TIAS 9581; 1182 UNTS 161.

Master data exchange agreement for the mutual development of weapons systems. Signed at Washington June 19, 1980; entered into force June 19, 1980.
TIAS 12376.

Cover agreement on the territorial command net, with annexes. Signed at Madrid July 24, 1980; entered into force July 24, 1980.
TIAS 10880; 1577 UNTS 297.

Agreement concerning the grant of defense articles and services under the military assistance program. Exchange of notes at Madrid August 28 and 29, 1981; entered into force August 29, 1981.
33 UST 3752; TIAS 10257; 1541 UNTS 121.

Agreement on friendship, defense and cooperation, with complementary agreements,[1] and exchanges of notes. Signed at Madrid July 2, 1982; entered into force May 14, 1983.
TIAS 10589.

Memorandum of understanding pertaining to installation of satellite ground terminal at Rota, Spain. Signed at Rota November 3, 1982; entered into force November 3, 1982.
TIAS 10566; 1871 UNTS 381.

General security of military information agreement, with protocol on security procedures for industrial operations with appendices. Signed at Washington March 12, 1984; entered into force March 12, 1984.
TIAS 10962.

Agreement on defense cooperation, with annexes and related letters. Signed at Madrid December 1, 1988; entered into force May 4, 1989.
TIAS

Memorandum of understanding concerning lease of equipment and exchange of technical information for the XXV Olympiad. Signed at Madrid October 19, 1990; entered into force October 19, 1990.
TIAS

Memorandum of understanding on the exchange of service personnel between the United States Navy and the Spanish Air Force and on the general conditions which will apply to the exchange of such personnel. Signed at Washington and Madrid July 20 and August 13, 1991; entered into force August 13, 1991.
NP

Memorandum of understanding on the exchange of service personnel between the United States Navy and the Spanish Navy and on the general conditions which will apply to the exchange of such personnel. Signed at Washington and Madrid August 5 and September 5, 1991; entered into force September 5, 1991.
NP

Memorandum of understanding regarding the exchange of scientists and engineers, with annexes. Signed at Madrid September 16, 1993; entered into force September 16, 1993.
NP

Acquisition and cross-servicing agreement. Signed at Madrid and Patch Barracks (Germany) May 6 and 19, 1999; entered into force May 19, 1999.
TIAS

NOTE:

[1] Complementary agreement seven concerns scientific, technological, cultural, educational and economic cooperation.

ECONOMIC AND TECHNICAL COOPERATION [1]

Economic aid agreement. Signed at Madrid September 26, 1953; entered into force September 26, 1953.
4 UST 1903; TIAS 2851; 207 UNTS 93.

Agreement relating to the waiver of the counterpart deposit requirement for certain categories of AID financed commodities. Exchange of notes at Madrid May 22, 1962; entered into force May 22, 1962.
13 UST 1830; TIAS 5131; 458 UNTS 304.

NOTE:

[1] See also complementary agreement seven to the agreement on friendship, defense and cooperation of July 2, 1982 (TIAS 10589).

EDUCATION [1]

Agreement for educational, cultural and scientific cooperation. Signed at Madrid October 27, 1994; entered into force April 26, 1995.
TIAS 12577; 1872 UNTS 287.

SPAIN (Cont'd)

NOTE:

[1] See also complementary agreement seven to the agreement on friendship, defense and cooperation of July 2, 1982 (TIAS 10589).

EMPLOYMENT

Agreement concerning the free pursuit of gainful employment by dependents of employees of diplomatic missions, consular posts or missions to international organizations, with exchange of notes. Signed at Madrid July 25, 1990; entered into force April 1, 1991.
TIAS

ENERGY

Memorandum of understanding for cooperation in energy research and development. Signed at Washington June 6, 1986; entered into force June 6, 1986.
TIAS 12128.

ENVIRONMENTAL COOPERATION

Agreement for cooperation in the Global Learning and Observations to Benefit the Environment (GLOBE) Program, with appendices. Signed at Madrid May 5, 1998; entered into force May 5, 1998.
TIAS

EXTRADITION

Treaty on extradition.[1] Signed at Madrid May 29, 1970; entered into force June 16, 1971.
22 UST 737; TIAS 7136; 796 UNTS 245.

Supplementary treaty on extradition. Signed at Madrid January 25, 1975; entered into force June 2, 1978.
29 UST 2283; TIAS 8938.

Second supplementary treaty on extradition. Signed at Madrid February 9, 1988; entered into force July 2, 1993.
TIAS

Third supplementary extradition treaty. Signed at Madrid March 12, 1996; entered into force July 25, 1999.
TIAS

NOTE:

[1] Applicable to all territories.

FINANCE

Agreement relating to the restitution of monetary gold looted by Germany. Exchange of notes at Madrid April 30 and May 3, 1948; entered into force May 3, 1948.
62 Stat. 4071; TIAS 2123; 11 Bevans 708; 132 UNTS 155.

FRIENDSHIP AND COOPERATION (See under DEFENSE)

INSULAR POSSESSIONS

Treaty for the cession to the United States of any and all islands of the Philippine Archipelago lying outside of the lines described in article III of the treaty of peace of December 10, 1898. Signed at Washington November 7, 1900; entered into force March 23, 1901.
31 Stat. 1942; TS 345; 11 Bevans 623.

JUDICIAL ASSISTANCE

Agreement exempting from authentication signatures attached to letters rogatory exchanged between Puerto Rico, the Philippine Islands, and Spain. Exchange of notes at Washington August 5, and at Manchester, Massachusetts, August 7, 1901, and declaration signed at Washington November 7, 1901; entered into force November 28, 1901.
TS 395; 11 Bevans 625.

Agreement on procedures for mutual assistance in connection with the Lockheed Aircraft Corporation matter, with annex. Signed at Washington July 14, 1976; entered into force July 14, 1976.
27 UST 3409; TIAS 8370.

Related agreement:
June 7 and July 22, 1977 (28 UST 7494; TIAS 8725).

Treaty on mutual legal assistance in criminal matters, with attachments. Signed at Washington November 20, 1990; entered into force June 30, 1993.
TIAS   ; 1730 UNTS 113.

MAPPING

Agreement concerning technical cooperation in cartography and geodesy. Signed at Madrid and Washington September 4 and October 27, 1986; entered into force October 27, 1986.
TIAS 11408.

Basic exchange and technical cooperation agreement for mapping, nautical and aeronautical charting, geodesy and geophysics, digital data and related materials, with appendix

and annexes. Signed at Madrid June 29, 1992; entered into force June 29, 1992.
NP

NARCOTIC DRUGS

Arrangement for the direct exchange of certain information regarding the traffic in narcotic drugs. Exchange of notes at Madrid February 3, March 10, and May 24, 1928; entered into force May 24, 1928.
11 Bevans 684.

Agreement on cooperation to reduce the demand for narcotic drugs. Signed at Madrid November 25, 1991; entered into force May 7, 1993.
TIAS 12443.

PACIFIC SETTLEMENT OF DISPUTES

Treaty for the settlement of disputes between the two countries. Signed at Washington September 15, 1914; entered into force December 21, 1914.
38 Stat. 1862; TS 605; 11 Bevans 661; 89 LNTS 427.

PATENTS

Agreement to facilitate interchange of patent rights and technical information for defense purposes. Exchange of notes at Madrid July 13 and 21, 1960; entered into force July 21, 1960.
11 UST 2187; TIAS 4588; 393 UNTS 289.

PEACE TREATIES

Treaty of peace. Signed at Paris December 10, 1898; entered into force April 11, 1899.
30 Stat. 1754; TS 343; 11 Bevans 615.

POSTAL MATTERS

Parcel post agreement.[1] Signed at Madrid July 16 and at Washington August 30, 1955; entered into force January 1, 1956.
7 UST 451; TIAS 3530; 270 UNTS 211.

International express mail agreement, with detailed regulations. Signed at Madrid October 18, 1982; entered into force April 1, 1983.
TIAS 10555; 1871 UNTS 341.

NOTE:

[1] Applicable to Puerto Rico, Guam, Samoa, the Virgin Islands, Andorra, and Spanish Territories of Africa.

SPAIN (Cont'd)

PUBLICATIONS

Agreement relating to the exchange of official publications. Exchange of notes at Madrid May 8, 1950; entered into force May 8, 1950.
1 UST 466; TIAS 2085; 98 UNTS 175.

SATELLITES

Agreement concerning a program of joint participation in intercontinental testing in connection with experimental communications satellites. Exchange of notes at Madrid September 18, 1964 and January 26, 1965; entered into force January 26, 1965.
16 UST 68; TIAS 5761; 542 UNTS 81.

SCIENTIFIC COOPERATION [1]

NOTE:
[1] See complementary agreement seven to the agreement on friendship, defense and cooperation of July 2, 1982 (TIAS 10589).

Agreement on scientific and technological cooperation, with annex. Signed at Madrid June 10, 1994; entered into force provisionally, June 10, 1994; definitively, January 18, 1996.
TIAS 12547.

Memorandum of understanding on scientific and technological cooperation in the field of water resources development. Signed at Madrid May 20, 1997; entered into force May 20, 1997.
TIAS

Implementing arrangement on cooperation in research on radiological evaluations. Signed at Madrid September 15, 1997; entered into force September 15, 1997.
TIAS

SEISMIC OBSERVATIONS

Memorandum of understanding concerning the Sonseca Seismographic Station, with annexes. Signed at Madrid January 18, 1996; entered into force January 18, 1996.
TIAS

SHIPPING

Agreement relating to jurisdiction over vessels utilizing the Louisiana Offshore Oil Port. Exchange of notes at Madrid November 5 and 22, 1983; entered into force October 19, 1984.
TIAS 10845.

SMUGGLING

Convention for the prevention of smuggling of alcoholic liquors. Signed at Washington February 10, 1926; entered into force November 17, 1926.
44 Stat. 2465; TS 749; 11 Bevans 676; 67 LNTS 131.

SOCIAL SECURITY

Agreement on social security, with administrative arrangement. Signed at Madrid September 30, 1986; entered into force April 1, 1988.
TIAS 12123.

SPACE COOPERATION

Agreement providing for a project in Spain to measure winds and temperatures at high altitudes and for continuing other cooperative space research projects. Exchange of notes at Washington April 14, 1966; entered into force April 14, 1966.
17 UST 493; TIAS 5992; 586 UNTS 79.

Agreement on space cooperation. Exchange of memoranda at Madrid August 31 and September 4, 1984; entered into force September 4, 1984.
TIAS 11067.

Extension:
March 13 and 31, 1989 (TIAS 12208).

Agreement on space cooperation. Signed at Madrid July 11, 1991; entered into force May 9, 1994.
TIAS   ; 1785 UNTS 393.

TAXATION

Tax relief annex attached to the mutual defense assistance agreement, and interpretative note. Signed at Madrid September 26, 1953; entered into force September 26, 1953.
4 UST 1876; TIAS 2849; 207 UNTS 61.

Convention for the avoidance of double taxation and the prevention of fiscal evasion with respect to taxes on income, with protocol. Signed at Madrid February 22, 1990; entered into force November 21, 1990.
TIAS   ; 1591 UNTS 41.

TELECOMMUNICATION

Agreement relating to the reciprocal granting of authorizations to permit licensed amateur radio operators of either country to operate their stations in the other country. Exchange of notes at Madrid December 11 and 20, 1979; entered into force December 20, 1979.
32 UST 517; TIAS 9721.

TRACKING STATIONS

Agreement providing for the establishment and operation of a tracking and data acquisition station. Exchange of notes at Madrid January 29, 1964; entered into force January 29, 1964.
15 UST 153; TIAS 5533; 511 UNTS 61.

Extensions and amendment:
October 11, 1965 (16 UST 1710; TIAS 5896; 574 UNTS 259).
February 1 and May 2, 1983 (TIAS 10717; 1607 UNTS 479).

TRADE AND COMMERCE

Agreement providing for consultations should exports of textiles or textile products from Spain cause market disruption in the United States. Exchange of notes at Madrid September 23, 1976; entered into force September 23, 1976.
28 UST 1308; TIAS 8512.

Agreement relating to the subsidization of exports in the context of the agreement on interpretation and application of articles VI, XVI, and XXIII (subsidies code) of the General Agreement on Tariffs and Trade (TIAS 9619). Exchange of letters at Washington April 13 and 14, 1982; entered into force April 14, 1982.
TIAS

Amendment:
January 16 and 29, 1985.

VISAS

Agreement relating to the reciprocal waiver of visa fees for nonimmigrants.[1] Exchange of notes at Madrid January 21, 1952; entered into force January 21, 1952; operative February 21, 1952.
3 UST 2927; TIAS 2471; 160 UNTS 63.

Amendment:
May 11 and July 5, 1963 (14 UST 1206; TIAS 5418; 488 UNTS 236).

NOTE:
[1] Applicable to all territories.

SRI LANKA

Article 6 of the External Affairs Agreement between the United Kingdom and Ceylon, signed at Colombo November 11, 1947, which entered into force on February 4, 1948, provides: "All obligations and responsibilities heretofore devolving on the Government of the United Kingdom which arise from any valid international instrument shall henceforth insofar as such instrument may be held to have application to Ceylon devolve upon the Government of Ceylon. The reciprocal rights and benefits heretofore enjoyed by the Government of

SRI LANKA (Cont'd)

the United Kingdom in virtue of the application of any such international instrument to Ceylon shall henceforth be enjoyed by the Government of Ceylon.''

AGRICULTURAL COMMODITIES

Agricultural commodities agreement. Signed at Washington June 18, 1958; entered into force June 18, 1958.
9 UST 611; TIAS 4042; 316 UNTS 15.

Amendments:
June 30, 1958 (9 UST 994; TIAS 4068; 321 UNTS 302).
August 24, 1961 (12 UST 1200; TIAS 4835; 418 UNTS 394).

Agricultural commodities agreement, with exchange of notes and related note. Signed at Colombo March 13, 1959; entered into force March 13, 1959.
10 UST 749; TIAS 4211; 342 UNTS 51.

Amendments:
May 28, 1959 (10 UST 1046; TIAS 4242; 346 UNTS 370).
December 1 and 8, 1959 (12 UST 1220; TIAS 4839; 418 UNTS 402).
August 24, 1961 (12 UST 1203; TIAS 4836; 418 UNTS 408).

Agricultural commodities agreement with exchange of notes. Signed at Colombo September 30, 1960; entered into force September 30, 1960.
11 UST 2140; TIAS 4576; 389 UNTS 221.

Agricultural commodities agreement with exchange of notes. Signed at Colombo July 19, 1962; entered into force July 19, 1962.
13 UST 1471; TIAS 5106; 454 UNTS 31.

Amendment:
March 30 and June 22, 1973 (24 UST 1658; TIAS 7671).

Agricultural commodities agreement with exchange of notes. Signed at Colombo March 12, 1966; entered into force March 12, 1966.
17 UST 190; TIAS 5971; 579 UNTS 117.

Amendments:
August 25, 1966 (17 UST 1192; TIAS 6079; 603 UNTS 342).
June 21, 1968 (19 UST 5447; TIAS 6528; 720 UNTS 292).

Agricultural commodities agreement with annex. Signed at Colombo October 27, 1967; entered into force October 27, 1967.
18 UST 3141; TIAS 6405.

Related agreements:
June 21, 1968 (19 UST 5379; TIAS 6521; 719 UNTS 95).

February 19, 1969 (20 UST 512; TIAS 6658; 707 UNTS 157).
September 27, 1970 (21 UST 2191; TIAS 6968; 764 UNTS 265).
March 10, 1971 (22 UST 403; TIAS 7074; 792 UNTS 405).
April 29, 1971 (22 UST 648; TIAS 7116; 792 UNTS 408).
October 12, 1971 (22 UST 1692; TIAS 7195; 807 UNTS 355).
December 20, 1971 (22 UST 2075; TIAS 7248; 882 UNTS 295).
November 3, 1972 (23 UST 3483; TIAS 7505; 898 UNTS 340).
November 23, 1973 (24 UST 2292; TIAS 7753; 938 UNTS 417).
January 18 and February 21, 1974 (25 UST 260; TIAS 7794; 944 UNTS 400).

Agricultural commodities agreement. Signed at Colombo March 25, 1975; entered into force March 25, 1975.
26 UST 1244; TIAS 8107.

Related agreements:
April 9, 1976 (27 UST 1453; TIAS 8256; 1049 UNTS 133).
April 30, 1976 (27 UST 2329; TIAS 8311; 1054 UNTS 376).
October 29, 1976 (28 UST 1280; TIAS 8510).
December 15, 1976 (28 UST 1280; TIAS 8510).
January 9, 1978 (29 UST 4164; TIAS 9052; 1135 UNTS 133).
April 12, 1978 (29 UST 4177; TIAS 9052; 1135 UNTS 144).
February 22, 1979 (30 UST 3631; TIAS 9418; 1171 UNTS 187).
March 18, 1980 (32 UST 898; TIAS 9737; 1222 UNTS 153).
May 21, 1980 (32 UST 1139; TIAS 9761; 1222 UNTS 160).
May 29, 1981 (33 UST 1983; TIAS 10162).
June 30, 1982 (TIAS 10478).
October 29, 1982 (TIAS 10596; 1871 UNTS 393).
April 20, 1983 (TIAS 10714).
December 12, 1983 (TIAS 10910; 1578 UNTS 149).
September 28, 1984 (NP).

Agricultural commodities agreement. Signed at Colombo October 23, 1985; entered into force October 23, 1985.
NP

Amendments:
January 10, 1986 (NP).
August 25, 1986 (NP).

Agricultural commodities agreement. Signed at Colombo November 13, 1986; entered into force November 13, 1986.
NP

Amendments:
April 28, 1987 (NP).
August 12, 1987 (NP).

Related agreements:
December 3, 1987 (NP).
May 20, 1988 (NP).
June 10, 1988 (NP).
September 30, 1988 (NP).
May 16, 1989 (NP).

July 26, 1989 (NP).
October 10, 1989 (NP).
July 24, 1990 (NP).
August 10, 1990 (NP).

AVIATION

Arrangement between the United States and the United Kingdom relating to pilot licenses to operate civil aircraft. Exchange of notes at Washington March 28 and April 5, 1935; entered into force May 5, 1935.
49 Stat. 3731; EAS 77; 12 Bevans 513; 162 LNTS 59.

CLAIMS

Agreement concerning a full and final settlement of the investment dispute between Enterprise Development International, Inc., formerly Enterprise Development Inc., and the Sri Lanka State Timber Corporation relating to Charlanka Company Ltd. Exchange of notes at Washington October 30, 1998; entered into force October 30, 1998.
NP

Agreement concerning a full and final settlement of the commercial dispute between Evans International Ltd. Co. and Centrepoint Colombo Ltd. Urban Development Authority of Sri Lanka, and the Government of the Democratic Socialist Republic of Sri Lanka relating to reconstruction of the Colombo financial district. Exchange of notes at Washington June 7, 1999; entered into force June 7, 1999.
NP

CONSULS

Convention to regulate commerce (article IV) between the United States and the United Kingdom. Signed at London July 3, 1815; entered into force July 3, 1815.
8 Stat. 228; TS 110; 12 Bevans 49.

COPYRIGHT (See APPENDIX)

DEFENSE

Agreement relating to the purchase by Ceylon of certain military equipment, materials, and services. Exchange of notes at Washington October 25 and November 2, 1956; entered into force November 2, 1956.
7 UST 3193; TIAS 3698; 282 UNTS 93.

Agreement regarding the status of U.S. military personnel and civilian employees of the Department of Defense who may be present in Sri Lanka for exercises or official duties. Exchange of notes at Colombo February 9 and

SRI LANKA (Cont'd)

May 16, 1995; entered into force May 16, 1995.
NP

Agreement regarding grants under the Foreign Assistance Act of 1961, as amended, and the furnishing of defense articles, related training, and other defense services from the United States of America to the Government of Sri Lanka. Exchange of notes at Colombo July 23 and August 4, 1998; entered into force August 4, 1998.
TIAS

ECONOMIC AND TECHNICAL COOPERATION

General agreement for technical cooperation. Signed at Colombo November 7, 1950; entered into force November 7, 1950.
1 UST 723; TIAS 2138; 92 UNTS 125.

Agreement relating to a development assistance program in Ceylon. Exchange of notes at Colombo April 28, 1956; entered into force April 28, 1956.
7 UST 751; TIAS 3554; 274 UNTS 35.

Agency for International Development:
November 9, 1977 (29 UST 3472; TIAS 9023; 1124 UNTS 15).
February 28, 1978 (30 UST 1737; TIAS 9284; 1152 UNTS 127).
February 28, 1978 (29 UST 4482; TIAS 9063; 1231 UNTS 379).
August 31, 1978 (30 UST 5493; TIAS 9512; 1231 UNTS 415).
August 31, 1978 (30 UST 5571; TIAS 9516).
August 31, 1978 (30 UST 5584; TIAS 9517).
July 21, 1988 (NP).

EDUCATION

Agreement for financing certain educational exchange programs. Signed at Colombo August 29, 1964; entered into force August 29, 1964.
15 UST 1699; TIAS 5645; 531 UNTS 93.

Amendment:
June 23 and August 13, 1998.

EMPLOYMENT

Agreement relating to the employment of dependents of official government employees. Exchange of notes at Colombo December 12, 1995; entered into force December 12, 1995.
TIAS 12710.

ENVIRONMENTAL COOPERATION

Agreement for cooperation in the Global Learning and Observations to Benefit the Environment (GLOBE) Program, with appendices. Signed at Colombo December 20, 1999; entered into force December 20, 1999.
TIAS

EXTRADITION

Extradition treaty between the United States and the United Kingdom. Signed at London December 22, 1931; entered into force June 24, 1935.
47 Stat. 2122; TS 849; 12 Bevans 482; 163 LNTS 59.

FINANCE

Agreement relating to investment guaranties. Exchange of notes at Colombo February 23, 1966; entered into force February 23, 1966.
17 UST 331; TIAS 5979; 586 UNTS 91.

INTELLECTUAL PROPERTY

Agreement on the protection and enforcement of intellectual property rights. Signed at Colombo September 20, 1991; entered into force October 20, 1991.
TIAS 12436.

INVESTMENT

Treaty concerning the encouragement and reciprocal protection of investment, with annex, protocol and exchange of letters. Signed at Colombo September 20, 1991; entered into force May 1, 1993.
TIAS

PEACE CORPS

Agreement relating to the establishment of a Peace Corps program in Sri Lanka. Exchange of notes at Colombo November 20, 1983; entered into force November 20, 1983.
TIAS 10844.

POSTAL MATTERS

Parcel post agreement and detailed regulations. Signed at Colombo July 18 and at Washington November 25, 1955; entered into force July 1, 1956.
7 UST 2871; TIAS 3670; 281 UNTS 295.

International express mail agreement, with detailed regulations. Signed at Colombo and Washington February 1 and 14, 1990; entered into force March 30, 1990.
TIAS 11716.

Postal money order agreement. Signed at Colombo and Washington April 9 and June 3, 1991; entered into force July 1, 1991.
TIAS 11819.

PROPERTY

Convention between the United States and the United Kingdom relating to tenure and disposition of real and personal property. Signed at Washington March 2, 1899; applicable to Ceylon February 9, 1901.
31 Stat. 1939; TS 146; 12 Bevans 246.

PUBLICATIONS

Agreement relating to the exchange of official publications. Exchange of notes at Colombo January 4 and 31, 1949; entered into force January 31, 1949.
63 Stat. 2356; TIAS 1894; 6 Bevans 515; 88 UNTS 21.

SCIENTIFIC COOPERATION

Agreement on cooperation in science and technology. Signed at Washington June 18, 1984; entered into force June 18, 1984.
TIAS 10992.

TELECOMMUNICATION

Agreement relating to the facilities of Radio Ceylon. Exchange of notes at Colombo May 12 and 14, 1951; entered into force May 14, 1951.
2 UST 1041; TIAS 2259; 141 UNTS 159.

Extensions and amendments:
July 14 and August 23, 1954 (11 UST 229; TIAS 4436; 314 UNTS 297).
April 30, 1962 (13 UST 972; TIAS 5037; 445 UNTS 319).
December 9, 1983 (TIAS 10856).
August 3, 1994.

TRADE AND COMMERCE

Arrangement relating to a visa system for exports of cotton, wool and man-made fiber apparel manufactured in Sri Lanka. Exchange of letters at Colombo March 12 and 23, 1979; entered into force March 23, 1979.
30 UST 3859; TIAS 9428; 1171 UNTS 201.

Agreement relating to trade in textiles and textile products, with annexes. Exchange of notes

SRI LANKA (Cont'd)

at Colombo May 23 and 24, 1988; entered into force May 24, 1988; effective June 1, 1988.
NP

Amendments and extensions:
November 17 and December 27, 1988 (NP).
October 2 and December 14, 1992 (NP).
April 7 and July 13, 1994 (NP).
March 22 and September 5, 1995 and April 17 and 23, 1996 (NP).

Related agreement:
January 13, 1994 (NP).

TRADE-MARKS

Declaration by the United States and the United Kingdom affording reciprocal protection to trade-marks. Signed at London October 24, 1877; entered into force October 24, 1877.
20 Stat. 703; TS 138; 12 Bevans 198.

VISAS

Agreement providing for the reciprocal reduction of nonimmigrant visa fees and issuance of multiple-entry nonimmigrant visas. Exchange of notes at Colombo August 25 and September 7, 1956; entered into force September 7, 1956; operative September 15, 1956.
8 UST 83; TIAS 3743; 280 UNTS 35.

SUDAN

AGRICULTURAL COMMODITIES

Agricultural commodities agreement with exchanges of notes. Signed at Khartoum November 14, 1961; entered into force November 14, 1961.
12 UST 3107; TIAS 4910; 434 UNTS 51.

Amendment:
January 12 and 18, 1966 (17 UST 311; TIAS 5976).

Agricultural commodities agreement. Signed at Khartoum January 31, 1963; entered into force January 31, 1963.
14 UST 1831; TIAS 5495; 494 UNTS 119.

Amendment:
January 12 and 18, 1966 (17 UST 311; TIAS 5976).

Agricultural commodities agreement with exchange of notes. Signed at Khartoum March 2, 1964; entered into force March 2, 1964.
15 UST 217; TIAS 5541; 524 UNTS 217.

Agricultural commodities agreement with exchange of notes. Signed at Khartoum April 13, 1966; entered into force April 13, 1966.
17 UST 502; TIAS 5994; 586 UNTS 39.

Agricultural commodities agreement with annex. Signed at Khartoum March 18, 1973; entered into force March 18, 1973.
24 UST 967; TIAS 7608.

Related agreement:
May 8, 1974 (25 UST 844; TIAS 7827).

Agricultural commodities agreement. Signed at Khartoum February 21, 1977; entered into force July 7, 1977.
29 UST 967; TIAS 8856.

Agricultural commodities agreement. Signed at Khartoum December 24, 1977; entered into force January 24, 1978.
29 UST 5873; TIAS 9157.

Related agreements:
February 8, 1979 (TIAS 10660).
January 19, 1981 (33 UST 906; TIAS 10075; 1275 UNTS 139).
August 27, 1981 (33 UST 3698; TIAS 10251).
February 13, 1982 (34 UST 275; TIAS 10352).
January 20, 1983 (TIAS 10660).
February 21, 1983 (TIAS 10660).
June 13, 1983 (TIAS 10660).
December 10, 1983 (TIAS 10909).

Agricultural commodities agreement, with annexes and agreed minutes. Signed at Khartoum December 22, 1979; entered into force December 22, 1979.
TIAS 10727.

Amendments:
August 7, 1980 (TIAS 10727).
February 14, 1981 (TIAS 10727).
April 29, 1982 (TIAS 10727).
June 13, 1983 (TIAS 10727).
August 9, 1984 (TIAS 10727).

Agricultural commodities agreement. Signed at Khartoum December 27, 1984; entered into force January 3, 1985.
NP

Amendments:
January 9, 1985 (NP).
May 12, 1985 (NP).
August 24, 1985 (NP).

Agricultural commodities agreement, with annexes. Signed at Khartoum January 26, 1986; entered into force January 26, 1986.
NP

Amendment:
July 16, 1986 (NP).

Agricultural commodities agreement. Signed at Khartoum March 12, 1987; entered into force March 12, 1987.
NP

Amendment:
June 18, 1987 (NP).

Agricultural commodities agreement. Signed at Khartoum February 28, 1988; entered into force February 28, 1988.
NP

Amendment:
March 31, 1988 (NP).

Agricultural commodities agreement. Signed at Khartoum June 8, 1989; entered into force June 8, 1989.
NP

Amendment:
July 28, 1989 (NP).

DEFENSE

Agreement relating to the deposit by Sudan of ten percent of the value of grant military assistance furnished by the United States. Exchange of notes at Khartoum April 27 and May 24, 1973; entered into force May 24, 1973.
24 UST 1740; TIAS 7677.

Mutual defense assistance agreement. Exchange of notes at Khartoum April 8 and 22, 1981; entered into force April 22, 1981.
34 UST 1000; TIAS 10389; 1560 UNTS 415.

Agreement concerning the grant of defense articles and services under the military assistance program. Exchange of notes at Khartoum August 24 and 30, 1981; entered into force August 30, 1981.
TIAS 10500.

Amendment:
August 30 and September 25, 1982 (TIAS 10500).

Agreement relating to the status of United States personnel temporarily stationed in Sudan. Exchange of letters at Khartoum November 12 and December 27, 1981; entered into force December 27, 1981.
33 UST 4513; TIAS 10322.

ECONOMIC AND TECHNICAL COOPERATION

Agreement providing for economic, technical and related assistance to the Sudan. Exchange of notes at Khartoum March 31, 1958; entered into force March 31, 1958.
9 UST 343; TIAS 4014; 308 UNTS 105.

Understanding interpreting the agreement of March 31, 1958. Exchange of notes at Khartoum July 1 and 12, 1958.
9 UST 1079; TIAS 4085; 335 UNTS 342.

Agency for International Development:
May 12, 1977 (29 UST 297; TIAS 8814).
December 31, 1979 (31 UST 5573; TIAS 9674; 1234 UNTS 73).

SUDAN (Cont'd)

FINANCE

Agreement relating to investment guaranties under section 413 (b)(4) of the Mutual Security Act of 1954, as amended. Exchange of notes at Khartoum March 17, 1959; entered into force March 17, 1959.
10 UST 408; TIAS 4201; 342 UNTS 13.

Amendment:
March 2, 1964 (15 UST 238; TIAS 5544; 524 UNTS 318).

Agreement regarding the consolidation and rescheduling of certain debts owed to, guaranteed or insured by the United States and its agencies, with annexes. Signed at Khartoum May 17, 1980; entered into force June 19, 1980.
32 UST 4373; TIAS 9952.

Agreement regarding the consolidation and rescheduling of payments due under P.L. 480 Title I agricultural commodity agreements. Signed at Khartoum August 18, 1980; entered into force August 18, 1980.
32 UST 4373; TIAS 9952.

Agreement regarding the consolidation and rescheduling of certain debts owed to, guaranteed or insured by the United States Government and its agencies, with annexes. Signed at Khartoum July 20, 1982; entered into force August 23, 1982.
TIAS 10437.

Agreement regarding the consolidation and rescheduling of certain debts owed to, guaranteed or insured by the United States Government and its agencies. Signed at Khartoum January 21, 1984; entered into force March 27, 1984.
TIAS 10981.

Agreement regarding the consolidation and rescheduling of certain debts owed to, guaranteed by or insured by the United States Government and its agencies, with annexes. Signed at Khartoum December 22, 1984; entered into force January 25, 1985.
NP

JUDICIAL ASSISTANCE

Agreement on procedures for mutual assistance in connection with matters relating to the Boeing Company. Signed at Washington September 23, 1977; entered into force September 23, 1977.
28 UST 7482; TIAS 8723.

POSTAL MATTERS

International express mail agreement, with detailed regulations. Signed at Khartoum and Washington October 22 and November 30, 1990; entered into force January 14, 1991.
TIAS 11768.

SUPREME ALLIED COMMANDER ATLANTIC (SACLANT)

DEFENSE

Acquisition and cross-servicing agreement concerning mutual logistic support, with annexes. Signed December 17 and 18, 1997; entered into force December 18, 1997.
TIAS

SUPREME HEADQUARTERS ALLIED POWERS EUROPE (SHAPE)

DEFENSE

Agreement concerning support of the allied tactical operations center at Sembach Air Base, Germany, with annexes. Signed at Heidelberg and Sembach Air Base August 28 and November 25, 1987; entered into force November 25, 1987; effective May 1, 1983.
TIAS

TELECOMMUNICATION

Mutual support agreement for telecommunications, with annex. Signed at Casteau and Vaihingen January 22 and February 25, 1985; entered into force February 25, 1985.
TIAS 11187.

SURINAME

On November 25, 1975 Suriname became an independent state. In a note dated November 29, 1975 to the Secretary-General of the United Nations, the Prime Minister made a statement reading in part as follows:

"The Government of the Republic of Surinam, conscious of the desirability of maintaining existing legal relationship, and conscious of its obligation under International Law to honour its treaty commitments, acknowledges that treaty rights and obligations of the Government of the Kingdom of the Netherlands in respect of Surinam were succeeded by the Republic of Surinam upon Independence by virtue of customary International Law.

"Since, however, it is likely that by virtue of customary International Law certain treaties may have lapsed at the date of Independence of Surinam, it seems essential that each treaty should be subjected to legal examination. It is proposed after this examination has been completed, to indicate which, if any, of the treaties which may have lapsed by customary International Law the Government of the Republic of Surinam wish to treat as having lapsed.

"It is desired that it be presumed that each treaty has been legally succeeded to by the Republic of Surinam and that action be based upon this presumption until a decision is reached that it should be regarded as having lapsed. Should the Government of the Republic of Surinam be of the opinion it has legally succeeded to a treaty but subsequently wish to terminate its operation, the Government will in due course give notice of termination in the terms thereof."

AVIATION

Agreement between the United States and the Netherlands providing for nonassertion of sovereign immunity from suit of air transport enterprises. Exchange of notes at Washington June 19, 1953; entered into force June 19, 1953.
4 UST 1610; TIAS 2828; 212 UNTS 249.

Air transport agreement between the United States and The Netherlands. Signed at Washington April 3, 1957; entered into force provisionally April 3, 1957; definitively May 31, 1957.
12 UST 837; TIAS 4782; 410 UNTS 193.

Amendment:
November 25, 1969 (20 UST 4070; TIAS 6797; 732 UNTS 316).

Memorandum of agreement concerning assistance in developing and modernizing the Suriname civil aviation infrastructure, with annexes. Signed at Washington and Paramaribo June 21 and August 27, 1990; entered into force August 27, 1990.
TIAS 11754.

COMMERCE

Treaty of friendship, commerce and navigation, with protocol and exchange of notes between the United States and the Netherlands. Signed at The Hague March 27, 1956; applicable to Suriname February 10, 1963.
8 UST 2043; TIAS 3942; 285 UNTS 231.

CONSULS

Convention between the United States and The Netherlands regarding consuls in the colonies of The Netherlands.[1] Signed at The Hague January 22, 1855; entered into force May 25, 1855.
10 Stat. 1150; TS 253; 10 Bevans 28.

SURINAME (Cont'd)

NOTE:

[1] American consular officers in colonies of the Netherlands have been instructed not to enforce that section of the convention relating to the arrest of deserters, as being in conflict with the Seamen's Act (38 Stat. 1164).

COPYRIGHT (See APPENDIX)

DEFENSE

Agreement concerning the provision of training related to defense articles under the United States International Military Education and Training (IMET) Program. Exchange of notes at Paramaribo August 22 and 25, 1980; entered into force August 25, 1980.
32 UST 3741; TIAS 9916; 1267 UNTS 155.

Agreement regarding the status of U.S. Special Forces Deployment for Training Exercise Mission. Exchange of notes at Paramaribo January 17 and February 2, 1996; entered into force February 2, 1996.
NP

ECONOMIC AND TECHNICAL COOPERATION

Economic cooperation agreement between the United States and The Netherlands. Signed at The Hague July 2, 1948; entered into force July 2, 1948.
62 Stat. 2477; TIAS 1791; 10 Bevans 240; 20 UNTS 91.

Amendments:
January 16 and February 2, 1950 (1 UST 665; TIAS 2126; 93 UNTS 361).
March 7 and April 3, 1951 (2 UST 1319; TIAS 2285; 141 UNTS 368).
November 28, 1952 (3 UST 5260; TIAS 2721; 173 UNTS 382).

General agreement between the United States and The Netherlands for technical cooperation for Suriname and Netherlands Antilles. Signed at The Hague January 22, 1954; entered into force April 21, 1954.
5 UST 819; TIAS 2982; 190 UNTS 207.

ENVIRONMENTAL COOPERATION

Agreement for cooperation in the Global Learning and Observations to Benefit the Environment (GLOBE) Program, with appendices. Signed at Paramaribo December 23, 1997; entered into force December 23, 1997.
TIAS

EXTRADITION

Convention between the United States and The Netherlands for the extradition of criminals. Signed at Washington June 2, 1887; entered into force July 11, 1889.
26 Stat. 1481; TS 256; 10 Bevans 47.

Treaty extending the extradition convention of June 2, 1887, between the United States and The Netherlands to their respective island possessions and colonies. Signed at Washington January 18, 1904; entered into force August 28, 1904.
33 Stat. 2257; TS 436; 10 Bevans 53.

FINANCE

Investment incentive agreement. Signed at Paramaribo May 28, 1993; entered into force February 20, 1996.
TIAS 12500.

JUDICIAL ASSISTANCE

Procedures for mutual assistance in connection with matters relating to the Reynolds Metals Company. Signed at Washington March 14, 1979; entered into force March 14, 1979.
30 UST 3864; TIAS 9429; 1171 UNTS 209.

MUTUAL SECURITY

Agreement between the United States and The Netherlands relating to the assurances required by the Mutual Security Act of 1951. Exchange of notes at The Hague January 8, 1952; entered into force January 8, 1952.
3 UST 4633; TIAS 2615; 173 UNTS 372.

NARCOTIC DRUGS

Agreement concerning cooperation in maritime law enforcement. Signed at Paramaribo December 31, 1998; entered into force August 26, 1999.
TIAS

PEACE CORPS

Agreement concerning the establishment of a Peace Corps program in Suriname. Exchange of notes at Paramaribo October 12, 1994 and January 5, 1995; entered into force January 5, 1995.
TIAS 12595.

POSTAL MATTERS

Parcel post convention. Signed at Paramaribo July 9 and at Washington August 18, 1930; operative September 1, 1930.
46 Stat. 2798; Post Office Department print; 125 LNTS 123.

Convention for the exchange of money orders. Signed at Paramaribo August 12 and at Washington September 16, 1930; operative November 1, 1930.
125 LNTS 147.

REFUGEES

Agreement terminating the memorandum of understanding of August 1, 1994, for the establishment within the territory of Suriname of facilities to provide temporary protection for nationals of Haiti and transferring certain facilities and equipment to Suriname. Exchange of notes at Paramaribo January 20 and 24, 1995; entered into force January 24, 1995.
TIAS 12600.

SCIENTIFIC COOPERATION

Memorandum of understanding concerning scientific and technical cooperation in the earth sciences, with annexes and related agreement. Signed at Paramaribo March 22, 1995; entered into force March 22, 1995.
TIAS 12619.

TELECOMMUNICATION

Agreement relating to the reciprocal granting of authorizations to permit licensed amateur radio operators of either country to operate their stations in the other country. Exchange of notes at Paramaribo October 3 and 12, 1978; entered into force October 12, 1978.
30 UST 2107; TIAS 9314.

VISAS

Agreement between the United States and the Netherlands relating to the reciprocal waiver of passport visa fees for nonimmigrants. Exchanges of notes at The Hague January 21, February 11, and March 5 and 13, 1946; entered into force April 15, 1946.
61 Stat. 3834; TIAS 1728; 10 Bevans 178; 84 UNTS 3.

SWAZILAND

In a note dated October 22, 1968 to the Secretary General of the United Nations, the Minister of State of Swaziland made a statement reading in part as follows: "[F]or a period of two years with effect from September 6, 1968,

SWAZILAND (Cont'd)

the Government of the Kingdom of Swaziland accepts all treaty rights and obligations entered into prior to independence by the British Government on behalf of the Kingdom of Swaziland, during which period the treaties and international agreements in which such rights and obligations are embodied will receive examination with a view to determining, at the expiration of that period of two years, which of those rights and obligations will be adopted, which will be terminated, and which of these will be adopted with reservations in respect of particular matters." In a further note dated October 30, 1970 it was stated that the Government of the Kingdom of Swaziland shall continue to apply the terms of these treaties within Swaziland, on a basis of reciprocity, for an indefinite period of time. This provisional arrangement should be deemed to continue in each case until the depositary is notified of the decision of the Government of the Kingdom of Swaziland either to accede definitively or to terminate its further adherence to the treaty.

COPYRIGHT (See APPENDIX)

DEFENSE

Agreement concerning the provision of training related to defense articles under the United States International Military Education and Training (IMET) Program. Exchange of notes at Mbabane January 10 and February 28, 1984; entered into force February 28, 1984.
TIAS 10952.

ECONOMIC AND TECHNICAL COOPERATION

General agreement on special development assistance. Signed at Mbabane June 3, 1970; entered into force June 3, 1970.
21 UST 1412; TIAS 6898; 756 UNTS 95.

Agreement for economic, technical and related assistance. Signed at Mbabane December 5, 1989; entered into force December 5, 1989.
TIAS 11733.

EXTRADITION

Extradition treaty between the United States and the United Kingdom. Signed at London December 22, 1931; entered into force June 24, 1935.
47 Stat. 2122; TS 849; 12 Bevans 482; 163 LNTS 59.

Agreement continuing in force between the United States and Swaziland the extradition treaty of December 22, 1931 (47 Stat. 2122), between the United States and the United Kingdom. Exchange of notes at Mbabane May 13 and July 28, 1970; entered into force July 28, 1970.
21 UST 1930; TIAS 6934; 756 UNTS 103.

FINANCE

Agreement relating to investment guaranties. Signed at Mbabane September 29, 1967; entered into force September 29, 1967.
18 UST 2510; TIAS 6350; 693 UNTS 167.

Agreement continuing in force the agreement of September 29, 1967 (TIAS 6350), relating to investment guaranties. Exchange of notes at Mbabane April 3 and July 28, 1970; entered into force July 28, 1970.
21 UST 2006; TIAS 6944; 763 UNTS 53.

PEACE CORPS

Agreement relating to the establishment of a Peace Corps program in Swaziland. Exchange of notes at Mbabane November 11, 1970; entered into force November 11, 1970.
21 UST 2487; TIAS 6989; 772 UNTS 173.

POSTAL MATTERS

International express mail agreement, with detailed regulations. Signed at Mbabane and Washington March 3 and April 6, 1988; entered into force May 1, 1988.
TIAS 11583.

TELECOMMUNICATION

Agreement relating to establishment of a Bureau of Foreign Broadcast Information Service (FBIS) in Swaziland. Signed at Mbabane August 3, 1981; entered into force August 3, 1981.
33 UST 3344; TIAS 10235.

Arrangement relating to radio communications between amateur stations on behalf of third parties. Exchange of notes at Mbabane April 12 and May 27, 1983; entered into force June 26, 1983.
TIAS 10718; 1607 UNTS 131.

SWEDEN

ATOMIC ENERGY

Agreement concerning a cooperative program in the field of management of radioactive wastes. Signed at Stockholm September 9, 1980; entered into force September 9, 1980.
TIAS 11337.

Amendment and extension:
September 13, 1990.

Agreement regarding participation in the USNRC international piping integrity research group, with appendices. Signed at Stockholm and Bethesda February 2 and March 3, 1987; entered into force March 3, 1987.
TIAS 12218.

Arrangement for the exchange of technical information and cooperation in nuclear safety matters, with patent addendum. Signed at Stockholm October 4, 1989; entered into force October 4, 1989.
TIAS 12229.

Agreement relating to participation in the USNRC program of severe accident research, with addendum and appendix. Signed at Rockville and Stockholm January 10 and April 24, 1995; entered into force April 24, 1995; effective January 1, 1994.
TIAS

AVIATION

Arrangement relating to pilot licenses to operate civil aircraft. Exchange of notes at Washington September 8 and 9, 1933; entered into force October 9, 1933.
48 Stat. 1799; EAS 48; 11 Bevans 788; 144 LNTS 171.

Agreement relating to air transport services. Exchange of notes at Washington December 16, 1944; entered into force January 1, 1945.
58 Stat. 1466; EAS 431; 11 Bevans 825; 6 UNTS 397.

Amendments:
August 6, 1954 (5 UST 1411; TIAS 3013; 222 UNTS 376).
June 16, 1995; (TIAS 12665).

Agreement relating to air service facilities in Sweden. Signed at Stockholm September 30, 1946; entered into force September 30, 1946.
61 Stat. 3893; TIAS 1742; 11 Bevans 832; 42 UNTS 213.

Agreement relating to airworthiness certifications. Exchange of notes at Stockholm April 24 and 26, 1973; entered into force April 26, 1973.
24 UST 997; TIAS 7611.

Agreement for the promotion of aviation safety. Signed at Stockholm February 9, 1998; entered into force February 9, 1998.
TIAS

CONSULS

Consular convention.[1] Signed at Washington June 1, 1910; entered into force March 18, 1911.
37 Stat. 1479; TS 557; 11 Bevans 730.

SWEDEN (Cont'd)

NOTE:
[1] Articles XI and XII abrogated as of March 18, 1921.

COPYRIGHT (See APPENDIX)

CUSTOMS

Arrangement relating to free entry, on a reciprocal basis, for goods imported by career consular representatives. Exchange of notes at Stockholm June 23 and 29, 1931; entered into force July 1, 1931.
11 Bevans 771.

Arrangement for the reciprocal exemption from duty of articles imported by diplomatic officers and all other persons belonging to missions, but not including personal servants. Exchange of notes at Washington January 5 and 17, 1933; entered into force January 17, 1933.
11 Bevans 776.

Agreement regarding mutual assistance in customs matters. Signed at Washington July 8, 1987; entered into force May 8, 1988.
TIAS 12122.

DEFENSE

Agreement relating to the procurement of reimbursable military equipment, materials, or services. Exchange of notes at Stockholm June 30 and July 1, 1952; entered into force July 1, 1952.
3 UST 2968; TIAS 2480; 187 UNTS 3.

Agreement concerning general security of military information. Exchange of notes at Washington December 4 and 23, 1981; entered into force December 23, 1981.
33 UST 4400; TIAS 10309.

Memorandum of understanding relating to the principles governing mutual cooperation in the defense procurement area, with related exchange of letters. Signed at Washington and Stockholm June 11 and 16, 1987; entered into force June 16, 1987.
TIAS

Memorandum of agreement concerning the exchange of engineers and scientists, with annexes. Signed at Washington and Stockholm June 9 and 15, 1992; entered into force June 15, 1992.
NP

Agreement for cooperative research and development efforts in the fields of aircrew protection and performance, with annexes. Signed at Stockholm April 23, 1993; entered into force April 23, 1993.
TIAS 12371.

Agreement for cooperation on environmental protection in defense matters. Signed at Stockholm April 24, 1995; entered into force April 24, 1995.
TIAS 12372.

Agreement for the bilateral cooperative program in electro-magnetic effects measurement and analysis (RF Effects Program). Signed at Washington June 2 and December 20, 1995; entered into force December 20, 1995.
TIAS 12373.

Agreement for technology research and development projects, with annex. Signed at Washington and Stockholm March 10 and April 22, 1997; entered into force April 22, 1997.
TIAS

Agreement regarding the exchange of engineers and scientists, with annexes. Signed at Stockholm and Washington October 7 and December 20, 1999; entered into force December 20, 1999.
NP

ECONOMIC AND TECHNICAL COOPERATION

Economic cooperation agreement. Signed at Stockholm July 3, 1948; entered into force July 21, 1948.
62 Stat. 2541; TIAS 1793; 11 Bevans 855; 23 UNTS 101.

Amendments:
January 5 and 17, 1950 (1 UST 181; TIAS 2034; 76 UNTS 254).
February 8 and 23, 1951 (3 UST 2800; TIAS 2448; 185 UNTS 326).

EDUCATION

Agreement for financing certain educational exchange programs. Signed at Stockholm November 20, 1952; entered into force November 20, 1952.
3 UST 4812; TIAS 2653; 177 UNTS 203.

Amendments:
November 20, 1959 (10 UST 1921; TIAS 4359; 360 UNTS 396).
June 28, 1963 (14 UST 985; TIAS 5389; 479 UNTS 358).
December 7, 1970 (21 UST 2732; TIAS 7018; 776 UNTS 330).

EMPLOYMENT

Arrangement relating to the employment of dependents of official government employees. Exchange of notes at Washington October 27 and 30, 1981; entered into force October 30, 1981.
33 UST 4148; TIAS 10291.

ENVIRONMENTAL COOPERATION

Agreement for cooperation in the Global Learning and Observations to Benefit the Environment (GLOBE) Program, with appendices. Signed at Stockholm August 23, 1995; entered into force August 23, 1995.
TIAS 12684.

EXTRADITION

Convention on extradition, with protocol.[1] Signed at Washington October 24, 1961; entered into force December 3, 1963.
14 UST 1845; TIAS 5496; 494 UNTS 141.

Supplementary convention on extradition. Signed at Stockholm March 14, 1983; entered into force September 24, 1984.
TIAS 10812.

NOTE:
[1] Protocol terminated January 1, 1965.

HIGHWAYS

Memorandum of understanding on highway management and technology. Signed at Borlange June 15, 1992; entered into force June 15, 1992.
TIAS 11870.

MAPPING

Basic exchange and cooperative agreement for global geospatial information and services, with annexes. Signed at Stockholm and Bethesda November 26 and December 14, 1998; entered into force December 14, 1998.
NP

MARITIME MATTERS

Arrangement relating to the reciprocal exemption of pleasure yachts from all navigation dues. Exchange of notes at Stockholm October 22 and 29, 1930; entered into force October 29, 1930.
47 Stat. 2655; EAS 21; 11 Bevans 763; 109 LNTS 181.

NATIONALITY

Convention relating to exemption from military service of persons having dual nationality. Signed at Stockholm January 31, 1933; entered into force May 20, 1935.
49 Stat. 3195; TS 890; 11 Bevans 778; 159 LNTS 261.

SWEDEN (Cont'd)

PACIFIC SETTLEMENT OF DISPUTES

Treaty for the advancement of peace. Signed at Washington October 13, 1914; entered into force January 11, 1915.
38 Stat. 1872; TS 607; 11 Bevans 741.

Agreement concerning compensation for commissioners designated under the treaty for advancement of peace signed October 13, 1914. Exchange of notes at Stockholm June 30, 1939; entered into force June 30, 1939.
53 Stat. 2428; EAS 154; 11 Bevans 821; 199 LNTS 203.

Treaty of arbitration. Signed at Washington October 27, 1928; entered into force April 15, 1929.
46 Stat. 2261; TS 783; 11 Bevans 760; 91 LNTS 225.

PATENTS

Agreement facilitating the interchange of patent rights and technical information for defense purposes. Exchange of notes at Washington October 4, 1962; entered into force October 4, 1962.
13 UST 2161; TIAS 5178; 462 UNTS 31.

Agreement approving the procedures for reciprocal filing of classified patent applications in the United States and Sweden. Exchange of notes at Washington October 20 and November 17, 1964; entered into force November 17, 1964.
15 UST 2086; TIAS 5690; 532 UNTS 378.

POSTAL MATTERS

Convention for the exchange of money orders. Signed at Stockholm December 27, 1884 and at Washington February 17, 1885; operative April 1, 1885.
23 Stat. 815.

Amendments:
May 23 and June 13, 1888 (NP).
November 11 and December 3, 1890 (NP).

Parcel post convention. Signed at Stockholm June 28 and at Washington July 11, 1932; operative July 1, 1932.
47 Stat. 2106; Post Office Department print.

International express mail agreement, with detailed regulations. Signed at Stockholm and Washington August 26 and 30, 1983; entered into force October 1, 1983.
TIAS 10780.

PUBLICATIONS

Agreement relating to exchange of official publications. Exchange of notes at Stockholm December 16, 1947; entered into force December 16, 1947.
61 Stat. 3605; TIAS 1688; 11 Bevans 843; 73 UNTS 65.

SCIENTIFIC COOPERATION

Memorandum of understanding concerning scientific and technical cooperation in the earth sciences, with annexes. Signed at Reston and Stockholm April 22 and June 1, 1994; entered into force June 1, 1994.
TIAS 12182.

SHIPPING

Agreement relating to jurisdiction over vessels utilizing the Louisiana Offshore Oil Port. Exchange of notes at Washington August 17 and 22, 1978; entered into force August 22, 1978.
30 UST 1698; TIAS 9277; 1153 UNTS 145.

SMUGGLING

Convention for the prevention of smuggling of intoxicating liquors. Signed at Washington May 22, 1924; entered into force August 18, 1924.
43 Stat. 1830; TS 698; 11 Bevans 750; 29 LNTS 421.

SOCIAL SECURITY

Agreement on social security, with administrative arrangement. Signed at Stockholm May 27, 1985; entered into force January 1, 1987.
TIAS 11266.

SPACE COOPERATION

Memorandum of understanding for cooperative sounding rocket activities. Signed at Washington and Stockholm May 17 and June 10, 1996; entered into force June 10, 1996.
TIAS

TAXATION

Arrangement relating to relief from double income tax on shipping profits. Exchange of notes at Washington March 31, 1938; entered into force March 31, 1938.
52 Stat. 1490; EAS 121; 11 Bevans 806; 189 LNTS 327.

Amendment:
June 26 and July 24, 1987 (TIAS 11286).

Convention for the avoidance of double taxation and the prevention of fiscal evasion with respect to taxes on estates, inheritances and gifts. Signed at Stockholm June 13, 1983; entered into force September 5, 1984.
TIAS 10826.

Convention for the avoidance of double taxation and the prevention of fiscal evasion with respect to taxes on income, with exchange of letters. Signed at Stockholm September 1, 1994; entered into force October 26, 1995.
TIAS

TELECOMMUNICATION

Agreement relating to the reciprocal granting of authorizations to permit licensed amateur radio operators of either country to operate their station in the other country. Exchange of notes at Stockholm May 27 and June 2, 1969; entered into force June 2, 1969.
20 UST 773; TIAS 6690; 715 UNTS 75.

TRADE AND COMMERCE

Agreement supplementary to the general agreement on tariffs and trade to provide concession as compensation to Sweden for spring clothespins escape clause action, and exchange of notes. Signed at Washington September 15, 1961; entered into force September 15, 1961.
12 UST 1271; TIAS 4847; 421 UNTS 241.

Agreement within the context of the multilateral trade negotiations concerning cheese and other agricultural products, and related letters of January 30 and February 19, 1980. Done at Geneva June 13, July 5 and 10, 1979; entered into force January 1, 1980.
32 UST 5512; TIAS 10003; 1266 UNTS 49.

VISAS

Agreement relating to passport visa fees for nonimmigrants. Exchange of notes at Washington April 10 and 30, 1947; entered into force April 30, 1947; operative June 1, 1947.
61 Stat. 4050; TIAS 1798; 11 Bevans 834; 84 UNTS 33.

SWITZERLAND

ATOMIC ENERGY

Agreement on research participation and technical exchange in the United States loss of fluid test program and the Swiss emergency core cooling systems-reflood program, with appendices. Signed at Washington and Wurenlingen June 15 and July 9, 1979; entered into force July 9, 1979.
31 UST 240; TIAS 9607.

SWITZERLAND (Cont'd)

Extension and amendment:
March 27 and May 2, 1984 (TIAS 11112).

Agreement on research participation and technical exchange in the United States heavy section steel technology program and the Swiss research program in fracture mechanics, with appendices. Signed at Washington and Wurenlingen June 15 and July 9, 1979; entered into force July 9, 1979.
31 UST 228; TIAS 9606.

Extension and amendment:
May 7 and 14, 1984 (TIAS 11194).

Agreement in the area of carbide fuel development, with appendices. Signed at Bern November 15, 1982; entered into force November 15, 1982.
TIAS 10608; 1871 UNTS 395.

Agreement in the field of radioactive waste management. Signed at Geneva April 19, 1985; entered into force April 19, 1985.
TIAS

Amendment and extensions:
August 8 and 15, 1990.
September 23, 1991.

Agreement on cooperation in radioactive waste management safety research, with appendix. Signed at Bethesda and Baden August 26 and September 26, 1986; entered into force September 26, 1986.
TIAS 11384.

Agreement regarding participation in the USNRC international piping integrity research group, with appendices. Signed at Bern and Bethesda February 3 and March 3, 1987; entered into force March 3, 1987.
TIAS 12219.

Arrangement for the exchange of technical information and cooperation in nuclear safety matters, with patent addendum. Signed at Vienna September 23, 1987; entered into force September 23, 1987.
TIAS 12224.

Agreement on cooperation in nuclear plant life extension research. Signed at Bern and Washington May 24 and June 13, 1989; entered into force June 13, 1989.
TIAS 12145.

Arrangment for the exchange of technical information and cooperation in nuclear safety matters, with addenda. Signed at Vienna September 30, 1997; entered into force September 30, 1997.
TIAS

Agreement for cooperation concerning peaceful uses of atomic energy, with agreed minute and annexes. Signed at Bern October 31, 1997; entered into force June 23, 1998.
TIAS

AVIATION

Exchange of notes approving the agreed minute of February 6, 1957 relating to an interpretation of the air transport agreement of August 3, 1945, as amended. Signed at Washington March 1 and 4, 1957; entered into force March 4, 1957.
8 UST 349; TIAS 3781; 279 UNTS 294.

Air service agreement relating to equipment at Cointrin Airport. Signed at Bern April 30, 1947; entered into force April 30, 1947.
61 Stat. 3859; TIAS 1736; 11 Bevans 957; 42 UNTS 235.

Agreement concerning the reciprocal acceptance of certificates of airworthiness for imported aircraft. Exchange of notes at Bern October 13, 1961; entered into force provisionally October 13, 1961, and definitively November 21, 1962.
13 UST 2479; TIAS 5214; 459 UNTS 219.

Amendment:
January 7, 1977 (28 UST 2446; TIAS 8563).

Air transport agreement, with annexes. Signed at Washington June 15, 1995; entered into force September 27, 1996.
TIAS 12662.

Agreement for promotion of aviation safety. Signed at Washington September 26, 1996; entered into force September 26, 1996.
TIAS

COMMERCE

Convention of friendship, commerce and extradition.[1] Signed at Bern November 25, 1850; entered into force November 8, 1855.
11 Stat. 587; TS 353; 11 Bevans 894.

NOTE:
[1] Articles 8-12 terminated March 23, 1900, as a result of notice given by the United States on March 23, 1899; articles 13-17 relating to extradition were superseded and expressly repealed by the extradition treaty signed May 14, 1900 (31 Stat. 1928; TS 354; 11 Bevans 904).

CONSULS (See COMMERCE)

COPYRIGHT (See APPENDIX)

DEFENSE

Memorandum of understanding for coproduction of the M109A1B self propelled 155 MM Howitzer. Signed at Washington July 18, 1988; entered into force July 18, 1988.
TIAS 11507.

Agreement amending the memorandum of understanding of February 25, 1988, as amended,

for the coproduction of the stinger post plus (stinger-RMP) weapon system. Signed at Washington and Berne March 23 and May 4, 1995; entered into force May 4, 1995.
TIAS 12642.

Agreement on the exchange of military personnel between the U.S. Navy and the Swiss Air Force and Anti-Aircraft Command. Signed at Bern and Washington July 5 and August 17, 1995; entered into force August 17, 1995.
NP

ENVIRONMENTAL COOPERATION

Agreement for cooperation in the Global Learning and Observations to Benefit the Environment (GLOBE) Program, with appendices. Signed at Berne April 22, 1998; entered into force April 22, 1998.
TIAS

EXTRADITION

Extradition treaty. Signed at Washington November 14, 1990; entered into force September 10, 1997.
TIAS

JUDICIAL ASSISTANCE

Treaty on mutual assistance in criminal matters with related notes. Signed at Bern May 25, 1973; entered into force January 23, 1977.
27 UST 2019; TIAS 8302; 1052 UNTS 61.

Related agreement:
November 3, 1993 (TIAS 12514).

MAPPING

Agreement concerning mapping, charting and geodesy cooperation. Signed at Fairfax August 5 and 11, 1992; entered into force August 11, 1992.
NP

NARCOTIC DRUGS

Arrangement for the direct exchange of certain information regarding the traffic in narcotic drugs. Exchange of notes at Bern November 15 and 16, 1929; entered into force November 16, 1929.
11 Bevans 917.

NATIONALITY

Convention relative to military obligations of certain persons having dual nationality. Signed

SWITZERLAND (Cont'd)

at Bern November 11, 1937; entered into force December 7, 1938.
53 Stat. 1791; TS 943; 11 Bevans 936; 193 LNTS 181.

PACIFIC SETTLEMENT OF DISPUTES

Treaty of arbitration and conciliation. Signed at Washington February 16, 1931; entered into force May 23, 1932.
47 Stat. 1983; TS 844; 11 Bevans 920; 129 LNTS 465.

PATENTS

Arrangement relating to reciprocal benefits under the patent laws of the two countries. Exchange of notes at Bern January 17 and 28, 1908; entered into force January 28, 1908.
11 Bevans 909.

POSTAL MATTERS

Agreement concerning the exchange of parcel post, and regulations of execution.[1] Signed at Washington April 1 and at Bern May 18, 1932; operative April 1, 1932.
47 Stat. 1997; Post Office Department print.

International express mail agreement, with detailed regulations. Signed at Bern and Washington December 7, 1978 and January 22, 1979; entered into force February 1, 1979.
32 UST 5549; TIAS 10008; 1265 UNTS 131.

NOTE:
[1] Applicable to Liechtenstein.

PRIVILEGES AND IMMUNITIES

Agreement concerning the status, privileges, and immunities of the SALT (START) delegation in Switzerland with annex. Exchange of notes at Bern November 21 and 22, 1972; entered into force November 22, 1972.
23 UST 3736; TIAS 7523.

Related agreement:
June 9, 1982 (TIAS 10414).

Agreement on rights, privileges and immunities of the United States-Union of Soviet Socialist Republics Standing Consultative Commission. Exchange of notes at Bern February 26 and March 5, 1973; entered into force March 5, 1973.
24 UST 772; TIAS 7582; 944 UNTS 95.

Agreement establishing rights, privileges and immunities of the delegation to the negotia-

tions concerning theater (intermediate range) nuclear forces. Exchange of letters at Bern October 17, 1980; entered into force October 17, 1980.
33 UST 610; TIAS 10056; 1265 UNTS 177.

Related agreement:
November 11 and 20, 1981 (33 UST 4237; TIAS 10298).

Agreement establishing rights, privileges and immunities of the United States delegation to the negotiations on nuclear and space arms. Exchange of notes at Bern March 1 and 5, 1985; entered into force March 5, 1985.
TIAS 11188.

PUBLICATIONS

Agreement relating to the exchange of official publications. Exchange of notes at Washington January 5 and February 24, 1950; entered into force February 24, 1950.
1 UST 396; TIAS 2058; 93 UNTS 3.

SOCIAL SECURITY

Agreement on social security, with final protocol. Signed at Washington July 18, 1979; entered into force November 1, 1980.
32 UST 2165; TIAS 9830; 1252 UNTS 127.

Amendment:
June 1, 1988 (TIAS 12126).

Administrative agreement for the implementation of the agreement on social security of July 18, 1979. Signed at Bern December 20, 1979; entered into force November 1, 1980.
32 UST 2165; TIAS 9830; 1252 UNTS 137.

TAXATION

Convention for the avoidance of double taxation with respect to taxes on estates and inheritances. Signed at Washington July 9, 1951; entered into force September 17, 1952.
3 UST 3972; TIAS 2533; 165 UNTS 51.

Convention for the avoidance of double taxation with respect to taxes on income, with protocol. Signed at Washington October 2, 1996; entered into force December 19, 1997.
TIAS

TELECOMMUNICATION

Agreement relating to the reciprocal granting of authorizations to permit licensed amateur radio operators of either country to operate their stations in the other country. Exchange of notes at Bern January 12 and May 16, 1967; entered into force May 16, 1967.
18 UST 554; TIAS 6264; 685 UNTS 319.

TRADE (See also COMMERCE)

Agreement within the context of the multilateral trade negotiations regarding motor vehicles, and related letter of November 19, 1980. Done at Bern April 11, 1979; entered into force January 1, 1980.
32 UST 5521; TIAS 10004; 1265 UNTS 181.

Arrangement within the context of the multilateral trade negotiations concerning cheeses, with exchange of letters, and related letter of November 19, 1980. Done at Geneva and Bern April 12, 1979; entered into force January 1, 1980.
32 UST 5527; TIAS 10005; 1265 UNTS 151.

Commitment of Switzerland within the context of the multilateral trade negotiations concerning access to its market for beef, and related letter of November 19, 1980. Done at Geneva and Bern April 12 and July 10, 1979; entered into force January 1, 1980.
32 UST 5539; TIAS 10006; 1265 UNTS 163.

Agreement within the context of the multilateral trade negotiations concerning the treatment of certain chemicals. Exchange of letters at Geneva and Washington December 18 and 21, 1979; entered into force December 21, 1979.
32 UST 5545; TIAS 10007; 1265 UNTS 171.

TRADE-MARKS

Agreement relating to the registration of trademarks. Exchange of notes at Washington April 27 and May 14, 1883; entered into force May 14, 1883.
TS 471; 11 Bevans 901.

VISAS

Agreement relating to the waiver of passport visa fees for nonimmigrants. Exchange of notes at Bern May 11, 1925; entered into force May 11, 1925; operative June 1, 1925.
11 Bevans 915.

Agreement relating to the waiver of passport visa fees for nonimmigrants. Exchanges of notes at Washington October 22 and 31 and November 4 and 13, 1947; entered into force November 13, 1947.
6 UST 93; TIAS 3172; 251 UNTS 79.

SYRIAN ARAB REPUBLIC

AGRICULTURAL COMMODITIES

Agreement between the United States and the United Arab Republic relating to the sale of agricultural commodities to the United Arab Republic (Northern Region). Signed at Cairo

SYRIAN ARAB REPUBLIC (Cont'd)

November 14, 1959; entered into force November 14, 1959.
10 UST 1908; TIAS 4357; 360 UNTS 311.

Agreement between the United States and the United Arab Republic relating to the sale of agricultural commodities to the United Arab Republic (Northern Region). Signed at Cairo August 9, 1960; entered into force August 9, 1960.
11 UST 1994; TIAS 4551; 388 UNTS 271.

Amendment:
September 17, 1960 (11 UST 2136; TIAS 4575; 389 UNTS 342).

Agricultural commodities agreement with exchange of notes. Signed at Damascus November 9, 1961; entered into force November 9, 1961.
13 UST 97; TIAS 4944; 435 UNTS 75.

Amendment:
February 24, 1962 (13 UST 376; TIAS 4993; 445 UNTS 389).

Agricultural commodities agreement with exchange of notes. Signed at Damascus November 18, 1963; entered into force November 18, 1963.
14 UST 1864; TIAS 5497; 494 UNTS 169.

Amendment:
December 28, 1963 (14 UST 1864; TIAS 5497; 494 UNTS 169).

Agricultural commodities agreement. Signed at Damascus November 20, 1974; entered into force November 20, 1974.
26 UST 1576; TIAS 8119; 1006 UNTS 57.

Related agreements:
April 20, 1976 (28 UST 7370; TIAS 8716).
May 11 and 16, 1976 (28 UST 7384; TIAS 8716).
June 2 and 3, 1976 (28 UST 7386; TIAS 8716).
September 28 and 29, 1976 (28 UST 7389; TIAS 8716).
March 3, 1977 (28 UST 7392; TIAS 8717).
May 3, 1978 (29 UST 5198; TIAS 9096; 1150 UNTS 47).
July 25, 1978 (29 UST 5211; TIAS 9096; 1150 UNTS 59).
May 2, 1979 (30 UST 7209; TIAS 9579).
June 23, 1979 (30 UST 7221; TIAS 9579).

CULTURAL RELATIONS

Cultural agreement. Signed at Damascus May 12, 1977; entered into force May 12, 1977.
28 UST 5321; TIAS 8634.

CUSTOMS

Agreement between the United States and France relating to customs privileges for educational, religious, and philanthropic institutions in Syria and Lebanon. Exchange of notes at Paris February 18, 1937; entered into force February 18, 1937.
51 Stat. 279; EAS 107; 7 Bevans 1017; 184 LNTS 479.

ECONOMIC AND TECHNICAL COOPERATION

Agreement between the United States and the United Arab Republic extending to the Syrian region of the United Arab Republic application of the general agreement for technical cooperation with Egypt of May 5, 1951, as amended, and the economic development program agreement of November 6, 1954. Exchange of notes at Cairo April 2, 1960; entered into force April 2, 1960.
11 UST 1500; TIAS 4492; 376 UNTS 422.

Agency for International Development:
February 27, 1975 (28 UST 575; TIAS 8477; 1068 UNTS 311).
February 27, 1975 (28 UST 809; TIAS 8482; 1068 UNTS 337).
February 27, 1975 (28 UST 595; TIAS 8478; 1068 UNTS 271).
June 30, 1975 (26 UST 3045; TIAS 8212).
June 30, 1975 (28 UST 624; TIAS 8478; 1068 UNTS 281).
July 22, 1976 (28 UST 1149; TIAS 8501; 1068 UNTS 369).
July 22, 1976 (28 UST 1174; TIAS 8502; 1068 UNTS 393).
September 30, 1976 (28 UST 3190; TIAS 8582).
September 20, 1977 (29 UST 3459; TIAS 9022; 1123 UNTS 233).
September 28, 1978 (30 UST 6296; TIAS 9554; 1234 UNTS 171).

FINANCE

Agreement relating to investment guaranties, with related letter. Exchange of notes at Damascus August 9, 1976; entered into force August 13, 1977.
28 UST 7122; TIAS 8707.

GENERAL RELATIONS

Convention between the United States and France relating to rights in Syria and Lebanon. Signed at Paris April 4, 1924; entered into force July 13, 1924.
43 Stat. 1821; TS 695; 7 Bevans 925.

Agreement relating to rights of American nationals. Exchange of notes at Damascus Sep-

tember 7 and 8, 1944; entered into force September 8, 1944.
58 Stat. 1491; EAS 434; 11 Bevans 970; 124 UNTS 251.

POSTAL MATTERS

Agreement with the United Arab Republic concerning the exchange of parcel post and regulations of execution. Signed at Cairo December 30, 1958 and at Washington January 13, 1959; entered into force October 1, 1959.
10 UST 1664; TIAS 4315; 358 UNTS 3.

International express mail agreement, with detailed regulations. Signed at Damascus and Washington September 26 and November 16, 1993; entered into force January 1, 1994.
NP

TELECOMMUNICATION

Agreement relating to reciprocal authorization for each Government to install and operate a lowpower radio station in the fixed service at or near its Embassy for transmission of official messages. Exchange of notes at Washington November 13, 1974 and May 15, 1975; entered into force May 15, 1975.
27 UST 3292; TIAS 8363; 1068 UNTS 359.

TAJIKISTAN

For agreements prior to December 31, 1991, see UNION OF SOVIET SOCIALIST REPUBLICS.

COPYRIGHT (See APPENDIX)

ECONOMIC AND TECHNICAL COOPERATION

Agreement regarding cooperation to facilitate the provision of humanitarian and technical economic assistance. Signed at Dushanbe September 13, 1993; entered into force September 13, 1993.
TIAS 12163.

FINANCE

Investment incentive agreement. Signed at Dushanbe June 25, 1992; entered into force June 25, 1992.
TIAS 12461.

TAJIKISTAN (Cont'd)

TRADE

Agreement on trade relations, with exchanges of letters. Signed at Dushanbe July 1, 1993; entered into force November 24, 1993.
TIAS

TANZANIA

On December 9, 1961 Tanganyika attained fully responsible status within the British Commonwealth. In a note dated December 9, 1961 to the Secretary-General of the United Nations from the Prime Minister, the Government of Tanganyika stated that it is willing to continue to apply, on a reciprocal basis, all such treaties validly applied or extended to it as a territory for a period of two years from the date of independence, that is to December 8, 1963, unless abrogated or modified earlier by mutual consent. On April 26, 1964 the Republic of Tanganyika and the People's Republic of Zanzibar were united as one Sovereign State under the name of the United Republic of Tanganyika and Zanzibar. In a note dated May 6, 1964 the United Republic of Tanganyika and Zanzibar informed the Secretary-General of the United Nations that "all international treaties and agreements in force between the Republic of Tanganyika or the People's Republic of Zanzibar and other States or international organizations will, to the extent that their implementation is consistent with the constitutional position established by the Articles of Union, remain in force within the regional limits prescribed on their conclusion and in accordance with the principles of international law." On October 29, 1964 the name of the Republic was changed to the United Republic of Tanzania.

AGRICULTURAL COMMODITIES

Agricultural commodities agreement. Signed at Dar es Salaam May 23, 1975; entered into force May 23, 1975.
26 UST 2290; TIAS 8158.

Agricultural commodities agreement. Signed at Dar es Salaam June 15, 1976; entered into force June 15, 1976.
27 UST 2314; TIAS 8310; 1055 UNTS 111.

Related agreements:
March 19, 1977 (29 UST 1; TIAS 8784).
April 28, 1978 (29 UST 6078; TIAS 9170).
March 19, 1980 (32 UST 890; TIAS 9736; 1222 UNTS 171).
June 9, 1980 (32 UST 1689; TIAS 9795).
May 5, 1981 (33 UST 1779; TIAS 10146; 1529 UNTS 379).

Agricultural commodities agreement, with minutes of negotiation. Signed at Dar es Salaam June 8, 1982; entered into force June 8, 1982. TIAS 10530.

Agreement for the sale of agricultural commodities, with minutes of negotiation. Signed at Dar es Salaam July 22, 1983; entered into force July 22, 1983.
TIAS 10758.

CONSULS

Consular convention and protocol of signature between the United States and the United Kingdom. Signed at Washington June 6, 1951; entered into force September 7, 1952.[1][2]
3 UST 3426; TIAS 2494; 165 UNTS 121.

NOTES:
[1] Paragraph 1 of article 7 is not applicable to Tanganyika.
[2] Treaty continued in force between the United States and Tanzania by the exchange of notes of November 30 and December 6, 1965 (16 UST 2066; TIAS 5946).

COPYRIGHT (See APPENDIX)

ECONOMIC AND TECHNICAL COOPERATION

Agreement providing for the furnishing of economic, technical, and related assistance. Exchange of notes at Dar es Salaam February 8, 1968; entered into force February 8, 1968.
19 UST 4614; TIAS 6448; 698 UNTS 67.

Agency for International Development:
August 12 and 13, 1975 (29 UST 9; TIAS 8786).
April 13, 1976 (29 UST 1003; TIAS 8861).
August 15, 1977 (29 UST 5276; TIAS 9104).
April 7, 1999.

ENVIRONMENTAL COOPERATION

Agreement for cooperation in the Global Learning and Observations to Benefit the Environment (GLOBE) Program, with appendices. Signed at Dar es Salaam April 1, 1997; entered into force April 1, 1997.
TIAS

EXTRADITION

Extradition treaty between the United States and the United Kingdom.[1] Signed at London December 22, 1931; entered into force June 24, 1935.
47 Stat. 2122; TS 849; 12 Bevans 482; 163 LNTS 59.

NOTE:
[1] Treaty continued in force between the United States and Tanzania by the exchange of notes of November 30 and December 6, 1965 (16 UST 2066; TIAS 5946).

FINANCE

Agreement relating to investment guaranties. Exchange of notes at Dar es Salaam November 14, 1963; entered into force November 14, 1963.
14 UST 1608; TIAS 5465; 493 UNTS 75.

Agreement regarding the consolidation and rescheduling of certain debts owed to, guaranteed by or insured by the United States Government, and its agencies, with annexes. Signed at Dar es Salaam March 18, 1987; entered into force April 27, 1987.
NP

Agreement regarding the consolidation and rescheduling of certain debts owed to, guaranteed by or insured by the United States Government and its agencies, with annexes. Signed at Dar es Salaam May 4, 1989; entered into force June 15, 1989.
NP

Agreement regarding the consolidation and rescheduling of certain debts owed to, guaranteed by, or insured by the United States Government and its agencies, with annexes. Signed at Dar es Salaam October 31, 1990; entered into force January 9, 1991.
NP

Agreement regarding the consolidation and rescheduling or refinancing of certain debts owed to, guaranteed by or insured by the United States Government and its agencies, with annexes. Signed at Dar es Salaam September 11, 1992; entered into force December 3, 1992.
NP

Investment incentive agreement. Signed at Dar es Salaam December 24, 1996; entered into force November 26, 1997.
TIAS

Agreement regarding the consolidation, reduction and rescheduling of certain debts owed to, guaranteed by, or insured by the United States Government and its Agency. Signed at Dar es Salaam January 16, 1998; entered into force March 27, 1998.
NP

PEACE CORPS

Agreement concerning the provision of Peace Corps volunteers in Tanzania. Signed at Dar es Salaam March 23, 1989; entered into force March 23, 1989.
TIAS 12110.

TANZANIA (Cont'd)

Extension:
February 11 and March 30, 1994 (TIAS 12110).

POSTAL MATTERS

Parcel post agreement and regulations of execution. Signed at Zanzibar October 20 and at Washington December 30, 1959; entered into force May 1, 1960.
11 UST 293; TIAS 4449.

International express mail agreement, with detailed regulations. Signed at Dar es Salaam and Washington December 30, 1987 and January 25, 1988; entered into force February 15, 1988.
TIAS 11886.

TREATY OBLIGATIONS

Agreement continuing in force between the United States and Tanzania the extradition treaty and the consular convention between the United States and the United Kingdom. Exchange of notes at Dar es Salaam November 30 and December 6, 1965; entered into force December 6, 1965; effective December 9, 1963.
16 UST 2066; TIAS 5946; 592 UNTS 53.

THAILAND

AGRICULTURAL COMMODITIES

Agricultural commodities agreement. Signed at Bangkok June 21, 1955; entered into force June 21, 1955.
6 UST 1169; TIAS 3260; 262 UNTS 87.

Amendment:
December 14, 1956 (7 UST 3463; TIAS 3722; 266 UNTS 436).

Agricultural commodities agreement with exchange of notes. Signed at Bangkok March 4, 1957; entered into force March 4, 1957.
8 UST 317; TIAS 3777; 279 UNTS 235.

Amendment:
March 12 and April 9, 1959 (10 UST 1242; TIAS 4261; 354 UNTS 416).

Agricultural commodities agreement with annex. Signed at Bangkok March 17, 1972; entered into force March 17, 1972.
23 UST 657; TIAS 7330.

Amendments:
May 11, 1973 (24 UST 1767; TIAS 7685).
May 23, 1974 (25 UST 1538; TIAS 7889).

AGRICULTURE

Memorandum of understanding for technical cooperation in agricultural development. Signed at Washington September 19, 1984; entered into force September 19, 1984.
TIAS 11034.

ATOMIC ENERGY

Agreement for cooperation concerning civil uses of atomic energy. Signed at Washington May 14, 1974; entered into force June 27, 1974.
25 UST 1181; TIAS 7850.

AVIATION

Agreement relating to air service facilities at Don Muang Airport and Bangkapi. Signed at Bangkok May 8, 1947; entered into force May 8, 1947.
61 Stat. 3855; TIAS 1735; 11 Bevans 1037; 42 UNTS 241.

Air transport agreement, with annex and memorandum of understanding. Signed at Bangkok May 8, 1996; entered into force May 8, 1996.
TIAS

COMMERCE

Treaty of amity and economic relations with exchanges of notes. Signed at Bangkok May 29, 1966; entered into force June 8, 1968.
19 UST 5843; TIAS 6540; 652 UNTS 253.

CONSULS (See COMMERCE)

COPYRIGHT (See APPENDIX)

DEFENSE (See also MUTUAL SECURITY)

Agreement respecting military assistance. Signed at Bangkok October 17, 1950; entered into force October 17, 1950.
3 UST 2675; TIAS 2434; 79 UNTS 41.

Agreement relating to the disposition of military equipment and materials furnished under the military assistance agreement. Exchange of notes at Bangkok July 6, 1955; entered into force July 6, 1955.
6 UST 2067; TIAS 3274; 258 UNTS 386.

Agreement concerning payment to the United States of net proceeds from the sale of defense articles furnished under the military assistance program. Exchange of notes at Bangkok Janu-

ary 3 and 17, 1975; entered into force January 17, 1975; effective July 1, 1974.
26 UST 80; TIAS 8010; 992 UNTS 105.

Memorandum of agreement on integrated communications system, with appendix. Signed at Bangkok January 10, 1977; entered into force January 10, 1977.
29 UST 591; TIAS 8837.

Memorandum of agreement relating to the storage of ammunition in Thailand. Signed at Bangkok March 22, 1977; entered into force March 22, 1977.
29 UST 743; TIAS 8850.

General security of military information agreement. Exchange of notes at Bangkok March 30 and April 5, 1983; entered into force April 5, 1983.
TIAS 10678.

Memorandum of understanding on logistic support. Signed at New York October 3, 1985; entered into force October 3, 1985.
TIAS 11232.

Extension:
September 26 and October 3, 1990 (TIAS 11508).

Agreement concerning the provision of training related to defense articles under the United States International Military Education and Training (IMET) Program. Exchange of notes at Bangkok April 15 and July 28, 1986; entered into force July 28, 1986.
TIAS 11385.

Agreement relating to a war reserve stockpile program in Thailand, with annexes. Signed at Bangkok January 9, 1987; entered into force March 22, 1988.
TIAS 12604.

Amendment and extension:
February 15, 1995 (TIAS 12604).

Agreement concerning measures to be taken for the transfer, security and safeguarding of technical information, software and equipment to the Ministry of Defense to enable industry to operate, maintain and expand Royal Thai Air Force air combat maneuvering instrumentation range facilities. Signed at Washington September 30, 1993; entered into force September 30, 1993.
TIAS 11509.

ECONOMIC AND TECHNICAL COOPERATION

Economic and technical cooperation agreement, with exchange of notes. Signed at Bangkok June 2, 1977; entered into force June 2, 1977.
28 UST 5210; TIAS 8622.

Agency for International Development:
December 11, 1975 (28 UST 397; TIAS 8474).
March 31, 1976 (29 UST 5454; TIAS 9122; 1228 UNTS 247).

THAILAND (Cont'd)

September 8, 1976 (28 UST 2209; TIAS 8539).
September 8, 1976 (28 UST 2214; TIAS 8540; 1071 UNTS 3).
May 31, 1977 (29 UST 1817; TIAS 8904).
May 4, 1978 (30 UST 3681; TIAS 9422; 1228 UNTS 289).

EDUCATION

Agreement for financing certain educational exchange programs. Signed at Bangkok May 24, 1963; entered into force May 24, 1963.
14 UST 770; TIAS 5355; 477 UNTS 123.

Amendment:
June 9 and July 9, 1970 (21 UST 1512; TIAS 6912; 753 UNTS 392).

EXTRADITION

Treaty relating to extradition. Signed at Washington December 14, 1983; entered into force May 17, 1991.
TIAS

FINANCE

Agreement relating to investment guaranties under section 413 (b)(4) of the Mutual Security Act of 1954. Exchange of notes at Washington August 27 and September 1, 1954; entered into force September 1, 1954.
5 UST 2258; TIAS 3086; 237 UNTS 209.

Amendment:
December 22, 1965 (16 UST 2041; TIAS 5940; 551 UNTS 292).

HEALTH

Agreement relating to the conversion of the Southeast Asia Treaty Organization cholera research project in Thailand to a SEATO medical research laboratory. Exchange of notes at Bangkok December 23, 1960; entered into force December 23, 1960.
11 UST 2683; TIAS 4665; 405 UNTS 135.

Agreement relating to the establishment and operation of a SEATO Clinical Research Center at the School of Graduate Studies of the University of Medical Sciences, with memorandum of understanding. Exchange of notes at Bangkok April 1 and 25, 1963; entered into force April 25, 1963.
14 UST 459; TIAS 5340; 476 UNTS 115.

Agreement modifying and continuing the agreements of December 23, 1960 and April 1 and 25, 1963, relating to the SEATO medical research project and the SEATO clinical re-

search centre. Exchange of notes at Bangkok January 19 and 28, 1977; entered into force July 1, 1977.
29 UST 643; TIAS 8840.

Agreement on research collaboration related to HIV infection and AIDS in Thailand, with annex. Signed at Bangkok and Atlanta July 24 and August 3 and 8, 1990; entered in force August 8, 1990.
TIAS 12419.

JUDICIAL ASSISTANCE

Treaty on mutual assistance in criminal matters, with attachments. Signed at Bangkok March 19, 1986; entered into force June 10, 1993.
TIAS

Agreement concerning an International Law Enforcement Academy. Signed at Bangkok September 30, 1998; entered into force September 30, 1998.
TIAS

MAPPING

Agreement providing for an aerial photographic mapping survey of Thailand. Exchange of notes at Bangkok November 8 and December 3, 1952; entered into force December 3, 1952.
3 UST 5893; TIAS 2759; 213 UNTS 91.

Memorandum of agreement concerning mapping, charting and geodesy. Signed at Bangkok and Fairfax February 27 and March 15, 1990; entered into force March 15, 1990.
NP

MUTUAL SECURITY

Agreement relating to the assurances required by the Mutual Security Act of 1951. Exchange of notes at Bangkok December 27 and 29, 1951; entered into force December 29, 1951.
3 UST 4653; TIAS 2619; 179 UNTS 113.

NARCOTIC DRUGS

Memorandum of understanding on cooperation in the narcotics field. Signed at Washington September 28, 1971; entered into force September 28, 1971.
22 UST 1587; TIAS 7185; 807 UNTS 49.

PEACE CORPS

Agreement relating to the establishment of a Peace Corps program in Thailand. Exchange of

notes at Bangkok November 20 and 28, 1961; entered into force November 28, 1961.
12 UST 3225; TIAS 4929; 434 UNTS 77.

POSTAL MATTERS

Agreement for the exchange of international money orders. Signed at Bangkok January 12 and at Washington February 21, 1962; entered into force July 1, 1962.
13 UST 1871; TIAS 5138; 459 UNTS 95.

Parcel post agreement. Signed at Bangkok May 31 and at Washington June 7, 1962; entered into force October 1, 1962.
13 UST 2209; TIAS 5188; 459 UNTS 135.

International express mail agreement, with detailed regulations. Signed at Bangkok and Washington November 14 and December 9, 1983; entered into force February 18, 1984.
TIAS 10847.

PRISONER TRANSFER

Treaty on cooperation in the execution of penal sentences. Signed at Bangkok October 29, 1982; entered into force December 7, 1988.
TIAS

PUBLICATIONS

Agreement relating to the exchange of official publications. Exchange of notes at Bangkok September 5, 1947; entered into force September 5, 1947.
61 Stat. 3154; TIAS 1654; 11 Bevans 1040; 73 UNTS 57.

SEISMIC OBSERVATIONS

Memorandum of understanding relating to Chiang Mai seismic research station. Signed at Bangkok December 29, 1976; entered into force December 29, 1976.
28 UST 8866; TIAS 8774; 1095 UNTS 191.

TAXATION

Convention for the avoidance of double taxation and the prevention of fiscal evasion with respect to taxes on income, with exchange of notes. Signed at Bangkok November 26, 1996; entered into force December 15, 1997.
TIAS

TELECOMMUNICATION

Agreement relating to the establishment of certain radio transmitting and receiving facilities in Thailand. Exchange of notes at Bangkok

THAILAND (Cont'd)

August 11, 1965; entered into force August 11, 1965.
23 UST 1158; TIAS 7378.

Extension and amendment:
February 28 and March 7, 1983 (TIAS 10751).

Agreement relating to the reciprocal granting of authorizations to permit licensed amateur radio operators of either country to operate their station in the other country. Exchange of notes at Bangkok October 11 and 30, 1990; entered into force December 14, 1990.
TIAS 12421.

TRADE (See also COMMERCE)

Memorandum of understanding concerning concessions and contributions to the multilateral trade negotiations, with related notes of September 28 and October 21, 1982. Signed at Geneva April 9, 1979; entered into force October 21, 1982; effective January 1, 1982.
TIAS 10897.

Agreement relating to trade in textiles and textile products, with annexes. Exchange of letters at Washington and Bangkok September 3, 1991; entered into force September 3, 1991; effective January 1, 1991.
NP

Amendments and extension:
May 28 and June 25, 1992 (NP).
October 9 and December 17, 1992 (NP).
June 3 and July 5, 1994 (NP).

VISAS

Arrangement relating to the waiver of passport visas and visa fees for nonimmigrants. Exchange of notes at Bangkok September 19, 1925; entered into force September 19, 1925.
11 Bevans 1014.

TOGO

COMMERCE

Treaty of amity and economic relations. Signed at Lome February 8, 1966; entered into force February 5, 1967.
18 UST 1; TIAS 6193; 680 UNTS 159.

COPYRIGHT (See APPENDIX)

DEFENSE

Agreement concerning the provision of training related to defense articles under the United States International Military Education and Training (IMET) Program. Exchange of notes at Lome March 10 and July 17, 1980; entered into force July 17, 1980.
32 UST 2642; TIAS 9866; 1274 UNTS 211.

ECONOMIC AND TECHNICAL COOPERATION

Agreement providing for economic, technical and related assistance. Exchange of notes at Lome December 22, 1960; entered into force December 22, 1960.
11 UST 2566; TIAS 4646; 401 UNTS 33.

Agency for International Development:
October 12, 1977 (29 UST 5286; TIAS 9106).

FINANCE

Agreement relating to investment guaranties. Signed at Washington March 20, 1962; entered into force March 20, 1962.
13 UST 321; TIAS 4983; 445 UNTS 79.

Agreement regarding the consolidation and rescheduling of certain debts owed to, guaranteed or insured by the United States Government and the Export-Import Bank of the United States, with annexes. Signed at Lome March 28, 1980; entered into force May 2, 1980.
32 UST 933; TIAS 9740; 1222 UNTS 225.

Agreement regarding the consolidation and rescheduling of certain debts owed to, or guaranteed by the United States Government through the Export-Import Bank of the United States, with annexes and agreed minute. Signed at Lome September 18, 1981; entered into force December 7, 1981.
NP

Agreement regarding the consolidation and rescheduling of certain debts owed to, or guaranteed by the United States Government through the Export-Import Bank. Signed at Lome November 29, 1983; entered into force January 31, 1984.
NP

JUDICIAL ASSISTANCE

Procedures for mutual assistance in connection with matters relating to the Gulfstream American Corporation, formerly known as Grumman American Aviation Corporation. Signed at

Washington January 30, 1979; entered into force January 30, 1979.
30 UST 3477; TIAS 9401; 1180 UNTS 199.

PEACE CORPS

Agreement relating to the establishment of a Peace Corps program in Togo. Exchange of notes at Lome August 1 and September 5, 1962; entered into force September 5, 1962.
13 UST 2251; TIAS 5191; 461 UNTS 47.

POSTAL MATTERS

International express mail agreement, with detailed regulations. Signed at Lome and Washington November 28, 1988 and January 6, 1989; entered into force January 30, 1989.
NP

SOCIAL SECURITY

Agreement relating to United States participation with respect to its eligible employees in the Togolese social security system. Exchange of notes at Lome March 17 and 26, 1971; entered into force March 26, 1971.
22 UST 526; TIAS 7094; 792 UNTS 223.

TONGA

On June 4, 1970 Tonga became an independent state. In a note dated June 18, 1970 to the Secretary-General of the United Nations, the Prime Minister of Tonga stated that each treaty validly made on behalf of the Kingdom of Tonga by the Government of the United Kingdom pursuant to and within the powers of the United Kingdom derived from certain instruments entered into between the United Kingdom and the Kingdom of Tonga, continues to bind the latter until validly terminated, that it is desired that it be presumed that each treaty continues to create rights and obligations, and that action be based on this presumption until a decision is reached that the treaty should be regarded as not having been validly made for the Kingdom of Tonga or as having lapsed. Should the Government of the Kingdom of Tonga be of the opinion that it continues to be legally bound by the treaty, and wishes to terminate the operation of the treaty, it will in due course give notice of termination in the terms thereof. With respect to duly ratified treaties which were entered into by the Kingdom of Tonga before the United Kingdom undertook the responsibility for the foreign relations thereof, the Government of the Kingdom of Tonga acknowledges that they remain in force to the extent to which their provisions were unaffected in virtue of international law by certain instruments entered into between the United Kingdom and the Kingdom of Tonga or by other events.

TONGA (Cont'd)

COMMERCE

Treaty of amity, commerce, and navigation.[1]
Signed at Nuku'alofa October 2, 1886; entered
into force September 18, 1888.
25 Stat. 1440; TS 357; 11 Bevans 1043.

NOTE:
[1] Entire treaty, with the exception of article
VI, terminated July 28, 1920.

CONSULS

Consular convention between the United States
and the United Kingdom. Signed at Washington June 6, 1951; entered into force September 7, 1952.
3 UST 3426; TIAS 2494; 165 UNTS 121.

DEFENSE

Agreement concerning the provision of training
related to defense articles under the United
States International Military Education and
Training (IMET) Program. Exchange of notes
at Suva and Nuku'alofa November 18 and 25,
1985; entered into force November 25, 1985.
TIAS 11101.

Agreement concerning the status of members
of the United States Armed Forces in the
Kingdom of Tonga. Signed at Suva July 20,
1992; entered into force July 20, 1992.
TIAS 12523.

EXTRADITION

Extradition treaty. Signed at London December
22, 1931; entered into force June 24, 1935; applicable to Tonga August 1, 1966.
47 Stat. 2122; TS 849; 12 Bevans 482; 163
LNTS 59.

Agreement continuing in force between the
United States and Tonga the extradition treaty
of December 22, 1931 between the United
States and the United Kingdom. Exchange of
notes at Nuku'alofa and Wellington March 14
and April 13, 1977; entered into force April
13, 1977.
28 UST 5290; TIAS 8628; 1087 UNTS 289.

FINANCE

Investment incentive agreement. Exchange of
notes at Suva and Nuku'alofa August 22, 1983
and November 26, 1984; entered into force
November 26, 1984.
TIAS 11000.

PEACE CORPS

Agreement relating to the establishment of a
Peace Corps program in Tonga with exchange
of letters. Exchange of notes at Suva and
Nuku'alofa May 17 and 27, 1968; entered into
force May 27, 1968.
19 UST 5486; TIAS 6534; 707 UNTS 71.

TRADE-MARKS

Declaration by the United States and the
United Kingdom affording reciprocal protection to trade-marks. Signed at London October
24, 1877; entered into force October 24, 1877.
20 Stat. 703; TS 138; 12 Bevans 198.

TRINIDAD and TOBAGO

On August 31, 1962 Trinidad and Tobago became independent. By an exchange of letters
on August 31, 1962 between the High Commissioner for the United Kingdom in Trinidad
and Tobago and the Prime Minister of Trinidad and Tobago, the Government of Trinidad
and Tobago agreed to assume all obligations
and responsibilities of the United Kingdom
which arise from any valid international instrument (including any such instrument made by
the Government of the Federation of the West
Indies by virtue of authority entrusted by the
Government of the United Kingdom). The
rights and benefits heretofore enjoyed by the
Government of the United Kingdom by virtue
of application of any such international instrument to Trinidad and Tobago shall henceforth
be enjoyed by the Government of Trinidad and
Tobago.

AVIATION

Arrangement between the United States and
the United Kingdom relating to pilot licenses
to operate civil aircraft. Exchange of notes at
Washington March 28 and April 5, 1935; entered into force May 5, 1935.
49 Stat. 3731; EAS 77; 12 Bevans 513; 162
LNTS 59.

Air transport agreement, with annexes. Signed
at Port-of-Spain May 23, 1990; entered into
force May 23, 1990.
TIAS 11724.

CLAIMS

Agreement between the United States and the
United Kingdom relating to claims for damages resulting from acts of armed forces or civilian personnel. Exchange of notes at Washington October 23, 1946 and January 23, 1947;
entered into force January 23, 1947; operative
from June 6, 1944.
61 Stat. 2876; TIAS 1622; 12 Bevans 805; 15
UNTS 281.

CONSULS

Consular convention between the United States
and the United Kingdom. Signed at Washington June 6, 1951; entered into force September 7, 1952.
3 UST 3426; TIAS 2494; 165 UNTS 121.

COPYRIGHT (See APPENDIX)

DEFENSE (See also MUTUAL SECURITY)

Agreement concerning the provision of training
related to defense articles under the United
States International Military Education and
Training (IMET) Program, with aide memoire.
Exchange of notes at Port of Spain December
29, 1983 and November 16, 1984; entered into
force November 16, 1984.
TIAS 10989.

Agreement concerning grants under the Foreign Assistance Act of 1961, as amended, and
the furnishing of defense articles, related training, and other defense services from the United
States to Trinidad and Tobago for counter-narcotics purposes. Exchange of notes at Port of
Spain February 4 and 13, 1998; entered into
force February 13, 1998.
TIAS

ECONOMIC AND TECHNICAL COOPERATION

Economic cooperation agreement between the
United States and the United Kingdom. Signed
at London July 6, 1948; applicable, with the
exception of article IV, to Trinidad and Tobago March 17, 1949.
62 Stat. 2596; TIAS 1795; 12 Bevans 874; 22
UNTS 263.

Amendments:
January 3, 1950 (1 UST 184; TIAS 2036; 84
UNTS 304).
May 25, 1951 (2 UST 1292; TIAS 2277; 99
UNTS 308).
February 23, 1953 (4 UST 1528; TIAS 2815;
172 UNTS 332).
June 26 and August 20, 1959 (11 UST 2680;
TIAS 4664; 405 UNTS 288).

Agreement between the United States and the
United Kingdom for technical cooperation in
respect of the territories for the international
relations of which the Government of the
United Kingdom are responsible. Signed at
London July 13, 1951; applicable to Trinidad
and Tobago August 14, 1954.
2 UST 1307; TIAS 2281; 105 UNTS 71.

TRINIDAD and TOBAGO (Cont'd)

EMPLOYMENT

Agreement relating to the employment of dependents of official government employees. Exchange of notes at Port of Spain May 15, 1990 and July 23, 1992; entered into force July 23, 1992.
TIAS 11924.

ENVIRONMENTAL COOPERATION

Agreement for cooperation in the Global Learning and Observations to Benefit the Environment (GLOBE) Program, with appendices. Signed at Port of Spain July 16, 1996; entered into force July 16, 1996.
TIAS

EXTRADITION

Extradition treaty. Signed at Port of Spain March 4, 1996; entered into force November 29, 1999.
TIAS

FINANCE

Agreement relating to investment guaranties. Exchange of notes at Port-of-Spain January 8 and 15, 1963; entered into force January 15, 1963.
14 UST 113; TIAS 5278; 471 UNTS 141.

Agreement regarding the consolidation and rescheduling of certain debts owed to, guaranteed by, or insured by the United States Government and its agencies. Signed at Port-of-Spain July 28, 1989; entered into force September 13, 1989.
NP

Agreement regarding the consolidation and rescheduling of certain debts owed to, guaranteed by, or insured by the United States Government and its agencies, with annexes. Signed at Port-of-Spain November 26, 1990; entered into force January 14, 1991.
NP

INVESTMENT

Treaty concerning the encouragement and reciprocal protection of investment, with annex and protocol. Signed at Washington September 26, 1994; entered into force December 26, 1996.
TIAS

JUDICIAL ASSISTANCE

Procedures for mutual assistance in the administration of justice in connection with matters relating to the investigation designated as MA-106. Signed at Washington June 7, 1982; entered into force June 7, 1982.
TIAS 10416.

Treaty on mutual legal assistance in criminal matters, with forms. Signed at Port of Spain March 4, 1996; entered into force November 29, 1999.
TIAS

MUTUAL SECURITY

Agreement between the United States and the United Kingdom relating to the assurances required under the Mutual Security Act of 1951. Exchange of notes at London January 8, 1952; entered into force January 8, 1952.
3 UST 4665; TIAS 2622; 126 UNTS 307.

NARCOTIC DRUGS

Agreement concerning maritime counter-drug operations. Signed at Port of Spain March 4, 1996; entered into force March 4, 1996.
TIAS

POSTAL MATTERS

Money order agreement. Signed at Port-of-Spain September 18 and at Washington October 23, 1891; operative January 1, 1891.
NP

Parcel post agreement with regulations of execution. Signed at Port-of-Spain and Washington March 9 and 18, 1968; entered into force May 1, 1968.
19 UST 4735; TIAS 6472; 698 UNTS 121.

International express mail agreement, with detailed regulations. Signed at Port of Spain and Washington November 3 and December 7, 1987; entered into force July 1, 1988.
TIAS 11558.

PROPERTY

Convention between the United States and the United Kingdom relating to the tenure and disposition of real and personal property. Signed at Washington March 2, 1899; applicable to Trinidad and Tobago February 9, 1901.
31 Stat. 1939; TS 146; 12 Bevans 246.

Supplementary convention relating to the tenure and disposition of real and personal property. Signed at Washington May 27, 1936; entered into force March 10, 1941.
55 Stat. 1101; TS 964; 5 Bevans 140; 203 LNTS 367.

TAXATION

Convention for the avoidance of double taxation, the prevention of fiscal evasion with respect to taxes on income, and the encouragement of international trade and investment with related notes.[1] Signed at Port-of-Spain January 9, 1970; entered into force December 30, 1970.
22 UST 164; TIAS 7047; 781 UNTS 99.

Agreement for the exchange of information with respect to taxes. Signed at Port of Spain January 11, 1989; entered into force February 9, 1990.
TIAS 11607.

NOTE:
[1] With reservation.

TELECOMMUNICATION

Agreement relating to the reciprocal granting of authorizations to permit licensed amateur radio operators of either country to operate their stations in the other country. Exchange of notes at Port-of-Spain January 14 and March 16, 1967; entered into force March 16, 1967.
18 UST 543; TIAS 6261; 685 UNTS 93.

Arrangement relating to radio communications between amateur stations on behalf of third parties. Exchange of notes at Port-of-Spain October 26 and November 18, 1971; entered into force December 18, 1971.
22 UST 2053; TIAS 7239.

TRADE AND COMMERCE

Agreement within the context of the multilateral trade negotiations, with related letter. Signed at Washington December 19, 1979; entered into force January 1, 1980.
31 UST 5909; TIAS 9694; 1222 UNTS 89.

Agreement relating to trade in cotton, wool and man-made fiber textiles and textile products, with annexes and administrative visa arrangement. Exchange of notes at Port of Spain October 15 and 23, 1986; entered into force October 23, 1986; effective October 1, 1986.
NP

Amendments and extension:
September 8, November 18 and 30, 1988 and July 19, 1990 (NP).
December 5, 1989 and November 8 and December 14, 1990 (NP).

Agreement on removal of trade distorting practices in steel trade, with appendices and exchange of letters. Exchange of letters at Washington and Port-of-Spain March 29 and April 12, 1990; entered into force April 12, 1990.
TIAS

TRINIDAD and TOBAGO (Cont'd)

TRADE-MARKS

Declaration by the United States and the United Kingdom affording reciprocal protection to trade-marks. Signed at London October 24, 1877; entered into force October 24, 1877.
20 Stat. 703; TS 138; 12 Bevans 198.

VISAS

Agreement relating to extended validity of passports issued by Trinidad and Tobago. Exchange of notes at Port-of-Spain October 28 and November 12, 1969; entered into force November 12, 1969.
21 UST 1995; TIAS 6942; 763 UNTS 9.

WEATHER STATIONS

Agreement for a cooperative meteorological observation program in Trinidad. Exchange of notes at Port-of-Spain October 7, 1970; entered into force October 7, 1970; effective January 1, 1968.
21 UST 2495; TIAS 6991; 772 UNTS 163.

TUNISIA

A general convention between France and Tunisia signed June 3, 1955, provided *inter alia* (1) for recognition of the primacy of international conventions and treaties over internal law (article 3) and (2) that Tunisia would take, within the framework of its internal autonomy, measures necessary for rendering applicable treaties concerning Tunisia and for assuring their execution (article 8).

The independence of Tunisia was recognized in a protocol between France and Tunisia signed March 20, 1956, recognizing Tunisia's exercise of its responsibilities in foreign affairs and providing for organization of interdependent cooperation in external relations.

AGRICULTURAL COMMODITIES

Agreement relating to a child-feeding program for Tunisia under Title II of the Agricultural Trade Development and Assistance Act of 1954, as amended. Exchange of notes at Tunis June 28, 1957; entered into force June 28, 1957.
8 UST 985; TIAS 3863; 289 UNTS 301.

Agricultural commodities agreement with exchange of notes. Signed at Tunis February 16, 1962; entered into force February 16, 1962.
13 UST 229; TIAS 4965; 442 UNTS 161.

Agricultural commodities agreement with exchange of notes. Signed at Tunis September 14, 1962; entered into force September 14, 1962.
13 UST 2238; TIAS 5190; 461 UNTS 31.

Amendments:
September 13, 1963 (14 UST 1275; TIAS 5430; 488 UNTS 318).
December 19, 1963 (14 UST 1878; TIAS 5498; 494 UNTS 338).

Agricultural commodities agreement with exchange of notes. Signed at Tunis April 7, 1964; entered into force April 7, 1964.
15 UST 300; TIAS 5556; 527 UNTS 3.

Amendment:
July 7, 1964 (15 UST 1453; TIAS 5620; 529 UNTS 387).

Agricultural commodities agreement with exchange of notes. Signed at Tunis February 17, 1965; entered into force February 17, 1965.
16 UST 97; TIAS 5767; 542 UNTS 125.

Amendments:
November 29, 1965 (16 UST 1770; TIAS 5908; 573 UNTS 352).
April 29, 1966 (17 UST 613; TIAS 6007; 592 UNTS 271).

Agricultural commodities agreement with exchange of notes. Signed at Tunis July 30, 1966; entered into force July 30, 1966.
17 UST 1108; TIAS 6067; 601 UNTS 133.

Amendment:
September 19, 1966 (17 UST 1401; TIAS 6098).

Agricultural commodities agreement with annexes. Signed at Tunis March 17, 1967; entered into force March 17, 1967.
18 UST 1777; TIAS 6323; 692 UNTS 155.

Related agreements:
November 6, 1967 (18 UST 2929; TIAS 6385; 701 UNTS 149).
May 17, 1968 (19 UST 4925; TIAS 6498; 698 UNTS 257).
December 24, 1968 (19 UST 7832; TIAS 6616; 714 UNTS 105).
July 11, 1969 (20 UST 2673; TIAS 6725; 720 UNTS 35).
December 18, 1969 (20 UST 4132; TIAS 6811; 732 UNTS 71).
March 17, 1971 (22 UST 507; TIAS 7090; 796 UNTS 325).
November 17, 1971 (22 UST 1772; TIAS 7215).
April 19, 1972 (23 UST 1477; TIAS 7427).
June 13, 1973 (24 UST 1661; TIAS 7672).

Agricultural commodities agreement. Signed at Tunis June 7, 1976; entered into force June 7, 1976.
28 UST 1233; TIAS 8506.

Amendments:
July 3, 1985 (NP).
June 11, 1986 (NP).

Related agreements:
January 21, 1977 (28 UST 5348; TIAS 8638; 1087 UNTS 145).
July 27 and 28, 1977 (29 UST 370; TIAS 8823; 1115 UNTS 365).
February 3, 1978 (32 UST 764; TIAS 9727; 1265 UNTS 79).
March 2, 1979 (32 UST 755; TIAS 9726; 1221 UNTS 113).
April 17, 1980 (TIAS 10527).
August 27, 1981 (TIAS 10470).
May 17, 1982 (34 UST 1003; TIAS 10390).
June 4, 1983 (TIAS 10743).
July 1, 1983 (TIAS 10743).
June 13, 1984 (NP).
July 3, 1985 (NP).
June 11, 1986 (NP).
September 4, 1986 (NP).
January 23, 1987 (NP).
June 13, 1987 (NP).
August 25, 1987 (NP).

Agricultural commodities agreement. Signed at Tunis March 16, 1988; entered into force March 16, 1988.
NP

Amendments:
May 12, 1988 (NP).
July 28, 1988 (NP).

Related agreements:
September 17, 1988 (NP).
May 10, 1989 (NP).
September 28, 1989 (NP).
November 1, 1990 (NP).

CONSULS

Consular convention. Signed at Tunis May 12, 1988; entered into force January 15, 1994.
TIAS

COPYRIGHT (See APPENDIX)

CULTURAL RELATIONS

Agreement concerning cultural cooperation. Signed at Tunis September 28, 1979; entered into force September 28, 1979.
31 UST 5027; TIAS 9653.

DEFENSE

Agreement concerning payment to the United States of net proceeds from the sale of defense articles furnished under the military assistance program. Exchange of notes at Tunis May 21 and June 29, 1974; entered into force July 1, 1974.
25 UST 1554; TIAS 7892.

TUNISIA (Cont'd)

Agreement relating to a program of grants of military equipment and material to Tunisia. Exchange of notes at Tunis September 12 and October 25, 1974; entered into force October 25, 1974; effective July 1, 1974.
25 UST 3051; TIAS 7964.

Memorandum of understanding for cooperation in the field of military medicine. Signed at Tunis August 14, 1985; entered into force August 14, 1985.
TIAS 12008.

Memorandum of understanding on the exchange of officers. Signed at Tunis and Washington February 14 and March 12, 1992; entered into force March 12, 1992.
NP

Agreement concerning mutual logistic support, with annexes. Signed at Tunis and Stuttgart-Vaihingen March 29 and April 29, 1994; entered into force April 29, 1994.
TIAS 12374.

ECONOMIC AND TECHNICAL COOPERATION

Agreement providing for economic, technical and related assistance. Exchange of notes at Tunis March 26, 1957; entered into force March 26, 1957.
8 UST 427; TIAS 3794; 283 UNTS 117.

Agreement regarding certain assurances by Tunisia supplementing the economic, technical, and related assistance agreement of March 26, 1957. Exchange of notes at Tunis October 8, 1958; entered into force October 8, 1958.
9 UST 1324; TIAS 4122; 336 UNTS 389.

Agreement relating to the commitment by the United States to Tunisia's three-year plan. Exchange of notes at Tunis September 28 and October 29, 1962; entered into force October 29, 1962.
13 UST 2667; TIAS 5239; 462 UNTS 201.

Agency for International Development:
December 29, 1977 (29 UST 4113; TIAS 9051; 1231 UNTS 187).
March 24, 1978 (29 UST 4557; TIAS 9068; 1231 UNTS 223).
August 31, 1978 (30 UST 6005; TIAS 9535; 1231 UNTS 249).

EDUCATION

Agreement for financing certain educational exchange programs. Signed at Tunis November 18, 1963; entered into force November 18, 1963.
14 UST 1881; TIAS 5499; 494 UNTS 193.

ENVIRONMENTAL COOPERATION

Agreement for cooperation in the Global Learning and Observations to Benefit the Environment (GLOBE) Program, with appendices. Signed at Washington July 27, 1995; entered into force July 27, 1995.
TIAS 12678.

FINANCE

Agreement relating to investment guaranties under section 413 (b)(4) of the Mutual Security Act of 1954, as amended. Exchange of notes at Tunis March 17 and 18, 1959; entered into force March 18, 1959.
10 UST 858; TIAS 4224; 344 UNTS 179.

Amendment:
January 22 and March 6, 1963 (14 UST 385; TIAS 5329; 474 UNTS 344).

GENERAL RELATIONS

Treaty between the United States and France for the determination of their relations in Tunis. Signed at Washington March 15, 1904; entered into force May 7, 1904.
33 Stat. 2263; TS 434; 7 Bevans 862.

INVESTMENT

Treaty concerning the reciprocal encouragement and protection of investment, with protocol. Signed at Washington May 15, 1990; entered into force February 7, 1993.
TIAS

MAPPING

Mapping, charting and geodesy cooperative and exchange agreement, with annexes. Signed at Tunis December 8, 1980; entered into force December 8, 1980.
TIAS 10698.

Amendment:
July 14 and August 31, 1982 (TIAS 10698).

OCEANOGRAPHIC RESEARCH

Agreement relating to the establishment and operation of a Mediterranean Marine Sorting Center in Tunisia. Exchange of notes at Tunis September 26, 1966; entered into force September 26, 1966.
17 UST 1412; TIAS 6101; 616 UNTS 259.

PEACE CORPS

Agreement relating to the establishment of a Peace Corps program in Tunisia. Exchange of notes at Tunis February 7 and 13, 1962; entered into force February 13, 1962.
13 UST 249; TIAS 4968; 442 UNTS 155.

POSTAL MATTERS

Convention relating to the exchange of money orders, and detailed regulations. Signed at Tunis November 4 and at Washington December 28, 1932; operative January 1, 1933.
NP

International express mail agreement, with detailed regulations. Signed at Tunis and Washington November 12, 1982 and January 4, 1983; entered into force April 1, 1983.
TIAS 10640.

Memorandum of understanding concerning the operation of the INTELPOST service, with details of implementation. Signed at Tunis and Washington December 19, 1989 and October 3, 1991; entered into force February 1, 1993.
TIAS 11903.

SCIENTIFIC COOPERATION

Agreement establishing principles for cooperation between American institutions conducting basic scientific research in Tunisia under Smithsonian Institution sponsorship and appropriate Tunisian institutions, organizations or governmental agencies. Exchange of notes at Tunis July 17, 1968; entered into force July 17, 1968.
19 UST 5900; TIAS 6543; 707 UNTS 127.

TAXATION

Convention for the avoidance of double taxation and the prevention of fiscal evasion with respect to taxes on income, with exchange of notes. Signed at Washington June 17, 1985; entered into force December 26, 1990.
TIAS

Supplementary protocol to the convention for the avoidance of double taxation and the prevention of fiscal evasion with respect to taxes on income of June 17, 1985. Signed at Tunis October 4, 1989; entered into force December 26, 1990.
TIAS

TELECOMMUNICATION

Agreement relating to the installation and operation of a radio transmitter by the Embassy of Tunisia. Exchange of notes at Washington May

TUNISIA (Cont'd)

28, 1975 and May 13, 1976; entered into force
May 13, 1976.
28 UST 2437; TIAS 8561.

VISAS

Arrangement between the United States and
France for the waiver by France of visa requirements for United States citizens visiting
Metropolitan France and certain French territories, and for the granting by the United
States of gratis passport visas to French citizens resident in those territories who enter the
United States as nonimmigrants. Exchange of
notes at Paris March 16 and 31, 1949; entered
into force March 31, 1949.
63 Stat. 2737; TIAS 1987; 7 Bevans 1311; 84
UNTS 283.

TURKEY

AGRICULTURAL
COMMODITIES

Agreement concerning lira deposits under the
agricultural commodities agreements of March
12, 1956, as amended, and November 12,
1956. Exchange of notes at Ankara November
23, 1956; entered into force November 23,
1956.
8 UST 1567; TIAS 3909; 290 UNTS 273.

Agricultural commodities agreement with exchange of notes. Signed at Ankara July 29,
1961; entered into force July 29, 1961.
12 UST 1098; TIAS 4819; 416 UNTS 151.

Amendments:
September 6, 1961 (12 UST 1628; TIAS 4874;
    426 UNTS 350).
December 8, 1961 (12 UST 3215; TIAS 4926;
    433 UNTS 394).
January 3, 1962 (13 UST 68; TIAS 4937; 433
    UNTS 398).
January 5, 1962 (13 UST 68; TIAS 4937; 433
    UNTS 402).
March 14, 1962 (13 UST 303; TIAS 4978; 445
    UNTS 370).
June 21, 1962 (13 UST 1283; TIAS 5077; 459
    UNTS 306).
October 11, 1962 (13 UST 2199; TIAS 5185;
    459 UNTS 310).
November 21, 1962 (13 UST 2638; TIAS
    5235; 462 UNTS 362).

Agricultural commodities agreement with exchange of notes. Signed at Ankara February
21, 1963; entered into force February 21, 1963.
14 UST 236; TIAS 5303; 473 UNTS 311.

Amendments:
April 4, 1963 (14 UST 364; TIAS 5324; 473
    UNTS 326).
January 22, 1965 (16 UST 66; TIAS 5760; 542
    UNTS 392).

Agricultural commodities agreement with exchange of notes. Signed at Ankara April 2,
1966; entered into force April 2, 1966.
17 UST 2301; TIAS 6173; 680 UNTS 183.

Agricultural commodities agreement with
annex. Signed at Ankara February 6, 1969; entered into force February 6, 1969.
20 UST 438; TIAS 6645; 714 UNTS 165.

Amendment:
July 22 and 24, 1969 (20 UST 2813; TIAS
    6751; 724 UNTS 400).

Related agreements:
November 3, 1969 (20 UST 3052; TIAS 6784;
    726 UNTS 241).
December 19, 1969 (20 UST 4096; TIAS
    6802; 732 UNTS 350).
March 16, 1970 (21 UST 1062; TIAS 6860;
    740 UNTS 295).
January 29, 1971 (22 UST 230; TIAS 7055;
    781 UNTS 195).

ATOMIC ENERGY

Agreement for cooperation on uses of atomic
energy for mutual defense purposes. Exchange
of notes at Ankara May 5, 1959; entered into
force July 27, 1959.
10 UST 1340; TIAS 4278; 355 UNTS 341.

Agreement continuing in effect safeguards and
guarantee provisions of the agreement of June
10, 1955, as amended, for cooperation concerning civil uses of atomic energy (TIAS
3320, 4748, 5828, 6040, 7122). Exchange of
notes at Ankara April 15 and June 9, 1981; entered into force June 9, 1981.
TIAS 10560; 1577 UNTS 403.

AVIATION

Air transport agreement, with annexes. Signed
at Washington November 7, 1990; entered into
force October 22, 1993.
TIAS 12423.

COMMERCE

Treaty of commerce and navigation. Signed at
Ankara October 1, 1929; entered into force
April 22, 1930.
46 Stat. 2743; TS 813; 11 Bevans 1122; 114
    LNTS 499.

Treaty of establishment and sojourn. Signed at
Ankara October 28, 1931; entered into force
February 15, 1933.
47 Stat. 2432; TS 859; 11 Bevans 1127; 138
    LNTS 345.

COPYRIGHT (See APPENDIX)

DEFENSE (See also MUTUAL
SECURITY)

Agreement relating to implementation of the
agreement between the parties to the North Atlantic Treaty regarding the status of their
forces of June 19, 1951 (4 UST 1792; TIAS
2846), with two minutes of understanding.
Signed at Ankara June 23, 1954; entered into
force June 23, 1954.
5 UST 1465; TIAS 3020; 233 UNTS 189.

Agreement amending the minute of under-
standing on paragraph 7 of the agreement of
June 23, 1954. Exchange of notes at Ankara
April 22 and July 21, 1955; entered into force
July 21, 1955.
6 UST 2917; TIAS 3337; 265 UNTS 418.

Agreement relating to redistributable and excess equipment and materials furnished pursuant to the mutual defense assistance program.
Exchange of notes at Ankara May 26, 1955;
entered into force May 26, 1955.
6 UST 2071; TIAS 3275; 262 UNTS 97.

Amendment:
August 10, 1962 (13 UST 2628; TIAS 5232;
    462 UNTS 350).

Agreement relating to a program of offshore
procurement, with memorandum of understanding and model contract attached, and exchange of notes. Exchange of notes at Ankara
June 29, 1955; entered into force June 29,
1955.
6 UST 3729; TIAS 3372.

Agreement of cooperation. Signed at Ankara
March 5, 1959; entered into force March 5,
1959.
10 UST 320; TIAS 4191; 327 UNTS 293.

Agreement relating to the introduction of mod-
ern weapons into NATO defense forces in Turkey. Exchange of notes at Ankara September
18 and October 28, 1959; entered into force
October 28, 1959.
10 UST 1866; TIAS 4350; 360 UNTS 265.

Agreement for the establishment of a facility
for repairing and rebuilding M-12 range find-
ers in Turkey. Exchange of notes at Ankara
November 30, 1959; entered into force November 30, 1959.
10 UST 2027; TIAS 4372; 361 UNTS 107.

Agreement relating to a weapons production
program. Exchange of notes at Ankara March
2, 1960; entered into force March 2, 1960.
11 UST 1322; TIAS 4465; 372 UNTS 37.

Agreement concerning duty certificates in implementation of article VII of the agreement
between the parties to the North Atlantic Treaty regarding the status of their forces. Exchange of notes at Ankara September 24,
1968; entered into force September 24, 1968.
19 UST 6317; TIAS 6582; 702 UNTS 235.

TURKEY (Cont'd)

Agreement concerning payment to the United States of net proceeds from the sale of defense articles furnished under the military assistance program. Exchange of notes at Ankara October 9 and 10, 1974; entered into force October 10, 1974; effective July 1, 1974.
25 UST 2494; TIAS 7933.

Agreement concerning the grant of defense articles and services under the military assistance program. Exchange of notes at Ankara August 15 and 31, 1979; entered into force August 31, 1979.
30 UST 7299; TIAS 9588; 1182 UNTS 93.

Amendment:
August 13 and September 24, 1982 (TIAS 10502).

Agreement for cooperation on defense and economy in accordance with articles II and III of the North Atlantic Treaty, with related note; supplementary agreement number 1 on defense support; supplementary agreement number 2 on defense industrial cooperation; and supplementary agreement number 3 on installations, with implementing agreements (annexes). Signed at Ankara March 29, 1980; entered into force December 18, 1980.
32 UST 3323; TIAS 9901.

Memorandum of understanding on cooperative measures for enhancing air defense capabilities of selected COBs in Turkey. Signed at Washington and Ankara November 14 and December 26, 1984; entered into force December 26, 1984.
TIAS

Agreement supplementing and extending the agreement of March 29, 1980 for cooperation on defense and economy. Exchange of letters at Washington March 16, 1987; entered into force March 16, 1987.
TIAS

Acquisition and cross-servicing agreement, with annexes. Signed at Ankara and Stuttgart July 26 and August 12, 1996; entered into force August 12, 1996.
TIAS

ECONOMIC AND TECHNICAL COOPERATION

Agreement on aid to Turkey. Signed at Ankara July 12, 1947; entered into force July 12, 1947.
61 Stat. 2953; TIAS 1629; 11 Bevans 1163; 7 UNTS 309.

Economic cooperation agreement. Signed at Ankara July 4, 1948; entered into force July 13, 1948.
62 Stat. 2566; TIAS 1794; 11 Bevans 1166; 24 UNTS 67.

Amendments:
January 31, 1950 (1 UST 188; TIAS 2037; 76 UNTS 258).
August 16, 1951 (3 UST 54; TIAS 2392; 152 UNTS 276).
December 30, 1952 (3 UST 5348; TIAS 2742; 185 UNTS 330).

Agreement concerning economic assistance to Turkey for the acquisition of prefabricated huts to be used as facilities for primary schools. Exchange of notes at Ankara May 26, 1959; entered into force May 26, 1959.
10 UST 1303; TIAS 4273; 354 UNTS 57.

Agency for International Development:
December 5, 1978 (30 UST 6615; TIAS 9571; 1182 UNTS 85).
November 1, 1979 (31 UST 4704; TIAS 9634; 1202 UNTS 325).
January 28, 1980 (31 UST 5612; TIAS 9678; 1234 UNTS 285).
November 20, 1981 (33 UST 4061; TIAS 10282).
December 17, 1982 (TIAS 10631).
April 22, 1983 (TIAS 10725; 1607 UNTS 113).
September 30, 1983 (TIAS 10725; 1607 UNTS 123).
December 24, 1984 (NP).
December 24, 1984 (NP).
December 29, 1986 (NP).
January 8, 1987 (NP).

EDUCATION

Agreement for the establishment of the United States Educational Commission in Turkey, and exchanges of notes. Signed at Ankara December 27, 1949; entered into force March 21, 1950.
1 UST 603; TIAS 2111; 98 UNTS 141.

Amendments:
January 8, 1957 (8 UST 41; TIAS 3737; 266 UNTS 404).
February 1, 1960 (11 UST 399; TIAS 4458; 371 UNTS 282).
April 21 and May 30, 1961 (12 UST 661; TIAS 4766; 409 UNTS 302).
April 26 and May 2, 1967 (18 UST 1654; TIAS 6307; 692 UNTS 400).

EMPLOYMENT

Agreement relating to the employment of dependents of official government employees. Exchange of notes at Ankara November 23, 1999; entered into force February 3, 2000.
TIAS

ENVIRONMENTAL COOPERATION

Memorandum of understanding concerning technical cooperation in the field of environmental protection. Signed at Ankara December

10, 1991; entered into force December 10, 1991.
TIAS 11982.

Agreement for cooperation in the Global Learning and Observations to Benefit the Environment (GLOBE) Program, with appendices. Signed at Ankara May 5, 1995; entered into force May 5, 1995.
TIAS 12643.

EXTRADITION

Treaty on extradition and mutual assistance in criminal matters. Signed at Ankara June 7, 1979; entered into force January 1, 1981.
32 UST 3111; TIAS 9891.

FINANCE

Agreement relating to assurances by the Government of Turkey with respect to guaranties to investors pursuant to article III of the economic cooperation agreement, as amended. Exchange of notes at Ankara November 15, 1951; entered into force November 15, 1951.
3 UST 3720; TIAS 2500; 177 UNTS 315.

Amendments:
January 15, 1957 (8 UST 202; TIAS 3761; 280 UNTS 79).
November 27, 1964 (15 UST 2197; TIAS 5704; 531 UNTS 322).

Agreement regarding ownership and use of local currency repayments made by Turkey to the Development Loan Fund. Exchange of notes at Ankara September 6, 1958; entered into force September 6, 1958.
9 UST 1251; TIAS 4111; 336 UNTS 85.

Agreements regarding the consolidation and rescheduling of certain debts owed to, guaranteed or insured by the United States Government and its agencies, with annexes. Signed at Washington and Ankara September 21 and December 5, 1978; entered into force December 7, 1978.
30 UST 2723; TIAS 9361; 1171 UNTS 3.

Agreement regarding the consolidation and rescheduling of certain debts owed to, guaranteed or insured by the United States Government and its agencies, with annexes. Signed at Ankara December 11, 1979; entered into force January 14, 1980.
32 UST 1461; TIAS 9783; 1234 UNTS 273.

Implementing agreement regarding the consolidation and rescheduling of certain debts owed to the Agency for International Development. Signed at Ankara April 22, 1980; entered into force April 22, 1980; effective January 14, 1980.
32 UST 1549; TIAS 9786; 1234 UNTS 293.

Agreement regarding the consolidation and rescheduling of certain debts owed to, guaranteed or insured by the United States Government and its agencies, with agreed minute and

TURKEY (Cont'd)

annexes. Signed at Ankara October 24, 1980; entered into force November 24, 1980.
32 UST 3674; TIAS 9909; 1267 UNTS 347.

Implementing agreement regarding the consolidation and rescheduling of certain debts owed to the Agency for International Development. Signed at Ankara February 7, 1981; entered into force February 7, 1981.
33 UST 1057; TIAS 10091; 1280 UNTS 437.

Agreement regarding the consolidation and rescheduling of payments due under P. L. 480 Title I agricultural commodity agreements, with annexes. Signed at Ankara March 27, 1981; entered into force March 27, 1981.
33 UST 1545; TIAS 10131.

Agreement regarding the consolidation and rescheduling of certain debts owed to, guaranteed or insured by the United States Government and its agencies, with annexes and agreed minute. Signed at Ankara September 24, 1981; entered into force November 2, 1981.
TIAS 10432.

Agreement regarding the consolidation and rescheduling of payments due under P.L. 480 Title I agricultural commodity agreements, with annexes. Signed at Ankara November 25, 1981; entered into force November 25, 1981.
TIAS 10432.

Implementing agreement regarding the consolidation and rescheduling of certain debts owed to the Agency for International Development. Signed at Ankara January 22, 1982; entered into force January 22, 1982.
TIAS 10432.

GENERAL RELATIONS

Agreement for the regularization of relations between the United States and Turkey. Exchange of notes at Ankara February 17, 1927; entered into force February 17, 1927.
Foreign Relations, 1927, Vol. III, p. 794 ff.; 11 Bevans 1109.

INVESTMENT

Treaty concerning the reciprocal encouragement and protection of investments, with protocol. Signed at Washington December 3, 1985; entered into force May 18, 1990.
TIAS

JUDICIAL ASSISTANCE (See EXTRADITION)

LEND-LEASE

Agreement on the principles applying to aid under the Act of March 11, 1941, and exchanges of notes. Signed at Ankara February 23, 1945; entered into force February 23, 1945.
59 Stat. 1476; EAS 465; 11 Bevans 1147; 121 UNTS 165.

Agreement on lend-lease and claims. Signed at Ankara May 7, 1946; entered into force May 25, 1946.
60 Stat. 1809; TIAS 1541; 11 Bevans 1158; 6 UNTS 293.

MUTUAL SECURITY

Agreement relating to the assurances required by the Mutual Security Act of 1951. Exchange of notes at Ankara January 7, 1952; entered into force January 7, 1952.
3 UST 4660; TIAS 2621; 179 UNTS 121.

NARCOTIC DRUGS

Arrangement for the direct exchange of certain information regarding the traffic in narcotic drugs. Exchange of notes at Constantinople and Angora February 18 and October 3, 1928; entered into force October 3, 1928.
11 Bevans 1117.

PATENTS

Agreement to facilitate interchange of patent rights and technical information for purposes of defense. Signed at Ankara May 18, 1956; entered into force April 2, 1957.
8 UST 597; TIAS 3809; 283 UNTS 167.

Agreement approving the procedures for reciprocal filing of classified patent applications in the United States and Turkey. Exchange of notes at Ankara March 17 and September 16, 1959; entered into force September 16, 1959.
11 UST 388; TIAS 4456; 371 UNTS 314.

PEACE CORPS

Agreement relating to the establishment of a Peace Corps program in Turkey. Exchange of notes at Ankara August 27, 1962; entered into force August 27, 1962.
13 UST 2263; TIAS 5193; 461 UNTS 55.

POSTAL MATTERS

Agreement concerning the exchange of parcel post, and regulations of execution. Signed at Washington July 2 and at Ankara May 25, 1935; entered into force August 1, 1935.
49 Stat. 3201; 164 LNTS 125.

International express mail agreement, with detailed regulations. Signed at Ankara and Washington October 16 and November 29, 1984; entered into force March 21, 1985.
TIAS 11012.

Memorandum of understanding concerning the operation of the BUREAUFAX service. Signed at Ankara and Washington February 14 and March 14, 1990; entered into force March 15, 1990.
TIAS 11712.

PRISONER TRANSFER

Treaty on the enforcement of penal judgments. Signed at Ankara June 7, 1979; entered into force January 1, 1981.
32 UST 3187; TIAS 9892.

REFUGEES

Agreement concerning the reimbursement of costs arising from the transit of United States Government employees and their families. Done at Ankara September 13, 1996; entered into force September 13, 1996.
TIAS

SCIENTIFIC COOPERATION

Memorandum of understanding for a cooperative program in strong-motion data acquisition and analysis. Signed at Ankara and Reston March 8 and April 16, 1984; entered into force April 16, 1984.
TIAS 11181.

Agreement relating to scientific and technological cooperation, with annexes. Signed at Ankara June 14, 1994; entered into force June 14, 1994.
TIAS 12185.

Extension:
May 28 and June 21, 1999.

Memorandum of understanding concerning scientific and technical cooperation in the earth sciences. Signed at Reston and Istanbul February 22 and April 2, 1999; entered into force April 2, 1999.
TIAS

TURKEY (Cont'd)

SHIPPING

Agreement relating to jurisdiction over vessels utilizing the Louisiana Offshore Oil Port. Exchange of notes at Washington April 9 and 10, 1984; entered into force April 10, 1984.
TIAS 11239.

SURPLUS PROPERTY

Agreement approving the procedures to be used in the sale of excess and/or scrap property in Turkey by the United States. Exchange of notes at Ankara October 6 and November 13, 1959; entered into force November 13, 1959.
10 UST 1990; TIAS 4366; 361 UNTS 3.

TAXATION

Agreement relating to relief from Turkish taxation on expenditures made by or on behalf of the United States for common defense, with annex and minute. Signed at Ankara June 23, 1954; entered into force June 23, 1954.
5 UST 1258; TIAS 2996; 222 UNTS 161.

Agreement for the avoidance of double taxation and the prevention of fiscal evasion with respect to taxes on income, with protocol. Signed at Washington March 28, 1996; entered into force December 19, 1997.
TIAS

TELECOMMUNICATIONS

Arrangement relating to radio communications between amateur stations on behalf of third parties. Exchange of notes at Ankara November 27, 1996; entered into force November 27, 1996.
TIAS

Agreement relating to the reciprocal granting of authorizations to permit licensed amateur radio operators of either country to operate their stations in the other country. Exchange of notes at Ankara November 27, 1996; entered into force November 27, 1996.
TIAS

TRADE (See also COMMERCE)

Agreement relating to subsidization of exports in the context of the agreement on interpretation and application of articles VI, XVI, and XXIII (subsidies code) of the general agreement on tariffs and trade (TIAS 9619). Exchange of letters at Washington February 25, 1985; entered into force February 25, 1985.
TIAS 11322.

Visa arrangement concerning textiles and textile articles, with annex. Exchange of letters at Washington and Ankara January 10, 1987; entered into force January 10, 1987; effective March 1, 1987.
NP

Amendments:
November 22 and 24, 1988 (NP).
June 29 and July 17, 1989 (NP).

Agreement concerning trade in cotton and man-made fiber textiles and textile products, with annexes. Exchange of notes at Ankara October 19 and November 16, 1988; entered into force November 16, 1988; effective July 1, 1988.
NP

Amendments and extensions:
June 30 and July 26, 1989 (NP).
July 29 and August 6, 1991 (NP).
April 27 and May 13, 1992 (NP).
October 31 and November 30, 1994 (NP).

VISAS

Agreement relating to passport visas and visa fees. Exchange of notes at Washington June 27, August 8, September 27, and October 11, 1955; entered into force October 11, 1955; operative December 1, 1955.
7 UST 337; TIAS 3508; 272 UNTS 145.

TURKMENISTAN

For agreements prior to December 31, 1991, see UNION OF SOVIET SOCIALIST REPUBLICS.

DEFENSE

Agreement concerning the provision of training related to defense articles under the United States International Military Education and Training (IMET) Program. Exchange of notes at Ashgabat November 29, 1993 and January 3, 1994; entered into force January 3, 1994.
NP

Agreement regarding grants under the Foreign Assistance Act of 1961, as amended, and the furnishing of defense articles, related training, and other defense services from the United States of America to the Government of Turkmenistan. Exchange of notes April 5 and 24, 1999; entered into force April 24, 1999.
TIAS

ECONOMIC AND TECHNICAL COOPERATION

Agreement regarding cooperation to facilitate the provision of assistance. Signed at Ashgabat

November 30, 1993; entered into force November 30, 1993.
TIAS 12518.

EMPLOYMENT

Agreement relating to the employment of dependents of official government employees. Exchange of notes at Ashgabat July 15 and 20, 1999; entered into force July 20, 1999.
TIAS

FINANCE

Investment incentive agreement. Signed at Ashgabat June 26, 1992; entered into force June 26, 1992.
TIAS 12462.

PEACE CORPS

Agreement concerning the program of the Peace Corps of the United States in Turkmenistan. Signed at Ashgabat February 26, 1993; entered into force February 26, 1993.
TIAS 11467.

TRADE AND COMMERCE

Agreement on trade relations, with exchanges of letters. Signed at Washington March 23, 1993; entered into force October 25, 1993.
TIAS 12491.

TUVALU

On October 1, 1978, Tuvalu became an independent state. In a note dated December 19, 1978, to the Secretary-General of the United Nations, the Prime Minister of Tuvalu made a statement reading in part as follows:

"2 The Government of Tuvalu, conscious of the desirability of maintaining existing international legal relationships, and conscious of its obligations under international law to honour its treaty commitments, acknowledges that many treaty rights and obligations of the Government of the United Kingdom in respect of the Gilbert and Ellice Islands Protectorate, the Gilbert and Ellice Islands Colony and Tuvalu were succeeded to by Tuvalu upon Independence by virtue of customary international law. Since, however, it is likely that by virtue of that law certain of such treaties may be said to have lapsed at the date of Tuvalu's Independence, it seems essential that each treaty purporting or deemed to bind Tuvalu before that date should be subjected to legal examination. The Government of Tuvalu proposes after such examination has been completed to indicate which, if any, of the treaties which may be said to have lapsed by virtue of

TUVALU (Cont'd)

customary international law it proposes to treat as having lapsed.

"3 The Government of Tuvalu desires that it should be presumed that each treaty purporting or deemed to bind Tuvalu before Independence has been legally succeeded to by Tuvalu and that action should be based on such presumption unless and until the Government of Tuvalu decides that any particular treaty should be treated as having lapsed. Should the Government of Tuvalu be of opinion that it has legally succeeded to any treaty, and wish to terminate the operation of such treaty, it will in due course give notice of termination in the terms thereof.

"4 For the avoidance of doubt, the Government of Tuvalu further declares that it does not regard itself as bound by the terms of any convention creating an international organisation to the extent that such convention requires the payment of any sum by any State, by virtue only of the accession of the Government of the United Kingdom to such convention.''

AVIATION

Agreement between the United States and the United Kingdom concerning air services with annexes and exchange of letters. Signed at Bermuda July 23, 1977; entered into force July 23, 1977.
28 UST 5367; TIAS 8641.

Amendment:
April 25, 1978 (29 UST 2680; TIAS 8965).

CONSULS

Consular convention between the United States and the United Kingdom. Signed at Washington June 6, 1951; entered into force September 7, 1952.
3 UST 3426; TIAS 2494; 165 UNTS 121.

EXTRADITION

Extradition treaty between the United States and the United Kingdom, with protocol of signature and exchange of notes. Signed at London June 8, 1972; entered into force January 21, 1977.
28 UST 227; TIAS 8468.

FRIENDSHIP

Treaty of friendship. Signed at Funafuti February 7, 1979; entered into force September 23, 1983.
TIAS 10776.

PEACE CORPS

Agreement relating to the establishment of a Peace Corps program in Tuvalu. Exchange of notes at Suva August 25, 1977; entered into force August 25, 1977.
29 UST 5428; TIAS 9119.

TELECOMMUNICATION

Agreement between the United States and the United Kingdom relating to the reciprocal granting of authorizations to permit licensed amateur radio operators of either country to operate their stations in the other country. Exchange of notes at London November 26, 1965; applicable to Tuvalu December 11, 1969.
16 UST 2047; TIAS 5941; 561 UNTS 193.

Agreement between the United States and the United Kingdom extending to certain territories the application of the agreement of November 26, 1965 relating to the reciprocal granting of authorizations to permit licensed amateur radio operators of either country to operate their stations in the other country. Exchange of notes at London December 11, 1969; entered into force December 11, 1969.
20 UST 4089; TIAS 6800; 732 UNTS 334.

TERRITORIAL SOVEREIGNTY (See FRIENDSHIP)

TRADE-MARKS

Declaration by the United States and the United Kingdom affording reciprocal protection to trade-marks. Signed at London October 24, 1877; entered into force October 24, 1877.
20 Stat. 703; TS 138; 12 Bevans 198.

TREATY OBLIGATIONS

Agreement relating to treaty obligations assumed by Tuvalu upon its independence. Exchange of notes at Suva and Funafuti January 29 and April 25, 1980; entered into force April 25, 1980.
32 UST 1310; TIAS 9770; 1222 UNTS 293.

UGANDA

AGRICULTURAL COMMODITIES

Agricultural commodities agreement. Signed at Kampala June 28, 1988; entered into force June 28, 1988.
NP

Related agreements:
February 2, 1989 (NP).
April 12, 1990 (NP).

COPYRIGHT (See APPENDIX)

DEFENSE

Agreement concerning the provision of training related to defense articles under the United States International Military Education and Training (IMET) Program. Exchange of notes at Kampala April 6, 1981 and June 15, 1984; entered into force June 15, 1984.
TIAS 10984.

Agreement regarding grants under the Foreign Assistance Act of 1961, as amended, and the furnishing of defense articles, related training and other defense services from the United States to Uganda. Exchange of notes at Kampala January 31 and March 25, 1994; entered into force March 25, 1994.
TIAS 11476.

Agreement regarding the status of U.S. military personnel and civilian employees of the Department of Defense temporarily in Uganda in connection with their official duties. Exchange of notes at Kampala July 25 and August 12, 1994; entered into force August 12, 1994.
NP

ECONOMIC AND TECHNICAL COOPERATION

Agreement relating to economic, technical and related assistance. Exchange of notes at Kampala December 3 and 11, 1971; entered into force December 11, 1971.
22 UST 1848; TIAS 7229.

EMPLOYMENT

Agreement relating to the employment of dependents of official government employees. Exchange of notes at Kampala October 8, 1998 and June 18, 1999; entered into force June 18, 1999.
TIAS

ENVIRONMENTAL COOPERATION

Agreement for cooperation on the Global Learning and Observations to Benefit the Environment (GLOBE) Program, with appendices. Signed at Kampala November 26, 1998; entered into force November 26, 1998.
TIAS

UGANDA (Cont'd)

FINANCE

Agreement relating to investment guaranties. Exchange of notes at Kampala May 29, 1965; entered into force May 29, 1965.
16 UST 827; TIAS 5818; 546 UNTS 209.

Agreement regarding the consolidation and rescheduling of certain debts owed to, guaranteed or insured by the United States Government and its agencies, with annexes. Signed at Kampala May 10, 1982; entered into force June 21, 1982.
NP

Agreements regarding the consolidation and rescheduling of certain debts owed to, or guaranteed by the United States Government and its agencies, with annexes, and implementing agreements regarding AID loans and agricultural commodity agreements. Signed at Kampala March 31, 1983; entered into force May 23, 1983.
NP

Agreement regarding the consolidation and rescheduling of certain debts owed to, guaranteed by, or insured by the United States Government and its agencies, with annexes. Signed at Kampala January 13, 1988; entered into force February 22, 1988.
NP

Agreement regarding the consolidation and rescheduling of certain debts owed to, guaranteed by, or insured by the United States Government and its agencies, with annexes. Signed at Kampala December 19, 1989; entered into force January 26, 1990.
NP

Agreement regarding the reduction and reorganization of certain debts owed to, guaranteed by, or insured by the United States Government and its Agency, with annexes. Signed at Kampala June 22, 1999; entered into force August 19, 1999.
NP

PEACE CORPS

Agreement relating to the establishment of a Peace Corps program in Uganda. Exchange of notes at Kampala November 16, 1964; entered into force November 16, 1964.
15 UST 2433; TIAS 5735; 586 UNTS 143.

POSTAL MATTERS

International express mail agreement, with detailed regulations. Signed at Kampala and Washington October 4 and November 3, 1988; entered into force December 15, 1988.
TIAS 11628.

UKRAINE

The following agreements include those between the United States and Ukraine, as well as those between the United States and the former Union of Soviet Socialist Republics that the United States and Ukraine have agreed remain in force between them. Bilateral arms limitation and related agreements between the United States and the former Union of Soviet Socialist Republics remain under review. No conclusion can be drawn from their absence from the following list.

AFGHANISTAN SETTLEMENT

Declaration between the United States and the Union of Soviet Socialist Republics on international guarantees (Afghanistan Settlement Agreement). Signed at Geneva April 14, 1988; entered into force May 15, 1988.
TIAS

ARMS LIMITATION

Agreement concerning assistance to Ukraine in the elimination of strategic nuclear arms and the prevention of proliferation of weapons of mass destruction. Signed at Kiev October 25, 1993; entered into force December 31, 1993.
TIAS

Agreement concerning development of state systems of control, accounting and physical protection of nuclear materials to promote the prevention of nuclear weapons proliferation from Ukraine. Signed at Washington December 18, 1993; entered into force December 31, 1993.
TIAS

Amendment and extension:
March 21, 1994.
July 7, 1999.

ATOMIC ENERGY

Agreement between the United States and the Union of Soviet Socialist Republics on scientific and technical cooperation in the field of peaceful uses of atomic energy, with annex. Signed at Washington June 1, 1990; entered into force June 1, 1990.
TIAS

Memorandum of cooperation between the United States and the Union of Soviet Socialist Republics in the fields of environmental restoration and waste management. Signed at Vienna September 18, 1990; entered into force September 18, 1990.
TIAS

Memorandum of cooperation between the United States and the Union of Soviet Socialist Republics in the field of magnetic confinement

fusion. Signed at Moscow July 5, 1991; entered into force July 5, 1991.
TIAS

Agreement concerning operational safety enhancements, risk reduction measures and nuclear safety regulation for civilian nuclear facilities in Ukraine, with exchange of notes. Signed at Kiev October 25, 1993; entered into force October 25, 1993.
TIAS 12513.

Extension:
July 22, 1998.

Agreement for cooperation concerning peaceful uses of nuclear energy, with annex and agreed minute. Signed at Kiev May 6, 1998; entered into force May 28, 1999.
TIAS

Agreement concerning the International Radioecology Laboratory of the International Chornobyl Center on Nuclear Safety, Radioactive Waste and Radioecology, with annex. Signed at Kiev July 22, 1998; entered into force July 22, 1998.
TIAS

Agreement on cooperation on research on health and environmental effects related to the Chernobyl accident. Signed at Washington December 8, 1999; entered into force December 8, 1999.
TIAS

Implementing agreement concerning the Ukraine Nuclear Fuel Qualification Project, with annex. Signed at Kiev June 5, 2000; entered into force June 5, 2000.
TIAS

AVIATION

Agreement between the United States and the Union of Soviet Socialist Republics supplementary to the 1966 civil air transport agreement (TIAS 6135), as amended by the agreement of February 13, 1986. Signed at Washington November 4, 1966; entered into force November 4, 1966.
17 UST 1936; TIAS 6135; 675 UNTS 24.

Air transport agreement, with annexes. Signed at Kiev June 5, 2000; entered into force June 5, 2000.
TIAS

CONSULS (See also PRIVILEGES AND IMMUNITIES)

Consular convention between the United States and the Union of Soviet Socialist Republics. Signed at Moscow June 1, 1964; entered into force July 13, 1968.
19 UST 5018; TIAS 6503; 655 UNTS 213.

UKRAINE (Cont'd)

COPYRIGHT (See APPENDIX)

CULTURAL HERITAGE

Agreement on the protection and preservation of cultural heritage. Signed at Washington March 4, 1994; entered into force March 4, 1994.
TIAS 11480.

CUSTOMS

Agreement regarding cooperation and mutual assistance between their customs services. Exchange of notes at Washington November 21, 1994; entered into force November 21, 1994.
TIAS 12582.

DEFENSE

Agreement between the United States and the Union of Soviet Socialist Republics on the prevention of dangerous military activities, with annexes and agreed statements. Signed at Moscow June 12, 1989; entered into force January 1, 1990.
TIAS

Agreement concerning the provision of training related to defense articles under the United States International Military Education and Training (IMET) Program. Exchange of notes at Kiev May 11 and 29, 1992; entered into force May 29, 1992.
NP

Agreement concerning the provision to Ukraine of material and services for the establishment of a government-to-government communications link, with annexes. Signed at Washington December 18, 1993; entered into force December 31, 1993.
TIAS

Agreement concerning the conversion of enterprises of the military-industrial complex. Signed at Kiev March 21, 1994; entered into force March 21, 1994.
TIAS

Amendment:
June 27, 1995.

Acquisition and cross-servicing agreement, with annexes. Signed at Stuttgart and Kiev November 17 and 19, 1999; entered into force November 19, 1999.
TIAS

Implementing arrangement concerning mutual logistic support, with annexes. Signed at Kiev and Stuttgart November 19 and December 7, 1999; entered into force December 7, 1999.
TIAS

ECONOMIC AND TECHNICAL COOPERATION

Agreement regarding humanitarian and technical economic cooperation. Signed at Washington May 7, 1992; entered into force May 7, 1992.
TIAS 11472.

Agency for International Development:
November 21, 1994 (NP).

EDUCATION

Agreement between the United States and the Union of Soviet Socialist Republics on expansion of undergraduate exchanges. Signed at Washington June 1, 1990; entered into force June 1, 1990.
TIAS

EMBASSY SITES

Agreement between the United States and the Union of Soviet Socialist Republics on the reciprocal allocation for use free of charge of plots of land in Moscow and Washington with annexes and exchanges of notes. Signed at Moscow May 16, 1969; entered into force May 16, 1969.
20 UST 789; TIAS 6693; 715 UNTS 33.

Agreement between the United States and the Union of Soviet Socialist Republics concerning dates for use of land for, and construction of, embassy complexes in Moscow and Washington. Exchange of notes at Moscow March 30, 1977; entered into force March 30, 1977.
28 UST 5293; TIAS 8629; 1087 UNTS 67.

EMERGENCY PREPAREDNESS

Memorandum of understanding on cooperation in natural and man-made technological emergency prevention and response. Signed at Kiev June 5, 2000; entered into force June 5, 2000.
TIAS

EMPLOYMENT

Agreement relating to the employment of dependents of official government employees. Exchange of notes at Washington November 21, 1994; entered into force November 21, 1994.
TIAS 12196.

ENVIRONMENTAL COOPERATION

Agreement on cooperation in the field of environmental protection. Signed at Washington May 7, 1992; entered into force May 7, 1992.
TIAS 11466.

Agreement concerning a regional environmental center in Ukraine. Signed at Washington December 8, 1999; entered into force December 8, 1999.
TIAS

FINANCE

Investment incentive agreement. Signed at Washington May 6, 1992; entered into force May 6, 1992.
TIAS 11475.

GENERAL RELATIONS

Arrangements between the United States and the Union of Soviet Socialist Republics relating to the establishment of diplomatic relations, nonintervention, freedom of conscience and religious liberty, legal protection, and claims. Exchanges of notes at Washington November 16, 1933; entered into force November 16, 1933.
Department of State Publication 528; European and British Commonwealth Series 2 [new series]; Eastern European Series No. 1 [old series]; 11 Bevans 1248.

HEALTH

Agreement between the United States and the Union of Soviet Socialist Republics on cooperation in artificial heart research and development. Signed at Moscow June 28, 1974; entered into force June 28, 1974.
25 UST 1331; TIAS 7867.

HOUSING

Memorandum of understanding between the United States and the Union of Soviet Socialist Republics on cooperation in housing and economic development. Signed at Moscow July 30, 1991; entered into force July 30, 1991.
TIAS

INVESTMENT

Treaty concerning the encouragement and reciprocal protection of investment, with annex and exchange of letters. Signed at Washington March 4, 1994; entered into force November 16, 1996.
TIAS

UKRAINE (Cont'd)

JUDICIAL ASSISTANCE

Agreement between the United States and the Union of Soviet Socialist Republics relating to the procedure to be followed in the execution of letters rogatory. Exchange of notes at Moscow November 22, 1935; entered into force November 22, 1935.
49 Stat. 3840; EAS 83; 11 Bevans 1262; 167 LNTS 303.

Memorandum of understanding concerning cooperation in the pursuit of Nazi war criminals. Signed at Washington August 26, 1993; entered into force August 26, 1993.
TIAS

LEND–LEASE

Preliminary agreement between the United States and the Union of Soviet Socialist Republics relating to principles applying to mutual aid in the prosecution of the war against aggression, and exchange of notes. Signed at Washington June 11, 1942; entered into force June 11, 1942.
56 Stat. 1500; EAS 253; 11 Bevans 1281; 105 UNTS 285.

Agreement between the United States and the Union of Soviet Socialist Republics regarding settlement of lend-lease, reciprocal aid and claims. Signed at Washington October 18, 1972; entered into force October 18, 1972.
23 UST 2910; TIAS 7478; 898 UNTS 297.

Agreement between the United States and the Union of Soviet Socialist Republics regarding settlement of lend-lease accounts. Exchange of letters at Washington June 1, 1990; entered into force June 1, 1990.
TIAS

MAPPING

Memorandum of understanding between the United States and the Union of Soviet Socialist Republics on cooperation in the mapping sciences, with annexes. Signed at Moscow May 14, 1991; entered into force May 14, 1991.
NP

MARITIME MATTERS

Agreement between the United States and the Union of Soviet Socialist Republics on the prevention of incidents on and over the high seas. Signed at Moscow May 25, 1972; entered into force May 25, 1972.
23 UST 1168; TIAS 7379; 852 UNTS 151.

Protocol between the United States and the Union of Soviet Socialist Republics to the agreement of May 25, 1972 (TIAS 7379) on the prevention of incidents on and over the high seas. Signed at Washington May 22, 1973; entered into force May 22, 1973.
24 UST 1063; TIAS 7624.

Memorandum of understanding between the United States and the Union of Soviet Socialist Republics regarding marine cargo insurance. Signed at London April 5, 1979; entered into force April 5, 1979.
30 UST 2194; TIAS 9326; 1171 UNTS 93.

Agreement regarding certain maritime matters, with annex. Signed at Washington January 23, 1997; entered into force January 23, 1997.
TIAS

Extension:
June 5, 2000.

MEDICAL ASSISTANCE

Agreement between the United States and the Union of Soviet Socialist Republics on emergency medical supplies and related assistance. Signed at Moscow July 30, 1991; entered into force July 30, 1991.
TIAS

NARCOTIC DRUGS

Memorandum of understanding between the United States and the Union of Soviet Socialist Republics on cooperation to combat illegal narcotics trafficking. Signed at Paris January 8, 1989; entered into force January 8, 1989.
TIAS 11436.

Agreement between the United States and the Union of Soviet Socialist Republics on a mutual understanding on cooperation in the struggle against the illicit traffic in narcotics. Signed at Washington January 31, 1990; entered into force January 31, 1990.
TIAS

NORTH ATLANTIC TREATY

Agreement to treat the agreement of June 19, 1995 among the States Parties to the North Atlantic Treaty and other states participating in the Partnership for Peace regarding the status of their forces as binding between the United States and Ukraine. Exchange of notes at Kiev May 28 and September 9, 1998; entered into force September 9, 1998.
TIAS

OCEANOGRAPHY

Agreement on cooperation between the United States and the Union of Soviet Socialist Republics on ocean studies, with annexes. Signed

at Washington June 1, 1990; entered into force June 1, 1990.
TIAS 11452.

PEACE CORPS

Agreement concerning the program of the Peace Corps of the United States in Ukraine. Signed at Washington May 6, 1992; entered into force May 6, 1992.
TIAS 11510.

POSTAL MATTERS

International express mail agreement, with detailed regulations. Signed at Kiev and Washington June 1 and November 8, 1993; entered into force January 1, 1994.
NP

PRISONERS OF WAR

Agreement between the United States and the Union of Soviet Socialist Republics relating to prisoners of war and civilians liberated by forces operating under Soviet command and forces operating under United States of America command. Signed at Yalta February 11, 1945; entered into force February 11, 1945;
59 Stat. 1874; EAS 505; 11 Bevans 1286; 68 UNTS 175.

PRIVILEGES AND IMMUNITIES

Agreement between the United States and the Union of Soviet Socialist Republics relating to privileges and immunities of all members of the Soviet and American embassies and their families, with agreed minute. Exchange of notes at Washington December 14, 1978; entered into force December 14, 1978; effective December 29, 1978.
30 UST 2341; TIAS 9340; 1171 UNTS 73.

Agreement between the United States and the Union of Soviet Socialist Republics relating to immunity of family members of consular officers and employees from criminal jurisdiction. Exchange of notes at Washington October 31, 1986; entered into force October 31, 1986.
TIAS 11432.

RULES OF WARFARE

Convention between the United States and the Union of Soviet Socialist Republics relating to the rights of neutrals at sea.[1] Signed at Washington July 22, 1854; entered into force October 31, 1854.
10 Stat. 1105; TS 300; 11 Bevans 1214.

UKRAINE (Cont'd)

NOTE:
[1] Declaration of accession by Nicaragua signed at Granada June 9, 1855 (7 Miller 139).

SCIENTIFIC COOPERATION

Memorandum of understanding between the United States and the Union of Soviet Socialist Republics on cooperation in the physical, chemical and engineering sciences, with annexes. Signed at Moscow May 13, 1991; entered into force May 13, 1991.
TIAS

Memorandum of understanding concerning scientific and technical cooperation in the earth sciences. Signed at Reston and Kiev August 13 and September 17, 1998; entered into force September 17, 1998.
TIAS

SEABED OPERATIONS

Agreement between the United States and the Union of Soviet Socialist Republics concerning the confidentiality of data on deep seabed areas, with related exchange of letters. Exchange of notes at Moscow December 5, 1986; entered into force December 5, 1986.
TIAS

Agreement between the United States and the Union of Soviet Socialist Republics relating to the agreement of August 14, 1987 on the resolution of practical problems with respect to deep seabed mining areas.[1] Exchange of notes at Moscow August 14, 1987; entered into force August 14, 1987.
TIAS 11438.

NOTE:
[1] Parties to the multilateral agreement of August 14, 1987 are Belgium, Canada, Italy, Netherlands and Union of Soviet Socialist Republics.

TAXATION

Convention between the United States and the Union of Soviet Socialist Republics on matters of taxation, with related letters. Signed at Washington June 20, 1973; entered into force January 29, 1976; effective January 1, 1976.
27 UST 1; TIAS 8225.

Convention for the avoidance of double taxation and the prevention of fiscal evasion with respect to taxes on income and capital, with protocol. Signed at Washington March 4, 1994; entered into force June 5, 2000.
TIAS

Agreement concerning the relationship between the Taxation Convention of March 4, 1994 and the General Agreement on Trade in Services with regard to the consultation, most-favored-nation and national treatment provisions. Exchange of notes at Washington May 26 and June 6, 1995; entered into force June 5, 2000.
TIAS

TECHNOLOGY TRANSFER

Agreement on technology safeguards associated with the launch by Ukraine of U.S.-licensed commercial spacecraft. Signed at Kiev March 6, 1998; entered into force December 22, 1998.
TIAS

Agreement on technology safeguards associated with Ukrainian launch vehicles, missile equipment and technical data for the "Sea Launch" Program. Signed at New York September 29, 1999; entered into force October 4, 2000.
TIAS

TRADE

Agreement between the United States and the Union of Soviet Socialist Republics regulating the position of corporations and other commercial associations. Signed at St. Petersburg June 25, 1904; entered into force June 25, 1904.
36 Stat. 2163; TS 526; 11 Bevans 1235.

Agreement on trade relations, with related exchanges of letters. Signed at Washington May 6, 1992; entered into force June 23, 1992.
TIAS

Agreement regarding international trade in commercial space launch services, with protocol, annex and exchange of letters. Signed at Washington February 21, 1996; entered into force February 21, 1996.
TIAS

Agreement on trade in textiles and apparel, with annexes. Signed at Kiev July 22, 1998; entered into force July 22, 1998; effective December 1, 1994.
NP

TRANSPORTATION

Agreement between the United States and the Union of Soviet Socialist Republics on cooperation in transportation science and technology, with annexes. Signed at Moscow May 31, 1988; entered into force May 31, 1988.
TIAS

TREATY SUCCESSION

Agreement concerning the succession of Ukraine to bilateral treaties between the United States and the former Union of Soviet Socialist Republics, with annex. Exchange of notes at Kiev May 10, 1995; entered into force May 15, 1995.
TIAS

VISAS

Agreement between the United States and the Union of Soviet Socialist Republics relating to the reciprocal issuance of multiple entry and exit visas to American and Soviet correspondents. Exchange of notes at Moscow September 29, 1975; entered into force September 29, 1975.
27 UST 4258; TIAS 8448.

WEAPONS

Agreement concerning the provision of assistance to Ukraine related to the establishment of an export control system to prevent the proliferation of weapons of mass destruction from Ukraine. Signed at Kiev December 5, 1993; entered into force December 31, 1993.
TIAS

Amendment:
June 27, 1995.

Agreement concerning the provision of material, services and related training to Ukraine in connection with the elimination of strategic nuclear arms, with annexes. Signed at Kiev December 5, 1993; entered into force December 31, 1993.
TIAS

Amendments:
December 18, 1993.
December 18, 1993.
March 21, 1994.
July 10, 1999.
July 24 and 28, 2000.

Agreement concerning the provision to Ukraine of emergency response equipment and related training in connection with the removal of nuclear warheads from Ukraine for destruction in the course of the elimination of strategic nuclear arms, with annex. Signed at Washington December 18, 1993; entered into force December 31, 1993.
TIAS

Agreement concerning cooperation in the elimination of infrastructure for weapons of mass destruction through provision to Ukraine of material, services and related training. Signed at Kiev June 27, 1995; entered into force June 27, 1995.
TIAS

Agreement concerning development of state systems of control, accounting and physical protection of nuclear materials to promote the prevention of nuclear weapons proliferation from Ukraine. Signed at Kiev June 27, 1995; entered into force June 27, 1995.
TIAS

UNION OF SOVIET SOCIALIST REPUBLICS

The Union of Soviet Socialist Republics dissolved December 25, 1991. As stated in the Alma Ata Declaration of December 21, 1991, ". . . The States participating in the Commonwealth guarantee in accordance with their constitutional procedures the discharge of the international obligations deriving from treaties and agreements concluded by the former Union of Soviet Socialist Republics. . ." In addition, the Russian Federation has informed the United States Government by a note dated January 13, 1992, that it ". . . continues to perform the rights and fulfil the obligations following from the international agreements signed by the Union of the Soviet Socialist Republics. . ."

Part 2 of Treaties in Force covers multilateral treaties and agreements. Where a multilateral treaty action was taken prior to dissolution, "Union of Soviet Socialist Republics" is retained; where a successor state has taken action it is listed separately.

The United States is reviewing the continued applicability of the agreements listed below. Bilateral agreements subsequent to December 31, 1991, are listed under individual country headings.

AFGHANISTAN SETTLEMENT

Declaration on international guarantees (Afghanistan Settlement Agreement). Signed at Geneva April 14, 1988; entered into force May 15, 1988.
TIAS

AGRICULTURE

Agreement on cooperation in the field of agriculture. Signed at Washington June 19, 1973; entered into force June 19, 1973.
24 UST 1439; TIAS 7650.

ARMS LIMITATION (See also NUCLEAR TEST LIMITATION and NUCLEAR WAR)

Treaty on the limitation of anti-ballistic missile systems. Signed at Moscow May 26, 1972; entered into force October 3, 1972.
23 UST 3435; TIAS 7503; 944 UNTS 13.

Memorandum of understanding regarding the establishment of a Standing Consultative Commission. Signed at Geneva December 21, 1972; entered into force December 21, 1972.
24 UST 238; TIAS 7545; 944 UNTS 27.

Protocol establishing and approving regulations governing procedures and other matters of the

Standing Consultative Commission with regulations. Signed at Geneva May 30, 1973; entered into force May 30, 1973.
24 UST 1124; TIAS 7637; 944 UNTS 30.

Basic principles of negotiation on the further limitation of strategic offensive arms. Signed at Washington June 21, 1973; entered into force June 21, 1973.
24 UST 1472; TIAS 7653; 944 UNTS 41.

Protocol to the treaty of May 26, 1972 on the limitation of anti-ballistic missile systems. Signed at Moscow July 3, 1974; entered into force May 24, 1976.
27 UST 1645; TIAS 8276.

Treaty on the limitation of underground nuclear weapon tests. Signed at Moscow July 3, 1974; entered into force December 11, 1990.
TIAS

Protocol to the treaty of July 3, 1974, on the limitation of underground nuclear weapon tests. Signed at Washington June 1, 1990; entered into force December 11, 1990.
TIAS

Treaty on the elimination of their intermediate-range and shorter-range missiles, with memorandum of understanding and protocols. Signed at Washington December 8, 1987; entered into force June 1, 1988.
TIAS

Agreement on notifications of launches of intercontinental ballistic missiles and submarine-launched ballistic missiles. Signed at Moscow May 31, 1988; entered into force May 31, 1988.
TIAS

Agreement on the conduct of a joint verification experiment, with annex. Signed at Moscow May 31, 1988; entered into force May 31, 1988.
TIAS

Agreement on principles of implementing trial verification and stability measures that would be carried out pending the conclusion of the U.S.-Soviet treaty on the reduction and limitation of strategic offensive arms. Signed at Jackson Hole, Wyoming, September 23, 1989; entered into force September 23, 1989.
TIAS 11459.

Memorandum of understanding regarding a bilateral verification experiment and data exchange related to prohibition of chemical weapons. Signed at Jackson Hole, Wyoming, September 23, 1989; entered into force September 23, 1989.
TIAS 11460.

Agreement concerning the conduct of reciprocal demonstrations of reentry vehicle inspection procedures, with appendix. Exchange of letters at Geneva January 22, 1990; entered into force March 23, 1990.
TIAS

Treaty on the reduction and limitation of strategic offensive arms, with annexes, protocols and memorandum of understanding.[1] Signed at

Moscow July 31, 1991; entered into force December 5, 1994.
TIAS

NOTE:
[1] For Protocol, see ARMS LIMITATION in multilateral section.

ATOMIC ENERGY

Memorandum of cooperation in the field of civilian nuclear reactor safety. Signed at Washington April 26, 1988; entered into force April 26, 1988.
TIAS 11486.

Agreement on scientific and technical cooperation in the field of peaceful uses of atomic energy, with annex. Signed at Washington June 1, 1990; entered into force June 1, 1990.
TIAS 11487.

Memorandum of cooperation in the fields of environmental restoration and waste management. Signed at Vienna September 18, 1990; entered into force September 18, 1990.
TIAS

AVIATION

Agreement supplementary to the 1966 civil air transport agreement (TIAS 6135), as amended by the agreement of February 13, 1986. Signed at Washington November 4, 1966; entered into force November 4, 1966.
17 UST 1936; TIAS 6135; 675 UNTS 24.

Memorandum of cooperation concerning air traffic control, with annexes. Signed at Washington February 16, 1990; entered into force February 16, 1990.
TIAS 11450.

Civil air transport agreement, with annexes. Signed at Washington June 1, 1990; entered into force June 1, 1990.[1]
TIAS 11461.

NOTE:
[1] Superseded by the agreement of January 14, 1994 as between the United States and the Russian Federation.

COMMERCE (See TRADE AND COMMERCE)

CONSERVATION

Convention concerning the conservation of migratory birds and their environment. Signed at Moscow November 19, 1976; entered into force October 13, 1978.
29 UST 4647; TIAS 9073; 1134 UNTS 97.

UNION OF SOVIET SOCIALIST REPUBLICS (Cont'd)

CONSULS (See also PRIVILEGES AND IMMUNITIES)

Consular convention. Signed at Moscow June 1, 1964; entered into force July 13, 1968.
19 UST 5018; TIAS 6503; 655 UNTS 213.

COPYRIGHT (See APPENDIX)

CULTURAL RELATIONS

General agreement on contacts, exchanges and cooperation in scientific, technical, educational, cultural and other fields. Signed at Geneva November 21, 1985; entered into force November 21, 1985.
TIAS

Program of cooperation and exchanges for 1986-1988, with annex. Signed at Geneva November 21, 1985; entered into force November 21, 1985.
TIAS

Program of cooperation and exchanges for 1989-1991, with annex. Signed at Moscow May 31, 1988; entered into force May 31, 1988; effective January 1, 1989.
TIAS 11454.

DEFENSE

Agreement on the prevention of dangerous military activities, with annexes and agreed statements. Signed at Moscow June 12, 1989; entered into force January 1, 1990.
TIAS 11485; 1566 UNTS 309.

ECONOMIC AND TECHNICAL COOPERATION

Long term agreement to facilitate economic, industrial, and technical cooperation. Signed at Moscow June 29, 1974; entered into force June 29, 1974.
25 UST 1782; TIAS 7910.

Extension:
June 15 and 27, 1984.

EDUCATION

Agreement on expansion of undergraduate exchanges. Signed at Washington June 1, 1990; entered into force June 1, 1990.
TIAS

EMBASSY SITES

Agreement on the reciprocal allocation for use free of charge of plots of land in Moscow and Washington with annexes and exchanges of notes. Signed at Moscow May 16, 1969; entered into force May 16, 1969.
20 UST 789; TIAS 6693; 715 UNTS 33.

Agreement on the conditions of construction of complexes of buildings of the U.S. Embassy in Moscow and the Russian Embassy in Washington with attachment. Signed at Washington December 4, 1972; entered into force December 4, 1972.
23 UST 3544; TIAS 7512.

Agreement concerning dates for use of land for, and construction of, embassy complexes in Moscow and Washington. Exchange of notes at Moscow March 30, 1977; entered into force March 30, 1977.
28 UST 5293; TIAS 8629; 1087 UNTS 67.

EMERGENCY PREPAREDNESS

Memorandum of understanding on cooperation in natural and man-made emergency prevention and response. Signed at Moscow July 30, 1991; entered into force July 30, 1991.
TIAS 11456.

ENVIRONMENTAL COOPERATION

Agreement on cooperation in the field of environmental protection. Signed at Moscow May 23, 1972; entered into force May 23, 1972.
23 UST 845; TIAS 7345.

FILMS (see HEALTH)

FISHERIES

Convention regarding navigation, fishing, and trading on the Pacific Ocean and along the northwest coast of America.[1] Signed at St. Petersburg April 17, 1824; entered into force January 11, 1825.
8 Stat. 302; TS 298; 11 Bevans 1205.

Agreement relating to the consideration of claims resulting from damage to fishing vessels or gear and measures to prevent fishing conflicts, with annex and protocol. Signed at Moscow February 21, 1973; entered into force February 21, 1973.
24 UST 669; TIAS 7575; 938 UNTS 38.

Amendment:
February 26, 1975 (26 UST 167; TIAS 8022).

Protocol to the agreement of February 21, 1973 (TIAS 7575), relating to the consideration of claims resulting from damage to fishing vessels or gear and measures to prevent fishing conflicts, with annex. Signed at Copenhagen June 21, 1973; entered into force June 21, 1973.
24 UST 1588; TIAS 7663; 938 UNTS 49.

Agreement on mutual fisheries relations, with annexes. Signed at Moscow May 31, 1988; entered into force October 28, 1988.
TIAS 11442.

NOTE:
[1] Article 3 obsolete by virtue of Alaska cession treaty (15 Stat. 539; TS 301); article 4 expired April 17, 1834.

GENERAL RELATIONS

Arrangements relating to the establishment of diplomatic relations, nonintervention, freedom of conscience and religious liberty, legal protection, and claims. Exchanges of notes at Washington November 16, 1933; entered into force November 16, 1933.
Department of State Publication 528; European and British Commonwealth Series 2 [new series]; Eastern European Series No. 1 [old series]; 11 Bevans 1248.

GRAINS

Agreement on the supply of grain. Signed at Washington June 1, 1990; entered into force June 1, 1990.
TIAS

HEALTH

Agreement relating to the exchange of medical films. Exchange of notes at Washington March 17 and September 5, 1955; entered into force September 5, 1955.
6 UST 3969; TIAS 3409; 256 UNTS 307.

Agreement on cooperation in the field of medical science and public health. Signed at Moscow May 23, 1972; entered into force May 23, 1972.
23 UST 836; TIAS 7344.

Agreement on cooperation in artificial heart research and development. Signed at Moscow June 28, 1974; entered into force June 28, 1974.
25 UST 1331; TIAS 7867.

UNION OF SOVIET SOCIALIST REPUBLICS (Cont'd)

HOUSING

Agreement on cooperation in the field of housing and other construction. Signed at Moscow June 28, 1974; entered into force June 28, 1974.
25 UST 1592; TIAS 7898.

Extension:
May 26 and July 11, 1989 (TIAS 11444).

Memorandum of understanding on cooperation in housing and economic development. Signed at Moscow July 30, 1991; entered into force July 30, 1991.
TIAS 11469.

JUDICIAL PROCEDURE

Agreement relating to the procedure to be followed in the execution of letters rogatory. Exchange of notes at Moscow November 22, 1935; entered into force November 22, 1935.
49 Stat. 3840; EAS 83; 11 Bevans 1262; 167 LNTS 303.

Memorandum of understanding concerning cooperation in the pursuit of Nazi war criminals. Signed at Moscow October 19, 1989; entered into force October 19, 1989.
TIAS 11462.

LEND-LEASE

Preliminary agreement relating to principles applying to mutual aid in the prosecution of the war against aggression, and exchange of notes. Signed at Washington June 11, 1942; entered into force June 11, 1942.
56 Stat. 1500; EAS 253; 11 Bevans 1281; 105 UNTS 285.

Agreement relating to the disposition of lend-lease supplies in inventory or procurement in the United States. Signed at Washington October 15, 1945; entered into force October 15, 1945.
7 UST 2819; TIAS 3662; 278 UNTS 151 and 315 UNTS 249.

Agreement regarding settlement of lend-lease, reciprocal aid and claims. Signed at Washington October 18, 1972; entered into force October 18, 1972.
23 UST 2910; TIAS 7478; 898 UNTS 297.

Agreement regarding settlement of lend-lease accounts. Exchange of letters at Washington June 1, 1990; entered into force June 1, 1990.
TIAS

MAPPING

Memorandum of understanding on cooperation in the mapping sciences, with annexes. Signed at Moscow May 14, 1991; entered into force May 14, 1991.
NP

MARITIME MATTERS

Declaration concerning the admeasurement of vessels. Signed at Washington June 6, 1884; entered into force August 1, 1884.
23 Stat. 789; TS 304; 11 Bevans 1223.

Agreement on the prevention of incidents on and over the high seas. Signed at Moscow May 25, 1972; entered into force May 25, 1972.
23 UST 1168; TIAS 7379; 852 UNTS 151.

Protocol to the agreement of May 25, 1972 (TIAS 7379) on the prevention of incidents on and over the high seas. Signed at Washington May 22, 1973; entered into force May 22, 1973.
24 UST 1063; TIAS 7624.

Memorandum of understanding regarding marine cargo insurance. Signed at London April 5, 1979; entered into force April 5, 1979.
30 UST 2194; TIAS 9326; 1171 UNTS 93.

Agreement on maritime search and rescue, with exchange of letters. Signed at Moscow May 31, 1988; entered into force July 3, 1989.
TIAS 11440.

Agreement to abide by terms of maritime boundary agreement of June 1, 1990, pending entry into force. Exchange of notes at Washington June 1, 1990; entered into force June 1, 1990; effective June 15, 1990.
TIAS 11451.

Agreement regarding certain maritime matters, with annexes. Signed at Washington June 1, 1990; entered into force October 1, 1990.
TIAS 11453.

MEDICAL ASSISTANCE

Agreement on emergency medical supplies and related assistance. Signed at Moscow July 30, 1991; entered into force July 30, 1991.
TIAS 11468.

NARCOTIC DRUGS

Memorandum of understanding on cooperation to combat illegal narcotics trafficking. Signed at Paris January 8, 1989; entered into force January 8, 1989.
TIAS 11436.

Agreement on a mutual understanding on cooperation in the struggle against the illicit traffic in narcotics. Signed at Washington January 31, 1990; entered into force January 31, 1990.
TIAS

NAVIGATION

Agreement on the establishment of joint Loran-C and Chayka radionavigation systems, with annex. Signed at Moscow May 31, 1988; entered into force March 2, 1989.
TIAS 11441.

NUCLEAR TEST LIMITATION

Treaty on underground nuclear explosions for peaceful purposes, with agreed minute. Signed at Washington and Moscow May 28, 1976; entered into force December 11, 1990.
TIAS   ; 1714 UNTS 387.

Protocol to the treaty of May 28, 1976, on underground nuclear explosions for peaceful purposes. Signed at Washington June 1, 1990; entered into force December 11, 1990.
TIAS   ; 1714 UNTS 440.

NUCLEAR WAR

Agreement on measures to reduce the risk of outbreak of nuclear war. Signed at Washington September 30, 1971; entered into force September 30, 1971.
22 UST 1590; TIAS 7186; 807 UNTS 57.

Agreement on the prevention of nuclear war. Signed at Washington June 22, 1973; entered into force June 22, 1973.
24 UST 1478; TIAS 7654.

Agreement on the establishment of nuclear risk reduction centers, with protocols. Signed at Washington September 15, 1987; entered into force September 15, 1987.
TIAS

Agreement on reciprocal advance notification of major strategic exercises. Signed at Jackson Hole, Wyoming, September 23, 1989; entered into force January 1, 1990.
TIAS 11458.

PACIFIC SETTLEMENT OF DISPUTES

Treaty for the settlement of disputes. Signed at Washington October 1, 1914; entered into force March 22, 1915.
39 Stat. 1622; TS 616; 11 Bevans 1239.

PASSPORTS

Agreement concerning mutual visits by inhabitants of the Bering Straits Region. Signed at

UNION OF SOVIET SOCIALIST REPUBLICS (Cont'd)

Jackson Hole, Wyoming September 23, 1989; entered into force July 10, 1991.
TIAS 11455.

POLLUTION

Agreement concerning cooperation in combatting pollution in the Bering and Chukchi Seas in emergency situations. Signed at Moscow May 11, 1989; entered into force August 17, 1989.
TIAS 11446.

POSTAL MATTERS

International express mail agreement, with detailed regulations. Signed at Moscow March 31, 1988; entered into force May 1, 1988.
TIAS 11439.

Memorandum of understanding concerning the operation of the INTELPOST service, with details of implementation. Signed at Moscow and Washington February 14 and March 9, 1989; entered into force April 3, 1989.
TIAS 11528.

PRISONERS OF WAR

Agreement relating to prisoners of war and civilians liberated by forces operating under Soviet command and forces operating under United States of America command. Signed at Yalta February 11, 1945; entered into force February 11, 1945.
59 Stat. 1874; EAS 505; 11 Bevans 1286; 68 UNTS 175.

PRIVILEGES AND IMMUNITIES

Agreement relating to privileges and immunities of all members of the Soviet and American embassies and their families, with agreed minute. Exchange of notes at Washington December 14, 1978; entered into force December 14, 1978; effective December 29, 1978.
30 UST 2341; TIAS 9340; 1171 UNTS 73.

Agreement relating to immunity of family members of consular officers and employees from criminal jurisdiction. Exchange of notes at Washington October 31, 1986; entered into force October 31, 1986.
TIAS 11432.

PUBLICATIONS

Memorandum of understanding to increase distribution of the magazines "America" and "Soviet Life". Signed at Washington June 2, 1990; entered into force June 2, 1990.
TIAS

REGIONAL COMMISSION

Agreement concerning the Bering Straits Regional Commission. Signed at Jackson Hole, Wyoming September 23, 1989; entered into force July 10, 1991.
TIAS 11448.

RULES OF WARFARE

Convention relating to the rights of neutrals at sea.[1] Signed at Washington July 22, 1854; entered into force October 31, 1854.
10 Stat. 1105; TS 300; 11 Bevans 1214.

NOTE:
[1] Declaration of accession by Nicaragua signed at Granada June 9, 1855 (7 Miller 139).

SCIENTIFIC COOPERATION

Agreement on cooperation in the field of basic scientific research, with annexes. Signed at Paris January 8, 1989; entered into force January 8, 1989.
TIAS 11443.

Memorandum of understanding on cooperation in geoscience, with annexes. Signed at Washington and Moscow May 6, 1989; entered into force May 6, 1989.
TIAS

Memorandum of understanding on cooperation in the field of basic scientific research, with annexes. Signed at Washington and Moscow May 6, 1989; entered into force May 6, 1989.
TIAS

Amendment:
May 7 and 14, 1991.

Memorandum of understanding on cooperation in the physical, chemical and engineering sciences, with annexes. Signed at Moscow May 13, 1991; entered into force May 13, 1991.
TIAS 11470.

SEABED OPERATIONS

Agreement concerning the confidentiality of data on deep seabed areas, with related exchange of letters. Exchange of notes at Moscow December 5, 1986; entered into force December 5, 1986.
TIAS

Agreement relating to the agreement of August 14, 1987 on the resolution of practical problems with respect to deep seabed mining areas.[1] Exchange of notes at Moscow August 14, 1987; entered into force August 14, 1987.
TIAS 11438.

NOTE:
[1] Parties to the multilateral agreement of August 14, 1987 are Belgium, Canada, Italy, Netherlands and Union of Soviet Socialist Republics.

SPACE COOPERATION

Agreement concerning cooperation in the exploration and use of outer space for peaceful purposes, with annex. Signed at Moscow April 15, 1987; entered into force April 15, 1987.
TIAS 11433.

Amendment:
May 31, 1988.

Implementing agreement concerning cooperation in the space flight of a Soviet Meteor-3 satellite employing a U.S. Total Ozone Mapping Spectrometer (TOMS). Signed at Moscow July 25, 1990; entered into force August 24, 1990.
TIAS

TAXATION

Convention on matters of taxation, with related letters. Signed at Washington June 20, 1973; entered into force January 29, 1976; effective January 1, 1976.
27 UST 1; TIAS 8225.

TELECOMMUNICATION

Agreement on the organization of commercial radio teletype communication channels. Signed at Moscow May 24, 1946; entered into force May 24, 1946.
60 Stat. 1696; TIAS 1527; 11 Bevans 1291; 4 UNTS 201.

Memorandum of understanding regarding the establishment of a direct communications ("hot-line") link, with annex. Signed at Geneva June 20, 1963; entered into force June 20, 1963.
14 UST 825; TIAS 5362; 472 UNTS 163.

Agreement on measures to improve the direct communications link, with annex. Signed at Washington September 30, 1971; entered into force September 30, 1971.
22 UST 1598; TIAS 7187; 806 UNTS 402.

Amendment:
March 20 and April 29, 1975 (26 UST 564; TIAS 8059; 991 UNTS 442).

Agreement relating to the memorandum of understanding of June 20, 1963 (TIAS 5362) and

UNION OF SOVIET SOCIALIST REPUBLICS (Cont'd)

the agreement of September 30, 1971, as amended (TIAS 7187, 8059), concerning the direct communications link. Exchange of notes at Washington July 17, 1984; entered into force July 17, 1984.
TIAS 11428.

Agreement modifying the memorandum of understanding of June 20, 1963, regarding the establishment of a direct communications link. Exchange of notes at Washington June 24, 1988; entered into force June 24, 1988.
TIAS

TERRITORIAL ACQUISITION

Convention ceding Alaska. Signed at Washington March 30, 1867; entered into force June 20, 1867.
15 Stat. 539; TS 301; 11 Bevans 1216.

TRADE AND COMMERCE

Agreement regulating the position of corporations and other commercial associations. Signed at St. Petersburg June 25, 1904; entered into force June 25, 1904.
36 Stat. 2163; TS 526; 11 Bevans 1235.

Agreement on the establishment of a U.S.-U.S.S.R. Commercial Commission. Communique issued at Moscow May 26, 1972; entered into force May 26, 1972.
26 UST 1334; TIAS 8116; 1006 UNTS 17.

Protocol relating to the possibility of establishing a U.S.-U.S.S.R. Chamber of Commerce. Signed at Washington June 22, 1973; entered into force June 22, 1973.
24 UST 1498; TIAS 7656.

Protocol relating to expansion and improvement of commercial facilities in Washington and Moscow. Signed at Washington June 22, 1973; entered into force June 22, 1973.
24 UST 1501; TIAS 7657; 938 UNTS 127.

Protocol relating to a Trade Representation of the U.S.S.R. in Washington and a Commercial Office of the U.S.A. in Moscow. Signed at Moscow October 3, 1973; entered into force October 3, 1973.
24 UST 2222; TIAS 7738; 938 UNTS 135.

Amendment:
May 21 and October 7, 1974 (27 UST 2987; TIAS 8356).

Agreement relating to the status of the Commercial Office of the United States in Moscow and the Trade Representation of the Soviet Union in Washington, with annexes. Exchange

of letters at Washington June 1, 1990; entered into force June 1, 1990.
TIAS

TRANSPORTATION

Agreement on cooperation in transportation science and technology, with annexes. Signed at Moscow May 31, 1988; entered into force May 31, 1988.
TIAS

VISAS

Agreement relating to the reciprocal waiver of visa fees to nonimmigrants. Exchange of notes at Moscow March 26 and August 11 and 20, 1958; entered into force August 20, 1958.
9 UST 1413; TIAS 4134; 336 UNTS 269.

Agreement relating to the reciprocal issuance of multiple entry and exit visas to American and Soviet correspondents. Exchange of notes at Moscow September 29, 1975; entered into force September 29, 1975.
27 UST 4258; TIAS 8448.

Agreement concerning diplomatic and other visas, with agreed minute and oral understanding. Exchange of notes at Moscow July 30, 1984; entered into force July 30, 1984.
TIAS

Agreement modifying the agreement of July 30, 1984 concerning diplomatic and other visas. Exchange of notes at Washington October 31, 1986; entered into force October 31, 1986.
TIAS

UNITED ARAB EMIRATES

AVIATION

Agreement on aviation security. Signed at Abu Dhabi December 26, 1993 and February 17, 1994; entered into force February 17, 1994.
TIAS

COPYRIGHT (See APPENDIX)

DEFENSE

Agreement relating to the sale of defense articles and services to the United Arab Emirates. Exchange of notes at Abu Dhabi June 15 and 21, 1975; entered into force June 21, 1975.
26 UST 1789; TIAS 8139; 1006 UNTS 251.

General security of military information agreement. Signed at Abu Dhabi May 23, 1987; entered into force May 23, 1987.
TIAS

ENVIRONMENTAL COOPERATION

Agreement for cooperation in the Global Learning and Observations to Benefit the Environment (GLOBE) Program, with appendices. Signed at Abu Dhabi June 6, 1999; entered into force June 6, 1999.
TIAS

FINANCE

Agreement on investment guaranties. Signed at Abu Dhabi September 29, 1991; entered into force April 22, 1992.
TIAS 12079.

POSTAL MATTERS

Memorandum of understanding for the exchange of international express mail, with details of implementation. Signed at Dubai and Washington December 31, 1984 and January 16, 1985; entered into force March 21, 1985.
TIAS 11149.

SCIENTIFIC COOPERATION

Memorandum of understanding concerning scientific and technical cooperation in the earth sciences. Signed at Abu Dhabi February 6, 1988; entered into force February 6, 1988.
TIAS 11647.

Amendment and extension:
June 26, 1993.
November 1, 1997.

TAXATION

Agreement regarding taxation of income derived from the international operation of ships or aircraft. Exchange of notes at Abu Dhabi October 7 and December 1, 1997; entered into force December 1, 1997; effective January 1, 1994.
TIAS

TRADE AND COMMERCE

Administrative arrangement concerning a textile visa system. Exchange of letters at Abu Dhabi February 4 and March 2, 1989; entered into force March 2, 1989.
NP

Agreement relating to trade in textiles and textile products, with annexes. Exchange of notes at Abu Dhabi January 26 and February 5, 1991; entered into force February 5, 1991; effective January 1, 1989.
NP

UNITED ARAB EMIRATES (Cont'd)

Amendment and extension:
March 29 and July 21, 1994 (NP).
December 30, 1995 and February 6, 1996 (NP).

UNITED KINGDOM

AMITY

Treaty of amity, commerce, and navigation (Jay Treaty).[1] Signed at London November 19, 1794; entered into force October 28, 1795.
8 Stat. 116; TS 105; 12 Bevans 13.

Treaty for an amicable settlement of all causes of differences between the two countries (Treaty of Washington).[2] Signed at Washington May 8, 1871; entered into force June 17, 1871.
17 Stat. 863; TS 133; 12 Bevans 170.

NOTES:
[1] Only articles 9 and 10 appear to remain in force between the United States and the United Kingdom. Article 3, so far as it relates to the right of Indians to pass across the border, appears to remain in force between the United States and Canada. But see *Akins v. U.S.*, 551 F.2d 1222 (1977).
[2] Articles I-XVII and XXXIV-XLII have been executed; articles XVIII-XXV, XXX, and XXXII terminated July 1, 1885; articles XXVIII and XXIX not considered in force.

ATOMIC ENERGY

Articles of agreement governing collaboration between the authorities of the United States of America and the United Kingdom in the matter of tube alloys. Signed at Quebec August 19, 1943; entered into force August 19, 1943.
5 UST 1114; TIAS 2993; 214 UNTS 341.

Agreement for cooperation on the uses of atomic energy for mutual defense purposes. Signed at Washington July 3, 1958; entered into force August 4, 1958.
9 UST 1028; TIAS 4078; 326 UNTS 3.

Amendments:
May 7, 1959 (10 UST 1274; TIAS 4267; 351 UNTS 458).
September 27, 1968 (20 UST 518; TIAS 6659).
October 16, 1969 (21 UST 1064; TIAS 6861).
July 22, 1974 (26 UST 110; TIAS 8014).
December 5, 1979 (31 UST 5853; TIAS 9688; 1203 UNTS 317).
June 5, 1984 (TIAS 11114).

Agreement in the field of liquid metal-cooled fast breeder reactors. Signed at Washington September 20, 1976; entered into force September 20, 1976.
33 UST 3080; TIAS 10213.

Amendment:
August 14 and 18, 1978 (33 UST 3099; TIAS 10213).

Agreement in the field of decommissioning nuclear facilities, with appendix. Signed at Washington March 1, 1985; entered into force March 1, 1985.
TIAS 11342.

Extension:
February 17 and March 6, 1989.

Agreement in the field of radioactive waste management technology. Signed at London October 30, 1986; entered into force October 30, 1986.
TIAS

Arrangement in the field of reactor safety research and development, with appendices and annex. Signed at Rockville and London April 3 and 4, 1995; entered into force April 4, 1995.
TIAS 12626.

Arrangement for the exchange of technical information and cooperation in nuclear safety matters, with addendum. Signed at Vienna September 18, 1996; entered into force September 18, 1996.
TIAS

AVIATION

Arrangement relating to pilot licenses to operate civil aircraft.[1] Exchange of notes at Washington March 28 and April 5, 1935; entered into force May 5, 1935.
49 Stat. 3731; EAS 77; 12 Bevans 513; 162 LNTS 59.

Agreement relating to the transfer and maintenance of radio range and SCS 51 equipment. Exchange of notes at London May 8 and July 31, 1946; entered into force July 31, 1946.
61 Stat. 4008; TIAS 1766; 12 Bevans 795; 42 UNTS 199.

Agreement concerning the opening of certain military air bases in the Caribbean area and Bermuda to use by civil aircraft and exchange of notes. Signed at Washington February 24, 1948; entered into force February 24, 1948.
62 Stat. 1860; TIAS 1717; 12 Bevans 850; 73 UNTS 143.

Agreement relating to the designation by the United States military authorities of an appropriate area within the boundaries of Kindley Air Force Base in Bermuda for civil airport facilities. Exchange of notes at Washington March 23 and April 25, 1951; entered into force April 25, 1951.
2 UST 1311; TIAS 2282; 99 UNTS 97.

Amendments:
May 25, 1960 (11 UST 1472; TIAS 4489).
June 4, 1968 (19 UST 5059; TIAS 6504; 649 UNTS 318).

Agreement providing for regular use by civil aircraft of certain facilities in the Bahama Islands Long Range Proving Ground for guided missiles. Exchange of notes at Washington July 11 and 22, 1955; entered into force July 22, 1955.
6 UST 3783; TIAS 3379; 218 UNTS 384.

Amendment:
December 6, 1956, and January 4, 1957 (8 UST 1; TIAS 3727; 266 UNTS 396).

Agreement relating to the reciprocal acceptance of airworthiness certifications. Exchange of notes at London December 28, 1972; entered into force December 28, 1972.
23 UST 4309; TIAS 7537.

Agreement concerning air services, with annexes and exchange of letters.[2] Signed at Bermuda July 23, 1977; entered into force July 23, 1977.
28 UST 5367; TIAS 8641.

Amendments:
April 25, 1978 (29 UST 2680; TIAS 8965; 1124 UNTS 437).
December 4, 1980 (33 UST 655; TIAS 10059).
February 20, 1985 (TIAS 11396).
May 25, 1989 (TIAS 11674; 1584 UNTS 445).
March 27, 1997.

Agreement relating to North Atlantic air fares. Exchange of letters at Washington March 17, 1978; entered into force March 17, 1978.
29 UST 2676; TIAS 8964.

Extension and amendment:
November 2 and 9, 1978 (30 UST 979; TIAS 9231; 1152 UNTS 473).

Memorandum of understanding concerning cooperation in the testing and development of anti-misting kerosene and related equipment, with appendix. Signed at Washington and London June 1 and 14, 1978; entered into force June 14, 1978.
30 UST 1369; TIAS 9256; 1153 UNTS 49.

Memorandum of agreement concerning the provision of equipment and services for the development of civil aeronautics. Signed at Washington and London June 29 and July 20, 1982; entered into force July 20, 1982.
TIAS 10874.

Amendment and extension:
September 12 and October 22, 1984 (TIAS 11405).
March 25 and April 15, 1986 (TIAS 11405).

Agreement concerning reciprocal recognition of airline fitness and citizenship determinations. Exchange of notes at Washington May 25, 1989; entered into force May 25, 1989.
TIAS 11675.

Agreement concerning settlement of the Heathrow Arbitration and the UK Arbitration and amending the air transport agreement of July 23, 1977, as amended. Exchange of notes at Washington March 11, 1994; entered into force March 11, 1994.
TIAS 12536.

UNITED KINGDOM
(Cont'd)

Agreement concerning the facilitation of air navigation services. Signed at London May 11, 1995; entered into force May 11, 1995.
TIAS 12645.

Agreement for the promotion of aviation safety. Signed at London December 20, 1995; entered into force December 20, 1995.
TIAS

NOTES:
[1] Applicable to American Samoa, Puerto Rico, Virgin Islands of the U.S., Bermuda, Falkland Is. and Dependencies, Gilbraltar, Hong Kong, Turks and Caicos Is. and the Cayman Is., Leeward Is., St. Helena and Ascension.
[2] Applicable to all territories.

BOUNDARIES

Convention respecting fisheries, boundary, and the restoration of slaves. Signed at London October 20, 1818; entered into force January 30, 1819.
8 Stat. 248; TS 112; 12 Bevans 57.

Treaty to settle and define the boundaries between the territories of the United States and the possessions of Her Britannic Majesty in North America; for the final suppression of the African slave trade, and for the giving up of criminals, fugitive from justice in certain cases (Webster-Ashburton treaty).[1] Signed at Washington August 9, 1842; entered into force October 13, 1842.
8 Stat. 572; TS 119; 12 Bevans 82.

Treaty establishing the boundary in the territory on the northwest coast of America lying westward of the Rocky Mountains (Oregon Treaty). Signed at Washington June 15, 1846; entered into force July 17, 1846.
9 Stat. 869; TS 120; 12 Bevans 95.

Declaration adopting maps of boundary prepared by the Joint Commission of the Northwest Boundary for surveying and marking the boundaries between the United States and British possessions on the forty-ninth parallel of north latitude, under the first article of the treaty of June 15, 1846 between the United States and the United Kingdom. Signed at Washington February 24, 1870; entered into force February 24, 1870.
TS 129; 12 Bevans 157.

Protocol of a conference respecting the northwest water boundary. Signed at Washington March 10, 1873; entered into force March 10, 1873.
18 Stat. (Pt. 2, Public Treaties) 369; TS 135; 12 Bevans 190.

Convention providing for the settlement of questions between the United States and the United Kingdom with respect to the boundary line between the territory of Alaska and the British possessions in North America.[2] Signed at Washington January 24, 1903; entered into force March 3, 1903.
32 Stat. 1961; TS 419; 12 Bevans 263.

Acceptance of the report of the commissioners to complete the award under the convention of January 24, 1903 respecting the boundary line between Alaska and the British North American possessions. Exchange of notes at Washington March 25, 1905; entered into force March 25, 1905.
TS 476; 12 Bevans 269.

Convention providing for the surveying and marking out upon the ground of the 141 degree of west longitude where said meridian forms the boundary line between Alaska and the British possessions in North America.[3] Signed at Washington April 21, 1906; entered into force August 16, 1906.
34 Stat. 2948; TS 452; 12 Bevans 276.

Agreement concerning the administration and lease of certain islands off the coast of Borneo by the British North Borneo Company. Exchange of notes at Intervale, New Hampshire, July 3 and at Washington July 10, 1907; entered into force July 10, 1907.
47 Stat. 2207; TS 856; 12 Bevans 287; 137 UNTS 314.

Treaty concerning the Canadian international boundary. Signed at Washington April 11, 1908; entered into force June 4, 1908.
35 Stat. 2003; TS 497; 12 Bevans 297.

Treaty relating to boundary waters and questions arising along the boundary between the United States and Canada.[4] Signed at Washington January 11, 1909; entered into force May 5, 1910.
36 Stat. 2448; TS 548; 12 Bevans 319.

Treaty concerning the boundary line in Passamaquoddy Bay. Signed at Washington May 21, 1910; entered into force August 20, 1910.
36 Stat. 2477; TS 551; 12 Bevans 341.

Treaty in regard to the boundary between the United States and Canada. Signed at Washington February 24, 1925; entered into force July 17, 1925.
44 Stat. 2102; TS 720; 6 Bevans 7; 43 LNTS 239.

Convention delimiting the boundary between the Philippine Archipelago and the State of North Borneo, and exchanges of notes dated January 2, 1930 and July 6, 1932. Signed at Washington January 2, 1930; entered into force December 13, 1932.
47 Stat. 2198; TS 856; 12 Bevans 473; 137 LNTS 297.

Treaty on the delimitation in the Caribbean of a maritime boundary relating to Puerto Rico/ U.S. Virgin Islands and the British Virgin Islands, with annex. Signed at London November 5, 1993; entered into force June 1, 1995.
TIAS

Treaty on the delimitation in the Caribbean of a maritime boundary relating to the U.S. Virgin Islands and Anguilla. Signed at London November 5, 1993; entered into force June 1, 1995.
TIAS

NOTES:
[1] Article X terminated June 24, 1935, upon entry into force of extradition convention signed December 22, 1931 (47 Stat. 2122; TS 849).
[2] Obsolete except for first paragraph of article VI.
[3] Obsolete except for article II.
[4] Paragraphs 3, 4, and 5 of article V terminated October 10, 1950 upon the entry into force of the treaty relating to uses of waters on the Niagara River (see under CANADA—BOUNDARY WATERS).

CANAL RIGHTS

Treaty to facilitate the construction of a ship canal. Signed at Washington November 18, 1901; entered into force February 21, 1902.
32 Stat. 1903; TS 401; 12 Bevans 258.

CLAIMS

Arrangement for the disposal of certain pecuniary claims arising out of World War I. Exchange of notes at Washington May 19, 1927; entered into force May 19, 1927.
TS 756; 12 Bevans 462; 64 LNTS 101.

Agreement relating to certain problems of marine transportation and litigation, and exchange of notes. Signed at London December 4, 1942; entered into force December 4, 1942.
56 Stat. 1780; EAS 282; 12 Bevans 631; 205 LNTS 33.

Amendments:
March 25 and May 7, 1946 (60 Stat. 1958; TIAS 1558; 12 Bevans 792; 6 UNTS 285).
June 17 and 27, 1947 (61 Stat. 3014; TIAS 1636; 12 Bevans 818; 16 UNTS 360).

Agreement relating to claims for damages resulting from acts of armed forces personnel. Exchange of notes at London February 29 and March 28, 1944; entered into force March 28, 1944.
61 Stat. 2728; TIAS 1602; 12 Bevans 660; 15 UNTS 413.

Amendment:
March 27, 1946 (60 Stat. 1525; TIAS 1509; 12 Bevans 745; 4 UNTS 2).

Agreement relating to mutual forbearance in claims resulting from acts of armed forces or civilian personnel. Exchange of notes at Washington October 23, 1946 and January 23, 1947; entered into force January 23, 1947; operative June 6, 1944.
61 Stat. 2876; TIAS 1622; 12 Bevans 805; 15 UNTS 281.

Agreement relating to the interpretation of paragraph 6 of the agreement on settlement of

UNITED KINGDOM (Cont'd)

intergovernmental claims of March 27, 1946 (60 Stat. 1534; TIAS 1509). Exchange of notes at Washington February 19 and 28, 1947; entered into force February 28, 1947.
61 Stat. 3012; TIAS 1635; 12 Bevans 812; 89 UNTS 368.

Agreement relating to indemnities on ammunition shipments in the United Kingdom or in British ships traveling to or from the United Kingdom. Exchange of notes at London October 27, 1966; entered into force October 27, 1966.
17 UST 2186; TIAS 6154; 597 UNTS 265.

COMMERCE

Convention to regulate commerce.[1] Signed at London July 3, 1815; entered into force July 3, 1815.
8 Stat. 228; TS 110; 12 Bevans 49.

Convention continuing in force indefinitely the convention of July 3, 1815. Signed at London August 6, 1827; entered into force April 2, 1828.
8 Stat. 361; TS 117; 12 Bevans 76.

NOTE:
[1] Article IV superseded from September 7, 1952 by consular convention of June 6, 1951 (3 UST 3426; TIAS 2494), including territories to which consular convention applies.

CONSULS

Consular convention and protocol of signature.[1] Signed at Washington June 6, 1951; entered into force September 7, 1952.
3 UST 3426; TIAS 2494; 165 UNTS 121.

NOTE:
[1] Applicable to all territories over which the United States has jurisdiction or international responsibility and to all British territories.

COPYRIGHT (See APPENDIX)

CUSTOMS

Declaration exempting commercial travelers' samples from customs inspection. Signed at Washington December 3 and 8, 1910; entered into force January 1, 1911.
TS 552; 12 Bevans 348.

Agreement relating to the prevention of abuses of customs privileges at certain leased naval and air bases. Exchange of notes at Washington January 18 and February 21, 1946; entered into force February 21, 1946.
61 Stat. 2637; TIAS 1592; 12 Bevans 739; 6 UNTS 137.

Understanding relating to the importation in bulk, free from customs duties, of certain articles for the use of the diplomatic staff of United States embassy and consular officers and other employees on duty in the United Kingdom. Exchange of notes at Washington February 16, 1949; entered into force February 16, 1949.
12 Bevans 928.

DEFENSE (See also MUTUAL SECURITY)

Arrangement relating to naval and air bases. Exchange of notes at Washington September 2, 1940; entered into force September 2, 1940.
54 Stat. 2405; EAS 181; 12 Bevans 551; 203 LNTS 201.

Protocol concerning the defense of Newfoundland. Signed at London March 27, 1941; entered into force March 27, 1941.
55 Stat. 1599; EAS 235; 12 Bevans 560; 204 LNTS 70.

Agreement regarding leased naval and air bases, and exchanges of notes.[1] Signed at London March 27, 1941; entered into force March 27, 1941.
55 Stat. 1560; EAS 235; 12 Bevans 560; 204 LNTS 15.

Amendments:
July 19 and August 1, 1950 (1 UST 585; TIAS 2105; 88 UNTS 273).
December 5 and 6, 1978 (30 UST 2683; TIAS 9359; 1179 UNTS 385).
March 7, 1985.

Mutual defense assistance agreement.[2] Signed at Washington January 27, 1950; entered into force January 27, 1950.
1 UST 126; TIAS 2017; 80 UNTS 261.

Agreement concerning a long-range proving ground for guided missiles to be known as "The Bahamas Long Range Proving Ground", and exchanges of note.[3] Signed at Washington July 21, 1950; entered into force July 21, 1950.
1 UST 545; TIAS 2099; 97 UNTS 193.

Amendment:
July 17, 1967 (18 UST 1657; TIAS 6308; 619 UNTS 330).

Related agreements:
February 24 and March 2, 1953 (4 UST 429; TIAS 2789; 172 UNTS 257).
July 11 and 22, 1955 (6 UST 3783; TIAS 3379; 218 UNTS 384).
December 6, 1956 and January 4, 1957 (8 UST 1; TIAS 3727; 266 UNTS 396).
April 1, 1957 (8 UST 493; TIAS 3803; 288 UNTS 364).

Agreement concerning the extension of the Bahamas Long Range Proving Ground by the establishment of additional sites in Ascension Island. Signed at Washington June 25, 1956; entered into force June 25, 1956.
7 UST 1999; TIAS 3603; 249 UNTS 91.

Amendment:
July 17, 1967 (18 UST 1657; TIAS 6308; 619 UNTS 330).

Agreement on administrative matters connected with the agreement of June 25, 1956 for the extension of the Bahamas Long Range Proving Ground by the establishment of additional sites in Ascension Island. Exchange of notes at Washington August 24 and 25, 1959; entered into force August 25, 1959.
10 UST 1453; TIAS 4296; 351 UNTS 438.

Agreement relating to the disposition of equipment and material furnished by the United States under the mutual defense assistance program and found surplus to the needs of the armed forces of the United Kingdom. Exchange of notes at London May 10 and 13, 1957; entered into force May 13, 1957.
8 UST 835; TIAS 3843; 291 UNTS 300.

Amendments:
December 17 and 30, 1958 (9 UST 1547; TIAS 4156; 340 UNTS 342).
November 7 and 10, 1961 (12 UST 2947; TIAS 4895; 431 UNTS 288).
August 28, 1963 (14 UST 1178; TIAS 5413; 486 UNTS 398).

Agreement for the establishment of oceanographic research stations in the Bahama Islands.[3] Signed at Washington November 1, 1957; entered into force November 1, 1957.
8 UST 1741; TIAS 3927; 299 UNTS 167.

Amendment:
May 12, 1960[3] (11 UST 1405; TIAS 4479; 372 UNTS 364).

Agreement relating to the supply by the United States to the United Kingdom of intermediate range ballistic missiles, with memorandum. Exchange of notes at Washington February 22, 1958; entered into force February 22, 1958.
9 UST 195; TIAS 3990; 307 UNTS 207.

Agreement relating to the establishment and operation of a ballistic missile early warning station at Fylingdales Moor, with memorandum. Exchange of notes at London February 15, 1960; entered into force February 15, 1960.
11 UST 156; TIAS 4425; 371 UNTS 45.

Amendment:
June 18, 1979 (30 UST 6045; TIAS 9536).

Agreement concerning the establishment in the Bahama Islands of a long range aid to navigation station.[3] Signed at Washington June 24, 1960; entered into force June 24, 1960.
11 UST 1587; TIAS 4502; 377 UNTS 63.

Agreement relating to rights of the United Kingdom in connection with the use of oceanographic research stations and parts of the Long Range Proving Ground.[4] Exchange of

UNITED KINGDOM (Cont'd)

notes at Port-of-Spain February 10, 1961; entered into force February 10, 1961.
12 UST 442; TIAS 4735; 409 UNTS 129.

Agreement on the setting up of a missile defense alarm system station in the United Kingdom, with memorandum. Exchange of notes at London July 18, 1961; entered into force July 18, 1961.
12 UST 1058; TIAS 4809; 404 UNTS 227.

Agreement relating to a weapons production program. Exchange of notes at London June 29, 1962; entered into force June 29, 1962.
13 UST 1318; TIAS 5087; 449 UNTS 286.

Agreement relating to the use of the airfield at Widewake in Ascension Island by aircraft of the Royal Air Force. Exchange of notes at Washington August 29, 1962; entered into force August 29, 1962.
13 UST 1917; TIAS 5148; 449 UNTS 177.

Polaris sales agreement. Signed at Washington April 6, 1963; entered into force April 6, 1963.
14 UST 321; TIAS 5313; 474 UNTS 49.

Agreement extending the Polaris sales agreement of April 6, 1963 (TIAS 5313) to cover the sale of Trident II weapon system. Exchange of notes at Washington October 19, 1982; entered into force October 19, 1982.
TIAS 10549.

Agreement for the establishment of an Atlantic Undersea Test and Evaluation Center in the Bahama Islands, with agreed minutes.[3] Signed at Washington October 11, 1963; entered into force October 11, 1963.
14 UST 1431; TIAS 5441; 483 UNTS 3.

Memorandum of arrangement between the United States, Australia, and the United Kingdom to cover re-entry experiments in Australia (Project Sparta). Signed at Canberra March 30, 1966; entered into force March 30, 1966.
17 UST 350; TIAS 5984; 593 UNTS 261.

Agreement concerning the availability of certain Indian Ocean Islands for the defense purposes of both governments.[5] Exchange of notes at London December 30, 1966; entered into force December 30, 1966.
18 UST 28; TIAS 6196; 603 UNTS 273.

Amendments:
June 22 and 25, 1976 (27 UST 3448; TIAS 8376).
November 16, 1987 (1576 UNTS 179).

Agreement for the construction, by Bermuda, of the proposed road through the United States Naval Air Station, Bermuda, with maps and related notes. Exchange of notes at London January 28, 1971; entered into force January 28, 1971.
22 UST 223; TIAS 7054; 792 UNTS 89.

Agreement relating to the transfer of certain real estate on Eleuthera Island to the United States Navy with annexes.[3] Exchange of notes at Nassau August 9, 1971 and February 17, 1972; entered into force February 17, 1972.
23 UST 155; TIAS 7286.

Understanding relating to the use by Bahamian organizations of certain land at the United States Navy Base, Georgetown, Great Exuma Island, with map and schedule.[3] Exchange of notes at Nassau June 19, September 12 and November 2, 1972; entered into force November 2, 1972.
23 UST 3688; TIAS 7514.

Agreement relating to the lease of certain land to the United States Navy on the Island of Anegada in the British Virgin Islands for use as a drone launching facility. Exchange of notes at Washington February 1, 1973; entered into force February 1, 1973.
24 UST 482; TIAS 7567.

Agreement relating to the expanded use of Ascension Island. Exchange of notes at London March 30, 1973; entered into force March 30, 1973.
24 UST 918; TIAS 7602.

Arrangement relating to the status of United States forces engaged in clearance of the Suez Canal which are using British Sovereign Base areas in Cyprus. Exchange of notes at London June 24 and July 4, 1974; entered into force July 4, 1974.
25 UST 2399; TIAS 7917.

Agreement concerning a United States naval support facility on Diego Garcia, British Indian Ocean Territory, with plan, related notes, and supplementary arrangement. Exchange of notes at London February 25, 1976; entered into force February 25, 1976.
27 UST 315; TIAS 8230; 1018 UNTS 372.

Related agreement:
December 13, 1982 (TIAS 10616).

Memorandum of understanding concerning the transfer of technical data relating to the JT-10D jet engine collaboration agreement to third countries. Signed at Washington December 30, 1976; entered into force December 30, 1976.
27 UST 4385; TIAS 8459; 1068 UNTS 437.

Letter of agreement concerning narrative record telecommunication interface arrangements, with appendices. Signed at Washington and London September 2 and 21, 1977; entered into force September 21, 1977.
TIAS 12252.

Agreement amending and supplementing the leased bases agreement of March 27, 1941, with regard to lands and facilities in Bermuda. Exchange of notes at Washington December 5 and 6, 1978; entered into force December 6, 1978.
30 UST 2683; TIAS 9359.

Agreement concerning United States defense areas in the Turks and Caicos Islands, with annex, memorandum of understanding and aide-memoire. Signed at Washington December 12, 1979; entered into force December 12, 1979; effective January 1, 1979.
32 UST 429; TIAS 9710.

Agreement concerning the turnover of the airfield at Grand Turk Auxiliary Air Base to the Government of the Turks and Caicos Islands and its use by the United States Government. Exchange of notes at Washington December 12, 1979; entered into force December 12, 1979.
32 UST 455; TIAS 9711.

Memorandum of agreement on the exchange of personnel between the United States Coast Guard and the Royal Navy. Signed at Washington August 29, 1980; entered into force August 29, 1980.
32 UST 2403; TIAS 9849; 1267 UNTS 187.

Memorandum of understanding concerning terrestrial radio site sharing, with annexes. Signed at Mildenhall and London August 19 and September 8, 1981; entered into force September 8, 1981.
33 UST 3767; TIAS 10260; 1541 UNTS 157.

Memorandum of understanding regarding support to the Royal Air Force detachment at Hickam Air Force Base. Signed at Honolulu April 21, 1981; entered into force April 21, 1981.
33 UST 998; TIAS 10084; 1285 UNTS 97.

Memorandum of understanding concerning the shared use of communications facilities in the northern Federal Republic of Germany, with annexes. Signed May 11 and June 2, 1981; entered into force June 2, 1981.
33 UST 2025; TIAS 10165; 1529 UNTS 415.

Memorandum of understanding on the exchange of personnel between the U.S. Coast Guard and the Royal Air Force. Signed at Washington November 14 and 16, 1983; entered into force November 16, 1983.
TIAS 10908.

Agreement regarding arrangements for continued United Kingdom access to and use of the Atlantic Undersea Test and Evaluation Centre (AUTEC) facility in The Bahamas. Exchange of notes at Washington April 5, 1984; entered into force April 5, 1984.
TIAS 11059.

Memorandum of understanding concerning the provision of mutual logistic support, supplies and services, with annexes. Signed at Vaihingen (Germany) and London October 5 and 11, 1984; entered into force October 11, 1984.
TIAS 11137.

Amendments:
June 29 and August 9, 1990 (TIAS 12198).
March 12 and April 2, 1991 (TIAS 12198).
March 15 and 18, 1996.

Agreement concerning certain communications facilities in the defense areas in the Turks and Caicos Islands. Exchange of notes at Washington December 18, 1984; entered into force December 18, 1984.
TIAS 11139.

UNITED KINGDOM (Cont'd)

Agreement relating to sharing facility construction costs on Ascension Island, with memoranda of agreement. Exchange of notes at London March 25, 1985; entered into force March 25, 1985.
TIAS 12383; 1443 UNTS 25.

Memorandum of understanding concerning the exchange of medical cadets between the British Army Medical Services and the Uniformed Services University of the Health Sciences. Signed at Washington and London March 25 and June 21, 1985; entered into force June 21, 1985.
TIAS 11109.

Memorandum of understanding concerning the exchange of medical cadets between the Royal Navy and the Uniformed Services University of the Health Sciences. Signed at Washington and London March 25 and October 7, 1985; entered into force October 7, 1985.
TIAS 11225.

Memorandum of understanding relating to the principles governing cooperation in research and development, production and procurement of defense equipment, with annex. Signed at London and Washington December 18 and 30, 1985; entered into force December 30, 1985.
TIAS 11235.

Memorandum of understanding for procurement of the RN ship-launched harpoon weapon system. Signed at London October 17, 1986; entered into force October 17, 1986.
TIAS 11381.

Amendment:
June 24 and July 9, 1996.

Memorandum of understanding for the procurement of an airborne early warning system for the Royal Air Force, with related letter. Signed at Washington February 25, 1987; entered into force February 25, 1987.
TIAS 11281.

Memorandum of understanding on the status of certain persons working for United States defense contractors in the United Kingdom, with annex. Signed at Washington July 7, 1987; entered into force July 7, 1987; effective for tax years beginning on or after April 6, 1987.
TIAS 11537.

Master information exchange arrangement, with annex. Signed at London September 6, 1988; entered into force September 6, 1988.
TIAS 11640.

Memorandum of understanding on the exchange of sub units. Signed at Washington October 5, 1988; entered into force October 5, 1988.
TIAS 11630.

Memorandum of understanding concerning a cooperative research project in imaging of the ocean using radar, with annexes. Signed at Arlington and London April 26 and May 5, 1989; entered into force May 5, 1989.
TIAS 12239.

Memorandum of understanding concerning the exchange of reserve officers. Signed at Washington September 11, 1989; entered into force September 11, 1989.
TIAS 11698.

Memorandum of understanding concerning cooperation in the development of a satellite communications modulator/demodulator and associated equipment resistant to electronic countermeasures and nuclear effects (Universal Modem), with annexes. Signed at Washington and London October 25 and December 8, 1989; entered into force December 8, 1989.
TIAS

Memorandum of understanding concerning the establishment of a radar site in the Cayman Islands as part of the Caribbean Basin Radar Network (CBRN). Signed at Washington February 26, 1990; entered into force February 26, 1990.
TIAS 12240.

Memorandum of understanding concerning measures to be taken for the transfer, security and safeguarding of classified technical information, software and equipment to the Ministry of Defence to enable industry to establish a North Sea ACMI range. Signed at Washington March 6, 1990; entered into force March 6, 1990.
TIAS 12248.

Memorandum of understanding concerning the provision, trial and operation of a relocatable over the horizon radar (ROTHR) in the United Kingdom, with annex. Signed at Washington April 20, 1990; entered into force April 20, 1990.
TIAS 12235.

Memorandum of understanding concerning the measures to be taken for the transfer to, and security and safeguarding of MK IV radar instrumentation system technical information, software and equipment in the United Kingdom. Signed at Washington February 6, 1991; entered into force February 6, 1991.
TIAS 11834.

Memorandum of understanding concerning the establishment of a portable radar tracking station in the Cayman Islands. Signed at Washington July 1, 1992; entered into force July 1, 1992.
TIAS 12241.

Agreement concerning defense cooperation arrangements. Exchange of notes at Washington May 27, 1993; entered into force May 27, 1993.
TIAS 12237; 1792 UNTS 145.

Memorandum of agreement concerning the exchange of military personnel. Signed at MacDill A.F.B. and London September 27 and October 6, 1993; entered into force October 6, 1993.
NP

Memorandum of understanding for the development testing, qualification testing and unconstrained enclosure development for the intercooled recuperated (ICR) gas turbine engine, with annex. Signed at Washington June 21, 1994; entered into force June 21, 1994.
TIAS 12257.

Amendments and extension:
March 6 and 11, 1997.
March 28 and November 6, 2000.

Memorandum of understanding concerning the cooperative outboard logistics update project (AN/SSQ–108–V()). Signed at London and Washington June 7 and July 1, 1994; entered into force July 1, 1994.
TIAS 12258.

Memorandum of understanding for the common affordable lightweight fighter, with annexes. Signed at London and Washington August 5 and 9, 1994; entered into force August 9, 1994.
TIAS 12251.

Memorandum of understanding concerning the exchange of scientists and engineers, with annexes. Signed at Washington and London July 27 and August 18, 1994; entered into force August 18, 1994.
NP

Memorandum of understanding concerning technology research and development projects, with annex. Signed at Washington November 18, 1994; entered into force November 18, 1994.
TIAS 12250.

Memorandum of understanding concerning exchange of research and development information, with appendix. Signed at Washington November 18, 1994; entered into force November 18, 1994.
TIAS 12249.

Agreement amending the agreement of November 29, 1973, as amended, to establish, operate and maintain line of communications and ancillary facilities in the United Kingdom for use under emergency conditions for logistic support of United States Armed Forces stationed in the European Command area in furtherance of the objectives of the North Atlantic Treaty. Exchange of notes at London November 20 and December 7, 1995; entered into force December 7, 1995.
TIAS

Agreement regarding U.S. approval for retransfer of U.S. defense articles and services to NATO for purposes of supporting the NATO-led Implementation Force (IFOR). Exchange of notes at Brussels December 18 and 19, 1995; entered into force December 19, 1995.
TIAS

Agreement amending and extending the memorandum of understanding of November 5, 1985 concerning ocean surveillance information system. Signed at Washington and London February 21 and March 15, 1996; entered into

UNITED KINGDOM (Cont'd)

force March 15, 1996; effective November 5, 1995.
TIAS

Memorandum of understanding for the cooperative development of technology upgrades to the AN/MSR-3(V) TACJAM–A Electronic Support (ES) Subsystem (Catalyst), with annexes. Signed at Washington and London July 26 and August 15, 1996; entered into force August 15, 1996.
TIAS

Memorandum of understanding concerning the framework for advanced concept technology demonstration (ACTD) cooperation, with annex. Signed at Washington and London August 12 and 16, 1996; entered into force August 16, 1996.
TIAS

Memorandum of understanding relating to information exchange on short range air-to-air missile technologies and systems. Signed at Washington and Bristol September 16 and 30, 1996; entered into force September 30, 1996.
TIAS

Memorandum of understanding for cooperation in the development of combined arms tactical training equipment. Signed at Alexandria and Abbey Wood December 6, 1996; entered into force December 6, 1996.
TIAS

Memorandum of understanding on the exchange of units between the United States Air Force and the Royal Air Force of the United Kingdom of Great Britain and Northern Ireland, with appendix. Signed at Washington and High Wycombe July 17 and August 6, 1997; entered into force August 6, 1997.
NP

Memorandum of understanding concerning the Trimaran Demonstrator Project, with annexes. Signed at Abbey Wood and Pyestock September 2 and 3, 1997; entered into force September 3, 1997.
TIAS

Memorandum of understanding concerning cooperation in the development, production and follow on support of an Armored Scout and Reconnaissance Vehicle (ASRV) system, with annexes. Signed at Washington and Bristol February 26 and July 7, 1998; entered into force July 7, 1998.
TIAS

Memorandum of understanding for the production of the Universal Modem System (UMS), with annexes. Signed at Bristol and Ft. Monmouth January 19 and 29, 1999; entered into force January 29, 1999.
TIAS

Memorandum of understanding for the Joint Anti-Armor Weapon System (JAAWS) Project.

Signed at Quantico and Abbey Wood September 20 and October 1, 1999; entered into force October 1, 1999.
TIAS

NOTES:
[1] See also agreement of December 5 and 6, 1978 (TIAS 9359). For use of bases by civil aircraft, see agreements of February 24, 1948 (TIAS 1717); March 23 and April 25, 1951 (TIAS 2282); and July 11 and 22, 1955 (TIAS 3379) under AVIATION.
[2] Article IV is applicable to Falkland Is., Gibraltar, Hong Kong, Leeward Is., St. Helena and Western Pacific Dependencies.
[3] See agreement of July 10 and 20, 1973 (TIAS 7688) between the United States and the Bahamas, under BAHAMAS—DEFENSE.
[4] This agreement relates to an agreement of the same date between the United States and the short-lived Federation of the West Indies (12 UST 408; TIAS 4734).
[5] See also agreement of February 25, 1976 concerning Diego Garcia, as amended (TIAS 8230, 10616).

DRUGS (See also NARCOTIC DRUGS)

Agreement relating to the synthesis of penicillin. Exchange of notes at Washington January 25, 1946; entered into force January 25, 1946; operative December 1, 1943.
60 Stat. 1485; TIAS 1506; 12 Bevans 713; 3 UNTS 209.

ECONOMIC AND TECHNICAL COOPERATION

Economic cooperation agreement.[1][2] Signed at London July 6, 1948; entered into force July 6, 1948.
62 Stat. 2596; TIAS 1795; 12 Bevans 874; 22 UNTS 263.

Amendments:
January 3, 1950 (1 UST 184; TIAS 2036; 86 UNTS 304).
May 25, 1951 (2 UST 1292; TIAS 2277; 99 UNTS 308).
February 25, 1953 (4 UST 1528; TIAS 2815; 172 UNTS 332).
June 26 and August 20, 1959 (11 UST 2680; TIAS 4664; 405 UNTS 288).

Agreement for technical cooperation in respect of the territories for the international relations of which the Government of the United Kingdom are responsible.[3] Signed at London July 13, 1951; entered into force July 13, 1951.
2 UST 1307; TIAS 2281; 105 UNTS 71.

Agreement relating to the use of the counterpart aid funds alloted to the United Kingdom[4] under section 115 (k) of the Economic Cooperation Act, as amended. Exchange of notes at London February 25, 1953; entered into force February 25, 1953.
4 UST 1532; TIAS 2816;

NOTES:
[1] Applicable to Channel Is., Falkland Is., Western Pacific High Commission territories, Gibraltar, British Virgin Is., Hong Kong, Isle of Man, St. Helena and Dependencies.
[2] Applicable, with the exception of article IV, to Turks and Caicos Is. and Cayman Is., Montserrat, and Anguilla.
[3] Applicable to British Virgin Is., Montserrat, Anguilla, Turks and Caicos Is. and Cayman Is.
[4] Including Isle of Man.

EDUCATION

Agreement for financing certain educational and cultural exchange programs.[1] Signed at London May 10, 1965; entered into force May 10, 1965.
16 UST 758; TIAS 5806; 545 UNTS 181.

Amendments:
February 16, 1967 (18 UST 297; TIAS 6232; 605 UNTS 394).
June 30, 1971 (22 UST 1629; TIAS 7190).
September 11 and 23, 1992 (1723 UNTS 270).

NOTE:
[1] Applicable to Bermuda, British Virgin Is., Falkland Is., Gibraltar, Hong Kong, Montserrat, Anguilla, St. Helena.

EMPLOYMENT

Arrangement relating to the employment of dependents of official government employees. Exchange of notes at Washington January 14 and 15, 1981; entered into force January 15, 1981.
32 UST 4581; TIAS 9971; 1267 UNTS 209.

ENERGY

Memorandum of understanding on collaboration in energy research and development. Signed at Washington June 11, 1990; entered into force June 11, 1990.
TIAS 12415.

ENVIRONMENTAL COOPERATION

Memorandum of understanding concerning cooperation in the field of environmental affairs. Signed at Washington June 2, 1986; entered into force June 2, 1986.
TIAS 11364.

EXTRADITION

Extradition treaty, with protocol of signature and exchange of notes.[1] Signed at London

UNITED KINGDOM (Cont'd)

June 8, 1972; entered into force January 21, 1977.
28 UST 227; TIAS 8468; 1049 UNTS 167.

Supplementary treaty to the extradition treaty of June 8, 1972, with annex. Signed at Washington June 25, 1985; entered into force December 23, 1986.[2]
TIAS 12050; 1556 UNTS 369.

NOTES:
[1] Applicable to all U.S. territories; Channel Is., Isle of Man, Bermuda, British Indian Ocean Territory, British Virgin Is., Cayman Is., Falkland Is. and Dependencies, Gibraltar, Hong Kong, Montserrat, Pitcairn, Henderson, Ducie and Oeno Is., Anguilla, St. Helena and Dependencies, Sovereign Base Areas of Akrotiri and Dhekelia in the Island of Cyprus, Turks and Caicos Is.
[2] With amendments.

FINANCE [1]

Debt funding agreement. Signed at Washington June 18, 1923; operative December 15, 1922.
Treasury Department print; 12 Bevans 397.

Agreement modifying the debt funding agreement of June 18, 1923. Signed at Washington June 4, 1932; operative July 1, 1931.
Treasury Department print; 12 Bevans 491.

Financial agreement. Signed at Washington December 6, 1945; entered into force July 15, 1946.
60 Stat. 1841; TIAS 1545; 12 Bevans 703; 126 UNTS 13.

Amendment:
March 6, 1957 (8 UST 2443; TIAS 3962; 303 UNTS 332).

Agreement concerning arrangements for the establishment of revolving loan funds in Uganda protectorate and Tanganyika with counterpart funds. Exchange of letters at London June 24, 1953; entered into force June 24, 1953.
5 UST 160; TIAS 2909; 224 UNTS 141.

Agreement on behalf of the Turks and Caicos Islands relating to investment guaranties. Signed at Washington April 20, 1999; entered into force April 20, 1999.
TIAS

NOTE:
[1] See also international fund for Ireland under FINANCE in multilateral section.

FISHERIES

Agreement adopting, with certain modifications, the rules and method of procedure recommended in the award of September 7, 1910, of the North Atlantic Coast Fisheries Arbitration. Signed at Washington July 20, 1912; entered into force November 15, 1912.
37 Stat. 1634; TS 572; 12 Bevans 357.

Reciprocal fisheries agreement, with agreed minute. Signed at London March 27, 1979; entered into force March 10, 1983.
TIAS 10545.

JUDICIAL ASSISTANCE

Agreement concerning the Cayman Islands and narcotics activities. Exchange of letters at London July 26, 1984; entered into force August 29, 1984.
TIAS

Extension:
February 27, 1990.

Treaty concerning the Cayman Islands relating to mutual legal assistance in criminal matters, with attachments, protocol and exchange of notes. Signed at Grand Cayman July 3, 1986; entered into force March 19, 1990.
TIAS   ; 1648 UNTS 179.

Agreement concerning the Turks and Caicos Islands and narcotics activities, with annex and forms. Exchange of letters at Washington September 18, 1986; entered into force October 21, 1986.
TIAS

Extension:
October 17, 1990 (1656 UNTS 570).

Agreement concerning Anguilla and narcotics activities, with annex and forms. Exchange of letters at Washington March 11, 1987; entered into force March 27, 1987.
TIAS 11686.

Extension:
September 26, 1990 (1656 UNTS 571).

Agreement concerning the British Virgin Islands and narcotics activities, with annex and forms. Exchange of letters at London April 14, 1987; entered into force August 12, 1987.
TIAS 11685; 1656 UNTS 3.

Extension:
August 9, 1990 (1681 UNTS 451).

Agreement concerning Montserrat and narcotics activities, with annex and forms. Exchange of letters at Washington May 14, 1987; entered into force June 1, 1987.
TIAS 11615; 1556 UNTS 23.

Extension:
February 26, 1991 (1670 UNTS 364).

Agreement concerning the investigation of drug trafficking offences and the seizure and forfeiture of proceeds and instrumentalities of drug trafficking, with attachment and exchange of notes. Signed at London February 9, 1988; entered into force April 11, 1989.
TIAS 11649.

Amendment and extensions:
January 6, 1994 (1863 UNTS 428).
June 19 and July 26, 1996 (1945 UNTS 406).

Agreement extending the application of the treaty of July 3, 1986, concerning the Cayman Islands relating to mutual legal assistance in criminal matters to Anguilla, the British Virgin Islands and the Turks and Caicos Islands. Exchange of notes at Washington November 9, 1990; entered into force November 9, 1990.
TIAS 11765.

Agreement extending application of the treaty of July 3, 1986, concerning the Cayman Islands relating to mutual legal assistance in criminal matters to Montserrat. Exchange of notes at Washington April 26, 1991; entered into force April 26, 1991.
TIAS 12429; 1670 UNTS 375.

Agreement for mutual assistance in administration of justice in connection with the Bank of Credit and Commerce International. Signed at London and Washington November 15 and December 4, 1991; entered into force December 4, 1991.
TIAS

Agreement extending application of the agreement of February 9, 1988, concerning the investigation of drug trafficking offences and seizure and forfeiture of proceeds and instrumentalities of drug trafficking to the Isle of Man. Exchange of notes at London September 30, 1992; entered into force September 30, 1992.
TIAS 12480; 1736 UNTS 424.

Agreement extending application of the agreement of February 9, 1988, concerning the investigation of drug trafficking offences and seizure and forfeiture of proceeds and instrumentalities of drug trafficking to Gibraltar. Exchange of notes at London September 30, 1992; entered into force September 30, 1992.
TIAS 12479; 1736 UNTS 424.

Treaty on mutual legal assistance in criminal matters, with appendices and related exchange of notes. Signed at Washington January 6, 1994; entered into force December 2, 1996.
TIAS

LEND-LEASE

Preliminary agreement regarding principles applying to mutual aid in the prosecution of the war against aggression. Signed at Washington February 23, 1942; entered into force February 23, 1942.
56 Stat. 1433; EAS 241; 12 Bevans 603.

Agreement relating to principles applying to the provision of aid to the armed forces of the United States. Exchange of notes at Wash-

UNITED KINGDOM (Cont'd)

ington September 3, 1942; entered into force September 3, 1942.
56 Stat. 1605; EAS 270; 12 Bevans 617.

LEND-LEASE SETTLEMENT

Joint statement regarding settlement for lend-lease, reciprocal aid, surplus war property, and claims. Dated at Washington December 6, 1945.
60 Stat. 1525; TIAS 1509; 12 Bevans 700; 4 UNTS 2.

Memorandum pursuant to joint statement of December 6, 1945, regarding settlement for lend-lease, reciprocal aid, surplus war property, and claims, with agreements annexed thereto. Signed at Washington March 27, 1946; entered into force March 27, 1946.
12 Bevans 745.

Agreement relating to settlement of the lend-lease interest in future sales of surplus stores in the Middle East. Signed at London January 7, 1948; entered into force January 7, 1948; operative July 15, 1947.
62 Stat. 1836; TIAS 1698; 12 Bevans 843; 89 UNTS 372.

Agreement relating to the settlement of the interests of the Government of the United States and the Government of the United Kingdom in joint installations in the Middle East. Signed at Washington July 12, 1948; entered into force July 12, 1948.
62 Stat. 2027; TIAS 1769; 12 Bevans 891; 71 UNTS 199.

Agreement relating to settlement of lend-lease and reciprocal aid accounts and intergovernmental claims. Signed at Washington July 12, 1948; entered into force July 12, 1948.
62 Stat. 2034; TIAS 1770; 12 Bevans 897; 71 UNTS 270.

Amendments:
April 28 and 30, 1952 (3 UST 4180; TIAS 2562; 134 UNTS 366).
April 24 and 25, 1957 (8 UST 771; TIAS 3834; 284 UNTS 362).

MAPPING

Agreement relating to cooperation in mapping, charting and geodesy. Signed at Feltham and Washington July 4 and 18, 1985; entered into force July 18, 1985.
TIAS 11530.

METEOROLOGICAL RESEARCH

Agreement providing for a meteorological research program in Barbados. Exchange of notes at Bridgetown January 7 and 15, 1963; entered into force January 15, 1963.
14 UST 109; TIAS 5276; 466 UNTS 181.

MILITARY CEMETERIES AND MONUMENTS

Agreement relating to the use of land at Madingley, near Cambridge, as a United States military cemetery. Exchange of notes at London June 21, 1954; entered into force June 21, 1954.
5 UST 1404; TIAS 3011; 209 UNTS 61.

MUTUAL SECURITY

Agreement relating to the assurances required under the Mutual Security Act of 1951.[1] Exchange of notes at London January 8, 1952; entered into force January 8, 1952.
3 UST 4665; TIAS 2622; 126 UNTS 307.

NOTE:
[1] Applicable to Falkland Is., Gibraltar, Hong Kong, Leeward Is., St. Helena, Western Pacific Is.

NARCOTIC DRUGS (See also JUDICIAL ASSISTANCE)

Arrangement for the direct exchange of certain information regarding the traffic in narcotic drugs. Exchange of notes at London December 23, 1927, and January 4 and 11, 1928; entered into force January 11, 1928.
12 Bevans 467.

Agreement to facilitate the interdiction by the United States of vessels of the United Kingdom suspected of trafficking in drugs. Exchange of notes at London November 13, 1981; entered into force November 13, 1981.
33 UST 4224; TIAS 10296; 1285 UNTS 197.

OCCUPIED TERRITORY

Agreement for the settlement of financial issues arising from the bizonal fusion agreement of December 2, 1946, as amended. Exchange of notes at Washington June 28, 1950; entered into force June 28, 1950.
1 UST 540; TIAS 2098; 88 UNTS 412.

OCEANOGRAPHY

Memorandum of understanding on the participation of the United Kingdom in the ocean drilling program as a regular member, with annexes. Signed at Swindon December 7, 1992; entered into force December 7, 1992; effective October 1, 1993.
TIAS

PACIFIC SETTLEMENT OF DISPUTES

Treaty for the advancement of peace. Signed at Washington September 15, 1914; entered into force November 10, 1914.
38 Stat. 1853; TS 602; 12 Bevans 370.

PATENTS

Agreement to facilitate the interchange of patent and technical information for defense purposes, and exchange of notes. Signed at London January 19, 1953; entered into force January 19, 1953.
4 UST 150; TIAS 2773; 161 UNTS 3.

PEACE TREATIES

Definitive treaty of peace.[1] Signed at Paris September 3, 1783; entered into force May 12, 1784.
8 Stat. 80; TS 104; 12 Bevans 8.

Treaty of peace and amity. Signed at Ghent December 24, 1814; entered into force February 17, 1815.
8 Stat. 218; TS 109; 12 Bevans 41.

NOTE:
[1] Only article 1 is in force.

POSTAL MATTERS

Agreement for the exchange of money orders. Signed at Washington July 4 and at London December 8, 1923; operative August 15, 1920.
23 LNTS 93.

Agreement for the direct exchange of parcels by parcel post. Signed at Washington October 1 and at London October 27, 1924; operative October 1, 1924.
43 Stat. 1854; Post Office Department print.

International express mail agreement, with detailed regulations. Signed at London and Washington November 6 and December 14, 1978; entered into force February 12, 1979; effective January 1, 1979.
30 UST 3357; TIAS 9395; 1180 UNTS 3.

International express mail agreement, with detailed regulations. Signed at Grand Cayman and Washington August 25 and September 9, 1986; entered into force November 26, 1986.
TIAS 11390.

UNITED KINGDOM
(Cont'd)

PROPERTY

Arrangement regarding the release of property seized under the American and British Trading With the Enemy Acts. Exchange of notes at London January 4 and February 23, 1927; entered into force February 23, 1927.
TS 754-A; 12 Bevans 457; 82 LNTS 17.

PROPERTY—REAL AND PERSONAL

Convention relating to tenure and disposition of real and personal property.[1] Signed at Washington March 2, 1899; entered into force August 7, 1900.
31 Stat. 1939; TS 146; 12 Bevans 246.

Supplementary convention extending the time within which notifications may be given of the accession of British colonies or foreign possessions to the convention of March 2, 1899, relating to the tenure and disposition of real and personal property. Signed at Washington January 13, 1902; entered into force April 2, 1902.
32 Stat. 1914; TS 402; 12 Bevans 261.

Supplementary convention providing for the accession of the Dominion of Canada to the real and personal property convention of March 2, 1899. Signed at Washington October 21, 1921; entered into force June 17, 1922.
42 Stat. 2147; TS 663; 12 Bevans 390; 12 LNTS 425.

Supplementary convention relating to the tenure and disposition of real and personal property. Signed at Washington May 27, 1936, by the United States, the United Kingdom, Australia, and New Zealand; entered into force March 10, 1941.
55 Stat. 1101; TS 964; 5 Bevans 140; 203 LNTS 367.

NOTE:
[1] Applicable to Puerto Rico, Ascension, Bermuda, Falkland Is., Gibraltar, Hong Kong, Leeward Is., St. Helena.

PUBLICATIONS

Agreement for the exchange of official publications. Exchange of notes at Washington July 13 and 30, 1951; entered into force July 30, 1951.
2 UST 1745; TIAS 2314; 105 UNTS 81.

SATELLITES

Agreement on cooperation in intercontinental testing in connection with experimental communications satellites. Exchange of notes at London March 29, 1961; entered into force March 29, 1961.
12 UST 246; TIAS 4704; 405 UNTS 107.

Agreement confirming a memorandum of understanding concerning the furnishing of launching and associated services by NASA for United Kingdom satellites, with annexes. Exchange of notes at Washington January 17, 1973; entered into force January 17, 1973.
24 UST 228; TIAS 7544; 881 UNTS 3.

Memorandum of understanding relating to a satellite-aided maritime distress alert system. Signed at Washington July 23, 1981; entered into force July 23, 1981.
33 UST 3303; TIAS 10229.

SCIENTIFIC COOPERATION

Agreement concerning the Annex on Intellectual Property Rights, with attachment. Exchange of notes at Washington November 29, 1995; entered into force November 29, 1995.
TIAS 12703; 1945 UNTS 295.

SHIPPING

Agreement relating to jurisdiction over vessels utilizing the Louisiana Offshore Oil Port. Exchange of notes at Washington May 14 and 25, 1979; entered into force May 25, 1979.
30 UST 5926; TIAS 9525; 1162 UNTS 351.

SMUGGLING

Convention for the prevention of smuggling of intoxicating liquors. Signed at Washington January 23, 1924; entered into force May 22, 1924.
43 Stat. 1761; TS 685; 12 Bevans 414; 27 LNTS 182.

SOCIAL SECURITY

Agreement on social security. Signed at London February 13, 1984; entered into force January 1, 1985, except for Part III which entered into force January 1, 1988.
TIAS 11086.

Administrative agreement for implementation of agreement on social security. Signed at London February 13, 1984; entered into force January 1, 1985.
TIAS 11086.

SPACE RESEARCH

Agreement relating to the establishment of a joint program of space research. Exchange of
notes at Washington September 8, 1961; entered into force September 8, 1961.
12 UST 1223; TIAS 4840; 418 UNTS 53.

TAXATION

Agreement relating to relief from taxation of United States Government expenditures in the United Kingdom for the common defense effort. Exchange of notes at London March 17 and 18, 1952; entered into force March 18, 1952.
3 UST 4158; TIAS 2559; 177 UNTS 33.

Convention for the avoidance of double taxation and the prevention of fiscal evasion with respect to taxes on income and capital gains.[1] Signed at London December 31, 1975; entered into force April 25, 1980.
31 UST 5668; TIAS 9682.

Amendments:
April 13, 1976 (31 UST 5692; TIAS 9682).
August 26, 1976 (31 UST 5704; TIAS 9682).
March 31, 1977 (31 UST 5707; TIAS 9682).
March 15, 1979 (31 UST 5709; TIAS 9682).

Convention for the avoidance of double taxation and the prevention of fiscal evasion with respect to taxes on estates of deceased persons and on gifts.[1] Signed at London October 19, 1978; entered into force November 11, 1979.
30 UST 7223; TIAS 9580; 1182 UNTS 83.

Convention (on behalf of the Government of Bermuda) relating to the taxation of insurance enterprises and mutual assistance in tax matters, with exchange of notes. Signed at Washington July 11, 1986; entered into force December 2, 1988.
TIAS 11676.

Agreement (on behalf of the Government of Bermuda) for the exchange of information with respect to taxes. Signed at Washington December 2, 1988; entered into force December 2, 1988.
TIAS 11986.

Agreement (on behalf of the Isle of Man) for the reciprocal exemption with respect to taxes on income from the international operation of ships. Exchange of notes at Washington August 1 and 15, 1989; entered into force August 15, 1989.
TIAS 11678.

NOTES:
[1] See article 28 for the circumstances under which the convention for the avoidance of double taxation and the prevention of fiscal evasion with respect to taxes on income of April 16, 1945 (60 Stat. 1377; TIAS 1546) would continue to have effect in the United Kingdom.
[2] See article 14 for the circumstances under which the convention for the avoidance of double taxation and the prevention of fiscal evasion with respect to taxes on the estates of deceased persons of April 16, 1945 (60 Stat. 1391; TIAS 1547) would continue to have effect in the United Kingdom.

UNITED KINGDOM (Cont'd)

TELECOMMUNICATION

Agreement on distance measuring equipment. Signed at Washington October 13, 1947; entered into force October 13, 1947.
61 Stat. 3131; TIAS 1652; 12 Bevans 824; 66 UNTS 269.

Agreement relating to the reciprocal granting of authorizations to permit licensed amateur radio operators of either country to operate their stations in the other country.[1] Exchange of notes at London November 26, 1965; entered into force November 26, 1965.
16 UST 2047; TIAS 5941; 561 UNTS 193.

Agreement extending to certain territories the application of the agreement of November 26, 1965 relating to the reciprocal granting of authorizations to permit licensed amateur radio operators of either country to operate their stations in the other country.[1] Exchange of notes at London December 11, 1969; entered into force December 11, 1969.
20 UST 4089; TIAS 6800; 732 UNTS 334.

NOTE:
[1] Applicable to all territories, for whose international relations the United States is responsible and the following British territories: Bermuda, British Virgin Is., Cayman Is., Falkland Is., Gibraltar, Hong Kong, Montserrat, St. Helena, Turks and Caicos Is.

TRACKING STATIONS

Agreement providing for the establishment and operation of a space vehicle tracking and communication station in Bermuda. Exchange of notes at Washington March 15, 1961; entered into force March 15, 1961.
12 UST 235; TIAS 4701; 404 UNTS 207.

Extensions and amendments:
September 23, 1963 (14 UST 1388; TIAS 5434; 486 UNTS 424).
January 17, 1968 (19 UST 4627; TIAS 6450; 642 UNTS 372).

Agreement providing for the establishment of a lunar and planetary spacecraft tracking facility on Ascension Island. Exchange of notes at London July 7, 1965; entered into force July 7, 1965.
16 UST 1183; TIAS 5864; 551 UNTS 221.

Agreement providing for the establishment and operation of space vehicle tracking and communications stations in the United Kingdom. Exchange of notes at London December 28, 1966 and January 1, 1967; entered into force January 1, 1967.
18 UST 129; TIAS 6208; 604 UNTS 3.

Agreement concerning the establishment and operation of a space vehicle tracking and communications station on Antigua. Exchange of notes at Washington January 17 and 23, 1967; entered into force January 23, 1967.
18 UST 112; TIAS 6207.

TRADE (See also COMMERCE)

Agreement supplementary to the general agreement on tariffs and trade. Signed at Washington June 27, 1957; schedule applicable June 29, 1957.
8 UST 890; TIAS 3851; 284 UNTS 75.

Agreement providing compensatory concessions under the general agreement on tariffs and trade for certain tariff actions taken by the United States. Exchange of notes at Geneva January 26 and February 16, 1962; entered into force February 16, 1962.
13 UST 954; TIAS 5032.

Agreement supplementary to the general agreement on tariffs and trade to compensate for escape clause actions to increase import duties on certain carpets and glass. Signed at Geneva December 10, 1962; entered into force December 10, 1962.
13 UST 3910; TIAS 5268; 471 UNTS 91.

Interim agreement relating to the renegotiation of Schedule XX (United States) to the general agreement on tariffs and trade. Signed at Washington April 5, 1966; entered into force April 5, 1966.
17 UST 254; TIAS 5975; 592 UNTS 61.

Amendment:
June 30, 1967 (18 UST 1753; TIAS 6318; 693 UNTS 366).

TRADE-MARKS

Declaration affording reciprocal protection to trade-marks.[1] Signed at London October 24, 1877; entered into force October 24, 1877.
20 Stat. 703; TS 138; 12 Bevans 198.

NOTE:
[1] Applicable to all territories.

VISAS

Agreement for the waiver of the visa requirements for United States citizens traveling to the United Kingdom and for the granting of gratis passport visas to British subjects entering the United States as nonimmigrants.[1] Exchange of notes at London November 9 and 12, 1948; entered into force November 12, 1948.
62 Stat. 3824; TIAS 1926; 12 Bevans 917; 84 UNTS 275.

NOTE:
[1] Applicable to all territories.

WEATHER STATIONS

Agreement for the continuation of a cooperative meteorological program in the Cayman Islands, with memorandum of arrangement. Exchange of notes at Washington April 6 and 13, 1976; entered into force April 13, 1976.
27 UST 1867; TIAS 8285.

ANGUILLA

FINANCE

Investment incentive agreement on behalf of Anguilla. Exchange of notes at London November 9, 1987; entered into force November 9, 1987.
TIAS 12045; 1556 UNTS 43.

PEACE CORPS

Agreement relating to the establishment of a Peace Corps program in Anguilla. Exchange of letters at Washington February 19 and June 24, 1981; entered into force June 24, 1981; effective May 1, 1981.
33 UST 2053; TIAS 10169; 1529 UNTS 429.

POSTAL MATTERS

Convention for the exchange of postal money orders with the British Colony of Saint Christopher, Nevis and Anguilla. Signed at Basseterre, St. Kitts, June 27 and at Washington September 14, 1959; entered into force February 1, 1960.
11 UST 1433; TIAS 4483.

Express mail agreement, with detailed regulations. Signed at Anguilla and Washington May 28, 1998 and January 8, 1999; entered into force April 15, 1999.
NP

BERMUDA

AVIATION

Agreement on preclearance for entry into the United States, with annex. Signed at Hamilton January 15, 1974; entered into force January 15, 1974.
25 UST 288; TIAS 7801.

Amendment:
August 28 and 29, 1979 (30 UST 7562; TIAS 9600; 1203 UNTS 365).

POLLUTION

Agreement concerning assistance to be rendered on a reimbursable basis by the United States Coast Guard in the event of major oil

UNITED KINGDOM
(Cont'd)

spills. Signed at Hamilton July 13, 1976; entered into force July 13, 1976.
27 UST 3788; TIAS 8396.

POSTAL MATTERS

Parcel post agreement. Signed at Washington December 13, 1906, and at Bermuda January 15, 1907; operative February 1, 1907.
34 Stat. 2983; Post Office Department print.

Money order agreement. Signed at Washington February 8 and at Hamilton May 20, 1907; operative July 1, 1907.
NP

International express mail agreement, with detailed regulations. Signed at Hamilton and Washington July 31 and August 13, 1979; entered into force September 1, 1979.
30 UST 6493; TIAS 9563; 1180 UNTS 47.

BRITISH VIRGIN ISLANDS

POSTAL MATTERS

Convention for the exchange of postal money orders with the Colony of British Virgin Islands. Signed at Road Town, Tortola, February 18 and at Washington March 14, 1957; entered into force July 1, 1957.
11 UST 1409; TIAS 4480.

GIBRALTAR

POSTAL MATTERS

Agreement for the exchange of parcel post and detailed regulations for the execution thereof. Signed at Gibraltar December 18, 1936, and at Washington January 5, 1937; operative January 1, 1937.
50 Stat. 1488; Post Office Department print; 177 LNTS 21.

LEEWARD ISLANDS

POSTAL MATTERS

Parcel post agreement. Signed at Antigua May 27 and at Washington July 11, 1929; operative September 1, 1929.
46 Stat. 2321; Post Office Department print; 98 LNTS 161.

MONTSERRAT

PEACE CORPS

Agreement relating to the establishment of a Peace Corps program in Montserrat. Exchange of letters at Bridgetown and Plymouth January 13 and February 9, 1981; entered into force February 9, 1981.
33 UST 1075; TIAS 10092; 1307 UNTS 415.

POSTAL MATTERS

Convention for the exchange of postal money orders with the British Colony of Montserrat. Signed at Montserrat March 15 and at Washington June 10, 1957; entered into force September 1, 1957.
11 UST 1417; TIAS 4481.

TURKS and CAICOS ISLANDS

DEFENSE

Memorandum of understanding concerning the establishment of a portable radar tracking station in the Turks and Caicos Islands. Signed at London July 24, 1987; entered into force July 24, 1987.
TIAS

PEACE CORPS

Agreement relating to the establishment of a Peace Corps program in the Turks and Caicos Islands. Exchange of letters at Washington April 17 and December 5, 1980; entered into force December 5, 1980.
32 UST 4235; TIAS 9945; 1267 UNTS 201.

REFUGEES

Memorandum of understanding to establish in the Turks and Caicos Islands a processing facility to determine the refugee status of boat people from Haiti, with related letter. Signed at Grand Turk June 18, 1994; entered into force June 18, 1994.
TIAS

Amendment:
July 13, 1994.

UNITED NATIONS

AGRICULTURAL COMMODITIES

Memorandum of understanding concerning a grant to the United Nations of Congo francs accruing to the United States under the agricultural commodities agreement of November 18, 1961 between the United States and the Republic of the Congo (Leopoldville). Signed at New York February 13, 1962; entered into force February 13, 1962.
13 UST 145; TIAS 4949; 494 UNTS 213.

Amendment:
August 25 and 26, 1964 (15 UST 1800; TIAS 5652; 529 UNTS 378).

DEFENSE

Agreement concerning the provision of assistance on a reimbursable basis in support of the United Nations operation in Somalia, with related annex. Signed at Washington and New York May 4 and 6, 1993; entered into force May 6, 1993.
TIAS

Agreement regarding the furnishing of defense articles and defense services by the United States to the United Nations for purposes of supporting the Rapid Reactor Force established pursuant to United Nations Security Council Resolution 998. Exchange of notes at New York July 28, 1995; entered into force July 28, 1995.
TIAS 12680.

DEVELOPMENT ASSISTANCE

Basic agreement governing grants by the United States to the United Nations Trust Fund for Africa. Signed at Washington June 17, 1976; entered into force June 17, 1976.
28 UST 6885; TIAS 8694.

ECONOMIC AND TECHNICAL COOPERATION

Agreement concerning technical assistance for Bangladesh in the field of statistical services. Signed at New York and Washington March 14 and May 2, 1978; entered into force May 2, 1978.
30 UST 1192; TIAS 9245.

HEADQUARTERS

Agreement regarding the headquarters of the United Nations. Signed at Lake Success June 26, 1947; entered into force November 21, 1947.
61 Stat. 3416; TIAS 1676; 12 Bevans 956; 11 UNTS 11.

Supplemental agreement regarding the headquarters of the United Nations. Signed at New York February 9, 1966; entered into force February 9, 1966.
17 UST 74; TIAS 5961; 554 UNTS 308.

UNITED NATIONS (Cont'd)

Amendment:
December 8, 1966 (17 UST 2319; TIAS 6176; 581 UNTS 362).

Second supplemental agreement regarding the headquarters of the United Nations. Signed at New York August 28, 1969; entered into force August 28, 1969.
20 UST 2810; TIAS 6750; 687 UNTS 408.

Third supplemental agreement regarding the headquarters of the United Nations. Signed at New York December 10, 1980; entered into force December 10, 1980.
32 UST 4414; TIAS 9955.

HUMANITARIAN ASSISTANCE

Agreement concerning reimbursement procedures for humanitarian relief operations in Somalia. Signed at New York January 29, 1993; entered into force January 29, 1993.
TIAS 11919.

Agreement concerning the provision of assistance on a reimbursable basis in support of the United Nations operation in Rwanda. Signed at New York June 6, 1994; entered into force June 6, 1994.
TIAS 12183.

Cooperation service agreement for the contribution of personnel to the International Tribunal for Rwanda, with annexes. Signed at New York September 6, 1995; entered into force September 6, 1995.
TIAS   ; 1887 UNTS 215.

Memorandum of understanding for the contribution of civilian personnel to the United Nations Transitional Administration for Eastern Slavonia, Baranja and Western Sirmium, with annexes. Signed at New York March 26, 1996; entered into force March 26, 1996; effective March 14, 1996.
TIAS

POSTAL MATTERS

Postal agreement. Signed March 28, 1951; entered into force October 24, 1951.
3 UST 369; TIAS 2399; 108 UNTS 231.

Amendments:
November 7 and 17, 1952 (3 UST 5164; TIAS 2711; 149 UNTS 414).
April 15 and 19, 1965 (16 UST 745; TIAS 5803; 531 UNTS 314).
June 20 and August 8, 1994 (1819 UNTS 497).

TAXATION

Agreement relating to a procedure for United States income tax reimbursement. Exchange of letters at New York June 30 and July 12, 1978; entered into force July 12, 1978.
30 UST 124; TIAS 9183; 1095 UNTS 307.

TELECOMMUNICATION

Agreement to permit the exchange of third-party messages between amateur stations of the United States and amateur station 4U1VIC of the Vienna International Amateur Radio Club. Exchange of letters at Vienna November 21 and December 3, 1985; entered into force January 2, 1986.
TIAS

TRUSTEESHIPS

Trusteeship agreement for the former Japanese mandated islands. Approved by the Security Council of the United Nations April 2, 1947, and by the United States July 18, 1947; entered into force July 18, 1947.
61 Stat. 3301; TIAS 1665; 12 Bevans 951; 8 UNTS 189.

Agreement relating to the provision of assistance by the United Nations Development Programme to the Trust Territory of the Pacific Islands, with exchange of notes. Signed at New York June 10, 1974; entered into force June 10, 1974.[1]
25 UST 1618; TIAS 7900.

WAR CRIMES

Cooperation service agreement for the contribution of personnel to the international criminal tribunal for the former Yugoslavia, with annexes. Signed at New York October 18, 1994; entered into force October 18, 1994.
TIAS

Amendments and extensions:
October 17, 1996 (1940 UNTS 392).
December 16 and 17, 1996.
March 18, 1997.
May 1, 1997.
September 30, 1997.
March 4, 1998.
May 19 and 22, 1998.
June 29, 1998.
December 23 and 24, 1998.
June 24 and 25, 1999.

Agreement for the provision of forensic specialists to the International Criminal Tribunal for the Former Yugoslavia, with attachment. Signed at New York July 2, 1999; entered into force July 2, 1999.
TIAS

NOTE:
[1] On December 22, 1990, the United Nations Security Council passed UNSC Resolution 683 (1990), which confirmed the termination of the Trusteeship Agreement as it applied to the Republic of the Marshall Islands, the Federated States of Micronesia, and the Commonwealth of the Northern Mariana Islands.

UNITED NATIONS CHILDREN'S FUND

ECONOMIC AND TECHNICAL COOPERATION

Agency for International Development:
April 29 and May 11, 1977 (29 UST 5266; TIAS 9101).
May 4 and 11, 1977 (29 UST 5263; TIAS 9100).
March 25, 1988 (NP).

UNITED NATIONS ENVIRONMENT PROGRAMME

REMOTE SENSING

Agreement concerning the operation of a Global Resource Information Database (GRID) facility. Signed at Nairobi December 16 and 18, 1997 and January 6, 1998; entered into force January 6, 1998.
TIAS

UNITED NATIONS HIGH COMMISSIONER FOR REFUGEES

ECONOMIC AND TECHNICAL COOPERATION

Agency for International Development:
June 29 and 30, 1978 (30 UST 3138; TIAS 9384; 1179 UNTS 13).

MIGRATION

Agreement concerning United States and UNHCR cooperation in providing assistance to the Cuban boat people. Exchange of letters at Washington September 29 and October 5, 1994; entered into force October 5, 1994.
TIAS

UNITED NATIONS HIGH COMMISSIONER FOR REFUGEES (Cont'd)

REFUGEE RELIEF

Grant agreement concerning assistance to displaced and uprooted persons in South Viet-Nam and Laos. Signed at Washington and Geneva November 13 and December 2, 1974; entered into force December 2, 1974.
26 UST 450; TIAS 8044; 991 UNTS 386.

Amendments:
December 16, 1974 (26 UST 457; TIAS 8044; 991 UNTS 392).
February 5 and 10, 1975 (26 UST 458; TIAS 8044; 991 UNTS 393).

Agreement relating to assistance with Cuban refugees. Done at Geneva May 16 and 21, 1980; entered into force May 21, 1980.
TIAS

UNIVERSAL POSTAL UNION

TAXATION

Tax reimbursement agreement, with annex. Signed at Bern January 12, 1995; entered into force January 12, 1995.
TIAS 12598.

URUGUAY

AGRICULTURAL COMMODITIES

Agricultural commodities agreement with exchange of notes. Signed at Montevideo February 20, 1959; entered into force February 20, 1959.
10 UST 161; TIAS 4179; 341 UNTS 201.

Amendments:
May 21, 1959 (10 UST 1023; TIAS 4238; 346 UNTS 358).
November 16, 1959 (10 UST 1904; TIAS 4356; 360 UNTS 428).
December 1, 1959 (10 UST 2067; TIAS 4375; 361 UNTS 372).
January 13, 1960 (11 UST 41; TIAS 4406; 368 UNTS 372).
September 13 and 16, 1960 (11 UST 2536; TIAS 4640; 401 UNTS 316).
October 14, 1960 (11 UST 2539; TIAS 4641; 401 UNTS 319).
September 18, 1961 (12 UST 1394; TIAS 4863; 433 UNTS 372).

Agricultural commodities agreement with exchanges of notes. Signed at Montevideo April 27, 1962; entered into force April 27, 1962.
13 UST 1018; TIAS 5044; 452 UNTS 25.

Agricultural commodities agreement with annex. Signed at Montevideo January 19, 1968; entered into force January 19, 1968.
19 UST 4534; TIAS 6445; 698 UNTS 3.

Amendments:
June 13 and 27, 1968 (19 UST 6048; TIAS 6564; 702 UNTS 418).
March 4 and 18, 1970 (21 UST 1141; TIAS 6868; 745 UNTS 345).

Related agreements:
May 7, 1968 (19 UST 4837; TIAS 6486; 698 UNTS 229).
July 8 and October 20, 1970 (21 UST 2256; TIAS 6976).
December 8 and 9, 1970 (21 UST 3102; TIAS 7033; 781 UNTS 356).
September 25, 1972 (23 UST 2905; TIAS 7477).

AVIATION

Air transport agreement. Signed at Montevideo December 14, 1946; entered into force provisionally December 14, 1946.
15 UST 2115; TIAS 5692; 532 UNTS 87.

Amendments:
July 9, 1976 and February 9, 1977 (28 UST 2442; TIAS 8562).
July 15, 1991 (TIAS 11806).

Memorandum of agreement relating to provision of Federal Aviation Administration services to the Government of Uruguay. Signed at Washington and Montevideo March 19 and 20, 1981; entered into force March 20, 1981.
33 UST 1461; TIAS 10122.

Memorandum of agreement concerning assistance in developing and modernizing Uruguay's civil aviation infrastructure. Signed at Washington and Montevideo September 25 and 30, 1997; entered into force September 30, 1997.
TIAS

COPYRIGHT (See APPENDIX)

CUSTOMS

Agreement providing more liberal exemptions from customs duties and related taxes for diplomatic and consular personnel. Exchange of notes at Washington October 31 and November 12, 1952; entered into force November 12, 1952.
5 UST 824; TIAS 2971; 231 UNTS 145.

DEFENSE

Military assistance agreement. Signed at Montevideo June 30, 1952; entered into force June 11, 1953.
4 UST 197; TIAS 2778; 207 UNTS 139.

Agreement providing for disposition of equipment and materials furnished by the United States under the military assistance agreement and no longer required by Uruguay. Exchange of notes at Montevideo June 1 and September 16, 1955, and note of April 20, 1956; entered into force September 16, 1955.
7 UST 831; TIAS 3562; 273 UNTS 259.

Agreement relating to the deposit by Uruguay of ten percent of the value of grant military assistance and excess defense articles furnished by the United States. Exchange of notes at Montevideo May 2, 1972; entered into force May 2, 1972; effective February 7, 1972.
23 UST 653; TIAS 7329.

Agreement relating to payment to the United States of net proceeds from the sale of defense articles furnished under the military assistance program. Exchange of notes at Montevideo December 11 and 30, 1974; entered into force December 30, 1974; effective July 1, 1974.
25 UST 3181; TIAS 7985; 991 UNTS 407.

Acquisition and cross-servicing agreement, with annexes. Signed at Montevideo March 29, 2000; entered into force March 29, 2000.
TIAS

ECONOMIC AND TECHNICAL COOPERATION

General agreement for a program of technical cooperation. Signed at Montevideo March 23, 1956; entered into force March 22, 1960.
11 UST 1489; TIAS 4491; 376 UNTS 311.

Agreement concerning the establishment of an Americas Fund and Administering Commission. Signed at Montevideo June 25, 1993; entered into force June 25, 1993.
TIAS 12503.

EDUCATION

Agreement for financing certain educational exchange programs. Exchange of notes at Montevideo March 22 and May 17, 1965; entered into force May 17, 1965.
16 UST 872; TIAS 5825; 564 UNTS 69.

EXTRADITION

Treaty on extradition and cooperation in penal matters. Signed at Washington April 6, 1973; entered into force April 11, 1984.
TIAS 10850.

URUGUAY (Cont'd)

FINANCE

Agreement relating to investment guaranties. Exchange of notes at Montevideo December 15, 1982; entered into force July 21, 1983.
TIAS 12038.

Agreement regarding the reduction of certain debts related to foreign assistance owed to the Government of the United States and its agencies, with appendices. Signed at Washington December 15, 1992; entered into force January 14, 1993.
NP

Agreement regarding the reduction of certain debts related to agriculture owed to the Government of the United States and its agencies, with appendices. Signed at Washington December 15, 1992; entered into force January 14, 1993.
NP

HIGHWAYS

Agreement concerning cooperation in highway technology. Signed at Washington June 18, 1986; entered into force June 18, 1986.
TIAS 11377.

JUDICIAL ASSISTANCE

Treaty on mutual legal assistance in criminal matters. Signed at Montevideo May 6, 1991; entered into force April 15, 1994.
TIAS

MAPPING

Cooperative mapping, charting and geodesy agreement. Signed at Montevideo and Fairfax August 27 and October 25, 1991; entered into force October 25, 1991.
NP

MISSIONS, AIR FORCE

Agreement relating to the appointment of officers and subordinate personnel to constitute an Air Force mission to Uruguay. Signed at Washington December 4, 1951; entered into force December 4, 1951.
2 UST 2517; TIAS 2369; 152 UNTS 41.

PACIFIC SETTLEMENT OF DISPUTES

Arbitration convention. Signed at Washington January 9, 1909; entered into force November 14, 1913.
38 Stat. 1741; TS 583; 12 Bevans 986.

Treaty for the advancement of peace. Signed at Washington July 20, 1914; entered into force February 24, 1915.
38 Stat. 1908; TS 611; 12 Bevans 988.

PEACE CORPS

Agreement relating to the establishment of a Peace Corps program in Uruguay. Exchange of notes at Montevideo March 19 and July 31, 1963; entered into force July 31, 1963.
14 UST 1455; TIAS 5443; 488 UNTS 3.

POSTAL MATTERS

International express mail agreement with detailed regulations. Signed at Washington September 22, 1983; entered into force February 15, 1984.
TIAS 10841.

TELECOMMUNICATION

Agreement relating to radio communications between radio amateurs on behalf of third parties. Exchange of notes at Montevideo September 12, 1961; entered into force September 26, 1966.
17 UST 1574; TIAS 6115; 607 UNTS 175.

Agreement relating to the reciprocal granting of authorizations to permit licensed amateur radio operators of either country to operate their stations in the other country. Exchange of notes at Montevideo May 28, 1971; entered into force May 28, 1971.
22 UST 701; TIAS 7129; 797 UNTS 23.

TRADE AND COMMERCE

Convention facilitating the work of traveling salesmen. Signed at Washington August 27, 1918; entered into force August 2, 1919.
41 Stat. 1663; TS 640; 12 Bevans 991.

Agreement concerning exports of certain textile products manufactured in Uruguay to the United States, with annexes. Exchange of notes at Montevideo December 30, 1983 and January 23, 1984; entered into force January 23, 1984; effective August 1, 1983.
NP

Amendments and extensions:
August 24 and September 13, 1984 (NP).
September 10 and 30, 1987 (NP).

September 10, 1987 and February 9, 1988 (NP).
November 14, 1988 and June 20, 1989 (NP).
November 9, 1988, January 18 and July 26, 1989 (NP).
June 9, July 27 and August 18, 1992 (NP).

Administrative arrangement for a visa system relating to trade in certain textile products. Exchange of notes at Montevideo August 24 and September 13, 1984; entered into force September 13, 1984.
NP

Amendments:
January 19 and July 11, 1988 (NP).
April 8, July 14 and October 4, 1988 (NP).
October 5, 1988 and April 25, 1989 (NP).

VISAS

Agreement relating to passport visas and fees for nonimmigrants. Exchange of notes at Montevideo November 3 and 8, 1949; entered into force November 10, 1949.
64 Stat. (3) B122; TIAS 2046; 12 Bevans 1035; 82 UNTS 45.

UZBEKISTAN

For agreements prior to December 31, 1991, see UNION OF SOVIET SOCIALIST REPUBLICS.

AVIATION

Air transport agreement, with annexes. Signed at Washington February 27, 1998; entered into force February 27, 1998.
TIAS

DEFENSE

Agreement concerning the provision of training under the United States International Military Education and Training (IMET) Program. Exchange of notes at Tashkent January 25 and February 21, 1995; entered into force February 21, 1995.
NP

Agreement regarding grants under the Foreign Assistance Act of 1961, as amended, and the furnishing of defense articles, related training, and other defense services to the Government of Uzbekistan. Exchange of notes at Tashkent March 18 and May 4, 1999; entered into force May 4, 1999.
TIAS

UZBEKISTAN (Cont'd)

ECONOMIC AND TECHNICAL COOPERATION

Agreement regarding cooperation to facilitate the provision of assistance. Signed at Tashkent March 1, 1994; entered into force March 1, 1994.
TIAS 12534.

FINANCE

Investment incentive agreement. Signed at Tashkent October 28, 1992; entered into force October 28, 1992.
TIAS

PEACE CORPS

Agreement concerning the activity of the Peace Corps of the United States in the Republic of Uzbekistan. Signed at Tashkent November 4, 1992; entered into force November 4, 1992.
TIAS 12083.

TRADE

Agreement on trade relations, with exchanges of letters. Signed at Tashkent November 5, 1993; entered into force January 13, 1994.
TIAS 12515.

WEAPONS

Agreement concerning cooperation in the area of the dismantlement of weapons of mass destruction, the prevention of proliferation of weapons of mass destruction, and the promotion of defense and military relations. Signed at Tashkent June 27, 1997; entered into force June 27, 1997.
TIAS

Agreement concerning cooperation in the area of demilitarization of chemical weapons associated facilities and the prevention of proliferation of chemical weapons technology. Signed at Tashkent May 25, 1999; entered into force May 25, 1999.
TIAS

VANUATU [1]

NOTE:
[1] Treaties and other agreements previously applicable to the New Hebrides are under review.

PEACE CORPS

Memorandum of understanding on the establishment of a Peace Corps program in Vanuatu. Signed at Port Vila October 2, 1989; entered into force October 2, 1989.
TIAS 12112.

POSTAL MATTERS

International express mail agreement, with detailed regulations. Signed at Port Vila and Washington May 23 and June 30, 1989; entered into force July 31, 1989.
TIAS 11668.

VATICAN

COPYRIGHT (See APPENDIX)

POSTAL MATTERS

Agreement for the exchange of international money orders. Signed at Vatican City November 24, 1955, and at Washington December 22, 1955; entered into force November 1, 1956.
7 UST 3205; TIAS 3700.

VENEZUELA

AGRICULTURAL COMMODITIES

Agricultural commodities agreement with exchange of notes. Signed at Washington May 17, 1962; entered into force May 17, 1962.
13 UST 1231; TIAS 5068; 456 UNTS 275.

Amendment:
June 18, 1962 (13 UST 1336; TIAS 5091; 459 UNTS 348).

AGRICULTURE

Agreement to establish a Venezuela-United States Agriculture Commission. Exchange of notes at Caracas December 26, 1984; entered into force December 26, 1984.
TIAS 11074.

Extension:
December 23, 1996 and January 6, 1997.

ATOMIC ENERGY

Agreement continuing in effect safeguards and guarantee provisions of the agreement of October 8, 1958, as amended (TIAS 4416, 6945), for cooperation concerning civil uses of atomic energy. Exchange of notes at Caracas February 18, 1981; entered into force February 18, 1981.
33 UST 1111; TIAS 10097; 1281 UNTS 3.

AVIATION

Air transport agreement with exchange of notes. Signed at Caracas August 14, 1953; entered into force August 22, 1953.
4 UST 1493; TIAS 2813; 213 UNTS 99.

Amendments:
February 11, 1972 (24 UST 271; TIAS 7549).
September 22, 1976 (27 UST 4111; TIAS 8433).
July 19 and October 10, 1990 (TIAS 11751).

Memorandum of agreement concerning the provision of technical assistance to develop and modernize Venezuela's civil aviation infrastructure, with annexes. Signed at Washington and Caracas February 1 and 4, 1977; entered into force February 4, 1977.
29 UST 5300; TIAS 9110.

Agreement for the provision of assistance in developing and modernizing Venezuela's civil aviation infrastructure. Signed at Washington June 29, 1998; entered into force June 29, 1998.
TIAS

BOUNDARIES

Maritime boundary treaty. Signed at Caracas March 28, 1978; entered into force November 24, 1980.
32 UST 3100; TIAS 9890.

COMMERCE

Treaty of peace, friendship, navigation and commerce.[1] Signed at Caracas January 20, 1836; entered into force May 31, 1836.
8 Stat. 466; TS 366; 12 Bevans 1038.

NOTE:
[1] Articles with respect to commerce and navigation terminated January 3, 1851.

CONSERVATION

Memorandum of understanding concerning the conservation of protected natural areas and their biodiversity. Signed at Caracas October 12, 1997; entered into force October 12, 1997.
TIAS

VENEZUELA (Cont'd)

COPYRIGHT (See APPENDIX)

CULTURAL HERITAGE

Memorandum of understanding on cooperation in management and protection of national parks and other protected natural and cultural heritage sites. Signed at Washington July 1, 1991; entered into force July 1, 1991.
TIAS 11807.

CUSTOMS

Agreement relating to duty-free entry privileges for nondiplomatic personnel. Exchange of notes at Caracas April 7 and 17, 1959; entered into force April 17, 1959.
10 UST 1715; TIAS 4323; 358 UNTS 83.

DEFENSE

Agreement relating to the deposit by Venezuela of ten percent of the value of grant military assistance furnished by the United States. Exchange of notes at Caracas July 19, 1972; entered into force July 19, 1972; effective February 7, 1972.
23 UST 1312; TIAS 7411.

Agreement relating to eligibility for United States military assistance and training pursuant to the International Security Assistance and Arms Export Control Act of 1976. Exchange of notes at Caracas June 16 and 30, 1977; entered into force June 30, 1977.
29 UST 1884; TIAS 8907.

General security of military information agreement. Signed at Caracas July 15, 1983; entered into force July 15, 1983.
TIAS 10747.

Agreement regarding grants under the Foreign Assistance Act of 1961, as amended, and the furnishing of defense articles, related training and other defense services from the United States to Venezuela. Exchange of letters at Caracas February 26 and 27, 1996; entered into force February 27, 1996.
TIAS

ECONOMIC AND TECHNICAL COOPERATION

Agreement relating to grants to Venezuelan nationals to facilitate their training in the United States. Exchange of notes at Caracas May 23 and June 7, 1951; entered into force June 7, 1951.
2 UST 1302; TIAS 2280; 141 UNTS 273.

Amendment:
December 20, 1951, and January 8 and April 8, 1952 (3 UST 4787; TIAS 2648; 205 UNTS 331).

General agreement on technical cooperation. Exchange of notes at Caracas September 29, 1952; entered into force September 29, 1952.
3 UST 5096; TIAS 2700; 186 UNTS 23.

EMPLOYMENT

Agreement concerning employment of dependents of official government employees. Exchange of notes at Caracas July 18 and 29, 1988; entered into force July 29, 1988, except with respect to dependents of employees of permanent missions to international organizations.
TIAS

ENERGY

Agreement in the field of energy research and development, with annex. Signed at Washington March 6, 1980; entered into force March 6, 1980.
32 UST 5679; TIAS 10012; 1267 UNTS 57.

Extension:
March 3 and 4, 1988 (TIAS 11326).

Agreement for energy cooperation, with annex. Signed at Caracas October 13, 1997; entered into force October 13, 1997.
TIAS

EXTRADITION

Treaty of extradition, and additional article. Signed at Caracas January 19 and 21, 1922; entered into force April 14, 1923.
43 Stat. 1698; TS 675; 12 Bevans 1128; 49 LNTS 435.

FINANCE

Agreement relating to investment guaranties. Exchange of notes at Caracas November 26 and 29, 1962; entered into force November 29, 1962.
14 UST 374; TIAS 5326; 474 UNTS 107.

Swap agreement between the United States Treasury and the Central Bank of Venezuela/Government of Venezuela, with related letter. Signed at Washington and Caracas March 10, 1989; entered into force March 10, 1989.
TIAS

Swap agreement among the United States Treasury and the Central Bank of Venezuela/Government of Venezuela, with memorandum of understanding. Signed at Washington and

Caracas March 16, 1990; entered into force March 16, 1990.
TIAS

Investment incentive agreement. Signed at Washington June 22, 1990; entered into force June 22, 1990.
TIAS 12098.

Agreement supplementing the investment incentive agreement of June 22, 1990, relating to the Export-Import Bank. Signed at Washington April 22, 1992; entered into force April 22, 1992.
TIAS 12098.

HEALTH

Agreement for scientific and technological cooperation in health. Signed at Caracas August 11, 1980; entered into force July 22, 1983.
TIAS 10651; 1647 UNTS 39.

Extension:
July 19 and 21, 1988.

JUDICIAL ASSISTANCE

Agreement on procedures for mutual assistance in connection with the Boeing Company matter. Signed at Washington May 31, 1977; entered into force May 31, 1977.
28 UST 5219; TIAS 8623.

Related agreement:
December 6 and 8, 1978 (30 UST 2254; TIAS 9333; 1171 UNTS 105).

Agreement regarding cooperation in the prevention and control of money laundering arising from illicit trafficking in narcotic drugs and psychotropic substances, with attachment. Signed at Washington November 5, 1990; entered into force January 1, 1991.
TIAS 12422.

Agreement for mutual assistance in administration of justice in connection with certain banking, financial and other institutions. Signed at Washington March 17, 1995; entered into force March 17, 1995.
TIAS 12615.

MAPPING

Agreement providing for a joint program of aerial photography in Venezuela. Exchange of notes at Caracas August 23 and September 24, 1957; entered into force September 24, 1957.
8 UST 1614; TIAS 3915; 293 UNTS 307.

Agreement governing cooperation in mapping, charting and geodesy. Signed at Washington and Caracas June 18 and November 26, 1985; entered into force November 26, 1985.
TIAS 11209.

VENEZUELA (Cont'd)

Basic exchange and cooperative agreement for topographic mapping, nautical and aeronautical charting and information, geodesy and geophysics, digital data and related mapping, charting and geodesy materials. Signed at Fairfax March 20, 1996; entered into force March 20, 1996.
NP

MARITIME MATTERS

Agreement for exemption of merchant vessels from requirements of admeasurement by port authorities. Signed at Caracas February 21, 1957; entered into force February 21, 1957.
8 UST 289; TIAS 3774; 279 UNTS 199.

MISSIONS, MILITARY

Agreement for the appointment of United States naval officers and personnel to constitute a naval mission to Venezuela. Signed at Washington August 23, 1950; entered into force August 23, 1950.
1 UST 573; TIAS 2104; 92 UNTS 341.

Extension and amendment:
March 31 and April 29, 1959 (10 UST 2120; TIAS 4382; 366 UNTS 392).

Agreement for appointment of an Army mission to Venezuela. Signed at Washington August 10, 1951; entered into force August 10, 1951.
2 UST 1570; TIAS 2299; 140 UNTS 345.

Extension and amendment:
March 31 and April 29, 1959 (10 UST 2117; TIAS 4381; 366 UNTS 405).

Agreement relating to an Air Force mission to Venezuela. Signed at Washington January 16, 1953; entered into force January 16, 1953.
4 UST 97; TIAS 2766; 199 UNTS 287.

Extension and amendment:
March 31 and April 29, 1959 (10 UST 2114; TIAS 4380; 361 UNTS 326).

NARCOTIC DRUGS

Agreement concerning the establishment and operation of a regional office of the Drug Enforcement Administration in Caracas. Exchange of notes at Caracas August 26, 1974; entered into force August 26, 1974.
25 UST 2440; TIAS 7925.

Memorandum of understanding concerning cooperation in the narcotics field. Signed at Caracas March 28, 1978; entered into force March 28, 1978.
30 UST 1012; TIAS 9235; 1152 UNTS 203.

Agreement to suppress illicit traffic in narcotic drugs and psychotropic substances by sea. Signed at Caracas November 9, 1991; entered into force November 9, 1991.
TIAS 11827.

Protocol to the agreement of November 9, 1991 to suppress illicit traffic in narcotic drugs and psychotropic substances by sea. Signed at Caracas July 23, 1997; entered into force July 23, 1997.
TIAS

PACIFIC SETTLEMENT OF DISPUTES

Treaty for the advancement of peace. Signed at Caracas March 21, 1914; entered into force February 12, 1921.
42 Stat. 1920; TS 652; 12 Bevans 1122.

PEACE CORPS

Agreement relating to the establishment of a Peace Corps program in Venezuela. Exchange of notes at Caracas April 14 and May 28, 1962; entered into force May 28, 1962.
13 UST 1326; TIAS 5089; 458 UNTS 249.

POSTAL MATTERS

International express mail agreement. Signed at Washington and Caracas August 10 and 15, 1984; entered into force December 1, 1984.
TIAS 11008.

SCIENTIFIC COOPERATION

Memorandum of understanding on cooperation in earth resources and geological phenomena. Signed at Washington and Caracas February 5 and 7, 1980; entered into force July 22, 1983.
TIAS 10650; 1647 UNTS 17.

Extension:
July 19 and 21, 1988.

Memorandum of understanding concerning scientific and technical cooperation in the earth and mapping sciences. Signed at Caracas January 15, 1992; entered into force January 15, 1992.
TIAS 11842.

Agreement for scientific and technological cooperation, with annexes. Signed at Caracas October 12, 1997; entered into force February 17, 1998.
TIAS

TAXATION

Agreement for the avoidance of double taxation with respect to shipping and air transport. Signed at Caracas December 29, 1987; entered into force August 10, 1988; effective with respect to taxable years beginning on or before January 1, 1987.
TIAS 11556.

Convention for the avoidance of double taxation and the prevention of fiscal evasion with respect to taxes on income and capital, with protocol. Signed at Caracas January 25, 1999; entered into force December 30, 1999.
TIAS

TELECOMMUNICATION

Arrangement for radio communications between amateur stations on behalf of third parties. Exchange of notes at Caracas November 12, 1959; entered into force December 12, 1959.
10 UST 3019; TIAS 4394; 367 UNTS 81.

Agreement relating to the reciprocal granting of authorizations to permit licensed amateur radio operators of either country to operate their stations in the other country. Exchange of notes at Caracas September 18, 1967; entered into force October 3, 1967.
18 UST 2499; TIAS 6348; 693 UNTS 109.

TOURISM

Agreement on the development and facilitation of tourism. Signed at New York September 27, 1989; entered into force September 27, 1989.
TIAS 12402.

TRADE (See also COMMERCE)

Convention facilitating the work of traveling salesmen. Signed at Caracas July 3, 1919; entered into force August 18, 1920.
41 Stat. 1719; TS 648; 12 Bevans 1125.

Reciprocal trade agreement.[1] Signed at Caracas November 6, 1939; entered into force provisionally December 16, 1939; definitively December 14, 1940.
54 Stat. 2375; EAS 180; 12 Bevans 1141; 203 LNTS 273.

Supplementary trade agreement.[1] Signed at Caracas August 28, 1952; entered into force October 11, 1952.
3 UST 4195; TIAS 2565; 178 UNTS 51.

Agreement relating to effectiveness of the United States revised tariff schedules to the trade agreement of November 6, 1939, as supplemented.[1] Exchange of notes at Caracas July 15 and 23, 1963; entered into force July 23, 1963.
14 UST 1901; TIAS 5502; 505 UNTS 316.

VENEZUELA (Cont'd)

Agreement terminating in part the reciprocal trade agreement of November 6, 1939, as supplemented. Exchange of notes at Caracas June 26, 1972; entered into force June 26, 1972.
23 UST 1213; TIAS 7387.

NOTE:
[1] Terminated in part June 30, 1972 by exchange of notes dated June 26, 1972.

VIETNAM [1]

NOTE:
[1] The agreements listed below were in force between the United States and the Republic of Viet-Nam (South Viet-Nam). The status of these agreements remains under review by the United States.

AGRICULTURAL COMMODITIES [1]

NOTE:
[1] Only the basic agricultural commodities agreements are listed hereunder. Amendments and related agreements, as listed in previous editions of *Treaties in Force,* are on file in the Office of the Assistant Legal Adviser for Treaty Affairs.

Agricultural commodities agreement with memorandum of understanding and exchange of notes. Signed at Saigon June 17, 1958; entered into force June 17, 1958.
9 UST 977; TIAS 4066; 321 UNTS 35.

Agricultural commodities agreement with exchange of notes. Signed at Saigon October 16, 1959; entered into force October 16, 1959.
10 UST 1868; TIAS 4351; 360 UNTS 271.

Agricultural commodities agreement. Signed at Saigon October 28, 1960; entered into force October 28, 1960.
11 UST 2518; TIAS 4637; 401 UNTS 3.

Agricultural commodities agreement with exchange of notes. Signed at Saigon March 25, 1961; entered into force March 25, 1961.
12 UST 350; TIAS 4722; 406 UNTS 187.

Agricultural commodities agreement with exchange of notes. Signed at Saigon July 14, 1961; entered into force July 14, 1961.
12 UST 1112; TIAS 4822; 416 UNTS 133.

Agricultural commodities agreement with exchange of notes. Signed at Saigon December 27, 1961; entered into force December 27, 1961.
12 UST 3169; TIAS 4920; 433 UNTS 185.

Agricultural commodities agreement with exchange of notes. Signed at Saigon November 21, 1962; entered into force November 21, 1962.
13 UST 3831; TIAS 5256; 469 UNTS 101.

Agricultural commodities agreement with exchange of notes. Signed at Saigon January 9, 1964; entered into force January 9, 1964.
15 UST 13; TIAS 5514; 505 UNTS 173.

Agricultural commodities agreement with exchange of notes. Signed at Saigon September 29, 1964; entered into force September 29, 1964.
15 UST 1973; TIAS 5674; 531 UNTS 183.

Agricultural commodities agreement with exchange of notes. Signed at Saigon May 26, 1965; entered into force May 26, 1965.
16 UST 838; TIAS 5821; 550 UNTS 3.

Agricultural commodities agreement with exchange of notes. Signed at Saigon March 21, 1966; entered into force March 21, 1966.
17 UST 129; TIAS 5968; 578 UNTS 165.

Agricultural commodities agreement with exchange of notes. Signed at Saigon December 15, 1966; entered into force December 15, 1966.
17 UST 2321; TIAS 6177; 681 UNTS 63.

Agricultural commodities agreement with annex. Signed at Saigon March 13, 1967; entered into force March 13, 1967.
18 UST 1219; TIAS 6271; 685 UNTS 71.

Agricultural commodities agreement with annex. Signed at Saigon July 8, 1970; entered into force July 8, 1970.
21 UST 2443; TIAS 6983; 775 UNTS 107.

Agricultural commodities agreement. Signed at Saigon October 8, 1974; entered into force October 8, 1974.
25 UST 2891; TIAS 7952.

CLAIMS

Agreement relating to mutual waiver of government claims for damages to government property and for injury or death of members of armed services. Exchange of notes at Saigon February 9, 1965; entered into force February 9, 1965.
16 UST 140; TIAS 5773; 542 UNTS 175.

Agreement concerning the settlement of certain property claims. Signed at Hanoi January 28, 1995; entered into force January 28, 1995.
TIAS 12602.

COMMERCE

Treaty of amity and economic relations. Signed at Saigon April 3, 1961; entered into force November 30, 1961.
12 UST 1703; TIAS 4890; 424 UNTS 137.

COPYRIGHT (See also APPENDIX)

Agreement on the establishment of copyright relations. Signed at Hanoi June 27, 1997; entered into force December 23, 1998.
TIAS

Amendment:
December 23, 1998.

DEFENSE

Agreement relating to the disposition of equipment and materials furnished by the United States found surplus to the needs of the Vietnamese armed forces. Exchange of notes at Saigon March 1 and May 10, 1955; entered into force May 10, 1955.
7 UST 837; TIAS 3563; 273 UNTS 157.

Agreement relating to the transfer of scrap to Viet-Nam as supplementary military assistance. Exchange of notes at Saigon November 8 and December 14, 1972; entered into force December 14, 1972.
23 UST 4263; TIAS 7534.

Amendment:
September 3 and October 14, 1974 (25 UST 2906; TIAS 7953).

ECONOMIC AND TECHNICAL COOPERATION

Economic cooperation agreement with exchange of notes. Signed at Saigon September 7, 1951; entered into force September 7, 1951.
2 UST 2205; TIAS 2346; 174 UNTS 165.

Amendment:
June 7, 1962 (13 UST 1279; TIAS 5076; 458 UNTS 300).

Agreement providing for additional direct economic assistance pursuant to the economic cooperation agreement of September 7, 1951. Exchange of notes at Saigon February 21 and March 7, 1955; entered into force March 7, 1955; operative from January 1, 1955.
7 UST 2507; TIAS 3640; 277 UNTS 285.

FINANCE

Agreement relating to investment guaranties under section 413 (b)(4) of the Mutual Security Act of 1954, as amended. Exchange of notes at Washington November 5, 1957; entered into force November 5, 1957.
8 UST 1869; TIAS 3932; 300 UNTS 23.

Amendment:
August 8, 1963 (14 UST 1210; TIAS 5419; 488 UNTS 270).

Agreement modifying the agreement of November 5, 1957, as amended, relating to in-

VIETNAM [1] (Cont'd)

vestment guaranties. Exchange of notes at Saigon December 16, 1969 and February 12, 1970; entered into force February 12, 1970.
21 UST 1148; TIAS 6869; 745 UNTS 312.

Agreement regarding the consolidation and rescheduling of certain debts owed to, guaranteed by, or insured by the United States Government and the Agency for International Development, with annexes. Signed at Hanoi April 7, 1997; entered into force June 23, 1997.
NP

Agreement regarding the operations of the Overseas Private Investment Corporation in Vietnam. Signed at Washington and Hanoi March 19 and 26, 1998; entered into force March 26, 1998.
TIAS

Project incentive agreement regarding the operations of the Export-Import Bank of the United States in Vietnam. Signed at Hanoi December 9, 1999; entered into force December 9, 1999.
TIAS

INFORMATIONAL MEDIA GUARANTIES

Agreement providing for an informational media guaranty program pursuant to section 1011 of the United States Information and Educational Exchange Act of 1948, as amended. Exchange of notes at Saigon October 11 and November 3, 1955; entered into force November 3, 1955.
6 UST 3940; TIAS 3402; 239 UNTS 195.

MUTUAL SECURITY

Agreement relating to the assurances required by the Mutual Security Act of 1951. Exchange of notes at Saigon December 18, 1951, and January 3, 16, and 19, 1952; entered into force January 3, 1952.
3 UST 4672; TIAS 2623; 205 UNTS 127.

POSTAL MATTERS

International express mail agreement, with detailed regulations. Signed at Seoul September 13, 1994; entered into force December 1, 1994.
NP

Postal money order agreement. Signed at Hanoi and Washington November 1 and December 4, 1995; entered into force February 1, 1996.
NP

PROPERTY

Agreement concerning the transfer of diplomatic properties, with appendices and amendment. Signed at Hanoi January 28, 1995; entered into force January 28, 1995.
TIAS

PUBLICATIONS

Agreement relating to the exchange of official publications. Exchange of notes at Saigon April 4, 1961; entered into force April 4, 1961.
12 UST 310; TIAS 4717; 405 UNTS 77.

REFUGEES

Agreement on the implementation of the special released reeducation center detainees resettlement program, with annex. Exchange of letters at Washington and Hanoi August 18 and 28, 1989; entered into force August 28, 1989.
TIAS

RELIEF SUPPLIES AND PACKAGES

Agreement relating to duty-free entry and defrayment of inland transportation charges on relief supplies and packages. Exchange of notes at Saigon August 20 and 26, 1954; entered into force August 26, 1954.
5 UST 2531; TIAS 3115; 234 UNTS 111.

SURPLUS PROPERTY

Agreement relating to the disposal of United States excess property in Viet-Nam. Exchange of notes at Saigon November 9, 1968; entered into force November 9, 1968.
19 UST 6703; TIAS 6586; 702 UNTS 293.

TAXATION

Agreement regarding income tax administration. Exchange of notes at Saigon March 31 and May 3, 1967; entered into force May 3, 1967.
18 UST 546; TIAS 6262; 685 UNTS 207.

TELECOMMUNICATION

Agreement relating to television broadcasting in Viet-Nam. Exchange of notes at Saigon January 3, 1966; entered into force January 3, 1966.
17 UST 44; TIAS 5954; 579 UNTS 99.

TRADE-MARKS

Declaration respecting the rights of nationals concerning trademark protection, with related note. Exchange of notes at Washington November 3, 1953, and October 25, 1954, and related note of November 22, 1954; entered into force October 25, 1954.
5 UST 2400; TIAS 3100; 235 UNTS 11.

WESTERN SAMOA

On January 1, 1962, Western Samoa became an independent state. In an exchange of letters dated November 30, 1962 between the Office of the High Commissioner for New Zealand and the Prime Minister of Western Samoa, the Government of Western Samoa agreed that "All obligations and responsibilities of the Government of New Zealand which arise from any valid international instrument are, from January 1, 1962, assumed by the Government of Western Samoa in so far as such instrument may be held to have application to or in respect of Western Samoa."

DEFENSE

Status of forces agreement. Signed at Apia June 25, 1990; entered into force June 25, 1990.
TIAS

Agreement concerning the provision of training related to defense articles under the United States International Military Education and Training (IMET) program. Exchange of notes at Apia December 1, 1992 and March 8, 1993; entered into force March 8, 1993.
NP

EMPLOYMENT

Agreement relating to the employment of dependents of official government employees. Exchange of notes at New York and Washington February 27 and March 15, 1995; entered into force March 15, 1995.
TIAS 12613.

FINANCE

Investment guaranty agreement. Signed at Wellington and Apia June 5 and July 22, 1969; entered into force July 22, 1969.
20 UST 2766; TIAS 6745; 720 UNTS 53.

PEACE CORPS

Agreement relating to the establishment of a Peace Corps program in Western Samoa. Ex-

WESTERN SAMOA (Cont'd)

change of notes at Wellington October 1, 1970; entered into force October 1, 1970.
21 UST 2186; TIAS 6967; 764 UNTS 281.

POSTAL MATTERS

International express mail agreement, with detailed regulations. Signed at Apia and Washington February 16 and March 18, 1993; entered into force May 1, 1993.
NP

WORLD FOOD PROGRAM

ECONOMIC AND TECHNICAL COOPERATION

Agency for International Development:
July 9 and 23, 1976 (29 UST 1001; TIAS 8860).

WORLD HEALTH ORGANIZATION

CHEMICAL SAFETY

Memorandum of understanding regarding U.S. Environmental Protection Agency collaboration in the international program on chemical safety. Signed at Washington and Geneva January 19 and March 19, 1981; entered into force March 19, 1981.
TIAS

WORLD INTELLECTUAL PROPERTY ORGANIZATION

INDUSTRIAL PROPERTY

Agreement relating to cooperation in the promotion of industrial property protection. Signed at Geneva September 26, 1980; entered into force September 26, 1980.
32 UST 4530; TIAS 9964; 1267 UNTS 247.

PATENTS

Agreement regarding the functioning of the United States Patent and Trademark Office as an international searching authority and international preliminary examining authority under the Patent Cooperation Treaty, with annexes.

Signed at Geneva October 1, 1997; entered into force January 1, 1998.
TIAS

TAXATION

Tax reimbursement agreement, with annex. Signed at Geneva December 5, 1988; entered into force December 5, 1988.
TIAS 11625.

WORLD METEOROLOGICAL ORGANIZATION

TAXATION

Agreement relating to a procedure for United States income tax reimbursement, with annex. Signed at Geneva January 23, 1987; entered into force January 23, 1987.
TIAS 11293.

WORLD TRADE ORGANIZATION

TAXATION

Tax reimbursement agreement, with annex. Signed at Geneva December 22, 2000; entered into force December 22, 2000.
TIAS

YEMEN

The People's Democratic Republic of Yemen and the Yemen Arab Republic merged into a single sovereign State on May 22, 1990 called the Republic of Yemen. In a note dated May 19, 1990, to the Secretary-General of the United Nations, it was stated that . . . "All treaties and agreements concluded between either the Yemen Arab Republic or the People's Democratic Republic of Yemen and other States and international organizations in accordance with international law which are in force on May 22, 1990 will remain in effect, and international relations existing on May 22, 1990 between the People's Democratic Republic of Yemen and the Yemen Arab Republic and other States will continue.''. . . .

These agreements are under review.

AGRICULTURAL COMMODITIES

Agricultural commodities agreement, with related letter. Signed at Sanaa June 19, 1984; entered into force June 19, 1984.
NP

Agricultural commodities agreement. Signed at Sanaa April 15, 1985; entered into force April 15, 1985.
NP

Amendment:
July 30, 1985 (NP).

Agricultural commodities agreement. Signed at Sanaa February 18, 1986; entered into force February 18, 1986.
NP

Amendment:
July 26, 1986 (NP).

Agricultural commodities agreement. Signed at Sanaa May 6, 1987; entered into force May 6, 1987.
NP

Amendments:
July 2, 1987 (NP).
August 1, 1987 (NP).

Related agreements:
March 9, 1988 (NP).
January 25, 1990 (NP).

Agricultural commodities agreement. Signed at Sanaa September 29, 1988; entered into force September 29, 1988.
NP

COMMERCE

Agreement relating to friendship and commerce. Exchange of notes at Sanaa May 4, 1946; entered into force May 4, 1946.
60 Stat. 1782; TIAS 1535; 12 Bevans 1223; 4 UNTS 165.

DEFENSE

Agreement concerning the provision of training related to defense articles under the United States International Military Education and Training (IMET) Program. Exchange of notes at Sanaa September 9, 1986 and May 19, 1987; entered into force May 19, 1987.
TIAS 12015.

ECONOMIC AND TECHNICAL COOPERATION

Economic, technical, and related assistance agreement, with related letter. Signed at Sanaa

YEMEN (Cont'd)

April 20, 1974; entered into force April 20, 1974.
25 UST 715; TIAS 7820.

Agency for International Development:
March 31, 1976 (29 UST 22; TIAS 8787; 1115 UNTS 35).

FINANCE

Agreement relating to investment guaranties. Exchange of notes at Sanaa October 22 and December 4, 1972; entered into force December 4, 1972.
24 UST 845; TIAS 7586.

Agreement regarding the consolidation and rescheduling of certain debts owed to, guaranteed by, or insured by the United States Government and its agencies, with annexes. Signed at Sanaa April 8, 1997; entered into force May 22, 1997.
TIAS

Agreement regarding consolidation and rescheduling of certain debts owed to, guaranteed by, or insured by the United States Government and its agency, with annexes. Signed at Sanaa May 19, 1998; entered into force August 10, 1998.
TIAS

PEACE CORPS

Agreement relating to the establishment of a Peace Corps program in the Yemen Arab Republic. Exchange of notes at Sanaa September 30, 1972 and January 29, 1973; entered into force January 29, 1973.
24 UST 853; TIAS 7588.

POSTAL MATTERS

International express mail agreement, with detailed regulations. Signed at Sanaa and Washington June 17 and July 23, 1992; entered into force September 21, 1992.
TIAS 11873.

Postal money order agreement. Signed at Sanaa and Washington January 29 and March 7, 1994; entered into force April 1, 1994.
NP

YUGOSLAVIA

Yugoslavia has dissolved. For agreements prior to dissolution, see below. Subsequent agreements are listed under individual country headings.

Part 2 of Treaties in Force covers multilateral treaties and agreements. Where a multilateral treaty action was taken prior to dissolution, "Yugoslavia" is retained; where a successor state has taken action it is listed separately.

The status of the agreements listed below is under review.

AGRICULTURAL COMMODITIES

Agricultural commodities agreement, and related letters. Signed at Belgrade January 5, 1955; entered into force January 5, 1955.
6 UST 45; TIAS 3167; 251 UNTS 29.

Amendments:
May 12, 1955 (6 UST 1141; TIAS 3253; 251 UNTS 422).
October 1, 1955 (6 UST 6011; TIAS 3446; 270 UNTS 408).
January 19, 1956 (7 UST 146; TIAS 3486; 268 UNTS 386).
September 10 and 11, 1958 (10 UST 155; TIAS 4177; 340 UNTS 376).
April 15, 1964 (15 UST 402; TIAS 5571; 524 UNTS 306).

Agreement providing for the furnishing of additional wheat to Yugoslavia. Exchange of notes at Belgrade May 12, 1955; entered into force May 12, 1955.
6 UST 1139; TIAS 3252; 251 UNTS 331.

Agricultural commodities agreement with exchanges of notes. Signed at Belgrade November 3, 1956; entered into force November 3, 1956.
7 UST 3093; TIAS 3688; 277 UNTS 119.

Amendments:
January 23 and 24, 1957 (8 UST 31; TIAS 3735; 277 UNTS 128).
March 22, 1957 (8 UST 375; TIAS 3785; 279 UNTS 360).
December 27, 1957 (8 UST 2489; TIAS 3970; 307 UNTS 316).
April 15, 1964 (15 UST 402; TIAS 5571; 524 UNTS 306).

Agricultural commodities agreement with exchanges of notes. Signed at Belgrade February 3, 1958; entered into force February 3, 1958.
9 UST 256; TIAS 4000; 304 UNTS 293.

Amendment:
June 26, 1958 (9 UST 949; TIAS 4060; 317 UNTS 370).

Agricultural commodities agreement with exchange of notes. Signed at Belgrade December 22, 1958; entered into force December 22, 1958.
9 UST 1513; TIAS 4153; 338 UNTS 243.

Amendments:
July 9, 1959 (10 UST 1291; TIAS 4270; 354 UNTS 438).
April 15, 1964 (15 UST 402; TIAS 5571; 524 UNTS 306).

Agricultural commodities agreement with exchanges of notes. Signed at Belgrade June 3, 1960; entered into force June 3, 1960.
11 UST 1524; TIAS 4497; 376 UNTS 243.

Amendment:
July 1, 1961 (12 UST 1282; TIAS 4850; 421 UNTS 344).

Agricultural commodities agreement with exchanges of notes. Signed at Belgrade April 28, 1961; entered into force April 28, 1961.
12 UST 600; TIAS 4756; 409 UNTS 171.

Amendments:
July 1, 1961 (12 UST 1093; TIAS 4817; 416 UNTS 378).
April 15, 1964 (15 UST 402; TIAS 5571; 524 UNTS 306).

Agricultural commodities agreement, and exchanges of notes. Signed at Belgrade December 28, 1961; entered into force December 28, 1961.
12 UST 3185; TIAS 4923; 434 UNTS 111.

Amendments:
April 21, 1962 (13 UST 458; TIAS 5009; 442 UNTS 348).
April 15, 1964 (15 UST 402; TIAS 5571; 524 UNTS 306).
May 21, 1965 (16 UST 782; TIAS 5810; 546 UNTS 388).

Agricultural commodities agreement with exchange of notes. Signed at Belgrade April 21, 1962; entered into force April 21, 1962.
13 UST 452; TIAS 5008; 442 UNTS 123.

Amendments:
May 18, 1962 (13 UST 1097; TIAS 5053; 451 UNTS 350).
November 28, 1962 (13 UST 2562; TIAS 5222; 460 UNTS 352).
December 20, 1968 (19 UST 7844; TIAS 6620; 714 UNTS 266).

Agricultural commodities agreement with exchanges of notes. Signed at Belgrade November 28, 1962; entered into force November 28, 1962.
13 UST 2578; TIAS 5224; 460 UNTS 185.

Amendments:
April 19 and May 9, 1963 (14 UST 905; TIAS 5376; 479 UNTS 412).
August 19 and November 3, 1965 (16 UST 1756; TIAS 5903; 573 UNTS 336).

Agricultural commodities agreement with exchange of notes. Signed at Belgrade April 27, 1964; entered into force April 27, 1964.
15 UST 372; TIAS 5566; 526 UNTS 73.

Agricultural commodities agreement with exchange of notes. Signed at Belgrade April 27, 1964; entered into force April 27, 1964.
15 UST 381; TIAS 5567; 526 UNTS 89.

Amendment:
December 20, 1968 (19 UST 7844; TIAS 6620; 714 UNTS 266).

YUGOSLAVIA (Cont'd)

Agricultural commodities agreement. Signed at Belgrade April 28, 1964; entered into force April 28, 1964.
15 UST 388; TIAS 5568; 526 UNTS 103.

Amendment:
December 29 and 30, 1965 (16 UST 2064; TIAS 5945; 574 UNTS 266).

Agricultural commodities agreement with exchange of notes. Signed at Belgrade October 28, 1964; entered into force October 28, 1964.
15 UST 2051; TIAS 5684; 533 UNTS 3.

Agricultural commodities agreement with exchange of notes. Signed at Belgrade October 29, 1964; entered into force October 29, 1964.
15 UST 2058; TIAS 5685; 533 UNTS 17.

Amendment:
December 29 and 30, 1965 (16 UST 2064; TIAS 5945; 574 UNTS 266).

Agricultural commodities agreement, with exchange of notes. Signed at Belgrade March 16, 1965; entered into force March 16, 1965.
16 UST 134; TIAS 5772; 542 UNTS 161.

Amendment:
December 20, 1968 (19 UST 7844; TIAS 6620; 714 UNTS 266).

Agricultural commodities agreement, with exchange of notes. Signed at Belgrade July 16, 1965; entered into force July 16, 1965.
16 UST 987; TIAS 5840; 549 UNTS 111.

Amendment:
December 20, 1968 (19 UST 7844; TIAS 6620; 714 UNTS 266).

Agricultural commodities agreement, with exchange of notes. Signed at Belgrade November 22, 1965; entered into force November 22, 1965.
16 UST 1775; TIAS 5910; 574 UNTS 211.

Amendment:
January 21, 1966 (17 UST 1; TIAS 5948; 574 UNTS 224).

Agricultural commodities agreement with exchange of notes. Signed at Belgrade April 11, 1966; entered into force April 11, 1966.
17 UST 771; TIAS 6031; 580 UNTS 239.

ATOMIC ENERGY

Agreement providing for a grant to assist in the acquisition of certain nuclear research and training equipment and materials. Exchange of notes at Belgrade April 19, 1961; entered into force April 19, 1961.
12 UST 398; TIAS 4731; 409 UNTS 163.

Arrangement for the exchange of technical information and cooperation in nuclear safety matters, with addenda. Signed at Belgrade September 19, 1985; entered into force September 19, 1985.
TIAS 12048.

AVIATION

Nonscheduled air service agreement, with annexes, and protocol. Signed at Belgrade September 27, 1973; entered into force provisionally September 27, 1973; definitively April 16, 1974.
25 UST 659; TIAS 7819.

Amendments:
December 15, 1977 (30 UST 4350; TIAS 9460; 1203 UNTS 369).
January 15 and July 6, 1987 (TIAS 11547).

Air transport agreement. Signed at Washington December 15, 1977; entered into force provisionally December 15, 1977; definitively May 15, 1979.
30 UST 2817; TIAS 9364; 1203 UNTS 205.

Amendment:
January 15 and July 6, 1987 (TIAS 11547).

CLAIMS

Agreement relating to the settlement of pecuniary claims against Yugoslavia, and accompanying aide memoire and notes. Signed at Washington July 19, 1948; entered into force July 19, 1948.
62 Stat. 2658; TIAS 1803; 12 Bevans 1277; 89 UNTS 43.

Agreement regarding claims of United States nationals, with exchange of notes and minute of interpretation. Signed at Belgrade November 5, 1964; entered into force January 20, 1965.
16 UST 1; TIAS 5750; 550 UNTS 31.

COMMERCE

Treaty of commerce. Signed at Belgrade October 2/14 1881; entered into force November 15, 1882.
22 Stat. 963; TS 319; 12 Bevans 1227.

CONSULS

Consular convention. Signed at Belgrade October 2 and 14, 1881; entered into force November 15, 1882.
22 Stat. 968; TS 320; 12 Bevans 1233.

Arrangement providing for the taking of testimony by consular officers. Exchange of notes at Belgrade October 17 and 24, 1938; entered into force October 24, 1938.
12 Bevans 1261.

COPYRIGHT (See APPENDIX)

CULTURAL RELATIONS

Memorandum of understanding relating to the establishment, maintenance, and operation of American reading rooms in Yugoslavia. Signed at Belgrade June 14, 1961; entered into force provisionally June 14, 1961; definitively December 28, 1961.
20 UST 2826; TIAS 6753; 723 UNTS 133.

Implementing agreements:
Ljubljana: June 5, 1970 (22 UST 398; TIAS 7073; 791 UNTS 293).
Skopje: April 13, 1972 (24 UST 457; TIAS 7564).
Sarajevo: July 18, 1973 (24 UST 2316; TIAS 7757).
Titograd: June 25, 1979 (31 UST 301; TIAS 9612; 1202 UNTS 173).

CUSTOMS

Agreement relating to reciprocal customs privileges for consular officers. Exchange of notes at Washington May 21, 1956; entered into force July 30, 1956.
7 UST 2234; TIAS 3622; 281 UNTS 93.

Agreement regarding mutual assistance between customs administrations. Signed at Belgrade April 11, 1990; entered into force November 18, 1990.
TIAS 12074.

DEFENSE

Memorandum of understanding relating to offshore procurement with standard contract and related notes. Signed at Belgrade October 18, 1954; entered into force October 18, 1954.
7 UST 849; TIAS 3567; 273 UNTS 163.

Agreement relating to the termination of military assistance furnished on a grant basis by the United States to Yugoslavia and amending the memorandum of October 18, 1954 relating to offshore procurement. Exchange of notes at Belgrade August 25, 1959; entered into force August 25, 1959.
10 UST 1468; TIAS 4300; 357 UNTS 77.

Agreement relating to the purchase by Yugoslavia of military equipment, materials, and services. Exchange of notes at Belgrade August 25, 1959; entered into force August 25, 1959.
10 UST 1474; TIAS 4301; 357 UNTS 87.

ECONOMIC AND TECHNICAL COOPERATION

Agreement relating to publicity for distribution program of emergency food assistance. Ex-

YUGOSLAVIA (Cont'd)

change of notes at Belgrade November 17 and 21, 1950; entered into force November 21, 1950.
1 UST 757; TIAS 2146; 93 UNTS 39.

Agreement governing the furnishing of assistance under the Yugoslav Emergency Relief Assistance Act of 1950. Signed at Belgrade January 6, 1951; entered into force January 6, 1951.
2 UST 13; TIAS 2174; 122 UNTS 137.

Economic cooperation agreement. Signed at Belgrade January 8, 1952; entered into force January 8, 1952.
3 UST 1; TIAS 2384; 152 UNTS 61.

Amendment:
February 25 and March 10, 1953 (4 UST 439; TIAS 2791; 207 UNTS 360).

EDUCATION

Agreement for financing certain educational exchange programs. Signed at Belgrade November 9, 1964; entered into force November 9, 1964.
15 UST 2081; TIAS 5689; 533 UNTS 39.

Amendment:
January 20, 1984 (TIAS 10980).

EXTRADITION

Extradition treaty. Signed at Belgrade October 25, 1901; entered into force June 12, 1902.
32 Stat. 1890; TS 406; 12 Bevans 1238.

FINANCE

Agreement relating to the funding of the indebtedness of Yugoslavia to the United States. Signed at Washington May 3, 1926; operative June 15, 1925.
12 Bevans 1246; Treasury Department print.

Counterpart release agreement, with annex. Signed at Belgrade April 16, 1954; entered into force April 16, 1954.
5 UST 2853; TIAS 3142; 237 UNTS 77.

Agreement relating to the disbursement of dinars made available for the procurement of certain agricultural commodities. Exchange of notes at Belgrade May 12, 1955; entered into force May 12, 1955.
6 UST 1144; TIAS 3254; 251 UNTS 343.

Amendment:
October 17, 1958 (9 UST 1499; TIAS 4150; 338 UNTS 392).

Agreement relating to the use of economic assistance funds for the financing of wheat pur-

chases. Exchange of notes at Belgrade May 12, 1955; entered into force May 12, 1955.
6 UST 1147; TIAS 3255; 251 UNTS 337.

Agreement providing for certain economic assistance on a loan basis pursuant to section 402 of the Mutual Security Act of 1954. Exchange of notes at Belgrade January 19, 1956; entered into force January 19, 1956.
7 UST 149; TIAS 3487; 240 UNTS 121.

Memorandum of agreement regarding the rescheduling of certain payments under agricultural commodities agreements and various AID loans with annexes and exchange of aide memoire. Signed at Belgrade October 15, 1971; entered into force March 30, 1972.
23 UST 222; TIAS 7298.

Agreement relating to investment guaranties, with aide memoire. Exchange of notes at Belgrade January 18, 1973; entered into force May 30, 1973.
24 UST 1091; TIAS 7630.

Swap agreement between the U.S. Treasury and the Central Bank of the Federated Republics of Yugoslavia, with related letter. Signed at Washington and Belgrade June 10, 1988; entered into force June 10, 1988.
TIAS

LEND-LEASE

Preliminary agreement regarding principles applying to mutual aid in the prosecution of the war against aggression. Signed at Washington July 24, 1942; entered into force July 24, 1942.
56 Stat. 1570; EAS 263; 12 Bevans 1263; 34 UNTS 361.

Agreement regarding settlement for lend-lease, military relief, and claims. Signed at Washington July 19, 1948; entered into force July 19, 1948.
62 Stat. 2133; TIAS 1779; 12 Bevans 1273; 34 UNTS 195.

MARITIME MATTERS

Agreement concerning the reciprocal recognition of tonnage certificates. Exchange of notes at Washington June 12 and 16, 1958; entered into force June 16, 1958.
9 UST 709; TIAS 4047; 317 UNTS 31.

NARCOTIC DRUGS

Arrangement for the direct exchange of certain information regarding traffic in narcotic drugs. Exchange of notes at Belgrade February 17, 1928, and May 8, 1930; entered into force May 8, 1930.
12 Bevans 1259.

PACIFIC SETTLEMENT OF DISPUTES

Treaty of arbitration. Signed at Washington January 21, 1929; entered into force June 22, 1929.
46 Stat. 2293; TS 790; 12 Bevans 1253; 93 LNTS 307.

Treaty of conciliation. Signed at Washington January 21, 1929; entered into force June 22, 1929.
46 Stat. 2297; TS 791; 12 Bevans 1256; 93 LNTS 301.

POSTAL MATTERS

Money order convention. Signed at Washington June 16, 1922, and at Belgrade October 29, 1923; operative January 1, 1924.
NP

Agreement concerning the exchange of parcel post and regulations of execution. Signed at Belgrade August 14 and at Washington September 1, 1950; entered into force January 1, 1950.
2 UST 2079; TIAS 2336; 137 UNTS 131.

International express mail agreement, with detailed regulations. Signed at Belgrade and Washington January 22 and March 1, 1990; entered into force March 30, 1990.
TIAS 11713.

PUBLICATIONS

Agreement relating to the exchange of official publications. Exchange of letters at Belgrade June 13 and 23, 1955; entered into force June 23, 1955.
TIAS

RELIEF SUPPLIES AND PACKAGES

Agreement for duty-free entry and defrayment of inland transportation and related costs of relief supplies and packages, and note of December 3, 1952. Signed at Belgrade December 3, 1952; entered into force December 3, 1952.
3 UST 5318; TIAS 2735; 185 UNTS 183.

TAXATION

Agreement relating to relief from taxation of United States Government expenditures in Yugoslavia for facilities, equipment, materials, or services. Exchange of letters at Belgrade July 23, 1953; entered into force July 23, 1953.
4 UST 2208; TIAS 2871; 221 UNTS 365.

YUGOSLAVIA (Cont'd)

TELECOMMUNICATION

Agreement relating to the reciprocal granting of authorization to permit licensed amateur radio operators who are citizens of either country to operate their stations in the other country. Exchange of notes at Belgrade October 31 and November 11, 1980; entered into force November 11, 1980.
32 UST 4173; TIAS 9936; 1267 UNTS 377.

TOURISM

Agreement on cooperation in the field of tourism. Signed at Washington February 2, 1984; entered into force June 18, 1984.
TIAS 10954.

TRADE (See also COMMERCE)

Agreement providing for consultations should exports of cotton, wool, and man-made fiber textiles and apparel products from Yugoslavia cause market disruption in the United States. Exchange of notes at Belgrade January 14, 1976; entered into force January 14, 1976.
27 UST 1622; TIAS 8271.

Agreement relating to trade in certain cotton, wool and man-made fiber textiles and textile products, with annexes. Exchange of notes at Belgrade December 5 and 26, 1986; entered into force December 26, 1986; effective January 1, 1987.[1]
NP

Amendments and extension:
April 15 and December 30, 1988 (NP).
December 19, 1989 and January 3, 1990 (NP).

NOTE:
[1] Although concluded as an extension of the textile agreement of October 26 and 27, 1978 (30 UST 4063; TIAS 9447), this agreement in effect replaces the earlier agreement.

VISAS

Agreement relating to the reduction of passport visa fees for nonimmigrants. Exchange of notes at Belgrade December 24 and 29, 1925; operative February 1, 1926.
12 Bevans 1243.

Understanding relating to entry and exit visas for American citizens visiting Yugoslavia. Exchange of notes at Belgrade March 23 and 25, 1950; entered into force March 25, 1950; operative April 1, 1950.
1 UST 471; TIAS 2087; 98 UNTS 195.

Agreement for the abolition of all nonimmigrant visa fees. Exchange of notes at Bel-grade December 30, 1963, March 27 and April 4, 1964; entered into force April 15, 1964.
15 UST 355; TIAS 5564; 526 UNTS 47.

ZAMBIA

On October 24, 1964, Zambia (former Northern Rhodesia) became an independent state. In a note dated September 1, 1965 to the Secretary General of the United Nations, the Minister of Foreign Affairs of Zambia made a Declaration reading in part as follows:

"I have the honour to inform you that the Government of Zambia, conscious of the desirability of maintaining existing legal relationships, and conscious of its obligations under international law to honour its treaty commitments acknowledges that many treaty rights and obligations of the Government of the United Kingdom in respect of Northern Rhodesia were succeeded to by Zambia upon independence by virtue of customary international law.

"Since, however, it is likely that in virtue of customary international law certain treaties may have lapsed at the date of independence of Zambia, it seems essential that each treaty should be subjected to legal examination. It is proposed after this examination has been completed, to indicate which, if any, of the treaties which may have lapsed by customary international law the Government of Zambia wishes to treat as having lapsed.

"The question of Zambia's succession to treaties is complicated by legal questions arising from the entrustment of external affairs powers to the former Federation of Rhodesia and Nyasaland. Until these questions have been resolved it will remain unclear to what extent Zambia remains affected by the treaties contracted by the former Federation.

"It is desired that it be presumed that each treaty has been legally succeeded to by Zambia and that action be based on this presumption until a decision is reached that it should be regarded as having lapsed. Should the Government of Zambia be of the opinion that it has legally succeeded to a treaty, and wishes to terminate the operation of the treaty, it will in due course give notice of termination in the terms thereof."

AGRICULTURAL COMMODITIES

Agricultural commodities agreement. Signed at Lusaka August 24, 1976; entered into force August 24, 1976.
27 UST 3451; TIAS 8377.

Agricultural commodities agreement, with minutes. Signed at Lusaka December 3, 1976; entered into force December 3, 1976.
28 UST 8768; TIAS 8771; 1095 UNTS 129.

Agricultural commodities agreement. Signed at Lusaka August 4, 1978; entered into force August 4, 1978.
TIAS 10590; 1871 UNTS 23.

Amendment:
September 11 and 12, 1978 (TIAS 10590; 1871 UNTS 23).

Related agreements:
July 19, 1979 (TIAS 10591; 1871 UNTS 25).
December 21, 1979 (TIAS 10592; 1871 UNTS 27).
July 22, 1981 (TIAS 10593; 1871 UNTS 29).
June 20, 1982 (TIAS 10594; 1871 UNTS 31).
July 16, 1982 (TIAS 10594; 1871 UNTS 31).
February 18, 1983 (TIAS 10662).

Agricultural commodities agreement. Signed at Lusaka July 17, 1984; entered into force July 17, 1984.
NP

Agricultural commodities agreement. Signed at Lusaka July 9, 1985; entered into force July 9, 1985.
NP

Related agreements:
May 23, 1986 (NP).
July 27, 1987 (NP).

Agricultural commodities agreement. Signed at Lusaka April 25, 1988; entered into force April 25, 1988.
NP

Related agreement:
March 10, 1989 (NP).

AVIATION

Arrangement between the United States and the United Kingdom relating to pilot licenses to operate civil aircraft. Exchange of notes at Washington March 28 and April 5, 1935; entered into force May 5, 1935.
49 Stat. 3731; EAS 77; 12 Bevans 513; 162 UNTS 59.

Agreement between the United States and the United Kingdom relating to air services. Signed at Bermuda February 11, 1946; entered into force February 11, 1946.
60 Stat. 1499; TIAS 1507; 12 Bevans 726; 3 UNTS 253.

Agreement on civil aviation security. Exchange of notes at Lusaka February 16 and March 28, 1988; entered into force March 28, 1988.
TIAS 11573.

CONSULS

Consular convention between the United States and the United Kingdom. Signed at Washington June 6, 1951; entered into force September 7, 1952.
3 UST 3426; TIAS 2494; 165 UNTS 121.

ZAMBIA (Cont'd)

COPYRIGHT (See APPENDIX)

DEFENSE

Agreement concerning the provision of training related to defense articles under the United States International Military, Education and Training (IMET) Program. Exchange of notes at Lusaka March 9, 1992; entered into force March 9, 1992.
NP

ECONOMIC AND TECHNICAL COOPERATION

Economic cooperation agreement between the United States and the United Kingdom. Signed at London July 6, 1948; applicable to Zambia July 20, 1948.
62 Stat. 2596; TIAS 1795; 12 Bevans 874; 22 UNTS 263.

Amendments:
January 3, 1950 (1 UST 184; TIAS 2036; 86 UNTS 304).
May 25, 1951 (2 UST 1292; TIAS 2277; 99 UNTS 308).
February 25, 1953 (4 UST 1528; TIAS 2815; 172 UNTS 332).

Agreement for technical cooperation in respect of the territories for the international relations of which the Government of the United Kingdom are responsible. Signed at London July 13, 1951; applicable to Federation of Rhodesia and Nyasaland April 8, 1960.
2 UST 1307; TIAS 2281; 105 UNTS 71.

Agency for International Development:
December 3, 1976 (28 UST 8751; TIAS 8770; 1095 UNTS 101).
March 30, 1978 (30 UST 1889; TIAS 9299; 1170 UNTS 65).
September 27, 1985 (NP).

EMPLOYMENT

Agreement relating to the employment of dependents of official government employees. Exchange of notes at Lusaka June 26, 1989 and January 4, 1990; entered into force January 4, 1990.
TIAS

EXTRADITION

Extradition treaty between the United States and the United Kingdom. Signed at London December 22, 1931; entered into force June 24, 1935.
47 Stat. 2122; TS 849; 12 Bevans 482; 163 LNTS 59.

FINANCE

Agreement regarding the consolidation and rescheduling of certain debts owed to, or guaranteed by the United States Government and its agencies, with annexes. Signed at Lusaka December 19, 1983; entered into force February 10, 1984.
TIAS 10941.

Agreement regarding the consolidation and rescheduling of certain debts owed to, guaranteed by or insured by the United States Government and its agencies, with annexes and implementing agreement. Signed at Lusaka December 15, 1984; entered into force January 22, 1985.
TIAS 11002.

Agreement regarding the consolidation and rescheduling of certain debts owed to, guaranteed by or insured by the United States Government and its agencies. Signed at Lusaka July 25, 1986; entered into force August 28, 1986.
NP

Agreement regarding the consolidation and rescheduling of certain debts owed to, guaranteed by or insured by the United States Government and its agencies, with annexes. Signed at Lusaka September 14, 1990; entered into force November 5, 1990.
NP

Agreement regarding the consolidation and rescheduling or refinancing of certain debts owed to, guaranteed by or insured by the U.S. Government and its agencies, with annexes and addendum. Signed at Lusaka March 23, 1993; entered into force August 11, 1993.
NP

Agreement regarding the consolidation, reduction, and rescheduling of certain debts owed to, guaranteed by, or insured by the United States Government and its agency, with annexes. Signed at Lusaka September 26, 1997; entered into force December 3, 1997.
NP

Investment incentive agreement. Signed at Lusaka June 23, 1999; entered into force July 2, 1999.
TIAS

Agreement regarding the reduction, consolidation, and rescheduling of certain debts owed to, guaranteed by, or insured by the United States Government and its Agency, with annexes. Signed at Lusaka November 19, 1999; entered into force February 23, 2000.
NP

MUTUAL SECURITY

Agreement relating to the assurances required under the Mutual Security Act of 1951. Exchange of notes at London January 8, 1952; entered into force January 8, 1952.
3 UST 4665; TIAS 2622; 126 UNTS 307.

POSTAL MATTERS

International express mail agreement, with detailed regulations. Signed at Ndola and Washington April 25 and May 16, 1988; entered into force June 15, 1988.
TIAS 11589.

PROPERTY

Convention between the United States and the United Kingdom relating to tenure and disposition of real and personal property. Signed at Washington March 2, 1899; applicable to Zambia May 29, 1947.
31 Stat. 1939; TS 146; 12 Bevans 246.

Supplementary convention relating to the tenure and disposition of real and personal property of March 2, 1899. Signed at Washington May 27, 1936; entered into force March 10, 1941.
55 Stat. 1101; TS 964; 5 Bevans 140; 203 LNTS 367.

TRADE-MARKS

Declaration by the United States and the United Kingdom affording reciprocal protection to trade-marks. Signed at London October 24, 1877; entered into force October 24, 1877.
20 Stat. 703; TS 138; 12 Bevans 198.

ZIMBABWE

On April 18, 1980, Zimbabwe became an independent state. In a note dated February 24, 1981 to the Secretary General of the United Nations, the Prime Minister made a statement reading in part as follows:

"My Government will continue to apply within its territory, on the basis of the principles of reciprocity and mutual respect for sovereign independence, all bilateral treaties validly concluded or recognised by the United Kingdom Government in respect of Southern Rhodesia for a period of three years from the date of independence, i.e. 18th April, 1980, unless such treaties are terminated or modified earlier by mutual consent. It is the intention of my Government during such period to subject all bilateral treaties to full examination for the purpose of determining whether such treaties require termination, revision or renegotiation in the light of Zimbabwe's sovereign status. It is the earnest hope of my Government that dur-

ZIMBABWE (Cont'd)

ing the aforementioned period the normal processes of diplomatic negotiation will enable it to reach satisfactory accord with the States concerned upon the possibility of the continuance, modification or termination of such treaties.

"At the end of the three year period referred to above my Government will regard such treaties whose continuance or modification have not been agreed as having terminated.

"As regards multilateral treaties validly concluded or recognised by the United Kingdom Government in respect of Southern Rhodesia, my Government proposes to review at least some of those treaties during a period of six years from the date of independence, i.e. 18th April, 1980. It will indicate to the depositaries in each case of review whether the Republic of Zimbabwe will confirm, seek to modify or terminate its obligations under the treaty concerned. During such period of review any party to a multilateral treaty which was validly applied or extended to Southern Rhodesia may, on the basis of reciprocity and respect for national independence, rely on the terms of such treaty until it is modified or terminated. At the expiration of the period of review treaties as modified, or which have not been terminated, shall continue fully in force as if they had been concluded by the Republic of Zimbabwe."

By note of April 14, 1983 to the Secretary-General of the United Nations, the Government of Zimbabwe extended the period of review of bilateral treaties to April 18, 1984. This period of review was further extended by a note dated April 11, 1984 in which the Prime Minister notified the Secretary General that ". . . my Government will continue to apply within its territory all such bilateral treaties until the 18th April 1985, unless terminated earlier or modified by mutual consent. Thereafter my Government will regard those treaties whose continuance or modification has not been agreed upon as having terminated."

In a further letter to the Secretary-General, received February 20, 1985, the Prime Minister stated in part:

"During the past four years my Government has reviewed all such bilateral treaties as were available to it or were brought to its attention and has also concluded a number of bilateral treaties with other governments with the effect that these instruments have superseded some of the earlier ones. It has become evident to my Government that many contracting parties prefer to enter into new arrangements with my Government rather than revive those treaties whose operations might have been suspended or terminated between 1965 and 1979 or which are now considered to be obsolete in the conduct of present-day international relations.

"Whilst it has not been practicable for my Government to re-negotiate and finalise all such agreements on which a willingness to

keep and maintain them in force was mutually indicated by my Government and other contracting parties, my Government has reached the stage at which it considers that legal continuity between itself and Other Contracting States has been achieved with an understanding either to revive, modify, re-negotiate, terminate or adopt such bilateral treaties and, accordingly, my Government now wishes to inform Your Excellency, and through you all Member States of the United Nations Organisation as follows:

"All bilateral treaties that were validly concluded or recognised by the United Kingdom Government in respect of Southern Rhodesia and continued to be applied and respected by my Government pursuant to the declaration aforementioned will now expire on 18 April 1985, UNLESS:

"(i) Either my Government has already communicated to the other contracting party its intention to maintain the continuance in force of the treaty or the process of re-negotiating its terms and provisions has been agreed upon; or

"(ii) The other contracting party notifies my Government before 18 April 1985 through normal diplomatic channels of its intention either to keep and maintain the continuance in force of the treaty concerned or to re-negotiate its terms and provisions, in which case, my Government will consider itself bound by that Treaty."

The United States presented Zimbabwe by diplomatic note of April 17, 1985 a list of international agreements which the Government of the United States intended to maintain in force.

AGRICULTURAL COMMODITIES

Agricultural commodities agreement. Signed at Harare April 1, 1985; entered into force April 1, 1985.
NP

AGRICULTURE

Memorandum of understanding on cooperation in the field of agricultural science and technology. Signed at Salisbury September 25, 1980; entered into force September 25, 1980.
33 UST 600; TIAS 10054; 1267 UNTS 237.

Extension:
October 12 and November 30, 1985.

AVIATION

Agreement between the United States and the United Kingdom concerning air services, with annexes and exchange of letters. Signed at

Bermuda July 23, 1977; entered into force July 23, 1977.
28 UST 5367; TIAS 8641.

Amendments:
April 25, 1978 (29 UST 2680; TIAS 8965).
December 27, 1979 (32 UST 524; TIAS 9722).

CONSULS

Consular convention between the United States and the United Kingdom. Signed at Washington June 6, 1951; entered into force September 7, 1952.
3 UST 3426; TIAS 2494; 165 UNTS 121.

COPYRIGHT (See APPENDIX)

DEFENSE

Agreement concerning the provision of training related to defense articles under the United States International Military Education and Training (IMET) Program. Exchange of notes at Harare September 2 and 17, 1981; entered into force September 17, 1981.
TIAS 10791.

ECONOMIC AND TECHNICAL COOPERATION

General agreement for economic, technical, and related assistance. Exchange of notes at Salisbury February 10 and March 22, 1982; entered into force March 22, 1982.
34 UST 194; TIAS 10348.

Agency for International Development:
April 7, 1982 (33 UST 4312; TIAS 10302).

EMPLOYMENT

Agreement relating to the employment of dependents of official government employees. Exchange of notes at Harare February 7, 1991 and March 7, 1992; entered into force March 7, 1992.
TIAS 11857.

EXTRADITION

Extradition treaty. Signed at Harare July 25, 1997; entered into force April 26, 2000.
TIAS

ZIMBABWE (Cont'd)

FINANCE

Investment incentive agreement. Signed at Harare June 20, 1990; entered into force June 20, 1990.
TIAS 12097.

PEACE CORPS

Agreement relating to the establishment of a Peace Corps in Zimbabwe. Signed at Harare March 18, 1991; entered into force March 18, 1991.
TIAS 12114.

POSTAL MATTERS

International express mail agreement, with detailed regulations. Signed at Harare and Washington February 15 and March 9, 1988; entered into force April 1, 1988.
TIAS 11569.

PROPERTY

Convention relating to tenure and disposition of real and personal property. Signed at Washington March 2, 1899; applicable to Southern Rhodesia July 27, 1901.
31 Stat. 1939; TS 146; 12 Bevans 246.

Supplementary convention relating to the tenure and disposition of real and personal property. Signed at Washington May 27, 1936; entered into force March 10, 1941.
55 Stat. 1101; TS 964; 5 Bevans 140; 203 LNTS 367.

SCIENTIFIC COOPERATION

Agreement for scientific and technical cooperation. Signed at Salisbury September 25, 1980; entered into force September 25, 1980.
32 UST 4543; TIAS 9967; 1267 UNTS 243.

Memorandum of understanding concerning scientific and technical cooperation in the earth sciences, with annexes. Signed at Reston and Harare August 12 and September 28, 1993; entered into force September 28, 1993.
TIAS 12164.

TRADE-MARKS

Declaration by the United States and the United Kingdom affording reciprocal protection to trade-marks. Signed at London October 24, 1877; entered into force October 24, 1877.
20 Stat. 703; TS 138; 12 Bevans 198.

CHINA (TAIWAN)

On January 1, 1979, the United States recognized the Government of the People's Republic of China as the sole legal Government of China. Within this context, the people of the United States maintain cultural, commercial and other unofficial relations with the people on Taiwan. The United States acknowledges the Chinese position that there is but one China and Taiwan is part of China. The United States does not recognize the "Republic of China" as a state or government.

Pursuant to Section 6 of the Taiwan Relations Act, (P.L. 96-8, 93 Stat. 14, 22 U.S.C. 3305) and Executive Order 12143, 44 F.R. 37191, the following agreements concluded with the Taiwan authorities prior to January 1, 1979, and any multilateral treaty or agreement relationship listed in Part II of this volume, are administered on a nongovernmental basis by the American Institute in Taiwan, a nonprofit District of Columbia corporation, and constitute neither recognition of the Taiwan authorities nor the continuation of any official relationship with Taiwan. The following bilateral agreements are on record as of January 1, 2001:

AGRICULTURAL COMMODITIES

Agricultural commodities agreement, with exchange of notes. Signed at Taipei August 31, 1962; entered into force August 31, 1962.
13 UST 1930; TIAS 5151; 460 UNTS 247.

Amendments:
January 15, 1963 (14 UST 131; TIAS 5282; 473 UNTS 380).
June 3, 1964 (15 UST 667; TIAS 5588; 526 UNTS 330).

ATOMIC ENERGY

Agreement for cooperation concerning civil uses of atomic energy. Signed at Washington April 4, 1972; entered into force June 22, 1972.
23 UST 945; TIAS 7364.

Extension and amendment:
March 15, 1974 (25 UST 913; TIAS 7834).

AVIATION

Memorandum of agreement relating to the provision of flight inspection services. Signed at Washington and Taipei August 21 and October 1, 1978; entered into force October 1, 1978.
30 UST 273; TIAS 9197; 1150 UNTS 271.

COMMERCE

Treaty of friendship, commerce, and navigation with accompanying protocol. Signed at Nanking November 4, 1946; entered into force November 30, 1948.
63 Stat. 1299; TIAS 1871; 6 Bevans 761; 25 UNTS 69.

ECONOMIC AND TECHNICAL COOPERATION

Agreement on technological advancement in connection with water resources, land utilization and various fields of irrigated agriculture. Signed at Taipei May 12, 1972; entered into force May 12, 1972.
23 UST 1135; TIAS 7374.

EDUCATION

Agreement for financing certain educational and cultural exchange programs. Signed at Taipei April 23, 1964; entered into force April 23, 1964.
15 UST 408; TIAS 5572; 524 UNTS 141.

FINANCE

Agreement relating to guaranties for projects in Taiwan proposed by nationals of the United States. Exchange of notes at Taipei June 25, 1952; entered into force June 25, 1952.
3 UST 4846; TIAS 2657; 136 UNTS 229.

Amendment:
December 30, 1963 (14 UST 2222; TIAS 5509; 505 UNTS 308).

Agreement regarding the ownership and use of local currency repayments made by China to the Development Loan Fund. Exchange of notes at Taipei December 24, 1958; entered into force December 24, 1958.
10 UST 16; TIAS 4162; 340 UNTS 251.

LEND-LEASE

Preliminary agreement regarding principles applying to mutual aid in the prosecution of the war against aggression. Signed at Washington June 2, 1942; entered into force June 2, 1942.
56 Stat. 1494; EAS 251; 6 Bevans 735; 14 UNTS 343.

Agreement under section 3 (c) of the Lend-Lease Act. Signed at Washington June 28, 1946; entered into force June 28, 1946.
61 Stat. 3895; TIAS 1746; 6 Bevans 758; 34 UNTS 121.

Agreement on the disposition of lend-lease supplies in inventory or procurement in the

CHINA (TAIWAN) (Cont'd)

United States. Signed at Washington June 14, 1946; operative September 2, 1945.
60 Stat. 1760; TIAS 1533; 6 Bevans 753; 4 UNTS 253.

MARITIME MATTERS

Agreement relating to the loan of small naval craft to China. Exchange of notes at Taipei May 14, 1954; entered into force May 14, 1954.
5 UST 892; TIAS 2979; 231 UNTS 165.

Extensions and amendments:
March 22 and 31, 1955 (6 UST 750; TIAS 3215; 251 UNTS 399).
June 18, 1955 (6 UST 2973; TIAS 3346; 265 UNTS 406).
May 16, 1957 (8 UST 787; TIAS 3837; 284 UNTS 380).
October 12, 1960 (11 UST 2233; TIAS 4597; 393 UNTS 320).
August 15, 1962 (13 UST 1924; TIAS 5150; 460 UNTS 237).
February 23, 1965 (16 UST 126; TIAS 5771; 542 UNTS 361).
December 16, 1970 and January 14, 1971 (22 UST 12; TIAS 7037; 776 UNTS 334).

NARCOTIC DRUGS

Arrangement for the direct exchange of certain information regarding the traffic in narcotic drugs. Exchanges of notes at Nanking March 12, June 21, July 28, and August 30, 1947; entered into force August 30, 1947.
6 Bevans 797.

PACIFIC SETTLEMENT OF DISPUTES

Treaty looking to the advancement of the cause of general peace. Signed at Washington September 15, 1914; entered into force October 22, 1915. Exchange of notes signed May 11 and 19, 1916.
39 Stat. 1642; TS 619 and 619-A; 6 Bevans 711.

Treaty of arbitration. Signed at Washington June 27, 1930; entered into force December 15, 1932.
47 Stat. 2213; TS 857; 6 Bevans 724; 140 LNTS 183.

POSTAL MATTERS

Agreement for the exchange of international money orders. Signed at Taipei October 8 and at Washington November 14, 1957; operative October 1, 1957.
9 UST 223; TIAS 3995; 304 UNTS 241.

Parcel post convention. Signed at Peking May 29, 1916, and at Washington July 11, 1916; entered into force August 1, 1916.
39 Stat. 1665; Post Office Department print.

Agreement for exchange of insured parcel post and regulations of execution. Signed at Taipei July 30 and at Washington August 19, 1957; entered into force November 1, 1957.
8 UST 2031; TIAS 3941; 300 UNTS 61.

International express mail agreement, with detailed regulations. Signed at Taipei and Washington September 11 and November 10, 1978; entered into force December 30, 1978; effective December 27, 1978.
30 UST 3277; TIAS 9392; 1179 UNTS 291.

RELIEF SUPPLIES AND PACKAGES

Agreement relating to duty-free entry of relief goods and relief packages and to the defrayment of transportation charges on such shipments. Exchange of notes at Nanking November 5 and 18, 1948; entered into force November 18, 1948.
3 UST 5462; TIAS 2749; 198 UNTS 287.

Amendments:
October 20 and December 12, 1952 (3 UST 5462; TIAS 2749; 198 UNTS 294).
July 12 and October 26, 1954 (5 UST 2930; TIAS 3151; 237 UNTS 337).

TRADE (See also COMMERCE)

Agreement relating to trade in textiles with letter dated April 10, 1974. Exchange of letters at Washington April 11, 1974; entered into force April 11, 1974.[1]
25 UST 720; TIAS 7821.

Agreement on trade matters, with annexes. Exchange of letters at Washington December 29, 1978; entered into force December 29, 1978.
30 UST 6439; TIAS 9561; 1179 UNTS 313.

NOTES:
[1] Exchange of letters dated April 11, 1974 terminated January 1, 1975. Letter dated April 10, 1974 remains in force.

VISAS

Agreement prescribing nonimmigrant visa fees and validity of nonimmigrant visas. Exchange of notes at Taipei December 20, 1955 and February 20, 1956; entered into force February 20, 1956; operative April 1, 1956.
7 UST 585; TIAS 3539; 275 UNTS 73.

Amendments:
July 11, October 17 and December 7, 1956 (18 UST 3167; TIAS 6410; 697 UNTS 256).
May 8, June 9 and 15, 1970 (21 UST 2213; TIAS 6972; 776 UNTS 344).

Pursuant to the Taiwan Relations Act and Executive Order 12143, 44 F.R. 37191, agreements concluded after January 1, 1979 by the American Institute in Taiwan, 1700 North Moore Street, Rosslyn, Virginia 22209, with its nongovernmental Taiwan counterpart, the Taipei Economic and Cultural Representative Office, are reported to the Congress as in effect under the law of the United States. A list of such agreements appears at 65 F.R. 81898.

PART 2: MULTILATERAL TREATIES AND OTHER AGREEMENTS

AFRICA

General Act for the repression of the African slave trade.[1] Signed at Brussels July 2, 1890; entered into force August 31, 1891; for the United States April 2, 1892.
27 Stat. 886; TS 383; 1 Bevans 134.
States which are parties:
Belgium [2]
Denmark
Ethiopia [3]
France [2][4]
Germany [2]
Iran
Italy [2]
Liberia
Netherlands [5]
Norway
Portugal [2]
Spain
Sweden
Tanzania [6]
Turkey [7]
Union of Soviet Socialist Reps. [8]
United Kingdom [2]
United States [2][7]

NOTES:
[1] Replaced, as between contracting parties to the later conventions, by the convention of September 10, 1919 (49 Stat. 3027; TS 877), except for the stipulations contained in article 1 of the 1919 convention, and by the convention of the same date on the subject of the liquor traffic in Africa (46 Stat. 2199; TS 779).
[2] Party to conventions of September 10, 1919.
[3] See note under ETHIOPIA in bilateral section.
[4] With exceptions.
[5] Applicable to Netherlands Antilles and Aruba.
[6] Applicable to Zanzibar. Application to that part of Tanzania which was formerly Tanganyika has apparently not been determined.
[7] With a statement.
[8] See note under UNION OF SOVIET SOCIALIST REPUBLICS in bilateral section.

Revision of the General Act of Berlin of February 26, 1885, and the General Act and Declaration of Brussels of July 2, 1890. Signed at St. Germain-en-Laye September 10, 1919; entered into force July 31, 1920; for the United States October 29, 1934.
49 Stat. 3027; TS 877; 2 Bevans 261; 8 LNTS 27.
States which are parties:
Australia
Belgium
Canada
Ethiopia [1][2]
France
Germany
India
Italy
New Zealand
Portugal
South Africa
United Kingdom
United States [3]

NOTES:
[1] Adhered to obligations formulated in article 11, paragraph 1, of convention.
[2] See note under ETHIOPIA in bilateral section.
[3] With an understanding.

Convention revising the duties imposed by the Brussels convention of June 8, 1899 on spirituous liquors imported into certain regions of Africa.[1] Signed at Brussels November 3, 1906; entered into force December 2, 1907.
35 Stat. 1912; TS 467; 1 Bevans 551.
States which are parties:
Belgium [2]
Denmark
France [2]
Germany [2]
Iran
Italy [2]
Netherlands
Norway
Portugal [2]
Spain
Sweden
Union of Soviet Socialist Reps. [3]
United Kingdom [2]
United States [2]

NOTES:
[1] Replaced by convention of September 10, 1919 (46 Stat. 2199; TS 779), as between contracting parties to the later convention.
[2] Party to convention of September 10, 1919.
[3] See note under UNION OF SOVIET SOCIALIST REPUBLICS in bilateral section.

Convention relating to the liquor traffic in Africa. Signed at St. Germain-en-Laye September 10, 1919; entered into force July 31, 1920; for the United States March 22, 1929.
46 Stat. 2199; TS 779; 2 Bevans 255; 8 LNTS 11.
States which are parties:
Australia
Belgium
Canada
Egypt
France
Germany
India
Italy
New Zealand
Portugal
South Africa
United Kingdom
United States [1]

NOTE:
[1] With reservation.

AFRICAN DEVELOPMENT BANK

(See under FINANCIAL INSTITUTIONS)

AGRICULTURAL DEVELOPMENT FUND

(See under FINANCE)

AGRICULTURE

(See also FOOD AND AGRICULTURE ORGANIZATION; PATENTS)

International agreement for the creation at Paris of an international office for epizootics, with annex. Done at Paris January 25, 1924; entered into force January 17, 1925; for the United States July 29, 1975.
26 UST 1840; TIAS 8141; 57 LNTS 135.
States which are parties:
Afghanistan
Albania *
Algeria
Angola
Argentina
Australia
Austria
Belgium
Benin
Bhutan
Botswana
Brazil
Bulgaria
Burkina Faso
Burma
Cambodia
Cameroon
Canada
Central African Rep.
Chad
Chile
China [1][2]
Colombia
Comoros
Congo *
Congo, Dem. Rep. *
Cote d'Ivoire
Croatia
Cuba
Cyprus
Czechoslovakia [3]
Denmark
Djibouti *
Ecuador
Egypt
Estonia
Ethiopia [4]
Finland
France [5]
Gabon
Georgia
German Dem. Rep. [6]
Germany, Fed. Rep. [6]
Ghana *
Greece
Guatemala
Guinea
Haiti
Hungary
India
Indonesia

AGRICULTURE (Cont'd)

Iran
Iraq
Ireland
Israel *
Italy
Japan
Jordan *
Kenya
Korea, Rep.
Kyrgyz Rep.
Laos
Latvia
Lebanon
Lesotho *
Libya
Lithuania
Luxembourg
Madagascar
Malawi
Malaysia *
Mali
Malta
Mauritania
Mexico
Monaco
Mongolia
Morocco
Mozambique *
Namibia
Netherlands
New Zealand
Niger
Nigeria *
Norway
Oman *
Pakistan
Panama
Paraguay
Peru *
Poland
Portugal
Romania
Saudi Arabia
Senegal
Sierra Leone
Slovak Rep.
Slovenia
Somalia
South Africa
Spain
Sri Lanka *
Sudan
Swaziland *
Sweden
Switzerland
Tajikistan
Tanzania *
Thailand
Togo *
Tunisia
Turkey
Turkmenistan
Uganda
Union of Soviet Socialist Reps. [7]
United Kingdom [8]
United States
Uruguay
Uzbekistan
Vanuatu
Venezuela
Vietnam [9]

Yugoslavia [10]
Zambia
Zimbabwe *

NOTES:
    * Listed as members by the International Office for Epizootics.
    [1] With statement.
    [2] The Taiwan authorities have also adhered to this agreement. See note under CHINA (Taiwan) in bilateral section.
    [3] See note under CZECHOSLOVAKIA in bilateral section.
    [4] See note under ETHIOPIA in bilateral section.
    [5] Extended to New Caledonia.
    [6] See note under GERMANY, FEDERAL REPUBLIC OF in bilateral section.
    [7] See note under UNION OF SOVIET SOCIALIST REPUBLICS in bilateral section.
    [8] Extended to Falkland Is.
    [9] The listing for Viet Nam, the Republic of Viet-Nam (South Viet-Nam), the Democratic Republic of Viet-Nam (North Viet-Nam), the Provisional Revolutionary Government of the Republic of South Viet-Nam, and the Socialist Republic of Vietnam are based on the last notice received by the United States Government from the depositary for the treaty or agreement in question. The United States has been informed by the Socialist Republic of Vietnam that ". . . in principle, the Government of the Socialist Republic of Vietnam is not bound by the treaties, agreements signed by the former Saigon administration. However . . . the Government of the Socialist Republic of Vietnam will consider the agreements, on an individual basis, and will examine adherence to those agreements, treaties which are in the interests of the Vietnamese people . . ."
    [10] See note under YUGOSLAVIA in bilateral section.

Amended constitution of the International Rice Commission. Approved at the 11th Session of the Conference of the Food and Agriculture Organization, Rome, November 23, 1961; entered into force November 23, 1961.
13 UST 2403; TIAS 5204; 418 UNTS 334.
States which are parties:
Australia
Bangladesh
Benin
Brazil
Burkina Faso
Burma
Cambodia
Cameroon
Chad
Colombia
Congo, Dem. Rep.
Cuba
Dominican Rep.
Ecuador
Egypt
France
Gambia, The
Ghana
Greece
Guatemala
Guinea
Guyana
Haiti
Hungary
India

Indonesia
Iran
Italy
Japan
Kenya
Korea
Laos
Liberia
Madagascar
Malaysia
Mali
Mauritania
Mexico
Mozambique
Nepal
Netherlands
Nicaragua
Nigeria
Pakistan
Panama
Paraguay
Peru
Philippines
Portugal
Senegal
Sierra Leone
Sri Lanka
Suriname
Thailand
Turkey
United Kingdom
United States
Uruguay
Venezuela
Vietnam, Socialist Rep.

Revised text of the international plant protection convention. Done at Rome November 28, 1979; entered into force April 4, 1991.
TIAS
States which are parties:
Algeria
Argentina [1]
Australia [2]
Austria
Bahrain
Bangladesh
Barbados
Belgium
Belize
Bhutan
Bolivia
Brazil
Bulgaria
Cambodia
Canada
Cape Verde
Chile
Colombia
Costa Rica
Cuba [1]
Czech Rep.
Denmark
Dominican Rep.
Ecuador
Egypt
El Salvador
Equatorial Guinea
Ethiopia [3]
Finland
France
German Dem. Rep. [4]
Germany, Fed. Rep. [4]
Ghana
Greece

AGRICULTURE (Cont'd)

Grenada
Guatemala
Guinea
Guyana
Haiti
Hungary
India
Indonesia [5]
Iran
Iraq
Ireland
Israel
Italy
Jamaica
Japan
Jordan
Kenya
Korea
Laos
Lebanon
Liberia
Libya
Luxembourg
Malawi
Malaysia
Mali
Malta
Mauritius
Mexico
Morocco
Nauru [6]
Netherlands
New Zealand [7]
Nicaragua
Niger
Nigeria
Norway
Oman
Pakistan
Panama
Papua New Guinea
Paraguay
Peru
Philippines
Portugal
Romania
Russian Fed.
St. Kitts & Nevis
Senegal
Sierra Leone
Slovak Rep.
Solomon Is.
South Africa
Spain
Sri Lanka
Sudan
Suriname
Sweden
Thailand
Togo
Trinidad & Tobago
Tunisia
Turkey
Union of Soviet Socialist Reps. [8]
United Kingdom [9]
United States [10]
Uruguay
Venezuela
Western Samoa [6]
Yemen [11]

Yugoslavia [12]
Zambia

NOTES:
[1] With reservation.
[2] Extended to Norfolk Is.
[3] See note under ETHIOPIA in bilateral section.
[4] See note under GERMANY, FEDERAL REPUBLIC OF in bilateral section.
[5] With declaration.
[6] See under country heading in the bilateral section for information concerning acceptance of treaty obligations.
[7] Extended to Cook Is. including Niue.
[8] See note under UNION OF SOVIET SOCIALIST REPUBLICS in bilateral section.
[9] Extended to Bailiwick of Guernsey, Isle of Man, and Jersey.
[10] Extended to all territories for the international relations of which the United States is responsible.
[11] See note under YEMEN in bilateral section.
[12] See note under YUGOSLAVIA in bilateral section.

North American plant protection agreement. Signed at Yosemite October 13, 1976; entered into force October 13, 1976.
28 UST 6223; TIAS 8680.

Cooperative agreement supplementary to the North American plant protection agreement of October 13, 1976. Signed at Alexandria October 20, 1991; entered into force October 20, 1991.
TIAS
States which are parties:
Canada
Mexico
United States

Convention on the Inter-American Institute for Cooperation on Agriculture.[1] Done at Washington March 6, 1979; entered into force December 8, 1980.
32 UST 3779; TIAS 9919.
States which are parties:
Antigua & Barbuda
Argentina
Bahamas
Barbados
Belize
Bolivia
Brazil
Canada
Chile
Colombia
Costa Rica
Dominica
Dominican Rep.
Ecuador
El Salvador
Grenada
Guatemala
Guyana
Haiti
Honduras
Jamaica
Mexico
Nicaragua
Panama
Paraguay
Peru

St. Kitts & Nevis
St. Lucia
Suriname
Trinidad & Tobago
United States
Uruguay
Venezuela

NOTE:
[1] Replaces as between contracting parties the convention on the Inter-American Institute of Agricultural Sciences of January 15, 1944 (58 Stat. 1169; TS 987; 3 Bevans 881; 161 UNTS 281). Cuba is a party to the 1944 convention only.

AIRCRAFT

(See AVIATION; TRADE AND COMMERCE)

ALIENS

Convention between the American Republics regarding the status of aliens in their respective territories. Signed at Habana February 20, 1928; entered into force August 29, 1929; for the United States May 21, 1930.
46 Stat. 2753; TS 815; 2 Bevans 710; 132 LNTS 301.
States which are parties:
Argentina
Brazil
Chile
Colombia
Costa Rica
Dominican Rep.
Ecuador
Guatemala
Haiti
Mexico [1]
Nicaragua
Panama
Peru
United States [2]
Uruguay

NOTES:
[1] With reservations. The United States does not accept the reservations made by Mexico and does not consider the convention to be in force between the United States and Mexico.
[2] With the exception of articles 3 and 4.

ANTARCTICA

(See also CONSERVATION)

Antarctic treaty. Signed at Washington December 1, 1959; entered into force June 23, 1961.
12 UST 794; TIAS 4780; 402 UNTS 71.
States which are parties:
Argentina [1]
Australia [1]
Austria
Belgium [1]
Brazil [1]
Bulgaria

ANTARCTICA (Cont'd)

Canada
Chile [1]
China [1][2]
Colombia
Cuba
Czech Rep.
Denmark
Ecuador [1]
Finland [1]
France [1]
German Dem. Rep. [1][3][4]
Germany, Fed. Rep. [1][4]
Greece
Guatemala
Hungary
India [1]
Italy [1]
Japan [1]
Korea, Dem. People's Rep.
Korea, Rep. of [1]
Netherlands [1][5]
New Zealand [1]
Norway [1]
Papua New Guinea
Peru [1]
Poland [1]
Romania [3]
Russian Fed.
Slovak Rep.
South Africa [1]
Spain [1]
Sweden [1]
Switzerland
Turkey
Ukraine
Union of Soviet Socialist Reps. [1][6]
United Kingdom [1]
United States [1]
Uruguay [1][3]
Venezuela

Measures approved under article IX:
Canberra July 24, 1961 (13 UST 1349; TIAS 5094).
Buenos Aires July 28, 1962 (14 UST 99; TIAS 5274).
Brussels June 2-13, 1964 (17 UST 991; TIAS 6058 and 10485).
Santiago November 18, 1966 (20 UST 614; TIAS 6668).
Paris November 29, 1968 (24 UST 1793; TIAS 7692).
Tokyo October 30, 1970 (25 UST 266; TIAS 7796).
Wellington November 10, 1972, except for Recommendation VII-5 (28 UST 1138; TIAS 8500).
Oslo June 20, 1975 (TIAS 10486).
London October 7, 1977 (TIAS 10735).
Washington October 5, 1979.
Buenos Aires July 7, 1981.

NOTES:
[1] Consultative members under article IX of the Treaty.
[2] Applicable to Hong Kong and Macao. See note under CHINA in bilateral section.
[3] With statement.
[4] See note under GERMANY, FEDERAL REPUBLIC OF in bilateral section.

[5] Applicable to Netherlands Antilles and Aruba.
[6] See note under UNION OF SOVIET SOCIALIST REPUBLICS in bilateral section.

Protocol on environmental protection to the Antarctic treaty, with schedule and annexes. [1] Signed at Madrid October 4, 1991; entered into force January 14, 1998.
TIAS
Parties:
Argentina [2]
Australia [3]
Belgium [3]
Brazil [3]
Bulgaria [3]
Chile [3]
China [3]
Ecuador
Finland [3]
France [3]
Germany [3]
Greece
India
Italy [3]
Japan [3]
Korea [3]
Netherlands
New Zealand [3]
Norway [3]
Peru [3]
Poland
Russian Fed.
South Africa [3]
Spain [3]
Sweden [3]
United Kingdom [3]
United States [3]
Uruguay [3]

NOTES:
[1] Annex V adopted October 17, 1991.
[2] With declaration(s).
[3] Accepts Annex V.

ANZUS PACT

(See Security Treaty under DEFENSE)

ARBITRATION

(See also CLAIMS; INVESTMENT DISPUTES; PACIFIC SETTLEMENT OF DISPUTES)

Convention on the recognition and enforcement of foreign arbitral awards. Done at New York June 10, 1958; entered into force June 7, 1959; for the United States December 29, 1970.
21 UST 2517; TIAS 6997; 330 UNTS 3.
States which are parties:
Algeria [1][2]
Antigua & Barbuda [1][2]
Argentina [1][2]
Armenia [1][2]
Australia [3]
Austria

Azerbaijan
Bahrain [1][2]
Bangladesh
Barbados [1][2]
Belarus [1][4]
Belgium [1]
Benin
Bolivia
Bosnia-Herzegovina [1][2][4]
Botswana [1][2]
Brunei
Bulgaria [1][4]
Burkina Faso
Cambodia
Cameroon
Canada [2]
Central African Rep. [1][2]
Chile
China [1][2][5]
Colombia
Costa Rica
Cote d'Ivoire
Croatia
Cuba [1][2][4]
Cyprus [1][2]
Czech Rep.
Denmark [1][2][6]
Djibouti
Dominica
Ecuador [1][2]
Egypt
El Salvador
Estonia
Finland
Former Yugoslav Republic of Macedonia
France [1][7]
Georgia
German Dem. Rep. [2][4][8]
Germany, Fed. Rep. [8]
Ghana
Greece [1][2]
Guatemala [1][2]
Guinea
Haiti
Holy See [1][2]
Honduras
Hungary [1][2]
India [1][2]
Indonesia [1][2]
Ireland [1]
Israel
Italy
Japan [1]
Jordan [9]
Kazakhstan
Kenya [1]
Korea [1][2]
Kuwait [1][9]
Kyrgyz Rep.
Laos
Latvia
Lebanon [1]
Lesotho
Lithuania
Luxembourg [1]
Madagascar [1][2]
Malaysia [1][2]
Mali
Malta
Mauritania
Mauritius
Mexico
Moldova
Monaco [1][2]
Mongolia [1][2]

ARBITRATION (Cont'd)

Morocco [1]
Mozambique [4]
Nepal [1 2]
Netherlands [1 10]
New Zealand [1 11]
Niger
Nigeria [1 2]
Norway [1 9]
Oman
Panama
Paraguay
Peru
Philippines [1 2]
Poland [1 2]
Portugal [4]
Romania [1 2 4]
Russian Fed.
St. Vincent & the Grenadines
San Marino
Saudi Arabia
Senegal
Singapore [1]
Slovak Rep.
Slovenia
South Africa
Spain
Sri Lanka
Sweden
Switzerland [1]
Syrian Arab Rep.
Tanzania [1]
Thailand
Trinidad & Tobago [1 2]
Tunisia [1 2]
Turkey [1 2]
Uganda [1]
Ukraine [1 4]
Union of Soviet Socialist Reps. [4 12]
United Kingdom [1 13]
United States [1 2 14]
Uruguay
Uzbekistan
Venezuela
Vietnam [1 2 4]
Yugoslavia [1 2 4 15]
Zimbabwe

NOTES:
[1] With declaration that it will apply the convention to the recognition and enforcement of awards made only in the territory of another contracting state.
[2] With declaration that it will apply the convention only to differences arising out of legal relationships, whether contractual or not, which are considered as commercial under its national law.
[3] Extended to all the external territories for the international relations of which Australia is responsible.
[4] With declaration.
[5] Applicable to Hong Kong. See note under CHINA in bilateral section.
[6] Extended to Faroe Is. and Greenland.
[7] Extended to all French territories.
[8] See note under GERMANY, FEDERAL REPUBLIC OF in bilateral section.
[9] With reservation.
[10] Applicable to Netherlands Antilles and Aruba.
[11] Not extended to Cook Is. and Niue.

[12] See note under UNION OF SOVIET SOCIALIST REPUBLICS in bilateral section.
[13] Extended to Anguilla, Bermuda, Cayman Is., Gibraltar, Guernsey, and Isle of Man.
[14] Extended to all territories for the international relations of which the United States is responsible.
[15] See note under YUGOSLAVIA in bilateral section.

Inter-American convention on international commercial arbitration. Done at Panama January 30, 1975; entered into force June 16, 1976; for the United States October 27, 1990.
TIAS
Parties:
Argentina
Bolivia
Brazil
Chile
Colombia
Costa Rica
Ecuador
El Salvador
Guatemala
Honduras
Mexico
Panama
Paraguay
Peru
United States [1]
Uruguay
Venezuela

NOTE:
[1] With reservation(s).

ARMISTICE AGREEMENTS

(See also KOREA)

Agreement concerning an armistice with Romania, with annex and protocol. Signed at Moscow September 12, 1944; entered into force September 12, 1944.
59 Stat. 1712; EAS 490; 3 Bevans 901.
States which are parties:
Romania
Union of Soviet Socialist Reps. [1]
United Kingdom
United States

NOTE:
[1] See note under UNION OF SOVIET SOCIALIST REPUBLICS in bilateral section.

Armistice agreement with Bulgaria, with protocol. Signed at Moscow October 28, 1944; entered into force October 28, 1944.
58 Stat. 1498; EAS 437; 3 Bevans 909; 123 UNTS 223.
States which are parties:
Bulgaria
Union of Soviet Socialist Reps. [1]
United Kingdom
United States

NOTE:
[1] See note under UNION OF SOVIET SOCIALIST REPUBLICS in bilateral section.

Armistice agreement with Hungary, with annex and protocol. Signed at Moscow January 20, 1945; entered into force January 20, 1945.
59 Stat. 1321; EAS 456; 3 Bevans 995; 140 UNTS 397.
States which are parties:
Hungary
Union of Soviet Socialist Reps. [1]
United Kingdom
United States

NOTE:
[1] See note under UNION OF SOVIET SOCIALIST REPUBLICS in bilateral section.

ARMS CONTROL

(See BIOLOGICAL WEAPONS; ENVIRONMENTAL MODIFICATION; GAS WARFARE; NUCLEAR FREE ZONE, TEST BAN, WEAPONS. See under SEABEDS; SPACE)

ARMS LIMITATION

Agreement regarding inspections relating to the treaty of December 8, 1987 between the United States and the Union of Soviet Socialist Republics on the elimination of their intermediate-range and shorter-range missiles, with annex. Signed at Brussels December 11, 1987; entered into force June 1, 1988.
TIAS   ; 1658 UNTS 363.
Parties:
Belgium [1]
Germany, Fed. Rep. [2]
Italy
Netherlands
United Kingdom
United States

NOTES:
[1] Provisional application.
[2] See note under GERMANY, FEDERAL REPUBLIC OF in bilateral section.

Protocol to the treaty of July 31, 1991, on the reduction and limitation of strategic offensive arms, with related letters. [1] Done at Lisbon May 23, 1992; entered into force December 5, 1994.
TIAS

NOTE:
[1] For Treaty, see ARMS LIMITATION under UNION OF SOVIET SOCIALIST REPUBLICS in bilateral section.

ARTISTIC EXHIBITIONS

(See CULTURAL RELATIONS)

ASIAN DEVELOPMENT BANK

(See under FINANCIAL INSTITUTIONS)

ASTRONAUTS

Agreement on the rescue of astronauts, the return of astronauts, and the return of objects launched into outer space. Done at Washington, London, and Moscow April 22, 1968; entered into force December 3, 1968.
19 UST 7570; TIAS 6599; 672 UNTS 119.
Parties:
Antigua & Barbuda
Argentina
Australia
Austria
Bahamas, The
Barbados
Belarus
Belgium
Bosnia-Herzegovina
Botswana
Brazil
Brunei [1]
Bulgaria
Cameroon
Canada
Chile
China [2][3]
Cuba
Cyprus
Czech Rep.
Denmark
Dominica [1]
Ecuador
Egypt
El Salvador
European Space Agency [4]
Fiji
Finland
France
Gabon
Gambia, The
German Dem. Rep. [5]
Germany, Fed. Rep. [5]
Greece
Grenada [1]
Guinea-Bissau
Guyana
Hungary
Iceland
India
Indonesia
Iran
Iraq
Ireland
Israel
Italy
Japan
Korea
Kuwait
Laos
Lebanon
Madagascar
Maldives
Mauritius
Mexico
Mongolia
Morocco
Nepal
Netherlands [6]
New Zealand
Niger
Nigeria
Norway
Pakistan
Papua New Guinea
Peru
Poland
Portugal
Romania
Russian Fed.
St. Kitts & Nevis [1]
St. Lucia [1]
San Marino
Seychelles
Singapore
Slovak Rep.
Slovenia
Solomon Is. [1]
South Africa
Swaziland
Sweden
Switzerland
Syrian Arab Rep.
Thailand
Tonga
Tunisia
Ukraine
Union of Soviet Socialist Reps. [7]
United Kingdom [8]
United States
Uruguay
Yugoslavia [9]
Zambia

NOTES:
[1] See under country heading in the bilateral section for information concerning acceptance of treaty obligations.
[2] The Taiwan authorities have also adhered to this agreement. See note under CHINA (Taiwan) in bilateral section.
[3] Applicable to Hong Kong and Macao. See note under CHINA in bilateral section.
[4] Declaration of acceptance.
[5] See note under GERMANY, FEDERAL REPUBLIC OF in bilateral section.
[6] Applicable to Netherlands Antilles and Aruba.
[7] See note under UNION OF SOVIET SOCIALIST REPUBLICS in bilateral section.
[8] Extended to Anguilla and territories under the territorial sovereignty of the United Kingdom.
[9] See note under YUGOSLAVIA in bilateral section.

ATLANTIC CHARTER

Joint Declaration, known as the Atlantic Charter, by the President of the United States and the Prime Minister of the United Kingdom, made on August 14, 1941.
55 Stat. 1600; EAS 236; 3 Bevans 686.
States which have signified their acceptance of the purposes and principles embodied in the Charter:
Australia
Belgium
Bolivia
Brazil
Canada
Chile
China [1]
Colombia
Costa Rica
Cuba
Czechoslovakia [2]
Dominican Rep.
Ecuador
Egypt
El Salvador
Ethiopia [3]
France
Greece
Guatemala
Haiti
Honduras
India
Iran
Iraq
Lebanon
Liberia
Luxembourg
Mexico
Netherlands
New Zealand
Nicaragua
Norway
Panama
Paraguay
Peru
Philippines
Poland
Saudi Arabia
Slovak Rep.
South Africa
Syrian Arab Rep.
Turkey
Union of Soviet Socialist Reps. [4]
United Kingdom
United States
Uruguay
Venezuela
Yugoslavia [5]

NOTES:
[1] Pre 1949 agreement, applicable only to Taiwan.
[2] See note under CZECHOSLOVAKIA in bilateral section.
[3] See note under ETHIOPIA in bilateral section.
[4] See note under UNION OF SOVIET SOCIALIST REPUBLICS in bilateral section.
[5] See note under YUGOSLAVIA in bilateral section.

ATOMIC ENERGY

(See also NORTH ATLANTIC TREATY ORGANIZATION; NUCLEAR MATERIALS; NUCLEAR TEST BAN; NUCLEAR WEAPONS—NONPROLIFERATION)

Agreed declaration on atomic energy by the President of the United States, the Prime Minister of the United Kingdom, and the Prime Minister of Canada. Signed at Washington November 15, 1945; entered into force November 15, 1945.
60 Stat. 1479; TIAS 1504; 3 Bevans 1304; 3 UNTS 123.

Agreement as to disposition of rights in atomic energy inventions. Signed at Washington September 24, 1956; entered into force September 24, 1956.
7 UST 2526; TIAS 3644; 253 UNTS 171.
States which are parties:
Canada
United Kingdom
United States

Statute of the International Atomic Energy Agency. Done at New York October 26, 1956; entered into force July 29, 1957.
8 UST 1093; TIAS 3873; 276 UNTS 3.
States which are parties:
Afghanistan
Albania
Algeria
Angola
Argentina [1]
Armenia
Australia
Austria
Bangladesh
Belarus
Belgium
Benin
Bolivia
Bosnia-Herzegovina
Brazil
Bulgaria
Burkina Faso
Burma
Cambodia
Cameroon
Canada
Chile
China [2]
Colombia
Congo, Dem. Rep.
Costa Rica
Cote d'Ivoire
Croatia
Cuba
Cyprus
Czech Rep.
Denmark
Dominican Rep.
Ecuador
Egypt
El Salvador
Estonia

Ethiopia [3]
Finland
Former Yugoslav Republic of Macedonia
France
Gabon
Georgia
German Dem. Rep.[4]
Germany, Fed. Rep.[4]
Ghana
Greece
Guatemala
Haiti
Hungary
Iceland
India
Indonesia
Iran
Iraq
Ireland
Israel
Italy
Jamaica
Japan
Jordan
Kazakhstan
Kenya
Korea, Rep.
Kuwait
Latvia
Lebanon
Liberia
Libya
Liechtenstein
Lithuania
Luxembourg
Madagascar
Malaysia
Mali
Malta
Marshall Is.
Mauritius
Mexico
Moldova
Monaco
Mongolia
Morocco
Namibia
Netherlands [5]
New Zealand
Nicaragua
Niger
Nigeria
Norway
Pakistan
Panama
Paraguay
Peru
Philippines
Poland
Portugal
Qatar
Romania
Saudi Arabia
Senegal
Sierra Leone
Singapore
Slovak Rep.
Slovenia
South Africa
Spain
Sri Lanka
Sudan
Sweden
Switzerland [1]
Syrian Arab Rep.

Tanzania
Thailand
Tunisia
Turkey
Uganda
Ukraine
Union of Soviet Socialist Reps. [6]
United Arab Emirates
United Kingdom
United States [7]
Uruguay
Uzbekistan
Vatican City
Venezuela
Vietnam, Socialist Rep.
Yemen [8]
Yugoslavia [9]
Zambia
Zimbabwe

Amendments:
October 4, 1961 (14 UST 135; TIAS 5284; 471 UNTS 334).
September 28, 1970 (24 UST 1637; TIAS 7668).
September 27, 1984.

NOTES:
[1] With reservation.
[2] Applicable to Hong Kong. See note under CHINA in bilateral section.
[3] See note under ETHIOPIA in bilateral section.
[4] See note under GERMANY, FEDERAL REPUBLIC OF in bilateral section.
[5] Applicable to Aruba and Netherlands Antilles.
[6] See note under UNION OF SOVIET SOCIALIST REPUBLICS in bilateral section.
[7] With an interpretation and understanding.
[8] See note under YEMEN in bilateral section.
[9] See note under YUGOSLAVIA in bilateral section.

Trilateral agreements signed at Vienna between the International Atomic Energy Agency, the United States, and other countries for the application of safeguards by the International Atomic Energy Agency to equipment, devices and materials supplied under the bilateral agreements for cooperation concerning civil uses of atomic energy between the United States and the following countries:
Argentina
    June 13, 1969; entered into force July 25, 1969.
    20 UST 2629; TIAS 6722; 694 UNTS 233.
Austria
    August 20, 1969; entered into force January 24, 1970.[1]
    21 UST 56; TIAS 6816; 798 UNTS 77.
Brazil
    March 10, 1967; entered into force October 31, 1968.
    19 UST 6322; TIAS 6583; 670 UNTS 109.
    Amendment:
    July 27, 1972 (23 UST 2526; TIAS 7440).
China (Taiwan)
    December 6, 1971; entered into force December 6, 1971.[2]
    22 UST 1837; TIAS 7228.
Colombia
    December 9, 1970; entered into force December 9, 1970.

ATOMIC ENERGY (Cont'd)

21 UST 2677; TIAS 7010; 795 UNTS 93.

Extension:
March 28, 1977 (28 UST 2404; TIAS 8556).
India
January 27, 1971; entered into force January 27, 1971.
22 UST 200; TIAS 7049; 798 UNTS 115.
Iran
March 4, 1969; entered into force August 20, 1969.[3]
20 UST 2748; TIAS 6741; 694 UNTS 163.
Israel
April 4, 1975; entered into force April 4, 1975.
26 UST 483; TIAS 8051.
Extension:
April 7, 1977 (28 UST 2397; TIAS 8554).
Korea
January 5, 1968; entered into force January 5, 1968.
19 UST 4404; TIAS 6435; 637 UNTS 123.
Amendment:
November 30, 1972 (24 UST 829; TIAS 7584).
Philippines
July 15, 1968; entered into force July 19, 1968.[4]
19 UST 5426; TIAS 6524; 650 UNTS 287.
Portugal
July 11, 1969; entered into force July 19, 1969.[5]
20 UST 2564; TIAS 6718; 694 UNTS 315.
South Africa
July 26, 1967; entered into force July 26, 1967.
18 UST 1643; TIAS 6306.
Amendment:
June 20, 1974 (25 UST 1175; TIAS 7848).
Spain
December 9, 1966; entered into force December 9, 1966.
17 UST 2351; TIAS 6182; 589 UNTS 55.
Amendment:
June 28, 1974 (25 UST 1261; TIAS 7856).
Sweden
March 1, 1972; entered into force March 1, 1972.
23 UST 195; TIAS 7295.[6]
Switzerland
February 28, 1972; entered into force February 28, 1972.[5]
23 UST 184; TIAS 7294.
Turkey
September 30, 1968; entered into force June 5, 1969.[7]
20 UST 780; TIAS 6692; 694 UNTS 139.
Extension:
June 30, 1981 (33 UST 2782; TIAS 10201; 1271 UNTS 360).
Venezuela
March 27, 1968; entered into force March 27, 1968.
19 UST 4385; TIAS 6433; 650 UNTS 195.[8]
Extension:
February 18, 1981 (33 UST 1106; TIAS 10096).

NOTES:
[1] Suspended by agreement signed September 21, 1971.
[2] See note under CHINA (Taiwan) in bilateral section.
[3] Suspended by agreement signed June 19, 1973.
[4] Suspended by agreement signed February 21, 1973.
[5] Suspended by agreement signed September 23, 1980.
[6] Suspended by agreement signed April 14, 1975.
[7] Suspended by agreement signed January 15, 1985.
[8] Suspended by agreement signed September 27, 1983.

Trilateral agreements signed at Vienna between the International Atomic Energy Agency, the United States, and other countries for the application of safeguards pursuant to the nonproliferation treaty of July 1, 1968 (21 UST 483; TIAS 6839; 729 UNTS 161) have been concluded with the following countries:
Australia
July 10, 1974; entered into force July 10, 1974.
25 UST 1325; TIAS 7865.
Austria *
September 21, 1971; entered into force July 23, 1972.
23 UST 1308; TIAS 7409.
Denmark
March 1, 1972; entered into force March 1, 1972.
23 UST 167; TIAS 7289; 873 UNTS 155.
Greece
March 1, 1972; entered into force March 1, 1972.
23 UST 169; TIAS 7290.
Iran *
June 19, 1973; entered into force May 15, 1974.
25 UST 853; TIAS 7829.
Norway
September 25, 1973; entered into force September 25, 1973.
24 UST 2046; TIAS 7721.
Philippines *
February 21, 1973; entered into force October 16, 1974.
25 UST 2967; TIAS 7957.
Portugal *
September 23, 1980; entered into force September 23, 1980.[1]
32 UST 3311; TIAS 9899; 1266 UNTS 382.
Sweden *
April 14, 1975; entered into force May 6, 1975.
26 UST 478; TIAS 8049.
Switzerland *
September 23, 1980; entered into force September 23, 1980.[1]
32 UST 3317; TIAS 9900.
Thailand
June 27, 1974; entered into force June 27, 1974.
25 UST 1178; TIAS 7849.
Turkey *
January 15, 1985; entered into force January 15, 1985.[1]
TIAS 11932.

Venezuela *
September 27, 1983; entered into force September 27, 1983.[1][2]
TIAS 10793.

NOTES:
* For suspension of previous agreements on safeguards, see entry above.
[1] Also pursuant to the United States–IAEA agreement of November 18, 1977 for the application of safeguards in the United States (32 UST 3059; TIAS 9889).
[2] Also pursuant to the treaty for the prohibition of nuclear weapons in Latin America (22 UST 762; TIAS 7137).

Agreements between the International Atomic Energy Agency, the United States, and other countries for the supply of nuclear material or equipment have been concluded with the following countries:[1]
Argentina–Peru
Vienna, May 9, 1978; entered into force May 9, 1978, with an exchange of notes signed at Buenos Aires and Washington March 31, April 7, May 10 and 22, 1978.
30 UST 1539; TIAS 9263; 1161 UNTS 305.
Canada–Jamaica
Vienna, January 25, 1984; entered into force January 25, 1984.
TIAS 10933.
Colombia
Vienna and Bogota, May 30, June 7 and 17, 1994; entered into force June 17, 1994.
TIAS
Indonesia
New Delhi, December 7, 1979; entered into force December 7, 1979.
32 UST 361; TIAS 9705.
Malaysia
Vienna, September 22, 1980; entered into force September 22, 1980.
32 UST 2610; TIAS 9863.
Amendment:
June 12 and July 22, 1981 (33 UST 2785; TIAS 10202).
Mexico
Vienna, December 18, 1963; entered into force December 18, 1963.
32 UST 3607; TIAS 9906; 490 UNTS 383.
Mexico City, October 4, 1972; entered into force October 4, 1972.
32 UST 3618; TIAS 9906; 874 UNTS 135.
Vienna, February 12, 1974; entered into force February 12, 1974.
TIAS 10705.
Vienna, June 14, 1974; entered into force June 14, 1974.
TIAS 10705.
Vienna, March 6, 1980; entered into force March 6, 1980.
32 UST 3628; TIAS 9906; 1267 UNTS 51.
Morocco
Vienna, December 2, 1983; entered into force December 2, 1983.
TIAS 10866.
Thailand
Vienna, September 30, 1986; entered into force September 30, 1986.
TIAS
Yugoslavia[2]
Vienna, June 14, 1974; entered into force June 14, 1974.
32 UST 773; TIAS 9728.

ATOMIC ENERGY (Cont'd)

Vienna, January 16, 1980; entered into force July 14, 1980.
32 UST 1228; TIAS 9767; 1266 UNTS 364.
Belgrade and Vienna, February 26, 1980; entered into force February 26, 1980.
32 UST 773; TIAS 9728.
Vienna, December 14, 15 and 20, 1982; entered into force December 20, 1982.
TIAS 10621.
Vienna, February 23, 1983; entered into force February 23, 1983.
TIAS 10664.

NOTES:
[1] Similar supply agreements, which have not been printed in the United States treaty series but are on file in the Office of Treaty Affairs, were concluded during the 1960's and early 1970's with the following countries: Argentina, Chile, Finland, Greece, India, Iran, Iraq, Norway, Pakistan, Philippines, Romania, Spain, Turkey, Venezuela, Yugoslavia, and Zaire.
[2] See note under YUGOSLAVIA in bilateral section.

Agreement concerning a joint project for planning, design, experiment preparation, performance and reporting of reactor safety experiments concerning containment response, with appendices. Dated January 24, 1975; entered into force for the United States February 20, 1975.
28 UST 629; TIAS 8479.
Parties:
Denmark
Finland
France
Germany, Fed. Rep.[1]
Japan [2]
Norway
Sweden
United States

NOTES:
[1] See note under GERMANY, FEDERAL REPUBLIC OF in bilateral section.
[2] Subject to approval of funds.

Agreement concerning a joint project for planning, design, experiment preparation, performance and reporting of reactor safety experiments concerning critical flow, with appendices. Dated April 14, 1977; entered into force June 17, 1977.
30 UST 129; TIAS 9184.
Parties:
Denmark
Finland
France
Netherlands
Norway
Sweden
United States

Agreement amending the agreement of February 11, 1977, between the United States and the Federal Republic of Germany in the field of gas-cooled reactor concepts and technology.[1] Done at Bonn September 30, 1977; entered into force September 30, 1977.
29 UST 4039; TIAS 9047; 1178 UNTS 198.

Parties:
France
Germany, Fed. Rep.[2]
Switzerland
United States

Extension:
January 20 and April 7, 1987.

NOTES:
[1] For the original bilateral agreement, see 29 UST 3983; TIAS 9046.
[2] See note under GERMANY, FEDERAL REPUBLIC OF in bilateral section.

Agreement on research participation and technical exchange in the in-pile CABRI and Annular Core Pulsed Reactor (ACPR) research programs related to fast reactor safety, with memorandum of understanding and appendices. Signed May 2, June 7 and 22, 1978; entered into force June 22, 1978.
30 UST 7545; TIAS 9603.
Parties:
France
Germany, Fed. Rep.[1]
United States

NOTE:
[1] See note under GERMANY, FEDERAL REPUBLIC OF in bilateral section.

Arrangement on research participation and technical exchange in a coordinated analytical and experimental study of the thermohydraulic behavior of emergency core coolant during the refill and reflood phase of a loss-of-coolant accident in the pressurized water reactor. Signed at Washington, Bonn and Tokyo January 25, March 20 and April 18, 1980; entered into force April 18, 1980.
32 UST 2275; TIAS 9835.
States which are parties:
Germany, Fed. Rep.[1]
Japan
United States

Amendment and extensions:
March 13, April 4 and 15, 1985 (TIAS 11120).
June 16, July 19 and August 14, 1989.

NOTE:
[1] See note under GERMANY, FEDERAL REPUBLIC OF in bilateral section.

Agreement regarding protection of information transferred into the United States in connection with the initial phase of a project for the establishment of a uranium enrichment installation in the United States based upon the gas centrifuge process developed within the three European countries. Signed at Washington April 11, 1990; entered into force April 11, 1990.
TIAS   ; 1640 UNTS 369.
Parties:
Germany, Fed. Rep.[1]
Netherlands
United Kingdom
United States

NOTE:
[1] See note under GERMANY, FEDERAL REPUBLIC OF in bilateral section.

Agreement on cooperation in the engineering design activities for the International Thermonuclear Experimental Reactor. Signed at Washington July 21, 1992; entered into force July 21, 1992.
TIAS
Parties:
European Atomic Energy Community
Japan
Russian Fed.
United States

Agreement regarding the establishment, construction and operation of a uranium enrichment installation in the United States, with annex and agreed minute. Signed at Washington July 24, 1992; entered into force February 1, 1995.
TIAS
Parties:
Germany
Netherlands
United Kingdom
United States

Agreement on the establishment of the Korean Peninsula Energy Development Organization. Done at New York March 9, 1995; entered into force March 9, 1995.
TIAS
Parties:
European Atomic Energy Community
Japan
Korea
United States

Amendment:
September 19, 1997.

Agreement on cooperation among the original members of the Korean Peninsula Energy Development Organization. Signed at Washington September 19, 1997; entered into force September 19, 1997.
TIAS
Parties:
Japan
Korea
United States

AUSTRIA

State treaty for the reestablishment of an independent and democratic Austria. Signed at Vienna May 15, 1955; entered into force July 27, 1955.
6 UST 2369; TIAS 3298; 217 UNTS 223.
States which are parties:
Australia
Austria
Brazil
Czechoslovakia [1]
France
Mexico
New Zealand
Poland
Union of Soviet Socialist Reps.[2]
United Kingdom
United States
Yugoslavia [3]

AUSTRIA (Cont'd)

NOTES:
[1] See note under CZECHOSLOVAKIA in bilateral section.
[2] See note under UNION OF SOVIET SOCIALIST REPUBLICS in bilateral section.
[3] See note under YUGOSLAVIA in bilateral section.

Memorandum concerning understandings supplementing the protection afforded by the provisions of the Austrian State Treaty with respect to United States and British owned property in Austria. Done at Vienna May 10, 1955; entered into force May 10, 1955.
7 UST 803; TIAS 3560; 273 UNTS 121.
States which are parties:
Austria
United Kingdom
United States

AUTOMOTIVE TRAFFIC

Convention on the regulation of inter-American automotive traffic, with annex.[1] Open for signature at the Pan American Union, Washington, December 15, 1943; entered into force July 25, 1944; for the United States October 29, 1946.
61 Stat. 1129; TIAS 1567; 3 Bevans 865.
States which are parties:
Argentina [2]
Brazil
Chile [2 3]
Colombia
Costa Rica
Dominican Rep.[2 3]
Ecuador [2]
El Salvador
Guatemala [2]
Haiti [2]
Honduras
Mexico [3]
Nicaragua
Panama
Paraguay [2]
Peru [2]
United States [2 4]
Uruguay
Venezuela [2 3]

NOTES:
[1] Replaced by convention of September 19, 1949 on road traffic (3 UST 3008; TIAS 2487), as between contracting parties to the later convention.
[2] Party to convention of September 19, 1949.
[3] With reservation.
[4] With an understanding and reservation.

Convention on road traffic, with annexes and protocol. Done at Geneva September 19, 1949; entered into force March 26, 1952.
3 UST 3008; TIAS 2487; 125 UNTS 22.
States which are parties:
Albania [1]
Algeria
Argentina

Australia [2]
Austria [3]
Bahamas, The [2 4]
Bangladesh
Barbados [1 2 5]
Belgium
Belize [1 2 4 5]
Benin
Botswana [2]
Bulgaria [1]
Cambodia
Canada
Central African Rep.
Chile [3]
China (Taiwan) [6]
Congo
Congo, Dem. Rep.
Cote d'Ivoire
Cuba
Cyprus [1 2 5]
Czech Rep.
Denmark [3]
Dominican Rep.[1 2]
Ecuador
Egypt
Fiji [1 2 5]
Finland [3 5]
France [5 7]
Georgia
Ghana [1 2]
Greece
Grenada [1 4]
Guatemala [1 3 5]
Guyana [1 2 4]
Haiti
Hong Kong [8]
Hungary
Iceland [3]
India [2]
Ireland [2 5]
Israel [3]
Italy
Jamaica [1 2 5]
Japan [3]
Jordan
Korea
Kyrgyz Rep.
Laos
Lebanon
Lesotho
Luxembourg
Macao [8]
Madagascar
Malawi [2]
Malaysia [2]
Mali
Malta [3]
Monaco [5]
Morocco
Namibia
Netherlands [7 9]
New Zealand [2]
Niger
Norway [3]
Papua New Guinea [1 2 5]
Paraguay
Peru
Philippines [3]
Poland
Portugal [5 10]
Romania [1]
Russian Fed.
Rwanda
St. Lucia [1 2 4 5]
St. Vincent & the Grenadines [1 2 4 5]

San Marino [3]
Senegal [3]
Seychelles [1 2 4 5]
Sierra Leone [1 2 5]
Singapore
Slovak Rep.
South Africa [2 11]
Spain [12]
Sri Lanka
Suriname [4 13]
Sweden [3]
Syrian Arab Rep.
Tanzania [4]
Thailand
Togo [5]
Trinidad & Tobago [2]
Tunisia
Turkey
Uganda
Union of Soviet Socialist Reps. [1 14]
United Kingdom [1 2 5 15]
United States [16]
Vatican City
Venezuela [1]
Vietnam, Rep. [17]
Western Samoa [2 4]
Yugoslavia [18]
Zimbabwe [2]

NOTES:
[1] With reservation(s).
[2] Excluding annexes 1 and 2.
[3] Excluding annex 1.
[4] See under country heading in the bilateral section for information concerning acceptance of treaty obligations.
[5] With a statement.
[6] See note under CHINA (Taiwan) in bilateral section.
[7] Applicable to all overseas territories and the Principality of Andorra.
[8] CHINA is not a party to this treaty but has made it applicable to Hong Kong and Macao.
[9] Applicable to Netherlands Antilles and Aruba.
[10] Applicable to all territories.
[11] Applicable to Namibia.
[12] Applicable to African localities and provinces.
[13] Excluding annex 2.
[14] See note under UNION OF SOVIET SOCIALIST REPUBLICS in bilateral section
[15] Applicable to Cayman Is., Gibraltar, Bailiwick of Guernsey, Isle of Man, States of Jersey.
[16] Applicable to all territories for the international relations of which the U.S. is responsible.
[17] According to *Multilateral Treaties Deposited with the Secretary-General: Status as at 31 December 1985:* "The Democratic Republic of Viet-Nam and the Republic of South Viet-Nam (the latter of which replaced the Republic of Viet-Nam) united on 2 July 1976 to constitute a new State, the Socialist Republic of Viet Nam (Viet Nam). . .

"At the time of preparing this publication no indication had been received from the Government of the Socialist Republic of Viet Nam regarding its position with respect to a possible succession." U.N. Doc. ST/LEG/SER.E/4.
[18] See note under YUGOSLAVIA in bilateral section.

AUTOMOTIVE TRAFFIC (Cont'd)

Convention concerning customs facilities for touring. Done at New York June 4, 1954; entered into force September 11, 1957.
8 UST 1293; TIAS 3879; 276 UNTS 230.
States which are parties:
Algeria [1]
Antigua & Barbuda [2]
Argentina
Australia
Austria
Barbados
Belgium
Belize [2]
Bosnia-Herzegovina
Brunei [2]
Bulgaria
Cambodia
Canada
Central African Rep.
Chile
Costa Rica
Croatia
Cuba [1]
Cyprus
Denmark [1]
Dominica [2]
Ecuador
Egypt [1]
El Salvador
Fiji
Finland [1]
France
Gambia, The [2]
Germany, Fed. Rep. [3]
Ghana [1]
Greece
Grenada [2]
Guyana [2]
Haiti [1]
Hong Kong [4]
Hungary [1]
India
Iran
Ireland
Israel
Italy
Jamaica
Japan
Jordan
Lebanon
Luxembourg
Macao [4]
Malaysia
Mali
Malta
Mauritius
Mexico
Morocco
Nepal
Netherlands [5]
New Zealand [6]
Nigeria
Norway
Peru
Philippines
Poland [1]
Portugal [7]
Romania [1]
Russian Fed.

Rwanda
St. Kitts & Nevis [2]
St. Vincent & the Grenadines [2]
Senegal [1]
Seychelles [2]
Sierra Leone
Slovenia
Solomon Is.
Spain
Sri Lanka
Suriname [2]
Sweden [1]
Switzerland [8]
Syrian Arab Rep. [1]
Tanzania [1]
Tonga
Trinidad & Tobago
Tunisia [1]
Turkey
Uganda [1]
Union of Soviet Socialist Reps. [1] [9]
United Kingdom [10]
United States [11]
Uruguay
Viet-Nam, Rep. [12]
Yugoslavia [13]

Amendment:
June 6, 1967 (19 UST 4684; TIAS 6461; 596 UNTS 542).

NOTES:
[1] With reservation.
[2] See under country heading in the bilateral section for information concerning acceptance of treaty obligations.
[3] See note under GERMANY, FEDERAL REPUBLIC OF in bilateral section.
[4] CHINA is not a party to this treaty but has made it applicable to Hong Kong and Macao.
[5] Applicable to Netherlands Antilles and Aruba.
[6] Extended to Cook Is., including Niue.
[7] Extended to overseas provinces.
[8] Applicable to Liechtenstein.
[9] See note under UNION OF SOVIET SOCIALIST REPUBLICS in bilateral section.
[10] Extended to Anguilla, Bermuda, British Virgin Is., Gibraltar, Montserrat, and St. Helena.
[11] Extended to Puerto Rico and the Virgin Is.
[12] See Vietnam footnote under AUTOMOTIVE TRAFFIC: convention of September 19, 1949 (3 UST 3008; TIAS 2487; 125 UNTS 22).
[13] See note under YUGOSLAVIA in bilateral section.

Customs convention on the temporary importation of private road vehicles. Done at New York June 4, 1954; entered into force December 15, 1957.
8 UST 2097; TIAS 3943; 282 UNTS 249.
States which are parties:
Algeria [1]
Antigua & Barbuda [2]
Australia
Austria
Barbados
Belgium
Belize [2]
Bosnia-Herzegovina
Brunei [2]
Bulgaria

Canada
Central African Rep.
Chile
Costa Rica
Croatia
Cuba [1]
Cyprus
Denmark
Dominica [2]
Ecuador
Egypt
El Salvador [1]
European Community
Fiji
Finland
Former Yugoslav Republic of Macedonia
France
Gambia, The [2]
Germany, Fed. Rep. [3]
Ghana
Grenada [2]
Guyana [2]
Haiti
Hong Kong [4]
Hungary [1]
India [1]
Iran
Ireland
Israel [1]
Italy
Jamaica
Japan
Jordan
Luxembourg
Malaysia
Mali
Malta
Mauritius
Mexico [1]
Morocco
Nepal
Netherlands [5]
New Zealand [6]
Nigeria
Norway
Peru
Philippines
Poland [1]
Portugal [7]
Romania [1]
Russian Fed.
Rwanda
St. Kitts & Nevis [2]
St. Vincent & the Grenadines [2]
Senegal [1]
Seychelles [2]
Sierra Leone
Singapore
Slovenia
Solomon Is.
Spain
Sri Lanka [1]
Suriname [2]
Sweden
Switzerland [8]
Syrian Arab Rep.
Tanzania
Tonga
Trinidad & Tobago
Tunisia [1]
Turkey
Uganda
Union of Soviet Socialist Reps. [1] [9]
United Kingdom [10]
United States [11]

AUTOMOTIVE TRAFFIC (Cont'd)

Viet-Nam, Rep. [12]
Yugoslavia [13]

Amendment:
July 2, 1984 (TIAS 11936).

NOTES:
[1] With reservation.
[2] See under country heading in the bilateral section for information concerning acceptance of treaty obligations.
[3] See note under GERMANY, FEDERAL REPUBLIC OF in bilateral section.
[4] CHINA is not a party to this treaty but has made it applicable to Hong Kong.
[5] Applicable to Netherlands Antilles and Aruba.
[6] Extended to Cook Is., including Niue.
[7] Applicable to all Portuguese territories.
[8] Applicable to Liechtenstein.
[9] See note under UNION OF SOVIET SOCIALIST REPUBLICS in bilateral section.
[10] Extended to Anguilla, British Virgin Is., Gibraltar, Montserrat, and St. Helena.
[11] Extended to Puerto Rico and the Virgin Is.
[12] See Vietnam footnote under AUTOMOTIVE TRAFFIC: convention of September 19, 1949 (3 UST 3008; TIAS 2487; 125 UNTS 22).
[13] See note under YUGOSLAVIA in bilateral section.

AVIATION

(See also INTERNATIONAL CIVIL AVIATION ORGANIZATION)

Convention for the unification of certain rules relating to international transportation by air, with additional protocol. Concluded at Warsaw October 12, 1929; entered into force February 13, 1933; for the United States October 29, 1934.
49 Stat. 3000; TS 876; 2 Bevans 983; 137 LNTS 11.
States which are parties: [1]
Afghanistan
Algeria
Angola
Armenia
Argentina
Australia [2]
Austria
Azerbaijan
Bahamas, The
Bahrain
Bangladesh
Barbados
Belarus
Belgium
Benin
Bolivia
Bosnia-Herzegovina
Botswana

Brazil
Brunei
Bulgaria
Burkina Faso
Burma
Cambodia
Cameroon
Canada [3]
Chile [3]
China [4]
Colombia
Comoros
Congo [3]
Congo, Dem. Rep.
Costa Rica
Cote d'Ivoire
Croatia
Cuba [3]
Cyprus
Czech Rep.
Denmark, not including Greenland
Dominican Rep.
Ecuador
Egypt
Equatorial Guinea
Estonia
Ethiopia [3][5]
Fiji
Federal Republic of Yugoslavia
Finland
Former Yugoslav Republic of Macedonia
France, including French colonies
Gabon
German Dem. Rep. [6]
Germany, Fed. Rep. [6]
Ghana
Greece
Guinea
Honduras
Hungary
Iceland
India
Indonesia
Iran
Iraq
Ireland
Israel
Italy
Japan
Jordan
Kenya
Korea, Dem. People's Rep.
Kuwait
Kyrgyzstan
Laos
Latvia
Lebanon
Lesotho
Liberia
Libya
Liechtenstein
Luxembourg
Madagascar
Malawi
Maldives
Malaysia
Mali
Malta
Mauritania
Mauritius
Mexico
Moldova
Mongolia
Morocco
Nauru

Nepal
Netherlands [7]
New Zealand
Niger
Nigeria
Norway
Oman
Pakistan [3]
Panama
Papua New Guinea
Paraguay
Peru
Philippines [3]
Poland
Portugal
Qatar
Romania
Rwanda
Saudi Arabia
Senegal
Seychelles
Sierra Leone
Slovak Rep.
Slovenia
Solomon Is.
South Africa [8]
Spain
Sri Lanka
Sudan
Sweden
Switzerland
Syrian Arab Rep.
Tanzania
Togo
Tonga
Trinidad & Tobago
Tunisia
Turkey
Turkmenistan
Uganda
Ukraine
Union of Soviet Socialist Reps. [9]
United Arab Emirates
United Kingdom [10]
United States [3]
Uruguay
Uzbekistan
Vanuatu
Venezuela
Vietnam, Socialist Rep.
Western Samoa
Yemen (Sanaa) [11]
Zambia
Zimbabwe

NOTES:
[1] The following states are parties to the convention, as amended, by reason of their adherence to the protocol done at The Hague on September 28, 1955 amending the convention (478 UNTS 371): El Salvador, Grenada, Korea (Rep.), Lithuania, Monaco and Swaziland. The United States is not a party to the 1955 protocol.
[2] Extended to Norfolk Is.
[3] With reservation.
[4] Applicable to Hong Kong and Macao. See note under CHINA in bilateral section.
[5] See note under ETHIOPIA in bilateral section.
[6] See note under GERMANY, FEDERAL REPUBLIC OF in bilateral section.
[7] Applicable to Aruba and Netherlands Antilles.
[8] Extended to Namibia.

AVIATION (Cont'd)

[9] See note under UNION OF SOVIET SOCIALIST REPUBLICS in bilateral section.

[10] Extended to Ascension Is., Bermuda, British Virgin Is., Cayman Is., Channel Is., Falkland Is. and dependencies, Gibraltar, Isle of Man, Montserrat, St. Helena, and Turks and Caicos Is.

[11] See note under YEMEN in bilateral section.

Montreal Protocol No. 4 to amend the Convention for the unification of certain rules relating to international carriage by air, signed at Warsaw on October 12, 1929, as amended by the Protocol, done at The Hague on September 28, 1955. Done at Montreal September 25, 1975; entered into force June 14, 1998; for the United States March 4, 1999.
TIAS
States which are parties:
Argentina [1]
Australia
Azerbaijan
Bahrain
Bosnia-Herzegovina
Brazil
Canada [5]
Colombia
Croatia
Cyprus
Denmark
Ecuador
Egypt
Estonia
Ethiopia
Federal Republic of Yugoslavia
Finland
Former Yugoslav Republic of Macedonia
Ghana
Greece
Guatemala
Guinea
Honduras
Hungary
Ireland
Israel
Italy
Japan
Jordan
Kenya
Kuwait
Lebanon
Mauritius
Nauru
Netherlands [2]
New Zealand [4]
Niger
Norway
Oman
Portugal
Singapore
Slovenia
Spain
Sweden
Switzerland [6]
Togo
Turkey
United Arab Emirates
United Kingdom [1] [3]
United States
Uzbekistan

NOTES:
[1] With declaration.
[2] Applicable to the Kingdom in Europe and the Netherlands Antilles.
[3] Extended to the Bailiwick of Jersey, the Bailiwick of Guernsey, the Isle of Man, Anguilla, Bermuda, British Antarctic Territory, British Indian Ocean Territory, British Virgin Is., Cayman Is., Falkland Is. and dependencies, Gibraltar, Hong Kong, Montserrat, Pitcairn, Henderson, Ducie and Oeno Is., Saint Helena and dependencies, Turks and Caicos Is., United Kingdom Sovereign Base Areas of Akrotiri and Dhekelia in the Island of Cyprus.
[4] Extended to Tokelau.
[5] With reservation in respect of Art. XXI, paragraph 1(a).
[6] With reservation in respect of Art. XXI, paragraph 1(b).

International air services transit agreement.[1] Signed at Chicago, December 7, 1944;[2] entered into force January 30, 1945; for the United States February 8, 1945.
59 Stat. 1693; EAS 487; 3 Bevans 916; 84 UNTS 389.
States which are parties:
Afghanistan
Albania
Algeria
Antigua & Barbuda
Argentina
Armenia
Australia
Austria
Azerbaijan
Bahamas, The
Bahrain
Bangladesh
Barbados
Belgium
Benin
Bolivia
Bosnia-Herzegovina
Brunei
Bulgaria
Burkina Faso
Burundi
Cameroon
Chile
Costa Rica
Cote d'Ivoire
Croatia
Cuba
Cyprus
Czech Rep.
Denmark
Ecuador
Egypt
El Salvador
Estonia
Ethiopia [3]
Fiji
Finland
Former Yugoslav Republic of Macedonia
France
Gabon
German Dem. Rep. [4]
Germany, Fed. Rep. [4]
Greece
Guatemala
Guinea
Guyana
Honduras
Hong Kong [5]

Hungary
Iceland
India
Iran
Iraq
Ireland
Israel
Italy
Jamaica
Japan
Jordan
Korea, Dem. People's Rep.
Korea, Rep.
Kuwait
Latvia
Lebanon
Lesotho
Liberia
Luxembourg
Macao [5]
Madagascar
Malawi
Malaysia
Mali
Malta
Mauritania
Mauritius
Mexico
Moldova
Monaco
Morocco
Nauru
Nepal
Netherlands
New Zealand
Nicaragua
Niger
Nigeria
Norway
Oman
Pakistan
Palau
Panama
Paraguay
Philippines [6]
Poland
Portugal
Rwanda
Senegal
Seychelles
Singapore
Slovak Rep.
Slovenia
Somalia
South Africa
Spain
Sri Lanka
Swaziland
Sweden
Switzerland
Thailand
Togo
Trinidad & Tobago
Tunisia
Turkey
United Arab Emirates
United Kingdom
United States [6]
Vanuatu
Venezuela
Yugoslavia [7]
Zambia

NOTES:
[1] Applicable to all territories.

AVIATION (Cont'd)

[2] For the convention on international civil aviation of the same date, see INTERNATIONAL CIVIL AVIATION ORGANIZATION (TIAS 1591).

[3] See note under ETHIOPIA in bilateral section.

[4] See note under GERMANY, FEDERAL REPUBLIC OF in bilateral section.

[5] CHINA is not a party to this treaty but has made it applicable to Hong Kong and Macao.

[6] With reservation.

[7] See note under YUGOSLAVIA in bilateral section.

Convention on the international recognition of rights in aircraft. Done at Geneva June 19, 1948; entered into force September 17, 1953.
4 UST 1830; TIAS 2847; 310 UNTS 151.
States which are parties: [1]
Algeria
Angola
Argentina
Azerbaijan
Bahrain
Bangladesh
Belgium
Bolivia
Bosnia-Herzegovina
Brazil
Cameroon
Central African Rep.
Chad
Chile
China [1]
Congo
Cote d'Ivoire
Croatia
Cuba
Czech Rep.
Denmark
Ecuador
Egypt
El Salvador
Estonia
Ethiopia [2]
Former Yugoslav Republic of Macedonia
France
Gabon
Gambia
Germany, Fed. Rep. [3]
Ghana
Greece
Grenada
Guatemala
Guinea
Haiti
Hungary
Iceland
Iraq
Italy
Kenya
Kuwait
Kyrgyz Rep.
Laos
Lebanon
Libya
Luxembourg
Madagascar
Maldives
Mali
Mauritania
Mauritius
Mexico [4]
Monaco
Morocco
Netherlands [4] [5]
Niger
Norway
Oman
Pakistan
Panama
Paraguay
Philippines
Portugal
Romania
Rwanda
Senegal
Seychelles
Slovenia
South Africa
Sri Lanka
Sweden
Switzerland
Tajikistan
Thailand
Togo
Tunisia
Turkmenistan
United States [4]
Uruguay
Uzbekistan
Vietnam
Yugoslavia [6]
Zimbabwe

NOTES:
[1] Applicable to Macao. See note under CHINA in bilateral section.

[2] See note under ETHIOPIA in bilateral section.

[3] See note under GERMANY, FEDERAL REPUBLIC OF in bilateral section.

[4] With reservation. The United States and The Netherlands are unable to accept the reservation made by Mexico and do not regard the convention as in force between Mexico and their governments.

[5] Only for the Kingdom in Europe.

[6] See note under YUGOSLAVIA in bilateral section.

Agreement on the joint financing of certain air navigation services in Iceland. Done at Geneva September 25, 1956; entered into force June 6, 1958.
9 UST 711; TIAS 4048; 334 UNTS 13.

Amendments:
March 27, 1975 (26 UST 1630; TIAS 8122).
September 27, 1979 (31 UST 5570; TIAS 9673).
November 3, 1982 (TIAS 11534).

Agreement on the joint financing of certain air navigation services in Greenland and the Faroe Islands. Done at Geneva September 25, 1956; entered into force June 6, 1958.
9 UST 795; TIAS 4049; 334 UNTS 89.
States which are parties:
Belgium
Canada
Cuba
Czechoslovakia [1]
Denmark
Finland
France
Germany, Fed. Rep. [2]
Greece
Iceland
Ireland
Italy
Japan [3]
Lebanon
Netherlands
Norway
Sweden
Switzerland
United Kingdom
United States [4]

Amendments:
June 4, 1963 (14 UST 874; TIAS 5369).
June 14, 1976 (27 UST 4013; TIAS 8421).
September 27, 1979 (31 UST 5570; TIAS 9673).
November 3, 1982. (TIAS 11533).

NOTES:
[1] See note under CZECHOSLOVAKIA in bilateral section.

[2] See note under GERMANY, FEDERAL REPUBLIC OF in bilateral section.

[3] With reservation(s)

[4] Subject to the availability of funds.

Convention on offenses and certain other acts committed on board aircraft. Done at Tokyo September 14, 1963; entered into force December 4, 1969.
20 UST 2941; TIAS 6768; 704 UNTS 219.
States which are parties:
Afghanistan
Albania
Algeria
Angola
Antigua & Barbuda
Argentina
Australia
Austria
Bahamas, The
Bahrain [1]
Bangladesh
Barbados
Belarus [1] [2]
Belgium
Belize
Bhutan
Bolivia
Bosnia-Herzegovina
Botswana
Brazil
Brunei
Bulgaria [3]
Burkina Faso
Burma
Burundi
Cambodia
Cameroon
Canada
Cape Verde
Central African Rep.
Chad
Chile
China [1] [2] [4] [5]
Colombia
Comoros
Congo
Congo, Dem. Rep.
Costa Rica
Cote d'Ivoire
Croatia

AVIATION (Cont'd)

Cyprus
Czech Rep.
Denmark
Djibouti
Dominican Rep.
Ecuador
Egypt [1]
El Salvador
Equatorial Guinea
Estonia
Ethiopia [1][6]
Fiji
Finland
Former Yugoslav Republic of Macedonia
France
Gabon
Gambia, The
Georgia
German Dem. Rep. [1][7]
Germany, Fed. Rep. [7]
Ghana
Greece
Grenada
Guatemala [1]
Guinea
Guyana
Haiti
Honduras
Hungary
Iceland
India [1]
Indonesia [1]
Iran
Iraq
Ireland
Israel
Italy
Jamaica
Japan
Jordan
Kazakhstan
Kenya
Korea, Dem. People's Rep. [1]
Korea, Rep.
Kuwait
Kyrgyz Rep.
Laos
Latvia
Lebanon
Lesotho
Libya
Lithuania
Luxembourg
Madagascar
Malawi
Malaysia
Maldives
Mali
Malta
Marshall Is. [8]
Mauritania
Mauritius
Mexico
Moldova
Monaco
Mongolia
Morocco [2]
Nauru
Nepal
Netherlands [9]
New Zealand

Nicaragua
Niger
Nigeria
Norway
Oman
Pakistan
Palau
Panama
Papua New Guinea [1]
Paraguay
Peru [1]
Philippines
Poland [1]
Portugal
Qatar
Romania [1]
Russian Fed.
Rwanda
St. Lucia
St. Vincent & the Grenadines
Saudi Arabia
Senegal
Seychelles
Sierra Leone
Singapore
Slovak Rep.
Slovenia
Solomon Is.
South Africa [1]
Spain
Sri Lanka
Sudan
Suriname
Swaziland
Sweden
Switzerland
Syrian Arab Rep. [1]
Tajikistan
Tanzania
Thailand
Togo
Trinidad & Tobago
Tunisia [1]
Turkey
Turkmenistan
Uganda
Ukraine [1][2]
Union of Soviet Socialist Reps. [1][2][10]
United Arab Emirates
United Kingdom [11]
United States
Uruguay [1]
Uzbekistan
Vanuatu
Venezuela [1]
Vietnam, Socialist Rep. [1]
Western Samoa
Yemen (Sanaa) [12]
Yugoslavia [13]
Zambia
Zimbabwe

NOTES:
[1] With reservation.
[2] With statement(s).
[3] With declaration.
[4] The Taiwan authorities have also adhered to this convention. See note under CHINA (Taiwan) in the bilateral section.
[5] Applicable to Hong Kong and Macao. See note under CHINA in bilateral section.
[6] See note under ETHIOPIA in bilateral section.
[7] See note under GERMANY, FEDERAL REPUBLIC OF in bilateral section.

[8] On October 15, 1986 the Compact of Free Association entered into force between the Government of the United States and the Government of the Republic of the Marshall Islands, effective October 21, 1986.
[9] Applicable to the Netherlands Antilles and Aruba.
[10] See note under UNION OF SOVIET SOCIALIST REPUBLICS in bilateral section.
[11] Extended to Anguilla.
[12] See note under YEMEN in bilateral section.
[13] See note under YUGOSLAVIA in bilateral section.

Convention for the suppression of unlawful seizure of aircraft. (Hijacking) Done at The Hague December 16, 1970; entered into force October 14, 1971.
22 UST 1641; TIAS 7192.
States which are parties:
Afghanistan
Albania
Algeria
Angola
Antigua & Barbuda
Argentina [1]
Australia
Austria
Azerbaijan
Bahamas, The
Bahrain [2]
Bangladesh
Barbados
Belarus [2]
Belgium
Belize
Benin
Bhutan
Bolivia
Bosnia-Herzegovina
Botswana
Brazil [2]
Brunei
Bulgaria [2]
Burkina Faso
Burma
Burundi
Cambodia
Cameroon
Canada
Cape Verde
Central African Rep.
Chad
Chile
China [1][2][3][4]
Colombia
Comoros
Congo
Congo, Dem. Rep.
Costa Rica
Cote d'Ivoire
Croatia
Cyprus
Czech Rep.
Denmark [5][6]
Djibouti
Dominican Rep.
Ecuador
Egypt [2]
El Salvador
Equatorial Guinea
Estonia
Ethiopia [2][7]
Fiji

AVIATION (Cont'd)

Finland
Former Yugoslav Republic of Macedonia
France
Gabon
Gambia, The
Georgia
German Dem. Rep. [8]
Germany, Fed. Rep. [8]
Ghana
Greece
Grenada
Guatemala
Guinea
Guinea-Bissau
Guyana
Haiti
Honduras [2]
Hungary
Iceland
India [2]
Indonesia [2]
Iran
Iraq
Ireland
Israel
Italy
Jamaica
Japan
Jordan
Kazakhstan
Kenya
Korea, Dem. People's Rep. [2]
Korea, Rep.
Kuwait
Kyrgyz Rep.
Laos
Latvia
Lebanon
Lesotho
Liberia
Libya
Lithuania
Luxembourg
Madagascar
Malawi [2]
Malaysia
Maldives
Mali
Malta
Marshall Is. [9]
Mauritania
Mauritius
Mexico
Moldova
Monaco
Mongolia [2]
Morocco [2]
Nauru
Nepal
Netherlands [10]
New Zealand
Nicaragua
Niger
Nigeria
Norway
Oman
Pakistan
Palau
Panama
Papua New Guinea [2]
Paraguay

Peru [2]
Philippines
Poland [2]
Portugal
Qatar [2]
Romania [2]
Rwanda
St. Lucia
Samoa
Saudi Arabia [2]
Senegal
Seychelles
Sierra Leone
Singapore
Slovak Rep.
Slovenia
South Africa [2]
Spain
Sri Lanka
Sudan
Suriname
Swaziland
Sweden
Switzerland
Syrian Arab Rep. [2]
Tajikistan
Tanzania
Thailand
Togo
Tonga
Trinidad & Tobago
Tunisia [2]
Turkey
Turkmenistan
Uganda
Ukraine [2]
Union of Soviet Socialist Reps. [2][11]
United Arab Emirates
United Kingdom [12]
United States
Uruguay
Uzbekistan
Vanuatu
Venezuela
Vietnam, Socialist Rep. [2]
Yemen (Aden) [13]
Yemen (Sanaa) [13]
Yugoslavia [14]
Zambia
Zimbabwe

NOTES:
[1] With statement.
[2] With reservation.
[3] The Taiwan authorities have also adhered to this convention. See note under CHINA (Taiwan) in the bilateral section.
[4] Applicable to Hong Kong and Macao. With declaration. See note under CHINA in bilateral section.
[5] Not extended to Faroe Is.
[6] Applicable to Greenland.
[7] See note under ETHIOPIA in bilateral section.
[8] See note under GERMANY, FEDERAL REPUBLIC OF in bilateral section.
[9] On October 15, 1986 the Compact of Free Association entered into force between the Government of the United States and the Government of the Republic of the Marshall Islands, effective October 21, 1986.
[10] Applicable to the Netherlands Antilles and Aruba.
[11] See note under UNION OF SOVIET SOCIALIST REPUBLICS in bilateral section.

[12] Extended to all territories under the territorial sovereignty of the United Kingdom.
[13] See note under YEMEN in bilateral section.
[14] See note under YUGOSLAVIA in bilateral section.

Convention for the suppression of unlawful acts against the safety of civil aviation. (Sabotage) Done at Montreal September 23, 1971; entered into force January 26, 1973.
24 UST 564; TIAS 7570.
States which are parties:
Afghanistan [1]
Albania
Algeria
Angola
Antigua & Barbuda
Argentina
Australia
Austria
Azerbaijan
Bahamas, The
Bahrain [1]
Bangladesh
Barbados
Belarus [1]
Belgium
Belize
Bhutan
Bolivia
Bosnia-Herzegovina
Botswana
Brazil [1]
Brunei
Bulgaria
Burkina Faso
Burma
Burundi
Cambodia
Cameroon [2]
Canada
Cape Verde
Central African Rep.
Chad
Chile
China [1][2][3][4]
Colombia
Comoros
Congo
Congo, Dem. Rep.
Costa Rica
Cote d'Ivoire
Croatia
Cyprus
Czech Rep.
Denmark [5]
Djibouti
Dominican Rep.
Ecuador
Egypt [1]
El Salvador
Equatorial Guinea
Estonia
Ethiopia [1][6]
Fiji
Finland
Former Yugoslav Republic of Macedonia
France [1]
Gabon
Gambia, The
Georgia
German Dem. Rep. [1][7]
Germany, Fed. Rep. [2][7]
Ghana

AVIATION (Cont'd)

Greece
Grenada
Guatemala [1]
Guinea
Guinea-Bissau
Guyana
Haiti
Honduras [1]
Hungary
Iceland
India [1]
Indonesia [1]
Iran
Iraq
Ireland
Israel
Italy
Jamaica
Japan
Jordan
Kazakhstan
Kenya
Korea, Dem. People's Rep. [1]
Korea, Rep.
Kuwait
Kyrgyz Rep.
Laos
Latvia
Lebanon
Lesotho
Liberia
Libya
Lithuania
Luxembourg
Madagascar
Malawi [1]
Malaysia
Maldives
Mali
Malta
Marshall Is. [8]
Mauritania
Mauritius
Mexico
Moldova
Monaco
Mongolia [1]
Morocco [1]
Nauru
Nepal
Netherlands [9]
New Zealand
Nicaragua
Niger
Nigeria
Norway
Oman [1]
Pakistan
Palau
Panama
Papua New Guinea [1]
Paraguay
Peru [1]
Philippines
Poland [1]
Portugal
Qatar [1]
Romania [1]
Rwanda
St. Lucia
St. Vincent & the Grenadines

Samoa
Saudi Arabia [1]
Senegal
Seychelles
Sierra Leone
Singapore
Slovak Rep.
Slovenia
Solomon Is.
South Africa [1]
Spain
Sri Lanka
Sudan
Suriname
Swaziland
Sweden
Switzerland
Syrian Arab Rep. [2]
Tajikistan
Tanzania
Thailand
Togo
Tonga
Trinidad & Tobago
Tunisia [1]
Turkey
Turkmenistan
Uganda
Ukraine [1]
Union of Soviet Socialist Reps. [1] [10]
United Arab Emirates
United Kingdom [11]
United States
Uruguay
Uzbekistan
Vanuatu
Venezuela [1]
Vietnam, Socialist Rep. [1]
Yemen (Aden) [1] [12]
Yemen (Sanaa) [12]
Yugoslavia [13]
Zambia
Zimbabwe

NOTES:
[1] With reservation.
[2] With declaration.
[3] The Taiwan authorities have also adhered to this convention. See note under CHINA (Taiwan) in the bilateral section.
[4] Applicable to Hong Kong and Macao. With declaration. See note under CHINA in bilateral section.
[5] Applicable to Faroe Is. and Greenland.
[6] See note under ETHIOPIA in bilateral section.
[7] See note under GERMANY, FEDERAL REPUBLIC OF in bilateral section.
[8] On October 15, 1986 the Compact of Free Association entered into force between the Government of the United States and the Government of the Republic of the Marshall Islands, effective October 21, 1986.
[9] Applicable to the Netherlands Antilles and Aruba.
[10] See note under UNION OF SOVIET SOCIALIST REPUBLICS in bilateral section.
[11] Extended to all territories under the territorial sovereignty of the United Kingdom.
[12] See note under YEMEN in bilateral section.
[13] See note under YUGOSLAVIA in bilateral section.

Memorandum of understanding regarding technical measures to improve the safety of civil aviation in the North Pacific. Done at Tokyo July 29, 1985; entered into force October 8, 1985.
TIAS 12066.
States which are parties:
Japan
Union of Soviet Socialist Reps. [1]
United States

NOTE:
[1] See note under UNION OF SOVIET SOCIALIST REPUBLICS in bilateral section.

Protocol for the suppression of unlawful acts of violence at airports serving international civil aviation, supplementary to the convention of September 23, 1971. Done at Montreal February 24, 1988; entered into force August 6, 1989; for the United States November 18, 1994.
TIAS
States which are parties:
Algeria
Argentina
Australia
Austria
Azerbaijan
Bahrain
Belarus
Belgium
Belize
Bosnia-Herzegovina
Botswana
Brazil
Brunei *
Bulgaria
Burkina Faso
Burma
Burundi
Cambodia
Canada
Central African Rep.
Chile
China [1]
Croatia
Czech Rep.
Denmark [2]
Egypt
El Salvador
Estonia
Ethiopia
Fiji
Finland
Former Yugoslav Republic of Macedonia
France [3]
Gambia
Georgia
Germany
Ghana
Greece
Guatemala
Guinea
Hungary
Iceland
India
Iraq
Ireland
Israel
Italy
Japan
Jordan
Kazakhstan
Kenya

AVIATION (Cont'd)

Korea
Korea, Dem. People's Rep.
Kuwait
Kyrgyz Rep.
Latvia
Lebanon
Libya
Lithuania
Madagascar
Maldives
Mali
Malta
Marshall Is.
Mauritius
Mexico
Moldova
Monaco
Mongolia
Netherlands [3]
New Zealand
Norway
Oman
Pakistan
Palau
Panama
Peru
Romania
Russian Fed.
St. Lucia
St. Vincent & the Grenadines
Samoa
Saudi Arabia
Singapore
Slovak Rep.
Slovenia
South Africa
Spain
Sri Lanka
Sudan
Sweden
Switzerland
Tajikistan
Thailand
Togo
Tunisia
Turkey
Turkmenistan
Uganda
Ukraine
United Arab Emirates
United Kingdom [3 4]
United States
Uruguay
Uzbekistan
Vietnam
Yugoslavia [5]

NOTES:
    * Enters into force for Brunei January 19, 2001.
    [1] Applicable to Hong Kong. See note under CHINA in bilateral section.
    [2] With reservation(s).
    [3] With declaration(s).
    [4] Applicable to Isle of Man.
    [5] See note under YUGOSLAVIA in bilateral section.

Convention on the marking of plastic explosives for the purpose of detection, with tech-nical annex. Done at Montreal March 1, 1991; entered into force June 21, 1998.
TIAS
Parties:
Algeria [1]
Argentina [2]
Austria [2]
Azerbaijan [2]
Bahrain [2]
Botswana [2]
Bulgaria [2]
Cameroon [2]
Canada [2]
Chile [2]
Czech Rep. [2]
Denmark [2 3]
Ecuador [2]
Egypt [2]
El Salvador [2]
Eritrea [2]
Estonia [2]
Former Yugoslav Republic of Macedonia [2]
France [2]
Gambia [2]
Georgia [2]
Germany [2]
Ghana [2]
Greece [2]
Guatemala [2]
Hungary [2]
India [1 2]
Japan [2]
Jordan [2]
Kazakhstan [2]
Kuwait [2]
Kyrgyz Rep. [2]
Latvia [2]
Lebanon [2]
Lithuania [2]
Maldives [2]
Mali [2]
Malta [2]
Mexico [2]
Moldova
Monaco [2]
Mongolia [2]
Morocco [2]
Netherlands [2]
Norway [2]
Panama [2]
Peru [1 2]
Qatar [2]
Romania [2]
Samoa [2]
Saudi Arabia [1 2]
Slovak Rep. [2]
Slovenia [2]
South Africa [2]
Spain [2]
Sudan [2]
Switzerland [2]
Tunisia [2]
Turkey [1 2]
Ukraine [2]
United Arab Emirates [2]
United Kingdom [2]
United States [2]
Uzbekistan [2]
Zambia [2]

NOTES:
    [1] With reservation(s).
    [2] With declaration(s).
    [3] Not applicable to the Faroe Is.

Agreement to ban smoking on international passenger flights. Done at Chicago November 1, 1994; entered into force March 1, 1995.
TIAS 12578.
Parties:
Australia
Canada
United States

Arrangement on the joint financing of a North Atlantic Height Monitoring System. Signed at Montreal July 31, August 11, 18 and 23, September 28, October 25 and December 12, 1995; entered into force December 12, 1995.
TIAS
Parties:
Canada
International Civil Aviation Organization
Iceland
Ireland
Portugal
United Kingdom
United States

BILLS OF LADING

(See under MARITIME MATTERS)

BIOLOGICAL WEAPONS

(See also GAS WARFARE)

Convention on the prohibition of the development, production and stockpiling of bacteriological (biological) and toxin weapons and on their destruction. Done at Washington, London and Moscow April 10, 1972; entered into force March 26, 1975.
26 UST 583; TIAS 8062; 1015 UNTS 163.
Parties:
Afghanistan
Albania
Argentina
Armenia
Australia
Austria [1]
Bahamas
Bahrain [1]
Bangladesh
Barbados
Belarus
Belgium
Belize
Benin
Bhutan
Bolivia
Bosnia-Herzegovina
Botswana
Brazil
Brunei [2]
Bulgaria
Burkina Faso
Cambodia
Canada
Cape Verde
Chile
China [3 4 5]
Colombia
Congo

BIOLOGICAL WEAPONS
(Cont'd)

Congo, Dem. Rep.
Costa Rica
Croatia
Cuba
Cyprus
Czech Rep.
Denmark
Dominica [2]
Dominican Rep.
Ecuador
El Salvador
Equatorial Guinea
Estonia
Ethiopia [6]
Fiji
Finland
Former Yugoslav Republic of Macedonia
France
Gambia
Georgia
German Dem. Rep. [7]
Germany, Fed. Rep. [7]
Ghana
Greece
Grenada
Guatemala
Guinea-Bissau
Honduras
Hungary
Iceland
India [4]
Indonesia
Iran
Iraq
Ireland
Italy
Jamaica
Japan
Jordan
Kenya
Korea, Dem. People's Rep.
Korea, Rep.
Kuwait [4]
Laos
Lebanon
Lesotho
Libya
Liechtenstein
Lithuania
Luxembourg
Malaysia [1]
Maldives
Malta
Mauritius
Mexico
Monaco
Mongolia
Netherlands [8]
New Zealand
Nicaragua
Niger
Nigeria
Norway
Oman
Pakistan
Panama
Papua New Guinea
Paraguay
Peru

Philippines
Poland
Portugal
Qatar
Romania
Russian Fed.
Rwanda
St. Kitts & Nevis
St. Lucia
St. Vincent & the Grenadines
San Marino
Sao Tome & Principe
Saudi Arabia
Senegal
Seychelles
Sierra Leone
Singapore
Slovak Rep.
Slovenia
Solomon Is. [2]
South Africa
Spain
Sri Lanka
Suriname
Swaziland
Sweden
Switzerland [4]
Thailand
Togo
Tonga
Tunisia
Turkey
Turkmenistan
Uganda
Ukraine
Union of Soviet Socialist Reps. [9]
United Kingdom [10]
United States
Uruguay
Uzbekistan
Vanuatu
Venezuela
Vietnam, Socialist Rep.
Yemen (Aden) [11]
Yugoslavia [12]
Zimbabwe

NOTES:

[1] With reservation.

[2] See under country heading in the bilateral section for information concerning acceptance of treaty obligations.

[3] The Taiwan authorities have also adhered to this convention. See note under CHINA (Taiwan) in bilateral section.

[4] With statement.

[5] Applicable to Hong Kong and Macao. See note under CHINA in bilateral section.

[6] See note under ETHIOPIA in bilateral section.

[7] See note under GERMANY, FEDERAL REPUBLIC OF in bilateral section.

[8] Applicable to Netherlands Antilles and Aruba.

[9] See note under UNION OF SOVIET SOCIALIST REPUBLICS in bilateral section.

[10] Extended to territories under the territorial sovereignty of the United Kingdom. Also extended to New Hebrides; continued application to Vanuatu not determined.

[11] See note under YEMEN in bilateral section.

[12] See note under YUGOSLAVIA in bilateral section.

BRIBERY

Convention on combating bribery of foreign public officials in international business transactions, with annex. Done at Paris December 17, 1997; entered into force February 15, 1999.
TIAS
Parties:
Australia
Austria
Belgium
Bulgaria
Canada
Czech Rep.
Finland
Germany
Greece
Hungary
Iceland
Japan
Korea
Mexico
Norway
Slovak Rep.
Spain
Sweden
Switzerland
United Kingdom
United States

CAMBODIA

Agreement on a comprehensive political settlement of the Cambodia conflict, with annexes. Done at Paris October 23, 1991; entered into force October 23, 1991.
TIAS

Agreement concerning the sovereignty, independence, territorial integrity and inviolability, neutrality and national unity of Cambodia. Done at Paris October 31, 1991; entered into force October 31, 1991.
TIAS

CHEMICAL WEAPONS

Convention on the prohibition of the development, production, stockpiling and use of chemical weapons and on their destruction, with annexes. Done at Paris January 13, 1993; entered into force April 29, 1997.
TIAS
Parties:
Albania
Algeria
Argentina
Armenia
Australia
Austria
Azerbaijan
Bahrain
Bangladesh
Belarus
Belgium
Benin
Bolivia
Bosnia-Herzegovina
Botswana
Brazil
Brunei

CHEMICAL WEAPONS
(Cont'd)

Bulgaria
Burkina Faso
Burundi
Cameroon
Canada
Chile
China [1] [2]
Colombia
Cook Is.
Costa Rica
Cote d'Ivoire
Croatia
Cuba [2]
Cyprus
Czech Rep.
Denmark
Ecuador
El Salvador
Equatorial Guinea
Eritrea
Estonia
Ethiopia
Fiji
Finland
Former Yugoslav Republic of Macedonia
France
Gabon
Gambia
Georgia
Germany
Ghana
Greece
Guinea
Guyana
Holy See
Hungary
Iceland
India
Indonesia
Iran
Ireland
Italy
Jamaica
Japan
Jordan
Kazakhstan
Kenya
Kiribati
Korea
Kuwait
Laos
Latvia
Lesotho
Liechtenstein
Lithuania
Luxembourg
Malawi
Malaysia
Maldives
Mali
Malta
Mauritania
Mauritius
Mexico
Micronesia
Moldova
Monaco
Mongolia
Morocco

Mozambique
Namibia
Nepal
Netherlands [3]
New Zealand
Nicaragua
Niger
Nigeria
Norway
Oman
Pakistan
Panama
Papua New Guinea
Paraguay
Peru
Philippines
Poland
Portugal
Qatar
Romania
Russian Fed.
St. Lucia
San Marino
Saudi Arabia
Senegal
Seychelles
Singapore
Slovak Rep.
Slovenia
South Africa
Spain
Sri Lanka
Sudan
Suriname
Swaziland
Sweden
Switzerland
Tajikistan
Tanzania
Togo
Trinidad & Tobago
Tunisia
Turkey
Turkmenistan
Ukraine
United Arab Emirates
United Kingdom
United States
Uruguay
Uzbekistan
Venezuela
Vietnam
Yemen
Yugoslavia
Zimbabwe

Proces-verbal of rectification of the Spanish original text of the convention on the prohibition of the development, production, stockpiling and use of chemical weapons and on their destruction of January 13, 1993. Done at New York January 10, 1994; entered into force January 10, 1994.
TIAS

NOTES:
  [1] Applicable to Hong Kong and Macao. See note under CHINA in bilateral section.
  [2] With declaration(s).
  [3] Applicable to Netherlands Antilles and Aruba.

CHINA

(Pre 1949 treaties, applicable only to Taiwan.)

Treaty relating to the principles and policies to be followed in matters concerning China. Signed at Washington February 6, 1922; entered into force August 5, 1925.
44 Stat. 2113; TS 723; 2 Bevans 375; 38 LNTS 278.
States which are parties:
Australia
Belgium
Bolivia
Canada
China
Denmark
France
India
Italy
Japan
Mexico
Netherlands
New Zealand
Norway
Portugal
South Africa
Sweden
United Kingdom
United States

Treaty relating to the Chinese customs tariff. Signed at Washington February 6, 1922; entered into force August 5, 1925.
44 Stat. 2122; TS 724; 2 Bevans 381; 38 LNTS 268.
States which are parties:
Australia
Belgium
Canada
China
Denmark
France
India
Italy
Japan
Netherlands
New Zealand
Norway
Portugal
South Africa
Spain
Sweden
United Kingdom
United States

CITIZENSHIP

(See NATIONALITY)

CLAIMS

(See also ARBITRATION; INVESTMENT DISPUTES; PACIFIC SETTLEMENT OF DISPUTES)

Convention for the arbitration of pecuniary claims. Signed at Buenos Aires August 11, 1910; entered into force January 1, 1913.
38 Stat. 1799; TS 594; 1 Bevans 763.
States which are parties:
Bolivia
Brazil
Costa Rica
Dominican Rep.
Ecuador
Guatemala
Honduras
Nicaragua
Panama
Paraguay
United States
Uruguay

Agreement relating to certain *Marechal Joffre* claims, with memorandum of understanding. Signed at Washington October 19, 1948; entered into force October 19, 1948.
62 Stat. 2841; TIAS 1816; 4 Bevans 783; 84 UNTS 201.
States which are parties:
Australia
France
United States

COLLISIONS AT SEA

(See under MARITIME MATTERS)

COMMERCE

(See CUSTOMS; TRADE AND COMMERCE)

COMMODITIES

(See COPPER; FOOD AID; RUBBER; WHEAT; WINE)

COMMUNICATIONS SYSTEMS

(See SATELLITE COMMUNICATIONS SYSTEMS; TELECOMMUNICATION)

CONCILIATION

(See PACIFIC SETTLEMENT OF DISPUTES)

CONSERVATION

(See also FISHERIES; POLAR BEARS; WHALING; WORLD HERITAGE)

Convention on nature protection and wildlife preservation in the Western Hemisphere, with annex. Done at the Pan American Union, Washington, October 12, 1940; entered into force April 30, 1942.
56 Stat. 1354; TS 981; 3 Bevans 630; 161 UNTS 193.
States which are parties:
Argentina [1]
Brazil
Chile
Costa Rica
Dominican Rep.
Ecuador
El Salvador
Guatemala
Haiti
Mexico
Nicaragua
Panama
Paraguay
Peru
Suriname
Trinidad & Tobago
United States
Uruguay
Venezuela

NOTE:
[1] With reservation.

Convention on international trade in endangered species of wild fauna and flora, with appendices. Done at Washington March 3, 1973; entered into force July 1, 1975.
27 UST 1087; TIAS 8249; 993 UNTS 243.
States which are parties:
Afghanistan
Algeria
Antigua & Barbuda
Argentina [1]
Australia
Austria
Azerbaijan
Bahamas, The
Bangladesh
Barbados
Belgium
Belize
Benin
Bolivia
Botswana
Brazil
Brunei
Bulgaria
Burkina Faso
Burundi
Cambodia

Cameroon
Canada
Central African Rep.
Chad
Chile
China [2]
Colombia
Comoros
Congo
Congo, Dem. Rep.
Costa Rica
Cote d'Ivoire
Croatia
Cuba
Cyprus
Czech Rep.
Denmark [3]
Djibouti
Dominican Rep.
Ecuador
Egypt
Equatorial Guinea
Eritrea
Estonia
Ethiopia [4]
Fiji
Finland
France
Gabon
Gambia, The
German Dem. Rep. [5]
Germany, Fed. Rep. [5]
Ghana
Greece
Guatemala
Guinea
Guinea-Bissau
Guyana
Honduras
Hungary
India
Indonesia
Iran
Israel
Italy
Japan
Jordan
Kenya
Kiribati [6]
Korea
Latvia
Liberia
Liechtenstein
Luxembourg
Madagascar
Malawi
Malaysia
Mali
Malta
Mauritius
Mexico
Monaco
Mongolia
Morocco
Mozambique
Namibia
Nepal
Netherlands
New Zealand
Nicaragua
Niger
Nigeria
Norway
Pakistan
Panama

CONSERVATION (Cont'd)

Papua New Guinea
Paraguay
Peru
Philippines
Poland
Portugal
Romania
Russian Fed.
Rwanda
St. Kitts & Nevis
St. Lucia
St. Vincent & the Grenadines
Saudi Arabia
Senegal
Seychelles
Sierra Leone
Singapore
Slovak Rep.
Somalia
South Africa
Spain
Sri Lanka
Sudan
Suriname [1]
Swaziland
Sweden
Switzerland
Tanzania
Thailand
Togo
Trinidad & Tobago
Tunisia
Tuvalu [6]
Uganda
Union of Soviet Socialist Reps. [7]
United Arab Emirates
United Kingdom [8]
United States
Uruguay
Uzbekistan
Vanuatu
Venezuela
Vietnam
Zambia
Zimbabwe

Amendment:
June 22, 1979 (TIAS 11079).

NOTES:
   [1] With statement.
   [2] Applicable to Hong Kong and Macao. With declaration. See note under CHINA in bilateral section.
   [3] Extended to Greenland and the Faroe Is. However, application as regards the Faroe Is. will only be accomplished at the time the authorities of the Faroe Is. will have enacted the appropriate legislation.
   [4] See note under ETHIOPIA in bilateral section.
   [5] See note under GERMANY, FEDERAL REPUBLIC OF in bilateral section.
   [6] See under country heading in the bilateral section for information concerning acceptance of treaty obligations.
   [7] See note under UNION OF SOVIET SOCIALIST REPUBLICS in bilateral section.

   [8] Applicable to the Bailiwick of Guernsey, the Bailiwick of Jersey, the Isle of Man, Bermuda, British Indian Ocean Territory, British Virgin Is., Falkland Is., Gibraltar, Montserrat, Pitcairn, St. Helena and dependencies (Tristan da Cunha, Ascension Is.), Cayman Is.

Convention on the conservation of Antarctic marine living resources, with annex for an arbitral tribunal. Done at Canberra May 20, 1980; entered into force April 7, 1982. 33 UST 3476; TIAS 10240.
States which are parties:
Argentina [1]
Australia
Belgium
Brazil
Bulgaria
Canada
Chile
European Economic Community
Finland
France [1]
German Dem. Rep. [2]
Germany, Fed. Rep. [2]
Greece
India
Italy
Japan
Korea
Netherlands
New Zealand
Norway
Peru
Poland
Russian Fed.
South Africa
Spain
Sweden
Union of Soviet Socialist Reps. [3]
United Kingdom
United States
Uruguay

NOTES:
   [1] With declaration.
   [2] See note under GERMANY, FEDERAL REPUBLIC OF in bilateral section.
   [3] See note under UNION OF SOVIET SOCIALIST REPUBLICS in bilateral section.

Convention on wetlands of international importance, especially as waterfowl habitat. Done at Ramsar February 2, 1971; entered into force December 21, 1975; for the United States December 18, 1986.
TIAS 11084; 996 UNTS 245.
States which are parties:
Albania
Algeria
Argentina
Armenia
Australia
Austria
Bahamas
Bahrain
Bangladesh
Belgium
Brazil
Bulgaria
Burkina Faso
Canada
Chad
Chile
China [1]

Colombia
Congo
Congo, Dem. Rep.
Costa Rica
Cote d'Ivoire
Croatia
Czechoslovakia [2]
Denmark
Ecuador
Egypt
Estonia
Finland
France
Gabon
Gambia, The
Georgia
German Dem. Rep. [3]
Germany, Fed. Rep. [3]
Greece
Guatemala
Guinea
Guinea-Bissau
Honduras
Hungary
Iceland
India
Indonesia
Iran
Ireland
Israel
Italy
Jamaica
Japan
Jordan
Kenya
Korea
Latvia
Libya
Liechtenstein
Lithuania
Luxembourg
Madagascar
Malawi
Mali
Malta
Mauritania
Mexico
Moldova
Monaco
Mongolia
Morocco
Namibia
Netherlands [4]
New Zealand
Nicaragua
Niger
Norway
Pakistan
Panama
Papua New Guinea
Paraguay
Peru
Philippines
Poland
Portugal
Romania
Russian Fed.
Senegal
Slovak Rep.
Slovenia
South Africa
Spain
Sri Lanka
Suriname
Sweden

CONSERVATION (Cont'd)

Switzerland
Tanzania
Thailand
Togo
Trinidad & Tobago
Tunisia
Turkey
Union of Soviet Socialist Reps. [5]
United Kingdom [6]
United States
Uruguay
Venezuela
Vietnam
Yugoslavia [7]
Zambia

Amendment:
December 3, 1982 (TIAS 11084).

NOTES:
[1] Applicable to Hong Kong. See note under CHINA in bilateral section.
[2] See note under CZECHOSLOVAKIA in bilateral section.
[3] See note under GERMANY, FEDERAL REPUBLIC OF in bilateral section.
[4] Applicable to Netherlands Antilles.
[5] See note under UNION OF SOVIET SOCIALIST REPUBLICS in bilateral section.
[6] Applicable to Anguilla, Bailiwick of Jersey, Bermuda, British Virgin Is., Cayman Is., Falkland Is. and dependencies, Gibraltar, Isle of Man, Montserrat, Pitcairn Is., St. Helena and dependencies, Turks and Caicos Is.
[7] See note under YUGOSLAVIA in bilateral section.

Convention for the conservation of Antarctic seals, with annex. Done at London June 1, 1972; entered into force March 11, 1978.
29 UST 441; TIAS 8826.
States which are parties:
Argentina
Australia
Belgium
Brazil
Canada
Chile
France
Germany, Fed. Rep. [1][2]
Italy
Japan
Norway
Poland
South Africa
Union of Soviet Socialist Reps. [3][4]
United Kingdom [5]
United States

Amendment:
September 12–16, 1988.

NOTES:
[1] See note under GERMANY, FEDERAL REPUBLIC OF in bilateral section.
[2] With declaration.
[3] With statement.
[4] See note under UNION OF SOVIET SOCIALIST REPUBLICS in bilateral section.

[5] Extended to Channel Is. and Isle of Man.

Convention for the protection of the natural resources and environment of the South Pacific Region, with annex. Done at Noumea November 24, 1986; entered into force August 22, 1990; for the United States July 10, 1991.
TIAS

Protocol for the prevention of pollution of the South Pacific Region by dumping, with annexes. Done at Noumea November 24, 1986; entered into force August 22, 1990; for the United States July 10, 1991.
TIAS

Protocol concerning cooperation in combatting pollution emergencies in the South Pacific Region. Done at Noumea November 24, 1986; entered into force August 22, 1990; for the United States July 10, 1991.
TIAS
Parties:
Australia
Cook Is.
Fiji
France [1]
Marshall Is.
Micronesia
New Zealand
Papua New Guinea
Solomon Is.
United States [2]
Western Samoa

NOTES:
[1] With reservation(s).
[2] With understanding(s).

CONSULS

Convention relating to the duties, rights, prerogatives, and immunities of consular agents. Signed at Habana February 20, 1928; entered into force September 3, 1929; for the United States February 8, 1932.
47 Stat. 1976; TS 843; 2 Bevans 714; 155 LNTS 291.
States which are parties:
Brazil
Colombia
Cuba
Dominican Rep. [1]
Ecuador
El Salvador
Haiti
Mexico
Nicaragua
Panama
Peru
United States
Uruguay

NOTE:
[1] With declaration.

Convention on consular relations. Done at Vienna April 24, 1963; entered into force March 19, 1967; for the United States December 24, 1969.
21 UST 77; TIAS 6820; 596 UNTS 261.
States which are parties:
Albania

Algeria
Andorra
Angola
Antigua & Barbuda
Argentina
Armenia
Australia
Austria
Azerbaijan
Bahamas, The
Bahrain [1]
Bangladesh
Barbados [1]
Belarus
Belgium
Benin
Bhutan
Bolivia
Bosnia-Herzegovina
Brazil
Bulgaria [1]
Burkina Faso
Burma [1][2]
Cameroon
Canada
Cape Verde
Chile
China [3]
Colombia
Congo, Dem. Rep.
Costa Rica
Croatia
Cuba [2]
Cyprus
Czech Rep.
Denmark [1][2]
Djibouti
Dominica
Dominican Rep.
Ecuador
Egypt [2]
El Salvador
Equatorial Guinea
Eritrea
Estonia
Fiji [2]
Finland [1][2]
Former Yugoslav Republic of Macedonia
France [1]
Gabon
Georgia
German Dem. Rep. [1][4]
Germany, Fed. Rep. [1][4]
Ghana
Greece
Grenada
Guatemala
Guinea
Guyana
Haiti
Holy See
Honduras
Hungary
Iceland [1]
India
Indonesia
Iran
Iraq [2]
Ireland
Italy [2]
Jamaica
Japan
Jordan
Kazakhstan
Kenya

CONSULS (Cont'd)

Kiribati
Korea, Dem. People's Rep.
Korea, Rep.
Kuwait [1]
Kyrgyz Rep.
Laos
Latvia
Lebanon
Lesotho [1]
Liberia
Libya
Liechtenstein
Lithuania
Luxembourg
Madagascar
Malawi
Malaysia
Maldives
Mali
Malta [2]
Marshall Is.
Mauritania
Mauritius
Mexico [2]
Micronesia
Moldova
Mongolia
Morocco [1] [2]
Mozambique [1]
Namibia
Nepal
Netherlands [1] [5]
New Zealand
Nicaragua
Niger
Nigeria
Norway [1]
Oman [1]
Pakistan
Panama
Papua New Guinea
Paraguay
Peru
Philippines
Poland
Portugal
Qatar [2]
Romania [1]
Russian Fed.
Rwanda
St. Kitts & Nevis [6]
St. Lucia
St. Vincent & the Grenadines [6]
Sao Tome & Principe
Saudi Arabia [2]
Senegal
Seychelles
Slovak Rep.
Slovenia
Solomon Is. [6]
Somalia
South Africa
Spain
Sudan
Suriname
Sweden [2]
Switzerland
Syrian Arab Rep. [2]
Tajikistan
Tanzania
Togo

Tonga
Trinidad & Tobago
Tunisia
Turkey
Turkmenistan
Tuvalu
Ukraine
United Arab Emirates [1]
United Kingdom [1] [7]
United States
Uruguay
Uzbekistan
Vanuatu
Venezuela
Vietnam, Socialist Rep. [2]
Viet-Nam, Rep. [8]
Western Samoa
Yemen (Sanaa) [2] [9]
Yugoslavia [10]
Zimbabwe

NOTES:
[1] With a statement.
[2] With reservation(s).
[3] Applicable to Hong Kong and Macao. See note under CHINA in bilateral section.
[4] See note under GERMANY, FEDERAL REPUBLIC OF in bilateral section.
[5] Applicable to Aruba and Netherlands Antilles.
[6] See under country heading in the bilateral section for information concerning acceptance of treaty obligations.
[7] Extended to Anguilla and territories under the sovereignty of the United Kingdom.
[8] See Vietnam footnote under AUTOMOTIVE TRAFFIC: convention of September 19, 1949 (3 UST 3008; TIAS 2487; 125 UNTS 22).
[9] See note under YEMEN in bilateral section.
[10] See note under YUGOSLAVIA in bilateral section.

Optional protocol to the convention on consular relations concerning the compulsory settlement of disputes. Done at Vienna April 24, 1963; entered into force March 19, 1967; for the United States December 24, 1969.
21 UST 325; TIAS 6820; 596 UNTS 487.
States which are parties:
Antigua & Barbuda [1]
Australia
Austria
Belgium
Bulgaria
Burkina Faso
Denmark
Dominica [1]
Dominican Rep.
Estonia
Finland
France
Gabon
Germany, Fed. Rep. [2]
Grenada [1]
Hungary
Iceland
India
Iran
Italy
Japan
Kenya
Korea, Rep.
Laos

Liechtenstein
Luxembourg
Madagascar
Malawi
Mauritius
Nepal
Netherlands [3]
New Zealand
Nicaragua
Niger
Norway
Oman
Pakistan
Panama
Paraguay
Philippines
St. Kitts & Nevis [1]
St. Lucia [1]
St. Vincent & the Grenadines [1]
Senegal
Seychelles
Slovak Rep.
Solomon Is. [1]
Suriname
Sweden
Switzerland
United Kingdom [4]
United States
Viet-Nam, Rep. [5]

NOTES:
[1] See under country heading in the bilateral section for information concerning acceptance of treaty obligations.
[2] See note under GERMANY, FEDERAL REPUBLIC OF in bilateral section.
[3] Applicable to Aruba and Netherlands Antilles.
[4] Extended to Anguilla and territories under the sovereignty of the United Kingdom.
[5] See Vietnam footnote under AUTOMOTIVE TRAFFIC: convention of September 19, 1949 (3 UST 3008; TIAS 2487; 125 UNTS 22).

CONTAINERS
(See also CUSTOMS)

International convention for safe containers (CSC), with annexes. Done at Geneva December 2, 1972; entered into force September 6, 1977; for the United States January 3, 1979.
29 UST 3707; TIAS 9037; 1064 UNTS 3.
States which are parties:
Afghanistan
Argentina
Australia
Austria
Bahamas, The
Barbados
Belarus [1]
Belgium
Benin
Bolivia
Brazil
Bulgaria [1]
Canada
Chile [2]
China [3]
Croatia
Cuba [1]

CONTAINERS (Cont'd)

Cyprus
Czech Rep.
Denmark [4]
Estonia
Finland
France [2]
Georgia
German Dem. Rep. [1][5]
Germany, Fed. Rep. [5]
Greece
Guinea
Guyana
Honduras
Hungary
Iceland
India
Indonesia
Israel
Italy
Japan
Kazakhstan
Kenya
Korea, Dem. People's Rep.
Korea, Rep.
Liberia
Lithuania
Luxembourg
Marshall Is.
Mexico
Morocco
Netherlands
New Zealand [6]
Norway
Pakistan
Peru
Poland
Portugal
Romania [1]
Russian Fed.
Saudi Arabia
Slovak Rep.
Slovenia
South Africa
Spain
Sweden
Ukraine [1]
Union of Soviet Socialist Reps. [1][7]
United Kingdom [2][8]
United States
Vanuatu
Yemen (Sanaa) [9]
Yugoslavia [10]

Amendments to annexes:
April 2, 1981 (33 UST 3238; TIAS 10220).
June 13, 1983 (TIAS 10914).
May 17, 1991.

NOTES:
[1] With statement.
[2] With reservation.
[3] Applicable to Hong Kong. See note under CHINA in bilateral section.
[4] Not applicable to Greenland and the Faroe Is.
[5] See note under GERMANY, FEDERAL REPUBLIC OF in bilateral section.
[6] Not applicable to Cook Is., Niue and Tokelau Is.
[7] See note under UNION OF SOVIET SOCIALIST REPUBLICS in bilateral section.

[8] Applicable to Bermuda, Guernsey and Isle of Man.
[9] See note under YEMEN in bilateral section.
[10] See note under YUGOSLAVIA in bilateral section.

CONTINENTAL SHELF

(See under MARITIME MATTERS)

COPPER

Terms of reference of the International Copper Study Group. Done at Geneva February 24, 1989; entered into force January 23, 1992.
TIAS
Parties:
Belgium *
Canada
Chile
China
European Economic Community
Finland
France
Germany
Greece
India
Indonesia
Italy
Japan
Luxembourg *
Mexico
Netherlands [1]
Norway
Peru
Poland
Portugal
Russian Fed.
Spain
United Kingdom *
United States
Zambia

Amendment:
June 26, 1992.

NOTES:
* Provisional application.
[1] For the Kingdom in Europe.

COPYRIGHT

(See also PHONOGRAMS; the Appendix)

Convention on literary and artistic copyrights.[1] Signed at Buenos Aires August 11, 1910; entered into force October 31, 1912.
38 Stat. 1785; TS 593; 1 Bevans 758.
States which are parties:
Argentina
Bolivia
Brazil
Chile
Colombia

Costa Rica
Dominican Rep.
Ecuador
Guatemala
Haiti
Honduras
Mexico
Nicaragua
Panama
Paraguay
Peru
United States
Uruguay

NOTE:
[1] Replaces the convention of January 27, 1902 (35 Stat. 1934; TS 491; 1 Bevans 339), which remains in force as between the contracting parties and El Salvador.

Universal copyright convention with three protocols annexed thereto. Done at Geneva September 6, 1952; entered into force September 16, 1955.
6 UST 2731; TIAS 3324; 216 UNTS 132.
States which are parties:
Algeria [1]
Andorra [2]
Argentina [3]
Australia
Austria
Azerbaijan [1]
Bahamas, The [1]
Bangladesh [3][4]
Barbados [1]
Belarus [1]
Belgium
Belize [1]
Bolivia
Bosnia-Herzegovina
Brazil
Bulgaria [1]
Cambodia
Cameroon [1]
Canada [4][5]
Chile [3][5]
China [1][6]
Colombia [1]
Costa Rica
Cuba [3]
Cyprus [3][4]
Czechoslovakia [5][7]
Denmark
Dominican Rep. [1]
Ecuador [3]
El Salvador [3][4]
Fiji [1]
Finland
Former Yugoslav Republic of Macedonia
France [8]
German Dem. Rep. [1][9][10]
Germany, Fed. Rep. [10]
Ghana
Greece
Grenada [11]
Guatemala
Guinea [3][4]
Guyana [11]
Haiti
Holy See
Hungary [3][5][9]
Iceland [1]
India
Ireland
Israel

COPYRIGHT (Cont'd)

Italy
Japan
Kazakhstan
Kenya
Korea [3 4]
Laos
Lebanon
Liberia [3]
Liechtenstein [3]
Luxembourg
Malawi [1]
Malta [1]
Mauritius
Mexico [3 5]
Moldova [1]
Monaco [3]
Morocco
Netherlands
New Zealand [12]
Nicaragua
Niger [3 4]
Nigeria [1]
Norway
Pakistan
Panama
Paraguay
Peru [3 4]
Philippines
Poland [3 4]
Portugal
Rwanda [3 4]
St. Lucia [11]
St. Vincent & the Grenadines [1]
Senegal [3 4]
Seychelles [11]
Slovak Rep. [5]
Slovenia
Spain [13]
Sri Lanka
Sweden
Switzerland [3]
Tajikistan [1]
Trinidad & Tobago [1]
Tunisia
Ukraine
Union of Soviet Socialist Reps. [1 14]
United Kingdom [15]
United States [16]
Uruguay
Venezuela
Yugoslavia [17]
Zambia [1]

NOTES:
[1] Party to convention only.
[2] An instrument of ratification deposited by the Spanish Ambassador on behalf of the Bishop of Urgel, Co-Prince of Andorra, does not include Protocol 1. An instrument of ratification deposited by the French Permanent Delegate to UNESCO on behalf of the President of the French Republic, Co-Prince of Andorra, did include Protocol 1.
[3] Not party to Protocol 3.
[4] Not party to Protocol 2.
[5] Not party to Protocol 1.
[6] China is a party to the convention only. However, the convention and the protocols are applicable to Hong Kong. With statement. Also applicable to Macao. See note under CHINA in bilateral section.

[7] See note under CZECHOSLOVAKIA in bilateral section.
[8] Extended to Guadeloupe, Martinique, French Guiana, and Reunion.
[9] With a statement.
[10] See note under GERMANY, FEDERAL REPUBLIC OF in bilateral section.
[11] See under country heading in the bilateral section for information concerning acceptance of treaty obligations.
[12] Extended to Cook Is. (including Niue) and Tokelau Is.
[13] With reservation to Protocol 1.
[14] See note under UNION OF SOVIET SOCIALIST REPUBLICS in bilateral section.
[15] Extended to Bermuda, British Virgin Is., Cayman Is., Falkland Is., Gibraltar, Isle of Man, Montserrat, and St. Helena.
[16] Extended to Guam, Puerto Rico and Virgin Is.
[17] See note under YUGOSLAVIA in bilateral section.

Universal copyright convention, as revised, with two protocols annexed thereto. Done at Paris July 24, 1971; entered into force July 10, 1974.
25 UST 1341; TIAS 7868.
States which are parties:
Algeria [1]
Australia
Austria
Bahamas, The [1]
Bangladesh
Barbados [1]
Bolivia [1 2]
Bosnia-Herzegovina
Brazil
Bulgaria [1]
Cameroon [1]
China [1 2 3]
Colombia [1]
Costa Rica [1]
Croatia
Cyprus
Czechoslovakia [4 5]
Denmark
Dominican Rep. [1]
Ecuador
El Salvador
Finland [1]
Former Yugoslav Republic of Macedonia
France
German Dem. Rep. [1 6]
Germany, Fed. Rep. [6]
Grenada [7]
Guinea
Hungary [4]
India
Italy [2]
Japan
Kenya
Korea
Liechtenstein
Mexico [1 2]
Moldova
Monaco
Morocco
Netherlands
Niger
Norway
Panama [1]
Peru
Poland
Portugal

Russian Fed.
Rwanda
St. Lucia [7]
St. Vincent & the Grenadines
Saudi Arabia
Senegal
Seychelles [7]
Slovak Rep. [4]
Slovenia
Spain [8]
Sri Lanka
Sweden
Switzerland
Trinidad & Tobago [1]
Tunisia
United Kingdom [9]
United States [10]
Uruguay
Vatican City
Venezuela
Yugoslavia [1 11]

NOTES:
[1] Not a party to the protocols.
[2] With statement.
[3] China is a party to the convention only. However, the convention and the protocols are applicable to Hong Kong. With statement. Also applicable to Macao. See note under CHINA in bilateral section.
[4] Not a party to protocol 1.
[5] See note under CZECHOSLOVAKIA in bilateral section.
[6] See note under GERMANY, FEDERAL REPUBLIC OF in bilateral section.
[7] See under country heading in the bilateral section for information concerning acceptance of treaty obligations.
[8] With reservation.
[9] Extended to British Virgin Is., Gibraltar, Isle of Man, and St. Helena.
[10] Extended to Guam, Puerto Rico and the Virgin Is.
[11] See note under YUGOSLAVIA in bilateral section.

Berne convention (with appendix) for the protection of literary and artistic works of September 9, 1886, completed at Paris May 4, 1896, revised at Berlin November 13, 1908, completed at Berne March 20, 1914, revised at Rome June 2, 1928, at Brussels June 26, 1948, at Stockholm July 14, 1967, and at Paris July 24, 1971, amended in 1979. Done at Paris July 24, 1971; entered into force for the United States March 1, 1989. [1]
TIAS
Parties:
Albania
Algeria [2]
Antigua & Barbuda
Argentina
Armenia
Australia
Austria
Azerbaijan
Bahamas, The [3]
Bahrain [2]
Bangladesh
Barbados
Belarus
Belgium
Belize
Benin
Bolivia

COPYRIGHT (Cont'd)

Bosnia-Herzegovina
Botswana
Brazil
Bulgaria
Burkina Faso
Cameroon
Canada
Cape Verde
Central African Rep.
Chad [3]
Chile
China [2 4]
Colombia
Congo
Congo, Dem. Rep.
Costa Rica
Cote d'Ivoire
Croatia
Cuba [2]
Cyprus
Czech Rep.
Denmark
Dominica
Dominican Rep.
Ecuador
Egypt
El Salvador
Equatorial Guinea
Estonia
Fiji [3]
Finland
Former Yugoslav Republic of Macedonia
France
Gabon
Gambia
Georgia
German Dem. Rep. [5]
Germany, Fed. Rep. [5]
Ghana
Greece
Grenada
Guatemala [2]
Guinea
Guinea-Bissau
Guyana
Haiti
Holy See
Honduras
Hungary
Iceland
India
Indonesia [2]
Ireland
Israel [3]
Italy
Jamaica
Japan
Jordan [2]
Kazakhstan
Kenya
Korea
Kyrgyz Rep.
Latvia
Lesotho [2]
Liberia [2]
Libya
Liechtenstein
Lithuania [2]
Luxembourg
Madagascar
Malawi

Malaysia
Mali
Malta [3]
Mauritania
Mauritius [2]
Mexico
Moldova [6]
Monaco
Mongolia [2]
Morocco
Namibia
Netherlands
New Zealand
Nicaragua
Niger
Nigeria
Norway [2]
Oman [2]
Pakistan [3]
Panama
Paraguay
Peru
Philippines
Poland
Portugal
Qatar
Romania
Russian Fed. [2]
Rwanda
St. Kitts & Nevis
St. Lucia
St. Vincent & the Grenadines
Senegal
Singapore [2]
Slovak Rep.
Slovenia
South Africa [3]
Spain
Sri Lanka [3]
Sudan
Suriname
Swaziland
Sweden
Switzerland
Tajikistan
Tanzania [2]
Thailand
Togo
Trinidad & Tobago
Tunisia
Turkey
Ukraine [2]
United Kingdom [7]
United States
Uruguay
Venezuela
Yugoslavia [8]
Zambia
Zimbabwe [3]

NOTES:
[1] See Appendix: International Copyright Relations of the United States, section under Proclamations, Treaties, and Conventions Establishing Copyright Relations Between the United States and Other Countries for applicable revision of the Berne convention to which any of the below listed countries are party.
[2] With declaration(s).
[3] Not a party to Articles 1–21.
[4] Applicable to Hong Kong and Macao. See note under CHINA in bilateral section.
[5] See note under GERMANY, FEDERAL REPUBLIC OF in bilateral section.
[6] With statement.

[7] Applicable to Isle of Man.
[8] See note under YUGOSLAVIA in bilateral section.

CORRUPTION

Inter-American convention against corruption. Done at Caracas March 29, 1996; entered into force March 6, 1997; for the United States October 29, 2000.
TIAS
Parties:
Argentina
Bahamas
Bolivia
Canada
Chile
Colombia
Costa Rica
Dominican Rep.
Ecuador
El Salvador
Honduras
Mexico
Nicaragua
Panama
Paraguay
Peru
Trinidad & Tobago
United States
Uruguay
Venezuela

CULTURAL PROPERTY

Statutes of the International Centre for the Study of the Preservation and Restoration of Cultural Property. Done at New Delhi November–December 1956, and revised April 24, 1963 and April 14–17, 1969; entered into force May 10, 1958; for the United States January 20, 1971.
22 UST 19; TIAS 7038.
States which are parties:
Albania
Algeria
Angola
Argentina
Australia
Austria
Barbados
Belgium
Benin
Bosnia-Herzegovina
Brazil
Bulgaria
Burkina Faso
Burma
Cambodia
Cameroon
Canada
Chad
Chile
China
Colombia
Cote d'Ivoire
Croatia
Cuba
Cyprus
Czech Rep.

CULTURAL PROPERTY
(Cont'd)

Denmark
Dominican Rep.
Ecuador
Egypt
Ethiopia [1]
Finland
Former Yugoslav Republic of Macedonia
France
Gabon
Germany, Fed. Rep. [2]
Ghana
Greece
Guatemala
Guinea
Guyana
Haiti
Honduras
Hungary
India
Iran
Iraq
Ireland
Israel
Italy
Japan
Jordan
Kenya
Korea, Dem. People's Rep.
Korea, Rep.
Kuwait
Lebanon
Libya
Lithuania
Luxembourg
Madagascar
Malaysia
Mali
Malta
Mauritius
Mexico
Morocco
Nepal
Netherlands
New Zealand
Nicaragua
Nigeria
Norway
Pakistan
Paraguay
Peru
Philippines
Poland
Portugal
Romania
Slovenia
Somalia
Spain
Sri Lanka
Sudan
Suriname
Sweden
Switzerland
Syrian Arab Rep.
Thailand
Tunisia
Turkey
Union of Soviet Socialist Reps. [3]
United Kingdom
United States

Vietnam
Yugoslavia [4]
Zimbabwe

NOTES:
[1] See note under ETHIOPIA in bilateral section.
[2] See note under GERMANY, FEDERAL REPUBLIC OF in bilateral section.
[3] See note under UNION OF SOVIET SOCIALIST REPUBLICS in bilateral section.
[4] See note under YUGOSLAVIA in bilateral section.

Convention on the means of prohibiting and preventing the illicit import, export and transfer of ownership of cultural property. Done at Paris November 14, 1970; entered into force April 24, 1972; for the United States December 2, 1983.
TIAS   ; 823 UNTS 231.
States which are parties:
Algeria
Angola
Argentina
Armenia
Australia [1]
Azerbaijan
Bahamas
Bangladesh
Belarus [2]
Belize
Bolivia
Bosnia-Herzegovina
Brazil
Bulgaria
Burkina Faso
Cambodia
Cameroon
Canada
Central African Rep.
China
Colombia
Congo, Dem. Rep.
Costa Rica
Cote d'Ivoire
Croatia
Cuba
Cyprus
Czech Rep.
Dominican Rep.
Ecuador
Egypt
El Salvador
Estonia
Finland
Former Yugoslav Republic of Macedonia
France [2]
Georgia
German Dem. Rep. [3]
Greece
Grenada
Guatemala
Guinea
Honduras
Hungary
India
Iran
Iraq
Italy
Jordan
Korea, Dem. People's Rep.
Korea, Rep.
Kuwait
Kyrgyz Rep.

Lebanon
Libya
Lithuania
Madagascar
Mali
Mauritania
Mauritius
Mexico
Mongolia
Nepal
Nicaragua
Niger
Nigeria
Oman
Pakistan
Panama
Peru
Poland
Portugal
Qatar
Romania
Russian Fed.
Saudi Arabia
Senegal
Slovak Rep.
Slovenia
Spain
Sri Lanka
Syrian Arab Rep.
Tajikistan
Tanzania
Tunisia
Turkey
Ukraine [2]
Union of Soviet Socialist Reps. [2][4]
United States [1]
Uruguay
Uzbekistan
Yugoslavia [5]
Zambia

NOTES:
[1] With reservation and understandings.
[2] With declaration.
[3] See note under GERMANY, FEDERAL REPUBLIC OF in bilateral section.
[4] See note under UNION OF SOVIET SOCIALIST REPUBLICS in bilateral section.
[5] See note under YUGOSLAVIA in bilateral section.

CULTURAL RELATIONS

(See also WORLD HERITAGE)

Treaty on the protection of artistic and scientific institutions and historic monuments. Signed at Washington April 15, 1935; entered into force August 26, 1935.
49 Stat. 3267; TS 899; 3 Bevans 254; 167 LNTS 279.
States which are parties:
Brazil
Chile
Colombia
Cuba
Dominican Rep.
El Salvador
Guatemala
Mexico
United States
Venezuela

CULTURAL RELATIONS (Cont'd)

Convention concerning artistic exhibitions. Signed at Buenos Aires December 23, 1936; entered into force December 7, 1937.
51 Stat. 206; TS 929; 3 Bevans 383; 188 LNTS 151.
States which are parties:
Brazil
Chile
Colombia
Costa Rica
Dominican Rep.
El Salvador
Guatemala
Haiti
Honduras
Mexico
Nicaragua
Panama
Peru
United States
Venezuela

Convention providing for creation of the Inter-American Indian Institute. Done at Mexico City November 1, 1940; entered into force December 13, 1941.
56 Stat. 1303; TS 978; 3 Bevans 661.
States which are parties:
Bolivia
Brazil
Chile
Colombia
Costa Rica
Ecuador
El Salvador
Guatemala
Honduras
Mexico
Nicaragua
Panama
Paraguay
Peru
United States
Venezuela

Agreement for facilitating the international circulation of visual and auditory materials of an educational, scientific and cultural character, with protocol. (Beirut agreement) Done at Lake Success July 15, 1949; entered into force August 12, 1954; for the United States January 12, 1967.
17 UST 1578; TIAS 6116; 197 UNTS 3.
States which are parties:
Bosnia-Herzegovina
Brazil
Cambodia
Canada
Congo
Costa Rica
Croatia
Cuba [1]
Cyprus
Czech Rep.
Denmark
El Salvador
Former Yugoslav Republic of Macedonia
Ghana
Greece

Haiti
Iran
Iraq
Jordan
Lebanon
Libya
Madagascar
Malawi
Malta
Morocco
Niger
Norway
Pakistan
Philippines
Slovak Rep.
Slovenia
Syrian Arab Rep.
Trinidad & Tobago
United States
Uruguay
Yugoslavia [2]

NOTES:
[1] With reservation.
[2] See note under YUGOSLAVIA in bilateral section.

Agreement on the importation of educational, scientific and cultural materials, with protocol. (Florence agreement) Done at Lake Success November 22, 1950; entered into force May 21, 1952; for the United States November 2, 1966.
17 UST 1835; TIAS 6129; 131 UNTS 25.
States which are parties:
Afghanistan
Antigua & Barbuda [1]
Australia
Austria
Bahamas, The [1]
Barbados
Belgium
Belize [1]
Bolivia
Bosnia-Herzegovina
Brunei [1]
Bulgaria
Burkina Faso
Cambodia
Cameroon
Congo
Congo, Dem. Rep.
Cote d'Ivoire
Croatia
Cuba
Cyprus
Czech Rep.
Denmark
Dominica [1]
Egypt
El Salvador
Fiji
Finland
Former Yugoslav Republic of Macedonia
France
Gabon
Gambia, The [1]
Germany, Fed. Rep. [2,3]
Ghana
Greece
Grenada [1]
Guatemala
Guyana [1]
Haiti
Hong Kong [4]

Hungary
Iran
Iraq
Ireland
Israel
Italy
Jamaica [1]
Japan
Jordan
Kazakhstan
Kenya [5]
Kiribati [1]
Laos
Libya
Liechtenstein
Lithuania
Luxembourg
Madagascar
Malawi
Malaysia
Malta
Mauritius
Moldova
Monaco
Morocco
Netherlands [6]
New Zealand [7]
Nicaragua
Niger
Nigeria
Norway
Oman
Pakistan
Philippines
Poland
Portugal
Romania
Russian Fed.
Rwanda
St. Kitts & Nevis [1]
St. Lucia [1]
St. Vincent & the Grenadines [1]
San Marino
Seychelles [1]
Sierra Leone
Singapore
Slovak Rep.
Slovenia
Solomon Is.
Spain
Sri Lanka
Suriname [1]
Sweden
Switzerland [5]
Syrian Arab Rep.
Tanzania
Thailand
Tonga
Trinidad & Tobago
Tunisia
Tuvalu [1]
Uganda
United Kingdom [8]
United States [5]
Uruguay
Vatican City
Venezuela
Viet Nam, Rep. [9]
Yugoslavia [10]
Zambia
Zimbabwe [1]

CULTURAL RELATIONS
(Cont'd)

NOTES:
[1] See under country heading in the bilateral section for information concerning acceptance of treaty obligations.
[2] With a statement.
[3] See note under GERMANY, FEDERAL REPUBLIC OF in bilateral section.
[4] CHINA is not a party to this treaty but has made it applicable to Hong Kong. With declaration.
[5] With reservation.
[6] Applicable to Netherlands Antilles and Aruba.
[7] Extended to Cook Is. (including Niue) and Tokelau Is.
[8] Extended to Anguilla, Ascension Is., British Virgin Is., Cayman Is., Channel Is., Christmas and Cocos (Keeling) Is., Falkland Is. (Colony and Dependencies), Gibraltar, Isle of Man, Montserrat, St. Helena, Tristan da Cunha, Turks and Caicos Is.
[9] See Vietnam footnote under AUTOMOTIVE TRAFFIC: convention of September 19, 1949 (3 UST 3008; TIAS 2487; 125 UNTS 22).
[10] See note under YUGOSLAVIA in bilateral section.

Convention for the promotion of inter-American cultural relations.[1] Signed at Caracas March 28, 1954; entered into force February 18, 1955; for the United States October 3, 1957.
8 UST 1903; TIAS 3936.
States which are parties:
Brazil
Costa Rica
Ecuador
Haiti
Panama
Paraguay
United States
Venezuela

NOTE:
[1] Replaces as between contracting parties the convention of December 23, 1936 (51 Stat. 178; TS 928; 3 Bevans 372; 188 LNTS 125). Parties to the 1936 convention not party to the 1954 convention are: Bolivia, Chile, Colombia, Cuba, Dominican Republic, Guatemala, Honduras, Mexico, Nicaragua and Peru.

Protocol revising the convention of November 22, 1928 relating to international expositions, with appendix and annex.[1] Done at Paris November 30, 1972; entered into force June 9, 1980.
32 UST 4283; TIAS 9948.
Parties:
Argentina
Australia
Austria
Belarus [2]
Belgium
Belize
Bolivia
Bulgaria [2]
Cambodia

Canada
Chile
China [3]
Costa Rica
Cuba
Czechoslovakia [2] [4]
Denmark
El Salvador
Finland
France
German Dem. Rep. [5]
Germany, Fed. Rep.[5]
Greece
Hungary [2]
Iceland
Italy
Jamaica
Japan
Laos
Latvia
Mexico
Monaco
Morocco
Netherlands
Nicaragua
Norway
Panama
Peru
Qatar
Romania [2]
St. Vincent & the Grenadines
Slovak Rep. [2]
South Africa
Spain
Sweden
Switzerland
Thailand
Tunisia
Ukraine [2]
Union of Soviet Socialist Reps. [2] [6]
United Kingdom
United States [2]
Uruguay
Venezuela

Amendment:
June 24, 1982.

NOTES:
[1] Replaces as between the contracting parties the convention of November 22, 1928, as amended. Parties to the 1928 convention that are not parties to the 1972 protocol are Haiti, Israel (with a reservation), Lebanon (with a reservation), Nigeria, Poland, and Portugal for which the 1928 convention remains in force as between the contracting parties.
[2] With reservations.
[3] Applicable to Hong Kong. See note under CHINA in bilateral section.
[4] See note under CZECHOSLOVAKIA in bilateral section.
[5] See note under GERMANY, FEDERAL REPUBLIC OF in bilateral section.
[6] See note under UNION OF SOVIET SOCIALIST REPUBLICS in bilateral section.

Protocol to the agreement on the importation of educational, scientific and cultural materials of November 22, 1950. Done at Nairobi November 26, 1976; entered into force January 2, 1982; for the United States November 15, 1989.
TIAS

Parties:
Australia
Austria [1]
Barbados
Belgium
Bosnia-Herzegovina
Bulgaria
Croatia
Cuba
Czech Rep.
Denmark
Egypt
Finland
Former Yugoslav Republic of Macedonia
France
Germany, Fed. Rep. [1] [2]
Greece
Holy See
Iraq [1]
Ireland
Italy
Kazakhstan
Lithuania [3]
Luxembourg [1]
Moldova
Netherlands [4]
Portugal[1]
Russian Fed.
San Marino
Slovak Rep.
Slovenia
Spain [1]
Sweden [3]
United Kingdom [1] [5]
United States [1]
Uruguay
Venezuela
Yugoslavia[6]

NOTES:
[1] With declaration.
[2] See note under GERMANY, FEDERAL REPUBLIC OF in bilateral section.
[3] With reservation.
[4] Applicable to Netherlands Antilles and Aruba.
[5] Extended to Anguilla, Bailiwicks of Guernsey and Jersey, Cayman Is., Falkland Is., Gibraltar, Isle of Man, Montserrat, St. Helena and dependencies, South Georgia and the South Sandwich Is., Turks and Caicos Is. and Sovereign Base Areas of Akrotiri and Dhekelia in the Island of Cyprus.
[6] See note under YUGOSLAVIA in bilateral section.

CUSTOMS

(See also AUTOMOTIVE TRAFFIC; CULTURAL RELATIONS; TRADE AND COMMERCE)

Convention concerning the formation of an International Union for the Publication of Customs Tariffs, regulations of execution, and final declarations. Signed at Brussels July 5, 1890; entered into force April 1, 1891.
26 Stat. 1518; TS 384; 1 Bevans 172.

CUSTOMS (Cont'd)

Protocol modifying the convention of July 5, 1890 relating to the creation of an International Union for the Publication of Customs Tariffs. Done at Brussels December 16, 1949; entered into force May 5, 1950; for the United States September 15, 1957.
8 UST 1669; TIAS 3922; 72 UNTS 3.
States which are parties:
Albania [1]
Algeria
Argentina [1]
Austria
Belgium
Bolivia [1]
Botswana
Brazil
Bulgaria
Burundi
Canada
Chile
China [1] [2]
Colombia
Congo, Dem. Rep.
Costa Rica
Cote d'Ivoire
Cuba
Cyprus
Czechoslovakia [3] [4]
Denmark [5]
Dominican Rep.
Ecuador [1]
Egypt
Estonia [1]
Finland
France [5]
Germany
Greece
Haiti
Hungary
Iceland
India
Indonesia
Iran
Iraq
Ireland
Israel
Italy
Japan
Jordan
Korea
Latvia [1]
Lebanon
Libya
Lithuania [1]
Luxembourg
Malaysia
Malta
Mexico
Morocco
Netherlands [5]
Nicaragua
Norway
Pakistan
Panama [1]
Philippines
Poland
Portugal [5]
Romania
Rwanda
Saudi Arabia
Senegal

Slovak Rep. [3]
South Africa [1]
Spain [5]
Sri Lanka
Sudan
Sweden
Switzerland
Syrian Arab Rep.
Tunisia
Turkey
Union of Soviet Socialist Reps. [6]
United States
Venezuela
Vietnam [7]
Yugoslavia[8]

NOTES:
[1] Not a party to Protocol.
[2] Pre 1949 convention, applicable only to Taiwan.
[3] Does not recognize that Germany, taken as a whole, is legally bound by signature affixed "for Germany".
[4] See note under CZECHOSLOVAKIA in bilateral section.
[5] Applicable to all territories.
[6] See note under UNION OF SOVIET SOCIALIST REPUBLICS in bilateral section.
[7] See Vietnam footnote under AGRICULTURE: agreement of January 25, 1924 (26 UST 1840; TIAS 8141; 57 LNTS 135).
[8] See note under YUGOSLAVIA in bilateral section.

Convention on publicity of customs documents. Signed at Santiago May 3, 1923; entered into force July 10, 1925.
44 Stat. 2547; TS 753; 2 Bevans 420; 33 LNTS 11.
States which are parties:
Brazil
Chile
Costa Rica
Cuba
Dominican Rep.
El Salvador
Haiti
Panama
Paraguay
United States
Uruguay

Convention establishing a Customs Co-operation Council, with annex and protocol. Done at Brussels December 15, 1950; entered into force November 4, 1952; for the United States November 5, 1970.
22 UST 320; TIAS 7063; 157 UNTS 129; 160 UNTS 267.
States which are parties:
Albania
Algeria
Angola
Argentina
Armenia
Australia [1]
Austria [2]
Azerbaijan
Bahamas, The
Bangladesh
Belgium [2]
Botswana
Brazil
Bulgaria
Burkina Faso

Burma
Burundi
Cameroon
Canada
Cape Verde
Central African Rep.
Chile
China [3]
Congo
Congo, Dem. Rep.
Cote d'Ivoire
Cuba
Cyprus
Czech Rep.
Denmark [2]
Ecuador
Egypt
Estonia
Ethiopia [4]
Finland
France [2]
Gabon
Gambia, The
German Dem. Rep. [5]
Germany, Fed. Rep.[2] [5]
Ghana
Greece [2]
Guatemala
Guinea
Guyana
Haiti
Hong Kong
Hungary
Iceland [2]
India
Indonesia
Iran
Iraq
Ireland [2]
Israel
Italy [2]
Jamaica
Japan
Jordan
Kazakhstan
Kenya
Korea
Kyrgyz Rep.
Latvia
Lebanon
Lesotho
Liberia
Libya
Lithuania
Luxembourg [2]
Madagascar
Malawi
Malaysia
Mali
Malta
Mauritania
Mauritius
Mexico
Mongolia
Morocco
Mozambique
Namibia
Nepal
Netherlands [2]
New Zealand
Niger
Nigeria
Norway [2]
Pakistan
Paraguay

CUSTOMS (Cont'd)

Peru
Philippines
Poland
Portugal [2]
Qatar
Romania
Rwanda
Saudi Arabia
Senegal
Sierra Leone
Singapore
Slovak Rep. [1]
Slovenia
South Africa
Spain [6]
Sri Lanka
Sudan
Swaziland
Sweden [2]
Switzerland [2]
Syrian Arab Rep.
Tanzania
Thailand
Togo
Trinidad & Tobago
Tunisia
Turkey [2]
Uganda
Ukraine
Union of Soviet Socialist Reps. [7]
United Arab Emirates [2]
United Kingdom [2]
United States [1] [2]
Uruguay
Uzbekistan
Yugoslavia [8]
Zambia
Zimbabwe

NOTES:
[1] With reservation.
[2] Also party to the protocol on the European Customs Union Study Group.
[3] Applicable to Macao. See note under CHINA in bilateral section.
[4] See note under ETHIOPIA in bilateral section.
[5] See note under GERMANY, FEDERAL REPUBLIC OF in bilateral section.
[6] Extended to Spanish possessions.
[7] See note under UNION OF SOVIET SOCIALIST REPUBLICS in bilateral section.
[8] See note under YUGOSLAVIA in bilateral section.

International convention to facilitate the importation of commercial samples and advertising material.[1] Done at Geneva November 7, 1952; entered into force November 20, 1955; for the United States October 17, 1957.
8 UST 1636; TIAS 3920; 221 UNTS 255.
States which are parties:
Antigua & Barbuda [2]
Australia
Austria
Barbados [2]
Belgium
Belize [2]
Bosnia-Herzegovina
Canada
Congo, Dem. Rep.

Croatia
Cuba [3]
Cyprus
Czech Rep.
Denmark
Dominica [2]
Egypt
Fiji
Finland
France
Gambia, The [2]
Germany, Fed. Rep. [3] [4]
Ghana
Greece
Grenada [2]
Guinea
Guyana [2]
Haiti
Hong Kong [5]
Hungary
Iceland
India [3]
Indonesia
Iran
Ireland
Israel
Italy
Jamaica
Japan
Kenya
Korea, Rep.
Luxembourg
Malaysia
Malta [6]
Mauritius
Mexico
Netherlands [7]
New Zealand [8]
Nigeria
Norway
Pakistan
Papua New Guinea [2]
Poland
Portugal
Romania [6]
Rwanda
St. Kitts & Nevis [2]
St. Lucia [2]
St. Vincent & the Grenadines [2]
Seychelles [2]
Sierra Leone
Singapore
Slovak Rep.
Slovenia
Spain
Sri Lanka
Suriname [2]
Sweden
Switzerland [9]
Tanzania [3]
Thailand
Tonga
Trinidad & Tobago [3]
Turkey
Uganda [3]
United Kingdom [10]
United States [11]
Western Samoa [2]
Yugoslavia [12]
Zimbabwe [2]

NOTES:
[1] Pursuant to articles 3(2) and 23 of the A.T.A. carnet convention of December 6, 1961 (TIAS 6631) the United States gave notice on May 19, 1969, effective June 30, 1969, of acceptance of A.T.A. carnets for goods temporarily imported under the 1952 samples convention.
[2] See under country heading in the bilateral section for information concerning acceptance of treaty obligations.
[3] With reservation.
[4] See note under GERMANY, FEDERAL REPUBLIC OF in bilateral section.
[5] CHINA is not a party to this treaty but has made it applicable to Hong Kong.
[6] With declaration.
[7] Applicable to Netherlands Antilles and Aruba.
[8] Extended to Cook Is. (including Niue) and the Tokelau Is.
[9] Applicable to Liechtenstein.
[10] Extended to Anguilla, British Virgin Is., Falkland Is., Gibraltar, Isle of Man, Montserrat, and St. Helena.
[11] Extended to all possessions except American Samoa, Guam, Kingman's Reef, Johnston Is., Midway Is., Virgin Is., and Wake Is.
[12] See note under YUGOSLAVIA in bilateral section.

Customs convention on containers, with annexes and protocol of signature.* Done at Geneva May 18, 1956; entered into force August 4, 1959; for the United States March 3, 1969. 20 UST 301; TIAS 6634; 338 UNTS 103.
States which are parties:
Algeria [1] **
Antigua & Barbuda
Australia [2] **
Austria **
Barbados [3]
Belgium
Bosnia-Herzegovina
Brunei [3]
Bulgaria **
Cambodia
Cameroon
Canada **
Croatia
Cuba [1] **
Cyprus [3]
Czech Rep. **
Denmark [4]
Dominica [3]
Finland **
France
Gambia, The [3]
Germany, Fed. Rep. [5]
Greece
Grenada [3]
Hungary **
Ireland
Israel
Italy
Jamaica
Japan
Kiribati [3]
Luxembourg
Malawi
Mauritius
Netherlands [6]
Norway
Papua New Guinea [3]
Poland [1] **

CUSTOMS (Cont'd)

Portugal
Romania [1] **
St. Kitts & Nevis [3]
St. Lucia [3]
St. Vincent & the Grenadines [3]
Sierra Leone
Singapore [3]
Slovak Rep. [1] **
Slovenia
Solomon Is.
Spain**
Sweden
Switzerland [7] **
Tanzania [3]
Trinidad & Tobago **
Tuvalu [3]
United Kingdom [8]
United States [9] **
Yugoslavia [10]

NOTES:
* Replaced as between the contracting parties by the customs convention on containers of December 2, 1972 (see below).
** Parties to the 1972 convention.
[1] With reservation.
[2] Extended to Christmas Is., Cocos (Keeling) Is., and Norfolk Is.
[3] See under country heading in the bilateral section for information concerning acceptance of treaty obligations.
[4] Extended to Danish customs area, which does not include Faroe Is. and Greenland.
[5] See note under GERMANY, FEDERAL REPUBLIC OF in bilateral section.
[6] Applicable to Netherlands Antilles and Aruba.
[7] Applicable to Principality of Liechtenstein so long as customs union treaty with Switzerland remains in force.
[8] Extended to Anguilla, Bermuda, Bailiwick of Guernsey, Falkland Is., Gibraltar, Isle of Man, Jersey, and Montserrat.
[9] Extended to the customs territory of the United States [which, at the present time, includes the States, the District of Columbia, and Puerto Rico].
[10] See note under YUGOSLAVIA in bilateral section.

Customs convention on the temporary importation of professional equipment, with annexes. Done at Brussels June 8, 1961; entered into force July 1, 1962; for the United States March 3, 1969.
20 UST 33; TIAS 6630; 473 UNTS 153.
States which are parties:
Algeria
Australia
Austria
Belgium
Bulgaria
Central African Rep.
Cuba
Cyprus
Czechoslovakia [1]
Denmark [2]
Egypt
Finland
France
Germany, Fed. Rep. [3]

Greece [4]
Hong Kong [5]
Hungary
Iceland
Iran
Ireland
Israel
Italy
Japan
Kenya
Korea
Lebanon
Lesotho
Luxembourg
Madagascar
Malta
Netherlands [6]
New Zealand
Niger
Norway
Poland
Portugal
Romania
Slovak Rep.
South Africa
Spain [4]
Sri Lanka
Sweden
Switzerland [7]
Trinidad & Tobago
Tunisia
Turkey
Uganda
United Kingdom [8]
United States [9]
Yugoslavia [10]
Zimbabwe

NOTES:
[1] See note under CZECHOSLOVAKIA in bilateral section.
[2] Extended to Danish customs area, which does not include Faroe Is. and Greenland.
[3] See note under GERMANY, FEDERAL REPUBLIC OF in bilateral section.
[4] Not bound by Annex C.
[5] CHINA is not a party to this treaty but has made it applicable to Hong Kong.
[6] Applicable to Netherlands Antilles and Aruba.
[7] Extended to Principality of Liechtenstein so long as customs union treaty with Switzerland remains in force.
[8] Extended to Bailiwick of Guernsey, Isle of Man, and Jersey.
[9] Extended to the customs territory of the United States [which, at the present time, includes the States, the District of Columbia, and Puerto Rico].
[10] See note under YUGOSLAVIA in bilateral section.

Customs convention on the A.T.A. carnet for temporary admission of goods, with annex. Done at Brussels December 6, 1961; entered into force July 30, 1963; for the United States March 3, 1969.
20 UST 58; TIAS 6631; 473 UNTS 219.
States which are parties:
Algeria
Australia
Austria
Belgium
Bulgaria
Canada

China [1]
Cote d'Ivoire
Cuba
Cyprus
Czechoslovakia [2]
Denmark [3]
Egypt
Finland
France
Germany, Fed. Rep. [4]
Greece
Hungary
Iceland
India
Iran
Ireland [5]
Israel
Italy
Japan
Korea
Lebanon
Lesotho
Luxembourg
Malaysia
Malta
Mauritius
Netherlands [6]
New Zealand
Niger
Nigeria [5]
Norway
Poland
Portugal
Romania
Senegal
Singapore
Slovak Rep.
South Africa [5]
Spain
Sri Lanka
Sweden
Switzerland [7]
Trinidad & Tobago
Tunisia
Turkey
United Kingdom [5] [8]
United States [5] [9]
Yugoslavia [10]

NOTES:
[1] Applicable to Hong Kong. See note under CHINA in bilateral section.
[2] See note under CZECHOSLOVAKIA in bilateral section.
[3] Not applicable to Faroe Is. and Greenland.
[4] See note under GERMANY, FEDERAL REPUBLIC OF in bilateral section.
[5] With reservation.
[6] Applicable to Netherlands Antilles and Aruba.
[7] Applicable to Principality of Liechtenstein so long as customs union treaty with Switzerland remains in force.
[8] Extended to Bailiwick of Guernsey, Gibraltar, Jersey, and Isle of Man.
[9] Extended to the customs territory of the United States [which at the present time, includes the States, the District of Columbia, and Puerto Rico].
[10] See note under YUGOSLAVIA in bilateral section.

Customs convention on containers, 1972, with annexes and protocol. [1] Done at Geneva De-

CUSTOMS (Cont'd)

cember 2, 1972; entered into force December 6, 1975; for the United States May 12, 1985. TIAS 12085; 988 UNTS 43.
States which are parties:
Algeria
Australia
Austria
Belarus [2]
Bulgaria
Burundi
Canada
China [3]
Cuba [2]
Czech Rep.
Finland
Georgia
German Dem. Rep. [2] [4]
Hungary
Indonesia
Korea
Morocco
New Zealand [5]
Poland
Romania
Russian Fed.
Slovak Rep.
Spain [6]
Switzerland [7]
Trinidad & Tobago
Turkey
Ukraine [2]
Union of Soviet Socialist Reps. [2] [8]
United States
Uzbekistan

NOTES:
[1] Replaces as between contracting parties the convention of May 18, 1956 (20 UST 301; TIAS 6634; 338 UNTS 103).
[2] With statement.
[3] Applicable to Hong Kong. See note under CHINA in bilateral section.
[4] See note under GERMANY, FEDERAL REPUBLIC OF in bilateral section.
[5] Not applicable to Cook Is., Niue and Tokelau Is.
[6] With reservation.
[7] Applicable to the Principality of Liechtenstein so long as customs union treaty with Switzerland remains in force.
[8] See note under UNION OF SOVIET SOCIALIST REPUBLICS in bilateral section.

International convention on the simplification and harmonization of customs procedures, with annexes.[1] Done at Kyoto May 18, 1973; entered into force September 25, 1974; for the United States January 28, 1984.
TIAS
Parties:
Algeria
Australia
Austria
Belgium
Bulgaria
Burundi
Cameroon
Canada
China
Congo, Dem. Rep.
Cote d'Ivoire

Cyprus
Denmark
European Communities
Finland
France
Gambia, The
Germany, Fed. Rep.[2]
Greece
Hungary
India
Ireland
Israel
Italy
Japan
Kenya
Korea
Lesotho
Luxembourg
Malaysia
Morocco
Netherlands
New Zealand
Nigeria
Norway
Pakistan
Poland
Portugal
Rwanda
Saudi Arabia
Senegal
South Africa
Spain
Sri Lanka
Sweden
Switzerland
Uganda
United Kingdom [3]
United States [1]
Yugoslavia [4]
Zambia
Zimbabwe

NOTES:
[1] The convention has thirty-one annexes, not all of which have entered into force and many of which are in force for only certain parties. The United States is not a party to certain annexes and has made reservations concerning others.
[2] See note under GERMANY, FEDERAL REPUBLIC OF in bilateral section.
[3] Extended to the Channel Is. and the Isle of Man.
[4] See note under YUGOSLAVIA in bilateral section.

Customs convention on the international transport of goods under cover of TIR carnets, with annexes.[1] Done at Geneva November 14, 1975; entered into force March 20, 1978; for the United States March 18, 1982.
TIAS
States which are parties:
Afghanistan [2]
Albania
Algeria [2]
Armenia
Austria
Azerbaijan
Belarus
Belgium
Bosnia-Herzegovina
Bulgaria
Canada
Chile

Croatia
Cyprus
Czech Rep.
Denmark [3]
Estonia
European Communities
Finland
Former Yugoslav Republic of Macedonia
France
Georgia
German Dem. Rep. [2] [4]
Germany, Fed. Rep. [4]
Greece
Hungary [2]
Indonesia
Iran
Ireland
Israel
Italy
Jordan
Kazakhstan
Korea
Kuwait [2]
Kyrgyz Rep.
Latvia
Lebanon
Lithuania
Luxembourg
Malta
Moldova
Morocco
Netherlands [5]
Norway
Poland [2]
Portugal
Romania [2]
Russian Fed.
Slovak Rep. [2]
Slovenia
Spain
Sweden
Switzerland [6]
Syria
Tajikistan
Tunisia
Turkey
Turkmenistan
Ukraine
Union of Soviet Socialist Reps. [2] [7]
United Kingdom [8]
United States
Uruguay
Uzbekistan
Yugoslavia [9]

Amendments to annexes:
October 20, 1978.
October 18, 1979.
July 3, 1980.
October 23, 1981.
October 28, 1983.
October 12, 1984.

NOTES:
[1] Replaces as between parties to the convention the customs convention of January 15, 1959 (20 UST 184; TIAS 6633). Japan is a party to the 1959 convention (with reservations) but not a party to the 1975 convention.
[2] With reservation(s).
[3] Extended to Faroe Is.
[4] See note under GERMANY, FEDERAL REPUBLIC OF in bilateral section.
[5] For the Kingdom in Europe, Netherlands Antilles and Aruba.

CUSTOMS (Cont'd)

⁶ Applicable to Liechtenstein.
⁷ See note under UNION OF SOVIET SO-
CIALIST REPUBLICS in bilateral section.
⁸ Applicable to the Bailiwicks of Guernsey
and Jersey, Gibraltar and the Isle of Man.
⁹ See note under YUGOSLAVIA in bilateral
section.

International convention on the harmonized
commodity description and coding system.
Done at Brussels June 14, 1983; entered into
force January 1, 1988; for the United States
January 1, 1989.
TIAS
Parties:
Algeria
Australia
Austria
Bangladesh
Belgium
Botswana
Brazil
Bulgaria
Burkina Faso
Cameroon
Canada
Chad
China
Congo, Dem. Rep.
Cote d'Ivoire
Czechoslovakia ¹
Denmark
European Economic Community
Finland
France
Germany, Fed. Rep. ²
Greece
Hungary
Iceland
India
Ireland
Israel
Italy
Japan
Jordan
Kenya
Korea
Lesotho
Luxembourg
Madagascar
Malawi
Malaysia
Malta
Mauritius
Mexico
Mongolia
Morocco
Netherlands
New Zealand
Niger
Nigeria
Norway
Pakistan
Portugal
Saudi Arabia
Senegal
Slovak Rep.
South Africa
Spain
Sri Lanka
Swaziland

Sweden
Switzerland
Thailand
Togo
Tunisia
Turkey
Uganda
United Kingdom
United States
Yugoslavia ³
Zambia
Zimbabwe

Amendment:
June 24, 1986.

NOTES:
¹ See note under CZECHOSLOVAKIA in
bilateral section.
² See note under GERMANY, FEDERAL
REPUBLIC OF in bilateral section.
³ See note under YUGOSLAVIA in bilateral
section.

DEFENSE

(See also GERMANY; NORTH ATLANTIC TREATY ORGANIZATION)

Convention on the provisional administration
of European colonies and possessions in the
Americas. Signed at Habana July 30, 1940; en-
tered into force January 8, 1942.
56 Stat. 1273; TS 977; 3 Bevans 623; 161
    UNTS 253.
States which are parties:
Argentina ¹
Brazil
Colombia
Costa Rica
Dominican Rep.
Ecuador
El Salvador
Guatemala
Haiti
Honduras
Mexico
Nicaragua
Panama
Peru
United States
Uruguay
Venezuela

NOTE:
¹ With reservation.

Act of Habana concerning the provisional ad-
ministration of European colonies and posses-
sions in the Americas. Signed at Habana July
30, 1940; entered into force July 30, 1940.
54 Stat. 2491; EAS 199; 3 Bevans 619.
States which are parties:
Argentina ¹
Bolivia
Brazil
Chile ¹
Colombia ¹
Costa Rica
Cuba

Dominican Rep.
Ecuador
El Salvador
Guatemala
Haiti
Honduras
Mexico
Nicaragua
Panama
Paraguay
Peru
United States
Uruguay ¹
Venezuela ¹

NOTE:
¹ With reservation.

Inter-American treaty of reciprocal assistance
(Rio Treaty). Done at Rio de Janeiro Sep-
tember 2, 1947; entered into force December
3, 1948.
62 Stat. 1681; TIAS 1838; 4 Bevans 559; 21
    UNTS 77.
States which are parties:
Argentina
Bahamas, The
Bolivia
Brazil
Chile
Colombia
Costa Rica
Cuba
Dominican Rep.
Ecuador ¹
El Salvador
Guatemala ¹ ²
Haiti
Honduras ²
Mexico
Nicaragua ²
Panama
Paraguay
Peru
Trinidad & Tobago
United States
Uruguay
Venezuela

NOTES:
¹ With declaration.
² With reservation.

Agreement for mutual defense assistance in
Indochina, with three annexes. Signed at Sai-
gon December 23, 1950; entered into force De-
cember 23, 1950.
3 UST 2756; TIAS 2447; 185 UNTS 3.
States which are parties:
Cambodia
France
Laos
United States
Vietnam ¹

NOTE:
¹ See Vietnam footnote under AGRI-
CULTURE: agreement of January 25, 1924
(26 UST 1840; TIAS 8141; 57 LNTS 135).

Security treaty (ANZUS Pact). Signed at San
Francisco September 1, 1951; entered into
force April 29, 1952.¹
3 UST 3420; TIAS 2493; 131 UNTS 83.

DEFENSE (Cont'd)

States which are parties:
Australia
New Zealand
United States

NOTE:
[1] As of September 17, 1986, the United States suspended obligations under the treaty as between the United States and New Zealand.

Southeast Asia collective defense treaty, with protocol (SEATO).[1] Signed at Manila September 8, 1954; entered into force February 19, 1955.
6 UST 81; TIAS 3170; 209 UNTS 28.
States which are parties:
Australia
France
New Zealand
Philippines
Thailand
United Kingdom
United States [2]

NOTES:
[1] By decision of the SEATO Council of September 24, 1975, the Organization ceased to exist as of June 30, 1977. The collective defense treaty remains in force.
[2] With an understanding.

The Pacific Charter. Signed at Manila September 8, 1954; entered into force September 8, 1954.
6 UST 91; TIAS 3171; 209 UNTS 23.
States which are parties:
Australia
France
New Zealand
Pakistan
Philippines
Thailand
United Kingdom
United States

Declaration relating to the Baghdad Pact (CENTO). Signed at London July 28, 1958; entered into force July 28, 1958.
9 UST 1077; TIAS 4084; 335 UNTS 205.
States which are parties:
Iran
Pakistan
Turkey
United Kingdom
United States

Memorandum of understanding on the co-production and sale of modular thermal imaging systems, with annex.[1] Signed at Washington July 11, 1985; entered into force July 11, 1985.
TIAS 11228.
States which are parties:
Germany, Fed. Rep. [2]
Switzerland
United States

NOTES:
[1] See also under NORTH ATLANTIC TREATY ORGANIZATION: COOPERATIVE AGREEMENTS.
[2] See note under GERMANY, FEDERAL REPUBLIC OF in bilateral section.

Memorandum of understanding concerning the four power air senior national representative cooperative long term technology projects. Signed at Washington and Paris April 11 and 27 and June 28, 1988; entered into force June 28, 1988.
TIAS

Agreement concerning the accession of Belgium, the Netherlands and the United Kingdom to the United States-German memorandum of understanding of March 10 and June 13, 1986 for cooperative software development and implementation for the EIFEL system. Signed at Bonn, Brussels, Washington, The Hague and London January 27, March 8, April 5, June 27 and July 19, 1988; entered into force July 19, 1988.
TIAS
Parties:
Belgium
Germany, Fed. Rep. [1]
Netherlands
United Kingdom
United States

NOTE:
[1] See note under GERMANY, FEDERAL REPUBLIC OF in bilateral section.

Memorandum of understanding concerning a cooperative program for full integration of a radar in the AV-8B weapon system and the production and life cycle support of a radar equipped AV-8B (AV-8B Harrier II Plus), with annexes. Signed at Rome, Washington and Madrid August 8 and 31 and September 28, 1990; entered into force September 28, 1990.
TIAS
Parties:
Italy
Spain
United States

Treaty on conventional armed forces in Europe, with protocols and annexes. Done at Paris November 19, 1990; entered into force November 9, 1992.
TIAS
Parties:
Armenia
Azerbaijan
Belarus
Belgium
Bulgaria
Canada
Czechoslovakia [1]
Denmark
France
Georgia
Germany, Fed. Rep. [2][3]
Greece [3]
Hungary
Iceland
Italy
Kazakhstan
Luxembourg
Moldova

Netherlands [4]
Norway
Poland
Portugal
Romania
Russian Fed.
Slovak Rep.
Spain [3]
Turkey [5]
Ukraine
United Kingdom [6]
United States

NOTES:
[1] See note under CZECHOSLOVAKIA in bilateral section.
[2] See note under GERMANY, FEDERAL REPUBLIC OF in bilateral section.
[3] With declaration(s).
[4] For the Kingdom in Europe.
[5] With reservation(s).
[6] Applicable to the Bailiwick of Jersey, the Bailiwick of Guernsey, the Isle of Man, the Dependent Territory of Gibraltar, UK Sovereign Base Areas of Akrotiri and Dhekelia in the Island of Cyprus.

Memorandum of understanding for exchanges of information regarding third-generation anti-tank guided missiles. Signed at Washington, London, Paris and Bonn January 30, February 13 and March 7, 1991; entered into force March 7, 1991.
TIAS
Parties:
France
Germany, Fed. Rep. [1]
United Kingdom
United States

NOTE:
[1] See note under GERMANY, FEDERAL REPUBLIC OF in bilateral section.

Program memorandum of understanding concerning general arrangements for the collaborative program on a multifunctional information distribution system, with supplement no. 1. Signed at Paris, Madrid, Washington, Rome and Bonn June 17, July 4, August 27 and October 4, 1991 and January 7, 1992; entered into force October 4, 1991.
TIAS

Memorandum of understanding on cooperative research, development and demonstration of internetworking technologies to improve communications systems network interoperability, with annex. Signed at Bonn, Washington, London and Paris October 22, November 7 and 14 and December 16, 1991; entered into force December 16, 1991.
TIAS
Parties:
Canada
France
Germany
Netherlands
United Kingdom
United States

Memorandum of understanding concerning a cooperative program for full integration of a radar in the AV-8B weapon system and the production, remanufacture and in-service sup-

DEFENSE (Cont'd)

port of a radar equipped AV-8B (AV-8B HARRIER II PLUS), with annexes and supplemental agreement. Signed at Rome and Washington February 7 and March 4, 1992; entered into force November 12, 1992.
TIAS
Parties:
Italy
Spain
United States

Memorandum of understanding concerning co-operation on an international military satellite for communications (INMILSAT) (Feasibility Study). Done at Washington, London and Paris December 30, 1993, January 6 and 28, 1994; entered into force January 28, 1994.
TIAS
Parties:
France
United Kingdom
United States

Memorandum of understanding for the development of synthetic aperture radar application to support coastal warfare and surface shipwake detection and characterization, with annexes. Signed at Washington, London and Kjeller August 12 and 25 and September 5, 1994; entered into force September 5, 1994.
TIAS
Parties:
Norway
United Kingdom
United States

Memorandum of understanding for the technical cooperation program, with appendices. Signed at Melbourne October 24, 1995; entered into force October 24, 1995.
TIAS 12700.

Memorandum of understanding for senior national representatives (ARMY) cooperation and exchanges of information, with attachments and an understanding. Signed at Washington, London, Paris and Bonn October 19, November 13 and 27, 1995 and January 9, 1996; entered into force January 9, 1996.
TIAS

Memorandum of understanding concerning multilateral exchange of research and development information, with appendix. Signed at Washington, Ottawa, London and Canberra October 20, November 15 and December 1, 1995 and January 30 and February 12, 1996; entered into force February 12, 1996.
TIAS

Memorandum of understanding concerning co-operation on project definition and validation of a medium extended air defense system, with annex. Signed at Washington, Rome and Bonn May 17, 24 and 28, 1996; entered into force May 28, 1996.
TIAS
Parties:
Germany
Italy
United States

Amendment:
December 16, 1996.

Document agreed among the States Parties to the Treaty on Conventional Armed Forces in Europe of November 19, 1990 ("the flank agreement"), with understanding. Adopted at Vienna May 31, 1996; entered into force May 15, 1997.
TIAS

Memorandum of understanding concerning multilateral exchange of military information, with appendix. Signed at Washington, London, Ottawa, Canberra and Wellington November 19, 1996, January 8, March 10 and 26, and April 18, 1997; entered into force April 18, 1997.
TIAS
Parties:
Australia
Canada
New Zealand
United Kingdom
United States

Memorandum of agreement concerning the Joint Strike Fighter (JSF) requirements validation project, with annex. Signed at Kjeller and Arlington June 10 and 11, 1997; entered into force June 11, 1997.
TIAS
Parties
Denmark
Netherlands
Norway
United States

Memorandum of understanding for the cooperative production of the Evolved Sea Sparrow Missile (ESSM), with annexes. Signed at Arlington, The Hague, Brussels, Copenhagen, Haakonsvern, Canberra, Lisbon, Rome, Athens, Ankara, Quebec, Madrid and Bonn August 7, 13, 14, 15, 21 and 23, September 8 and 22, October 10, November 7, December 19 and 26, 1997 and January 2, 1998; entered into force December 26, 1997.
TIAS

Agreement for the High speed Anti-Radiation Missile (HARM) AGM-88 upgrade, with annexes. Signed at Washington, Bonn and Rome October 14, 1997, February 5 and March 7, 1998; entered into force March 7, 1998.
TIAS
Parties:
Germany
Italy
United States

DIPLOMATIC AGENTS

(See under TERRORISM)

DIPLOMATIC RELATIONS

Vienna convention on diplomatic relations. Done at Vienna April 18, 1961; entered into force April 24, 1964; for the United States December 13, 1972.
23 UST 3227; TIAS 7502; 500 UNTS 95.
States which are parties:
Afghanistan
Albania
Algeria
Andorra
Angola
Argentina
Armenia
Australia [1]
Austria
Azerbaijan
Bahamas, The [1]
Bahrain [2]
Bangladesh
Barbados
Belarus [1,2]
Belgium [1]
Benin
Bhutan
Bolivia
Bosnia-Herzegovina
Botswana [2]
Brazil
Bulgaria [1,2]
Burkina Faso
Burma
Burundi
Cambodia [2]
Cameroon
Canada [1]
Cape Verde
Central African Rep.
Chad
Chile
China [2,3,4]
Colombia
Congo
Congo, Dem. Rep.
Costa Rica
Cote d'Ivoire
Croatia
Cuba [2]
Cyprus
Czech Rep.
Denmark [1]
Djibouti
Dominica
Dominican Rep.
Ecuador
Egypt [2]
El Salvador
Equatorial Guinea
Eritrea
Estonia
Ethiopia [5]
Fiji
Finland
Former Yugoslav Republic of Macedonia
France [1]
Gabon
Georgia
German Dem. Rep. [1,2,6]
Germany, Fed. Rep. [1,6]
Ghana
Greece [1]
Grenada
Guatemala [1]
Guinea
Guinea-Bissau
Guyana
Haiti [1]
Holy See

DIPLOMATIC RELATIONS
(Cont'd)

Honduras
Hungary [1]
Iceland
India
Indonesia
Iran
Iraq [2]
Ireland [1]
Israel
Italy
Jamaica
Japan [1]
Jordan
Kazakhstan
Kenya
Kiribati
Korea, Dem. People's Rep.
Korea, Rep.
Kuwait [1,2]
Kyrgyz Rep.
Laos
Latvia
Lebanon
Lesotho
Liberia
Libya [2]
Liechtenstein
Lithuania
Luxembourg [1]
Madagascar
Malawi
Malaysia
Mali
Malta [1,2]
Marshall Is.
Mauritania
Mauritius
Mexico
Micronesia
Moldova
Mongolia [1,2]
Morocco [2]
Mozambique
Namibia
Nauru
Nepal [2]
Netherlands [1,7]
New Zealand [1]
Nicaragua
Niger
Nigeria
Norway
Oman [1]
Pakistan
Panama
Papua New Guinea
Paraguay
Peru
Philippines
Poland [1]
Portugal
Qatar [2]
Romania [1]
Russian Fed. [1,2]
Rwanda
St. Lucia
St. Vincent & the Grenadines
San Marino
Sao Tome & Principe

Saudia Arabia [2]
Senegal
Seychelles
Sierra Leone
Slovak Rep. [1]
Slovenia
Somalia
South Africa
Spain
Sri Lanka
Sudan [2]
Suriname
Swaziland
Sweden
Switzerland
Syrian Arab Rep. [2]
Tajikistan
Tanzania [1]
Thailand
Togo
Tonga [1]
Trinidad & Tobago
Tunisia
Turkey
Turkmenistan
Tuvalu
Uganda
Ukraine [1,2]
United Arab Emirates [1]
United Kingdom [1]
United States
Uruguay
Uzbekistan
Venezuela [2]
Vietnam, Socialist Rep. [2]
Western Samoa
Yemen (Aden) [1,2,8]
Yemen (Sanaa) [2,8]
Yugoslavia [9]
Zambia
Zimbabwe

NOTES:
[1] With statement(s).
[2] With reservation(s).
[3] The Taiwan authorities have also adhered to this convention. See note under CHINA (Taiwan) in the bilateral section.
[4] Applicable to Hong Kong and Macao. See note under CHINA in bilateral section.
[5] See note under ETHIOPIA in bilateral section.
[6] See note under GERMANY, FEDERAL REPUBLIC OF in bilateral section.
[7] Applicable to Netherlands Antilles and Aruba.
[8] See note under YEMEN in bilateral section.
[9] See note under YUGOSLAVIA in bilateral section.

Optional protocol to the Vienna convention on diplomatic relations concerning the compulsory settlement of disputes. Done at Vienna April 18, 1961; entered into force April 24, 1964; for the United States December 13, 1972.
23 UST 3374; TIAS 7502; 500 UNTS 241.
States which are parties:
Australia
Austria
Bahamas, The
Belgium
Bosnia-Herzegovina
Botswana
Bulgaria

Cambodia
Central African Rep.
Congo, Dem. Rep.
Costa Rica
Denmark
Dominican Rep.
Ecuador
Estonia
Fiji
Finland
Former Yugoslav Republic of Macedonia[1]
France
Gabon
Germany, Fed. Rep. [2]
Guinea
Hungary
Iceland
India
Iran
Iraq
Italy
Japan
Kenya
Korea
Kuwait
Laos
Liechtenstein
Luxembourg
Madagascar
Malawi
Malaysia
Malta
Mauritius
Nepal
Netherlands [3]
New Zealand
Nicaragua
Niger
Norway
Oman
Pakistan
Panama
Paraguay
Philippines
Seychelles
Slovak Rep.
Slovenia
Sri Lanka
Suriname
Sweden
Switzerland
Tanzania
United Kingdom
United States
Yugoslavia [4]

NOTES:
[1] With declaration.
[2] See note under GERMANY, FEDERAL REPUBLIC OF in bilateral section.
[3] Applicable to Netherlands Antilles and Aruba.
[4] See note under YUGOSLAVIA in bilateral section.

DISPUTES

(See INVESTMENT DISPUTES; PACIFIC SETTLEMENT OF DISPUTES)

DRUGS

(See HEALTH; NARCOTIC DRUGS)

ECONOMIC AND TECHNICAL COOPERATION AND DEVELOPMENT

Convention on the Organization for Economic Cooperation and Development, with supplementary protocols nos. 1 and 2 and memorandum of understanding on the application of Article 15. Signed at Paris December 14, 1960; entered into force September 30, 1961.
12 UST 1728; TIAS 4891; 888 UNTS 179.
States which are parties:
Australia [1]
Austria
Belgium
Canada
Czech Rep.
Denmark
Finland [1]
France
Germany, Fed. Rep.[2]
Greece
Hungary
Iceland
Ireland
Italy
Japan [1]
Korea
Luxembourg
Mexico
Netherlands
New Zealand [1]
Norway
Poland
Portugal
Slovak Rep.
Spain
Sweden
Switzerland
Turkey
United Kingdom
United States [3]

NOTES:
[1] Not party to memorandum of understanding.
[2] See note under GERMANY, FEDERAL REPUBLIC OF in bilateral section.
[3] With interpretation and explanation.

Agreement for economic and technical assistance to the programs of Central American Integration. Signed at Guatemala October 30, 1965; entered into force September 28, 1967.
18 UST 2770; TIAS 6362.
States which are parties:
Costa Rica
El Salvador
Guatemala
Honduras
Nicaragua
United States

Agreement for the establishment of the International Development Law Institute. Signed at Rome February 5, 1988; entered into force April 28, 1989.
TIAS
Parties:
China
France
Philippines
Sudan
United States

EDUCATION

(See under CULTURAL RELATIONS)

ENDANGERED SPECIES

(See CONSERVATION)

ENERGY

(See also ATOMIC ENERGY)

Agreement concerning the establishment of a coordinating group to direct and coordinate development of international cooperation in the field of energy, and related matters. Communique issued at Washington February 13, 1974; entered into force February 13, 1974.
25 UST 223; TIAS 7791.
Parties:
Belgium
Canada
Denmark
European Community
France [1]
Germany, Fed. Rep.[2]
Ireland
Italy
Japan
Luxembourg
Netherlands
Norway
Organization for Economic Cooperation and Development
United Kingdom
United States

NOTES:
[1] France does not accept point 9 and first three paragraphs of point 10.
[2] See note under GERMANY, FEDERAL REPUBLIC OF in bilateral section.

Memorandum of understanding concerning cooperative information exchange relating to the development of solar heating and cooling systems in buildings. Formulated at Odeillo, France October 1-4, 1974; entered into force July 1, 1975.
26 UST 2932; TIAS 8202.
Parties:
Australia
Belgium
Canada
Denmark

France
Germany, Fed. Rep.[1]
Greece
Israel
Italy
Jamaica
Netherlands
New Zealand
Spain
United Kingdom
United States

NOTE:
[1] See note under GERMANY, FEDERAL REPUBLIC OF in bilateral section.

Agreement on an international energy program, including establishment of the International Energy Agency. Done at Paris November 18, 1974; entered into force provisionally November 18, 1974; definitively January 19, 1976.
27 UST 1685; TIAS 8278.
States which are parties: [1]
Australia
Austria
Belgium
Canada
Denmark
Finland
France
Germany, Fed. Rep.[2][3]
Greece
Hungary
Ireland
Italy
Japan
Luxembourg
Netherlands
New Zealand
Portugal
Spain
Sweden
Switzerland
Turkey
United Kingdom [5]
United States

Amendment:
February 5, 1975 (27 UST 1817; TIAS 8278).

NOTES:
[1] Although not a party to the agreement, Norway participates in the work of the Agency in accordance with an agreement of November 7, 1974 between the Government of Norway and the International Energy Agency.
[2] See note under GERMANY, FEDERAL REPUBLIC OF in bilateral section.
[3] With declaration.
[4] Extended to The Bailiwick of Guernsey and the Isle of Man.

Long-term cooperation program in the field of energy. Done at Paris January 30, 1976; entered into force March 8, 1976.
27 UST 231; TIAS 8229.
States which are parties:
Australia
Austria
Belgium
Canada
Denmark
Germany, Fed. Rep.[1]
Greece
Ireland

ENERGY (Cont'd)

Italy
Japan
Luxembourg
Netherlands
New Zealand
Norway
Portugal
Spain
Sweden
Switzerland
Turkey
United Kingdom
United States

NOTE:
[1] See note under GERMANY, FEDERAL REPUBLIC OF in bilateral section.

Implementing agreement for the establishment of a project on the fluidised combustion of coal, with annexes. Done at Paris November 20, 1975; entered into force November 20, 1975.
33 UST 2131; TIAS 10177.
Parties:
Germany, Fed. Rep.[1]
United Kingdom
United States

NOTE:
[1] See note under GERMANY, FEDERAL REPUBLIC OF in bilateral section.

Implementing agreement for the establishment of the economic assessment service for coal, with annex. Done at Paris November 20, 1975; entered into force November 20, 1975.
32 UST 1337; TIAS 9775.
Parties:
Australia
Canada
Denmark
Germany, Fed. Rep.[1]
Ireland
Italy
Japan
Netherlands
Spain
Sweden
United Kingdom
United States

NOTE:
[1] See note under GERMANY, FEDERAL REPUBLIC OF in bilateral section.

Implementing agreement for a program of research and development on energy conservation in buildings and community systems, with annexes. Done at Paris March 16, 1977; entered into force March 16, 1977.
TIAS 10553.
Parties:
Australia
Belgium
Canada
Denmark
Germany, Fed. Rep.[1]
Greece
Italy
Netherlands

New Zealand
Norway
Sweden
Switzerland
Turkey
United Kingdom
United States

NOTE:
[1] See note under GERMANY, FEDERAL REPUBLIC OF in bilateral section.

Implementing agreement for a program of research and development on energy conservation in heat transfer and heat exchangers, with annexes. Done at Paris June 28, 1977; entered into force June 28, 1977.
TIAS
Parties:
Sweden
Switzerland
United Kingdom
United States

Implementing agreement for a program of research and development on man-made geothermal energy systems, with annex. Done at Paris October 6, 1977; entered into force October 6, 1977.
33 UST 2157; TIAS 10178.
Parties:
Germany, Fed. Rep.[1]
Japan
Sweden
Switzerland
United Kingdom
United States

NOTE:
[1] See note under GERMANY, FEDERAL REPUBLIC OF in bilateral section.

Implementing agreement for a program of research and development of plasma wall interaction in textor, with annex. Done at Paris October 6, 1977; entered into force October 6, 1977.
33 UST 2181; TIAS 10179.
Parties:
Canada
European   Atomic   Energy   Community   (EURATOM)
Japan
Turkey
United States

Implementing agreement for a program of research and development on superconducting magnets for fusion power, with annex. Done at Paris October 6, 1977; entered into force October 6, 1977.
33 UST 2201; TIAS 10180.
Parties:
European   Atomic   Energy   Community   (EURATOM)
Japan
Switzerland
United States

Implementing agreement for a program of research and development on the production of hydrogen from water, with annexes. Done at Paris October 6, 1977; entered into force October 6, 1977.
TIAS

Parties:
Belgium
Canada
Commission of the European Communities
Germany, Fed. Rep.[1]
Italy
Japan
Netherlands
Sweden
Switzerland
United Kingdom
United States

NOTE:
[1] See note under GERMANY, FEDERAL REPUBLIC OF in bilateral section.

Implementing agreement for the establishment of a project on small solar power systems, with annexes. Done at Paris October 6, 1977; entered into force October 6, 1977.
TIAS
Parties:
Austria
Belgium
Germany, Fed. Rep.[1]
Greece
Italy
Spain
Sweden
Switzerland
United Kingdom
United States

NOTE:
[1] See note under GERMANY, FEDERAL REPUBLIC OF in bilateral section.

Supplement to the implementing agreement of October 6, 1977 for the establishment of a project on small solar power systems, with annex. Done at Paris May 22, 1979; entered into force May 22, 1979.
TIAS
Parties:
Belgium
Germany, Fed. Rep.[1]
Greece
Italy
Spain
Sweden
United States

NOTE:
[1] See note under GERMANY, FEDERAL REPUBLIC OF in bilateral section.

Implementing agreement for a program of research and development on wind energy conversion systems, with annexes. Done at Paris October 6, 1977; entered into force October 6, 1977.
TIAS
Parties:
Canada
Denmark
Germany, Fed. Rep.[1]
Ireland
Japan
Netherlands
New Zealand
Norway
Sweden
United Kingdom
United States

ENERGY (Cont'd)

NOTE:
[1] See note under GERMANY, FEDERAL REPUBLIC OF in bilateral section.

Implementing agreement for cooperation in the development of large scale wind energy conversion systems. Done at Paris October 6, 1977; entered into force October 6, 1977.
TIAS
Parties:
Denmark
Germany, Fed. Rep.[1]
Sweden
United States

NOTE:
[1] See note under GERMANY, FEDERAL REPUBLIC OF in bilateral section.

Implementing agreement for the establishment of a project on the treatment of coal gasifier effluent liquors, with annexes. Done at Paris October 17, 1977; entered into force October 17, 1977, effective October 1, 1976.
33 UST 2229; TIAS 10181.
Parties:
Netherlands
United Kingdom
United States

Implementing agreement for a program of research and development on wave power, with annex. Done at Tokyo April 13, 1978; entered into force April 13, 1978.
33 UST 2253; TIAS 10182.
Parties:
Canada
Ireland
Japan
United Kingdom
United States

Implementing agreement for a program of research, development and demonstration on forestry energy, with annex. Done at Tokyo April 13, 1978; entered into force April 13, 1978.
TIAS
Parties:
Belgium
Canada
Denmark
Ireland
New Zealand
Norway
Sweden
Switzerland
United Kingdom
United States

Implementing agreement for the establishment of the biomass conversion technical information service. Done at Paris May 24, 1978; entered into force May 24, 1978.
TIAS
Parties:
Belgium
Canada
Commission of the European Communities
Germany, Fed. Rep.[1]
Ireland
Italy

Japan
New Zealand
Sweden
United Kingdom
United States

NOTE:
[1] See note under GERMANY, FEDERAL REPUBLIC OF in bilateral section.

Implementing agreement for a program of research and development on advanced heat pump systems, with annex. Done at Paris July 27, 1978; entered into force July 27, 1978.
33 UST 2279; TIAS 10183.
Parties:
Belgium
Canada
Denmark
Germany, Fed. Rep.[1]
Italy
Japan
Netherlands
Spain
Sweden
United Kingdom
United States

NOTE:
[1] See note under GERMANY, FEDERAL REPUBLIC OF in bilateral section.

Implementing agreement for a program of research and development for energy conservation in cement manufacture, with annex. Done at Paris July 27, 1978; entered into force July 27, 1978.
33 UST 2305; TIAS 10184.
Parties:
Germany, Fed. Rep.[1]
New Zealand
Sweden
United Kingdom
United States

NOTE:
[1] See note under GERMANY, FEDERAL REPUBLIC OF in bilateral section.

Implementing agreement for a program of research and development on energy conservation through energy storage, with annex. Done at Paris September 22, 1978; entered into force September 22, 1978; for the United States February 21, 1979.
33 UST 2325; TIAS 10185.
Parties:
Belgium
Commission of the European Communities
Denmark
Germany, Fed. Rep.[1]
Netherlands
Sweden
United States [2]

NOTES:
[1] See note under GERMANY, FEDERAL REPUBLIC OF in bilateral section.
[2] With an understanding.

Implementing agreement for a program of research, development and demonstration on geothermal equipment. Done at Paris May 22, 1979; entered into force May 22, 1979.
33 UST 2359; TIAS 10186.

Parties:
Italy
Mexico
New Zealand
United States

Implementing agreement for a program of research, development and demonstration on enhanced recovery of oil, with annex. Done at Paris May 22, 1979; entered into force May 22, 1979.
TIAS
Parties:
Austria
Canada
Germany, Fed. Rep.[1]
Japan
Norway
United Kingdom
United States

NOTE:
[1] See note under GERMANY, FEDERAL REPUBLIC OF in bilateral section.

Implementing agreement for a program of research and development on high temperature materials for automotive engines, with annex. Done at Paris May 22, 1979; entered into force May 22, 1979.
33 UST 2383; TIAS 10187.
Parties:
Germany, Fed. Rep.[1]
United States

NOTE:
[1] See note under GERMANY, FEDERAL REPUBLIC OF in bilateral section.

Implementing agreement for a program of research, development, and demonstration on hot dry rock technology, with annex. Done at Paris September 18, 1979; entered into force October 1, 1979.
33 UST 2408; TIAS 10188.
Parties:
Germany, Fed. Rep.[1]
Japan
United States

Extension:
September 19, 1983.

NOTE:
[1] See note under GERMANY, FEDERAL REPUBLIC OF in bilateral section.

Implementing agreement for the establishment of a project on control of nitrogen oxides emissions during coal combustion, with annexes. Done at Paris March 21, 1980; entered into force March 21, 1980.
32 UST 5725; TIAS 10014.
Parties:
Canada
Denmark
Sweden
United States

Implementing agreement for a program of research and development on radiation damage in fusion materials, with annexes. Done at Paris October 21, 1980; entered into force October 21, 1980.
TIAS

ENERGY (Cont'd)

Parties:
Canada
European Atomic Energy Community
Japan
Switzerland
United States

Implementing agreement for a program of energy technology systems analysis, with annex. Done at Paris November 13, 1980; entered into force November 13, 1980.
TIAS
Parties:
Australia
Belgium
Commission of the European Communities
Denmark
Germany, Fed. Rep.[1]
Italy
Norway
Sweden
Switzerland
United States

NOTE:
[1] See note under GERMANY, FEDERAL REPUBLIC OF in bilateral section.

Implementing agreement for a program of research and development and demonstration on energy conservation in the pulp and paper industry, with annexes. Done at Paris February 18, 1981; entered into force February 18, 1981.
TIAS 10525.
Parties:
Belgium
Canada
Japan
Netherlands
Norway
Spain
Sweden
United Kingdom
United States

Implementing agreement for a program of research, development and demonstration on coal/oil mixtures. Done at Paris March 23, 1981; entered into force March 23, 1981.
TIAS
Parties:
Canada
Japan
Netherlands
Spain
Sweden
United States

Memorandum of understanding concerning the exchange of energy-related information. Done July 27-September 24, 1987; entered into force September 24, 1987.
TIAS
Parties:
Denmark
Finland
Norway
Sweden
United States

ENVIRONMENT

United Nations framework convention on climate change, with annexes. Done at New York May 9, 1992; entered into force March 21, 1994.
TIAS
Parties:
Albania
Algeria
Angola
Antigua & Barbuda
Argentina
Armenia
Australia
Austria
Azerbaijan
Bahamas
Bahrain
Bangladesh
Barbados
Belarus
Belgium
Belize
Benin
Bhutan
Bolivia
Bosnia-Herzegovina
Botswana
Brazil
Bulgaria[1]
Burkina Faso
Burma
Burundi
Cambodia
Cameroon
Canada
Cape Verde
Central African Rep.
Chad
Chile
China[2]
Colombia
Comoros
Congo
Congo, Dem. Rep.
Cook Is.
Costa Rica
Cote d'Ivoire
Croatia[1]
Cuba[1]
Cyprus
Czech Rep.
Denmark
Djibouti
Dominica
Dominican Rep.
Ecuador
Egypt
El Salvador
Equatorial Guinea
Eritrea
Estonia
Ethiopia
European Economic Community[1]
Fiji
Finland
Former Yugoslav Republic of Macedonia
France
Gabon
Gambia
Georgia
Germany

Ghana
Greece
Grenada
Guatemala
Guinea
Guinea-Bissau
Guyana
Haiti
Honduras
Hungary[1]
Iceland
India
Indonesia
Iran
Ireland
Israel
Italy
Jamaica
Japan
Jordan
Kazakhstan
Kenya
Kiribati
Korea, Dem. People's Rep.
Korea, Rep.
Kuwait
Kyrgyz Rep.
Laos
Latvia
Lebanon
Lesotho
Libya
Liechtenstein
Lithuania
Luxembourg
Madagascar
Malawi
Malaysia
Maldives
Mali
Malta
Marshall Is.
Mauritania
Mauritius
Mexico
Micronesia
Moldova
Monaco[1]
Mongolia
Morocco
Mozambique
Namibia
Nauru
Nepal
Netherlands[3]
New Zealand
Nicaragua
Niger
Nigeria
Niue
Norway
Oman
Pakistan
Palau
Panama
Papua New Guinea[1]
Paraguay
Peru
Philippines
Poland
Portugal
Qatar
Romania
Russian Fed.
Rwanda

ENVIRONMENT (Cont'd)

St. Kitts & Nevis
St. Lucia
St. Vincent & the Grenadines
Samoa
San Marino
Sao Tome & Principe
Saudi Arabia
Senegal
Seychelles
Sierra Leone
Singapore
Slovak Rep.
Slovenia
Solomon Is. [1]
South Africa
Spain
Sri Lanka
Sudan
Suriname
Swaziland
Sweden
Switzerland
Syria
Tajikistan
Tanzania
Thailand
Togo
Tonga
Trinidad & Tobago
Tunisia
Turkmenistan
Tuvalu
Uganda
Ukraine
United Arab Emirates
United Kingdom [4]
United States
Uruguay
Uzbekistan
Vanuatu
Venezuela
Vietnam
Yemen
Yugoslavia
Zambia
Zimbabwe

Amendment:
December 11, 1997.

NOTES:
[1] With declaration(s).
[2] Applicable to Macao. See note under CHINA in bilateral section.
[3] For the Kingdom in Europe.
[4] Applicable to Bailiwick of Jersey and Isle of Man.

Agreement establishing the Inter-American Institute for Global Change Research. Done at Montevideo May 13, 1992; entered into force March 12, 1994.
TIAS
Parties:
Argentina
Brazil
Canada
Chile
Colombia
Costa Rica
Cuba

Dominican Rep.
Ecuador
Guatemala
Jamaica
Mexico
Panama
Paraguay
Peru
United States
Uruguay
Venezuela

North American agreement on environmental cooperation, with annexes. Signed at Mexico, Washington and Ottawa September 8, 9, 12 and 14, 1993; entered into force January 1, 1994.
TIAS
Parties:
Canada
Mexico
United States

ENVIRONMENTAL MODIFICATION

Convention on the prohibition of military or any other hostile use of environmental modification techniques, with annex. Done at Geneva May 18, 1977; entered into force October 5, 1978; for the United States January 17, 1980.
31 UST 333; TIAS 9614.
States which are parties:
Afghanistan
Algeria
Antigua & Barbuda
Argentina [1]
Australia
Austria
Bangladesh
Belarus
Belgium
Benin
Brazil
Brunei [2]
Bulgaria
Canada
Cape Verde
Chile
Costa Rica
Cuba
Cyprus
Czech Rep.
Denmark
Dominica
Egypt
Finland
German Dem. Rep. [3]
Germany, Fed. Rep. [3]
Ghana
Greece
Guatemala [4]
Hungary
India
Ireland
Italy
Japan
Korea, Dem. People's Rep.
Korea, Rep.
Kuwait
Laos

Malawi
Mauritius
Mongolia
Netherlands [5]
New Zealand [6]
Niger
Norway
Pakistan
Papua New Guinea
Poland
Romania
Russian Fed.
St. Kitts & Nevis [2]
St. Lucia
St. Vincent & the Grenadines
Sao Tome & Principe
Slovak Rep.
Solomon Is.
Spain
Sri Lanka
Sweden
Switzerland [4]
Tajikistan
Tunisia
Ukraine
Union of Soviet Socialist Reps. [7]
United Kingdom [8]
United States
Uruguay
Uzbekistan
Vietnam, Socialist Rep.
Yemen (Aden) [9]
Yemen (Sanaa) [9]

NOTES:
[1] With declaration.
[2] See under country heading in the bilateral section for information concerning acceptance of treaty obligations.
[3] See note under GERMANY, FEDERAL REPUBLIC OF in bilateral section.
[4] With reservation(s).
[5] Applicable to the Netherlands Antilles and Aruba.
[6] Extended to Cook Is. and Niue.
[7] See note under UNION OF SOVIET SOCIALIST REPUBLICS in bilateral section.
[8] Extended to Anguilla, Sovereign Base Areas of Akrotiri and Dhekelia in the Island of Cyprus and territories under the territorial sovereignty of the United Kingdom.
[9] See note under YEMEN in bilateral section.

EPIZOOTICS

(See under AGRICULTURE)

EUROPEAN COLONIES AND POSSESSIONS

(See under DEFENSE)

EVIDENCE

(See under JUDICIAL PROCEDURE)

EXHIBITIONS AND EXPOSITIONS

(See under CULTURAL RELATIONS)

EXTRADITION

Convention on extradition.[1] Signed at Montevideo December 26, 1933; entered into force January 25, 1935.
49 Stat. 3111; TS 882; 3 Bevans 152; 165 LNTS 45.
States which are parties:
Argentina
Chile [2]
Colombia
Dominican Rep.
Ecuador [2]
El Salvador [2]
Guatemala
Honduras [2]
Mexico [2]
Nicaragua
Panama
United States [2]

NOTES:
[1] Article 21 provides that the convention "does not abrogate or modify the bilateral or collective treaties, which at the present date are in force between the signatory States. Nevertheless, if any of said treaties lapse, the present Convention will take effect and become applicable immediately among the respective States . . . ." The United States has bilateral extradition treaties with each of the other parties which antedate the convention, except for those with Argentina, Colombia and Mexico.
[2] With reservation.

FINANCE

(See also FINANCIAL INSTITUTIONS; INVESTMENT DISPUTES; REPARATIONS)

North American framework agreement between the United States Treasury, the Banco de Mexico/Government of Mexico and the Bank of Canada. Signed at Mexico April 22 and 26, 1994; entered into force April 26, 1994.
TIAS
Parties:
Canada
Mexico
United States

WORLD WAR II RELATED AGREEMENTS

Accord relating to the liquidation of German property in Switzerland. Exchange of notes at Washington May 25, 1946; entered into force June 27, 1946.
13 UST 1118; TIAS 5058.
States which are parties:
France
Switzerland
United Kingdom
United States

Agreement concerning German property in Switzerland, with related notes. Signed at Bern August 28, 1952; entered into force March 19, 1953.
13 UST 1131; TIAS 5059; 175 UNTS 69.
States which are parties:
France
Switzerland
United Kingdom
United States

Agreement relating to German assets in Sweden. Exchanges of letters at Washington July 18, 1946; entered into force March 28, 1947.
61 Stat. 3191; TIAS 1657; 4 Bevans 88; 125 UNTS 119.
States which are parties:
France
Sweden
United Kingdom
United States

Memorandum of understanding regarding German assets in Italy. Signed at Washington August 14, 1947; entered into force August 14, 1947.
61 Stat. 3292; TIAS 1664; 4 Bevans 552; 138 UNTS 111.
States which are parties:
France
Italy
United Kingdom
United States

Memorandum of understanding regarding German assets in Italy, with exchange of notes. Signed at Rome March 29, 1957; entered into force March 29, 1957.
8 UST 445; TIAS 3797; 283 UNTS 137.
States which are parties:
France
Italy
United Kingdom
United States

Protocol relating to the transfer to the Italian Government of gold captured by the Allied military forces at Fortezza. Signed at London October 10, 1947; effective September 15, 1947.
61 Stat. 3239; TIAS 1658; 4 Bevans 637; 54 UNTS 193.
States which are parties:
Italy
United Kingdom
United States

Agreement relating to the resolution of conflicting claims to German enemy assets. Done at Brussels December 5, 1947; entered into force for the United States January 24, 1951.
2 UST 729; TIAS 2230.
States which are parties:
Belgium
Canada
Cuba

Denmark
Haiti
Honduras
Luxembourg
Netherlands
Nicaragua
United States [1]

Extensions and amendments:
February 3, 1949 (2 UST 785; TIAS 2230).
May 10, 1950 (2 UST 791; TIAS 2230).
January 24, 1951 (2 UST 795; TIAS 2230).
April 30, 1952 (3 UST 4254; TIAS 2569).

NOTE:
[1] With reservation.

Protocol terminating obligations arising from the accord of May 10, 1948 (62 Stat. 2061; TIAS 1773) regarding German assets in Spain, with exchange of notes. Signed at Madrid August 9, 1958; entered into force July 2, 1959.
11 UST 2274; TIAS 4606; 351 UNTS 398.
States which are parties:
France
Spain
United Kingdom
United States

Agreement relating to the restitution of gold looted by Germany and transferred to the Bank for International Settlements. Effected by exchanges of letters at Washington May 13, 1948, between the Chairman of the Bank for International Settlements and representatives of the United States, United Kingdom, and France; entered into force May 13, 1948.
62 Stat. 2672; TIAS 1805; 4 Bevans 754; 140 UNTS 187.

Agreement relating to prewar external debts of the German Reich and the debt arising out of economic assistance furnished since May 8, 1945. Exchange of letters at Bonn March 6, 1951; entered into force March 6, 1951.
2 UST 1249; TIAS 2274; 106 UNTS 141.
States which are parties:
France
Germany, Fed. Rep.[1]
United Kingdom
United States

NOTE:
[1] See note under GERMANY, FEDERAL REPUBLIC OF in bilateral section.

Agreement for the submission to an arbitrator of certain claims with respect to gold looted by the Germans from Rome in 1943. Signed at Washington April 25, 1951; entered into force April 25, 1951.
2 UST 991; TIAS 2252; 91 UNTS 21; 100 UNTS 304.
States which are parties:
France
United Kingdom
United States

Agreement on German external debts. Signed at London February 27, 1953; entered into force September 16, 1953.
4 UST 443; TIAS 2792; 333 UNTS 3.
States which are parties:
Argentina
Australia [1]

FINANCE (Cont'd)

Austria
Belgium
Cambodia
Canada
Chile
Denmark
Egypt
Finland
France [2]
Germany, Fed. Rep. [3]
Greece
Iran
Ireland
Israel
Italy
Liechtenstein
Luxembourg
Malta [4]
Morocco [4]
Nauru [4]
Netherlands [5]
New Zealand [6]
Norway
Pakistan
Papua New Guinea [4]
Peru
South Africa [7]
Spain
Sri Lanka
Suriname [4]
Sweden
Switzerland [8]
Syrian Arab Rep.
Tanzania [4]
Thailand
Tunisia [4]
United Kingdom [9]
United States [10]
Western Samoa [4]
Yugoslavia [11]
Zambia [4]
Zimbabwe [4]

NOTES:
[1] Extended to Norfolk Is.
[2] Extended to all French overseas territories.
[3] See note under GERMANY, FEDERAL REPUBLIC OF in bilateral section.
[4] See under country heading in the bilateral section for information concerning acceptance of treaty obligations.
[5] Applicable to Netherlands Antilles and Aruba.
[6] Extended to Cook Is., including Niue, and Tokelau Is.
[7] Extended to Namibia.
[8] With a statement.
[9] Extended to Channel Is., Falkland Is., and Gibraltar.
[10] Extended to all territories for the international relations of which the United States is responsible.
[11] See note under YUGOSLAVIA in bilateral section.

Letter-agreement relating to restitution and liquidation of confiscated property recovered in Italy from German forces ("Rome Treasure"). Letter of April 27, 1954, from Administrator, Paris Reparation Refugee Fund, to the American Ambassador, Rome, accepted by the

United States, the United Kingdom, and Italy on July 23, 1954; entered into force July 23, 1954.
5 UST 2170; TIAS 3080.

Administrative agreement concerning the Arbitral Tribunal and the Mixed Commission under the agreement on German external debts, with annex and exchange of letters. Signed at Bonn December 1, 1954; entered into force December 1, 1954.
6 UST 865; TIAS 3233; 210 UNTS 197.
States which are parties:
France
Germany, Fed. Rep. [1]
United Kingdom
United States

Amendments:
November 30, 1956 (7 UST 3442; TIAS 3717; 265 UNTS 380).
August 29, 1960 (11 UST 2324; TIAS 4609; 385 UNTS 378).
June 26, 1969 (20 UST 2867; TIAS 6762).

NOTE:
[1] See note under GERMANY, FEDERAL REPUBLIC OF in bilateral section.

Agreement relating to external debts of the City of Berlin and of public utility enterprises owned or controlled by Berlin. Exchange of notes at Bonn between the United States and the Federal Republic of Germany February 29 and March 2, 1956, with related notes of August 13 and 29, 1955; entered into force March 2, 1956.[1]
7 UST 635; TIAS 3545; 273 UNTS 209.

NOTE:
[1] Notes were exchanged *mutatis mutandis* by the Federal Republic of Germany with France and the United Kingdom.

Memorandum agreement relating to the disposition of certain German assets in Thailand. Signed at Bangkok January 31, 1957; entered into force January 31, 1957.
8 UST 129; TIAS 3747; 278 UNTS 105.
States which are parties:
France
Thailand
United Kingdom
United States

Agreement relating to the disposition of certain accounts in Thailand under article 16 of the treaty of peace with Japan. Signed at Washington July 30, 1953; entered into force July 30, 1953.
4 UST 1778; TIAS 2844; 215 UNTS 97.
States which are parties:
Thailand
United Kingdom
United States

Agreement relating to German assets in Portugal and to certain claims regarding monetary gold. Signed at Lisbon October 27, 1958; entered into force October 24, 1959.
351 UNTS 303.
States which are parties:
France
Portugal

United Kingdom
United States

MULTILATERAL FUNDS

Indus Basin Development Fund agreement, with annexes. Done at Karachi September 19, 1960; entered into force January 12, 1961; effective from April 1, 1960.
12 UST 19; TIAS 4671; 444 UNTS 259.

Supplemental agreement, 1964. Done at Washington March 31, 1964; entered into force April 6, 1964.
15 UST 396; TIAS 5570; 503 UNTS 388.
Parties:
Australia
Canada
Germany, Fed. Rep. [1]
International Bank for Reconstruction and Development
New Zealand
Pakistan
United Kingdom
United States

NOTE:
[1] See note under GERMANY, FEDERAL REPUBLIC OF in bilateral section.

Tarbela Development Fund agreement. Done at Washington May 2, 1968; entered into force May 2, 1968.
19 UST 4866; TIAS 6492; 637 UNTS 4.

Supplemental agreement, 1975. Done at Washington August 15, 1975; entered into force August 15, 1975.
26 UST 2751; TIAS 8193.
Parties:
Canada
France [1]
International Bank for Reconstruction and Development
International Development Association [2]
Italy
Pakistan
United Kingdom
United States

NOTES:
[1] Not a party to the supplemental agreement.
[2] Party to the supplemental agreement only.

Agreement establishing the African Development Fund, with schedules. Done at Abidjan November 29, 1972; entered into force June 30, 1973; for the United States November 18, 1976.
28 UST 4547; TIAS 8605.
Parties:
African Development Bank
Argentina
Austria
Belgium
Brazil
Canada
Denmark [1]
Finland
France
Germany, Fed. Rep. [2]

FINANCE (Cont'd)

Italy
Japan
Korea, Rep.
Kuwait
Netherlands
Norway [1]
Saudi Arabia
Spain
Sweden [1]
Switzerland
United Arab Emirates
United Kingdom
United States [1]
Yugoslavia [3]

NOTES:
 [1] With declaration.
 [2] See note under GERMANY, FEDERAL REPUBLIC OF in bilateral section.
 [3] See note under YUGOSLAVIA in bilateral section.

Agreement establishing the International Fund for Agricultural Development. Done at Rome June 13, 1976; entered into force November 30, 1977.
28 UST 8435; TIAS 8765.
States which are parties:
Afghanistan
Albania
Algeria
Angola
Antigua & Barbuda
Argentina
Armenia
Australia
Austria
Azerbaijan
Bangladesh
Barbados
Belgium
Belize
Benin
Bhutan
Bolivia
Bosnia-Herzegovina
Botswana
Brazil
Burkina Faso
Burma
Burundi
Cambodia
Cameroon
Canada
Cape Verde
Central African Rep.
Chad
Chile
China
Colombia
Comoros
Congo
Congo, Dem. Rep.
Cook Is.
Costa Rica
Cote d'Ivoire
Croatia
Cuba [1] [2]
Cyprus
Denmark
Djibouti

Dominica
Dominican Rep.
Ecuador
Egypt
El Salvador
Equatorial Guinea
Eritrea
Ethiopia [3]
Fiji
Finland
Former Yugoslav Republic of Macedonia
France [2]
Gabon
Gambia, The
Georgia
Germany, Fed. Rep.[4]
Ghana
Greece
Grenada
Guatemala
Guinea
Guinea-Bissau
Guyana
Haiti
Honduras
India
Indonesia
Iran
Iraq
Ireland
Israel
Italy
Jamaica
Japan
Jordan
Kazakhstan
Kenya
Korea, Dem. People's Rep.
Korea, Rep.
Kuwait
Kyrgyz Rep.
Laos
Lebanon
Lesotho
Liberia
Libya
Luxembourg
Madagascar
Malawi
Malaysia
Maldives
Mali
Malta
Mauritania
Mauritius
Mexico
Moldova
Mongolia
Morocco
Mozambique
Namibia
Nepal
Netherlands [5]
New Zealand
Nicaragua
Niger
Nigeria
Norway
Oman
Pakistan
Panama
Papua New Guinea
Paraguay
Peru
Philippines

Portugal
Qatar
Romania [1] [2]
Rwanda
St. Kitts & Nevis
St. Lucia
St. Vincent & the Grenadines
Sao Tome & Principe
Saudi Arabia
Senegal
Seychelles
Sierra Leone
Solomon Is.
Somalia
South Africa
Spain [1]
Sri Lanka
Sudan
Suriname
Swaziland
Sweden
Switzerland
Syrian Arab Rep.
Tajikistan
Tanzania
Thailand
Togo
Tonga
Trinidad & Tobago
Tunisia
Turkey
Uganda
United Arab Emirates
United Kingdom [1]
United States
Uruguay
Venezuela [2]
Vietnam, Socialist Rep.
Western Samoa
Yemen (Aden) [6]
Yemen (Sanaa) [6]
Yugoslavia [7]
Zambia
Zimbabwe

Amendment:
December 11, 1986 (TIAS 12068).

NOTES:
 [1] With statement.
 [2] With reservation.
 [3] See note under ETHIOPIA in bilateral section.
 [4] See note under GERMANY, FEDERAL REPUBLIC OF in bilateral section.
 [5] Applicable to Netherlands Antilles and Aruba.
 [6] See note under YEMEN in bilateral section.
 [7] See note under YUGOSLAVIA in bilateral section.

Agreement concerning the international fund for Ireland, with annexes. Done at Washington September 26, 1986; entered into force September 26, 1986.
TIAS 11401.
Parties:
Ireland
United Kingdom
United States

FINANCIAL INSTITUTIONS

(See also FINANCE)

Articles of agreement of the International Monetary Fund, formulated at the Bretton Woods Conference July 1–22, 1944.[1] Opened for signature at Washington December 27, 1945; entered into force December 27, 1945.
60 Stat. 1401; TIAS 1501; 3 Bevans 1351; 2 UNTS 39.
States which are parties:
Afghanistan
Albania
Algeria
Angola
Antigua & Barbuda
Argentina
Armenia
Australia
Austria
Azerbaijan
Bahamas, The
Bahrain
Bangladesh
Barbados
Belarus
Belgium
Belize
Benin
Bhutan
Bolivia
Botswana
Brazil
Brunei
Bulgaria
Burkina Faso
Burma
Burundi
Cambodia
Cameroon
Canada
Cape Verde
Central African Rep.
Chad
Chile
China [2]
Colombia
Comoros
Congo
Congo, Dem. Rep.
Costa Rica
Cote d'Ivoire
Cyprus
Czechoslovakia [3]
Denmark
Djibouti
Dominica
Dominican Rep.
Ecuador
Egypt
El Salvador
Equatorial Guinea
Eritrea
Estonia
Ethiopia [4]
Fiji
Finland
France
Gabon
Gambia, The

Georgia
Germany, Fed. Rep. [5]
Ghana
Greece
Grenada
Guatemala
Guinea
Guinea-Bissau
Guyana
Haiti
Honduras
Hungary
Iceland
India
Indonesia
Iran
Iraq
Ireland
Israel
Italy
Jamaica
Japan
Jordan
Kazakhstan
Kenya
Kiribati
Korea
Kuwait
Kyrgyz Rep.
Laos
Latvia
Lebanon
Lesotho
Liberia
Libya
Lithuania
Luxembourg
Madagascar
Malawi
Malaysia
Maldives
Mali
Malta
Marshall Is.
Mauritania
Mauritius
Mexico
Micronesia
Moldova
Mongolia
Morocco
Mozambique
Namibia
Nepal
Netherlands
New Zealand
Nicaragua
Niger
Nigeria
Norway
Oman
Pakistan
Palau
Panama
Papua New Guinea
Paraguay
Peru
Philippines
Poland
Portugal
Qatar
Romania
Russian Fed.
Rwanda
St. Kitts & Nevis

St. Lucia
St. Vincent & the Grenadines
San Marino
Sao Tome & Principe
Saudi Arabia
Senegal
Seychelles
Sierra Leone
Singapore
Solomon Is.
Somalia
South Africa
Spain
Sri Lanka
Sudan
Suriname
Swaziland
Sweden
Switzerland
Syrian Arab Rep.
Tajikistan
Tanzania
Thailand
Togo
Tonga
Trinidad & Tobago
Tunisia
Turkey
Turkmenistan
Uganda
Ukraine
United Arab Emirates
United Kingdom
United States
Uruguay
Uzbekistan
Vanuatu
Venezuela
Vietnam, Socialist Rep.
Western Samoa
Yemen (Aden) [6]
Yemen (Sanaa) [6]
Yugoslavia [7]
Zambia
Zimbabwe

Amendments:
May 31, 1968 (20 UST 2775; TIAS 6748).
April 30, 1976 (29 UST 2203; TIAS 8937).
June 28, 1990 (TIAS 11898).

NOTES:
[1] Applicable to all territories.
[2] Applicable to Hong Kong and Macao. See note under CHINA in bilateral section.
[3] See note under CZECHOSLOVAKIA in bilateral section.
[4] See note under ETHIOPIA in bilateral section.
[5] See note under GERMANY, FEDERAL REPUBLIC OF in bilateral section.
[6] See note under YEMEN in bilateral section.
[7] See note under YUGOSLAVIA in bilateral section.

Articles of agreement of the International Bank for Reconstruction and Development, formulated at the Bretton Woods Conference July 1–22, 1944.[1] Opened for signature at Washington December 27, 1945; entered into force December 27, 1945.
60 Stat. 1440; TIAS 1502; 3 Bevans 1390; 2 UNTS 134.

FINANCIAL INSTITUTIONS (Cont'd)

States which are parties:
Afghanistan
Albania
Algeria
Angola
Antigua & Barbuda
Argentina
Armenia
Australia
Austria
Azerbaijan
Bahamas, The
Bahrain
Bangladesh
Barbados
Belarus
Belgium
Belize
Benin
Bhutan
Bolivia
Bosnia-Herzegovina
Botswana
Brazil
Brunei
Bulgaria
Burkina Faso
Burma
Burundi
Cambodia
Cameroon
Canada
Cape Verde
Central African Rep.
Chad
Chile
China [2]
Colombia
Comoros
Congo
Congo, Dem. Rep.
Costa Rica
Cote d'Ivoire
Croatia
Cyprus
Czech Rep.
Denmark
Djibouti
Dominica
Dominican Rep.
Ecuador
Egypt
El Salvador
Equatorial Guinea
Eritrea
Estonia
Ethiopia [3]
Fiji
Finland
Former Yugoslav Republic of Macedonia
France
Gabon
Gambia, The
Georgia
Germany, Fed. Rep.[4]
Ghana
Greece
Grenada
Guatemala

Guinea
Guinea-Bissau
Guyana
Haiti
Honduras
Hungary
Iceland
India
Indonesia
Iran
Iraq
Ireland
Israel
Italy
Jamaica
Japan
Jordan
Kazakhstan
Kenya
Kiribati
Korea
Kuwait
Kyrgyz Rep.
Laos
Latvia
Lebanon
Lesotho
Liberia
Libya
Lithuania
Luxembourg
Madagascar
Malawi
Malaysia
Maldives
Mali
Malta
Marshall Is.
Mauritania
Mauritius
Mexico
Micronesia
Moldova
Mongolia
Morocco
Mozambique
Namibia
Nepal
Netherlands
New Zealand
Nicaragua
Niger
Nigeria
Norway
Oman
Pakistan
Palau
Panama
Papua New Guinea
Paraguay
Peru
Philippines
Poland
Portugal
Qatar
Romania
Russian Fed.
Rwanda
St. Kitts & Nevis
St. Lucia
St. Vincent & the Grenadines
Sao Tome & Principe
Saudi Arabia
Senegal
Seychelles

Sierra Leone
Singapore
Slovak Rep.
Slovenia
Solomon Is.
Somalia
South Africa
Spain
Sri Lanka
Sudan
Suriname
Swaziland
Sweden
Switzerland
Syrian Arab Rep.
Tajikistan
Tanzania
Thailand
Togo
Tonga
Trinidad & Tobago
Tunisia
Turkey
Turkmenistan
Uganda
Ukraine
United Arab Emirates
United Kingdom
United States
Uruguay
Uzbekistan
Vanuatu
Venezuela
Vietnam, Socialist Rep.
Western Samoa
Yemen (Aden) [5]
Yemen (Sanaa) [5]
Yugoslavia [6]
Zambia
Zimbabwe

Amendment:
August 25, 1965 (16 UST 1942; TIAS 5929).

NOTES:
  [1] Applicable to all territories.
  [2] Applicable to Hong Kong and Macao. See note under CHINA in bilateral section.
  [3] See note under ETHIOPIA in bilateral section.
  [4] See note under GERMANY, FEDERAL REPUBLIC OF in bilateral section.
  [5] See note under YEMEN in bilateral section.
  [6] See note under YUGOSLAVIA in bilateral section.

Articles of agreement of the International Finance Corporation. Done at Washington May 25, 1955; entered into force July 20, 1956. 7 UST 2197; TIAS 3620; 264 UNTS 117.
States which are parties:
Afghanistan
Albania
Algeria
Angola
Antigua & Barbuda
Argentina
Armenia
Australia
Austria
Azerbaijan
Bahamas, The
Bahrain
Bangladesh

FINANCIAL INSTITUTIONS (Cont'd)

Barbados
Belarus
Belgium
Belize
Benin
Bolivia
Bosnia-Herzegovina
Botswana
Brazil
Bulgaria
Burkina Faso
Burma
Burundi
Cambodia
Cameroon
Canada
Cape Verde
Central African Rep.
Chad
Chile
China [1]
Colombia
Comoros
Congo
Congo, Dem. Rep.
Costa Rica
Cote d'Ivoire
Croatia
Cyprus
Czech Rep.
Denmark
Djibouti
Dominica
Dominican Rep.
Ecuador
Egypt
El Salvador
Equatorial Guinea
Eritrea
Estonia
Ethiopia [2]
Fiji
Finland
Former Yugoslav Republic of Macedonia
France
Gabon
Gambia, The
Georgia
Germany, Fed. Rep. [3]
Ghana
Greece
Grenada
Guatemala
Guinea
Guinea-Bissau
Guyana
Haiti
Honduras
Hungary
Iceland
India
Indonesia
Iran
Iraq
Ireland
Israel
Italy
Jamaica
Japan

Jordan
Kazakhstan
Kenya
Kiribati
Korea
Kuwait
Kyrgyz Rep.
Laos
Latvia
Lebanon
Lesotho
Liberia
Libya
Lithuania
Luxembourg
Madagascar
Malawi
Malaysia
Maldives
Mali
Marshall Is.
Mauritania
Mauritius
Mexico
Micronesia
Moldova
Mongolia
Morocco
Mozambique
Namibia
Nepal
Netherlands
New Zealand
Nicaragua
Niger
Nigeria
Norway
Oman
Pakistan
Palau
Panama
Papua New Guinea
Paraguay
Peru
Philippines
Poland
Portugal
Romania
Russian Fed.
Rwanda
St. Kitts & Nevis
St. Lucia
Saudi Arabia
Senegal
Seychelles
Sierra Leone
Singapore
Slovak Rep.
Slovenia
Solomon Is.
Somalia
South Africa
Spain
Sri Lanka
Sudan
Swaziland
Sweden
Switzerland
Syrian Arab Rep.
Tajikistan
Tanzania
Thailand
Togo
Tonga
Trinidad & Tobago

Tunisia
Turkey
Turkmenistan
Uganda
Ukraine
United Arab Emirates
United Kingdom
United States
Uruguay
Uzbekistan
Vanuatu
Venezuela
Vietnam, Socialist Rep.
Western Samoa
Yemen (Sanaa) [4]
Yugoslavia [5]
Zambia
Zimbabwe

Amendments:
September 1, 1961 (12 UST 2945; TIAS 4894; 439 UNTS 318).
August 25, 1965 (24 UST 1760; TIAS 7683).

NOTES:
[1] Applicable to Hong Kong. See note under CHINA in bilateral section.
[2] See note under ETHIOPIA in bilateral section.
[3] See note under GERMANY, FEDERAL REPUBLIC OF in bilateral section.
[4] See note under YEMEN in bilateral section.
[5] See note under YUGOSLAVIA in bilateral section.

Agreement establishing the Inter-American Development Bank, with annexes. Done at Washington April 8, 1959; entered into force December 30, 1959.
10 UST 3029; TIAS 4397; 389 UNTS 69.
States which are parties:
Argentina
Austria
Bahamas
Barbados
Belgium
Belize
Bolivia
Brazil
Canada
Chile
Colombia
Costa Rica
Denmark
Dominican Rep.
Ecuador
El Salvador
Finland
France [1]
Germany, Fed. Rep. [1] [2]
Guatemala
Guyana
Haiti
Honduras
Israel
Italy
Jamaica
Japan
Mexico
Netherlands [3]
Nicaragua
Norway
Panama
Paraguay

FINANCIAL INSTITUTIONS (Cont'd)

Peru
Portugal
Spain
Suriname
Sweden
Switzerland
Trinidad & Tobago
United Kingdom [1]
United States
Uruguay
Venezuela
Yugoslavia [4]

Amendments:
January 28, 1964 (21 UST 1570; TIAS 6920).
March 31, 1968 (19 UST 7381; TIAS 6591).
March 23, 1972 (23 UST 2455; TIAS 7437; 851 UNTS 283).
June 1, 1976 (27 UST 3547; TIAS 8383).
January 27, 1977.

NOTES:
[1] With statements.
[2] See note under GERMANY, FEDERAL REPUBLIC OF in bilateral section.
[3] Applicable to Aruba and Netherlands Antilles.
[4] See note under YUGOSLAVIA in bilateral section.

Articles of agreement of the International Development Association.[1] Done at Washington January 26, 1960; entered into force September 24, 1960.
11 UST 2284; TIAS 4607; 439 UNTS 249.
States which are parties:
Afghanistan
Albania
Algeria
Angola
Argentina
Armenia
Australia
Austria
Azerbaijan
Bangladesh
Barbados
Belgium
Belize
Benin
Bhutan
Bolivia
Bosnia-Herzegovina
Botswana
Brazil
Burkina Faso
Burma
Burundi
Cambodia
Cameroon
Canada
Cape Verde
Central African Rep.
Chad
Chile
China [2]
Colombia
Comoros
Congo

Congo, Dem. Rep.
Costa Rica
Cote d'Ivoire
Croatia
Cyprus
Czech Rep.
Denmark
Djibouti
Dominica
Dominican Rep.
Ecuador
Egypt
El Salvador
Equatorial Guinea
Eritrea
Ethiopia [3]
Fiji
Finland
Former Yugoslav Republic of Macedonia
France
Gabon
Gambia, The
Georgia
Germany, Fed. Rep.[4]
Ghana
Greece
Grenada
Guatemala
Guinea
Guinea-Bissau
Guyana
Haiti
Honduras
Hungary
Iceland
India
Indonesia
Iran
Iraq
Ireland
Israel
Italy
Japan
Jordan
Kazakhstan
Kenya
Kiribati
Korea
Kuwait
Kyrgyz Rep.
Laos
Latvia
Lebanon
Lesotho
Liberia
Libya
Luxembourg
Madagascar
Malawi
Malaysia
Maldives
Mali
Marshall Is.
Mauritania
Mauritius
Mexico
Micronesia
Moldova
Mongolia
Morocco
Mozambique
Nepal
Netherlands
New Zealand
Nicaragua

Niger
Nigeria
Norway
Oman
Pakistan
Palau
Panama
Papua New Guinea
Paraguay
Peru
Philippines
Poland
Portugal
Russian Fed.
Rwanda
St. Kitts & Nevis
St. Lucia
St. Vincent & the Grenadines
Sao Tome & Principe
Saudi Arabia
Senegal
Sierra Leone
Slovak Rep.
Slovenia
Solomon Is.
Somalia
South Africa
Spain
Sri Lanka
Sudan
Swaziland
Sweden
Switzerland
Syrian Arab Rep.
Tajikistan
Tanzania
Thailand
Togo
Tonga
Trinidad & Tobago
Tunisia
Turkey
Uganda
United Arab Emirates
United Kingdom
United States
Uzbekistan
Vanuatu
Vietnam, Socialist Rep.
Western Samoa
Yemen (Aden) [5]
Yemen (Sanaa) [5]
Yugoslavia [6]
Zambia
Zimbabwe

NOTES:
[1] Applicable to all territories.
[2] Applicable to Hong Kong. See note under CHINA in bilateral section.
[3] See note under ETHIOPIA in bilateral section.
[4] See note under GERMANY, FEDERAL REPUBLIC OF in bilateral section.
[5] See note under YEMEN in bilateral section.
[6] See note under YUGOSLAVIA in bilateral section.

Articles of agreement establishing the Asian Development Bank, with annexes. Done at Manila December 4, 1965; entered into force August 22, 1966.
17 UST 1418; TIAS 6103; 571 UNTS 123.

FINANCIAL INSTITUTIONS (Cont'd)

Parties:
Afghanistan
Australia [1] [2]
Austria
Bangladesh
Belgium
Bhutan
Burma
Cambodia
Canada [1]
China [3]
Cook Is.
Denmark [4]
Fiji
Finland
France [1]
Germany, Fed. Rep. [1] [5]
Hong Kong
India [1]
Indonesia
Italy [1]
Japan [1]
Kiribati
Korea [1]
Laos
Malaysia [1]
Maldives
Nepal
Netherlands [1] [6]
New Zealand [1]
Norway [1]
Pakistan
Papua New Guinea
Philippines [1]
Singapore [1]
Solomon Is.
Spain
Sri Lanka [1]
Sweden [4]
Switzerland
Thailand
Tonga
United Kingdom [1] [4]
United States [1]
Uzbekistan
Vanuatu
Vietnam, Socialist Rep.
Western Samoa

NOTES:
[1] With reservation.
[2] With declaration.
[3] Following the accession of the People's Republic of China, the President of the Bank in letter dated March 15, 1986 declared that "the Republic of China" (which had ratified the Bank's articles of agreement on September 22, 1966 and had maintained its membership thereafter) would be "referred to by the Bank as 'Taipei, China'."
[4] With a statement.
[5] See note under GERMANY, FEDERAL REPUBLIC OF in bilateral section.
[6] Extended only to Kingdom in Europe.

Proces-verbal of rectification of the agreement establishing the Asian Development Bank. Signed at New York November 2, 1967.
18 UST 2935; TIAS 6387; 608 UNTS 380.

Agreement amending the agreement establishing the African Development Bank, [1] with annexes. Adopted by the Board of Governors at Abidjan May 17, 1979; [2] entered into force May 7, 1982; for the United States January 31, 1983.
TIAS
States which are parties:
Angola
Argentina
Austria [3]
Belgium [3]
Benin
Botswana
Brazil [3]
Burkina Faso
Burundi
Cameroon
Canada [3] [4]
Cape Verde
Central African Rep.
Chad
China
Comoros
Congo
Congo, Dem. Rep.
Cote d'Ivoire
Denmark [3] [5]
Djibouti
Egypt
Equatorial Guinea
Ethiopia [6]
Finland [3]
France [3]
Gabon
Gambia, The
Germany, Fed Rep. [3] [4] [7]
Ghana
Guinea
Guinea-Bissau
India [3] [4]
Italy [3] [4]
Japan [3] [4]
Kenya
Korea, Rep. [3]
Kuwait [3]
Lesotho
Liberia
Madagascar
Malawi
Mali
Mauritania
Mauritius
Morocco
Mozambique
Namibia
Netherlands [3] [4]
Niger
Nigeria
Norway [3] [4] [5]
Portugal [3]
Rwanda
Sao Tome & Principe
Saudi Arabia [3]
Senegal
Seychelles
Sierra Leone
Somalia
South Africa
Spain [3]
Sudan
Swaziland
Sweden [3] [4] [5]
Switzerland [3] [4]
Tanzania

Togo
Tunisia
Uganda
United Kingdom [3] [4] [5]
United States [3] [4]
Yugoslavia [3] [8]
Zambia
Zimbabwe

NOTES:
[1] The agreement establishing the African Development Bank, done at Khartoum, August 4, 1963, entered into force September 10, 1964 (510 UNTS 3 and 569 UNTS 353 (corr.)).
[2] The amendments to the agreement, which provide for non-regional membership, were adopted at Abidjan by resolution 05–09 of May 17, 1979 of the Board of Governors and concluded at Lusaka on May 7, 1982. Algeria and Libya are parties to the agreement establishing the Bank but not parties to the 1979 amendments.
[3] Non-regional members.
[4] With reservation(s).
[5] With declaration(s).
[6] See note under ETHIOPIA in bilateral section.
[7] See note under GERMANY, FEDERAL REPUBLIC OF in bilateral section.
[8] See note under YUGOSLAVIA in bilateral section.

Agreement establishing the Inter-American Investment Corporation, with annex. Done at Washington November 19, 1984; entered into force March 23, 1986.
TIAS 12087.
States which are parties:
Argentina
Austria
Bahamas
Barbados
Bolivia
Brazil
Chile
Colombia
Costa Rica
Dominican Rep.
Ecuador
El Salvador
France
Germany, Fed. Rep. [1]
Guatemala
Guyana
Haiti
Honduras
Israel
Italy
Jamaica
Japan
Mexico
Netherlands
Nicaragua
Panama
Paraguay
Peru
Spain
Switzerland
Trinidad & Tobago
United States
Uruguay
Venezuela

FINANCIAL
INSTITUTIONS (Cont'd)

NOTE:

[1] See note under GERMANY, FEDERAL REPUBLIC OF in bilateral section.

Convention establishing the Multilateral Investment Guarantee Agency (MIGA) with annexes and schedules. Done at Seoul October 11, 1985; entered into force April 12, 1988. TIAS 12089.
Parties:
Albania
Algeria
Angola
Argentina
Armenia
Australia
Austria
Azerbaijan
Bahamas
Bahrain
Bangladesh
Barbados
Belarus
Belgium
Belize
Benin
Bolivia
Bosnia-Herzegovina
Botswana
Brazil
Bulgaria
Burkina Faso
Burundi
Cambodia
Cameroon
Canada
Cape Verde
Chile
China [1]
Colombia
Congo
Congo, Dem. Rep.
Costa Rica
Cote d'Ivoire
Croatia
Cyprus
Czech Rep.
Denmark
Dominica
Dominican Rep.
Ecuador
Egypt
El Salvador
Equatorial Guinea
Eritrea
Estonia
Ethiopia [2]
Fiji
Finland
Former Yugoslav Republic of Macedonia
France
Gambia
Georgia
Germany, Fed. Rep.[3]
Ghana
Greece
Grenada
Guatemala
Guinea

Guyana
Haiti
Honduras
Hungary
Iceland
India
Indonesia
Ireland
Israel
Italy
Jamaica
Japan
Jordan
Kazakhstan
Kenya
Korea
Kuwait
Kyrgyz Rep.
Laos
Latvia
Lebanon
Lesotho
Libya
Lithuania
Luxembourg
Madagascar
Malawi
Malaysia
Mali
Malta
Mauritania
Mauritius
Micronesia
Moldova
Mongolia
Morocco
Mozambique
Namibia
Nepal
Netherlands
Nicaragua
Nigeria
Norway
Oman
Pakistan
Palau
Panama
Papua New Guinea
Paraguay
Peru
Philippines
Poland
Portugal
Qatar
Romania
Russian Fed.
St. Kitts & Nevis
St. Lucia
St. Vincent & the Grenadines
Saudi Arabia
Senegal
Seychelles
Sierra Leone
Singapore
Slovak Rep.
Slovenia
South Africa
Spain
Sri Lanka
Sudan
Swaziland
Sweden
Switzerland
Tanzania
Thailand

Togo
Trinidad & Tobago
Tunisia
Turkey
Turkmenistan
Uganda
Ukraine
United Arab Emirates
United Kingdom
United States
Uruguay
Uzbekistan
Vanuatu
Venezuela
Vietnam
Western Samoa
Yemen
Yugoslavia [4]
Zambia
Zimbabwe

NOTES:

[1] Applicable to Hong Kong. See note under CHINA in bilateral section.

[2] See note under ETHIOPIA in bilateral section.

[3] See note under GERMANY, FEDERAL REPUBLIC OF in bilateral section.

[4] See note under YUGOSLAVIA in bilateral section.

Agreement establishing the European Bank for Reconstruction and Development, with annexes. Done at Paris May 29, 1990; entered into force March 28, 1991.
TIAS
Parties:
Albania
Armenia
Australia
Austria
Azerbaijan
Belarus
Belgium
Bosnia-Herzegovina
Bulgaria
Canada
Croatia
Cyprus
Czech Rep.
Denmark
Egypt
Estonia
European Community
European Investment Bank
Finland
Former Yogoslav Republic of Macedonia
France
Georgia
Germany
Greece
Hungary
Iceland
Ireland
Israel
Italy
Japan
Kazakhstan
Korea
Kyrgyz Rep.
Latvia
Liechtenstein
Lithuania
Luxembourg
Malta

FINANCIAL INSTITUTIONS (Cont'd)

Mexico
Moldova
Mongolia
Morocco
Netherlands
New Zealand
Norway
Poland
Portugal
Romania
Russian Fed.
Slovak Rep.
Slovenia
Spain
Sweden
Switzerland
Tajikistan
Turkey
Turkmenistan
Ukraine
United Kingdom
United States
Uzbekistan

FISHERIES

(See also CONSERVATION; WHALING)

Convention for the establishment of an Inter-American Tropical Tuna Commission, with exchange of notes of March 3, 1950. Signed at Washington May 31, 1949; entered into force March 3, 1950.
1 UST 230; TIAS 2044; 80 UNTS 3.
States which are parties:
Costa Rica
Ecuador
El Salvador
France
Japan
Mexico
Nicaragua
Panama
United States
Vanuatu
Venezuela

Convention on fishing and conservation of living resources of the high seas. Done at Geneva April 29, 1958; entered into force March 20, 1966.
17 UST 138; TIAS 5969; 559 UNTS 285.
States which are parties:
Australia
Belgium
Bosnia-Herzegovina
Burkina Faso
Cambodia
Colombia
Denmark [1]
Dominican Rep.
Fiji
Finland
France
Haiti

Jamaica
Kenya
Lesotho
Madagascar
Malawi
Malaysia
Mauritius
Mexico
Netherlands [2]
Nigeria
Portugal
Senegal
Sierra Leone
Solomon Is.
South Africa
Spain [3]
Switzerland
Thailand
Tonga
Trinidad & Tobago
Uganda
United Kingdom [3]
United States [4]
Venezuela
Yugoslavia [5]

NOTES:
[1] With reservation.
[2] Applicable to Netherlands Antilles and Aruba.
[3] With a statement.
[4] With an understanding.
[5] See note under YUGOSLAVIA in bilateral section.

Amended agreement for the establishment of the Indo-Pacific Fisheries Commission.[1] Approved at the 11th Session of the Conference of the Food and Agriculture Organization, Rome, November 23, 1961; entered into force November 23, 1961.
13 UST 2511; TIAS 5218; 418 UNTS 348.
Parties:
Australia
Bangladesh
Burma
Cambodia
France
Hong Kong
India
Indonesia
Japan
Korea
Malaysia
Nepal
New Zealand
Pakistan
Philippines
Sri Lanka
Thailand
United Kingdom
United States
Vietnam, Socialist Rep.

NOTE:
[1] Formerly the Indo-Pacific Fisheries Council.

International convention for the conservation of Atlantic tunas. Done at Rio de Janeiro May 14, 1966; entered into force March 21, 1969.
20 UST 2887; TIAS 6767; 673 UNTS 63.
States which are parties:
Angola
Benin

Brazil
Canada
Cape Verde
China
Cote d'Ivoire
Croatia
Cuba
Equatorial Guinea
European Community
France
Gabon
Ghana
Guinea
Italy
Japan ·
Korea
Libya
Morocco
Namibia
Panama
Portugal
Russian Fed.
Sao Tome & Principe
Senegal
South Africa
Spain
Trinidad & Tobago
Tunisia
Union of Soviet Socialist Reps.[1][2]
United Kingdom
United States
Uruguay
Venezuela

NOTES:
[1] With statement.
[2] See note under UNION OF SOVIET SOCIALIST REPUBLICS in bilateral section.

Convention on future multilateral cooperation in the northwest Atlantic fisheries. Done at Ottawa October 24, 1978; entered into force January 1, 1979; for the United States November 29, 1995.
TIAS
Parties:
Bulgaria
Canada
Cuba
Denmark [1]
Estonia
European Economic Community
European Union
France [2]
Iceland
Japan
Korea
Latvia
Lithuania
Norway
Poland
Portugal
Romania
Russian Fed.
Spain
Union of Soviet Socialist Reps.[3][4]
United States

NOTES:
[1] Applicable to Faroe Is.
[2] Applicable to St. Pierre and Miquelon.
[3] With declaration(s).
[4] See note under UNION OF SOVIET SOCIALIST REPUBLICS in bilateral section.

FISHERIES (Cont'd)

Convention for the conservation of salmon in the North Atlantic. Done at Reykjavik March 2, 1982; entered into force October 1, 1983. TIAS 10789.
Parties:
Canada
Denmark [1]
European Communities
Finland
Iceland
Norway
Sweden
Union of Soviet Socialist Reps. [2]
United States

NOTES:
[1] For the Faroe Is.
[2] See note under UNION OF SOVIET SOCIALIST REPUBLICS in bilateral section.

Memoranda of understanding concerning salmonid research and enforcement of the international convention for the high seas fisheries of the North Pacific Ocean. Signed at Vancouver April 9, 1986; entered into force April 9, 1986.
TIAS
States which are parties:
Canada
Japan
United States

Treaty on fisheries, with annexes and agreed statement. Done at Port Moresby April 2, 1987; entered into force June 15, 1988. TIAS 11100.
Parties:
Australia
Cook Is.
Fiji
Kiribati
Marshall Is.[1]
Micronesia [2]
Nauru
New Zealand [3]
Niue
Palau
Papua New Guinea
Solomon Is.
Tonga
Tuvalu
United States
Western Samoa

Amendment:
May 14, 1992.

NOTES:
[1] On October 15, 1986 the Compact of Free Association entered into force between the Government of the United States and the Government of the Republic of the Marshall Islands, effective October 21, 1986.
[2] On October 24, 1986 the Compact of Free Association entered into force between the Government of the United States and the Government of the Federated States of Micronesia, effective November 3, 1986.
[3] Applicable to Tokelau.

Convention for the prohibition of fishing with long driftnets in the South Pacific. Done at Wellington November 24, 1989; entered into force May 17, 1991; for the United States February 28, 1992.
TIAS
Parties:
Cook Is.
Kiribati
Micronesia
New Zealand
Palau
Tokelau
United States

Convention for the conservation of anadromous stocks in the North Pacific Ocean, with annex. Done at Moscow February 11, 1992; entered into force February 16, 1993. TIAS 11465.
Parties:
Canada
Japan
Russian Fed.
United States

Convention on the conservation and management of pollock resources in the central Bering Sea, with annex. Done at Washington June 16, 1994; entered into force December 8, 1995. TIAS
Parties:
China
Japan
Korea
Poland
Russian Fed.
United States

Agreement on the international dolphin conservation program, with annexes. Done at Washington May 21, 1998; entered into force February 15, 1999.
TIAS
Parties
Ecuador
Mexico
Nicaragua
Panama
United States
Venezuela

FOOD AID

Food aid convention, 1986.[1] Done at London March 13, 1986; entered into force July 1, 1986; definitively for the United States January 27, 1988.
TIAS
Parties:
Argentina
Australia
Austria
Belgium
Canada
Denmark
European Economic Community
Finland
France
Germany, Fed. Rep.[2]
Greece
Ireland

Italy
Japan
Luxembourg
Netherlands [3]
Norway
Portugal
Spain
Sweden
Switzerland
United Kingdom [4]
United States

Extension:
June 27, 1991.

NOTES:
[1] Part of the international wheat agreement, 1986. See also wheat trade convention under WHEAT.
[2] See note under GERMANY, FEDERAL REPUBLIC OF in bilateral section.
[3] For the Kingdom in Europe.
[4] Applicable to the British Virgin Islands and St. Helena.

FOOD AND AGRICULTURE ORGANIZATION

(See also AGRICULTURE; FISHERIES; POPLAR COMMISSION)

Constitution of the United Nations Food and Agriculture Organization. Signed at Quebec October 16, 1945; entered into force October 16, 1945.

Composite Text, as amended to 1957: 12 UST 980; TIAS 4803.
States which are parties:
Afghanistan
Albania
Algeria
Angola
Antigua & Barbuda
Argentina
Australia
Austria
Bahamas, The
Bahrain
Bangladesh
Barbados
Belgium
Belize
Benin
Bhutan
Bolivia
Botswana
Brazil
Bulgaria
Burkina Faso
Burma
Burundi
Cambodia
Cameroon
Canada
Cape Verde
Central African Rep.
Chad

FOOD AND AGRICULTURE ORGANIZATION (Cont'd)

Chile
China [1]
Colombia
Comoros
Congo
Congo, Dem. Rep.
Cook Is.
Costa Rica
Cote d'Ivoire
Cuba
Cyprus
Czechoslovakia [2]
Denmark
Djibouti
Dominica
Dominican Rep.
Ecuador
Egypt
El Salvador
Equatorial Guinea
Eritrea
Estonia
Ethiopia [3]
Fiji
Finland
France
Gabon
Gambia, The
Germany, Fed. Rep. [4]
Ghana
Greece
Grenada
Guatemala
Guinea
Guinea-Bissau
Guyana
Haiti
Honduras
Hungary
Iceland
India
Indonesia
Iran
Iraq
Ireland
Israel
Italy
Jamaica
Japan
Jordan
Kenya
Korea, Dem. People's Rep.
Korea, Rep.
Kuwait
Laos
Latvia
Lebanon
Lesotho
Liberia
Libya
Lithuania
Luxembourg
Madagascar
Malawi
Malaysia
Maldives
Mali

Malta
Mauritania
Mauritius
Mexico
Mongolia
Morocco
Mozambique
Namibia
Nepal
Netherlands
New Zealand
Nicaragua
Niger
Nigeria
Norway
Oman
Pakistan
Panama
Papua New Guinea
Paraguay
Peru
Philippines
Poland
Portugal
Puerto Rico [5]
Qatar
Romania
Rwanda
St. Kitts & Nevis
St. Lucia
St. Vincent & the Grenadines
Sao Tome & Principe
Saudi Arabia
Senegal
Seychelles
Sierra Leone
Slovak Rep.
Solomon Is.
Somalia
Spain
Sri Lanka
Sudan
Suriname
Swaziland
Sweden
Switzerland
Syrian Arab Rep.
Tanzania
Thailand
Togo
Tonga
Trinidad & Tobago
Tunisia
Turkey
Uganda
United Arab Emirates
United Kingdom [6]
United States
Uruguay
Vanuatu
Venezuela
Vietnam, Socialist Rep.
Western Samoa
Yemen (Aden) [7]
Yemen (Sanaa) [7]
Yugoslavia [8]
Zambia
Zimbabwe

Amendments:
October 30–November 24, 1961 (13 UST 2616; TIAS 5229).
November 16–December 5, 1963 (14 UST 2203; TIAS 5506).

November 20–December 9, 1965 (17 UST 457; TIAS 5987).
November 4–23, 1967 (18 UST 3273; TIAS 6421).
October 30–November 27, 1969 (21 UST 1464; TIAS 6902).
November 6–25, 1971 (23 UST 74; TIAS 7274).
November 16–26, 1973 (25 UST 928; TIAS 7836).
November 26, 1975 (27 UST 2381; TIAS 8318).
November 29, 1977 (29 UST 2868; TIAS 8982).
November 18, 1991 (TIAS 12134).

NOTES:
[1] Applicable to Hong Kong. See note under CHINA in bilateral section.
[2] See note under CZECHOSLOVAKIA in bilateral section.
[3] See note under ETHIOPIA in bilateral section.
[4] See note under GERMANY, FEDERAL REPUBLIC OF in bilateral section.
[5] Associate member.
[6] Including all colonies and overseas territories.
[7] See note under YEMEN in bilateral section.
[8] See note under YUGOSLAVIA in bilateral section.

FORESTRY

Establishment agreement for the Center for International Forestry Research (CIFOR), with constitution. Done at Canberra March 5, 1993; entered into force March 5, 1993; for the United States May 3, 1993.
TIAS 11960.
Parties:
Australia
Sweden
Switzerland
United States

GAS WARFARE

Protocol for the prohibition of the use in war of asphyxiating, poisonous or other gases, and of bacteriological methods of warfare. Done at Geneva June 17, 1925; entered into force February 8, 1928; for the United States April 10, 1975.
26 UST 571; TIAS 8061; 94 LNTS 65.
States which are parties:
Afghanistan
Angola [1]
Antigua & Barbuda
Argentina
Australia
Austria
Bahamas, The [1][2]
Bahrain [1]
Bangladesh [1]
Barbados
Belgium
Belize [1][2]
Benin

GAS WARFARE (Cont'd)

Bhutan
Bolivia
Botswana [1] [2]
Brazil
Bulgaria [1]
Burkina Faso
Burma [1]
Cambodia
Cameroon
Canada [1]
Cape Verde
Central African Rep.
Chile [1]
China [1] [3] [4]
Cote d'Ivoire
Cuba
Cyprus
Czechoslovakia [1] [5]
Denmark
Dominica [1] [2]
Dominican Rep.
Ecuador
Egypt
Equatorial Guinea
Estonia [1]
Ethiopia [6]
Fiji [1]
Finland
France [1] [7]
Gambia, The
German Dem. Rep. [8]
Germany, Fed. Rep. [8]
Ghana
Greece
Grenada
Guatemala
Guinea-Bissau
Guyana [1] [2]
Holy See
Hungary
Iceland
India [1]
Indonesia
Iran
Iraq [1]
Ireland
Israel [1]
Italy
Jamaica
Japan
Jordan [1]
Kenya
Kiribati [1] [2]
Korea, Dem. People's Rep. [9]
Korea, Rep. [1]
Kuwait [1]
Laos
Latvia
Lebanon
Lesotho
Liberia
Libya [1]
Liechtenstein
Lithuania
Luxembourg
Madagascar
Malawi
Malaysia
Maldives
Mali
Malta

Mauritius
Mexico
Monaco
Mongolia [1]
Morocco
Nepal
Netherlands [10]
New Zealand
Nicaragua
Niger
Nigeria [1]
Norway
Pakistan
Panama
Papua New Guinea [1]
Paraguay
Peru
Philippines
Poland
Portugal [1]
Qatar
Romania [1]
Rwanda
St. Kitts & Nevis [1] [2]
St. Lucia
St. Vincent & the Grenadines [1]
Saudi Arabia
Seychelles [1] [2]
Sierra Leone
Singapore [1] [2]
Slovak Rep. [1]
Solomon Is. [1] [2]
South Africa
Spain [1]
Sri Lanka
Sudan
Suriname [1] [2]
Swaziland [1] [2]
Sweden
Switzerland
Syrian Arab Rep. [1]
Tanzania
Thailand
Togo
Tonga
Trinidad & Tobago
Tunisia
Turkey
Tuvalu [1] [2]
Uganda
Union of Soviet Socialist Reps. [1] [11]
United Kingdom [1] [12]
United States [1]
Uruguay
Venezuela
Vietnam, Socialist Rep. [1]
Yemen (Aden) [13]
Yemen (Sanaa) [13]
Yugoslavia [1] [14]
Zambia [1] [2]
Zimbabwe [1] [2]

NOTES:
[1] With reservation(s).
[2] See under country heading in the bilateral section for information concerning acceptance of treaty obligations.
[3] The Taiwan authorities have also adhered to this protocol. See note under CHINA (Taiwan) in the bilateral section.
[4] Applicable to Hong Kong and Macao. See note under CHINA in bilateral section.
[5] See note under CZECHOSLOVAKIA in bilateral section.

[6] See note under ETHIOPIA in bilateral section.
[7] Applicable to all French territories.
[8] See note under GERMANY, FEDERAL REPUBLIC OF in bilateral section.
[9] With declaration(s).
[10] Extended to Curaçao.
[11] See note under UNION OF SOVIET SOCIALIST REPUBLICS in bilateral section.
[12] It does not bind India or any British Dominion which is a separate member of the League of Nations and does not separately sign or adhere to the protocol. It is applicable to colonies. See footnote 2 above.
[13] See note under YEMEN in bilateral section.
[14] See note under YUGOSLAVIA in bilateral section.

GENEVA CONVENTIONS

(See RED CROSS CONVENTIONS; RULES OF WARFARE)

GENOCIDE

Convention on the prevention and punishment of the crime of genocide. Done at Paris December 9, 1948; entered into force January 12, 1951; for the United States February 23, 1989.
TIAS
Parties:
Afghanistan
Albania [1] [2]
Algeria [1] [2]
Antigua & Barbuda
Argentina [1] [2]
Armenia
Australia
Austria
Azerbaijan
Bahamas
Bahrain
Bangladesh [2]
Barbados
Belarus [2]
Belgium
Belize
Bosnia-Herzegovina
Brazil
Bulgaria [2]
Burkina Faso
Burma [1] [2]
Burundi
Cambodia
Canada
Chile
China [1] [3] [4]
Colombia
Congo, Dem. Rep. [5]
Costa Rica
Cote d'Ivoire
Croatia
Cuba
Cyprus
Czech Rep.
Denmark
Ecuador

GENOCIDE (Cont'd)

Egypt
El Salvador
Estonia
Ethiopia [6]
Fiji [5]
Finland [7]
Former Yugoslav Republic of Macedonia
France
Gabon
Gambia, The
Georgia
German Dem. Rep. [1][2][8]
Germany, Fed. Rep. [8]
Ghana
Greece
Guatemala
Guinea
Haiti
Honduras
Hungary
Iceland
India [1]
Iran
Iraq
Ireland
Israel
Italy
Jamaica
Jordan
Kazakhstan
Korea, Dem. People's Rep.
Korea, Rep.
Kuwait
Kyrgyz Rep.
Laos
Latvia
Lebanon
Lesotho
Liberia
Libya
Liechtenstein
Lithuania
Luxembourg
Malaysia
Maldives
Mali
Mexico
Moldova
Monaco
Mongolia [2]
Morocco [1][2]
Mozambique
Namibia
Nepal
Netherlands [9]
New Zealand
Nicaragua
Norway
Pakistan
Panama
Papua New Guinea
Peru
Philippines [1][2]
Poland [1][2]
Portugal
Romania [1][2]
Russian Fed.
Rwanda [1]
St. Vincent & the Grenadines
Saudi Arabia
Senegal

Seychelles
Singapore
Slovak Rep. [1][2]
Slovenia
South Africa
Spain [1]
Sri Lanka
Sweden
Switzerland
Syria
Tanzania
Togo
Tonga
Tunisia
Turkey
Uganda
Ukraine [2]
Union of Soviet Socialist Reps. [2][10]
United Kingdom [11]
United States [1][7]
Uruguay
Uzbekistan
Venezuela [1][2]
Vietnam [1][2][12]
Yemen (Aden) [1][2][13]
Yemen (Sanaa) [13]
Yugoslavia [14]
Zimbabwe

NOTES:
[1] With reservation(s).
[2] With declaration(s).
[3] The Taiwan authorities have also adhered to this convention. See note under CHINA (Taiwan) in bilateral section.
[4] Applicable to Hong Kong and Macao. With declaration. See note under CHINA in bilateral section.
[5] Considers itself bound by application extended to its territory before attainment of independence.
[6] See note under ETHIOPIA in bilateral section.
[7] With understanding(s).
[8] See note under GERMANY, FEDERAL REPUBLIC OF in bilateral section.
[9] Applicable to Netherlands Antilles and Aruba.
[10] See note under UNION OF SOVIET SOCIALIST REPUBLICS in bilateral section.
[11] Applicable to Bermuda, British Virgin Is., Channel Is., Dominica, Falkland Is., Gibraltar, Grenada, Isle of Man, Pitcairn, Seychelles, St. Helen and Dependencies, St. Lucia, Turks and Caicos Is.
[12] See Vietnam footnote under AGRICULTURE: agreement of January 25, 1924 (26 UST 1840; TIAS 8141; 57 LNTS 135).
[13] See note under YEMEN in bilateral section.
[14] See note under YUGOSLAVIA in bilateral section.

GERMANY

(See also FINANCE; PATENTS; REPARATIONS)

Act of military surrender. Terms between the United States and other Allied Powers and Germany. Signed at Rheims May 7 and at Berlin May 8, 1945; effective May 8, 1945.
59 Stat. 1857; EAS 502; 3 Bevans 1123.

Agreements relating to basic principles for merger of the three western German zones of occupation and other matters. Signed at Washington April 8, 1949; entered into force April 8, 1949.
63 Stat. 2817; TIAS 2066; 4 Bevans 832; 140 UNTS 196.
States which are parties:
France
United Kingdom
United States

Agreement relating to the lifting of restrictions imposed since March 1, 1948 on communications, transportation, and trade with Berlin. Done at New York May 4, 1949; entered into force May 4, 1949.
63 Stat. 2410; TIAS 1915; 4 Bevans 843; 138 UNTS 123.
States which are parties:
France
Union of Soviet Socialist Reps. [1]
United Kingdom
United States

NOTE:
[1] See note under UNION OF SOVIET SOCIALIST REPUBLICS in bilateral section.

Protocol of agreements reached between the Allied High Commissioners and the Chancellor of the German Federal Republic. Signed at Bonn November 22, 1949; entered into force November 22, 1949.
3 UST 2714; TIAS 2439; 185 UNTS 307.
States which are parties:
France
Germany, Fed. Rep. [1]
United Kingdom
United States

NOTE:
[1] See note under GERMANY, FEDERAL REPUBLIC OF in bilateral section.

Convention on the settlement of matters arising out of the war and the occupation, with annex. [1] Signed at Bonn May 26, 1952.
6 UST 4411; TIAS 3425; 332 UNTS 219.
Accessions to Annex (Charter of the Arbitral Commission):
Belgium
Denmark
Greece
Italy
Luxembourg
Netherlands
Norway

NOTE:
[1] This instrument, as amended by the protocol of October 23, 1954 (TIAS 3425), entered into force simultaneously with the protocol.

Protocol to correct certain textual errors in the convention on relations between the Three Powers and the Federal Republic of Germany and the related conventions signed at Bonn

GERMANY (Cont'd)

May 26, 1952.[1] Signed at Bonn June 27, 1952.
6 UST 5381; TIAS 3425.

NOTE:
[1] This instrument, as amended by the protocol of October 23, 1954 (TIAS 3425), entered into force simultaneously with the protocol.

Agreement relating to certain German libraries and properties in Italy. Signed at Rome April 30, 1953; entered into force May 1, 1953.
4 UST 376; TIAS 2785; 175 UNTS 89.
States which are parties:
France
Germany, Fed. Rep.[1]
Italy
United Kingdom
United States

NOTE:
[1] See note under GERMANY, FEDERAL REPUBLIC OF in bilateral section.

Agreement concerning storage of, access to, and release of information from the archives of the Allied High Commission and connected tripartite agencies, with exchanges of notes relating to the Bipartite Coal Control Group. Signed at Bonn June 30, 1954; entered into force June 30, 1954.
5 UST 1598; TIAS 3036; 204 UNTS 99.
States which are parties:
France
United Kingdom
United States

Tripartite agreement on the exercise of retained rights in Germany. Signed at Paris October 23, 1954; entered into force May 5, 1955.
6 UST 5703; TIAS 3427.
States which are parties:
France
United Kingdom
United States

Protocol on the termination of the occupation regime in the Federal Republic of Germany, with five schedules and related letters.[2] Signed at Paris October 23, 1954; entered into force May 5, 1955.
6 UST 4117; TIAS 3425; 331 UNTS 253.
States which are parties:
France
Germany, Fed. Rep.[3]
United Kingdom
United States

NOTES:
[1] Schedules II, III, and V terminated July 1, 1963 by the agreement of August 3, 1959 (TIAS 5351, p. 156). Schedule I as it relates to postal matters and telecommunications terminated November 1, 1968.
[2] See also agreements of May 26, 1952 (TIAS 3425).
[3] See note under GERMANY, FEDERAL REPUBLIC OF in bilateral section.

Convention on the presence of foreign forces in the Federal Republic of Germany. Signed at Paris October 23, 1954; entered into force May 6, 1955.
6 UST 5689; TIAS 3426; 334 UNTS 3.
States which are parties:
Belgium
Canada
Denmark
France
Germany, Fed. Rep.[1]
Luxembourg
Netherlands
United Kingdom
United States

NOTE:
[1] See note under GERMANY, FEDERAL REPUBLIC OF in bilateral section.

Penal administrative agreement with exchanges of notes dated November 1 and December 20, 1955, and notes of the German Chancellor dated October 14 and November 7, 1953. Done at Bonn September 29, 1955; entered into force May 5, 1955.
7 UST 663; TIAS 3549.
States which are parties:
France
Germany, Fed. Rep.[1]
United Kingdom
United States

NOTE:
[1] See note under GERMANY, FEDERAL REPUBLIC OF in bilateral section.

Agreement relating to the return of captured files and archives of the former German Foreign Office at present in the territory of the United Kingdom. Exchange of notes between the United States and the Federal Republic of Germany at Bonn March 14 and April 18, 1956; entered into force April 18, 1956.[1]
7 UST 2119; TIAS 3613; 271 UNTS 319.

NOTE:
[1] Notes were exchanged *mutatis mutandis* between the Federal Republic of Germany and France and the United Kingdom.

Memorandum of understanding regarding German trademarks in Italy. Signed at Rome July 5, 1956; entered into force July 5, 1956.
7 UST 1989; TIAS 3601; 258 UNTS 371.
States which are parties:
France
Italy
United Kingdom
United States

Administrative agreement concerning the Arbitration Tribunal and the Arbitral Commission on property, rights, and interests in Germany. Signed at Bonn July 13, 1956; entered into force July 13, 1956; operative from May 5, 1955.
7 UST 2129; TIAS 3615; 281 UNTS 3.
States which are parties:
France
Germany, Fed. Rep.[1]
United Kingdom
United States

NOTE:
[1] See note under GERMANY, FEDERAL REPUBLIC OF in bilateral section.

Agreement relating to the waiver of immunity from legal process of members of the Arbitration Tribunal and the Arbitral Commission on property, rights and interests in Germany under the administrative agreement of July 13, 1956. Exchange of notes between the United States and the Federal Republic of Germany at Bonn July 24 and 27, 1956; entered into force July 27, 1956.[1]
7 UST 2773; TIAS 3657; 278 UNTS 3.

NOTE:
[1] Notes were exchanged *mutatis mutandis* between the Federal Republic of Germany and France and the United Kingdom.

Protocol modifying the agreement concerning storage of, access to, and release of information from the archives of the Allied High Commission and connected tripartite agencies of June 30, 1954. Signed at Bonn March 5, 1959; entered into force March 5, 1959.
10 UST 341; TIAS 4195; 341 UNTS 386.
States which are parties:
France
United Kingdom
United States

Agreement on the abrogation of the convention on rights and obligations of foreign forces and their members in the Federal Republic of Germany, the agreement on the tax treatment of the forces and their members, and the finance convention, all signed May 26, 1952, as amended by the protocol of October 23, 1954 on the termination of the occupation regime in Germany. Signed at Bonn August 3, 1959; entered into force July 1, 1963.
14 UST 686; TIAS 5351; 481 UNTS 591.
States which are parties:
France
Germany, Fed. Rep.[1]
United Kingdom
United States

NOTE:
[1] See note under GERMANY, FEDERAL REPUBLIC OF in bilateral section.

Agreement concerning the administration of the archives of the Arbitral Commission on property, rights and interests in Germany. Exchange of notes at Bonn and Bad Godesberg August 12 and 26, 1971; entered into force December 31, 1971.
23 UST 590; TIAS 7317.
States which are parties:
France
Germany, Fed. Rep.[1]
United Kingdom
United States

NOTE:
[1] See note under GERMANY, FEDERAL REPUBLIC OF in bilateral section.

Treaty on the final settlement with respect to Germany, with agreed minute and related letters. Done at Moscow September 12, 1990; entered into force March 15, 1991.
TIAS   ; 1696 UNTS 115.

GERMANY (Cont'd)

Agreement concerning the convention of October 23, 1954, on the presence of foreign forces in the Federal Republic of Germany. Exchange of notes at Bonn September 25, 1990; entered into force September 25, 1990.
TIAS

Amendment:
September 12, 1994.

Agreement regarding the status of foreign forces in the former territory of the German Democratic Republic. Exchange of notes at Bonn September 25, 1990; entered into force October 3, 1990.
TIAS

Agreement concerning the convention of May 26, 1952, as amended, on relations between the Three Powers and the Federal Republic of Germany and the convention of May 26, 1952, as amended, on settlement of matters arising out of the war and the occupation. Exchange of notes at Bonn September 27 and 28, 1990; entered into force September 28, 1990.
TIAS   ; 1656 UNTS 29.

Declaration suspending the operation of quadripartite rights and responsibilities. Signed at New York October 1, 1990; entered into force October 3, 1990.
TIAS

Agreement terminating the agreement of September 25, 1990, concerning the presence and status of Allied Forces in Berlin. Exchange of notes at Bonn September 12, 1994; entered into force September 12, 1994.
TIAS

GRAINS

(See FOOD AID; WHEAT)

HAGUE CONVENTIONS

(See under JUDICIAL PROCEDURE; PACIFIC SETTLEMENT OF DISPUTES; RULES OF WARFARE)

HEALTH

The Pan American sanitary code.[1] Signed at Habana November 14, 1924; entered into force June 26, 1925.
44 Stat. 2031; TS 714; 2 Bevans 483; 86 LNTS 43.

Additional protocol amending the Pan American sanitary code of November 14, 1924.

Signed at Lima October 19, 1927; entered into force July 3, 1928.
45 Stat. 2613; TS 763; 2 Bevans 648; 87 LNTS 453.
States which are parties:
Argentina
Bolivia [2]
Brazil
Chile
Colombia [3]
Costa Rica [2]
Cuba
Dominican Rep.[3]
Ecuador
El Salvador [2]
Guatemala [2]
Haiti [2]
Honduras [2]
Mexico [4]
Panama [3]
Paraguay [2]
Peru
United States
Uruguay
Venezuela

NOTES:
[1] Articles 2, 9, 10, 11, 16 to 53 inclusive, 61 and 62 replaced by the international health regulations, adopted at Boston July 25, 1969 (TIAS 7026).
[2] Not a party to additional protocol.
[3] With memorandum of interpretation.
[4] With reservation.

Constitution of the World Health Organization. Done at New York July 22, 1946; entered into force April 7, 1948; for the United States June 21, 1948.
62 Stat. 2679; TIAS 1808; 4 Bevans 119; 14 UNTS 185.
Parties:
Afghanistan
Albania
Algeria
Andorra
Angola
Antigua & Barbuda
Argentina
Armenia
Australia
Austria
Azerbaijan
Bahamas, The
Bahrain
Bangladesh
Barbados
Belarus
Belgium
Belize
Benin
Bhutan
Bolivia
Bosnia-Herzegovina
Botswana
Brazil
Brunei
Bulgaria
Burkina Faso
Burma
Burundi
Cambodia
Cameroon
Canada
Cape Verde

Central African Rep.
Chad
Chile
China [1]
Colombia
Comoros
Congo
Congo, Dem. Rep.
Cook Is.
Costa Rica
Cote d'Ivoire
Croatia
Cuba
Cyprus
Czech Rep.
Denmark
Djibouti
Dominica
Dominican Rep.
Ecuador
Egypt
El Salvador
Equatorial Guinea
Eritrea
Estonia
Ethiopia [2]
Fiji
Finland
Former Yugoslav Republic of Macedonia
France
Gabon
Gambia, The
Georgia
German Dem. Rep. [3]
Germany, Fed. Rep. [3]
Ghana
Greece
Grenada
Guatemala
Guinea
Guinea-Bissau
Guyana
Haiti
Honduras
Hungary
Iceland
India
Indonesia
Iran
Iraq
Ireland
Israel
Italy
Jamaica
Japan
Jordan
Kazakhstan
Kenya
Kiribati
Korea, Dem. People's Rep.
Korea, Rep.
Kuwait
Kyrgyz Rep.
Laos
Latvia
Lebanon
Lesotho
Liberia
Libya
Lithuania
Luxembourg
Madagascar
Malawi
Malaysia
Maldives

HEALTH (Cont'd)

Mali
Malta
Marshall Is.
Mauritania
Mauritius
Mexico
Micronesia
Moldova
Monaco
Mongolia
Morocco
Mozambique
Namibia [4]
Nauru
Nepal
Netherlands [5]
New Zealand
Nicaragua
Niger
Nigeria
Niue
Norway
Oman
Pakistan
Palau
Panama
Papua New Guinea
Paraguay
Peru
Philippines
Poland
Portugal
Qatar
Romania
Russian Fed.
Rwanda
St. Kitts & Nevis
St. Lucia
St. Vincent & the Grenadines
San Marino
Sao Tome & Principe
Saudi Arabia
Senegal
Seychelles
Sierra Leone
Singapore
Slovak Rep.
Slovenia
Solomon Is.
Somalia
South Africa
Spain
Sri Lanka
Sudan
Suriname
Swaziland
Sweden
Switzerland
Syrian Arab Rep.
Tajikistan
Tanzania
Thailand
Togo
Tonga
Trinidad & Tobago
Tunisia
Turkey
Turkmenistan
Tuvalu
Uganda
Ukraine

United Arab Emirates
United Kingdom
United States [6]
Uruguay
Uzbekistan
Vanuatu
Venezuela
Vietnam, Socialist Rep.
Western Samoa
Yemen (Aden) [7]
Yemen (Sanaa) [7]
Yugoslavia [8]
Zambia
Zimbabwe

Amendments:
May 23, 1967 (26 UST 990; TIAS 8086).
May 22, 1973 (28 UST 2088; TIAS 8534).
May 17, 1976 (TIAS 10930).
May 12, 1986 (TIAS 12049).

NOTES:
[1] Applicable to Hong Kong and Macao. See note under CHINA in bilateral section.
[2] See note under ETHIOPIA in bilateral section.
[3] See note under GERMANY, FEDERAL REPUBLIC OF in bilateral section.
[4] Associate member.
[5] Applicable to Netherlands Antilles and Aruba.
[6] With statement.
[7] See note under YEMEN in bilateral section.
[8] See note under YUGOSLAVIA in bilateral section.

World Health Organization nomenclature regulations, 1967.[1] Adopted at Geneva May 22, 1967; entered into force January 1, 1968.
18 UST 3003; TIAS 6393.

NOTE:
[1] In force for all members of the World Health Organization with the exception of the Federal Republic of Germany which has made a reservation that the nomenclature regulations, 1967, will not enter into force in the Federal Republic until the Director-General of the World Health Organization has been notified that the domestic prerequisites have been fulfilled. The World Health Organization Regulations No. 1 of July 24, 1948 (7 UST 79; TIAS 3482) regarding nomenclature remain in force as regards parties to them which are not yet parties to the 1967 regulations.

International health regulations, with appendices. Adopted at Boston July 25, 1969; entered into force January 1, 1971.[1][2]
21 UST 3003; TIAS 7026; 764 UNTS 3.

Additional regulations amending articles 1, 21, 63 to 71, 92, and appendix 2 of the international health regulations. Adopted at Geneva May 23, 1973; entered into force January 1, 1974.[3]
25 UST 197; TIAS 7786.

Additional amendments to the international health regulations. Adopted at Geneva May 20, 1981; entered into force January 1, 1982.[4]
33 UST 4436; TIAS 10314.

NOTES:
[1] Replaces as between States bound by these regulations the international sanitary conventions and regulations listed in article 99 of the regulations.
[2] In force for all members of the World Health Organization except as follows: Not bound—Australia, Singapore, and South Africa. Bound with reservations—Egypt, India, Pakistan, and Suriname. Position not defined—Holy See and Nauru.
[3] In force for all members of the World Health Organization except as follows: Not bound—Australia, Egypt, Iran, Italy, Libya, Madagascar, Singapore, and South Africa. Position not defined—Holy See and Nauru.
[4] In force for all members of the World Health Organization except as provided in article 22 of the Constitution of the Organization.

Protocol for the termination of the Brussels agreement for the unification of pharmacopoeial formulas for potent drugs. Done at Geneva May 20, 1952; entered into force May 20, 1952.
3 UST 5067; TIAS 2692; 219 UNTS 55.
States which are parties:
Antigua & Barbuda [1]
Australia
Austria
Bahamas, The [1]
Barbados [1]
Belgium
Belize [1]
Botswana [1]
Brunei [1]
Cyprus [1]
Denmark
Dominica [1]
Egypt
Fiji [1]
Finland
France [2]
Gambia, The [1]
Germany, Fed. Rep. [3]
Greece
Grenada [1]
Guyana [1]
Iceland
Italy
Jamaica [1]
Kenya [1]
Kiribati [1]
Lesotho [1]
Luxembourg
Malaysia [1]
Malta [1]
Mauritius [1]
Netherlands
Nigeria [1]
Norway
St. Kitts & Nevis [1]
St. Lucia [1]
St. Vincent & the Grenadines [1]
Seychelles [1]
Sierra Leone [1]
Singapore [1]
Solomon Is. [1]
South Africa
Spain
Swaziland [1]
Sweden
Switzerland
Tanzania [1]
Trinidad & Tobago [1]

HEALTH (Cont'd)

Tuvalu [1]
United Kingdom [2] [4]
United States
Yugoslavia [5]
Zambia [1]

NOTES:
[1] See under country heading in the bilateral section for information concerning acceptance of treaty obligations.
[2] Extended to New Hebrides; continued application to Vanuatu not determined.
[3] See note under GERMANY, FEDERAL REPUBLIC OF in bilateral section.
[4] Extended to Anguilla, Bermuda, Montserrat, and St. Helena.
[5] See note under YUGOSLAVIA in bilateral section.

Statute of International Agency for Research on Cancer. Done at Geneva May 20, 1965; entered into force September 15, 1965.
16 UST 1239; TIAS 5873.
States which are parties:
Australia
Belgium
Canada
France
Germany, Fed. Rep.[1]
Italy
Japan
Netherlands
Sweden
Union of Soviet Socialist Reps. [2]
United Kingdom
United States

Amendment:
May 19, 1970 (21 UST 1567; TIAS 6919).

NOTES:
[1] See note under GERMANY, FEDERAL REPUBLIC OF in bilateral section.
[2] See note under UNION OF SOVIET SOCIALIST REPUBLICS in bilateral section.

Agreement for phase I of the project for the strengthening of public health delivery system in Central and West Africa. Dated March 26, 1975; entered into force April 17, 1975, effective April 19, 1975.
28 UST 3743; TIAS 8597.
Parties:
Agency for International Development
Benin
Burkina Faso
Cameroon
Central African Rep.
Chad
Congo
Cote d'Ivoire
Gabon
Gambia, The
Ghana
Guinea
Liberia
Mali
Mauritania
Niger
Senegal
Sierra Leone

Togo
World Health Organization

Amendment:
June 22, 1976 (28 UST 3772; TIAS 8597).

HIJACKING
(See under AVIATION)

HOSTAGES
(See under TERRORISM)

HUMAN RIGHTS

International covenant on civil and political rights. Done at New York December 16, 1966; entered into force March 23, 1976; for the United States September 8, 1992.
TIAS
Parties:
Afghanistan
Albania
Algeria
Angola
Argentina
Armenia
Australia [1]
Austria
Azerbaijan
Bangladesh
Barbados
Belarus
Belgium
Belize
Benin
Bolivia
Bosnia-Herzegovina [1]
Botswana
Brazil
Bulgaria
Burkina Faso
Burundi
Cambodia
Cameroon
Canada
Cape Verde
Central African Rep.
Chad
Chile
Colombia
Congo
Congo, Dem. Rep.
Costa Rica
Cote d'Ivoire
Croatia [1]
Cyprus
Czech Rep.
Denmark
Dominica
Dominican Rep.
Ecuador
Egypt
El Salvador
Equatorial Guinea
Estonia
Ethiopia [2]

Finland
Former Yugoslav Republic of Macedonia
France
Gabon
Gambia
Georgia
German Dem. Rep. [3]
Germany, Fed. Rep. [1] [3]
Ghana
Greece
Grenada
Guatemala
Guinea
Guyana [1]
Haiti
Honduras
Hong Kong [4]
Hungary
Iceland
India
Iran
Iraq
Ireland
Israel
Italy
Jamaica
Japan
Jordan
Kenya
Korea, Dem. People's Rep.
Korea, Rep.
Kuwait
Kyrgyz Rep.
Latvia
Lebanon
Lesotho
Libya
Liechtenstein [1] [5]
Lithuania
Luxembourg
Macao [4]
Madagascar
Malawi
Mali
Malta
Mauritius
Mexico
Moldova
Monaco
Mongolia
Morocco
Mozambique
Namibia
Nepal
Netherlands [6]
New Zealand
Nicaragua
Niger
Nigeria
Norway
Panama
Paraguay
Peru
Philippines
Poland
Portugal
Romania
Russian Fed.
Rwanda
St. Vincent & the Grenadines
San Marino
Senegal
Seychelles
Sierra Leone
Slovak Rep. [1]

HUMAN RIGHTS (Cont'd)

Slovenia
Somalia
South Africa
Spain
Sri Lanka
Sudan
Suriname
Sweden
Switzerland [1] [5]
Syria
Tajikistan
Tanzania
Thailand
Togo
Trinidad & Tobago
Tunisia [1]
Turkmenistan
Uganda
Ukraine [1]
Union of Soviet Socialist Reps. [7]
United Kingdom
United States [1] [8]
Uruguay
Uzbekistan
Venezuela
Viet Nam
Yemen (Aden) [9]
Yugoslavia [10]
Zambia
Zimbabwe [1]

NOTES:
   [1] With declaration(s).
   [2] See note under ETHIOPIA in bilateral section.
   [3] See note under GERMANY, FEDERAL REPUBLIC OF in bilateral section.
   [4] CHINA is not a party to this treaty but has made it applicable to Hong Kong and Macao.
   [5] With reservation(s).
   [6] Applicable to Netherlands Antilles and Aruba.
   [7] See note under UNION OF SOVIET SOCIALIST REPUBLICS in bilateral section.
   [8] With understanding(s).
   [9] See note under YEMEN in bilateral section.
   [10] See note under YUGOSLAVIA in bilateral section.

HYDROGRAPHY

Convention on the International Hydrographic Organization, with annexes. Done at Monaco May 3, 1967; entered into force September 22, 1970.
21 UST 1857; TIAS 6933; 751 UNTS 41.
States which are parties:
Argentina
Australia
Belgium
Brazil
Canada
Chile
China [1]
Colombia
Congo, Dem. Rep.
Cuba

Cyprus
Denmark
Dominican Rep.
Ecuador
Egypt
Fiji
Finland
France
German Dem. Rep. [2]
Germany, Fed. Rep. [2] [3]
Greece
Guatemala
Iceland
India
Indonesia
Iran
Italy
Japan
Korea, Dem. People's Rep.
Korea, Rep.
Malaysia
Monaco
Mozambique
Netherlands
New Zealand
Nigeria
Norway
Oman
Pakistan
Papua New Guinea
Peru
Philippines
Poland
Portugal
Singapore
South Africa
Spain
Sri Lanka
Suriname
Sweden
Syrian Arab Rep.
Thailand
Trinidad & Tobago
Tunisia [3]
Turkey
Ukraine
Union of Soviet Socialist Reps. [3] [4]
United Kingdom
United States
Uruguay
Venezuela
Yugoslavia [5]

NOTES:
   [1] Applicable to Hong Kong. See note under CHINA in bilateral section.
   [2] See note under GERMANY, FEDERAL REPUBLIC OF in bilateral section.
   [3] With reservation.
   [4] See note under UNION OF SOVIET SOCIALIST REPUBLICS in bilateral section.
   [5] See note under YUGOSLAVIA in bilateral section.

INDUSTRIAL PROPERTY

(See also INTELLECTUAL PROPERTY; PATENTS)

Convention for the protection of inventions, patents, designs and industrial models. Signed at Buenos Aires August 20, 1910; entered into force July 31, 1912.
38 Stat. 1811; TS 595; 1 Bevans 767; 155 LNTS 179.
States which are parties:
Bolivia
Brazil
Costa Rica
Cuba
Dominican Rep.
Ecuador
Guatemala
Haiti
Honduras
Nicaragua
Paraguay
United States
Uruguay

General inter-American convention for trademark and commercial protection.[1] Signed at Washington February 20, 1929; entered into force April 2, 1930; for the United States February 17, 1931.
46 Stat. 2907; TS 833; 2 Bevans 751; 124 LNTS 357.
States which are parties:
Colombia
Cuba
Guatemala
Haiti
Honduras
Nicaragua
Panama
Paraguay
Peru
United States

NOTE:
   [1] Replaces as between contracting parties the convention of August 20, 1910 (39 Stat. 1675; TS 626; 1 Bevans 772) and the convention of April 28, 1923 (44 Stat. 2494; TS 751; 2 Bevans 395). Parties to the 1923 convention not party to the 1929 convention are: Brazil, Dominican Republic and Uruguay. Parties to the 1910 convention not party to the subsequent conventions are: Bolivia and Ecuador.

Convention revising the Paris convention of March 20, 1883, as revised, for the protection of industrial property.[1] [2] Done at Stockholm July 14, 1967; entered into force April 26, 1970; for the United States September 5, 1970 except for Articles 1 through 12 which entered into force May 19, 1970; for the United States August 25, 1973.
21 UST 1583; 24 UST 2140; TIAS 6923, 7727.

NOTES:
   [1] Originally called the Convention of the Union of Paris.
   [2] Replaces as between contracting parties the (Lisbon) convention of October 31, 1958 (13 UST 1; TIAS 4931; 828 UNTS 107) and the (London) convention of June 2, 1934 (53 Stat. 1748; TS 941; 3 Bevans 223) which in turn replaced the (Hague) convention of November 6, 1925 (47 Stat. 1789; TS 834; 2 Bevans 524) and the (Washington) convention of June 2, 1911 (38 Stat. 1645; TS 579; 1 Bevans 791).

INDUSTRIAL PROPERTY
(Cont'd)

States which are parties	1911	1925	1934	1958	1967
Albania					X
Algeria				X	X [1]
Antigua & Barbuda					X
Argentina				X	X [2]
Armenia					X
Australia	X	X	X		X
Austria	X	X	X	X	X
Azerbaijan					X
Bahamas, The				X	X [2]
Bahrain					X
Bangladesh					X [1]
Barbados					X
Belarus					X
Belgium	X	X	X	X	X
Belize					X
Benin		X		X	X
Bhutan					X
Bolivia					X
Bosnia-Herzegovina					X
Botswana					X
Brazil	X	X			X [1]
Bulgaria	X	X	X	X	X [1]
Burkina Faso		X		X	X
Burundi					X
Cambodia					X
Cameroon		X		X	X
Canada	X	X	X		X
Central African Rep.		X		X	X
Chad		X		X	X
Chile					X
China					X [1] [3]
Colombia					X
Congo		X		X	X
Congo, Dem. Rep.					X
Costa Rica					X
Cote d'Ivoire		X		X	X
Croatia					X
Cuba	X			X	X [1]
Cyprus				X	X
Czech Rep.					X
Denmark	X	X	X		X [4]
Dominica					X
Dominican Rep.	X	X			
Ecuador					X [5]
Egypt			X		X [1]
El Salvador					X
Equatorial Guinea					X
Estonia	X				X
Finland	X		X		X
Former Yugoslav Republic of Macedonia					X
France	X	X	X	X	X [6]
Gabon				X	X
Gambia					X
Georgia					X
German Dem. Rep.			X	X	X [7]
Germany, Fed. Rep.			X	X	X [7]
Ghana					X
Greece	X		X		X
Grenada					X
Guatemala					X
Guinea					X
Guinea-Bissau					X
Guyana					X
Haiti			X	X	X
Honduras					X
Hungary	X	X	X	X	X [1]

INDUSTRIAL PROPERTY
(Cont'd)

States which are parties	1911	1925	1934	1958	1967
Iceland			X [2]		X
India					X [5]
Indonesia			X		X
Iran			X	X	X [5]
Iraq					X [1]
Ireland	X		X	X	X
Israel			X	X	X
Italy	X	X	X	X	X
Jamaica					X
Japan	X	X	X	X	X
Jordan					X
Kazakhstan					X
Kenya				X	X
Korea, Dem. People's Rep.					X
Korea, Rep.					X
Kyrgyz Rep.					X
Laos					X [5]
Latvia	X				X
Lebanon	X	X	X		X [1] [2]
Lesotho					X
Liberia					X
Libya					X [1]
Liechtenstein		X	X		X
Lithuania					X
Luxembourg	X		X		X
Madagascar		X		X	X
Malawi				X	X
Malaysia					X
Mali					X
Malta		X	X	X	X [1] [2]
Mauritania		X		X	X
Mauritius					X
Mexico	X	X	X	X	X
Moldova					X
Monaco			X	X	X
Mongolia					X
Morocco	X	X	X	X	X
Mozambique					X
Netherlands	X	X	X		X [8]
New Zealand	X	X	X		X [2] [9]
Nicaragua					X [1]
Niger		X		X	X
Nigeria				X	
Norway	X		X	X	X
Oman					X [5]
Panama					X
Papua New Guinea					X
Paraguay					X
Peru					X
Philippines				X	X [2]
Poland	X	X			X [1]
Portugal	X	X	X		X
Qatar					X
Romania	X	X	X	X	X [1]
Russian Fed.					X
Rwanda					X
St. Kitts & Nevis					X
St. Lucia					X [1]
St. Vincent & the Grenadines					X
San Marino			X		X
Sao Tome					X
Senegal		X		X	X
Sierra Leone					X
Singapore					X
Slovak Rep.	X	X	X	X	X [1]
Slovenia					X

INDUSTRIAL PROPERTY
(Cont'd)

States which are parties	1911	1925	1934	1958	1967
South Africa			X	X	X [1]
Spain	X	X	X		X
Sri Lanka	X		X		X [2]
Sudan					X
Suriname			X		X
Swaziland					X
Sweden	X	X	X		X
Switzerland	X	X	X	X	X
Syrian Arab Rep.	X	X	X		
Tajikistan					X
Tanzania				X	X [2]
Togo				X	X
Trinidad & Tobago	X	X		X	X
Tunisia	X	X	X		X [1]
Turkey	X	X	X		X
Turkmenistan					X
Uganda				X	X
Ukraine					X
United Arab Emirates					X
United Kingdom	X	X	X	X	X [10]
United States	X	X	X	X	X [11]
Uruguay				X	X
Uzbekistan					X
Vatican City			X		X
Venezuela					X
Viet Nam			X		X [1]
Yugoslavia	X	X	X	X	X [1] [12]
Zambia			X	X	X [2]
Zimbabwe					X

NOTES to chart:
[1] With reservation under article 28.
[2] Not a party to articles 1–12; bound by relevant provisions of previous conventions.
[3] Applicable to Hong Kong and Macao. With declarations. See note under CHINA in bilateral section.
[4] Extended to Faroe Is.
[5] With declaration(s).
[6] Including all Overseas Departments and Territories.
[7] See note under GERMANY, FEDERAL REPUBLIC OF in bilateral section.
[8] Applicable to Netherlands Antilles and Aruba.
[9] Applicable to Cook Is., Niue and Tokelau.
[10] Extended to Isle of Man.
[11] Extended to all the territories and possessions of the United States, including Puerto Rico.
[12] See note under YUGOSLAVIA in bilateral section.

INDUSTRIAL PROPERTY
(Cont'd)

Nice agreement, as revised, concerning the international classification of goods and services for the purposes of the registration of marks.[1] Done at Geneva May 13, 1977; entered into force February 6, 1979; for the United States February 29, 1984.
TIAS
States which are parties:
Algeria
Australia
Austria
Barbados
Belarus
Belgium
Benin
Bosnia-Herzegovina
Bulgaria *
China [2]
Croatia
Cuba [3]
Czech Rep.
Denmark
Dominica
Estonia
Finland
Former Yugoslav Republic of Macedonia
France [4]
German Dem. Rep.[5]
Germany, Fed. Rep.[5]
Greece
Guinea
Hungary
Iceland
Ireland
Israel
Italy
Japan
Korea, Dem. People's Rep.
Korea, Rep.
Kyrgyz Rep.
Latvia
Lebanon
Liechtenstein
Lithuania
Luxembourg
Malawi
Moldova
Monaco
Morocco
Netherlands
Norway
Poland
Portugal
Romania
Russian Fed.
Singapore
Slovak Rep.
Slovenia
Spain
Suriname
Sweden
Switzerland
Tajikistan
Tanzania
Trinidad & Tobago
Tunisia
Turkey
Ukraine
Union of Soviet Socialist Reps. [6]

United Kingdom
United States
Uruguay
Yugoslavia

Amendment:
October 2, 1979.

NOTES:
  * Enters into force for Bulgaria February 27, 2001.
  [1] The 1977 agreement replaces as between contracting parties the agreement concerning the international classification of goods and services to which trade marks apply done at Nice June 15, 1957 (23 UST 1336; TIAS 7418; 550 UNTS 45), as revised at Stockholm July 14, 1967 (23 UST 1353; TIAS 7419; 828 UNTS 191). Parties to the 1967 revision not parties to the 1977 revision include: Algeria, Israel, Morocco and Yugoslavia. Lebanon and Tunisia are parties to the agreement of 1957 but are not parties to the subsequent revisions.
  [2] Applicable to Macao. See note under CHINA in bilateral section.
  [3] With declaration.
  [4] Extended to Overseas Departments and Territories.
  [5] See note under GERMANY, FEDERAL REPUBLIC OF in bilateral section.
  [6] See note under UNION OF SOVIET SOCIALIST REPUBLICS in bilateral section.

Trademark law treaty and regulations. Done at Geneva October 27, 1994; entered into force August 1, 1996; for the United States August 12, 2000.
TIAS
Parties:
Australia
Cyprus
Czech Rep.
Denmark [1]
Egypt
Hungary
Indonesia
Ireland
Japan
Latvia
Liechtenstein
Lithuania
Moldova
Monaco
Romania
Russian Fed.
Slovak Rep.
Spain
Sri Lanka
Switzerland
Trinidad & Tobago
Ukraine
United Kingdom
United States
Uzbekistan
Yugoslavia

NOTE:
  [1] Not applicable to the Faroe Is. or to Greenland.

INSULAR POSSESSIONS

Convention to adjust amicably questions between the United States, Germany, and the United Kingdom in respect of the Samoan group of islands.[1] Signed at Washington December 2, 1899; entered into force February 16, 1900.
31 Stat. 1878; TS 314; 1 Bevans 276.
States which are parties:
United Kingdom
United States

NOTE:
  [1] The German Samoan islands became a mandate of New Zealand on May 7, 1919, Germany having renounced rights and titles to them, effective August 4, 1919 (articles 22, 119, and 288, treaty of peace with Germany signed at Versailles June 28, 1919). Subsequently these islands were administered by New Zealand, first under a League of Nations mandate, then as a United Nations Trust Territory. On January 1, 1962, Western Samoa acquired the status of an independent state.

Treaty relating to insular possessions and insular dominions in the region of the Pacific Ocean, with declaration. Signed at Washington December 13, 1921; entered into force August 17, 1923.
43 Stat. 1646; TS 669; 2 Bevans 332; 25 LNTS 184.

Agreement supplementary to the treaty relating to insular possessions and insular dominions in the region of the Pacific Ocean. Signed at Washington February 6, 1922; entered into force August 17, 1923.
43 Stat. 1652; TS 670; 2 Bevans 372; 25 LNTS 196.
States which are parties:
France
Japan
United Kingdom
United States [1]

NOTE:
  [1] With reservation and understanding.

INTELLECTUAL PROPERTY

Convention establishing the World Intellectual Property Organization. Done at Stockholm July 14, 1967; entered into force April 26, 1970; for the United States August 25, 1970.
21 UST 1749; TIAS 6932; 828 UNTS 3.
States which are parties:
Albania
Algeria
Andorra
Angola
Antigua & Barbuda
Argentina
Armenia
Australia
Austria
Azerbaijan
Bahamas, The

INTELLECTUAL PROPERTY (Cont'd)

Bahrain
Bangladesh
Barbados
Belarus
Belgium
Belize
Benin
Bhutan
Bolivia
Bosnia-Herzegovina
Botswana
Brazil
Brunei
Bulgaria
Burkina Faso
Burundi
Cambodia
Cameroon
Canada
Cape Verde
Central African Rep.
Chad
Chile
China [1]
Colombia
Congo
Congo, Dem. Rep.
Costa Rica
Cote d'Ivoire
Croatia
Cuba
Cyprus
Czech Rep.
Denmark
Dominica
Dominican Rep.
Ecuador
Egypt
El Salvador
Equatorial Guinea
Eritrea
Estonia
Ethiopia
Fiji
Finland
Former Yugoslav Republic of Macedonia
France
Gabon
Gambia, The
Georgia
German Dem. Rep. [2]
Germany, Fed. Rep. [2]
Ghana
Greece
Grenada
Guatemala
Guinea
Guinea-Bissau
Guyana
Haiti
Holy See
Honduras
Hungary
Iceland
India
Indonesia
Iraq
Ireland
Israel

Italy
Jamaica
Japan
Jordan
Kazakhstan
Kenya
Korea, Dem. People's Rep.
Korea, Rep.
Kuwait
Kyrgyz Rep.
Laos
Latvia
Lebanon
Lesotho
Liberia
Libya
Liechtenstein
Lithuania
Luxembourg
Madagascar
Malawi
Malaysia
Mali
Malta
Mauritania
Mauritius
Mexico
Moldova
Monaco
Mongolia
Morocco
Mozambique
Namibia
Nepal
Netherlands [3]
New Zealand [4]
Nicaragua
Niger
Nigeria
Norway
Oman
Pakistan
Panama
Papau New Guinea
Paraguay
Peru
Philippines
Poland
Portugal
Qatar
Romania
Russian Fed.
Rwanda
St. Kitts & Nevis
St. Lucia
St. Vincent & the Grenadines
San Marino
Sao Tome & Principe
Saudi Arabia
Senegal
Seychelles
Sierra Leone
Singapore
Slovak Rep.
Slovenia
Somalia
South Africa
Spain
Sri Lanka
Sudan
Suriname
Swaziland
Sweden
Switzerland
Tajikistan

Tanzania
Thailand
Togo
Trinidad & Tobago
Tunisia
Turkey
Turkmenistan
Uganda
Ukraine
United Arab Emirates
United Kingdom
United States
Uruguay
Uzbekistan
Venezuela
Viet-Nam
Western Samoa
Yemen (Aden) [5]
Yemen (Sanaa) [5]
Yugoslavia [6]
Zambia
Zimbabwe

Amendment:
October 2, 1979.

NOTES:
[1] Applicable to Hong Kong and Macao. See note under CHINA in bilateral section.
[2] See note under GERMANY, FEDERAL REPUBLIC OF in bilateral section.
[3] Applicable to Netherlands Antilles and Aruba.
[4] Applicable to Cook Is., Niue and Tokelau.
[5] See note under YEMEN in bilateral section.
[6] See note under YUGOSLAVIA in bilateral section.

INTER-AMERICAN DEVELOPMENT BANK

(See under FINANCIAL INSTITUTIONS)

INTER-AMERICAN (RIO) TREATY OF RECIPROCAL ASSISTANCE

(See under DEFENSE)

INTERGOVERNMENTAL MARITIME CONSULTATIVE ORGANIZATION

(See INTERNATIONAL MARITIME ORGANIZATION)

INTERNATIONAL ATOMIC ENERGY AGENCY

(See under ATOMIC ENERGY)

INTERNATIONAL BANK FOR RECONSTRUCTION AND DEVELOPMENT

(See under FINANCIAL INSTITUTIONS)

INTERNATIONAL CIVIL AVIATION ORGANIZATION

(See also AVIATION)

Convention on international civil aviation.[1] Done at Chicago December 7, 1944; entered into force April 4, 1947.
61 Stat. 1180; TIAS 1591; 3 Bevans 944; 15 UNTS 295.

Protocol on the authentic trilingual text of the convention on international civil aviation with annex.[2] Done at Buenos Aires September 24, 1968; entered into force October 24, 1968.
19 UST 7693; TIAS 6605; 740 UNTS 21.

Proces-verbal of rectification to the protocol of September 24, 1968 on the authentic trilingual text of the convention on international civil aviation. Done at Washington April 8, 1969; entered into force April 8, 1969.
20 UST 718; TIAS 6681.

Protocol on the authentic quadrilingual text of the convention on international civil aviation, with annex.[2] Done at Montreal September 30, 1977; entered into force September 16, 1999.
TIAS
States which are parties:
Afghanistan [3]
Albania
Algeria [3]
Angola
Antigua & Barbuda
Argentina
Armenia
Australia
Austria
Azerbaijan
Bahamas, The
Bahrain
Bangladesh
Barbados
Belarus
Belgium
Belize
Benin [3]
Bhutan
Bolivia [3]
Bosnia-Herzegovina

Botswana
Brazil
Brunei
Bulgaria
Burkina Faso
Burma [3]
Burundi [3]
Cambodia [3]
Cameroon
Canada
Cape Verde
Central African Rep.[3]
Chad
Chile
China [4] [5]
Colombia
Comoros
Congo [3]
Congo, Dem. Rep. [3]
Cook Is.
Costa Rica
Cote d'Ivoire
Croatia
Cuba
Cyprus
Czech Rep.
Denmark
Djibouti
Dominican Rep.[3]
Ecuador
Egypt
El Salvador [3]
Equatorial Guinea
Eritrea
Estonia
Ethiopia [3] [6]
Fiji
Finland
Former Yugoslav Republic of Macedonia
France
Gabon
Gambia, The
Georgia
German Dem. Rep [7]
Germany, Fed. Rep.[7]
Ghana [3]
Greece
Grenada
Guatemala
Guinea [3]
Guinea-Bissau
Guyana [3]
Haiti [3]
Honduras [3]
Hungary
Iceland [3]
India
Indonesia [3]
Iran
Iraq
Ireland
Israel
Italy
Jamaica
Japan [3]
Jordan
Kazakhstan
Kenya [3]
Kiribati
Korea, Dem. People's Rep.
Korea, Rep.
Kuwait
Kyrgyz Rep.
Laos [3]
Latvia

Lebanon
Lesotho
Liberia [3]
Libya [3]
Lithuania
Luxembourg [3]
Madagascar
Malawi
Malaysia [3]
Maldives
Mali
Malta [3]
Marshall Is.[8]
Mauritania
Mauritius
Mexico
Micronesia [9]
Moldova
Monaco
Mongolia
Morocco [3]
Mozambique
Namibia
Nauru
Nepal [3]
Netherlands
New Zealand
Nicaragua [3]
Niger
Nigeria
Norway
Oman
Pakistan
Palau
Panama [4]
Papua New Guinea
Paraguay [3]
Peru
Philippines [3]
Poland
Portugal
Qatar
Romania
Russian Fed.
Rwanda
St. Lucia
St. Vincent & the Grenadines
San Marino
Sao Tome & Principe
Saudi Arabia [4]
Senegal [3]
Seychelles
Sierra Leone [3]
Singapore [3]
Slovak Rep.
Slovenia
Solomon Is.
Somalia [3]
South Africa
Spain
Sri Lanka [3]
Sudan [3]
Suriname
Swaziland
Sweden
Switzerland [10]
Syrian Arab Rep.
Tajikistan
Tanzania
Thailand [3]
Togo
Tonga
Trinidad & Tobago [3]
Tunisia
Turkey

INTERNATIONAL CIVIL AVIATION ORGANIZATION (Cont'd)

Turkmenistan
Uganda [3]
Ukraine
United Arab Emirates
United Kingdom
United States
Uruguay
Uzbekistan
Vanuatu
Venezuela
Vietnam, Socialist Rep.
Western Samoa
Yemen (Aden) [11]
Yemen (Sanaa) [3] [11]
Yugoslavia *
Zambia
Zimbabwe

NOTES:

* Enters into force for Yugoslavia January 13, 2001.

[1] Applicable to all territories.

[2] States becoming parties to the convention after the entry into force of the protocol are deemed parties to the protocol.

[3] Not a party to the protocol.

[4] With a statement.

[5] Applicable to Hong Kong and Macao. With declaration. See note under CHINA in bilateral section.

[6] See note under ETHIOPIA in bilateral section.

[7] See note under GERMANY, FEDERAL REPUBLIC OF in bilateral section.

[8] On October 15, 1986 the Compact of Free Association entered into force between the Government of the United States and the Government of the Republic of the Marshall Islands, effective October 21, 1986.

[9] On October 24, 1986 the Compact of Free Association entered into force between the Government of the United States and the Government of the Federated States of Micronesia, effective November 3, 1986.

[10] Applicable to Liechtenstein as long as the customs treaty of March 29, 1923 between Switzerland and Liechtenstein remains in force.

[11] See note under YEMEN in bilateral section.

Amendments: [1]
June 14, 1954 (8 UST 179; TIAS 3756; 320 UNTS 21).
September 15, 1962 (26 UST 2374; TIAS 8162; 1008 UNTS 213).
July 7, 1971 (26 UST 1061; TIAS 8092).
October 16, 1974 (32 UST 322; TIAS 9702). [2]
September 30, 1977.
September 30, 1977.
October 6, 1980.

NOTES:

[1] Protocols of amendment to the convention are legally binding only on those states which ratify or otherwise accept them; however, the above amendments are all of an organizational character and thus in effect for all ICAO members. The United States is not a party to the protocols of May 27, 1947 (418 UNTS 161) and June 14, 1954 (320 UNTS 209).

[2] This amendment increasing the size of the ICAO council supersedes the protocols of June 21, 1961 (13 UST 2105; TIAS 5170; 514 UNTS 209) and March 12, 1971 (24 UST 1019; TIAS 7616).

INTERNATIONAL COURT OF JUSTICE

Statute of the International Court of Justice annexed to the Charter of the United Nations. All Members of the United Nations are *ipso facto* parties to the Statute (article 93, UN Charter). 59 Stat. 1055; TS 993; 3 Bevans 1153.

In addition, the following countries not members of the UN have become parties to the Statute pursuant to resolutions adopted by the General Assembly:
Nauru
Switzerland (17 UNTS 111)

INTERNATIONAL DEVELOPMENT LAW INSTITUTE

(See under ECONOMIC AND TECHNICAL COOPERATION AND DEVELOPMENT)

INTERNATIONAL ENERGY AGENCY

(See under ENERGY)

INTERNATIONAL LABOR ORGANIZATION

(See under LABOR)

INTERNATIONAL MARITIME ORGANIZATION

Convention on the Intergovernmental Maritime Consultative Organization.* Signed at Geneva March 6, 1948; entered into force March 17, 1958.
9 UST 621; TIAS 4044; 289 UNTS 48.

States which are parties:
Albania
Algeria
Angola
Antigua & Barbuda
Argentina
Australia
Austria
Azerbaijan
Bahamas, The
Bahrain
Bangladesh
Barbados
Belgium
Belize
Benin
Bolivia
Bosnia-Herzegovina
Brazil
Brunei
Bulgaria
Burma
Cambodia [1]
Cameroon
Canada
Cape Verde
Chile
China
Colombia
Congo
Congo, Dem. Rep.
Costa Rica
Cote d'Ivoire
Croatia
Cuba [1]
Cyprus
Czech Rep.
Denmark [1]
Djibouti
Dominica
Dominican Rep.
Ecuador [1]
Egypt
El Salvador
Equatorial Guinea
Eritrea
Estonia
Ethiopia [2]
Fiji
Finland [1]
Former Yugoslav Republic of Macedonia
France
Gabon
Gambia, The
Georgia
German Dem. Rep. [1] [3]
Germany, Fed. Rep. [3]
Ghana
Greece [1]
Grenada
Guatemala
Guinea
Guinea-Bissau
Guyana
Haiti
Honduras
Hong Kong [4]
Hungary
Iceland [1]
India [1]
Indonesia [1]
Iran
Iraq [1]
Ireland
Israel

INTERNATIONAL MARITIME ORGANIZATION (Cont'd)

Italy
Jamaica
Japan
Jordan
Kazakhstan
Kenya
Korea, Dem. People's Rep.
Korea, Rep.
Kuwait
Latvia
Lebanon
Liberia
Libya
Lithuania
Luxembourg
Macao [4]
Madagascar
Malawi
Malaysia [1]
Maldives
Malta
Marshall Is.
Mauritania
Mauritius
Mexico [1]
Monaco
Mongolia
Morocco [1]
Mozambique
Namibia
Nepal
Netherlands [5]
New Zealand
Nicaragua
Nigeria
Norway [1]
Oman
Pakistan
Panama
Papua New Guinea
Paraguay
Peru
Philippines
Poland [1]
Portugal
Qatar
Romania
Russian Fed.
St. Lucia
St. Vincent & the Grenadines
Samoa
Sao Tome & Principe
Saudi Arabia
Senegal
Seychelles
Sierra Leone
Singapore
Slovak Rep.
Slovenia
Solomon Is.
Somalia
South Africa
Spain [1]
Sri Lanka [1]
Sudan
Suriname
Sweden [1]

Switzerland [1]
Syrian Arab Rep.
Tanzania
Thailand
Togo
Tonga
Trinidad & Tobago
Tunisia
Turkey [1]
Turkmenistan
Ukraine
Union of Soviet Socialist Reps. [6]
United Arab Emirates
United Kingdom
United States [1]
Uruguay
Vanuatu
Venezuela
Vietnam
Yemen (Aden) [7]
Yemen (Sanaa) [7]
Yugoslavia [8]

Amendments:
September 15, 1964 (18 UST 1299; TIAS 6285; 607 UNTS 276).
September 28, 1965 (19 UST 4855; TIAS 6490; 649 UNTS 334).
October 17, 1974 (28 UST 4607; TIAS 8606).
November 14, 1975 (34 UST 497; TIAS 10374).
November 17, 1977 (TIAS 11094).
November 15, 1979 (TIAS 11094).

NOTES:
* The title of the Convention was changed to the Convention on the International Maritime Organization by amendment adopted by the Organization November 14, 1975, effective May 22, 1982.
[1] With declaration.
[2] See note under ETHIOPIA in bilateral section.
[3] See note under GERMANY, FEDERAL REPUBLIC OF in bilateral section.
[4] Associate Member.
[5] Applicable to Netherlands Antilles and Aruba.
[6] See note under UNION OF SOVIET SOCIALIST REPUBLICS in bilateral section.
[7] See note under YEMEN in bilateral section.
[8] See note under YUGOSLAVIA in bilateral section.

INTERNATIONAL MONETARY FUND

(See under FINANCIAL INSTITUTIONS)

INTERNATIONAL TRACING SERVICE

Agreement constituting an International Commission for the International Tracing Service.

Signed at Bonn June 6, 1955; entered into force May 5, 1955.
6 UST 6186; TIAS 3471, pp. 18-37; 219 UNTS 79.
States which are parties:
Belgium
France
Germany, Fed. Rep. [1]
Greece
Israel
Italy
Luxembourg
Netherlands
United Kingdom
United States

Extensions and amendments:
August 23, 1960 (12 UST 463; TIAS 4736, pp. 18-24; 377 UNTS 402).
April 27, 1972.

Related agreements

Agreement relating to the operation of the International Tracing Service. Exchange of notes between the United States and the Federal Republic of Germany at Bonn and Bonn-Bad Godesberg June 6, 1955; operative May 5, 1955.[2]
6 UST 6169; TIAS 3471, pp. 2-6; 315 UNTS 155.

Extensions and amendments:
April 28 and May 5, 1960 (12 UST 445; TIAS 4736, pp. 2-5).
May 24, 1968.

Agreement providing for the administration and direction of the International Tracing Service by the International Committee of the Red Cross. Exchange of notes between the United States and the President of the International Committee of the Red Cross at Bonn–Bad Godesberg and Geneva June 6, 1955; entered into force May 5, 1955.[3]
6 UST 6175; TIAS 3471, pp. 7-17.

Extensions and amendments:
May 9 and 12, 1960 (12 UST 452; TIAS 4736, pp. 5-18).
May 31 and July 25, 1968.

NOTES:
[1] See note under GERMANY, FEDERAL REPUBLIC OF in bilateral section.
[2] Notes were exchanged *mutatis mutandis* by the Federal Republic of Germany with France and the United Kingdom.
[3] Notes were exchanged *mutatis mutandis* by the International Committee of the Red Cross with France, the Federal Republic of Germany, and the United Kingdom. See also agreement signed at Bonn June 6, 1955 by the Chairman of the International Commission and a representative of the International Committee of the Red Cross (6 UST 6207; TIAS 3471, pp. 39-54; 219 UNTS 96), as extended and amended September 30 and October 7, 1960 (12 UST 471; TIAS 4736, pp. 2533); December 22, 1972.

INVESTMENT DISPUTES

Convention on the settlement of investment disputes between states and nationals of other states.[1] Done at Washington March 18, 1965; entered into force October 14, 1966.
17 UST 1270; TIAS 6090; 575 UNTS 159.
States which are parties:
Afghanistan
Albania
Algeria
Argentina
Armenia
Australia
Austria
Azerbaijan
Bahamas
Bahrain
Bangladesh
Barbados
Belarus
Belgium
Benin
Bolivia
Bosnia-Herzegovina
Botswana
Burkina Faso
Burundi
Cameroon
Central African Rep.
Chad
Chile
China [2]
China, People's Rep. [3]
Colombia
Comoros
Congo
Congo, Dem. Rep.
Costa Rica
Cote d'Ivoire
Croatia
Cyprus
Czech Rep.
Denmark [4]
Ecuador
Egypt
El Salvador
Estonia
Fiji
Finland
Former Yugoslav Republic of Macedonia
France
Gabon
Gambia, The
Georgia
Germany, Fed. Rep.[5]
Ghana
Greece
Grenada
Guinea
Guyana
Honduras
Hungary
Iceland
Indonesia
Ireland
Israel
Italy
Jamaica
Japan
Jordan
Kenya
Korea

Kuwait
Latvia
Lesotho
Liberia
Lithuania
Luxembourg
Madagascar
Malawi
Malaysia
Mali
Mauritania
Mauritius
Micronesia
Mongolia
Morocco
Mozambique
Nepal
Netherlands [6]
New Zealand
Nicaragua
Niger
Nigeria
Norway
Oman
Pakistan
Panama
Papua New Guinea
Paraguay
Peru
Philippines
Portugal
Romania
Rwanda
St. Kitts & Nevis
St. Lucia
Saudi Arabia
Senegal
Seychelles
Sierra Leone
Singapore
Slovak Rep.
Slovenia
Solomon Is.
Somalia
Spain
Sri Lanka
Sudan
Swaziland
Sweden
Switzerland
Tanzania
Togo
Tonga
Trinidad & Tobago
Tunisia
Turkey
Turkmenistan
Uganda
Ukraine
United Arab Emirates
United Kingdom [7]
United States
Uruguay
Uzbekistan
Venezuela
Western Samoa
Yugoslavia [8]
Zambia
Zimbabwe

NOTES:
[1] The convention is applicable to all territories for whose international relations a Contracting State is responsible, except those which are excluded by such State by written notice to the depositary . . .'' (Article 70).
[2] On October 2, 1980, the Administrative Council decided that ''the Republic of China be removed from the list of Contracting States and noted that, pending study by the Government of the People's Republic of the possibility of becoming a party to the Convention, China is not a Contracting State.''
[3] Applicable to Hong Kong and Macao. See note under CHINA in bilateral section.
[4] Extended to Faroe Is.
[5] See note under GERMANY, FEDERAL REPUBLIC OF in bilateral section.
[6] Applicable to Netherlands Antilles and Aruba.
[7] Extended to all territories for whose international relations it is responsible except British Indian Ocean Territory, Pitcairn Islands, and Sovereign Base Areas of Cyprus.
[8] See note under YUGOSLAVIA in bilateral section.

JUDICIAL PROCEDURE

INTER-AMERICAN AGREEMENTS

Convention for the establishment of an International Commission of Jurists. Signed at Rio de Janeiro August 23, 1906; entered into force August 26, 1907; for the United States March 9, 1908.
37 Stat. 1554; TS 565; 1 Bevans 547.
States which are parties:
Argentina
Brazil
Chile
Colombia
Costa Rica
Dominican Rep.
Ecuador
El Salvador
Guatemala
Honduras
Mexico
Nicaragua
Panama
Peru
United States
Uruguay

Protocol embodying a declaration on the juridical personality of foreign companies. Done at the Pan American Union, Washington, June 25, 1936; entered into force for the United States July 10, 1941.
55 Stat. 1201; TS 973; 3 Bevans 274; 161 UNTS 217.
States which are parties:
Chile [1]
Dominican Rep.[1]
Ecuador
El Salvador
Nicaragua
Peru

JUDICIAL PROCEDURE (Cont'd)

United States [2]
Venezuela

NOTES:
  [1] With a statement.
  [2] With understandings.

Protocol on uniformity of powers of attorney which are to be utilized abroad. Done at the Pan American Union, Washington, February 17, 1940; entered into force for the United States April 16, 1942.
56 Stat. 1376; TS 982; 3 Bevans 612; 161 UNTS 229.
States which are parties:
Brazil
Colombia [1]
El Salvador [1]
Mexico [1]
United States
Venezuela [1]

NOTE:
  [1] With reservation.

Inter-American convention on letters rogatory. Done at Panama January 30, 1975; entered into force January 16, 1976; for the United States August 27, 1988.
TIAS

Additional protocol to the Inter-American convention on letters rogatory, with annex. Done at Montevideo May 8, 1979; entered into force June 14, 1980; for the United States August 27, 1988.
TIAS
Parties:
Argentina*
Brazil*
Chile* [1]
Colombia*
Costa Rica
Ecuador*
El Salvador [1][2]
Guatemala*
Honduras
Mexico* [1]
Panama*
Paraguay*
Peru* [1]
Spain [3]
United States* [2]
Uruguay* [3]
Venezuela* [2]

NOTES:
  * The United States has a treaty relationship only with these countries which are a party to the Convention and the Additional Protocol.
  [1] With declaration(s).
  [2] With reservation(s).
  [3] Designation of Central Authority in accordance with Article 4.

HAGUE CONVENTIONS [1]

NOTE:
  [1] Adopted under the auspices of the Hague Conference on International Law. (See under LAW, PRIVATE INTERNATIONAL.)

Convention abolishing the requirement of legalisation for foreign public documents, with annex. Done at The Hague October 5, 1961; entered into force January 24, 1965; for the United States October 15, 1981.
33 UST 883; TIAS 10072; 527 UNTS 189.
States which are parties: [1]
Andorra
Antigua & Barbuda
Argentina
Armenia
Australia
Austria
Bahamas, The
Barbados
Belarus
Belgium
Belize
Bosnia-Herzegovina
Botswana
Brunei
Croatia
Cyprus
Czech Rep.
El Salvador
Fiji
Finland
Former Yugoslav Republic of Macedonia
France [2]
Germany, Fed. Rep. [3]
Greece
Hong Kong [4]
Hungary
Ireland
Israel
Italy
Japan
Latvia
Lesotho
Liberia
Liechtenstein
Lithuania
Luxembourg
Macao [4]
Malawi
Malta
Marshall Is.
Mauritius
Mexico
Netherlands [5]
Niue
Norway
Panama [1]
Portugal [2]
Russian Fed.
St. Kitts & Nevis
Samoa
San Marino
Seychelles
Slovenia
South Africa
Spain
Suriname
Swaziland
Sweden
Switzerland
Tonga

Turkey
Union of Soviet Socialist Reps. [6]
United Kingdom [7]
United States [8][9]
Venezuela
Yugoslavia [10]

NOTES:
  [1] With designation(s).
  [2] Applicable to all overseas departments and territories.
  [3] See note under GERMANY, FEDERAL REPUBLIC OF in bilateral section.
  [4] CHINA is not a party to this treaty but has made it applicable to Hong Kong and Macao. With declaration.
  [5] Applicable to the Kingdom in Europe, the Netherlands Antilles, and Aruba.
  [6] See note under UNION OF SOVIET SOCIALIST REPUBLICS in bilateral section.
  [7] Applicable to Anguilla, Jersey, the Bailiwick of Guernsey, Isle of Man, Bermuda, Cayman Is., Falkland Is., Gibraltar, Montserrat, St. Helena, Turks and Caicos Is. and the British Virgin Is.
  [8] Extended to those territories for the foreign relations of which the United States is responsible.
  [9] With statement(s).
  [10] See note under YUGOSLAVIA in bilateral section.

Convention on the service abroad of judicial and extrajudicial documents in civil or commercial matters. Done at The Hague November 15, 1965; entered into force February 10, 1969.
20 UST 361; TIAS 6638; 658 UNTS 163.
States which are parties: [1]
Antigua & Barbuda
Bahamas
Barbados
Belarus
Belgium [2]
Botswana [2]
Canada [2]
China [1][2][3]
Cyprus [2]
Czech Rep.
Denmark [2]
Egypt
Estonia [2]
Finland [2]
France [2]
Germany, Fed. Rep. [2][4]
Greece [2]
Ireland [2]
Israel [2]
Italy
Japan [2]
Latvia
Luxembourg [2]
Malawi
Netherlands [2][5]
Norway [2]
Pakistan
Poland [2]
Portugal [2]
Seychelles [2]
Slovak Rep.
Spain [2]
Sweden [2]
Switzerland [2]
Turkey [2]

JUDICIAL PROCEDURE (Cont'd)

United Kingdom [2][6]
United States [2][7]
Venezuela [2]

NOTES:
[1] With designation(s).
[2] With declaration(s).
[3] Applicable to Hong Kong and Macao. With declarations. See note under CHINA in bilateral section.
[4] See note under GERMANY, FEDERAL REPUBLIC OF in bilateral section.
[5] Extended to Aruba.
[6] Extended to Anguilla, Bermuda, British Virgin Is., Cayman Is., Central and Southern Line Is., Falkland Is. and dependencies, Gibraltar, Guernsey, Isle of Man, Jersey, Montserrat, Pitcairn, St. Helena and dependencies, Turks and Caicos Is.
[7] Extended to the Commonwealth of the Northern Mariana Is., the District of Columbia, Guam, Puerto Rico, and the Virgin Is.

Convention on the taking of evidence abroad in civil or commercial matters. Done at The Hague March 18, 1970; entered into force October 7, 1972.
23 UST 2555; TIAS 7444; 847 UNTS 231.
States which are parties: [1]
Argentina [2][3]
Australia [2][3]
Barbados
China [2][3][4]
Cyprus
Czech Rep.
Denmark [2][3]
Estonia [2]
Finland [2][3]
France [2][5]
Germany, Fed. Rep. [2][3][6]
Israel [2]
Italy [2]
Latvia
Luxembourg [2][3]
Mexico [2][3]
Monaco [2][3]
Netherlands [7]
Norway [2][3]
Poland
Portugal [2][3]
Singapore [2][3]
Slovak Rep.
South Africa [2][3]
Spain [2][3]
Sweden [2]
Switzerland [2][3]
United Kingdom [2][3][8]
United States [2][9]
Venezuela

NOTES:
[1] With designation(s).
[2] With declaration(s).
[3] With reservation(s).
[4] Applicable to Hong Kong and Macao. With declarations. See note under CHINA in bilateral section.
[5] Applicable to all territories of the French Republic.

[6] See note under GERMANY, FEDERAL REPUBLIC OF in bilateral section.
[7] Extended to Aruba.
[8] Extended to Anguilla, Cayman Is., Falkland Is. and dependencies, Gibraltar, Guernsey, Isle of Man, Jersey, and the Sovereign Base Areas of Akrotiri and Dhekelia on the Island of Cyprus.
[9] Extended to Guam, Puerto Rico, and the Virgin Is.

Convention on the civil aspects of international child abduction. Done at The Hague October 25, 1980; entered into force December 1, 1983; for the United States July 1, 1988.
TIAS 11670.
Parties:
Argentina [1]
Australia [2]
Austria [1]
Bahamas
Belize [3]
Bosnia-Herzegovina
Burkina Faso
Canada [3][4][5]
Chile [4]
Colombia
Croatia
Cyprus
Czech Rep.
Denmark [1][4]
Ecuador
Finland [4]
Former Yugoslav Republic of Macedonia
France [3][4]
Germany, Fed. Rep. [1][3][6]
Greece [3][4]
Honduras
Hong Kong [7]
Hungary [1]
Iceland
Ireland
Israel [3]
Italy
Luxembourg [4]
Macao [7]
Mauritius [3]
Mexico
Monaco [3]
Netherlands [3][8]
New Zealand [3]
Norway [3]
Panama
Poland [3]
Portugal [1]
Romania
St. Kitts & Nevis [3]
Slovak Rep.
Slovenia
South Africa
Spain [1]
Sweden [3]
Switzerland [1]
Turkey
United Kingdom [3][4][9]
United States [1][3]
Venezuela [3]
Yugoslavia [10]
Zimbabwe

NOTES:
[1] With designation(s).
[2] Extended to legal system applicable only in Australian states and mainland territories.
[3] With reservation(s).

[4] With declaration(s).
[5] Extended to Alberta, Newfoundland, Northwest Territories, Nova Scotia, Prince Edward Is., Quebec, Saskatchewan and Yukon Territory.
[6] See note under GERMANY, FEDERAL REPUBLIC OF in bilateral section.
[7] CHINA is not a party to this treaty but has made it applicable to Hong Kong and Macao. With declarations.
[8] Applicable to Kingdom in Europe.
[9] Extended to Isle of Man.
[10] See note under YUGOSLAVIA in bilateral section.

KOREA

Joint declaration of policy on Korea. Signed at Washington July 27, 1953.
4 UST 230; TIAS 2781.
States which are parties:
Australia
Belgium
Canada
Colombia
Ethiopia [1]
France
Greece
Luxembourg
Netherlands
New Zealand
Philippines
South Africa
Thailand
Turkey
United Kingdom
United States

NOTE:
[1] See note under ETHIOPIA in bilateral section.

Agreement concerning a military armistice in Korea, with annex. Signed at Panmunjom July 27, 1953, by the Commander-in-Chief, United Nations Command; the Supreme Commander of the Korean People's Army; and the Commander of the Chinese People's Volunteers; entered into force July 27, 1953.
4 UST 234; TIAS 2782.

Temporary agreement supplementary to the armistice agreement in Korea. Signed at Panmunjom July 27, 1953, by the Commander-in-Chief, United Nations Command; the Supreme Commander of the Korean People's Army; and the Commander of the Chinese People's Volunteers; entered into force July 27, 1953.
4 UST 346; TIAS 2782.

Agreement regarding the status of the United Nations forces in Japan, with agreed official minutes. Signed at Tokyo February 19, 1954; entered into force June 11, 1954.
5 UST 1123; TIAS 2995; 214 UNTS 51.
States which are parties:
Australia
Canada
France
Italy
Japan
New Zealand

KOREA (Cont'd)

Philippines
South Africa
Thailand
Turkey
United Kingdom
United States

LABOR

Instrument for the amendment of the constitution of the International Labor Organization. Dated at Montreal October 9, 1946; entered into force April 20, 1948; reentered into force for the United States February 18, 1980.[1]
62 Stat. 3485; TIAS 1868; 4 Bevans 188; 15 UNTS 35.
Members of the International Labor Organization:
Afghanistan
Algeria
Angola
Antigua & Barbuda
Argentina
Armenia
Australia
Austria
Azerbaijan
Bahamas, The
Bahrain
Bangladesh
Barbados
Belarus
Belgium
Belize
Benin
Bolivia
Bosnia-Herzegovina
Botswana
Brazil
Bulgaria
Burkina Faso
Burma
Burundi
Cambodia
Cameroon
Canada
Cape Verde
Central African Rep.
Chad
Chile
China[2]
Colombia
Comoros
Congo
Congo, Dem. Rep.
Costa Rica
Cote d'Ivoire
Croatia
Cuba
Cyprus
Czech Rep.
Denmark
Djibouti
Dominica
Dominican Rep.
Ecuador
Egypt
El Salvador

Equatorial Guinea
Eritrea
Estonia
Ethiopia[3]
Fiji
Finland
Former Yugoslav Republic of Macedonia
France
Gabon
Georgia
German Dem. Rep.[4]
Germany, Fed. Rep.[4]
Ghana
Greece
Grenada
Guatemala
Guinea
Guinea-Bissau
Guyana
Haiti
Honduras
Hungary
Iceland
India
Indonesia
Iran
Iraq
Ireland
Israel
Italy
Jamaica
Japan
Jordan
Kazakhstan
Kenya
Korea
Kuwait
Kyrgyz Rep.
Laos
Latvia
Lebanon
Lesotho
Liberia
Libya
Lithuania[5]
Luxembourg
Madagascar
Malawi
Malaysia
Mali
Malta
Mauritania
Mauritius
Mexico
Moldova
Mongolia
Morocco
Mozambique
Namibia
Nepal
Netherlands
New Zealand
Nicaragua
Niger
Nigeria
Norway
Oman
Pakistan
Panama
Papua New Guinea
Paraguay
Peru
Philippines
Poland
Portugal

Qatar
Romania
Rwanda
St. Lucia
San Marino
Sao Tome & Principe
Saudi Arabia
Senegal
Seychelles
Sierra Leone
Singapore
Slovak Rep.
Slovenia
Solomon Is.
Somalia
South Africa
Spain
Sri Lanka
Sudan
Suriname
Swaziland
Sweden
Switzerland
Syrian Arab Rep.
Tajikistan
Tanzania
Thailand
Togo
Trinidad & Tobago
Tunisia
Turkey
Turkmenistan
Uganda
Ukraine
Union of Soviet Socialist Reps.[6]
United Arab Emirates
United Kingdom
United States
Uruguay
Uzbekistan
Venezuela
Vietnam, Socialist Rep.
Yemen (Aden)[7]
Yemen (Sanaa)[7]
Yugoslavia[8]
Zambia
Zimbabwe

Amendments:
June 25, 1953 (7 UST 245; TIAS 3500; 191 UNTS 143).
June 22, 1962 (14 UST 1039; TIAS 5401; 466 UNTS 323).
June 22, 1972 (25 UST 3253; TIAS 7987).

NOTES:
[1] The Constitution of the ILO instrument of amendment, 1946, entered into force for the United States April 20, 1948. By letter dated November 5, 1975 the United States informed the Director-General of the ILO of its intention to withdraw from the organization. The withdrawal became effective November 6, 1977. By letter dated February 15, 1980 the United States informed the Director-General of its decision to resume membership in the organization and accordingly accepted the obligations of the ILO Constitution; which became effective February 18, 1980.
[2] Applicable to Hong Kong and Macao. See note under CHINA in bilateral section.
[3] See note under ETHIOPIA in bilateral section.
[4] See note under GERMANY, FEDERAL REPUBLIC OF in bilateral section.

LABOR (Cont'd)

[5] With statement.

[6] See note under UNION OF SOVIET SO-
CIALIST REPUBLICS in bilateral section.

[7] See note under YEMEN in bilateral section.

[8] See note under YUGOSLAVIA in bilateral
section.

Convention (ILO No. 53) concerning the min-
imum requirement of professional capacity for
masters and officers on board merchant ships.
Adopted at the 21st session of the General
Conference of the International Labor Organi-
zation, Geneva, October 24, 1936; entered into
force March 29, 1939; for the United States
October 29, 1939.
54 Stat. 1683; TS 950; 3 Bevans 281; 40
    UNTS 153.
States which are parties:
Argentina
Belgium
Bosnia-Herzegovina
Brazil
Bulgaria
Croatia [1]
Cuba
Denmark [1]
Djibouti
Egypt
Estonia
Finland
Former Yugoslav Republic of Macedonia
France [2]
Germany [3]
Ireland
Israel
Italy
Liberia
Libya
Luxembourg
Mauritania
Mexico
New Zealand
Norway
Panama
Peru
Philippines
Slovenia
Spain
Syrian Arab Rep.
United States [4] [5]
Yugoslavia [6]

NOTES:
[1] Extended to all Danish territories except
Greenland.
[2] Extended to Guadeloupe, Martinique,
French Guiana, and Reunion.
[3] See note under GERMANY, FEDERAL
REPUBLIC OF in bilateral section.
[4] With understandings.
[5] Extended to all territories over which the
United States has jurisdiction.
[6] See note under YUGOSLAVIA in bilateral
section.

Convention (ILO No. 55) concerning the liabil-
ity of the shipowner in case of sickness, injury
or death of seamen. Adopted at the 21st ses-
sion of the General Conference of the Inter-
national Labor Organization, Geneva, October
24, 1936; entered into force October 29, 1939.
54 Stat. 1693; TS 951; 3 Bevans 287; 40
    UNTS 169.
States which are parties:
Belgium
Bulgaria
Djibouti
Egypt
France [1]
Greece
Italy
Liberia
Luxembourg
Mexico
Morocco
Panama
Peru
Spain
Tunisia
United States [2] [3]

NOTES:
[1] Extended to Guadeloupe, Martinique,
French Guiana, and Reunion.
[2] With understandings.
[3] Extended to all territories over which the
United States has jurisdiction.

Convention (ILO No. 58) fixing the minimum
age for the admission of children to employ-
ment at sea (revised 1936). Adopted at the
22nd session of the General Conference of the
International Labor Organization, Geneva, Oc-
tober 24, 1936; entered into force April 11,
1939; for the United States October 29, 1939.
54 Stat. 1705; TS 952; 3 Bevans 294; 40
    UNTS 205.
Parties:
Argentina
Australia
Belize
Bermuda [1]
Brazil
Brunei
Canada
Djibouti
Fiji
Ghana
Grenada
Guatemala
Hong Kong [2]
Jamaica
Japan
Lebanon
Liberia
Mauritania
Mexico
New Zealand
Nigeria
Panama
Peru
Seychelles
Sierra Leone
Sri Lanka
Tanzania:
    Zanzibar
Union of Soviet Socialist Reps. [3]
United States [4] [5]
Yemen (Aden) [6]

NOTES:
[1] Applied by the United Kingdom with
modifications for Bermuda.

[2] CHINA is not a party to this treaty but has
made it applicable to Hong Kong.
[3] See note under UNION OF SOVIET SO-
CIALIST REPUBLICS in bilateral section.
[4] With understandings.
[5] Extended to all territories over which the
United States has jurisdiction.
[6] See note under YEMEN in bilateral section.

Convention (ILO No. 74) concerning the cer-
tification of able seamen. Adopted at the 28th
session of the General Conference of the Inter-
national Labor Organization, Seattle, June 29,
1946; entered into force July 14, 1951; for the
United States April 9, 1954.
5 UST 605; TIAS 2949; 94 UNTS 11.
States which are parties:
Algeria
Angola
Barbados
Belgium
Bosnia-Herzegovina
Canada
Croatia
Egypt
Former Yugoslav Republic of Macedonia
France [1]
Ghana
Guinea-Bissau
Hong Kong [2]
Ireland
Italy
Lebanon
Luxembourg
Macao [2]
Mauritius
Netherlands [3]
New Zealand
Panama
Poland
Portugal
Slovenia
Spain
United Kingdom [4]
United States [5] [6]
Yugoslavia [7]

NOTES:
[1] Extended to Guadeloupe, Martinique,
French Guiana, and Reunion.
[2] CHINA is not a party to this treaty but has
made it applicable to Hong Kong and Macao.
[3] Applicable to Netherlands Antilles and
Aruba.
[4] Extended to Isle of Man, Jersey, and
Guernsey.
[5] With understandings.
[6] Extended to Puerto Rico, Virgin Is., and
Guam.
[7] See note under YUGOSLAVIA in bilateral
sections.

Convention (ILO No. 80) for the partial revision of the conventions adopted by the General
Conference of the International Labor Organization at its first twenty-eight sessions (Final
articles revision convention, 1946). Adopted at
the 29th session of the General Conference of
the International Labor Organization, Montreal,
October 9, 1946; entered into force May 28,
1947; for the United States June 24, 1948.
62 Stat. 1672; TIAS 1810; 4 Bevans 183; 38
    UNTS 3.

LABOR (Cont'd)

States which are parties:
Algeria
Argentina
Australia [1]
Austria
Bangladesh
Belgium
Bosnia-Herzegovina
Brazil
Bulgaria
Canada
Chile
Colombia
Cuba
Czech Rep.
Denmark
Dominican Rep.
Egypt
Ethiopia [2]
Finland
Former Yugoslav Republic of Macedonia
France
Greece
Guatemala
India
Iraq
Ireland
Italy
Japan
Lithuania
Luxembourg
Mexico
Morocco
Netherlands
New Zealand
Norway
Pakistan
Panama
Peru
Poland
Slovak Rep.
Slovenia
South Africa
Spain
Sri Lanka
Sweden
Switzerland
Syrian Arab Rep.
Thailand
Turkey
United Kingdom
United States
Uruguay
Venezuela
Viet-Nam [3]
Yugoslavia [4]

NOTES:
[1] Extended to Norfolk Is.
[2] See note under ETHIOPIA in bilateral section.
[3] See Vietnam footnote under AGRICULTURE: agreement of January 25, 1924 (26 UST 1840; TIAS 8141; 57 LNTS 135).
[4] See note under YUGOSLAVIA in bilateral section.

Convention (ILO No. 105) concerning the abolition of forced labor. Adopted at the 40th session of the General Conference of the International Labor Organization, Geneva, June 25, 1957; entered into force January 17, 1959; for the United States September 25, 1992.
TIAS   ; 320 UNTS 291.
Parties:
Afghanistan
Albania
Algeria
Angola
Antigua & Barbuda
Argentina
Australia [1]
Austria
Bahamas
Bahrain
Bangladesh
Barbados
Belarus
Belgium
Belize
Benin
Bolivia
Botswana
Brazil
Bulgaria
Burkina Faso
Burundi
Cambodia
Cameroon
Canada
Cape Verde
Central African Rep.
Chad
Chile
Colombia
Comoros
Congo
Costa Rica
Cote d'Ivoire
Croatia
Cuba
Cyprus
Czech Rep.
Denmark
Djibouti
Dominica
Dominican Rep.
Ecuador
Egypt
El Salvador
Estonia
Ethiopia
Fiji
Finland
France
Gabon
Georgia
Germany [2]
Ghana
Greece
Grenada
Guatemala
Guinea
Guinea-Bissau
Guyana
Haiti
Honduras
Hong Kong [3]
Hungary
Iceland
Indonesia
Iran
Iraq
Ireland
Israel
Italy

Jamaica
Jordan
Kenya
Kuwait
Kyrgyz Rep.
Latvia
Lebanon
Liberia
Libya
Lithuania
Luxembourg
Macao [3]
Malawi
Mali
Malta
Mauritania
Mauritius
Mexico
Moldova
Morocco
Mozambique
Netherlands
New Zealand [1]
Nicaragua
Niger
Nigeria
Norway
Pakistan
Panama
Papua New Guinea
Paraguay
Peru
Philippines
Poland
Portugal
Romania
Russian Fed.
Rwanda
St. Lucia
St. Vincent & the Grenadines
San Marino
Saudi Arabia
Senegal
Seychelles
Sierra Leone
Slovak Rep.
Slovenia
Somalia
South Africa
Spain
Sudan
Suriname
Swaziland
Sweden
Switzerland
Syrian Arab Rep.
Tajikistan
Tanzania
Thailand
Togo
Trinidad & Tobago
Tunisia
Turkey
Turkmenistan
Uganda
United Arab Emirates
United Kingdom
United States
Uruguay
Uzbekistan
Venezuela
Yemen [4]
Zambia
Zimbabwe

LABOR (Cont'd)

NOTES:

[1] With declaration(s).

[2] See note under GERMANY, FEDERAL REPUBLIC OF in bilateral section.

[3] CHINA is not a party to this treaty but has made it applicable to Hong Kong and Macao.

[4] See note under YEMEN in bilateral section.

Convention (ILO No. 144) concerning tripartite consultations to promote the implementation of international labor standards. Adopted at the 61st session of the General Conference of the International Labor Organization, Geneva, June 21, 1976; entered into force May 16, 1978.
TIAS
Parties:
Albania
Algeria
Argentina
Australia
Austria
Azerbaijan
Bahamas
Bangladesh
Barbados
Belarus
Belgium
Botswana
Brazil
Bulgaria
Burundi
Chad
Chile
China [1]
Colombia
Congo
Costa Rica
Cote d'Ivoire
Cyprus
Denmark
Dominican Rep.
Ecuador
Egypt
El Salvador
Estonia
Fiji
Finland
France
Gabon
Germany, Fed. Rep. [2]
Greece
Grenada
Guatemala
Guinea
Guyana
Hungary
Iceland
India
Indonesia
Iraq
Ireland
Italy
Jamaica
Kenya
Korea
Latvia
Lesotho
Lithuania
Madagascar
Malawi

Mauritius
Mexico
Moldova
Mongolia
Mozambique
Namibia
Nepal
Netherlands
New Zealand
Nicaragua
Nigeria
Norway
Pakistan
Philippines
Poland
Portugal
Romania
San Marino
Sao Tome & Principe
Sierra Leone
Slovak Rep.
Spain
Sri Lanka
Suriname
Swaziland
Sweden
Syria
Tanzania
Togo
Trinidad & Tobago
Turkey
Uganda
Ukraine
United Kingdom
United States
Uruguay
Venezuela
Zambia
Zimbabwe

NOTES:

[1] Applicable to Hong Kong and Macao. See note under CHINA in bilateral section.

[2] See note under GERMANY, FEDERAL REPUBLIC OF in bilateral section.

Convention (ILO No. 147) concerning minimum standards in merchant ships. Adopted at the 62nd session of the General Conference of the International Labor Organization, Geneva, October 13, 1976; entered into force November 28, 1981.
TIAS
Parties:
Azerbaijan
Barbados
Belgium
Brazil
Canada
Costa Rica
Croatia
Cyprus
Denmark
Egypt
Finland
France
Germany, Fed. Rep. [1]
Greece
Hong Kong [2]
Iceland
India
Iraq
Ireland
Israel
Italy

Japan
Kyrgyz Rep.
Latvia
Lebanon
Liberia
Luxembourg
Morocco
Netherlands
Norway
Poland
Portugal
Russian Fed.
Slovenia
Spain
Sweden
Tajikistan
Trinidad & Tobago
Ukraine
United Kingdom
United States

NOTES:

[1] See note under GERMANY, FEDERAL REPUBLIC OF in bilateral section.

[2] CHINA is not a party to this treaty but has made it applicable to Hong Kong.

Convention (ILO No. 150) concerning labor administration: role, functions and organization. Adopted at the 64th session of the General Conference of the International Labor Organization, Geneva, June 26, 1978; entered into force October 11, 1980; for the United States March 3, 1996.
TIAS
Parties:
Algeria
Australia
Belarus
Burkina Faso
Cambodia
Congo
Congo, Dem. Rep.
Costa Rica
Cuba
Cyprus
Denmark
Dominican Rep.
Egypt
Finland
Gabon
Germany
Ghana
Greece
Guinea
Guyana
Hong Kong [1]
Iraq
Israel
Italy
Jamaica
Korea
Latvia
Malawi
Mexico
Namibia
Netherlands
Norway
Portugal
Russian Fed.
San Marino
Seychelles
Spain
Suriname
Sweden

LABOR (Cont'd)

Switzerland
Tunisia
United Kingdom
United States
Uruguay
Venezuela
Zambia
Zimbabwe

NOTE:
   [1] CHINA is not a party to this treaty but has made it applicable to Hong Kong.

Convention (ILO No. 160) concerning labor statistics. Adopted at the 71st session of the General Conference of the International Labor Organization, Geneva, June 25, 1985; entered into force April 24, 1988; for the United States June 11, 1991.
TIAS
Parties:
Australia
Austria
Azerbaijan
Belarus
Bolivia
Brazil
Canada
Colombia
Cyprus
Czech Rep.
Denmark
El Salvador
Finland
Germany
Greece
Guatemala
Hong Kong [1]
India
Ireland
Italy
Korea
Kyrgyz Rep.
Latvia
Lithuania
Mauritius
Mexico
Netherlands
Norway
Panama
Poland
Portugal
Russian Fed.
San Marino
Slovak Rep.
Spain
Sri Lanka
Swaziland
Sweden
Switzerland
Tajikistan
Ukraine
United Kingdom
United States

NOTE:
   [1] CHINA is not a party to this treaty but has made it applicable to Hong Kong.

North American agreement on labor cooperation, with annexes. Signed at Mexico, Wash-

ington and Ottawa September 8, 9, 12 and 14, 1993; entered into force January 1, 1994.
TIAS
Parties:
Canada
Mexico
United States

Convention (ILO No. 182) concerning the prohibition and immediate action for the elimination of the worst forms of child labor. Adopted at the 87th session of the General Conference of the International Labor Organization, Geneva, June 17, 1999; entered into force November 19, 2000; for the United States December 2, 2000.
TIAS
Parties:
Ireland
Malawi
Seychelles
Slovak Rep.
United States

LAND-LOCKED STATES

(See under TRADE AND COMMERCE)

LAOS

Declaration and protocol on the neutrality of Laos. Signed at Geneva July 23, 1962; entered into force July 23, 1962.
14 UST 1104; TIAS 5410; 456 UNTS 301.
Governments or regimes which are parties:
Burma
Cambodia
Canada
China, People's Rep.
France
India
Laos [1]
Poland
Thailand
Union of Soviet Socialist Reps. [2]
United Kingdom
United States
Viet-Nam, Dem. Rep. [3]
Viet Nam, Rep. [3]

NOTES:
   [1] Party to protocol only.
   [2] See note under UNION OF SOVIET SOCIALIST REPUBLICS in bilateral section.
   [3] See Vietnam footnote under AGRICULTURE: agreement of January 25, 1924 (26 UST 1840; TIAS 8141; 57 LNTS 135).

LAW, PRIVATE INTERNATIONAL

(See also JUDICIAL PROCEDURE)

Statute of The Hague Conference on Private International Law. Done at the 7th session of

the Conference at The Hague October 9–31, 1951; entered into force July 15, 1955; for the United States October 15, 1964.
15 UST 2228; TIAS 5710; 220 UNTS 121.
States which are parties:
Argentina
Australia
Austria
Belgium
Bulgaria
Canada
Chile
China [1]
Croatia
Cyprus
Czech Rep.
Denmark
Egypt
Estonia
Finland
Former Yugoslav Republic of Macedonia
France
Germany, Fed. Rep. [2]
Greece
Hungary
Ireland
Israel
Italy
Japan
Korea
Latvia
Luxembourg
Malta
Mexico
Monaco
Morocco
Netherlands
Norway
Poland
Portugal
Romania [3]
Slovak Rep.
Slovenia
Spain
Suriname
Sweden
Switzerland
Turkey
United Kingdom
United States
Uruguay
Venezuela
Yugoslavia [4]

NOTES:
   [1] Applicable to Macao. See note under CHINA in bilateral section.
   [2] See note under GERMANY, FEDERAL REPUBLIC OF in bilateral section.
   [3] With designation(s).
   [4] See note under YUGOSLAVIA in bilateral section.

Statute of the International Institute for the Unification of Private Law. Done at Rome March 15, 1940; entered into force July 15, 1955; for the United States March 13, 1964.
15 UST 2494; TIAS 5743.
States which are parties:
Argentina
Australia
Austria
Belgium
Bolivia
Brazil

LAW, PRIVATE INTERNATIONAL (Cont'd)

Bulgaria
Canada
Chile
China
Colombia
Croatia
Cuba
Cyprus
Czech Rep.
Denmark
Egypt
Finland
France
German Dem. Rep.[1]
Germany, Fed. Rep.[1]
Greece
Holy See
Hungary
India
Iran
Iraq
Ireland
Israel
Italy
Japan
Korea
Luxembourg
Malta
Mexico
Netherlands
Nicaragua
Nigeria
Norway
Pakistan
Paraguay
Poland
Portugal
Romania
Russian Fed.
San Marino
Slovak Rep.
Slovenia
South Africa
Spain
Sweden
Switzerland
Tunisia
Turkey
United Kingdom
United States
Uruguay
Venezuela
Yugoslavia[2]

Amendments:
June 15-16, 1965 (19 UST 7802; TIAS 6611).
December 18, 1967 (20 UST 2529; TIAS 6716).
February 18, 1969 for articles 5, 11 and 16 (30 UST 5663; TIAS 9519).

NOTES:
[1] See note under GERMANY, FEDERAL REPUBLIC OF in bilateral section.
[2] See note under YUGOSLAVIA in bilateral section.

LAW OF SEA

(See under FISHERIES; MARITIME MATTERS; SEABEDS)

LOAD LINES

(See under MARITIME MATTERS)

MARINE POLLUTION

International convention for the prevention of pollution of the sea by oil, with annexes.* Done at London May 12, 1954; entered into force July 26, 1958; for the United States December 8, 1961.
12 UST 2989; TIAS 4900; 327 UNTS 3.
States which are parties:
Algeria
Argentina[1 2]
Austria
Bahamas, The[1 2]
Bahrain**
Bangladesh**
Belgium
Canada
Chile[2]
Congo**
Cote d'Ivoire
Cyprus
Denmark
Djibouti
Dominican Rep.**
Egypt
Fiji[1 2]**
Finland
France[1]
German Dem Rep.[2 3]
Ghana
Greece
Guinea**
Iceland
India
Israel
Italy[2]
Japan
Jordan**
Kenya
Korea, Rep.
Kuwait**
Lebanon
Liberia[2]
Libya**
Madagascar**
Maldives**
Malta
Mexico
Monaco
Morocco
New Zealand
Nigeria**
Norway[1]
Panama
Papua New Guinea
Philippines**

Poland[2]
Portugal[2]
Qatar**
Saudi Arabia[2]**
Senegal
Slovenia
Spain
Sri Lanka**
Suriname
Sweden
Switzerland
Syrian Arab Rep.
Tunisia[2]
Union of Soviet Socialist Reps.[2 4]
United Arab Emirates**
United Kingdom[5]
United States[1 6 7]
Uruguay
Vanuatu
Venezuela
Yemen (Aden)[8]**
Yemen (Sanaa)[8]**
Yugoslavia[9]

Amendments:
April 11, 1962 (17 UST 1523; TIAS 6109; 600 UNTS 332).
October 21, 1969 (28 UST 1205; TIAS 8505).

NOTES:
* Superseded by the 1978 protocol relating to the international convention for the prevention of pollution from ships as between parties to that protocol.
** Not party to the 1978 protocol.
[1] With a statement.
[2] With reservation(s).
[3] See note under GERMANY, FEDERAL REPUBLIC OF in bilateral section.
[4] See note under UNION OF SOVIET SOCIALIST REPUBLICS in bilateral section.
[5] Extended to Bermuda.
[6] Extended to American Samoa, Guam, Midway, Wake and Johnston Is., Trust Territories of the Pacific Is., Puerto Rico, and the Virgin Is.
[7] With an understanding and a recommendation.
[8] See note under YEMEN in bilateral section.
[9] See note under YUGOSLAVIA in bilateral section.

International convention relating to intervention on the high seas in cases of oil pollution casualties, with annex. Done at Brussels November 29, 1969; entered into force May 6, 1975.
26 UST 765; TIAS 8068.
States which are parties:
Argentina[1]
Australia[2]
Bahamas, The
Bangladesh
Barbados
Belgium
Benin
Bulgaria
Cameroon
Chile
China[3]
Cote d'Ivoire
Croatia
Cuba[2]
Denmark

MARINE POLLUTION
(Cont'd)

Djibouti
Dominican Rep.
Ecuador
Egypt
Equatorial Guinea
Fiji
Finland
France [4]
Gabon
Georgia
German Dem. Rep. [5]
Germany, Fed. Rep. [5]
Ghana
Guyana
Iceland
India
Iran
Ireland
Italy
Jamaica
Japan [4]
Kuwait
Lebanon
Liberia
Marshall Is.
Mauritania
Mexico
Monaco
Morocco
Netherlands [6]
New Zealand
Nicaragua
Norway
Oman
Pakistan
Panama
Papua New Guinea
Poland
Portugal
Qatar
Russian Fed.
St. Vincent & the Grenadines
Senegal
Slovenia
South Africa
Spain
Sri Lanka
Suriname
Sweden
Switzerland
Syrian Arab Rep.
Tonga
Trinidad & Tobago
Tunisia
Ukraine
Union of Soviet Socialist Reps. [7]
United Arab Emirates
United Kingdom [4][8]
United States [9]
Vanuatu
Yemen (Sanaa) [10]
Yugoslavia [11]

NOTES:
[1] With reservation.
[2] With declaration.
[3] Applicable to Hong Kong. See note under CHINA in bilateral section.
[4] With statements.

[5] See note under GERMANY, FEDERAL REPUBLIC OF in bilateral section.
[6] Applicable to Netherlands Antilles and Aruba.
[7] See note under UNION OF SOVIET SOCIALIST REPUBLICS in bilateral section.
[8] Extended to Anguilla, Bermuda, British Virgin Is., Cayman Is., Falkland Is. and dependencies, Isle of Man, Montserrat, Pitcairn, Henderson, Ducie and Oeno Is., St. Helena and dependencies, Turks and Caicos Is., United Kingdom Sovereign Base Areas of Akrotiri and Dhekelai on the Island of Cyprus.
[9] Extended to American Samoa, Guam, Puerto Rico, Trust Territories of the Pacific Is., and the Virgin Is.
[10] See note under YEMEN in bilateral section.
[11] See note under YUGOSLAVIA in bilateral section.

Convention on the prevention of marine pollution by dumping of wastes and other matter, with annexes. Done at Washington, London, Mexico City and Moscow December 29, 1972; entered into force August 30, 1975.
26 UST 2403; TIAS 8165; 1046 UNTS 120.
Parties:
Afghanistan
Antigua & Barbuda
Argentina [1]
Australia
Azerbaijan
Barbados
Belarus
Belgium [1]
Belize [2]
Brazil
Canada
Cape Verde
Chile
China [3]
Congo, Dem. Rep.
Costa Rica
Cote d'Ivoire
Croatia
Cuba
Cyprus
Denmark [4]
Dominican Rep.
Egypt
Finland
France [1][5]
Gabon
German Dem. Rep. [1][6]
Germany, Fed. Rep. [6]
Greece [5]
Guatemala
Haiti
Honduras
Hungary
Iceland
Iran
Ireland
Italy [1]
Jamaica
Japan
Jordan
Kenya
Kiribati
Korea
Libya
Luxembourg
Malta
Mexico

Monaco
Morocco
Nauru
Netherlands [7]
New Zealand [8]
Nigeria
Norway
Oman
Pakistan
Panama
Papua New Guinea
Philippines
Poland
Portugal
Russian Fed.
St. Lucia
Seychelles
Slovenia
Solomon Is.
South Africa
Spain
Suriname
Sweden
Switzerland
Tonga
Tunisia
Tuvalu [2]
Ukraine
Union of Soviet Socialist Reps. [9]
United Arab Emirates
United Kingdom [10]
United States
Vanuatu
Yugoslavia [11]

Amendment:
    November 12, 1993.

NOTES:
[1] With statement.
[2] See under country heading in the bilateral section for information concerning acceptance of treaty obligations.
[3] Applicable to Hong Kong and Macao. With declarations. See note under CHINA in bilateral section.
[4] Extended to Faroe Is.
[5] With reservation.
[6] See note under GERMANY, FEDERAL REPUBLIC OF in bilateral section.
[7] Applicable to Netherlands Antilles and Aruba.
[8] Not applicable to Cook Is., Niue, and Tokelau Is.
[9] See note under UNION OF SOVIET SOCIALIST REPUBLICS in bilateral section.
[10] Extended to Bailiwick of Guernsey, Bermuda, British Indian Ocean Territory, British Virgin Is., Cayman Is., Ducie and Oeno Is., Falkland Is. and dependencies, Henderson, Isle of Man, Bailiwick of Jersey, Montserrat, Pitcairn, St. Helena and dependencies, Turks and Caicos Is., and United Kingdom Sovereign Base Areas of Akrotiri and Dhekelia on the Island of Cyprus.
[11] See note under YUGOSLAVIA in bilateral section.

Protocol relating to intervention on the high seas in cases of pollution by substances other than oil. Done at London November 2, 1973; entered into force March 30, 1983.
TIAS 10561.
States which are parties:
Australia [1]

MARINE POLLUTION (Cont'd)

Bahamas, The
Barbados
Belgium
Chile
China [2]
Croatia
Denmark
Egypt
Finland
France [3]
Georgia
Germany, Fed. Rep. [4]
Iran
Ireland
Italy
Jamaica
Liberia
Marshall Is.
Mauritania
Mexico
Netherlands [5]
Nicaragua
Norway
Oman
Pakistan
Poland
Portugal
Russian Fed.
St. Vincent & the Grenadines
Slovenia
South Africa
Spain
Sweden
Switzerland
Tonga
Tunisia
Union of Soviet Socialist Reps. [6]
United Kingdom [1] [7]
United States
Vanuatu
Yemen (Sanaa) [8]
Yugoslavia [9]

Amendment:
July 10, 1996.

NOTES:
[1] With declaration(s).
[2] Applicable to Hong Kong. See note under CHINA in bilateral section.
[3] With reservation(s).
[4] See note under GERMANY, FEDERAL REPUBLIC OF in bilateral section.
[5] Applicable to Netherlands Antilles and Aruba.
[6] See note under UNION OF SOVIET SOCIALIST REPUBLICS in bilateral section.
[7] Extended to Anguilla, Bermuda, British Virgin Is., Cayman Is., Falkland Is. and dependencies, Isle of Man, Montserrat, Pitcairn, Henderson, Ducie and Oeno Is., St. Helena and dependencies, Sovereign Base Areas of Akrotiri and Dhekelia on the Island of Cyprus, and Turks and Caicos Is.
[8] See note under YEMEN in bilateral section.
[9] See note under YUGOSLAVIA in bilateral section.

Protocol of 1978 relating to the international convention for the prevention of pollution from ships, 1973, with annexes and protocols. [1] Done at London February 17, 1978; entered into force October 2, 1983.
TIAS
States which are parties:
Algeria [2]
Antigua & Barbuda
Argentina [3]
Australia
Austria
Bahamas, The
Barbados
Belgium [2]
Belize
Brazil [3]
Brunei [4] [5]
Bulgaria [2]
Burma [4] [5]
Cambodia
Canada [2] [4] [5]
Chile [5]
China [6]
Colombia
Comoros *
Cote d'Ivoire
Croatia
Cuba [4] [5]
Cyprus [4]
Czech Rep.
Denmark [2] [7]
Djibouti [4] [5]
Ecuador
Egypt
Equatorial Guinea
Estonia
Finland
France [2]
Gabon
Gambia
Georgia
German Dem. Rep. [8]
Germany, Fed. Rep. [8]
Ghana [4] [5]
Greece
Guatemala
Guyana
Hungary
Iceland
India [4] [5]
Indonesia [2] [4] [5]
Ireland [2]
Israel [5]
Italy [9]
Jamaica
Japan [3]
Kazakhstan
Kenya
Korea, Dem. People's Rep.
Korea, Rep.
Latvia
Lebanon
Liberia
Lithuania
Luxembourg
Malaysia [2] [4]
Malta [4] [5]
Marshall Is. [10]
Mauritania
Mauritius
Mexico [4]
Monaco
Morocco
Netherlands [2] [11]

New Zealand [2]
Norway [9]
Oman [2]
Pakistan
Panama
Papua New Guinea
Peru
Poland
Portugal
Romania
St. Kitts & Nevis [3]
St. Vincent & the Grenadines
Sao Tome & Principe
Senegal
Seychelles [4] [5]
Singapore
Slovak Rep.
Slovenia
South Africa
Spain
Suriname
Sweden [9]
Switzerland
Syria [3] [4] [5]
Togo
Tonga
Tunisia
Turkey [4]
Tuvalu
Ukraine
Union of Soviet Socialist Reps. [12]
United Kingdom [3] [13]
United States [2]
Uruguay
Vanuatu
Venezuela
Vietnam [4] [5]
Yugoslavia [14]

Amendments:
September 7, 1984.
December 5, 1985.
December 5, 1985.
December 1, 1987.
October 17, 1989.
November 16, 1990.
July 4, 1991.
July 4, 1991.
March 6, 1992.
October 30, 1992.
October 30, 1992.
September 14, 1995.
July 10, 1996.
July 10, 1996.
July 10, 1996.
September 25, 1997.

NOTES:
* Enters into force for Comoros February 22, 2001.
[1] The 1978 protocol incorporates with modifications the provisions of the international convention for the prevention of pollution from ships, including its annexes and protocol, signed at London November 2, 1973. The 1973 convention is not intended to enter into force and be applied on its own. Accordingly, as of October 2, 1983 the regime to be applied by the states parties to the 1978 protocol will be the regime contained in the 1973 convention as modified by the 1978 protocol.
Annex III entered into force July 1, 1992; Annex IV to the convention is not in force; Annex V entered into force December 31, 1988.

MARINE POLLUTION (Cont'd)

The 1978 protocol supersedes the international convention for the prevention of pollution of the sea by oil of May 12, 1954 (TIAS 4900) as between the contracting parties to the 1978 protocol.

[2] With declaration(s).

[3] With reservation(s).

[4] Not a party to Annex III.

[5] Not a party to Annex V.

[6] Applicable to Hong Kong and Macao. See note under CHINA in bilateral section.

[7] Extended to Faroe Is.

[8] See note under GERMANY, FEDERAL REPUBLIC OF in bilateral section.

[9] With statement(s).

[10] On October 15, 1986 the Compact of Free Association entered into force between the Government of the United States and the Government of the Republic of the Marshall Islands, effective October 21, 1986.

[11] For the Kingdom in Europe, the Netherlands Antilles and Aruba.

[12] See note under UNION OF SOVIET SOCIALIST REPUBLICS in bilateral section.

[13] Applicable to Bermuda, the Cayman Is., Falkland Is., Gibraltar, and Isle of Man.

[14] See note under YUGOSLAVIA in bilateral section.

Convention for the protection and development of the marine environment of the wider Caribbean region, with annex. Done at Cartagena March 24, 1983; entered into force October 11, 1986.
TIAS 11085.

Protocol concerning cooperation in combating oil spills in the wider Caribbean region, with annex. Done at Cartagena March 24, 1983; entered into force October 11, 1986.
TIAS 11085.
States which are parties:
Antigua & Barbuda
Barbados
Colombia
Cuba
Dominica
France [1]
Grenada
Guatemala
Jamaica
Mexico [1]
Netherlands [2]
Panama
St. Kitts & Nevis
St. Lucia [3]
St. Vincent & the Grenadines
Trinidad & Tobago
United Kingdom [1][4]
United States
Venezuela

NOTES:

[1] With declaration(s).

[2] Applicable to Aruba and Netherlands Antilles.

[3] Not a party to the protocol.

[4] Applicable to British Virgin Is., Cayman Is. and Turks and Caicos Is.

International convention on oil pollution preparedness, response and co-operation, 1990. Done at London November 30, 1990; entered into force May 13, 1995.
TIAS
Parties:
Antigua & Barbuda
Argentina
Australia
Brazil
Canada
Chile
China
Comoros
Croatia
Denmark
Djibouti
Egypt
El Salvador
Finland
France
Georgia
Germany
Greece
Guyana
Iceland
India
Iran
Israel
Italy
Jamaica
Japan
Kenya
Korea
Liberia
Malaysia
Marshall Is.
Mauritania
Mauritius
Mexico
Monaco
Netherlands
New Zealand
Nigeria
Norway
Pakistan
Romania
Senegal
Seychelles
Singapore
Spain
Sweden
Switzerland
Thailand
Tonga
Trinidad & Tobago
Tunisia
United Kingdom
United States
Uruguay
Vanuatu
Venezuela

MARINE SCIENCE

Convention for a North Pacific Marine Science Organization (PICES). Done at Ottawa December 12, 1990; entered into force March 24, 1992.
TIAS
Parties:
Canada
China
Japan
Korea
Russian Fed.
United States

MARITIME MATTERS

(See also INTERNATIONAL MARITIME ORGANIZATION; LABOR; MARINE POLLUTION; RED CROSS CONVENTIONS; RULES OF WARFARE; SEABEDS)

Convention for the unification of certain rules of law with respect to assistance and salvage at sea. Signed at Brussels September 23, 1910; entered into force March 1, 1913.
37 Stat. 1658; TS 576; 1 Bevans 780.
States which are parties:
Algeria
Antigua & Barbuda [1]
Argentina
Australia [2]
Austria
Bahamas, The [1]
Barbados [1]
Belgium
Belize [1]
Brazil
Canada
Congo, Dem. Rep.
Croatia
Cyprus [1]
Dominica [1]
Dominican Rep.
Egypt
Estonia
Fiji
Finland
France
Gambia, The [1]
German Dem. Rep.[3]
Germany, Fed. Rep.[3][4]
Ghana [1]
Greece
Grenada [1]
Guyana [1]
Haiti
Hong Kong [5]
Hungary
India
Iran
Italy
Jamaica [1]
Japan
Kiribati [1]
Latvia
Luxembourg
Macao [5]
Madagascar
Malaysia [1]
Malta [1]
Mauritius [1]
Mexico
New Zealand
Nigeria [1]
Norway
Oman

MARITIME MATTERS (Cont'd)

Papua New Guinea
Paraguay
Poland
Portugal[6]
Romania
St. Kitts & Nevis[1]
St. Lucia[1]
St. Vincent & the Grenadines[1]
Seychelles[1]
Sierra Leone[1]
Singapore
Solomon Is.
Spain
Sri Lanka
Switzerland
Syrian Arab Rep.
Tonga
Trinidad & Tobago[1]
Turkey
Tuvalu[1]
Union of Soviet Socialist Reps.[7]
United States
Uruguay
Yugoslavia[8]

NOTES:

[1] See under country heading in the bilateral section for information concerning acceptance of treaty obligations.

In addition, the depositary (Belgium) lists as "countries involved" the following states to which the convention was extended prior to their independence: Angola, Cape Verde, Guinea-Bissau, Ireland, Kenya, Mozambique, Sao Tome & Principe and Somalia.

[2] Extended to Norfolk Is.

[3] See note under GERMANY, FEDERAL REPUBLIC OF in bilateral section.

[4] Convention applicable to the Federal Republic of Germany except for relations with Hungary, New Zealand, Poland, Romania, Union of Soviet Socialist Republics, and Uruguay.

[5] CHINA is not a party to this treaty but has made it applicable to Hong Kong and Macao.

[6] Extended to all Portuguese territories.

[7] See note under UNION OF SOVIET SOCIALIST REPUBLICS in bilateral section.

[8] See note under YUGOSLAVIA in bilateral section.

International convention for the unification of certain rules relating to bills of lading for the carriage of goods by sea, with protocol of signature. Done at Brussels August 25, 1924; entered into force June 2, 1931; for the United States December 29, 1937.
51 Stat. 233; TS 931; 2 Bevans 430; 120 LNTS 155.
States which are parties:
Algeria
Antigua & Barbuda[1]
Argentina
Bahamas, The[1]
Barbados[1]
Belgium[2]
Belize[1]
Bolivia
Congo, Dem. Rep.

Cote d'Ivoire[2]
Croatia
Cuba[2]
Cyprus[1]
Dominica[1]
Ecuador
Egypt[2]
Fiji[2]
France[3]
Gambia, The[1]
German Dem. Rep.[4]
Germany, Fed. Rep.[2 4 5]
Ghana[1]
Grenada[1]
Guyana[1]
Hong Kong[6]
Hungary
Iran
Ireland[2]
Israel
Jamaica[1]
Kiribati[1]
Kuwait[2 7]
Lebanon
Luxembourg
Macao[6]
Madagascar
Malaysia[1]
Mauritius
Monaco
Nauru[1]
Nigeria[1]
Papua New Guinea[1]
Paraguay
Peru
Poland
Portugal[8]
Romania
St. Kitts & Nevis[1]
St. Lucia[1]
St. Vincent & the Grenadines[1]
Senegal
Seychelles[1]
Sierra Leone[2]
Singapore
Slovenia
Solomon Is.
Spain
Sri Lanka
Switzerland
Syrian Arab Rep.
Tanzania
Tonga
Trinidad & Tobago[1]
Turkey
Tuvalu[1]
United Kingdom[2 9]
United States[7 10]
Yugoslavia[11]

NOTES:

[1] See under country heading in the bilateral section for information concerning acceptance of treaty obligations.

In addition, the depositary (Belgium) lists as "countries involved", the following states to which the convention was extended prior to their independence: Angola, Cape Verde, Guinea-Bissau, Kenya, Mozambique, Sao Tome & Principe and Somalia.

[2] With reservation.

[3] Not including colonies, possessions or overseas territories.

[4] See note under GERMANY, FEDERAL REPUBLIC OF in bilateral section.

[5] Convention applicable to the Federal Republic of Germany except for relations with Hungary, Poland, and Romania.

[6] CHINA is not a party to this treaty but has made it applicable to Hong Kong and Macao.

[7] The United States is unable to accept the reservation made by Kuwait and does not regard the convention as in force between the United States and Kuwait.

[8] Including all territories.

[9] Extended to Ascension Is. and St. Helena.

[10] With understandings.

[11] See note under YUGOSLAVIA in bilateral section.

Agreement regarding financial support of the North Atlantic ice patrol. Opened for signature at Washington January 4, 1956; entered into force July 5, 1956.
7 UST 1969; TIAS 3597; 256 UNTS 171.
States which are parties:
Belgium
Canada
Denmark
Finland
France
Germany, Fed. Rep.[1]
Greece
Italy
Japan
Netherlands[2]
Norway
Panama
Poland
Spain
Sweden
United Kingdom
United States
Yugoslavia[3]

NOTES:

[1] See note under GERMANY, FEDERAL REPUBLIC OF in bilateral section.

[2] Applicable to Netherlands Antilles and Aruba.

[3] See note under YUGOSLAVIA in bilateral section.

Convention on the high seas. Done at Geneva April 29, 1958; entered into force September 30, 1962.
13 UST 2312; TIAS 5200; 450 UNTS 82.
States which are parties:
Afghanistan
Albania[1 2]
Australia[3]
Austria
Belarus[1 2]
Belgium
Bosnia-Herzegovina
Bulgaria[1 2]
Burkina Faso
Cambodia
Central African Rep.
Costa Rica
Croatia
Cyprus
Czech Rep.[2]
Denmark[3]
Dominican Rep.
Fiji[3]
Finland
German Dem. Rep.[1 2 4]
Germany, Fed. Rep.[3 4]
Guatemala

MARITIME MATTERS
(Cont'd)

Haiti
Hungary [1] [2]
Indonesia [1]
Israel [3]
Italy
Jamaica
Japan [3]
Kenya
Latvia
Lesotho
Madagascar [3]
Malawi
Malaysia
Mauritius
Mexico [1]
Mongolia [2]
Nepal
Netherlands [3] [5]
Nigeria
Poland [1] [2]
Portugal [3]
Romania [1] [2]
Russian Fed.
Senegal
Sierra Leone
Slovak Rep. [1] [2]
Slovenia
Solomon Is.
South Africa
Spain [2]
Swaziland
Switzerland
Thailand [3]
Tonga [3]
Trinidad & Tobago
Uganda
Ukraine [1] [2]
Union of Soviet Socialist Reps. [1] [2] [6]
United Kingdom [3]
United States [3]
Venezuela
Yugoslavia [7]

NOTES:
   [1] With reservation.
   [2] With declaration.
   [3] With a statement.
   [4] See note under GERMANY, FEDERAL REPUBLIC OF in bilateral section.
   [5] Applicable to Netherlands Antilles and Aruba.
   [6] See note under UNION OF SOVIET SOCIALIST REPUBLICS in bilateral section.
   [7] See note under YUGOSLAVIA in bilateral section.

Convention on the continental shelf. Done at Geneva April 29, 1958; entered into force June 10, 1964.
15 UST 471; TIAS 5578; 499 UNTS 311.
States which are parties:
Albania
Australia
Belarus
Bosnia-Herzegovina
Bulgaria
Cambodia
Canada [1] [2]
China (Taiwan) [3] [4]

Colombia
Costa Rica
Croatia
Cyprus
Czech Rep.
Denmark
Dominican Rep.
Fiji [2]
Finland
France [1] [3]
German Dem. Rep. [5]
Greece [3]
Guatemala
Haiti
Israel
Jamaica
Kenya
Latvia
Lesotho
Madagascar
Malawi
Malaysia
Malta
Mauritius
Mexico
Netherlands [2] [6]
New Zealand
Nigeria
Norway [2]
Poland
Portugal
Romania
Russian Fed.
Senegal
Sierra Leone
Slovak Rep.
Solomon Is.
South Africa
Spain [1] [2]
Swaziland
Sweden
Switzerland
Thailand [2]
Tonga [2]
Trinidad & Tobago
Uganda
Ukraine
Union of Soviet Socialist Reps. [7]
United Kingdom [2]
United States [2]
Venezuela [3]
Yugoslavia [2] [3] [8]

NOTES:
   [1] With declaration.
   [2] With a statement.
   [3] With reservation.
   [4] See note under CHINA (Taiwan) in bilateral section.
   [5] See note under GERMANY, FEDERAL REPUBLIC OF in bilateral section.
   [6] Applicable to Netherlands Antilles and Aruba.
   [7] See note under UNION OF SOVIET SOCIALIST REPUBLICS in bilateral section.
   [8] See note under YUGOSLAVIA in bilateral section.

Convention on the territorial sea and contiguous zone. Done at Geneva April 29, 1958; entered into force September 10, 1964.
15 UST 1606; TIAS 5639; 516 UNTS 205.
States which are parties:
Australia [1]
Belarus [2]

Belgium
Bosnia-Herzegovina
Bulgaria [2]
Cambodia
Croatia
Czech Rep. [3]
Denmark [1]
Dominican Rep.
Fiji [1]
Finland
German Dem. Rep. [2] [4]
Haiti
Hungary [2]
Israel [1]
Italy [2]
Jamaica
Japan [1]
Kenya
Latvia
Lesotho
Lithuania
Madagascar [1]
Malawi
Malaysia
Malta
Mauritius
Mexico [2]
Netherlands [1] [5]
Nigeria
Portugal [1]
Romania [2]
Russian Fed.
Senegal
Sierra Leone [3]
Slovak Rep. [2]
Slovenia
Solomon Is.
South Africa
Spain [3]
Swaziland
Switzerland
Thailand [1]
Tonga [1]
Trinidad & Tobago
Uganda
Ukraine [2]
Union of Soviet Socialist Reps. [2] [6]
United Kingdom [1]
United States [1]
Venezuela [2]
Yugoslavia [7]

NOTES:
   [1] With a statement.
   [2] With reservation.
   [3] With a declaration.
   [4] See note under GERMANY, FEDERAL REPUBLIC OF in bilateral section.
   [5] Applicable to Netherlands Antilles and Aruba.
   [6] See note under UNION OF SOVIET SOCIALIST REPUBLICS in bilateral section.
   [7] See note under YUGOSLAVIA in bilateral section.

International agreement regarding the maintenance of certain lights in the Red Sea. Done at London February 20, 1962; entered into force October 28, 1966.
17 UST 2145; TIAS 6150.
States which are parties:
China
Denmark
Egypt
Germany, Fed. Rep. [1]

MARITIME MATTERS
(Cont'd)

Italy
Kuwait
Liberia
Netherlands
Norway
Pakistan
Portugal
Sweden
Union of Soviet Socialist Reps. [2]
United Kingdom
United States

NOTES:
[1] See note under GERMANY, FEDERAL REPUBLIC OF in bilateral section.
[2] See note under UNION OF SOVIET SOCIALIST REPUBLICS in bilateral section.

Inter-American convention on facilitation of international waterborne transportation, with annex. Signed at Mar del Plata June 7, 1963; entered into force January 11, 1981.
TIAS 12064.
States which are parties:
Argentina
Chile [1][2]
Costa Rica
Dominican Rep.
Ecuador
Guatemala
Mexico
Panama
Paraguay
Peru [1]
United States
Uruguay

NOTES:
[1] With reservation(s).
[2] With statement(s).

Convention on facilitation of international maritime traffic, with annex. Done at London April 9, 1965; entered into force March 5, 1967; for the United States May 16, 1967.
18 UST 411; TIAS 6251; 591 UNTS 265.
States which are parties:
Algeria
Argentina
Australia
Austria
Bahamas, The
Bangladesh
Barbados
Belgium
Benin
Brazil
Bulgaria
Burundi
Cameroon
Canada
Cape Verde
Chile
China [1]
Colombia
Cote d'Ivoire
Croatia
Cuba
Czech Rep.

Denmark
Dominican Rep.
Ecuador
Egypt [2]
Fiji
Finland
France
Gambia
Georgia
Germany, Fed. Rep. [3]
Ghana
Greece
Guinea
Guyana
Hungary
Iceland
India
Iran
Iraq
Ireland
Israel
Italy
Jordan
Korea, Dem. People's Rep.
Latvia
Liberia
Lithuania
Luxembourg
Madagascar
Marshall Is.
Mauritius
Mexico
Monaco
Netherlands [4]
New Zealand
Nigeria
Norway
Peru
Poland
Portugal
Russian Fed.
Senegal
Seychelles
Singapore
Slovak Rep.
Slovenia
Spain
Sri Lanka
Suriname
Sweden
Switzerland
Syrian Arab Rep.
Thailand
Trinidad & Tobago
Tunisia
Ukraine
Union of Soviet Socialist Reps. [5]
United Kingdom
United States [6]
Uruguay [7]
Vanuatu
Yemen (Sanaa) [8]
Yugoslavia [9]
Zambia

Amendments:
November 19, 1973 (TIAS 11092).
November 10, 1977.

NOTES:
[1] Applicable to Hong Kong. See note under CHINA in bilateral section.
[2] With reservation.
[3] See note under GERMANY, FEDERAL REPUBLIC OF in bilateral section.

[4] Applicable to Netherlands Antilles and Aruba.
[5] See note under UNION OF SOVIET SOCIALIST REPUBLICS in bilateral section.
[6] Extended to American Samoa, Guam, Midway, Wake and Johnston Is., Trust Territories of the Pacific Is., Puerto Rico, and the Virgin Is.
[7] With declaration(s).
[8] See note under YEMEN in bilateral section.
[9] See note under YUGOSLAVIA in bilateral section.

Convention for the International Council for the Exploration of the Sea. Done at Copenhagen September 12, 1964; entered into force July 22, 1968; for the United States April 18, 1973.
24 UST 1080; TIAS 7628; 652 UNTS 237.
States which are parties:
Belgium
Canada
Denmark
Estonia
Finland
France
German Dem. Rep. [1]
Germany, Fed. Rep. [1]
Iceland
Ireland
Netherlands
Norway
Poland
Portugal
Spain
Sweden
Union of Soviet Socialist Reps. [2]
United Kingdom
United States

Amendment:
August 13, 1970 (27 UST 1022; TIAS 8238).

NOTES:
[1] See note under GERMANY, FEDERAL REPUBLIC OF in bilateral section.
[2] See note under UNION OF SOVIET SOCIALIST REPUBLICS in bilateral section.

International convention on load lines, 1966. Done at London April 5, 1966; entered into force July 21, 1968.
18 UST 1857; TIAS 6331; 640 UNTS 133.

States which are parties:
Algeria
Angola
Antigua & Barbuda
Argentina
Australia
Austria
Azerbaijan
Bahamas, The
Bahrain
Bangladesh
Barbados
Belarus
Belgium
Belize
Benin
Bolivia
Brazil
Brunei
Bulgaria

MARITIME MATTERS
(Cont'd)

Burma
Cambodia
Cameroon
Canada
Cape Verde
Chile
China [1] [2] [3] [4]
Colombia
Comoros *
Congo
Congo, Dem. Rep.
Cote d'Ivoire
Croatia
Cuba
Cyprus
Czech Rep.
Denmark
Djibouti
Dominica
Dominican Rep.
Ecuador
Egypt [2]
Equatorial Guinea
Eritrea
Estonia
Ethiopia [5]
Fiji
Finland
France
Gabon
Gambia
Georgia
German, Dem. Rep.[6]
Germany, Fed. Rep.[6]
Ghana
Greece
Guatemala
Guinea
Guyana
Haiti
Honduras
Hungary
Iceland
India
Indonesia
Iran
Ireland
Israel
Italy
Jamaica
Japan
Jordan
Kazakhstan
Kenya
Korea, Dem. People's Rep.
Korea, Rep.
Kuwait
Latvia
Lebanon
Liberia
Libya
Lithuania
Luxembourg
Madagascar
Malaysia
Maldives
Malta
Marshall Is.[7]
Mauritania

Mauritius
Mexico
Monaco
Morocco
Mozambique
Netherlands [8]
New Zealand
Nicaragua
Nigeria
Norway
Oman
Pakistan
Panama
Papua New Guinea
Peru
Philippines
Poland
Portugal
Qatar
Romania
Russian Fed.
St. Vincent & the Grenadines
Sao Tome & Principe
Saudi Arabia
Senegal
Seychelles
Sierra Leone
Singapore
Slovak Rep.
Slovenia
Somalia
South Africa
Spain
Sri Lanka
Sudan
Suriname
Sweden
Switzerland
Syrian Arab Rep.
Tanzania
Thailand
Togo
Tonga
Trinidad & Tobago
Tunisia
Turkey
Tuvalu
Ukraine
Union of Soviet Socialist Reps. [9]
United Arab Emirates
United Kingdom [10]
United States [11]
Uruguay
Vanuatu
Venezuela
Vietnam
Western Samoa
Yemen (Aden) [12]
Yemen (Sanaa) [12]
Yugoslavia [13]
Zambia

Proces-verbal of rectification of the international convention on load lines, 1966. Signed at London January 30, 1969.
20 UST 17; TIAS 6629.

Proces-verbal of rectification of the international convention on load lines, 1966. Signed at London May 5, 1969.
20 UST 2577; TIAS 6720.

NOTES:
  *Enters into force for Comoros February 22, 2001.

[1] With reservation.
[2] With a statement.
[3] The Taiwan authorities have also adhered to this convention. See note under CHINA (Taiwan) in the bilateral section.
[4] Applicable to Hong Kong. See note under CHINA in bilateral section.
[5] See note under ETHIOPIA in bilateral section.
[6] See note under GERMANY, FEDERAL REPUBLIC OF in bilateral section.
[7] On October 15, 1986 the Compact of Free Association entered into force between the Government of the United States and the Government of the Republic of the Marshall Islands, effective October 21, 1986.
[8] Applicable to Netherlands Antilles and Aruba.
[9] See note under UNION OF SOVIET SOCIALIST REPUBLICS in bilateral section.
[10] Extended to Bermuda, Cayman Is., Gibraltar, and Isle of Man.
[11] Extended to American Samoa, Guam, Midway, Wake and Johnston Is., Trust Territories of the Pacific Is., Puerto Rico, and the Virgin Is.
[12] See note under YEMEN in bilateral section.
[13] See note under YUGOSLAVIA in bilateral section.

International convention on tonnage measurement of ships, 1969, with annexes. Done at London June 23, 1969; entered into force July 18, 1982; for the United States February 10, 1983.
TIAS 10490.
States which are parties:
Algeria
Antigua & Barbuda
Argentina
Australia
Austria
Azerbaijan
Bahamas
Bahrain
Bangladesh
Barbados
Belgium
Belize
Benin
Bolivia
Brazil
Brunei
Bulgaria
Burma
Cambodia
Canada
Chile [1]
China [2]
Colombia
Comoros *
Cote d'Ivoire
Croatia
Cuba
Cyprus
Czech Rep.
Denmark
Dominica
Ecuador
El Salvador
Equatorial Guinea
Eritrea
Estonia
Ethiopia [3]

MARITIME MATTERS
(Cont'd)

Fiji
Finland
France [1]
Gambia
Georgia
German Dem. Rep.[4]
Germany, Fed. Rep.[4]
Ghana
Greece
Guinea
Guyana
Haiti
Honduras
Hungary
Iceland
India
Indonesia
Iran
Iraq
Ireland
Israel
Italy
Jamaica
Japan
Jordan
Kazakhstan
Kenya
Korea, Dem. People's Rep.
Korea, Rep.
Kuwait
Latvia
Lebanon
Liberia
Lithuania
Luxembourg
Malaysia
Maldives
Malta
Marshall Is.[5]
Mauritania
Mauritius
Mexico
Monaco
Morocco
Mozambique
Namibia *
Netherlands [6]
New Zealand [7]
Nicaragua
Nigeria
Norway
Oman
Pakistan
Panama
Papua New Guinea
Peru
Philippines
Poland
Portugal
Qatar
Romania
Russian Fed.
St. Vincent & the Grenadines
Sao Tome & Principe
Saudi Arabia
Senegal
Singapore
Slovak Rep.
Slovenia

South Africa
Spain
Sri Lanka
Sweden
Switzerland
Syrian Arab Rep.
Thailand
Togo
Tonga
Trinidad & Tobago
Tunisia
Turkey
Tuvalu
Ukraine
Union of Soviet Socialist Reps. [8]
United Arab Emirates
United Kingdom [9]
United States [10]
Uruguay
Vanuatu
Venezuela
Vietnam
Yemen (Sanaa) [11]
Yugoslavia [12]

NOTES:
* Enters into force for Comoros February 22, 2001; for Namibia February 27, 2001.
[1] With reservation.
[2] Applicable to Hong Kong. See note under CHINA in bilateral section.
[3] See note under ETHIOPIA in bilateral section.
[4] See note under GERMANY, FEDERAL REPUBLIC OF in bilateral section.
[5] On October 15, 1986 the Compact of Free Association entered into force between the Government of the United States and the Government of the Republic of the Marshall Islands, effective October 21, 1986.
[6] Applicable to Netherlands Antilles and Aruba.
[7] Not extended to Cook Is., Niue and Tokelau.
[8] See note under UNION OF SOVIET SOCIALIST REPUBLICS in bilateral section.
[9] Extended to Bermuda, Cayman Is., Falkland Is., Gibraltar, Guernsey, and Isle of Man.
[10] With understanding.
[11] See note under YEMEN in bilateral section.
[12] See note under YUGOSLAVIA in bilateral section.

Convention on the international regulations for preventing collisions at sea, 1972.* Done at London October 20, 1972; entered into force July 15, 1977.
28 UST 3459; TIAS 8587.
States which are parties:
Algeria
Angola
Antigua & Barbuda
Argentina [1]
Australia
Austria
Azerbaijan
Bahamas, The
Bahrain
Bangladesh
Barbados
Belarus
Belgium
Belize [2]
Benin

Bolivia
Brazil
Brunei
Bulgaria
Burma
Cambodia
Cameroon
Canada [1]
Cape Verde
Chile
China [3]
Colombia
Comoros
Congo
Congo, Dem. Rep.
Cote d'Ivoire
Croatia
Cuba
Cyprus
Czech Rep.
Denmark
Djibouti
Dominica
Dominican Rep.
Ecuador
Egypt
El Salvador
Equatorial Guinea
Eritrea
Estonia
Ethiopia [4]
Fiji
Finland
France
Gabon
Gambia
Georgia
German Dem. Rep. [5]
Germany, Fed. Rep. [5]
Ghana
Greece
Guatemala
Guinea
Guyana
Honduras
Hungary
Iceland
India
Indonesia
Iran
Ireland
Israel
Italy
Jamaica
Japan
Jordan
Kazakhstan
Kenya
Kiribati [2]
Korea, Dem. People's Rep.
Korea, Rep.
Kuwait
Latvia
Liberia
Lithuania
Luxembourg
Malaysia
Maldives
Malta
Marshall Is.[6]
Mauritania
Mauritius
Mexico
Monaco
Morocco

MARITIME MATTERS (Cont'd)

Mozambique
Namibia
Netherlands [7]
New Zealand
Nicaragua
Nigeria
Norway
Oman
Pakistan
Panama
Papua New Guinea
Peru
Poland
Portugal
Qatar
Romania
Russian Fed.
St. Vincent & the Grenadines
Sao Tome & Principe
Saudi Arabia
Senegal
Seychelles
Singapore
Slovak Rep.
Slovenia
Solomon Is.
South Africa
Spain
Sri Lanka
Sweden
Switzerland
Syrian Arab Rep.
Thailand
Togo
Tonga
Trinidad & Tobago
Tunisia
Turkey
Tuvalu
Ukraine
Union of Soviet Socialist Reps. [8]
United Arab Emirates
United Kingdom [9]
United States [10]
Uruguay
Vanuatu
Venezuela
Vietnam
Western Samoa
Yemen (Sanaa) [11]
Yugoslavia [12]

Amendments:
November 19, 1981 (TIAS 10672).
November 19, 1987.
October 19, 1989.

NOTES:
*The 1972 convention replaces and abrogates the international regulations for preventing collisions at sea, 1960 (16 UST 794; TIAS 5813). Parties to the 1960 regulations not parties to the 1972 convention are: Lebanon, Libya, Madagascar, Paraguay, Philippines, and Suriname.
[1] With statement.
[2] Provisional application.
[3] Applicable to Hong Kong and Macao. See note under CHINA in bilateral section.

[4] See note under ETHIOPIA in bilateral section.
[5] See note under GERMANY, FEDERAL REPUBLIC OF in bilateral section.
[6] On October 15, 1986 the Compact of Free Association entered into force between the Government of the United States and the Government of the Republic of the Marshall Islands, effective October 21, 1986.
[7] Applicable to Netherlands Antilles and Aruba.
[8] See note under UNION OF SOVIET SOCIALIST REPUBLICS in bilateral section.
[9] Extended to Bailiwick of Guernsey, Bailiwick of Jersey, Bermuda, British Virgin Is., Cayman Is., Falkland Is. and dependencies, Gibraltar, Isle of Man, Montserrat, Pitcairn Is. group, St. Helena and dependencies, Turks and Caicos Is.
[10] Extended to American Samoa, Baker Is., Guam, Howland Is., Jarvis Is., Johnston Is., Kingman Reef, Midway, Navassa Is., Palmyra Is., Puerto Rico, Trust Territory of the Pacific Is., Virgin Is., and Wake Is.
[11] See note under YEMEN in bilateral section.
[12] See note under YUGOSLAVIA in bilateral section.

International convention for the safety of life at sea, 1960.* Done at London June 17, 1960; entered into force May 26, 1965.
16 UST 185; TIAS 5780; 536 UNTS 27.
States which are parties:
Algeria
Australia [1]
Austria
Bahamas, The [1]
Bangladesh
Belgium
Brazil
Burma
Cambodia
Canada [1]
Chile [2]
China [2]
Congo, Dem. Rep. [3]
Cote d'Ivoire
Cuba
Cyprus
Czechoslovakia [4]
Denmark [1]
Ecuador
Egypt
Equatorial Guinea
Fiji [1]
Finland
France [1]
Gabon
Gambia, The
German Dem. Rep.[5]
Germany, Fed. Rep.[1] [5]
Ghana
Greece [1]
Guinea
Haiti
Honduras
Hungary [1]
Iceland
India
Indonesia
Iran
Iraq
Ireland [1]
Israel

Italy
Jamaica
Japan [1]
Kenya [3]
Korea
Kuwait [1]
Lebanon
Liberia
Libya
Madagascar [1]
Malaysia
Maldives
Mauritania
Mexico
Monaco
Morocco
Nauru [3]
Netherlands [6]
New Zealand
Nicaragua [3]
Nigeria
Norway [1]
Oman
Pakistan [1]
Panama
Papua New Guinea [1]
Paraguay [3]
Peru
Philippines
Poland
Portugal
Qatar
Romania
Saudi Arabia
Senegal
Seychelles
Singapore
Slovak Rep.
Somalia [3]
South Africa
Spain
Sri Lanka
Sweden
Switzerland
Syrian Arab Rep.[3]
Tonga
Trinidad & Tobago
Tunisia
Turkey
Union of Soviet Socialist Reps. [7]
United Kingdom [1] [8]
United States [1] [9]
Uruguay
Venezuela
Viet-Nam, Rep.[10]
Western Samoa
Yemen (Aden) [3] [11]
Yemen (Sanaa) [11]
Yugoslavia [12]
Zambia [3]

Proces-verbal of rectification of Annexes to the international convention for the safety of life at sea, 1960. Signed at London February 15, 1966.
18 UST 1289; TIAS 6284.

NOTES:
*Replaced and abrogated by the 1974 convention for the safety of life at sea as between contracting governments.
[1] With a statement.
[2] The Taiwan authorities have also adhered to this convention. See note under CHINA (Taiwan) in the bilateral section.

MARITIME MATTERS
(Cont'd)

[3] Not a party to the 1974 convention.

[4] See note under CZECHOSLOVAKIA in bilateral section.

[5] See note under GERMANY, FEDERAL REPUBLIC OF in bilateral section.

[6] Applicable to Netherlands Antilles and Aruba.

[7] See note under UNION OF SOVIET SOCIALIST REPUBLICS in bilateral section.

[8] Extended to Bermuda.

[9] Extended to American Samoa, Guam, Midway, Wake and Johnston Is., Trust Territories of the Pacific Is., Puerto Rico, and the Virgin Is.

[10] See Vietnam footnote under AGRICULTURE: agreement of January 25, 1924 (26 UST 1840; TIAS 8141; 57 LNTS 135).

[11] See note under YEMEN in bilateral section.

[12] See note under YUGOSLAVIA in bilateral section.

International convention for the safety of life at sea, 1974, with annex.[1] Done at London November 1, 1974; entered into force May 25, 1980.
32 UST 47; TIAS 9700.
States which are parties:

Algeria
Angola
Antigua & Barbuda
Argentina
Australia
Austria
Azerbaijan
Bahamas, The
Bahrain
Bangladesh
Barbados
Belarus
Belgium
Belize
Benin
Bolivia
Brazil
Brunei
Bulgaria
Burma
Cambodia
Cameroon
Canada
Cape Verde
Chile
China [2] [3]
Colombia
Comoros *
Congo
Cote d'Ivoire
Croatia
Cuba
Cyprus
Czech Rep.
Denmark
Djibouti
Dominica
Dominican Rep.
Ecuador
Egypt
Equatorial Guinea

Eritrea
Estonia
Ethiopia [4]
Fiji
Finland
France [2]
Gabon
Gambia
Georgia
German Dem. Rep. [5]
Germany, Fed. Rep. [5]
Ghana
Greece
Guatemala
Guinea
Guyana
Haiti
Honduras
Hungary
Iceland
India
Indonesia
Iran
Iraq
Ireland
Israel
Italy
Jamaica
Japan
Jordan
Kazakhstan
Kenya
Korea, Dem. People's Rep.
Korea, Rep.
Kuwait
Latvia
Lebanon
Liberia
Libya
Lithuania
Luxembourg
Madagascar
Malawi
Malaysia
Maldives
Malta
Marshall Is. [6]
Mauritania
Mauritius
Mexico
Monaco
Morocco
Mozambique
Namibia *
Netherlands [7]
New Zealand [8]
Nigeria
Norway
Oman
Pakistan
Panama
Papua New Guinea
Peru
Philippines
Poland
Portugal
Qatar
Romania
Russian Fed.
St. Vincent & the Grenadines
Samoa
Sao Tome & Principe
Saudi Arabia
Senegal
Seychelles

Sierra Leone
Singapore
Slovak Rep.
Slovenia
South Africa
Spain
Sri Lanka
Sudan
Suriname
Sweden
Switzerland
Thailand
Togo
Tonga
Trinidad & Tobago
Tunisia
Turkey
Tuvalu
Ukraine
Union of Soviet Socialist Reps. [9]
United Arab Emirates
United Kingdom [10]
United States
Uruguay
Vanuatu
Venezuela
Vietnam
Yemen (Sanaa) [11]
Yugoslavia [12]

Proces-verbal of rectification to the international convention for the safety of life at sea, 1974. Done at London December 22, 1982.
TIAS 10626.

Amendments:
November 20, 1981.
June 17, 1983.
April 21, 1988.
October 28, 1988.
November 9, 1988.
April 11, 1989.
May 25, 1990.
May 23, 1991.
May 23, 1991.
April 10, 1992.
April 10, 1992.
December 11, 1992.
May 23, 1994.
May 23, 1994.
May 24, 1994.
May 16, 1995.
June 4, 1996.
June 4, 1996.
June 4, 1996.
June 4, 1996.

NOTES:
*Enters into force for Comoros February 22, 2001; for Namibia February 27, 2001.

[1] Replaces convention of 1960 as between contracting parties.

[2] With reservation.

[3] Applicable to Hong Kong and Macao. See note under CHINA in bilateral section.

[4] See note under ETHIOPIA in bilateral section.

[5] See note under GERMANY, FEDERAL REPUBLIC OF in bilateral section.

[6] On October 15, 1986 the Compact of Free Association entered into force between the Government of the United States and the Government of the Republic of the Marshall Islands, effective October 21, 1986.

MARITIME MATTERS
(Cont'd)

[7] Applicable to Netherlands Antilles and Aruba.

[8] With declaration.

[9] See note under UNION OF SOVIET SOCIALIST REPUBLICS in bilateral section.

[10] Extended to Bermuda, Cayman Is., Gibraltar, and Isle of Man.

[11] See note under YEMEN in bilateral section.

[12] See note under YUGOSLAVIA in bilateral section.

Protocol of 1978 relating to the international convention for the safety of life at sea, 1974. Done at London February 17, 1978; entered into force May 1, 1981.
32 UST 5577; TIAS 10009.
States which are parties:
Algeria
Angola
Antigua & Barbuda
Argentina
Australia
Austria
Bahamas, The
Barbados
Belgium
Belize
Benin
Bolivia
Brazil
Brunei '
Bulgaria
Burma
Cambodia
Chile
China [1]
Colombia
Comoros *
Cote d'Ivoire
Croatia
Cuba
Cyprus
Czech Rep.
Denmark
Dominica
Egypt
Equatorial Guinea
Estonia
Ethiopia [2]
Finland
France
German Dem. Rep.[3]
Germany, Fed. Rep.[3]
Ghana
Greece
Guyana
Honduras
Hungary
Iceland
India
Indonesia
Iran
Ireland
Israel
Italy
Japan
Kazakhstan
Korea, Dem. People's Rep.

Korea, Rep.
Kuwait
Lebanon
Liberia
Libya
Lithuania
Luxembourg
Malaysia
Malta
Marshall Is.[4]
Mauritania
Mexico
Namibia *
Netherlands [5]
New Zealand [6]
Nigeria
Norway
Oman
Pakistan
Panama
Peru
Poland
Portugal
Russian Fed.
St. Vincent & the Grenadines
Samoa
Sao Tome & Principe
Saudi Arabia
Senegal
Seychelles
Singapore
Slovak Rep.
Slovenia
South Africa
Spain
Sweden
Switzerland
Togo
Tunisia
Ukraine
Union of Soviet Socialist Reps. [7]
United Arab Emirates
United Kingdom [8]
United States
Uruguay
Vanuatu
Viet Nam
Yugoslavia [9]

Amendments:
November 20, 1981.
November 10, 1988.

NOTES:
*Enters into force for Comoros February 22, 2001; for Namibia February 27, 2001.

[1] Applicable to Hong Kong and Macao. See note under CHINA in bilateral section.

[2] See note under ETHIOPIA in bilateral section.

[3] See note under GERMANY, FEDERAL REPUBLIC OF in bilateral section.

[4] On October 15, 1986 the Compact of Free Association entered into force between the Government of the United States and the Government of the Republic of the Marshall Islands, effective October 21, 1986.

[5] Applicable to Netherlands Antilles and Aruba.

[6] With declaration.

[7] See note under UNION OF SOVIET SOCIALIST REPUBLICS in bilateral section.

[8] Applicable to Bermuda, Cayman Is., Gilbraltar, and Isle of Man.

[9] See note under YUGOSLAVIA in bilateral section.

International convention on standards of training, certification and watchkeeping for seafarers, 1978. Done at London July 7, 1978; entered into force April 28, 1984; for the United States October 1, 1991.
TIAS
Parties:
Algeria
Angola
Antigua & Barbuda
Argentina
Australia [1]
Austria
Azerbaijan
Bahamas
Bahrain
Bangladesh
Barbados
Belgium
Belize
Benin
Bolivia
Brazil
Brunei
Bulgaria
Burma
Cameroon
Canada [2]
Cape Verde
Chile [2]
China, People's Rep. [3]
Colombia
Comoros
Congo, Dem. Rep.
Cote d'Ivoire
Croatia
Cuba
Cyprus
Czech Rep.
Denmark [1] [2]
Dominica
Ecuador
Egypt
Equatorial Guinea
Eritrea
Estonia
Ethiopia [4]
Fiji
Finland
France
Gabon
Gambia
Georgia
German, Dem. Rep. [5]
Germany, Fed. Rep. [5] [6]
Ghana
Greece
Guinea
Guyana
Haiti
Honduras
Hungary
Iceland
India
Indonesia
Iran
Ireland
Israel
Italy
Jamaica
Japan
Jordan

MARITIME MATTERS
(Cont'd)

Kazakhstan
Kenya
Kiribati
Korea, Dem. People's Rep.
Korea, Rep.
Kuwait
Latvia
Lebanon
Liberia
Libya
Lithuania
Luxembourg
Madagascar
Malawi
Malaysia
Maldives
Malta
Marshall Is.
Mauritania
Mauritius
Mexico
Micronesia
Morocco
Mozambique
Netherlands [7]
New Zealand [8]
Nigeria
Norway
Oman
Pakistan
Panama
Papua New Guinea
Peru
Philippines
Poland
Portugal
Romania
Russian Fed.
St. Vincent & the Grenadines
Sao Tome & Principe
Saudi Arabia
Senegal
Seychelles
Sierra Leone
Singapore
Slovak Rep.
Slovenia
Solomon Is.
South Africa
Spain
Sri Lanka
Sudan
Sweden
Switzerland
Tanzania
Thailand
Togo
Tonga
Trinidad & Tobago
Tunisia
Turkey
Tuvalu
Ukraine
Union of Soviet Socialist Reps. [9]
United Arab Emirates
United Kingdom [2] [10]
United States
Uruguay
Vanuatu

Venezuela
Vietnam
Western Samoa
Yugoslavia [11]

Amendments:
May 22, 1991.
May 23, 1994.

NOTES:
[1] With a statement.
[2] With a reservation.
[3] Applicable to Hong Kong. See note under CHINA in bilateral section.
[4] See note under ETHIOPIA in bilateral section.
[5] See note under GERMANY, FEDERAL REPUBLIC OF in bilateral section.
[6] With a declaration.
[7] Applicable to Netherlands Antilles and Aruba.
[8] Applicable to Cook Is. and Nieu.
[9] See note under UNION OF SOVIET SOCIALIST REPUBLICS in bilateral section.
[10] Applicable to Bermuda, Cayman Is., and Isle of Man.
[11] See note under YUGOSLAVIA in bilateral section.

International convention on maritime search and rescue, 1979, with annex. Done at Hamburg April 27, 1979; entered into force June 22, 1985.
TIAS 11093.
States which are parties:
Algeria
Argentina
Australia [1]
Barbados
Belgium
Belize [2]
Brazil
Bulgaria
Cameroon
Canada
Chile [1]
China [1] [3]
Cote d'Ivoire
Croatia
Cuba
Cyprus
Denmark
Ecuador
Finland
France
Gambia
Georgia
German Dem. Rep.[4]
Germany, Fed. Rep.[4]
Greece [5]
Hungary
Iceland
Iran
Ireland
Italy
Jamaica
Japan
Kenya
Korea
Latvia
Luxembourg
Mauritius
Mexico
Monaco
Morocco

Mozambique
Netherlands
New Zealand [6]
Norway
Oman
Pakistan
Papua New Guinea
Peru
Poland
Portugal
Romania
Russian Fed.
St. Kitts & Nevis [2]
Senegal
Singapore
South Africa
Spain
Sweden
Trinidad & Tobago [1]
Tunisia
Turkey
Ukraine
Union of Soviet Socialist Reps.[7] [8]
United Arab Emirates
United Kingdom [9]
United States
Uruguay
Vanuatu
Venezuela

NOTES:
[1] With declaration.
[2] Provisional application.
[3] Applicable to Hong Kong. See note under CHINA in bilateral section.
[4] See note under GERMANY, FEDERAL REPUBLIC OF in bilateral section.
[5] With reservation.
[6] Applicable to Cook Is. and Niue.
[7] With statement.
[8] See note under UNION OF SOVIET SOCIALIST REPUBLICS in bilateral section.
[9] Extended to Anguilla, the Bailiwicks of Guernsey and Jersey, Bermuda, British Virgin Is., Gibraltar, and Isle of Man.

Convention for the suppression of unlawful acts against the safety of maritime navigation. Done at Rome March 10, 1988; entered into force March 1, 1992; for the United States March 6, 1995.
TIAS
Parties:
Algeria [1]
Argentina [1]
Australia
Austria
Barbados
Botswana
Bulgaria
Canada
Chile
China [1]
Cyprus
Denmark
Egypt
Finland
France [1] [2]
Gambia
Germany
Greece
Hungary
India
Italy
Japan

MARITIME MATTERS
(Cont'd)

Lebanon
Liberia
Marshall Is.
Mexico
Netherlands [1]
New Zealand
Norway
Oman
Pakistan
Poland
Portugal
Romania
Seychelles
Spain
Sri Lanka
Sudan
Sweden
Switzerland
Trinidad & Tobago
Tunisia [2]
Turkey [1]
Turkmenistan
Ukraine
United Kingdom [2]
United States
Uzbekistan
Vanuatu
Yemen

NOTES:
   [1] With reservation(s).
   [2] With declaration(s).

Protocol of 1988 relating to the international convention on load lines, 1966, with annexes. Done at London November 11, 1988; entered into force February 3, 2000.
TIAS
Parties:
Antigua & Barbuda
Argentina
Australia
Bahamas
Barbados
Chile
China
Croatia
Cyprus
Denmark
Dominica
Egypt
Equatorial Guinea
Eritrea
Finland
France
Germany
Greece
Iceland
India
Italy
Japan
Korea
Liberia
Luxembourg
Malta
Marshall Is.
Mexico
Netherlands
Nicaragua

Norway
Oman
Russian Fed.
Seychelles
Singapore
Slovak Rep.
Slovenia
Spain
Sweden
Tonga
Tunisia
United Kingdom
United States
Vanuatu
Venezuela

Protocol of 1988 relating to the international convention for the safety of life at sea, 1974, with annex. Done at London November 11, 1988; entered into force February 3, 2000.
TIAS
Parties:
Antigua & Barbuda
Argentina
Australia
Bahamas
Barbados
Chile
China
Croatia
Cyprus
Denmark
Dominica
Egypt
Equatorial Guinea
Eritrea
Finland
France
Georgia
Germany
Greece
Guatemala
Iceland
India
Italy
Japan
Korea
Latvia
Liberia
Luxembourg
Malta
Marshall Is.
Mexico
Netherlands [1]
Norway
Oman
Portugal
Russian Fed.
Seychelles
Singapore
Slovak Rep.
Slovenia
Spain
Sweden
Tonga
Tunisia
United Kingdom
United States
Vanuatu
Venezuela

NOTE:
   [1] Applicable to the Kingdom in Europe, the Netherlands Antilles and Aruba.

Protocol for the suppression of unlawful acts agains the safety of fixed platforms located on the continental shelf. Done at Rome March 10, 1988; entered into force March 1, 1992; for the United States March 6, 1995.
TIAS
Parties:
Australia
Austria
Barbados
Botswana
Bulgaria
Canada
Chile
China [1]
Cyprus
Denmark [2]
Egypt
Finland
France [1] [3]
Germany [1]
Greece
Hungary
India
Italy
Japan
Lebanon
Liberia
Marshall Is.
Mexico
Netherlands [1]
New Zealand
Norway
Oman
Pakistan
Poland
Portugal
Romania
Seychelles
Spain
Sudan
Sweden
Switzerland
Trinidad & Tobago
Tunisia
Turkey [1]
Turkmenistan
Ukraine
United Kingdom [3] [4]
United States
Uzbekistan
Vanuatu
Yemen

NOTES:
   [1] With reservation(s).
   [2] Not applicable to the Faroe Is. nor to Greenland.
   [3] With declaration(s).
   [4] Extended to Isle of Man.

International convention on salvage, 1989. Done at London April 28, 1989; entered into force July 14, 1996.
TIAS
Parties:
Australia
Canada [1]
China [1] [2]
Croatia [1]
Denmark
Egypt
Georgia
Greece
Guyana

MARITIME MATTERS
(Cont'd)

India
Iran [1]
Ireland [1]
Italy
Jordan
Kenya
Latvia
Lithuania
Marshall Is.
Mexico [1][3]
Netherlands [1]
Nigeria
Norway [1]
Oman
Russian Fed. [1]
Saudi Arabia [1]
Sweden [1]
Switzerland
Tunisia [1]
United Arab Emirates
United Kingdom [1][4]
United States
Vanuatu

NOTES:
[1] With reservation(s).
[2] Applicable to Hong Kong. With declaration. See note under CHINA in bilateral section.
[3] With declaration(s).
[4] Extended to Anguilla, the Bailiwick of Jersey, the Antarctic Territory, the Indian Ocean Territory, the Cayman Is., the Isle of Man, Falkland Is., Montserrat, Pitcairn, Henderson, Ducie and Oeno Is., St. Helena and its Dependencies, South Georgia, South Sandwich Is., Turks & Caicos Is., and the Virgin Is.

METEOROLOGY

(See WORLD METEOROLOGICAL ORGANIZATION)

METROLOGY

(See under WEIGHTS AND MEASURES)

MIGRATION

Constitution of the Intergovernmental Committee for Migration. Adopted at Venice October 19, 1953; entered into force November 30, 1954.
6 UST 603; TIAS 3197; 207 UNTS 189.
States which are parties:
Argentina
Australia
Austria
Belgium

Bolivia
Chile
Colombia
Costa Rica
Cyprus
Denmark
Dominican Rep.
Ecuador
El Salvador
Germany, Fed. Rep. [1]
Greece
Guatemala
Honduras
Israel
Italy
Kenya
Luxembourg
Netherlands
Nicaragua
Norway
Panama
Paraguay
Peru
Portugal
Switzerland
Thailand
United States
Uruguay
Venezuela

Amendment:
May 20, 1987.

NOTE:
[1] See note under GERMANY, FEDERAL REPUBLIC OF in bilateral section.

MOROCCO

Convention for the establishment of the right of protection in Morocco. [1] Signed at Madrid July 3, 1880; entered into force May 1, 1881; for the United States March 9, 1882; effective July 3, 1880.
22 Stat. 817; TS 246; 1 Bevans 71.
States which are parties:
Belgium
Denmark
France
Italy
Morocco
Netherlands
Norway
Portugal
Spain
Sweden
Union of Soviet Socialist Reps. [2]
United Kingdom
United States

NOTES:
[1] Extraterritorial jurisdiction in Morocco relinquished by the United States October 6, 1956. Article 15 relating to Moroccan nationality is obsolete and without effect.
[2] See note under UNION OF SOVIET SOCIALIST REPUBLICS in bilateral section.

General act of the international conference at Algeciras, with an additional protocol. [1] Signed at Algeciras (Spain) April 7, 1906; entered into force December 31, 1906.
34 Stat. 2905; TS 456; 1 Bevans 464.

States which are parties:
Belgium
France
Italy
Morocco
Netherlands
Portugal
Spain
Sweden
Union of Soviet Socialist Reps. [2]
United Kingdom
United States [3]

NOTES:
[1] Extraterritorial jurisdiction in Morocco relinquished by the United States October 6, 1956.
[2] See note under UNION OF SOVIET SOCIALIST REPUBLICS in bilateral section.
[3] With reservation and understanding.

Declaration and protocol of the conference on the status of Tangier. Signed at Tangier October 29, 1956; entered into force October 29, 1956.
7 UST 3035; TIAS 3680; 263 UNTS 165.
States which are parties:
Belgium
France
Italy
Morocco
Netherlands
Portugal
Spain
Sweden
United Kingdom
United States

MOSCOW AGREEMENT

(See under WORLD WAR II)

NARCOTIC DRUGS

Single convention on narcotic drugs, 1961. Done at New York March 30, 1961; entered into force December 13, 1964; for the United States June 24, 1967. [1]
18 UST 1407; TIAS 6298; 520 UNTS 204.

Protocol amending the single convention on narcotic drugs, 1961. Done at Geneva March 25, 1972; entered into force August 8, 1975.
26 UST 1439; TIAS 8118; 976 UNTS 3.
States which are parties:
Afghanistan*
Algeria* [2]
Antigua & Barbuda
Argentina [2][3]
Australia [4]
Austria [5]
Azerbaijan *
Bahamas, The
Bangladesh [2]
Barbados
Belarus * [2]
Belgium [6]
Belize [7]
Benin
Botswana

NARCOTIC DRUGS
(Cont'd)

Brazil [6]
Brunei
Bulgaria
Burkina Faso *
Burma* [2]
Cameroon
Canada [6]
Chad*
Chile
China (Taiwan) [2 8]
Colombia
Congo, Dem. Rep.
Costa Rica
Cote d'Ivoire
Croatia
Cuba [6]
Cyprus
Czech Rep. [2]
Denmark
Dominica
Dominican Rep.
Ecuador
Egypt
El Salvador *
Ethiopia [9]
Fiji
Finland
Former Yugoslav Republic of Macedonia
France [2 10]
Gabon *
Gambia, The *
German Dem. Rep.[2 11]
Germany, Fed. Rep.[11]
Ghana *
Greece [6]
Grenada [7]
Guatemala
Guinea *
Guinea-Bissau
Haiti
Holy See
Honduras
Hong Kong* [12]
Hungary [2]
Iceland
India [2 6]
Indonesia [2]
Iran*
Iraq
Ireland
Israel [6]
Italy
Jamaica
Japan
Jordan
Kazakhstan
Kenya
Kiribati [7]
Korea
Kuwait
Kyrgyz Rep. *
Laos*
Latvia
Lebanon
Lesotho
Liberia *
Libya
Liechtenstein
Lithuania *

Luxembourg
Macao* [12]
Madagascar
Malawi
Malaysia
Mali
Marshall Is. *
Mauritius
Mexico [6]
Micronesia *
Moldova
Monaco
Mongolia
Morocco *
Mozambique *
Nauru [2 7]
Netherlands [13]
New Zealand [14]
Nicaragua *
Niger
Nigeria *
Norway
Oman *
Pakistan [2]
Panama [6]
Papua New Guinea [2]
Paraguay
Peru [6]
Philippines
Poland [2]
Portugal
Romania [2 6]
Russian Fed.
St. Kitts & Nevis
St. Lucia *
San Marino
Sao Tome & Principe*
Saudi Arabia *
Senegal
Seychelles [7]
Singapore
Slovak Rep. [2]
Solomon Is. *
Somalia *
South Africa [2]
Spain
Sri Lanka
Sudan
Suriname
Sweden
Switzerland
Syrian Arab Rep.
Thailand
Togo
Tonga
Trinidad & Tobago
Tunisia
Turkey *
Turkmenistan *
Tuvalu [7]
Uganda
Ukraine * [2]
Union of Soviet Socialist Reps.* [2 15]
United Kingdom [16]
United States [17]
Uruguay
Venezuela
Viet-Nam [18]
Yugoslavia [6 19]
Zambia
Zimbabwe *

NOTES:
   *Not a party to the 1972 protocol.

[1] The single convention on narcotic drugs replaced as between the contracting parties the following conventions to which the United States is a party:
   (a) Convention of January 23, 1912 relating to the suppression of the abuse of opium and other drugs (38 Stat. 1912; TS 612; 1 Bevans 855; 8 LNTS 187), as amended by the protocol of December 11, 1946 (61 Stat. 2230, 62 Stat. 1796; TIAS 1671, 1859; 4 Bevans 267; 12 UNTS 179).
   (b) Convention of July 13, 1931 for limiting the manufacture and regulating the distribution of narcotic drugs (48 Stat. 1543; TS 863; 3 Bevans 1; 139 LNTS 301), as amended by the protocol of December 11, 1946 (61 Stat. 2230, 62 Stat. 1796; TIAS 1671, 1859; 4 Bevans 267; 12 UNTS 179).
   (c) Protocol bringing under international control drugs outside the scope of the convention of July 13, 1931, as amended (see above) (2 UST 1629; TIAS 2308; 44 UNTS 277).
   (d) Protocol for limiting and regulating the cultivation of the poppy plant, the production of, international and wholesale trade in, and use of opium (14 UST 10; TIAS 5273; 456 UNTS 3).
Parties to (or otherwise obligated under) the above conventions and protocols which are not parties to the single convention of 1961 include: Albania (1912, 1931, 1948); Cambodia (1912, 1931, 1953); Central African Republic (1912, 1931, 1948, 1953); Congo (1912, 1931, 1948, 1953); Estonia (1912, 1931); Tanzania (1931, 1948); Western Samoa (1948, 1953).
   [2] With reservation(s).
   [3] With statement.
   [4] Applicable to the non-metropolitan territories for the international relations of which Australia is responsible.
   [5] With declaration(s).
   [6] With reservation(s) to the 1972 protocol.
   [7] See under country heading in the bilateral section for information concerning acceptance of treaty obligations.
   [8] The Taiwan authorities have adhered to the 1961 convention. See note under CHINA (Taiwan) in bilateral section.
   [9] See note under ETHIOPIA in bilateral section.
   [10] Applicable to the whole of the territory of the French Republic.
   [11] See note under GERMANY, FEDERAL REPUBLIC OF in bilateral section.
   [12] CHINA is not a party to these treaties but has made them applicable to Hong Kong and Macao.
   [13] Applicable to Netherlands Antilles and Aruba.
   [14] Applicable to the Cook Is. (including Niue) and Tokelau Is.
   [15] See note under UNION OF SOVIET SOCIALIST REPUBLICS in bilateral section.
   [16] Applicable to Anguilla, Bailiwicks of Guernsey and Jersey, Bermuda, British Virgin Is., Cayman Is., Falkland Is. and dependencies, Gibraltar, Isle of Man, Montserrat, St. Helena, Turks and Caicos Is.
   [17] Applicable to all areas for the international relations of which the United States is responsible.

NARCOTIC DRUGS
(Cont'd)

[18] See Vietnam footnote under AUTO-MOTIVE TRAFFIC: convention of September 19, 1949 (3 UST 3008; TIAS 2487; 125 UNTS 22).

[19] See note under YUGOSLAVIA in bilateral section.

Convention on psychotropic substances. Done at Vienna February 21, 1971; entered into force August 16, 1976; for the United States July 15, 1980.
32 UST 543; TIAS 9725; 1019 UNTS 175.
States which are parties:
Afghanistan [1]
Algeria
Antigua & Barbuda
Argentina [1]
Armenia
Australia
Austria
Azerbaijan
Bahamas
Bahrain [1]
Bangladesh
Barbados
Belarus [1]
Belgium
Benin
Bolivia
Bosnia-Herzegovina
Botswana
Brazil [1]
Brunei
Bulgaria
Burkina Faso
Burma
Burundi
Cameroon
Canada [1]
Cape Verde
Chad
Chile
China [1][2]
Colombia
Comoros
Congo, Dem. Rep.
Costa Rica
Cote d'Ivoire
Croatia
Cuba [1]
Cyprus
Czech Rep.
Denmark
Dominica
Dominican Rep.
Ecuador
Egypt [1]
El Salvador
Estonia
Ethiopia [3]
Fiji
Finland
Former Yugoslav Republic of Macedonia
France [1][4]
Gabon
Gambia
Georgia
German Dem. Rep. [1][5]
Germany, Fed. Rep. [1][5]

Ghana
Greece
Grenada
Guatemala
Guinea
Guinea-Bissau
Guyana
Hungary [1]
Iceland
India [1]
Indonesia
Iran
Iraq [1]
Ireland
Israel
Italy
Jamaica
Japan
Jordan
Kazakhstan
Kenya
Korea, Rep.
Kuwait
Kyrgyz Rep.
Laos
Latvia
Lebanon
Lesotho
Libya [1]
Liechtenstein
Lithuania
Luxembourg
Madagascar
Malawi
Malaysia
Maldives
Mali
Malta
Marshall Is.
Mauritania
Mauritius
Mexico [1]
Micronesia
Moldova
Monaco
Mongolia
Morocco
Mozambique
Namibia
Netherlands
New Zealand [6]
Nicaragua
Niger
Nigeria
Norway
Oman [7]
Pakistan
Palau
Panama
Papua New Guinea [1]
Paraguay
Peru [1]
Philippines
Poland [1]
Portugal
Qatar
Romania
Russian Fed.
Rwanda
St. Kitts & Nevis
San Marino
Sao Tome & Principe
Saudi Arabia
Senegal
Seychelles

Sierra Leone
Singapore
Slovak Rep.
Slovenia
Somalia
South Africa [1]
Spain
Sri Lanka
Sudan
Suriname
Swaziland
Sweden
Switzerland
Syrian Arab Rep.
Tajikistan
Tanzania
Thailand
Togo
Tonga
Trinidad & Tobago
Tunisia [1]
Turkey [1]
Turkmenistan
Uganda
Ukraine [1]
United Arab Emirates
United Kingdom [8]
United States [1]
Uruguay
Uzbekistan
Vatican City
Venezuela
Viet Nam
Yemen
Yugoslavia [1][9]
Zambia
Zimbabwe

NOTES:
[1] With reservation(s).
[2] Applicable to Hong Kong and Macao. With declaration. See note under CHINA in bilateral section.
[3] See note under ETHIOPIA in bilateral section.
[4] Applicable throughout the territory of the French Republic (European and overseas departments and territories).
[5] See note under GERMANY, FEDERAL REPUBLIC OF in bilateral section.
[6] Applicable to Niue and Tokelau.
[7] With declaration(s).
[8] Extended to Anguilla, Bermuda, British Antarctic Territory, Cayman Is., Falkland Is., Gibraltar, Montserrat, South Georgia and South Sandwich Is., and Turks and Caicos Is.
[9] See note under YUGOSLAVIA in bilateral section.

United Nations convention against illicit traffic in narcotic drugs and psychotropic substances, with annex and final act. Done at Vienna December 20, 1988; entered into force November 11, 1990.
TIAS
Parties:
Afghanistan
Algeria
Andorra
Antigua & Barbuda
Argentina
Armenia
Australia
Austria [1]
Azerbaijan

NARCOTIC DRUGS
(Cont'd)

Bahamas
Bahrain [2]
Bangladesh
Barbados
Belarus
Belgium
Belize
Benin
Bhutan
Bolivia [2]
Bosnia-Herzegovina
Botswana
Brazil
Brunei [2]
Bulgaria
Burkina Faso
Burma [2]
Burundi
Cameroon
Canada
Cape Verde
Chad
Chile
China [1] [3]
Colombia
Comoros
Costa Rica
Cote d'Ivoire
Croatia
Cuba
Cyprus [1]
Czech Rep.
Denmark [1]
Dominica
Dominican Rep.
Ecuador
Egypt
El Salvador
Estonia
Ethiopia
European Economic Community
Fiji
Finland
Former Yugoslav Republic of Macedonia
France [2]
Gambia
Georgia
German Dem. Rep. [4]
Germany [1] [4]
Ghana
Greece
Grenada
Guatemala
Guinea
Guinea-Bissau
Guyana
Haiti
Honduras
Hungary
Iceland
India
Indonesia
Iran
Iraq
Ireland
Italy
Jamaica
Japan
Jordan

Kazakhstan
Kenya
Korea
Kuwait
Kyrgyz Rep.
Latvia
Lebanon
Lesotho
Libya
Lithuania [1] [2]
Luxembourg
Madagascar
Malawi
Malaysia [1]
Maldives
Mali
Malta
Mauritania
Mexico
Moldova
Monaco
Morocco
Mozambique
Nepal
Netherlands [2] [5]
New Zealand
Nicaragua
Niger
Nigeria
Norway
Oman
Pakistan
Panama
Paraguay
Peru
Philippines
Poland
Portugal
Qatar
Romania
Russian Fed.
St. Kitts & Nevis
St. Lucia
St. Vincent & the Grenadines
San Marino
Sao Tome & Principe
Saudi Arabia [2]
Senegal
Seychelles
Sierra Leone
Singapore [1] [2]
Slovak Rep.
Slovenia
South Africa
Spain
Sri Lanka
Sudan
Suriname
Swaziland
Sweden [1]
Syria [1]
Tajikistan
Tanzania
Togo
Tonga
Trinidad & Tobago
Tunisia
Turkey
Turkmenistan
Uganda
Ukraine
United Arab Emirates
United Kingdom [2] [6]
United States [1]
Uruguay

Uzbekistan
Venezuela [1]
Viet Nam
Yemen
Yugoslavia [7]
Zambia
Zimbabwe

NOTES:
[1] With declaration(s).
[2] With reservation(s).
[3] Applicable to Hong Kong and Macao. With declaration. See note under CHINA in bilateral section.
[4] See note under GERMANY, FEDERAL REPUBLIC OF in bilateral section.
[5] For the Kingdom in Europe.
[6] Extended to Isle of Man.
[7] See note under YUGOSLAVIA in bilateral section.

Declaration of Cartagena concerning the production of, trafficking in and demand for illicit drugs. Signed at Cartagena February 15, 1990; entered into force February 15, 1990.
TIAS 12411.
Parties:
Bolivia
Colombia
Peru
United States

Memorandum of understanding concerning cooperation in the fight against illicit trafficking of narcotic drugs through the use of equipment and personnel based at Great Inagua and such other bases as may be established in the Turks and Caicos Islands, with annexes. Signed at Washington July 12, 1990; entered into force July 12, 1990.
TIAS
Parties:
Bahamas
Turks & Caicos Is.
United States

NATIONALITY

Protocol relating to military obligations in certain cases of double nationality. Concluded at The Hague April 12, 1930; entered into force May 25, 1937.
50 Stat. 1317; TS 913; 2 Bevans 1049; 178 LNTS 227.
States which are parties:
Australia [1]
Austria
Belgium
Brazil
Burma
Colombia
Cuba [2]
Cyprus
El Salvador
Fiji
India [2]
Kiribati
Lesotho
Malawi
Malta
Mauritania
Mauritius

NATIONALITY (Cont'd)

Netherlands [3]
Niger
Nigeria
South Africa [2]
Swaziland
Sweden
United Kingdom [4]
United States

NOTES:
[1] Extended to Norfolk Is.
[2] With reservation.
[3] Extended to Curacao.
[4] Extended to all parts of the British Empire not separate members of League of Nations.

Convention on the nationality of women. Signed at Montevideo December 26, 1933; entered into force August 29, 1934.
49 Stat. 2957; TS 875; 3 Bevans 141.
States which are parties:
Argentina
Brazil
Chile
Colombia
Costa Rica
Cuba
Dominica
Ecuador
Guatemala
Honduras [1]
Mexico [1]
Nicaragua
Panama
United States [1]
Uruguay

NOTE:
[1] With reservation.

NORTH ATLANTIC ICE PATROL

(See under MARITIME MATTERS)

NORTH ATLANTIC TREATY ORGANIZATION (NATO) (See also PATENTS)

For parties to following agreements, see chart.

North Atlantic Treaty. Signed at Washington April 4, 1949; entered into force August 24, 1949.
63 Stat. 2241; TIAS 1964; 4 Bevans 828; 34 UNTS 243.

Protocol to the North Atlantic Treaty on the accession of Greece and Turkey. Done at London October 17, 1951; entered into force February 15, 1952.
3 UST 43; TIAS 2390; 126 UNTS 350.

Protocol to the North Atlantic Treaty on the accession of the Federal Republic of Germany. Signed at Paris October 23, 1954; entered into force May 5, 1955.
6 UST 5707; TIAS 3428; 243 UNTS 308.

Protocol to the North Atlantic Treaty on the accession of Spain. Signed at Brussels December 10, 1981; entered into force May 29, 1982.
TIAS 10564.

Protocol to the North Atlantic Treaty on the accession of the Czech Republic. Signed at Brussels December 16, 1997; entered into force December 4, 1998.
TIAS

Protocol to the North Atlantic Treaty on the accession of Hungary. Signed at Brussels December 16, 1997; entered into force December 4, 1998.
TIAS

Protocol to the North Atlantic Treaty on the accession of Poland. Signed at Brussels December 16, 1997; entered into force December 4, 1998.
TIAS

Agreement between the parties to the North Atlantic Treaty regarding the status of their forces. Signed at London June 19, 1951; entered into force August 23, 1953.
4 UST 1792; TIAS 2846; 199 UNTS 67.

Agreement to supplement the agreement of June 19, 1951 between the parties to the North Atlantic Treaty regarding the status of their forces with respect to foreign forces stationed in the Federal Republic of Germany, with protocol of signature.[1] Signed at Bonn August 3, 1959; entered into force July 1, 1963.
14 UST 531; TIAS 5351; 481 UNTS 262.

Amendments:
October 21, 1971 (24 UST 2355; TIAS 7759).
May 18, 1981 (34 UST 405; TIAS 10367).[2]
March 18, 1993.
March 18, 1993.
May 16, 1994.

Agreement on the status of the North Atlantic Treaty Organization, national representatives, and international staff.[3] Done at Ottawa September 20, 1951; entered into force May 18, 1954.
5 UST 1087; TIAS 2992; 200 UNTS 3.

Protocol on the status of International Military Headquarters. Signed at Paris August 28, 1952; entered into force April 10, 1954.
5 UST 870; TIAS 2978; 200 UNTS 340.

NOTES:
[1] For the agreement implementing paragraph 5 of article 45, see 14 UST 670; TIAS 5351; 481 UNTS 551. For administrative agreement to article 60, see 14 UST 677; TIAS 5351; 481 UNTS 565. See also TIAS 5352 under GERMANY-DEFENSE in bilateral section.
[2] Effective April 1, 1974.
[3] See also NORTH ATLANTIC TREATY ORGANIZATION in bilateral section.

NORTH ATLANTIC TREATY ORGANIZATION (NATO) (See also PATENTS) (Cont'd)

States which are parties	North Atlantic Treaty	Protocol Greece Turkey	Protocol Germany Fed. Rep.	Protocol Spain	Protocols Czech Rep., Hungary and Poland	Status of Forces	Status of Forces in Germany	Status of Organization	International Military Hdqrs.
Belgium	X	X	X	X	X	X	X	X	X
Canada	X	X	X	X	X	X	X	X	
Czech Rep.	X					X		X	X
Denmark	X	X	X	X	X	X		X	X
France	X	X	X	X	X	X	X	X	
Germany, Fed. Rep.[1]	X			X	X	X	X	X	X
Greece	X		X	X[2]	X	X		X	X
Hungary	X					X		X	X
Iceland	X	X	X	X	X			X	X
Italy	X	X	X	X	X	X		X	X
Luxembourg	X	X	X	X	X	X		X	X
Netherlands	X	X	X	X	X	X	X	X	X
Norway	X	X	X	X	X	X		X	X
Poland	X					X		X	X
Portugal	X	X	X	X	X	X[2]		X[2]	X
Spain	X				X	X		X	X
Turkey	X		X	X	X	X		X	X
United Kingdom	X	X	X	X	X	X[3]	X	X	X
United States	X	X	X	X	X	X[2]	X	X	X

NOTES:
[1] See note under GERMANY, FEDERAL REPUBLIC OF in bilateral section.
[2] With a statement.
[3] Extended to Isle of Man.

INTERNATIONAL MILITARY HEADQUARTERS—FEDERAL REPUBLIC OF GERMANY

Agreement on the special conditions applicable to the establishment and operation of the International Military Headquarters in the Federal Republic of Germany, with protocol and exchange of notes. Signed at Paris March 13, 1967 by the Federal Republic of Germany and the Chairman of the Delegation of the Supreme Headquarters Allied Powers in Europe; entered into force December 21, 1969.
29 UST 879; TIAS 8854.

Agreement regarding making available by the armed forces of the United States and the United Kingdom of accommodation to International Military Headquarters of North Atlantic Treaty Organization in the Federal Republic of Germany. Done at Bonn February 7, 1969; entered into force December 21, 1969.
20 UST 4050; TIAS 6791; 737 UNTS 175.
States which are parties:
Germany, Fed. Rep.[1]
United Kingdom
United States

NOTE:
[1] See note under GERMANY, FEDERAL REPUBLIC OF in bilateral section.

Agreement regarding the status of personnel of sending states attached to an International Military Headquarters of North Atlantic Treaty Organization in the Federal Republic of Germany. Done at Bonn February 7, 1969; entered into force December 21, 1969.
20 UST 4055; TIAS 6792; 737 UNTS 161.
States which are parties:
Belgium
Canada
Germany, Fed. Rep.[1]
Netherlands
United Kingdom
United States

NOTE:
[1] See note under GERMANY, FEDERAL REPUBLIC OF in bilateral section.

COOPERATIVE AGREEMENTS (See also PATENTS)

Agreement between the parties to the North Atlantic Treaty for cooperation regarding atomic information. Done at Paris June 18, 1964; entered into force March 12, 1965.
16 UST 109; TIAS 5768; 542 UNTS 145.
States which are parties:
Belgium
Canada
Czech Rep.

Denmark
France
Germany, Fed. Rep.[1]
Greece
Hungary
Iceland
Italy
Luxembourg
Netherlands
Norway
Portugal
Turkey
United Kingdom
United States

NOTE:
[1] See note under GERMANY, FEDERAL REPUBLIC OF in bilateral section.

North Atlantic Treaty Organization agreement on the communication of technical information for defense purposes. Done at Brussels October 19, 1970; entered into force February 7, 1971.
22 UST 347; TIAS 7064; 800 UNTS 5.
States which are parties:
Belgium
Canada
Czech Rep.
Denmark
France [1]
Germany, Fed. Rep.[2]
Greece
Hungary

NORTH ATLANTIC TREATY ORGANIZATION (NATO) (See also PATENTS) (Cont'd)

Italy
Netherlands [3]
Norway
Poland
Spain
Turkey
United Kingdom
United States

NOTES:
[1] With statement.
[2] See note under GERMANY, FEDERAL REPUBLIC OF in bilateral section.
[3] Applicable to Netherlands Antilles and Aruba.

Memorandum of understanding for the international development of the North Atlantic Treaty Organization sea gnat system, with annexes. Dated December 8, 1976; entered into force January 10, 1977.
28 UST 8897; TIAS 8776.
States which are parties:
Germany, Fed. Rep. [1]
Norway
United Kingdom
United States

NOTE:
[1] See note under GERMANY, FEDERAL REPUBLIC OF in bilateral section.

Memorandum of understanding No. 2 creating a multilateral organization for the definition and implementation of common interests with regard to the weapon system, ROLAND. Done at Bonn, Washington and Paris January 25, May 31 and June 22, 1977; entered into force June 22, 1977.
TIAS
States which are parties:
France
Germany, Fed. Rep. [1]
United States

NOTE:
[1] See note under GERMANY, FEDERAL REPUBLIC OF in bilateral section.

Memorandum of understanding for the co-operative support of the NATO seasparrow surface missile system, with exhibit. Done May 20, 1977; entered into force May 31, 1977.
29 UST 1103; TIAS 8870.
States which are parties:
Belgium
Denmark
Germany, Fed. Rep. [1]
Italy
Netherlands
Norway
United States

NOTE:
[1] See note under GERMANY, FEDERAL REPUBLIC OF in bilateral section.

Agreement to provide for the accession of Spain to the memorandum of understanding of May 20, 1977, for the cooperative support of the NATO seasparrow surface missile system. Signed at Hamburg October 4, 8 and 14, 1991; entered into force October 14, 1991.
TIAS
Parties:
Australia
Belgium
Canada
Denmark
Germany
Greece
Italy
Netherlands
Norway
Portugal
Spain
Turkey
United States

Addendum to the memorandum of understanding of May 20, 1977 for cooperative support of the NATO seasparrow surface missile system concerning the cooperative engineering and manufacturing development of the evolved seasparrow missile, with annexes and related letter. Signed at Washington April 26 and June 16, 1995; entered into force June 16, 1995.
TIAS

Agreement concerning helicopter pilot training in the United States under the scope of EURO/NATO training, with annexes. Signed at Washington July 14, Bonn August 10, The Hague September 1, Copenhagen September 27 and Oslo October 10, 1977; entered into force October 10, 1977.
29 UST 5555; TIAS 9128.
States which are parties:
Denmark
Germany, Fed. Rep. [1]
Netherlands
Norway
United States

NOTE:
[1] See note under GERMANY, FEDERAL REPUBLIC OF in bilateral section.

Memorandum of understanding for international collaboration on the NATO explosion resistant multi-influence sweep system (ERMISS). Done April 5, 1978; entered into force April 25, 1978; for the United States August 24, 1978.
30 UST 1170; TIAS 9244.
States which are parties:
France
Germany, Fed. Rep. [1]
Netherlands
United Kingdom
United States

NOTE:
[1] See note under GERMANY, FEDERAL REPUBLIC OF in bilateral section.

Memorandum of understanding concerning cooperative full-scale engineering development of an advanced surface-to-air missile system, with annexes. Signed April 24, May 9, 18 and July 6, 1979; entered into force July 6, 1979.
TIAS 12256.

States which are parties:
Denmark
Germany, Fed. Rep. [1]
United States

NOTE:
[1] See note under GERMANY, FEDERAL REPUBLIC OF in bilateral section.

Memorandum of understanding for the cooperative support of the 76/62 OTO Melara Compact Gun (OMCG), with annexes. Done October 24, 1978; entered into force October 24, 1978; for the United States July 17, 1979.
TIAS
States which are parties:
Denmark
Germany, Fed. Rep. [1]
Greece
Italy
Netherlands
Turkey
United States

Amendments:
May 30, June 22, August 24 and November 8, 1990.
June 14, July 5, October 9 and December 3, 1991 and February 5, 1992.

NOTE:
[1] See note under GERMANY, FEDERAL REPUBLIC OF in bilateral section.

Memorandum of understanding concerning the EURO-NATO Joint Jet Pilot Training (ENJJPT) Program. Signed at Brussels December 9, 1980; entered into force December 9, 1980.
32 UST 4259; TIAS 9947.
States which are parties:
Belgium
Canada
Denmark
Germany, Fed. Rep. [1]
Greece
Italy
Netherlands
Norway
Portugal
Turkey
United Kingdom
United States

Amendments:
December 6, 1991.
January 31, March 20, April 9, May 5, July 17, August 14, September 9, October 19 and November 3, 1992, January 15, March 16 and April 15, 1993.
November 3, 1993, January 11, February 4 and 16, April 1 and 28, May 11 and 25, June 6 and 28, July 20 and October 4, 1994.
March 17, 29 and 30, April 27, June 16 and 30, July 27 and September 19, 1995 (TIAS 12692).

NOTE:
[1] See note under GERMANY, FEDERAL REPUBLIC OF in bilateral section.

Memorandum of understanding for coproduction and sale of modular thermal imaging systems (MOD FLIR) and their components, with annex.[1] Signed at Bonn, The Hague and Wash-

NORTH ATLANTIC TREATY ORGANIZATION (NATO) (See also PATENTS) (Cont'd)

ington February 12, May 21 and December 22, 1981; entered into force December 22, 1981.
TIAS 10877.
States which are parties:
Germany, Fed. Rep.[2]
Netherlands
United States

NOTES:
[1] See also under GERMANY, FED. REP–DEFENSE in bilateral section.
[2] See note under GERMANY, FEDERAL REPUBLIC OF in bilateral section.

Memorandum of understanding concerning a cooperative study of the surface effect ship 200. Signed at Ottawa, Bonn, London, Madrid, Washington and Paris, November 26, December 6, 10, 19 and 23, 1985 and February 7, 1986; entered into force February 7, 1986.
TIAS
Parties:
Canada
France
Germany, Fed. Rep.[1]
Spain
United Kingdom
United States

NOTE:
[1] See note under GERMANY, FEDERAL REPUBLIC OF in bilateral section.

Memorandum of understanding concerning general arrangements for the collaborative development and production of a modular stand-off weapon system. Signed June 12-July 24, 1987; entered into force July 24, 1987.
TIAS
Parties:
Canada
France
Germany, Fed. Rep.[1]
Italy
Spain
United Kingdom
United States

NOTE:
[1] See note under GERMANY, FEDERAL REPUBLIC OF in bilateral section.

Memorandum of understanding concerning a NATO anti-air warfare system (NAAWS), with annex. Signed September 11–October 19, 1987; entered into force October 19, 1987.
TIAS
Parties:
Canada
Germany, Fed. Rep.[1]
Netherlands
Spain
United Kingdom
United States

NOTE:
[1] See note under GERMANY, FEDERAL REPUBLIC OF in bilateral section.

Memorandum of understanding for the project definition phase of a NATO frigate replacement for the 1990s (NFR 90). Signed October 20, 1987 and January 23 and 25, 1988; entered into force January 25, 1988.
TIAS
Parties:
Canada
France
Germany, Fed. Rep.[1]
Italy
Netherlands
Spain
United Kingdom
United States

NOTE:
[1] See note under GERMANY, FEDERAL REPUBLIC OF in bilateral section.

Memorandum of understanding concerning a cooperative project for the establishment and operation of a pilot NATO insensitive munitions information center, with annexes. Signed at Brussels April 26 and 28 and May 26, 1988; entered into force May 26, 1988.
TIAS 12400.
Parties:
France
Netherlands
Norway
United Kingdom
United States

Amendment:
April 18 and June 6, 1989 (TIAS 12400).

Memorandum of understanding concerning a cooperative project for the establishment, operation, management and support of the NATO Insensitive Munitions Information Center (NIMIC), with annexes. Signed at Brussels October 24, 1990; entered into force October 24, 1990.
TIAS

Amendments:
October 6, 12, 17 and 25 and November 2, 1994.
March 15, 28 and 29, 1995.
March 15, 28 and 29 and April 4 and 10, 1995.
March 15, 28 and 29 and April 4 and 12, 1995.
March 29, April 2, 9, 16, 18, 22 and 30 and June 13, 1996.
April 7, 20, 21, 26 and 27 and May 6, 18 and 21, 1999.

Agreement on the status of missions and representatives of third states to the North Atlantic Treaty Organization. Done at Brussels September 14, 1994; entered into force March 28, 1997.
TIAS
Parties:
Belgium
Canada
Czech Rep.
Denmark
Germany[1]

Hungary
Italy
Netherlands
Norway
Poland
Spain
Turkey
United Kingdom
United States

NOTE:
[1] With declaration(s).

Agreement among the States Parties to the North Atlantic Treaty and other States participating in the Partnership for Peace regarding the status of their forces. Done at Brussels June 19, 1995; entered into force January 13, 1996.
TIAS 12666.
Parties:
Albania
Austria [1]
Azerbaijan
Belgium
Bulgaria
Canada
Czech Rep.
Denmark [2]
Estonia
Finland [3]
Former Yugoslav Republic of Macedonia
France
Georgia
Germany [4]
Hungary
Italy
Kazakhstan
Latvia
Lithuania
Moldova
Netherlands [5][6]
Norway [6]
Poland
Portugal
Romania
Slovak Rep.
Slovenia
Spain
Sweden [6]
Turkey
Ukraine
United Kingdom [6]
United States
Uzbekistan

NOTES:
[1] With statement(s).
[2] Not applicable to the Faroe Is. or to Greenland.
[3] With declaration(s).
[4] With understanding(s).
[5] For the Kingdom in Europe.
[6] With reservation(s).

Memorandum of understanding on the establishment and operation of the International Planning and Coordination Staff for the Multinational Reaction Forces (Air) of NATO – Reaction Force Air Staff, with annexes. Signed at Casteau July 20, 24, 25 and 28 and August 1, 10 and 15, 1995; entered into force August 15, 1995.
TIAS

NORTH ATLANTIC TREATY ORGANIZATION (NATO) (See also PATENTS) (Cont'd)

Memorandum of understanding concerning the establishment, mission, financing, administration and status of Headquarters 5 Allied Tactical Air Force (HQ 5 ATAF), with annexes. Signed at Casteau September 25, 26, 29 and October 2, 1995; entered into force October 2, 1995; effective January 1, 1994.
TIAS 12694.

Memorandum of understanding concerning the manning, funding and support of NATO Southern Region Maritime Sub-Principal Subordinate Command Headquarters of Commander Gibraltar Mediterranean (HQ GIBMED), Commander Maritime Air Forces Mediterranean (HQ MARAIRMED), Commander Central Mediterranean (HQ MEDCENT), Commander Eastern Mediterranean (HQ MEDEAST), Commander Northeast Mediterranean (HQ MEDNOREAST) and Commander Submarines Mediterranean (HQ SUBMED), with annexes. Signed at Casteau September 27 and October 2, 1995; entered into force October 2, 1995; effective January 1, 1994.
TIAS 12695.

Memorandum of understanding covering a feasibility study for a NATO submarine rescue system (NSRS). Signed at Bristol, Oslo, Washington, Rome and Paris February 21 and 29, March 15 and 22 and June 12, 1996; entered into force June 12, 1996.
TIAS
Parties:
France
Italy
Norway
United Kingdom
United States

Memorandum of understanding covering subphase two of the design and development phase of the NATO improved link eleven (NILE) project, with annex and related letter. Signed at Quebec, Bristol, Rome, Bonn, The Hague, Washington and Paris May 24, June 5, 6 and 11 and July 2 and 8, 1996; entered into force July 2, 1996.
TIAS
Parties:
Canada
France
Germany
Italy
Netherlands
United Kingdom
United States

Administrative agreement to implement article 60 of the agreement of August 3, 1959, as amended, to supplement the agreement between the parties to the North Atlantic Treaty regarding the status of their forces with respect to foreign forces stationed in the Federal Re-

public of Germany. Done at Bonn March 18, 1993; entered into force March 29, 1998.
TIAS

Agreement between the parties to the North Atlantic Treaty for the security of information, with annexes. Done at Brussels March 6, 1997; entered into force August 16, 1998.
TIAS
Parties:
Canada
Czech Rep.
Hungary
Netherlands [1]
Poland
United States

NOTE:
[1] For the Kingdom in Europe.

NUCLEAR ACCIDENTS

Convention on early notification of a nuclear accident. Done at Vienna September 26, 1986; entered into force October 27, 1986; for the United States October 20, 1988.
TIAS
Parties:
Argentina [1]
Armenia
Australia
Austria
Bangladesh
Belarus [1]
Belgium
Bosnia-Herzegovina
Brazil
Bulgaria [1]
Burma
Canada
China [1]
Costa Rica
Croatia
Cuba [1]
Cyprus
Czech Rep.
Denmark
Egypt [1]
Estonia
Finland
Food and Agriculture Organization [1]
Former Yugoslav Republic of Macedonia
France [1]
German Dem. Rep. [1][2]
Germany, Fed. Rep. [1][2]
Greece
Guatemala
Hungary
Iceland
India [1]
Indonesia [1]
Iran
Iraq [1]
Ireland
Israel [1]
Italy [1]
Japan
Jordan
Korea
Latvia
Lebanon
Liechtenstein

Lithuania
Luxembourg
Malaysia [1]
Mauritius [1]
Mexico
Moldova
Monaco [1]
Mongolia
Morocco
Netherlands
New Zealand
Nicaragua [1]
Nigeria
Norway
Pakistan [1]
Panama
Peru [1]
Philippines
Poland [1]
Portugal
Romania [1]
Russian Fed. [1]
Saudi Arabia [1]
Singapore
Slovak Rep. [1]
Slovenia
South Africa [1]
Spain [1]
Sri Lanka [1]
Sweden
Switzerland
Thailand [1]
Tunisia
Turkey [1]
Ukraine [1]
Union of Soviet Socialist Reps. [1][3]
United Arab Emirates [1]
United Kingdom [1]
United States [1]
Uruguay
Vietnam, Socialist Rep. [1]
World Health Organization [1]
World Meteorological Organization [1]
Yugoslavia [4]

NOTES:
[1] With declaration(s).
[2] See note under GERMANY, FEDERAL REPUBLIC OF in bilateral section.
[3] See note under UNION OF SOVIET SOCIALIST REPUBLICS in bilateral section.
[4] See note under YUGOSLAVIA in bilateral section.

Convention on assistance in the case of a nuclear accident or radiological emergency. Done at Vienna September 26, 1986; entered into force February 26, 1987; for the United States October 20, 1988.
TIAS
Parties:
Argentina [1]
Armenia
Australia [1]
Austria [1]
Bangladesh
Belarus [1]
Belgium
Bosnia-Herzegovina
Brazil
Bulgaria [1]
China [1]
Costa Rica
Croatia
Cuba [1]

NUCLEAR ACCIDENTS (Cont'd)

Cyprus
Czech Rep.
Egypt [1]
Estonia
Finland [1]
Food and Agriculture Organization [1]
Former Yugoslav Republic of Macedonia
France [1]
German Dem. Rep.[1][2]
Germany, Fed. Rep.[1][2]
Greece
Guatemala
Hungary
India [1]
Indonesia [1]
Iran
Iraq [1]
Ireland
Israel [1]
Italy [1]
Japan [1]
Jordan
Korea [1]
Latvia
Lebanon
Libya
Liechtenstein
Lithuania
Luxembourg
Malaysia [1]
Mauritius [1]
Mexico
Moldova
Monaco [1]
Mongolia
Morocco
Netherlands
New Zealand [1]
Nicaragua [1]
Nigeria
Norway
Pakistan [1]
Panama
Peru [1]
Philippines
Poland [1]
Romania [1]
Russian Fed.[1]
Saudi Arabia [1]
Singapore
Slovak Rep.
Slovenia
South Africa [1]
Spain [1]
Sri Lanka [1]
Sweden [1]
Switzerland
Thailand [1]
Tunisia
Turkey [1]
Ukraine [1]
Union of Soviet Socialist Reps. [1][3]
United Arab Emirates [1]
United Kingdom [1]
United States [1]
Uruguay
Vietnam, Socialist Rep.[1]
World Health Organization [1]
World Meteorological Organization [1]
Yugoslavia [4]

NOTES:
    [1] With declaration(s).
    [2] See note under GERMANY, FEDERAL REPUBLIC OF in bilateral section.
    [3] See note under UNION OF SOVIET SOCIALIST REPUBLICS in bilateral section.
    [4] See note under YUGOSLAVIA in bilateral section.

NUCLEAR ENERGY

(See ATOMIC ENERGY)

NUCLEAR FREE ZONE— LATIN AMERICA [1]

NOTE:
    [1] The United States is not a party to the treaty for the prohibition of nuclear weapons in Latin America (the Treaty of Tlatelolco). For the English text of the treaty, see 22 UST 762; TIAS 7137; for the text in other languages, see 634 UNTS 281.

Additional protocol I to the treaty of February 14, 1967 for the prohibition of nuclear weapons in Latin America. Done at Mexico February 14, 1967; entered into force December 11, 1969; for the United States November 23, 1981.
33 UST 1792; TIAS 10147; 634 UNTS 362.
States which are parties:
France
Netherlands [1]
United Kingdom [2]
United States [3]

NOTES:
    [1] With statement(s).
    [2] Applicable to Anguilla, British Virgin Is., Cayman Is., Falkland Is., Montserrat, Turks and Caicos Is.
    [3] With understanding and declarations.

Additional protocol II to the treaty of February 14, 1967 for the prohibition of nuclear weapons in Latin America. Done at Mexico February 14, 1967; entered into force December 11, 1969; for the United States May 12, 1971.
22 UST 754; TIAS 7137; 634 UNTS 364.
States which are parties:
China [1][2]
France [1]
Union of Soviet Socialist Rep.[1][3]
United Kingdom [4][5]
United States [6]

NOTES:
    [1] With statement.
    [2] Applicable to Hong Kong and Macao. See note under CHINA in bilateral section.
    [3] See note under UNION OF SOVIET SOCIALIST REPUBLICS in bilateral section.
    [4] With declaration.
    [5] Applicable to Anguilla, British Virgin Is., Cayman Is., Falkland Is., Montserrat, Turks and Caicos Is.
    [6] With understandings and declarations.

NUCLEAR MATERIALS

Convention on the physical protection of nuclear materials, with annex. Done at Vienna October 26, 1979; entered into force February 8, 1987.
TIAS 11080.
States which are parties:
Antigua & Barbuda
Argentina [1]
Armenia
Australia
Austria
Belarus [1]
Belgium
Bosnia-Herzegovina
Botswana
Brazil
Bulgaria
Canada
Chile [1]
China [1]
Croatia
Cuba
Cyprus
Czech Rep.
Denmark
Ecuador
Estonia
European Atomic Energy Community [1]
Finland
Former Yugoslav Republic of Macedonia
France [1]
German Dem. Rep.[2][3]
Germany, Fed. Rep. [3]
Greece
Guatemala
Hungary
Indonesia [1]
Ireland
Italy [1]
Japan
Korea [2]
Lebanon
Libya
Liechtenstein
Lithuania
Luxembourg
Mexico
Moldova
Monaco
Mongolia
Netherlands [2]
Norway
Pakistan
Panama
Paraguay
Peru [2]
Philippines
Poland [2]
Portugal
Romania
Russian Fed.[2]
Slovak Rep.
Slovenia
Spain [2]
Sudan
Sweden
Switzerland
Tajikistan
Tunisia
Turkey [2]
Ukraine

NUCLEAR MATERIALS (Cont'd)

Union of Soviet Socialist Reps. [2][4]
United Kingdom
United States
Uzbekistan
Yugoslavia [5]

NOTES:
[1] With declaration(s).
[2] With reservation(s).
[3] See note under GERMANY, FEDERAL REPUBLIC OF in bilateral section.
[4] See note under UNION OF SOVIET SOCIALIST REPUBLICS in bilateral section.
[5] See note under YUGOSLAVIA in bilateral section.

NUCLEAR SAFETY

Convention on nuclear safety. Done at Vienna September 20, 1994; entered into force October 24, 1996; for the United States July 10, 1999.
TIAS
Parties:
Argentina
Armenia
Australia
Austria
Bangladesh
Belarus
Belgium
Brazil
Bulgaria
Canada
Chile
China
Croatia
Cyprus
Czech Rep.
Denmark [1]
European Atomic Energy Community
Finland
France
Germany
Greece
Hungary
Ireland
Italy
Japan
Korea
Latvia
Lebanon
Lithuania
Luxembourg
Mali
Mexico
Moldova
Netherlands [2]
Norway
Pakistan
Peru
Poland
Portugal
Romania
Russian Fed.
Singapore
Slovak Rep.

Slovenia
South Africa
Spain
Sri Lanka
Sweden
Switzerland
Turkey
Ukraine [1]
United Kingdom [3]
United States

NOTES:
[1] With reservation(s)/declaration(s).
[2] For the Kingdom in Europe.
[3] For the United Kingdom of Great Britain and Northern Ireland, the Bailiwick of Guernsey, the Bailiwick of Jersey and the Isle of Man.

NUCLEAR TEST BAN

Treaty banning nuclear weapon tests in the atmosphere, in outer space and under water. Done at Moscow August 5, 1963; entered into force October 10, 1963.
14 UST 1313; TIAS 5433; 480 UNTS 43.
Parties:
Afghanistan
Antigua & Barbuda
Argentina
Armenia
Australia
Austria
Bahamas, The
Bangladesh
Belarus
Belgium
Benin
Bhutan
Bolivia
Bosnia-Herzegovina
Botswana
Brazil
Bulgaria
Burma
Canada
Cape Verde
Central African Rep.
Chad
Chile
China (Taiwan) [1]
Colombia
Congo, Dem. Rep.
Costa Rica
Cote d'Ivoire
Croatia
Cyprus
Czech Rep.
Denmark
Dominican Rep.
Ecuador
Egypt
El Salvador
Fiji
Finland
Gabon
Gambia, The
German Dem. Rep. [2]
Germany, Fed. Rep. [2]
Ghana
Greece
Guatemala

Honduras
Hungary
Iceland
India
Indonesia
Iran
Iraq
Ireland
Israel
Italy
Jamaica
Japan
Jordan
Kenya
Korea
Kuwait
Laos
Lebanon
Liberia
Libya
Luxembourg
Madagascar
Malawi
Malaysia
Malta
Mauritania
Mauritius
Mexico
Mongolia
Morocco
Nepal
Netherlands [3]
New Zealand
Nicaragua
Niger
Nigeria
Norway
Pakistan
Panama
Papua New Guinea
Peru
Philippines
Poland
Romania
Russian Fed.
Rwanda
San Marino
Senegal
Seychelles
Sierra Leone
Singapore
Slovak Rep.
Slovenia
South Africa
Spain
Sri Lanka
Sudan
Suriname
Swaziland
Sweden
Switzerland
Syrian Arab Rep.
Tanzania
Thailand
Togo
Tonga
Trinidad & Tobago
Tunisia
Turkey
Uganda
Ukraine
Union of Soviet Socialist Reps. [4][5]
United Kingdom [4]
United States [4]
Uruguay

NUCLEAR TEST BAN
(Cont'd)

Venezuela
Western Samoa
Yemen (Aden)[6]
Yugoslavia[7]
Zambia

NOTES:
[1] See note under CHINA (Taiwan) in bilateral section.
[2] See note under GERMANY, FEDERAL REPUBLIC OF in bilateral section.
[3] Applicable to Netherlands Antilles and Aruba.
[4] Original Party.
[5] See note under UNION OF SOVIET SOCIALIST REPUBLICS in bilateral section.
[6] See note under YEMEN in bilateral section.
[7] See note under YUGOSLAVIA in bilateral section.

NUCLEAR WEAPONS— NON-PROLIFERATION

(See also SEABEDS)

Treaty on the non-proliferation of nuclear weapons. Done at Washington, London and Moscow July 1, 1968; entered into force March 5, 1970.
21 UST 483; TIAS 6839; 729 UNTS 161.
States which are parties:
Afghanistan
Albania
Algeria
Andorra
Angola
Antigua & Barbuda
Argentina
Armenia
Australia
Austria
Azerbaijan
Bahamas, The
Bahrain
Bangladesh
Barbados
Belarus
Belgium
Belize
Benin
Bhutan
Bolivia
Bosnia-Herzegovina
Botswana
Brazil
Brunei
Bulgaria
Burkina Faso
Burma
Burundi
Cambodia
Cameroon
Canada
Cape Verde
Central African Rep.

Chad
Chile
China[1][2]
Colombia
Comoros
Congo
Congo, Dem. Rep.
Costa Rica
Cote d'Ivoire
Croatia
Cyprus
Czech Rep.
Denmark
Djibouti
Dominica
Dominican Rep.
Ecuador
Egypt[3]
El Salvador
Equatorial Guinea
Eritrea
Estonia
Ethiopia[4]
Fiji
Finland
Former Yugoslav Republic of Macedonia
France
Gabon
Gambia, The
Georgia
German Dem. Rep.[5]
Germany, Fed. Rep.[3][5]
Ghana
Greece
Grenada
Guatemala
Guinea
Guinea-Bissau
Guyana
Haiti
Holy See[3]
Honduras
Hungary
Iceland
Indonesia[3]
Iran
Iraq
Ireland
Italy[3]
Jamaica
Japan[3]
Jordan
Kazakhstan
Kenya
Kiribati
Korea, Dem. People's Rep.
Korea, Rep.
Kuwait
Kyrgyz Rep.
Laos
Latvia
Lebanon
Lesotho
Liberia
Libya
Liechtenstein[3]
Lithuania
Luxembourg
Madagascar
Malawi
Malaysia
Maldives
Mali
Malta
Marshall Is.

Mauritania
Mauritius
Mexico[3]
Micronesia
Moldova
Monaco
Mongolia
Morocco
Mozambique
Namibia
Nauru
Nepal
Netherlands[6]
New Zealand
Nicaragua
Niger
Nigeria
Norway
Oman
Palau
Panama
Papua New Guinea
Paraguay
Peru
Philippines
Poland
Portugal
Qatar
Romania
Russian Fed.
Rwanda
St. Kitts & Nevis
St. Lucia
St. Vincent & the Grenadines
San Marino
Sao Tome & Principe
Saudi Arabia
Senegal
Seychelles
Sierra Leone
Singapore
Slovak Rep.
Slovenia
Solomon Is.
Somalia
South Africa
Spain
Sri Lanka
Sudan
Suriname
Swaziland
Sweden
Switzerland[3]
Syrian Arab Rep.
Tajikistan
Tanzania
Thailand
Togo
Tonga
Trinidad & Tobago
Tunisia
Turkey[3]
Turkmenistan
Tuvalu
Uganda
Ukraine
United Arab Emirates
United Kingdom[7]
United States
Uruguay
Uzbekistan
Vanuatu
Venezuela
Vietnam, Socialist Rep.
Western Samoa

NUCLEAR WEAPONS— NON-PROLIFERATION (Cont'd)

Yemen (Aden) [8]
Yemen (Sanaa) [8]
Yugoslavia [3] [9]
Zambia
Zimbabwe

NOTES:

[1] The Taiwan authorities have also adhered to this treaty. See note under CHINA (Taiwan) in bilateral section.

[2] Applicable to Hong Kong and Macao. See note under CHINA in bilateral section.

[3] With statement.

[4] See note under ETHIOPIA in bilateral section.

[5] See note under GERMANY, FEDERAL REPUBLIC OF in bilateral section.

[6] Applicable to Netherlands Antilles and Aruba.

[7] Extended to Anguilla and territories under the territorial sovereignty of the United Kingdom.

[8] See note under YEMEN in bilateral section.

[9] See note under YUGOSLAVIA in bilateral section.

OCEAN DUMPING

(See MARINE POLLUTION)

OCEANOGRAPHIC RESEARCH

Agreement concerning the continuation of marine geoscientific research and mineral resource studies in the South Pacific region, with annex. Signed at Washington September 10, 1990; entered into force September 10, 1990.
TIAS 11750.
Parties:
Australia
New Zealand
United States

OIL POLLUTION

(See MARINE POLLUTION)

OPIUM

(See NARCOTIC DRUGS)

ORGANIZATION FOR ECONOMIC COOPERATION AND DEVELOPMENT

(See under ECONOMIC AND TECHNICAL COOPERATION AND DEVELOPMENT)

ORGANIZATION OF AMERICAN STATES

Charter of the Organization of American States. Signed at Bogota April 30, 1948; entered into force December 13, 1951.
2 UST 2394; TIAS 2361; 119 UNTS 3.
States which are parties:
Antigua & Barbuda
Argentina
Bahamas, The
Barbados
Belize
Bolivia
Brazil
Canada
Chile
Colombia
Costa Rica
Cuba
Dominica
Dominican Rep.
Ecuador
El Salvador
Grenada
Guatemala [1]
Guyana
Haiti
Honduras
Jamaica
Mexico
Nicaragua
Panama
Paraguay
Peru [1]
St. Kitts & Nevis
St. Lucia
St. Vincent & the Grenadines
Suriname
Trinidad & Tobago
United States [1]
Uruguay
Venezuela

Amendment:
February 27, 1967 (21 UST 607; TIAS 6847).

NOTE:
[1] With reservation.

PACIFIC CHARTER

(See under DEFENSE)

PACIFIC SETTLEMENT OF DISPUTES

(See also ARBITRATION; INVESTMENT DISPUTES)

HAGUE CONVENTIONS (See also RULES OF WARFARE)

Convention for the pacific settlement of international disputes.[1] Signed at The Hague July 29, 1899; entered into force September 4, 1900.
32 Stat. 1779; TS 392; 1 Bevans 230.

Convention for the pacific settlement of international disputes. Signed at The Hague October 18, 1907; entered into force January 26, 1910.
36 Stat. 2199; TS 536; 1 Bevans 577.
Parties:
Argentina [2]
Australia
Austria
Belarus [3]
Belgium
Bolivia
Brazil [4]
Bulgaria [2]
Burkina Faso
Cambodia
Cameroon
Canada
Chile [4]
China [5] [6]
Colombia
Congo, Dem. Rep.
Costa Rica [7]
Croatia
Cuba
Cyprus [7]
Czech Rep [7]
Denmark
Dominican Rep.
Ecuador [2]
Egypt [7]
El Salvador
Eritrea
Fiji [2]
Finland [7]
France
German Dem. Rep.[8]
Germany, Fed. Rep.[8]
Greece [2]
Guatemala
Guyana
Haiti
Honduras
Hungary
Iceland
India [2]
Iran [2]
Iraq
Israel [7]
Italy [2]
Japan [4]
Kyrgyz Rep.
Laos
Lebanon
Libya [7]

PACIFIC SETTLEMENT OF DISPUTES (Cont'd)

Liechtenstein [7]
Luxembourg
Malta [7]
Mauritius [2]
Mexico
Netherlands
New Zealand [2]
Nicaragua
Nigeria [7]
Norway
Pakistan [2]
Panama
Paraguay
Peru [2]
Poland [7]
Portugal
Romania [4]
Senegal
Singapore
Slovak Rep. [7]
Slovenia [2]
South Africa
Spain
Sri Lanka [2]
Sudan [7]
Suriname
Swaziland [7]
Sweden
Switzerland [4]
Thailand
Turkey [2][4]
Uganda [7]
Ukraine [3]
Union of Soviet Socialist Reps. [3][9]
United Kingdom [10]
United States [4][11]
Uruguay [2]
Venezuela [2]
Yugoslavia [4][12]
Zambia [7]
Zimbabwe [2]

NOTES:
[1] Replaced by convention of October 18, 1907 as between contracting parties to the later convention. The parties to the 1899 and/or 1907 conventions comprise the members of the Permanent Court of Arbitration.
[2] Not a party to the 1907 convention.
[3] With statement(s).
[4] With reservation(s).
[5] The Administrative Council of the Permanent Court of Arbitration decided on April 6, 1972 that the designation of the ''Republic of China,'' as well as the names of the arbitrators previously listed under that designation, should be omitted from the Annual Report pending consultation of the contracting parties by the Government of the Netherlands, which is the depositary for the conventions of 1899 and 1907.
[6] Applicable to Hong Kong and Macao. See note under CHINA in bilateral section.
[7] Not a party to the 1899 convention.
[8] See note under GERMANY, FEDERAL REPUBLIC OF in bilateral section.
[9] See note under UNION OF SOVIET SOCIALIST REPUBLICS in bilateral section.

[10] Extended to Anguilla and territories under the territorial sovereignty of the United Kingdom.
[11] With understanding.
[12] See note under YUGOSLAVIA in bilateral section.

Convention respecting the limitation of the employment of force for the recovery of contract debts. Signed at The Hague October 18, 1907; entered into force January 26, 1910.
36 Stat. 2241; TS 537; 1 Bevans 607.
States which are parties:
Australia
Austria
Canada
China [1]
Denmark
El Salvador [2]
Finland
France
Germany
Guatemala [2]
Haiti
Hungary
India
Ireland
Japan
Laos
Liberia
Netherlands
New Zealand
Nicaragua [2]
Norway
Pakistan
Panama
Philippines [3]
Portugal
South Africa
Spain
Sri Lanka
Union of Soviet Socialist Reps. [4][5]
United Kingdom
United States [3]

NOTES:
[1] Pre 1949 convention, applicable only to Taiwan.
[2] With reservation.
[3] With an understanding.
[4] With statement.
[5] See note under UNION OF SOVIET SOCIALIST REPUBLICS in bilateral section.

INTER-AMERICAN CONVENTIONS (See also ORGANIZATION OF AMERICAN STATES)

Convention for the establishment of International Commissions of Inquiry. Signed at Washington February 7, 1923; entered into force June 13, 1925.
44 Stat. 2070; TS 717; 2 Bevans 387.
States which are parties:
Costa Rica
Guatemala
Honduras
Nicaragua
United States

Treaty to avoid or prevent conflicts between the American States. Signed at Santiago May 3, 1923; entered into force October 8, 1924.
44 Stat. 2527; TS 752; 2 Bevans 413; 33 LNTS 25.
States which are parties:
Brazil
Chile
Colombia
Costa Rica
Cuba
Dominican Rep.
Ecuador
El Salvador
Guatemala
Haiti
Honduras
Mexico
Nicaragua
Panama
Paraguay
Peru
United States
Uruguay [1]
Venezuela

NOTE:
[1] With reservation.

General treaty of inter-American arbitration and protocol of progressive arbitration. Signed at Washington January 5, 1929; entered into force October 28, 1929; for the United States April 16, 1935.
49 Stat. 3153; TS 886; 2 Bevans 737; 130 LNTS 135.
States which are parties:
Brazil
Chile [1]
Colombia [1]
Cuba
Dominican Rep. [1]
Ecuador [1]
El Salvador [1]
Guatemala [1]
Haiti
Honduras [1]
Mexico [1]
Nicaragua
Panama
Peru
United States [2]

NOTES:
[1] With reservation.
[2] With an understanding.

General convention of inter-American conciliation. Signed at Washington January 5, 1929; entered into force November 15, 1929.
46 Stat. 2209; TS 780; 2 Bevans 745; 100 LNTS 401.

Additional protocol to the general convention of inter-American conciliation. Signed at Montevideo December 26, 1933; entered into force March 10, 1935.
49 Stat. 3185; TS 887; 3 Bevans 161.
States which are parties:
Brazil
Chile [1]
Colombia [1]
Cuba
Dominican Rep. [1]
Ecuador

PACIFIC SETTLEMENT OF DISPUTES (Cont'd)

El Salvador
Guatemala [1]
Haiti
Honduras [1]
Mexico [1]
Nicaragua
Panama [1]
Paraguay [1]
Peru
United States [1]
Uruguay
Venezuela [1] [2]

NOTES:
   [1] Party to the 1933 protocol.
   [2] With reservation.

Anti-war treaty of nonaggression and conciliation.[1] Signed at Rio de Janeiro October 10, 1933; entered into force November 13, 1935.
49 Stat. 3363; TS 906; 3 Bevans 135; 163 LNTS 395.
States which are parties:
Argentina
Brazil
Bulgaria [2]
Chile [2]
Colombia [2]
Cuba
Czechoslovakia [2] [3]
Dominican Rep.
Ecuador [2]
El Salvador [2]
Finland [2]
Greece [2]
Guatemala
Haiti
Honduras [2]
Italy [2]
Mexico
Nicaragua
Norway [2]
Panama
Paraguay
Peru [2]
Portugal
Romania [2]
Slovak Rep. [2]
Spain
Turkey [2]
United States [2]
Uruguay
Venezuela
Yugoslavia [2] [4]

NOTES:
   [1] The treaty was "open to the adherence of all states."
   [2] With reservation.
   [3] See note under CZECHOSLOVAKIA in bilateral section.
   [4] See note under YUGOSLAVIA in bilateral section.

Convention for the maintenance, preservation, and reestablishment of peace. Signed at Buenos Aires December 23, 1936; entered into force August 25, 1937.
51 Stat. 15; TS 922; 3 Bevans 338; 188 LNTS 9.
States which are parties:
Brazil
Chile
Colombia
Costa Rica
Cuba
Dominican Rep.
Ecuador [1]
El Salvador
Guatemala
Haiti
Honduras [2]
Mexico
Nicaragua
Panama
Paraguay [2]
United States
Venezuela

NOTES:
   [1] With declaration.
   [2] With reservation.

Additional protocol relative to non-intervention. Signed at Buenos Aires December 23, 1936; entered into force August 25, 1937.
51 Stat. 41; TS 923; 3 Bevans 343; 188 LNTS 31.
States which are parties:
Brazil
Chile
Colombia
Costa Rica
Cuba
Dominican Rep.
Ecuador [1]
El Salvador
Guatemala
Haiti
Honduras
Mexico
Nicaragua
Panama
United States
Venezuela

NOTE:
   [1] With declaration.

Treaty on the prevention of controversies. Signed at Buenos Aires December 23, 1936; entered into force July 29, 1937.
51 Stat. 65; TS 924; 3 Bevans 357; 188 LNTS 53.
States which are parties:
Chile
Colombia
Costa Rica
Cuba
Dominican Rep.
Ecuador
El Salvador
Guatemala [1]
Haiti
Honduras
Mexico
Nicaragua
Panama
United States

NOTE:
   [1] With reservation.

Inter-American treaty on good offices and mediation. Signed at Buenos Aires December 23, 1936; entered into force July 29, 1937.
51 Stat. 90; TS 925; 3 Bevans 362; 188 LNTS 75.
States which are parties:
Brazil
Chile
Colombia
Costa Rica
Cuba
Dominican Rep.
Ecuador
El Salvador
Guatemala
Haiti
Honduras [1]
Mexico
Nicaragua
Panama
United States

NOTE:
   [1] With reservation.

Convention to coordinate, extend and assure the fulfillment of the existing treaties between the American States. Signed at Buenos Aires December 23, 1936; entered into force November 24, 1938.
51 Stat. 116; TS 926; 3 Bevans 348; 195 LNTS 229.
States which are parties:
Brazil
Chile
Colombia [1]
Cuba
Dominican Rep.
Ecuador
El Salvador [1]
Guatemala
Haiti
Honduras [1]
Mexico
Nicaragua
Panama
United States [2]

NOTES:
   [1] With reservation.
   [2] With declaration.

PAN AMERICAN HIGHWAY

Convention on the Pan American highway. Signed at Buenos Aires December 23, 1936; entered into force July 29, 1937.
51 Stat. 152; TS 927; 3 Bevans 367; 188 LNTS 99.
States which are parties:
Bolivia
Chile
Colombia
Costa Rica
El Salvador
Guatemala
Honduras
Mexico

PAN AMERICAN HIGHWAY (Cont'd)

Nicaragua
Panama
Peru
United States

PAN AMERICAN UNION

(See ORGANIZATION OF AMERICAN STATES)

PANAMA CANAL

(See in bilateral section PANAMA: CANALS)

PATENTS

(See also INDUSTRIAL PROPERTY; INTELLECTUAL PROPERTY; PHONOGRAMS)

Accord relating to the treatment of German-owned patents. Done at London July 27, 1946; entered into force November 30, 1946.
3 UST 552; TIAS 2415; 90 UNTS 229.

Protocol amending the accord relating to the treatment of German-owned patents of July 27, 1946. Done at London July 17, 1947; entered into force July 17, 1947.
3 UST 560; TIAS 2415; 90 UNTS 246.
States which are parties:
Belgium
Belize [1]
Bolivia
Canada
Chile
Cuba [2]
Czechoslovakia [3]
Denmark
Dominica [1]
Dominican Rep.
Ecuador
Egypt [2]
El Salvador [2]
Ethiopia [2][4]
France
Ghana [1]
Grenada [1]
Guatemala
Guyana [1]
Haiti [2]
Honduras [2]
India
Iran
Iraq
Jamaica [1]
Lebanon
Luxembourg
Malaysia (Sarawak) [1]
Malta [1]

Netherlands
New Zealand
Nicaragua
Nigeria [1]
Norway
Panama [2]
Paraguay
Poland
St. Lucia [1]
St. Vincent & the Grenadines [1]
Saudi Arabia [2]
Singapore [1]
Slovak Rep.
South Africa
Sri Lanka
Syrian Arab Rep.
Tanzania [1]
Trinidad & Tobago [1]
Turkey
United Kingdom [5]
United States
Venezuela
Western Samoa [1]
Yugoslavia [6]
Zambia [1]
Zimbabwe [1]

NOTES:
  [1] See under country heading in the bilateral section for information concerning acceptance of treaty obligations.
  [2] Party pursuant to provisions of article 2 of the protocol of July 17, 1947 (TIAS 2415).
  [3] See note under CZECHOSLOVAKIA in bilateral section.
  [4] See note under ETHIOPIA in bilateral section.
  [5] Extended to Falkland Is.
  [6] See note under YUGOSLAVIA in bilateral section.

Agreement relating to German-owned patents in Italy. Signed at Rome November 29, 1950; entered into force November 29, 1950.
2 UST 553; TIAS 2204; 88 UNTS 221.
States which are parties:
Canada
France
India
Italy
Norway
United Kingdom
United States

Agreement among parties to the North Atlantic Treaty for the mutual safeguarding of secrecy of inventions relating to defense and for which applications for patents have been made. Done at Paris September 21, 1960; entered into force January 12, 1961.
12 UST 43; TIAS 4672; 394 UNTS 3.

First revision of implementing procedures. Done at Paris March 15, 1967; entered into force March 15, 1967; for the United States September 3, 1969.
20 UST 3062; TIAS 6786.

Second revision of implementing procedures. Done at Brussels September 5, 1973; entered into force September 5, 1973.
25 UST 1203; TIAS 7853.
States which are parties:
Belgium
Canada

Czech Rep. [1]
Denmark
France
Germany, Fed. Rep. [2]
Greece
Hungary [1]
Italy [1]
Luxembourg
Netherlands [3]
Norway
Poland [1]
Portugal
Spain [1]
Turkey
United Kingdom
United States

NOTES:
  [1] Not parties to implementing procedures.
  [2] See note under GERMANY, FEDERAL REPUBLIC OF in bilateral section.
  [3] Applicable to Netherlands Antilles and Aruba.

Patent cooperation treaty, with regulations. Done at Washington June 19, 1970; entered into force January 24, 1978.
28 UST 7645; TIAS 8733.
States which are parties:
Albania
Algeria [1]
Antigua & Barbuda
Armenia
Australia
Austria
Azerbaijan
Barbados
Belarus
Belgium
Belize
Benin
Bosnia-Herzegovina
Brazil
Bulgaria
Burkina Faso
Cameroon
Canada
Central African Rep.
Chad
China [2]
Colombia *
Congo
Costa Rica
Cote d'Ivoire
Croatia
Cuba [1]
Cyprus
Czech Rep.
Denmark [3]
Dominica
Estonia
Finland [4]
Former Yugoslav Republic of Macedonia
France [1][5]
Gabon
Gambia
Georgia
Germany, Fed. Rep. [6]
Ghana
Greece
Grenada
Guinea
Guinea-Bissau
Hungary [1]
Iceland

PATENTS (Cont'd)

India [1]
Indonesia [1]
Ireland
Israel
Italy
Japan [7]
Kazakhstan
Kenya
Korea, Dem. People's Rep.
Korea, Rep.
Kyrgyz Rep.
Latvia
Lesotho
Liberia
Liechtenstein
Lithuania
Luxembourg
Madagascar [7]
Malawi
Mali
Mauritania
Mexico
Moldova
Monaco
Mongolia
Morocco
Mozambique
Netherlands [7 8]
New Zealand
Niger
Norway [3]
Poland [1]
Portugal
Romania [1 4 7]
Russian Fed.
St. Lucia [1]
Senegal
Sierra Leone
Singapore
Slovak Rep.
Slovenia
South Africa [1]
Spain
Sri Lanka
Sudan
Swaziland
Sweden [7]
Switzerland
Tajikistan
Tanzania
Togo
Trinidad & Tobago
Turkey
Turkmenistan
Uganda
Ukraine
United Arab Emirates
United Kingdom [9]
United States [7 10]
Uzbekistan
Viet Nam
Yugoslavia
Zimbabwe

Amendment:
October 2, 1979.

NOTES:
    *Enters into force for Colombia February
28, 2001.
    [1] With declaration(s).

    [2] Applicable to Hong Kong. With declarations. See note under CHINA in bilateral section.
    [3] Not bound by provisions of Chapter II.
    [4] With reservation.
    [5] Extended to the territory of the French Republic including the overseas departments and territories.
    [6] See note under GERMANY, FEDERAL REPUBLIC OF in bilateral section.
    [7] With statement.
    [8] Applicable to Netherlands Antilles and Aruba.
    [9] Extended to Isle of Man.
    [10] Extended to all areas for which the United States has international responsibility.

Strasbourg agreement concerning the international patent classification. Done at Strasbourg March 24, 1971; entered into force October 7, 1975.
26 UST 1793; TIAS 8140.
States which are parties:
Australia [1]
Austria
Belarus
Belgium [1]
Brazil
Canada
China [2]
Croatia
Cuba [2]
Czech Rep.
Denmark
Egypt
Estonia
Finland [1]
France [1]
German Dem. Rep. [1 3]
Germany, Fed. Rep. [3]
Greece
Guinea [2]
Ireland [1]
Israel
Italy [1]
Japan
Korea
Kyrgyz Rep.
Luxembourg [1]
Malawi
Moldova
Monaco [1]
Netherlands [4]
Norway [1]
Poland
Portugal
Romania
Russian Fed.
Slovak Rep. [1]
Spain [1]
Suriname
Sweden
Switzerland
Tajikistan
Trinidad & Tobago
Turkey
Union of Soviet Socialist Reps. [1 5]
United Kingdom [1]
United States
Uruguay

Amendment:
October 2, 1979.

NOTES:
    [1] With statement.
    [2] With reservation(s).
    [3] See note under GERMANY, FEDERAL REPUBLIC OF in bilateral section.
    [4] Applicable to Netherlands Antilles and Aruba.
    [5] See note under UNION OF SOVIET SOCIALIST REPUBLICS in bilateral section.

Budapest treaty on the international recognition of the deposit of microorganisms for the purposes of patent procedure, with regulations. Done at Budapest April 28, 1977; entered into force August 19, 1980.
32 UST 1241; TIAS 9768.
States which are parties:
Australia
Austria
Belgium
Bulgaria
Canada
China
Croatia
Cuba
Czech Rep.
Denmark
Estonia
Finland
France
German Dem. Rep. [1]
Germany, Fed. Rep. [1]
Greece
Hungary
Iceland
Ireland
Israel
Italy
Japan
Korea
Latvia
Liechtenstein
Lithuania
Moldova
Monaco
Netherlands [2]
Norway
Philippines
Poland
Portugal
Romania
Russian Fed.
Singapore
Slovak Rep.
Slovenia
South Africa
Spain
Sweden
Switzerland
Tajikistan
Trinidad & Tobago
Turkey
Ukraine
Union of Soviet Socialist Reps. [3]
United Kingdom
United States
Yugoslavia

Amendments:
September 26, 1980.
January 20, 1981 (33 UST 955; TIAS 10078).

NOTES:
    [1] See note under GERMANY, FEDERAL REPUBLIC OF in bilateral section.

PATENTS (Cont'd)

[2] Extended to Netherlands Antilles and Aruba.

[3] See note under UNION OF SOVIET SOCIALIST REPUBLICS in bilateral section.

International convention for the protection of new varieties of plants of December 2, 1961, as revised. Done at Geneva March 19, 1991; entered into force April 24, 1998; for the United States February 22, 1999. *
TIAS
Parties
Argentina
Australia *
Austria
Belgium
Bolivia
Brazil
Bulgaria *
Canada
Chile
China [1]
Colombia
Czech Rep.
Denmark[2] *
Ecuador
Estonia *
Finland
France [3]
Germany *
Hungary
Ireland
Israel *
Italy
Japan *
Kenya
Kyrgyz Rep. *
Mexico
Moldova *
Netherlands [4] *
New Zealand
Norway
Panama
Paraguay
Poland
Portugal
Russian Fed. *
Slovak Rep.
Slovenia *
South Africa
Spain
Sweden *
Switzerland
Trinidad & Tobago
Ukraine [5]
United Kingdom *
United States [6] *
Uruguay

NOTES:
* Those countries marked with an asterisk are parties to the 1991 Act; the remainder are party to the 1978 Act.

[1] Not applicable to Hong Kong. See Note under CHINA in bilateral section.

[2] Not applicable to Greenland and the Faroe Is.

[3] Applicable to the territory of the French Republic, including the Oversea Departments and Territories.

[4] For the Kingdom in Europe.

[5] With declaration.
[6] With reservation(s).

PEACE TREATIES

(See also VIET-NAM)

Treaty of peace with Italy.[1] Signed at Paris February 10, 1947; entered into force September 15, 1947.
61 Stat. 1245; TIAS 1648; 4 Bevans 311; 49 and 50 UNTS.
States which are parties:
Albania
Australia
Belgium
Brazil
Canada
China [2]
Czechoslovakia [3]
Ethiopia [4]
France
Greece
India
Iraq
Italy
Mexico
Netherlands
New Zealand
Pakistan
Poland
Slovak Rep.
South Africa
Union of Soviet Socialist Reps. [5]
United Kingdom
United States
Yugoslavia [6]

NOTES:
[1] For agreements between the United States and Italy regarding implementation of the peace treaty and release of Italy from certain of its obligations thereunder, see under ITALY, PEACE TREATIES in bilateral section.

[2] Pre 1949 treaty, applicable only to Taiwan.

[3] See note under CZECHOSLOVAKIA in bilateral section.

[4] See note under ETHIOPIA in bilateral section.

[5] See note under UNION OF SOVIET SOCIALIST REPUBLICS in bilateral section.

[6] See note under YUGOSLAVIA in bilateral section.

Protocol on the establishment of a four power naval commission, the disposal of excess units of the Italian fleet, and the return by the Soviet Union of warships on loan. Signed at Paris February 10, 1947; entered into force February 10, 1947.
61 Stat. 3846; TIAS 1733; 4 Bevans 306; 140 UNTS 111.
States which are parties:
France
Union of Soviet Socialist Reps. [1]
United Kingdom
United States

NOTE:
[1] See note under UNION OF SOVIET SOCIALIST REPUBLICS in bilateral section.

Memorandum of understanding regarding the free territory of Trieste, with two annexes. Initialed at London October 5, 1954; entered into force October 5, 1954.
5 UST 2386; TIAS 3099; 235 UNTS 99.
States which are parties:
Italy
United Kingdom
United States
Yugoslavia [1]

NOTE:
[1] See note under YUGOSLAVIA in bilateral section.

Treaty of peace with Romania. Signed at Paris February 10, 1947; entered into force September 15, 1947.
61 Stat. 1757; TIAS 1649; 4 Bevans 403; 42 UNTS 3.
States which are parties:
Australia
Canada
Czechoslovakia [1]
India
New Zealand
Romania
Slovak Rep.
South Africa
Union of Soviet Socialist Reps. [2]
United Kingdom
United States

NOTES:
[1] See note under CZECHOSLOVAKIA in bilateral section.

[2] See note under UNION OF SOVIET SOCIALIST REPUBLICS in bilateral section.

Treaty of peace with Bulgaria. Signed at Paris February 10, 1947; entered into force September 15, 1947.
61 Stat. 1915; TIAS 1650; 4 Bevans 429; 41 UNTS 21.
States which are parties:
Australia
Bulgaria
Czechoslovakia [1]
Greece
India
New Zealand
Slovak Rep.
South Africa
Union of Soviet Socialist Reps. [2]
United Kingdom
United States
Yugoslavia [3]

NOTES:
[1] See note under CZECHOSLOVAKIA in bilateral section.

[2] See note under UNION OF SOVIET SOCIALIST REPUBLICS in bilateral section.

[3] See note under YUGOSLAVIA in bilateral section.

Treaty of peace with Hungary. Signed at Paris February 10, 1947; entered into force September 15, 1947.
61 Stat. 2065; TIAS 1651; 4 Bevans 453; 41 UNTS 135.
States which are parties:
Australia
Canada
Czechoslovakia [1]

PEACE TREATIES (Cont'd)

Hungary
India
New Zealand
Slovak Rep.
South Africa
Union of Soviet Socialist Reps. [2]
United Kingdom
United States
Yugoslavia [3]

NOTES:
    [1] See note under CZECHOSLOVAKIA in bilateral section.
    [2] See note under UNION OF SOVIET SOCIALIST REPUBLICS in bilateral section.
    [3] See note under YUGOSLAVIA in bilateral section.

Treaty of peace with Japan. Signed at San Francisco September 8, 1951; entered into force April 28, 1952.
3 UST 3169; TIAS 2490; 136 UNTS 45.
States which are parties:
Argentina
Australia
Belgium
Bolivia
Brazil
Cambodia
Canada
Chile
Costa Rica
Cuba
Dominican Rep.
Ecuador [1]
Egypt
El Salvador [1]
Ethiopia [2]
France
Greece
Guatemala
Haiti
Honduras
Iran
Iraq
Japan
Laos
Lebanon
Liberia
Mexico
Netherlands
New Zealand
Nicaragua
Norway
Pakistan
Panama
Paraguay
Peru
Philippines
Saudi Arabia
South Africa
Sri Lanka
Syrian Arab Rep.
Turkey
United Kingdom
United States [1]
Uruguay
Venezuela
Vietnam [3]

NOTES:
    [1] With declaration.
    [2] See note under ETHIOPIA in bilateral section.
    [3] See Vietnam footnote under AGRICULTURE: agreement of January 25, 1924 (26 UST 1840; TIAS 8141; 57 LNTS 135).

Declaration by Japan with respect to the treaty of peace. Signed at San Francisco September 8, 1951.
3 UST 3306; TIAS 2490; 136 UNTS 146, 160.

Agreement for the settlement of disputes arising under article 15(a) of the treaty of peace with Japan. Done at Washington June 12, 1952; entered into force June 12, 1952; for the United States June 19, 1952.
3 UST 4054; TIAS 2550; 138 UNTS 183.
States which are parties:
Argentina
Australia
Belgium
Cambodia
Canada
Chile
Cuba
Dominican Rep.
France
Greece
Haiti
Iraq
Japan
Lebanon
Liberia
Mexico
Netherlands [1]
New Zealand
Norway
Pakistan
South Africa
Sri Lanka
Turkey
United Kingdom
United States
Venezuela

NOTE:
    [1] Applicable to Netherlands Antilles and Aruba.

PEACEKEEPING [1]

Agreement concerning United States participation in the Multinational Force and Observers established by Egypt and Israel. Exchanges of letters at Washington August 3, 1981; entered into force August 3, 1981.
TIAS 10556.
States which are parties:
Egypt
Israel
United States

NOTE:
    [1] See also PEACEKEEPING under EGYPT, ISRAEL and MULTINATIONAL FORCE AND OBSERVERS in bilateral section.

PHONOGRAMS

Convention for the protection of producers of phonograms against unauthorized duplication of their phonograms. Done at Geneva October 29, 1971; entered into force April 18, 1973; for the United States March 10, 1974.
25 UST 309; TIAS 7808; 866 UNTS 67.
States which are parties:
Argentina
Australia
Austria
Barbados
Brazil
Bulgaria
Burkina Faso
Chile
China [1]
Colombia
Congo, Dem. Rep.
Costa Rica
Croatia
Cyprus
Czech Rep.
Denmark
Ecuador
Egypt
El Salvador
Estonia
Fiji
Finland [2]
Former Yugoslav Republic of Macedonia
France
Germany, Fed. Rep. [3]
Greece
Guatemala
Holy See
Honduras
Hungary
India
Israel
Italy [2]
Jamaica
Japan
Kenya
Korea
Latvia
Liechtenstein
Lithuania
Luxembourg
Mexico
Moldova
Monaco
Netherlands [4]
New Zealand
Nicaragua
Norway
Panama
Paraguay
Peru
Romania
Russian Fed.
St. Lucia [5]
Seychelles [5]
Slovak Rep.
Slovenia
Spain
Sweden
Switzerland
Trinidad & Tobago
Ukraine
United Kingdom [6]
United States

PHONOGRAMS (Cont'd)

Uruguay
Venezuela

NOTES:
[1] Applicable to Hong Kong. See note under CHINA in bilateral section.
[2] With statement.
[3] See note under GERMANY, FEDERAL REPUBLIC OF in bilateral section.
[4] Applicable to the Kingdom in Europe.
[5] See under country heading in the bilateral section for information concerning acceptance of treaty obligations.
[6] Extended to Bermuda, British Virgin Is., Cayman Is., Gibraltar, Isle of Man, and Montserrat.

POLAR BEARS

Agreement on the conservation of polar bears. Done at Oslo November 15, 1973; entered into force May 26, 1976; for the United States November 1, 1976.
27 UST 3918; TIAS 8409.
States which are parties:
Canada [1]
Denmark
Norway
Union of Soviet Socialist Reps. [2]
United States

NOTES:
[1] With statement.
[2] See note under UNION OF SOVIET SOCIALIST REPUBLICS in bilateral section.

POLLUTION

(See also MARINE POLLUTION)

Convention on long-range transboundary air pollution. Done at Geneva November 13, 1979; entered into force March 16, 1983.
TIAS 10541.

Protocol on long-term financing of the co-operative programme for monitoring and evaluation of the long-range transmission of air pollutants in Europe (EMEP). Done at Geneva September 28, 1984; entered into force January 28, 1988.
TIAS 12086.

Protocol to the 1979 convention on long-range transboundary air pollution concerning the control of emissions of nitrogen oxides or their transboundary fluxes, with annex. Done at Sofia October 31, 1988; entered into force February 14, 1991.
TIAS 12086.
Parties:
Armenia * **
Austria
Belarus
Belgium
Bosnia-Herzegovina **

Bulgaria
Canada
Croatia **
Cyprus **
Czech Rep.
Denmark [1]
Estonia *
European Economic Community
Finland
Former Yugoslav Republic of Macedonia * **
France
Georgia * **
German Dem. Rep.[2]
Germany, Fed. Rep.[2]
Greece
Hungary
Iceland * **
Ireland
Italy
Kyrgyz Rep. * **
Latvia **
Liechtenstein
Lithuania * **
Luxembourg
Malta **
Moldova * **
Monaco **
Netherlands
Norway
Poland **
Portugal **
Romania * **
Russian Fed.
Slovak Rep.
Slovenia **
Spain
Sweden
Switzerland
Turkey **
Ukraine
Union of Soviet Socialist Reps. [3]
United Kingdom [4]
United States
Yugoslavia ** [5]

NOTES:
*Not a party to the 1984 protocol.
**Not a party to the 1988 protocol.
[1] Not applicable to the Faroe Is. or Greenland.
[2] See note under GERMANY, FEDERAL REPUBLIC OF in bilateral section.
[3] See note under UNION OF SOVIET SOCIALIST REPUBLICS in bilateral section.
[4] Applicable to the Bailiwick of Jersey and Guernsey, Isle of Man, Gibraltar and the United Kingdom Sovereign Base Areas of Akrotiri and Dhekelia on the island of Cyprus.
[5] See note under YUGOSLAVIA in bilateral section.

Convention for the protection of the ozone layer, with annexes. Done at Vienna March 22, 1985; entered into force September 22, 1988.
TIAS 11097.
Parties:
Albania
Algeria
Angola
Antigua & Barbuda
Argentina [1]
Armenia
Australia
Austria
Azerbaijan

Bahamas
Bahrain
Bangladesh
Barbados
Belarus
Belgium
Belize
Benin
Bolivia
Bosnia-Herzegovina
Botswana
Brazil
Brunei
Bulgaria
Burkina Faso
Burma
Burundi
Cameroon
Canada
Central African Rep.
Chad
Chile [1]
China [2]
Colombia
Comoros
Congo
Congo, Dem. Rep.
Costa Rica
Cote d'Ivoire
Croatia
Cuba
Cyprus
Czech Rep.
Denmark
Djibouti
Dominica
Dominican Rep.
Ecuador
Egypt
El Salvador
Equatorial Guinea
Estonia
Ethiopia
European Economic Community
Fiji
Finland
Former Yugoslav Republic of Macedonia
France
Gabon
Gambia, The
Georgia
German Dem. Rep.[3]
Germany, Fed. Rep.[3]
Ghana
Greece
Grenada
Guatemala
Guinea
Guyana
Haiti
Honduras
Hungary
Iceland
India
Indonesia
Iran
Ireland
Israel
Italy
Jamaica
Japan
Jordan
Kazakhstan
Kenya
Kiribati

POLLUTION (Cont'd)

Korea, Dem. People's Rep.
Korea, Rep.
Kuwait
Kyrgyz Rep.
Laos
Latvia
Lebanon
Lesotho
Liberia
Libya
Liechtenstein
Lithuania
Luxembourg
Madagascar
Malawi
Malaysia
Maldives
Mali
Malta
Marshall Is.
Mauritania
Mauritius
Mexico
Micronesia
Moldova
Monaco
Mongolia
Morocco
Mozambique
Namibia
Nepal
Netherlands [1]
New Zealand [4]
Nicaragua
Niger
Nigeria
Norway
Oman
Pakistan
Panama
Papua New Guinea
Paraguay
Peru
Philippines
Poland
Portugal
Qatar
Romania
Russian Fed.
St. Kitts & Nevis
St. Lucia
St. Vincent & the Grenadines
Samoa
Saudi Arabia
Senegal
Seychelles
Singapore
Slovak Rep.
Slovenia
Solomon Is.
South Africa
Spain
Sri Lanka
Sudan
Suriname
Swaziland
Sweden [1]
Switzerland
Syria
Tajikistan
Tanzania

Thailand
Togo
Tonga
Trinidad & Tobago
Tunisia
Turkey
Turkmenistan
Tuvalu
Uganda
Ukraine
United Arab Emirates
United Kingdom [5]
United States
Uruguay
Uzbekistan
Vanuatu
Venezuela
Vietnam
Yemen
Yugoslavia [6]
Zambia
Zimbabwe

NOTES:
  [1] With declaration(s).
  [2] Applicable to Hong Kong and Macao. See note under CHINA in bilateral section.
  [3] See note under GERMANY, FEDERAL REPUBLIC OF in bilateral section.
  [4] For New Zealand, Cook Is. and Niue.
  [5] For the United Kingdom of Great Britain and Northern Ireland, the Bailiwicks of Guernsey and Jersey, the Isle of Man, Anguilla, Bermuda, British Antarctic Territory, British Indian Ocean Territory, British Virgin Is., Cayman Is., Falkland Is., Gibraltar, Montserrat, Pitcairn, Henderson, Ducie and Oeno Is., St. Helena, St. Helena Dependencies, South Georgia and South Sandwich Is., Turks and Caicos Is., and United Kingdom Sovereign Base Areas of Akrotiri and Dhekelia in Cyprus.
  [6] See note under YUGOSLAVIA in bilateral section.

Montreal protocol on substances that deplete the ozone layer, with annexes. Done at Montreal September 16, 1987; entered into force January 1, 1989.
TIAS
Parties:
Albania
Algeria
Angola
Antigua & Barbuda
Argentina
Armenia
Australia
Austria
Azerbaijan
Bahamas
Bahrain
Bangladesh
Barbados
Belarus
Belgium
Belize
Benin
Bolivia
Bosnia-Herzegovina
Botswana
Brazil
Brunei
Bulgaria
Burkina Faso
Burma

Burundi
Cameroon
Canada
Central African Rep.
Chad
Chile
China [1]
Colombia
Comoros
Congo
Congo, Dem. Rep.
Costa Rica
Cote d'Ivoire
Croatia
Cuba
Cyprus
Czech Rep.
Denmark [2]
Djibouti
Dominica
Dominican Rep.
Ecuador
Egypt
El Salvador
Estonia
Ethiopia
European Economic Community
Fiji
Finland
Former Yugoslav Republic of Macedonia
France
Gabon
Gambia, The
Georgia
German Dem. Rep. [3]
Germany, Fed. Rep. [3]
Ghana
Greece
Grenada
Guatemala
Guinea
Guyana
Haiti
Honduras
Hungary
Iceland
India
Indonesia
Iran
Ireland
Israel
Italy
Jamaica
Japan
Jordan
Kazakhstan
Kenya
Kiribati
Korea, Dem. People's Rep.
Korea, Rep.
Kuwait
Kyrgyz Rep.
Laos
Latvia
Lebanon
Lesotho
Liberia
Libya
Liechtenstein
Lithuania
Luxembourg
Madagascar
Malawi
Malaysia
Maldives

POLLUTION (Cont'd)

Mali
Malta
Marshall Is.
Mauritania
Mauritius
Mexico
Micronesia
Moldova
Monaco
Mongolia
Morocco
Mozambique
Namibia
Nepal
Netherlands [4]
New Zealand
Nicaragua
Niger
Nigeria
Norway
Oman
Pakistan
Panama
Papua New Guinea
Paraguay
Peru
Philippines
Poland
Portugal
Qatar
Romania
Russian Fed.
St. Kitts & Nevis
St. Lucia
St. Vincent & the Grenadines
Samoa
Saudi Arabia
Senegal
Seychelles
Singapore
Slovak Rep.
Slovenia
Solomon Is.
South Africa
Spain
Sri Lanka
Sudan
Suriname
Swaziland
Sweden
Switzerland
Syria
Tajikistan
Tanzania
Thailand
Togo
Tonga
Trinidad & Tobago
Tunisia
Turkey
Turkmenistan
Tuvalu
Uganda
Ukraine
United Arab Emirates
United Kingdom [5]
United States
Uruguay
Uzbekistan
Vanuatu
Venezuela

Vietnam
Yemen
Yugoslavia [6]
Zambia
Zimbabwe

Amendments and adjustments:
June 29, 1990.
June 29, 1990.
June 19-21, 1991.
November 23–25, 1992.
November 23–25, 1992.
December 7, 1995.
September 15-17, 1997.

NOTES:
[1] Applicable to Hong Kong and Macao. With declaration. See note under CHINA in bilateral section.
[2] Not applicable to the Faroe Is.
[3] See note under GERMANY, FEDERAL REPUBLIC OF in bilateral section.
[4] For the Kingdom in Europe, the Netherlands Antilles and Aruba.
[5] Extended to the Bailiwicks of Guernsey and Jersey, the Isle of Man, Anguilla, Bermuda, British Antarctic Territory, British Indian Ocean Territory, British Virgin Is., Cayman Is., Falkland Is., Gibraltar, Montserrat, Pitcairn, Henderson, Ducie and Oeno Is., St. Helena, St. Helena Dependencies, South Georgia and the South Sandwich Is., Turks and Caicos Is.
[6] See note under YUGOSLAVIA in bilateral section.

OECD Council decision on the control of transfrontier movements of wastes destined for recovery operations. Adopted at Paris March 30, 1992; entered into force March 30, 1992.
TIAS
Parties:
Australia
Austria
Belgium
Canada
Denmark
Finland
France
Germany
Greece
Iceland
Ireland
Italy
Luxembourg
Netherlands
New Zealand
Norway
Portugal
Spain
Sweden
Switzerland
Turkey
United Kingdom
United States

POPLAR COMMISSION

Convention placing the International Poplar Commission within the framework of the Food and Agricultural Organization. Approved at the 10th Session of the Conference of the Food

and Agricultural Organization, Rome, November 19, 1959; entered into force September 26, 1961; for the United States August 13, 1970. UST 2060; TIAS 6952; 410 UNTS 155.
States which are parties:
Argentina
Austria
Belgium
Bulgaria [1]
Canada
Chile
China
Croatia
Egypt
Finland
France
Germany, Fed. Rep. [2]
Hungary
India
Iran
Iraq
Ireland
Italy
Japan
Korea
Lebanon
Morocco
Netherlands
New Zealand [3]
Pakistan
Portugal
Romania
South Africa
Spain
Sweden
Switzerland
Syrian Arab Rep.
Tunisia
Turkey
United Kingdom [4]
United States
Yugoslavia [5]

Amendments:
October 30, 1967 (21 UST 2060; TIAS 6952; 634 UNTS 433).
November 15, 1977 (29 UST 5579; TIAS 9130).

NOTES:
[1] With reservation.
[2] See note under GERMANY, FEDERAL REPUBLIC OF in bilateral section.
[3] Not extended to territories.
[4] Extended to Channel Is. and Isle of Man.
[5] See note under YUGOSLAVIA in bilateral section.

POSTAL ARRANGEMENTS

Constitution of the Universal Postal Union, with Final Protocol. Done at Vienna July 10, 1964; entered into force January 1, 1966.
16 UST 1291; TIAS 5881; 611 UNTS 7.

Additional protocol to the constitution of the Universal Postal Union of July 10, 1964. Done at Tokyo November 14, 1969; entered into force July 1, 1971, except for Article V which entered into force January 1, 1971.
22 UST 1056; TIAS 7150; 810 UNTS 7.

POSTAL ARRANGEMENTS (Cont'd)

Second additional protocol to the constitution of the Universal Postal Union of July 10, 1964. Done at Lausanne July 5, 1974; entered into force January 1, 1976; definitively for the United States April 14, 1976.
27 UST 345; TIAS 8231; 1005 UNTS 9.

Third additional protocol to the constitution of the Universal Postal Union of July 10, 1964, general regulations with annex, and the universal postal convention with final protocol and detailed regulations. Done at Hamburg July 27, 1984; entered into force January 1, 1986; definitively for the United States June 6, 1986.
TIAS

Fourth additional protocol to the constitution of the Universal Postal Union of July 10, 1964, general regulations and the universal postal convention with final protocol. Done at Washington December 14, 1989; entered into force January 1, 1991.
TIAS

Fifth additional protocol to the constitution of the Universal Postal Union of July 10, 1964, with general regulations and the universal postal convention with final protocol. Done at Seoul September 14, 1994; entered into force January 1, 1996; for the United States May 20, 1998.*
TIAS
States which are parties:
Afghanistan [1 2]
Albania **
Algeria
Angola
Antigua & Barbuda [1 2]
Argentina
Armenia
Australia [3]
Austria
Azerbaijan [1 2]
Bahamas, The [4]
Bahrain
Bangladesh
Barbados **
Belarus **
Belgium
Belize
Benin
Bhutan
Bolivia
Bosnia-Herzegovina [1 2]
Botswana
Brazil
Brunei [1 2]
Bulgaria
Burkina Faso
Burma
Burundi
Cambodia
Cameroon
Canada
Cape Verde
Central African Rep.
Chad
Chile

China [5]
Colombia
Comoros [1 2]
Congo
Congo, Dem. Rep.
Costa Rica
Cote d'Ivoire
Croatia
Cuba
Cyprus
Czech Rep.
Denmark
Djibouti
Dominica [1]
Dominican Rep.
Ecuador
Egypt
El Salvador [1 2]
Equatorial Guinea
Eritrea
Estonia
Ethiopia [6]
Fiji
Finland
Former Yugoslav Republic of Macedonia [1]
France
Gabon
Gambia, The [1]
Georgia ** [1 2]
German Dem. Rep. [7]
Germany, Fed. Rep. [7]
Ghana
Greece
Grenada
Guatemala [1 2]
Guinea
Guinea-Bissau [1]
Guyana
Haiti [1 2]
Honduras
Hungary
Iceland
India **
Indonesia
Iran
Iraq [1 2]
Ireland
Israel
Italy
Jamaica [1]
Japan
Jordan
Kazakhstan
Kenya
Kiribati [1 2]
Korea, Dem. People's Rep. [1 2]
Korea, Rep.
Kuwait
Kyrgyz Rep. **
Laos [1 2]
Latvia **
Lebanon
Lesotho **
Liberia
Libya [1]
Liechtenstein
Lithuania [1 2]
Luxembourg **
Madagascar
Malawi
Malaysia
Maldives
Mali
Malta
Mauritania

Mauritius
Mexico
Moldova [1 2]
Monaco
Mongolia
Morocco
Mozambique
Namibia ** [1]
Nauru
Nepal
Netherlands
Netherlands Antilles [8]
New Zealand [9]
Nicaragua [1]
Niger [1 2]
Nigeria
Norway
Oman
Pakistan
Panama
Papua New Guinea
Paraguay
Peru
Philippines
Poland
Portugal
Qatar
Romania
Russian Fed.
Rwanda [1 2]
St. Kitts & Nevis [1 2]
St. Lucia
St. Vincent & the Grenadines
San Marino
Sao Tome & Principe [1]
Saudi Arabia
Senegal
Seychelles
Sierra Leone
Singapore
Slovak Rep.
Slovenia [1 2]
Solomon Is.
Somalia [1 2]
South Africa
Spain
Sri Lanka
Sudan **
Suriname
Swaziland
Sweden
Switzerland
Syrian Arab Rep.
Tajikistan
Tanzania
Thailand
Togo
Tonga
Trinidad & Tobago ** [1]
Tunisia
Turkey
Turkmenistan
Tuvalu [1]
Uganda
Ukraine **
United Arab Emirates
United Kingdom [10]
United States [11]
Uruguay
Uzbekistan
Vanuatu
Vatican City
Venezuela **
Vietnam, Socialist Rep.
Western Samoa

POSTAL ARRANGEMENTS (Cont'd)

Yemen (Aden) [12]
Yemen (Sanaa) [12]
Yugoslavia [1][2][13]
Zambia
Zimbabwe

NOTES:

*Unless otherwise indicated all states parties to the Constitution of the Universal Postal Union signed the Final Acts of the Universal Postal Congress, Seoul, 1994; those marked with a double asterisk (**) have also deposited instruments of ratification/approval. The general regulations and universal postal convention adopted at Seoul replaced those adopted at Washington December 14, 1989 which in turn replaced those adopted at previous postal congresses.

[1] Not a signatory to the Acts of the 1994 Seoul Congress.

[2] Not a party to the 1994 Seoul Protocol.

[3] Applicable to all territories.

[4] With a declaration.

[5] Applicable to Hong Kong and Macao. See note under CHINA in bilateral section.

[6] See note under ETHIOPIA in bilateral section.

[7] See note under GERMANY, FEDERAL REPUBLIC OF in bilateral section.

[8] Applicable to Aruba as a separate entity as of January 1, 1986.

[9] Extended to Cook Is., including Niue and the Tokelau Is.

[10] Extended to Channel Is., Isle of Man, Anguilla, Bermuda, British Indian Ocean Territory, British Virgin Islands, Cayman Islands, Falkland Islands, Gibraltar, Montserrat, Ducie and Oeno Islands, St. Helena, St. Helena Dependencies, South Georgia and South Sandwich Islands, Turks and Caicos Islands.

[11] Extended to the territories of the United States, and all areas for the international relations of which it is responsible.

[12] See note under YEMEN in bilateral section.

[13] See note under YUGOSLAVIA in bilateral section.

Money orders agreement. Done at Seoul September 14, 1994; entered into force January 1, 1996; for the United States May 20, 1998.
TIAS
Parties:
Albania
Algeria
Argentina
Armenia
Austria
Bangladesh
Belgium
Benin
Bolivia
Brazil
Bulgaria
Burkina Faso
Burundi
Cambodia
Cameroon
Cape Verde

Central African Rep.
Chad
Chile
China
Congo
Congo, Dem. Rep.
Cote d'Ivoire
Croatia
Cyprus
Czech Rep.
Denmark
Djibouti
Ecuador
Egypt
Equatorial Guinea
Fiji
Finland
Former Yugoslav Republic of Macedonia
France
Gabon
Georgia
Germany, Fed. Rep. [1]
Ghana
Greece
Grenada
Guinea
Guyana
Hungary
Iceland
Indonesia
Iran
Italy
Japan
Jordan
Kenya
Korea
Kuwait
Lebanon
Liberia
Liechtenstein
Luxembourg
Madagascar
Maldives
Mali
Mauritania
Mexico
Monaco
Morocco
Mozambique
Namibia
Netherlands [2]
Nigeria
Norway
Panama
Papua New Guinea
Paraguay
Peru
Philippines
Poland
Portugal
Qatar
Romania
St. Lucia
St. Vincent & the Grenadines
San Marino
Senegal
Sierra Leone
Slovak Rep.
Solomon Is.
Spain
Sri Lanka
Sudan
Suriname
Sweden
Switzerland

Syria
Thailand
Togo
Tunisia
Turkey
Uganda
United Arab Emirates
United States
Uruguay
Vanuatu
Vatican City
Vietnam
Western Samoa
Yemen (Aden) [3]
Yemen (Sanaa) [3]
Yugoslavia [4]
Zambia
Zimbabwe

NOTES:

[1] See note under GERMANY, FEDERAL REPUBLIC OF in bilateral section.

[2] Applicable to Netherlands Antilles and Aruba.

[3] See note under YEMEN in bilateral section.

[4] See note under YUGOSLAVIA in bilateral section.

Postal parcels agreement, with final protocol. Done at Seoul September 14, 1994; entered into force January 1, 1996; for the United States May 20, 1998.
TIAS
Parties:
Albania
Algeria
Angola
Argentina
Armenia
Austria
Bahamas
Bahrain
Bangladesh
Barbados
Belarus
Belgium
Belize
Benin
Bhutan
Bolivia
Botswana
Brazil
Bulgaria
Burkina Faso
Burma
Burundi
Cambodia
Cameroon
Canada
Cape Verde
Central African Rep.
Chad
Chile
China
Colombia
Congo
Congo, Dem. Rep.
Costa Rica
Cote d'Ivoire
Croatia
Cuba
Cyprus
Czech Rep.
Denmark

POSTAL ARRANGEMENTS (Cont'd)

Djibouti
Dominican Rep.
Ecuador
Egypt
Equatorial Guinea
Eritrea
Estonia
Ethiopia [1]
Fiji
Finland
Former Yugoslav Republic of Macedonia
France
Gabon
Georgia
German Dem. Rep.[2]
Germany, Fed. Rep.[2]
Ghana
Greece
Grenada
Guinea
Guyana
Honduras
Hungary
Iceland
India
Indonesia
Iran
Ireland
Israel
Italy
Japan
Jordan
Kazakhstan
Kenya
Korea
Kuwait
Kyrgyz Rep.
Latvia
Lebanon
Lesotho
Liberia
Liechtenstein
Luxembourg
Madagascar
Malawi
Malaysia
Maldives
Mali
Malta
Mauritania
Mauritius
Mexico
Monaco
Mongolia
Morocco
Mozambique
Namibia
Nauru
Nepal
Netherlands [3]
New Zealand
Nigeria
Norway
Oman
Pakistan
Panama
Papua New Guinea
Paraguay
Peru

Philippines
Poland
Portugal
Qatar
Romania
Russian Fed.
St. Lucia
St. Vincent & the Grenadines
San Marino
Saudi Arabia
Senegal
Seychelles
Sierra Leone
Singapore
Slovak Rep.
Solomon Is.
Spain
Sri Lanka
Sudan
Suriname
Swaziland
Sweden
Switzerland
Syria
Tajikistan
Tanzania
Thailand
Togo
Tonga
Trinidad & Tobago
Tunisia
Turkey
Turkmenistan
Uganda
Ukraine
Union of Soviet Socialist Reps. [4]
United Arab Emirates
United Kingdom [5]
United States
Uruguay
Uzbekistan
Vanuatu
Vatican City
Venezuela
Viet Nam
Western Samoa
Yemen (Aden) [6]
Yemen (Sanaa) [6]
Zambia
Zimbabwe

NOTES:
   [1] See note under ETHIOPIA in bilateral section.
   [2] See note under GERMANY, FEDERAL REPUBLIC OF in bilateral section.
   [3] Applicable to Netherlands Antilles and Aruba.
   [4] See note under UNION OF SOVIET SOCIALIST REPUBLICS in bilateral section.
   [5] Applicable to all territories.
   [6] See note under YEMEN in bilateral section.

Constitution of the Postal Union of the Americas and Spain, with final protocol. Done at Santiago November 26, 1971; entered into force for the United States July 1, 1972.
23 UST 2924; TIAS 7480.

Additional protocol to the constitution of the Postal Union of the Americas and Spain. Done at Lima March 18, 1976; entered into force October 1, 1976.
30 UST 337; TIAS 9206.

Second additional protocol to the constitution of the Postal Union of the Americas and Spain, with general regulations. Done at Managua August 28, 1981; entered into force January 1, 1982.*
TIAS
States which are parties:
Argentina [1]
Bolivia
Brazil [2]
Canada
Chile
Colombia
Costa Rica [2]
Cuba [2][3]
Dominican Rep.[2]
Ecuador
El Salvador
Guatemala [2]
Haiti [4]
Honduras [2]
Mexico
Nicaragua [2]
Panama [2]
Paraguay [2]
Peru [2]
Spain
Suriname
United States [5]
Uruguay
Venezuela [2]

NOTES:
   * While the United States has acceded to the second additional protocol most of the other parties have not yet done so. Even though not formally ratified, these agreements are customarily applied administratively.
   [1] With statement.
   [2] 1976 protocol provisionally in force.
   [3] With reservation.
   [4] Not a signatory to the 1976 protocol.
   [5] Extended to all the territories of the United States including the Trust Territory of the Pacific Is.

POTSDAM AGREEMENT

(See under WORLD WAR II)

PRISONER TRANSFER

Convention on the transfer of sentenced persons. Done at Strasbourg March 21, 1983; entered into force July 1, 1985.
TIAS 10824.
States which are parties:
Albania [1]
Andorra
Austria [1]
Bahamas [1]
Belgium [1]
Bulgaria [1]
Canada
Chile
Costa Rica
Croatia [1]
Cyprus
Czech Rep.
Denmark [1][2]

PRISONER TRANSFER (Cont'd)

Estonia [1]
Finland [1]
Former Yugoslav Republic of Macedonia
France [1]
Georgia [1]
Germany [1]
Greece [1]
Hungary [1]
Iceland [1]
Ireland [1][3]
Israel [1]
Italy [1]
Latvia [1]
Liechtenstein [1]
Lithuania [1]
Luxembourg [1]
Malta [1]
Netherlands [1][4]
Norway [1][5]
Panama [1]
Poland [1]
Portugal [1]
Romania [1]
Slovak Rep. [1]
Slovenia
Spain [1]
Sweden [1]
Switzerland [1]
Tonga
Trinidad & Tobago
Turkey [1]
Ukraine
United Kingdom [1][6]
United States [1]

NOTES:
   [1] With declaration(s).
   [2] Applicable to Faroe Is. and entire Kingdom of Denmark with exception of Greenland.
   [3] With reservation(s).
   [4] For the Kingdom in Europe, Netherlands Antilles and Aruba.
   [5] Extended to Bouvet Is., Peter I's Is. and Queen Maud Land.
   [6] Extended to Anguilla, British Indian Ocean Territory, British Virgin Is., Cayman Is., Falkland Is., Gibraltar, Isle of Man, Montserrat, Pitcairn, Henderson, Ducie and Oeno Is., St. Helena and dependencies, and the Sovereign Base Areas of Akrotiri and Dhekelia on the Island of Cyprus.

PRISONERS OF WAR

(See RED CROSS CONVENTIONS; RULES OF WARFARE)

PRIVATE INTERNATIONAL LAW

(See LAW, PRIVATE INTERNATIONAL)

PUBLICATIONS

Convention for the international exchange of official documents, scientific and literary publications. Concluded at Brussels March 15, 1886; entered into force January 14, 1889.
25 Stat. 1465; TS 381; 1 Bevans 107.

Convention for the immediate exchange of the official journals, parliamentary annals, and documents. Concluded at Brussels March 15, 1886; entered into force January 14, 1889.
25 Stat. 1469; TS 382; 1 Bevans 110.
States which are parties:
Argentina [1]
Belgium
Brazil
China [1][2]
Czechoslovakia [3]
Dominican Rep.
Egypt
Hungary
Italy
Latvia
Paraguay [1]
Poland
Portugal
Romania
Slovak Rep.
Spain
Switzerland [1]
United States
Uruguay
Yugoslavia [4]

NOTES:
   [1] Not a party to convention on official journals, parliamentary annals, and documents (25 Stat. 1469; TS 382; 1 Bevans 110).
   [2] Pre 1949 convention, applicable only to Taiwan.
   [3] See note under CZECHOSLOVAKIA in bilateral section.
   [4] See note under YUGOSLAVIA in bilateral section.

Convention relating to the exchange of official, scientific, literary and industrial publications. Signed at Mexico January 27, 1902; entered into force July 16, 1902.
TS 491-A; 1 Bevans 335.
States which are parties:
Colombia
Costa Rica
Cuba
El Salvador
Guatemala
Honduras
Mexico
Nicaragua
United States

Agreement for the repression of the circulation of obscene publications. Signed at Paris May 4, 1910; entered into force September 15, 1911.
37 Stat. 1511; TS 559; 1 Bevans 748.

Protocol amending the agreement for the suppression of the circulation of obscene publications signed at Paris May 4, 1910, with annex. Done at Lake Success May 4, 1949; entered

into force May 4, 1949; for the United States August 14, 1950.
1 UST 849; TIAS 2164; 30 UNTS 3.
States which are parties:
Afghanistan [1]
Albania [2]
Antigua & Barbuda [3]
Australia [4]
Austria
Bahamas, The [3]
Barbados [3]
Belgium
Belize [3]
Botswana [3]
Brazil [2]
Brunei [3]
Bulgaria [2]
Burma [1]
Cambodia
Canada
China [5]
Colombia [1]
Congo, Dem. Rep.
Cuba
Cyprus
Czech Rep.
Denmark
Dominica [3]
Egypt
El Salvador [1]
Estonia [2]
Fiji
Finland
France
Gambia, The [3]
German Dem. Rep. [6]
Germany, Fed. Rep. [1][6]
Ghana
Greece [1]
Grenada [3]
Guatemala [1]
Guyana [3]
Haiti [1]
Hong Kong [1][7]
Hungary [2]
Iceland
India
Iran
Iraq
Ireland
Italy
Jamaica [1]
Japan [1]
Jordan [1]
Kiribati [3]
Latvia [2]
Lesotho
Luxembourg
Madagascar
Malawi
Malaysia
Malta
Mauritius
Mexico
Monaco [2]
Morocco [1]
Nauru [3]
Netherlands [8]
New Zealand
Nigeria
Norway
Pakistan
Papua New Guinea [3]
Paraguay [1]
Poland [2]

PUBLICATIONS (Cont'd)

Portugal [2]
Romania
Russian Fed.
St. Kitts & Nevis [3]
St. Lucia [3]
St. Vincent & the Grenadines [3]
San Marino [2]
Seychelles [3]
Sierra Leone
Singapore [3]
Slovak Rep.
Solomon Is.
South Africa [9]
Spain [2]
Sri Lanka
Suriname [3]
Swaziland [3]
Switzerland
Tanzania
Thailand [2]
Trinidad & Tobago
Turkey
Tuvalu [3]
Union of Soviet Socialist Reps. [10]
United Kingdom [11]
United States
Western Samoa [3]
Yugoslavia [12]
Zambia
Zimbabwe [3]

NOTES:

[1] Bound by virtue of ratification or adherence to, or application of, the convention for the suppression of the circulation of and the traffic in obscene publications signed at Geneva September 12, 1923 (27 LNTS 213) and amended by the protocol signed at Lake Success, New York November 12, 1947 (46 UNTS 201).

[2] Not a party to the protocol.

[3] See under country heading in the bilateral section for information concerning acceptance of treaty obligations.

[4] Applicable to Norfolk Is.

[5] Pre 1949 agreement, applicable only to Taiwan.

[6] See note under GERMANY, FEDERAL REPUBLIC OF in bilateral section.

[7] CHINA is not a party to this treaty but has made it applicable to Hong Kong.

[8] Applicable to Aruba and Netherlands Antilles.

[9] Applicable to Namibia.

[10] See note under UNION OF SOVIET SOCIALIST REPUBLICS in bilateral section.

[11] Applicable to Bermuda, British Virgin Is., Falkland Is., Gibraltar, Montserrat, St. Helena, and Turks and Caicos.

[12] See note under YUGOSLAVIA in bilateral section.

Convention on interchange of publications. Signed at Buenos Aires December 23, 1936; entered into force April 1, 1938; for the United States October 23, 1939.
54 Stat. 1715; TS 954; 3 Bevans 378; 201 LNTS 295.
States which are parties:
Brazil
Colombia

Costa Rica
Dominican Rep.
El Salvador
Guatemala
Haiti
Honduras
Nicaragua
Panama
Peru
United States [1]
Venezuela

NOTE:
[1] With an understanding.

Convention concerning the international exchange of publications. Adopted at Paris December 3, 1958; entered into force November 23, 1961; for the United States June 9, 1968.
19 UST 4449; TIAS 6438; 416 UNTS 51.

Convention concerning the exchange of official publications and government documents between States. Adopted at Paris December 3, 1958; entered into force May 30, 1961; for the United States June 9, 1968.
19 UST 4467; TIAS 6439; 398 UNTS 9.
States which are parties:
Antigua & Barbuda [1]
Australia
Bahamas, The [1]
Barbados [1]
Belarus
Belgium
Brazil [2]
Bulgaria
Central African Rep. [3]
China (Taiwan) [4]
Cuba
Czechoslovakia [5]
Denmark
Dominica
Dominican Rep.
Ecuador
Egypt
Finland
France
Georgia
German Dem. Rep. [6]
Germany, Fed. Rep. [6]
Ghana
Grenada [1]
Guatemala
Guyana [1]
Hungary
Indonesia
Iraq [3]
Israel
Italy
Jamaica [1]
Japan
Kiribati [1]
Libya
Lithuania [2]
Luxembourg
Malawi [2]
Malta
Morocco
Netherlands [2] [7]
New Zealand
Nigeria
Norway
Panama
Poland
Romania

St. Kitts & Nevis [1]
St. Lucia [1]
St. Vincent & the Grenadines [1]
Seychelles [1] [3]
Singapore [1]
Slovak Rep.
Solomon Is. [3]
Spain
Sri Lanka [3]
Suriname [1]
Sweden
Tajikistan
Trinidad & Tobago [1]
Tuvalu [1]
Ukraine
Union of Soviet Socialist Reps. [8]
United Kingdom [9]
United States
Zambia [1]
Zimbabwe [1]

NOTES:

[1] See under country heading in the bilateral section for information concerning acceptance of treaty obligations.

[2] Not a party to the convention on official publications.

[3] Party to convention on official publications only.

[4] See note under CHINA (Taiwan) in bilateral section.

[5] See note under CZECHOSLOVAKIA in bilateral section.

[6] See note under GERMANY, FEDERAL REPUBLIC OF in bilateral section.

[7] Applicable to Netherlands Antilles and Aruba.

[8] See note under UNION OF SOVIET SOCIALIST REPUBLICS in bilateral section.

[9] Extended to Anguilla, Bermuda, British Virgin Is., Bailiwick of Guernsey, Isle of Man, Jersey, and Montserrat.

Proces-verbal relating to the convention concerning the exchange of official publications and government documents between States. Signed at Paris October 18, 1960.
19 UST 4485; TIAS 6439.

Statutes of the International Center for the Registration of Serial Publications. Done at Paris November 14, 1974, and amended October 11 and 12, 1976; entered into force January 21, 1976; provisionally for the United States March 31, 1978.
TIAS
States which are parties:
Argentina
Belgium
Brazil
Bulgaria
Canada
Chile
Cyprus
Denmark
Ecuador
Finland
Georgia
Germany, Fed. Rep. [1]
Hungary
Jamaica
Korea
Libya
Lithuania
Nigeria

PUBLICATIONS (Cont'd)

Norway
Philippines
Poland
Romania
Senegal
Slovenia
Spain
Sweden
Switzerland
Turkey
United Kingdom
United States
Uruguay

NOTE:
    [1] See note under GERMANY, FEDERAL REPUBLIC OF in bilateral section.

RACIAL DISCRIMINATION

International convention on the elimination of all forms of racial discrimination. Done at New York December 21, 1965; entered into force January 4, 1969; for the United States November 20, 1994.
TIAS   ; 660 UNTS 195.
Parties:
Afghanistan
Albania
Algeria [1]
Antigua & Barbuda
Argentina
Armenia
Australia [1]
Austria
Azerbaijan
Bahamas
Bahrain
Bangladesh
Barbados
Belarus
Belgium
Bolivia
Bosnia–Herzegovina
Botswana
Brazil
Bulgaria [1]
Burkina Faso
Burundi
Cambodia
Cameroon
Canada
Cape Verde
Central African Rep.
Chad
Chile [1]
China [2 3 4]
Colombia
Congo
Congo, Dem. Rep.
Costa Rica [1]
Cote d'Ivoire
Croatia
Cuba [1 3]
Cyprus [1]
Czech Rep.
Denmark [1]

Dominican Rep.
Ecuador [1]
Egypt
El Salvador
Estonia
Ethiopia
Fiji
Finland
Former Yugoslav Republic of Macedonia
France [1]
Gabon
Gambia
Georgia
Germany
Ghana
Greece
Guatemala
Guinea
Guyana [1]
Haiti
Holy See
Hungary [1]
Iceland [1]
India [3]
Indonesia
Iran
Iraq [3]
Ireland
Israel [3]
Italy [1]
Jamaica [3]
Japan
Jordan
Kazakhstan
Korea
Kuwait [2]
Kyrgyz Rep.
Laos
Latvia
Lebanon [3]
Lesotho
Liberia
Libya [3]
Liechtenstein
Lithuania
Luxembourg [1]
Madagascar [3]
Malawi
Maldives
Mali
Malta [2]
Mauritania
Mauritius
Mexico
Moldova
Monaco
Mongolia
Morocco [3]
Mozambique [3]
Namibia
Nepal [2 3]
Netherlands [1 5]
New Zealand
Nicaragua
Niger
Nigeria
Norway [1]
Pakistan
Panama
Papua New Guinea [3]
Peru [1]
Philippines
Poland [2 3]
Portugal
Qatar

Romania
Russian Fed. [1]
Rwanda [3]
St. Lucia
St. Vincent & the Grenadines
Saudi Arabia
Senegal [1]
Seychelles
Sierra Leone
Slovak Rep. [1]
Slovenia
Solomon Is.
Somalia
South Africa
Spain [1 3]
Sri Lanka
Sudan
Suriname
Swaziland
Sweden [1]
Switzerland
Syria [3]
Tajikistan
Tanzania
Togo
Tonga
Trinidad & Tobago
Tunisia
Turkmenistan
Uganda
Ukraine [1]
United Arab Emirates [2]
United Kingdom [2 6]
United States [1 2 3]
Uruguay [1]
Uzbekistan
Venezuela
Vietnam [2 3]
Yemen [3 7]
Yugoslavia [8]
Zambia
Zimbabwe

NOTES:
    [1] With declaration(s).
    [2] With statement(s).
    [3] With reservation(s).
    [4] Applicable to Hong Kong and Macao. With declarations. See note under CHINA in bilateral section.
    [5] Applicable to Netherlands Antilles and Aruba.
    [6] Applicable to Dominica, St. Kitts & Nevis, Brunei and territories under territorial sovereignty of the United Kingdom.
    [7] See note under YEMEN in bilateral section.
    [8] See note under YUGOSLAVIA in bilateral section.

RADIO

(See TELECOMMUNICATION)

RECIPROCAL ASSISTANCE, INTER-AMERICAN

(See under DEFENSE)

RED CROSS CONVENTIONS

(See also INTERNATIONAL TRACING SERVICE; RULES OF WARFARE)

Convention for the amelioration of the condition of the wounded and sick in armed forces in the field. [1] Dated at Geneva August 12, 1949; entered into force October 21, 1950; for the United States February 2, 1956.
6 UST 3114; TIAS 3362; 75 UNTS 31.

Convention for the amelioration of the condition of the wounded, sick, and shipwrecked members of armed forces at sea. Dated at Geneva August 12, 1949; entered into force October 21, 1950; for the United States February 2, 1956.
6 UST 3217; TIAS 3363; 75 UNTS 85.

Convention relative to the treatment of prisoners of war. [1] Dated at Geneva August 12, 1949; entered into force October 21, 1950; for the United States February 2, 1956.
6 UST 3316; TIAS 3364; 75 UNTS 135.

Convention relative to the protection of civilian persons in time of war. Dated at Geneva August 12, 1949; entered into force October 21, 1950; for the United States February 2, 1956.
6 UST 3516; TIAS 3365; 75 UNTS 287.
States which are parties:
Afghanistan
Albania [2]
Algeria
Andorra
Angola
Antigua & Barbuda
Argentina
Australia [3]
Austria
Bahamas, The
Bahrain
Bangladesh
Barbados [3]
Belarus [2]
Belgium
Belize
Benin
Bolivia
Botswana
Brazil
Brunei
Bulgaria
Burkina Faso
Burma
Burundi
Cambodia
Cameroon
Canada
Cape Verde
Central African Rep.
Chad
Chile
China [2] [4]
Colombia
Comoros
Congo

Congo, Dem. Rep.
Costa Rica
Cote d'Ivoire
Croatia
Cuba
Cyprus
Czechoslovakia [2] [5]
Denmark
Djibouti
Dominica
Dominican Rep.
Ecuador
Egypt
El Salvador
Equatorial Guinea
Eritrea
Ethiopia [6]
Fiji
Finland
Former Yugoslav Republic of Macedonia
France
Gabon
Gambia, The
Georgia
German Dem. Rep. [2] [7]
Germany, Fed. Rep. [3] [7]
Ghana
Greece
Grenada
Guatemala
Guinea
Guinea-Bissau [2]
Guyana
Haiti
Holy See
Honduras
Hungary
Iceland
India
Indonesia
Iran
Iraq
Ireland
Israel [8] [9] [10]
Italy
Jamaica
Japan
Jordan
Kazakhstan
Kenya
Kiribati
Korea, Dem. People's Rep. [2]
Korea, Rep. [10] [11]
Kuwait
Kyrgyz Rep.
Laos
Latvia
Lebanon
Lesotho
Liberia
Libya
Liechtenstein
Lithuania
Luxembourg
Madagascar
Malawi
Malaysia
Maldives
Mali
Malta
Mauritania
Mauritius
Mexico
Micronesia
Monaco

Mongolia
Morocco
Mozambique
Namibia, U.N. Council for
Nepal
Netherlands [12]
New Zealand [3]
Nicaragua
Niger
Nigeria
Norway
Oman
Pakistan [10]
Palau
Panama
Papua New Guinea
Paraguay
Peru
Philippines
Poland [2]
Portugal [2]
Qatar
Romania [2]
Russian Fed.
Rwanda
St. Kitts & Nevis
St. Lucia
St. Vincent & the Grenadines
San Marino
Sao Tome & Principe
Saudi Arabia
Senegal
Seychelles
Sierra Leone
Singapore
Slovak Rep. [2]
Slovenia
Solomon Is.
Somalia
South Africa
Spain
Sri Lanka
Sudan
Suriname [10]
Swaziland
Sweden
Switzerland
Syrian Arab Rep.
Tajikistan
Tanzania
Thailand
Togo
Tonga
Trinidad & Tobago
Tunisia
Turkey
Turkmenistan
Tuvalu
Uganda
Ukraine [2]
Union of Soviet Socialist Reps. [2] [13]
United Arab Emirates
United Kingdom [3] [14]
United States [3] [8] [10] [15]
Uruguay [10] [11]
Uzbekistan
Vanuatu
Venezuela
Vietnam, Socialist Rep. [2] [15]
Western Samoa
Yemen (Aden) [16]
Yemen (Sanaa) [16]
Yugoslavia [2] [17]
Zambia
Zimbabwe

RED CROSS CONVENTIONS (Cont'd)

NOTES:

[1] The 1949 conventions on the amelioration of the condition of the armed forces in the field and on prisoners of war replaced the conventions of July 27, 1929 (47 Stat. 2021 and 2074; TS 846 and 847) as between contracting parties. Estonia is not a party to the later conventions.

[2] With reservations to all four conventions.

[3] With statement.

[4] Applicable to Hong Kong and Macao. See note under CHINA in bilateral section.

[5] See note under CZECHOSLOVAKIA in bilateral section.

[6] See note under ETHIOPIA in bilateral section.

[7] See note under GERMANY, FEDERAL REPUBLIC OF in bilateral section.

[8] With reservation to "field" convention.

[9] With reservation to "sea" convention.

[10] With reservation to "civilians" convention.

[11] With reservation to "prisoners-of-war" convention.

[12] Applicable to Netherlands Antilles and Aruba.

[13] See note under UNION OF SOVIET SOCIALIST REPUBLICS in bilateral section.

[14] Extended to all territories for the international relations of which the United Kingdom is responsible.

[15] With reference to the notification by the Federal Political Department of the Swiss Confederation dated November 8, 1976, that the Socialist Republic of Vietnam continues the participation of the Democratic Republic of Vietnam and the Provisional Revolutionary Government of the Republic of South Vietnam, together with the reservations enunciated by both, the United States made clear its position on these previous accessions and specifically rejected all of these reservations in its Notes to the Federal Political Department of the Swiss Confederation dated September 17, 1957 and December 31, 1974.

[16] See note under YEMEN in bilateral section.

[17] See note under YUGOSLAVIA in bilateral section.

REFUGEES

Protocol relating to the status of refugees. [1] Done at New York January 31, 1967; entered into force October 4, 1967; for the United States November 1, 1968.
19 UST 6223; TIAS 6577; 606 UNTS 267.
States which are parties:
Albania
Algeria
Angola [2]
Antigua & Barbuda
Argentina
Armenia
Australia
Austria [3]
Azerbaijan

Bahamas, The [2]
Belgium [3]
Belize
Benin
Bolivia
Bosnia-Herzegovina
Botswana [2 3]
Brazil [3]
Bulgaria
Burkina Faso
Burundi [2]
Cambodia
Cameroon
Canada [3]
Cape Verde [2]
Central African Rep.
Chad
Chile [2]
China [2 4]
Colombia
Congo [2]
Congo, Dem. Rep.
Costa Rica
Cote d'Ivoire
Croatia
Cyprus [3]
Czech Rep.
Denmark [3]
Djibouti
Dominica
Dominican Rep.
Ecuador [3]
Egypt [3]
El Salvador [2]
Equatorial Guinea
Estonia
Ethiopia [2 5]
Fiji [3]
Finland [3]
Former Yugoslav Republic of Macedonia
France [3 6]
Gabon
Gambia, The [3]
Germany, Fed. Rep. [7]
Ghana [2]
Georgia
Greece [3]
Guatemala [3]
Guinea
Guinea-Bissau
Haiti
Holy See [3]
Honduras [2]
Hungary
Iceland
Iran [3]
Ireland [3]
Israel [3]
Italy [3]
Jamaica [2 3]
Japan
Kazakhstan
Kenya
Kiribati [8]
Korea [2 3]
Kyrgyz Rep.
Latvia [9]
Lesotho
Liberia
Liechtenstein [3]
Lithuania
Luxembourg [3]
Malawi [2]
Mali
Malta [3]

Mauritania [2]
Mexico
Morocco
Mozambique
Netherlands [3 10]
New Zealand [3]
Nicaragua
Niger
Nigeria
Norway [3]
Panama
Papua New Guinea
Paraguay
Peru
Philippines
Poland
Portugal [3 6]
Romania
Russian Fed.
Rwanda [2]
St. Lucia [8]
Samoa
Sao Tome & Principe
Senegal
Seychelles
Sierra Leone
Slovak Rep.
Slovenia
Solomon Is.
Somalia [2 3]
South Africa
Spain [3]
Sudan [3]
Suriname
Swaziland [2]
Sweden [3]
Switzerland [3]
Tajikistan
Tanzania [2]
Togo
Tunisia
Turkey [3]
Turkmenistan [9]
Tuvalu [3]
Uganda [3]
United Kingdom [3 11]
United States [2]
Uruguay
Venezuela [2]
Yemen (Sanaa) [12]
Yugoslavia [13]
Zambia [3]
Zimbabwe

NOTES:

[1] Protocol incorporates articles 2 through 34 of the convention relating to the status of refugees of July 28, 1951 (189 UNTS 150). States parties to the convention not parties to the protocol are: Madagascar and Monaco. The United Kingdom also extended application of the convention to various territories for the international relations of which it was responsible.

[2] With reservation(s).

[3] With reservations and declarations to the convention.

[4] Applicable to Macao. See note under CHINA in bilateral section.

[5] See note under ETHIOPIA in bilateral section.

[6] Without geographical limitations.

[7] See note under GERMANY, FEDERAL REPUBLIC OF in bilateral section.

REFUGEES (Cont'd)

[8] See under country heading in the bilateral section for information concerning acceptance of treaty obligations.

[9] With declaration(s).

[10] Applicable to Netherlands Antilles and Aruba.

[11] Extended to Jersey and Montserrat.

[12] See note under YEMEN in bilateral section.

[13] See note under YUGOSLAVIA in bilateral section.

RENUNCIATION OF WAR

Treaty providing for the renunciation of war as an instrument of national policy. Signed at Paris August 27, 1928; entered into force July 24, 1929.
46 Stat. 2343; TS 796; 2 Bevans 732; 94 LNTS 57.
States which are parties:
Afghanistan
Albania
Antigua & Barbuda
Australia
Austria
Barbados
Belgium
Bosnia-Herzegovina
Brazil
Bulgaria
Canada
Chile
China [1]
Colombia
Costa Rica
Cuba
Czech Rep.
Czechoslovakia [2]
Denmark
Dominica
Dominican Rep.
Ecuador
Egypt
Estonia
Ethiopia [3]
Fiji
Finland
France
Germany
Greece
Guatemala
Haiti
Honduras
Hungary
Iceland
India
Iran
Iraq
Ireland
Italy
Japan
Latvia
Liberia
Lithuania
Luxembourg
Mexico
Netherlands

New Zealand
Nicaragua
Norway
Panama
Paraguay
Peru
Poland
Portugal
Romania
Saudi Arabia
Slovenia
South Africa
Spain
Sweden
Switzerland
Thailand
Turkey
Union of Soviet Socialist Reps. [4]
United Kingdom
United States
Venezuela
Yugoslavia [5]

NOTES:
[1] Pre 1949 convention, applicable only to Taiwan.

[2] See note under CZECHOSLOVAKIA in bilateral section.

[3] See note under ETHIOPIA in bilateral section.

[4] See note under UNION OF SOVIET SOCIALIST REPUBLICS in bilateral section.

[5] See note under YUGOSLAVIA in bilateral section.

REPARATIONS

(See also FINANCE: WORLD WAR II RELATED AGREEMENTS)

Protocol on the talks between the Heads of the three governments at the Crimea Conference on the question of the German reparation in kind. Signed at Yalta February 11, 1945; entered into force February 11, 1945.
Foreign Relations of the United States: "The Conferences at Malta and Yalta, 1945," pp. 968-975. 3 Bevans 1020.
States which are parties:
Union of Soviet Socialist Reps. [1]
United Kingdom
United States

NOTE:
[1] See note under UNION OF SOVIET SOCIALIST REPUBLICS in bilateral section.

Agreement on reparation from Germany, on the establishment of an inter-Allied reparation agency and on the restitution of monetary gold. Concluded at Paris January 14, 1946; entered into force January 24, 1946.
61 Stat. 3157; TIAS 1655; 4 Bevans 5; 555 UNTS 69.
States which are parties:
Albania
Australia
Belgium
Canada

Czechoslovakia [1]
Denmark
Egypt
France
Greece
India
Luxembourg
Netherlands
New Zealand
Norway
Pakistan [2]
Slovak Rep.
South Africa
United Kingdom
United States
Yugoslavia [3]

NOTES:
[1] See note under CZECHOSLOVAKIA in bilateral section.

[2] See protocol of March 15, 1948 (62 Stat. 2613; TIAS 1797; 4 Bevans 701; 555 UNTS 104).

[3] See note under YUGOSLAVIA in bilateral section.

Agreement on a plan for allocation of a reparation share to nonrepatriable victims of German action, with annex. Signed at Paris June 14, 1946; entered into force June 14, 1946.
61 Stat. 2649; TIAS 1594; 4 Bevans 75.
States which are parties:
Czechoslovakia [1]
France
Slovak Rep.
United Kingdom
United States
Yugoslavia [2]

NOTES:
[1] See note under CZECHOSLOVAKIA in bilateral section.

[2] See note under YUGOSLAVIA in bilateral section.

Protocol relating to Austrian participation in the restitution of monetary gold looted by Germany, as provided in the reparation agreement of January 14, 1946. Signed at London November 4, 1947; entered into force November 4, 1947.
61 Stat. 3571; TIAS 1683; 4 Bevans 689; 93 UNTS 61.
States which are parties:
Austria
France
United Kingdom
United States

Protocol relating to participation by Italy in the restitution of monetary gold looted by Germany, as provided in the reparation agreement of January 14, 1946. Signed at London December 16, 1947; effective September 15, 1947.
61 Stat. 3729; TIAS 1707; 4 Bevans 692; 82 UNTS 237.
States which are parties:
France
Italy
United Kingdom
United States

Protocol relating to participation by Poland in the restitution of monetary gold looted by Ger-

REPARATIONS (Cont'd)

many, as provided in the reparation agreement signed at Paris January 14, 1946. Signed at London July 6, 1949; entered into force July 6, 1949.
63 Stat. 2677; TIAS 1970; 4 Bevans 850.
States which are parties:
France
Poland
United Kingdom
United States

RICE COMMISSION, INTERNATIONAL

(See under AGRICULTURE)

RIGHTS AND DUTIES OF STATES

(See STATES, RIGHTS AND DUTIES)

RIO TREATY

(See under DEFENSE)

ROAD TRAFFIC

(See under AUTOMOTIVE TRAFFIC)

RUBBER

International natural rubber agreement, 1994. Done at Geneva February 17, 1995; entered into force provisionally, February 6, 1997; definitively, February 14, 1997.
TIAS
Parties:
Austria
Belgium *
China
Cote d'Ivoire
Denmark *
European Community *
Finland *
France
Germany * [1]
Greece
Indonesia
Ireland
Italy
Japan
Luxembourg *

Netherlands [2]
Nigeria *
Spain
Sweden
United Kingdom [3]
United States

NOTES:
  * Provisional application.
  [1] With declaration.
  [2] For the Kingdom in Europe.
  [3] In respect of the United Kingdom of Great Britain and Northern Ireland.

RULES OF WARFARE

(See also RED CROSS CONVENTIONS; WAR CRIMINALS)

Convention regarding the rights of neutrals at sea. Signed at Washington July 22, 1854; entered into force October 31, 1854.
10 Stat. 1105; TS 300; 11 Bevans 1214.
States which are parties:
Nicaragua [1]
Union of Soviet Socialist Reps. [2]
United States

NOTES:
  [1] Declaration of accession by Nicaragua signed at Granada June 9, 1855 (7 Miller 139).
  [2] See note under UNION OF SOVIET SOCIALIST REPUBLICS in bilateral section.

Convention with respect to the laws and customs of war on land, with annex of regulations. [1] Signed at The Hague July 29, 1899; entered into force September 4, 1900; for the United States April 9, 1902.
32 Stat. 1803; TS 403; 1 Bevans 247.
States which are parties:
Argentina
Australia [2]
Austria [2]
Belgium [2]
Bolivia [2]
Brazil [2]
Bulgaria
Canada [2]
Chile
China [2][3]
Colombia
Cuba [2]
Denmark [2]
Dominican Rep. [2]
Ecuador
El Salvador [2]
France [2]
Germany [2]
Greece
Guatemala [2]
Haiti [2]
Honduras
Hungary [2]
India [2]
Iran
Ireland [2]
Italy
Japan [2]

Korea
Laos [2]
Luxembourg [2]
Mexico [2]
Netherlands [2]
New Zealand [2]
Nicaragua [2]
Norway [2]
Pakistan [2]
Panama [2]
Paraguay
Peru
Philippines [2]
Portugal [2]
Romania [2]
South Africa [2]
Spain
Sri Lanka [2]
Sweden [2]
Switzerland [2]
Thailand [2]
Turkey
Union of Soviet Socialist Reps. [2][4]
United Kingdom [2]
United States [2]
Uruguay
Venezuela
Yugoslavia [5]

NOTES:
  [1] Replaced by convention of October 18, 1907 (36 Stat. 2277; TS 539), as between contracting parties to the later convention. Sections II and III of the regulations are supplemented by convention of August 12, 1949 (6 UST 3516; TIAS 3365), relative to protection of civilians in time of war, as between contracting parties to both conventions; chapter II of the regulations is complemented by convention of August 12, 1949 (6 UST 3316; TIAS 3364), relative to treatment of prisoners of war, as between contracting parties to both conventions.
  [2] Party to convention of October 18, 1907.
  [3] Pre 1949 convention, applicable only to Taiwan.
  [4] See note under UNION OF SOVIET SOCIALIST REPUBLICS in bilateral section.
  [5] See note under YUGOSLAVIA in bilateral section.

Convention for the exemption of hospital ships, in time of war, from the payment of all dues and taxes imposed for the benefit of the state. Done at The Hague December 21, 1904; entered into force March 26, 1907.
35 Stat. 1854; TS 459; 1 Bevans 430.
States which are parties:
Austria
Belgium
China [1]
Cuba
Denmark
France
Germany [2]
Greece
Guatemala
Iran
Italy
Japan
Korea
Luxembourg
Mexico
Netherlands
Norway

RULES OF WARFARE
(Cont'd)

Peru
Poland, including Free City of Danzig
Portugal
Romania [1]
Spain
Sweden
Switzerland
Thailand
Turkey
Union of Soviet Socialist Reps. [3]
United States

NOTES:
[1] Pre 1949 convention, applicable only to Taiwan.
[2] With reservation.
[3] See note under UNION OF SOVIET SOCIALIST REPUBLICS in bilateral section.

Convention relative to the opening of hostilities. Signed at The Hague October 18, 1907; entered into force January 26, 1910.
36 Stat. 2259; TS 538; 1 Bevans 619.
States which are parties:
Australia
Austria
Belgium
Bolivia
Brazil
Canada
China [1]
Denmark
El Salvador
Ethiopia [2]
Finland
France
Germany
Guatemala
Haiti
Hungary
India
Ireland
Japan
Laos
Liberia
Luxembourg
Mexico
Netherlands
New Zealand
Nicaragua
Norway
Pakistan
Panama
Philippines
Poland
Portugal
Romania
South Africa
Spain
Sri Lanka
Sweden
Switzerland
Thailand
Union of Soviet Socialist Reps. [3]
United Kingdom
United States

NOTES:
[1] Pre 1949 convention, applicable only to Taiwan.
[2] See note under ETHIOPIA in bilateral section.
[3] See note under UNION OF SOVIET SOCIALIST REPUBLICS in bilateral section.

Convention respecting the laws and customs of war on land, with annex of regulations. [1] Signed at The Hague October 18, 1907; entered into force January 26, 1910.
36 Stat. 2277; TS 539; 1 Bevans 631.
States which are parties:
Australia
Austria [2]
Belgium
Bolivia
Brazil
Canada
China [3]
Cuba
Denmark
Dominican Rep.
El Salvador
Ethiopia [4]
Finland
France
Germany [2]
Guatemala
Haiti
Hungary [2]
India
Ireland
Japan [2]
Laos
Liberia
Luxembourg
Mexico
Netherlands
New Zealand
Nicaragua
Norway
Pakistan
Panama
Philippines
Poland
Portugal
Romania
South Africa
Sri Lanka
Sweden
Switzerland
Thailand
Union of Soviet Socialist Reps. [2] [5]
United Kingdom
United States

NOTES:
[1] Sections II and III of the regulations are supplemented by convention of August 12, 1949 (6 UST 3516; TIAS 3365), relative to protection of civilians in time of war, as between contracting parties to both conventions; chapter II of the regulations is complemented by convention of August 12, 1949 (6 UST 3316; TIAS 3364), relative to treatment of prisoners of war, as between contracting parties to both conventions.
[2] With reservation.
[3] Pre 1949 convention, applicable only to Taiwan.
[4] See note under ETHIOPIA in bilateral section.

[5] See note under UNION OF SOVIET SOCIALIST REPUBLICS in bilateral section.

Convention respecting the rights and duties of neutral powers and persons in case of war on land. Signed at The Hague October 18, 1907; entered into force January 26, 1910.
36 Stat. 2310; TS 540; 1 Bevans 654.
States which are parties:
Austria
Belgium
Bolivia
Brazil
China [1]
Cuba
Denmark
El Salvador
Ethiopia [2]
Finland
France
Germany
Guatemala
Haiti
Hungary
Japan
Laos
Liberia
Luxembourg
Mexico
Netherlands
Nicaragua
Norway
Panama
Philippines
Poland
Portugal
Romania
Spain
Sweden
Switzerland
Thailand
Union of Soviet Socialist Reps. [3]
United States

NOTES:
[1] Pre 1949 convention, applicable only to Taiwan.
[2] See note under ETHIOPIA in bilateral section.
[3] See note under UNION OF SOVIET SOCIALIST REPUBLICS in bilateral section.

Convention relative to the laying of automatic submarine contact mines. Signed at The Hague October 18, 1907; entered into force January 26, 1910.
36 Stat. 2332; TS 541; 1 Bevans 669.
States which are parties:
Australia [1]
Austria
Belgium
Brazil
Canada [1]
China [2]
Denmark
El Salvador
Ethiopia [3]
Finland
France [1]
Germany [1]
Guatemala
Haiti
Hungary
India [1]
Ireland [1]

RULES OF WARFARE
(Cont'd)

Japan
Laos [1]
Liberia
Luxembourg
Mexico
Netherlands
New Zealand [1]
Nicaragua
Norway
Pakistan [1]
Panama
Philippines
Romania
South Africa [1]
Sri Lanka [1]
Switzerland
Thailand [1]
United Kingdom [1]
United States

NOTES:
[1] With reservation.
[2] Pre 1949 convention, applicable only to Taiwan.
[3] See note under ETHIOPIA in bilateral section.

Convention concerning bombardment by naval forces in time of war. Signed at The Hague October 18, 1907; entered into force January 26, 1910.
36 Stat. 2351; TS 542; 1 Bevans 681.
States which are parties:
Australia [1]
Austria
Belgium
Bolivia
Brazil
Canada [1]
China [1] [2]
Cuba
Denmark
El Salvador
Ethiopia [3]
Finland
France [1]
Germany [1]
Guatemala
Haiti
Hungary
India [1]
Ireland [1]
Japan [1]
Laos [1]
Liberia
Luxembourg
Mexico
Netherlands
New Zealand [1]
Nicaragua
Norway
Pakistan [1]
Panama
Philippines
Poland
Portugal
Romania
South Africa [1]
Spain

Sri Lanka [1]
Sweden
Switzerland
Thailand
Union of Soviet Socialist Reps. [4]
United Kingdom [1]
United States

NOTES:
[1] With reservation.
[2] Pre 1949 convention, applicable only to Taiwan.
[3] See note under ETHIOPIA in bilateral section.
[4] See note under UNION OF SOVIET SOCIALIST REPUBLICS in bilateral section.

Convention relative to certain restrictions with regard to the exercise of the right of capture in naval war. Signed at The Hague October 18, 1907; entered into force January 26, 1910.
36 Stat. 2396; TS 544; 1 Bevans 711.
States which are parties:
Australia
Austria
Belgium
Brazil
Canada
China [1]
Denmark
El Salvador
Ethiopia [2]
Finland
France
Germany
Guatemala
Haiti
Hungary
India
Ireland
Japan
Laos
Liberia
Luxembourg
Mexico
Netherlands
New Zealand
Nicaragua
Norway
Pakistan
Panama
Philippines
Poland
Portugal
Romania
South Africa
Spain
Sri Lanka
Sweden
Switzerland
Thailand
United Kingdom
United States

NOTES:
[1] Pre 1949 convention, applicable only to Taiwan.
[2] See note under ETHIOPIA in bilateral section.

Convention concerning the rights and duties of neutral powers in naval war. Signed at The Hague October 18, 1907; entered into force

January 26, 1910; for the United States February 1, 1910.
36 Stat. 2415; TS 545; 1 Bevans 723.
States which are parties:
Austria
Belgium
Brazil
China [1] [2]
Denmark
El Salvador
Ethiopia [3]
Finland
France
Germany [1]
Guatemala
Haiti
Hungary
Japan [1]
Laos
Liberia
Luxembourg
Mexico
Netherlands
Nicaragua
Norway
Panama
Philippines [4]
Portugal
Romania
Sweden
Switzerland
Thailand [1]
Union of Soviet Socialist Reps. [5]
United States [4]

NOTES:
[1] With reservation.
[2] Pre 1949 convention, applicable only to Taiwan.
[3] See note under ETHIOPIA in bilateral section.
[4] With reservation and understanding.
[5] See note under UNION OF SOVIET SOCIALIST REPUBLICS in bilateral section.

Declaration prohibiting the discharge of projectiles and explosives from balloons. Signed at The Hague October 18, 1907; entered into force November 27, 1909.
36 Stat. 2439; TS 546; 1 Bevans 739.
States which are parties:
Australia
Belgium
Bolivia
Brazil
Canada
China [1]
El Salvador
Ethiopia [2]
Finland
Haiti
India
Ireland
Liberia
Luxembourg
Netherlands
New Zealand
Nicaragua
Norway
Pakistan
Panama
Philippines
Portugal
South Africa
Sri Lanka

RULES OF WARFARE
(Cont'd)

Switzerland
Thailand
United Kingdom
United States

NOTES:
[1] Pre 1949 convention, applicable only to Taiwan.
[2] See note under ETHIOPIA in bilateral section.

Convention on maritime neutrality. Signed at Habana February 20, 1928; entered into force January 12, 1931; for the United States March 22, 1932.
47 Stat. 1989; TS 845; 2 Bevans 721; 135 LNTS 187.
States which are parties:
Bolivia
Colombia
Dominican Rep.
Ecuador
Haiti
Nicaragua
Panama
United States [1]

NOTE:
[1] With reservation.

Treaty for the limitation and reduction of naval armament. Signed at London April 22, 1930; entered into force December 31, 1930.
46 Stat. 2858; TS 830; 2 Bevans 1055; 112 LNTS 65.

All provisions of this treaty with the exception of Part IV, which relates to rules of international law in regard to the operations of submarines or other war vessels with respect to merchant vessels, expired on December 31, 1936. Under the terms of article 23, Part IV "shall remain in force without limit of time".

States which are parties to Part IV:
Afghanistan
Albania
Australia
Austria
Belgium
Brazil
Bulgaria
Canada
Costa Rica
Czechoslovakia [1]
Denmark
Egypt
El Salvador
Estonia
Finland
France
Germany
Greece
Guatemala
Haiti
Holy See
Hungary
India
Indonesia

Iran
Iraq
Ireland
Italy
Japan
Latvia
Lithuania
Mexico
Nepal
Netherlands, including Curacao
New Zealand
Norway
Panama
Peru
Poland
Saudi Arabia
Slovak Rep.
South Africa
Sweden
Switzerland
Thailand
Turkey
Union of Soviet Socialist Reps. [2]
United Kingdom
United States
Yugoslavia [3]

NOTES:
[1] See note under CZECHOSLOVAKIA in bilateral section.
[2] See note under UNION OF SOVIET SOCIALIST REPUBLICS in bilateral section.
[3] See note under YUGOSLAVIA in bilateral section.

SABOTAGE

(See under AVIATION)

SAFETY AT SEA

(See under MARITIME MATTERS)

SALE OF GOODS

(See under TRADE AND COMMERCE)

SATELLITE COMMUNICATIONS SYSTEMS

Agreement on cooperation in inter-continental testing in connection with experimental communications satellites. Exchanges of notes at Stockholm July 5 and 25, 1963, at Oslo July 8 and September 11, 1963, and at Copenhagen July 2 and September 14, 1963; entered into force September 14, 1963.
14 UST 1278; TIAS 5431; 488 UNTS 121.
States which are parties:
Denmark
Norway

Sweden
United States

Agreement relating to the International Telecommunications Satellite Organization (INTELSAT), with annexes. Done at Washington August 20, 1971; entered into force February 12, 1973.
23 UST 3813; TIAS 7532.

Operating agreement relating to the International Telecommunications Satellite Organization (INTELSAT), with annex. Done at Washington August 20, 1971; entered into force February 12, 1973.
23 UST 4091; TIAS 7532.
Parties: [1]
Afghanistan
Algeria
Angola
Argentina
Armenia
Australia
Austria
Azerbaijan
Bahamas, The
Bahrain
Bangladesh
Barbados
Belgium
Benin
Bhutan
Bolivia
Bosnia-Herzegovina
Botswana
Brazil
Brunei
Bulgaria
Burkina Faso
Cameroon
Canada
Cape Verde
Central African Rep.
Chad
Chile
China [2]
Colombia
Comoros
Congo
Congo, Dem. Rep.
Costa Rica
Cote d'Ivoire
Croatia
Cuba
Cyprus
Czechoslovakia [3]
Denmark
Dominican Rep.
Ecuador
Egypt
El Salvador
Equatorial Guinea
Ethiopia [4]
Fiji
Finland
France
Gabon
Georgia
Germany, Fed. Rep. [5]
Ghana
Greece
Guatemala
Guinea
Haiti
Honduras

SATELLITE COMMUNICATIONS SYSTEMS (Cont'd)

Hungary
Iceland
India
Indonesia
Iran
Iraq
Ireland
Israel
Italy
Jamaica
Japan
Jordan
Kazakhstan
Kenya
Korea
Kuwait
Kyrgyz Rep.
Lebanon
Libya
Liechtenstein
Luxembourg
Madagascar
Malawi
Malaysia
Mali
Malta
Mauritania
Mauritius
Mexico
Micronesia
Monaco
Mongolia
Morocco
Mozambique
Namibia
Nepal
Netherlands [6]
New Zealand
Nicaragua
Niger
Nigeria
Norway
Oman
Pakistan
Panama
Papua New Guinea
Paraguay
Peru
Philippines
Poland
Portugal
Qatar
Romania
Russian Fed.
Rwanda
Saudi Arabia
Senegal
Singapore
Slovak Rep.
Somalia
South Africa
Spain
Sri Lanka
Sudan
Swaziland
Sweden
Switzerland

Syrian Arab Rep.
Tajikistan
Tanzania
Thailand
Togo
Trinidad & Tobago
Tunisia
Turkey
Uganda
Union of Soviet Socialist Reps. [7]
United Arab Emirates
United Kingdom
United States
Uruguay
Uzbekistan
Vatican City
Venezuela
Vietnam, Socialist Rep.
Yemen (Sanaa) [8]
Yugoslavia [9]
Zambia
Zimbabwe

NOTES:

[1] Parties to the INTELSAT agreement may designate a "telecommunications entity" as the "signatory" to the Operating Agreement. The Communications Satellite Corporation (COMSAT) has been so designated by the United States. A list of the other entities so designated is on file in the Office of the Assistant Legal Adviser for Treaty Affairs, Department of State.

[2] Applicable to Hong Kong and Macao. See note under CHINA in bilateral section.

[3] See note under CZECHOSLOVAKIA in bilateral section.

[4] See note under ETHIOPIA in bilateral section.

[5] See note under GERMANY, FEDERAL REPUBLIC OF in bilateral section.

[6] Applicable to Netherlands Antilles and Aruba.

[7] See note under UNION OF SOVIET SOCIALIST REPUBLICS in bilateral section.

[8] See note under YEMEN in bilateral section.

[9] See note under YUGOSLAVIA in bilateral section.

Convention relating to the distribution of programme-carrying signals transmitted by satellite. Done at Brussels May 21, 1974; entered into force August 25, 1979; for the United States March 7, 1985.
TIAS 11078.
States which are parties:
Armenia
Australia
Austria
Bosnia-Herzegovina
Costa Rica
Croatia
Former Yugoslav Republic of Macedonia
Germany, Fed. Rep. [1] [2]
Greece
Italy [1]
Jamaica
Kenya
Mexico
Morocco
Nicaragua
Panama
Peru
Portugal

Russian Fed.
Slovenia
Switzerland
Trinidad & Tobago [1]
Union of Soviet Socialist Reps. [3]
United States
Yugoslavia [4]

NOTES:
[1] With declaration(s).
[2] See note under GERMANY, FEDERAL REPUBLIC OF in bilateral section.
[3] See note under UNION OF SOVIET SOCIALIST REPUBLICS in bilateral section.
[4] See note under YUGOSLAVIA in bilateral section.

Convention on the International Maritime Satellite Organization (INMARSAT), with annex. Done at London September 3, 1976; entered into force July 16, 1979.
31 UST 1; TIAS 9605.

Operating agreement on the International Maritime Satellite Organization (INMARSAT), with annex. Done at London September 3, 1976; entered into force July 16, 1979.
31 UST 135; TIAS 9605.
Parties: [1]
Algeria
Argentina
Australia
Bahamas
Bahrain
Bangladesh
Belarus
Belgium
Bosnia-Herzegovina
Brazil
Brunei
Bulgaria
Cameroon
Canada
Chile
China [2]
Colombia
Comoros
Costa Rica
Croatia
Cuba
Cyprus
Czech Rep.
Denmark
Egypt
Finland
France
Gabon
German Dem. Rep. [3]
Germany, Fed. Rep. [3]
Ghana
Greece
Hungary
Iceland
India
Indonesia [4]
Iran
Iraq
Israel
Italy
Japan
Kenya
Korea
Kuwait
Latvia
Lebanon

SATELLITE COMMUNICATIONS SYSTEMS (Cont'd)

Liberia
Libya
Malaysia
Malta
Marshall Is.
Mauritius
Mexico
Monaco
Morocco
Mozambique
Netherlands [5]
New Zealand
Nigeria
Norway
Oman
Pakistan
Panama
Peru
Philippines
Poland
Portugal
Qatar
Romania
Russian Fed.
Saudi Arabia
Senegal
Singapore
Slovak Rep.
South Africa
Spain
Sri Lanka
Sweden
Switzerland
Tanzania
Thailand
Tunisia
Turkey
Ukraine
Union of Soviet Socialist Reps. [6]
United Arab Emirates
United Kingdom [7]
United States
Vietnam
Yugoslavia [8]

Amendments:
October 16, 1985.
January 19, 1989.

NOTES:
[1] Parties to the convention may designate a "competent entity, public or private, subject to the jurisdiction of that Party" as the "signatory" to the Operating Agreement. The Communications Satellite Corporation (COMSAT) has been so designated by the United States.
[2] Applicable to Hong Kong. See note under CHINA in bilateral section.
[3] See note under GERMANY, FEDERAL REPUBLIC OF in bilateral section.
[4] With statement.
[5] Applicable to Netherlands Antilles and Aruba.
[6] See note under UNION OF SOVIET SOCIALIST REPUBLICS in bilateral section.
[7] Extended to Bermuda.
[8] See note under YUGOSLAVIA in bilateral section.

Understanding concerning participation by Norway in an investigation of the demonstration and evaluation of an experimental satellite-aided search and rescue system. Signed at Ottawa, Paris, Washington and Oslo September 25 and 30, October 19 and November 13, 1981; entered into force November 13, 1981.
TIAS 12378.
States which are parties:
Canada
France
Norway
United States

International COSPAS-SARSAT program agreement. Done at Paris July 1, 1988; entered into force August 30, 1988.
TIAS
Parties:
Canada
France
Union of Soviet Socialist Reps. [1]
United States

NOTE:
[1] See note under UNION OF SOVIET SOCIALIST REPUBLICS in bilateral section.

Memorandum of agreement concerning the SARSAT Space Segment. Done at Washington September 11, 1995; entered into force November 10, 1995.
TIAS 12690.
Parties:
Canada
France
United States

SCIENTIFIC COOPERATION

Memorandum of understanding for collaboration on advanced materials and standards. Signed January 30, 1986-April 2, 1987; entered into force April 2, 1987.
TIAS 12018.
Parties:
Canada
European Communities
France
Germany, Fed. Rep. [1]
Italy
Japan
United Kingdom
United States

NOTE:
[1] See note under GERMANY, FEDERAL REPUBLIC OF in bilateral section.

Agreement to establish a science and technology center in Ukraine. Done at Kiev October 25, 1993; entered into force July 16, 1994.
TIAS
Parties:
Canada
Ukraine
United States

Agreement establishing the Middle East Desalination Research Center. Signed at Muscat

December 22, 1996; entered into force December 22, 1996.
TIAS
Parties:
Israel
Japan
Korea
Oman
United States

SEA, LAW OF

(See under FISHERIES; MARITIME MATTERS)

SEABEDS

Treaty on the prohibition of the emplacement of nuclear weapons and other weapons of mass destruction on the seabed and the ocean floor and in the subsoil thereof. Done at Washington, London and Moscow February 11, 1971, entered into force May 18, 1972.
23 UST 701; TIAS 7337; 955 UNTS 115.
Parties:
Afghanistan
Algeria
Antigua & Barbuda
Argentina
Australia
Austria
Bahamas, The
Belarus
Belgium
Benin
Bosnia-Herzegovina
Botswana
Brazil [1,2]
Brunei [3]
Bulgaria
Canada [2]
Cape Verde
Central African Rep.
China [2,4]
China (Taiwan) [5]
Congo
Cote d'Ivoire
Croatia
Cuba
Cyprus
Czech Rep.
Denmark
Dominica [3]
Dominican Rep.
Ethiopia [6]
Finland
German Dem. Rep. [7]
Germany, Fed. Rep. [7]
Ghana
Greece
Grenada [3]
Guatemala
Guinea-Bissau
Hungary
Iceland
India [2]
Iran
Iraq
Ireland
Italy [2]

SEABEDS (Cont'd)

Jamaica
Japan
Jordan
Korea
Laos
Latvia
Lesotho
Liechtenstein
Luxembourg
Malaysia
Malta
Mauritius
Mexico [2]
Mongolia
Morocco
Nepal
Netherlands [8]
New Zealand
Nicaragua
Niger
Norway
Panama
Philippines
Poland
Portugal
Qatar
Romania
Rwanda
St. Kitts & Nevis [3]
St. Lucia [3]
St. Vincent & the Grenadines
Sao Tome & Principe
Saudi Arabia
Seychelles
Singapore
Slovak Rep.
Slovenia
Solomon Is. [3]
South Africa
Spain
Swaziland
Sweden
Switzerland
Togo
Tunisia
Turkey [2]
Ukraine
Union of Soviet Socialist Reps. [9]
United Kingdom [10]
United States
Vietnam, Socialist Rep. [2]
Yemen (Aden) [11]
Yugoslavia [12]
Zambia

NOTES:
[1] With understanding(s).
[2] With declaration.
[3] See under country heading in the bilateral section for information concerning acceptance of treaty obligations.
[4] Applicable to Hong Kong and Macao. See note under CHINA in bilateral section.
[5] See note under CHINA (Taiwan) in bilateral section.
[6] See note under ETHIOPIA in bilateral section.
[7] See note under GERMANY, FEDERAL REPUBLIC OF in bilateral section.
[8] Applicable to Netherlands Antilles and Aruba.

[9] See note under UNION OF SOVIET SOCIALIST REPUBLICS in bilateral section.
[10] Extended to Anguilla, and territories under the territorial sovereignty of the United Kingdom.
[11] See note under YEMEN in bilateral section.
[12] See note under YUGOSLAVIA in bilateral section.

Agreement concerning interim arrangements relating to polymetallic nodules of the deep sea bed. Done at Washington September 2, 1982; entered into force September 2, 1982.
TIAS 10562; 1871 UNTS 275.
States which are parties:
France
Germany, Fed. Rep. [1]
United Kingdom
United States

NOTE:
[1] See note under GERMANY, FEDERAL REPUBLIC OF in bilateral section.

Provisional understanding regarding deep sea-bed matters, with memorandum of implementation, joint record, and related exchanges of notes. Signed at Geneva August 3, 1984; entered into force September 2, 1984.
TIAS 11066.
States which are parties:
Belgium [1]
France
Germany, Fed. Rep. [2]
Italy [1]
Japan
Netherlands [1] [3]
United Kingdom
United States

NOTES:
[1] With declaration.
[2] See note under GERMANY, FEDERAL REPUBLIC OF in bilateral section.
[3] For the Kingdom in Europe only.

Memorandum of understanding on the avoidance of overlaps and conflicts relating to deep seabed areas, with annexes. Signed at New York February 22, 1991; entered into force February 22, 1991.
TIAS

Memorandum of understanding on the avoidance of overlaps and conflicts relating to deep sea-bed areas, with annexes. Done at New York August 20, 1991; entered into force August 28, 1991; effective August 20, 1991.
TIAS 11825.
Parties:
Canada
Czech Rep.
Germany
Italy
Poland
Union of Soviet Socialist Reps. [1]
United Kingdom
United States

NOTE:
[1] See note under UNION OF SOVIET SOCIALIST REPUBLICS in bilateral section.

SHIPPING

(See under MARITIME MATTERS; RULES OF WARFARE)

SLAVERY

(See also TRAFFIC IN WOMEN AND CHILDREN)

Convention to suppress the slave trade and slavery. Concluded at Geneva September 25, 1926; entered into force March 9, 1927; for the United States March 21, 1929.
46 Stat. 2183; TS 778; 2 Bevans 607; 60 LNTS 253.

Protocol amending the slavery convention signed at Geneva on September 25, 1926, with annex. Done at New York December 7, 1953; entered into force December 7, 1953; for the United States March 7, 1956.
7 UST 479; TIAS 3532; 182 UNTS 51.

Supplementary convention on the abolition of slavery, the slave trade and institutions and practices similar to slavery. Done at Geneva September 7, 1956; entered into force April 30, 1957; for the United States December 6, 1967.
18 UST 3201; TIAS 6418; 266 UNTS 3.
States which are parties:
Afghanistan
Albania
Algeria
Antigua & Barbuda
Argentina [1]
Australia [2]
Austria
Azerbaijan
Bahamas, The
Bahrain
Bangladesh
Barbados
Belarus
Belgium
Belize [3]
Benin [4]
Bolivia
Bosnia-Herzegovina
Botswana [3]
Brazil
Brunei [3]
Bulgaria
Burma [5]
Cambodia [1]
Cameroon
Canada
Central African Rep.
Chile
China (Taiwan) [6]
Congo
Congo, Dem. Rep. [1]
Cote d'Ivoire
Croatia
Cuba
Cyprus
Czech Rep.

SLAVERY (Cont'd)

Denmark
Djibouti [1]
Dominica
Dominican Rep. [1]
Ecuador
Egypt
Estonia [4]
Ethiopia [7]
Fiji
Finland
Former Yugoslav Republic of Macedonia
France [8]
Gambia, The [3]
German Dem. Rep. [9]
Germany, Fed. Rep. [9]
Ghana
Greece
Grenada [3]
Guatemala
Guinea
Guyana [3]
Haiti
Hong Kong [10]
Hungary
Iceland [1]
India [5]
Iran
Iraq
Ireland
Israel
Italy
Jamaica
Jordan
Kiribati [3]
Kuwait
Kyrgyz Rep.
Laos [1]
Latvia
Lebanon [4]
Lesotho
Liberia [4]
Libya
Luxembourg [1]
Macao [10]
Madagascar
Malawi
Malaysia [1]
Mali
Malta
Mauritania
Mauritius
Mexico
Monaco
Mongolia
Morocco
Nauru [3]
Nepal
Netherlands [11]
New Zealand [12]
Nicaragua
Niger
Nigeria
Norway
Pakistan
Papua New Guinea [4]
Philippines
Poland
Portugal
Romania
Russian Fed.
St. Kitts & Nevis [3]

St. Lucia
St. Vincent & the Grenadines
San Marino [1]
Saudi Arabia
Senegal
Seychelles [3]
Sierra Leone
Singapore [1]
Slovak Rep.
Slovenia [1]
Solomon Is.
South Africa [4] [13]
Spain
Sri Lanka
Sudan
Suriname
Swaziland [3]
Sweden
Switzerland
Syrian Arab Rep.
Tanzania
Togo
Tonga [3]
Trinidad & Tobago
Tunisia
Turkey
Turkmenistan
Tuvalu [3]
Uganda
Ukraine
Union of Soviet Socialist Reps. [14]
United Kingdom [15]
United States [5] [16]
Viet-Nam [4] [17]
Yemen (Aden) [18]
Yugoslavia [19]
Zambia
Zimbabwe [3]

NOTES:

[1] Party to Supplementary Convention only.

[2] Extended to all non-selfgoverning territories and other non-metropolitan territories for the international relations of which Australia is responsible.

[3] See under country heading in the bilateral section for information concerning acceptance of treaty obligations.

[4] Party only to the Convention.

[5] With reservation to the Convention.

[6] Convention and Protocol are pre 1949 agreements applicable only to Taiwan. See also note under CHINA (Taiwan) in bilateral section.

[7] See note under ETHIOPIA in bilateral section.

[8] Extended to all overseas departments and territories.

[9] See note under GERMANY, FEDERAL REPUBLIC OF in bilateral section.

[10] CHINA is not a party to this treaty but has made it applicable to Hong Kong and Macao.

[11] Applicable to Netherlands Antilles and Aruba.

[12] Extended to Cook Is. (including Niue) and the Tokelau Is.

[13] Extended to Namibia.

[14] See note under UNION OF SOVIET SOCIALIST REPUBLICS in bilateral section.

[15] Extended to Bermuda, British Virgin Is., Channel Is., Falkland Is., Gibraltar, Isle of Man, Montserrat, and St. Helena.

[16] Extended to all territories for the international relations of which the United States is responsible.

[17] See Vietnam footnote under AUTOMOTIVE TRAFFIC: convention of September 19, 1949 (3 UST 3008; TIAS 2487; 125 UNTS 22).

[18] See note under YEMEN in bilateral section.

[19] See note under YUGOSLAVIA in bilateral section.

SOUTH PACIFIC COMMISSION

Agreement establishing the South Pacific Commission. Signed at Canberra February 6, 1947; entered into force July 29, 1948.
2 UST 1787; TIAS 2317; 97 UNTS 227.
Parties:
Australia
Cook Is.
Fiji
France
Nauru
New Zealand
Niue
Papua New Guinea
Solomon Is.
Tuvalu
United Kingdom
United States
Western Samoa

Amendments:
November 7, 1951 (3 UST 2851; TIAS 2458; 124 UNTS 320).
April 5, 1954 (5 UST 639; TIAS 2952; 201 UNTS 374).
October 6, 1964 (16 UST 1055; TIAS 5845; 542 UNTS 350).
October 2, 1974 (26 UST 1606; TIAS 8120).
October 20, 1976 (33 UST 585; TIAS 10051).
October 7-12, 1978 (33 UST 590; TIAS 10052).

SOUTHEAST ASIA TREATY ORGANIZATION (SEATO)

(See under DEFENSE)

SPACE

(See also ASTRONAUTS)

Treaty on principles governing the activities of states in the exploration and use of outer space, including the moon and other celestial bodies. Done at Washington, London, and Moscow January 27, 1967; entered into force October 10, 1967.
18 UST 2410; TIAS 6347; 610 UNTS 205.
Parties:
Afghanistan
Algeria

SPACE (Cont'd)

Antigua & Barbuda
Argentina
Australia
Austria
Bahamas, The
Bangladesh
Barbados
Belarus
Belgium
Benin
Brazil [1]
Brunei [2]
Bulgaria
Burkina Faso
Burma
Canada
Chile
China [3] [4]
Cuba
Cyprus
Czech Rep.
Denmark
Dominica [2]
Dominican Rep.
Ecuador
Egypt
El Salvador
Fiji
Finland
France
German Dem. Rep. [5]
Germany, Fed. Rep. [5]
Greece
Grenada [2]
Guinea-Bissau
Hungary
Iceland
India
Iraq
Ireland
Israel
Italy
Jamaica
Japan
Kenya
Korea
Kuwait
Laos
Lebanon
Libya
Madagascar [1]
Mali
Mauritius
Mexico
Mongolia
Morocco
Nepal
Netherlands [6]
New Zealand
Niger
Nigeria
Norway
Pakistan
Papua New Guinea
Peru
Poland
Romania
Russian Fed.
St. Kitts & Nevis [2]
St. Lucia [2]
San Marino

Saudi Arabia
Seychelles
Sierra Leone
Singapore
Slovak Rep.
Solomon Is. [2]
South Africa
Spain
Sri Lanka
Swaziland [2]
Sweden
Switzerland
Syrian Arab Rep.
Thailand
Togo
Tonga
Tunisia
Turkey
Uganda
Ukraine
Union of Soviet Socialist Reps. [7]
United Kingdom [8]
United States
Uruguay
Venezuela
Vietnam, Socialist Rep.
Yemen (Aden) [9]
Zambia

NOTES:
[1] With a statement.
[2] See under country heading in the bilateral section for information concerning acceptance of treaty obligations.
[3] The Taiwan authorities have also adhered to this treaty. See note under CHINA (Taiwan) in bilateral section.
[4] Applicable to Hong Kong and Macao. See note under CHINA in bilateral section.
[5] See note under GERMANY, FEDERAL REPUBLIC OF in bilateral section.
[6] Applicable to Netherlands Antilles and Aruba.
[7] See note under UNION OF SOVIET SOCIALIST REPUBLICS in bilateral section.
[8] Extended to Anguilla and to the territories under the territorial sovereignty of the United Kingdom.
[9] See note under YEMEN in bilateral section.

Agreement for a cooperative program concerning the development, procurement and use of a space laboratory in conjunction with the space shuttle system, with memorandum of understanding between the National Aeronautics and Space Administration and the European Space Research Organization. Done at Neuilly-sur-Seine August 14, 1973; entered into force August 14, 1973.
24 UST 2049; TIAS 7722.
States which are parties:
Belgium
Denmark
France
Germany, Fed. Rep. [1]
Italy
Netherlands
Spain
Switzerland
United Kingdom
United States

NOTE:
[1] See note under GERMANY, FEDERAL REPUBLIC OF in bilateral section.

Convention on international liability for damage caused by space objects. Done at Washington, London, and Moscow March 29, 1972; entered into force September 1, 1972; for the United States October 9, 1973.
24 UST 2389; TIAS 7762; 961 UNTS 187.
Parties:
Antigua & Barbuda
Argentina
Australia
Austria [1]
Belarus
Belgium
Benin
Bosnia-Herzegovina
Botswana
Brazil
Bulgaria
Canada [1]
Chile
China [2] [3]
Cuba
Cyprus
Czech Rep.
Denmark [1]
Dominica [4]
Dominican Rep.
Ecuador
European Space Agency [5]
European Telecommunications Satellite Organization [5]
Fiji
Finland
France
Gabon
German Dem. Rep. [6]
Germany, Fed. Rep. [6]
Greece
Grenada [4]
Hungary
India
Indonesia
Iran
Iraq
Ireland [1]
Israel
Italy
Japan
Kenya
Korea, Rep.
Kuwait
Laos
Liechtenstein
Luxembourg
Mali
Malta
Mexico
Mongolia
Morocco
Netherlands [7]
New Zealand [1]
Niger
Pakistan
Panama•
Papua New Guinea
Poland
Qatar
Romania
Russian Fed.
St. Kitts & Nevis [4]
St. Lucia [4]

SPACE (Cont'd)

St. Vincent & the Grenadines [4]
Saudi Arabia
Senegal
Seychelles
Singapore
Slovak Rep.
Slovenia
Solomon Is. [4]
Spain
Sri Lanka
Sweden [1]
Switzerland
Syrian Arab Rep.
Togo
Trinidad & Tobago
Tunisia
Ukraine
Union of Soviet Socialist Reps. [8]
United Arab Emirates
United Kingdom [9]
United States
Uruguay
Venezuela
Yugoslavia [10]
Zambia

NOTES:
[1] With a declaration.
[2] The Taiwan authorities have also adhered to this convention. See note under CHINA (Taiwan) in bilateral section.
[3] Applicable to Hong Kong. See note under CHINA in bilateral section.
[4] See under country heading in bilateral section for information concerning acceptance of treaty obligations.
[5] Declaration of acceptance in accordance with Art. XXII.
[6] See note under GERMANY, FEDERAL REPUBLIC OF in bilateral section.
[7] Applicable to the Kingdom in Europe, Netherlands Antilles, and Aruba.
[8] See note under UNION OF SOVIET SOCIALIST REPUBLICS in bilateral section.
[9] Extended to Anguilla and territories under the territorial sovereignty of the United Kingdom.
[10] See note under YUGOSLAVIA in bilateral section.

Convention on registration of objects launched into outer space. Done at New York January 14, 1975; entered into force September 15, 1976.
28 UST 695; TIAS 8480; 1023 UNTS 15.
Parties:
Antigua & Barbuda
Argentina
Australia
Austria
Belarus
Belgium
Brunei [1]
Bulgaria
Canada
Chile
China [2]
Cuba
Cyprus
Czech Rep.
Denmark

Dominica [1]
European Organization for the Exploitation of Meteorological Satellites
European Space Agency
France
German Dem. Rep. [3]
Germany, Fed. Rep. [3]
Hungary
India
Indonesia
Japan
Korea, Rep.
Liechtenstein
Mexico
Mongolia
Netherlands [4]
Niger
Norway
Pakistan
Peru
Poland
Russian Fed.
St. Kitts & Nevis [1]
St. Lucia [1]
St. Vincent & the Grenadines
Seychelles
Slovak Rep.
Solomon Is. [1]
Spain
Sweden
Switzerland
Ukraine
Union of Soviet Socialist Reps. [5]
United Arab Emirates
United Kingdom [6]
United States
Uruguay
Yugoslavia [7]

NOTES:
[1] See under country heading in the bilateral section for information concerning acceptance of treaty obligations.
[2] Applicable to Hong Kong. See note under CHINA in bilateral section.
[3] See note under GERMANY, FEDERAL REPUBLIC OF in bilateral section.
[4] Applicable to Netherlands Antilles and Aruba.
[5] See note under UNION OF SOVIET SOCIALIST REPUBLICS in bilateral section.
[6] Applicable to Anguilla and territories under the territorial sovereignty of the United Kingdom.
[7] See note under YUGOSLAVIA in bilateral section.

Arrangement concerning application of the space station intergovernmental agreement pending its entry into force. Done at Washington September 29, 1988; entered into force September 29, 1988.
TIAS
Parties:
Belgium
Canada
Denmark
France
Germany, Fed. Rep. [1]
Italy
Netherlands
Norway
Spain
United Kingdom
United States

NOTE:
[1] See note under GERMANY, FEDERAL REPUBLIC OF in bilateral section.

Agreement on cooperation in the detailed design, development, operation and utilization of the permanently manned civil space station, with annex. Done at Washington September 29, 1988; entered into force January 30, 1992.
TIAS
Parties:
Japan
United States

Arrangement concerning application of the space station intergovernmental agreement pending its entry into force. Signed at Washington January 29, 1998; entered into force January 29, 1998.
TIAS

SPITZBERGEN

Treaty relating to Spitzbergen (Svalbard), with annex. Done at Paris February 9, 1920; entered into force August 14, 1925.
43 Stat. 1892; TS 686; 2 Bevans 269; 2 LNTS 7.
States which are parties:
Afghanistan
Albania
Argentina
Australia
Austria
Belgium
Bulgaria
Canada
Chile
China [1]
Czechoslovakia [2]
Denmark
Dominican Rep.
Egypt
Estonia
Finland
France
German Dem. Rep. [3]
Greece
Hungary
India
Italy
Japan
Monaco
Netherlands
New Zealand
Norway
Poland
Portugal
Romania
Slovak Rep.
South Africa
Spain
Sweden
Switzerland
Union of Soviet Socialist Reps. [4]
United Kingdom
United States
Venezuela
Yugoslavia [5]

NOTES:
[1] Pre 1949 treaty, applicable only to Taiwan.

SPITZBERGEN (Cont'd)

[2] See note under CZECHOSLOVAKIA in bilateral section.
[3] See note under GERMANY, FEDERAL REPUBLIC OF in bilateral section.
[4] See note under UNION OF SOVIET SOCIALIST REPUBLICS in bilateral section.
[5] See note under YUGOSLAVIA in bilateral section.

STATES, RIGHTS AND DUTIES

Convention on the rights and duties of states in the event of civil strife. Done at Habana February 20, 1928; entered into force May 21, 1929; for the United States May 21, 1930.
46 Stat. 2749; TS 814; 2 Bevans 694; 134 LNTS 45.
States which are parties:
Argentina
Bolivia
Brazil
Colombia
Costa Rica
Cuba
Dominican Rep.
Ecuador
El Salvador
Haiti
Honduras
Mexico
Nicaragua
Panama
Paraguay
Peru
United States [1]
Uruguay

NOTE:
[1] With an understanding.

Convention on rights and duties of states. Done at Montevideo December 26, 1933; entered into force December 26, 1934.
49 Stat. 3097; TS 881; 3 Bevans 145; 165 LNTS 19.
States which are parties:
Brazil
Chile
Colombia
Costa Rica
Cuba
Dominican Rep.
Ecuador
El Salvador
Guatemala
Haiti
Honduras
Mexico
Nicaragua
Panama
United States [1]
Venezuela

NOTE:
[1] With reservation.

SUBMARINE CABLES

(See under TELECOMMUNICATION)

TANGIER, STATUS OF

(See MOROCCO)

TAXATION

Convention on mutual administrative assistance in tax matters. Signed at Strasbourg January 25, 1988; entered into force April 1, 1995.
TIAS
Parties:
Denmark [1]
Finland
Iceland [1]
Netherlands [1]
Norway
Poland [1]
Sweden
United States [1]

NOTE:
[1] With reservation(s) and declaration(s).

Agreement on state and local taxation of foreign employees of public international organizations. Done at Washington April 21, 1992; entered into force May 24, 1994.
TIAS 12135.
Parties:
Eastern Caribbean Investment Promotion Service
European Space Agency
Food and Agriculture Organization of the United Nations
Inter-American Defense Board
Inter-American Institute for Cooperation on Agriculture
International Committee of the Red Cross
International Food Policy Research Institute
International Maritime Satellite Organization
International Telecommunications Satellite Organization
Inter-Parliamentary Union
Organization for Economic Cooperation and Development
Organization of American States
Pan American Health Organization
United States
World Health Organization

TECHNOLOGY TRANSFER

Agreement on technological safeguards associated with the launch of the INMARSAT-3 satellite. Signed at Washington February 14, 1994; entered into force August 19, 1994.
TIAS
Parties:
Kazakhstan
Russian Fed.
United States

TELECOMMUNICATION

(See also SATELLITE COMMUNICATIONS SYSTEMS)

Convention for protection of submarine cables, signed at Paris March 14, 1884. [1] Declaration respecting the interpretation of articles II and IV, signed at Paris December 1, 1886; Final Protocol of agreement fixing May 1, 1888 as the date of effect of the convention, signed at Paris July 7, 1887; entered into force May 1, 1888.
24 Stat. 989; 25 Stat. 1424; TS 380, 380 1 and 2, 380-3; 1 Bevans 89, 112, 114.
States which are parties:
Algeria
Argentina
Australia
Austria
Belgium
Brazil
Canada
Costa Rica
Czechoslovakia [2]
Denmark
Dominican Rep.
El Salvador
Fiji
France
German Dem. Rep.[3]
Germany, Fed. Rep.[3]
Greece
Guatemala
Hong Kong [4]
Hungary
Italy
Japan
Luxembourg
Macao [4]
Malta
Morocco
Netherlands [5]
New Zealand
Norway
Poland
Portugal
Romania
Slovak Rep.
South Africa
Spain
Sweden
Tunisia
Turkey
Union of Soviet Socialist Reps. [6]
United Kingdom
United States
Uruguay
Yugoslavia [7]

NOTES:
[1] Applicable to all territories.
[2] See note under CZECHOSLOVAKIA in bilateral section.
[3] See note under GERMANY, FEDERAL REPUBLIC OF in bilateral section.
[4] CHINA is not a party to this treaty but has made it applicable to Hong Kong and Macao.
[5] Extended to Curacao.
[6] See note under UNION OF SOVIET SOCIALIST REPUBLICS in bilateral section.
[7] See note under YUGOSLAVIA in bilateral section.

TELECOMMUNICATION (Cont'd)

Inter-American Agreements

Inter-American radiocommunications convention, with annexes.[1] Signed at Habana December 13, 1937; entered into force July 1, 1938; for the United States July 21, 1938 for Parts One, Three, and Four; April 17, 1939 for Part Two.
53 Stat. 1576; TS 938; 3 Bevans 462.
States which are parties:
Bahamas, The
Brazil [2]
Canada
Cuba
Dominican Rep.
Haiti
Mexico
Panama
Paraguay [3]
United States

NOTES:
    [1] Part 2 of the convention (Inter-American Radio Office) terminated for all parties December 20, 1958.
    [2] With reservation.
    [3] In force provisionally.

Regional radio convention for Central America, Panama, and the Canal Zone. Signed at Guatemala December 8, 1938; entered into force October 8, 1939.
54 Stat. 1675; TS 949; 3 Bevans 529; 202 LNTS 49.
States which are parties:
Guatemala
Nicaragua
United States

Inter-American radio agreement, with annex, appendices, declaration, resolutions, and recommendations.[1] Done at Washington July 9, 1949; entered into force April 13, 1952.
3 UST 3064; TIAS 2489; 168 UNTS 143.
States which are parties:
Costa Rica
Cuba
Dominican Rep.
Haiti
Honduras
Nicaragua
Paraguay
United States

NOTE:
    [1] The 1949 agreement replaces the agreement of January 26, 1940 (55 Stat. 1482; EAS 231; 3 Bevans 611) which in turn replaced the arrangement of December 13, 1937 (54 Stat. 2514; EAS 200; 3 Bevans 480). The 1940 agreement remains in force as between the contracting parties (including the United States) and Brazil, Canada (with reservation), Chile and Venezuela. The 1937 arrangement remains in force as between the contracting parties and Peru and Panama.

Multilateral declaration to denounce Part Two (Inter-American Radio Office) of the inter-American radiocommunications convention of December 13, 1937.[1] Signed at Washington December 20, 1957; entered into force December 20, 1957.
9 UST 1037; TIAS 4079.
States which are parties:
Brazil
Canada
Cuba
Dominican Rep.
Haiti
Mexico
Nicaragua
Panama
United States

NOTE:
    [1] A contract on the exchange of notifications of radio broadcasting frequencies between the Pan American Union and the Governments of Canada, Cuba, the Dominican Republic, Haiti, Jamaica, Mexico, and the United States was signed at Washington on December 20, 1957, effective January 1, 1958. (For text see 9 UST 1050; TIAS 4079.)

North American regional broadcasting agreement, with final protocol. Signed at Washington November 15, 1950; entered into force April 19, 1960.
11 UST 413; TIAS 4460.
States which are parties:
Bahamas, The
Dominican Rep.
United States

Inter-American convention on amateur radio service. Done at Lima August 14, 1987; entered into force September 13, 1987; for the United States March 20, 1991.
TIAS
Parties:
Argentina
Bolivia
Brazil
Canada
Chile
Colombia
Guatemala
Haiti
Mexico
Paraguay
Peru
Suriname
United States
Venezuela

British Commonwealth Agreements

Agreement revising the telecommunications agreement signed at Bermuda December 4, 1945.[1] Annexed to the Final Act of the United States–Commonwealth telecommunications meeting signed at London August 12, 1949; entered into force February 24, 1950.
3 UST 2686; TIAS 2435; 87 UNTS 131.
States which are parties:
Antigua & Barbuda [2]
Australia
Bahamas, The [2]
Barbados [2]
Belize [2]
Botswana [2]
Canada
Cyprus [2]

Dominica [2]
Fiji
Gambia, The [2]
Ghana [2]
Grenada [2]
Guyana [2]
India
Jamaica [2]
Kiribati [2]
Lesotho [2]
Malaysia [2]
Malta [2]
Mauritius [2]
Nauru [2]
New Zealand
Nigeria [2]
Pakistan
Papua New Guinea [2]
St. Kitts & Nevis [2]
St. Lucia [2]
St. Vincent & the Grenadines [2]
Seychelles [2]
Sierra Leone [2]
Singapore [2]
South Africa
Sri Lanka
Swaziland [2]
Tanzania [2]
Tonga [2]
Trinidad & Tobago [2]
Tuvalu [2]
United Kingdom
United States
Western Samoa [2]
Zambia [2]
Zimbabwe [2]

Amendment:
October 1, 1952 (3 UST 5140; TIAS 2705; 151 UNTS 378).

NOTES:
    [1] Applicable to all territories.
    [2] See under country heading in the bilateral section for information concerning acceptance of treaty obligations.

International Telecommunication Union

Radio regulations, with appendices and final protocol. Done at Geneva December 6, 1979; entered into force January 1, 1982; definitively for the United States October 27, 1983.*
TIAS

Partial revisions of Radio Regulations (Geneva, 1979):

Relating to mobile services. Done at Geneva March 18, 1983; entered into force January 15, 1985; for the United States April 6, 1993.
TIAS

On the use of the geostationary-satellite orbit and on the planning of space services utilizing it. Done at Geneva September 15, 1985; entered into force October 30, 1986; for the United States April 6, 1993.
TIAS

Relating to mobile services. Done at Geneva October 17, 1987; entered into force October 3, 1989; for the United States April 6, 1993.
TIAS

TELECOMMUNICATION (Cont'd)

it. Done at Geneva October 6, 1988; entered into force March 16, 1990; for the United States April 6, 1993.
TIAS

On the use of the geostationary-satellite orbit and on the planning of space services utilizing

States which are parties:*	Radio Regs. Geneva, 1979	1983 Rev. Mobile Serv- ices	1985 Rev. Geostationary Orbit	1987 Rev. Mobile Serv- ices	1988 Rev. Geostationary Orbit
Afghanistan	X	X	X	X	X
Albania	X				
Algeria	X	X	X	X	X
Andorra	X	X	X	X	X
Angola	X	X	X		
Antigua & Barbuda	X	X	X		
Argentina	X	X	X	X	X
Armenia	X	X	X	X	X
Australia	X	X	X	X	X
Austria	X	X	X	X	X
Azerbaijan	X	X	X	X	X
Bahamas	X	X	X	X	X
Bahrain	X	X	X	X	X
Bangladesh	X	X	X	X	X
Barbados	X	X	X	X	X
Belarus	X	X	X	X	X
Belgium	X	X	X	X	X
Belize	X	X	X	X	X
Benin	X	X	X	X	X
Bhutan	X	X	X	X	X
Bolivia	X	X	X	X	X
Bosnia-Herzegovina	X	X	X	X	X
Botswana	X	X			
Brazil	X	X	X	X	X
Brunei	X	X	X	X	X
Bulgaria	X	X	X	X	X
Burkina Faso	X	X	X	X	X
Burma	X	X			
Burundi	X	X	X		
Cambodia	X	X	X	X	X
Cameroon	X	X	X	X	X
Canada	X	X	X	X	X
Cape Verde	X	X	X		
Central African Rep.	X	X	X	X	X
Chad	X	X	X	X	X
Chile	X	X			
China	X	X	X	X	X
Colombia	X	X	X	X	X
Comoros	X	X	X	X	X
Congo	X	X	X	X	X
Congo, Dem. Rep.	X	X	X		
Costa Rica					
Cote d'Ivoire	X	X	X	X	X
Croatia	X	X	X	X	X
Cuba	X	X	X	X	X
Cyprus	X	X	X	X	X
Czech Rep.	X	X	X	X	X
Denmark	X	X	X	X	X
Djibouti	X	X	X	X	X
Dominica	X	X	X	X	X
Ecuador	X	X	X	X	X
Egypt	X	X	X	X	X
El Salvador	X	X			
Equatorial Guinea	X	X			
Eritrea	X	X	X	X	X
Estonia	X	X	X	X	X
Ethiopia	X	X	X	X	X
Fiji	X	X			
Finland	X	X	X	X	X
Former Yugoslav Republic of Macedonia	X	X	X	X	X
France	X	X	X	X	X
Gabon	X	X	X	X	X

States which are parties:*	Radio Regs. Geneva, 1979	1983 Rev. Mobile Services	1985 Rev. Geostationary Orbit	1987 Rev. Mobile Services	1988 Rev. Geostationary Orbit
Gambia, The	X	X	X		
Georgia	X	X	X	X	X
Germany	X	X	X	X	X
Ghana	X	X	X	X	X
Greece	X	X			
Grenada					
Guatemala	X	X	X		
Guinea	X	X	X	X	X
Guinea-Bissau					
Guyana	X	X	X	X	X
Haiti	X	X	X	X	X
Honduras	X	X			
Hungary	X	X	X	X	X
Iceland	X	X	X	X	X
India	X	X	X	X	X
Indonesia	X	X	X	X	X
Iran	X	X	X	X	X
Iraq	X	X			
Ireland	X	X	X	X	X
Israel	X	X	X	X	X
Italy	X	X	X	X	X
Jamaica	X	X			
Japan	X	X	X	X	X
Jordan	X	X	X	X	X
Kazakhstan	X	X	X	X	X
Kenya	X	X	X	X	X
Kiribati	X	X	X		
Korea, Dem. People's Rep.	X	X	X	X	X
Korea, Rep.	X	X	X	X	X
Kuwait	X	X	X	X	X
Kyrgyz Rep.	X	X	X	X	X
Laos	X	X	X	X	X
Latvia	X	X	X	X	X
Lebanon	X	X	X		
Lesotho	X	X			
Liberia	X	X	X		
Libya	X	X	X		
Liechtenstein	X	X	X	X	X
Lithuania	X	X	X	X	X
Luxembourg	X	X	X	X	X
Madagascar	X	X	X	X	X
Malawi	X	X			
Malaysia	X	X	X	X	X
Maldives	X	X	X	X	X
Mali	X	X	X	X	X
Malta	X	X	X	X	X
Marshall Is.	X	X	X	X	X
Mauritania	X	X	X		
Mauritius	X	X	X	X	X
Mexico	X	X	X	X	X
Micronesia	X	X	X	X	X
Moldova	X	X	X	X	X
Monaco	X	X	X	X	X
Mongolia	X	X	X	X	X
Morocco	X	X	X	X	X
Mozambique	X	X	X	X	X
Namibia	X	X	X	X	X
Nauru					
Nepal	X	X	X	X	X
Netherlands	X	X	X	X	X
New Zealand	X	X	X	X	X
Nicaragua	X	X	X		
Niger	X				
Nigeria	X	X			
Norway	X	X	X	X	X
Oman	X	X	X	X	X

States which are parties:*	Radio Regs. Geneva, 1979	1983 Rev. Mobile Serv- ices	1985 Rev. Geostationary Orbit	1987 Rev. Mobile Serv- ices	1988 Rev. Geostationary Orbit
Pakistan	X	X	X	X	X
Panama	X	X			
Papua New Guinea	X	X	X	X	X
Paraguay	X	X	X	X	X
Peru	X	X	X	X	X
Philippines	X	X	X	X	X
Poland	X	X	X	X	X
Portugal	X	X	X	X	X
Qatar	X	X			
Romania	X	X	X	X	X
Russian Fed.	X	X	X	X	X
Rwanda	X	X			
San Marino	X	X	X	X	X
Sao Tome & Principe	X	X	X	X	X
Saudi Arabia	X	X	X	X	X
Senegal	X	X	X	X	X
Sierra Leone	X	X			
Singapore	X	X	X	X	X
Slovak Rep.	X	X	X	X	X
Solomon Is.	X	X	X		
South Africa	X	X	X	X	X
Spain	X	X	X	X	X
St. Lucia	X	X	X	X	X
St. Vincent & the Grenadines	X	X	X	X	X
Suriname	X	X	X	X	X
Swaziland	X	X	X	X	X
Sweden	X	X	X	X	X
Switzerland	X	X	X	X	X
Syria	X	X	X	X	X
Tajikistan	X	X	X	X	X
Tanzania	X	X	X		
Thailand	X	X	X	X	X
Togo	X	X	X	X	X
Tonga	X	X	X	X	X
Trinidad & Tobago	X	X	X	X	X
Tunisia	X	X	X	X	X
Turkey	X	X			
Turkmenistan	X	X	X	X	X
Tuvalu	X	X	X	X	X
Uganda	X	X	X	X	X
Ukraine	X	X	X	X	X
United Arab Emirates	X	X	X	X	X
United Kingdom	X	X	X	X	X
United States	X	X	X	X	X
Uruguay	X	X	X	X	X
Uzbekistan	X	X	X	X	X
Vanuatu	X	X	X		
Vatican City	X	X	X	X	X
Venezuela	X	X	X	X	X
Vietnam, Socialist Rep.	X	X	X	X	X
Western Samoa	X	X	X	X	X
Yemen (Sanaa) [1]	X	X	X		
Zambia	X	X			
Zimbabwe	X	X	X	X	X

TELECOMMUNICATION
(Cont'd)

NOTES to Chart:

*The 1979 Radio Regulations abrogate and replace the Radio Regulations adopted at Geneva December 21, 1959 (12 UST 2377; TIAS 4893) and partial revisions thereto: November 8, 1963 (15 UST 887; TIAS 5603); April 29, 1966 (18 UST 2091; TIAS 6332); November 3, 1967 (19 UST 6717; TIAS 6590); July 17, 1971 (23 UST 1527; TIAS 7435); June 8, 1974 (28 UST 3909); and March 5, 1978 (32 UST 3821; TIAS 9920), as between parties to the later Regulations. The 1959 Radio Regulations were considered as annexed to the international telecommunication conventions of 1965 (Montreux) and 1973 (Malaga-Torremolinos) and as such binding upon parties to those conventions (see Notes to the international telecommunication convention 1982 (Nairobi) below.) The Taiwan authorities also adhered to the 1959 Radio Regulations and the 1963, 1966 and 1967 revisions thereto (see Note under CHINA (Taiwan) in bilateral section).

[1] See note under YEMEN in bilateral section.

International telecommunication convention, with annexes and protocols. Done at Nairobi November 6, 1982;[1] entered into force January 1, 1984; definitively for the United States January 10, 1986.*
TIAS
States which are parties:
Afghanistan [2]
Albania [2]
Angola
Azerbaijan
Barbados
Brazil
Burma
Burundi
Cape Verde
Chile [2]
Comoros
Congo, Dem. Rep.
El Salvador
Equatorial Guinea
Fiji
Gabon
Gambia, The
Ghana
Greece [2]
Guatemala
Honduras
Iraq
Jamaica
Kiribati
Lebanon
Lesotho
Liberia
Libya
Lithuania
Malawi
Mauritania
Niger
Nigeria
Panama
Qatar [2]
Rwanda
Sierra Leone
Solomon Is.[2]

Somalia
Swaziland [2]
Tanzania
Turkey
Uruguay [2]
Vanuatu
Yemen (Sanaa) [3]

NOTES:

*The 1982 convention has been abrogated and replaced in relations between contracting parties by the Constitution and Convention of the International Telecommunication Union adopted at Geneva December 22, 1992 (see below). Only those states parties to the 1982 convention that are not parties to the 1992 Constitution and Convention are listed here.

[1] The 1982 international telecommunications convention replaced the Malaga-Torremolinos convention of October 25, 1973 (28 UST 2495; TIAS 8572), as between contracting parties to the later convention. Costa Rica, Grenada, Guinea-Bissau, Nauru, and Yugoslavia (see note under YUGOSLAVIA in bilateral section) are parties to the 1973 convention but not parties to the later conventions. The Dominican Republic is a party to the Montreux convention of November 12, 1965 (18 USC 575; TIAS 6267) but not a party to later conventions.

[2] With reservation(s)/declaration(s).

[3] See note under YEMEN in bilateral section.

Regional agreement for the medium frequency broadcasting service in Region 2, with annexes and final protocol. Done at Rio de Janeiro December 19, 1981; entered into force July 1, 1983; for the United States April 6, 1993.
TIAS
States which are parties:
Argentina [1]
Brazil
Canada
Denmark
France
Netherlands [2]
Suriname
United Statest

NOTES:
[1] With statement(s).
[2] For the Netherlands Antilles and Aruba.

Regional agreement tor the use of the band 1605–1705kHz in Region 2, with annexes and final protocol. Done at Rio de Janeiro June 8, 1988; entered into force July 1, 1990; for the United States April 6, 1993.
TIAS
States which are parties:
Canada
Denmark
France
Netherlands [1]
United States [2]

NOTES:
[1] For the Netherlands Antilles and Aruba.
[2] With declarations.

International telecommunications regulations [telegraph and telephone], with appendices and final protocol. Done at Melbourne December

9, 1988; entered into force July 1, 1990; definitively for the United States April 6, 1993.*
TIAS

NOTE:
*Ratification of or accession to the Constitution and Convention of the International Telecommunication Union adopted at Geneva December 22, 1992 (see article 54 of the Constitution), and predecessor international telecommunication conventions (Nairobi, 1982; Malaga-Torremolinas, 1973) typically involves acceptance of the telegraph and telephone regulations which are considered annexed thereto. The 1988 regulations replace the 1973 regulations (28 UST 3293; TIAS 8586) as between the contracting parties. The 1958 regulations (10 UST 2423; TIAS 4390) remain in force as between the contracting parties and the Dominican Republic. The Taiwan authorities have also adhered to the 1958 regulations (see note under CHINA (Taiwan) in bilateral section).

Constitution and Convention of the International Telecommunication Union, with annexes. Done at Geneva December 22, 1992; entered into force July 1, 1994; definitively for the United States October 26, 1997.*
TIAS
States which are parties:
Algeria [1]
Andorra
Argentina [1]
Armenia
Australia [1]
Austria [1]
Bahamas
Bahrain
Bangladesh
Belarus [1]
Belgium
Belize
Benin
Bhutan
Bolivia
Bosnia-Herzegovina
Brunei
Bulgaria
Burkina Faso
Cambodia
Cameroon
Canada [1]
Central African Rep.
Chad [1]
China [1] [2]
Colombia [1]
Congo
Cote d'Ivoire
Croatia
Cuba
Cyprus
Czech Rep.
Denmark
Djibouti
Dominica
Ecuador
Egypt
Eritrea
Estonia
Ethiopia
Finland [1]
Former Yugoslav Republic of Macedonia
France
Georgia
Germany

TELECOMMUNICATION
(Cont'd)

Guyana
Guinea
Haiti
Hungary
Iceland
India [1]
Indonesia [1]
Iran
Ireland
Israel
Italy [1]
Japan
Jordan
Kazakhstan
Kenya
Korea, Dem. People's Rep.
Korea, Rep.
Kuwait
Kyrgyz Rep.
Laos
Liechtenstein [1]
Luxembourg
Madagascar
Malaysia
Maldives
Mali
Malta [1]
Marshall Is.
Mauritius
Mexico [1]
Micronesia
Moldova
Monaco
Mongolia
Morocco
Mozambique
Namibia [1]
Nepal
Netherlands
New Zealand
Norway [1]
Oman
Pakistan
Papua New Guinea
Paraguay
Peru [1]
Philippines
Poland
Portugal [1]
Romania
Russia
San Marino
Sao Tome & Principe
Saudi Arabia [1]
Senegal
Singapore
Slovak Rep.
Slovenia
South Africa
Spain [1]
Sri Lanka
St. Lucia
St. Vincent & the Grenadines
Sudan
Suriname
Sweden
Switzerland [1]
Syria
Tajikistan
Thailand
Togo

Tonga
Trinidad & Tobago
Tunisia
Turkmenistan
Tuvalu
Uganda
Ukraine
United Arab Emirates
United Kingdom
United States [1]
Uzbekistan
Vatican City [1]
Venezuela [1]
Vietnam, Socialist Rep.
Western Samoa
Zimbabwe

Amendment:
October 14, 1994.

NOTES:
  *The 1992 Constitution and Convention replace the international telecommunication convention adopted at Nairobi November 6, 1982, as between contracting parties to the Constitution and Convention. For the position of states which have signed but not ratified the Constitution and Convention, see article 52 of the Constitution. The following states parties to the Nairobi Convention have neither signed nor acceded to the 1992 Constitution and Convention: Antigua & Barbuda, Equatorial Guinea, Guatemala, Iraq, Kiribati, Libya, Rwanda, Sierra Leone, Solomon Is., Somalia and Vanuatu.
  [1] With reservation(s)/statement(s).
  [2] Applicable to Hong Kong and Macao. See note under CHINA in bilateral section.

TERRORISM

Convention to prevent and punish the acts of terrorism taking the form of crimes against persons and related extortion that are of international significance. Done at Washington February 2, 1971; entered into force October 16, 1973, for the United States October 20, 1976. 27 UST 3949; TIAS 8413.
States which are parties:
Brazil
Colombia
Costa Rica
Dominican Rep.
El Salvador
Guatemala
Mexico
Nicaragua
Panama
Peru
United States
Uruguay
Venezuela

Convention on the prevention and punishment of crimes against internationally protected persons, including diplomatic agents. Done at New York December 14, 1973; entered into force February 20, 1977.
28 UST 1975; TIAS 8532; 1035 UNTS 167.
States which are parties:
Algeria
Antigua & Barbuda
Argentina [1]

Armenia
Australia
Austria
Bahamas
Barbados
Belarus [1]
Belize [2]
Bhutan
Bosnia-Herzegovina
Botswana
Brazil
Brunei
Bulgaria [1]
Burundi [1]
Cameroon
Canada
Chile
China [1][3]
Colombia [1]
Congo, Dem. Rep. [1]
Costa Rica
Croatia
Cuba [1]
Cyprus
Czech Rep.
Denmark [4]
Dominican Rep.
Ecuador [1]
Egypt
El Salvador [1]
Estonia
Finland [1]
Former Yugoslav Republic of Macedonia
Gabon
German Dem. Rep. [1][5]
Germany, Fed. Rep. [5][6]
Ghana [1]
Greece
Guatemala
Haiti
Hungary
Iceland
India [1]
Iran
Iraq [1]
Israel [1][6]
Italy [6]
Jamaica [1]
Japan
Jordan
Kazakhstan
Kiribati [2]
Korea, Dem. People's Rep. [6]
Korea, Rep.
Kuwait
Latvia
Lebanon
Liberia
Libya
Liechtenstein
Malawi [1]
Maldives
Mauritania
Mexico
Moldova
Mongolia [1]
Nepal
Netherlands [1]
New Zealand [7]
Nicaragua
Niger
Norway
Oman
Pakistan [1]
Panama

TERRORISM (Cont'd)

Paraguay
Peru [1]
Philippines
Poland [6]
Portugal [1]
Qatar
Romania [1]
Russian Fed.
Rwanda
St. Vincent & the Grenadines
Seychelles
Slovak Rep. [1]
Slovenia
Spain
Sri Lanka
Sudan
Sweden
Switzerland
Syria
Togo
Trinidad & Tobago [1]
Tunisia [1]
Turkey
Turkmenistan
Ukraine [1]
Union of Soviet Socialist Reps. [1 8]
United Kingdom [6 9]
United States
Uruguay
Uzbekistan
Yemen (Aden) [10]
Yugoslavia [11]

NOTES:
   [1] With reservation.
   [2] See under country heading in the bilateral section for information concerning acceptance of treaty obligations.
   [3] Applicable to Hong Kong and Macao. See note under CHINA in bilateral section.
   [4] Applicable to Faroe Is. and Greenland.
   [5] See note under GERMANY, FEDERAL REPUBLIC OF in bilateral section.
   [6] With statement.
   [7] Applicable to Cook Is. and Niue.
   [8] See note under UNION OF SOVIET SO-CIALIST REPUBLICS in bilateral section.
   [9] Extended to Bailiwick of Jersey, Bailiwick of Guernsey, Isle of Man, Bermuda, British Indian Ocean Territory, British Virgin Is., Cayman Is., Falkland Is. and Dependencies, Gibraltar, Montserrat, the Pitcairn, Henderson, Ducie and Oeno Is., St. Helena and Dependencies, Turks and Caicos Is., United Kingdom Sovereign Base Areas of Akrotiri and Dhekelia in the Island of Cyprus.
   [10] See note under YEMEN in bilateral section.
   [11] See note under YUGOSLAVIA in bilateral section.

International convention against the taking of hostages. Done at New York December 17, 1979; entered into force June 3, 1983; for the United States January 6, 1985.
TIAS 11081.
States which are parties:
Algeria [1]
Antigua & Barbuda
Argentina
Australia

Austria
Azerbaijan
Bahamas, The
Barbados
Belarus [1 2]
Belgium
Bhutan
Bolivia
Bosnia-Herzegovina
Botswana
Brazil
Brunei
Bulgaria
Cameroon [1 2]
Canada
Chile [2]
China [1 3]
Cote d'Ivoire
Cyprus
Czech Rep.
Denmark
Dominica
Ecuador
Egypt
El Salvador [1]
Finland
Former Yugoslav Republic of Macedonia
France
German Dem. Rep. [1 2 4]
Germany, Fed. Rep. [4]
Ghana
Greece
Grenada
Guatemala
Haiti
Honduras
Hungary
Iceland
India [1]
Italy
Japan
Jordan
Kazakhstan
Kenya [1]
Korea
Kuwait
Lebanon [2]
Lesotho
Libya
Liechtenstein
Luxembourg
Malawi
Mali
Mauritania
Mauritius
Mexico
Mongolia
Nepal
Netherlands [1 2 5]
New Zealand [6]
Norway
Oman
Pakistan
Panama
Philippines
Poland
Portugal
Romania
Russian Fed.
St. Kitts & Nevis
St. Vincent & the Grenadines
Saudi Arabia
Senegal
Slovak Rep. [1]
Slovenia

Spain
Sri Lanka
Sudan
Suriname
Sweden
Switzerland
Togo
Trinidad & Tobago
Tunisia
Turkey [1]
Turkmenistan
Ukraine [1 2]
Union of Soviet Socialist Reps. [1 2 7]
United Kingdom [8]
United States
Uzbekistan
Venezuela [2]
Yugoslavia [9]

NOTES:
   [1] With reservation.
   [2] With declaration.
   [3] Applicable to Hong Kong and Macao. See note under CHINA in bilateral section.
   [4] See note under GERMANY, FEDERAL REPUBLIC OF in bilateral section.
   [5] Applicable to the Kingdom in Europe, the Netherlands Antilles and Aruba.
   [6] Applicable to Cook Is. and Niue.
   [7] See note under UNION OF SOVIET SO-CIALIST REPUBLICS in bilateral section.
   [8] Applicable to territories under the territorial sovereignty of the United Kingdom.
   [9] See note under YUGOSLAVIA in bilateral section.

TEXTILES

(See under TRADE AND COMMERCE)

TIMBER

International tropical timber agreement, 1994, with annexes. Done at Geneva January 26, 1994; entered into force provisionally, January 1, 1997.
TIAS:
Parties:
Australia
Austria
Belgium *
Bolivia
Brazil
Burma
Cambodia
Cameroon *
Canada
Central African Rep. *
China
Colombia
Congo *
Congo, Dem. Rep. *
Cote d'Ivoire
Denmark
Ecuador
Egypt
European Community * [1]
Fiji *
Finland *

TIMBER (Cont'd)

France *
Gabon *
Germany *
Ghana
Greece
Guyana
Honduras *
India
Indonesia
Ireland
Italy
Japan
Korea
Liberia
Luxembourg *
Malaysia
Nepal *
Netherlands * [2]
New Zealand
Norway
Panama
Papua New Guinea
Peru
Philippines *
Portugal
Spain
Suriname
Sweden
Switzerland
Thailand
Togo
Trinidad & Tobago
United Kingdom *
United States
Vanuatu
Venezuela

NOTES:
  *Provisional application.
  [1] With declaration(s).
  [2] For the Kingdom in Europe.

TONNAGE MEASUREMENT

(See under MARITIME MATTERS)

TORTURE

Convention against torture and other cruel, in-human or degrading treatment or punishment. Done at New York December 10, 1984; entered into force June 26, 1987; for the United States November 20, 1994.
TIAS
Parties:
Afghanistan [1]
Albania
Algeria [2]
Antigua & Barbuda
Argentina
Armenia
Australia [2]
Austria [2]

Azerbaijan
Bahrain [1]
Bangladesh [2]
Belarus [1][2]
Belgium
Belize
Benin
Bolivia
Bosnia-Herzegovina
Botswana
Brazil
Bulgaria [1][2]
Burkina Faso
Burundi
Cambodia
Cameroon
Canada [2]
Cape Verde
Chad
Chile [1]
China [1][3]
Colombia
Congo, Dem. Rep.
Costa Rica
Cote d'Ivoire
Croatia [2]
Cuba [2]
Cyprus
Czech Rep. [2]
Denmark [2]
Ecuador [1][2]
Egypt
El Salvador
Estonia
Ethiopia
Finland [2]
Former Yugoslav Republic of Macedonia
France [1][2]
Gabon
Georgia
Germany
Ghana
Greece [2]
Guatemala
Guinea
Guyana
Honduras
Hungary
Iceland [2]
Indonesia [1][2]
Israel [1]
Italy [2]
Japan
Jordan
Kazakhstan
Kenya
Korea
Kuwait [1]
Kyrgyz Rep.
Latvia
Lebanon
Libya
Liechtenstein
Lithuania
Luxembourg [2]
Malawi
Mali
Malta
Mauritius
Mexico
Moldova
Monaco
Morocco [1]
Mozambique
Namibia

Nepal
Netherlands [2][4]
New Zealand [1]
Niger
Norway [2]
Panama [1]
Paraguay
Peru
Philippines
Poland [2]
Portugal [2]
Qatar
Romania
Russian Fed.
Saudi Arabia
Senegal [2]
Seychelles
Slovak Rep. [2]
Slovenia [2]
Somalia
South Africa
Spain [2]
Sri Lanka
Sweden
Switzerland [2]
Tajikistan
Togo [2]
Tunisia [2]
Turkey [1][2]
Turkmenistan
Uganda
Ukraine [1][2]
United Kingdom [2][5]
United States [1][2]
Uruguay [2]
Uzbekistan
Venezuela [2]
Yemen
Yugoslavia [6]
Zambia

NOTES:
  [1] With reservation(s).
  [2] With declaration(s).
  [3] Applicable to Hong Kong and Macao. With declaration. See note under CHINA in bilateral section.
  [4] For the Kingdom in Europe, the Netherlands Antilles and Aruba.
  [5] Applicable to Anguilla, Bailiwicks of Guernsey and Jersey, Bermuda, British Virgin Is., Cayman Is., Falkland Is., Gibraltar, Isle of Man, Montserrat, Pitcairn, Henderson, Ducie and Oeno Is., St. Helena, St. Helena dependencies and Turks & Caicos Is.
  [6] See note under YUGOSLAVIA in bilateral section.

TRADE AND COMMERCE

(See also CUSTOMS)

Agreement to refrain from invoking the obligations of most-favored-nation clause in respect of certain multilateral economic conventions. Done at the Pan American Union, Washington, July 15, 1934; entered into force September 12, 1935.
49 Stat. 3260; TS 898; 3 Bevans 252; 165 LNTS 9.
States which are parties:
Cuba

TRADE AND COMMERCE (Cont'd)

Greece
United States

Convention on transit trade of land-locked states. Done at New York July 8, 1965; entered into force June 9, 1967; for the United States November 28, 1968.
19 UST 7383; TIAS 6592; 597 UNTS 42.
States which are parties:
Australia
Belarus [1]
Belgium [1]
Burkina Faso
Burundi
Central African Rep.
Chad
Chile [1]
Croatia
Czech Rep.
Denmark
Finland
Georgia
Hungary [1]
Laos
Lesotho
Malawi
Mali
Mongolia
Nepal
Netherlands [2]
Niger
Nigeria
Norway
Russian Fed.
Rwanda
San Marino
Senegal
Slovak Rep. [1]
Swaziland
Sweden
Turkey
Ukraine [1]
Union of Soviet Socialist Reps. [1] [3]
United States
Uzbekistan
Yugoslavia [4]
Zambia

NOTES:
[1] With reservation.
[2] Applicable to Netherlands Antilles and Aruba.
[3] See note under UNION OF SOVIET SOCIALIST REPUBLICS in bilateral section.
[4] See note under YUGOSLAVIA in bilateral section.

Convention on the limitation period in the international sale of goods. Done at New York June 12, 1974; entered into force August 1, 1988; for the United States December 1, 1994.
TIAS
Parties:
Argentina
Belarus
Bosnia-Herzegovina
Burundi
Cuba
Czech Rep.

Dominican Rep.
Egypt
German Dem. Rep. [1]
Ghana
Guinea
Hungary
Mexico
Moldova
Norway [2]
Poland
Romania
Slovak Rep.
Slovenia
Uganda
Ukraine
United States [3]
Uruguay
Yugoslavia [4]
Zambia

Amendment:
April 11, 1980.

NOTES:
[1] See note under GERMANY, FEDERAL REPUBLIC OF in bilateral section.
[2] With reservation(s).
[3] With declaration(s).
[4] See note under YUGOSLAVIA in bilateral section.

Agreement on trade in civil aircraft. Done at Geneva April 12, 1979; entered into force January 1, 1980.
31 UST 619; TIAS 9620; 1186 UNTS 170.
Parties:
Austria
Belgium
Bulgaria
Canada
Denmark [1]
Egypt
European Economic Community
France
Germany, Fed. Rep. [2]
Greece
Ireland
Italy
Japan
Luxembourg
Macao
Netherlands [3]
Norway
Portugal
Romania
Spain
Sweden
Switzerland
United Kingdom [4]
United States

Amendments (annex):
January 17, 1983 (TIAS 10673).
January 27, 1984 (TIAS 11531).
January 1, 1985 (TIAS 11531).
December 2, 1986.

NOTES:
[1] Not applicable to Faroe Is.
[2] See note under GERMANY, FEDERAL REPUBLIC OF in bilateral section.
[3] Applicable provisionally to the Kingdom in Europe, the Netherlands Antilles and Aruba pending approval.

[4] Accepted in respect of the territories for which it has international responsibility except for: Bermuda, Cayman Is., Montserrat, Sovereign Base Areas Cyprus, British Virgin Is.

United Nations convention on contracts for the international sale of goods. Done at Vienna April 11, 1980; entered into force January 1, 1988.
TIAS
States which are parties:
Argentina [1]
Australia [2]
Austria
Belarus [1]
Belgium
Bosnia-Herzegovina
Bulgaria
Burundi
Canada [3]
Chile [1]
China [1]
Croatia
Cuba
Czech Rep.
Denmark [1]
Ecuador
Egypt
Estonia [1]
Finland [4]
France
Georgia
German Dem. Rep. [5]
Germany, Fed. Rep. [1] [5]
Greece
Guinea
Hungary [1]
Iraq
Italy
Kyrgyz Rep.
Latvia
Lesotho
Lithuania
Luxembourg
Mauritania
Mexico
Moldova
Mongolia
Netherlands
New Zealand
Norway [4]
Peru
Poland
Romania
Russian Fed. [1]
St. Vincent & the Grenadines
Singapore
Slovak Rep.
Slovenia
Spain
Sweden [4]
Switzerland
Syria
Uganda
Ukraine [1]
Union of Soviet Socialist Reps. [1] [6]
United States [1]
Uruguay
Uzbekistan
Yugoslavia [7]
Zambia

NOTES:
[1] With declaration(s).

TRADE AND COMMERCE (Cont'd)

[2] Applicable to "all Australian States and mainland territories and to all external territories except the territories of Christmas Island, the Cocos (Keeling) Islands and the Ashmore and Cartier Islands."

[3] Applicable to Alberta, British Columbia, Prince Edward Island, Manitoba, New Brunswick, Nova Scotia, Ontario, Newfoundland, Northwest Territories, Quebec, Saskatchewan, and the Territory of the Yukon.

[4] With reservation(s).

[5] See note under GERMANY, FEDERAL REPUBLIC OF in bilateral section.

[6] See note under UNION OF SOVIET SOCIALIST REPUBLICS in bilateral section.

[7] See note under YUGOSLAVIA in bilateral section.

North American free trade agreement, with notes and annexes. Signed at Washington, Ottawa and Mexico December 8, 11, 14 and 17, 1992; entered into force January 1, 1994.
TIAS
Parties:
Canada
Mexico
United States

Marrakesh agreement establishing the World Trade Organization (WTO). Done at Marrakesh April 15, 1994; entered into force January 1, 1995.
TIAS

Related agreements were done at Marrakesh April 15, 1994; entered into force January 1, 1995:
General Agreement on Tariffs and Trade 1994.
TIAS
Agreement on agriculture.
TIAS
Agreement on the application of sanitary and phytosanitary measures.
TIAS
Agreement on textiles and clothing.
TIAS
Agreement on technical barriers to trade.
TIAS
Agreement on trade-related investment measures.
TIAS
Agreement on implementation of Article VI (Anti-Dumping) of the General Agreement on Tariffs and Trade 1994.
TIAS
Agreement on implementation of Article VII (Customs Valuation) of the General Agreement on Tariffs and Trade 1994.
TIAS
Agreement on preshipment inspection.
TIAS
Agreement on rules of origin.
TIAS
Agreement on import licensing procedures.
TIAS
Agreement on subsidies and countervailing measures.
TIAS

Agreement on safeguards.
TIAS
General agreement on trade in services and annexes.
TIAS
Agreement on trade-related aspects of intellectual property rights.
TIAS
Understanding on rules and procedures governing the settlement of disputes.
TIAS
Trade policy review mechanism.
TIAS
Parties:
Albania
Angola
Antigua & Barbuda
Argentina
Australia
Austria
Bahrain
Bangladesh
Barbados
Belgium
Belize
Benin
Bolivia
Botswana
Brazil
Brunei
Bulgaria
Burkina Faso
Burma
Burundi
Cameroon
Canada
Central African Rep.
Chad
Chile
Colombia
Congo
Congo, Dem. Rep.
Costa Rica
Cote d'Ivoire
Croatia
Cuba
Cyprus
Czech Rep.
Denmark
Djibouti
Dominica
Dominican Rep.
Ecuador
Egypt
El Salvador
Estonia
European Community
Fiji
Finland
France
Gabon
Gambia
Georgia
Germany
Ghana
Greece
Grenada
Guatemala
Guinea
Guinea-Bissau
Guyana
Haiti
Honduras
Hong Kong
Hungary

Iceland
India
Indonesia
Ireland
Israel
Italy
Jamaica
Japan
Jordan
Kenya
Korea
Kuwait
Kyrgyz Rep.
Latvia
Lesotho
Liechtenstein
Luxembourg
Macao
Madagascar
Malawi
Malaysia
Maldives
Mali
Malta
Mauritania
Mauritius
Mexico
Mongolia
Morocco
Mozambique
Namibia
Netherlands [1]
New Zealand
Nicaragua
Niger
Nigeria
Norway
Oman
Pakistan
Panama
Papua New Guinea
Paraguay
Peru
Philippines
Poland
Portugal
Qatar
Romania
Rwanda
St. Kitts & Nevis
St. Lucia
St. Vincent & the Grenadines
Senegal
Sierra Leone
Singapore
Slovak Rep.
Slovenia
Solomon Is.
South Africa
Spain
Sri Lanka
Suriname
Swaziland
Sweden
Switzerland
Tanzania
Thailand
Togo
Trinidad & Tobago
Tunisia
Turkey
Uganda
United Arab Emirates
United Kingdom
United States

TRADE AND COMMERCE (Cont'd)

Uruguay
Venezuela
Zambia
Zimbabwe

NOTE:
[1] For the Kingdom in Europe and for the Netherlands Antilles.

Agreement on government procurement. Done at Marrakesh April 15, 1994; entered into force January 1, 1996.
TIAS
Parties:
Austria
Belgium
Canada
Denmark
European Community
Finland
France
Germany
Greece
Hong Kong
Ireland
Israel
Italy
Japan
Korea
Liechtenstein
Luxembourg
Netherlands [1]
Norway
Portugal
Singapore
Spain
Sweden
Switzerland
United Kingdom
United States

NOTE:
[1] For the Kingdom in Europe and for Aruba.

TRADE-MARKS

(See INDUSTRIAL PROPERTY)

TRAFFIC IN WOMEN AND CHILDREN

Agreement for the suppression of the white slave traffic. Signed at Paris May 18, 1904; entered into force July 18, 1905; for the United States June 6, 1908.
35 Stat. 1979; TS 496; 1 Bevans 424; 1 LNTS 83.
States which are parties:
Algeria
Antigua & Barbuda [1]
Australia [2]
Austria
Bahamas, The

Barbados [1]
Belgium
Belize [1]
Benin
Brazil
Bulgaria
Burma [1]
Cameroon [3]
Canada
Central African Rep.
Chile [3]
China [3][4]
Colombia
Congo
Cote d'Ivoire
Cuba [3]
Cyprus
Czech Rep.
Denmark
Dominica [1]
Egypt [3]
Estonia [3]
Fiji
Finland [3]
France [2]
Gambia, The [1]
German Dem. Rep. [5]
Germany, Fed. Rep. [5]
Ghana
Grenada [1][3]
Guyana [1]
Hong Kong [6]
Hungary
Iceland [7]
India [3]
Iran [3]
Iraq [3]
Ireland [3]
Italy
Jamaica
Japan [3]
Kiribati [1]
Lebanon
Lithuania [3]
Luxembourg
Madagascar
Malawi
Malaysia [1]
Mali
Malta
Mauritius
Mexico
Monaco [3]
Morocco
Nauru [1][3]
Netherlands [8]
New Zealand
Niger
Nigeria
Norway
Pakistan
Papua New Guinea [1][3]
Poland
Portugal
Russian Fed.
St. Kitts & Nevis [1]
St. Lucia [1][3]
St. Vincent & the Grenadines [1][3]
Senegal
Seychelles [1]
Sierra Leone
Singapore
Slovak Rep.
Solomon Is. [1]
South Africa [3]

Spain
Sri Lanka
Sudan [3]
Suriname [1]
Sweden
Switzerland
Tanzania [1][3]
Thailand [3]
Trinidad & Tobago
Tunisia [3]
Turkey [3]
Tuvalu [1]
Union of Soviet Socialist Reps. [9]
United Kingdom [10]
United States
Uruguay [3]
Yugoslavia [3][11]
Zambia
Zimbabwe [1]

NOTES:
[1] See under country heading in the bilateral section for information concerning acceptance of treaty obligations.
[2] Extended to all territories.
[3] Party by virtue of ratification or adherence to the international convention for the suppression of the white slave traffic signed at Paris May 4, 1910 (3 LNTS 278) or the protocol of May 4, 1949 (2 UST 1997; TIAS 2332).
[4] Pre 1949 agreement, applicable only to Taiwan.
[5] See note under GERMANY, FEDERAL REPUBLIC OF in bilateral section.
[6] CHINA is not a party to this treaty but has made it applicable to Hong Kong.
[7] Included in ratification by Denmark.
[8] Extended to Curacao.
[9] See note under UNION OF SOVIET SOCIALIST REPUBLICS in bilateral section.
[10] Extended to Bermuda, British Virgin Is., Falkland Is., Gibraltar, Guernsey, Isle of Man, Jersey, Montserrat, and St. Helena.
[11] See note under YUGOSLAVIA in bilateral section.

Protocol amending the international agreement for the suppression of the white slave traffic, signed at Paris May 18, 1904, and the international convention for the suppression of the white slave traffic, signed at Paris May 4, 1910. Done at Lake Success May 4, 1949; entered into force May 4, 1949; for the United States August 14, 1950; annex amending 1904 agreement entered into force June 21, 1951.
2 UST 1997; TIAS 2332; 92 UNTS 19.

TRANSPORTATION— FOODSTUFFS

Agreement on the international carriage of perishable foodstuffs and on the special equipment to be used for such carriage (ATP), with annexes. Done at Geneva September 1, 1970; entered into force November 21, 1976; for the United States January 20, 1984.
TIAS   ; 1028 UNTS 121.
States which are parties:
Austria
Azerbaijan
Belgium
Bosnia-Herzegovina

TRANSPORTATION— FOODSTUFFS (Cont'd)

Bulgaria [1]
Croatia
Czech Rep.
Denmark
Estonia
Finland
Former Yugoslav Republic of Macedonia
France [2]
Georgia
German Dem. Rep. [1][3]
Germany, Fed. Rep. [3]
Greece
Hungary [1]
Ireland
Italy [2]
Kazakhstan
Luxembourg
Morocco
Netherlands [4]
Norway
Poland [1]
Portugal
Romania
Russian Fed.
Slovak Rep. [1]
Slovenia
Spain
Sweden
Switzerland
Union of Soviet Socialist Reps. [1][5]
United Kingdom
United States [2]
Uzbekistan
Yugoslavia [6]

NOTES:
[1] With reservation(s).
[2] Objections by France and Italy to the United States declaration under Article 10 have not been accepted by the United States.
[3] See note under GERMANY, FEDERAL REPUBLIC OF in bilateral section.
[4] For the Kingdom in Europe.
[5] See note under UNION OF SOVIET SOCIALIST REPUBLICS in bilateral section.
[6] See note under YUGOSLAVIA in bilateral section.

TRIESTE

(See under PEACE TREATIES)

UNITED NATIONS

Declaration by United Nations. Signed at Washington January 1, 1942; entered into force January 1, 1942.
55 Stat. 1600; EAS 236; 3 Bevans 697.
States which are parties:
Australia
Belgium
Bolivia
Brazil
Canada
Chile

China [1]
Colombia
Costa Rica
Cuba
Czechoslovakia [2]
Dominican Rep.
Ecuador
Egypt
El Salvador
Ethiopia [3]
France
Greece
Guatemala
Haiti
Honduras
India
Iran
Iraq
Lebanon
Liberia
Luxembourg
Mexico
Netherlands
New Zealand
Nicaragua
Norway
Panama
Paraguay
Peru
Philippines
Poland
Saudi Arabia
Slovak Rep.
South Africa
Syrian Arab Rep.
Turkey
Union of Soviet Socialist Reps. [4]
United Kingdom
United States
Uruguay
Venezuela
Yugoslavia [5]

NOTES:
[1] Pre 1949 agreement, applicable only to Taiwan.
[2] See note under CZECHOSLOVAKIA in bilateral section.
[3] See note under ETHIOPIA in bilateral section.
[4] See note under UNION OF SOVIET SOCIALIST REPUBLICS in bilateral section.
[5] See note under YUGOSLAVIA in bilateral section.

Charter of the United Nations with the Statute of the International Court of Justice annexed thereto. [1] Signed at San Francisco June 26, 1945; entered into force October 24, 1945.
59 Stat. 1031; TS 993; 3 Bevans 1153.
States which are parties:
Afghanistan
Albania
Algeria
Andorra
Angola
Antigua & Barbuda
Argentina
Armenia
Australia
Austria
Azerbaijan
Bahamas, The
Bahrain
Bangladesh

Barbados
Belarus
Belgium
Belize
Benin
Bhutan
Bolivia
Bosnia-Herzegovina
Botswana
Brazil
Brunei
Bulgaria
Burkina Faso
Burma
Burundi
Cambodia
Cameroon
Canada
Cape Verde
Central African Rep.
Chad
Chile
China [2]
Colombia
Comoros
Congo
Congo, Dem. Rep.
Costa Rica
Cote d'Ivoire
Croatia
Cuba
Cyprus
Czech Rep.
Denmark
Djibouti
Dominica
Dominican Rep.
Ecuador
Egypt
El Salvador
Equatorial Guinea
Eritrea
Estonia
Ethiopia [3]
Fiji
Finland
Former Yugoslav Republic of Macedonia
France
Gabon
Gambia, The
Georgia
German Dem. Rep. [4]
Germany, Fed. Rep. [4]
Ghana
Greece
Grenada
Guatemala
Guinea
Guinea-Bissau
Guyana
Haiti
Honduras
Hungary
Iceland
India
Indonesia
Iran
Iraq
Ireland
Israel
Italy
Jamaica
Japan
Jordan
Kazakhstan

UNITED NATIONS (Cont'd)

Kenya
Korea
Kuwait
Kyrgyz Rep.
Laos
Latvia
Lebanon
Lesotho
Liberia
Libya
Liechtenstein
Luxembourg
Madagascar
Malawi
Malaysia
Maldives
Mali
Malta
Marshall Is.
Mauritania
Mauritius
Mexico
Micronesia
Moldova
Monaco
Mongolia
Morocco
Mozambique
Namibia
Nepal
Netherlands
New Zealand
Nicaragua
Niger
Nigeria
Norway
Oman
Pakistan
Palau
Panama
Papua New Guinea
Paraguay
Peru
Philippines
Poland
Portugal
Qatar
Romania
Russian Fed.
Rwanda
St. Kitts & Nevis
St. Lucia
St. Vincent & the Grenadines
San Marino
Sao Tome & Principe
Saudi Arabia
Senegal
Seychelles
Sierra Leone
Singapore
Slovak Rep.
Slovenia
Solomon Is.
Somalia
South Africa
Spain
Sri Lanka
Sudan
Suriname
Swaziland
Sweden

Syrian Arab Rep.
Tajikistan
Tanzania
Thailand
Togo
Trinidad & Tobago
Tunisia
Turkey
Turkmenistan
Uganda
Ukraine
United Arab Emirates
United Kingdom
United States
Uruguay
Uzbekistan
Vanuatu
Venezuela
Vietnam, Socialist Rep.
Western Samoa
Yemen (Aden) [5]
Yemen (Sanaa) [5]
Yugoslavia [6]
Zambia
Zimbabwe

Amendments:
December 17, 1963 (16 UST 1134; TIAS 5857; 557 UNTS 143).
December 20, 1965 (19 UST 5450; TIAS 6529).
December 20, 1971 (24 UST 2225; TIAS 7739).

NOTES:
[1] For parties to the Statute, not parties to the Charter, see INTERNATIONAL COURT OF JUSTICE.
[2] Applicable to Hong Kong and Macao. See note under CHINA in bilateral section.
[3] See note under ETHIOPIA in bilateral section.
[4] See note under GERMANY, FEDERAL REPUBLIC OF in bilateral section.
[5] See note under YEMEN in bilateral section.
[6] See note under YUGOSLAVIA in bilateral section.

Convention on the privileges and immunities of the United Nations. Done at New York February 13, 1946, entered into force September 17, 1946; for the United States April 29, 1970. 21 UST 1418; TIAS 6900; 1 UNTS 16.
States which are parties:
Afghanistan
Albania [1]
Algeria [1]
Angola
Antigua & Barbuda
Argentina
Australia
Austria
Azerbaijan
Bahamas, The
Bahrain [2]
Bangladesh
Barbados
Belarus [1]
Belgium
Bolivia
Bosnia-Herzegovina
Brazil
Bulgaria [1]
Burkina Faso

Burma
Burundi
Cambodia
Cameroon
Canada [1]
Central African Rep.
Chile
China [1] [3]
Colombia
Congo
Congo, Dem. Rep.
Costa Rica
Cote d'Ivoire
Croatia
Cuba
Cyprus
Czech Rep.
Denmark
Djibouti
Dominica
Dominican Rep.
Ecuador
Egypt
El Salvador
Estonia
Ethiopia [4]
Fiji
Finland
Former Yugoslav Republic of Macedonia
France
Gabon
Gambia, The
German Dem. Rep. [1] [5]
Germany, Fed. Rep. [5]
Ghana
Greece
Guatemala
Guinea
Guyana
Haiti
Honduras
Hungary [1]
Iceland
India
Indonesia [1]
Iran
Iraq
Ireland
Israel
Italy
Jamaica
Japan
Jordan
Kazakhstan
Kenya
Korea
Kuwait
Kyrgyz Rep.
Laos [1]
Latvia
Lebanon [6]
Lesotho
Liberia
Libya
Liechtenstein
Lithuania [1]
Luxembourg
Madagascar
Malawi
Malaysia
Mali
Malta
Mauritius
Mexico [1]
Moldova

UNITED NATIONS (Cont'd)

Mongolia
Morocco
Nepal [1]
Netherlands [7]
New Zealand
Nicaragua
Niger
Nigeria
Norway
Pakistan
Panama
Papua New Guinea
Paraguay
Peru
Philippines
Poland
Portugal [1]
Romania [1]
Russian Fed.
Rwanda
St. Lucia
Senegal
Seychelles
Sierra Leone
Singapore
Slovak Rep. [1]
Slovenia
Somalia
Spain
Sudan
Sweden
Syrian Arab Rep.
Tanzania
Togo
Trinidad & Tobago
Tunisia
Turkey [1]
Ukraine [1]
Union of Soviet Socialist Reps. [1] [8]
United Kingdom [6]
United States [1]
Uruguay
Venezuela
Vietnam [1]
Yemen (Sanaa) [9]
Yugoslavia [10]
Zambia
Zimbabwe

NOTES:
[1] With reservation(s).
[2] With declaration(s).
[3] Applicable to Hong Kong and Macao. See note under CHINA in bilateral section.
[4] See note under ETHIOPIA in bilateral section.
[5] See note under GERMANY, FEDERAL REPUBLIC OF in bilateral section.
[6] With statement.
[7] Applicable to Netherlands Antilles and Aruba.
[8] See note under UNION OF SOVIET SOCIALIST REPUBLICS in bilateral section.
[9] See note under YEMEN in bilateral section.
[10] See note under YUGOSLAVIA in bilateral section.

VIET-NAM

Act of the International Conference on Viet-Nam. Done at Paris March 2, 1973; entered into force March 2, 1973.
24 UST 485; TIAS 7568; 935 UNTS 405.
Parties:
Canada
China, People's Rep.
France
Hungary
Indonesia
Poland
Provisional Revolutionary Government of Rep. of South Viet-Nam [1]
Union of Soviet Socialist Reps. [2]
United Kingdom
United States
Viet-Nam, Dem. Rep. [1]
Viet-Nam, Rep. [1]

NOTES:
[1] See Vietnam footnote under AGRICULTURE: agreement of January 25, 1924 (26 UST 1840; TIAS 8141; 57 LNTS 135).
[2] See note under UNION OF SOVIET SOCIALIST REPUBLICS in bilateral section.

WAR

(See RED CROSS CONVENTIONS; RENUNCIATION OF WAR; RULES OF WARFARE; WORLD WAR II)

WAR CRIMINALS

(See also RULES OF WARFARE)

Agreement for the prosecution and punishment of the major war criminals of the European Axis. Signed at London August 8, 1945; entered into force August 8, 1945.
59 Stat. 1544; EAS 472; 3 Bevans 1238; 82 UNTS 279.
States which are parties:
Australia
Belgium
Czechoslovakia [1]
Denmark
Ethiopia [2]
France
Greece
Haiti
Honduras
India
Luxembourg
Netherlands
New Zealand
Norway
Panama
Paraguay
Poland
Slovak Rep.
Union of Soviet Socialist Reps. [3]

United Kingdom
United States
Uruguay
Venezuela
Yugoslavia [4]

NOTES:
[1] See note under CZECHOSLOVAKIA in bilateral section.
[2] See note under ETHIOPIA in bilateral section.
[3] See note under UNION OF SOVIET SOCIALIST REPUBLICS in bilateral section.
[4] See note under YUGOSLAVIA in bilateral section.

Charter of the International Military Tribunal for the Far East. Dated at Tokyo January 19, 1946, amended April 26, 1946.
TIAS 1589; 4 Bevans 20.

WARSAW CONVENTION

(See under AVIATION)

WEAPONS

Convention on prohibitions or restrictions on the use of certain conventional weapons which may be deemed to be excessively injurious or to have indiscriminate effects. Adopted at Geneva October 10, 1980; entered into force December 2, 1983; for the United States September 24, 1995.
TIAS

Protocol on non-detectable fragments (Protocol I). Adopted at Geneva October 10, 1980; entered into force December 2, 1983; for the United States September 24, 1995.
TIAS

Protocol on prohibitions or restrictions on the use of mines, booby-traps and other devices (Protocol II). Adopted at Geneva October 10, 1980; entered into force December 2, 1983; for the United States September 24, 1995. [1]
TIAS
Parties:
Argentina
Australia
Austria
Bangladesh
Belarus
Belgium
Benin [2]
Bosnia-Herzegovina
Brazil
Bulgaria
Cambodia
Canada [3]
Cape Verde
China [4]
Colombia
Costa Rica
Croatia
Cuba
Cyprus
Czech Rep.
Denmark

WEAPONS (Cont'd)

Djibouti
Ecuador
El Salvador
Estonia [2]
Finland
Former Yugoslav Republic of Macedonia
France
Georgia
Germany
Greece
Guatemala
Holy See
Hungary
India
Ireland
Israel
Italy
Japan
Jordan [2]
Laos
Latvia
Lesotho
Liechtenstein
Lithuania [2]
Luxembourg
Maldives [2]
Malta
Mauritius
Mexico
Moldova
Monaco [2]
Mongolia
Netherlands
New Zealand
Nicaragua [2]
Niger
Norway
Pakistan
Panama
Peru [2]
Philippines
Poland
Portugal
Romania
Russian Fed.
Senegal [5]
Seychelles
Slovak Rep.
Slovenia
South Africa
Spain
Sweden
Switzerland
Tajikistan
Togo
Tunisia
Uganda
Ukraine
United Kingdom [3]
United States [3 6 7]
Uruguay
Uzbekistan
Yugoslavia [8]

Amendment:
May 3, 1996.

NOTES:
[1] Protocols III and IV are not yet in force for the United States.
[2] Not a party to Protocol II.

[3] With declaration(s).
[4] Applicable to Hong Kong and Macao. See note under CHINA in bilateral section.
[5] Not a party to Protocols I and II.
[6] With reservation(s).
[7] With understanding(s).
[8] See note under YUGOSLAVIA in bilateral section.

WEIGHTS AND MEASURES

Convention concerning the creation of an international office of weights and measures, regulations and transient provisions. Signed at Paris May 20, 1875; entered into force January 1, 1876; for the United States August 2, 1878. 20 Stat. 709; TS 378; 1 Bevans 39.

Convention amending the convention relating to weights and measures. Dated at Sevres October 6, 1921; entered into force June 23, 1922; for the United States October 24, 1923. 43 Stat. 1686; TS 673; 2 Bevans 323; 17 LNTS 45.
States which are parties:
Argentina [1]
Australia
Austria
Belgium
Brazil
Bulgaria
Cameroon
Canada
Chile [1]
China [2]
Czechoslovakia [3]
Denmark
Dominican Rep.
Egypt
Finland
France
German Dem. Rep. [4]
Germany, Fed. Rep. [4]
Hungary
India
Indonesia
Iran
Ireland
Italy
Japan
Korea, Dem. People's Rep.
Korea, Rep.
Mexico
Netherlands
Norway
Pakistan
Poland
Portugal
Romania
Slovak Rep.
South Africa
Spain
Sweden
Switzerland
Thailand
Turkey
Union of Soviet Socialist Reps. [5]
United Kingdom
United States
Uruguay

Venezuela
Yugoslavia [6]

NOTES:
[1] Not a party to the 1921 convention.
[2] The Taiwan authorities have also adhered to these conventions. See note under CHINA (Taiwan) in the bilateral section.
[3] See note under CZECHOSLOVAKIA in bilateral section.
[4] See note under GERMANY, FEDERAL REPUBLIC OF in bilateral section.
[5] See note under UNION OF SOVIET SOCIALIST REPUBLICS in bilateral section.
[6] See note under YUGOSLAVIA in bilateral section.

Convention establishing an International Organization of Legal Metrology. Done at Paris October 12, 1955; entered into force May 28, 1958; for the United States October 22, 1972 as amended January 18, 1968. 23 UST 4233; TIAS 7533; 560 UNTS 3.
Parties:
Algeria
Arab Organization of Standardization and Metrology [1]
Australia
Austria
Belarus
Belgium
Brazil
Bulgaria
Cameroon
Canada
China
Cuba
Cyprus
Czechoslovakia [2]
Denmark
Egypt
Ethiopia [3]
Finland
France [4]
German Dem. Rep. [5]
Germany, Fed. Rep. [5]
Greece
Guinea
Hungary
India
Indonesia
Ireland
Israel
Italy
Jamaica [1]
Japan
Jordan [1]
Kazakhstan
Kenya
Korea, Dem. People's Rep.
Korea, Rep.
Lebanon
Luxembourg [1]
Monaco
Morocco
Nepal [1]
Netherlands
New Zealand [1]
Norway
Pakistan
Poland
Portugal
Romania
Saudi Arabia
Slovak Rep.

WEIGHTS AND MEASURES (Cont'd)

Spain
Sri Lanka
Sweden
Switzerland
Tanzania
Tunisia
Turkey [1]
Union of Soviet Socialist Reps. [6]
United Kingdom [7]
United States
Venezuela
Yugoslavia [8]
Zambia

NOTES:
[1] Corresponding Member.
[2] See note under CZECHOSLOVAKIA in bilateral section.
[3] See note under ETHIOPIA in bilateral section.
[4] Extended to the French overseas territories.
[5] See note under GERMANY, FEDERAL REPUBLIC OF in bilateral section.
[6] See note under UNION OF SOVIET SOCIALIST REPUBLICS in bilateral section.
[7] Extended to the British Virgin Is., Gibraltar, Montserrat, Turks and Caicos Is.
[8] See note under YUGOSLAVIA in bilateral section.

WETLANDS

(See under CONSERVATION)

WHALING

Convention for the regulation of whaling. Concluded at Geneva September 24, 1931; entered into force January 16, 1935.
49 Stat. 3079; TS 880; 3 Bevans 26; 155 LNTS 349.
States which are parties:
Antigua & Barbuda [1]
Austria
Bahamas, The [1]
Barbados [1]
Belize [1]
Brazil
Brunei [1]
Canada
Cyprus [1]
Czechoslovakia [2]
Denmark, including Greenland
Dominica [1]
Ecuador
Egypt
Fiji [1]
Finland
France
Gambia, The [1]
Ghana [1]
Grenada [1]
Guyana [1]
Ireland

Italy [3]
Jamaica [1]
Kiribati [1]
Latvia
Malaysia [1]
Malta [1]
Mauritius [1]
Mexico
Monaco
Netherlands [4]
New Zealand
Nicaragua
Nigeria [1]
Norway
Poland
St. Kitts & Nevis [1]
St. Lucia [1]
St. Vincent & the Grenadines [1]
Seychelles [1]
Sierra Leone [1]
Slovak Rep.
Solomon Is. [1]
South Africa
Spain
Sri Lanka [1]
Sudan
Suriname [1]
Switzerland
Tanzania [1]
Tonga [1]
Trinidad & Tobago [1]
Turkey
Tuvalu [1]
United Kingdom [5]
United States
Yugoslavia [6]

NOTES:
[1] See under country heading in the bilateral section for information concerning acceptance of treaty obligations.
[2] See note under CZECHOSLOVAKIA in bilateral section.
[3] With reservation.
[4] Extended to Curacao.
[5] Extended to Ascension Is., Bermuda, British Virgin Is., Cayman Is., Falkland Is. and dependencies, Gibraltar, Montserrat, St. Helena, Turks and Caicos Is.
[6] See note under YUGOSLAVIA in bilateral section.

International convention for the regulation of whaling with schedule of whaling regulations. Signed at Washington December 2, 1946; entered into force November 10, 1948.
62 Stat. 1716; TIAS 1849; 4 Bevans 248; 161 UNTS 72.

Protocol to the international convention for the regulation of whaling. Done at Washington November 19, 1956; entered into force May 4, 1959.
10 UST 952; TIAS 4228; 338 UNTS 366.
States which are parties:
Antigua & Barbuda
Argentina [1]
Australia
Austria
Brazil
Chile [1]
China [2] [3]
Costa Rica
Denmark
Dominica

Ecuador [1] *
Finland
France
Germany, Fed. Rep. [2] [4]
Grenada
India
Ireland
Italy
Japan
Kenya
Korea
Mexico
Monaco
Netherlands [5]
New Zealand
Norway [2]
Oman
Peru [2]
St. Kitts & Nevis
St. Lucia
St. Vincent & the Grenadines
Senegal
Seychelles
Solomon Is.
South Africa
Spain
Sweden
Switzerland
Union of Soviet Socialist Reps. [6]
United Kingdom
United States
Venezuela

Amendments to the Schedule:
June 7, 1949 (1 UST 506; TIAS 2092; 161 UNTS 100).
July 21, 1950 (2 UST 11; TIAS 2173; 161 UNTS 108).
July 27, 1951 (3 UST 2999; TIAS 2486; 177 UNTS 396).
June 6, 1952 (3 UST 5094; TIAS 2699; 181 UNTS 364).
June 26, 1953 (4 UST 2179; TIAS 2866; 252 UNTS 316).
July 23, 1954 (6 UST 645; TIAS 3198; 252 UNTS 324).
July 23, 1955 (7 UST 657; TIAS 3548; 252 UNTS 330).
July 20, 1956 (8 UST 69; TIAS 3739; 278 UNTS 278).
June 28, 1957 (8 UST 2203; TIAS 3944; 300 UNTS 376).
June 27, 1958 (10 UST 330; TIAS 4193; 337 UNTS 408).
July 1, 1959 (11 UST 32; TIAS 4404; 361 UNTS 272).
June 24, 1960 (13 UST 493; TIAS 5014; 435 UNTS 324).
June 23, 1961 (13 UST 497; TIAS 5015; 435 UNTS 328).
July 6, 1962 (14 UST 112; TIAS 5277; 495 UNTS 254).
July 5, 1963 (14 UST 1690; TIAS 5472; 495 UNTS 256).
June 26, 1964 (15 UST 2547; TIAS 5745; 586 UNTS 248).
July 2, 1965 (17 UST 35; TIAS 5953; 586 UNTS 252).
July 1, 1966 (17 UST 1640; TIAS 6120; 675 UNTS 384).
June 30, 1967 (18 UST 2391; TIAS 6345; 723 UNTS 280).
June 28, 1968 (19 UST 6030; TIAS 6562; 723 UNTS 282).
June 27, 1969 (20 UST 4063; TIAS 6794).

WHALING (Cont'd)

June 26, 1970 (21 UST 2460; TIAS 6985; 772 UNTS 442).
June 25, 1971 (23 UST 179; TIAS 7293).
June 30, 1972 (23 UST 2820; TIAS 7471).
June 29, 1973 (25 UST 2591; TIAS 7936).
June 28, 1974 (25 UST 2978; TIAS 7960).
June 27, 1975 (27 UST 1885; TIAS 8286).
June 25, 1976 (27 UST 4015; TIAS 8422).
June 24, 1977 (29 UST 1452; TIAS 8886).
December 7, 1977 (29 UST 2874; TIAS 8983).
June 30, 1978 (30 UST 1639; TIAS 9271).
December 20, 1978 (30 UST 2852; TIAS 9366).
July 13, 1979 (31 UST 4815; TIAS 9642).
July 26, 1980 (32 UST 4241; TIAS 9946).
July 25, 1981.
July 24, 1982.
July 23, 1983.
June 22, 1984.
July 19, 1985.
June 13, 1986.
June 26, 1987 (TIAS 11951).
June 3, 1988 (TIAS 11951).
June 16, 1989 (TIAS 11951).
July 6, 1990 (TIAS 11951).
May 31, 1991 (TIAS 11951).
July 3, 1992 (TIAS 11951).
May 14, 1993.

NOTES:
[1] With reservation.
[2] With statement.
[3] Applicable to Hong Kong. See note under CHINA in bilateral section.
[4] See note under GERMANY, FEDERAL REPUBLIC OF in bilateral section.
[5] Applicable to the Netherlands Antilles and Aruba.
[6] See note under UNION OF SOVIET SOCIALIST REPUBLICS in bilateral section.

WHEAT

Agricultural commodities agreement for the sale of wheat, with memorandum of understanding. Signed at Dar-es-Salaam February 18 and at Nairobi February 19 and 22 and March 4, 1966; entered into force March 4, 1966.
17 UST 628; TIAS 6010; 578 UNTS 57.
Parties:
East African Common Services Organization
Kenya
Tanzania
Uganda
United States

Wheat trade convention, 1986.[1] Done at London March 13, 1986; entered into force July 1, 1986; definitively for the United States January 27, 1988.
TIAS
Parties:
Algeria
Argentina
Australia
Austria
Barbados
Belgium
Bolivia
Brazil*
Canada
Cuba
Denmark
Ecuador
Egypt
El Salvador*
European Economic Community
Finland
France
Germany, Fed. Rep.[2]
Greece
Hungary
India
Iraq
Ireland
Israel
Italy
Japan
Korea
Luxembourg
Malta
Mauritius
Morocco*
Netherlands[3]
Norway
Pakistan
Panama*
Portugal
Russian Fed.
South Africa
Spain
Sweden
Switzerland
Tunisia
Turkey
Union of Soviet Socialist Reps.[4]
United Kingdom[5]
United States
Vatican City

Extension:
June 26, 1991.

NOTES:
* Provisional application.
[1] Part of the international wheat agreement, 1986. See also FOOD AID.
[2] See note under GERMANY, FEDERAL REPUBLIC OF in bilateral section.
[3] For the Kingdom in Europe.
[4] See note under UNION OF SOVIET SOCIALIST REPUBLICS in bilateral section.
[5] Applicable to British Virgin Islands, Gibraltar and St. Helena.

WHITE SLAVE TRAFFIC

(See TRAFFIC IN WOMEN AND CHILDREN)

WILDLIFE PRESERVATION

(See CONSERVATION; FISHERIES; POLAR BEARS; WHALING)

WINE

Agreement for the creation, in Paris of an International Wine Office.[1] Done at Paris November 29, 1924; entered into force October 29, 1927; for the United States July 24, 1984.
80 LNTS 293.
States which are parties:
Algeria
Argentina
Australia[2]
Austria
Belgium
Bulgaria
Chile
Cyprus
Czechoslovakia[3]
Denmark
Finland
France
Germany, Fed. Rep.[4]
Greece
Hungary
Israel
Italy
Luxembourg
Moldova
Morocco
Netherlands
Norway
Portugal
Romania
Slovak Rep.
South Africa
Spain
Switzerland
Syrian Arab Rep.
Tunisia
Ukraine
Union of Soviet Socialist Reps.[5]
United Kingdom
United States[2]
Uruguay
Yugoslavia[6]

NOTES:
[1] Renamed International Vine and Wine Office in 1958.
[2] With reservation.
[3] See note under CZECHOSLOVAKIA in bilateral section.
[4] See note under GERMANY, FEDERAL REPUBLIC OF in bilateral section.
[5] See note under UNION OF SOVIET SOCIALIST REPUBLICS in bilateral section.
[6] See note under YUGOSLAVIA in bilateral section.

WOMEN—POLITICAL RIGHTS

(See also NATIONALITY)

Inter-American convention on the granting of political rights to women. Done at Bogota May 2, 1948; entered into force March 17, 1949; for the United States May 24, 1976.
27 UST 3301; TIAS 8365.
States which are parties:
Argentina

WOMEN—POLITICAL RIGHTS (Cont'd)

Brazil
Canada
Chile
Colombia
Costa Rica
Cuba
Dominica
Dominican Rep.
Ecuador
El Salvador
Guatemala
Haiti
Honduras
Mexico
Nicaragua
Panama
Paraguay
Peru
Suriname
United States
Uruguay
Venezuela

Convention on the political rights of women.
Done at New York March 31, 1953; entered
into force July 7, 1954; for the United States
July 7, 1976.
27 UST 1909; TIAS 8289; 193 UNTS 135.
States which are parties:
Afghanistan
Albania [1][2]
Angola
Antigua & Barbuda [1]
Argentina [1]
Australia [1]
Austria [1]
Bahamas, The
Bangladesh [2]
Barbados
Belarus [1][2]
Belgium
Belize [3]
Bolivia
Bosnia-Herzegovina
Brazil
Brunei [3]
Bulgaria [2]
Burundi
Canada [1][4]
Central African Rep.
Chile
China (Taiwan) [4][5]
Colombia
Congo
Congo, Dem. Rep.
Costa Rica
Cote d'Ivoire
Croatia
Cuba
Cyprus
Czech Rep.
Denmark [1][4]
Dominica [3]
Dominican Rep.[4]
Ecuador [1]
Egypt
Ethiopia [4][6]
Fiji [1]
Finland [1]

Former Yugoslav Republic of Macedonia
France
Gabon
German Dem. Rep.[1][2][7]
Germany, Fed. Rep.[1][7]
Ghana
Greece
Grenada [3]
Guatemala [1]
Guinea
Haiti
Hong Kong [8]
Hungary [2]
Iceland
India [1]
Indonesia [1]
Ireland [1]
Israel [4]
Italy [1]
Jamaica
Japan
Jordan
Kazakhstan
Kiribati [3]
Korea [4]
Kyrgyz Rep.
Laos
Latvia
Lebanon
Lesotho [1]
Libya
Luxembourg
Madagascar
Malawi
Mali
Malta [1]
Mauritania
Mauritius [1]
Mexico
Moldova
Mongolia [2]
Morocco [1]
Nepal [1]
Netherlands [1]
New Zealand [1]
Nicaragua
Niger
Nigeria
Norway [4]
Pakistan [1][4]
Papua New Guinea
Paraguay
Peru
Philippines [4]
Poland [1][2]
Romania [1][2]
Russian Fed.
St. Kitts & Nevis [3]
St. Lucia [3]
St. Vincent & the Grenadines
Senegal
Seychelles [3]
Sierra Leone [1]
Slovak Rep. [1][2][4]
Slovenia
Solomon Is.[1]
Spain [2]
Suriname [3]
Swaziland [1]
Sweden [4]
Tajikistan
Tanzania
Thailand
Tonga [3]
Trinidad & Tobago

Tunisia [1]
Turkey
Turkmenistan
Tuvalu [3]
Uganda
Ukraine [1][2]
Union of Soviet Socialist Reps.[1][2][9]
United Kingdom [1][10]
United States
Uzbekistan
Venezuela [1]
Yemen (Aden) [11]
Yugoslavia [4][12]
Zambia
Zimbabwe

NOTES:
  [1] With reservation(s).
  [2] With declaration(s).
  [3] See under country heading in the bilateral
section for information concerning acceptance
of treaty obligations.
  [4] With statement(s).
  [5] See note under CHINA (Taiwan) in bilateral section.
  [6] See note under ETHIOPIA in bilateral section.
  [7] See note under GERMANY, FEDERAL
REPUBLIC OF in bilateral section.
  [8] CHINA is not a party to this treaty but has
made it applicable to Hong Kong.
  [9] See note under UNION OF SOVIET SO-
CIALIST REPUBLICS in bilateral section.
  [10] Extended to territories under the territorial sovereignty of the United Kingdom.
  [11] See note under YEMEN in bilateral section.
  [12] See note under YUGOSLAVIA in bilateral section.

WORLD BANK

(See under FINANCIAL INSTITUTIONS)

WORLD HEALTH ORGANIZATION

(See HEALTH)

WORLD HERITAGE

Convention concerning the protection of the
world cultural and natural heritage. Done at
Paris November 23, 1972; entered into force
December 17, 1975.
27 UST 37; TIAS 8226.
States which are parties:
Afghanistan
Albania
Algeria
Andorra
Angola
Antigua & Barbuda
Argentina
Armenia
Australia

WORLD HERITAGE
(Cont'd)

Austria
Azerbaijan
Bahrain
Bangladesh
Belarus
Belgium
Belize
Benin
Bolivia
Bosnia-Herzegovina
Botswana
Brazil [1]
Bulgaria [1]
Burkina Faso
Burma
Burundi
Cambodia
Cameroon
Canada
Cape Verde [2]
Central African Rep.
Chile
China [3]
Colombia
Comoros
Congo
Congo, Dem. Rep.
Costa Rica
Cote d'Ivoire
Croatia
Cuba
Cyprus
Czech Rep.
Denmark [1]
Dominica
Dominican Rep.
Ecuador
Egypt
El Salvador
Estonia
Ethiopia [4]
Fiji
Finland
Former Yugoslav Republic of Macedonia
France [1]
Gabon
Gambia
Georgia
German Dem. Rep. [5]
Germany, Fed. Rep. [5]
Ghana
Greece
Grenada
Guatemala
Guinea
Guyana
Haiti
Honduras
Hungary
Iceland
India
Indonesia
Iran
Iraq
Ireland
Israel
Italy
Jamaica
Japan

Jordan
Kazakhstan
Kenya
Kiribati
Korea, Dem. People's Rep.
Korea, Rep.
Kyrgyz Rep.
Laos
Latvia
Lebanon
Libya
Lithuania
Luxembourg
Madagascar
Malawi
Malaysia
Maldives
Mali
Malta
Mauritania
Mauritius
Mexico
Monaco
Mongolia
Morocco
Mozambique
Namibia
Nepal
Netherlands [6]
New Zealand [7]
Nicaragua
Niger
Nigeria
Norway [1]
Oman [1]
Pakistan
Panama
Papau New Guinea
Paraguay
Peru
Philippines
Poland
Portugal
Qatar
Romania
Russian Fed.
St. Kitts & Nevis
St. Lucia
San Marino
Saudi Arabia
Senegal
Seychelles
Slovak Rep.
Slovenia
Solomon Is.
South Africa [8]
Spain
Sri Lanka
Sudan
Suriname
Sweden
Switzerland
Syrian Arab Rep. [2]
Tajikistan
Tanzania
Thailand
Togo
Tunisia
Turkey
Turkmenistan
Uganda
Ukraine
Union of Soviet Socialist Reps. [9]
United Kingdom [10]
United States [1]

Uruguay
Uzbekistan
Vatican City
Venezuela
Vietnam
Yemen (Aden) [11]
Yemen (Sanaa) [11]
Yugoslavia [12]
Zambia
Zimbabwe

NOTES:
  [1] With reservation.
  [2] With statement.
  [3] Applicable to Hong Kong and Macao. See note under CHINA in bilateral section.
  [4] See note under ETHIOPIA in bilateral section.
  [5] See note under GERMANY, FEDERAL REPUBLIC OF in bilateral section.
  [6] For the Kingdom in Europe, the Netherlands Antilles and Aruba.
  [7] Extended to Cook Is. and Niue.
  [8] With declaration(s).
  [9] See note under UNION OF SOVIET SOCIALIST REPUBLICS in bilateral section.
  [10] Extended to the Isle of Man, Anguilla, Bailiwick of Jersey, Bermuda, British Virgin Is., Cayman Is., Falkland Is. and dependencies, Gibraltar, Montserrat, Pitcairn, Henderson, Ducie and Oeno Is., St. Helena and dependencies, Turks and Caicos Is., and United Kingdom Sovereign Base Areas of Akrotiri and Dhekelia on the Island of Cyprus.
  [11] See note under YEMEN in bilateral section.
  [12] See note under YUGOSLAVIA in bilateral section.

WORLD INTELLECTUAL PROPERTY ORGANIZATION

(See INTELLECTUAL PROPERTY)

WORLD METEOROLOGICAL ORGANIZATION

Convention of the World Meteorological Organization, with related protocol. Done at Washington October 11, 1947; entered into force March 23, 1950.
1 UST 281; TIAS 2052; 77 UNTS 143.
Members:
Afghanistan
Albania
Algeria
Angola
Antigua & Barbuda
Argentina
Armenia
Australia [1]
Austria
Azerbaijan
Bahamas, The
Bahrain

WORLD METEOROLOGICAL ORGANIZATION (Cont'd)

Bangladesh
Barbados
Belarus
Belgium
Belize
Benin
Bolivia
Bosnia-Herzegovina
Botswana
Brazil
British Caribbean Territories
Brunei
Bulgaria
Burkina Faso
Burma
Burundi
Cambodia
Cameroon
Canada
Cape Verde
Central African Rep.
Chad
Chile
China [2] [3]
Colombia
Comoros
Congo
Congo, Dem. Rep.
Cook Is.
Costa Rica
Cote d'Ivoire
Croatia
Cuba
Cyprus
Czech Rep.
Denmark [4]
Djibouti
Dominica
Dominican Rep.
Ecuador
Egypt
El Salvador
Eritrea
Estonia
Ethiopia [5]
Fiji
Finland
Former Yugoslav Republic of Macedonia
France [6]
French Polynesia
Gabon
Gambia, The
Georgia
German Dem. Rep. [7]
Germany, Fed. Rep. [7]
Ghana
Greece
Guatemala
Guinea
Guinea-Bissau
Guyana
Haiti
Honduras
Hong Kong
Hungary
Iceland
India

Indonesia
Iran
Iraq
Ireland
Israel
Italy
Jamaica
Japan
Jordan
Kazakhstan
Kenya
Korea, Dem. People's Rep.
Korea, Rep.
Kuwait
Kyrgyz Rep.
Laos
Latvia
Lebanon
Lesotho
Liberia
Libya
Lithuania
Luxembourg
Madagascar
Malawi
Malaysia
Maldives
Mali
Malta
Mauritania
Mauritius
Mexico
Micronesia
Moldova
Monaco
Mongolia
Morocco
Mozambique
Namibia
Nepal
Netherlands
Netherlands Antilles (Curacao) [8]
New Caledonia
New Zealand
Nicaragua
Niger
Nigeria
Niue
Norway
Oman
Pakistan
Panama
Papua New Guinea
Paraguay
Peru
Philippines
Poland
Portugal [9]
Qatar
Romania
Rwanda
St. Lucia
Sao Tome & Principe
Saudi Arabia
Senegal
Seychelles
Sierra Leone
Singapore
Slovak Rep.
Slovenia
Solomon Is.
Somalia
South Africa [10]
Spain [11]
Sri Lanka

Sudan
Suriname
Swaziland
Sweden
Switzerland
Syrian Arab Rep.
Tajikistan
Tanzania
Thailand
Togo
Tonga
Trinidad & Tobago
Tunisia
Turkey
Uganda
Ukraine
Union of Soviet Socialist Reps. [12]
United Arab Emirates
United Kingdom [13]
United States
Uruguay
Uzbekistan
Vanuatu
Venezuela
Vietnam, Socialist Rep.
Western Samoa
Yemen (Aden) [14]
Yemen (Sanaa) [14]
Yugoslavia [15]
Zambia
Zimbabwe

Amendments:
April 11, 1963 (16 UST 2069; TIAS 5947).
April 27, 1963 (16 UST 2073; TIAS 5947).
April 11 and 26, 1967 (18 UST 2795; TIAS 6364).
April 26, 1967 (18 UST 2800; TIAS 6364).
April 28–May 25, 1975 (26 UST 2580; TIAS 8175).

NOTES:
[1] Extended to Norfolk Is.
[2] With reservation.
[3] Applicable to Macao. See note under CHINA in bilateral section.
[4] Including Greenland.
[5] See note under ETHIOPIA in bilateral section.
[6] Extended to French Guiana, French West Indies, Reunion, Valleys of Andorra, St. Pierre and Miquelon.
[7] See note under GERMANY, FEDERAL REPUBLIC OF in bilateral section.
[8] Also applicable to Aruba.
[9] Extended to all Portuguese territories.
[10] Extended to Namibia.
[11] Extended to African territories and Valleys of Andorra.
[12] See note under UNION OF SOVIET SOCIALIST REPUBLICS in bilateral section.
[13] Extended to Falkland Is. and dependencies, Gibraltar.
[14] See note under YEMEN in bilateral section.
[15] See note under YUGOSLAVIA in bilateral section.

WORLD WAR II

(See also ARMISTICE AGREEMENTS; PEACE TREATIES; REPARATIONS; WAR CRIMINALS)

Agreement regarding Japan. Signed at Yalta February 11, 1945; entered into force February 11, 1945.
59 Stat. 1823; EAS 498; 3 Bevans 1022.

Protocol of the proceedings of the Crimea conference. Signed at Yalta February 11, 1945; entered into force February 11, 1945.
3 Bevans 1013; *Foreign Relations: The Conferences at Malta and Yalta*, 1945, p. 975 ff.

Protocol of the proceedings of the Berlin conference. Signed at Berlin August 2, 1945; entered into force August 2, 1945.
3 Bevans 1207; *Foreign Relations: Conference of Berlin (Potsdam) 1945*, Vol. II, p. 1478 ff.

Communique on the Moscow conference of Foreign Ministers. Signed at Moscow December 27, 1945; entered into force December 27, 1945.
60 Stat. 1899; TIAS 1555; 3 Bevans 1341; 20 UNTS 259.
States which are parties:
Union of Soviet Socialist Reps. [1]
United Kingdom
United States

NOTE:
[1] See note under UNION OF SOVIET SOCIALIST REPUBLICS in bilateral section.

APPENDIX

INTERNATIONAL
COPYRIGHT   RELATIONS
OF   THE   UNITED   STATES

APPENDIX

By virtue of Presidential proclamations, treaties, and conventions, the United States has established copyright relations with various other countries. This appendix is an attempt to present a complete and annotated list of those countries. Treaties and conventions on the subject of copyright relations are also included in the preceding pages under appropriate country or subject headings.

Proclamations by the President of the United States extending copyright protection upon compliance with the provisions of the United States copyright law, to the works of foreign authors prior to July 1, 1909, were issued pursuant to the Act of March 3, 1891 (26 Stat. 1106) and those issues subsequent to July 1, 1909, were issued under the provisions of the Act of March 4, 1909 (35 Stat. 1075), as amended by the Act of December 18, 1919 (41 Stat. 368) and the Act of September 25, 1941 (55 Stat. 732). The Act of March 4, 1909, as amended, became Title 17 of the United States Code when it was codified and enacted into positive law by the Act of July 30, 1947 (61 Stat. 652). Title 17 of the United States Code was completely revised by the Act of October 19, 1976, (Public Law 94–553, 90 Stat. 2541), which became fully effective on January 1, 1978. A number of the proclamations were preceded or accompanied by exchanges of diplomatic notes which served as the basis for their issuance. Such exchanges of notes, if printed in the official pamphlet series, may be included in the preceding pages under appropriate country and subject heading.

The period for compliance with the conditions and formalities prescribed by the copyright law was extended by proclamation with respect to certain works in the case of a number of countries because of the disruption or suspension of facilities essential for such compliance during World War I and World War II. In the case of World War I, this period for compliance was extended by proclamations issued under the Act of December 18, 1919 (41 Stat. 368) to fifteen months after the proclamation, as to works published after August 1, 1914, and before the proclamation of peace. In the case of World War II, this period was extended by proclamations issued under the Act of September 25, 1941 (55 Stat. 732) until such time as terminated or suspended, either by the terms of the proclamation itself or by the issuance of a subsequent proclamation. A number of the proclamations issued under the 1919 Act and all of the proclamations issued under the 1941 Act refer to rights previously granted.

It is important to note the provisions of section 104 of the Act of October 19, 1976, which, as amended by the Act of October 31, 1988 (Public Law 100–568, 102 Stat. 2853, 2855), read as follows:

"*Subject matter of copyright: National Origin*

(a) UNPUBLISHED WORKS.—The works specified by sections 102 and 103, while unpublished, are subject to protection under this title without regard to the nationality or domicile of the author.

(b) PUBLISHED WORKS.—The works specified by sections 102 and 103, when published, are subject to protection under this title if—

(1) on the date of first publication, one or more of the authors is a national or domiciliary of the United States, or is a national, domiciliary, or sovereign authority of a foreign nation that is a party to a copyright treaty to which the United States is also a party, or is a stateless person, wherever that person may be domiciled; or

(2) the work is first published in the United States or in a foreign nation that, on the date of first publication, is a party to the Universal Copyright Convention; or

(3) the work is first published by the United Nations or any of its specialized agencies, or by the Organization of American States; or

(4) the work is a Berne Convention work; or

(5) the work comes within the scope of a Presidential proclamation. Whenever the President finds that a particular foreign nation extends, to works by authors who are nationals or domiciliaries of the United States or to works that are first published in the United States, copyright protection on substantially the same basis as that on which the foreign nation extends protection to works of its own nationals and domiciliaries and works first published in that nation, the President may by proclamation extend protection under this title to works of which one or more of the authors is, on the date of first publication, a national, domiciliary, or sovereign authority of that nation, or which was first published in that nation. The President may revise, suspend, or revoke any such proclamation or impose any conditions or limitations on protection under that proclamation.

(c) EFFECT OF BERNE CONVENTION.—No right or interest in a work eligible for protection under this title may be claimed by virtue of, or in reliance upon, the provisions of the Berne Convention, or the adherence of the United States thereto. Any rights in a work eligible for protection under this title that derive from this title, other Federal or State statutes, or the common law, shall not be expanded or reduced by virtue of, or in reliance upon, the provisions of the Berne Convention, or the adherence of the United States thereto."

Also, the Act of October 19, 1976, specifies, in section 104 of the TRANSITIONAL AND SUPPLEMENTARY PROVISIONS thereof (90 Stat. 2541, 2599), that all proclamations issued by the President under the U.S. copyright law "as it existed on December 31, 1977, or under previous copyright statutes of the United States shall continue in force until terminated, suspended, or revised by the President."

KEY TO SYMBOLS

PROCLAMATIONS

P Proclamation issued pursuant to the Act of March 3, 1891, the Act of March 4, 1909, and as amended, or Title 17 of the United States Code.

Pm Proclamation including mechanical reproduction rights for musical works under the United States copyright law.

Px Proclamation providing an extension of time under the Act of December 18, 1919, for compliance with the conditions and formalities prescribed by the United States copyright law.

Pmx Proclamation specifically including provisions similar to those contained in both "Pm" and "Px" proclamations.

Pxx Proclamation providing an extension of time under the Act of September 25, 1941, for compliance with the conditions and formalities prescribed by the United States copyright law.

Po Proclamation specifically issued for the purpose of terminating a proclamation issued under the Act of September 25, 1941.

TREATIES AND CONVENTIONS

BAC Buenos Aires Convention. Convention on literary and artistic copyright between the United States and other American Republics, signed at the Fourth International Conference of American States at Buenos Aires August 11, 1910. U.S. ratification deposited on May 1, 1911. Convention proclaimed by the President of the United States on July 13, 1914.

Berne The Berne Convention for the Protection of Literary and Artistic Works of September 9, 1886, as revised at Paris on July 24, 1971. Appearing within parentheses is the latest Act[27] of the Convention to which the listed country is party. The Berne Convention, as revised at Paris on July 24, 1971, and amended on October 2, 1979, did not enter into force with respect to the United States until March 1, 1989.

MCC Mexico City Convention. Convention on literary and artistic copyrights signed at the Second International Conference of American States at Mexico City, January 27, 1902, effective June 30, 1908, to which the United States became a party, effective on that same date. As regards copyright relations with the United States, this convention is considered to have been superseded by adherence of the foreign country and the United States to the Buenos Aires Convention of August 11, 1910.

UCC Universal Copyright Convention. Done at Geneva September 6, 1952. Came into force on September 16, 1955. United States became a party, effective on that same date.

UCC rev. Universal Copyright Convention revised. Done at Paris July 24, 1971. Came into force on July 10, 1974. United States became a party, effective on that same date.

C Bilateral convention.

Cm Bilateral convention including provisions covering mechanical reproduction rights for musical works.

T Treaty relating in part to copyright.

Pg Convention for the Protection of Producers of Phonograms Against Unauthorized Duplication of Their Phonograms. Done at Geneva October 29, 1971. Entered into force with respect to the United States on March 10, 1974.

Pcss Convention Relating to the Distribution of Programme-Carrying Signals Transmitted by Satellite. Done at Brussels May 21, 1974. Entered into force with respect to the United States on March 7, 1985.

WTO   Member of the World Trade Organization, established pursuant to the Marrakesh Agreement of April 15, 1994, to implement the Uruguay Round Agreements. These Agreements affect, among other things, intangible property rights, including copyright and other intellectual property rights. The effective date of United States membership in the WTO is January 1, 1995. A country's membership in the World Trade Organization is effective as of the date indicated.

PROCLAMATIONS, TREATIES, AND CONVENTIONS ESTABLISHING COPYRIGHT RELATIONS BETWEEN THE UNITED STATES AND OTHER COUNTRIES

Country	Document	Date of Document	Effective Date for Party [28]	Reference
Albania	Berne (Paris)	July 24, 1971	Mar. 6, 1994	T. Doc. 99–27
Algeria	UCC	Sept. 6, 1952	Aug. 28, 1973	6 UST 2731
	UCC rev.	July 24, 1971	July 10, 1974	25 UST 1341
	Berne (Paris)	July 24, 1971	Apr. 19, 1998	T. Doc. 99–27
Andorra	UCC	Sept. 6, 1952	Sept. 16, 1955	6 UST 2731
Angola	WTO	Apr. 15, 1994	Nov. 23, 1996	33 ILM 15
Antigua and Barbuda	WTO	Apr. 15, 1994	Jan. 1, 1995	33 ILM 15
	Berne (Paris)	July 24, 1971	Mar. 17, 2000	T. Doc. 99–27
Argentina	Pm	Aug. 23, 1934	Aug. 23, 1934	49 Stat. 3413
	BAC	Aug. 11, 1910	Apr. 19, 1950	38 Stat. 1785
	UCC	Sept. 6, 1952	Feb. 13, 1958	6 UST 2731
	Berne (Paris)	July 24, 1971	Oct. 8, 2000	T. Doc. 99–27
	Pg [32]	Oct. 29, 1971	June 30, 1973	25 UST 309
	WTO	Apr. 15, 1994	Jan. 1, 1995	33 ILM 15
Armenia	Pcss	May 21, 1974	Dec. 13, 1993	T. Doc. 98–31
	Berne (Paris)	July 24, 1971	Oct. 19, 2000	T. Doc. 99–27
Australia [1]	Pm	Apr. 3, 1918	Mar. 15, 1918	40 Stat. 1764
	Pxx [2]	Dec. 29, 1949	Dec. 29, 1949	64 Stat. A385
	UCC	Sept. 6, 1952	May 1, 1969	6 UST 2731
	Pg	Oct. 29, 1971	June 22, 1974	25 UST 309
	UCC rev.	July 24, 1971	Feb. 28, 1978	25 UST 1341
	Berne (Paris)	July 24, 1971	Mar. 1, 1978	T. Doc. 99–27
	Pcss	May 21, 1974	Oct. 26, 1990	T. Doc. 98–31
	WTO	Apr. 15, 1994	Jan. 1, 1995	33 ILM 15
Austria [3]	P	Sept. 20, 1907	Sept. 20, 1907	35 Stat. 2155
	P	Apr. 9, 1910	July 1, 1909	36 Stat. 2685
	Px	May 25, 1922	May 25, 1922	42 Stat. 2273
	Pm	Mar. 11, 1925	Aug. 1, 1920	44 Stat. 2571
	Pxx	June 15, 1960	June 15, 1960	74 Stat. C69
	UCC	Sept. 6, 1952	July 2, 1957	6 UST 2731
	Pcss [31]	May 21, 1974	Aug. 6, 1982	T. Doc. 98–31
	UCC rev.	July 24, 1971	Aug. 14, 1982	25 UST 1341
	Pg	Oct. 29, 1971	Aug. 21, 1982	25 UST 309
	Berne (Paris)	July 24, 1971	Aug. 21, 1982	T. Doc. 99–27
	WTO	Apr. 15, 1994	Jan. 1, 1995	33 ILM 15
Azerbaijan	UCC	Sept. 6, 1952	May 27, 1973	6 UST 2731
	Berne (Paris)	July 24, 1971	June 4, 1999	T. Doc. 99–27
Bahamas, The	Berne (Brussels)	June 26, 1948	July 10, 1973	331 UNTS 217
	UCC	Sept. 6, 1952	Oct. 13, 1976	6 UST 2731
	UCC rev.	July 24, 1971	Dec. 27, 1976	25 UST 1341

(Footnote references appear at end of chart).

PROCLAMATIONS, TREATIES, AND CONVENTIONS ESTABLISHING COPYRIGHT RELATIONS BETWEEN THE UNITED STATES AND OTHER COUNTRIES (Cont'd)

Country	Document	Date of Document	Effective Date for Party [28]	Reference
Bahrain	WTO	Apr. 15, 1994	Jan. 1, 1995	33 ILM 15
	Berne (Paris)	July 24, 1971	Mar. 2, 1997	T. Doc. 99–27
Bangladesh	UCC	Sept. 6, 1952	Aug. 5, 1975	6 UST 2731
	UCC rev.	July 24, 1971	Aug. 5, 1975	25 UST 1341
	Berne (Paris)	July 24, 1971	May 4, 1999	T. Doc. 99–27
	WTO	Apr. 15, 1994	Jan. 1, 1995	33 ILM 15
Barbados	UCC	Sept. 6, 1952	June 18, 1983	6 UST 2731
	UCC rev.	July 24, 1971	June 18, 1983	25 UST 1341
	Pg	Oct. 29, 1971	July 29, 1983	25 UST 309
	Berne (Paris)	July 24, 1971	July 30, 1983	T. Doc. 99–27
	WTO	Apr. 15, 1994	Jan. 1, 1995	33 ILM 15
Belarus	UCC	Sept. 6, 1952	May 27, 1973	6 UST 2731
	Berne (Paris)	July 24, 1971	Dec. 12, 1997	T. Doc. 99–27
Belgium	P	July 1, 1891	July 1, 1891	27 Stat. 981
	P	Apr. 9, 1910	July 1, 1909	36 Stat. 2685
	Pm	June 14, 1911	July 1, 1909	37 Stat. 1688
	Berne (Brussels)	June 26, 1948	Aug. 1, 1951	331 UNTS 217
	UCC	Sept. 6, 1952	Aug. 31, 1960	6 UST 2731
	WTO	Apr. 15, 1994	Jan. 1, 1995	33 ILM 15
Belize	UCC [20]	Sept. 6, 1952	Dec. 1, 1982	6 UST 2731
	WTO	Apr. 15, 1994	Jan. 1, 1995	33 ILM 15
	Berne (Paris)	July 24, 1971	June 17, 2000	T. Doc. 99–27
Benin	Berne (Paris)	July 24, 1971	Mar. 12, 1975	T. Doc. 99–27
	WTO	Apr. 15, 1994	Feb. 22, 1996	33 ILM 15
Bolivia	BAC	Aug. 11, 1910	May 15, 1914	38 Stat. 1785
	UCC	Sept. 6, 1952	Mar. 22, 1990	6 UST 2731
	UCC rev.	July 24, 1971	Mar. 22, 1990	25 UST 1341
	Berne (Paris)	July 24, 1971	Nov. 4, 1993	T. Doc. 99–27
	WTO	Apr. 15, 1994	Sept. 13, 1995	33 ILM 15
Bosnia – Herzegovina	UCC	Sept. 6, 1952	May 11, 1966	6 UST 2731
	UCC rev.	July 24, 1971	July 10, 1974	25 UST 1341
	Berne (Paris)	July 24, 1971	Mar. 6, 1992	T. Doc. 99–27
	Pcss	May 21, 1974	Mar. 6, 1992	T. Doc. 98–31
Botswana	WTO	Apr. 15, 1994	May 31, 1995	33 ILM 15
	Berne (Paris)	July 24, 1971	Apr. 15, 1998	T. Doc. 99–27
Brazil	BAC	Aug. 11, 1910	Aug. 31, 1915	38 Stat. 1785
	Pm	Apr. 2, 1957	Apr. 2, 1957	8 UST 424
	UCC	Sept. 6, 1952	Jan. 13, 1960	6 UST 2731
	Berne (Paris)	July 24, 1971	Apr. 20, 1975	T. Doc. 99–27
	Pg	Oct. 29, 1971	Nov. 28, 1975	25 UST 309
	UCC rev.	July 24, 1971	Dec. 11, 1975	25 UST 1341
	WTO	Apr. 15, 1994	Jan. 1, 1995	33 ILM 15

(Footnote references appear at end of chart).

PROCLAMATIONS, TREATIES, AND CONVENTIONS ESTABLISHING COPYRIGHT RELATIONS BETWEEN THE UNITED STATES AND OTHER COUNTRIES (Cont'd)

Country	Document	Date of Document	Effective Date for Party [28]	Reference
Brunei	WTO	Apr. 15, 1994	Jan. 1, 1995	33 ILM 15
Bulgaria	Berne (Paris)	July 24, 1971	Dec. 4, 1974	T. Doc. 99–27
	UCC	Sept. 6, 1952	June 7, 1975	6 UST 2731
	UCC rev.	July 24, 1971	June 7, 1975	25 UST 1341
	Pg	Oct. 29, 1971	Sept. 6, 1995	25 UST 309
	WTO	Apr. 15, 1994	Dec. 1, 1996	33 ILM 15
Burkina Faso	Berne (Paris)	July 24, 1971	Jan. 24, 1976	T. Doc. 99–27
	Pg	Oct. 29, 1971	Jan. 30, 1988	25 UST 309
	WTO	Apr. 15, 1994	June 3, 1995	33 ILM 15
Burma	WTO	Apr. 15, 1994	Jan. 1, 1995	33 ILM 15
Burundi	WTO	Apr. 15, 1994	July 23, 1995	33 ILM 15
Cambodia [6]	UCC	Sept. 6, 1952	Sept. 16, 1955	6 UST 2731
Cameroon	UCC	Sept. 6, 1952	May 1, 1973	6 UST 2731
	UCC rev.	July 24, 1971	July 10, 1974	25 UST 1341
	Berne (Paris)	July 24, 1971	Oct. 10, 1974	T. Doc. 99–27
	WTO	Apr. 15, 1994	Dec. 13, 1995	33 ILM 15
Canada [1]	Pm	Dec. 27, 1923	Jan. 1, 1924	43 Stat. 1932
	Berne (Rome)	June 2, 1928	Apr. 10, 1928	123 LNTS 232
	UCC	Sept. 6, 1952	Aug. 10, 1962	6 UST 2731
	WTO	Apr. 15, 1994	Jan. 1, 1995	33 ILM 15
	Berne (Paris)	July 24, 1971	June 26, 1998	T. Doc. 99–27
Cape Verde	Berne (Paris)	July 24, 1971	July 7, 1997	T. Doc. 99–27
Central African Republic	Berne (Paris)	July 24, 1971	Sept. 3, 1977	T. Doc. 99–27
	WTO	Apr. 15, 1994	May 31, 1995	33 ILM 15
Chad	Berne (Brussels)	June 26, 1948	Nov. 25, 1971	331 UNTS 217
	WTO	Apr. 15, 1994	Oct. 19, 1996	33 ILM 15
Chile	P	May 25, 1896	May 25, 1896	29 Stat. 880
	P	Apr. 9, 1910	July 1, 1909	36 Stat. 2685
	Pm	Nov. 18, 1925	July 1, 1925	44 Stat. 2590
	BAC	Aug. 11, 1910	June 14, 1955	38 Stat. 1785
	UCC	Sept. 6, 1952	Sept. 16, 1955	6 UST 2731
	Berne (Paris)	July 24, 1971	July 10, 1975	T. Doc. 99–27
	Pg	Oct. 29, 1971	Mar. 24, 1977	25 UST 309
	WTO	Apr. 15, 1994	Jan. 1, 1995	33 ILM 15

(Footnote references appear at end of chart).

PROCLAMATIONS, TREATIES, AND CONVENTIONS ESTABLISHING COPYRIGHT RELATIONS BETWEEN THE UNITED STATES AND OTHER COUNTRIES (Cont'd)

Country	Document	Date of Document	Effective Date for Party [28]	Reference
China	T	Oct. 8, 1903	Jan. 13, 1904	33 Stat. 2208
	T	Nov. 4, 1946	Nov. 30, 1948	63 Stat. 1299
	P [4]	Mar. 17, 1992	Mar. 17, 1992	57 F.Reg 9647
	Berne (Paris)	July 24, 1971	Oct. 15, 1992	T. Doc. 99–27
	UCC	Sept. 6, 1952	Oct. 30, 1992	6 UST 2731
	UCC rev.	July 24, 1971	Oct. 30, 1992	25 UST 1341
	Pg	Oct. 29, 1971	Apr. 30, 1993	25 UST 309
Colombia	BAC	Aug. 11, 1910	Dec. 23, 1936	38 Stat. 1785
	UCC	Sept. 6, 1952	June 18, 1976	6 UST 2731
	UCC rev.	July 24, 1971	June 18, 1976	25 UST 1341
	Berne (Paris)	July 24, 1971	Mar. 7, 1988	T. Doc. 99–27
	Pg	Oct. 29, 1971	May 16, 1994	25 UST 309
	WTO	Apr. 15, 1994	Apr. 30, 1995	33 ILM 15
Congo	Berne (Paris)	July 24, 1971	Dec. 5, 1975	T. Doc. 99–27
	WTO	Apr. 15, 1994	Mar. 27, 1997	33 ILM 15
Congo, Democratic Republic of (formerly Zaire)	Berne (Paris)	July 24, 1971	Jan. 31, 1975	T. Doc. 99–27
	Pg	Oct. 29, 1971	Nov. 29, 1977	25 UST 309
	WTO	Apr. 15, 1994	Jan. 1, 1997	33 ILM 15
Costa Rica	P	Oct. 19, 1899	Oct. 19, 1899	31 Stat. 1955
	P	Apr. 9, 1910	July 1, 1909	36 Stat. 2685
	MCC	Jan. 27, 1902	June 30, 1908	35 Stat. 1934
	BAC	Aug. 11, 1910	Nov. 30, 1916	38 Stat. 1785
	UCC	Sept. 6, 1952	Sept. 16, 1955	6 UST 2731
	Berne (Paris)	July 24, 1971	June 10, 1978	T. Doc. 99–27
	UCC rev.	July 24, 1971	Mar. 7, 1980	25 UST 1341
	Pg	Oct. 29, 1971	June 17, 1982	25 UST 309
	WTO	Apr. 15, 1994	Jan. 1, 1995	33 ILM 15
	PCSS	May 21, 1974	June 25, 1999	T. Doc. 98–31
Cote d'Ivoire	Berne (Paris)	July 24, 1971	Oct. 10, 1974	T. Doc. 99–27
	WTO	Apr. 15, 1994	Jan. 1, 1995	33 ILM 15
Croatia	UCC	Sept. 6, 1952	May 11, 1966	6 UST 2731
	UCC rev.	July 24, 1971	July 10, 1974	25 UST 1341
	Berne (Paris)	July 24, 1971	Oct. 8, 1991	T. Doc. 99–27
	Pcss	May 21, 1974	Oct. 8, 1991	T. Doc. 98–31
	Pg	Oct. 29, 1971	Apr. 20, 2000	25 UST 309
Cuba	P	Nov. 17, 1903	Nov. 17, 1903	33 Stat. 2324
	P	Apr. 9, 1910	July 1, 1909	36 Stat. 2685
	Pm	Nov. 27, 1911	May 29, 1911	37 Stat. 1721
	UCC	Sept. 6, 1952	June 18, 1957	6 UST 2731
	WTO	Apr. 15, 1994	Apr. 20, 1995	33 ILM 15
	Berne (Paris)	July 24, 1971	Feb. 20, 1997	T. Doc. 99–27

(Footnote references appear at end of chart).

PROCLAMATIONS, TREATIES, AND CONVENTIONS ESTABLISHING COPYRIGHT RELATIONS BETWEEN THE UNITED STATES AND OTHER COUNTRIES (Cont'd)

Country	Document	Date of Document	Effective Date for Party [28]	Reference
Cyprus	Berne (Paris)	July 24, 1971	July 27, 1983	T. Doc. 99–27
	UCC	Sept. 6, 1952	Dec. 19, 1990	6 UST 2731
	UCC rev.	July 24, 1971	Dec. 19, 1990	25 UST 1341
	Pg	Oct. 29, 1971	Sept. 30, 1993	25 UST 309
	WTO	Apr. 15, 1994	July 30, 1995	33 ILM 15
Czech Republic [33]	UCC	Sept. 6, 1952	Jan. 6, 1960	6 UST 2731
	UCC rev.	July 24, 1971	Apr. 17, 1980	25 UST 1341
	Berne (Paris)	July 24, 1971	Jan. 1, 1993	T. Doc. 99–27
	Pg	Oct. 29, 1971	Jan. 1, 1993	25 UST 309
	WTO	Apr. 15, 1994	Jan. 1, 1995	33 ILM 15
Czechoslovakia [34] [35]	Pm	Apr. 27, 1927	Mar. 1, 1927	45 Stat. 2906
Danzig	Pm	Apr. 7, 1934	Apr. 7, 1934	48 Stat. 1737
Denmark [5]	P	May 8, 1893	May 8, 1893	28 Stat. 1219
	P	Apr. 9, 1910	July 1, 1909	36 Stat. 2685
	Pmx	Dec. 9, 1920	Dec. 9, 1920	41 Stat. 1810
	Pxx	Feb. 4, 1952	Feb. 4, 1952	66 Stat. C20
	UCC	Sept. 6, 1952	Feb. 9, 1962	6 UST 2731
	Pg	Oct. 29, 1971	Mar. 24, 1977	25 UST 309
	Berne (Paris)	July 24, 1971	June 30, 1979	T. Doc. 99–27
	UCC rev.	July 24, 1971	July 11, 1979	25 UST 1341
	WTO	Apr. 15, 1994	Jan. 1, 1995	33 ILM 15
Djibouti	WTO	Apr. 15, 1994	May 31, 1995	33 ILM 15
Dominica	WTO	Apr. 15, 1994	Jan. 1, 1995	33 ILM 15
	Berne (Paris)	July 24, 1971	Aug. 7, 1999	T. Doc. 99–27
Dominican Rep.	MCC	Jan. 27, 1902	June 30, 1908	35 Stat. 1934
	BAC	Aug. 11, 1910	Oct. 31, 1912	38 Stat. 1785
	UCC	Sept. 6, 1952	May 8, 1983	6 UST 2731
	UCC rev.	July 24, 1971	May 8, 1983	25 UST 1341
	WTO	Apr. 15, 1994	Mar. 9, 1995	33 ILM 15
	Berne (Paris)	July 24, 1971	Dec 24, 1997	T. Doc. 99–27
Ecuador	BAC	Aug. 11, 1910	Aug. 31, 1914	38 Stat. 1785
	UCC	Sept. 6, 1952	June 5, 1957	6 UST 2731
	Pg	Oct. 29, 1971	Sept. 14, 1974	25 UST 309
	UCC rev.	July 24, 1971	Sept. 6, 1991	25 UST 1341
	Berne (Paris)	July 24, 1971	Oct. 9, 1991	T. Doc. 99–27
	WTO	Apr. 15, 1994	Jan. 21, 1996	33 ILM 15
Egypt	Berne (Paris)	July 24, 1971	June 7, 1977	T. Doc. 99–27
	Pg	Oct. 29, 1971	Apr. 23, 1978	25 UST 309
	WTO	Apr. 15, 1994	June 30, 1995	33 ILM 15

(Footnote references appear at end of chart).

PROCLAMATIONS, TREATIES, AND CONVENTIONS ESTABLISHING COPYRIGHT RELATIONS BETWEEN THE UNITED STATES AND OTHER COUNTRIES (Cont'd)

Country	Document	Date of Document	Effective Date for Party[28]	Reference
El Salvador	MCC	Jan. 27, 1902	June 30, 1908	35 Stat. 1934
	Pg	Oct. 29, 1971	Feb. 9, 1979	25 UST 309
	UCC	Sept. 6, 1952	Mar. 29, 1979	6 UST 2731
	UCC rev.	July 24, 1971	Mar. 29, 1979	25 UST 1341
	Berne (Paris)	July 24, 1971	Feb. 19, 1994	T. Doc. 99–27
	WTO	Apr. 15, 1994	May 7, 1995	33 ILM 15
Equatorial Guinea	Berne (Paris)	July 24, 1971	June 26, 1997	T. Doc. 99–27
Estonia	Berne (Paris)	July 24, 1971	Oct. 26, 1994	T. Doc. 99–27
	Pg	Oct. 29, 1971	May 28, 2000	25 UST 309
	WTO	Apr. 15, 1994	Nov. 13, 1999	33 ILM 15
European Community	WTO	Apr. 15, 1994	Jan. 1, 1995	33 ILM 15
Fiji	UCC	Sept. 6, 1952	Mar. 13, 1972	6 UST 2731
	Berne (Brussels)	June 26, 1948	Dec. 1, 1971	331 UNTS 217
	Pg[32]	Oct. 29, 1971	Apr. 18, 1973	25 UST 309
	WTO	Apr. 15, 1994	Jan. 14, 1996	33 ILM 15
Finland	Pm	Dec. 15, 1928	Jan. 1, 1929	45 Stat. 2980
	Pxx	Nov. 16, 1951	Nov. 16, 1951	66 Stat. C5
	UCC	Sept. 6, 1952	Apr. 16, 1963	6 UST 2731
	Pg[32]	Oct. 29, 1971	Apr. 18, 1973	25 UST 309
	Berne (Paris)	July 24, 1971	Nov. 1, 1986	T. Doc. 99–27
	UCC rev.	July 24, 1971	Nov. 1, 1986	25 UST 1341
	WTO	Apr. 15, 1994	Jan. 1, 1995	33 ILM 15
Former Yugoslav Republic of Macedonia	Berne (Paris)	July 24, 1971	Sept. 8, 1991	T. Doc. 99–27
	Pcss	May 21, 1974	Nov. 17, 1991	T. Doc. 98–31
	UCC	Sept. 6, 1952	July 30, 1997	6 UST 2731
	UCC rev.	July 24, 1971	July 30, 1997	25 UST 1341
	Pg	Oct. 29, 1971	Mar. 2, 1998	25 UST 309
France[6]	P	July 1, 1891	July 1, 1891	27 Stat. 981
	P	Apr. 9, 1910	July 1, 1909	36 Stat. 2685
	Pm	May 24, 1918	May 24, 1918	40 Stat. 1784
	Pxx	Mar. 27, 1947	Mar. 27, 1947	61 Stat. 1057
	Po	May 26, 1950	Dec. 29, 1950	64 Stat. A413
	UCC	Sept. 6, 1952	Jan. 14, 1956	6 UST 2731
	Pg[32]	Oct. 29, 1971	Apr. 18, 1973	25 UST 309
	UCC rev.	July 24, 1971	July 10, 1974	25 UST 1341
	Berne (Paris)	July 24, 1971	Oct. 10, 1974	T. Doc. 99–27
	WTO	Apr. 15, 1994	Jan. 1, 1995	33 ILM 15
Gabon	Berne (Paris)	July 24, 1971	June 10, 1975	T. Doc. 99–27
	WTO	Apr. 15, 1994	Jan. 1, 1995	33 ILM 15
Gambia, The	Berne (Paris)	July 24, 1971	Mar. 7, 1993	T. Doc. 99–27
	WTO	Apr. 15, 1994	Oct. 23, 1996	33 ILM 15

(Footnote references appear at end of chart).

PROCLAMATIONS, TREATIES, AND CONVENTIONS ESTABLISHING COPYRIGHT RELATIONS BETWEEN THE UNITED STATES AND OTHER COUNTRIES (Cont'd)

Country	Document	Date of Document	Effective Date for Party [28]	Reference
Georgia	Berne (Paris)	July 24, 1971	May 16, 1995	T. Doc. 99–27
	WTO	Apr. 15, 1994	June 14, 2000	33 ILM 15
Germany [3 29 36]	P	Apr. 15, 1892	Apr. 15, 1892	27 Stat. 1021
	P	Apr. 9, 1910	July 1, 1909	36 Stat. 2685
	Pm	Dec. 8, 1910	Dec. 8, 1910	36 Stat. 2761
	Px	May 25, 1922	May 25, 1922	42 Stat. 2271
	UCC	Sept. 6, 1952	Sept. 16, 1955	6 UST 2731
	Pxx	July 12, 1967	July 12, 1967	18 UST 2369
	Pg	Oct. 29, 1971	May 18, 1974	25 UST 309
	UCC rev.	July 24, 1971	July 10, 1974	25 UST 1341
	Berne (Paris)	July 24, 1971	Oct. 10, 1974	T. Doc. 99–27
	Pcss [31]	May 21, 1974	Aug. 25, 1979	T. Doc. 98–31
	WTO	Apr. 15, 1994	Jan. 1, 1995	33 ILM 15
Ghana	UCC	Sept. 6, 1952	Aug. 22, 1962	6 UST 2731
	Berne (Paris)	July 24, 1971	Oct. 11, 1991	T. Doc. 99–27
	WTO	Apr. 15, 1994	Jan. 1, 1995	33 ILM 15
Greece	Pm	Feb. 23, 1932	Mar. 1, 1932	47 Stat. 2502
	UCC	Sept. 6, 1952	Aug. 24, 1963	6 UST 2731
	Berne (Paris)	July 24, 1971	Mar. 8, 1976	T. Doc. 99–27
	Pcss	May 21, 1974	Oct. 22, 1991	T. Doc. 98–31
	Pg	Oct. 29, 1971	Feb. 9, 1994	25 UST 309
	WTO	Apr. 15, 1994	Jan. 1, 1995	33 ILM 15
Grenada	WTO	Apr. 15, 1994	Feb. 22, 1996	33 ILM 15
	Berne (Paris)	July 24, 1971	Sept. 22, 1998	T. Doc. 99–27
Guatemala	MCC	Jan. 27, 1902	June 30, 1908	35 Stat. 1934
	BAC	Aug. 11, 1910	Mar. 28, 1913	38 Stat. 1785
	UCC	Sept. 6, 1952	Oct. 28, 1964	6 UST 2731
	Pg	Oct. 29, 1971	Feb. 1, 1977	25 UST 309
	WTO	Apr. 15, 1994	July 21, 1995	33 ILM 15
	Berne (Paris)	July 24, 1971	July 28, 1997	T. Doc. 99–27
Guinea	Berne (Paris)	July 24, 1971	Nov. 20, 1980	T. Doc. 99–27
	UCC	Sept. 6, 1952	Nov. 13, 1981	6 UST 2731
	UCC rev.	July 24, 1971	Nov. 13, 1981	25 UST 1341
	WTO	Apr. 15, 1994	Oct. 25, 1995	33 ILM 15
Guinea-Bissau	Berne (Paris)	July 24, 1971	July 22, 1991	T. Doc. 99–27
	WTO	Apr. 15, 1994	May 31, 1995	33 ILM 15
Guyana	Berne (Paris)	July 24, 1971	Oct. 25, 1994	T. Doc. 99–27
	WTO	Apr. 15, 1994	Jan. 1, 1995	33 ILM 15
Haiti	BAC	Aug. 11, 1910	Nov. 27, 1919	38 Stat. 1785
	UCC	Sept. 6, 1952	Sept. 16, 1955	6 UST 2731
	Berne (Paris)	July 24, 1971	Jan. 11, 1996	T. Doc. 99–27
	WTO	Apr. 15, 1994	Jan. 30, 1996	33 ILM 15

(Footnote references appear at end of chart).

PROCLAMATIONS, TREATIES, AND CONVENTIONS ESTABLISHING COPYRIGHT RELATIONS BETWEEN THE UNITED STATES AND OTHER COUNTRIES (Cont'd)

Country	Document	Date of Document	Effective Date for Party [28]	Reference
Holy See (See entry under Vatican City)				
Honduras	MCC	Jan. 27, 1902	June 30, 1908	35 Stat. 1934
	BAC	Aug. 11, 1910	Apr. 27, 1914	38 Stat. 1785
	Berne (Paris)	July 24, 1971	Jan. 25, 1990	T. Doc. 99–27
	Pg	Oct. 29, 1971	Mar. 6, 1990	25 UST 309
	WTO	Apr. 15, 1994	Jan. 1, 1995	33 ILM 15
Hong Kong	WTO	Apr. 15, 1994	Jan. 1, 1995	33 ILM 15
Hungary [3]	Cm [7]	Jan. 30, 1912	Oct. 16, 1912	37 Stat. 1631
	Px	June 3, 1922	June 3, 1922	42 Stat. 2277
	T [8][9]	Feb. 10, 1947	Sept. 15, 1947	61 Stat. 2065
	UCC	Sept. 6, 1952	Jan. 23, 1971	6 UST 2731
	UCC rev.	July 24, 1971	July 10, 1974	25 UST 1341
	Berne (Paris)	July 24, 1971	Oct. 10, 1974	T. Doc. 99–27
	Pg	Oct. 29, 1971	May 28, 1975	25 UST 309
	WTO	Apr. 15, 1994	Jan. 1, 1995	33 ILM 15
Iceland	Berne (Rome)	June 2, 1928	Sept. 7, 1947	123 LNTS 232
	UCC	Sept. 6, 1952	Dec. 18, 1956	6 UST 2731
	WTO	Apr. 15, 1994	Jan. 1, 1995	33 ILM 15
India [1][10]	Pm	Oct. 21, 1954	Aug. 15, 1947	5 UST 2529
	UCC	Sept. 6, 1952	Jan. 21, 1958	6 UST 2731
	Pg	Oct. 29, 1971	Feb. 12, 1975	25 UST 309
	Berne (Paris)	July 24, 1971	May 6, 1984	T. Doc. 99–27
	UCC rev.	July 24, 1971	Apr. 7, 1988	25 UST 1341
	WTO	Apr. 15, 1994	Jan. 1, 1995	33 ILM 15
Indonesia	P	July 31, 1989	Aug. 1, 1989	103 Stat. 3069
	WTO	Apr. 15, 1994	Jan. 1, 1995	33 ILM 15
	Berne (Paris)	July 24, 1971	Sept. 5, 1997	T. Doc. 99–27
Ireland [1]	Pm [11]	Sept. 28, 1929	Oct. 1, 1929	46 Stat. 3005
	UCC	Sept. 6, 1952	Jan. 20, 1959	6 UST 2731
	Berne (Brussels)	June 26, 1948	July 5, 1959	331 UNTS 217
	WTO	Apr. 15, 1994	Jan. 1, 1995	33 ILM 15
Israel [12]	Pm	May 4, 1950	May 15, 1948	64 Stat. A402
	Berne (Brussels)	June 26, 1948	Aug. 1, 1951	331 UNTS 217
	UCC	Sept. 6, 1952	Sept. 16, 1955	6 UST 2731
	Pg	Oct. 29, 1971	May 1, 1978	25 UST 309
	WTO	Apr. 15, 1994	Apr. 21, 1995	33 ILM 15

(Footnote references appear at end of chart).

PROCLAMATIONS, TREATIES, AND CONVENTIONS ESTABLISHING COPYRIGHT RELATIONS BETWEEN THE UNITED STATES AND OTHER COUNTRIES (Cont'd)

Country	Document	Date of Document	Effective Date for Party [28]	Reference
Italy	P [13]	Oct. 31, 1892	Oct. 31, 1892	27 Stat. 1043
	P	Apr. 9, 1910	July 1, 1909	36 Stat. 2685
	Pm [13]	May 1, 1915	May 1, 1915	39 Stat. 1725
	Px	June 3, 1922	June 3, 1922	42 Stat. 2276
	T [9] [14]	Feb. 10, 1947	Sept. 15, 1947	61 Stat. 1245
	Pxx	Dec. 12, 1951	Dec. 12, 1951	66 Stat. C13
	UCC	Sept. 6, 1952	Jan. 24, 1957	6 UST 2731
	Pg	Oct. 29, 1971	Mar. 24, 1977	25 UST 309
	Berne (Paris)	July 24, 1971	Nov. 14, 1979	T. Doc. 99–27
	UCC rev.	July 24, 1971	Jan. 25, 1980	25 UST 1341
	Pcss [31]	May 21, 1974	July 7, 1981	T. Doc. 98–31
	WTO	Apr. 15, 1994	Jan. 1, 1995	33 ILM 15
Jamaica	Berne (Paris)	July 24, 1971	Jan. 1, 1994	T. Doc. 99–27
	Pg	Oct. 29, 1971	Jan. 11, 1994	25 UST 309
	WTO	Apr. 15, 1994	Mar. 9, 1995	33 ILM 15
	Pcss	May 21, 1974	Jan. 12, 2000	T. Doc. 98–31
Japan	C [15]	Nov. 10, 1905	May 10, 1906	34 Stat. 2890
	C [16]	May 19, 1908	Aug. 6, 1908	35 Stat. 2044
	T [17]	Sept. 8, 1951	Apr. 28, 1952	3 UST 3169
	Pm [18]	Nov. 10, 1953	Apr. 28, 1952	5 UST 118
	UCC	Sept. 6, 1952	Apr. 28, 1956	6 UST 2731
	Berne (Paris)	July 24, 1971	Apr. 24, 1975	T. Doc. 99–27
	UCC rev.	July 24, 1971	Oct. 21, 1977	25 UST 1341
	Pg	Oct. 29, 1971	Oct. 14, 1978	25 UST 309
	WTO	Apr. 15, 1994	Jan. 1, 1995	33 ILM 15
Jordan	Berne (Paris)	July 24, 1971	July 28, 1999	T. Doc. 99–27
	WTO	Apr. 15, 1994	Apr. 11, 2000	33 ILM 15
Kazakhstan	UCC	Sept. 6, 1952	May 27, 1973	6 UST 2731
	Berne (Paris)	July 24, 1971	Apr. 12, 1999	T. Doc. 99–27
Kenya	UCC	Sept. 6, 1952	Sept. 7, 1966	6 UST 2731
	UCC rev.	July 24, 1971	July 10, 1974	25 UST 1341
	Pg	Oct. 29, 1971	Apr. 21, 1976	25 UST 309
	Pcss [31]	May 21, 1974	Aug. 25, 1979	T. Doc. 98–31
	Berne (Paris)	July 24, 1971	June 11, 1993	T. Doc. 99–27
	WTO	Apr. 15, 1994	Jan. 1, 1995	33 ILM 15
Korea	C [19]	May 19, 1908	Aug. 6, 1908	35 Stat. 2041
Korea, Republic of	UCC	Sept. 6, 1952	Oct. 1, 1987	6 UST 2731
	UCC rev.	July 24, 1971	Oct. 1, 1987	25 UST 1341
	Pg	Oct. 29, 1971	Oct. 10, 1987	25 UST 309
	WTO	Apr. 15, 1994	Jan. 1, 1995	33 ILM 15
	Berne (Paris)	July 24, 1971	Aug. 21, 1996	T. Doc. 99–27
Kuwait	WTO	Apr. 15, 1994	Jan. 1, 1995	33 ILM 15

(Footnote references appear at end of chart).

PROCLAMATIONS, TREATIES, AND CONVENTIONS ESTABLISHING COPYRIGHT RELATIONS BETWEEN THE UNITED STATES AND OTHER COUNTRIES (Cont'd)

Country	Document	Date of Document	Effective Date for Party [28]	Reference
Kyrgyz Rep.	WTO	Apr. 15, 1994	Dec. 20, 1998	33 ILM 15
	Berne (Paris)	July 24, 1971	July 8, 1999	T. Doc. 99–27
Laos [6]	UCC	Sept. 6, 1952	Sept. 16, 1955	6 UST 2731
Latvia	Berne (Paris)	July 24, 1971	Aug. 11, 1995	T. Doc. 99–27
	Pg	Oct. 29, 1971	Aug. 23, 1997	25 UST 309
	WTO	Apr. 15, 1994	Feb. 10, 1999	33 ILM 15
Lebanon	Berne (Rome)	June 2, 1928	Sept. 30, 1947	123 LNTS 232
	UCC	Sept. 6, 1952	Oct. 17, 1959	6 UST 2731
Lesotho	Berne (Paris)	July 24, 1971	Sept. 28, 1989	T. Doc. 99–27
	WTO	Apr. 15, 1994	May 31, 1995	33 ILM 15
Liberia	UCC	Sept. 6, 1952	July 27, 1956	6 UST 2731
	Berne (Paris)	July 24, 1971	Mar. 8, 1989	T. Doc. 99–27
Libya	Berne (Paris)	July 24, 1971	Sept. 28, 1976	T. Doc. 99–27
Liechtenstein	Berne (Brussels)	June 26, 1948	Aug. 1, 1951	331 UNTS 217
	UCC	Sept. 6, 1952	Jan. 22, 1959	6 UST 2731
	WTO	Apr. 15, 1994	Sept. 1, 1995	33 ILM 15
	UCC rev.	July 24, 1971	Nov. 11, 1999	25 USt 1341
	Pg	Oct. 29, 1971	Oct. 12, 1999	25 UST 309
Lithuania	Berne (Paris)	July 24, 1971	Dec. 14, 1994	T. Doc 99–27
Luxembourg	P	June 29, 1910	June 29, 1910	36 Stat. 2716
	Pm	June 14, 1911	June 29, 1910	37 Stat. 1689
	UCC	Sept. 6, 1952	Oct. 15, 1955	6 UST 2731
	Berne (Paris)	July 24, 1971	Apr. 20, 1975	T. Doc. 99–27
	Pg	Oct. 29, 1971	Mar. 8, 1976	25 UST 309
	WTO	Apr. 15, 1994	Jan. 1, 1995	33 ILM 15
Macao	WTO	Apr. 15, 1994	Jan. 1, 1995	33 ILM 15
Madagascar	Berne (Brussels)	June 26, 1948	Jan. 1, 1966	331 UNTS 217
	WTO	Apr. 15, 1994	Nov. 17, 1995	33 ILM 15
Malawi	UCC	Sept. 6, 1952	Oct. 26, 1965	6 UST 2731
	Berne (Paris)	July 24, 1971	Oct. 12, 1991	T. Doc. 99–27
	WTO	Apr. 15, 1994	May 31, 1995	33 ILM 15
Malaysia	Berne (Paris)	July 24, 1971	Oct. 1, 1990	T. Doc. 99–27
	WTO	Apr. 15, 1994	Jan. 1, 1995	33 ILM 15
Maldives	WTO	Apr. 15, 1994	May 31, 1995	33 ILM 15
Mali	Berne (Paris)	July 24, 1971	Dec. 5, 1977	T. Doc. 99–27
	WTO	Apr. 15, 1994	May 31, 1995	33 ILM 15

(Footnote references appear at end of chart).

PROCLAMATIONS, TREATIES, AND CONVENTIONS ESTABLISHING COPYRIGHT RELATIONS BETWEEN THE UNITED STATES AND OTHER COUNTRIES (Cont'd)

Country	Document	Date of Document	Effective Date for Party [28]	Reference
Malta	Berne (Rome)	June 2, 1928	Sept. 21, 1964	123 LNTS 232
	UCC	Sept. 6, 1952	Nov. 19, 1968	6 UST 2731
	WTO	Apr. 15, 1994	Jan. 1, 1995	33 ILM 15
Mauritania	Berne (Paris)	July 24, 1971	Feb. 6, 1973	T. Doc. 99–27
	WTO	Apr. 15, 1994	May 31, 1995	33 ILM 15
Mauritius	UCC	Sept. 6, 1952	Mar. 12, 1968	6 UST 2731
	Berne (Paris)	July 24, 1971	May 10, 1989	T. Doc. 99–27
	WTO	Apr. 15, 1994	Jan. 1, 1995	33 ILM 15
Mexico	P	Feb. 27, 1896	Feb. 27, 1896	29 Stat. 877
	P	Apr. 9, 1910	July 1, 1909	36 Stat. 2685
	UCC	Sept. 6, 1952	May 12, 1957	6 UST 2731
	BAC	Aug. 11, 1910	Apr. 24, 1964	38 Stat. 1785
	Pg [32]	Oct. 29, 1971	Dec. 21, 1973	25 UST 309
	Berne (Paris)	July 24, 1971	Dec. 17, 1974	T. Doc. 99–27
	UCC rev.	July 24, 1971	Oct. 31, 1975	25 UST 1341
	Pcss [31]	May 21, 1974	Aug. 25, 1979	T. Doc. 98–31
	WTO	Apr. 15, 1994	Jan. 1, 1995	33 ILM 15
Moldova	Berne (Paris)	July 24, 1971	Nov. 2, 1995	T. Doc 99–27
	UCC	Sept. 6, 1952	July 18, 1997	6 UST 2731
	Pg	Oct. 29, 1971	July 17, 2000	25 UST 309
Monaco	Pm	Oct. 15, 1952	Oct. 15, 1952	67 Stat. C16
	UCC	Sept. 6, 1952	Sept. 16, 1955	6 UST 2731
	Berne (Paris)	July 24, 1971	Nov. 23, 1974	T. Doc. 99–27
	Pg	Oct. 29, 1971	Dec. 2, 1974	25 UST 309
	UCC rev.	July 24, 1971	Dec. 13, 1974	25 UST 1341
	WTO	Apr. 15, 1994	Jan. 29, 1997	33 ILM 15
Mongolia	Berne (Paris)	July 24, 1971	Mar. 12, 1998	T. Doc. 99–27
	WTO	Apr. 15, 1994	Jan. 29, 1997	33 ILM 15
Morocco	UCC	Sept. 6, 1952	May 8, 1972	6 UST 2731
	UCC rev.	July 24, 1971	Jan. 28, 1976	25 UST 1341
	Pcss [31]	May 21, 1974	June 30, 1983	T. Doc. 98–31
	Berne (Paris)	July 24, 1971	May 17, 1987	T. Doc. 99–27
	WTO	Apr. 15, 1994	Jan. 1, 1995	33 ILM 15
Mozambique	WTO	Apr. 15, 1994	Aug. 26, 1995	33 ILM 15
Namibia	Berne (Paris)	July 24, 1971	Mar. 21, 1990	T. Doc. 99–27
	WTO	Apr. 15, 1994	Jan. 1, 1995	33 ILM 15

(Footnote references appear at end of chart).

PROCLAMATIONS, TREATIES, AND CONVENTIONS ESTABLISHING COPYRIGHT RELATIONS BETWEEN THE UNITED STATES AND OTHER COUNTRIES (Cont'd)

Country	Document	Date of Document	Effective Date for Party[28]	Reference
Netherlands and Possessions	P	Nov. 20, 1899	Nov. 20, 1899	31 Stat. 1961
	P	Apr. 9, 1910	July 1, 1909	36 Stat. 2685
	Pm	Feb. 26, 1923	Oct. 2, 1922	42 Stat. 2297
	UCC	Sept. 6, 1952	June 22, 1967	6 UST 2731
	UCC rev.	July 24, 1971	Nov. 30, 1985	25 UST 1341
	Berne (Paris)	July 24, 1971	Jan. 30, 1986	T. Doc. 99–27
	Pg	Oct. 29, 1971	Oct. 12, 1993	25 UST 309
	WTO	Apr. 15, 1994	Jan 1, 1995	33 ILM 15
New Zealand[1]	Pm	Feb. 9, 1917	Dec. 1, 1916	39 Stat. 1815
	Px	May 25, 1922	May 25, 1922	42 Stat. 2274
	Pxx	Apr. 24, 1947	Apr. 24, 1947	61 Stat. 1065
	Berne (Rome)	June 2, 1928	Dec. 4, 1947	123 LNTS 232
	Po	May 26, 1950	Dec. 29, 1950	64 Stat. A414
	UCC	Sept. 6, 1952	Sept. 11, 1964	6 UST 2731
	Pg	Oct. 29, 1971	Aug. 13, 1976	25 UST 309
	WTO	Apr. 15, 1994	Jan. 1, 1995	33 ILM 15
Nicaragua	MCC	Jan. 27, 1902	June 30, 1908	35 Stat. 1934
	BAC	Aug. 11, 1910	Dec. 15, 1913	38 Stat. 1785
	UCC	Sept. 6, 1952	Aug. 16, 1961	6 UST 2731
	Pcss[31]	May 21, 1974	Aug. 25, 1979	T. Doc. 98–31
	WTO	Apr. 15, 1994	Sept. 3, 1995	33 ILM 15
	Berne (Paris)	July 24, 1971	Aug. 23, 2000	T. Doc. 99–27
Niger	Berne (Paris)	July 24, 1971	May 21, 1975	T. Doc. 99–27
	UCC	Sept. 6, 1952	May 15, 1989	6 UST 2731
	UCC rev.	July 24, 1971	May 15, 1989	25 UST 1341
	WTO	Apr. 15, 1994	Dec. 13, 1996	33 ILM 15
Nigeria	UCC	Sept. 6, 1952	Feb. 14, 1962	6 UST 2731
	Berne (Paris)	July 24, 1971	Sept. 14, 1993	T. Doc. 99–27
	WTO	Apr. 15, 1994	Jan. 1, 1995	33 ILM 15
Norway	P	July 1, 1905	July 1, 1905	34 Stat. 3111
	P	Apr. 9, 1910	July 1, 1909	36 Stat. 2685
	Pm	June 14, 1911	Sept. 9, 1910	37 Stat. 1687
	UCC	Sept. 6, 1952	Jan. 23, 1963	6 UST 2731
	Berne (Paris)	July 24, 1971	Oct. 11, 1995	T. Doc. 99–27
	UCC rev.	July 24, 1971	Aug. 7, 1974	25 UST 1341
	Pg	Oct. 29, 1971	Aug. 1, 1978	25 UST 309
	WTO	Apr. 15, 1994	Jan. 1, 1995	33 ILM 15
Oman	Berne (Paris)	July 24, 1971	July 14, 1999	T. Doc. 99–27
Pakistan[1]	Berne (Rome)	June 2, 1928	July 5, 1948	123 LNTS 232
	UCC	Sept. 6, 1952	Sept. 16, 1955	6 UST 2731
	WTO	Apr. 15, 1994	Jan. 1, 1995	33 ILM 15

(Footnote references appear at end of chart).

PROCLAMATIONS, TREATIES, AND CONVENTIONS ESTABLISHING COPYRIGHT RELATIONS BETWEEN THE UNITED STATES AND OTHER COUNTRIES (Cont'd)

Country	Document	Date of Document	Effective Date for Party [28]	Reference
Palestine (excluding Trans-Jordan)	Pm	Sept. 29, 1933	Oct. 1, 1933	48 Stat. 1713
	Pxx [12]	Mar. 10, 1944	Mar. 10, 1944	58 Stat. 1129
	Po [12]	May 26, 1950	Dec. 29, 1950	64 Stat. A412
Panama	BAC	Aug. 11, 1910	Nov. 25, 1913	38 Stat. 1785
	UCC	Sept. 6, 1952	Oct. 17, 1962	6 UST 2731
	Pg	Oct. 29, 1971	June 29, 1974	25 UST 309
	UCC rev.	July 24, 1971	Sept. 3, 1980	25 UST 1341
	Pcss	May 21, 1974	Sept. 25, 1985	T. Doc. 98–31
	Berne (Paris)	July 24, 1971	June 8, 1996	T. Doc. 99–27
	WTO	Apr. 15, 1994	Sept. 6, 1997	33 ILM 15
Papua New Guinea	WTO	Apr. 15, 1994	June 9, 1996	33 ILM 15
Paraguay	BAC	Aug. 11, 1910	Sept. 20, 1917	38 Stat. 1785
	UCC	Sept. 6, 1952	Mar. 11, 1962	6 UST 2731
	Pg	Oct. 29, 1971	Feb. 13, 1979	25 UST 309
	Berne (Paris)	July 24, 1971	Jan. 2, 1992	T. Doc. 99–27
	WTO	Apr. 15, 1994	Jan. 1, 1995	33 ILM 15
Peru	BAC	Aug. 11, 1910	Apr. 30, 1920	38 Stat. 1785
	UCC	Sept. 6, 1952	Oct. 16, 1963	6 UST 2731
	UCC rev.	July 24, 1971	July 22, 1985	25 UST 1341
	Pcss	May 21, 1974	Aug. 7, 1985	T. Doc. 98–31
	Pg	Oct. 29, 1971	Aug. 24, 1985	25 UST 309
	Berne (Paris)	July 24, 1971	Aug. 20, 1988	T. Doc. 99–27
	WTO	Apr. 15, 1994	Jan. 1, 1995	33 ILM 15
Philippines	Pm	Oct. 21, 1948	Oct. 21, 1948	62 Stat. 1568
	UCC [21]	Sept. 6, 1952	Nov. 19, 1955	6 UST 2731
	WTO	Apr. 15, 1994	Jan. 1, 1995	33 ILM 15
	Berne (Paris)	July 24, 1971	June 18, 1997	T. Doc. 99–27
Poland	Pm	Feb. 14, 1927	Feb. 16, 1927	44 Stat. 2634
	UCC	Sept. 6, 1952	Mar. 9, 1977	6 UST 2731
	UCC rev.	July 24, 1971	Mar. 9, 1977	25 UST 1341
	Berne (Paris)	July 24, 1971	Oct. 22, 1994	T. Doc. 99–27
	WTO	Apr. 15, 1994	July 1, 1995	33 ILM 15
Portugal	P	July 20, 1893	July 20, 1893	28 Stat. 1222
	P	Apr. 9, 1910	July 1, 1909	36 Stat. 2685
	UCC	Sept. 6, 1952	Dec. 25, 1956	6 UST 2731
	Berne (Paris)	July 24, 1971	Jan. 12, 1979	T. Doc. 99–27
	UCC rev.	July 24, 1971	July 30, 1981	25 UST 1341
	WTO	Apr. 15, 1994	Jan. 1, 1995	33 ILM 15
	Pcss	May 21, 1974	Mar. 11, 1996	T. Doc. 98–31
Qatar	WTO	Apr. 15, 1994	Jan. 13, 1996	33 ILM 15
	Berne (Paris)	July 24, 1971	July 5, 2000	T. Doc. 99–27

(Footnote references appear at end of chart).

PROCLAMATIONS, TREATIES, AND CONVENTIONS ESTABLISHING COPYRIGHT RELATIONS BETWEEN THE UNITED STATES AND OTHER COUNTRIES (Cont'd)

Country	Document	Date of Document	Effective Date for Party [28]	Reference
Romania	Pm [22]	May 14, 1928	May 14, 1928	45 Stat. 2949
	T⁹ [23]	Feb. 10, 1947	Sept. 15, 1947	61 Stat. 1757
	WTO	Apr. 15, 1994	Jan. 1, 1995	33 ILM 15
	Berne (Paris)	July 24, 1971	Sept. 9, 1998	T. Doc. 99–27
	Pg	Oct. 29, 1971	Oct. 1, 1998	25 UST 309
Russian Federation	UCC	Sept. 6, 1952	May 27, 1973	6 UST 2731
	Pcss [30]	May 21, 1974	Dec. 25, 1991	T. Doc. 98–31
	UCC rev.	July 24, 1971	Mar. 9, 1995	25 UST 1341
	Berne (Paris)	July 24, 1971	Mar. 13, 1995	T. Doc. 99–27
	Pg	Oct. 29, 1971	Mar. 13, 1995	25 UST 309
Rwanda	Berne (Paris)	July 24, 1971	Mar. 1, 1984	T. Doc. 99–27
	UCC	Sept. 6, 1952	Nov. 10, 1989	6 UST 2731
	UCC rev.	July 24, 1971	Nov. 10, 1989	25 UST 1341
	WTO	Apr. 15, 1994	May 22, 1996	33 ILM 15
St. Kitts and Nevis	Berne (Paris)	July 24, 1971	Apr. 9, 1995	T. Doc. 99–27
	WTO	Apr. 15, 1994	Feb. 21, 1996	33 ILM 15
Saint Lucia	Berne (Paris)	July 24, 1971	Aug. 24, 1993	T. Doc. 99–27
	WTO	Apr. 15, 1994	Jan. 1, 1995	33 ILM 15
Saint Vincent and the Grenadines	UCC	Sept. 6, 1952	Apr. 22, 1985	6 UST 2731
	UCC rev.	July 24, 1971	Apr. 22, 1985	25 UST 1341
	WTO	Apr. 15, 1994	Jan. 1, 1995	33 ILM 15
	Berne (Paris)	July 24, 1971	Aug. 29, 1995	T. Doc. 99–27
Saudi Arabia	UCC	Sept. 6, 1952	July 13, 1994	6 UST 2731
	UCC rev.	July 24, 1971	July 13, 1994	25 UST 1341
Senegal	UCC	Sept. 6, 1952	July 9, 1974	6 UST 2731
	UCC rev.	July 24, 1971	July 10, 1974	25 UST 1341
	Berne (Paris)	July 24, 1971	Aug. 12, 1975	T. Doc. 99–27
	WTO	Apr. 15, 1994	Jan. 1, 1995	33 ILM 15
Sierra Leone	WTO	Apr. 15, 1994	July 23, 1995	33 ILM 15
Singapore	P	May 18, 1987	May 18, 1987	101 Stat. 2134
	WTO	Apr. 15, 1994	Jan. 1, 1995	33 ILM 15
	Berne (Paris)	July 24, 1971	Dec. 21, 1998	T. Doc. 99–27
Slovakia [37]	UCC	Sept. 6, 1952	Jan. 6, 1960	6 UST 2731
	UCC rev.	July 24, 1971	Apr. 17, 1980	25 UST 1341
	Berne (Paris)	July 24, 1971	Jan. 1, 1993	T. Doc. 99–27
	Pg	Oct. 29, 1971	Jan. 1, 1993	25 UST 309
	WTO	Apr. 15, 1994	Jan. 1, 1995	33 ILM 15

(Footnote references appear at end of chart).

PROCLAMATIONS, TREATIES, AND CONVENTIONS ESTABLISHING COPYRIGHT RELATIONS BETWEEN THE UNITED STATES AND OTHER COUNTRIES (Cont'd)

Country	Document	Date of Document	Effective Date for Party [28]	Reference
Slovenia	UCC	Sept. 6, 1952	May 11, 1966	6 UST 2731
	UCC rev.	July 24, 1971	July 10, 1974	25 UST 1341
	Berne (Paris)	July 24, 1971	June 25, 1991	T. Doc. 99–27
	Pcss	May 21, 1974	June 25, 1991	T. Doc 98–31
	WTO	Apr. 15, 1994	July 30, 1995	33 ILM 15
	Pg	Oct. 29, 1971	Oct. 15, 1996	25 UST 309
Solomon Islands	WTO	Apr. 15, 1994	July 26, 1996	33 ILM 15
South Africa [1]	Pm	June 26, 1924	July 1, 1924	43 Stat. 1957
	Berne (Brussels)	June 26, 1948	Aug. 1, 1951	331 UNTS 217
	WTO	Apr. 15, 1994	Jan. 1, 1995	33 ILM 15
Spain [5]	P [24]	July 10, 1895	July 10, 1895	29 Stat. 871
	P	Apr. 9, 1910	July 1, 1909	36 Stat. 2685
	Pm	Oct. 10, 1934	Oct. 10, 1934	49 Stat. 3420
	UCC	Sept. 6, 1952	Sept. 16, 1955	6 UST 2731
	UCC rev.	July 24, 1971	July 10, 1974	25 UST 1341
	Pg	Oct. 29, 1971	Aug. 24, 1974	25 UST 309
	Berne (Paris)	July 24, 1971	Oct. 10, 1974	T. Doc. 99–27
	WTO	Apr. 15, 1994	Jan. 1, 1995	33 ILM 15
Sri Lanka (formerly Ceylon)	Berne (Rome)	June 2, 1928	July 20, 1959	123 LNTS 232
	UCC	Sept. 6, 1952	Jan. 25, 1984	6 UST 2731
	UCC rev.	July 24, 1971	Jan. 25, 1984	25 UST 1341
	WTO	Apr. 15, 1994	Jan. 1, 1995	33 ILM 15
Sudan	Berne (Paris)	July 24, 1971	Dec. 28, 2000	T. Doc. 99–27
Suriname	Berne (Paris)	July 24, 1971	Feb. 23, 1977	T. Doc. 99–27
	WTO	Apr. 15, 1994	Jan. 1, 1995	33 ILM 15
Swaziland	WTO	Apr. 15, 1994	Jan. 1, 1995	33 ILM 15
	Berne (Paris)	July 24, 1971	Dec. 14, 1998	T. Doc. 99–27
Sweden	P	May 26, 1911	June 1, 1911	37 Stat. 1682
	Pm	Feb. 27, 1920	Feb. 1, 1920	41 Stat. 1787
	UCC	Sept. 6, 1952	July 1, 1961	6 UST 2731
	Pg [32]	Oct. 29, 1971	Apr. 18, 1973	25 UST 309
	UCC rev.	July 24, 1971	July 10, 1974	25 UST 1341
	Berne (Paris)	July 24, 1971	Oct. 10, 1974	T. Doc. 99–27
	WTO	Apr. 15, 1994	Jan. 1, 1995	33 ILM 15
Switzerland	P	July 1, 1891	July 1, 1891	27 Stat. 981
	P	Apr. 9, 1910	July 1, 1909	36 Stat. 2685
	Pm	Nov. 22, 1924	July 1, 1923	43 Stat. 1976
	UCC	Sept. 6, 1952	Mar. 30, 1956	6 UST 2731
	UCC rev.	July 24, 1971	Sept. 21, 1993	25 UST 1341
	Pcss	May 21, 1974	Sept. 24, 1993	T. Doc. 98–31
	Berne (Paris)	July 24, 1971	Sept. 25, 1993	T. Doc. 99–27
	Pg	Oct. 29, 1971	Sept. 30, 1993	25 UST 309
	WTO	Apr. 15, 1994	July 1, 1995	33 ILM 15

(Footnote references appear at end of chart).

PROCLAMATIONS, TREATIES, AND CONVENTIONS ESTABLISHING COPYRIGHT RELATIONS BETWEEN THE UNITED STATES AND OTHER COUNTRIES (Cont'd)

Country	Document	Date of Document	Effective Date for Party [28]	Reference
Tajikistan	UCC	Sept. 6, 1952	May 27, 1973	6 UST 2731
	Berne (Paris)	July 24, 1971	Mar. 9, 2000	T. Doc. 99–27
Tanzania (United Republic of)	Berne (Paris)	July 24, 1971	July 25, 1994	T. Doc. 99–27
	WTO	Apr. 15, 1994	Jan. 1, 1995	33 ILM 15
Thailand	T [25]	Dec. 16, 1920	Sept. 1, 1921	42 Stat. 1928
	T [25]	Nov. 13, 1937	Oct. 1, 1938	53 Stat. 1731
	T [25]	May 29, 1966	June 8, 1968	19 UST 5843
	WTO	Apr. 15, 1994	Jan. 1, 1995	33 ILM 15
	Berne (Paris)	July 24, 1971	Sept. 2, 1995	T. Doc. 99–27
Togo	Berne (Paris)	July 24, 1971	Apr. 30, 1975	T. Doc. 99–27
	WTO	Apr. 15, 1994	May 31, 1995	33 ILM 15
Trinidad and Tobago	Berne (Paris)	July 24, 1971	Aug. 16, 1988	T. Doc. 99–27
	UCC	Sept. 6, 1952	Aug. 19, 1988	6 UST 2731
	UCC rev.	July 24, 1971	Aug. 19, 1988	25 UST 1341
	Pg	Oct. 29, 1971	Oct. 1, 1988	25 UST 309
	WTO	Apr. 15, 1994	Mar. 1, 1995	33 ILM 15
	Pcss	May 21, 1974	Nov. 1, 1996	T. Doc. 98–31
Tunisia	P [26]	Oct. 4, 1912	Oct. 4, 1912	37 Stat. 1765
	UCC	Sept. 6, 1952	June 19, 1969	6 UST 2731
	UCC rev.	July 24, 1971	June 10, 1975	25 UST 1341
	Berne (Paris)	July 24, 1971	Aug. 16, 1975	T. Doc. 99–27
	WTO	Apr. 15, 1994	Mar. 29, 1995	33 ILM 15
Turkey	Berne (Paris)	July 24, 1971	Jan. 1, 1996	T. Doc 99–27
	WTO	Apr. 15, 1994	Mar. 26, 1995	33 ILM 15
Uganda	WTO	Apr. 15, 1994	Jan. 1, 1995	33 ILM 15
Ukraine	UCC	Sept. 6, 1952	May 27, 1973	6 UST 2731
	Berne (Paris)	July 24, 1971	Oct. 25, 1995	T. Doc. 99–27
United Arab Emirates	WTO	Apr. 15, 1994	Apr. 10, 1996	33 ILM 15
United Kingdom [1]	UCC	Sept. 6, 1952	Sept. 27, 1957	6 UST 2731
	Pg [32]	Oct. 29, 1971	Apr. 18, 1973	25 UST 309
	UCC rev.	July 24, 1971	July 10, 1974	25 UST 1341
	Berne (Paris)	July 24, 1971	Jan. 2, 1990	T. Doc. 99–27
	WTO	Apr. 15, 1994	Jan. 1, 1995	33 ILM 15
United Kingdom and Possessions [1]	P	July 1, 1891	July 1, 1891	27 Stat. 981
	P	Apr. 9, 1910	July 1, 1909	36 Stat. 2685

(Footnote references appear at end of chart).

PROCLAMATIONS, TREATIES, AND CONVENTIONS ESTABLISHING COPYRIGHT RELATIONS BETWEEN THE UNITED STATES AND OTHER COUNTRIES (Cont'd)

Country	Document	Date of Document	Effective Date for Party [28]	Reference
United Kingdom and the British Dominions, Colonies and Possessions with the exception of Canada, Australia, New Zealand, South Africa and Newfoundland [1]	Pm Pmx	Jan. 1, 1915 Apr. 10, 1920	Jan. 1, 1915 Feb. 2, 1920	38 Stat. 2044 41 Stat. 1790
United Kingdom, including certain British Territories [1] and Palestine [12]	Pxx Po	Mar. 10, 1944 Mar. 26, 1950	Mar. 10, 1944 Dec. 29, 1950	58 Stat. 1129 64 Stat. A412
Uruguay	BAC Berne (Paris) Pg UCC UCC rev. WTO	Aug. 11, 1910 July 24, 1971 Oct. 29, 1971 Sept. 6, 1952 July 24, 1971 Apr. 15, 1994	Dec. 17, 1919 Dec. 28, 1979 Jan. 18, 1983 Apr. 12, 1993 Apr. 12, 1993 Jan. 1, 1995	38 Stat. 1785 T. Doc. 99–27 25 UST 309 6 UST 2731 25 UST 1341 33 ILM 15
Vatican City (Holy See)	UCC Berne (Paris) Pg UCC rev.	Sept. 6, 1952 July 24, 1971 Oct. 29, 1971 July 24, 1971	Oct. 5, 1955 Apr. 24, 1975 July 18, 1977 May 6, 1980	6 UST 2731 T. Doc. 99–27 25 UST 309 25 UST 1341
Venezuela	UCC Pg Berne (Paris) WTO UCC rev.	Sept. 6, 1952 Oct. 29, 1971 July 24, 1971 Apr. 15, 1994 July 24, 1971	Sept. 30, 1966 Nov. 18, 1982 Dec. 30, 1982 Jan. 1, 1995 Feb. 11, 1997	6 UST 2731 25 UST 309 T. Doc. 99–27 33 ILM 15 25 UST 1341
Vietnam	P[38]	Dec. 23, 1998	Dec. 23, 1998	63 F.Reg. 71571
Yugoslavia [39]	UCC UCC rev. Berne (Paris) Pcss [31]	Sept. 6, 1952 July 24, 1971 July 24, 1971 May 21, 1974	May 11, 1966 July 10, 1974 Sept. 2, 1975 Aug. 25, 1979	6 UST 2731 25 UST 1341 T. Doc. 99–27 T. Doc. 98–31
Zambia	UCC Berne (Paris) WTO	Sept. 6, 1952 July 24, 1971 Apr. 15, 1994	June 1, 1965 Jan. 2, 1992 Jan. 1, 1995	6 UST 2731 T. Doc. 99–27 33 ILM 15
Zimbabwe	Berne (Rome) WTO	June 2, 1928 Apr. 15, 1994	Apr. 18, 1980 Mar. 3, 1995	123 LNTS 232 33 ILM 15

(Footnote references appear at end of chart).

References:

[1] The proclamations of July 1, 1891 and April 9, 1910, apply to "Great Britain and the British possessions," but the proclamations of January 1, 1915 and April 10, 1920, specifically except Australia, Canada, Newfoundland, New Zealand, and South Africa. The proclamations of March 10, 1944 and May 26, 1950, enumerate the various British territories to which they apply; the enumeration does not mention the areas specifically excepted in the proclamations of 1915 and 1920. Proclamations establishing individual copyright relations with Australia, Canada, Ireland, New Zealand, Palestine, and South Africa are listed separately. See also footnotes 2, 11, and 12. The proclamation of December 27, 1923, regarding Canada is considered as applying to Newfoundland at the present time.

The copyright proclamations of July 1, 1891, April 9, 1910, January 1, 1915, April 10, 1920, and March 10, 1944, regarding Great Britain and possessions each applied when issued to the areas now within the boundaries of Burma, Ceylon, India, and Pakistan. See footnote 10 with respect to India. No announcement has been made as to the application of the proclamations to Burma, Ceylon, and Pakistan since they acquired their new status.

[2] The proclamation of December 29, 1949, extends for one year from its date the period of time for compliance by citizens of Australia with the conditions and formalities prescribed by the copyright law of the United States.

[3] The United States entered into treaties restoring friendly relations with Austria, Germany, and Hungary at Vienna on August 24, 1921 (42 Stat. 1946; TS 659), at Berlin on August 25, 1921 (42 Stat. 1939; TS 658); and at Budapest on August 29, 1921 (42 Stat. 1951; TS 610). By virtue of these treaties the United States became entitled to the benefits of the provisions relative to copyright protection in the treaties of peace signed by Austria, Germany, and Hungary at Saint-Germain-en-Laye on September 10, 1919, at Versailles on June 28, 1919, and at Trianon on June 4, 1920, respectively. See also footnote 7.

[4] Bilateral copyright relations between the People's Republic of China and the United States of America were established, effective March 17, 1992, by a Presidential Proclamation of the same date, under the authority of section 104 of title 17 of the United States Code, as amended by the Act of October 31, 1988 (Public Law 100–568, 102 Stat. 2853, 2855).

[5] Treaties and conventions containing provisions relative to copyright protection in territories ceded to the United States are not included in this table: for example, the Treaty of Peace with Spain signed at Paris, December 10, 1898 (30 Stat. 1754; TS 343), and the Convention with Denmark for the Cession to the United States of the Danish West Indies, signed at New York, August 4, 1916 (39 Stat. 1706; TS 629).

[6] The Department of State has made no announcement as to the application of the proclamations of July 1, 1891, April 9, 1910, May 24, 1918, and March 27, 1947, to Cambodia, Laos, and Viet-Nam.

[7] Copyright convention signed at Budapest January 30, 1912 (TS 571). This convention was continued in force following World War I by notice given by the United States on May 27, 1922, to Hungary in pursuance of Article 224 of the Treaty of Trianon concluded on June 4, 1920 (III Redmond 3539), to the benefits of which the United States became entitled by the Treaty of August 29, 1921, establishing friendly relations between the United States and Hungary (42 Stat. 1951; TS 660). The convention of 1912 was kept in force or revived following World War II by notice given on March 9, 1948, by the United States to Hungary pursuant to Article 10 of the Treaty of Peace with Hungary (61 Stat. 2065; Department of State Bulletin, March 21, 1948, p. 382).

[8] Treaty of Peace with Hungary (Annex IV A) dated at Paris, February 10, 1947 (TIAS 1651).

[9] Except with respect to rights of third parties, the provisions relating to protection of copyright in the annexes to the Treaties of Peace with Hungary, Italy, and Romania dated at Paris, February 10, 1947, are bilateral in character. For example, the provisions of Annex IV A of the Treaty of Peace with Hungary relate, in general, to copyright relations between Hungary, on the one hand, and each of the other ratifying or adhering States, on the other. Those provisions do not pertain to copyright relations between those other States, except for third party rights. Annex IV of the Treaty of Peace with Bulgaria dated at Paris, February 10, 1947 (61 Stat. 1915; TIAS 1650) contains similar provisions. See also footnote 13.

[10] The proclamation of October 21, 1954, affirms the existence of copyright relations with India after August 15, 1947 (the effective date of the Indian Independence Act). See also footnote 1.

[11] The Department of State has determined that the entry into force on April 18, 1949, of the Republic of Ireland Act had no effect upon the proclamation of September 28, 1929, regarding the Irish Free State (Eire). Copyright relations with Ireland are therefore governed by that proclamation. See also footnote 1.

[12] The proclamations of March 10, 1944 and May 26, 1950, regarding Great Britain and possessions, also specifically refer to Palestine (excluding Trans-Jordan). See also footnote 1.

[13] The exchanges of notes between the United States and Italy, on the basis of which the proclamations of October 31, 1892 and May 1, 1915, were issued, were the subject of a note delivered on March 12, 1948, to the Italian Foreign Office by the American Embassy at Rome with respect to pre-war bilateral treaties and other international agreements which the United States desired to keep in force or revive pursuant to Article 44 of the Treaty of Peace with Italy. The note stated in part ''that the Government of the United States of America wishes to include the reciprocal copyright arrangement between the United States and Italy effected pursuant to the exchange of notes signed at Washington October 28, 1892, and the exchanges of notes signed at Washington September 2, 1914, February 12, March 4, and March 11, 1915, among the pre-war bilateral treaties and other international agreements with Italy which the United States desires to keep in force or revive. Accordingly, it is understood that the aforementioned arrangement will continue in force and that the Government of each country will extend to the nationals of the other country treatment as favorable with respect to copyrights as was contemplated at the time the arrangement was entered into by the two countries.'' (Department of State Bulletin, April 4, 1948, p. 455).

[14] Treaty of Peace with Italy (Annex XV A) dated at Paris, January 10, 1947 (TIAS 1648).

[15] Copyright convention, signed at Tokyo, November 10, 1905 (TS 450). This convention is considered as having been abrogated on April 22, 1953, pursuant to the provisions of Article 7 of the Treaty of Peace which Japan signed at San Francisco, September 8, 1951 (TIAS 2490), since it was not included in the notification which was given on behalf of the United States Government to the Japanese Government on April 22, 1953, indicating the pre-war bilateral treaties or conventions which the United States wished to continue in force or revive.

[16] Convention between the United States and Japan for reciprocal protection of inventions, designs, trademarks, and copyrights in China and other countries where either contracting party may exercise extraterritorial jurisdiction, signed at Washington, May 19, 1908 (TS 507). This convention is considered as having been abrogated on April 22, 1953, pursuant to the provisions of Article 7 of the Treaty of Peace with Japan signed at San Francisco, September 8, 1951 (TIAS 2490), since it was not included in the notification which was given on behalf of the United States Government to the Japanese Government on April 22, 1953, indicating the pre-war bilateral treaties or conventions which the United States wished to continue in force or revive.

[17] Treaty of Peace with Japan (Articles 12, 14, and 15) signed at San Francisco, September 8, 1951 (TIAS 2490). See also footnotes 15, 16, 18, and 19.

[18] The proclamation of November 10, 1953, extends benefits under the copyright law for a period of four years from the coming into force of the Treaty of Peace with Japan (TIAS 2490). That period expired April 28, 1956.

[19] Copyright convention with Japan for reciprocal protection in Korea of inventions, designs, trademarks, and copyrights, signed at Washington, May 19, 1908 (TS 506). This convention is considered as having been abrogated on April 22, 1953, pursuant to the provisions of Article 7 of the Treaty of Peace with Japan signed at San Francisco, September 8, 1951 (TIAS 2490), since it was not included in the notification which was given on behalf of the United States Government to the Japanese Government on April 22, 1953, indicating the pre-war bilateral treaties or conventions which the United States wished to continue in force or revive.

[20] Belize notified the Director-General of UNESCO on December 1, 1982, of its decision to apply ''provisionally, and on the basis of reciprocity'' the Universal Copyright Convention as adopted at Geneva on September 6, 1952, the application of which had been extended to its territory before the attainment of independence from the United Kingdom on September 21, 1981.

[21] An instrument of accession was deposited by the Philippine Government August 19, 1955. In a communication received by the State Department January 17, 1956, UNESCO stated that by a note dated November 14, 1955, the Philippine Government informed the Director-General of UNESCO that "the President of the . . . Philippines has directed the withdrawal of the . . . accession . . . to the Universal Copyright Convention prior to the date of November 19, 1955, at which time the Convention would become effective" for the Philippines. The Director-General notified the Philippine Government that he "proposed to submit their communication to the States concerned, upon whom it is incumbent to declare what legal inference they intend to draw from it."

[22] In a note delivered February 26, 1948, to the Romanian Minister for Foreign Affairs by the American Minister at Bucharest with respect to pre-war bilateral treaties and other international agreements which the United States desired to keep in force or revive pursuant to Article 10 of the Treaty of Peace with Romania, the following statement was made regarding the proclamation of May 14, 1928, and the exchange of notes on which it is based: "It shall be understood that the reciprocal copyright arrangement between the United States and Rumania effected pursuant to the exchanges of notes signed at Bucharest May 13 and October 21, 1927 and at Washington May 12 and 19, 1928 and the proclamation issued May 14, 1928 by the President of the United States of America will continue in force." (Department of State Bulletin, March 14, 1948, p. 356). See also footnote 9.

[23] Treaty of Peace with Romania, dated at Paris, February 10, 1947 (TIAS 1649).

[24] The proclamation of July 10, 1895, regarding Spain was based upon an arrangement between the United States and Spain effected by an exchange of notes signed at Washington, July 6 and 15, 1895. An agreement restoring the arrangement of July 6 and 15, 1895, was effected by an exchange of notes signed at Madrid, January 29 and November 18 and 26, 1902 (II Malloy 1710), following the Treaty of Peace between the United States and Spain signed at Paris, December 10, 1898 (30 Stat. 1754; TS 343). The latter treaty also contains in Article XIII the following provisions: "The rights of property secured by copyrights and patents acquired by Spaniards in the Island of Cuba, and in Puerto Rico, the Philippines and other ceded territories, at the time of the exchange of ratifications of this treaty, shall continue to be respected. Spanish scientific, literary and artistic works, not subversive of public order in the territories in question, shall continue to be admitted free of duty into such territories, for the period of ten years, to be reckoned from the date of the exchange of ratification of this treaty."

[25] Treaty of friendship, commerce and navigation, protocol and exchanges of notes, signed at Bangkok, November 13, 1937 (TS 940). This treaty replaces the treaty of friendship, commerce and navigation between the United States and Thailand signed at Washington, December 16, 1920 (TS 655), Article XII of which contains provisions relating to copyright protection. The treaty of amity and economic relations, with three exchanges of notes between the United States and Thailand signed at Bangkok, May 29, 1966 (TIAS 6540), replaces the treaty of November 13, 1937. Article V.2 contains provisions relating to copyright.

[26] The proclamation of October 4, 1912, stated, in effect, that the law "in Tunis" extended to U.S. citizens protection substantially equal to the protection secured under the copyright law of the United States and declared that "the subjects of Tunis" were entitled to the benefits of the Act of March 4, 1909, as amended, except copyright controlling the mechanical reproduction of a copyrighted musical work.

[27] "Paris" means the Berne Convention for the Protection of Literary and Artistic Works as revised at Paris on July 24, 1971 (Paris Act); "Stockholm" means the said Convention as revised at Stockholm on July 14, 1967 (Stockholm Act); "Brussels" means the said Convention as revised at Brussels on June 26, 1948 (Brussels Act); "Rome" means the said Convention as revised at Rome on June 2, 1928 (Rome Act); "Berlin" means the said Convention as revised at Berlin on November 13, 1908 (Berlin Act). NOTE: In each case the reference to Act signifies adherence to the substantive provisions of such Act only, *e.g.*, Articles 1 to 21 and the Appendix of the Paris Act.

[28] The effective date is the date on which the designated State became party to the Convention or Treaty named, or in the case of the Berne Convention, the date on which the latest Act of the Convention to which such State is party entered into force with respect to that State.

[29] The dates of adherence by Germany to multilateral treaties include adherence by the Federal Republic of Germany when that country was divided into the Federal Republic of Germany and the German Democratic Republic. However, through the accession, effective October 3, 1990, of the German Democratic Republic to the Federal Republic of Germany, in accordance with the German Unification Treaty of August 31, 1990, the German Democratic Republic ceased, on the said date, to be a sovereign state. Previously, the German Democratic Republic had become party to the Paris Act of the Berne Convention for the Protection of Literary and Artistic Works on February 18, 1978, but ceased to be a party to the said Convention on October 3, 1990. The German Democratic Republic had also been a member of the Universal Copyright Convention, having become party to the Geneva text of the said Convention on October 5, 1973, and party to the revised Paris text of the same Convention on December 10, 1980.

[30] The Union of Soviet Socialist Republics (or Soviet Union) was a party to the Convention Relating to the Distribution of Programme-Carrying Signals Transmitted by Satellite from January 20, 1989, through December 24, 1991.

[31] The Convention Relating to the Distribution of Programme-Carrying Signals Transmitted by Satellite done at Brussels on May 21, 1974, did not enter into force with respect to the United States until March 7, 1985.

[32] The Convention for the Protection of Producers of Phonograms Against Unauthorized Duplication of Their Phonograms done at Geneva on October 29, 1971, did not enter into force with respect to the United States until March 10, 1974.

[33] For 1992 and prior years, see CZECHOSLOVAKIA.

[34] See also Czech Republic, Slovak Republic, and Slovakia.

[35] See note under CZECHOSLOVAKIA in bilateral section.

[36] See note under GERMANY, FEDERAL REPUBLIC OF in bilateral section.

[37] Also known as Slovak Republic. For 1992 and prior years, see Czechoslovakia.

[38] Bilateral copyright relations between the Socialist Republic of Vietnam and the United States of America were established effective December 23, 1998, by a Presidential Proclamation of that same date, under the authority of sections 104(b)(5) and 104A(g) of title 17 of the United States Code, as amended.

[39] See note under YUGOSLAVIA in bilateral section.